DATE DUE

			PRINTED IN U.S.A.

CLASSICAL AND MEDIEVAL LITERATURE CRITICISM

Guide to Gale Literary Criticism Series

For criticism on	Consult these Gale series
Authors now living or who died after December 31, 1959	*CONTEMPORARY LITERARY CRITICISM (CLC)*
Authors who died between 1900 and 1959	*TWENTIETH-CENTURY LITERARY CRITICISM (TCLC)*
Authors who died between 1800 and 1899	*NINETEENTH-CENTURY LITERATURE CRITICISM (NCLC)*
Authors who died between 1400 and 1799	*LITERATURE CRITICISM FROM 1400 TO 1800 (LC)* *SHAKESPEAREAN CRITICISM (SC)*
Authors who died before 1400	*CLASSICAL AND MEDIEVAL LITERATURE CRITICISM (CMLC)*
Authors of books for children and young adults	*CHILDREN'S LITERATURE REVIEW (CLR)*
Dramatists	*DRAMA CRITICISM (DC)*
Poets	*POETRY CRITICISM (PC)*
Short story writers	*SHORT STORY CRITICISM (SSC)*
Black writers of the past two hundred years	*BLACK LITERATURE CRITICISM (BLC)*
Hispanic writers of the late nineteenth and twentieth centuries	*HISPANIC LITERATURE CRITICISM (HLC)*
Native North American writers and orators of the eighteenth, nineteenth, and twentieth centuries	*NATIVE NORTH AMERICAN LITERATURE (NNAL)*
Major authors from the Renaissance to the present	*WORLD LITERATURE CRITICISM, 1500 TO THE PRESENT (WLC)*

ISSN 0896-0011

R

Volume 31

CLASSICAL AND MEDIEVAL LITERATURE CRITICISM

Excerpts from Criticism of the Works of World
Authors from Classical Antiquity through the
Fourteenth Century, from the First Appraisals
to Current Evaluations

Jelena O. Krstović
Editor

DETROIT • SAN FRANCISCO • LONDON • BOSTON • WOODBRIDGE, CT

Contents

Preface vii

Acknowledgments xi

Preface

Since its inception in 1988, *Classical and Medieval Literature Criticism* has been a valuable resource for students and librarians seeking critical commentary on the writers and works of these periods in world history. Major reviewing sources have assessed *CMLC* as "useful" and "extremely convenient," noting that it "adds to our understanding of the rich legacy left by the ancient period and the Middle Ages," and praising its "general excellence in the presentation of an inherently interesting subject." No other single reference source has surveyed the critical reaction to classical and medieval literature as thoroughly as *CMLC*.

Scope of the Series

CMLC is designed to serve as an introduction for students and advanced readers of the works and authors of antiquity through the fourteenth century. The great poets, prose writers, dramatists, and philosophers of this period form the basis of most humanities curricula, so that virtually every student will encounter many of these works during the course of a high school and college education. By organizing and reprinting an enormous amount of commentary written on classical and medieval authors and works, *CMLC* helps students develop valuable insight into literary history, promotes a better understanding of the texts, and sparks ideas for papers and assignments. Each entry in *CMLC* presents a comprehensive survey of an author's career, an individual work of literature, or a literary topic, and provides the user with a multiplicity of interpretations and assessments. Such variety allows students to pursue their own interests; furthermore, it fosters an awareness that literature is dynamic and responsive to many different opinions.

CMLC continues the survey of criticism of world literature begun by Gale's *Contemporary Literary Criticism (CLC)*, *Twentieth-Century Literary Criticism (TCLC)*, *Nineteenth-Century Literature Criticism (NCLC)*, *Literature Criticism from 1400 to 1800 (LC)*, and *Shakespearean Criticism (SC)*. For additional information about these and Gale's other criticism series, users should consult the Guide to Gale Literary Criticism Series preceding the title page in this volume.

Coverage

Each volume of *CMLC* is carefully compiled to present:

* criticism of authors, works, and topics which represent a variety of genres, time periods, and nationalities

* both major and lesser-known writers and works of the period (such as non-Western authors and literature, increasingly read by today's students)

* 4-6 authors, works, or topics per volume

* individual entries that survey the critical response to each author, work, or topic, including early criticism, later criticism (to represent any rise or decline in reputation), and current retrospective analyses. The length of each author, work, or topic entry also indicates relative importance, reflecting the amount of critical attention the author, work, or topic has received from critics writing in English, and from foreign criticism in translation.

An author may appear more than once in the series if his or her writings have been the subject of a substantial amount of criticism; in these instances, specific works or groups of works by the author will be covered in separate entries. For example, Homer will be represented by three entries, one devoted to the *Iliad,* one to the *Odyssey,* and one to the Homeric Hymns.

Starting with Volume 10, *CMLC* will also occasionally include entries devoted to literary topics. For example, *CMLC*-10 focuses on Arthurian Legend and includes general criticism on that subject as well as individual entries on writers or works central to that topic—Chrétien de Troyes, Gottfried von Strassburg, Layamon, and the Alliterative *Morte Arthure*. Presocratic Philosophy is the focus of *CMLC*-22, which includes general criticism as well as essays on Greek philosophers Anaximander, Heraclitus, Parmenides, and Pythagoras.

Organization of the Book

An author entry consists of the following elements: author heading, biographical and critical introduction, principal works, principal English translations or editions, excerpts of criticism (each preceded by a bibliographic citation and an annotation), and a bibliography of further reading.

• The **Author Heading** consists of the author's most commonly used name, followed by birth and death dates. If the entry is devoted to a work, the heading will consist of the most common form of the title in English translation (if applicable), and the original date of composition. Located at the beginning of the introduction are any name or title variations.

• A **Portrait** of the author is included when available. Many entries also feature illustrations of materials pertinent to the author or work, including manuscript pages, book illustrations, and representations of people, places, and events important to a study of the author or work.

• The **Biographical and Critical Introduction** contains background information that concisely introduces the reader to the author, work, or topic.

• The list of **Principal Works** and **English Translations** or **Editions** is chronological by date of first publication and is included as an aid to the student seeking translated versions or editions of these works for study. The list will focus primarily on twentieth-century translations, selecting those works most commonly considered the best by critics.

• **Criticism** is arranged chronologically in each entry to provide a useful perspective on changes in critical evaluation over the years. All titles by the author featured in the critical entry are printed in boldface type to enable the user to ascertain without difficulty the works being discussed. Also for purposes of easier identification, the critic's name and the publication date of the essay are given at the beginning of each piece of criticism. Anonymous criticism is preceded by the title of the journal in which it appeared. Publication information (such as publisher names and book prices) and parenthetical numerical references (such as footnotes or page and line references to specific editions of works) have been deleted at the editors' discretion to provide smoother reading of the text. Many critical entries in *CMLC* also contain translations to aid the users. Footnotes that appear with previously published pieces of criticism are reprinted at the end of each essay or excerpt. In the case of excerpted criticism, only those footnotes that pertain to the excerpted text are included.

• A complete **Bibliographic Citation** provides original publication information for each piece of criticism.

• Critical excerpts are also prefaced by **Annotations** providing the reader with information about both the critic and the criticism, the scope of the excerpt, the growth of critical controversy, or changes in critical trends regarding an author or work. In some cases, these notes include cross-references to excerpts by critics who discuss each other's commentary. Dates in parentheses within the annotation refer to a book publication date when they follow a book title, and to an essay date when they follow a critic's name.

• An annotated bibliography of **Further Reading** appears at the end of each entry and lists additional secondary sources on the author or work. In some cases it includes essays for which the editors could not obtain reprint rights. When applicable, the Further Reading is followed by references to additional entries on the author in other literary reference series published by Gale.

Topic Entries are subdivided into several thematic rubrics in which criticism appears in order of descending scope.

Cumulative Indexes

Each volume of *CMLC* includes a cumulative **author index** listing all authors who have appeared in Gale's Literary Criticism Series, along with cross references to such biographical series as *Contemporary Authors* and *Dictionary of Literary Biography.* For readers' convenience, a complete list of Gale titles included appears on the page prior to the author index. Useful for locating an author within the various series, this index is particularly valuable for those authors who are identified with a certain period but who, because of their death date, are placed in another, or for those authors whose careers span two periods. For example, Geoffrey Chaucer, who is usually considered a medieval author, is found in *Literature Criticism from 1400 to 1800* because he died after 1399.

Beginning with the tenth volume, *CMLC* includes a cumulative index listing all topic entries that have appeared in the Gale Literary Criticism Series *Classical and Medieval Literature Criticism, Contemporary Literary Criticism, Literature Criticism from 1400 to 1800, Nineteenth-Century Literature Criticism,* and *Twentieth-Century Literary Criticism.*

Beginning with the second volume, *CMLC* also includes a cumulative nationality index. Authors and/or works are grouped by nationality, and the volume in which criticism on them may be found is indicated.

Title Index

Each volume of *CMLC* also includes an index listing the titles of all literary works discussed in the series. Foreign language titles that have been translated are followed by the titles of the translations—for example, *Slovo o polku Igorove (The Song of Igor's Campaign).* Page numbers following these translated titles refer to all pages on which any form of the title, either foreign language or translated, appears. Titles of novels, dramas, nonfiction books, and poetry, short story, or essay collections are printed in italics, while those of all individual poems, short stories, and essays are printed in roman type within quotation marks. In cases where the same title is used by different authors, the author's name or surname is given in parentheses after the title, e.g. *Collected Poems* (Horace) and *Collected Poems* (Sappho).

Critic Index

An index to critics, which cumulates with the second volume, is another useful feature of *CMLC.* Under each critic's name are listed the authors and/or works on whom the critic has written and the volume and page number where criticism may be found.

A Note to the Reader

When writing papers, students who quote directly from any volume in the Literary Criticism Series may use the following general forms to footnote reprinted criticism. The first example pertains to material drawn from a periodical, the second to material reprinted from books.

Rollo May, "The Therapist and the Journey into Hell," *Michigan Quarterly Review,* XXV, No. 4 (Fall 1986), 629-41; excerpted and reprinted in *Classical and Medieval Literature Criticism,* Vol. 3, ed. Jelena O. Krstovic (Detroit: Gale Research, 1989), pp. 154-58.

Dana Ferrin Sutton, *Self and Society in Aristophanes* (University of Press of America, 1980); excerpted and reprinted in *Classical and Medieval Literature Criticism,* Vol. 4, ed. Jelena O. Krstovic (Detroit: Gale Research, 1990), pp. 162-69.

Suggestions Are Welcome

Readers who wish to make suggestions for future volumes, or who have other comments regarding the series, are cordially invited to write or call the editors (1-800-347-GALE; Fax: (248) 699-8049).

Acknowledgments

The editors wish to thank the copyright holders of the excerpted criticism included in this volume and the permissions managers of many book and magazine publishing companies for assisting us in securing reproduction rights. We are also grateful to the staffs of the Detroit Public Library, the Library of Congress, the University of Detroit Mercy Library, Wayne State University Purdy/Kresge Library Complex, and the University of Michigan Libraries for making their resources available to us. Following is a list of the copyright holders who have granted us permission to reproduce material in this volume of *CMLC*. Every effort has been made to trace copyright, but if omissions have been made, please let us know.

COPYRIGHTED MATERIAL IN *CMLC*, VOLUME 31, WERE REPRODUCED FROM THE FOLLOWING PERIODICALS:

American Philosophical Quarterly, v. 18, October, 1981. Reproduced by permission.—*British Journal of Aesthetics,* v. 24, Spring, 1984. Reproduced by permission.—*Interpretation: A Journal of Political Philosophy,* v. 9, September, 1981 for "The Rationality of Political Speech: An Interpretation of Aristotle's *Rhetoric*" by Larry Arnhart. Copyright 1981 Interpretation. Reproduced by permission of the publisher and the author.—*The Journal of Aesthetics and Art Criticism,* v. XXVIII, Fall, 1969. Copyright © 1969 by The American Society for Aesthetics. Reproduced by permission.—*Philosophy,* v. XL, 1965, for "The Final Good in Aristotle's *Ethics*" by W. F. R. Hardie. Reproduced by permission of the Cambridge University Press and the Literary Estate of W. F. R. Hardie.—*The Review of Metaphysics: A Philosophical Quarterly,* v. 46, December, 1992. Copyright 1992 by *The Review of Metaphysics*. Reproduced by permission.—*Western Journal of Speech Communication,* v. 54, 1990. Reproduced by permission.

COPYRIGHTED MATERIAL IN *CMLC*, VOLUME 31, WERE REPRODUCED FROM THE FOLLOWING BOOKS:

Berns, Laurence. From "Aristotle's *Poetics*" in *Ancients and Moderns: Essays on the Tradition of Political Philosophy in Honor of Leo Strauss.* Edited by Joseph Cropsey. Basic Books Inc., Publishers, 1964. Copyright (c)1964 by Basic Books Inc., Publishers. Reproduced by permission of HarperCollins Publishers.—Bolotin, David. From *An Approach to Aristotle's Physics: With Particular Attention to the Role of His Manner of Writing.* State University of New York Press, 1998. © 1998 State University of New York. All rights reserved. Reproduced by permission of the State University of New York Press.—Brentano, Franz. From *On the Several Senses of Being in Aristotle.* By Franz Brentano. Edited by Rolf George. Translated by Rolf George. © 1975 by The Regents of the University of California. Reproduced by permission of the translator.—Chroust, Anton-Hermann. From *Aristotle: New Light on His Life and on Some of His Lost Works, Vol. II.* Routledge & Kegan Paul Ltd., 1973. © 1973 by Anton-Hermann Chroust. Reproduced by permission of the publisher and the Literary Estate of Anton-Hermann Chroust.—Crem, Theresa M. From "The Definition of Rhetoric According to Aristotle" in *Aristotle: The Classical Heritage of "Rhetoric."* Edited by Keith V. Erickson. The Scarecrow Press, Inc., 1974. Copyright 1974 by Keith V. Erickson. Reproduced by permission.—Devereux, Daniel T. From "Aristotle on the Essence of Happiness" in *Studies in Aristotle.* Edited by Dominic J. O'Meara. The Catholic University of America Press, 1981. Copyright © 1981 by The Catholic University of America Press. All rights reserved. Reproduced by permission.—Edel, Abraham. From *Aristotle and His Philosophy.* The University of North Carolina Press, 1982. Copyright © 1982 University of North Carolina Press. All rights reserved. Used by permission.—Erickson, Keith V. From *Aristotle's Rhetoric: Five Centuries of Philological Research.* The Scarecrow Press, Inc., 1975. Copyright 1975 by Keith V. Erickson. Reproduced by permission.—Fortenbaugh, W. W. From "Aristotle on Slaves and Women" in *Articles on Aristotle : 2. Ethics and Politics.* Edited by Jonathan Barnes, Malcolm Schofield, and Richard Sorabji. Duckworth, 1977. © 1977 by Gerald Duckworth & Company Limited. All rights reserved. Reprinted by permission of Gerald Duckworth and Co. Ltd.—Gulley, Norman. From "Aristotle on the Purposes of Literature" in *Articles on Aristotle : 4. Psychology and Aesthetics.* Edited by Jonathan Barnes, Malcolm Schofield, and Richard Sorabji. Duckworth, 1979. © 1979 by Gerald Duckworth & Company Limited. All rights reserved. Reprinted by permission of Gerald Duckworth and Co. Ltd.—Halliwell, Stephen. From *Aristotle's "Poetics."* Duckworth, 1986. © 1986 by Stephen Halliwell. All rights reserved. Reprinted by permission of Gerald Duckworth and

PHOTOGRAPHS AND ILLUSTRATIONS APPEARING IN *CMLC,* VOLUME 31, WERE RECEIVED FROM THE FOLLOWING SOURCES:

Aristotle

384 B. C.-322 B. C.

Greek philosopher and scientist.

GENERAL INTRODUCTION

Aristotle wrote on a multitude of topics including metaphysics, biology, psychology, logic, and physics. While earlier and contemporary philosophers are believed to have influenced Aristotle's views, he is credited with systematizing entire fields of ideas and with providing the methodology for future philosophic and scientific studies.

Biographical Information

Born in the Ionian colony of Stagira in Macedonia, Aristotle lost his parents at an early age. Little is known about them, but scholars have recorded that his father, Nicomachus, served as the court physician to the King of Macedon. When Aristotle was seventeen, his guardian sent him to study in Athens, under Plato. Aristotle spent twenty years at the Academy and left after Plato's death in 347 B.C. After a period of travel, Aristotle married Pythias, with whom he had a daughter and probably a son, Nicomachus. In 342, Aristotle was appointed tutor to Philip II's thirteen-year-old son, Alexander (later known as Alexander the Great). After remaining in the Macedonian court at Pella for some time, Aristotle probably retired to Stagira in 340, when Alexander became his father's regent. Not long after, in 335, Aristotle returned to Athens and founded a school, the Lyceum. Here, Aristotle lectured, conducted research, and established a library. Upon Alexander's death in 323, the anti-Macedonian party grew strong in Athens. Some of its officials charged him with impiety and prosecuted him. Following this incident, Aristotle left the directorship of his school to Theophrastus and departed Athens for the last time. He retired to Chalcis and died in the next year, 322.

Major Works

Aristotle's major works are typically grouped into the following categories: primary philosophy, practical science, logic, natural philosophy, rhetoric, and poetics. (The works on rhetoric and poetics are sometimes classified as practical science.) Such rubrics may seem a bit confusing to modern students of Aristotle; what Aristotle referred to as "practical science" includes his

writings on ethics and politics (works we might think of as simply "philosophy"); what he classified as "natural philosophy" includes his works in the areas of physics, psychology, and biology (topics we would refer to as "science"). This volume attempts to group Aristotle's works in a manner reflective of critical consensus, as well as to provide entry headings which would both guide users according to modern conceptions of the terms "science" and "philosophy" and honor traditional classifications. The entry **Philosophy** includes coverage of *Metaphysics, Ethics,* and *Politics;* the entry **Rhetoric** covers *Rhetoric;* the entry **Science** covers the works on logic (including, for example, *Categories* and *Posterior Analytics*), biological works (such as *On the Generation of Animals*), and psychological works (such as *De Anima* [*On the Soul*]). This entry also includes coverage of *Physics*. Finally, the entry **Poetics** focuses on Aristotle's *Poetics*. Each entry's introduction provides a more detailed account of the primary works in that field of study; a brief overview of the textual history of those works; and a survey of the critical reception and interpretation of those works.

Philosophy

INTRODUCTION

Major Works

Aristotle's *Metaphysics* deals with what he referred to as "primary philosophy" or "first principles." The field of metaphysics studies cosmology and ontology, and in Aristotle's *Metaphysics,* both areas are investigated through an analysis of the nature of being. Cosmology is concerned with the origin and nature of the universe, and ontology with the nature of existence.

Aristotle refers to the philosophical inquiry into ethics and politics as "practical science," as it is concerned with the individual's actions. His *Nicomachean Ethics,* often referred to simply as the *Ethics,* offers a close study of Greek ideals, of the notion of "the good" and the best way of life, of the nature of virtue, and of social problems and conflicts. The shorter *Eudemian Ethics* covers similar material but with different emphases. *Politics* approaches political science from the viewpoint of the state, or city-state. Consisting of eight books (the order of which is still a matter of debate), *Politics* covers such topics as the nature and structure of the state and of society, civic virtue, education, and class roles and distinctions.

Textual History

Little is known about the fate of Aristotle's works after his death. It is believed by some scholars that for about two hundred years the works were either lost or hidden. They were discovered by Sulla (178-38 B.C.) and brought to Rome. Modern editions of Aristotle's works derive from Roman editions dating back to the late first century B.C. In the Middle Ages, Latin and Arabic translations broadened the influence of Aristotle's teachings and his philosophy was studied extensively by St. Thomas Aquinas (c. 1225-74) and later by Francis Bacon (1561-1626). As relatively few of Aristotle's works can be dated with any degree of accuracy, the focus of nineteenth- and twentieth-century scholars has been on determining the chronological order of the works.

Critical Reception

Modern criticism of *Metaphysics* has focused on Aristotle's intended meaning, as well as on the iden-

tification of, and attempts to resolve, apparent inconsistencies within the text. Joseph Owens has discussed the various interpretations regarding the nature of being made by medieval metaphysicians, noting that there are two distinct ways in which this doctrine may be understood. Owens has observed that medieval Christian thinkers attempted to unify these two concepts; he has also presented the views of later critics who either attack or support such a unification. Franz Brentano has examined a different aspect of the nature of being, studying Aristotle's analysis of "potential" and "actual" being. Brentano has pointed to some apparent difficulties with the definitions Aristotle provides, and has offered an interpretation which elucidates the two concepts and the relationship between potential and actual being. The concepts of substance and form as Aristotle presents them in *Metaphysics* have also generated much criticism. Wilfrid Sellars and Richard Rorty have both approached these issues, but from different angles. Sellars has noted the ways in which Aristotle's *Categories* (discussed in the *Science* section of this volume), particularly the theory of predication found there, can aid one's understanding of the nature of substance, form, and matter as presented in *Metaphysics*. Rorty has argued that, by giving more credence to Aristotle's claim that genus is matter, the difficulties encountered when studying substance and form are reduced.

The most salient issues for modern critics with regard to *Ethics* have included Aristotle's doctrine of "the good" and the related issue of happiness—"the good" being the single end at which one aims throughout one's life, and happiness being a result of that quest. W. F. R. Hardie and Daniel T. Devereux have addressed the critical debate concerning the nature of the good and whether Aristotle views it as a dominant or inclusive end. Hardie has asserted that Aristotle presents the final good as dominant, but that the philosopher at the same time suggests its inclusive nature. Hardie has concluded that the doctrine of the good focuses on the power of man to "reflect on his own abilities and desires and to conceive and choose for himself a satisfactory way of life." Devereux has asserted, however, that the issues of dominance and inclusiveness are far removed from Aristotle's views on the subject of the good. Devereux has stated that the *Ethics* outlines two different types of happiness, both of which are "implicitly inclusive." Perfect happiness, Devereux has noted, is associated by Aristotle with a life of philosophical contemplation, and a secondary degree of happiness may be achieved through a life of moral virtue. Aristide Tessitore has also stressed Aristotle's proposition that perfect, complete happiness can only be found through philosophic contemplation. Yet Tessitore has emphasized as well that Aristotle encourages a life of virtue for non-philosophers by linking them, through the concept of moral decency, to philosophers.

---

*PRINCIPAL WORKS

Ethica Eudemia [*Eudemian Ethics*] (philosophy)

Ethica Nicomachea [*Nicomachean Ethics*] (philosophy)

Metaphysica [*Metaphysics*] (philosophy)

Politica [*Politics*] (philosophy)

*Since the dates of Aristotle's treatises are unknown, his works are listed here in alphabetical order.

PRINCIPAL ENGLISH TRANSLATIONS

The Works of Aristotle Translated into English [edited by J. A. Smith and W. D. Ross] 1910-52

Aristotle's Eudemian Ethics, Books I, II, and VIII [translated by Michael Woods] 1982

The Politics [translated by Carnes Lord] 1984

Aristotle: Nicomachean Ethics [translated by Terence C. Irwin] 1985

CRITICISM

PRIMARY PHILOSOPHY

Franz Brentano (essay date 1862)

SOURCE: "Potential and Actual Being," in *On the Several Senses of Being in Aristotle,* by Franz Brentano, edited by Rolf George, translated by Rolf George, University of California Press, 1975, pp. 27-48.

[*In the following essay, originally published in 1862, Brentano discusses the nature of potential and actual being as analyzed by Aristotle in* Metaphysics. *Brentano examines Aristotle's definitions of potential and actual being and presents readings of them designed to resolve some difficulties within them. Finally, he explores the relationship between the two concepts, maintaining that "movement is the actuality of the potentiality."*]

The two senses of being . . . , namely, being which is divided into the categories and potential and actual being, belong together and are intimately connected with each other.[1] Thus they have in common that the science of being, metaphysics, is concerned in the same way with one as with the other,[2] while, as we saw, both accidental being and being in the sense of being true were excluded from it. Since being, as the most general, is asserted of everything,[3] it follows for the subject of metaphysics that it comprises everything insofar as it has extramental being which is one with it and belongs to it essentially. Hence it follows that, just as the being which divides into the categories, being in the sense now under discussion is being that is independent and outside the mind [*on kath' hauto exo tes dianoias*].

> 1. The kind of being which is divided into actual [*on energeia*] and potential [*on dynamei*] is being in the sense in which this name is applied not only to that which is realized, that which exists, the really-being, but also to the mere real possibility of being.

Potential being [*on dynamei*] plays a large role in the philosophy of Aristotle, as does the concept of matter [*hyle*]. Indeed, these two concepts are coextensive,[4] while actual being [*on energeia*] is either pure form or is actualized by form.

There is a great difference between what we here mean by the potential [the *dynaton* or *dynamei on*] and what in more recent times is meant by calling something possible in contrast with real, where the necessary is added as a third thing. This is a possibility which completely abstracts from the reality of that which is called possible, and merely claims that something could exist if its existence did not involve a contradiction. It does not exist in things but in the objective concepts and combinations of concepts of the thinking mind; it is a merely rational thing.

Aristotle was quite familiar with the concept of possibility so understood, as we can see from *De interpretatione,* but it bears no relation to what he calls potential being, since otherwise it would have to be excluded from the subject of metaphysics along with being as being true. So that no doubt may remain, he mentions in *Met.* [*Metaphysics*] V. 12, as well as in IX. 1, the impossible whose contrary is necessarily true [*adynaton hou to enantion ex anankes alethes*] (*Met.* V. 12. 1019b23). The possible object [*dynaton*] which is associated with this impossibility is distinguished from the potential object [*dynaton*] which bears this name because it stands in relation to a power [*dynamis*]. It is the same only in name[5] and must be distinguished from this potentiality along with the powers of mathematics, a², b³, etc., which are powers only in a metaphorical sense [*kata metaphoran*].[6] Thus he speaks here of something which really has potential being. This is based upon his peculiar view that a non-real, something which has, properly speaking, non-being *(me on)*[7], in a manner or speaking exists insofar as it is potentially, and it is this which leads him to a special wide sense of real being, which comprises as well that which potentially is.

Now, what is this potential thing which, being real, belongs to the object of metaphysics, and which has potential being as opposed to actual being? Aristotle defines it in the third chapter of the ninth book as follows: "a thing is possible if there is nothing impossible in its having the actuality of that of which it is said to have the potentiality."[8] Two things are to be noted about this definition: (1) that Aristotle seems to define a thing through itself, since he defines the possible in terms of the impossible, and (2) the definition is based upon the concept of actuality whose understanding is therefore presupposed.

The first difficulty can be resolved as follows: the impossible [*adynaton*] in question is the contradictory. It is opposed to the possible in the logical sense which we have just discussed and not to the potential [*dynaton*] which we are now trying to comprehend.

The second difficulty forces us to direct our attention initially to actuality [*energeia*]. Potential being cannot be defined except with the aid of the concept of actuality, for the latter is prior in both concept and substance, as we are told in *Met.* IX. 8: "Actuality," he says, "is prior to potentiality both in concept and in essence." Further on he continues, "It is necessary that concept and cognition of the former precede that of the latter."[9] "Actuality" [*energeia, Wirklichkeit*] derives from "to act" *(ergo, wirken)*, a verb having to do with motion, since, as he says, it is especially motion which seems to be an actuality.[10] But the extension of the concept does not stop here.[11] What then is actuality? Aristotle does not give us a definition and declares explicitly that we should not demand one, since the concept of actuality is so basic and simple that it does not permit definition but can be clarified only inductively through examples.[12] As one of these he adduces the knower, if we mean by this expression a person who is presently engaged in an act of cognition; hence, this person is *actually* cognizing. Furthermore, a statue of Hermes is actual if it is completely sculpted, finished, and not raw wood or a marble block to which the artist has not yet put his hand. If someone knows something but is not presently engaged in the act of cognition, or if a block is rough and unsculpted, then the former is not actually cognizing, even if he could perform the act of cognition, and the latter is not actually a statue, even if it is one potentially.[13] Thus we see that we are led back to potential being; it is best to clarify the concept of actuality through the relation between actuality and potentiality. They are related "as that which is actually building to that which is capable of building, as that which is awake to that which is

asleep, as that which is seeing to that which has eyes shut, but has the power of sight, and as that which is formed from matter is to matter, and as the finished article to the raw material. In this contrast let one member be assigned to actuality, the other to potentiality."[14] We can see from this collection of examples that something is actual if it exists in complete reality; potential being lacks this reality, although "nothing impossible will result if potential being achieves the actuality of which it is said to be capable." (see above). Thus Aristotle often uses the designation "actuality" [*energeia*] and "entelechy" [*entelecheia*] interchangeably[15] where the latter means the same as consummation *(teleiotes)*,[16] as was correctly noted by Alexander and Simplicus.[17] But how? A mere potentiality in things, a merely potential thing which exists, is that not a thing which exists and yet does not have existence? Is this not a contradiction and impossibility? The Megarians did indeed see a contradiction here, as often happens if one withdraws the basis of being from contradictions which ought to be resolved. Thus they denied the merely potential, and that a thing is capable of something which is not already actual in the thing. But it is not difficult, says Aristotle,[18] to reduce such an assertion to absurdity. For then there would not be a builder who is not presently engaged in building, and no one would have an enduring ability. But it is certain that a person who has exercised an art does not at once lose his knowledge and his capability, and that he does not have to learn and acquire them for every new use, and it is equally certain that the artist remains an artist, even if he rests from his activity. Furthermore, nothing would be cold or hot, and Protagoras would be correct in his claim that all truth depends upon subjective sensation and opinion.[19] Furthermore, the man with healthy eyes and ears would often become blind and deaf during a day since, when he closes his eyes and ceases actually to see he would, on this theory, no longer see potentiality, i.e., he would have lost the very capacity to see.[20] Finally, all coming to be and passing away of things would have become a complete impossibility, for everything would be what it can be, and what it cannot be it could never become, and whatever one might say of past and future things would be a lie.[21]

In this way, Aristotle rebuts the Megarians and clarifies for us the existence and justification of his potential being. The additional examples which he adduces in this context serve to remove all doubt about the meaning of "potential being." But perhaps it is possible to employ in addition a manner of illucidation which we have used above in the determination of accidental being [*on kata symbebekos*]. I have in mind the enumeration of the different kinds of potential being, or rather of the different ways in which various things participate in this name. This can be done since "potential being" is not used univocally, but applies to the concepts which fall under it merely with a certain unity of analogy. In **Met.** V. 12. four modes are indicated in which something can be called potential. They all agree in that they are origins of something,[22] and all of them are reduced to a single principle from which they receive the name, and therein consists their analogy.[23] The first mode of potentiality which Aristotle distinguishes is the origin of motion or change in another, insofar as it is another.[24] The last clause is added on since the active principle could possibly be contained in the subject, as when something moves itself. Even then it is not moving and moved, active and passive, in one and the same respect; one and the same thing acts and receives action, but not insofar as it is the same, but insofar as it is another.[25] The second mode is the passive capacity, which is the principle whereby something is moved by another insofar as it is another.[26] Again, the last clause is added for similar reasons, since if something is passive with respect to itself, it is active not insofar as it is the same thing but insofar as it is another. The third mode of potentiality is impassivity [*hexis apatheias*], as he calls it in **Met.** IX. 1. 1046a11. This is the disposition of a thing which makes it altogether incapable of suffering or change, or at least which makes it difficult for it to change for the worse. It is the so-called capacity of resisting.[27] Finally, the fourth mode in which something is called a potentiality is the principle not just of doing or suffering something, but of doing it well and according to desire. Thus, for example, if somebody limps or stutters we do not describe him as one who can walk or talk; rather, we use these words for those who can do these things without stumbling and error. Similarly, green wood is called non-flammable, while dry wood is called flammable, etc.[28]

Corresponding to these four modes of potentiality, there are four kinds of things capable,[29] which are most adequately described not as "possible" [*moeglich*] nor as "powerful" [*maechtig*], but rather as "capable" [*vermoegend*] or "able" [*faehig*]. All of these are called capable relative to a capacity [*kata dynamin*], which does not hold for the concept which logicians connect with the word "possible" [*dynaton*].[30] As analogous concepts all of them can be reduced to the first mode of things capable and of potentiality, to the source of change in another insofar as it is another [*arche metaboles en hetero he heteron*], from which they also receive their name.[31] It is a question whether the here-indicated modes of potentiality [*dynamis*] and of things capable [*dynaton*] will attain our purpose, which was to ascertain the various modes of potential being. Is it perhaps the case that our potential being [*dynamei on*] is one and the same as the thing capable [*dynaton*] which was just mentioned? We must deny this if we wish to retain the concept of potential being [*dynamei on*], which was introduced with sufficient clarity above. Both physics and metaphysics agree that the first principle of motion is to be sought in God, but God, though certainly a thing capable [*dynaton*], is in no way a

potential being, since he is an actual being [*on energeia*] in the fullest sense of the word.[32] Hence this kind of thing capable [*dynaton*], which occupies the third position in the above order, shows us that we should not seek the modes of potential being [*dynamei on*] in those of the things capable [*dynaton*]. But how? Is there only one mode of potential being [*dynamei on*] and is this the concept of a genus in which all things designated by that name participate in the same manner? What will be the method by which we gain knowledge of the various modes of potential being?

The third chapter of the ninth book speaks of a thing capable [*dynaton*]; the entire context and the examples themselves show clearly that in this case it is identical with potential being [*dynamei on*], and it is said that it is found in every category.[33] The same holds, of course, also of actual being [*on energeia*]; thus the tenth chapter of the same book and the seventh chapter of the fifth claim that in every category some objects are said to be in actuality, others in potentiality.[34] If this is so, then it is clear that potential as well as actual being is said in many ways and can be called one only by analogy. This is necessarily the case with everything that reaches beyond the extension of any one category, as Aristotle clearly indicates in **Eth. Nic. [Nicomachean Ethics]** I.4. 1096a19 and other places. We, too, shall give a detailed demonstration of this point, and shall recognize the principles upon which it rests.[35] Consequently, Aristotle also asserts explicitly of actual being that "not everything is said to have actual being in the same, but only in an analogous way: as one is in or to a second, so a third is in or to a fourth; for some are related as operation to potency, others as form to some sort of matter."[36] And with respect to potential being [*dynamei on*] it is a major objection to Plato and the Platonists that they did not realize how every category presupposes as a different mode of being a certain determination and mode of potentiality.[37] We have already touched upon the close relation between potential and actual and being which is divided into the categories,[38] and we shall encounter a consequence of this fact, viz. the variegation of the concepts of potential as well as actual being. There are as many modes of potential being and actual being as there are categories; through the latter we shall understand the number of, and differences between, the former.

But something remains to be done for the complete determination of potential being [*dynamei on*]. The question is *at what time* is something potentially; the analogous question with respect to actual being does not occasion any doubts. It would certainly be incorrect to say of a newborn child that he is capable of speaking, of walking, or even of investigating the deepest principles of science. It is necessary that he should first grow in strength, that the germ of his talent should unfold so that he may acquire the ability, which he still lacks, to do all these things. Thus it is not correct to

Plato and Aristotle in debate, by Luca della Robbia.

say that earth is a potential statue, for one cannot make such a statue of it until its nature has been changed, and it has become, for example, ore.[39] But how, in general, can one determine when something is a potential being?

Anything which is potentially something else does not in reality become this thing except through the influence of an efficient cause. Thus to every potential being there corresponds a certain efficient cause and its activity, whether it be artificial, where the principle of realization is external to the potential being, or natural, where it resides within the latter. Anything has potential being if either nature or art can make it actual through a single action. It is potential through art if the artist can actualize it whenever he wants to, provided only that there is no external hindrance; thus, for example, something is called potentially healthy (curable) if it can become healthy through one application of medical art. Something is potential through nature if it can be lead to actuality by its peculiar active principle or its inherent natural power, provided only that no external hindrance stands in the way. In this manner, something is potentially healthy if there is nothing in the sick body which must be removed before nature can exercise her healing force. But wherever other changes are presupposed before the proper process of actualization can begin, there is no potential being. Trees which must first be felled and dressed, or the stuff which must first transform itself into a tree, these are not potentially a house; but when the beams from which it can be erected are finished, then one can say that the house has potential being. Thus the earth is not potentially a man, and even the semen is not, but if the foetus can become an actual man through its peculiar active principle, then it is already potentially a man.[40]

All this confirms anew the determinations given above of the concepts of actual being [*on energeia*] and potential being [*on dynamei*] so that there can be no further doubt about the sense which Aristotle connects with the word 'being' [*on*], insofar as he comprehends under it not only fully actualized, but also unactualized being, which is only potentially whatever it is, and strives toward and desires its form, as it were.[41]

> 2. Connections between states of potentiality and actuality. Movement [*kinesis*] as actuality which constitutes a thing as being in a state of potentiality.

In the previous section we have considered what Aristotle meant by actual being [*on energeia*] and potential being [*on dynamis*]. The latter appeared as being which was as such incomplete, and this is the reason why the perfect separate substance, God, does not in any way partake of potential being, but is pure actuality. On the other hand, if a thing is composed of substance and accident, matter and form, then this imperfection results in its not being free of potentiality; for such a thing actual being consists of a union of potential being with actuality.[42] This is not inconsistent, as can be seen from the definition of potential being itself.

But aside from the *what* of potential and actual being we have also noted a *when* for both. For potential being we did so following Aristotle, while it is of itself clear that for actual being the state of its actualization through form must correspond to its completion. But while there is no doubt that this union of potential and actual being actually occurs, a union of the *states* which correspond to one or the other does not seem possible since the state corresponding to unactualized potential being is a state prior to actualization which, however, can be brought about through a single process of becoming. . . . Yet even their union is in a sense not inconsistent; of course, we do not here speak of a simultaneous union, for if a body is now potentially and later actually white, then this union in the subject is not properly called a union of states, and there are no problems with respect to this matter. A simultaneous union, however, is possible in this way: something which is actually ore is in a state of potentiality with respect to a certain figure, etc. This is a union no different from those occuring between something that has actual being with a second and a third thing which has actual being, as when one and the same subject is actually a body, actually large, actually green, etc. In this case, the actuality of that which actually is does not belong to the potential object as such; for example, the actuality of the ore belongs to the ore as ore but not as potential statue.[43] In the same manner we can explain the union of something actually alive with the potential corpse, etc. But there is a second manner in which both states can be united, and this occurs in the state of becoming, *on kinesei,* as Aristotle calls it.

In **Met.** XI. 9 he gives the following remarkable definition of motion [*kinesis*], which is not easily comprehensible in spite of everything he has already taught us about potentiality and actuality. He says this: "The actuality *(energeia)* of the potential *(tou dynamei ontos)* as such I call movement." Similarly, in the first chapter of Book III of the **Physics:** "Since being of every kind is divided into actual and potential being, the actuality *(entelecheia)* of potential being as such is motion." And farther down: "It is obvious that the actuality of what is potential as potential is movement."[44]

This definition makes it clear, first of all, that by potential being or the potential (*dynamei on, dynaton*), we are to understand that which is in a state of potentiality; for if we were to take it in the sense in which all matter as such, even after its union with form, is to be called something merely potential, then aside from the separate substances, every form would have to be called an actuality of a potential being, and nothing peculiar to movement would have been indicated.

But there is something else which causes problems: the words "the actuality of potential being" can be interpreted in two ways, as can be seen in the following: every form or actuality which is not a separate substance can be called an actuality of something in two ways: (1) as the actuality of the substratum, for example when we say of the soul that it is the actuality of the physical body which is potentially alive;[45] and (2) as the actuality of the composite which was formed from matter through its union with form, for example when we say of the soul that it is the actuality of the living being. Since in our definition movement was described as the actuality of something, viz., of potential being, the question is whether this potential being is to be construed as subject or as something which is constituted through movement. Each interpretation, despite the difference, gives a true sense which agrees with what has been said so far, and which therefore ultimately coincides with the other. Let us show this by looking at both of them more closely. According to the first interpretation, which is adopted by most commentators,[46] our definition would determine movement to be a form which has the following characteristics: as it brings its subject from the corresponding state of potentiality to [the] actuality [of movement], it leaves it in a state of potentiality to another thing. This other thing is such that the subject was in a state of potentiality to it by virtue of being in a state of potentiality to the actuality of the movement itself.

To understand this, we must remember what was said in the preceding section in answer to the question at what time something is a potential being. Something has potentiality if nature or art can make it an actuality through a single action, hence if it can be actualized through a single becoming. But this becoming, even if it must be single, does not have to be momentary. If a black body becomes white through a single change, it does not follow that it changes suddenly. Thus becoming and consummation do not coincide here; first the subject partakes in becoming, and then achieves its completion. Hence, here the subject has a double potentiality, viz. (1) to the becoming of the form, and (2) to the form itself. Yet this double state of potentiality is in itself and in its concept only a single one. For if a black body is capable of becoming white through a single becoming (hence as a potentiality to the becoming-of-the-form), it is obviously in a state of potentiality to whiteness. Now, if a subject is transferred from this state of potentiality to actuality with respect to becoming, then it is also transferred to a new and heightened state of potentiality with respect to the form which is the consummation of becoming.[47] It is a heightened state insofar as the state of becoming is that from which the subject immediately achieves complete actuality, while the state before the state of becoming must

first be changed into the state of becoming so that the subject may thereafter be transferred into a state of consummate actuality. Hence commentators have described this state as a third, intervening, state between mere potentiality and actuality;[48] this state of an actual tendency after the act is being qua movement [*on kinesei*], while movement [*kinesis*] is that becoming which actualizes but does not completely exhaust potentiality.

Thus there are no further difficulties in understanding the definition. The kind of thing something is [*he toiouton esti*] distinguishes this kind of union between states of potentiality and actuality from the one mentioned above in which, for example, the actuality of the ore as ore coexisted with the potentiality of being a statue.[49]

The authority of almost all commentators speaks for this interpretation; yet, as mentioned above, there is still another possible interpretation which has its own advantages. The first interpretation made good sense with respect to movement [*kinesis*], yet it does not seem free of inaccuracies. For if the double potentiality of the subject were really only *one,* both in itself and according to the concept (*haplos kai kata ton logon,* **Physics** III. 1. 201a32), then it would be impossible for this state to be terminated with respect to one of them, and to continue with respect to the other. For if it is terminated with respect to whatever, then it is completely terminated, hence for both. And if only the becoming of the form has become actual, while the form itself is still potentiality, it has not remained in the previous, but in a new and more advanced state of potentiality, viz. precisely its state of becoming. Thus in a sense a subject has remained in a state of potentiality, just as I can say of something which is now white and then red that it has remained in a state of actuality with respect to color, although it is now colored by virtue of a different state of actuality than before; but in the strict sense the subject has not *remained* in a state of potentiality; rather, it has been transferred from one state of potentiality to a second state which aims at the same form, i.e., it is in a state of becoming, which is constituted by movement.

Thus, if the great authority of the men who maintained the first interpretation did not make me hesitate, I would unquestionably prefer the second, according to which the definition determines as follows: Movement is the actuality of the potential as such, just as the form of the ore is the actuality of the ore as such, i.e., it is the actuality *(energeia)* which makes something that is potentially *(tou dynamei ontos)* into that which it is *(he toiouton esti),* viz. into this potential being. In other words, it constitutes and forms a potential (it constitutes and forms something which is in a state of potentiality as being in this state). After what has been said, the definition when put this way has no further difficulties. This interpretation has the advantage that it makes the definition not only more precise, but also simpler. Let the following contribute to its comprehensibility, where we make constant reference to the appropriate passages in Aristotle to show that our argumentation agrees with his meaning. We shall show (1) that there are potentialities which are constituted as such through some actuality, (2) that this is not the case with all potential states, and (3) that where it is the case, the constituting actuality is a movement.

The first point is likely to provoke the most doubt and opposition, hence we want to treat it with special care. Thus we shall conduct our proof as follows: we shall show (1) that in many cases there are two different states of potentiality which are related to the same state of actuality; and (2) that, where there is such a multiplicity of potential states, at least one of them must be constituted (or formed) by some actuality. We begin by referring back to the previous section, in which we saw that aside from that which is in a state of actuality [the *energeia on*], there is also being in the state of potentiality [*on dynamei*].[50] But in virtue of what is something constituted an actual being [*on energeia*]? Obviously, through a form or actuality. But what about a potential being? Is it, too, constituted (formed) as such by something? It is indeed difficult to believe that a state of potentiality as such can be constituted through a form, which is, after all, an actuality;[51] yet this is the case, provided only that there is a double state of potentiality with respect to the same form, as we have just said. . . .

Let us again consider and confirm this fact. We have said that there is often a double state of potentiality with respect to the same actuality, and this was derived from another truth which was proved earlier (p. 37), viz. that there are double states of potentiality, i.e., that there are things which, by virtue of one and the same state (one and the same in itself and in concept *(haplos kai kata ton logon),* have potentiality to two different actualities. For example, something which is potentially white has potentiality for whiteness and also for becoming-white by virtue of one and the same state, since a single operation, namely white-making, actualizes both (see above). From this we have concluded that if both actualities could occur only one after the other, the first of them would have to terminate the state of potentiality with respect to the second, for the two states of potentiality are one and the same. But since the subject maintained the potentiality to the second form, it could do so only by virtue of a second, new state of potentiality to this form. . . . It follows from this that there are two states of potentiality corresponding to this actuality. Hence there is a double state of potentiality with respect to the same actuality.

We can support this argument by a second one. If there is a state of potentiality with respect to a form from which and by virtue of which the subject can immediately attain possession of actuality, and if there is a state of potentiality with respect to the same form, from which and by virtue of which the subject cannot immediately attain possession of actuality, then these two states are distinct and there is a double state of potentiality with respect to one and the same form. But the antecedent of this conditional proposition is true, hence also the consequent. For it is true that a stone which is thrown is capable (has potentiality) of reaching a certain location toward which it has been thrown, and that from the state in which it is now, viz. the state of a-thing-being-thrown, it immediately attains a state of rest having reached its target. And it is true that a stone which rests in a certain location is capable of attaining another location since it can get there through a single throw, and yet it cannot immediately get there from the state in which it is before the throw; it must first attain the state of being-thrown. Here we have an example of two states of potentiality with respect to the same actuality. We take this argument from Aristotle himself when he says, in the second book of the **Metaphysics,** that there is a double way in which something comes from something, as a man from a boy who matured to manhood, or the air from water; in the first case, that which is becoming changes into that which has become, out of that which is in the process of completion (actualization) there arises the completed (the actual). "For," he says, "there is always an intermediate: just as becoming is between being and nonbeing, so that which is becoming is between what is and what is not."[52]

We take a further confirmation of our claim from the same passage: that we have here two different states follows from the fact that there is a characteristic which is peculiar to one of them, but which the other lacks. Something can pass from a state of becoming into a state of actuality, but not vice versa; for what is already white cannot become white. But from the state of potentiality prior to becoming, a thing attains the state of actuality, and conversely; for the black is potentially white, and after it has actually become white, it is potentially black and can therefore return to this state.[53]

But wherever such a multiplicity of potential states is found, at least *one* must as such be constituted (formed) through an actuality. This is perfectly clear and certain. For privation as such does not constitute anything. It is itself only accidental being [*on kata symbebekos*] and, taken by itself, has no existence at all;[54] while matter, as such, is undifferentiated, and since it receives all its determinations from the form through which it is what it is, there can be only *one* matter with respect to one and the same form.[55] Hence, how could this matter produce the difference between the state of becoming and the state of the potentiality to the same form prior to becoming? Impossible! Rather, only one thing is possible, viz. that the difference between the two states of potentiality is produced by a form, so that at least one of the two states as such is constituted (formed) through an actuality. And this is what we had wanted to prove in the first place, and what at first sight is liable to occasion considerable doubt, i.e., that there are states of potentiality which are constituted as such through an actuality.

One can also show this in another way once the above established proposition has been secured, i.e., that one and the same state of potentiality (one and the same both in itself and in concept, see above p. 37) is a state of potentiality with respect to two actualities. For if the two actualities considered by themselves are two, then they must be one in their relation [*in der Ordnung*] to this state of potentiality, and so one of them must be a function of the other [*zur andern hingeordnet sein*], hence must give the subject an actual tendency toward itself, i.e., toward a new state of potentiality which is closer to it, an intermediate state between the first and actuality.[56]

Now we come to the second point. If the preceding investigation has made it clear that many things which are in a state of potentiality are constituted as such through a form, this is not to say that this must be the case with everything that is in a state of potentiality. On the contrary, this, too, would be an error; consequently, we find Aristotle opposing it in the third book of the ***Physics*** and the corresponding part of the eleventh book of the ***Metaphysics.*** Let us now give a somewhat more complete version of his argumentation. If something is in a state of potentiality, and is constituted as such by an actuality, then (1) it must be in a state of actuality, and (2) it must, as such, have a form, and therefore an essence and a concept which determines this form, for each form issues in an essence. From this it follows, for instance, that a motionless waxen ball, which is potentially a cube, is not constituted by an actuality as being in that particular state [of potentiality]. For, of all the forms which are in a wax ball, it can only be the actuality of the wax as wax, or the softness of the wax, which lend it a certain disposition that facilitates reshaping it. But when the wax ball has become a cube, the form of the wax as wax, hence also its softness, hence everything through which the wax was formerly constituted remains; now, if this were a state of potentiality, hence a state prior to actuality, then the cube which has come about would not yet be a cube, which is contradictory. Hence, one would have to believe that it is the form of the wax ball as a sphere which constitutes the potentiality of becoming a cube; for it is indeed true that whatever has the shape of a sphere cannot at the same time be a cube. But against this a second argument can be advanced which is also decisive with respect to the previously mentioned form of the wax. The wax ball is a potentiality not only to the form of the cube but to a thousand

other shapes as well. Hence, all these states of potentiality would have to be constituted through the form of the ball (or the wax) if the wax ball as sphere (or as wax) were indeed presently in a state of potentiality, and hence they would have to be identical with the sphere (with the wax) as such (i.e., in themselves and in this essence and concept). But this is impossible; for if two are identical with the same third thing, then they are identical with each other, and hence the innumerable different states of potentiality to become a cube, a tetrahedron, a dodecahedron, a icosahedron and other regular and irregular forms would have to be both in themselves and in concept [*haplos kai kata ton logon*] identical, although they are as different as these forms themselves which diverge from each other in a number of directions. Hence, it has been established that the wax ball by being constituted as wax through the actuality of the wax, and as a sphere through the spherical figure, is not constituted through any of its actualities as having a state of potentiality to become a cube. Hence it has a potentiality to be in this state without being constituted in this respect by any of its actualities.[57]

We come to the third point. Having seen that there are two kinds of states of potentiality, one of which is constituted as such by an actuality while the other is not, the question now is which states of potentiality are constituted by an actuality or, what comes to the same, which actualities constitute potential states as such.

All potential being as such stands in a relation to an active principle; for the subject is potentially something if it can become an actuality through a single act of an active principle. Thus we must also examine those states of potentiality which are constituted as such through an actuality in their relation to an active principle and its operation. Thus a state of potentiality to become something exists in a subject either before the operation, or during the operation, or after the operation of the force through whose activity it is transformed into a state of actuality. But it can obviously not exist *after* the activity, for if the activity has passed nothing remains that can be realized through this activity; what this activity was capable of actualizing either exists now or has existed in actuality. With respect to this activity at least it does certainly not exist in potentiality, whether or not the latter be constituted through a form. Hence, it remains to consider the states of the subject prior to and during the activity. But the state of potentiality which exists in the subject *prior to* the activity cannot be constituted through an actuality. For at that point there are only three forms in the subject which must be considered. One is to be envisaged as the *terminus a quo* for the change, as for example the spherical figure of the wax which is to be transformed into a cube. A second, which is the most deceptive and is therefore the only one considered by Aristotle, is the form which constitutes the subject as that which it actually is. In the case of the wax ball, this is the actuality which constitutes the wax as wax. Finally, there is a third form, in the case of the wax it is softness, which lends a certain disposition to the subject.[58] But in considering the second point we have already shown that none of these forms constitutes a potential being as such. Hence the latter, as such, does not possess any actuality. On the other hand, the state of potentiality in which the subject is *during* the activity of the active principle is indeed a state which is constituted, as such, through an actuality. For the principle acts only to the extent in which the subject receives an influence, i.e., something actual. Now, if the subject is still in a state of potentiality with respect to this force and its activity, then this is due to a further state of potentiality: we have shown this above when we discussed the first point, and everything else said there applies here as well.

The only remaining question is what we should call those states of potentiality which exist during the activity of the acting principle and what to call those actualities which potentialize the subject, as it were. We commonly call them states of becoming or movement,[59] and as movement they must be considered actualities which constitute a potential thing as potential. Induction shows this. While the builder builds, that with which he builds is in a state of potentiality which is constituted by actuality, but the building material as such was only a potentiality with respect to house construction and to the edifice. Either the actuality of constructing or the actuality of the edifice must therefore be that which constitutes that higher state of potentiality. But not that of the edifice, for the edifice as such is no longer a potentiality with respect to the builder and this building activity of his; hence, the actuality in question must be the building activity *(oikodomesis),* and this is indeed a movement *(kinesis).* One can give a similar demonstration with respect to all other movements.[60] If that which is potentially a building is constituted as such through an actuality, then it is presently in the process of being erected, and just this is house construction, hence movement. The same occurs when something heals, when there is a revolution, a jump, etc.[61] Hence, movement is the actuality of that which is in a state of potentiality as such, the actuality of the potential as potential. For example, the movement toward a quality *(alloiosis)* constitutes that which is becoming a *quale (poion)* in this state of potentiality toward a quality; similarly, the movement toward quantity *(auxesis kai phthisis)* constitutes that which is about to become a quantum *(poson)* in this state of potentiality toward a quantity; furthermore, locomotion *(phora)* constitutes that which moves toward a goal in this state of potentiality for a location. Now, if there is such an intermediate state of potentiality also in the domain of the substantial, then the state of substantial becoming and passing away through generation and corruption *(genesis kai phthora)*

must be formally constituted in the same way, and these, too, will be movements.[62]

Aristotle, after he has advanced and positively supported his view of movement, seeks to support it further by a polemic against definitions of earlier philosophers, which seems to be aimed especially at Plato;[63] he does so in the *Physics* III.2. and the corresponding part of the eleventh book of the *Metaphysics.* Here as elsewhere his polemic is never unfruitful, since it always manages to find and isolate what is correct in a mistaken position. He notes that earlier attempts had defined movement as otherness, as inequality, and as non-being. None of these definitions describe the essence of movement, for none of these need to be moved, neither that which is other, nor that which is unequal, nor that which has non-being. It is peculiar to the state of becoming that that which is in the state of becoming has a potentiality to acquire the state of that which has become, while that which has become does not have a state of potentiality to acquire that particular state of becoming from which it arose, as we have seen above,[64] while, on the other hand, the equal passes into the unequal, as well as the unequal into the equal, and being into non-being, as well as non-being into being, etc.[65] But what occasioned these mistaken definitions? There is indeed something in the nature of movement which could lead one to put it into the order[66] of privation. Since becoming does not form a special species of things, but must be reduced to the species of accomplished being,[67] as that which is growing large to largeness, and that which is in the process of acquiring a certain characteristic to that characteristic, one is inclined to take it for something indeterminate, something lacking form. What else is one to make of movement? The potentiality *(dynamis)* by virtue of which something is potentially is not movement, and what is actually [*energeia*] something is also not in motion; thus the only thing left seems to declare motion to be an unfinished actuality [*energeia*], an accomplished reality [*entelecheia*] for which there is no completion, which, unless we envisage it as a privation, seems to be a contradiction. But the puzzle is resolved in this way: as actualization [*energeia*], movement constitutes something as being in a state of potentiality as such, and the potential is of course incomplete;[68] hence, that which completes [*vollendet*] is indeed a state of incompleteness;[69] it actualizes a state which is prior to actuality. "Therefore," says Aristotle, "it is difficult to grasp what movement is, for one either thinks that it either has to be defined as a privation or as a potentiality, or simply as an actuality; yet none of these seem possible. Hence the indicated way is the only one that remains, namely that it is an actuality, but the kind we have described, which is difficult to grasp, but nonetheless possible."[70]

Thus it becomes clear how, under this interpretation of the definition, everything Aristotle teaches about movement agrees. For what we have just touched upon, viz. that movement does not form a special species of being, but follows the various species as does actuality as such, and potentiality as well, is also fully consonant with this. Movement as actuality constitutes a state of potentiality. Since the states of potentiality belong to the same genus as the corresponding states of actuality, just as the possible body belongs, with the actual body, to the genus of substance, and the potentially white belongs, with the actually white, to the genus of color and of quality, etc., in the same way the thing-in-motion [*on kinesei*] and motion [*kinesis*] must be reduced to the particular species of that which comes about through this motion, and must belong to the same genera as the complete being. This is not to say that there is a motion [*kinesis*] in every species of being, as there is a potentiality [*dynamis*] and an actuality [*energeia*]. A state of becoming, i.e., a second state of potentiality which is to be formed by the proper movement, can occur only where there is gradual, continuous becoming, and this can be found only where there are contrary concepts, and hence intermediate states, which are absent where there is an opposition of contradictories. The transformation from non-being to being can only be sudden and momentary. After having declared in **Physics** III. 1 and **Met.** XI. 9[71] that "there are as many kinds of movement and change as there are kinds of being," Aristotle delineates these matters at some length in the third book of the **Physics** (and the corresponding part of the eleventh book of the **Metaphysics**[72]) and makes the qualification that proper movement is to be restricted to the three categories of quality, quantity and location, where alone the requisite conditions are satisfied, as he shows by a careful investigation.[73]

Still and all, we do not actually wish to contest the first interpretation; despite the considerable formal difference of the two interpretations they do not, in the end, differ essentially, as we have already pointed out. We note that according to both of them the thing in motion [*on kinesei*] exemplifies a peculiar mode of union of a potential and an actual state. The second interpretation allows this union to be very clearly indicated in the definition of motion, by saying that motion is an actuality which, by producing its actual state, constitutes a state of potentiality, i.e., constitutes the potential as potential. We see that here, too, the subject which is in the state of becoming occupies an intermediate state between a more distant potentiality and actuality; but by being in this one state, it has simultaneously a state of actuality with respect to becoming, movement; it has potentiality with respect to the form which is approached through movement.

This middle state is also attained by potentialities which have the peculiar characteristic that there cannot be a complete reality corresponding to the potentiality. Just as the concept of movement has something in it which

is difficult to grasp, and which at first occasions astonishment and doubts concerning the correctness of the definition (cf. **Met.** I. 2; 983a14), many will find it difficult to admit, initially, that there can be a potentiality to which no actuality corresponds, at least not one which exists *in rebus* though perhaps one which is thought and comprised within its concept since, they will say, something is called potential only in relation to an actuality. Yet such is the case, as the example of any line and of any solid clearly shows. The line, which in actuality is one, can be halved, and thus is potentially two, and since the half is capable of further division, it is potentially four; hence, it is potentially two, four, eight, sixteen, etc. But what is the limit of this potentiality? It does not have a limit; while it is in actuality one, it is potentially infinitely many. But this potentiality is never exhausted by an actuality. The infinitely many lines which are now contained as parts in one line will never actually exist as infinitely many actual lines. Here, and wherever else we are concerned with bodies,[74] the infinite exists always only in a state of potentiality, either as a state of potentiality prior to movement (one line has infinitely many parts), or as thing in motion *(on kinesei),* when a division into infinity is attempted. Similar considerations hold for surfaces, bodies, and other things.[75]

So much for being insofar as it comprises real potentiality, becoming, and that which is in a state of complete being, being in the sense of potential and actual being [*on dynamei kai energeia*].

Notes

[1] Cf. Brandis, *op. cit.,* III, 1, 46, n. 85 and the passage from Prantl quoted there.

[2] Books VII and VIII deal with the being [*on*] of the categories and of substance [*ousia*] respectively, Book IX of potential and actual being [*dynamei kai energeia on*].

[3] See above p. 1.

[4] Cf. Zeller, *Philosophie der Griechen,* II, 2, p. 238, n. 5. Matter [*hyle*] must of course be taken in a wider sense in which it includes, in addition to primary matter [*prote hyle*], also the subjects of the accidents. Then Zeller's remark is correct that "a thing is potentially [*dynamei*] only insofar as it has matter [*hyle*] within itself." *Met.* XIV. 1. 1088b1: "The matter of each thing must be that which is potentially of the nature in question."

[5] *Met.* V. 12. 1019b21: "Some things, then, are called *adynata* [not potent] in virtue of this kind of incapacity, while others are so in another sense; i.e., both *dynaton* and *adynaton* are used as follows, etc." As belonging to this merely rational possibility [*dynaton*]

he enumerates: "The possible, then, in one sense, means that which is not of necessity false; in one that which is true; in one, that which may be true." Cf. *Met.* IX. 1. 1046a8.

[6] *Met.* V. 12. 1019b33: "A 'potency' or 'power' in geometry is so-called by a change of meaning." Cf. *Met.* IX. 1. 1046a7: "Some are called so by analogy." The similarity consists in this: that just as potential being turns into actual being, so from the multiplication of the root with itself is generated the magnitude whose root it is.

[7] *Met.* XIV. 2. 1089a28.

[8] *Met.* IX. 3. 1047a24: "And a thing is capable of doing something if there will be nothing impossible in its having the actuality of that of which it is said to have the capacity. I mean, for instance, if a thing is capable of sitting and it is open to it to sit, there will be nothing impossible in its actually sitting; and similarly if it is capable of being moved or moving, or of standing or of making to stand, or of being or coming to be, or of not-being or not coming to be."

[9] *Met.* IX. 8. 1049b10: "To all such potency, then, actuality is prior both in formula and in substantiality . . . so that the formula and the knowledge of the one must precede the knowledge of the other."

[10] *Met.* IX. 3. 1047a30: "The word 'actuality', which we connect with 'complete reality', has, in the main, been extended from movements to other things; for actuality in the strict sense is thought to be identical with movement."

[11] *Ibid.,* 6. 1048a25.

[12] *Ibid.,* a35: "Our meaning can be seen in the particular cases by induction, and we must not seek a definition of everything."

[13] *Ibid.,* a30: "Actuality, then, is the existence of a thing not in the way which we express by 'potentially'; we say that potentially, for instance, a statue of Hermes is in the block of wood and the half-line is in the whole, because it might be separated out, and we call even the man who is not studying a man of science, if he is capable of studying; the thing that stands in contrast to each of these exists actually."

[14] *Met.* IX. 6. 1048a36: "And we must not seek a definition of everything but be content to grasp the analogy, that it is as that which is building is to that which is capable of building, and the waking to the sleeping, and that which is seeing to that which has its eyes shut but has sight, and that which has been shaped out of the matter to the matter, and that which has been wrought up to the unwrought. Let actuality be defined by one member of this antithesis, and the potential by the other." Cf. Schwegler concerning the reading of this passage.

[15] Cf. Schwegler, *Metaphysik des Aristoteles,* 4, 222.

[16] Ancient as well as recent commentators are in disagreement concerning the distinction between *"energeia"* and *"entelecheia",* but the difference between their opinions is much larger than the difference between the concepts that are designated by these two names. They are indeed applied to different things. It is not so much the case that they differ from one another, but that each differs from itself in different uses [contexts]; for "actual being" [*on energeia*] is not a univocally, but an analogously used name, as we shall see when the categories are discussed. Thus it could happen that commentators came to opposing views depending on the passage upon which they focussed. Many attribute more consummate reality to *entelecheia* than to *energeia,* while Schwegler claims *(op. cit.)* "*energeia* is the activity (self-employment) in consummate being, while *entelecheia* is striving activity connected with *dynamis.*" *On energeia* as well as *on entelecheia* mean that which is realized and completed through form. But while the designation *"entelecheia"* expresses this through the very word, the name *"energeia"* is taken from movements (as Aristotle teaches, cf. above, n. 10) not because that which is in motion is *energeia* in the fullest sense, but of all realities movement strikes our eye first. Movement is not asserted of anything that is not real, while other predicates, such as thinkable and desirable, also apply to non-being (Arist., *ibid*).

[17] In connection with *Physics* 358a19 ff.

[18] *Met.* IX. 3. 1046b29: "There are some who say, as the Megaric school does, that a thing 'can' act only when it is acting and when it is not acting it 'cannot' act, e.g., that he who is not building cannot build, but only he who is building, when he is building; and so in all other cases. It is not hard to see the absurdities that attend this view. For it is clear that on this view a man will not be a builder unless he is building (for to be a builder is to be able to build)."

[19] *Met.* IX. 3. 1047a4.

[20] *Ibid.,* a7.

[21] *Ibid.,* a10.

[22] *Met.* IX. 1. 1046a9: "All are originative sources of some kind."

[23] See below chap. 5, sect. 3.

[24] *Met.* V. 12. 1019a15: "'potency' means a source of

movement or change, which is in another thing than the thing moved or in the same thing *qua* other, etc."

[25] Cf. below chap. 5, sect. 13.

[26] *Met.* V. 12. 1019a20. "'Potency' then means the source of change or movement by another thing or by itself qua other."

[27] *Ibid.,* a26: "The states in virtue of which things are absolutely impassive or unchangeable, or not easily changed for the worse, are called potencies; for things are broken and crushed and bent and in general destroyed, not by having a potency but by not having one and by lacking something, and things are impassive with respect to such processes if they are scarcely and slightly affected by them because of a 'potency' and because they 'can' do something and are in some positive state."

[28] *Met.* V. 12. 1019a23: "The capacity of performing this well or according to intention . . . so too, in the case of passivity." This kind of potentiality [*dynamis*] is here actually mentioned in the third place. According to the order which is used in IX. 1, which we have followed, and which corresponds to the order of things capable [*dynata*], we have introduced it as the fourth.

[29] *Ibid.,* a32 ff.

[30] See above, n. 5.

[31] *Ibid.,* b35: "But the senses which involve a reference to potency all refer to the primary kind of potency; and this is a source of change in another thing or in the same thing *qua* other. For other things are called 'capable', because something else has such a potency over them, some because it has not, some because it has it in a particular way, etc."

[32] In order for something to be a potential being [*dynamei on*] it does not suffice that the principle of an activity should be found in it; doing [*poiein*] must also belong to it as a proper accident (see below, chap. 5, sect. 13). This is not the case with God.

[33] *Met.* IX. 3. 1047a20: "So that it is possible that a thing may be capable of being and not *be,* and capable of not-being and yet *be,* and similarly with the other kinds of predicates; it may be capable of walking and yet not walk or capable of not walking and yet walk."

[34] *Met.* IX. 10. 1051a34: "The terms 'being' and 'non-being' are employed firstly with reference to the categories, and secondly with reference to the potency or actuality of these or their non-potency or non-actuality." V. 7. 1017a35: "Again, 'being' and 'that which is' mean that some of the things we have mentioned 'are' potentially, others in complete reality." (At this point he has already discussed the categories.) Cf. also *De anima* II. 1. 412a6.

[35] See below chap. 5, sect. 3.

[36] *Met.* IX. 6. 1048b6: "But all things are not said in the *same sense* to exist actually, but only by analogy—as A is in B or to B, C is in D or to D; (for this reading cf. Bonitz, *Observationes criticae in Aristotelis libros Metaphysicae* [Berlin, 1842]). Some are as movement to potency, and the others as substance to some sort of matter." Cf. below, chap. 5, sect. 13.

[37] *Met.* XIV. 2. 1089a34: "Now it is strange to enquire how being in the sense of 'what' is many, and not how either qualities or quantities are many." b15: "What is the reason, then, why there is a plurality of these? It is necessary, then, as we say, to presuppose for each thing that which it is potentially." See *Met.* X. 3. 1054b28.

[38] Cf. the beginning of this chapter.

[39] *Met.* IX. 7. 1049a17: "Just as earth is not yet potentially a statue (for it must first change in order to become brass)."

[40] *Met.* IX. 7. 1049a3: "Just as not everything can be healed by the medical art or by luck, but there is a certain kind of thing which is capable of it, and only this is potentially healthy. And (1) the delimiting mark of that which as a result of *thought* comes to exist in complete reality from having existed potentially is that if the agent has willed it it comes to pass if nothing external hinders, while the condition on the other side—viz. in that which is healed—is that nothing in it hinders the result. It is on similar terms that we have what is potentially a house; if nothing in the thing acted on—i.e., in the matter—prevents it from becoming a house, and if there is nothing which must be added or taken away or changed, this is potentially a house; and the same is true of all other things the source of whose becoming is external. And (2) in the cases in which the source of the becoming is in the very thing which comes to be, a thing is potentially all those things which it will be of itself if nothing external hinders it. E.g., the seed is not yet potentially a man; for it must be deposited in something other than itself and undergo a change. But when through its own motive principle it has already got such and such attributes, in this state it is already potentially a man; while in the former state it needs another motive principle, just as earth is not yet potentially a statue (for it must first change in order for it to become brass)."

[41] Cf. *Physics* I. 9. 192b16.

[42] E.g., *De anima,* II. 1. 412a6: "We are in the habit of recognizing, as one determinate kind of what is, substance, and that in several senses, (a) in the sense of

matter or that which in itself is not 'a this', and (b) in the sense of form or essence which is that precisely in virtue of which a thing is called 'a this', and thirdly (c) in the sense of that which is compounded of both (a) and (b). Now matter is potentiality, form, actuality."

[43] Cf. *Physics* III. 1. 201a29. *Ibid.,* 21.

[44] *Met.* XI. 9. 1065b16: "I call the actuality of the potential as such, movement." *Physics* III. 1. 201a9: "We have now before us the distinctions in the various classes of being between what is fully real and what is potential. *The fulfillment of what exists potentially, insofar as it exists potentially, is motion.*" *Ibid.* b4: "Clearly it is the fulfillment of what is potential *as* potential that is motion."

[45] *De anima,* II. 1. 412a19: "Hence this soul must be a substance in the sense of the form of a natural body having life potentially within it. But substance is actuality, and thus soul is the actuality of a body as above characterized."

[46] E.g., Simplicius, *In Aristotelis Physicorum commentarium,* ed. Hermann Diels, *Com. in Arist. Gr.,* IX (Berlin 1882), 414: "Whenever a thing changes from potentiality to actuality, with the potentiality remaining in the thing, we say it moves." Similarly Themistius and otheo.

[47] Philiponus, *In Aristotelis Physicorum libros tres priores commentaria,* ed. Hieronymus Vitelli, *Com. in Arist. Gr.* 16 (Berlin 1887), 351: "They explain motion (Themistius changed this somewhat) as the first entelechy of potential being as such; for the final entelechy is the transition to the form in which it remains thereafter; by contrast, the first entelechy is the passage toward the form; and this is motion."

[48] *Simplicius, loc. cit.:* "Therefore, insofar as something is in actuality, it moves not at all. Also insofar as something potential remains potential and merely capacity, we would not say that it moves. But when it changes from potentiality to actuality, and the potentiality remains in it, then we say it moves."

[49] *Physics* III. 1. 201a29. Also *Met.* XI. 9.

[50] *Physics* III. 1. 201a9: "The distinctions in the various classes of being between what is fully real and what is potential. . . . " Similarly *Met.* XI. 9.

[51] *De anima,* II. 1. 412a8: "Now matter is potentiality, form actuality." *Met.* VIII. 2. 1043a27: "One kind of it [is substance] as matter, another as form or actuality."

[52] *Met.* II. 2. 994a22: "For one thing comes *from* another in two ways—not in the sense in which 'from' means 'after' (as we say 'from the Isthmian games

come the Olympian'), but either (1) as the man comes from the boy, by the boy's changing or (2) as air comes from water. By 'as the man comes from the boy' we mean 'as that which has come to be from that which is coming to be. Or as that which is finished from that which is being achieved' (for as becoming is between being and not being, so that which is becoming is always between that which is and that which is not; for the learner is a man of science in the making, and this is what is meant when we say that *from* a learner a man of science is being made); on the other hand, coming from another thing as water comes from air implies the destruction of the other thing."

[53] *Met.* II. 2. 994a31: "This is why changes of the former kind are not reversible, and the boy does not come from the man (for it is not that which comes to be something that comes to be as a result of coming to be, but that which exists after the coming to be; for it is thus that the day, too, comes from the morning—in the sense that it comes after the morning; which is the reason why the morning cannot come from the day); but changes of the other kind are reversible."

[54] See above, pp. 8f.

[55] *Met.* VIII. 2. 1043a12: "The actuality or the formula is different when the matter is different."

[56] *Met.* II. 2. See above, n. 52.

[57] *Physics* III. 1. 201a31: "For 'to be bronze' and 'to be a certain potentiality [for motion]' are not the same. . . . (This is obvious in contraries. 'To be capable of health' and 'to be capable of illness' are not the same, for if they were there would be no difference between being ill and being well. Yet the *subject* both of health and of sickness—whether it is humor or blood—is one and the same.) We can distinguish, then, between the two just as, to give another example, 'color' and 'visible' are different, and clearly it is the fulfillment of what is potential *as* potential that is motion."

[58] *Physics* III. 1. Cf. the preceding note.

[59] *Physics* III. 1. 201a27: "[the fulfillment of] a potential thing, as thing moved, is motion, whenever this fully real being is in the process of bringing about (either itself or another)." [Brentano relies on a different reading than Ross for this difficult passage. We translate the Brentano version. The quotation continues:] "what I mean by 'as' is this: bronze is potentially a statue. But it is not the fulfillment of bronze as *bronze* which is motion. For 'to be bronze' and 'to be a certain potentiality' are not the same."

[60] *Physics* III. 1. 201b5: "further it is evident that motion is an attribute of a thing just *when* it is fully real in this way, and neither before nor after. For each thing of

this kind is capable of being at one time actual, at another not. Take for instance the buildable as buildable. The actuality of the buildable as buildable is the process of building. For the actuality of the buildable must be either this or the house. But when there is a house, the buildable is no longer buildable. On the other hand it *is* the buildable which is *being* built. The process then of being built must be the kind of actuality required. But building is a kind of motion, and the same account will apply to the other kinds also."

[61] *Ibid.,* a15: "Examples will illucidate this definition of motion. When the buildable, insofar as it is just *that,* is fully real, it is *being built,* and this is *building.* Similarly, learning, doctoring, rolling, leaping, ripening, aging."

[62] *Physics* III. 1. 201b4: "Clearly it is the fulfillment of what is potential *as* potential that is motion." *Ibid.* a10: "The fulfillment of what exists potentially, insofar as it exists potentially, is motion—namely, of what is alterable *qua* alterable, *alteration:* of what can be increased and its opposite what can be decreased (there is no common name), *increase* and *decrease:* of what can come to be and can pass away, *coming to be* and *passing away:* of what can be carried along, *locomotion.*"

[63] Cf. Alexander Aphrodisiensis, *In Aristotelis Metaphysica Commentaria, Com. in Arist. Gr.,* I (Berlin 1891), 396.

[64] *Met.* II. 2; See above, n. 53.

[65] *Physics* III. 2. 201b19: "This is plain if we consider where some people put it; they identify motion with 'difference' or 'inequality' or 'not being'; but such things are not necessarily moved, whether they are 'different' or 'unequal' or 'non-existent'; nor is change either *to* or from *these,* rather to or from their opposites."

[66] According to the order of the Pythagoreans; cf. C. A. Brandis, ed. *Scholia in Aristotelem* (Berlin 1836), pp. 360a8 and 360a15.

[67] *Physics* III. 2. 201b24: "The reason why I put motion into these genera is that it is thought to be something indefinite, and the principles in the second column are indefinite because they are privative: none of them is either 'this' or 'such' or comes under any of the other modes of predication." *Ibid.,* 1. 200b32: "There is no such thing as motion *over and above* the things. It is always with respect to substance or to quantity or to quality or to place that what changes changes. But it is impossible, as we assert, to find anything *common* to these which is neither 'this' nor *quantum* nor *quale* nor any of the other predicates. Hence neither will motion and change have reference

to something over and above the things mentioned, for there is nothing over and above them."

[68] *Physics* III. 2. 201b27: "The reason in turn why motion is thought to be indefinite is that it cannot be classed simply as a potentiality or as an actuality—a thing that is merely *capable* of having a certain size is not undergoing change, nor yet a thing that is *actually* of a certain size, and motion is thought to be a source of *actuality,* but incomplete, the reason for this view being that the potential whose actuality it is is incomplete." *De anima* III. 7. 431a6: "Movement, is as we saw, an activity of what is imperfect."

[69] In following the first interpretation one encounters the difficulty (cf. Brandis, *op. cit.,* p. 358a19) that Aristotle describes movement [*kinesis*] not only as actuality [*energeia*] but also as consummate reality [*entelecheia*] which implies a consummation [*teleiotes,* see above sect. 1]. It is easy for us to explain this. Just as motion [*kinesis*] constitutes a state of becoming, and realizes this state, for which reason it is actuality [*energeia*], so it also consummates it *as such* and is therefore called a consummate reality [*entelecheia*]. It thus produces a more advanced, higher, and as it were, more consummate state of potentiality.

[70] *Physics* III. 2. 201b33: "This is why it is hard to grasp what motion is. It is necessary to class it with privation or with potentiality or with sheer actuality, yet none of this seems possible. There remains then the suggested mode of definition, namely, that it is a sort of actuality, or actuality of the kind described, hard to grasp, but not incapable of existing."

[71] *Physics* III. 1. 201a8: "Hence there are as many types of motion or change as there are meanings of the word 'is'." See also *Met.* XI. 9.

[72] Cf. *Met.* XI. 11. 1067b14ff. Likewise *Physics* III.

[73] *Met.* XI. 12. 1068a8: "If the categories are classified as substance, quality, place, acting or being acted on, relation, quantity, there must be three kinds of movement—of quality, of quantity, of place." Similarly *Physics* III. For those things which do not allow an intermediate state between the state prior to becoming and actuality and for which consequently there is not motion [*kinesis*], (hence, as we are told, for all categories outside of quality, quantity, and place [*poion, poson,* and *pou*]) the state of potentiality prior to becoming, which is not constituted by any form as such, is to be described as a state of most proximate potentiality. The state of their becoming is the state of actuality at the first moment.

[74] Cf. *Physics* III. 5. 204a8.

[75] *Met.* IX. 6. 1048b9: "But also the infinite and the

void and all similar things are said to exist potentially and actually in a different sense from that which applies to many other things, e.g., to that which sees or walks or is seen. For of the latter class these predicates can at some time be also truly asserted without qualification; for the seen is so called sometimes because it is being seen, sometimes because it is capable of being seen. But the infinite does not exist potentially in the sense that it will ever actually have separate existence; it exists potentially only for knowledge. For the fact that the process of dividing never comes to an end ensures that this activity exists potentially, but not that the infinite exists separately."

Wilfrid Sellars (essay date 1957)

SOURCE: "Substance and Form in Aristotle," in *Journal of Philosophy,* Vol. LIV, No. 22, October 24, 1957, pp. 688-99.

[*In the following essay, Sellars reviews the nature of substance, form, and matter as discussed by Aristotle, noting ways in which* Categories, *particularly statements regarding the theory of predication, can help one understand the concepts expressed in* Metaphysics.]

I

In *Categories* 2 b 4 ff., Aristotle writes, "Everything except primary substance is either predicated of primary substances or is present in them, and if these last did not exist, it would be impossible for anything else to exist."[1] By "everything except primary substances" he presumably means, in this context, everything which is either a secondary substance, or belongs in one of the other categories. And he is telling us that while items other than primary substances may legitimately be said to exist, their existence is essentially bound up with the fact that they are either 'predicated of' or 'present in' primary substances.

What, exactly, does Aristotle mean by these two technical expressions? Leaving 'predicated of' aside, for the moment, let us note some distinctive features of his account of 'present in'. "By being 'present in a subject' I do not mean present as parts are in a whole, but being incapable of existence apart from the said subject" (1 a 24-5). He then tells us (2 a 25 ff.) that "with respect to those things . . . which are present in a subject, it is generally the case that neither the name nor the definition is predicable of that in which they are present," to which he adds that "though the *definition* is *never* predicable, there is nothing, in certain cases, to prevent the *name* being used" (italics mine). He has just been pointing out that both the name and the definition of the species Man are predicable of the individual,—thus, 'Socrates is a man' and 'Socrates is a two-footed, terrestrial animal'. If we coin the expres-

sions 'nominal predication' and 'full predication' to stand for the difference Aristotle has in mind, the question arises as to what sorts of things are fully predicable of primary substances. The list includes not only the species, but also the genera, proximate and remote. It also includes the differentiae, thus, *two-footed* and *terrestrial.* Does it include anything else? Aristotle continues the above quoted passage by giving an example of something which is *nominally* but not *fully* predicable of a primary substance. "For instance, white being present in a body, [the word] 'white' is predicated of that in which it is present; the definition, however, of white is never predicated of the body."[2]

In *Categories* 4 a 10 ff. Aristotle tells us that "the most distinctive mark of substance appears[3] to be that while remaining numerically the same, it is capable of admitting contrary qualities." The question naturally arises, Is Aristotle contrasting materiate substances with items in other categories of being which, also remaining numerically the same, are *incapable* of admitting contrary qualities? And to this the answer is, Yes. "Thus," he continues, "one and the same color cannot be both white and black. Nor can the same action be both good and bad."

It should now be quite clear that by 'one and the same color'—'a color which is numerically one'—Aristotle does *not* mean a shade of color, that is to say, a repeatable or universal which is common to many individual things, but a *particular,* an *instance* of a shade of color. If we call this particular 'Tom', the idea is that Tom is, say, *a white* as Socrates is *a man,* not as Man is an Animal. The doctrine is that of the *Phaedo,* where (102 D ff.) distinguishing between the large thing, the large in the thing, and The Large Itself. Plato tells us that while the large thing may become small (by losing the large which is in it and, sharing in The Small Itself, acquiring *a* small to be *the* small which replaces it), the large in the thing can never be small, nor the small in the thing large.

The view which emerges from these passages is one according to which all predication is built on one fundamental form, namely 'X is a Y'. If X is a primary substance, Y is a secondary substance or thing-kind. But there are other examples of this form—thus, 'Tom is a white'. Here Tom would be a quality in a 'primary' sense which corresponds to the 'primary' sense of 'substance'. A similar distinction is to be drawn in each of the other categories.[4] We shall call items such as Tom, *qualia,* and primary instances of the category of Quantity, *quanta.*[5]

There are, then, for Aristotle, at least two dimensions in which the being of items other than primary substances is dependent on the being of primary substances. In one dimension the 'is' of 'This white is' stands to the 'is' of 'This man is' as 'inseparable' to 'separate'.[6]

What they have in common can be represented by saying that they share the form 'X is a Y'. A second dimension in which beings other than primary substances are dependent on primary substances is concerned with the being of universals. This dimension is brought out by the formula

Man is = Some primary substances are men.

'Man is' is traced to 'This (substance) is a man'. In these terms the significant difference between Plato and Aristotle is that whereas the former takes 'man' to be *primarily* the *proper* name of a single entity, Aristotle takes it to be primarily a *common* name of many individual men (thus, **Categories** 3 b 15-17) and consequently refuses to treat even its derivative use in, say, 'Man is an animal' as that of a proper name.[7]

II

What light does the teaching of the **Categories** throw on Aristotle's analysis of changing substances into matter and form in the **Metaphysics**? One thinks right away of the fact that if anything is clear about an Aristotelian form it is that its primary mode of being is to be a *this*. Certainly the form of a materiate substance is not a *universal*, for, as Aristotle reiterates, the form is 'the substance of' the composite, and the substance of a *this* must be of the nature of a *this* and never a universal.[8] Two questions obviously arise: (1) Is the form of a materiate substance not only a *this*, as contrasted with a *universal*, but a 'primary substance' in the sense of the **Categories**[9]? (2) To what extent does the sense in which the form is present in either the composite or the matter correspond to the sense in which, e.g., the white-in-the-thing is *present in* the white substance?

That the form of a materiate substance is *in some sense* an 'individual' or 'this' is clear. Does it follow that since it is not a universal, it must be a 'primary substance' in the sense of the **Categories?** No; for, as we shall see, it can be 'substance' in a *derivative* sense as being the immanent principle or cause of a primary substance. It can be a *this* which is a substance as being that by virtue of which the substance in which it is present is a substance in the primary or underivative sense of the term.[10] Indeed, it can even be a *this* in a derivative sense *without being a universal,* which, after all, is the heart of the matter.

But if a form is a *this* which is a *this* and *substance* only in a derivative sense, what is it in its own character? To use Aristotle's own example, medicine is healthy *qua* capable of restoring health, but in its own character, it is, say, a concoction of juices. The answer which leaps to mind, though it won't do as it stands, is that the form is, in its own character, a quale (or quantum, or combination of these or other particulars from categories other than substance), but that it is a

form not *qua quale,* but *qua* that by virtue of which the primary substance in which it is present *is a separate being of a certain kind.* We seem to find something like this account in Aristotle's treatment of artifacts. Of particular interest in this connection is a passage in the **Categories** where he writes (3 b 18 ff.):

> Yet species and genus do not merely indicate quality, like the term 'white'; 'white' indicates quality and nothing further, but species and genus determine quality with reference to a substance; they signify substance qualitatively differentiated.

To this passage should be related **Metaphysics** 1042 b 9 ff.,—in which he tells us that the 'principles of the beings of things' are to be found in the attributes with respect to which the various kinds of things or substances differ from one another. To this he adds the necessary reminder that the principle of the being of a substance cannot be found *simply* in a category other than substance, e.g., quality: " . . . none of these differentiae is substance, even when coupled with matter, yet it is what is analogous to substance in each case." This remark is, in the first instance, a reference to the view that the difference is to the genus as form to matter; that is to say, the genus is a determinable which the difference makes determinate much as *plane figure* is made determinate by *bounded by three straight lines,* and still more determinate by specifying that the lines are equally long. But of even greater significance is the fact that the difference is a *difference* of a kind of substance, as opposed to "a quality and nothing further," by determining *a way of being a* substance. For it clearly won't do to treat the category of substance as the highest determinable under which the difference falls, if the difference is construed simply as a quality, for then the category of substance would simply be the category of quality.

How is this to be understood? Aristotle, like all philosophers who take substance seriously, faced a dilemma. This dilemma concerns the relation of thing-kinds or secondary substances to the criteria which things must satisfy in order to belong to these kinds. It is important to see that this dilemma depends in no way on the Socratic-Aristotelian distinction between qualities and qualia, quantities and quanta, etc., though failure to escape between the horns of the dilemma may suggest this multiplication of particulars.

On the one hand, there is a strong temptation to *identify* 'S_1 is a K' with 'S_1 is Q_1 . . . Qn', which identification might be expressed by the equation (where S_1 is an individual substance, Q_1 . . . Qn its criterion qualities),

$$S_1 \text{ is a } K = S_1 \text{ is } Q_1 \ldots Qn.$$

The violence this does to our conceptual framework is

brought out by the fact that it doesn't make sense to say 'S_1 is *a* Q_1'. And no matter how 'complex' we make the adjective 'Q_1' it still doesn't make sense to say 'S_1 is *a* Q_1'. Even if 'S_1 is Q_1' were equivalent in meaning to 'S_1 is $Q_1 \ldots Qn$', the question 'What kind of thing is S_1?' i.e., 'S_1 is a *what?*' is no more answered by 'S_1 is Q_1' (save by implication) than, as Urmson has pointed out, 'Is this apple good?' is answered by 'This apple is XYZ', where 'XYZ' is the descriptive term which specifies the criteria for good apples.

In particular, it won't do to equate 'S_1 is a man' with 'S_1 is human', for, outside of the textbooks, 'S_1 is human' means 'S_1 is like a man' (cf. 'Fido is almost human') or, more usually, like a good man (in some respect relevant to the discussion). Thus 'S_1 is human', far from illuminating 'S_1 is a man', presupposes it.

Since the question 'S_1 is a what?' will not down, the attempt to reduce thing-kind expressions to complex adjectives leads to the introduction of a new (and pseudo-) thing-kind expression, namely 'Substratum'. It is 'a substratum' which is $Q_1 \ldots Qn$. The substratum is a "bare substratum" in that though 'S_1 is a substratum' professes to answer the question *'Of what kind is the object which is $Q_1 \ldots Qn$?'* it fails to do so. Clearly it is words like 'man', 'horse', 'shoe', etc. which properly play this role.[11]

On the other hand (the second horn of the dilemma) the attempt to distinguish between the thing-kind and its criteria may lead to equally desperate expedients. For if we insist that to say of S_1 that it is *a K* is to *characterize* S_1 in a way which does not amount to characterizing it as $Q_1 \ldots Qn$, we are open at once to the challenge 'Is it then *logically possible* for there to be a K which isn't $Q_1 \ldots Qn$ (although the latter are granted to be the criteria for being a K)?'; while to take the line that 'K' as distinguished from the criteria simply *characterizes* S as "thingish" or "substantial" is to return to the "bare substratum" of the first horn.

Now the genius of Aristotle (as well as his limitations) is nowhere better illustrated than in his treatment of substance. This becomes clear once we discover how to run between the horns of the above dilemma. And, indeed, all we need to do is face up to the fact that thing-kind words are *common names* and not a peculiar kind of adjective. Thus, while 'S_1 is a K' *implies* that S is $Q_1 \ldots Qn$, 'K' is by no means "logical shorthand" for "being $Q_1 \ldots Qn$". $Q_1 \ldots Qn$ are criteria for the application of 'K' without being "the meaning of 'K'" as XYZ, say, is the criterion for the application of 'good' to apples without being *the meaning of* 'good' as applied to apples. The point is not simply that there is "free play", "vagueness", or "open texture" in the connection between *being a K* and the qualities $Q_1 \ldots Qn$. The connection could be ever so

tight, so tight that there is a definite set of conditions separately necessary and jointly sufficient to establish that something was a K and still 'K' would play a unique role in discourse, a role which is quite other than that of a complex adjective. Words for thing-kinds are no more shorthand for their criteria, than proper names are shorthand for definite descriptions, which serve as their criteria (cf. Wittgenstein, *Investigations*, 79).

I have emphasized that thing-kind words are common names. By this I mean that they are common names of individuals, not proper names of universals; and as I have already indicated, I believe that Aristotle saw this and saw it clearly. It is just because 'man' is the common *name* of individual men that it can "cover the whole being of individual men". ('Man' is no more the name of a part of the individuals it names, than 'Julius Caesar' is the name of a part of Julius Caesar.) Also clearly reflected in his account is the fact that while a shoe may at one time be polished and at another time scuffed, which we may represent by the form

S_1 is Q-at-t

thing-kind words do not have the form

S_1 is a K-at-t.

A shoe is not *a shoe at a time*. Certainly there is a sense in which a piece of paper may be *now* a letter, *now* a (toy) aeroplane. But while the paper may come to be arranged in that way which makes it an aeroplane, and continue to be arranged in that way, and then cease to be arranged in that way, the aeroplane simply comes to be, exists throughout the stretch of time, and then ceases to be. To say that the paper is *now* an aeroplane is to say that the name 'aeroplane' is *now* appropriately applied to the paper. And since 'aeroplane' is the name of pieces of paper *qua* arranged in that manner, the name comes to be applicable to the piece of paper (the aeroplane comes to be) when the paper becomes so arranged, and ceases to be applicable (the aeroplane ceases to be) when the paper ceases to be so arranged.

We might put this by saying that *aeroplane* is predicable of the paper *qua arranged,* but the material mode of speech and the term 'predicable' should not deceive us. We can, if we like, say that 'aeroplane' means *the character of being an aeroplane,* and that this *character* is *attributable* to the paper *qua* arranged. The important thing is not to be misled by this manner of speaking into assimilating 'being an aeroplane' to 'being white'.

But not only are thing-kinds not reducible to the qualities which are their criteria, these qualities have, as criteria, their own logical peculiarities. We saw above that a shoe is not a shoe-at-t. It can now be pointed out that not only are animals not animals-at-t but to be a two-footed animal is not to be an animal which is two-footed-at-t. Again when a certain quality, say white, is a criterion quality, its character as criterion for the thing-kind name is reflected in the fact that it has the form 'white-thing' or 'white substance', where these phrases are *not* to be understood in terms of such contexts as 'What is that white thing over there?' To refer to something as 'a white thing' in the sense of this question is not to imply that the object would cease to be the thing it is if it ceases to be white. For the question has the force of

> That thing over there, which is (now) white, of what kind is it? it is *a what?*

On the other hand, as the form of the criterion-predicate, 'white substance' indicates not only that to be white in this sense is not to be white-at-a-time, but implies that something which was not in this sense white would not be a thing of the relevant kind, i.e., that 'being white' in this sense is a criterion for the applicability of the corresponding common name.

III

Let us apply these considerations to Aristotle's account of artifacts, for example, a shoe. 'Shoe', then, is a common noun applicable to pieces of leather *qua* qualified by certain criterion qualities. 'Shoe' is not a complex adjective, nor is it defined by qualities, but by qualities 'determined with reference to substance'. A shoe is a *this* in that it is *a shoe.* For to be a *this* in the primary Aristotelian sense is to be not simply *not a universal,* but to be an instance of a thing kind.[12]

It is against this background that we can understand Aristotle's denial that matter is (save in a derivative sense) a *this.* For while the matter of which a shoe is made is a particular in a broad sense as contrasted with a universal, it is not a *this* in the sense of 'a K'. Notice that we speak of 'a shoe' but of 'a *piece of* leather'; 'a statue' but 'a *chunk of* marble'; and so on. 'Leather', 'marble', 'bronze' are not thing-kind words, and Aristotle's distinction between *thises* and *the matter for thises* reflects an important distinction. What Aristotle has in mind is that when you have said of something that it is a piece of leather, you have not classified it under a secondary substance, and that even when you say 'a piece of leather of such and such a size and shape' you have not yet characterized it as a *this,* though you will have done so *by implication* if by virtue of being a piece of leather thus qualified, it conforms to the criteria for a thing-kind, e.g., shoe.[13]

Now if the shoe 'as a whole' is the instance of the secondary substance *shoe* (a fact which reflects the role of 'shoe' as a common name), what is the *form* of the shoe as contrasted with its matter? Among the conditions to be met by an answer are the following: (1) The form is not a universal, yet it is not *simply* a *this* or primary substance. (2) The form is not a quale, quantum, etc., nor any combination of these, for it is that by virtue of which the shoe is a primary *substance;* yet it cannot be explained without reference to categories other than substance. The answer, as far as I see, is to be found by a more careful analysis of the secondary substance *shoe.* We have been representing it (in the material mode, so to speak) as *such and such qualities determined to substance.* Would we not, however, better reflect the above analysis if we represented it by *such and such qualities determined to substance in* leather? If so, it springs to the attention that shoes, after all, can be made of other materials, for the attributes which justify the application of the name 'shoe' to a piece of leather can, at least in principle, be present in these other materials. Thus, the form of shoes taken universally is the secondary substance *shoe* as represented immediately above ('leathern shoe') without the specification of the material in which the criterion qualities are to be present. On the other hand, the form (taken universally) is not these qualities *simpliciter,* but these qualities determined with reference to substance (i.e., as criterion qualities for a thing-kind name) *in some appropriate material or other.* Thus Aristotle can say that the form of *this shoe* is, in a certain sense, the shoe itself. For, to follow up the above line of thought, the form of *this shoe* is the shoe itself *qua* a foot-covering made of *some* appropriate kind of matter. The form is *in this disjunctive sense* (indicated by 'some') more 'abstract' than the shoe, but it is not for this reason a *universal.* Furthermore, the form, in this 'abstract' (disjunctive) way includes the whole being of the individual shoe. The form *qua form* is incapable of separate existence as disjunctive facts are incapable of existing apart from "basic" facts, but it is not 'present in' the shoe as a quale is present in a primary substance. For the form taken universally is fully predicable of the subject. S1 is not only a covering for the feet made of *leather,* it is a covering for the feet made of *some appropriate material or other.* The sense, therefore, in which the form of the shoe is present in the shoe, and is an *incomplete* entity incapable of separate existence, is not to be simply identified with the sense in which qualia, quanta, etc. are present in primary substances, nor is it to be identified with the sense in which universals are incapable of separate existence.[14]

It is, I think, clear, that something like the above distinctions can be drawn without a commitment to the theory of predication of the ***Categories.*** As far as I can see, however, Aristotle remained committed to this theory throughout his career.[15] And this is the occasion to admit that Aristotle sometimes seems to think of the form of a materiate substance as a substance which is more truly substance than the substance of which it is the form—particularly in the case of living things, where Human Soul, for example, seems at times to be a thing-kind which is more truly a thing-kind than the materiate universal Man; the soul of Socrates to be in a *primary* sense a *this,* and Socrates a *this* in a derivative sense as having a primary *this* within him. To be sure, the soul of Socrates would not be primary substance in the full sense of the *Categories,* for it is incapable of separate existence. But, then, is any being truly capable of separate existence save those incorporeal intelligences which everlastingly think on thought?

That Aristotle *could* think along these lines was made possible by the fact that his theory of predication provides a built-in way of going from 'this matter is [. . .]' to 'a [. . .] in this matter'. Is this not the key to Aristotle's claim that whereas 'to be man' is not identical with the essence of man, 'to be soul' *is* identical with the essence of soul'? For the latter treats souls as items which are not only the essence of the living things to which they belong, *but themselves have an essence.* What essence? Do we not have here an echo of the *Phaedo*? of the idea that souls are essentially alive and as alive make the composites to which they belong derivatively alive?[16]

Notes

[1] I have found Joseph Owen's important book *The Doctrine of Being in the Aristotelian Metaphysics* (Toronto: Pontifical Institute of Medieval Studies, 1957) and Ellen Stone Haring's analysis of *Metaphysics Z* ("Substantial Form in Aristotle's *Metaphysics Z,*" *Review of Metaphysics,* Vol. 10, 1957) helpful and suggestive, although I ran into the latter too late to give it more than a careful first reading.

[2] The Oxford translation, which I have modified slightly, reads: "For instance, 'white' being present in a body is predicated of that in which it is present, for a body is called white: the definition, however, of the color 'white' is never predicable of the body."

[3] The "appears" is undoubtedly a tacit reference to the existence of unchanging, immaterial substances. Strictly speaking, however, it is probably incorrect to say that immaterial substances are substances in the sense of the Categories, i.e., in the sense in which substances are contrasted with the qualities, quantities, etc. by which they are characterized. They are, however, beings which 'exist apart'—indeed, more truly apart than the primary substances of the *Categories.*

[4] Cf. Ross, *Aristotle,* Second Edition, p. 24.

[5] A no less explicit and, in certain respects, more interesting formulation of this theory of predication is to be found in *Topics* 102 b 20 ff. Two points require to be made about the translation: (1) 'White' in 103 b 32 should be 'the (presented) white' *(to ekkeimenon leu-*

kon) to parallel 'the (presented) man' *(to ekkeimenon anthropon)* which the translator renders simply by 'a man'. (2) 'Essence' is here the translation of *'ti esti'* and has the sense of the 'what it is' or 'identity' of something. To give something's *ti esti* is to identify it as, say, 'a man' or 'an animal'—or, and this is the crux of the matter, 'a white (quale)' or 'a color (quale)'. In 102 a 32 ff. Aristotle writes, "We should treat as predicates in the category of essence *(ti esti)* all such things as it would be appropriate to mention in reply to the question 'What is the object before you?'" Notice that the distinction between the first class of predicates and the remaining nine which is drawn in this passage is not that between *substance* and the various sorts of thing that can be said of substances, but rather between the *identity,* the *ti esti* of *an item of whatever category in the more familiar sense,* and the sort of things that can be said of it.

[6] While changeable things must have qualia present in them, and in this sense cannot exist apart from qualia, they can exist *apart* in the specific sense in which qualia cannot; for primary substances are not *present in* a subject.

[7] The argument of the *Categories* implies that while we might begin to explicate 'White exists' by saying 'White is = Some primary substances are white', the analysis would not be complete until we said something like 'White is = Some qualia are whites', though Aristotle nowhere explicitly undertakes this reduction.

[8] It is perhaps worth nothing that the unmoved movers are with equal certainty not universals. Of what would they be predicated?

[9] As contrasted with the use of this and related expressions in other contexts. Thus in *Metaphysics* VII, 1032 b 1, 1037 a 5, and 1037 b 1, this expression is applied to the form of a materiate substance as the principle by virtue of which the latter is a substance. The form is 'primary' as not itself consisting of matter and form, and as prior to the concrete individual which does consist of matter and form. Yet that the form of a materiate substance in some sense includes its matter will be argued below.

[10] It is essential to realize that the idea that the concrete individual is a substance in the *primary* sense of 'substance' (as having separate existence) is *not* incompatible with the idea that there is an entity which though a substance in a *derivative* sense, is nevertheless *prior* to the concrete individual as a principle of its being.

[11] The realization that 'substratum' is a stone where there should be bread, combined with the fact that the question 'S₁ is a what?' will not down, soon generates a more subtle scheme. By the simple expedient of coining a new usage according to which the adjective

'white' rests on a postulated common name 'white' so that we can speak of 'a white', and, in general, of 'a Q', bare substrata are avoided by turning S_1 into a bundle consisting of a Q_1, a Q_2 . . . and a Qn. Since it is a fundamental feature of logic of a set of thing-kind expressions belonging to a given universe of discourse, that no object belongs to more than one kind (unless these kinds are related as genus to species) the introduction of qualia soon leads to the feeling that no quale can be of two kinds which are not related as determinable to determinate. I have trodden this road myself in "Particulars," *Philosophy and Phenomenological Research,* Vol. 13, 1952, and "The Logic of Complex Particulars," *Mind,* Vol. 58, 1949. My mistake was in thinking that in the language we actually use things that are complex particulars, and 'thing-kind' words 'abstract' references to sets of simple particulars. I remain convinced, however, that there is a sense in which an ideal description of the world would be in a language of this form. In any event, Aristotle's recognition of *whites* in addition to *white things* and *whiteness* is clearly not motivated by a desire to avoid substrata. Nor was his doctrine of prime matter motivated by logical puzzles relating to predication. That opposite (e.g., *a* hot) cannot act directly on opposite (e.g., *a* cold) but only qualified substratum on qualified substratum is a fundamental principle of his *Physics*. And the very claim that first matter is, as such, 'blank' and incapable of separate existence rather than an empirical stuff such as fire or air, is argued on natural philosophical rather than narrowly logical grounds.

[12] In *Metaphysics* 1049 a 19-b 2, which begins with the familiar characterization of prime matter as "that which is no longer with reference to something else called 'thaten',," Aristotle distinguishes between predication in which the subject is a 'this' (a concrete individual) and predication in which the subject is not a 'this' but, rather, matter. He writes: "For the subject or substratum is differentiated by being a 'this' or not being one; i.e., the substratum of *modifications* is, e.g., a man, i.e. a body and a soul, while the modification is 'musical' or 'pale'. . . . Wherever this is so, then, the ultimate subject is a substance; but when this is not so but the predicate is a form and a 'this', the ultimate subject is matter and material substance." The concluding sentence is likely to be misinterpreted and to lead to unnecessary puzzlement unless it is realized that "the predicate is a form and a 'this'" has the sense of "the predicate is 'a K' (e.g., 'a man', 'a shoe', etc.)."

[13] It might be thought that 'piece of leather' is a thing-kind expression, even if 'leather' is not. Let me indicate, in an Aristotelian mood, why it is only "in a sense" that this is so. Artifacts are purpose servers. The purpose of shoes, for example—to protect and embellish the feet—is part of the very 'meaning' of 'shoe'. But pieces of leather *as such* are purpose-servers only by being raw material for direct purpose-servers. The context 'piece of . . .', 'chunk of . . .', etc., so characteristic of *recipes,* turn words for kinds of material ('leather', 'marble', etc.) into expressions which, as far as purpose is concerned, imply at most that their designata can be the material cause of items which, as correctly designated by a proper thing-kind expression (in the universe of discourse of artifacts), are direct purpose-servers. A shoe can, indeed, be part of the matter for, e.g., a store window dummy; yet it remains a purpose-server in its own right. But something which is *merely* 'a piece of . . . ' is *only* a purpose-server in a derivative sense. The fact that leather is *made* doesn't mean that pieces of leather are artifacts in the *primary* sense of this important Aristotelian expression. Aristotle views even the elements in the context of craftsmanship (including the 'craftsmanship' of living things). It is for this reason that he views pieces of earth, air, etc. as *thises* only in a derivative sense.

[14] That the form component of the materiate universal (secondary substance) *man* might also be found in other materials is suggested by Metaphysics 1036 a 31 ff.

[15] See, for example, *Metaphysics* 1077 b 5 and 1087 a 17; also 991 a 14.

Joseph Owens (essay date 1957)

SOURCE: "The Problem of Being," in *The Doctrine of Being in the Aristotelian "Metaphysics,"* Pontifical Institute of Metaphysical Studies, 1957, pp. 35-68.

[*In the following essay, Owens studies how Medieval metaphysicians interpreted Aristotle's* Metaphysics. *Owens observes that the two apparently contradictory notions of being identified in* Metaphysics (being *as either an abstract, empty concept and being as related to the concept of God) were often merged by Medieval Christian thinkers, and he reviews the debate among later critics regarding the possibility of unifying the two concepts.*]

To determine whether the notion of Being in Alexander of Hales is Aristotelian or Platonic, a recent historian seeks his criterion in "the gradual separation of the Aristotelian views from the essential and fundamental teachings of Plato."[1] He arrives at a clear-cut norm: "Therefore the essential difference between a Platonic and an Aristotelian conception of Being consists in this, that for the former conception, Being as Being is the *ens perfectissimum;* while for the latter, Being as Being is the *ens commune.*"[2]

In its application to the mediaeval thinker, the norm places two alternatives. The one question is: "Does Alexander give the concept of Being a sense that makes it the proper concept of God?"[3] If so, his notion of Being is Platonic. The opposite query runs: "Does our author see in the concept of Being the concept most abstract and most empty of content, which, because it has the least content, has the widest extension?"[4] In this case his doctrine is properly Aristotelian.

Back of the criterion lies an easily recognizable view of the Aristotelian Primary Philosophy.[5]

Towards the close of the nineteenth century, Natorp called attention—apparently for the first time—to an "insufferable contradiction" in the traditional *Metaphysics.* He distinguished two series of texts. These expressed "mutually exclusive" conceptions of the Primary Philosophy. Natorp proceeded to excise the one set of these texts as Platonizing additions inserted by early Peripatetics.[6]

In strong reaction to so violent a method, Zeller pointed out that the contradiction emerged from the most fundamental of the Stagirite's doctrines. It was too deeply rooted in the whole Aristotelian philosophy to be set aside by philological criticism of certain texts.[7]

In the present century, Jaeger has sought a more reasonable and primarily philosophical[8] solution. The Platonizing character of the texts becomes a mark of their authenticity.[9] The two contradictory notions of the Primary Philosophy are actually present in the course of Aristotle's own development. There is an earlier view, which is Platonic; and there is a later one, which is properly Aristotelian. In the earlier stage, the 'object'[10] of the science is a particular kind of Being—namely, supersensible or immobile Being. In the later conception, the object is not a particular type of Being, but Being in general, applicable to sensible and supersensible Being alike.[11]

Should this theory of the Primary Philosophy be historically correct, it will necessarily have important repercussions in any estimate of mediaeval metaphysics.

What are the consequences involved?

They seem quite evident. If a philosopher of the middle ages conceives metaphysics as the science of the Being richest in comprehension, he is thinking in a Platonic direction. If, on the other hand, he agrees that Being as Being means the Being which is widest in extension but most empty in comprehension, he is following the later and properly Aristotelian lead. The historical background restricts the question to the interpretation in the West of the newly-acquired Aristotelian text. For the study of metaphysics as a distinct science in the university circles of the middle ages was occasioned by the spread of that text in Latin translation during the first three quarters of the thirteenth century.[12] In a comparatively short time the influence of the Stagirite had altered the whole external structure and technique of Christian thought.[13] Accordingly, if a Christian metaphysician working in this milieu took for the subject of his science Being in general—in the sense of the 'most abstract and empty of concepts,' he was drawing the properly Aristotelian inspiration out of the texts from which he was learning his technique. But if—helped largely by the influence of traditional Augustinian thought—he equated the subject of metaphysics with the concept of God, he was interpreting the text according to the Stagirite's earlier and Platonic leanings. Such, at least, seems the way in which the above-mentioned criterion has been applied to Alexander of Hales.[14]

Some serious misgivings arise after a little reflection on this situation. How could any mediaeval thinker look upon Being as "the concept most abstract and most empty of content"? To the mentality of the age, untouched by Idealism, Being in some way included everything. Nothing could be added to it, neither difference nor accident. It included all its differences. In this sense the mediaeval philosophers interpreted Aristotle's doctrine that Being is not a genus.[15] Unlike a generic concept, Being for these thinkers did not decrease in content according to its increase in extension. Besides enjoying the widest possible extension, it possessed in one way or another the greatest possible comprehension. It was far from being an 'empty' concept.[16]

On the other hand, was any Christian thinker of the middle ages free to identify the subject of metaphysics with the God of his religious faith?

Etienne Gilson has pointed out the profound difference between the Greek and the Christian notions of Being.[17] The mediaeval philosophers, as they approached the Aristotelian treatises, were already equipped with the belief in a God whose very name was Being. *I am who am* was the way in which He had revealed Himself to Moses.[18] For the Christian thinker, God was the primary and perfect instance of Being.

But this supreme instance of Being, besides being triune, was an omnipotent and sovereignly free Creator.[19] In the natural as well as in the supernatural order, the nature of the First Being transcended human comprehension. Such a Being could hardly be conceived as forming the subject of a specifically human science.[20] The subject of metaphysics, when brought formally to the attention of a Christian philosopher, required location in a kind of Being other than the proper nature of the primary and all-perfect type.

Neither, then, of the opposite conceptions of the Primary Philosophy seems acceptable in the mediaeval world.

In point of historical fact, the leading metaphysicians of the middle ages agreed in declaring that Being as Being was the subject of their science. They understood it to include in some way all the differences of Being. It was not an 'empty' concept. But they distinguished it sharply from the primary Being.[21] They knew that Aristotle had spoken of the Primary Philosophy as the science of the highest causes and as the science of the separate Entities. They felt obliged to justify their position and to explain in various ways these other formulae of the Stagirite.

Albert the Great, for instance, had no patience with the Latin thinkers who tried to combine into one the three conceptions of metaphysics.[22] The theory that God is the subject of this science he considered frankly Platonic and false.[23]

St. Thomas Aquinas explained that while the science treats of the first causes and the separate substances, *ens commune* alone can be its subject.[24]

Siger of Brabant declared, after considering the three views, that "the principles of a thing are sometimes not the principles of its discipline." God, though the first principle of Being, is not "the principle of *Being according as it is Being*."[25]

Duns Scotus discusses at considerable length the problems involved in the different conceptions.[26] The interpretation of metaphysics as the science of Being *qua* Being—in the sense of Being *in communi*[27]—is for him, as for Siger, the view of Avicenna;[28] while the doctrine that God and the separate substances are the subject of the science, is regarded as the position of Averroes.[29] Scotus also discusses the view that metaphysics is the science of substance.[30] The notion of the primary causes as the subject seems to merge for him in the conception of Being *in communi*.[31] This latter view is the one to which he himself adheres.[32]

Nor does William of Ockham think differently on this particular point, as far as can be gathered from his teaching about human knowledge of God and substance. Both are known through *ens communissimum*.[33]

These mediaeval philosophers, consequently, were well aware of the different conceptions regarding the Aristotelian Primary Philosophy. If they were concerned merely with the neatest formula to delineate the science of metaphysics, they would not be raising any specially important issue. But if they were encountering trouble in expressing their Christian notion of Being in Aristotelian terms, might they not be facing a much more serious problem? Might they not be forcing their own conception of Being into formulae which could not contain it, and which under the pressure burst open in various ways?

In point of fact, the different Christian thinkers of the thirteenth and fourteenth centuries developed radically divergent metaphysics.[34] Yet all learned their technique from Aristotle, and all couched their theses in his formulae. They held in common the doctrine of God and creatures taught by their faith. How can the all-pervasive differences in their metaphysics be explained? An adequate explanation must be given if the mediaeval controversies are to be understood. And not only the lack of agreement in mediaeval procedure, but also the subsequent discouraging history of the science up to the present day seems rooted in these diverging interpretations of the Aristotelian text at the critical period in the inauguration of Western metaphysics.

The first step in solving this problem must be a clear understanding of the doctrine of Being actually contained in the text which confronted the mediaeval thinkers.

In the **Metaphysics** itself, the study of Being is expressed in various ways. Sometimes the Primary Philosophy is described as the science that treats of the highest principles and causes of things.[35] More specifically it seems designated as the inquiry into the causes of Being *qua* Being.[36] It is called the science which deals universally with Being *qua* Being, and not with particular Being.[37] Again, it is delimited to divine and immobile Being, and named 'theology'.[38] In this sense it deals with Being *qua* Being, which now seems to become the equivalent of separate Being.[39] In other places the Primary Philosophy is the science of *ousia*,[40] of the primary *ousia*,[41] of the causes of *ousiae*,[42] or of the causes of the visible divine things.[43] Again, it is the science of truth.[44] In the **Physics** it is the science of form.[45]

Can all these different modes of expression denote the same doctrine of Being?

Aristotle himself appears conscious of no inconsistency or contradiction in these various designations. Even when raising a question that today seems to bring an antinomy to the fore, he writes as though unaware of any real difficulty.[46] He does not seem in the least perturbed by what many modern commentators find embarrassing if not impossible.

Yet the texts have given rise to considerable difficulty in the history of Aristotelian interpretation. A glance over the Greek and the modern presentations of these formulae will help articulate the problem back of the mediaeval efforts to determine precisely the subject of metaphysics.

The long tradition of the Greek commentators seems to have been quite unanimous in interpreting the Aristotelian Being. As studied by the Primary Philosophy, Being *qua* Being,—Being in its own proper nature—

somehow referred to a definite type of Being and ultimately meant divine and separate Being.

The Greek tradition may be studied as far back as Theophrastus and Eudemus, both disciples of Aristotle.

Theophrastus was the friend and heir of the Stagirite. He was not a commentator on Aristotle. But in the short treatise known as his *Metaphysics,* he deals with some of the leading problems of the Primary Philosophy.[47] As the immediate successor of his master in the Peripatetic school, he is a witness of the Aristotelian tradition in its earliest stages.

> How, and by what distinguishing marks, should we delimit the study of first principles? . . . the study of first principles is definite and unchanging; which is the reason also why men describe it as concerned with objects of reason, not of sense, on the ground that these are unmovable and unchangeable, and why, in general, too, they think it a more dignified and greater study.

> . . . It is, at all events, more reasonable to suppose that there is a connexion and that the universe is not a mere series of episodes, but some things are, so to speak, prior and others posterior—some, ruling principles, and others, subordinate to them—as eternal things are prior to and ruling principles of those that are perishable. If this *is* so, what is their nature and in what sort of things are they found? . . . But if there is another reality prior and superior to the objects of mathematics, we ought to try to specify this and say whether it is a single reality in number or in species or in genus. It is, at all events, more reasonable to suppose that, having the nature of a ruling principle, they should be found only in a few things and things of no ordinary kind, if not, indeed, only in things that are primary, and in the first of all things. What, at any rate, this reality is, or what these realities are, if they are more than one, we must try to indicate somehow or other, whether in virtue of an analogy or of some other comparison . . . . for, the ruling principle of all things, through which all things both are and endure, *is* divine.[48]

The Being with which the science of the 'firsts'—there is no noun in the Greek text—deals, is for Theophrastus the divine Being. It is something definite and determined. It is not an abstract or most general concept. It is located in a determined type of Being.

Theophrastus does not employ the expression 'Being *qua* Being' in the extant text.[49] But there is no doubt that he considers the study of the first principles of all things to be the science of the unchangeable Being, in the sense of the divine Being. Through that Being all things *are.*

Eudemus of Rhodes poses the problem of how the science of the first principles can be the science of those subordinated to it.

If there is to be a term to the process, and there are to be some sciences or even one proper science of the principles, this science will inquire into and seek an account of why it is the science of those subordinated to it as well as of its own principles, while the others are not.[50]

The problem seems intelligible only if the first principles are looked upon as a definite nature. If the primary science merely considered the principles of the other sciences in a more abstract and general way, it would hardly give rise to any problem in this regard.[51] Not much definite information, however, can be gathered from this brief statement of Eudemus.

Alexander of Aphrodisias, the first of the Greek commentators on the **Metaphysics,** regards 'philosophy' as a generic science. The Primary Philosophy, one of its species, is the science of the divine. This Primary Philosophy is universal, because it deals with what is primary in the sense of causing Being to all other things.

> There is the genus, that is, the common nature of Being, knowable by the common and generic philosophy, and the parts of Being knowable by the parts of philosophy. In this way each of these latter— namely, the sciences which come under philosophy as a generic science—will be the science of one of the species of Being. . . . At the same time he also showed us in these words how philosophy is a single science—for it is so by being universal. Its species are as many as those of Being. For its species are:— 1) The Primary Philosophy, which is also called in an eminent sense wisdom, being the science of the eternal and immobile and divine things. For wisdom is the universal and primary science, as it is the one concerned with Being *qua* Being but not particular Being. There is under it

> (1) the Primary Philosophy, which deals with the primary Entities,[52]

> (2) Natural Philosophy, which deals with natural things, in which are found movement and change,

> (3) the science which treats of things done; for some Beings are of this nature.

> That the philosophy which treats of Being *qua* Being is one in genus, he explained also through what he said at the very beginning of the Book: 'This science is identical with none of those which are called particular'—namely, the science which deals with the principles and the first causes and Entity. It is at the same time primary and universal; for in things that are denominated from one thing and in reference to one thing, the primary instance is also universal, by reason of its being the cause of Being to the others also, as he himself will say in Book E of this treatise.[53]

According to this statement of Alexander, the Primary Philosophy deals with the immobile and primary Entities. These divine Entities seem to be equated with 'Being *qua* Being' and distinguished from particular Being. The science is universal, because what it treats of is universal as the *cause of Being* to the other things.

In the earliest of the commentators, accordingly, the universality of the Aristotelian 'Being *qua* Being' is the universality of the divine Entities. This Being is universal by way of reference, for it is the cause of all other Being. The Being treated of by the Primary Philosophy, therefore, does not seem to be regarded as universal after the manner of an abstract concept.

Pseudo-Alexander[54] has the same general doctrine. He distinguishes explicitly the two kinds of universality, and excludes the ordinary type from the Primary Philosophy. He feels obliged to defend the Stagirite's use of the term 'universal' in the case of things expressed by way of reference to a common cause. Aristotle designated the primary instances in such things, he thinks, as 'universal' in order to conform to accepted custom.

> But if there is also another Entity which is immobile and separate, this Entity will be prior to the physical, and the science dealing with it will be philosophy and the primary science of all, and universal as by reference to the others—not as comprehending them, but as primary; and it will be the office of this science to investigate and treat of Being *qua* Being, and what the nature of Being is, . . . And I think that when he asked whether the Primary Philosophy is universal, he was not asking about the universality which we understand as comprehending the others,[55] but universality in the sense of 'belonging to the better things' and 'having greater worth'.[56]

> . . . It is also clear that when he called Being in the eminent sense of Being—I mean, the first principle—universal, he did not so designate this principle as being predicated universally of many things, but as involving in its own removal the removal of the other principles. But for what reason at all does he call the present science and its principle 'universal'? The reason is that we are accustomed to call things that involve in their own removal the removal of others 'more universal' than the things thereby removed. . . . In following this custom he called them 'universal.'[57]

'Being *qua* Being' seems in this explanation of Pseudo-Alexander to coincide with the Being of the immobile and separate Entities, as the nature treated of by the Primary Philosophy. The problem of its universality is carefully articulated in terms taken from the Stagirite's own text. Universality in the sense of 'comprehending' its inferiors is not found in 'Being *qua* Being.'

Syrianus collates the question with the doctrine expressed in Book a of the **Metaphysics.**

> For if the highest knowledge is that of the highest Being, and if a thing excels to the same extent in truth and clarity of knowledge as in worth, as has been said in the lesser of the *alphas,* there will be a science of Being *qua* Being, and not merely that, but even the fairest and best of sciences . . . . for the primary science may rightly be held to deal with what is primary, and the best with what is best, and the all-embracing with what is all-embracing.[58]

The species of philosophy seem related to the genus in the same way as with Alexander.

> In fact, however, just as the one and all-embracing philosophy is related to all Entities, so also are its species to the species of Entities. The Primary Philosophy, then, will deal with intelligible Entity, that concerned with the heavens will treat of the Entity that is eternal though mobile, and another with the Entity that is in the process of generation and corruption.[59]

In this explanation also, 'Being *qua* Being' seems to be equated with one kind of Entity as the theme of the Primary Philosophy. This is intelligible Entity, the highest and richest in content.

Asclepius similarly introduces the Aristotelian metaphysics as the science which treats of the divine.

> And finally, in this treatise he discourses to us about the entirely immobile things. This is theology; for such a consideration corresponds to the divine things. For this reason it has also been entitled 'Metaphysics', . . . [60]

'Being *qua* Being,' accordingly, is meant by Aristotle to stand for 'Being *par excellence,*' namely the intelligible Beings.

> In these words Aristotle wishes to show us that there is a science which is that of *Being according as it is Being,* in the sense of Being *par excellence.* This Being *par excellence* he calls good and primary and having fertile power; and from it do all other things proceed. . . . It is evident that from Being *par excellence* and simply such, that is, the absolutely primary Entity, Being proceeded to these things, because of its fertility. . . . Absolutely primary Entity, for instance, are the Intelligibles which are Beings, after them are sensible things, which hold the second place, third are the accidents, as even these are Beings.[61]

The universality of the science is explained by its 'primary' nature.

If there is also an immobile Entity, as indeed there is, this is the prior and primary philosophy, and for this reason universal, since it is primary in so far as it has the principles of all things in itself.[62]

He who knows the principles knows also the things which follow from the principles.[63]

Knowing the primary Entity, metaphysics knows all the others.

... he has now added what that science is—that it is indeed the universal philosophy, differing from the others in so far as each of those deals with particular Being, while philosophy deals universally with Being in so far as it is Being, not with particular Being. In every case, therefore, science deals eminently with the primary instance, just as in the case of reference to man; for knowledge is of the man and not of the statue, for instance, that is, of the image; for these are because of the man. If, likewise, in the present case all other things are because of the absolutely primary Entity, and all things depend upon it, of this kind of Entity then must we seek out the principles and the causes.[64]

For Asclepius the knowledge of all Being is the knowledge of the primary Being. Just as it is the man himself that is contemplated in his statue or image, so it is the Being of the immobile Entities that is studied in all other types of Being.

With Eustratius, in the early twelfth century, Being *qua* Being likewise means the Being of the immobile Entities.

Wisdom is the science of Beings *qua* Beings—the Beings that are immobile and unchanging and always remaining the same, and forever abiding in immo-bility and possessing in this immobility Being in all truth.[65]

A patristic witness to the Greek tradition is found in Clement of Alexandria. Speaking of 'theological' study, he says: "Aristotle calls this type metaphysics."[66] No one in ancient times, as Natorp admits,[67] doubted that the Primary Philosophy and 'theology' were one for Aristotle. On into the twelfth century, the apparently unanimous tradition of Greek thought seems to have equated the Aristotelian 'Being *qua* Being' with the Being of the separate Entities, as the theme treated by the Primary Philosophy.

It is true that the philosophy of Theophrastus is not necessarily that of the Stagirite. With Alexander, who lived five centuries afterwards, the notion of the Primary Philosophy need not be presumed to correspond in all details to the original Aristotelian conception. The long period of time between the two different ages may easily have had its corroding effects. In the later Greek commentators other viewpoints played an im-

portant role. Syrianus and Asclepius, for instance, were under strong Neoplatonic influence. But at least these writers are witnesses that the Greek tradition throughout all these centuries considered the Stagirite's 'Being *qua* Being,' as the theme of the Primary Philosophy, to mean ultimately the divine and separate and immobile Being.

During the Christian middle ages, on the other hand, and down to the beginning of the modern era, the Aristotelian formula 'Being *qua* Being' was interpreted as *ens commune* in a sense opposed to the divine Being. It meant the Being with the widest possible extension, and included in some way the greatest possible comprehension; but it was clearly and consciously distinguished from the Being of God.

The nineteenth century revival of interest in the Aristotelian text did not at first bring this problem to the fore.

Ravaisson, for instance, seems aware of no special difficulty.

Being *qua* Being does not allow itself to be confined to any one class; its causes are not diverse and particular, but universal and uniform; it can be the object only of a universal science.

The science of the first principles, First Philosophy can therefore be defined 'the universal science of being *qua* being.'[68]

The pioneer French commentator locates this Being in the divine thought which appears universally in all things.

Each particular Being or each nature is an imperfect act, or a movement, of which the Thought is the cause, the purpose, and the essence; or, to reduce movement to its principle, it is the desire by which the divine Thought, present to all the potencies which matter includes, makes them come to existence and to life ...

One and the same Being, which is none other than the Thought or the intuition of itself, appearing in the different potencies of matter, under countless forms and in countless different operations ... such is the general conception in which is summed up the whole of Metaphysics.[69]

This interpretation follows the general line of the Greek tradition. It also accentuates the role of final causality in the Aristotelian notion of Being.

Schwegler, after a penetrating study of Aristotle's analysis of sensible Being, comes to the following conclusion:

"The only true *ousia* . . . is the divinity. . . . God is the *ousia* . . . that metaphysics seeks. The idea of God is therefore the theme, the end, and the driving motive of the whole Aristotelian metaphysics . . . From what has been said it is doubly clear how far metaphysics is for Aristotle a theology."[70]

This conception, too, approaches the spirit of the Greek interpreters. Being *qua* Being is the divine Being.

Bonitz repeats the language of the early commentators, without calling attention to any special problem concealed under the phrasing.

> The universal genus of philosophy pertains to the universal genus of Beings, just as in other cases also the same genus, in either the sensible or the knowable order, pertains to the same genus either of sensation or of knowledge; and each of the species of being . . . is comprised by one of the species or branches of philosophy.[71]

> Therefore theology is the primary discipline, and in so far as it is the first of all, it can be called universal, since all the others have to seek their first principle in it.[72]

Zeller seemed conscious of no *special* difficulty lying under this phraseology of the **Metaphysics.**

> The science of the ultimate grounds of things must go through the whole world of things, and must take them back, not to finite principles, but to their eternal causes, and, in the last resort, to that which is unmoved and incorporeal, from which proceeds all movement and formation in the corporeal world. This science is the First Philosophy, which Aristotle also names Theology, and its task is to investigate all actuality and the ultimate grounds thereof, which, as being ultimate, are necessarily also the most universal, and concern, not any part of the actual, but the whole.[73]

In reply to Natorp's critique of the **Metaphysics,** Zeller pushed the problem further back. He still maintained that Aristotle actually united the two conceptions of the science. But the union does involve a fundamental contradiction. Its roots lie in the double sense of the Aristotelian *ousia.*

> In Aristotle's orbit of thought, therefore, there is between the metaphysical ontology and the theology not only no opposition, but, on the contrary, a connection so close that both belong to one and the same science. In accordance with its content, this science can be called both the science of Being and the science of the Divine. Aristotle considers as pure Being . . . only the immaterial, and therefore unchangeable, Being. Another question, deserving of separate treatment, is whether this view can be maintained without contradiction. This question can

be answered only in the negative. But the difficulties arising here have their roots too deep in the whole of the Aristotelian system to be set aside by the critical methods of philology, through the excision of particular sections and an altered interpretation of single passages. For its ultimate reason lies in that double sense of the concept of [*ousia*] which permeates the whole of the **Metaphysics.** This consists in the fact that finally, as in Plato, only form without matter can be something actual in the fullest sense, an [*ousia*] or an [*energeiaon*]; while, on the other hand, actuality can be so little denied to individual things and to matter, that only the indi-viduals may in fact be [*prōte ousia*]. According to the first viewpoint the investigation of [*ousia*] must limit itself to immaterial and unchangeable Being, the [*theīa*]; according to the other it must embrace on equal footing all Being, including the corporeal.[74]

Zeller, accordingly, places the contradiction at the very root of the Aristotelian Being—in its *ousia* or 'Being-ness.' This denotes on the one hand pure form, on the other the individual. These two conceptions, which were ultimately one in Schwegler's interpretation,[75] are for Zeller mutually exclusive.

Grote sees no problem in uniting the Aristotelian descriptions of the Primary Philosophy.

> The highest and most universal of all theoretical Sciences is recognized by Aristotle as Ontology (First Philosophy, sometimes called by him Theology) which deals with all *Ens* universally *quatenus Ens,* and with the *Prima Moventia,* themselves immovable, of the entire Kosmos.[76]

With Natorp the serious implications of the two-fold interpretation of the **Metaphysics** come to light.

Natorp first shows that the Aristotelian 'Being as Being' is the most abstract, i.e., most empty of notions.

> The [*prōtai arkhai kai aitiai*] form its object. The word [*prōtos*] here has, naturally, Aristotle's hardened, technical sense of the conceptually fundamental, of what lies at the basis of everything. It is a question therefore of the most universal, the most abstract, in whatever can be the object of scientific examination. This highest, because the most universal and most abstract object, is, however, as we will learn from *Gamma* 1, the fundamental concept of 'object in general. . . . '[77]

After treating of the other way in which Aristotle is considered to have spoken of the science, namely, as dealing with supersensible entity, Natorp continues:

> That this ambiguous conception of the theme of the [*prōtē philosophia*] contains an insufferable contradiction, . . . does not seem up to the present time to

have been made clear. A science which treats of Being in general and as such, must be superior in exactly the same manner to all those sciences which deal with any particular sphere of Being. This science cannot at the same time be identical with any one of them, be it the most important and the most excellent . . . On these premises, from which our chapter took its point of departure, it is impossible to have as a result that the [prōtē philosophia] should in fact on the one hand be the universal science, the science that is basic for all, but on the other hand be one and the same as the science of immaterial, unchangeable Being, as of the most excellent class of Being.[78]

Natorp considers that he is calling attention to a point that up to his own time had not been brought out clearly. This point is that the two views of the Aristotelian *Metaphysics* are mutually exclusive and contradictory.

In Natorp, then, for the first time in the history of modern Aristotelian criticism, there appears the realization of a serious problem behind the different formulae.

Natorp proceeds to show that metaphysics cannot be identified in Aristotle with 'theology.' . . . [79]

In establishing his view that Being in the most abstract sense is the 'genuinely Aristotelian concept'[80] of the object of metaphysics, Natorp excises the texts which state the opposite conception.[81] In order to explain a number of other texts[82] he must also admit a frequent use by Aristotle of the word 'first' in a sense quite different from what he has isolated as 'the hardened technical sense of the conceptually fundamental.'[83] He is fully conscious that the entire Greek tradition definitely held the view which he is destroying, namely, that the Primary Philosophy is the science of supersensible Being.[84] This view he considers to date from very close to the time of Aristotle. Its origin and the consequent textual interpolations are to be sought among minor Peripatetics.[85]

Clodius Piat, writing at the beginning of the present century, still sees no difficulty in unifying the different Aristotelian formulae.

'First Philosophy' has for its object Being considered as such. . . . In this way, metaphysics is the science of the principles and the causes of Being taken as such. By that very fact it is the science of the first principles and the first causes; . . . it is the perfect science. And one may add that it is also the most noble. It is proper, then, to regard as such the science that finds in God both its ideal development and its highest term . . .

If God is not only the metaphysician *par excellence,* but also the supreme object of metaphysics, this

science merits a name more precise than those which have been given it previously. It was defined at first:—The science of Being; then:—The science of the first causes and the first principles. We can now provide a more concrete notion of it:—Metaphysics is theology.[86]

Gomperz, on the other hand, sees the same fundamental contradiction as Zeller in the Aristotelian Being. He considers it hopeless.

In different passages of his **'Metaphysics'** Aristotle has, in truth, adopted fundamentally different attitudes towards this question; he has defined the truly existent, . . . now in the one, now in the other sense. The contradiction is glaring, and, in fact, generally recognized. No attempt to minimize its significance could possibly succeed. Followed into its consequences, the conflict is between the recognition of the world of experience on the one hand, and the transcendental world on the other.[87]

Apelt reduced the various senses of the Aristotelian Being to the copula. . . . [88]

This Being is an empty notion.[89] . . .

Hermann Dimmler, writing about the same time as Piat, employed, like Apelt, a grammatical approach to the Aristotelian problem of Being. The entire doctrine of Being was based on the function of the copula in a sentence.

The investigation was limited to the 'is' predication. This consists in predicating that what is asserted in the subject of the sentence *is* that which is designated in its predicate. This predication takes place by means of the copula . . .

Accordingly, the whole Aristotelian doctrine of Being is built up on the concept of Being as expressed in the form of the copula.[91]

For G. Rodier, the Aristotelian 'Being' pertains to things by reference to substance and by analogy. These two ways of conceiving Being are ultimately identical.

Thus the two conceptions of Being basically coalesce. For, according to the first, all that which is not substance itself is something pertaining to substance. According to the second, every part of substance is to its contrary or to its privation what complete substance is to its contrary or to its privation . . . In other words, complete Being is substance, and all other things of which one asserts Being are not comprised under the extension of *ousia* as its species, but in its comprehension as its parts.[92]

The Aristotelian 'Being' is therefore far from 'empty' in comprehension. It is individual; but the only complete individuality, pursues Rodier, is that of pure act. Yet matter must be real. This is the only inconsistency in Aristotle; but it is radical and grave.[93]

Octave Hamelin blames the confusion rather on a faulty notion which is prevalent in regard to Aristotle's epistemology. Hamelin identifies the notions of substance and Being as they are treated of by metaphysics.

> The treatment of substance as substance or of Being as Being is a science apart, the supreme science, the one which Aristotle calls first philosophy and which after his time has been called metaphysics.[94]

Hamelin then enters into a long discussion about the nature of the universal in Aristotle.[95] Only the element of *comprehension* is essential to the Aristotelian universal, he finds, and not the element of extension.[96]

> . . . science does not require as object in the eyes of Aristotle universals properly so-called. It can get along perfectly without the extensive element in the genera, it can get along even without the genera.[97]

In fact, the universal, in the ordinary acceptation, cannot be the object studied by any science whose subject matter is real.

> . . . for that which is common to several things is not, as such, enclosed in any one of them. For Aristotle, you have precisely there a character which prevents it from being a reality.[98]

The Aristotelian form, then, has a universality that is not of the same type as the commonly accepted notion of the universal. This peculiar doctrine of form enables the object of first philosophy to be an individual.

> Besides, even if the role of the form were not as manifestly preponderant in the reality of the composite substances, this would be of slight importance, since these substances are still not the realization of what is most substantial; and, according to Aristotle, Being as Being is not to be sought among them, nor even, to speak properly, at the root of any one of them. The object of first philosophy, says Aristotle, is Being as Being. But it must not be believed that Being as Being is a universal, a character common to all Beings . . . If Being, insofar as it regards all Beings, can be called universal, it is by a particular kind of universality. It is universal because it is primary and the foundation of analogy. Being as Being, because primary, becomes a type, it is imitated by other Beings. Each of these models itself upon it. But it is apart from them all, and that in a real, not logical, sense; and the true name of first philosophy is Theology. In a word, the object of first philosophy is an individual. Now this individual, as Aristotle repeats unceasingly in different ways of expression, is a pure form. It is a pure form, because its function is to explain the

other Beings and because the true explanation consists in calling upon the end, and, in the last analysis, the form. The form explains all the rest and is self-sufficient in its own right.[99]

Hamelin's interpretation follows the general lines of the ancient Greek commentators. He emphasizes the resolution of Aristotle's notion of Being into that of form. In calling attention to the peculiar nature of the form's universality, he suggests that the root of the trouble is the misunderstanding of the phrase 'Being as Being' in the sense of a universal object.

Werner Jaeger's well-known thesis maintains that the different ways of expressing the object of metaphysics indicate two mutually contradictory conceptions of the science in Aristotle.

> This gloss does not remove the contradiction. On the contrary, it only makes it more obvious. In attempting here to combine the two definitions he understands by a universal science a science of the 'first' object, which is a principle in a more comprehensive sense than are the other kinds of being; but in [G] 1 and the beginning of E universal meant that which does not refer to any particular part of being at all, and Aristotle could not and does not assert that the immaterial movers of the stars are not 'particular beings' nor 'one sort of being.' . . .

> These two accounts of the nature of metaphysics certainly did not arise out of one and the same act of reflection. Two fundamentally different trains of thought are here interwoven. It is obvious at once that the theological and Platonic one is the older of the two, . . . When metaphysics is defined as the study of being as being, on the other hand, reality is regarded as one single, unified series of levels, and this therefore is the more Aristotelian account of the two, that is to say, the one that corresponds to the last and most characteristic stage of his thought.[100]

In the earlier or Platonic stage, Aristotle merely replaced the Ideas by the prime mover. The earlier metaphysics was exclusively the science of supersensible Being, and not of Being as such.[101]

This theory makes the *Metaphysics* fragmentary from a doctrinal as well as from a literary point of view. The treatises contain two contradictory conceptions of the Primary Philosophy.

Jaeger's theory draws its strength from the brilliant manner in which it is supported by years of painstaking historical and philological research. Jaeger seems simply to take for granted, however, that the primary notion of the phrase 'Being as Being' is the concept of abstract, universal Being. He does not consider the possibility that its original and primary meaning in

Aristotle may have been something radically different. Nor does he take into account the peculiar nature of the Aristotelian universal as pointed out by Hamelin.

Sir David Ross admits two 'genuinely Aristotelian' views.

> Aristotle has in the main two ways of stating the subject-matter of metaphysics. In one set of passages it is stated as . . . the whole of being as such. This view is expressed throughout Book [G], and occasionally elsewhere; it is implied also in the description of [*sofia*] as being occupied with the first causes and principles, *sc.* of reality as a whole. But more frequently metaphysics is described as studying a certain part of reality, viz. that which . . . (exists independently) . . . In *E* an attempt is made to reconcile the two views. . . . In studying the nature of pure being, form without matter, philosophy is in effect coming to know the nature of being as a whole.

> Both views are genuinely Aristotelian, but the narrower view of the scope of metaphysics is that which is more commonly present in his works, and more in keeping with the distrust of a universal science expressed in the **Posterior Analytics.**[102]

The description of metaphysics as the study of first causes and principles is reduced by Ross to the conception of the science as the study of 'the whole of being, as such.' Jaeger, on the contrary, reduces this formulation to the earlier or 'theological' stage of Aristotle's reflection.[103]

Carlini notes the problem, without accepting any particular solution.[104]

Hans v. Arnim refuses to admit any real difference in the two descriptions of the Primary Philosophy as separated by Jaeger.

> I do not, in fact, admit that in *K* (and in [*G*] and *E*) any contamination of two contradictory conceptions regarding the object of metaphysics, which must arise out of two different sources of thought, is to be seen.[105]

> We find neither an earlier nor a later conception in Aristotle . . . , but always this one only, which we must recognize as the carefully weighed conviction of the philosopher. Whenever the Primary Philosophy is signalized as the science of the eternal, the separate, the immobile, this is a designation *a parte potiori.* It in no way excludes the other and secondary types of Being—insofar as they stand in relation to this primary Being through which they are called Beings—from treatment in this science. Only the first Being, the godhead, joins in itself the Eleatic characteristics of true Being—independent self-subsistence, eternity, and immobility.[106]

In v. Arnim's view there is only one Being in Aristotle which meets the requirements of Parmenides. All other things are called Beings through reference to it. The science that studies Being as such is therefore the science of separate Being. The different designations of the Primary Philosophy denote the one single science.

Endre v. Ivanka likewise sees no contradiction in the science of the supersensible as the universal science of Being, nor does he notice any greater emphasis of either formulation in the different treatises.

> There never was an Aristotelian metaphysics which did not proceed from the analysis of sensible substance and acquire the concept of its object—supersensible Being as the highest and first Being—from the comparative study of the different specific levels of Being. (This was the only way possible after the Platonic identification of the most perfect with the most universal). In this way it was the universal science of Being. Just as little was there ever a metaphysics that dealt with sensible substance for its own sake, . . . And even if . . . the one viewpoint actually were more strongly emphasized in the earlier parts and the other in the later, still an internal contradiction of the two conceptions would never result, . . . [107]

But Emilio Oggioni, in the wake of Jaeger, still finds successive stages of development in the **Metaphysics.** In the earliest, metaphysics was conceived as the science of the Platonic supersensibles, which were devastatingly criticized. In the second stage, it was the science of the causes. As such it was shown to be impossible. Then it was determined as the science of Being *qua* Being.[108] But within the notion of Being *qua* Being, Oggioni finds three different though closely related significations.

> The expression 'science of Being *qua* Being' receives, in these Aristotelian writings, three different and closely connected significations. If they are not kept clearly distinct, they render the progress of the thought particularly difficult to understand.

> I) The science of Being *qua* Being specifies, in some 'real' or being, the necessary conditions of reality or of actual existence—that is, the 'minimum' required for its cognoscibility in reality, all its determinations which remain when cognition prescinds from all that it can prescind from, without altogether ceasing to have an object. In this case the science of Being *qua* Being is a purely formal science, insofar as it determines the necessary conditions which render possible the real, or actual being in general, without, however, pronouncing on its actual reality. In this case the science of Being *qua* Being is a formal ontology. . . .

> II) The science of Being *qua* Being determines the totality of sufficient conditions regarding the actual

existence of one, some, or all the 'reals' or Beings, that is, the objects of actual or possible cognition. In opposition to the preceding case, the science of Being *qua* Being has now a character of reality. It is metaphysics in the current sense of the word. . . .

> III) Insofar, finally, as Aristotle determines the metaphysical principles of the real (which are evident for him through actual cognition) by the more mediate concepts, . . . he then conceives—though rarely and secondarily—the science of Being *qua* Being as that which deals with the ontological determinations which, according to his doctrine, explain the real in its actual metaphysical nature.[109]

'Being *qua* Being,' according to this analysis, can mean in the Aristotelian treatises either I) Being in general, II) substance, or III) (rarely and secondarily) substance determined by accidents.

Léon Robin, like Hamelin, finds the solution of the question in the peculiar nature of the Aristotelian universal.

> However, if it is indeed the truth that Being 'as Being' is not a genus, is it not true, on the other hand, as we have seen, that it is a universal attribute? Consequently, Being 'as Being' would be *the universality of Being;* in short, a universal of which philosophy would be the science. Now, such a way of presenting things is very plain in the *Metaphysics,* . . . But, on the other hand, assertions . . . which assign to philosophy as its object those Beings which are the stars and that separate and immobile Being which is God,—suppose an entirely different conception.[110]

Robin terms this a "capital problem."[111] Aristotle's solution, on the basis of the primacy of the First Being, calls for explanation. The 'analogy' of Being provides the answer.

> That is how Being 'as Being' is at the same time an individual and a universal, the supreme universal because it is the supreme individual and because it has the power to make itself universal in repeating itself, but with an exactitude that is always weaker. Its universality, however, is founded, it must be well understood, on its necessity, . . . and, if all the existences in which it repeats itself and which imitate it do not receive it in the same degree, nevertheless *they are all related to it.* In this manner its universality is, in them, but an identity of *relation* or an 'analogy.'[112]

In the same manner, each category in the sensible individual 'imitates' the fundamental category of substance.[113] In this way the unity of the First Substance is extended to all things.

> The *individual* unity of the first substance is found *universally,* through analogy, in all these singular things.[114]

A still more recent comment admits that the object of metaphysics is much wider than the supersensible world. It professes, however, to see no inconsistency in Aristotle's different ways of expressing this object.

> In the first Book of his *Metaphysics,* Aristotle describes first philosophy as the science of the ultimate causes of the whole of reality. . . . As a result, the supersensible world, which is the proper domain of first philosophy in this sense that it is studied by no other science, is not identified purely and simply with the object of metaphysics: This latter is much more vast. . . . In other places Aristotle insists rather on the supersensible character of the object of metaphysics, because that is a domain which is properly reserved to first philosophy. W. Jaeger is wrong then in considering these two conceptions as irreconcilable. The manner in which they are found mingled with each other in the work of the Stagirite indicates clearly that the author did not conceive them as opposed one to the other. Besides, this is what he expressly affirms in *Methaph.* VI, 1, 1026a22-32 and IX, 7, 1064b14: the priority of metaphysics over the other sciences involves necessarily the universal character of its object.[115]

Quite similarly, Giovanni di Napoli admits Jaeger's twofold conception,[116] but asserts that the two notions radically imply each other in Aristotle's thought. Only by studying sensible things precisely as Being can human thought attain the Immobile.

> This means that in the thought of Aristotle the two views of metaphysics radically imply each other: metaphysics as the science of Being *qua* Being conditions metaphysics as the science of the Immobile; only by transcending the physical level (and that means considering not only that which is, but Being *qua* Being) is it possible to reach the Immobile.[117]

A. H. Armstrong, on the other hand, returns to the ancient Greek view. The First Philosophy studies Being at its highest level, and in this way treats Being as such.

> It is therefore Substance which Metaphysics studies . . . Furthermore, there are different grades of Substance. Besides the separate substantial individual beings which are subject to change, . . . there are, Aristotle says, separate substances which are free from change, pure actualities with no potency in them at all. These are the highest class of substantial being, the most completely real things that exist. It is therefore on them that Metaphysics concentrates, because by studying being at its most perfect and complete it obtains the fullest possible knowledge of being as such. It is therefore First Philosophy because it studies the primary forms of being and Theology because these primary beings are divine.[118]

The results of the long centuries of interpretation regarding the Aristotelian 'Being *qua* Being' may now be briefly summed up.

In the Greek tradition, 'Being *qua* Being' seems to be ultimately identified with the Being of the separate Entities. Among the Arabs there appears with Avicenna its interpretation as *Ens commune*. In this sense the Aristotelian phrase was understood in the mediaeval universities. It was not considered as an 'empty' concept, yet it was sharply distinguished from the most perfect Being. These two general interpretations, though understood in various ways, have been revived in the present era. Some moderns have professed to see an incurable contradiction between the two conceptions. Others think they follow with perfect consistency from Aristotle's fundamental doctrines of *ousia* and of the universal. Apparently, then, a thorough investigation, unprejudiced by any positions adopted in advance, is alone adequate for the inquiry. Only after such a study will one be in a position to declare what notion of Being actually lay in the texts before the mediaeval thinkers during the all-important formative period of Western metaphysics.

As recent writers have advocated such different approaches to the problem, and since the approach has considerable influence on the solution, the proper method of entering upon the investigation should first be determined.

This in itself is no easy task. Yet the manner in which the centuries have unfolded the problem should furnish at least some guidance. What light does the historical sketch that has just been concluded throw upon the situation? Does it indicate the correct way in which the Aristotelian treatment of Being should be approached?

The problem, as the historical survey should make evident, will center upon the Aristotelian universal in relation to Being, and still more ultimately upon the relation of form to individual thing. the controversy in the wake of Natorp and Jaeger emphasizes the first consideration. Is the universal synonymous with the real for the Stagirite? Or are the two opposed to each other? Does a thing increase in reality as it becomes more universal? Or, on the contrary, does universality involve abstraction, and so make the most universal the most abstract and therefore the least real? In a word, is there any abstraction in the Primary Philosophy? Back of these queries, as appears from the reflections of writers like Zeller and Hamelin, is the still more fundamental relation of form and individual. Is the Aristotelian form individual of its very nature, or does it require a further principle as matter to individuate it? The form can be seen quite readily as the principle of universality. Is it also the principle of individuality? If it is both, then the universal and the indi-

vidual should coincide not only in the supersensible, but in all Beings. The greater the universality, the higher would be the degree of reality and Being. But the difficulties in conceiving the form as the principle of individuation in sensible things seem evident. If matter, accordingly, must be the individuating principle, then the universal will be abstract. The greater the universality, the less will be the reality and the degree of Being. The problem therefore hinges ultimately upon the character of the Aristotelian form, and its relations to the universal and the singular. But all these operative notions—universal, singular, individual, matter, form—have been understood in various senses throughout the long history of Aristotelian influence. Their rendition in other languages and in different philosophical background has often obscured their sense. Yet to grasp precisely what they meant for the Stagirite is essential for the study of Being. Through these notions must the problem be approached. But how is one to arrive at their original signification in the Lyceum?

The only means at hand today are Aristotle's own writings and the available historical and philological knowledge of the setting in which these were composed. The correct approach, accordingly, will necessitate an investigation of the nature of the Stagirite's writings and their immediate background, his use of terms and concepts, and the exact rendition of his thought in the English language. Such preliminary considerations of technique may seem laborious. But they are indispensable if the problem of Aristotelian Being is to be adequately studied in the setting which history has imposed upon it, namely, in terms of the universal and the real, and ultimately in function of the form and the individual.

Notes

[1] "Schon in der Gegenstandsbestimmung der Metaphysik zeigt sich das allmähliche Loslösen der aristotelischen Anschauungen von wesentlichen und grundlegenden Lehren Platos." Johann Fuchs, *Die Proprietäten des Seins bei Alexander von Hales,* p. 45.

[2] "Darin besteht also der wesentliche Unterschied zwischen platonischer und aristotelischer Seinsauffassung, dass für erstere das Sein als Sein das *ens perfectissimum* ist, während für letztere Sein als Sein das *ens commune* ist." *Ibid.,* p. 48.

[3] "Die Frage lässt sich konkret so formulieren: Gibt Alexander dem Seinsbegriff einen Sinn, der ihn zum eigentlichen Gottesbegriff macht und der darum alles endliche und veränderliche Sein nur im Sinne einer unvollkommenen Erfüllung, einer Erfüllung *per participationem* umfasst?" *Ibid.,* p. 49.

[4] "Sieht unser Autor im Seinsbegriff den Inhaltsleersten und abstraktesten Begriff, der, weil den geringsten

Inhalt, den weitesten Umfang hat?" *Ibid.,* p. 49.

[5] Fuchs (*ibid.,* p. 46, n. 1) cites Jaeger for this interpretation of the *Metaphysics.*

[6] Texts and references *infra,* pp. 53-55, nn. 77-85.

[7] Text, *infra,* p. 52, n. 74.

[8] Cf. W. Jaeger, *Aristoteles,* p. 5 (trans. Robinson, p. 7).

[9] Cf. *op. cit.,* p. 217 (trans. Robinson, p. 210).

[10] Aristotle does not speak of the 'object' of a science. He merely names what the science treats, either in the accusative case after a verb, or in the genitive after a noun; or, more frequently, with the preposition 'about.' The Arabians—in accord with their general usage of the passive participle for the object of any activity—employed the participle MAWDŪ, meaning 'that which is posited.' This was the same term which they used for the *subject* of predication (cf. A-M Goichon, *Lexique,* pp. 438-439; *Vocabulaires,* p. 40a). The Latins translated the term in both cases by *subjectum.* They spoke accordingly of the 'subject' of a science. At *K* 4, 1061b31, Aristotle uses the corresponding Greek word . . . , in the plural, for the things of which a science treats. Zabarella, a leading representative of the Peripatetic tradition in the late Renaissance, still uses *subjectum.* Cf. *De Natura Logicae,* I, 14; *Opera Logica* (1594), col. 33 ff. But among the Scholastics there appears with the close of the thirteenth century the term *objectum.* Duns Scotus, while using both words in practice, considers *objectum* the more proper term. "Sed loquimur de materia *circa quam* est scientia, quae dicitur a quibusdam subjectum scientiae, vel magis proprie objectum, sicut et illud circa quod est virtus, dicitur objectum virtutis proprie, non subjectum." *Quaest. Metaph.,* Prologus, 10; in *Op. Om.,* VII, 7a.

The transition from *subjectum* to *objectum,* as may be seen in the above text, was not difficult. 'Objectum' had been used for the object of the generic 'habitus' as well as for the object of a faculty. This was the Aristotelian . . . [subject] (cf. H. Bonitz, *Ind. Arist.,* 64a18-35). St. Thomas Aquinas, however, seems careful in using *subjectum* in regard to science, even while employing *objectum* in reference to the more generic 'habitus'. " . . . sic enim se habet subjectum ad scientiam, sicut objectum ad potentiam vel habitum." *Summa Th.,* I, 1, 7c; 7a2-4. Cf. L. Schütz, *Thomas-Lexikon,* pp. 536; 725.

On account of possible doctrinal implications, it is safer when dealing with the different writers to retain the particular mode of expression that was customary at the time.

I am indebted to Dr. Emil Fackenheim, of the University of Toronto, for the information here and elsewhere regarding the usage of arabic terms.

[11] W. Jaeger, *Aristoteles,* pp. 222-228 (trans. Robinson, pp. 214-219).

[12] Cf. M. Grabmann, *Die lateinischen Aristotelesübersetzungen des 13. Jahrhunderts,* pp. 1-169.

[13] *Ibid.,* pp. 1-2.

[14] Cf. J. Fuchs, *op. cit.,* pp. 48-49.

[15] E.g., "Sed enti non potest addi aliquid quasi extranea natura, per modum quo differentia additur generi, vel accidens subjecto; quia quaelibet natura essentialiter est ens; ut etiam probat Philosophus in III Metaphys. (comm. 1), quod ens non potest esse genus." St. Thomas Aquinas, *De Veritate,* I, 1c.

[16] G. Rodier describes—without accepting—the different tendency of the more modern approach. "Si nous demandons, en effet, à Aristote ce qu'il faut entendre par l'être, ce qu'il y a de plus immédiatement saisissable dans sa réponse est à peu près ceci: L'être n'est qu'un terme vide, qui ne correspond à aucune réalité et à aucun concept." *L'Année Philosophique,* XX (1909), 1. Being is not even a concept, but merely an empty term. R. G. Collingwood (*An Essay on Metaphysics,* pp. 6-20), for instance, interprets the Aristotelian Being *qua* Being in this sense. Being so understood is the equivalent of 'nothing.' *Ibid.,* p. 14. On the gradual 'emptying' of the notion of Being during the late mediaeval and post-Scholastic periods, cf. André Marc, *L'Idée de l'Etre,* pp. 1-11; E. Gilson, *L'Etre et l'Essence,* pp. 121-212; *Being and Some Philosophers,* pp. 76-137.

It is true that *ex professo* commentators remain as a rule too close to the text of the *Metaphysics* to use the term 'empty' in describing the Stagirite's Being *qua* Being. Apelt, however, writes of the Aristotelian Being: "Das 'Seiende' ist also für sich genommen noch gar nichts weiter als ein leeres, weisses Blatt, auf das erst etwas geschrieben werden muss, wenn es Bedeutung bekommen soll." *Beiträge zur Geschichte der Griechischen Philosophie,* p. 112. But others, though more cautious in their language, tend towards the same conception. Natorp (text *infra,* p. 53, n. 77) considers the Aristotelian Being *qua* Being as the "most abstract object" and as "object in general," somewhat in the Kantian sense. Jaeger denies in it any "determined Being". . . . *Aristoteles,* p. 227 (cf. trans. Robinson, p. 218; text *infra,* pp. 59-60). On the Kantian background involved in this approach cf. C. Arpe, . . . *Aristoteles,* p. 8, n. 2.

[17] E. Gilson, *The Spirit of Mediaeval Philosophy* (trans. A. H. C. Downes), pp. 64-107.

[18] *Exod.,* III, 14 (Vulgate). Cf. E. Gilson, *op. cit.,* pp. 51-52.

[19] William of Auvergne has the merit of focusing mediaeval attention upon this difference between the Greek and the Christian conceptions. In the still early stages of the Aristotelian influence in the university circles, the militant theologian-bishop of Paris designated clearly the fundamental point of cleavage. "De tribus causis, quae videntur in errorem praemissum Aristotelem, et alios induxisse,—*Causae autem erroris istius videntur potissimum fuisse tres. Harum prima fuit ignorantia eorum, qua non intellexerunt verbum creatoris, neque virtutem ipsius verbi.* Est enim non solum enunciativum, ut ita loquamur sed etiam imperativum imperiositate forti in ultimitate fortitudinis propter quod ejus imperio obediunt non solum ea quae sunt, sed etiam ea, quae non sunt, et non solum in faciendo, et non faciendo, quae mandaverit, aut prohibuerit, sed etiam in essendo, et non essendo, in fiendo, et non fiendo; . . . *Secunda causa fuit ignorantia libertatis ipsius creatoris,* qua operatur absque eo, quod prohiberi possit ullo modorum ab eo, quod vult, aut cogi ad id, quod non vult: *ipsi autem opinari nixi sunt sicut praedixi tibí,* quod operaretur per modum naturae, et juxta ordinem ipsius, cum ipse operetur per electionem, et voluntatem liberrimam. . . . *Tertia causa fuit opinio eorum erronea, qua putaverunt elongationem posse aliquid apud creatorem,* et aestimaverunt creatorum longe esse a quibusdam, et prope quibusdam, et propter hoc ipsum non operari per se, aut minus operari. *Non intellexerunt igitur supereminentiam creatoris,* et amplitudinem, ac fortitudinem virtutis ejus, qua attingit a summo universi usque deorsum, et a primo creatorum usque ad novissimum, omnia continens, tenens, et retinens, prout vult, et quamdiu vult, alioquin reciderent in non esse, unde educta sunt ab ipso, et per ipsum." William of Auvergne, *De Universo,* I-Iae, 27; ed. Orleans (1674), I, 623b-624a. Cf. *ibid.,* cc. 17-30, pp. 611-629.

From the Greek side, Galen had expressed the same view. "It was not in itself sufficient merely to will that they should come to be made of this nature. For if he had wished to make the stone instantly into a man, it was not in his power. And it is here that our own doctrine, and that of Plato and of all the Greeks who have correctly undertaken the treatment of nature, differs from that of Moses. For Moses, it suffices that God willed that matter be given a formation, and thereupon it has received that formation. He considers that all things are possible to God, even if He wishes to make ashes into a horse or an ox. We do not think that way, but say that some things are impossible by nature, and these God does not even attempt. He only chooses the best from among the things that were possible to be made." C. Galen, *De Usu Partium,* XI, 14,905-906; ed. Helmreich, II, 158.17-159.3.

These two appraisals, by a Christian and a Greek respectively, agree in signalizing the same fundamental difference between the doctrine of Genesis and the tradition of the Greeks. In the Christian teaching, the power of God is infinite; for the Greeks, it is finite. Perfect Being for the Greeks meant limitation and finitude; for the Christians, the perfect Being is infinite. Limitation for the Christians denotes imperfection; while for the Greeks, imperfection was implied by infinity. Cf. J. Chevalier, *La Notion du Nécessaire chez Aristote,* pp. 187-188; F. M. Cornford, *Plato's Cosmology,* p. 36. H. Guyot, in concluding a survey (*L'Infinité Divine depuis Philon le Juif jusqu'à Plotin,* pp. 1-32) of the Greek notion of infinity up to Philo, writes: "En somme, l'esprit grec aima trop la mesure et la proportion pour s'être résolu à voir dans l'Infinité le comble de la perfection . . . En tout cas, le Principe premier—Eau, Fini, Atome, Idée, Pensée—est conçu dès l'origine et par la suite comme déterminé." *Ibid.,* p. 31.

Origen, at the meeting-point of Greek philosophy and Christian revelation, encountered serious difficulty owing to the Greek equation of finitude with perfection and knowability. "For if the divine power were infinite, it would of necessity not know itself; for by its nature the infinite is incomprehensible." *De Principiis,* II, 9, 1; ed. Koetschau, p. 164.5-6.

[20] E.g. "Metaphysica vero, ut est nobis possibilis nunc, non est principaliter scientia, *propter quid* de Deo; . . . Aliter potest dici, quod passio prius conclusa *quia,* de Deo semper est posterior et remotior ab ejus essentia, quia propinquoir effectui, ex quo concluditur, ita quod semper in passionibus proceditur *quia;* cujus signum est, quia Trinitas, quae illi essentiae singularissimae inest, ex nullo effectu concluditur." John Duns Scotus, *Quaest. Metaph.,* 1, 1, 45; in *Op. Om.,* VII, 34b-35a. Cf. *Op. Ox.,* Prologus I, 2, 13 (14); ed. Garcia, I, 14-15.

At best, according to Scotus, a metaphysics with the *primum ens* as its subject could be only *per accidens* of God. " . . . igitur Metaphysica et naturalis scientia sunt de eodem per accidens; sed de Deo est naturalis magis per accidens, quia summa descriptio, ad quam pervenit de ipso, quasi remotior est a quiddidate Dei, quam summa Metaphysici." *Quaest. Metaph.,* I, 1, 49; *Op. Om.,* VII, 37a. Cf. J. Owens, *Mediaeval Studies* X (1948), 175-176. Scotus describes the different status of a metaphysics in God or in the angels, *Quaest. Metaph.,* I, 1, 40; v. VII, p. 32a.

[21] For a general conspectus of the Scholástics on this question, cf. Francisco Suarez, *Disputationes Metaphysicae,* I, 1; in *Op. Om.,* XXV, 2-12; especially

no. 26, p. 11a.

22 " . . . et hi more Latinorum, qui omnem distinctionem solutionem esse reputant dicentes subjectum tribus modis dici in scientia, scilicet quod communius subjicitur, aut certius, aut in scientia dignius: et primo modo dicunt ens in ista subjici scientia, et secundo causam, et tertio modo Deum: et hanc scientiam non a toto, sed a quadam sui parte dignissima vocari divinam. Sed ego tales logicas consequentias in scientiis de rebus abhorreo, eo quod ad multos deducunt errores." Albertus Magnus, *Metaph.*, I, 1, 2; in *Op. Om.*, VI, 6b.

23 *Ibid.*, pp. 4a-5b; 6a.

24 "Ex quo apparet, quod quamvis ista scientia praedicta tria consideret, non tamen considerat quodlibet eorum ut subjectum, sed ipsum solum ens commune." St. Thomas Aquinas, *in Metaph.*, Prooemium; ed. Cathala, p. 2b. Cf. J. D. Robert, *Divus Thomas* (Piacenza), L (1947), 220-221.

25 "Dicendum quod haec scientia debet considerare de per se consequentibus ad ens, quae sunt enti propria; cuiusmodi sunt partes seu species et passiones quae non faciunt ens cuiusmodi sunt partes esse aliquid scientiae particularis. Nunc autem principium est de consequentibus ad ens, non communius ente neque aequale, nec collocat ens in aliquo genere particulare; quare, etc.

Et de Primo Principio essendi debet haec scientia inquirere passiones non reales: cuiusmodi sunt perfectionum causa et sic de aliis; multitudo enim attributorum Deo nihil est extra intellectum.

Videndum etiam est quid est et si est. Tamen entis, secundum quod ens, non est principium qui a tunc omne ens haberet principium.

Ad rationes cum arguitur, dicendum quod aliquando principia rei non sunt principia doctrinae, . . ." Siger of Brabant, *Quaest. Metaph.*, 2; ed. Graiff, p. 5.8-22.

26 John Duns Scotus, *Quaest. Metaph.*, I, 1; *Op. Om.*, VII, 11-37.

27 *Ibid.*, nos. 21-27; pp. 21-25.

28 Cf. "Dico ergo impossibile esse ut ipse Deus sit subjectum hujus scientiae, quia subjectum omnis scientiae est res quae conceditur esse, et ipsa scientia non inquirit nisi dispositiones illius subjecti." Avicenna, *Metaph.*, I, 1; fol. 70rl-2. Cf. trans. Horten, p. 7. Also: "Oportebit tunc ut ens in quantum est ens sit subjectum: quod est convenientius. Monstrata est igitur destructio illius opinionis qua dicitur quod subjectum hujus scientiae sunt causae ultimae. Sed tamen debes scire quod haec sunt completio et quaesitum ejus." *Ibid.*, I,

1, fol. 70 vl; Horten trans. p. 14. Cf. Siger of Brabant, *op. cit.*, pp. 3-4.

29 Duns Scotus, *Quaest. Metaph.*, I, 1, 4; VII, 13. Cf. Averroes: "Naturalis consyderat de formis materialibus, secunda autem de formis simplicibus abstractis a materia, et est illa Scientia, quae consyderat de ente simpliciter. Sed notandum est, quod istud genus entium, esse, scilicet, separatum a materia, non declaratur nisi in hac scientia naturali. Et qui dicit quod prima Philosophia nititur declarare entia separabilia esse, peccat. Haec enim entia sunt subjecta primae Philosophiae, . . ." Averroes, *Physica,* I, 83FG; Venice (1562), fol. 47r2-vl.

30 John Duns Scotus, *loc. cit.*, nos. 28-33; pp. 25-28.

31 *Ibid.*, no. 21; p. 21a.

32 Cf. *Adnotatio* of M. de Portu, in *Duns Scoti Op. Om.*, VII, 37b-39b; C. L. Shircel, *The Univocity of the Concept of Being in the Philosophy of Duns Scotus,* pp. 90-94.

33 "Secundo dico, quod communissimum quod potest apprehendi a nobis est ens quod est univocum omni enti reali. Aliter non possemus habere aliquam cognitionem nec de deo nec de substantia." William of Ockham, *in Sent.* I, 3, 8E. Cf. *ibid.*, Prologus, III, 7S.

34 " . . . une extrême diversité de points de vue se fait jour sur presque toutes les questions." E. Gilson, *La Philosophie au Moyen Age,* (1944), p. 413.

35 Aristotle, *Metaph.*, A 1,982a1-3; 2,982b9-10.

36 [*G*] 1,1003a26-32; *E* 1,1025b3-4; *K* 1,1059a18-20.

37 [*G*] 1,1003a21-24; *K* 3,1060b31-32.

38 *E* 1,1026a19-23; *K* 7,1064b1-6.

39 *E* 1,1026a23-32; *K* 7,1064b6-14.

40 *B* 2,996b31; 997a1-2; 11; *Z* 1,1028b4-7; [*L*] 1,1069a18.

41 [*G*] 3,1005a35.

42 *Ibid.*, 2,1003b18; *H* 1,1042a5; [*L*] 1,1069a18-19.

43 *E* 1,1026a16-18.

44 *A* 3,983b2-3. Cf. W. D. Ross, *Arist. Metaph.*, I, 128.

45 *Ph.*, I 9,192a34-36; cf. II 2,194b14-15.

46 "One might be in aporia about whether the science of Being *qua* Being is to be regarded as universal or

not . . . . if there is another nature and Entity, separate and immobile, the knowledge of it must be different and prior to natural philosophy, and universal by being prior." *K* 8,1064b6-14. Cf. *E* 1,1026a23-32.

[47] Cf. W. D. Ross, *Theophrastus Metaph.,* pp. xi-xxi.

[48] Theophrastus, *Metaphysics,* I, 1-4; trans. Ross-Fobes, pp. 2.2-4.5.

[49] Natorp (*Philos. Monatsh.,* XXIV, 1888, pp. 546-548) claims that Theophrastus intends in this document to deal with only one part of the Primary Philosophy.—The text seems to offer no grounds for such a distinction. For general interpretation of the document, cf. A. M. J. Festugière, *Rev. Néoscol.* XXXIII (1931), 40-49; on the relation of document to the Aristotelian *Metaphysics,* cf. E. Zeller, *Abh. Berl. Akad.* (1877), 146-150.

[50] Eudemus of Rhodes, *Fr.* 4; ed. Mullach, *Fragmenta Philos. Graec.,* III, 224 (Wehrli, *Fr.* 34, p. 23.27-29). On the interpretation of the fragment, see P. Merlan, *From Platonism to Neoplatonism* (2nd ed., 1960), pp. 208-209.

[51] Natorp (*loc. cit.,* p. 548) interprets the text of Eudemus in the 'abstract' sense. On the historical origin of this modern contrast of 'ontology' with the particular branches of philosophy, cf. E. Conze, *Der Begriff der Metaphysik bei Franciscus Suarez,* p. 65. In such a conception no problem can arise in the mutual relations of their respective objects. "Hier wird kein Verbindungsglied zwischen dem Sein und den immateriellen Substanzen mehr gesucht, sie werden einfach gegenüber gestellt, wie der allgemeine Teil dem besonderen." E. Conze, *ibid.,* pp. 64-65.

[52] 'Entity' is used here to translate *ousia.* Cf. *infra,* Chapter Four, pp. 138-153.

[53] Alexander of Aphrodisias, *in Metaph.,* 245.29-246.13. On the lines introducing the three-fold division, cf. trans. Sepulveda (1551), fol. 43rl: "Prima enim philosophia, quae proprie sapientia nuncupatur, quaeque de sempiternis ac immobilibus divinisque considerat, *philosophiae pars* est. Itaque sapientia *licet* universalis et prima *sit,* ut quae de ente in eo quod est ens, non de aliquo ente contempletur, *subjicitur tamen philosophiae;* sub hac itaque collocatur tum prima philosophia, . . ." Italics mine, indicating words added or changed in the interpretation of the difficult Greek text. Cf. Alexander, *op. cit.* (ed. Hayduck), pp. 18.8-11; 171.5-10; 250.30-32; 266.2-14.

Alexander (*ibid.,* p. 245.23-24) explains the [*tō genei*] at line 6 of the passage just cited, in a way that makes it a Dative of Respect. On this Dative in the original Aristotelian text, cf. *infra,* Chapter Seven, a), n. 55.

[54] The commentaries on Books *E-N* which have come down under Alexander's name are by a much later writer. Cf. F. Ueberweg, *Geschichte der Philosophie,* I, 564; W. D. Ross, *Arist. Metaph.,* II, 347.

[55] Cf. [*D*] 26,1023b29-32.

[56] Alexander, *op. cit.,* p. 447.22-32; cf. A. Mansion, *Rev. Néoscol.* XXIX (1927), 329.

[57] *Ibid.,* p. 661.33-39.

[58] Syrianus, *in Metaph.,* p. 55.3-16.

[59] *Ibid.,* p. 58.12-15.

[60] Asclepius, *in Metaph.,* p. 1.17-20; cf. pp. 2.9-20; 3.25-4.3. Asclepius (*ibid.,* pp. 235.13-236.6) explains the Primary Philosophy as genus (p. 235.15) and as species (p. 236.1-2), using to a considerable extent the words of Alexander quoted above, n. 53. As with Alexander, the divine Being seems distinguished from 'particular Being'—"Wisdom is therefore the *par excellence* science of the immobile and eternal and divine things, and it deals with Being *qua* Being, but not particular Being." *Ibid.,* pp. 235.33-236.1.

[61] *Ibid.,* pp. 225.14-226.25.

[62] *Ibid.,* p. 364.22-25; cf. p. 226.2-5.

[63] *Ibid.,* p. 235.12-13; cf. p. 364.17-19.

[64] *Ibid.,* p. 232.4-11.

[65] Eustratius, *in Eth. Nic.,* p. 42.10-12.

[66] *Stromata,* I, 28, 176; *PG* VIII, 924A.

[67] P. Natorp, *Philos. Monatsh.,* XXIV (1888), 63-64.

[68] "L'être en tant qu'être ne se laisse circonscrire dans aucune classe; les causes n'en sont pas diverses et particulières, mais universelles et uniformes; il ne peut être l'objet que d'une science universelle.

La science des premiers principes, la philosophie premiere peut donc être définie 'la science universelle de l'être en tant qu'être'." F. Ravaisson, *Essai,* I, 354; cf. I, 378-379

[69] "Chaque être particulier ou chaque nature c'est un acte imparfait, ou un mouvement, dont la Pensée est la cause, la fin, et l'essence; ou, pour réduire le mouvement à son principe, c'est le désir par lequel la divine Pensée, présente à toutes les puissances que la matière enferme, les fait venir à l'existence et à la vie. . . .

Un seul et même Etre, qui n'est autre que la Pensée ou l'intuition de lui-même, apparaissant dans les puissances différentes de la matière, sous mille formes et en mille opérations différentes, . . . telle est la conception générale dans laquelle se résume toute la Métaphyique." *Ibid.,* II, 564-565.

[70] . . . A. Schwegler, *Metaph. Arist.,* IV, 35.

[71] "Pertinet autem universum genus philosophiae ad universum genus entium, sicut alibi etiam idem genus vel sensibile vel scibile eidem generi vel sensus vel scientiae subiicitur; singulae autem species entis . . . singulis speciebus sive doctrinis philosophiae continentur . . ." H. Bonitz, *Arist. Methaph.,* II, 174.

[72] "Igitur theologia prima est doctrina, et quatenus prima est omnium, universalis potest dici, quum reliquae omnes ex illa summum debeant repetere principium." *Ibid.,* II, 285.

Other writers of the same period likewise saw no difficulty in combining the different Aristotelian formulae. E.g., "Da nun die Metaphysik das Seyende als solches in Betrachtung zieht, so hat sie zu ihrem Gegenstande vorzugsweise die ursprünglichen, unveränderlichen Wesenheiten." Franz Biese, *Philosophie des Aristoteles,* I, 364. Cf. also W. Christ, *Studia in Aristotelis Libros Metaph.,* pp. 98-99; W. Luthe, *Begriff und Aufgabe der Metaphysik des Aristoteles,* p. 15. J. Glaser (*Die Metaphysik des Aristoteles,* pp. 58-61) encounters no trouble, but for another reason—the different formulae seem in Hegelian fashion to express different moments of the metaphysical object. Cf. *ibid.,* pp. 244-249.

[73] Edward Zeller, *Aristotle and the Earlier Peripatetics,* (trans. Costelloe and Muirhead, London: 1897), I, 291-292. Cf. *ibid.,* pp. 290-295.

[74] . . . E. Zeller, *AGP,* II (1889), 270-271.

[75] . . . A. Schwegler, *Metaph. Arist.,* IV, 118.

[76] G. E. Grote, *Aristotle* (1883), p. 423.

[77] . . . P. Natorp, *Philos. Monatsh.,* XXIV (1888), 39. In a footnote, Natorp calls attention to the deepseated difference, from the epistemological viewpoint, between the Aristotelian and Kantian notions. Aristotle does not make the investigation concern the conditions and laws of the objectivity of *knowledge.* The Aristotelian Being is not intended as a mere condition of knowledge. *Ibid.,* p. 39, n. 5.

The one reference given by Natorp (*ibid.,* p. 39, n. 3) for his interpretation of Being as in the sense of the 'most abstract' is A 2,982a26.

[78] . . . *Ibid.,* pp. 49-50.

[79] . . . *Ibid.,* 52-53.

[80] *Op. cit.,* p. 548.

[81] Cf. *op. cit.,* pp. 51-52; 55; 549-554.

[82] *Op. cit.,* pp. 542; 544-545; 547. Cf. pp.39; 53; 54-55.

[83] *Op. cit.,* pp. 39. Cf. note 51, *supra.*

[84] *Op. cit.,* pp. 63-64.

[85] *Op. cit.,* pp. 64-65; 546; 548-549. Aurelio Covotti reacted to Natorp on this point in practically the same way as Zeller (cf. *supra,* n. 74). . . . A. Covotti, *Rivista di Filologia,* XXIV (1896), 350-351. (In *Da Aristotele ai Bizantini,* pp. 55-56).

For Covotti, the two conceptions of the Primary Philosophy are in fact contradictory, because the Aristotelian Being *qua* Being has two mutually contradictory senses, the one universal, the other individual. This expresses clearly the contrasts involved in the modern problem of interpreting the Aristotelian Being. One side appears as universal, and, in Zeller's *(loc. cit.)* words, pure form and object of pure knowledge. The other side is the singular, the concrete, and the real. Covotti sees the contradiction running through both the earlier and later parts of the *Metaphysics,* as he divides the treatises. Cf. A. Covotti, *op. cit.,* p. 73.

[86] "La 'philosophie première' a pour objet l'être considéré comme tel. Chacune des autres sciences n'embrasse qu'une portion définie de la réalité; . . .

Ainsi, la métaphysique est la science des principes et des causes de l'être pris comme tel. Par là même, c'est celle des premiers principes et des premières causes; . . . c'est la science parfaite. Et l'on peut ajouter que c'est aussi la plus noble. Il convient, en effet, de regarder comme telle la science qui trouve en Dieu et son développement idéal et son terme le plus élevé. . . .

Si Dieu est non seulement le métaphysicien par excellence, mais encore l'objet suprême de la métaphysique, cette science mérite un nom plus précis que ceux qu'on lui a donnés précédemment. On l'a d'abord définie; la science de l'être; puis: la science des premières causes et des premiers principes. On peut en fournir maintenant une notion plus concrète: la métaphysique, c'est la théologie." Clodius Piat, *Aristote,* pp. 1-5.

Eugen Rolfes took the same view. "So sucht denn auch die Metaphysik die Gründe des Seienden als solchen zu erkennen. . . . Die Metaphysik hat also zweierlei zu betrachten, einmal das Seiende im allgemeinen nach den ihm zukommenden Bestimmungen und dann die letzten Gründe alles Seienden. Es sind das aber keine zwei getrennten Objekte, sondern das zweite ist mit dem ersten gegeben, insofern ja nichts ohne seine Gründe gewusst sein kann: . . ." E. Rolfes, *Aristoteles' Metaphysik* (1904), p. 1. Similarly also P. Alfaric, *Aristote,* pp. 11-13.

[87] T. Gomperz, *Greek Thinkers* (trans. G. G. Berry, 1912), IV, 77.

[88] . . . O. Apelt, *Beiträge zur Geschichte der griechischen Philosophie,* p. 128.

[89] Cf. *supra,* n. 16. . . .

[91] "Die Untersuchung beschränkte sich auf die Ist-Aussage. Diese besteht darin, dass ausgesagt wird, das im Satzubjekt Angegebene *sei* das im Satzprädikat Bezeichnete. Diese Aussage erfolgt mittelst der Kopula . . .

Die ganze aristotelische Seinslehre baut sich demgemäss auf dem Seinsbegriff auf, wie er in der Form der Kopula zum Ausdruck kommt." H. Dimmler, *Ousia-Lehre,* p. 49. Cf. *Festgabe G. v. Hertling,* pp. 64-67.

An approach from the viewpoint of logic may be seen in R. Demos, *Philosophy and Phenomenological Research,* V (1944-1945), 255-268.

[92] . . . G. Rodier, *L'Année Philosophique,* XX (1909), 5. For P. Eusebietti, writing about the same time as Rodier, the object of the Primary Philosophy was the supreme pair of contraries. "A me basta aver messo in rilievo questo che nessuno ancora . . . a fatto notare; che secondo Aristotele la filosofia prima ha per obietto la suprema coppia di contrarii, l'essere ed il non essere, alla quale qualisivoglia altra coppia si riconduce: . . ." *AGP,* XXII (1909), 541; cf. pp. 536-539. Cf. *infra,* Chapter Nineteen, n. 38.

[93] G. Rodier, *op. cit.,* p. 11.

[94] "La théorie de la substance comme substance ou de l'être en tant qu'être est une science à part, la science suprême, celle qu'Aristote appelle la philosophie première et qu'on a appelée après lui la métaphysique." O. Hamelin, *Le Système d'Aristote,* p. 394.

[95] *Op. cit.,* pp. 394-400.

[96] *Ibid.,* p. 396. Cf. G. Rodier, *Aristote: Traité de l'Ame,* II, 19.

[97] " . . . la science ne réclame pas pour objet aux yeux d'Aristote des universaux proprement dits. Elle se passe parfaitement de l'élément extensif dans les genres, et

elle se passe même aussi des genres." O. Hamelin, *op. cit.,* p. 398.

[98] " . . . car ce qui est commun à plusieurs choses n'est, comme tel, enfermé dans aucune d'elles. Pour Aristote, c'est précisément là un caractère qui l'empêche d'être une réalité." *Ibid.,* p. 400. Cf. L. Robin, text *infra,* n. 112. Schwegler had already pointed out the tendency of the Aristotelian philosophy to identify the universal and the individual in the highest instance of each, namely in the divinity. Cf. *supra,* n. 75.

[99] "Quand même d'ailleurs la part de la forme ne serait pas aussi manifestement prépondérante dans la réalité des substances composées, cela serait de peu d'importance, puisque ces substances ne sont pas encore ce qu'il y a de plus substantiel et que, selon Aristote, l'être en tant qu'être ne doit pas être cherché parmi elles, ni même, à proprement parler, au fond d'aucune d'entre elles. L'objet de la philosophie première, dit Aristote, est l'être en tant qu'être. Mais il ne faut pas croire que l'être en tant qu'être est un universel, un caractère commun à tous les êtres . . . Si l'être, en tant qu'il se retrouve à propos de tous les êtres peut être dit universel, c'est d'un genre particulier d'universalité: il est universel parce qu'il est premier et fondement d'analogie. L'être en tant qu'être, étant premier, devient un type, il est imité par d'autres êtres. Chacun d'eux se règle sur lui. Mais il est à part d'eux tous, et cela réellement, non logiquement; et le vrai nom de la philosophie première, c'est la Théologie (*E,* 1.1026a18). En un mot, l'objet de la philosophie première est un individu. Or cet individu, comme Aristote le répète sans cesse avec des expressions diverses, est une pure forme. Il est une pure forme, parce que sa fonction est d'expliquer les autres êtres et que la véritable explication consiste à invoquer la fin, et, en dernière analyse, la forme. La forme explique tout le reste et se suffit à elle-même." O. Hamelin, *op. cit.,* pp. 404-405, (texts cited by courtesy of *Presses Universitaires de France*). Similarly, J. Chevalier: " . . . l'être en tant qu'être est à la fois *en soi* et universel." *La Notion du Nécessaire chez Aristote,* p. 172.

[100] W. Jaeger, *Aristotle* (trans. Robinson), pp. 218-219. Cf. pp. 216-218 (*Aristoteles,* pp. 226-228).

[101] *Aristoteles,* p. 228 (trans. Robinson, p. 219).

[102] W. D. Ross, *Arist. Metaph.,* I, 252-253.

[103] W. Jaeger, *Aristoteles,* pp. 197-198; 226 (trans. Robinson, pp. 191-192; 217).

[104] Carlini ends his critique of the double conception of the Primary Philosophy: "In fine: che A. stesso adattasse con un mero accomodamento esteriore una sua precedente trattazione a un intendimento addirittura opposto a quella ch'essa realmente aveva, è, per lo

meno, una congettura che lascia molto perplessi." *Arist. Metaf.,* pp. xxv-xxvi. Cf. *ibid.,* pp. 193-194, n. 1, . . . *Estratti,* p. 104, n. 3. Cf. *ibid.,* p. 65, n. 1, for Carlini's reduction of the science of the causes and of truth to that of 'Being *qua* Being.'

M. Gentili, *Rivista di Filosofia Neoscolastica,* Suppl. XXVII (July 1935), 25-30, following Jaeger's interpretation, distinguishes three different positions of the problem of Being in the *Metaphysics;* first as immobile Being, then as Being in general, and finally as the immanent act in sensible Becoming. The link between the first and third positions was not perfectly achieved by Aristotle, though it is demanded by the exigencies of his thought and still remains a living problem. "Tra le due posizioni la saldatura non è speculativamente perfetta; ma la sua perfezione è richiesta dall'intima energia del pensiero aristotelico e costituisce quindi compito e problema vivo per chi consideri l'aristotelismo come la prima posizione storicamente sistematica dei problemi della filosofia." *Ibid.,* pp. 28-29.

[105] "Ich gebe nämlich nicht zu, dass im *K* (und im [*G*] und *E*) bezüglich des Gegenstandes der Metaphysik Contamination zweier widersprechender Auffassungen anzuerkennen ist, die aus zwei verschiedenen geistigen Schöpfungsakten stammen müssen." H. v. Arnim, *Wien. Stud.,* XLVI (1928), 20.

[106] . . . *Ibid.,* p. 32, Cf. *Gotteslehre,* pp. 3; 46.

In *ZH,* accordingly, *ousia* does not mean for v. Arnim, an abstract generic notion as Jaeger understands it, but an individual Being. . . . *Wien. Stud.,* XLVI (1928), 45.

[107] "Ebensowenig wie es eine aristotelische Metaphysik gegeben hat, die nicht von der Analyse der sinnlichen Substanz ausgegangen ist und die den Begriff ihres Gegenstandes, des übersinnlichen Seins als des obersten und ersten Seins, nicht aus der vergleichenden Betrachtung der Stufenreihe der verschiedenen Seinsarten gewonnen hatte (was ja auch der einzig mögliche Weg war, seit dem die platonische Identifizierung des Volkommensten mit dem Allgemeinsten gefallen war) und die nicht in diesem Sinn Allgemeinwissenschaft vom Sein gewesen wäre, ebensowenig hat es je eine Metaphysik gegeben, die die sinnliche Substanz um ihrer selbst willen behandelt hätte . . . Und selbst wenn wirklich . . . in den früheren Teilen der eine, in den späteren Teilen der andere Gesichtspunkt stärker betont würde, so würde daraus noch immer nicht ein innerer Gegensatz der beiden Auffassungen folgen, . . ." E. v. Ivánka, *Scholastik,* VII (1932), 23-24.

[108] Cf. *infra,* pp. 102-104.

[109] "L'espressione 'scienza del ente in quanto ente' riceve, in questi scritti aristotelici, tre significati diversi e strettamente connessi, che per non essere tenuti chiaramente distinti, rendono particolarmente difficile la comprensione del procedimento del pensiero.

I) La scienza dell'ente in quanto ente individua in qualche reale o ente le condizioni necessarie della realtà o dell' esistenza attuale, cioè il 'minimum' richiesto per la conoscibilità di esso reale, tutte quelle determinazioni di esso che rimangono qualora la conoscenza prescinda da tutte quelle da cui può prescindere, senza tuttavia cessare di avere un qualche oggetto. In questo caso la scienza dell' ente in quanto ente è una scienza puramente formale, inquanto essa determina le condizioni necessarie che rendono possibile il reale o l'ente attuale in genere, senza tuttavia pronunciarsi sulla sua effettiva realtà. In questo caso, la scienza dell' ente in quanto ente è un' ontologia formale . . .

II) La scienza dell' ente in quanto ente determina la totalità delle condizioni sufficienti che spiegano l'esistenza attuale di uno, più o tutti i reali o gli enti, cioè gli oggetti di conoscenza attuale o possibile. In opposizione al caso precedente, la scienza del ente in quanto ente, ha ora un carattere reale, è una metafisica nel senso corrente della parola . . .

III) In quanto finalmente Aristotele determina i principi metafisici del reale, di cui gli consta per effettiva conoscenza, per lo più mediante concetti, . . . egli concepisce talora, benchè più raramente e in via secondaria, la scienza dell' ente in quanto ente, come quella che si riferisce alle determinazioni ontologiche che, secondo la sua dottrina, spiegano il reale nella sua effettiva natura metafisica." Emilio Oggioni, *La 'Filosofia Prima' di Aristotele,* pp. 64-65.

[110] "Cependant, si c'est bien la vérité que l'être 'en tant qu'être' n'est pas un genre, n'est-il pas vrai, d'autre part, on l'a vu, que c'est un attribut universel? De la sorte, l'être 'en tant qu'être' serait l'*universalité de l'être,* bref, un universel duquel la philosophie serait la science. Or, une telle façon de présenter les choses est très nette dans la *Métaphysique,* . . . Mais, d'un autre côté, des assertions . . . qui assignent à la philosophie pour objet ces êtres que sont les Astres et cet être séparé et immobile qu'est Dieu,—supposent une conception toute différente; . . ." L. Robin, *Aristote,* pp. 106-107.

[111] *Ibid.,* p. 107.

[112] "Voilà comment l'être 'en tant qu'être' est à la fois un individu et un universel, l'universel suprême parce qu'il est l'individu suprême et qu'il a le pouvoir de se faire universel en se répétant, mais avec une exactitude toujours plus faible. Son universalité, toutefois, se fonde, il importe de le bien comprendre, sur sa nécessité, . . . et, si toutes les existences dans lesquelles

il se répète et qui l'imitent ne le reçoivent pas au même degré, *elles se rapportent néanmoins toutes à lui,* de telle sorte que son universalité n'est, en elles, qu'une identité *de rapport* ou une 'analogie': . . ." *Ibid.,* p. 108. Cf. *supra,* nn. 97-99.

[113] L. Robin, *op. cit.,* pp. 108-109.

[114] "L'unité *individuelle* de la substance première se retrouve *universellement,* grâce à l'analogie, en toutes ces choses singulières." *Ibid.,* p. 109. Robin stresses the feature of 'imitation' in the Stagirite's doctrine of Being. This view and the resultant 'analogy' may be also seen in Hamelin, *supra,* n. 99.

[115] "Au livre I de sa *Métaphysique,* Aristote décrit la philosophie première comme la science des causes ultimes de la réalité entière. . . . Il en résulte que le monde suprasensible, qui est le domaine propre de la philosophie première en ce sens qu'il n'est étudié par aucune autre science, ne se confond pas cependant purement et simplement avec l'objet de la Métaphysique: celui-ci est beaucoup plus vaste. . . . A d'autres endroits Aristote insiste plutôt sur le caractère suprasensible de l'objet métaphysique, parce que c'est là un domaine qui est réservé en propre à la philosophie première. W. Jaeger a donc tort de considérer ces deux conceptions comme inconciliables: la manière dont elles se trouvent entremêlées dans l'œuvre du Stagirite indique clairement que l'auteur ne les conçoit pas comme opposées l'une à l'autre; c'est ce qu'il affirme d'ailleurs de façon explicite dans *Métaph.* VI, 1,1026a22-32 et XI, 7,1064b14: La priorité de la métaphysique sur les autres sciences entraîne nécessairement le caractère universel de son objet." Gerard Verbeke, *Revue Philosophique de Louvain,* XLIV (1946), 206, n. 3.

[116] G. di Napoli, *rivista di Filosofia Neoscolastica,* XXXIX (1947), 220.

[117] "Il che vuol dire che nel pensiero di Aristotele le due visuali della metafisica si implicano radicalmente: la metafisica come scienza dell' essere in quanto essere condiziona la metaficisa come scienza dell' Immobile; soltanto superando il piano fisico (e cioè: studiando non solo ciò che è, ma l' ente in quanto ente) è possibile arrivare all' Immobile." *Ibid.*

[118] A. H. Armstrong, *An Introduction to Ancient Philosophy,* p. 87. For more recent surveys of the problem, see S. Gómez Nogales, *Horizonte de la Metafisica Aristotelica* (1955), pp. 173-196; V. Décarie, *L'Object de la Métaphysique selon Aristote* (1961), pp. xxvii-xxviii; P. Aubenque, *Le Problème de l'Être chez Aristote* (1962), pp. 1-13.

The writings of Aristotle and of Plato are cited with the abbreviated titles given in Liddel and Scott, *A Greek-English Lexicon* (1940), I, xix and xxxiii respectively, except that *Rep.* is used for Plato's *Republic.* Outside the *Metaphysics,* the Books of the Aristotelian treatises are quoted by Roman, and the chapters by Arabic, numerals. In view of the four different ways of enumerating the Books of the *Metaphysics* (cf. synoptic tables in A. Mansion, *Rev. Néoscol.,* XXIX, 1927, p. 307, n. 2; A. Nolte, *Het Godsbegrip bij Aristoteles,* p. 5, n. 9), the most convenient policy is to use the traditional Greek letters. This manner of citation allows the title *Metaph.* to be omitted, except in immediate sequence to citations from other Aristotelian treatises.

The text of Plato is quoted according to the Stephanus pagination. Aristotle, the Greek commentators, and the *Index Aristotelicus* of Bonitz are cited by page and line of the Prussian Academy editions.

The following abbreviations for periodicals and collections are used:—

AGP—Archiv für Geschichte der Philosophie.

AJP—American Journal of Philology.

Abh. Bayr. Akad.—Abhandlungen der Philosophisch-historischen Classe der Bayerischen Akademie der Wissenschaften.

Abh. Berl. Akad.—Abhandlungen der Preussischen Akademie der Wissenschaften zu Berlin, Philos.-histor. Classe.

Bayr. Sitzb.—Sitzungsberichte der Philos.-histor. Classe der Bayerischen Akademie der Wissenschaften.

Berl. Sitzb.—Sitzungsberichte der Preussischen Akademie der Wissenschaften zu Berlin, Philos.-histor. Classe.

CQ.—Classical Quarterly.

CR.—Classical Review.

CSEL.—Corpus Scriptorum Ecclesiasticorum Latinorum.

Class. Phil.—Classical Philology.

Encyc. Brit.—Encyclopaedia Britannica.

JP.—Journal of Philology.

PG.—Patrologia Graeca (Migne).

PL.—Patrologia Latina (Migne).

Philol.—Philologus.

Philos. Monatsh.—Philosophische Monatshefte.

Rev. Néoscol.—Revue Néoscolastique de Philosophie.

Rh. Mus.—Rheinisches Musäum für Philologie.

Wien. Sitzb.—Sitzungsberichte der Akademie der Wissenschaften in Wien, Philosophisch-historische Klasse.

Wien. Stud.—Wiener Studien.

Monographs are cited with full title or with easily recognizable shorter form. The few strongly abbreviated titles used are italicized in parentheses immediately before the full title given in the *Bibliography,* pp. 475 ff.

Richard Rorty (essay date 1973)

SOURCE: "Genus as Matter: A Reading of *Metaphysics* Z-H," in *Exegesis and Argument: Studies in Greek Philosophy Presented to Gregory Vlastos,* edited by E. N. Lee, A. P. D. Mourelatos, R. M. Rorty, Van Gorcum & Company B. V., 1973, pp. 393-420.

[*In the following essay, Rorty reviews what he describes as a significant difficulty in the reading of* Metaphysics, *namely that it appears to lack unity and a conclusion. Rorty locates the primary source of the substance-form puzzle in Book Z, and argues that by understanding Aristotle's claim that genus is matter, a claim not often taken seriously, certain difficulties in Book Z are eliminated.*]

One difficulty in reading the **Metaphysics** is to locate the conclusion of the argument.[1] The difficulty is so great that many have concluded that there is no conclusion, and no unity to the treatise. Now, it may well be that what we call a "treatise" is in fact a collection of scraps. Perhaps all that we shall be able to find is variations on a theme, rather than a sustained argument. Nevertheless the only way to tell how much unity there is is to try out various unifying schemes and see how soon they fail. Two such schemes are fairly familiar. Both take the question which the treatise is supposed to answer to be "What is substance?" and both take the conclusion to be that substance is form. One scheme (Ross's) thinks this to be established at the end of Z, and regards H, [*O*], and I as appendices, with [*L*] introducing a new subject—theology.[2] The other scheme (the Thomistic view typified by Owens) takes the end of Z as expressing a problem (how *can* substance be form?) which is only resolved in [*L*]. On this latter view, finding out about the pure actualities which are the Unmoved Movers is necessary in order to understand what substance is, because only thus do we get the [*en*] to which all other senses of "substance" are related by [*pros en*] equivocity.[3]

The problems with both of these unifying schemes are as familiar as the schemes themselves. In the Ross scheme, it is hard to say just what we have learned when we learn that substance is form. We knew long before the end of Z that "form" was *one* sense of substance; what light is shed by telling us that it is the *primary* sense? Further, it looks as if Aristotle would like to say that an individual thing is the same as its form, but Z, 17 gives us no help in seeing how this might be possible. In the Owens scheme, we have to say that we do not really understand what a horse is unless we understand what God is, and we also have to make sense of a form which is the form of no matter and of an actuality which is the actualization of no potentiality. Again, neither scheme seems to allow enough weight to H, [*O*] and I. On both, the only really important passage in all three books is the claim in [*O*] that actuality is prior to potentiality—a claim which underlines unhelpfully the conclusion of Z, 17.

In this paper, I want to suggest how one might read the central books as centering on the end of H rather than of Z—so that the conclusion of the treatise comes in the last lines of that book:

> The reason is that people look for a unifying formula, and a difference, between potency and complete reality. But, as has been said, the proximate matter and the form are one and the same thing, the one potentially, and the other actually. Therefore it is like asking what in general is the cause of unity and of a thing's being one; for each thing is a unity, and the potential and the actual are somehow one. Therefore there is no other cause here unless there is something which caused the movement from potency into actuality. And all things which have *no* matter are *without qualification* essentially unities.[4]

This interpretive scheme is not original; something like it has been suggested often by Randall, McKeon, and others. But I think that it needs to be backed up by fairly detailed analysis of how this conclusion relates to the topics discussed in Z, and this is what I propose to do here. I shall claim that the plausibility of saying that substance is form only appears when this is taken together with the claim that proximate matter and form are identical. I shall be arguing, further, that to understand this latter claim one needs to take Aristotle's claim that genus is matter more seriously than it is usually taken. Roughly, I construe Aristotle as saying that the unity of genus and differentia in the definition somehow mirrors the special sort of unity which is the unity of form with proximate matter, and that appreciating this fact clears up the puzzles of Z. In order to make this out, however, I shall have to give an account of these puzzles. This account will necessarily be brief and dogmatic.

In imagining Aristotle's motives for writing the **Metaphysics,** one runs least risk of anachronism if one views him as primarily concerned with refuting his predecessors. Whatever else the question "What is Being?" might have meant to Aristotle, it certainly at least meant "What is wrong with the sort of thing Plato and Democritus said about what really exists?" Accordingly, I think that the question "What is substance?" which begins Z should be seen as meaning at least "What is wrong with the kinds of reductionisms discussed in A—the over-emphasis by Pythagoreans and Platonists on formal causality, or by materialists on material causality, which produces the notion that only forms are real, or the notion that only matter is real?" This way of putting it, however, suggests that there is no problem about substance until technical philosophical senses of terms like [eidos] and [hulē] have been mastered. A better way of putting the question, I think, is as follows: "How shall we reconcile the division within common sense which on the one hand suggests that practically every noun refers to a substance and on the other hand suggests that only relatively few nouns refer to substances?" Or, putting it another way: "How shall we reconcile the common-sensical notion (expressed at, e.g., **Categories** 2b27) that everything that is neither predicable of nor present in another thing is *equally* a substance with the fact that scientific explanation suggests that certain substances or putative substances (the four elements, atoms, numbers, Forms) are the realities behind the appearances?" The temptation to say that only a few things are substances, and that these things are far from common sense, is just the same temptation which leads present-day readers of *The Scientific American* to say that science has shown that only elementary particles are real. We may assume that this reductionistic temptation was as current then as now. The primary purpose of the **Metaphysics,** in my view, and especially of Z-H, is to guard against such temptations.

We may state the temptation a bit more exactly, and relate it to the opposition between Platonists and materialists, as follows. Aristotle acknowledges two broad, and conflicting, sets of criteria for substantiality. The first is the one laid down in the **Categories,** out of which I shall pick as basic the notion of *determinability*—a notion which Aristotle expresses as follows:

> It seems most distinctive of substance that what is numerically one and the same is able to receive contraries.[5]

I shall call this the "logical" criterion of substance. I do not think that this criterion can be made precise,

since there seems no neat way to explain why "the white thing" . . . could not admit such contraries as being now here and now there, or being now a sock and later (when torn into strips and knotted together) a tourniquet. So it is not clear why, on *this* criterion, calling something a dog or a sock is a predication in the category of substance whereas calling it white is not. There certainly is an intuition that when we call it a dog or a sock we are saying what kind of thing it is, but not when we call it white—but I doubt that this intuition is capable of precise analysis which would deal with borderline cases.[6]

Contrasted to this logical criterion, there is what I shall call the "physical" criterion of substantiality—the criterion of *self-reliance*. The *locus classicus* for this criterion is in Z, 16:

> Evidently even of the things that are thought to be substances, most are only potencies—both the parts of animals (for none of them exist separately; and when they *are* separated, then too they exist, all of them, merely as matter) and earth and fire and air; for none of them is a unity, but as it were a mere heap, till they are worked up and some unity is made out of them.[7]

This latter sort of criterion comes out in the places where Aristotle says that a thing is "*one in a still higher degree*" if it is "naturally continuous" . . . and that only immaterial substances are "one without qualification". . . . It is this criterion which supports the Thomist reading according to which the Unmoved Movers are the only substances in the full sense of the term. This criterion, like the criterion of determinability, cannot be made precise, nor does Aristotle try to do so. It is thoroughly unclear whether, on this criterion, only a full-fledged cultured adult male counts as a substance or whether babies also count. Mules do not make the grade (cf. 1034a1, a passage I shall discuss more fully later) but perhaps an amoeba would. Aristotle does not, as far as I know, invoke this criterion anywhere except in the middle of the **Metaphysics**—and it comes in there only for certain dialectical reasons which I shall be talking about later. What I want to emphasize here is not that Aristotle is torn by conflict between self-reliance and determinability as criteria for identifying [ousia] but simply that both are criteria which he feels able to appeal to without argument. The bland [phaneron de hoti] which begins the passage just quoted, in spite of the fact that the passage flatly contradicts the standard list of paradigm cases of substance given at [D] 8 and Z, 2, shows that the notion that only a few so-called substances might really be substances was a philosophical commonplace which Aristotle was not prepared to reject out of hand.

These two criteria of substantiality can conflict (as they do in the cases of mules and detached human hands) but it is important to see how they also complement each other. A thing has to have *some* degree of self-reliance—some ability to persist despite whatever other forces are at work in the universe—in order to have determinability. If there were such a thing as prime matter, it would be a *bare* substratum which would let itself be called by the name of whatever accidental quality it exhibited at the moment; it would not be capable of alteration—for this is change against a background, and there would be no enduring features to provide such a background. Only what is strong enough to possess a nature, and retain it through some period of time, can be passive enough to undergo alteration. So the two criteria go together naturally up to the point at which we begin asking what counts as nature, and begin to look askance at common-sensical distinctions between essential nature and accidental qualities. We ask such questions, and begin to wonder whether common-sense is drawing lines in the right places, when we realize that certain borderline cases of substance present exceptionally attractive opportunities for gaining certainty, or explanatory power, or both. When it turns out that such peculiar entities as geometrical shapes or atoms can be known with more certainty than common-sense entities, or can be used to explain common-sense entities better than common-sense entities explain themselves, then two things happen: first, efforts are made to show that these entities are better examples of substance than more familiar examples, and second, the original substance-accident distinction begins to be dropped in favor of the distinction between reality and appearance.

Aristotle is notable among Greek philosophers for his refusal to invoke the appearance-reality distinction—for his unwillingness to go against common sense. The *Metaphysics,* on the view I am offering, is an attempt to show that we can do justice to scientific knowledge without adopting what Strawson would call a "revisionary metaphysics"—a reductionism of either the Platonist or the materialist sort. These reductionisms start by pushing one or the other of the two criteria of substantiality beyond its proper limits. The Platonist form of reductionism seizes on such abstractions as the Good, the Equal, and the Circle and notes that they satisfy the "physical" criterion of substantiality to an eminent degree. The claim of the Platonic Forms to be more real than common-sense things is based on their eminent self-reliance—their immunity to pressure from other things, their immutability and eternity. The reasons which impel one to think that Socrates is a better example of a substance than a drop of water impel one also to think of the Form of Man, if such there be, as an even better example. From this point of view, the whole sensible world can come to look like merely so much matter—or, if this seems too paradoxical, so much appearance. The materialist form of reductionism, on the other hand, works with the logical criterion of substantiality—determinability. Let us, the materialist says, press the notion of substance as that which receives contraries a little farther. We do not say that it is the red which changes between crimson and vermillion, but, say, the red *book.* But why stop with the book? It is the same stuff that was once a tree and is now a book. So let us look down to the ultimate determinables—the elements or the atoms. There we will find the determinable in an eminent degree, and we shall consign all the usual paradigms of substance to the role of transitory accidents of this more profound substratum or, if this seems too paradoxical, to the role of mere appearance.

Now one way to deal with these promotions of borderline cases of substance to the status of paradigms would be just to distinguish sharply between questions about what is real, about what is knowable with most certainty, and about what is the most powerful tool of scientific explanation. One could then insist that these questions have nothing in particular to do with each other. But this is not the line Aristotle takes. He is convinced, for better or worse, that there is a powerful case to be made for departing from common-sense paradigms and proclaiming that substance really is substratum, and another powerful case for proclaiming that it really is form. He thinks that the only way to defeat the reductionists is to find some way in which the common-sense paradigms of substance can *be* both form and substrate, rather than constructs out of these, or combinations of these, or appearances of these. Aristotle could simply, like an ordinary-language philosopher, have appealed to paradigm cases and then gone on to argue that the reductionists were misusing words like "one" when, for example, they insisted that abstractions like the Platonic Forms were more clearly unities than any sensible thing. Again, he could have distinguished the question "Which things are substances?" from the question "What is it about substances which makes them substances?" and accused the reductionists of confounding these questions. But he did neither. Instead, he takes the view that the [*sunolon*]—the composite of form and matter—can only be called a substance if it can somehow be shown to be identical both with form and with matter; if it is a third thing distinct from both form and matter, it will not make the grade. Still another tactic which he might have adopted is the Strawsonian sort of "parasitism" argument—in which one would say to both varieties of reductionists that the unfamiliar notions (separable forms, or invisible substrata) which they employ could only have been given sense by reference to the so called "composites" which are the common-sense paradigms of substance. But he does not do that either. Instead, he takes the technical philosophical notions of "substrate" and "form" as, if anything, more intelligible and better understood than the familiar notion that Socrates is a substance. He tries to clarify the latter by reference to the former.

Given this set of tactics, the central question for defending the common-sense notion of substance against reductionist attack is how to construe the relation between matter (the ground of the composite's determinability) and form (the ground of the composite's self-reliance) in some way *other* than as the relation between the composite itself and its accidents. If we do use this latter model, we either turn the matter into an accident of form ("Plato thought nature but a spume that plays/ Upon a ghostly paradigm of things") or else, with the materialists, turn form into an accident of matter. Either way of looking at the composite will deprive the composite itself of the status of substance and force us to regard it as some other ("underlying") substance plus assorted accidents. So the defense of substance against reductionist attack ultimately depends upon being able to provide a different sort of connection between the formal and the material aspects of a substance than either the connection between that substance and its attributes, or the connection between that substance and its parts.

The need for a special connection here is a recurrent theme in Aristotle. Consider the following texts, one from the **Categories,** one from Z, and one from [*G*]:

> Yet genus and species do not merely indicate quality, like the term "white"; "white" indicates quality and nothing further, but species and genus determine the quality with reference to a substance; they signify substance qualitatively differentiated.[8]

> Nothing, then, which is not a species of a genus will have an essence—only species will have it, for these are thought to imply not merely that the subject participates in the attribute and has it as an affection, or has it by accident.[9]

> In general, those who talk like this (denying the principle of contradiction) do away with substance and essence. For they must say that all attributes are accidents, and that there is no such thing as "being essentially a man" or "an animal" . . . but if *all* statements are accidental, there will be nothing primary about which they are made, if the accidental always implies predication about a subject. The predication, then, must go on *ad infinitum.*[10]

The first and second of these passages merely say that there is something special which distinguishes the relation between the name or the formula of a species and that to which it applies from the relation between any other sort of name or formula and that to which *it* applies. The third passage should, I think, be read in the light of Anscombe's point that Aristotle in his discussion of the law of contradiction in [*G*] is talking not about what is ordinarily so-called but about a principle that says "If [*fa*], '[*f*]' being a predicate in the category of substance, then 'not [*fa*]' is an impossible proposi-

tion."[11] It should be contrasted with Aristotle's occasional suggestion that "substance is predicated of matter."[12] This latter notion is tempting but insidious, since it would cut off the infinite regress suggested by the third passage cited only at the cost of a fatal concession to what I have been calling reductionism. If we were to admit that to call something a man is to be saying it is what stands to the thing's matter as the man's paleness stands to the man. Aristotle's program would be hopeless. If we take the third passage together with the second, we can see the problem presented as looking like this: "When we say that something is a man, we are saying something about what form this matter has, but we cannot be predicating qualities of a bit of matter. Nor can we be predicating form of a bit of matter, for the *matter* doesn't *exemplify* the form—only the *composite* does. So in order to avoid an infinite regress, and to avoid agreeing with Anaxagoras that all things are together ([*G*], 4) and with Protagoras that all opinions are true (*G*, 5) we must find some way of saying something about the matter which is not ordinary predication." This search for a new logical relation . . . is not distinguished by Aristotle from the search for a new sort of metaphysical relation distinct from "being present in a subject" . . . which will link form and matter. Both searches are, I suggest, assimilated to the question of Z, 12: What is the relation between "animal" and "two-footed" in the definition of "man" which will permit this definition to attribute one characteristic rather than two? The answer to all three problems Aristotle takes to be given, in one way or another, by the potentiality-actuality distinction. So this latter distinction will, if it works, solve problems about predication left over from the **Categories** as well as refuting the metaphysical reductionists.

So far I have been giving a general description of what I take to be the central theme in Aristotle's over-all philosophical program. I want now to make things a little more concrete and to go through some of the chapters of Z in order to show how this program gets worked into a form which leads up naturally to the question about unity posed in Z, 12 and the answer offered to this question at H, 6. This will be a matter of picking out texts like plums and, by focusing on just a few texts, hoping to exhibit an order in the discussion which is hardly apparent when one reads straight through. I shall start with the insistence on the identity between the individual substance . . . and what it is to be that substance . . . in chapter 6, since I want to read the remainder of Z (and H) as an answer to the question, "How is this identification possible?"

The general argument for this identification is that without it we have an infinite regress. Aristotle first trots out a reminder of the third man argument (1031a3 ff.) in connection with Platonic Forms, and then generalizes the argument by saying that

The absurdity of the separation (between an individual thing and its essence) would appear also if one were to assign a name to each of the essences; for there would be yet another essence besides the original one, e.g. to the essence of horse there will belong a second essence.[13]

I take this to be saying: if every true subject-predicate statement expressed a relation between two things, then an infinite regress of predication would ensue. In particular, if we unwisely called the essence of X "Y," then the statement "X is Y" would *look like* an expression of a relation between two things. The regress (essences of essences of essences with, presumably, a new substrate for each new essence to inhere in) of Z, 6 would thus be engendered by the same mistake as was the regress (substrates . . . of substrates of substrates, each substrate having its own essence) of [*G*], 4. In both cases, we would err in assuming that the logical relation between subject . . . and predicate must mirror a relation between an independently characterizable substrate and an essence or form. Ordinary language wisely calls both Socrates and his essence . . ."man," and wisely calls the accidental feature . . . which is being a white man "being a white man," rather than using a snappy one-word expression like "cloak" (as he suggests we might in Z, 4.1029b28 ff.). The connection between the two regresses emerges when we see that predicating "man" does *not* signify a relation between two things in the way in which predicating "white man" does—even though to truly apply *either* expression requires that some character be embodied in some substrate. If "man" were taken as an ellipsis for "such and such features inhering in such and such a substrate," then each of the two things related would themselves split into "what it is to be X" and "the substrate of which 'X' is a character," and *these* two will split, and so on—engendering ramified regresses in both directions. Aristotle thinks that we stop all such regresses by realizing, first, that mere qualities don't have essences (1030a12-14 again) and, second, that not every predication can be the predication of a mere feature. . . . If this were the only sort of predication there were, he thinks, predication would never get started, because the question "What are you talking about? Where is the subject . . . ?" would never get answered.

This is Aristotle's master argument for "substance" being a distinct category irreducible to "quality" or anything else. It is a bad argument because it confuses the sound point that, in Anscombe's words, one cannot "identify a thing without identifying it as a *such-and-such*"[14] with the unproven Strawsonian claim that a language-game which contained only quality-terms and demonstratives could not be played. But I do not want to criticize it here—only to emphasize that the insistence on the identity of a thing with its essence is no momentary whim on Aristotle's part, but rather a doc-

trine which he thinks we must cling to at all costs unless we are to fall into the arms of Anaxagoras and Protagoras. To deny this identification is to make everything (or at least every common-sense thing) an "accidental" . . . entity, that is, an entity which is really two entities tacked together by what Aristotle calls "mere juxtaposition". . . . So it seems at least prima facie reasonable to take this identification as the object of concern throughout Z.

Going on now from Z, 6 to 7-9, the discussion formed by these three chapters begins by identifying essence . . . and form . . . : "By form I mean the essence of each thing and its primary substance,"[15] So it looks as if we could treat "substance," "form," and "essence" as synonyms. But if we do, Aristotle point out, we run into paradox. For particular substances, or at least sublunary ones, are generated out of matter, and "contain" matter, in the sense that they are "capable of being and not being" (1032a15-23). But specific forms don't get generated nor have such a capacity. So how can we avoid thinking of the form as "just a part of" the individual substance? Aristotle begins to tackle this question at 1033a2, where he asks whether "matter is part of the formula . . . of a thing," and concludes that "the brazen sphere has matter in its formula" (1033a6). A bit later, in chapter 8, he decides that "'man' and 'animal'" correspond to "brazen sphere in general. . . . "[16] The point of both passages seems to be that we should not think of form as a list of qualities which, if stuck onto "matter," will produce an exemplar of the species in question. Rather, it must be thought of as those qualities which, if used to transform certain particular sorts of substance (e.g. brass in the case of the sphere, flesh in the case of the man), will produce such an exemplar. So to know the "formula" . . . of a given "form" . . . , we have to know which sorts of substance are appropriate proximate material causes of instances of that form. Since a definition . . . is the formula . . . of an essence (1031a13), and since form and essence have just been identified, we now seem to be saying that to know what a given form is you have to know what sort of matter it fits—but more, that the form *includes* the matter in some generalized, [*holōs*] way. Aristotle does not *present* this conclusion as a solution to the puzzle of how we can avoid thinking of form and matter as two distinct parts, but it seems to show that "part" is the wrong word. We have not yet solved the problem of how the ungenerated can be identical with the generated, but we have at least smuggled in a reference to generability in the definition of the ungenerated. We still do not know how to identify a "this" . . . with a "such" . . . (1033b22) but at least we see that you cannot, *pace* Platonists, know what a "such" is (for most cases of "such") without knowing that it is the sort of thing which gets exemplified in a "this."

The next three chapters—10 to 12—seem like so many independent treatments of the same problem: viz. the formula which tells us what makes a given substance the substance it is is going to tell us about the form of the substance, but it has to do so by telling us just enough about the matter to prevent the Platonist reductionism decried in chapter 9, while not enough to lead us back into the materialist reductionism decried in chapter 3. Consider the three questions which lead off these three chapters:

> ch. 10: must the formula of the parts be present in the formula of the whole or not? (1034b23-24)

> ch. 11: what sort of parts belong to the form and what sort not to the form but to the concrete thing? (1036a26-27)

> ch. 12: wherein can consist the unity of that, the formula of which we call a definition, as for instance, in the case of man, "two-footed animal", for let this be the formula of man, why then is this one and not many, viz. "animal" *and* "two-footed"? (1037b11-14).

Chapters 10 and 11, I think, are inconclusive discussions of the difficulties presented by the upshot of chapters 7-9, and it is only in chapter 12 that a breakthrough is made. In chapter 10 we gloss the point that "man" corresponds to "brazen sphere" in general by the notion that forms considered as universal . . . are not substances but rather are "something composed . . . of this particular formula . . . and this particular matter . . . treated as universal . . ." 1035b27-30). This suggestion will, if my interpretation is right, be taken up in chapter 12 in the notion of genus-as-matter. But here in chapter 10 it is pushed aside in favor of the Platonist notion that "only the parts of the form . . . are parts of the formula . . ." (1035b35) and that matter is "unknowable in itself". . . . More generally, it is pushed aside in favor of a distinction between parts of the composite . . . and parts of the form (1035a30-32). If one read chapter 10 as Aristotle's last word on the subject, one would conclude that he had given up on the attempt announced in chapter 6 to identify a substance with its form. But going on to chapter 11 we find an anti-Platonist polemic (1036b8 ff.) culminating in the remark that "to reduce all things to Forms and to eliminate the matter is useless labor; for some things surely are particular forms in a particular matter"—a remark which is explicated by noting that "an animal is something perceptible, and it is not possible to define it . . . without reference to movement—nor, therefore, without reference to the parts being in a certain state" (1036b22 f., 28 f.). Chapter 10 and 11 taken together leave the status of the project of getting the individual and the essence together up in the air.

In Z, 12, on the other hand, we get the first clue about how we might develop the notion of "matter treated as universal" which came up in chapter 10. In chapter 12,

we are told that, despite what has been said in chapter 10 about the distinction between parts of the composite and parts of the form, still

> surely all the attributes in the definition must be one; for the definition is a single formula and a formula of substance, so that it must be a formula of some one thing; for substance means a "one" and a "this," as we maintain.[14]

This suggests that the program of chapter 6—identifying the particular . . . and the essence—is still alive. Aristotle, in other words, is not yet willing to say that the definition gives the form qua immaterial and that matter only comes in at the level of the composite. Somehow we have to get matter into the form, and immediately following the passage just quoted we take up the topic of the *genus*—a topic of which little has been heard so far in Z. The relevance of the topic comes out at 1038a6 where we get the notion of the genus "existing as matter." The full passage is:

> If then the genus absolutely does not exist apart from the species-of-a-genus, or if it exists but exists as matter (for the voice is genus and matter, but its differentiae make the species, i.e. the letters, out of it) clearly the definition is the formula which comprises the differentiae.[18]

Now this passage is in one way grist for my mill and in another way very embarrassing. What I want to argue is that Aristotle thinks that we can get matter into the form by taking the genus, which on anybody's account is a component of the definition, as representing the matter of the composite. But if this is what Aristotle were up to, one would not expect him to conclude the sentence just quoted by saying that the definition is the formula which comprises the *differentia*. Saying this suggests that because the genus is a sort of matter it does not count for purposes of giving a definition. I have to explain away this suggestion as best I can by noting that Aristotle restricts his consideration in the passage just quoted to "definitions reached by the method of division" . . . As Ross notes, the contrast seems to be with definitions which give "components" . . . , a contrast drawn at 998b13 and at 1043a20. In the latter passage, Aristotle says the "division"-definitions tell us about the *logos* of the form and the actuality . . . whereas "component"-definitions tell us about matter. So since Aristotle in chapter 12 says he is going to talk *first* about the former sort of definitions, we might assume that he was going on to tell us about the other sort of definition, and would there have given the genus its due weight. But I am not happy about this, because the distinction between the two sorts of definitions, if my over-all interpretation is right, is a phony one—one which breaks the unity which Aristotle at the very outset of chapter 12 says he is concerned with (the unity between animal and two-footed) by speaking as if each component got treated in a separate sort of definition.

All that I really need to claim for chapter 12, however, is something non-controversial: i.e. that there Aristotle asks the question which he answers in what I am viewing as the *dénouement* of the central books—H, 6. The question posed at the beginning of chapter 12 is answered there as follows. Aristotle begins the chapter by saying that we shall now return to the difficulty about how definitions and numbers can be one, and then goes on to say

> What then is it that makes man one; why is he one and not many, e.g. animal plus biped, especially if there are, as some say, an animal-itself and a biped-itself? . . . Clearly, then, if people proceed thus in their usual manner of definition and speech, they cannot explain and solve the difficulty. But if, as we say, one element is matter and another is form, and one is potentially and the other actually, the question will no longer be thought a difficulty. For this difficulty is the same as would arise if "round bronze" were the definition of "cloak"; for this word would be a sign of the definitory formula, so that the question is, what is the cause of the unity of "round" and "bronze"? The difficulty disappears, because the one is matter, the other form. What, then, causes this—that which was potentially to be actually—except, in the case of things which are generated, the agent?[19]

Now for my purposes it would be much nicer if Z had ended with 12 and we had gone on to H immediately. For my interpretation requires one to treat the remainder of Z (chapters 13-17) as a collection of miscellaneous ruminations on various topics; I cannot find any way to treat them as contributing to the swelling theme which seems to me to connect Z, 12 with H. So let me quickly go on to make two small remarks about these last five chapters, and then get down to business by explaining how I think Aristotle might have thought that the passage just quoted from H answered the problems of Z.

The first remark is that the surprising "physical" definition of "substance" at the beginning of Z, 16 (which I quoted earlier) fits in fairly well with the notion that Aristotle was getting ready to take the notion of genus-as-matter seriously. If he is going to say that there is matter in the definition of a substance because reference to the genus is reference to the matter, then, since he is very clear that substances can't be composed of other substances, or at least not of other *actual* substances . . . , he might well be nervous of thinking of the material causes of substances (e.g. the four elements, flesh and bone, etc.) as substances. He might be saying to himself something like this: "if the genus 'animal' in the definition of 'man' is a way of referring to the matter of men—the kind of flesh and bones

which are common to men and horses—then flesh and bones shouldn't be given the status of substance in their own right." This line of thought might explain why here in Z, 16 and again in H, 3 (cf. 1043b20 ff.) he says that they are not substances but are mere potencies. He does not, I think, *need* to say this; he could just say that a piece of flesh was a perfectly good actual substance viewed in its own right and a perfectly good potentiality viewed in a relational . . . way, as material cause of a man. What Aristotle ought to have said was that something can be actually X and potentially Y, and that the question "Is it a mere potency or does it exist in actuality?" is misguided. This is, in fact, the line he tacitly takes in most of his discussions of matter as "that out of which" . . . —though, never, as far as I know, explicitly. But in Z, 16, in what seems to be the throes of an anti-materialist polemic thrown in to balance the anti-Platonist polemic of chapters 14-15, he insists that the elements, parts of animals, etc. are not substances—thus betraying a good deal of his over-all project—while at H, 3 he casually tosses out artifacts as substances, thus making all the talk about brazen spheres wildly misleading.

My second remark about these last five chapters is that Z, 17, despite many commentators, simply does not look like the conclusion of anything. Aristotle does say there that the answer to the question "Why is the matter so-and-so?" is "because of the form" and adds that form is substance (1041b5 ff.). But this is no news, and saying this doesn't solve any of the problems about how substance *can* be form which have taken up most of the previous chapters. In the very last lines of the chapter we are told that substance is nature . . . which is not an *element* . . . but rather a *principle . . . ,* and presumably we can identify [*eidos*] and nature, in this context (1041b30 ff.). But what we want to know is how something *can* be a principle without being an element, for this is precisely the puzzle about the unity of substance and of definition which was raised back at chapter 12 and is still unresolved. Owens rightly thinks of Z as ending by saying "Substance must, somehow, be form—but we still have to see how it can be."

So much for the remainder of Z. I come now to my main point, which is that the passages which I have quoted from H, 6 are supposed to solve the problems of Z. Ross says that Aristotle goes from a "static" treatment of substance in Z to a "dynamic" treatment of *change* in H.[20] What he has in mind is that in H Aristotle introduces the potentiality-actuality distinction which has been practically absent in Z. But this suggests that the treatment of substance is over, whereas at the beginning of H, 1 and again at the beginning of H, 2 it is explicitly substance and its nature which is announced as the topic. On my view, it would be closer to the truth to say that Z was a "philosophical" or "logical" or "verbal" . . . treatment of substance whereas H was a "physical" or "scientific" . . . treatment of the same topic, although Aristotle himself uses [*logikōs*] to refer simply to the first two-thirds of Z, 4.[21] In H, it is as if Aristotle had said to his students, "All right now, *outside* of metaphysics class, what answer would you give to the question of what ties form and matter together?" The answer is, of course, that the efficient cause does. (What unites the lump of bronze with the spherical form? The sculptor does.) Viewed in this light, matter is no longer the name for a special sort of quasi-substance, which is in some funny way "a part" of every generated substance, but rather is the proximate material cause. Various different substances are the proximate material causes of other substances, and not every substance can be matter for every other substance. ("Each thing has some matter which is proper . . . for it," Aristotle says at H, 4.[22]) To put it another way, a substance is the proximate material cause of another substance only when it *is* that substance potentially: "the proximate material cause . . . and the form . . . are one and the same thing . . ."—the passage I quoted at the very beginning (1045b18 ff.). Seen in this light, the question of Z, 12—what unifies the genus with the differentia?—becomes pointless. "It is," as Aristotle says, "like asking what in general is the cause of unity . . . the potential and the actual are somehow one. Therefore there is no other cause here unless there is something which caused the movement from potentiality to actuality" (1045b19-23).

This approach to the problem, however, seems to confuse the history of the genesis of a particular exemplar of a specific form with the definition of that form. After all, isn't the definition supposed simply to signify the formal cause, rather than summing up the whole causal situation within which the formal cause works? In answer to this, Aristotle has to say something which he never says explicitly but which he must maintain if he is to regard H, 6 as his answer to the question of Z, 12. He has to say that genus, in a definition by genus and differentia, somehow signifies the material cause of the individuals of the species defined. In other words, he has to say that, e.g., animality stands to rationality as the brass of the statue stands to its shape. The proximate material cause of a man is that sort of organic material which can be called "animal" but cannot be called "human." As he puts it at I, 8:

> The matter is indicated by negation, and the genus is the matter of that of which it is called the genus.[23]

If we do *not* think of the genus of an individual as telling us about its proximate material cause, the claim in H, 6 that the unity of definitions is simply the sort of unity which unites the proximate material cause with the form will have to be taken as merely a loose analogy. On that view, H, 6 would simply be saying "the relation between the term referring to the genus and the term referring to the differentia in the definition is like the relation between proximate material cause and

form simply in that both pairs express the determination of the relatively indeterminate. In the loose sense in which we can identify what exists potentially with the indeterminate and what exists actually with the determinate, we can identify the unity of the first two with the unity of the second two." But on the view I want to present, Aristotle is saying more than this, both in H, 6 and in the various passages (such as the one just quoted) where he speaks of genus as matter. All these latter passages can, at a pinch, be taken as expressing merely a loose analogy between two sorts of things which have the feature of indeterminacy in common. But I think that Aristotle had more than a loose analogy in mind, and that the way to flesh out the notion of genus-as-matter is to think of him as saying that the genus is a name for the sort of thing that an exemplar of a species of that genus can be made out of.

Now all this may seem a little wild, for we are used to thinking of the genus as a universal, as an abstraction. Although Aristotle does sometimes explicitly contrast these two notions . . . —e.g. at 1028b35—there are other occasions where he seems to bring them together. Thus at 1038b33 ff. he says that because there cannot be a particular animal existing apart from some particular species of animal, and because the differentia cannot exist separately either, we see that "no universal attribute is a substance."[24] Again, in the familiar passage from ***Categories*** 2b7 ff., we are told that genus is less substance than species, because it is further from primary substance. This latter passage, is, I think, often unconsciously interpreted as meaning that "animal" is a more abstract term than "man," and thus less capable of being used to refer to a particular. But this line of thinking neglects the fact that Aristotle didn't have the notion of "an abstraction" and that his use of the term "universal" . . . is so baffling that it is very difficult to back up any claim that he thought of certain things as universals and others as particulars. All that Aristotle says in defense of his claim about genus in the ***Categories*** passage is that it is less informative to tell somebody that Socrates is an animal than to say that he is a man, but this leaves wide open the question whether the genus may not be used to refer to a class of what we, if not Aristotle, would call particulars. To put all this another way, when *we* want to disparage something ontologically we call it a mere abstraction, whereas when Aristotle wants to disparage something ontologically he calls it "indeterminate" or "indefinable" . . . or "just a potentiality. . . . " Aristotle's main objection to calling a genus "substance" is not that it has a merely notional existence, nor that is just a group of the thing's qualities arbitrarily marked off from another group of qualities called the differentiae, but rather that it's just a substrate . . . , just a sort of matter. . . . It is worth nothing that in his formal definition of "genus" in [D] there is no trace of the notion of genus-as-universal; rather he distinguishes genus as "race," genus as the first mover of the race (as in the Hellenes as descendants of Helen), and then lumps all the other senses of "genus" under "matter"— "For," as he says, "that to which the differentia or quality belongs is the substrate, which we call matter."[25]

But still, it might be objected, Aristotle seems perfectly clear in the passage cited from Z, 13 about a particular animal that nothing exemplifies a genus without exemplifying one of the species of that genus. So how can one say that to refer to a genus is to refer to a proximate material cause, or to any sort of particular? Here I have two separate replies to make. The first is that when discussing mules (and other freaks . . .) Aristotle seems to be saying that you *can* have things that fall in genera but not in any species. The second point is something I have touched on previously—the fact that Aristotle is hopelessly torn on the questions of whether something which is a potentiality . . . also counts as a "this" . . . , and of whether the sort of thing which is a proximate material cause for something else is also a particular in its own right.

To begin with the mules, Aristotle says at 1033b-1034a2 that the "genus next above them" common to horses and asses is in both horse and ass, just as the mule is: "For that which would be common to horse and ass, the genus next above them, has not received a name but it would doubtless be both, in fact, something like a mule."[26] It is far from clear what "both" adds to "common to horse and ass," and the context of the passage does not, as far as I can see, offer any clear direction. The context is the claim that "that which generates is of the same kind as what is generated, in the sense of having the same form," and Aristotle seems to be saying that even in the case of "unnatural" generations . . . , freaks, the principle is preserved because just as in the normal case the sire and the colt have the same form so in the freakish case the sire and mule share the same "genus next above." But this still does not tell us how to take "both." I think, however, that Ross's note on the passage probably tells us all that Aristotle has in mind. He says:

> Aristotle's account is that the form of the mule is not the same as that of its sire, the horse, since this has failed to master the opposition offered by the material element coming from the dam, the ass; but it is identical with the generic form of the sire, since this is also the generic form of the dam and thus has no opposition to conquer. *Thus the mule is a sort of abstract universal,* with the generic qualities common to horse and ass but without (or at least not having all) the specific qualities of either. (Italics added.)[27]

My only hesitation over Ross's interpretation concerns the claim that the mule is a sort of abstract universal. This seems to me to be pushing Aristotle's brief and

temporary identification of genus and universal in Z, 13 beyond its proper bounds. Rather, the point is that the mule is a potentiality . . . —one of those heaps . . . discussed in the "physical" definition of "substance" in Z, 16. It is a heap that walks like a substance, so to speak, but we can tell that it is *not* a substance because, like all freaks, it cannot reproduce and, pathetically enough, has no "prime" . . . [28] It is "incomplete" or "unfinished" . . . , like a severed part of an animal— Aristotle's paradigm of a heap.[29]

On the strength of this passage about mules, I am prepared to claim that though Aristotle may have held that no *substance* exemplifies a genus without exemplifying a species . . . , he also held that some *things*[30] . . . can do so. To see how he could have held this doctrine, however, one has to recognize his embarrassment in the face of the question: which, if any, things are "thises" without being substances? Here the tension which appeared in the employment of both the logical and the physical definitions of "substance" shows up again with a vengeance. The trouble may be put as follows: we start out in the **Categories** and the **Topics** with the notion that there are two sorts of things in the world—[ousiai] and [sumbebekota], essential unities like Socrates and accidental unities like "white man." This seems to engender no metaphysical perplexity because the accidental unities are always firmly attached to primary substances. But when we come to matter, potentiality, and similar indeterminate . . . things, we can't fit them under either of these two headings. A piece of dirt is not an accidental unity . . . , and it is not a substance either, according to the physical definition. Such pieces of matter cannot be called "thises" . . . , even though they look for all the world like particulars. So one can imagine Aristotle reconciling the passage concerned with particular animals with the passage about mules (1038b38 ff. with 1033a34ff.) by saying, "But a mule isn't even a 'this' . . . and so can hardly be a 'particular animal'. . . . " If he takes this line, he has to say that nine-tenths of the world is "matter," "potentiality," "indefinite," and so on. But this is embarrassing, for the natural scientist ought to know the matter of things . . . as well as their shapes (cf. **Physics** B, 2). More generally, it is embarrassing to say that matter is "unknowable in itself" (1036a8-9, quoted above), for this means that nine-tenths of the world is unknowable, including all the processes of coming-to-be of natural things.

One might think that Aristotle can avoid embarrassment by saying, as I suggested earlier he might, that anything that is a potentiality is also actually a something-or-other. On this view, everything that is called "potentiality" or "matter" would be a primary substance viewed in some special, functional . . . way. I think that this line would indeed have saved Aristotle a lot of trouble, but I have a hunch about why he takes it only tacitly and never explicitly. The reason, I think, is that he was afraid that if one began seeing a "this" possessing a form . . . and thus falling within a species . . . everywhere there was a material cause . . . , then the distinction between substances and accidental unities would begin to give way. This point may be brought out by noticing the discussion in [*O*], 7 of the question "Is earth potentially a man?" His answer is "No, but rather when it has already become seed . . . and perhaps not even then" (1049a1-2). He goes on to say that something is a house potentially . . . only if "nothing in the thing acted upon—i.e. in the matter—prevents it from becoming a house."[31] This is a slippery slope, because it suggests that instead of having the world neatly blocked out into species of substance which can be matter for one another we get a potential X . . . only after a whole series of accidental changes (alternations . . .) have brought a Y just to the brink of toppling over into being an X. So we cannot say that primary substances which are in species Y are the proximate material causes for the coming-to-be of primary substances which are in species X, but rather those Y's which have been worked up a lot. I think that Aristotle may have noticed that pressing the question "When is Y a potential X?" seemed to "substantify" accidental states of bodies, and dimly saw that if one once began to chop up the realm of the indefinite into quasi-unities one would be well on the road to, as we would put it, a law-event framework of scientific explanation as opposed to a thing-nature framework. So I think he may have subconsciously decided to play it safe by accepting the embarrassments I listed above—those brought on by the physical definition of substance. More generally, he may have recognized that if he once admitted the relevance of accidental change . . . to substantial change . . . he would have betrayed his whole anti-reductionist program, and may have recognized further that looking too closely at material causes would have made this relevance obvious; so he preferred to save the program by condemning nine-tenths of the world to the realm of the potential, the accidental, and the unintelligible. (He got away with this move until, with the rise of the law-event framework in the New Science of the Renaissance, Descartes remarked that it wasn't what Aristotle called "accidental" that was unintelligible, it was Aristotle's notion of "potentiality" itself.[32]

If we assume that the first set of embarrassments were the ones Aristotle preferred, at least while he was writing the central books of the **Metaphysics,** then I can sum up my interpretation of the relevance of H, 6 to Z, 12 as follows. Aristotle should be thought of as saying something like this. Substances look as if they have two parts, form and matter. But actually the matter is just the sort of thing that the genus-term in the definition refers to—something that is not a "this" at all, some indefinite stuff. So it isn't a real part of the substance at all—it is just the substance potentially. So the reason why a man is one thing, and why "two-footed animal" is the definition of one thing, is the

same: that what looked like two "thises" (or, worse yet, two "suches") was really just one. "Two-footed" doesn't refer to one batch of qualities and "animal" to another. Rather, "animality" is different in horses and in men—there really isn't anything *common* at all, for even what we call "common" is different.[33] The fact that there isn't anything common reflects the fact that the material cause of the substance was not a "this," but just undifferentiated animal goo. We only thought that there was a problem about the unity of definition and the unity of substance because we thought that "two-footed" stood to "animal" as "white" stands to "man"—but the former relation is actualization, which is not, like predication, a dyadic relation between two things but a pseudo-relation between one thing and one non-thing.

This ends my account of what Aristotle must have had in mind if he intended H, 6 to be the conclusion of the discussion begun in Z. I shall conclude the paper by noting what is wrong with Aristotle's solution to his putative problem. The first difficulty lies on the surface. If the genus refers to the proximate material cause, it does so because there is a difference between different pieces of matter—some can become an X and some can't. Animalish stuff can become a man and watery stuff cannot. Genus-species definitions are only going to work if genera draw real lines in nature; but if matter is not a "this," is not a substance viewed in a functional way, there are no lines to be drawn. We would not even be able to say that a mule is an animal, for example. Aristotle's solution depends upon saying that terms signifying genera do not stand for collections of qualities, but if they do not then there will be no way of giving meaning to genus-terms.

The second difficulty emerges when we remember that all this was supposed in the end to answer the question, "How can the particular and its essence be the same thing—as Z, 6 said they were?" The answer we have developed to this question has proceeded through the following steps:

(1) Form does not exclude matter; rather there must be reference to the matter in the definition.

(2) Including the genus-term in the form makes the formula of the form, which is also the formula of the essence, be the formula of matter as well as of shape-as-opposed-to-matter.

(3) So since the only apparent difference between the particular and its essence was that there was matter in one and not, as we had thought, in the other, we are now, given a better understanding of essence, in a position to understand their identity.

Put this way, the sophistry is obvious. The most we can get out of the reference to matter which the genus-term gives us is the fact that we should expect *some* accidental features or other in the particular. That is, the best face we can put on (3) is to interpret it as saying that anything which has a given form will also have some other features—accidental features like paleness, snub-nosedness, and so on. I think that Aristotle did have something like this in mind. He may have thought that he had finished the job once he had shown that anybody who understands the definition of "man" will expect there to be something indefinite about a man, because he understands that the reference to indefinite animality in the definition implies that men are generated—and generated things have that funny "capacity for being and not being" (1032a21 ff.) which is their matter, and which makes it possible to tell different exemplars of a form apart. But all this amounts to is the point that if you know what a man is you will know that there are more things to know about men than that they are men. We still do not have any way of making sense of the claim that Socrates, who is pale, and was generated, is the same as the form *man* which is not pale and was not generated.

However, if we go back to the problem for the sake of which the claim about the identity of the particular and the essence was made, things may look a bit better. The problem was that if "Socrates is a man" expresses a relation between two things, one of them will be a substrate and the other will be something predicated of that substrate—but the substrate will have an essence which is predicated of it, other than man. Thus an infinite descending regress will be engendered. In terms of this problem, we may think of Aristotle as saying: this only appears a problem because people think of the matter in the composite as forming a substrate of which the essence is predicated, but we have now seen that that matter was (a) never a "this" in the first place, and so never had an essence, and (b) doesn't exist any more anyway, since it is only what the substance was *potentially*. But this solution just dodges the real issue. We can set up the infinite regress without using the notion of "matter" at all. As long as we have a distinction between essence and a collection of accidents, it doesn't matter whether the substance was generated out of proximate matter or not. The problem is the accidents, not the matter. For the friend of the infinite regress can simply say: we predicate the essence not of some mysterious thing called "matter," but simply of something characterized as "that there white and short," for example. If, *pace* Aristotle and Anscombe, we think that for purposes of getting a language-game going "white and short thing" is just as good as "man," we can dismiss the spectre of an infinite regress simply by saying, first, that sentences get meaning by being used in connection with other sentences, not by any language-world relation, and second that even if a "foundational" view of language or of knowledge were correct, there is no special virtue in "man" which "white and short" lacks; either would be an equally good

candidate for being taken as "identical" with the thing of which it is said.

To sum up these criticisms of Aristotle, I am arguing that he makes the following identifications in the hope of backing up his conviction that the essence-accident distinction is real and important. He identifies the *ensemble* of accidents in a particular substance with the matter "in" it and the matter in it with the proximate material cause of its generation. He then says one or the other of two things, depending on the context and his mood: either that the material cause isn't a "this" at all, but merely a potentiality, or that though perhaps the material cause *was* a full-fledged substance it now, having perished in the course of the genesis of the new substance, does not exist. But this is a conjuring trick. Aristotle moves from saying that the substance has accidents because it came from a material cause which was not quite mastered by form to saying that insofar as it has accidents it somehow still is that old material cause. But this amounts to saying that insofar as something has—*actually* has—certain qualities it is merely a potentiality. This makes no sense at all. All of Aristotle's complicated moves about the unity of the particular composite substance and the unity of the formula of the essence are just one long attempt to find a way of saying that accidents do not count. But he might as well have said this in the first place, and spared us the argument of Z-H, for the upshot is the absurdity that a set of actual features of Socrates are simply Socrates *qua* potential.[34]

One last criticism of Aristotle and I shall stop. I have argued that Aristotle thinks that actualization is a unique sort of metaphysical glue, distinct from inherence, just as the relation between "animal" and "two-footed" is a unique sort of logical glue, distinct from predication. But he turns right around and spoils this by talking about potentialities for accidental change, matter for quality and quantity as well as for substance, and so on.[35] He becomes so infatuated by the potentiality-actuality distinction, so to speak, that he forgets that the whole point of it was to keep the substance-accident distinction sharp and begins to apply it all over the place. In the end, he is reduced to saying such things as that the "primary" sense of "matter" is "matter for generation," and that matter for alteration and locomotion is only a derivate notion,[36] just as he's said in Z,4 that only substances have definitions and an essence in the strict sense, but that accidents do in derivative senses.[37] But this strict-vs.-derivative distinction is just whistling in the dark; for Aristotle to resort to it is for him to insist that his reductionist opponents are wrong without arguing that they are wrong.

The interpretation I have offered here has two obvious defects: it fastens on certain texts and turns a blind eye to others, and it presents Aristotle as offering what may well seem an awkward and verbal solution to a pseudo-problem. All I can say in its defense is that it is hard to find an interpretation of Z-H which has neither of these faults, and that I think that this one ties together some interesting passages which many other interpretations leave dangling.

Notes

1 This paper was read (under the title "Two Concepts of Mules," suggested to me by Elliot Skinner) at the Summer Institute in Greek Philosophy and Science held in Colorado Springs in the summer of 1970. I am grateful to the audience on that occasion, and especially to Bernard Williams, for helpful criticisms. I am also grateful for some very acute criticism to Edward Lee and to John Robertson, and to Gregory Vlastos for kind encouragement and advice.

2 Cf. W. D. Ross, *Aristotle's* Metaphysics (Oxford, 1958), vol. 1, pp. xci-cxiv; *Aristotle* (New York, 1959), pp. 168-70. For a more detailed and careful defense of the view, see Ellen Haring, "Substantial Form in Aristotle's *Metaphysics Z*," *Review of Metaphysics,* 10 (1956-57), 308-32, 482-501, 698-713.

3 Cf. Joseph Owens, *The Doctrine of Being in the Aristotelian* Metaphysics (Toronto, 1951), pp. 374-77, and also chapters 16 and 19.

4 1045b17-24.

5 4a10-11.

6 For attempts to firm up this intuition, see Manley Thompson, "On the Distinction between Thing and Property," in *The Return to Reason,* ed. John Wild (Chicago, 1953), pp. 125-51, and G. E. M. Anscombe and P. Geach, *Three Philosophers* (Oxford, 1961), esp. pp. 18, 34. Whether one can firm up the distinction between kinds of things and properties of things depends upon whether one is allowed to use such terms as "thing" or "object" rather than dismissing them as "pseudo-concepts" (cf. Anscombe and Geach, p. 36). To put it another way, it depends upon whether Greek phrases. . . are permitted to stand on their own feet rather than immediately giving rise to the question "The white *what?*" It is not clear to me what could settle this sort of issue, largely because it is not clear to me what could settle the larger issue between those who think that essence and necessity are relative to descriptions and those who think that they are not. On the latter, see Kripke's attempt to revive an Aristotelian outlook, *pace* Quine and Wittgenstein, in "Naming and Necessity," *Semantics of Natural Language,* ed. Davidson and Harman (Dordrecht, 1972), esp. pp. 264 ff. with n. 12. See also the exchange between Sellars and Strawson in a symposium on "Logical Subjects and Physical Objects," *Philosophy and Phenomenological Research,* 17 (1957), 441-87.

7 1040b5-10.

8 3b18-20.

9 1030a12-14.

10 1007a20-23, 33 ff.

11 Anscombe and Geach, p. 44.

12 For a discussion of six texts in the *Metaphysics* in which this notion occurs, see Richard J. Blackwell, "Matter as a Subject of Predication in Aristotle," *The Modern Schoolman,* 33 (1955), 19-30. Three of these (988a8-13; 995b36; 999a32-b2) are relatively easily dismissed as occurring in passages in which Aristotle is interpreting Plato, or setting up a problem in Platonic terms, and this is the line Blackwell follows. The fourth (1029a20-25) is, I think, rightly treated by Blackwell as a corollary of the claim that "substance is matter," which is the alternative discussed and rejected in Z.3. I am not sure that either of the other two passages (1043a3-7 and 1049a34-b1) can be set aside in the ways in which Blackwell attempts. The former (in H.2) might be viewed as occurring in the same sort of context as the Z.3 passage—since these two chapters both advertise themselves as concerned with substance-as-matter. But H.2 is sufficiently mysterious, in various ways, as to require extended treatment. The sixth last passage occurs in [O].7—a chapter which I argue below (pp. 415-16) shows Aristotle in the throes of a problem ("when does an X become a potential Y?") which threatens the whole scheme he has erected at the end of H. The problems connected with this last chapter tend to be discussed in terms of the notion of "prime matter," of which, I think, the most thorough exploration is in papers by Owens, McMullin, Fisk, Nielsen, and Sellars in *The Concept of Matter,* ed. E. McMullin (Notre Dame, 1963). The view presented by Owens permits one both to take the notion of prime matter seriously and to give the notion that "substance is predicated of matter" a respectable place among basic Aristotelian doctrines. I do not think it should be given such a place, but to argue the point would require debating some of Owens' fundamental methodological and interpretive assumptions.

13 1031b28-31.

14 Anscombe and Geach, p. 10.

15 1032b2-3. I do not know whether Aristotle has just forgotten his use of [*prōtē ousia*] in the *Categories,* or whether he remembers it and is invoking the identification made in the previous chapters.

16 1033b24-6: I take [*kai*] to mean "or" here, so that Aristotle is saying that both "man" and "animal" stand to "brazen sphere in general" as Callias stands to some

given individual brazen sphere, not that "man-and-animal" is the parallel to "brazen sphere in general."

[17] 1037b24-27.

[18] 1038a5-9.

[19] 1045a14-17, 20-31.

[20] Ross, *Aristotle's* Metaphysics, vol. 1, p. cxxiv.

[21] Cf. 1029b13, with 1030a27 ff.

[22] 1044a18 ff.; cf. *Physics* 194b8 ff.

[23] 1058a23-24.

[24] 1038b35.

[25] 1024b8-9. . . . For other genus-as-matter passages, cf. (in addition to 1058a23 ff., previously quoted) 1057b38 ff. and 1038a8.

[26] 1033b34-34a2. . . .

[27] Ross, vol. 2, p. 189.

[28] Cf. *De Anima* 432b22 ff.

[29] Note the etymological connection between being [*ateles*] and existing [*ouk entelekheia*]. On freaks as incomplete, note the use of [*pērōsis*] in the [*sōros*] passage (1040b9 ff.) previously cited from Z, 16. There may be a confirmation of the Whorf hypothesis in the fact that the Greek for "mule" is "half-ass". . . . The English pun is not present in Greek, but nevertheless those accustomed to putting down mules in this way may be more ready to assign them a low rank in the scale of beings.

[30] Cf. 1041b29.

[31] 1049a9 ff.

[32] See, for example, Descartes' sneer at the definition of motion as "the actualization of the potential, *qua* potential" (*Oeuvres,* ed. Adam et Tannery, vol. 10, p. 426, Haldane and Ross translation, vol. 1, p. 46).

[33] 1058a2-5. . . .

[34] Those familiar with Anscombe's treatment of matter as principle of individuation ("The Principle of Individuation," *Proceedings of the Aristotelian Society,* supplementary volume 27 (1953), pp. 83-96, esp. pp. 92 ff.) will realize that I would take issue with her claim that Aristotle thinks of a thing's matter as something distinct from the *ensemble* of its accidents, and that he wants a principle of individuation which is

something other than that *ensemble*. But I cannot discuss the issue in the present space.

[35] Cf., e.g., the use of [*hulē topikē*] at 1042b6.

[36] *De Gen. et Corr.* 320a2 ff.

[37] 1030a18-b14.

Abraham Edel (essay date 1982)

SOURCE: "The Character of Aristotle's Thought and His Philosophic Method," in *Aristotle and His Philosophy,* The University of North Carolina Press, 1982, pp. 30-39.

[*In the following essay, Edel reviews Aristotle's method of philosophical analysis, noting its strengths and weaknesses. Edel states that Aristotle's "mode of inquiry" is characterized by a common-sense attitude, by pluralistic contextualism (that is, the notion that an idea must be understood within a specific, rather than universal, context), and by his treatment of the world as possessing a single order of nature.*]

The analytic character of Aristotle's thought is inherent in his method. He does not first get an idea, work out its implications, and then go looking for evidence. Instead, he first assembles a wide array of opinion and information in the form of common beliefs *(endoxa),* including previous theories, common linguistic usage, and reported observations. He then takes the greatest pains with the formulation of a problem and with a systematic breakdown of its issues. Here especially he develops the difficulties and puzzles and apparent contradictions that have emerged in traditional beliefs. Then he sifts thoroughly for what can hold up and what cannot and makes distinctions, offering solutions that will reconcile or harmonize the divergent elements in the theories, usages, and observations that have not been rejected or wholly reinterpreted.

Aristotle is not, however, merely analytical. His thought is also structural and systematic. There is always a systematic concern operative in his thinking, in two senses. First, he constantly employs a whole framework or network of concepts, in terms of which he formulates the problems of a given field. (The analysis of these concepts is, of course, a great part of his philosophical work.) And second, in working in any one domain he seems to carry with him a web of specific theory developed in other domains, so that the ramifications of one part of knowledge on other parts of knowledge are always near the surface. For example, he considers the suggestion that the world is elliptical in shape and revolves around one central point within itself; this, he notes, means we will have to allow some empty space for it to revolve through, whereas if it is spherical we will not need such an assumption—and he has earlier already rejected the possibility of empty space. In general, he is sensitive to the biological presuppositions of ethics and politics, the physical assumptions of metaphysics, and the psychological assumptions of the theory of knowledge. The cross-references in the corpus are not merely an editor's delight, but integral to his structural way of thinking. Whether the result is an Aristotelian "system" need not concern us now. This stress on structure sharply differentiates Aristotle from Socrates, who will plunge in anywhere and seems content with digging up any contradiction that will stimulate the mind of the interlocutor and shed light on a particular interest.

Besides the ability to analyze and to deal in structures, two other qualities usually found in outstanding philosophers are speculative capacity and originality. If "speculative" indicates ranging insightfully over wide problems, then of course Aristotle is a speculative thinker. If, however, it be taken in the sense of a soaring mind that leaps to imagine possible worlds, that constantly asks for alternatives to the principles it has settled on and speculates what the world would be like if that rather than this were so, then Aristotle either does not have this capacity in high degree or else he mutes it. He often seems too earthbound and too ready to accept as final the principles of order that have emerged from his inquiry, too ready to dismiss possibilities for which there are no existent specimens to examine. On the other hand, his creative originality should not go unrecognized simply because he seems to be extracting his conclusions from the examination of his predecessors and adding on to their work. In fact he is the great master in original concept formation, and he plays with traditions as a great musician works up older themes into a novel pattern. The concepts Aristotle fashioned, and the way of looking at the world they embodied, provided a framework for sophisticated thought in which men could for a time make advances in understanding their world and themselves.

Whether the works bear the stamp of a great scientist as well as a great philosopher is more debatable. The biological writings have won admiration not only for their scope and foundational character but also for their detail of observation. In comparative studies Aristotle shows tremendous insight in ordering descriptive materials and in sensing useful analogies. Again, he is quick to theorize and ready to offer explanations. Indeed, sometimes he jumps for explanations too quickly, without waiting to check the fact he is setting out to explain. Thus he gives the example, cited above, that the surface of a mirror becomes clouded red when a menstruating woman looks into it (and he adds, "If the mirror is a new one the stain is not easy to remove"), and he goes on right away to offer complex explanations in terms of his theory of vision why this should happen.[1] On many occasions there is an element of

credulity in his acceptance of alleged facts, even where, as in this case, he could have arranged for tests. But there is no gainsaying his ingenuity in fashioning alternative explanations on the basis of his own hypotheses, even in relatively unsuccessful domains such as meteorology, as well as in his treatments of psychological and political phenomena (he was a political scientist, not merely a political philosopher). Take, for example, his complex reckoning with prophecy in dreams.[2] He notes first that small stimuli in waking life may go unnoticed because competing greater impulses crowd them out, but that in sleeping, with the competition cut off, a faint echo may be heard, like distant thunder and lightning. The problem of explaining successful prophecies is then posed as showing the relation of small stimuli to large events. Aristotle suggests three relations: signal, cause, and coincidence. A person might prophesy his coming illness because its first beginnings reverberated loudly in sleep and so signaled its coming. Or he might foresee doing something because the small beginnings of intention had come in a dream, and so begotten the action. Where the dreamer does not initiate an event, what happens is best understood as coincidence; most dreams do not coincide with what happens, so it is not surprising that an occasional one does.

In general, then, Aristotle's strength lay on the observational side in gathering and systematizing data. It was perhaps too early for controlled experiment. On the theoretical side it lay in ingenuity of explanation, but he sometimes pressed general theories into particular explanations without sufficient precision to test them against alternative possibilities.

It is not easy to decide which of the shortcomings of Aristotelian science are to be attributed to lack of specific qualities of scientific intellect. Some may follow either from immature development of specific sciences in his day, or from a lack of precision in instruments, or simply a lack of instruments (he did complain that insects were too small for observation), or an insufficient development of mathematical tools. The growing field of the philosophical history of science has not yet sufficiently explored these questions.

There are further specific attitudes that stand out in Aristotle's mode of inquiry: a stubborn commonsense attitude, a sensitivity to contextual differences, and a special kind of one-world outlook. These also require our preliminary attention.

Aristotle is often extraordinarily commonsensical. He has an essentially realistic orientation to the phenomena of a field and a stubborn how-is-it-used attitude to the meaning of terms. He has little patience with those who raise dialectical difficulties about the reality of initial phenomena. If a man denies motion (says Aristotle in the ***Physics***), no physicist will have anything to do with him. More precisely, his point is that such disputes do not fall within the work of the physicist, but concern another scientist—the metaphysician. We shall see later how he deals with Zeno's paradoxes that seem to impugn the reality of motion. Again, if a philosopher wants to elevate Being into an ultimate One which is the reality of all that is, Aristotle sometimes invokes minute logical objections stemming from his logical views. More often he simply says that there are many senses of *being (is)* as well as many senses of *one;* in fact, things can be one by being of the same material, or by being instances of the same form, or by being continuous—as when they are stuck together by glue! Such calculated commonsensicality has the same sobering effect as Socrates' talk of carpenters and doctors and things of the marketplace, and of course like Socrates' method it goes through the commonplace to deal with difficult and complex problems.[3]

Sometimes, however, Aristotle's realism leads him into dogmatism. Thus, maintaining that not every doubt deserves inquiry, he says, "Those in doubt whether one ought to honor the gods and love one's parents or not, are in need of punishment, while those who doubt whether snow is white or not, lack perception."[4] Again, in the **Physics** he takes it to be obvious that things have natures. Yet this, far from being an obvious phenomenon, is a very sophisticated thesis. There is thus the danger that his sense of realism, while salutary in many contexts, may in others be blind to possible differences of interpretation when one interpretation is already built into the alleged phenomenon.

A commonsensical attitude may, even more, be a way in which significant philosophical views are introduced and taken for granted. It is one thing to attack as near madness the doctrine that all is one and immovable ("no madman is so out of his senses as to think that fire and ice are one; but in dealing with things that are fine and things that through habit appear fine, some people on account of madness seem to find no difference");[5] it is quite another to let such a passionate devotion to common sense establish the epistemological principle that whatever contradicts sense-perception is erroneous, or the ontological principle that whatever physical account may be given of sense-qualities, their observational properties are not to be denied or their reality impugned by "reduction." Indeed, we shall see that at a number of critical points—in analyzing the infinite, continuity, and the properties of motion, as well as the relation of potentiality to determinism—the commonsensical attitude becomes almost a technical philosophical instrument. In the light of the range of the commonsensical we shall therefore have to pay close attention to the occasions of its use in different contexts and see both its strengths and its weaknesses.

The second important attitude in Aristotle's mode of inquiry may be described as a kind of pluralistic contextualism: the meaning of an idea has to be understood in a specific context of inquiry; there is no universal context, and hence no possibility of dispensing with contextual reference. This attitude emerges clearly in his treatment of philosophical ideas, in the so-called philosophical lexicon of **Metaphysics** 5. Take, for instance, the term *principle (archē)*. This has a sonorous sound; it conveys the idea of what is basic or fundamental in the area under investigation. Philosophy generally takes the notion for granted. Yet what, after all, is a principle? It is refreshing to see Aristotle dip down to the ordinary meaning of the Greek term, which is simply "beginning" or "starting point." He illustrates with the examples that the starting point of a journey is the beginning of travel and that the keel of a ship is the beginning of its construction, carefully pointing out that the latter is an internal part of what is constructed. Once we recognize the basic contextualism we find it hard thereafter to make philosophical sense of the use of a concept or a principle without specifying the kind of activity or inquiry involved. Principles or judgments of priority or primacy unavoidably pinpoint relations in some ordering. They are context-bound. (Even the sense "governing principle" comes from an ordinary usage—*archai* could also mean the rulers of government.) Of course some contexts become standardized for philosophical inquiry. Aristotle distinguishes repeatedly between the order of learning and the order of logical demonstration; in the one, perceived particulars will provide the starting point, in the other, primary premises. The contextual reference is usually not far below the surface. It may involve terms that are needed to enter into a basic definition in the field, or initial phenomena for investigation that are not to be denied, or regular starting points for understanding development, and so on. For example, a house is logically prior to the process of building because the account or statement *(logos)* of the process refers to the house, but the account of the house does not include the process of building.[6] (Of course, the particular process is temporally prior to the particular house.)

Such contextualism does not necessarily guarantee that the outcomes will be different. The contexts may be different, but the principles or starting points specified may turn out on investigation to be related or to converge in various ways on a single outcome. Any discovered unity would thus be subsequent to the inquiry, not laid down in advance.

There is a sense—and this is the third fundamental attitude in Aristotle's inquiries—in which he does approach the world as one world. He treats it as a single order of nature with no impassable barriers, with none of the cleavages that have characterized modern thought at least since the seventeenth century, and modern philosophy since Descartes: the partition of man from nature, spirit from matter, mind from its objects, in one or another explicit or subtle form. Aristotle asks questions we would not dream of asking, which at first seem odd and then shock us out of our presuppositions. Thus he wants to know whether, if a house grew up by nature, it would grow up in the same way as we would build it. He decides it would—for is not man in his crafts only imitating natural processes? Does not the doctor cure by trying to reproduce nature's operations? Aristotle's favorite paradigm of nature's operations is the doctor curing himself as patient—that is, nature raised to a conscious level. Now we moderns may find Aristotle's doctrinal view of the architecture of house-building archaically limited; we may suspect that he is having nature imitate man rather than the reverse. Yet there may be much to learn from his easy passage from one to the other. Think how much effort we spend today on the similar question whether the brain is a machine, some of us ingeniously multiplying the powers of the machine to approximate the variegated powers of man, and others, fearful of the continuity of man and machine, insisting on the uniqueness of consciousness. Whatever Aristotle's specific scientific errors and naïvetés, we cannot dismiss his one-world attitude as an immature pre-Cartesianism. It is a genuine, sophisticated philosophical alternative that he can help us understand and that we may today be better able to evaluate. After all, how can one simply settle by postulation whether spirit is or is not a separate stuff out of which thoughts and feelings are constituted? The answer has to be the cumulative outcome of investigation into one field after another, of psychological investigation added to physical and biological investigation.

In considering Aristotle's one-world attitude as a characteristic mode of thought we have passed from qualities of thought to principles of philosophical outlook. There are accordingly other matters that would clamor at this point for a place in our inventory—e.g., his attitude toward change, toward evolution and history, as contrasted with the search for a rational eternal order. Such questions can best be considered in relation to his philosophical concepts, to which we turn shortly. There is, however, one general matter in his method that has wide ramifications and ought to be considered before we go on, namely his attitude toward language and the place of language analysis in philosophizing. Precisely because linguistic analysis looms large in contemporary philosophy and because there has been some tendency to look back to Aristotle as having been engaged in a comparable practice, it is important to see both what he says on the question and what he does in his actual philosophizing.

There is, of course, a close relation in Aristotelian writing between logic, reason, and speech. The term *logos* (plural *logoi*) is kin to *legein* (to speak) and refers to a proposition, an account or formula, and becomes extended to mean a rational explanation or

theory. On occasions Aristotle contrasts the adverb *logikōs* with *phusikōs,* or sometimes *logoi* with *pragmata*. The first may set off a logical or dialectical argument against a scientific one, but the scientific one could be of the order of theoretical results as well as an appeal to observational fact. Sometimes when Aristotle contrasts *logikōs* and *phusikōs* it is almost as if he were contrasting theoretical considerations with factual ones. The distinction between *logoi* and *pragmata* is more often one between the conclusion of an argument based on assumptions, and the obvious reality (how things stand).[7] The exact shade of contrast in both formulations doubtless varies with the context. We shall have occasion to examine specific contexts later.

We have already seen that Aristotle includes what people say and think or believe among the data or received opinions *(endoxa)* he records at the outset of an inquiry and that he follows this up by exploring shades of usage. It is perfectly clear that he expects to learn a great deal from the analysis of linguistic usages. Now this is a trap for modern interpreters, for modern linguistic thought has been intensely concerned with specifying a *general* relation between the structure of language and the structure of reality. It has been easy (much too easy) to say that for Aristotle speech embodies reason and reason grasps the structure of things, so that the structure of speech is the structure of the real—that, for example, because speech takes a subject-predicate form, therefore reality consists of substances and their properties. Such a generalization, we shall see, is misleading. It is not even to be assumed that for Aristotle the logical—linguistic is a separate order from the real or that its correspondence with the real poses a general problem. They may just be two modes of investigation or inquiry, one logical or dialectical, the other physical or scientific. Talking about things is itself a natural phenomenon; things get talked about just as they get played upon in other ways in this world, and so how we think about them and how we embody that thought in speech may give us clues to what they are like. Both our thoughts and our speech are therefore part of the evidence in any inquiry.[8] There will be all sorts of occasions on which linguistic formulations may be misleading. While there are appropriate names to distinguish some processes, such as "drizzle" when drops are small and "rain" when they are large, there are other cases in which the physical analysis clarifies the linguistic: Aristotle analyzes the process of boiling and then points out that the (apparently) common use of the term *boiling* to mean heating gold or wood is only metaphorical since the process is physically different.[9] Similarly, linguistic form may mislead us on appropriate category: "to flourish" has the same verbal form as "to cut" or "to build," but the first denotes a quality, while the others denote actions.[10] Again, there are cases in which Aristotle seems to be giving a linguistic analysis but is really drawing on linguistic corroboration for a physical analysis. In discussing growth and the addition of one thing to another, he wonders why when mixing water and wine we say we have more wine as a result rather than more water. It is clear that we do so because the function *(ergon)* of the mixture is to serve as wine; later on he points out that when we put in too much water the result is water.[11]

On critical occasions, when a conflict arises, Aristotle is quite explicit. In **Metaphysics** 7, when he is failing to solve the problem of substance in purely logical terms, he says, "We should certainly inquire how we should speak on each point, but not more than how the facts actually stand."[12] Further on in the same inquiry he says, "It is clear that if people go on in their customary way of defining and speaking it is not possible to answer and resolve the difficulty."[13]

If we look not for a correspondence of structures but to the simple fact that he spends much time analyzing what we ordinarily say and showing complex patterns of usage with a high degree of sensitivity, we have again to note that he does this to offer *partial* evidence for one or another thesis. For example, presenting the view that body has three dimensions, he points out that we say "both" of two things or two people, but not "all," whereas of three we say "all"; thus we are following nature, since three dimensions give us a complete body, and "complete" and "all" do not differ in form.[14] Linguistic usages are thus part of phenomena and so can serve evidentially for a thesis. Linguistic analysis, then, although it does play a large part in his inquiry when he wants greater precision or feels it necessary to fashion a technical term, is not for Aristotle a separate mode of analysis. But he does end with a set of highly refined terms that he uses in carrying out analyses in special fields from physics to politics. What, then, is the relation of his refined technical language to the ordinary language he uses?

We can distinguish three different levels of concepts conveyed by his terminology. At the top are the highly general concepts—*matter, form, nature, potentiality, actuality, substance,* and so on. These are very technical, and Aristotle is obliging enough occasionally to show how he has fashioned them. In the middle are concepts with only a moderate amount of fashioning, often expressed by ordinary words standardized for the purpose—for example, most of what he calls the "categories" (*quality, quantity, place, time, action,* etc.), and change and its species. At the bottom are concepts conveyed by the little words. These are not necessarily the imposing little words such as *the what-is* or *the one,* for these, in the guise of Being and Unity, already had an exalted metaphysical place in Platonic construction, and we have suggested that Aristotle in a commonsensical way tried to prick the Platonic balloon of inflated concepts. They have their place in

Aristotle too, but chiefly as problems at the top. The heavy work at the bottom is done by the little words of ordinary discourse, such as *from, out of, in, having, prior, now,* and the like. Of course, there are also the little words that are used as a source for middle-rank terms like some of the category terms and the four causes: *how big, what sort, when, where, out of, what, whence, for the sake of,* and so on. Actually, we find an even wider range of little words in specific analyses throughout the corpus. They are especially resorted to at critical points in the analysis of more complex conceptions. Not only are *in* and *now* used in analyzing *place* and *time,* but subtle problems of mathematical continuity rest on a basic consideration of *together, apart, touching, next,* and so on. Problems of the motion of physical elements involve *up, down, right, left, front,* and *back.* Biological questions such as the order of development of parts of the body and functional relations therein prompt an aside on the meanings of *prior,* just as the relation of offspring to seed leads Aristotle to reflect on the meaning of one thing's *coming from* another. The question as to what constitutes a single physical movement necessitates an account of the different senses of *one.*

Of course, such a distinction between levels does not mean that some terms may not operate in different ways on different levels. *Matter* and *form* in the sense of material and shape are certainly ordinary terms. As a relative distinction on the middle level, Aristotle turns them into two of the four causes. *Matter* in a basic sense and especially *form* as *essence* become high-level. Similarly, *place* is an ordinary word, but as a category it is elevated to at least middle rank.

There is no simple uniform relation in Aristotle between ordinary language and technical language. The latter is not built up in a formal way out of the former, as complex definitions may be constructed out of simple elements. Nor is it one-directional; that is, no technical term on every occasion of its use is analyzable as a combination of elements in ordinary (bottom-level) language, with (of course) contextual differentiation. In fact, Aristotle is occasionally ready to refine the smaller, ordinary word by the more technical ones. In discussing the order of development of bodily parts, he distinguishes the meanings of *prior* first by applying his technical distinction between final cause and efficient or generative cause and then by breaking the latter into agent and instrument.[15] Similarly, in *Metaphysics* 5, *prior* seems to be explicated by reference to already established technical terms. Again, in discussing the relation of body and psyche, two senses of *for the sake of* are distinguished—one the end or purpose for which, and the other the person for whom.[16]

We cannot classify Aristotle in the modern sense as either a formalist or an informalist; he does not fashion his philosophical terms by precise combinations, logically explicit, out of simpler elements, nor does he use them merely as pointers to variegated contexts of ordinary language. He seems to have achieved something different, a kind of conceptual network, generated out of ordinary uses to be sure, but presupposing always some factual picture, some governing purposes, and sometimes a specific model of construction. The resulting network is different from either the formalist's system or the informalist's studied pluralism. Each concept reaches over to the others and only gradually becomes intelligible as its relations to the others and their grounding in existent phenomena are revealed. . . .

Notes

[1] *On Dreams* 459b27 ff.

[2] *On Prophecy in Sleep* 1.

[3] The complex problems on this point are dealt with in chapter 7 below. There are important differences of direction between Socrates and Aristotle here. In one sense, Socrates is trying to rouse the mind of the hearer through the material into a flight to ideas, whereas Aristotle is using the ordinary material to keep the flight responsible. Socratic method has long challenged philosophers who attempt to locate its effect and its logic as well as its charm; see Nelson 1949; Vlastos 1956, introduction; and Edel 1963, ch. 4.

[4] *Top.* 105a3 ff.

[5] *Gen. Corr.* 325a19-23.

[6] *Part. An.* 646a25-29.

[7] See, for example, *Gen. Corr.* 325a13-19 (the passage just preceding the one in n. 5 above). Aristotle reports the argument—from initial general assumptions—of those who reach such conclusions as that motion does not exist. He says they go further and disregard observation as necessary to following *logos*. Their beliefs seem to follow in terms of the *logoi*, but to believe them in view of the *pragmata* is near madness.

[8] It is important at the outset to contrast this interpretation of Aristotle, which sees the linguistic as furnishing partial evidence, with some current interpretations that draw sharp distinctions between the linguistic and the empirical. The latter want to decide precisely where Aristotle is engaging in a linguistic inquiry (and so "doing philosophy"), and where an empirical inquiry (and so "doing science"). This attitude is a familiar one in contemporary linguistic analysis, which has made serious contributions to Aristotelian studies by sharpening our linguistic sensitivity and occasionally by furnishing modern linguistic tools, but at some points it creates obstacles by applying its own doctrines of language rather than looking through Aristotle's eyes

at how he saw language. Some of the issues involved will be discussed later in this book, but one fundamental point should be noted in a kind of preview. This is that Aristotle looks at words from the point of view of things, not things from the point of view of words. At the beginning of the *Categories,* when he defines *homonymy* and *synonymy,* he says that *things* are homonymous if they share the same name but the name has a different definition in the two cases, and synonymous if they share the same name and its definition is in both cases the same. (If this sounds outrageous to modern ears, please remember Aristotle was there first—we are the ones who *re*defined it.) We are more linguistically oriented when we start with *words* and call the words equivocal or univocal, and speak of the words as synonymous. Ackrill 1963, p. 71, in his comment on the same passage in the *Categories,* explains this whole point clearly and adds, "It is encumbent on the translator not to conceal this, and, in particular, not to give a misleadingly linguistic appearance to Aristotle's statements by gratuitously supplying inverted commas in all the places where *we* might feel that it is linguistic expressions that are under discussion." We shall have occasion to come back to this important topic in several different contexts later on.

The significance of this fundamental point is that Aristotle does not have to segregate language in general from things in general as a sharply distinct order. Of course there are the different inquiries mentioned—one *logikōs,* a dialectical inquiry, and one *physikōs,* a scientific inquiry—but we would be hard put to construe the first as pure language and the second as pure observation. There is for Aristotle, then, no general or metaphysical question of the correspondence of language and reality, or whether the structure of language mirrors the structure of reality, such as modern philosophers like to raise about language and about Aristotle. (There are notions of correspondence in his theory of truth, but that is another matter.) It is doubtless a perfectly reasonable question to raise on some presuppositions, but not on Aristotle's.

Some illustrations of the effect of these modern approaches on interpretations of Aristotle will be found later when we compare different modern philosophical viewpoints on specific passages and issues in the corpus.

[9] *Meteor.* 347a11f., 380b28ff.

[10] *Soph. Ref.* 166b16 f.

[11] *Gen. Corr.* 321a29-b2, 322a31 f.

[12] *Meta.* 7, 1030a27 ff. "How the facts actually stand" translates *to pōs echei.* The "fact," in this context, turns out to be a reiteration, no matter which way we choose to speak, that in a primary sense definition and essence

belong to substance. "How things stand" has here, then, more of the character of an established principle from which usage must not detract.

[13] *Meta.* 8, 1045a20 ff.

[14] *Heav.* 268a16 ff.

[15] *Gen. An.* 742a19 ff.

[16] *Psych.* 415b20 f.

Aristotle's Works: Titles, Abbreviations, and Translations

Wherever possible, the English titles have been used rather than the Latin versions, except for *Historia Animalium, Parva Naturalia,* and *Magna Moralia,* whose Latin titles seem firmly entrenched. In the case of Aristotle's chief psychological work (Latin, *De Anima*), the current English translation, *On the Soul,* seems likely to mislead; I have resorted to *On the Psyche,* staying close to the original Greek term, which has become an established English word. . . . Where abbreviation is desirable the following are used:

Top.	*Topics*
Soph. Ref.	*On Sophistical Refutations*
Heav.	*On the Heavens*
Gen. Corr.	*On Generation and Corruption*
Meteor.	*Meteorology*
Psych.	*On the Psyche*
Part. An.	*Parts of Animals*
Gen. An.	*Generation of Animals*
Meta.	*Metaphysics*

Bibliography

Edel, Abraham. 1963. *Method in Ethical Theory.* Indianapolis: Bobbs-Merrill.

Nelson, Leonard. 1949. "The Socratic Method." In his *Socratic Method and Critical Philosophy,* chapter 1. Translated by Thomas K. Brown, III. New Haven: Yale University Press.

Vlastos, Gregory. 1956. *Plato's Protagoras.* New York: Liberal Arts Press.

PRACTICAL SCIENCE: ETHICS AND POLITICS

G. R. G. Mure (essay date 1932)

SOURCE: "Practical Man: *Politics,*" in *Aristotle,* Ernest Benn Limited, 1932, pp. 157-62.

[*In the following excerpt, Mure surveys Aristotle's* Politics, *asserting that Aristotle criticizes and completes the "broad outline of Platonic theory." Mure notes Aristotle's views on the role of the state, classes, and citizenship, and comments on the similarities and differences between Aristotle's and Plato's political philosophies.*]

. . . Aristotle's **Politics** contains several sets of lectures, and some of them are fragmentary.[1] But no other work of his displays more clearly the vast masses of fact which he mastered and analysed in order both to criticise and to complete the broad outline of Platonic theory. In history and politics he is as acute and comprehensive an observer as he is in the animal world. We can here only sketch his political views as a part of his whole system, but scarcely a chapter of the **Politics** has failed directly or indirectly to influence subsequent political thought.

We have already seen . . . that for Aristotle as for Plato the state exists by nature as the real *prius* of the individual, and that in consequence the main function of government is to promote the [*endaimonia*] of the citizens by making them virtuous: "Those may be expected to lead the best life who are governed in the best manner of which their circumstances admit" (**Pol.** [**Politics**] 1323a17).

Aristotle, like Plato, conceives political philosophy as normative, and the construction of an ideal state as an essential part of its task. He agrees too that in the ideal state the naturally better[2] rules the naturally worse for the good—and the freedom—of the whole state. But he distinguishes sharply the statesman's activity from the philosopher's . . . , and he takes the view that Plato has over-simplified the structure of the state. To give to the state the unity of the sentient organism, which feels as its own the pains and pleasures of each several member, Plato had allowed no differentiation below the three classes of husbandmen, warriors, and rulers; and within the two latter classes he had abolished the family and private property as a menace to the loyalty of the citizen. In the *Republic,* justice, scarcely distinguished from friendship, culminates in a single [*filia*] in which love of self, kinsman, friend, and city is one undivided passion. Aristotle replies that the strength of love depends on limitation, and that the extension of family feeling to coincide with patriotism could only result in its proportionate dilution. The state is "a community of communities." Man takes to himself a wife and a slave, being fitted by nature to rule both of them;

his wife as his delegate within the household, for she can deliberate; his slave, who can only obey, as "a living tool for the conduct of life," whose inferior natural function is to serve a master for their mutual benefit. Several families unite to form a village, several villages to constitute a state, which "comes to be for the sake of life, but *is* for the sake of the good life."[3] The state is like all works of nature and man: its quantitative proportions must be precisely right. It must be neither too small to be self-sufficient, nor too great to be controlled: "Of an exceeding great multitude who shall be the general, or who the herald save a Stentor?" (*ibid.* 1236ᵇ5). The ideal territorial conditions can be determined accordingly.

The classes necessary to the proper functioning of the state are the serfs, the husbandmen, the mechanics, the traders, the warriors, the rich who bear costly public burdens, the rulers and officials, and the priests. But the warriors are those who are to become officials and rulers in middle age, and priests when they grow old; and they alone are to own the land. Hence the four latter classes, which are thus genetically one, are the sole organic parts of the state; the remainder, though they differ in degree of importance, are mere *sine quibus non* of the well-being of the citizen community.[4] Aristotle implies that the happiness of the state requires an order of external goods, which descends through the slave—"the living tool"—to the physical features of the city's locality. This order is analogous to that according to which within rational man the nutritive ranks below the sensory-appetitive soul, and itself requires an external nutriment. Some men in fact are by nature inferior in virtue to others, just as in different degrees obedience is the virtue of children and women. Aristotle does not regard their common rationality as qualifying men for political equality, though he concedes that the son of a natural slave need not be one himself, and he condemns enslavement by right of conquest.

He does not, like Plato, favour a communistic system. Private property affords an extension of personality, and is not only a source of legitimate pleasure but also a means to generosity. Its *use,* however, should be common, and its excessive accumulation is an evil. But the remedy for this evil is not to equalise property by legislation which the mere increase of the population will nullify; the solution is "rather to educate the nobler natures not to desire more, and to prevent the lower from getting more" (*ibid.* 1267ᵇ5). Sharing the usual Greek view of trade as an illiberal pursuit, he even regards barter as less natural than use, though inevitable up to a point. The exchange of goods for money, which leads to usury, seems to him definitely unnatural, despite the convenience of currency. It must be remembered that economic organisations with large resources of invested capital were no more necessary than representative government in the small city-states

of Greece. The public spirit of a few rich individuals could take the place of the one, and primary self-government of the other, to an extent impossible in the cumbrous nation-states of our day.

In actual states qualification for citizenship varies, but in general—and reasonably—the citizen is he who can claim a share in legislative and judicial functions. Yet if a man greater and better than his fellows should arise, it were well that he alone should rule. The ideal state is in fact monarchical, and the monarch's care of his subjects reflects paternal love. But the ideal monarch, as Plato had held in the *Politicus,* will rule as the embodiment of law. Though Aristotle distinguishes the legislative, the judicial, and the executive elements in the state, Athenian politics had taught him how dangerous the process of particularising the law's generality by *ad hoc* enactment rather could become, and he minimises the executive function.

Monarchy perverted becomes—as in Persia—tyranny, which is analogous to a dominion of master over slave for the sole benefit of the master. Failing the wise autocrat, let the best men of the state form an aristocracy, reflecting the household ruled by a wise master partly through his wife. Aristocracy perverted becomes oligarchy, the rule of a rich minority, sometimes found in actual fact ameliorated by good breeding and education; and this answers to the rule in a household of a master who interferes by force where he should not, or of an heiress who rules by "virtue" of her wealth. The most practicable ideal for actual states is polity—government by a large middle class, based on free birth and a moderate property qualification. This reflects the friendship of brothers, and its perversion, democracy, is like a family where the head of the house is weak, and all the sons claim an equal share of control irrespective of age or merit.[5]

Thus polity is the worst of the good constitutions; tyranny the worst, and democracy the least bad, of the perversions. Polity is possible where "there naturally exists a large warrior class able to rule and to obey in turn according to a law which gives office to the well-to-do in proportion to their desert."[6] If a large middle class holds the balance between rich and poor, they will mistrust each other too much to combine against it, and polity thus has the merit of "consisting in a mean."[7] To democracy, which is based on the idea of liberty and equality for all, Aristotle grants the possible advantages that a number of ordinary men may be collectively better than a few good ones, and less liable to be all moved by passion at once; and, further, that if the people are allowed to choose and dismiss their rulers, it is at all events the consumer who is made the judge. On the whole, his view of democracy, which elaborates Plato's rather than differs from it, is that it illustrates the resistance of matter to form—it is something indeterminate rather than actively vicious—

and his contention that democracy is the least bad, tyranny the worst, of the perverted constitutions, accords with his own theory of evil in *EN* [*Nicomachean Ethics*] and with Plato's. . . .

In an unfinished sketch of ideal education (*Pol.* VIII), Aristotle observes that the training of youth is commonly left in private hands, and that opinion differs as to whether it should be intellectual, moral, or utilitarian. His own view is that the education of the ideal citizen will be the concern of the state. For the citizen belongs not to himself but to the state, and education is a training for the practice of virtue—the sole end for which the state exists. Sparta, despite her wrong-headed militarism, has rightly taken this view. The citizen is to be trained for leisure—neither, that is, to make a living, nor for war and politics as ultimate ends, but for self-sufficing rational activity. But Bk. VIII ends without a discussion of intellectual training, and only treats of eugenics and of the earlier stages of a liberal education. Of these the principle is that a boy must learn to obey in order that he may learn to rule. Of the subjects customarily taught Aristotle allows the need of some gymnastic—since the body must be trained before the soul; of reading and writing; of drawing, because it teaches one to appreciate the beauty of the human form. To music, a very important factor in Greek education, of which he speaks at some length, he accords a recreational, a moral . . . and even perhaps . . . a specifically aesthetic pleasure. But the type of melody must be carefully selected on moral grounds, and, though boys should be taught to play an instrument well enough to become tolerable critics of skill in execution, to be a professional player is vulgar.

For Aristotle's analysis of actually existent constitutions (*Pol.* III) and the right methods of governing even the worst of them by a "mean" policy (*Pol.* VI), and for his diagnosis of the causes and cure of revolution (*Pol.* V), we have no space but to say that he puts at the disposal of the practical statesman a knowledge and insight which have never been approached.

Notes

[1] And probably written at different periods of his life and thought. The *a priori* and empirical elements do not seem in complete harmony, and Books VII and VIII on the ideal state were very likely composed before IV-VI, which deal with actual constitutions: see pp. 265 ff.

[2] The reader of the *Politics* must always remember what human goodness means to Aristotle.

[3] Pol. 1252^{b}29. Aristotle is here describing the genesis of the state within history as we know it. In *reality* the state, in which alone the individual is actualised, is prior to him. Aristotle maintains that ultimately the actual is prior to the potential temporally as well as really; see note 1, p. 92.

[4] The doctrine is that of the *Republic,* save that the rulers do not lead the speculative life in old age. Presumably Aristotle's priests do not know God as the philosopher knows him: cp. Ch. VIII, sect. 1.

[5] With this order of constitutions and their domestic analogues compare the order of constitutions and corresponding *individuals* in *Republic,* IX. See also *Politicus,* 297c ff., where Plato is nearer to Aristotle.

[6] Pol. 1288^{a}12. Aristotle has in mind the Athenian constitution of 411, in which the 5000 hoplites dominated.

[7] That the worst of the good constitutions illustrates the mean *par excellence,* confirms the view of the mean taken in Chap. VII, sect. 3.

David Ross (lecture date 1957)

SOURCE: "The Development of Aristotle's Thought," in *Aristotle and Plato in the Mid-Fourth Century: Papers of the Symposium Aristotelicum at Oxford in August, 1957,* edited by Düring and G. E. L., Göteborg, 1960, pp. 1-18.

[*In the following essay, originally delivered as a lecture in 1957, Ross traces the contributions of various critics toward understanding the development of Aristotle's doctrines. Ross notes some of the difficulties in the sketchy chronology outlined by some critics, and discusses in particular Aristotle's plan for* Politics *as developed and articulated in* Ethics. *He also argues that Aristotle's concept of the "unmoved first mover" appeared in successive stages through a number of works, including* Metaphysics.]

It is only within the last forty years or so that a determined effort has been made to discover the line of development of Aristotle's thought; until forty years ago the tendency of scholars had been to treat the great majority of the works that bear his name as forming one single mass of doctrine, articulated into parts by his own recognition of the various branches of philosophy and science as separate studies, but bearing within itself few signs of development.[1] Where works included within the traditional corpus did differ markedly in doctrine from the general mass, there was a tendency to regard this as showing that they were not genuine works of the master at all. Thus for instance Valentinus Rose, to whose work we owe most of our knowledge of the fragments of Aristotle, was so much impressed by the differences of doctrine between the dialogues and the extant works that he treated the dialogues as spurious; and the scholars who studied the

Eudemian Ethics were led, by noting the difference of doctrine between this work and the *Nicomachean Ethics,* to treat the *Eudemian Ethics* as the work not of Aristotle but of Eudemus. Similarly the *De Interpretatione,* in which the theory of judgement was different from that which underlay the *Analytics,* was for that reason rejected as not being by Aristotle.

We may in this country take some pride in the fact that, as Lewis Campbell had been the pioneer in showing the way to a true chronology of Plato's dialogues, a British scholar was the pioneer in showing the way towards not only a chronology of Aristotle's works but also the tracing of a development of doctrine within them. This scholar was Thomas Case, Professor of Moral and Political Philosophy at Oxford from 1894 to 1904, and President of Corpus from 1904 to 1924. As a metaphysician, Case stood quite aloof from the Kantian and Hegelian tendencies which were dominant at Oxford through the earlier part of that period. In other matters his general attitude is tersely summed up in the *Concise Dictionary of National Biography,* in the remark that he 'opposed changes in church, state, and University'. In Aristotelian studies he stood outside of the general stream of Oxford scholarship; he was not one of the faithful band which met under Bywater's roof to study the Master's work. He was working on his own lines, and in 1910 he wrote for the *Encyclopaedia Britannica* the article on Aristotle. Partly because it was buried in this decent obscurity, and partly because he had few, if any, disciples, his account of Aristotle received little recognition. But in it he traced, in three departments, a line of development which is now pretty generally accepted. (1) He vindicated the authenticity of the dialogues, and showed them to be natural, both in form and in doctrine, as the work of one gradually emerging, as Aristotle must be supposed to have done, from Platonism into a system of his own. (2) He showed that the *De Interpretatione* expresses a theory of judgment akin to that expressed in Plato's *Sophistes,* and therefore in the same way natural to one emerging from discipleship into independence. And (3) he showed that the *Eudemian Ethics* stands nearer to the Platonic ethics than the *Nicomachean Ethics* does. Thus he not only vindicated the authenticity of the dialogues, the *De Interpretatione,* and the *Eudemian Ethics,* but placed them in their true place in the development of Aristotle's doctrine.

In the same year, 1910, another important new chapter in the discussion of the chronology of Aristotle's works was opened by D'Arcy Thompson in the preface to his translation of the *Historia Animalium.* He there called attention to the frequent references in that work, and (though to a less extent) in other biological works of Aristotle, to the island of Lesbos and to places in or near it. There are references to Arginussa, Lectum, Mitylene, Pordoselene, Pyrrha, and the Pyrrhaean

Euripus, and perhaps to Malia, the south-eastern promontory of Lesbos. There are also references to Macedonia and to places on the coast of Asia Minor all the way from the Bosporus to the Carian coast. There are virtually none to Athens or its neighbourhood.

How does this fit into the pattern of Aristotle's life? His life falls into four roughly equal periods. There is first his boyhood in Chalcidice and in Macedonia from 384 to 367. Secondly, there is the period of his membership of the Platonic Academy from 367 to Plato's death in 348 or 347. Thirdly, there is the period of his life at Assos in the Troad, in the island of Lesbos, and at Pella in Macedonia, from 348 or 347 to 335 or 334. Finally, there is the period of his headship of the Lyceum, from 335 or 334 to his death in 322. Ignoring for our present purpose his boyhood, we may speak of his early period, his middle period, and his late period.

'I think it can be shown', D'Arcy Thompson said, 'that Aristotle's natural history studies were carried on, or mainly carried on, in middle age, between his two periods of residence in Athens: that the calm, landlocked lagoon at Pyrrha was one of his favourite hunting-grounds.' He adds that 'Aristotle's work in natural history was antecedent to his more strictly philosophical work, and it would follow that we might proceed definitely to interpret the latter in the light of the former'. This last opinion is perhaps too broadly expressed; but there can hardly be any doubt of the correctness of Thompson's main thesis, that in all probability the biological works of Aristotle were written during the middle period of his life, probably partly at Assos, partly in Pella, but mainly in Lesbos. It may be added that these works—the genuine parts of the *Historia Animalium,* the *De Partibus Animalium,* the *De Motu Animalium,* the *De Incessu Animalium,* and the *De Generatione Animalium*—occupy more than a fifth of the genuine Aristotelian corpus—a sufficient volume of work to have filled at least half of these thirteen years.

This line of thought has been carried on by the scholar François Nuyens, who published in 1939 his work on the evolution of Aristotle's psychology. He took as his central subject Aristotle's view of the relation between soul and body. He points out that in the dialogues (which are no doubt early works) Aristotle describes the soul as the prisoner of the body, and death as a welcome release from this imprisonment, a release which leaves the soul free to live its own life. He points out that throughout the biological works (except the *De Generatione Animalium,* which is probably the latest of them) a second view is found. The soul is no longer the prisoner of the body, but it is still a distinct entity which inhabits the body, and has its seat in a particular organ, the heart; and soul and body are described as acting on one another. This account Nuyens supports by many quotations which amply prove his point. These works, then, belong to a period later than that of the dialogues. But they are not the final stage in Aristotle's thought about soul and body; for in the *De Anima,* Book II, the soul has ceased to be a separate entity. It has become the form or first entelechy of the body, or as we might say, the organizing principle of the body. The acquisition of the faculties of soul by a body is the first stage in its development, the second stage or second entelechy being the *exercise* of the various faculties—the nutritive, the sensitive, the appetitive, the active, the intellectual, which together form the soul. This last-named theory, being the farthest from the early, Platonic view expressed in the dialogues, must (Nuyens argued) be the latest. He points out that the middle view characterizes not only the biological works but also most of the psychological treatises which form the *Parva Naturalia;* but he assigns two of these, the *De Sensu* and the *De Memoria,* to the third period.

There can, to my mind, be little doubt about the correctness of his main point, that the biological writings (the *De Generatione* excepted) and some of the psychological writings belong to the middle period. But he speaks too widely, I think, in assigning the *De Anima* as a whole, and the treatises on sense and on memory, to the third period. For the entelecheia view of soul is found only in *part* of the *De Anima*—in Book II and the first eight chapters of Book III. It is absent not only from Book I[2]) (which signifies little, since Aristotle says little there about his own views), but also from the latter part of Book III. Also I have, after fairly careful study of the *De Sensu* and the *De Memoria,* found no trace of the entelecheia view in them, and considerable evidence of the two-substance view.[3]) It would seem, then, that the whole of the psychological writings, except the central part of the *De Anima,* belong to the biological period, and that adds another large number of pages to those we have already assigned conjecturally to the middle period of Aristotle's activity as a writer.

This would seem to push the central part of the *De Anima,* and the *De Generatione Animalium,* into the final period, or at least towards the end of the middle period. The question arises, how much more of Aristotle's writing must be pushed forward with these works. We do not expect to find much in the *Metaphysics* dealing with the relation of soul to body; for that is not his subject there. But let us look at such evidence as we can find in the *Metaphysics.* In *M* 1077 a 32-34 the view that soul is the form of the living body—what we may call for short the hylemorphic view—is put forward tentatively: 'How can lines be substances? Neither as a form or shape, as the soul *perhaps* [my italics] is, nor as matter, as the body is'. Compare this with the language of *De An.* 2. 412 a 19-21, 'Hence the soul must be a substance in the sense of the form of a natural body having life potentially

within it.' The same view is stated quite clearly in *Met.* Z 1035 b 14-16, 'Since the soul of animals (for this is the substance of a living being) is their substance according to the formula, i. e. the form and the essence of a body of a certain kind', and again Z 1037 a 5-7, 'It is clear also that the soul is the primary substance and the body is matter and the man or the animal is the compound of both taken universally', and again, more explicitly, in *H* 1043 a 29-36, and once more in [*L*] 1075 b 34-36. It would seem, then, that four of the principal books of the *Metaphysics*—Z, H, [L], M—in their present form at least are later than the whole series of biological and psychological writings, except the *De Generatione* and the central part of the *De Anima,* and must be dated, at earliest, only shortly before Aristotle's return to Athens as head of the Lyceum, and are just as likely to belong to the Lyceum period itself.

I turn now to the most brilliant Aristotelian of our time. In 1912 Professor Jaeger published a remarkable study of the *Metaphysics* in which he pointed out differences of doctrine between different parts of that work, and treated these as examples of development in Aristotle's view. He pointed to the fact that in the first book Aristotle uses the first person plural in the sense of 'we Platonists', while in a part of Book *M* which covers much the same ground he uses the third person when speaking of the Platonists. The first book, he pointed out, thus belongs to a time when Aristotle was still a member of the Platonic school, though a critical member, while Book *M* belongs to a time when he had ceased to be a member of the school. He pointed out that Aristotle in the first book uses the name Coriscus as we might use the name John Smith, and reminded us that Coriscus was a member of a school of Platonists with whom Aristotle probably had associations while at the court of Hermeias at Assos in the years 347 to 344; and he dated the first book early accordingly. This conclusion is almost certainly true, but lest anyone should be tempted to do what Jaeger does *not* do, to assign to this period every work in which Coriscus occurs, I may point out that he occurs similarly, as Aristotle's John Smith, in the *Prior Analytics,* in the *Sophistici Elenchi,* in the *De Partibus,* the *De Generatione Animalium,* the *De Memoria* and the *De Insomniis,* books [D]EZ of the *Metaphysics,* and the *Eudemian Ethics.* It would be impossible to fit all these works into three years. Nor was Aristotle's association with Coriscus confined to Assos; for in the *Physics* 219 b 21 we find the phrase 'Coriscus in the Lyceum', in Aristotle's own school at Athens. I think, therefore, that references to Coriscus are not useful for the purpose of dating works of Aristotle.

In this same book Jaeger made an exhaustive and excellent analysis of the contents of the *Metaphysics,* assigning them to different periods of Aristotle's life; I shall say something later on this subject.

Jaeger carried his research much farther in his general book on Aristotle, published in 1923, in which he unfolded a whole theory of the development of the Master's views. He gave us in this book a striking study of the more important fragments of the dialogues, whose authenticity he effectively vindicated. He showed that in the **Eudemus** Aristotle expressed a purely Platonic theory of the soul, as an entity independent of the body and in some measure hostile to it. Of the **Protrepticus,** also, he gave an excellent account, showing that it too was thoroughly Platonic in character. He showed that in the **De Philosophia** Aristotle had in many respects become critical of Platonism. Broadly speaking, he gave a valuable account of these early writings; it remains the best account we have of this period of Aristotle's thought. The only other parts of the Aristotelian corpus with which he dealt in detail are the **Metaphysics,** the two works on ethics, and the **Politics.** I will begin with his study of the works on ethics. He vindicates the traditional view which includes the **Eudemian Ethics** among the works of Aristotle, against that which considers it to be the work of Eudemus, and, like Case, he treats the **Eudemian Ethics** as earlier than the better-known **Nicomachean Ethics.** Further, he treats the **Protrepticus,** which is purely Platonic in its views, the less Platonic and less theological **Eudemian Ethics,** and the still less Platonic **Nicomachean Ethics,** as showing a continuous development in Aristotle's views about ethics. This general view he supports by detailed discussion of passages from the three works, a discussion which I find convincing.

Before discussing Jaeger's views about the **Politics,** I shall deal with a question which has been much discussed, and to which I believe that a definite answer can be given, the question of the proper order of the books of the **Politics.**

The contents of the eight books of the **Politics** may be briefly stated as follows, taking them in the order in which they appear in all the manuscripts. The first book describes the city-state as the highest form of community, and as formed by the coalescence of villages, which in turn are formed by the coalescence of households; and it proceeds to discuss two main themes—slavery, which is an element in the Greek household, and property, of which slaves are a part. The second book discusses the ideal commonwealths described by Plato, Phaleas, and Hippodamus, and the best states existing in the world known to the Greeks of Aristotle's day. The third deals with the definition of citizenship, the classification of constitutions, and the varieties of one of them—monarchy. The fourth discusses variations in the five other types of constitution recognized by Aristotle, and the three institutions regarded by him as essential to a state—the deliberative assembly, the executive, and the law-courts. The fifth discusses revolutions and their causes, and the means of preventing

them. The sixth discusses the proper organization of two inferior forms of state—democracies and oligarchies. The seventh and eighth form a continuous but unfinished discussion of the ideal state.

This is a very curious and an apparently ill-arranged, though always impressive, study in political philosophy. It raises in the mind of any attentive reader a question that has been much debated—whether the order in which we have the books is that intended by Aristotle.

Two changes in the order have been advocated. One consists of placing the sixth book before the fifth. But few scholars have adopted this change, and it is negatived by four clear references in the sixth book to the fifth (1316 b 34-36, 1317 a 37-38, 1319 b 4-6, 37-38). The other change—one which has been adopted by many scholars—consists in placing the last two books after the third. This finds some support in the fact that at the end of the third book all the manuscripts have a sentence (followed in some by a fragment of a second sentence) which seems to herald an immediate discussion of the ideal state, a discussion which we do not actually find until we come to the last two books. By means of this change, it has been maintained, we get five idealistic books followed by three realistic books. As *against* the change we have the fact that *all* the manuscripts place Books 4-6 *before* Books 7 and 8.

I believe that this question can be settled by considering the final words of the **Nicomachean Ethics,** which read as follows: "Our predecessors have left the subject of legislation to us unexamined; it is perhaps best, therefore, that we should ourselves study it, and in general study the question of the constitution, in order to complete, to the best of our ability, our philosophy of human nature. First, then, if anything has been said well in detail by earlier thinkers, let us try to review it'—that is just what Aristotle does in Book 2, 1-8 of the **Politics**—'then in the light of the constitutions we have collected let us study what sorts of influence preserve and destroy states, and what sorts preserve or destroy the particular kinds of constitution, and to what causes it is due that some are well and some are ill administered'—that is just what Aristotle does in the fifth and sixth books. 'When these matters have been studied we shall perhaps be more likely to see with a comprehensive view which constitution is best, and how each must be ordered, and what laws and customs it must use, if it is to be at its best'—that is just what Aristotle begins to do, but does not finish doing, in Books 7 and 8. Thus when he wrote the **Ethics** he contemplated a **Politics** to which Books 2 (chapters 1-8), 5-6, 7-8, in that order, correspond. In carrying out his scheme he added a preliminary book—Book 1—dealing in the main with the household, as the unit out of which the state emerged. He added, as a natural appendix to the account of the ideal constitutions of

Plato and others, an account of what he considered the best existing constitutions (Book 2, 9-12). And, most important of all, he added his classification and description of constitutions (Books 3 and 4). Thus he carried out the scheme laid down in the *Ethics*, in the order laid down in the *Ethics*, but with additions—Books 1, 2. 9-12, 3, 4—the necessity of which he saw in the course of carrying out his plan.[4] Any one who studies this passage of the *Ethics* is bound to say that if the *Politics* in its traditional order is not Professor Susemihl's idea of a *Politics*, it is at least Aristotle's idea of one.

The question of the proper order of the books of the *Politics* has been much bedevilled by the labelling of some books as realistic and of others as idealistic, and by the assumption that Aristotle passed from an idealistic period to a realistic one. Both in the adumbration of the scheme, in the execution of it, and in the additions made to it, idealism and realism are in fact present hand in hand. Aristotle knew that any sketch of an ideal state will be nothing worth if it is not based on a knowledge of human nature and of the ways in which different types of constitution work out in practice.

On the question of the proper order of the books I note with pleasure that Jaeger does not adopt the changes in the order that have been proposed.

The second general question which faces us in studying the *Politics* is the question when the various parts of the work were written. Jaeger thinks that there was an earlier form of the *Politics*, which was much more Platonic and idealistic in character, and which rested on the *Eudemian Ethics*, as the work in its present form rests on the *Nicomachean Ethics*. Time does not permit me to deal with this view in detail; I must content myself with pointing out the facts which seem to me to tell against it. It must be noted, to begin with, that in the passage of the *Nicomachean Ethics* which I have quoted Aristotle speaks of the *Politics* as a work not yet existing: there is no suggestion there that he has already written a book on the subject. Next we note that in the same passage he refers to 'the constitutions that have been collected' (*Eth. Nic.* 1181 b 17). I agree with Jaeger in thinking that this is a reference to the famous collection of the constitutions of 158 Greek states or cities, of which the only survivor is the *Athenaion Politeia*. This collection could not be made until Aristotle had a school of disciples, during his headship of the Lyceum, from 335-4 to his death in 322; indeed, to allow time for this collection to be made, we must date the formulation of the scheme in the *Ethics*, and its execution in the *Politics*, in the *second half* of that period.

The conclusion that the main scheme of the *Politics*—that which is sketched in the *Ethics*—was carried out during Aristotle's headship of the Lyceum is slightly

confirmed by one or two details. Book 5, 1311 b 1-3 refers to the death of Philip of Macedon, which took place in 336. Newman, the learned editor of the *Politics*, suggests that Book 5, 1312 b 6-7, should perhaps be dated about the year 330. As Sir Ernest Barker has pointed out, Book 7, 1330 b 32-1331 a 18, which refers to the defences to be used against modern siege engines, may well be a reference to the strengthening of the walls of Athens carried out by Lycurgus between 338 and 326 B. C. The reference to guardhouses in the countryside in Book 7, 1331 b 16, may well be a reference to Lycurgus' system of military training established in that last period of Aristotle's life. We cannot be so sure about the late date of the parts of the *Politics* which *do not* fall within the programme stated in the *Ethics*, but there are indications that some of them at least were written at this late date. Newman suggests that the events at Andros mentioned in Book 2, 1270 b 11-13, happened in the year 333, and that the reference in Book 4, 1299 a 14-19 was probably written after 329. Thus there is evidence both that the scheme adumbrated in the *Ethics*, in the order there adopted, was carried out during Aristotle's headship of the Lyceum, i.e. within the last thirteen years of his life, and that the additions to this scheme were also written within that period. This being so, I find it difficult to accept Jaeger's view that parts of the *Politics* were written at an earlier date and during a more Platonic period of Aristotle's life. Instead of supposing that the passages written with more eloquence than those which precede them or those which follow them were written earlier, I incline to think that Aristotle's style alters as he approaches a different part of his subject, a part in which eloquence is more in place.

I turn now to say something about Jaeger's discussion of the *Metaphysics*. It had long been known, and is indeed obvious, upon the most cursory examination, that the *Metaphysics* as it stands is not a consecutive whole. In the main Jaeger followed the admirable lead given long before by Bonitz, treating *AB[G]* and part of *E, ZH[O] I, MN* as the main blocks in a planned but never completed whole, and *A, [D], K,* and *[L]* as genuine Aristotelian works but not as parts of that whole. Jaeger's chief innovation lay in his dating of the various books. The earlier tendency had been to date the whole of the *Metaphysics*, like most of the other major works, in the latest period of Aristotle's life, that of his headship of the Lyceum. Jaeger dated *A, B,* and *N* in the Assos period, and the remaining parts of the *Metaphysics* in the ten years after this, when Aristotle was in Macedonia. As regards *A, B,* and *N*, he is in all probability right. In *A* and *B* Aristotle is still saying 'we' in the sense of 'we Platonists'; but he begins to be a very critical Platonist, in particular a critic of Plato's transcendent ideas. With regard to the remaining books, Jaeger is less convincing. His view is that Aristotle's mind moved steadily away from interest in philosophy to interest in natural science and in the organization of research, such as the accounts of the constitutions of 158 Greek states, lists of victors in the Olympic games, and such-like matters. On this basis Jaeger leaves for the final or Lyceum period comparatively few of Aristotle's extant works. We may ask whether it is really likely that the metaphysical interest which appears so clearly in every book of the *Metaphysics* ever faded away into nothingness, or into such antiquarian pursuits as the compilation of the lists of victors in the games. If we were dealing with an ordinary man, we *might* suppose that an interest in metaphysics could not have coexisted with an interest in scientific, political, and antiquarian research; but we are dealing with no ordinary man. There were, it would seem, two strains in Aristotle which coexisted throughout his life. He was born into an Asclepiad, that is to say a medical, family, and into the Ionian race, and he inherited the Ionian interest in nature and the Asclepiad interest in medicine, and therefore in biology; in the first chapter, and again in the last chapter, of the *Parva Naturalia* he points out how the study of nature furnishes medical practice with its first principles. But he was for nineteen years a member of Plato's school, at first an enthusiastic member, as the *Eudemus* and the *Protrepticus* show, later a critical member, as the *De Philosophia* and the earliest parts of the *Metaphysics* show; but in becoming a critic of Plato he by no means became a deserter from philosophy to science or to antiquarianism. It is far more likely that while he was head of the Lyceum he delegated most of the detailed research to pupils, and himself continued to lecture on philosophical subjects, and in particular that the writing of the *Metaphysics* lasted on into that period.

This can be seen from a consideration of chapter 8 of Book *[L]*. Aristotle there refers to the astronomical theory of Callippus; now Callippus lived from about 370 to about 300, and his theory is believed to have been put forward about 330-325; and Aristotle refers to it in the imperfect tense—'Callippus used to maintain', so that we must suppose Aristotle to be writing, at the very earliest, not before 330, when he was head of the Lyceum and within eight years of his death. Jaeger contrasts this chapter very strongly with the other chapters of *[L]*. He stresses the amplitude of its style with the brevity of the other chapters. He thinks that the doctrine set out in chapter 8, the doctrine of the separate 'intelligences' that move the celestial spheres, is inconsistent with the doctrine of the prime mover as set forth in chapters 7 and 9. Chapter 8 may very well be later than the rest of *[L]*; at least we know that it is very late, and we have nothing to show that the rest of the book is so. But chapter 8 itself shows that it was intended by Aristotle to fit in at this point; for the words with which it starts, 'we must not ignore the question whether we have to suppose one such substance or more than one, and if the latter, how many', clearly refer back to the words of the previous chapter,

'it is clear then from what has been said that there is a substance which is eternal and unmoveable and separate from sensible things', and would be unintelligible apart from these words, and chapter 8 itself repeats the doctrine of the first mover; 'the first principle or primary being', Aristotle says, 'is not moveable either in itself or accidentally, but produces the primary, eternal, and single movement' (1073 a 23-25); the position is stated again quite clearly a few lines later (1073 a 28-34), 'since we see that besides the simple movement of the universe, which we maintain to be actuated by the first, the unmoved substance, there are other eternal movements, those of the planets, each of these movements also must be actuated by a substance both unmoved itself and eternal.'

The position, then, is plain. In this chapter, which belongs to the very last years of Aristotle's life, he retains the doctrine of the prime mover. But the researches of Eudoxus and Callippus had shown the movements of the sun, moon, and planets, to be not simple circular movements as those of the other stars *appeared* to be, but highly complex, involving more than one circular movement. Aristotle accepts these findings, but retains his belief in the prime mover which moves the *non*-planetary stars and gives their *daily* movements to sun, moon, and planets. Thus the chapter is not, as Jaeger appears to hold, a fragment found by Aristotle's editors and fitted by them into Book *[L]* but an addition made by Aristotle himself in view of the theories of Eudoxus and Callippus—an addition which he thought to be in no way contradictory of the view he still maintained, that the diurnal movement of the heavens, the movement common to the sun and moon and planets and to the other stars, requires a single, eternal, unmoved mover. The agent which causes this movement clearly stands on a higher plane than the departmental movers assigned to sun, moon, and to each of the planets; and so Aristotle is able to retain his triumphant conclusion to the book, 'The rule of many is not good; one ruler let there be.'

This problem of the cause of motion of the heavenly bodies is one in which it seems to be possible to trace pretty exactly the development of Aristotle's views. In what follows I shall be in the main following the arguments put forward by Professor Guthrie in his edition of the *De Caelo* (pages xxix-xxxi). Plato, we know from the *Laws,* believed in the possibility of self-movement, and ascribed it to the stars, which he regarded as living beings. In the *De Philosophia,* according to the account of it in Cicero's *De Natura Deorum,* Aristotle said that there are three causes of motion—nature, force, and free will. The motion of the stars could not be natural, since natural movement is not circular, but either upward or downward; nor could it be impressed by force, since there cannot be any force greater than that of the stars, which could move them contrary to their nature. Therefore, it must be voluntary. This ascription of voluntary movement to the stars agrees well with the ascription to them of sense-perception, intelligence, and divinity, which, like the ascription of voluntary movement to them, we learn of from the *De Natura Deorum.* This is the first stage in Aristotle's thought on the subject.

In the *De Caelo,* itself probably a fairly early work, a different account is given. In this the contrast between a voluntary self-movement of the stars and the natural movement of the four elements has disappeared. It is as natural for the ether, the substance of the heavenly bodies, to move in a circle as it is for earth to move down and for fire to move up. The references in the *De Caelo* to a transcendent non-moving mover of the stars are few in number, and inconsistent with the main drift of the argument; they are probably best regarded as later additions, made when Aristotle had altered his view. On the other hand, as Professor Guthrie has pointed out, there are several passages which definitely exclude any source of movement transcending the stars; e.g. 279 a 30-b 3, where the heavenly system is itself described as the highest deity, and it is added that there is nothing more powerful, nothing that could move it.

The third stage comes in *Physics* 7 and 8, where the movement of the heavens is explained by the introduction of an unmoving mover which causes movement not as one body moves another, by imparting its own movement to it, but 'as an object of desire', by inspiring desire to imitate as far as possible its eternal life—Dante's 'l'amor che muove il sole e l'altre stelle'.

The final stage comes in *Metaphysics [L],* where this explanation is retained, but in consequence of the recent discoveries of Eudoxus and Callippus the machinery of the transmission of movement to the heavenly bodies has become very complicated. Thus the belief in an unmoved first mover is not an early belief but Aristotle's last word on the subject; the *De Philosophia,* the *De Caelo,* the *Physics,* and the *Metaphysics* reveal the successive stages in the development of Aristotle's view.

If at some points I have been rather critical of some of Jaeger's views I should not like to fail to express my high admiration of the originality of his work, and of the flood of light which he has shed on many dark places in Aristotle's writings. The general attitude I have been led to adopt towards his account of Aristotle is that, while I accept his belief that Aristotle moved from a Platonic, other-wordly view for which the physical world was of little interest, and super-sensual reality was all that mattered, to one for which the problems of the physical world mattered a great deal, the movement of his mind proceeded neither so far nor so fast as Jaeger describes it as having proceeded. The clearest evidence of this is Aristotle's retention of the

prime unmoved mover as the mainspring of his system in the very last years of his life. But we have also seen that, while Aristotle's conception of the soul went through three distinct phases, in the last of which it had ceased to be for him an entity distinct from the body, the physical activities of living things remained for him a matter of great interest. In ethics we find the same story. The *Nicomachean Ethics,* by general consent a late work, breathes as high an idealism as any of his works. The same is true of the *Politics;* the so-called idealistic parts of it, in their present form, at least, are in all probability, no less than its other parts, to be dated near the end of his life.

In this connexion it is important to consider the significance of a passage to which Jaeger rightly attaches much importance—the fifth chapter of the first book of the *De Partibus Animalium.* I will quote the passage which he quotes: (1, 644 b 22-645 a 36).

> Of things constituted by nature some are ungenerated, imperishable, and eternal, while others are subject to generation and decay. The former are excellent beyond compare and divine, but less accessible to knowledge. The evidence that might throw light on them, and on the problems which we long to solve respecting them, is furnished but scantily by sensation; whereas respecting perishable plants and animals we have abundant information, living as we do in their midst, and ample data may be collected concerning all their various kinds, if only we are willing to take sufficient pains. Both departments, however, have their special charm. The scanty conceptions to which we can attain of celestial things give us, from their excellence, more pleasure than all our knowledge of the world in which we live; just as a half-glimpse of persons that we love is more delightful than a leisurely view of other things, whatever their number and dimensions. On the other hand, in certitude and in completeness our knowledge of terrestrial things has the advantage. Moreover, their greater nearness and affinity to us balances somewhat the loftier interest of the heavenly things that are the objects of the higher philosophy. Having already treated of the celestial world, as far as our conjectures could reach, we proceed to treat of animals, without omitting, to the best of our ability, any member of the kingdom, however ignoble. For if some have no graces to charm the sense, yet even these, by disclosing to intellectual perception the artistic spirit which designed them, give immense pleasure to all who can trace links of causation and are inclined to philosophy. Indeed, it would be strange if mimic representations of them were attractive, because they disclose the mimetic skill of the painter or sculptor, and the original realities themselves were not more interesting, to all, at any rate, who have eyes to discern the reasons that determined their formation. We therefore must not recoil with childish aversion from the examination of the humbler animals. Every realm of nature is marvellous . . . we should venture on the study of every kind of animal without distaste;

for each and all will reveal to us something natural and something beautiful. Absence of haphazard and conduciveness of everything to an end are to be found in nature's works in the highest degree, and the resultant end of her generations and combinations is a form of the beautiful. If anyone thinks the examination of the rest of the animal kingdom an unworthy task, he must hold in like disesteem the study of man. For no one can look at the primordia of the human frame—blood, flesh, bones, vessels, and the like—without much repugnance. Moreover, when any one of the parts or structures, be it which it may, is under discussion, it must not be supposed that it is its material composition to which attention is being directed, or which is the object of the discussion, but the relation of each part to the total form. Similarly, the true object of architecture is not bricks, mortar, or timber, but the house; and so the principal object of natural philosophy is not the material objects, but their composition, and the totality of the form, inde-pendently of which they have no existence.

This is a beautiful passage, and of all passages in Aristotle's works it is perhaps that in which he, generally so severely objective, most clearly strikes a personal note. Professor Jaeger treats it as implying an almost complete abandonment of interest in metaphysics, as placing, to use his words, 'metaphysics completely in the background', and 'reading like a programme for research and instruction in the Peripatetic School'. But anyone who considers the passage without prejudice will, I think, not read it so. It is a noble vindication of biological research, but it recognizes in so many words that both departments, both the study of things eternal and the study of living, perishable organisms have their own charm and attraction. The contrast Aristotle draws is not between biology and philosophy, but between biology and astronomy, what he here calls the study of celestial things; and it is a plea not for the abandonment of astronomy but for the study of biology as well.

The study of the development of Aristotle's philosophy must depend largely on the view to be taken of the comparative dates of his various works; and there is one way of studying this question which has never been strongly followed. That is by studying the references in one book to another. This would be a long task, since the references are very numerous, and it could be a dry task; but it would certainly be one worth attacking, and if I should live long enough I should feel inclined to have a try at it: it is quite possible that a clear order of the various works, and therefore of the views expressed in them, might emerge.

In his recent book *The Hedgehog and the Fox,* Mr. Berlin[5] has described Aristotle as being, in contrast with Plato, a fox. The hedgehog is a creature with only one means of defence, the fox has several, and Mr. Berlin uses them as corresponding to the thinkers who

are interested in a single all-embracing world-view and those whose interest is in the multiplicity and variety of the empirical facts that lie before them. His subject is Tolstoi, and his reading of Tolstoi is that he was a natural fox trying without much success to be a hedgehog, a man intensely interested in the detail of human life, but aiming without success at a philosophy; and no one who has been, as I have been, enthralled by the narrative of *War and Peace,* and bored to extinction by the philosophy in it, can fail to agree with Mr. Berlin's diagnosis. But when we come to Plato and Aristotle I am not so sure of the truth of his dictum, which is, after all, only thrown off in passing. I agree that Plato had little of the fox in him; his effort is always towards generalization, and he shows little of the interest in detailed fact of which Aristotle's biological works, for example, afford so much evidence. But I think that Aristotle had a great deal of the hedgehog in him, as well as of the fox. He is striving all the time, and certainly not without success, to generalize; he is, if anything, too ready to apply his great general notions, like those of matter and form, of potentiality and actuality, to the solution of particular problems. But he did establish a general system which held the field for many centuries, and is still deserving of the closest study. Still less can I agree with Jaeger's view, that, having during the greater part of his life tried to be a hedgehog, Aristotle in the end realized that he was only a fox, and abandoned the pursuit of general ideas for the tabulation of hard facts, for such things as the descriptions of the constitutions of Greek cities and the cataloguing of Olympic victors.

Notes

[1] Delivered as the Dawes Hicks lecture on Philosophy to the British Academy on 6 February, 1957.

[2] Except for one passage, 402 a 26.

[3] The word [*entelekheia*] occurs nowhere in the *Parva Naturalia.*

[4] It is possible that the most important of these additions—Books 3 and 4—formed originally a separate larger course, the [*Politeia*] (two books) of Ptolemy's Aristotle's works.

[5] Now Sir Isaiah Berlin.

W. F. R. Hardie (essay date 1965)

SOURCE: "The Final Good in Aristotle's Ethics," in *Aristotle: A Collection of Critical Essays,* edited by J. M. E. Moravcsik, Anchor Books, 1967, pp. 297-322.

[*In the following essay, originally written in 1965, Hardie highlights the ambiguity of Aristotle's doctrine of the final good, noting that Aristotle represents the final good as a dominant end, but that he also seems to suggest its inclusive nature. Hardie concludes that the doctrine of the final good centers on man's power to reflect on his abilities and desires and to choose a satisfactory course in life.*]

Aristotle maintains that every man has, or should have, a single end . . . , a target at which he aims. The doctrine is stated in *NE* I 2. 'If, then, there is some end of the things we do which we desire for its own sake (everything else being desired for the sake of this), and if we do not choose everything for the sake of something else (for at that rate the process would go on to infinity, so that our desire would be empty and vain), clearly this must be the good and the chief good. Will not the knowledge of it, then, have a great influence on life? Shall we not, like archers who have a mark to aim at, be more likely to hit upon what is right?'[1] (1094a18-24). Aristotle does not here *prove*, nor need we understand him as claiming to prove, that there is only *one* end which is desired for itself. He points out correctly that, if there are objects which are desired but not desired for themselves, there must be *some* object which is desired for itself. The passage further suggests that, if there were *one* such object and one only, this fact would be important and helpful for the conduct of life.

The same doctrine is stated in *EE* A 2. But, whereas in the *NE* the emphasis is on the concern of political science, statesmanship, with the human good conceived as a single end, the *EE* speaks only of the planning by the individual of his own life. 'Everyone who has the power to live according to his own choice . . . should dwell on these points and set up for himself some object for the good life to aim at, whether honour or reputation or wealth or culture, by reference to which he will do all that he does, since not to have one's life organised in view of some end is a sign of great folly. Now above all we must first define to ourselves without hurry or carelessness in which of our possessions the good life consists, and what for men are the conditions of its attainment' (1214b6-14). Here, then, we are told that lack of practical wisdom is shown in a man's failure to plan and organise his life for the attainment of a single end. Aristotle omits to say, but says elsewhere, that lack of practical wisdom is shown also in a man's preference for a bad or inadequate end, say pleasure or money. We learn in *NE* VI 9 that the man of practical wisdom has a true conception of the end which is best for him as well as the capacity to plan effectively for its realisation (1141b31-33).

How far do men in fact plan their lives, as Aristotle suggests they should, for the attainment of a single end? As soon as we ask this question, we see that there is a confusion in Aristotle's conception of the single end. For the question confuses two questions: first, how far do men plan their lives; and, secondly, so far as they do, how far do they, in their plans, give a central and dominating place to a single desired object, money or fame or science? To both these questions the answer that first suggests itself is that some men do and some do not. Take the second question first. It is exceptional for a life to be organised to achieve the satisfaction of one ruling passion. If asked for examples we might think of Disraeli's political ambition or of Henry James' self-dedication to the art of the novel. But exceptional genius is not incompatible with a wide variety of interests. It seems plain that very few men can be said, even roughly, to live their lives under the domination of a single end. Consider now the first question. How far do men plan their lives? Clearly some do so who have no single dominant aim. It is possible to have a plan based on priorities, or on equal consideration, as between a number of objects. It is even possible to plan not to plan, to resolve never to cross bridges in advance. Hobbes remarked that there is no '*finis ultimus,* utmost aim, nor *summum bonum,* greatest good, as is spoken of in the books of the old moral philosophers. . . . Felicity is a continual progress of the desire, from one object to another, the attaining of the former being still but the way to the latter' (*Leviathan,* ch. xi). But even such a progress may be planned, although the plan may not be wise. Every man has, and knows that he has, a number of independent desires, i.e. desires which are not dependent on other desires in the way in which desire for a means is dependent on desire for an end. Every man is capable, from time to time, of telling himself that, if he pursues one particular object too ardently, he may lose or imperil other objects also dear to him. So it may be argued that every man capable, as all men are, of reflection is, even if only occasionally and implicitly, a planner of his own life.

We can now distinguish the two conceptions which are confused or conflated in Aristotle's exposition of the doctrine of the single end. One of them is the conception of what might be called the inclusive end. A man, reflecting on his various desires and interests, notes that some mean more to him than others, that some are more, some less, difficult and costly to achieve, that the attainment of one may, in different degrees, promote or hinder the attainment of others. By such reflection he is moved to plan to achieve at least his most important objectives as fully as possible. The following of such a plan is roughly what is sometimes meant by the pursuit of happiness. The desire for happiness, so understood, is the desire for the orderly and harmonious gratification of desires. Aristotle sometimes, when he speaks of the final end, seems to be fumbling for the idea of an inclusive end, or comprehensive plan, in this sense. Thus in *NE* I 2 he speaks of the end of politics as 'embracing' other ends (1094b6-7). The aim of a science which is 'architectonic' (1094a26-27; cf. *NE* VI 8, 1141b24-26) is a second-order aim. Again in

NE I 7 he says that happiness must be 'most desirable of all things, without being counted as one good thing among others since, if it were so counted, it would be made more desirable by the addition of even the least of goods . . .' (1097b16-20). Such considerations ought to lead Aristotle to define happiness as a secondary end, the full and harmonious achievement of primary ends. This is what he ought to say. It is not what he says. His explicit view, as opposed to his occasional insight, makes the supreme end not inclusive but dominant, the object of one prime desire, philosophy. This is so even when, as in *NE* I 7, he has in mind that, *prima facie,* there is not only one final end: ' . . . if there are more than one, the most final of these will be what we are seeking' (1097a30). Aristotle's mistake and confusion are implicit in his formulation in *EE* A 2 of the question in *which* of our possessions does the good life consist (1214b12-13). For to put the question thus is to rule out the obvious and correct reply; that the life which is best for a man cannot lie in gaining only *one* of his objects at the cost of losing all the rest. This would be too high a price to pay even for philosophy.

The ambiguity which we have found in Aristotle's conception of the final good shows itself also in his attempt to use the notion of a 'function' . . . which is 'peculiar' to man as a clue to the definition of happiness. The notion of function cannot be defended and should not be pressed, since a man is not designed for a purpose. The notion which Aristotle in fact uses is that of the specific nature of man, the characteristics which primarily distinguish him from other living things. This notion can be given a wider interpretation which corresponds to the inclusive end or a narrower interpretation which corresponds to the dominant end. In *NE* I 7, seeking what is peculiar to man (1097b33-34), Aristotle rejects first the life of nutrition and growth and secondly the life of perception which is common to 'the horse, the ox and every animal' (1098a2-3). What remains is 'an active life of the element that has a rational principle' (1098a3-4). This expression need not, as commentators point out, be understood as excluding theoretical activity. 'Action' can be used in a wide sense, as in the *Politics* VII 3 (1325b16-23), to include contemplative thinking. But what the phrase specifies as the proper function of man is clearly wider than theoretical activity and includes activities which manifest practical intelligence and moral virtue. But the narrower conception is suggested by a phrase used later in the same chapter. 'The good for man turns out to be the activity of soul in accordance with virtue, and if there are more than one virtue in accordance with the best and most complete' (1098a16-18). The most complete virtue must be theoretical wisdom, although this is not made clear in *NE* I.

The doctrine that only in theoretical activity is man really happy is stated and defended explicitly in X 7

and 8. Theoretical reason, the divine element in man, more than anything else is man (1177b27-28, 1178a6-7). 'It would be strange, then, if he were to choose not the life of his self but that of something else. And what we said before will apply now; that which is proper to each thing is by nature best and most pleasant for each thing' (1178a3-6). Man is truly human only when he is more than human, godlike. 'None of the other animals is happy, since they in no way share in contemplation' (1178b27-28). This statement makes obvious the mistake involved in the conception of the end as dominant rather than inclusive. It is no doubt true that man is the only theoretical animal. But the capacity of some men for theory is very small. And theory is not the only activity in respect of which man is rational as no other animal is rational. There is no logic which leads from the principle that happiness is to be found in a way of living which is common and peculiar to men to the narrow view of the final good as a dominant end. What is common and peculiar to men is rationality in a general sense, not theoretical insight which is a specialised way of being rational. A man differs from other animals not primarily in being a natural metaphysician, but rather in being able to plan his life consciously for the attainment of an inclusive end.

The confusion between an end which is final because it is inclusive and an end which is final because it is supreme or dominant accounts for much that critics have rightly found unsatisfactory in Aristotle's account of the thought which leads to practical decisions. It is connected with his failure to make explicit the fact that practical thinking is not always or only the finding of means to ends. Thought is needed also for the setting up of an inclusive end. But, as we have seen, Aristotle fails to make explicit the concept of an inclusive end. This inadequacy both confuses his statement in *NE* I 1 and 2 of the relation of politics to subordinate arts and leads to his giving an incomplete account of deliberation.

I have represented Aristotle's doctrine as primarily a doctrine about the individual's pursuit of his own good, his own welfare. . . . But something should be said at this point about the relation between the end of the individual and the 'greater and more complete' end of the state. 'While it is worth while to attain the end merely for one man, it is finer and more godlike to attain it for a nation or for city-states' *NE* I 2, 1094b7-10). This does not mean more than it says: if it is good that Smith should be happy, it is even better that Brown and Robinson should be happy too.

What makes it inevitable that planning for the attainment of the good for man should be political is the simple fact that a man needs and desires social community with others. This is made clear in *NE* I 7 where Aristotle says that the final good must be sufficient by itself. 'Now by self-sufficient we do not mean that which is sufficient for a man by himself, for one who lives a solitary life, but also for parents, children, wife and in general for his friends and fellow-citizens, since man is born for citizenship' (1097b7-11). That individual end-seeking is primary, that the state exists for its citizens, is stated in Ch. 8 of *NE* VI, one of the books common to both treatises. 'The man who knows and concerns himself with his own interests is thought to have practical wisdom, while politicians are thought to be busybodies. . . . Yet perhaps one's own good cannot exist without household management, nor without a form of government' (1142a1-10). The family and the state, and other forms of association as well, are necessary for the full realisation of any man's capacity for living well.

The statesman aims, to speak roughly, at the greatest happiness of the greatest number. He finds his own happiness in bringing about the happiness of others (*NE* X 7, 1177b14), especially, if Aristotle is right, the happiness of those capable of theoretical activity. Speaking in terms of the end as dominant Aristotle, in *NE* VI 13, sets a limit to the authority of political wisdom. 'But again it is not supreme over philosophic wisdom, i.e. over the superior part of us, any more than the art of medicine is over health; for it does not use it but provides for its coming into being; it issues orders, then, for its sake but not to it' (1145a6-9). This suggestion that science and philosophy are insulated in principle from political interference cannot be accepted. The statesman promotes science but also uses it, and may have to restrict the resources to be made available for it. If the secondary and inclusive end is the harmonisation and integration of primary ends, no primary end can be sacrosanct. But, even if Aristotle had held consistently the extravagant view that theoretical activity is desired only for itself and is the only end desired for itself, he would not have been right to conclude that there could be no occasion for the political regulation of theoretical studies. For the unrestricted pursuit of philosophy might hinder measures needed to make an environment in which philosophy could flourish. It might be necessary to order an astronomer to leave his observatory, or a philosopher his school, in order that they should play their parts in the state. Similarly the individual who plans his life so as to give as large a place as possible to a single supremely desired activity must be ready to restrain, not only desires which conflict with his ruling passion, but the ruling passion itself when it is manifested in ways which would frustrate its own object.

In *NE* I 1 and 2 Aristotle expounds the doctrine that statesmanship has authority over the arts and sciences which fall under it, are subordinate to it. An art, A, is under another art, B, if there is a relation of means to end between A and B. If A is a productive art, like bridle-making, its product may be used by a superior art, riding. Riding is not a productive activity, but it falls under generalship in so far as generals use cavalry, and generalship in turn falls under the art of the statesman, the art which is in the highest degree architectonic (1094a27; cf. VI 8, 1141b23-25). Thus the man of practical wisdom, the statesman or legislator, is compared by Aristotle to a foreman, or clerk of the works, in charge of technicians and workmen of various kinds, all engaged in building an observatory to enable the man of theoretical wisdom to contemplate the starry heavens. In the *Magna Moralia* the function of practical wisdom is said to be like that of a steward whose business it is so to arrange things that his master has leisure for his high vocation (A 34, 1198b12-17). Perhaps the closest parallel to the function of the statesman as conceived by Aristotle is the office of the Bursar in a college at Oxford or Cambridge.

This account of statesmanship as aiming at the exercise of theoretical wisdom by those capable of it is an extreme expression of the conception of the end as dominant and not inclusive. The account, as it stands, is a gross over-simplification of the facts. When he speaks of a subordinate art as pursued 'for the sake of' a superordinate or architectonic art (1094a15-16), Aristotle should make explicit the fact that the subordinate activity, in addition to serving other objects, may be pursued for its own sake. Riding, for example, has non-military uses and can be a source of enjoyment. Again two arts, or two kinds of activity, may each be subordinate, in Aristotle's sense, to the other. Riders use bridles, and bridle-makers may ride to their work. The engineer uses techniques invented by the mathematician, but also promotes the wealth and leisure in which pure science can flourish. Aristotle does not fail to see and mention the fact that an object may be desired both independently for itself and dependently for its effects (*NE* I 6, 1097a30-34). He was aware also that theoretical activity is not the only kind of activity which is independently desired. But he evidently thought that an activity which was never desired except for itself would be intrinsically desirable in a higher degree than an activity which, in addition to being desired for itself, was also useful. It is, so to say, beneath the dignity of the most godlike activities that they should be useful. Aristotle is led in this way, and also by other routes, to give a narrow and exclusive account of the final good, to conceive of the supreme end as dominant and not inclusive.

Aristotle describes deliberation, the thinking of the wise man, as a process which starts from the conception of an end and works back, in a direction which reverses the order of causality, to the discovery of a means. Men do not, he asserts, deliberate about ends. 'They assume the end and consider how and by what means it is to be attained; and if it seems to be produced by several means they consider by which it is most easily and best produced, while, if it is achieved by one only, they consider how it will be achieved by this and by what means *this* will be achieved, till they come to the first cause, which in the order of discovery is last' (*NE* III 3, 1112b15-20). Such an investigation is compared to the method of discovering by analysis the solution of a geometrical problem. Again in VI 2 practical wisdom is said to be shown in finding means to a good end. 'For the syllogisms which deal with acts to be done are things which involve a starting-point, viz. "since the end, i.e. what is best, is of such and such a nature" . . .' (1144a31-33).

This is Aristotle's official account of deliberation. But here again, as in his account of the relation between political science and subordinate sciences, a too narrow and rigid doctrine is to some extent corrected elsewhere, although not explicitly, by the recognition of facts which do not fit into the prescribed pattern. Joseph, in *Essays in Ancient and Modern Philosophy,* pointed out that the process of deciding between alternative means, by considering which is easiest and best, involves deliberation which is not comparable to the geometer's search (pp. 180-81). But he remarks that Aristotle does not 'appear to see' this. What the passage suggests is that the agent may have to consider the intrinsic goodness, or badness, of the proposed means as well as its effectiveness in promoting a good end. A less incidental admission that there is more in deliberation than the finding of means is involved in Aristotle's account of 'mixed actions' in *NE* III 1. Aristotle recognises that, if the means are discreditable, the end may not be important enough to justify them. 'To endure the greatest indignities for no noble end or for a trifling end is the mark of an inferior person' (1110a22-23). 'It is difficult sometimes to determine what should be chosen at what cost, and what should be endured in return for what gain' (1110a29-30). Alcmaeon's decision to kill his mother, on his father's instruction, rather than face death himself is given as an example of a patently wrong answer to a question of this kind. This kind of deliberation is clearly not the regressive or analytic discovery of means to a preconceived end. It is rather the determination of an ideal pattern of behaviour, a system of priorities, from which the agent is not prepared to depart. It is what we described earlier as the setting up of an inclusive end. It is a kind of practical thinking which Aristotle cannot have had in his mind when he asserted in *NE* III 3 that 'we deliberate not about ends but about means' (1112b11-12).

I have argued that Aristotle's doctrine of the final human good is vitiated by his representation of it as dominant rather than inclusive, and that this mistake underlies his too narrow account of practical thinking as the search for means. But to say that the final good is inclusive is not to deny that within it there are certain dominant ends corresponding to the major interests of developed human nature. One of these major interests is the interest in theoretical sciences. Of these,

according to Aristotle, there are three; theology or first philosophy, mathematics and physics (*Metaphysics* E 1, 1026a18-19, cf. *NE* VI 8, 1142a16-18). His account of contemplation in the Ethics, based on the doctrine of reason as the divine or godlike element in man (*NE* X 7, 1177a13-17; 8, 1178a20-23), exalts the first and makes only casual mention of the other two. Elsewhere, in the *De Partibus Animalium* I 5, he admits that physics has attractions which compensate for the relatively low status of the objects studied. 'The scanty conceptions to which we can attain of celestial things give us, from their excellence, more pleasure than all our knowledge of the world in which we live; just as a half-glimpse of persons that we love is more delightful than a leisurely view of other things, whatever their number and dimensions. On the other hand, in certitude and in completeness our knowledge of terrestrial things has the advantage. Moreover their greater nearness and affinity to us balances somewhat the loftier interest of the heavenly things that are the object of the higher philosophy' (644b31-645a4).

I cannot here discuss the theological doctrines which led Aristotle to place 'the higher philosophy' on the summit of human felicity. But there is an aspect of his account of the theoretic life which has an immediate connection with my main topic. He remarks in *NE* VII 14 that 'there is not only an activity of movement but an activity of immobility, and pleasure is found more in rest than in movement' (1154b26-28). This doctrine that there is no 'movement' in theoretical contemplation, and the implication that its immobility is a mark of its excellence, is determined primarily by Aristotle's conception of the divine nature. The latest commentators on the *NE,* Gauthier and Jolif, say, with justification, that he here excludes discovery from the contemplative life. 'On pourrait même dire que l'idéal, pour le contemplatif aristotélicien—et cet idéal le Dieu d'Aristote le rélise—ce serait de ne jamais étudier et de ne jamais découvrir . . .' (855-56). In *NE* X 7 we are told that 'philosophy is thought to offer pleasures marvellous for their purity and their enduringness' and that it is 'reasonable to suppose that those who know will pass their time more pleasantly than those who enquire' (1177a25-27). It is not reasonable at all. It is a startling paradox. I shall now suggest that Aristotle's apparent readiness to accept this paradox, like his confusion between the dominant and the inclusive end, is to be explained, at least in part, by his failure to give any explicit or adequate analysis of the concept of end and means.

Aristotle states in *NE* I that an end may be either an activity or the product of an activity. 'But a certain difference is to be found among ends; some are activities, others are products apart from the activities that produce them. Where there are ends apart from the actions, it is the nature of the products to be better than the activities' (1094a3-6). The suggestion here is that, when an activity leads to a desired result, as medicine produces health or shipbuilding a ship or enquiry knowledge, the end-seeking activity is not itself desired. As he says (untruly) in the **Metaphysics,** 'of the actions which have a limit none is an end' ([O]. 6, 1048b18). But an activity which aims at producing a result may be an object either of aversion or of indifference or of a positive desire which may be less or greater than the desire for its product. It is necessary to distinguish between 'end' in the sense of a result intended and planned and 'end' in the sense of a result, or expected result, which, in addition to being intended and planned, is also desired for itself while the process of reaching it is not. It is true that travel may be unattractive, but it may also be more attractive that arrival. A golfer plays to win. But, if he loses, he does not feel that his day has been wasted, that he has laboured in vain, as he would if his only object in playing were to win a prize or to mortify his opponent or just to win. Doing crossword puzzles may be a waste of time, but what makes it a waste of time is not the fact that we rarely get one out. It would be a greater waste of time if we never failed to finish them. In short, the fact that an activity is progressive towards a planned result leaves quite open the question whether it is the process or the result which is desired, and, if both, which primarily. If Aristotle had seen and said this, he might have found it more difficult than he does to suggest that the pleasures of discovery are not an essential element in science as a major human interest. Philosophy would be less attractive than it is if only results mattered. God's perfection requires that his thinking should be unprogressive. But men, who fall short of perfect simplicity, need, to make them happy, the pleasures of solving problems and of learning something new and of being surprised. For them the best way of life leads, in the words of Meredith,

'through widening chambers of surprise to where throbs rapture near an end that aye recedes'.

We have seen that Aristotle's doctrine of the final human good needs clarification in terms of a distinction between an end which is inclusive, a plan of life, and an end which is dominant as the satisfaction of theoretical curiosity may be dominant in the life of a philosopher. No man has only one interest. Hence an end which is to function as a target, as a criterion for deciding what to do and how to live, must be inclusive. But some men have ruling passions. Hence some inclusive ends will include a dominant end. I shall now try to look more closely at these Aristotelian notions, and to suggest some estimate of their relevance and value in moral philosophy.

It will be best to face at once and consider a natural and common criticism of Aristotle; the criticism that his virtuous man is not moral at all but a calculating egoist whose guiding principle is not duty but pru-

dence, Bishop Butler's 'cool self-love'. Aristotle is in good company as claiming that rationality is what makes a man ideally good. But his considered view, apart from incidental insights, admits, it is said, only the rationality of prudent self-interest and not the rationality of moral principle. Thus Professor D. J. Allan, in *The Philosophy of Aristotle,* tells us that Aristotle "takes little or no account of the motive of moral obligation" and that "self-interest, more or less enlightened, is assumed to be the motive of all conduct and choice" (p. 189). Similarly the late Professor Field, a fair and sympathetic critic of Aristotle, remarked that, whereas morality is 'essentially unselfish', Aristotle's idea of the final end or good makes morality 'ultimately selfish' (*Moral Theory,* pp. 109, 111).

When a man is described as selfish what is meant primarily is that he is moved to act, more often and more strongly than most men, by desires which are selfish. The word 'selfish' is also applied to a disposition so to plan one's life as to give a larger place than is usual or right to the gratification of selfish desires. But what is it for a desire to be selfish? Professor Broad, in his essay 'Egoism as a theory of human motives' (in *Ethics and the History of Philosophy*), makes an important distinction between two main kinds of 'self-regarding' desires. There are first desires which are 'self-confined', which a man could have even if he were alone in the world, e.g. desires for certain experiences, the desire to preserve his own life, the desire to feel respect for himself. Secondly there are self-regarding desires which nevertheless presuppose that a man is not alone in the world, e.g. desires to own property, to assert or display oneself, to inspire affection. Broad further points out that desires which are 'other-regarding' may also be 'self-referential', e.g. desires for the welfare of *one's own* family, friends, school, college, club, nation.

A man might perhaps be called selfish if his other-regarding motives were conspicuously and exclusively self-referential, if he showed no interest in the welfare of anyone with whom he was not personally connected. But usually 'selfish' refers to the prominence of self-regarding motives, and different kinds of selfishness correspond to different self-regarding desires. The word, being pejorative, is more readily applied to the less reputable of the self-regarding desires. Thus a man strongly addicted to the pursuit of his own pleasures might be called selfish even if his other-regarding motives were not conspicuously weak. A man whose ruling passion was science or music would not naturally be described as selfish unless to convey that there was in him a reprehensible absence or failure of other-regarding motives, as shown, say, by his neglect of his family or of his pupils.

The classification of desires which I have quoted from Broad assumes that their nature is correctly represented by what we ordinarily think and say about them. *Prima facie* some of our desires are self-regarding; and, of the other-regarding desires, some are and some are not self-referential. But there have been philosophers who have questioned or denied the reality of these apparent differences. One doctrine, psychological egoism, asserts in its most extreme form that the only possible objects of a man's first-order independent desires are experiences, occurrent states of his own consciousness. Thus my desire to be liked is really a desire to know that I am liked; and my desire that my children should be happy when I am dead is really a desire for my present expectation that they will be happy. The obvious criticism of this doctrine is that it is preposterous and self-defeating: I must first desire popularity and the happiness of my children if I am to find gratifying my thought that I am popular and that my children will be happy. To most of us it seems that introspective self-scrutiny supports the validity of this dialectic. We can, therefore, reject psychological egoism. *A fortiori* we can reject psychological hedonism which asserts that the *only* experiences which can be independently desired are pleasures, feelings of enjoyment. This further doctrine was stated as follows by the late Professor Prichard. 'For the enjoyment of something which we enjoy, e.g. the enjoyment of seeing a beautiful landscape, is related to the thing we enjoy, not as a quality but as an effect, being something excited by the thing we enjoy, so that, if it be said that we desire some enjoyment for its own sake, the correct statement must be that we desire the experience, e.g. the seeing of some beautiful landscape, for the sake of the feeling of enjoyment which we think it will cause, this feeling being really what we are desiring for its own sake' (*Moral Obligation,* p. 116). Surely most of us would be inclined to say that we *can* desire for its own sake 'the seeing of some beautiful landscape' and that we do not detect a distinct 'feeling of enjoyment'.

Was Aristotle a psychological egoist or a psychological hedonist? A crisp answer would have been possible only if Aristotle had explicitly formulated these doctrines as I have defined them. So far as I can see, he did not do so even in his long, but not always lucid, treatment of friendship and self-love in *NE* IX. This being so, he cannot be classed as a psychological egoist in respect of his account of first-order desires. When Aristotle confronts the fact of altruism, he does not refuse to accept benevolent desires at their face value (*NE* VIII 2, 1155b31; 3, 1156b9-10; 7, 1159a8-12). But he shows acuteness in detecting self-referential elements in benevolence. Thus he compares the feelings of benefactors to beneficiaries with those of parents for their children and of artists for their creations. 'For that which they have treated well is their handiwork, and therefore they love this more than the handiwork does its maker' (*NE* IX 7, 1167b31-1168a5).

The nearest approach which Aristotle makes to the formulation of psychological hedonism is, perhaps, in the following passage in *NE* II 3. 'There being three objects of choice and three of avoidance, the noble, the advantageous, the pleasant, and their contraries, the base, the injurious, the painful, about all of these the good man tends to go right and the bad man to go wrong, and especially about pleasure; for this is common to the animals, and also it accompanies all objects of choice; for even the noble and the advantageous appear pleasant' (1104b30-1105a1). But there are passages in his discussion of pleasure in *NE* X which show that, even if he had accepted psychological egoism, he would not have accepted psychological hedonism. 'And there are many things we should be keen about even if they brought no pleasure, e.g. seeing, remembering, knowing, possessing the virtues. If pleasures necessarily do accompany these, that makes no odds; we should choose them even if no pleasure resulted' (1174a4-8). This reads like a direct repudiation of the doctrine in my quotation from Prichard. In *NE* X 4 he asks, without answering, the question whether we choose activity for the sake of the attendant pleasure or vice versa (1175a18-21). The answer which his doctrine requires is surely that neither alternative can be accepted, since both the activity and the attendant pleasure are desired for their own sake. But it is open to question whether, when we speak of a state or activity, such as 'the seeing of some beautiful landscape', as pleasant, we are referring to a feeling distinct from the state or activity itself.

The charge against Aristotle that his morality is a morality of self-interest is directed primarily against his doctrine of the final good, the doctrine which I have interpreted as a conflation of the distinct notions of the 'inclusive end' and the 'dominant end'. But the critic may also wish to suggest that Aristotle overstates the efficacy of self-regarding desires in the determination of human conduct. To this the first answer might well be that it is not easy to overstate their efficacy. The term 'self-regarding' applies, as we have seen, to a wide variety of motives; and there is a 'self-referential' factor in the most potent of the other-regarding motives. Altruism which is pure, not in any way self-regarding or self-referential, is a rarity. The facts support the assertion that man is a selfish animal. But the criticism can be met directly. Aristotle does not ignore other-regarding motives. Thus, while he points out that the philosopher, unlike those who exercise practical virtue, does not need other men 'towards whom and with whom he shall act', he admits that the pleasures of philosophy are enhanced by interest in the work of colleagues. 'He perhaps does better if he has fellow-workers, but still he is the most self-sufficient' (*NE* X 7, 1177a27-b1). When, in the *EE,* Aristotle speaks of philosophy as the service of God, he seems to imply that the love of wisdom is not directed merely to the lover's own conscious states (1249b20). Again, in *NE*

IX 8, he can attribute to the 'lover of self' conduct which is, in the highest degree, altruistic and self-sacrificing. 'For reason always chooses what is best for itself, and the good man obeys his reason. It is true of the good man too that he does many acts for the sake of his friends and his country, and, if necessary, dies for them; for he will throw away both wealth and honours and in general the goods that are objects of competition, gaining for himself nobility . . . since he would prefer a short period of intense pleasure to a long one of mild enjoyment, a twelvemonth of noble life to many years of humdrum existence, and one great and noble action to many trivial ones. Now those who die for others doubtless attain this result; it is, therefore, a great prize that they choose for themselves' (1169a17-26).

But it is not enough, if we are to do justice to the criticism that Aristotle makes morality selfish, to quote this passage, or the passage in *NE* I 10 where Aristotle speaks of the shining beauty of the virtue shown in bearing disasters which impair happiness (1100b30-33). Such passages, it may be said, show Aristotle's moral sensibility and moral insight. But the question can still be asked whether their commendation of the ultimate self-sacrifice, and of endurance in suffering, is consistent with Aristotle's doctrine of the final human good. Perhaps he is speaking more consistently with his own considered views when, again in *NE* IX 8, he makes the suggestion (or is it a joke?) that a man may show the finest self-sacrifice, the truest love, by surrendering to his friend the opportunity of virtuous action (1169a33-34). Perhaps Aristotle's commendation of the surrender, in a noble cause, of life itself needs to be qualified, from his own point of view, as it was qualified by Oscar Wilde:

> And yet, and yet
> Those Christs that die upon the barricades,
> God knows it I am with them, in some ways.

To this question I now turn. My answer must and can be brief.

We have found two main elements in Aristotle's doctrine of the final good for man. There is, first, the suggestion that, as he says in *EE* A 2, it is a sign of 'great folly' not to 'have one's life organised in view of some end'. Perhaps it would be better to say that it is impossible not to live according to some plan, and that it is folly not to try to make the plan a good one. The inevitability of a plan arises from the fact that a man both has, and knows that he has, a number of desires and interests which can be adopted as motives either casually and indiscriminately or in accordance with priorities determined by the aim of living the kind of life which he thinks proper for a man like himself. But in an agent naturally reflective the omission to make such a plan is not completely undesigned: the

minimal plan is a plan not to plan. To this side of Aristotle's doctrine I have applied the term 'inclusive end', inclusive because there is no desire or interest which should not be regarded as a candidate, however unpromising, for a place in the pattern of life. Wisdom finds a place even for folly. The second element which we have found in Aristotle's doctrine is his own answer to the question what plan will be followed by a man who is most fully a man, as high as a man can get on the scale from beast to god. Aristotle's answer is that such a man will make theoretical knowledge, his most godlike attribute, his main object. At a lower level, as a man among men, he will find a place for the happiness which comes from being a citizen, from marriage and from the society of those who share his interests. I have called this the doctrine of the dominant end. The question whether Aristotle's doctrine of the final good can be reconciled with the morality of altruism and self-sacrifice must be asked with reference both to the inclusive end and to the dominant end.

To say that a man acts, or fails to act, with a view to an inclusive end is to say nothing at all about the comparative degrees of importance which he will ascribe to his various aims. His devotion to his own good, in the sense of his inclusive end, need not require him to prefer self-regarding desires to other-regarding desires, or one kind of self-regarding desire to another. All desires have to be considered impartially as candidates for places in the inclusive plan. To aim at a long life in which pleasures, so far as possible, are enjoyed and pains avoided it is a possible plan, but not the only possible plan. That a man seeks an inclusive end leaves open the question whether he is an egoist or an altruist, selfish or unselfish in the popular sense.[2]

While a man seeking his inclusive end need not be selfish, he can be described as self-centred in at least three different ways. First and trivially his desire to follow his inclusive plan is his own desire; it is self-owned. Secondly, a man can think of a plan as being for his own good only if he thinks about himself, thinks of himself as the one owner of many desires. His second-order desire for his own good is self-reflective. Thirdly, this second-order desire, being a desire about desires, an interest in interests, can be gratified only through the gratification of his first-order desires. Even the martyr plans to do what he wants to do. We can express this by saying that the pursuit of the final good is self-indulging as well as self-reflective. But 'self-indulgence' as applied to a way of life in which pleasures may be despised and safety put last carries no pejorative sense. That action in pursuit of an inclusive end is self-centred in these ways does not mean that the agent is self-regarding or self-seeking in any sense inconsistent with the most heroic or saintly self-sacrifice.

To the question whether the pursuit of the human good, understood in terms of Aristotle's conception of the dominant end, can be reconciled with the morality of altruism, and in particular the extreme altruism of the man who gives his life for his friends or his country, a different answer must be given. Here reconciliation is not possible. In order to see this it is necessary only to reflect on Aristotle's definition in *NE* I 7 of the dominant end, which he calls happiness, and to compare this definition with what is said about the self-love of the man who nobly gives up his own life. 'Human good turns out to be activity of soul in accordance with virtue, and if there are more than one virtue, in accordance with the best and most complete. But we must add "in a complete life." For one swallow does not make a summer nor does one day; and so too one day or a short time does not make a man blessed and happy' (1098a16-20). How then can the man who, to gain nobility . . . for himself, gives his life for his friends or his country be said to achieve happiness? Aristotle's answer, as we have seen, is that such a man prefers 'a short period of intense pleasure to a long one of mild enjoyment, a twelvemonth of noble life to many years of humdrum existence, and one great and noble action to many trivial ones' (1169a22-25). But the scales are being loaded. For why should it be supposed that the man who declines to live the final, if crowded, hour of glorious life will survive to gain only 'mild' enjoyments and a 'humdrum' or 'trivial' existence? If such existence is, or seems, humdrum *because* the 'intense pleasure' of self-sacrifice has been missed, then Aristotle's thought here is circular and self-stultifying. The intensity of the brief encounter, it is suggested, is such that by contrast the remainder of life would be humdrum. But, unless the alternative would be humdrum in its own right, the encounter would not be intense enough to compensate for the curtailment of life and happiness. A 'complete life' either is, or is not, a necessary condition of happiness. Aristotle as a theorist cannot justify the admiration which, as a man, he no doubt feels for the 'one great and noble action'. Confronted with the facts he would have to admit that the man who, whether by good fortune or design, survives a revolution or a war may live to experience intense enjoyments and to perform activities in accordance with the best and most complete virtue. He may become a professor of philosophy or at least a prime minister. We must conclude, therefore, that Professor Field was right: the doctrine of the good for man, as developed by Aristotle in his account of the dominant end, does make morality 'ultimately selfish' (*Moral Theory,* pp. 109, 111).

Aristotle offers us in his *Ethics* a handbook on how to be happy though human. To some it may seem that a treatise on conduct with an aim so practical and so prudential can do little to clarify the concepts with which moral philosophy is mainly concerned, the concepts of duty and of moral worth. 'He takes little or no account', Professor Allan tells us, 'of the motive of moral obligation' (*The Philosophy of Aristotle,* p. 189). Perhaps not. The topic is too large for a concluding paragraph. Certainly most men feel moral obligations which cannot be subsumed under the obligation, if there is one, to pursue their own happiness by planning for the orderly satisfaction of their self-regarding desires. But 'obligation' and 'duty' are words with many meanings, meanings variously related to the concept of moral worth. Perhaps Aristotle is not wrong, as he is not alone, in connecting the concept of moral worth with the fact that man is not just the plaything of circumstance and his own irrational nature but also the responsible planner of his own life. This aspect of Aristotle's teaching is what I have called his doctrine of the 'inclusive end', and I have argued that there is no necessity for the doctrine to be specified and developed as a recommendation of calculated egoism. Aristotle himself, as we have seen, does not adhere consistently to his own exaltation of self-regarding aims. He is, indeed, always ready to notice facts which are awkward for his own theories. Thus in *NE* I 10 he recognises that the actual achievement of happiness, virtuous activity, is largely outside a man's control. 'A multitude of great events if they turn out well will make life happier . . . while if they turn out ill they crush and maim happiness; for they both bring pain with them and hinder many activities' (1100b25-30). He adds that, even when disaster strikes, 'nobility shines through, when a man bears with resignation many great misfortunes, not through insensibility to pain but through nobility and greatness of soul' (1100b30-33). 'The man who is truly good and wise', he goes on to say, 'bears all the chances of life becomingly and always makes the best of circumstances as a good shoemaker makes the best shoes out of the hides that are given to him' (1100b35-1101a5). The suggestion of this passage is that a man's worth lies not in his actual achievement, which may be frustrated by factors outside his own control, but in his striving towards achievement. In an earlier chapter (5) of *NE* I he speaks of the good as something which 'we divine to be proper to a man and not easily taken from him' (1095b25-26). Aristotle's doctrine of the final good is a doctrine about what is 'proper' to a man, the power to reflect on his own abilities and desires and to conceive and choose for himself a satisfactory way of life. What 'cannot be taken from him' is his power to keep on trying to live up to such a conception. Self-respect, thus interpreted, is *a* principle of duty. If moral philosophy must seek *one* comprehensive principle of duty, what other principle has a stronger claim to be regarded as *the* principle of duty?

Notes

¹ Here, and in quoting other passages, I have reproduced the Oxford translation. I refer to the *Nicomachean Ethics as NE* and to the *Eudemian Ethics as EE.*

[2] I owe this point, and less directly much else in my discussion of the criticism of Aristotle's ethical system as egoistic, to Professor C. A. Campbell's British Academy Lecture (1948), "Moral Intuition and the Principle of Self-Realisation" (especially pp. 17-25). Professor Campbell's lecture discusses the ethical theory of T. H. Green and F. H. Bradley, and I do not know whether he would think of his arguments as being relevant to the interpretation of Aristotle. But I have found his defence of 'self-realisation' as a moral principle helpful in my attempt to separate the strands of thought in Aristotle's doctrine of the final good.

Daniel T. Devereux (essay date 1981)

SOURCE: "Aristotle on the Essence of Happiness," in *Studies in Aristotle,* edited by Dominic O'Meara, The Catholic University of America Press, 1981, pp. 247-60.

[*In the following essay, Devereux responds to critics who have maintained that Aristotle's doctrine of the good is either dominant or inclusive, and who have noted that inconsistencies resulting from characterizing the good in this manner are apparent in the doctrine. Devereux asserts that neither view coincides with Aristotle's doctrine of the good and he suggests that Aristotle's ideas need not be understood as inconsistent.*]

I

Recent discussions of Aristotle's doctrine of the good often take up the question whether his doctrine is inclusive or dominant. The distinction between an "inclusive" and a "dominant" conception of the final good can be briefly explained as follows. Let us suppose, first, that A, B, and C are the only goods which are desirable for their own sake and, second, that A is more desirable than B or C. According to the "dominant" conception, the final good will be identical with A, and one who seeks to be happy should devote all of his energies to the pursuit of A. On the "inclusive" conception, the good will consist of A, B, and C together, and one can achieve a happy life only by pursuing all three of these goods, paying special attention to A on account of its superiority.

W. F. R. Hardie, who first introduced this distinction some years ago, argued that Aristotle did not have a clear grasp of it, and, as a result, the discussion of the final good in Book I of the *Nicomachean Ethics* (*NE* I) suffers from a basic confusion.[1] In some passages Aristotle speaks of the good as if it were an inclusive end, but in other places he clearly treats it as a dominant end. Hardie's view has been challenged by J. L. Ackrill, who tries to show that Aristotle's conception

of the good in *NE* I is consistently inclusive.[2] Ackrill believes (as does Hardie) that in *NE* X Aristotle commits himself to a dominant conception, but he finds no evidence of this conception in the rest of the treatise. Hardie and Ackrill are thus in agreement that Aristotle's account of the good is inconsistent. They disagree about the location of the inconsistency, Ackrill holding that it is between *NE* X and the rest of the treatise while Hardie thinks it can be found in *NE* I itself. As if to round out the picture, Anthony Kenny has recently argued that in both *NE* I and X Aristotle consistently adheres to a dominant conception of the end.[3] Surprisingly enough, the passages he bases his argument on are the very ones appealed to by Hardie and Ackrill.

I shall not take sides in this debate, for I believe that the question at issue is ill conceived. Asking whether Aristotle's conception of the good is inclusive or dominant presents us with two models, neither of which really fits his view. If there are inconsistencies in the discussion of happiness in the *NE,* they do not have to do with the contrast between dominant and inclusive conceptions of the end. Before attempting to explain and substantiate these sweeping claims, let me begin with an examination of the passages in *NE* I and X which have given rise to the controversy.

II

In an important and difficult passage in *NE* I, 7 Aristotle asserts that the final good is "self-sufficient." The tail end of this passage is cited by both Hardie and Ackrill as evidence of the inclusive conception of the end. Kenny, however, claims that the very same passage commits Aristotle to the dominant conception. As might be expected, their preferred translations differ markedly. I shall first give the translation favored by Hardie and Ackrill.[4]

> And further we think it [happiness] most desirable of all things, without being counted together with others . . . if it were countable along with other goods, it would clearly be made more desirable by the addition of even the least of goods (1097b16-18).

As Hardie and Ackrill understand the passage, Aristotle's point can be explicated in the following way. Goods like health, honor, and friendship are apparently such that they can be "counted together" with other goods; they are like discrete quantities, and we can say, e.g., that health plus friendship is more desirable than health by itself. The passage implies that happiness differs from other goods in this respect—it cannot be made more desirable by the addition of other goods. If happiness were identical with a single good like philosophical contemplation, the addition of other goods *would* seem to make it more desirable: philosophical contemplation plus the possession of good friends would surely be more desirable than philosophical contemplation by itself. Only if happiness includes or presupposes the other goods could it *not* be made more desirable by the addition of other goods. Taken in this way, the passage clearly indicates that Aristotle was here thinking of happiness as an inclusive and not a dominant end.

The translation favored by Kenny differs mainly in the second part (the part following the semicolon).

> . . . clearly if it is counted together with others, it is more desirable with even the least additional good.[5]

On this reading, happiness *can* be "counted together" with other goods, and if other goods are added to happiness, the sum is more desirable than happiness by itself. Happiness is thus the most desirable of all goods, *taken singly*. If the passage is understood in this way, it implies that happiness is just one good among others and, therefore, presupposes a dominant rather than inclusive conception of the end.

Kenny's translation seems possible, but there are strong reasons in favor of the standard translation preferred by Hardie and Ackrill. In *NE* X, 2 we find a parallel passage in which Aristotle says quite clearly that the final good (or happiness) cannot be made more desirable by the addition of any other good. I shall quote the passage in full.

> And so it is by an argument of this kind that Plato proves the good *not* to be pleasure; he argues that the pleasant life is more desirable with wisdom than without, and that if the mixture is better, pleasure is not the good; for the good cannot become more desirable by the addition of anything to it. Now it is clear that nothing else, any more than pleasure, can be the good if it is made more desirable by the addition of any of the things that are good in themselves. What, then, is there that satisfies this criterion, which at the same time we can participate in? It is something of this sort that we are looking for (1172b28-35, Ross's translation).[6]

This passage is clearly designed to make the same point as the self-sufficiency passage in I, 7. But if we accept Kenny's translation of the latter, we have a glaring contradiction between the two passages. This is, I think, a clear and decisive reason in favor of the standard translation. And given that translation, we can safely affirm that Aristotle, at least at one point in *NE* I, was thinking of happiness as an inclusive end.

III

However, Aristotle's official definition of happiness, as Hardie points out[7], evidently exemplifies the domi-

nant rather than the inclusive conception. The definition, which is formulated near the end of I, 7, reads as follows.

> Happiness . . . is activity of soul in accordance with virtue, and if there are more virtues than one, in accordance with the best and most perfect . . . (1098a16-18).

Of course, it does turn out that there are more virtues than one, so the last clause effectively tells us that happiness should be identified with one particular kind of activity—that in accordance with the best and most perfect virtue. In *NE* X, 7, resuming his discussion of happiness, Aristotle says: "If happiness is activity in accordance with virtue, it is reasonable that it should be in accordance with the highest . . . virtue; and this will be that of the best thing in us. . . . That this activity is contemplative we have already said" (1177a12-18). Here the activity of the best or most perfect virtue is identified as philosophical contemplation; in the following lines Aristotle tells us that the best virtue is philosophic wisdom (1177a22-25).

In view of the close relationship between this passage in X, 7 and the definition in I, 7, most commentators have supposed that Aristotle must have had philosophical contemplation in mind when he formulated his definition of happiness. In other words, Aristotle deliberately sets up an equation between happiness and the activity of contemplation in I, 7, but the reader can only see this in retrospect. If this is true, Aristotle's definition seems to exemplify a dominant rather than inclusive conception of the good; instead of a combination of goods, happiness turns out to be the single good of contemplation. So, as Hardie points out, within a couple of pages of I, 7, we find Aristotle first thinking of happiness as an inclusive end in the self-sufficiency passage but then committing himself to the dominant conception near the end of the chapter.

Ackrill believes that this common way of understanding the definition of happiness is based on a mistake. We need not assume that when Aristotle speaks of the "most perfect" or "most final" virtue he means some one, single virtue. Ackrill draws our attention to a passage earlier in I, 7 in which the same superlative, "most final" . . . , is used in talking about ends (1097a28-34);[8] here a "most final" end is one which is "final without qualification," and Aristotle uses the phrase to refer to the comprehensive end which includes all partial ends. With this passage as a guide, we may understand the phrase "most final virtue" in the definition of happiness as referring to *comprehensive* virtue—the combination of all the virtues.

Ackrill further points out that in the parallel passage in the ***Eudemian Ethics*** Aristotle defines happiness as "activity in accordance with complete virtue" . . . , and it is clear from the context that "complete virtue" here means the combination of all the virtues (1219a34-39)[9]. Towards the end of *NE* I, there is a passage which apparently refers back to the definition in I, 7 in the following way: "Since happiness is an activity of soul in accordance with complete virtue . . . , we must investigate virtue" (1102a5-6). Aristotle here seems to treat the definition in *NE* I, 7 as having the same meaning as the definition in the **Eudemian Ethics.** So this passage, taken together with the definition in the **Eudemian Ethics,** provides confirmation of Ackrill's suggestion that by "most final virtue" Aristotle means comprehensive or total virtue.

On Ackrill's interpretation, Aristotle's definition of happiness in *NE* I, 7 represents an inclusive conception of the good. If Ackrill is right, the conception of happiness throughout *NE* I is consistently inclusive. However, there are several difficulties with Ackrill's interpretation of the definition of happiness. First of all, in the passage in which Aristotle talks about the "most final" end, although he does seem to be referring to an end which is comprehensive and includes other ends, this is not what he *means* by saying it is most final. According to his explicit account, an end which is "most final" is one which is always chosen simply for its own sake and never for the sake of anything else (1098a28-34). This account does not imply that a "most final" end must include other ends. So the appeal to what Aristotle means by "most final" in this passage does not give us a basis for understanding the "most final virtue" as comprehensive virtue, i.e., the combination of all the virtues.[10]

More importantly, we should notice that Aristotle does not simply say "in accordance with the most final virtue" but "in accordance with *the best* and most final virtue." He is implying, in other words, that if there are several virtues and not just one, we should determine which of these is best, and happiness will be identical with the activity of this one virtue. The use of "best" implies that we should rank the virtues and single out the one which is first or highest.[11] Still another difficulty for Ackrill's interpretation is posed by the following passage in *NE* I, 8.

> Happiness then is the best, noblest, and most pleasant thing, and these attributes are not severed as in the inscription at Delos, . . . For all these properties belong to the best activities; and these, or one—the best—of these, we identify with happiness (1099a24-31).[12]

The upshot of this passage is clear and unambiguous: happiness should be identified not with a combination of activities but with one single activity—the best. In the light of this passage, it seems obvious that the definition of happiness in I, 7 exemplifies a dominant conception of the good.[13]

Ackrill thinks that Aristotle consistently adheres to an inclusive conception of the end in *NE* I-IX but that he then switches to a dominant conception in *NE* X. I have argued that the apparent inconsistency in *NE* I cannot be eliminated in the way that he proposes. It is interesting to note that the same apparent inconsistency also crops up in *NE* X. In X, 7-8 Aristotle singles out philosophical contemplation as the activity which constitutes "perfect" happiness, and all the commentators agree that this commits him to the dominant view. But in X, 2, in the passage quoted above (in which Aristotle says that the good cannot be made more desirable by the addition of any of the things that are good in themselves), we find clear evidence of the inclusive conception. Just as we cannot say that *NE* I consistently adheres to an inclusive conception, so we cannot say that *NE* X consistently adheres to a dominant conception.

IV

We seem to be forced back to Hardie's view: there is an inconsistency in Aristotle's doctrine which runs right through the *NE,* from beginning to end. However, I think there is a way of understanding the doctrine which does not saddle Aristotle with this inconsistency. I said at the outset that I believe the distinction between inclusive and dominant conceptions presents us with two models, neither of which really fits Aristotle's view. Let me now try to spell out what I have in mind.

As Hardie understands the distinction, the various goods which might be ingredients in an inclusive conception of the end are "separable" in the sense that one could possess any one of them without possessing the others. One who pursues a dominant end concentrates exclusively on one of these goods and forgoes the rest; this would only be possible if the goods were independent of each other.[14] But it is clear that Aristotle does *not* think that goods are separable in this way. In I, 9, for instance, he says:

> Happiness was said to be a certain kind of activity in accordance with virtue; of the remaining goods, some belong [to the definiens] necessarily, while the others are in their nature helpmates and useful as instruments (1099b26-28).[15]

Aristotle is in effect denying that virtuous activity is independent of other goods; he is claiming that we cannot possess this good without possessing certain other goods. One of the chief aims of I, 8 is to show that the definiens, "virtuous activity," guarantees possession of the most important goods commonly thought to be essential to happiness. Earlier in I, 7, virtue, intellect, honor, and pleasure were mentioned as primary examples of intrinsic goods (1097b2-4). In I, 8 Aristotle first points out that virtue and wisdom are implicit in his definition (1098b22-31). He then argues that another intrinsic good, pleasure, necessarily accompanies virtuous activity; moreover, the kind of pleasure associated with virtuous activity is of the best and most satisfying kind (1099a7-21).[16] Finally he speaks of certain goods which are instrumentally necessary, or at least useful, for the performance of a full range of virtuous activities.

> Yet evidently, as we said, it needs the external goods as well; for it is impossible, or not easy, to do noble acts without the proper equipment. In many actions we use friends and riches and political power as instruments (1099a31-b2; cf. 1099b27-28).

Insofar as one's ability to carry out virtuous activity is impeded if one lacks friends or is very poor, the goods of friendship and moderate means are also presupposed by Aristotle's defining formula, "virtuous activity."[17]

The general point Aristotle argues for in I, 8 is that most of the goods commonly thought to be ingredients in a happy life are entailed by his definition. We might say that his definition of happiness, as he understands it, is *implicitly* inclusive. Why doesn't he make it explicitly inclusive? To answer this question, it will be helpful to draw attention to some general and, I hope, uncontroversial points concerning Aristotle's theory of definition and essence.

V

A definition, for Aristotle, is a formula giving the essence of the thing defined. Fortunately we do not need to try to explain here what an Aristotelian essence is; a few very brief comments will be sufficient for our limited purposes. An essence is a necessary attribute of a thing and one in virtue of which other necessary attributes belong to that thing. Thus, Aristotle speaks of using the essence to demonstrate various properties of a thing.[18] One of the most important functions of an essence, then, is explanatory: ideally one should be able to explain by means of the essence why a thing has various necessary properties.

In some places Aristotle argues that it is not possible to distinguish certain types of entities from their essences;[19] in the case of such entities, it seems clear that all of their necessary properties will either be included in or entailed by their essence. But with entities which are distinguishable from their essences, it seems that not all their necessary properties need be entailed by their essences. For instance, Aristotle considers it possible that the intellect is the essence of a human being, while at the same time recognizing that a human being cannot exist without certain biological capacities and that these capacities are not entailed by possession of intellect—God possesses intellect but no biological capacities.[20] The key point, however, is that the essence of a thing does not include all of the properties

which are severally necessary and jointly sufficient for the existence of the thing.[21] A definition which consisted of a list of such properties would be considered defective by Aristotle insofar as it would fail to indicate the important explanatory relations among the necessary properties of the thing.

In view of these general considerations about definition and essence, we would not expect Aristotle to mention all of the necessary ingredients of a happy life in his definition of happiness. A definition of happiness should single out that attribute which best explains how other necessary attributes are involved in a happy life. Aristotle's definiens meets this requirement: other goods such as pleasure, friendship, and external prosperity either follow from or support virtuous activity, or are related to it in some other way. An explicitly inclusive definition would treat happiness as simply a collection of goods; a formula which singles out the essence, on the other hand, points to a unity and structure among the goods which are necessary features of the happy life.

In the preceding section, we pointed out that Aristotle's definition of happiness, as he understands it, is implicitly inclusive. In this section we have noted some general points about Aristotle's theory of definition which show why he would not approve of an explicitly inclusive definition. The general lesson is clear: the fact that only one good is mentioned in the definition of happiness does not mean that Aristotle is recommending pursuit of one single good to the exclusion of all others.

VI

In trying to show how Aristotle's definition of happiness is implicitly inclusive, we construed his definition—as he does himself in I, 8—in terms of the active life involving the exercise of the moral virtues. The goods which are implicit in the definition are goods related in one way or another to *morally* virtuous activity. But in taking the definition in this way, we are ignoring the factor which originally led Hardie and others to claim that it exemplifies a dominant conception of the end. We have agreed that the final clause of the definition sets up an equation between happiness and a life of philosophical contemplation. Thus, unless we can show that the contemplative life, as Aristotle understands it, includes more than the single good of philosophical contemplation, we shall have to admit after all that the definition of happiness does exemplify a dominant conception of the final good.

There is one line of reasoning in *NE* X, 7-8 which seems to presuppose a dominant conception of the good. Aristotle contends that contemplation is the characteristic activity of god, and he says that we partake of this activity insofar as we have a share of the divine in us

(1178b8-22). Aristotle's god is a supremely happy being, and his happiness apparently involves nothing but contemplation; it would be absurd, he says, to attribute moral virtues and other goods to god. Clearly Aristotle subscribes to a dominant conception of god's happiness.

Now if the philosophical life is modelled after the supremely happy life of god, it would appear that this life must consist of the single activity of contemplation. Of course, the philosopher is not a god; he must live with other men and, therefore, must practice the virtues and partake of other human goods (1178b5-7). Although these other goods are ingredients in the happiness associated with the active life, perhaps they need not be considered parts of the philosopher's happiness.[22] Some scholars have argued that in *NE* X, 7 Aristotle identifies each person with his theoretical intellect;[23] the activity of the intellect would then be the only activity which is truly the person's own. Activities of other faculties (e.g., morally virtuous activity) would properly belong to some other being with whom the person is somehow associated (cf. 1178a3-4). The happiness of the philosopher would then have the same simplicity and purity as the life of god. And it would be true after all that the definition of happiness in *NE* I, 7 expresses a dominant conception of the end insofar as it equates happiness with philosophical contemplation.

Although this is a plausible way of reading *some* of Aristotle's remarks in X, 7-8, it does not make for a satisfactory interpretation of his general position in these chapters. We should note, first of all, that Aristotle's very tentative suggestion that the individual might be identical with his intellect[24] is effectively cancelled a few lines later when he says " . . . if this [the intellect] *most of all* is man."[25] He is surely not saying both (a) that an individual is a composite of several elements and (b) that an individual is identical with one of these elements. The wording suggests that an individual is made up of several different elements and that one of these elements is more responsible than any of the others for the whole entity being a man. Other passages in these chapters clearly imply that an individual human being is not simply identical with his theoretical intellect.[26]

In his praise of the self-sufficiency of the philosophical life, Aristotle is sometimes taken to be claiming that the philosopher can and should emulate god by living apart from other men and spending all his time philosophizing. Actually, he says that the philospher (in contrast to god) will be better off if he spends his time with friends and associates (1177a34). However, if the philosopher should suffer the misfortune of being separated from friends, he will still be able to philosophize and derive satisfaction from that activity. In this respect, the philosopher's happiness is less dependent on external factors, and therefore more self-sufficient, than the happiness of the active life (1177a27-b1).

If the philosopher is happier spending time with friends than living by himself, then his friendships with others will be a part of his happiness. These friendships will presumably be of the best kind—the kind which presupposes possession of the moral virtues and is expressed by morally virtuous actions.[27] The philosopher will therefore partake of the goods associated with the active life of moral virtue, and insofar as (a) he is a human being and not just pure intellect and (b) these goods are desirable (for human beings at least) for their own sake, they will make up a part of his happiness.[28]

As I understand Aristotle's last words on the good for man in *NE* X, 7-8, there are two forms of happiness, one associated with the active life of moral virtue and the other with the contemplative life. The latter he characterizes as "perfect happiness," the former as "happiness of a secondary degree."[29] Both of these forms of happiness are implicitly inclusive, though in different ways. The essence of the secondary form of happiness is morally virtuous activity. Aristotle holds that this activity by its very nature depends upon and produces other goods, and thus the life of morally virtuous activity must include a variety of other goods. The essence of what Aristotle calls "perfect happiness" is contemplation. Now it is not true that this activity by its very nature presupposes a variety of other goods; as we have seen, Aristotle's god engages in this activity and is in no way handicapped by lacking other goods like friends and moral virtue. But a human being who pursues a contemplative life *will* be handicapped if he lacks friends and moral virtue. It is not the activity of contemplation itself which presupposes other goods but, rather, this activity as engaged in by human beings.

Notes

[1] W. F. R. Hardie, "The Final Good in Aristotle's Ethics," *Philosophy* (1965): 277-95. Hardie's article has been reprinted in *Aristotle, A Collection of Critical Essays,* ed. J. M. E. Moravcsik (Garden City, 1967). I shall refer to page numbers of the reprint. A condensed version of the article appears as part of chapter II of Hardie's book, *Aristotle's Ethical Theory* (Oxford, 1968).

[2] J. L. Ackrill, "Aristotle on *Eudaimonia,*" *Proceedings of the British Academy,* vol. 60 (1974): 339-59.

[3] Anthony Kenny, *The Aristotelian Ethics* (Oxford, 1978), pp. 204-6.

[4] Ackrill translates [*mē sunarithmoumenen*] as "not being counted as one good thing among others" (op. cit.,

348). I have changed this slightly in order to make it more neutral; this way attention can be focussed on the second clause, for *it* is the real locus of disagreement between Kenny on the one hand and Hardie and Ackrill on the other. Another point about translation: throughout the paper I use "happiness" as a translation of [*eudaimonia*] and this is criticized by Ackrill (op. cit., 348-9) and others. Richard Kraut has recently given a very persuasive defense of the traditional translation in his article "Two Conceptions of Happiness," *Philosophical Review* (1979): 167-97. However, I should note that I have tried to use "happiness" simply as a stand-in for [*eudaimonia*] nothing that I say depends upon the correctness of Kraut's contentions.

[5] Kenny, op. cit., 204.

[6] This passage is not mentioned by Kenny. Gauthier and Jolif in their commentary (*L'Ethique à Nicomaque* [Louvain, 1970]) see the relevance of this passage in X, 2 to the self-sufficiency passage in I, 7; cf. II, 1, on 1097b16-20. This passage incidentally indicates that the goods which happiness must include are not any and all goods but rather the intrinsic goods. Cf. also 1169b5-10.

[7] Hardie, op. cit., 299-300.

[8] Ackrill, op. cit., 353.

[9] Ackrill, op. cit., 353-4.

[10] Even if we understand the definition in the way that Ackrill proposes, it would still not be inclusive in the required sense. To be inclusive in the way sketched by the self-sufficiency passage and 1172b28-35, the good would have to include all intrinsic goods; activity in accordance with "complete" or "comprehensive" virtue would apparently fall short of being inclusive in this way; if not, we need some explanation of how the other intrinsic goods are entailed by activity in accordance with complete virtue.

[11] This point is mentioned by Kenny (op. cit., p. 205); cf. also John Cooper, *Reason and Human Good in Aristotle* (Cambridge, Mass., 1975), p. 100, n. 10.

[12] Cf. 1153b9-12 and 1176a26-27.

[13] Ackrill also points out that the definition of happiness is put forward as the conclusion of an argument appealing to man's characteristic activity and that if the last clause of the definition is understood as a reference to philosophical contemplation, the conclusion of the argument becomes a *non sequitur;* nothing in the argument justifies restricting man's characteristic activity to the exercise of the theoretical intellect (op. cit., 351-52). Ackrill's claim is justified only if the definition is understood as a *simple* identification of

happiness and philosophical contemplation. But Aristotle formulates the definition in such a way that it can be construed as referring to the active life involving the exercise of the moral virtues, and this is the way in which he understands it in I, 8. From the vantage point of X, 7-8, taking the definition as a reference to the active life turns out to be a mistake but not a complete missing of the mark; the active life *is* a form of happiness, though not the highest form. So in the usual way of understanding the definition in I, 7, it both is and is not a *non sequitur*. In any case, the evidence is overwhelming that the final clause of the definition is a reference to philosophical contemplation.

[14] Cf. Hardie, op. cit., p. 300: " . . . to put the question thus is to rule out the obvious and correct reply; that the life which is best for a man cannot lie in gaining only one of his objects at the cost of losing all the rest. This would be too high a price to pay even for philosophy."

[15] In defense of my insertion of "to the definiens," it should be noted that this passage refers back to points made earlier, and the earlier points concern the necessary tie between *virtuous activity* and various other goods; cf. 1098b22-31, 1099a7-21, 1099a31-b2.

[16] Honor is apparently omitted from the list because Aristotle does not actually believe that it is an intrinsic good; cf. 1159a16-27.

[17] Cf. 1153b14-25. When Aristotle says at 1099b1-2 that "we use friends . . . as instruments," he might be taken to mean that friends are *mere* instruments to the good man. Later in his discussion of friendship, he makes it clear that in his view the best type of friendship—that in which friends value each other partly for their good moral qualities—is desirable for its own sake. Moral virtue is a necessary condition of this kind of friendship, and the friendship is expressed at least partly through the exercise of the virtues. Cf. *NE* IX, 9.

[18] This is implied by the doctrine that definitions are "first principles" . . . of demonstrations; cf. *Posterior Analytics* 72a14-24, 72b23-25, 89a16-19, 90b24-27, 96b21-25; cf. Joan Kung, "Aristotle on Essence and Explanation," *Philosophical Studies* (1977): 361-83.

[19] *Metaphysics* VII, 6; cf. 1036a16-25, 1043b1-4, *De Anima* 429b10-22.

[20] Cf. *NE* 1178a6-7, 1178b22-28 and 33-35.

[21] Cf. *Eudemian Ethics* 1214b11-27 where Aristotle distinguishes between factors which should be included in the definition of happiness and necessary conditions which are often confused with the former; cf. *Politics* 1328a21-35.

[22] I am assuming that the active and contemplative lives

are two alternative lives, not to be combined in a single best life. I have tried to give some support to this view in "Aristotle on the Active and Contemplative Lives," *Philosophy Research Archives* 3, no. 1138 (1977).

[23] Cooper, op. cit., pp. 174-76; G. Rodier, *Etudes de philosophie grecque* (Paris, 1926), pp. 213-17.

[24] Note the use of [*doxeie*] " . . . this *would seem* to be each individual."

[25] 1178a7; compare the very similar formulations at 1166a22-23 and 1169a2. Cooper claims that there is a very important difference between these passages in *NE* IX and the passage in X, 7 about the intellect (op. cit., pp. 169-75). In the former passages, Aristotle is thinking of the intellect primarily as a practical faculty—a faculty which guides action and makes decisions—but in X, 7 he is thinking of it exclusively as a theoretical faculty. He says " . . . Aristotle in the tenth book sharply separates the practical from the theoretical reason, associating the former with the *syntheton*, the living body, while making the latter a godlike thing apart" (op. cit., p. 175). Cooper seems to overlook 1177a12-15: "Whether it be reason [or intellect . . . or something else that is this element which is thought to be our natural ruler and guide and to take thought of things noble and divine. . . . " Here intellect cannot be understood as a purely theoretical faculty. Gauthier and Jolif seem closer to the mark: "Au-dessous de cette activité [contemplation] qui est son activité propre, l'intellect a une autre activité, qu'il n'exerce pas en tant qu'il est lui-même, mais en tant qu'il est uni au corps: c'est de commander à la bête, de régler les passions, de diriger la partie irrationnelle (cf 1177a14-15)" (op. cit., II, 2, p. 895). The [*syntheton*] which Aristotle refers to at 1177b28 and 1178a20, need not be understood as the living body; it may be taken, as Gauthier and Jolif suggest (ibid.), as the combination of the intellect and the other elements in human nature.

[26] For instance, the following passages speak of intellect as an element in man: 1177a15-17, 1177b27-28, 1177b34; cf. 1178b5-7, and 1178b33-35.

[27] Cf. 1170b10-19, 1156b6-24.

[28] Ackrill would apparently agree that the contemplative life includes these other goods (op. cit., 356-57); it is therefore puzzling that he regards the conception of happiness in *NE* X as dominant (cf. 340-41).

[29] 1177a17, 1177b24, 1178b8, 1178a7-10.

Terence Irwin (essay date 1985)

SOURCE: An introduction to *Nichomachean Ethics*, Hackett Publishing Company, 1985, pp. xi-xxii.

[*In the following essay, Irwin describes the content of Aristotle's* Nicomachean Ethics, *noting that the work analyzes traditional Greek ideals regarding the good life, the virtues necessary to be deemed an "acceptable and admirable" member of Greek society, as well as social problems and conflicts. Irwin also responds to common objections readers have had to* Ethics.]

*Why Read the **Ethics**?*

Aristotle's ethical works matter to the student of moral behaviour. Aristotle provides the closest and most detailed analysis of Greek attitudes and aspirations, modified and criticized from his own point of view. Traditional Greek ideals of the best life (i 5); the canon of virtues that made someone an acceptable and admirable member of society (iii-v); the problems and conflicts of social life (viii 13-ix 3)—all these are examined by a dispassionate and careful observer.

For the historian of moral theory Aristotle's ethics is important as a primary source of mediaeval, and hence of modern, ethical thought. The **Ethics** provide the framework of Aquinas' account of the moral virtues; they have been read and cited as an influence by modern theorists—in the nineteenth century by Henry Sidgwick, in the twentieth by John Rawls, among many others.

But what has Aristotle to offer the contemporary reader interested in moral problems and in reflective thinking about them? The concrete detail that makes him interesting to the historian of Greece may seem to remove him from our concerns and interests. We do not readily value all the Aristotelian virtues; we will not be immediately inclined to find the magnanimous person (iv 3) as admirable as Aristotle finds him. And if Aristotle has been influential in moral theory, has his contribution been absorbed and superseded?

First of all, the contemporary student can learn from Aristotle's treatment of some problems of contemporary interest. His account of voluntary action and conditions for responsibility (iii 1,5); of purposive action and practical inference (iii 2-3, vii 3); of the nature and variety of pleasure (vii 11-14, x 1-5)—these have been justly admired for their stimulus to further thought on these issues.

However, Aristotle is important to the contemporary philosopher most of all because he does not share exactly our immediate concerns in moral theory. He does not ask the questions we would find it natural to ask about ethics—the contents of the **Ethics** look rather different from the contents of modern works on ethics. But when we take the trouble to understand Aristotle's questions, we can see that they are worth asking.

Aristotle's Life and Works

Aristotle was born in Stagira in Macedon, in 384, and

hence was never a citizen of Athens, where he spent most of his life. He was a member of Plato's Academy from 367 to Plato's death in 347, when he left Athens, first for the eastern Aegean islands, and then for Macedon. Here he was a tutor of Alexander, the son of Philip the king of Macedon. He returned to Athens in 334 and founded his own school in the Lyceum. In 323 Alexander died, and Aristotle—apparently because of anti-Macedonian feeling in Athens—left for Chalcis, where he died in 322.

Aristotle was a Macedonian, and associated with the rising Macedonian dynasty that eventually founded an empire ruling over the previously independent city-states of Greece, and then over much of western Asia. Historians like to see here the transition from the age of the city-states to the age of empire, first the Macedonian and then (after 146) the Roman. It is surprising to some that this transition leaves no mark in Aristotle's ethical and political works. Aristotle still thinks of a Greek city as the natural and desirable form of community, and of the virtues of the citizen of such a city as the virtues needed for the best life. Probably we should not be surprised. Aristotle and his contemporaries did not know that the Macedonian empire would last and would be replaced by the Roman; and the rise of Macedon probably made little difference to the character of Greek social life or to individual and collective attitudes.

One major intellectual interest of Aristotle's is empirical inquiry and theory in biology—this is the subject of about a quarter of the extant Aristotelian corpus. Aristotle's biological works reflect his emphasis on detailed observation and comparison of circumstances, structure and behaviour of different animals. We may see some of the same interests in his classification and description of the virtues and the corresponding types of people.

A further major influence on Aristotle is Plato. Aristotle takes over Plato's interest in dialectic, logic, metaphysics and ethics. He is a keen critic of Plato (i 6); and Plato's concerns lead Aristotle to quite un-Platonic conclusions. In ethics Aristotle agrees rather closely with Plato's main aims and lines of argument.

It is easy, but seriously misleading, to present the 'empirical' and the 'Platonic' aspects of Aristotle as two sides of a conflict, or at least a tension, in his thought. In fact they are very closely connected. Aristotle examines nature, and interprets the empirical evidence, in the light of his own theoretical conceptions, especially his conceptions of form, matter . . . and end. . . . The clearest statements of his programme, especially relevant to the study of human nature in the *Ethics,* are *Phys.* [*Physics*] ii and *PA* i, 1.

Aristotle's works can be divided into groups:
(1) Logic and dialectic have no specific subject-matter, but are relevant in principle to all areas of inquiry. They examine the proper forms of argument for different purposes—dialectic, syllogistic and demonstrative . . . *Categories, De Interpretatione, Analytics, Topics* (together usually called the *Organon*) are in this group.

(2) Philosophy of nature considers the principles required for understanding movement and change in general, especially for living organisms with souls. *Physics, De Caelo, De Generatione et Corruptione, De Anima, Parva Naturalia, De Partibus Animalium, De Generatione Animalium, De Motu Animalium* are in this group.

(3) First philosophy considers being in general, both unchanging (theology) and changing (hence the principles also used in natural philosophy). The *Metaphysics* addresses these matters.

(4) Practical science considers action (in the narrow sense), and hence includes the *Ethics* and *Politics.*

(5) Productive science is concerned with production, including the *Rhetoric* and *Poetics.*

It is easy to see that some of the same questions about the same things might belong to more than one area of inquiry, and that (4) and (5) introduce an apparently different principle of division from (1)-(3). . . .

Aristotle does not obtrude the rest of his philosophy into ethical questions (see note to 1155b1). But the reader who has read *Phys.* ii, *PA* i 1, *DA* ii 1-4, and *Met.* ix 1-8, will understand the arguments better in e.g. i 7, ii 5, vii 3, ix 9, x 4-8. Aristotle's account of dialectic is presupposed in his method in ethics. . . .

Background

Aristotle faces questions partly set by 'the many and the wise' . . . , both common views and more or less systematic reflection on them. Some of his sources may be briefly indicated. . . .

A traditional conception of happiness and the good person finds the ideal life in a Homeric hero, displaying strength and bravery in battle, leadership in political life and receiving honour as his reward. However, this life is dangerous; success is precarious, liable to the sort of reversal of fortune presented in, e.g., Sophocles' *Ajax.*

At the same time Greek moralists want to encourage justice and concern for others as a virtue that is no less fine and admirable than bravery and strength. This may require restraint on the single-minded pursuit of success and honour. It seems to require sacrifice of my own interests for the sake of other people's. When appeals to divine rewards and punishments seemed unconvincing, moralists looked for some reason to persuade someone concerned with his own happiness to be just.

Dangers and difficulties in traditional ideals provoked different reactions:

(1) 'Avoid the dangerous ambitions of the hero; live a quiet, unambitious and secure life, and then happiness won't be so easily lost.' (See Herodotus, iii 39-42, v 92.)

(2) 'Avoid the dangers of justice. The rules of justice are nothing but conventional norms imposed by the laws and expectations of society. They are irrelevant to human nature, which is best satisfied by the satisfaction of our immediate desires.' (See Plato, *Gorg.* 482c-492c.)

(3) 'Avoid the dangers of bravery and justice and turn to higher things, to the life of pure thought and study, away from the vicissitudes of the world.' (See Plato, *Rep.* 493b-e, *Tht.* 172d-177b.)

Aristotle wants to answer the criticism of the traditional virtues that makes them irrelevant to a rational person's conception of his happiness. He does not retain the traditional views unmodified; but bravery, restraint of appetites, concern for honour and other-regarding aims are all defended as parts of happiness. Their relation is clearest in the account of magnanimity (iv 3) and friendship (esp. ix 8-9). Here Aristotle's aim is very similar to Plato's in the *Republic*.

Misunderstandings of Aristotle

Objection: When Aristotle makes my happiness my ultimate end, he is accepting psychological hedonism. But he is wrong. I can value lots of things for their own sake apart from my pleasure or contentment.

Reply: Aristotle's conception of happiness does not identify happiness with pleasure.

Objection: When Aristotle requires me to aim at my own happiness above all, he endorses an immoral and objectionable version of egoism. Surely I can, and justifiably do, value, e.g., the welfare of other people for its own sake, not simply as a means to my happiness. Doesn't Aristotle make genuine altruism impossible?

Reply: The objection rests on a mistake about the relation between happiness and other intrinsic goods. . . .

Objection: Aristotle claims that virtue of character requires a mean or intermediate state, moderation that avoids extremes. But sometimes extremes are good and

moderation bad. Sometimes, for instance, it is good to be extremely angry, not just moderately angry, and sometimes it is good to give away a lot of money, not just a moderate amount.

Reply: The doctrine of the mean does not advise this sort of moderation. . . .

Objection: Aristotle leaves no place for distinctively moral reasoning. The only practical function of reason that he allows is deliberation about means to ends. The only reasoning he allows is quasi-technical calculation about how to get what we want. He allows no reasoning about whether the ends we are pursuing are the morally right ones.

Reply: Aristotle's conception of decision and of 'things promoting ends' does not imply this sort of restriction. . . .

Objection: By making the judgements of the intelligent person the ultimate standard of the morally virtuous action Aristotle commits himself to a conservative view of morality. To know what the virtuous action is we must ask an intelligent person. But how do we recognize one except by relying on the conventional judgements of our society?

Reply: The intelligent person need not accept all of conventional morality. Since he deliberates about the components of happiness . . . , he may well form a conception of the good and of the virtues that differs from the conventional conception. To the extent that we can do some of the right deliberation ourselves, we can see that the intelligent person is right if he disagrees with conventional judgements.

Objection: The virtues Aristotle describes are perhaps suitable for a Greek gentleman wanting to act according to his station in life. But they are irrelevant to us when we live in different conditions and most of us do not think so highly of these aristocratic values.

Reply: The types of actions belonging to each virtue are, not surprisingly, suitable primarily for the social and historical conditions familiar to Aristotle. But it does not follow that the states and attitudes corresponding to the different virtues are historically limited in the same way. . . .

Questions about Aristotle

While some natural objections to Aristotle's theory have been found to rest on misunderstandings that can be dispelled by closer study, some related objections and questions are not to be dismissed so easily. Often Aristotle's own argument is brief, inexplicit and incomplete on some important issues.

Is happiness a reasonable first principle for ethics? Happiness is supposed to be the ultimate end which any rational agent has good reason to refer to when he decides how to live, what sort of person to be, what states of character to acquire. But can any conception of an ultimate end provide the right sort of guidance here? Should we perhaps decide what to do on moral grounds, without reference to some further end?

How informative is Aristotle's own conception of happiness? He argues that happiness is activity according to virtue. How then do we tell what states are virtues? If we are not simply to follow conventional judgements, we must apparently turn again to happiness—but what sort of answer will we find here?

How does the intelligent person know what promotes happiness? This question raises again our previous question about the informativeness of Aristotle's conception of happiness. The reader can best answer this question by asking how each of the particular virtues could be shown to promote happiness as Aristotle conceives it. . . . Aristotle answers the question most fully in his defence of friendship, ix 9.

Does Aristotle show that we have reason to be moral? One task of the *Ethics* is to support Plato's claim in the *Republic* that we are better off being just, concerned with the interests of others, than being unjust. Aristotle does not face this question explicitly in Book v, on justice. He comes nearest to an answer in his account of friendship.

How much practical guidance does Aristotle really offer? Despite his emphasis on the practical function of ethics, . . . he does not offer many specific moral rules. He discusses e.g. few of the questions that have divided utilitarians from non-utilitarians in modern ethics. . . . Here we should remember:

(i) Aristotle is more concerned with identifying the right states of character than with specifying the range of actions associated with them.

(ii) He thinks detailed ethical instructions require reference to social and political conditions; and these are discussed in the *Politics.*

The Structure of the **Ethics**

The work translated here and often called 'Aristotle's **Ethics'** is the **Nicomachean Ethics** (**Ethica Nicomachea,** or **EN**), one of three detailed treatises on ethics in the Aristotelian corpus; the others are the **Eudemian Ethics** and the *Magna Moralia.* (Nicomachus and Eudemus may have been the original editors of the works named after them, after Aristotle's death, or he may have dedicated the works to them.) The *MM* is generally agreed not to have been written by Aristotle. It may still contain genuine Aristotelian doctrine identical to the doctrine of neither the **EN** nor the **EE.** The **EE** is by Aristotle, and is generally (but not universally) supposed to predate the **EN.** All three works cover many of the same topics in interestingly different ways, and comparative study is often rewarding. A special puzzle is raised by the three books common to the **EN** and the **EE.** . . .

Probably the **EN** we have was not intended for publication in exactly its present form. Like most of the Aristotelian corpus, it is probably Aristotle's lecture notes, perhaps edited after his death. This origin would explain why the argument is often compressed (e.g. in i 6)—perhaps intended for oral elaboration—and why the order of topics within a book is not always easy to follow. The order is in any case fairly loose—Aristotle takes up topics as they naturally lead into each other, and then resumes his main topic. . . .

Aristide Tessitore (essay date 1996)

SOURCE: "Making the City Safe for Philosophy, Book X," in *Reading Aristotle's "Ethics,"* State University of New York Press, 1996, pp. 97-117.

[*In the following essay, Tessitore examines Book X of* Ethics, *arguing that in this final book of the treatise, Aristotle offers a concluding statement with regard to happiness. Tessitore notes that Aristotle's conclusion—that perfect happiness may be found in philosophic contemplation, while the practice of ethical virtue offers only a secondary degree of happiness—may seem to conflict with earlier statements Aristotle presented in Book VII. Suggesting that this teaching has been implied throughout the work, Tessitore argues that its harshness is tempered by Aristotle's effort to connect philosophers and non-philosophers through the concept of moral decency, and by his emphasis on the significance of ethical virtue to non-philosophers.*]

It is only in the final book of his treatise that Aristotle explicitly presents a teaching that he has intimated in different ways at various points in his study: Complete or perfect happiness is to be found in the philosophic activity of contemplation; the practice of ethical virtue is happy in a secondary degree (10.7.1177a12-18; 10.8.1178a9-10). The discussion that follows traces the rhetorical dimension of this final assessment of the relative standing of philosophic and ethical excellence by focusing on the artfulness of the argument in the concluding book of the **Ethics.** I will attempt to demonstrate that the harshness of this conclusion is mitigated by the rhetorical framework within which it has been placed. The inquiry in Book X proceeds through four themes: pleasure, happiness, the best way of life, and the turn to politics, each of which is considered in sequence.

Pleasure and Moral Education

Scholars have long recognized discrepancies in the double treatment of pleasure (7.11-14; 10.1-5) but, for the most part, have neglected to observe the very different horizons within which these two accounts are offered. As we have already observed, the initial treatment of pleasure in Book VII began by recommending it as a subject worthy of study for political philosophers (7.11.1152b1-3). This contrasts sharply with the didactic concern that guides the second consideration in Book X (10.1.1172a19-25). The subject of pleasure is reintroduced because of its critical influence on the moral education of the young. Pleasure and pain extend throughout the whole of life and are of particular import for the development of virtue and the attainment of happiness.

The approach to pleasure in Book X is consistent with Aristotle's approach to the study of ethical virtue as a whole. He mediates a debate between two extreme and influential positions with a view to directing his readers toward a salutary mean. On the one hand, Eudoxus taught that pleasure was the good, a philosophic stance that gained acceptance because it was combined with a personal reputation for exceptional moderation. Eudoxus did not appear to advocate this view because he wished to indulge in pleasure and, as a result, people assumed that he must be speaking the truth. Aristotle comments that the influence of Eudoxus's position was, however, more a reflection of his good character than the quality of his arguments (10.2.1172b16-17). On the other hand, Speussipus and members of the Academy maintained that pleasure was entirely base. Among those who adopted this second position, some really believed it to be true, whereas others maintained this view because they wanted to encourage the practice of virtue. They argued that the natural inclination toward pleasure among human beings makes it advisable to point most persons in the opposite direction, with the hope that this will bring them closer to the mean.

Aristotle takes issue with this approach, not with its aim (10.1.1172a33-b7). He explains that in matters involving feeling and action, a particular theory or position is despised or dismissed whenever it appears to be inconsistent with the most readily perceived facts. If those who condemn pleasure are, even on occasion, seen to enjoy it, their arguments become implausible because it is assumed that, contrary to their stated position, they really believe pleasure to be the good. The arguments are discredited not necessarily because they are untrue, but because most *(hoi polloi)* lack the capacity to discriminate *(to diorizein)*. For most human beings, actions speak louder than words. A further consequence is that the truth itself is undermined because of the loss of credibility occasioned by the deeds of those who may in fact be speaking it. Hence, to the extent that it is possible to bring theory into harmony

with practice, the theories in question will prove more useful for the conduct of life. This practical aim characterizes Aristotle's reconsideration of pleasure in Book X and distinguishes it from his more theoretical treatment in Book VII. His attempt to harmonize theory and practice is intended to "encourage" *(protrepō)* those capable of understanding ethical arguments to live better lives (10.1.1172b3-7). A reconsideration of pleasure is made necessary by a concern for the education of decent, although not necessarily philosophic, readers.

Aristotle's New Description of Pleasure

Aristotle lists the particular arguments used by Eudoxus and members of the Academy to support their respective positions, and in most cases supplies an immediate rejoinder (chs. 2-3).[1] He then goes on to offer an account of his own (chs. 4-5). The following summary focuses on those aspects of the treatment of pleasure in Book X that distinguish it most sharply from the earlier account in Book VII.

In Book VII, Aristotle defines pleasure as "unimpeded activity" and leaves open the possibility that pleasure is both the highest good and something divine. Book X offers not so much a redefinition as a new description of pleasure. Pleasure "perfects" or "completes" *(telei)* activity (10.4.1174b23). The activities of both sense perception and thought have corresponding pleasures that become most acute when the activity is executed in the best possible way. These pleasures do not inhere in the activities themselves, but rather "come to be in addition" *(epigignomenon)* (10.4.1174b31-33). Pleasure is a kind of unlooked for bonus that enhances activity, perfecting and increasing the capacity for action. In this new view, pleasure belongs to or depends upon activity. In Book VII, pleasure is defined as activity of a certain kind. In Book X, while maintaining that pleasure and activity are inextricably bound together, Aristotle indicates that they are nevertheless distinct. The consequences of this key difference in the two treatments of pleasure will become increasingly apparent.

The most immediate and primary corollary to follow from the new distinction is that it makes possible an independent standard by which pleasures can be ranked and judged. Activity, not pleasure, is the fundamental thing, for the latter depends upon the former. On this basis, Aristotle is able to bolster a widespread opinion among the decent that pleasure is good but not the only or supreme good. If pleasure comes from or belongs to activity, the supreme good cannot be pleasure; rather, it would belong to the best activity. With the help of this distinction, readers are now provided with edifying explanations for some of the more strident suggestions and puzzles raised by the discussion in Book VII.

Aristotle begins by returning to the question with which he had concluded his account of pleasure in Book VII: Why is it that no one is able to feel pleasure continuously (10.4.1175a3-10)? He now points out that no human faculty is characterized by uninterrupted activity, an observation that he illustrates with the example of sight. The pleasure enjoyed in seeing something depends upon looking at it intently. As the activity of looking becomes less vigorous and attention relaxes, the pleasure also fades. Book VII had emphasized an absolute limit to pleasure imposed by the composite nature of human being, a limit that emerged by means of a contrast with the single simple pleasure enjoyed perpetually by god. This teaching is not retracted in the present context, although the emphasis is different: pleasure increases or decreases in the measure that one increases or decreases effort with respect to the activity from which the pleasure arises. In a book that is intended to encourage readers to take pleasure in what they ought, Aristotle's example implies that the effort necessary for excellence in any activity is not without a certain bonus in pleasure.

He next turns his attention to the initial observation of Book X; namely, that pleasure and pain extend throughout the whole of human life (10.4.1175a12-21). It turns out that human beings have good reason to pursue pleasure, for this perfects activities and, therefore, life itself. The musician and the lover of learning are given as examples. The activity of each one is sharpened, prolonged, and improved by the pleasure that belongs to that activity. Hence, pleasure perfects the life of each one by making a person a better musician or philosopher. The argument concludes with the assertion that, for the present, we ought to dismiss the question whether life is for the sake of pleasure or pleasure for the sake of life (10.4.1175a18-19). Whatever the answer, pleasure and life appear to be inseparably yoked together *(suzeugnumi)*;[2] for pleasure does not exist apart from activity, nor is there perfect activity without pleasure (10.4.1175a19-21).

It is especially in the next stages of the argument that the practical consequences of the new description of pleasure become most apparent. In contrast to an earlier puzzling suggestion that all might actually seek a single pleasure, the distinction between pleasure and activity in Book X is used to explain that pleasures differ in kind (10.5.1175a21-76a29). It is because activities differ in kind that the pleasures that belong to and augment them are seen to differ as well. In fact, pleasures derived from one activity can impede other activities. Someone may be distracted from philosophy by hearing music if the latter activity is more pleasurable. This leads to reflection upon the vast array of pleasures arising from the multiplicity of activities undertaken by different species of animals. If some maintain that each species has its own proper pleasure corresponding to its particular work or activity

(10.5.1176a3-9), this view cannot be applied in an unqualified way to the human species (10.5.1176a10-29). Human beings enjoy a bewildering variety of pleasures. Some indication of the problem is evidenced by the fact that the same things delight some people and cause pain to others. Feverish and healthy persons find different things to be sweet, and the same temperature is both painful and pleasant to the weak and the robust. The more serious difficulty, however, concerns the different kinds of pleasure sought out and cultivated by human beings. The three most conspicuous have been anticipated since the outset of the *Ethics,* namely, the different kinds of pleasures connected with the senses, with honors and political offices, and, less frequently but no less emphatically, with study. How is one to find an appropriate standard by which to rank these pleasures? Given the variation and irregularity that characterizes human affairs, is it even possible to speak of a distinctively human pleasure?

It is here that the ethical bearing of the distinction between pleasure and activity becomes explicit (10.5.1175b24-29). Since activity is the fundamental thing, it is possible not only to distinguish various pleasures, but to do so by determining the moral worth of the activities to which they correspond. On the basis of this distinction, pleasures accompanying morally serious activities *(spoudaiai)* are differentiated from those that are base *(phauloi)*. In all cases, the thing is as it appears to the morally serious person *(ho spoudaios)* (10.5.1176a15-16). Moreover, if we wish to know what constitutes the distinctively human pleasure or pleasures, we should look to the best activity or activities of "the perfect and blessed man" *(tou teleiou kai makariou andros)*. All other pleasures sought by human beings are "human" in secondary and even more tenuous ways, depending upon the activities from which they arise (10.5.1176a24-29).

More precisely, Aristotle writes that the perfect and blessed person reveals the pleasure or pleasures that are human in the most authoritative *(kuriōs)* sense, that other pleasures are human in a secondary *(deuterōs)* degree, and still others are even more remotely *(pollostōs)* connected with distinctively human activity (10.5.1176a26-29). Although *deuterōs kai pollostōs* is sometimes taken as a single idiomatic expression, it is helpful to call attention to the distinct meanings of these adverbs. Taken literally, this passage articulates the threefold hierarchy that provides the rhetorical framework for the argument of Book X. Aristotle's distinctions between primary, secondary, and remotely human pleasures correspond to the three views of happiness that he had introduced in Book I and to which he is about to return. The life of study, the moral-political life, and the life devoted to sensual pleasure are each given their proper weight as the *Ethics* approaches its denouement.

Before turning to the final thematic treatment of happiness, we should not allow a persistent ambiguity to pass without comment: Who, precisely, is the morally serious human being? Is Aristotle thinking of the magnanimous person or the philosopher when he speaks of the perfect and blessed person? Despite the obvious importance of this question, Aristotle has not at this point provided his readers with a definitive answer. He does not even call attention to the question; rather, he seems intent upon retaining a certain ambiguity. Indeed, such ambiguity is not without practical effect, since it is apt to elicit greater openness on the part of decent readers who are able and likely to find in these expressions recognition of the fact that they do, or at least should, provide the standard for all who fall below them. Such a reading is not incorrect but, as will become clear in the sequel, it is incomplete.

Happiness and the Pleasures of the Powerful

Whereas Book I provided an outline or sketch of the relationship between happiness and ethical virtue, Book X returns to this subject in a thematic way. It begins by recapitulating some of the initial conclusions about happiness from Book I (10.6.1176a30-76b9). Happiness is not a disposition, but some form of activity that is chosen for its own sake and is lacking in nothing. This way of describing happiness is also believed to describe the nature of virtuous actions, since noble and virtuous deeds are desirable for their own sake. The implicit identification of happiness and ethical virtue is taken over from Book I and constitutes the perspective that, with a few notable exceptions, has been adopted and clarified throughout the study. Only in Book X does Aristotle address in a serious way a problem that challenges the special or authoritative status such a view confers on morally serious persons. The pleasures of play also appear to be desirable for their own sake (10.6.1176b9-17).[3] So simple an assertion is not so simply dismissed. Not only are such amusements thought by many *(hoi polloi)* to constitute happiness; but also and especially, those in positions of absolute power *(turannoi)* are seen to devote themselves to such pastimes. The life styles of the rich and famous undermine the meritorious belief that happiness is to be found in the morally serious activities of decent human beings.[4]

Aristotle responds with five arguments, all of which demonstrate the unique capacity of philosophy to defend and clarify the dignity of moral virtue despite the weight of actual political practice (10.6.1176b17-77a11): (1) It is a lack of experience in mature pleasures that leads many, like children, to think that more accessible but lesser pleasures are best. (2) The serious work that fills human life is not for the sake of fleeting moments of play. Rather, the opposite is the case; play is a form of rest that is for the sake of further activity. (3) In the measure that happiness requires virtue, it will be found in serious activities rather than amusements. (4) Things that are taken seriously are better than funny or amusing things, and happiness engages the better part of the soul. (5) The fact that no one would deem slaves happy despite their ability to enjoy bodily pleasures indicates that happiness involves activities of a different kind.

Each of these five arguments advances the claim that the example of the powerful should be judged by a more authoritative standard furnished by the activities of morally serious persons. The particular arguments used to reinforce this claim are prefaced with a general statement that reveals something of the strategy employed in this section as a whole. Since virtue *(aretē)* and intelligence *(nous)* give rise to the most pure *(eilikrinē s)* and liberal *(eleutherios)* pleasures, happiness cannot consist in the pleasures of play, but in activities in accordance with the virtue and intelligence of morally serious persons (10.6.1176b18-28).

The arguments in this section combine the natural standard of pleasure with a standard furnished by decent opinion. Aristotle does this in two ways. First, he relies on the earlier distinction between pleasure and activity to rule out a priori the possibility that pleasure could provide an independent standard for human conduct. It should be noticed, however, that the claim that pleasure furnishes such a standard is reflected in the pastime activities of the powerful. Second, by including both virtue and intelligence within the single category of activities that give rise to pure and liberal pleasures, Aristotle does not call attention to the ambiguous meaning of these words. Virtue *(aretē)* explicitly embraces both ethical and intellectual excellence, and although intelligence *(nous),* strictly speaking, designates a theoretical activity, it has also been used, as we have seen, to refer to the activity of practical reason as well. Aristotle minimizes the extent to which different activities falling within the categories of *aretē* and *nous,* and the pleasures arising from them, can lead to radically different ways of life.[5] There is, of course, some warrant for this conflation, since, as the discussion of intellectual excellence in Book VI has already made apparent, the life of ethical virtue also involves reason.[6] Aristotle's argument in the present context is consistent with his earlier lack of precision in this matter. Instead of emphasizing that the activities of virtue and intelligence can lead to two different ways of life, he uses both as attributes to describe the activity of the "morally serious person," an expression that is itself laden with ambiguity.

The argument effectively forges an alliance between the philosopher and the nonphilosopher. They are united in opposing the opinion of the many and even the authority of sovereigns who, by their example, teach that happiness consists in the pleasures of play. Morally decent persons possess greater authority on this issue than the rich and famous because they experience pleasures that are purer, more liberal, more serious, and, in general, more specifically human, than those typically desired by the many and indulged by the powerful.

Happiness and the Best Way of Life

It is only after eliciting this sense of solidarity among morally serious persons that Aristotle clarifies the exact relationship between ethical and intellectual excellence as it bears on the all-important question of happiness. As we have anticipated, the final book of the **Ethics** confronts its readers with a surprising demotion of moral virtue in light of the superior happiness of the contemplative life. If happiness consists in activity in accordance with virtue, it is reasonable that it should be activity in accordance with the best virtue. Unlike his initial and open-ended presentation of this argument in Book I (1.7.1098a16-18), Aristotle now specifies that the best and most perfect virtue consists in the godlike activity of contemplation. Happiness is coextensive in its range with contemplative excellence; the exercise of moral virtue is happy in a secondary way (10.7.1177a12-18; 10.8.1178b28-32; 10.8.1178a9-10).

This conclusion, in some way the culmination of the entire book, is oddly out of step with the rest of Aristotle's study. It is incompatible with the earlier and dominant teaching of the **Ethics,** one that emphasized the intrinsic value of both moral virtue and friendship for a flourishing human life. Moreover, apart from the dissonances of which the reader of this book is especially aware, this conclusion is in large measure unanticipated. The prominence given in Aristotle's treatise to both excellences of character (Bks. II-V) and friendship (Bks. VIII-IX) leads more readily to the conclusion that human happiness is a composite of activities involving character, friendship, and reflection. This expected conclusion is, however, unexpectedly derailed by Aristotle's elevation of the theoretical life and subsequent deflation of moral virtue.

The incongruent character of the conclusion of the **Ethics** returns us to the starting point for the current study. The apparent incompatibility of X.7-8 with the rest of the treatise has led scholars to the various critical assessments summarized in chapter 1. As should by now be clear, I do not think it is necessary to conclude that the **Ethics** is marred by a fundamental incoherence or that the arguments of X.7-8 have been carelessly grafted onto the trunk of the **Ethics** by Aristotle or a later editor. Rather, these chapters espouse a position that has in fact been present throughout the entire study, with two notable differences. First, whereas this argument has been kept in the background as an alternative to the dominant teaching of the **Ethics,** it is now

given a position of preeminence. Indeed, it is made into the climax of the book as a whole. Secondly, as we shall see, this shift is accompanied by another. Aristotle's most explicit endorsement of the philosophic life mutes rather than emphasizes the extent to which a life devoted to philosophic inquiry conflicts radically with the demands of moral-political excellence. This, I shall argue, is achieved by presenting a beautiful, if rarified, image of philosophic activity that is in important respects both similar and complementary to the moral-political excellence of the *kalos k'agathos.*

Aristotle's concluding teaching on the surpassing happiness of the philosophic life is supported by six arguments (10.7.1177a18-b26): (1) Contemplation is the best *(kratistē)* activity because it involves the best thing in us. (2) It is the most continuous activity in which human beings can engage. (3) It is held to contain pleasures of marvelous purity and permanence. (4) It is the most self-sufficient activity, for the wise need not depend upon others in order to contemplate. (5) It is loved for its own sake and produces no result beyond itself. (6) It is an activity of leisure par excellence. On the basis of these six arguments, Aristotle concludes that contemplation is the highest activity in accordance with virtue and, consequently, that complete human happiness consists in a life of study. He also anticipates the objection that such a life exceeds human capacity (10.7.1177b26-78a2). If the intellect *(nous)* is something divine in comparison to human capacity, then the life of the intellect would describe a divine, not a human, life. Against this objection, Aristotle urges that we must not follow those who enjoin that mortals should have thoughts of mortality. Rather, as far as possible, we ought to be immortal, and do all that we can to live in accordance with the best thing in us. In sharp contrast to the sober teaching of Book VII on the composite nature of human being, Aristotle concludes his study with a seemingly Platonic exhortation to cultivate the most divine aspect of the human soul. Human happiness is not identified with a range of activities reflecting the composite nature of human being but with the most godlike activity of which human beings are capable.

The argument of these chapters invokes a conception of philosophic activity that stands in sharp contrast to the understanding of political philosophy that Aristotle has discretely but persistently exhibited throughout his study. It suffices to recall the more jarring aspects of his teaching to bring this difference into full view. In the course of his inquiry, Aristotle has suggested the dependence of ethical virtue on *orthos logos,* the circular or ungrounded character of prudence from which *orthos logos* arises, persistent and unresolved tensions between different peaks of ethical excellence (most notably magnanimity and justice), the instrumental character of prudence for the attainment of wisdom, the possibility that pleasure could be the highest good, and the nature and limits of friendship in light of a necessary concern with self-love. I have emphasized the extent to which Aristotle's consideration of each of these issues is left deliberately open ended. It would be inaccurate to confer the status of 'ethical doctrine" upon any of these points. Quite the contrary, it is the intractable character of these problems that reveals, in a way that has yet to be fully appreciated, the essentially dialectical ground in which Aristotle's more familiar ethical and political doctrines are embedded.

In contrast to the kind of political philosophy exhibited in Aristotle's text, his concluding endorsement of philosophy is tame.[7] The final image of philosophic activity is idealized in the sense that it is removed from, and therefore less apparently in conflict with, the exigencies of moral and political life. Philosophy is presented as a thing apart, a god-like activity that does not threaten decent sensibilities because it is not preoccupied with the necessities that constrain civic life. Aristotle's final teaching about the dignity of the philosophic life reflects his concern for nonphilosophic readers: His most explicit endorsement of the surpassing value of contemplation extols a domesticated version of philosophy, one in which philosophic activity is reduced to a largely private or academic enterprise, shorn of the unwieldy and disruptive political consequences that inevitably attend a life of radical inquiry.

Aristotle's arguments for the superiority of the philosophic life confront readers in an unambiguous way with a truth that many of them would necessarily find disconcerting. However, unlike Platonic versions of this teaching, which are almost invariably met by anger or ridicule on the part of Socrates' interlocutors, Aristotle has reason to expect that his presentation of the dignity of the philosophic life will be neither dismissed nor ridiculed by the majority of his nonphilosophic readers. Not only has he painstakingly clarified the horizon of ethical virtue on its own terms in the first half of the *Ethics* and pointed to a relatively innocuous version of theoretical excellence in the concluding chapters of his study, but, as we shall see, even this most explicit teaching on the superiority of the philosophic life is offered within a broader context that emphasizes the similar and even complementary character of ethical and intellectual virtue.

One Consistent Teaching: Similar and Complementary Ways of Life

The similarity between philosophic and ethical excellence is suggested by the particular arguments used to establish the superior happiness of the contemplative life. All six of these arguments apply, to some extent at least, to ethical excellence as well. It is possible to argue that a life characterized by the practice of ethical virtue is superior to, and happier than, a life given over to the enjoyment of bodily pleasures and amusements,

the example of sovereigns notwithstanding, for precisely the reasons used to demonstrate the ultimate superiority of the philosophic life.

These arguments, or variants of them, are in fact applied by Aristotle to ethical virtue. With respect to the six propositions enumerated above, one should consider the following Aristotelian assertions: (1) Justice is considered the best *(kratistē)* of the virtues (5.1.1129b27-28). (2) Friendship, based on the practice of moral virtue, facilitates the continuous activity characteristic of happiness (9.9.1170a5-11). (3) Pure and liberal pleasures are found in the activities of virtue and intelligence (10.6.117b18-21). Less broadly, generosity in particular and virtuous action in general are accompanied by pleasure (4.1.1120a24-31). (4) Self-sufficiency is characteristic of the magnanimous person (4.3.1125a11-12). (5) The repeated insistence that noble actions are desirable for their own sake is one of the leitmotifs of the *Ethics* (e.g., 3.7.1115b11-13; 4.1.1120a23-25; 4.2.1122b6-7; 10.6.1176b6-9). (6) Justice and moderation are cited as activities appropriate to leisure (*Pol.* 7.15.1334a11-34).

The reason for calling attention to these statements is not to question Aristotle's final evaluation of the theoretical life. Rather, it is to make clear that the very arguments used to substantiate its superiority simultaneously suggest a similarity between philosophic and moral excellence. The philosophic life is happier than the moral life not because it is radically different from it, but because it offers to a greater and more perfect degree the very things that decent persons both seek and enjoy for themselves. It is within the broader framework of several propositions bearing on both philosophic and moral excellence that Aristotle presents his most explicit teaching on the superiority of the philosophic life.

This affirmation of the superiority of contemplative excellence necessitates some further consideration of ethical virtue. The issue is confronted in chapter 8, where ethical virtue is also said to result in happiness, but in some lesser way than the godlike activity of philosophic contemplation. However, as we shall see, the argument of this chapter as a whole also suggests that ethical and intellectual virtues are not mutually exclusive but rather complementary forms of excellence for human beings.

Moral virtue is reduced to a secondary rank because it is an activity limited by a need for, and dependence upon, others (10.8.1178a9-b7). By way of contrast, the happiness of contemplation requires less "external equipment," an expression that, in Aristotle's usage, includes other human beings. In fact, the kind of equipment necessary for doing virtuous deeds, especially great ones, might in some cases prove to be a hindrance to contemplation (10.8.1178b1-5). If this argument is more forthcoming about a dissimilarity and possible tension between the moral and contemplative ways of life, such candor is immediately restrained by asserting that the philosopher, since he lives in society, also chooses to engage in virtuous actions (10.8. 1178b5-7).

If, as Aristotle has argued in the preceding chapter, morally decent persons ought to look up to the philosopher as the exemplar of the best way of life, he now indicates that the philosopher is not, or at least should not be, indifferent to the moral-political concerns that are the special preoccupation of the city and those who bear primary responsibility for its welfare. The philosopher is human *(anthr peuesthai)* and for that reason needs to live among other human beings (10.8.1178b5-7; see 7.14.1154b20-31). We are thus brought to consider the possibility of a complementary relationship between theoretical and moral virtue. Whereas the life of the philosopher discloses the fullest possibility of happiness for human beings, morally decent persons embody the kind of excellence necessary to live well in the polis. The two kinds of excellence complement each other because of the essentially political character of composite beings who are able to appreciate but not sustain godlike simplicity.

Although ethical virtue is reduced to a secondary status because of its dependence upon external goods, Aristotle's final argument on this subject softens without denying this diminution (10.8.1178b33-79a9). Since human nature is not self-sufficient with respect to contemplation, even philosophers must concern themselves with external well-being. However, as the life of philosophy reveals, happiness does not require an abundance of external goods. In this respect, it is possible for the practitioner of moral virtue to imitate the philosopher, since one can also undertake virtuous actions with modest resources. It is possible, Aristotle writes, to do noble deeds without being a ruler of land and sea (10.8.1179a4-5). Indeed, he observes that private citizens are more likely to act in accord with the requirements of virtue than those in positions of political authority. This conclusion is supported by drawing from the sayings of Solon and Anaxagoras—a wise statesman and a philosopher (10.8.1179a9-17). Both citations give added authority to the final edifying teaching of the *Ethics* on happiness: Contrary to what most believe, happiness is not to be found in the excesses of the powerful but rather in imitating, as much as possible, the materially unencumbered activity of philosophers.[8]

This emphasis on the similar and complementary character of ethical and philosophic excellence points to a single consistent teaching on the best life for a human being. The argument suggests that ethical and philosophic excellence, though distinct, are not incompatible. The tentative character of the argument in Book

I gives way to greater, though still incomplete, specificity in Book X. The happiness of each individual, nonphilosopher and potential philosopher alike, depends upon the full development of the soul, a development that gives first but not exclusive priority to whatever theoretical capacity one might possess. The reader is led to conclude that one should give paramount importance to the life of study, depending upon ability and circumstances, while at the same time developing the more generally accessible ethical virtues.

Two Inconsistent Teachings: Persistent Tension

We should, however, be careful to observe that although Aristotle does not emphasize dissimilarity or dissonance in the relationship between ethical and theoretical virtue in Book X, neither does he deny it.[9] Indeed, he weaves into the argument of his concluding book three striking indications of persistent tension: (1) the unanswered question whether life is for the sake of pleasure (10.4.1175a18-19), (2) the suggestion that the practice of the greatest and most noble moral virtues impedes the highest human excellence (10.81178b1-5), and (3) the apparently insignificant character of moral virtue in light of divine activity (10.81178b7-23). Each of these passages is briefly discussed below.

(1) As we have already noted, in the course of his reconsideration of pleasure, Aristotle raises a crucial theoretical question: Is life for the sake of pleasure or pleasure for the sake of life? Gauthier and Jolif point out that the decision to put this question aside as inappropriate in the present context has occasioned a great deal of comment on the part of those who are uncomfortable with Aristotle's willingness to turn away from such a crucial issue. They observe that most major commentators (Alexander of Aphrodisias, Michael of Ephesus, St. Albert, St. Thomas, et al.) have not been able to resist the temptation to try to resolve a question that the text leaves in suspense. Gauthier and Jolif, finding some support in Burnet, proceed to argue that such efforts are misguided since, whatever the answer to this question, Aristotle is here arguing that the contemplative "activity-pleasure" *(le bloc opération-plaisir)* constitutes the ultimate end for human beings.[10] Although they are surely correct in maintaining that this constitutes the overall argument in Book X, their explanation does not adequately account for the passage in question, which explicitly raises the question whether life is for the sake of pleasure or pleasure for the sake of life. The discomfort of earlier commentators seems more justified than the effort to minimize a deliberately open-ended question by subordinating it to the most obvious conclusion of the *Ethics* as a whole.

The dismissal of a question that he has nevertheless put into the minds of his readers in some sense draws attention to the question itself and, in so doing, to the central difference between Books VII and X. What constitutes the fundamental standard for human beings? Is it pleasure or a kind of life that is characterized by noble disregard for questions of this sort? The disturbing character of Aristotle's failure to resolve this question in the concluding book of the ***Ethics*** is augmented by the fact that he had earlier cited with apparent approval, the belief that nothing prevents pleasure from being the supreme good (7.13. 1153b7-8), a view that implies that life is for the sake of pleasure. Without going so far as to suggest that Aristotle advocates a kind of philosophic hedonism, it is sufficient to observe that the unanswered question about pleasure in Book X, together with the arguments from Book VII (11-14) that it recalls, evidences the continuing presence of a perspective that is alien to the teaching on ethical virtue for which the ***Ethics*** is rightly famous.

(2) In his final discussion of happiness, Aristotle suggests that the external equipment necessary for great and noble actions may constitute an impediment to the life of study (10.8.1178b1-5). Although he does not elaborate the problem here, it is easily clarified in light of his earlier discussions. Peak moral virtues such as magnificence and magnanimity presuppose an abundance of external goods, something that in turn requires attentiveness to the economic and political circumstances that make these virtues possible and appropriate. A preoccupation with these concerns and with the constantly shifting circumstances from which they arise reduces both suitability and appreciation for a life given over to the contemplation of the unchanging beings of nature.

Moreover, whereas the pleasure associated with each activity enhances that activity, it has the further effect of impeding other activities (10.5.1175a29-b24). Given the morally edifying horizon that prevails in Book X, it is not surprising that Aristotle fails to apply this principle directly to the different activities of ethical and philosophic excellence. He restricts himself to the considerably less controversial observation that the pleasures arising from musical harmony can be an obstacle to the activity of philosophy. It is, however, difficult to imagine that someone who has experienced the nearly divine pleasures of contemplation would not find the pleasures associated with ethical virtue to be in some respect diminished.[11]

(3) In the course of his final assessment of ethical virtue, Aristotle turns once again to the question of divine activity (10.8.1178b7-23). It is here that the problematic relationship between ethical and intellectual virtue becomes most apparent. In what does the happiness of the gods consist? It would be ludicrous to try to conceive of them as practicing moral virtue, since all forms of virtuous conduct are "trifling and unworthy" *(mikra kai anaxia)* of gods (10.8.1178b17-18). The only possible activity appropriate to deities is some

form of contemplation. This description of the gods, one that echoes the earlier account in Book VII (7.14.1154b26-31), is Aristotle's most severe and most explicit criticism of the human tendency to project a concern for ethical virtue onto the divine. He argues instead that happiness is coextensive in its range with contemplation (10.8.1178b28-32). Given the essentially political character of human beings, human imitation of divine indifference toward moral virtue would be reprehensible. Nevertheless, an appropriate human approximation of divine detachment expresses itself in the cultivation of ethical virtue as a means to the godlike activity of contemplation, not as an end in itself.

By way of contrast, the happiness of the *kalos k'agathos* is limited, not only by a need for those external goods necessary for the practice of moral virtue, but because the most sublime happiness turns out to belong to another kind of activity. Aristotle's depiction of divine disinterestedness, together with his identification of human happiness and the godlike activity of contemplation, points to the existence of a still unresolved tension between ethical and philosophic excellence. This problem is exacerbated by Aristotle's further undeveloped suggestion that the activity of *nous*, more than anything else, constitutes the identity of a human being (10.7.1178a5-8), a suggestion that undercuts his earlier insistence on the composite nature of human being as the most salient aspect of human identity and therefore happiness.

Whereas the dominant argument of Book X establishes the superior happiness of the philosophic life within a context emphasizing the similar and complementary character of ethical and intellectual excellence, these three brief but pointed remarks suggest that the exact relationship between them remains problematic. Those most attuned to these notes of discord are likely to detect in the ***Ethics*** the presence of two inconsistent teachings on the best way to live as a human being.

Concluding Arguments: Gods, Moral Nobility, and the City

The sharpness of the conflict between the requirements and sensibilities of moral and contemplative virtue is reflected no human and divine activity in Books VII and X (7.14.1154b20-31; 10.8.1178b7-23). This teaching, however, is at odds with the final argument of the ***Ethics*** on this subject (10.8.1179a22-29). Aristotle maintains that if, as is generally held, the gods exercise some concern over human affairs, they are likely to benefit those who most love and honor godlike excellence in themselves. Those who cultivate intelligence *(nous)* and undertake "right and noble deeds" *(orthōs te kai kalōs prattontas)* are most beloved by the gods and recompensed with godlike happiness. The premise of this argument flatly contradicts Aristotle's previous description of the gods. Divine indifference to moral virtue has given way to a more consoling preoccupation with and concern for correct and noble human actions.

The contradiction, however, does not lie in Aristotle's thinking, since this final argument about the gods is explicitly drawn from a pervasive and decent opinion rather than from Aristotle himself. Thus, without actually retracting his theoretical speculations about divine activity, he overlays them with a concluding and morally edifying argument about the gods. The gods reward those who practice moral virtue and honor intelligence. Despite the profound *theoretical* differences that separate the two portrayals of the divine in this chapter, it is important to observe that, taken together, these accounts direct readers to a single consistent *practical* teaching: One ought to imitate the gods as much as possible and, depending upon one's abilities and circumstances, this means giving a privileged place to intelligence in either its theoretical or practical manifestations. Whereas the contemplative activity of theoretical intelligence enables one to *experience* godlike happiness, Aristotle's concluding argument holds out the *promise* of such happiness to those who honor intelligence by performing noble deeds. The fulfillment of this promise depends upon the veracity of the pervasive and decent opinion about divine solicitude for human affairs. Although attentive readers might be more impressed by the distance between human and divine concerns and what that implies about the best way of life for a human being, the final reference to the gods in the *Ethics* encourages all readers to live in accordance with the best thing in them and to revere rather than disparage those who most embody the peculiar excellence of philosophic contemplation.

The concluding chapter of the *Ethics* returns to a theme that has implicitly informed the study as a whole and explicitly guided the consideration in Book X, namely, the moral education of the young. Although speech may be sufficient to encourage generous youths to pursue a life of moral nobility *(kalokagathia),* speech by itself is unlikely to awaken a similar desire in the majority of human beings (10.9. 1179b7-10). Since most are ruled by passions, compulsion and punishment are more effective than the appeal to reason and the noble (10.9. 1180a3-5). Hence, there arises a need for laws that take their bearings from moral nobility but are also backed by the strong arm of the civic body. The application of force is necessary not only for the city in that it establishes the rudiments of political order, but also and especially for individual citizens since it encourages them to live in accordance with the best thing in them.

If the argument of the preceding two chapters demotes the life of moral virtue in light of the most perfectly happy life of philosophy, the concluding chapter of the *Ethics* draws upon the broader context within which

that argument has been framed. The extent to which these two ways of life are similar and complementary is most evident when they are contrasted to the lower and more pervasive alternative that dominates actual political practice. Aristotle's sober evaluation of the nature and limits of the majority of human beings directs our attention to the third component of the threefold hierarchy that has been especially prominent in Book X. Those whose lives are susceptible to the influence of reason and the noble define *orthos logos* for the majority of human beings whose lives are circumscribed by passion. Aristotle concludes his study of ethics and introduces the study of politics in a way that allows the resplendent character of moral virtue to stand together with philosophic contemplation as the authoritative standard for the laws of the city. In so doing, he emphasizes the dignity of a life characterized by the practice of moral virtue, its practical importance for politics, and the need that all those who bear primary responsibility for the city have for the philosopher, who—in the person of Aristotle—promises to help his readers gain a better understanding of the crucial relationship between virtue and actual political practice in the second half of his "philosophy concerning the human things."

Consistent Inconsistency

The continuing controversy over Aristotle's teaching on the precise relationship between moral and theoretical excellence is well grounded in the text. I have attempted to show that the ambiguity of this treatment is due, at least in part, to the fact that he provides two different accounts of this relationship, a fact that is itself attributable to the different audiences to which the book is addressed.

For the majority of Aristotle's decent, reflective, but not essentially philosophic, readers, ethical virtue is presented on its own terms and with a degree of clarity and precision that is appropriate to its subject matter. Although he argues for the existence of something higher than the life of ethical virtue, the overarching teaching of Book X takes issue with the widespread human tendency to identify happiness with the pleasures of play by pointing to the greater satisfactions to be derived from the practice of moral virtue. Moreover, the emphasis on a similar and complementary relationship between ethical and philosophic excellence directs readers away from the seductive extremes of unreflective patriotism and political domination. By subordinating passion to intelligence and intelligence to contemplation, Aristotle points toward that aspect of human activity that offers the greatest possibility of happiness. Insofar as decent persons are more concerned to cultivate the life of the mind than amass money, power, and prestige, they are able to experience something of the godlike happiness of the philosopher.

To those who are most attracted to the theoretical life, Aristotle's treatment offers a second, more problematic ground for serious concern with ethical virtue. The *Ethics* urges attentiveness to the practice of moral virtue, not as an end in itself or as something that provides the greatest happiness but as a means to the end of contemplation. This argument is double edged. Whereas it is reassuring to learn that philosophers are or should be concerned about moral virtue, the argument simultaneously raises a question as to whether their motivation is consistent with the requirements of moral virtue itself.

A harsh expression of this so-called intellectualist argument is found in *Magna Moralia,* where ethical virtue is reduced to the status of a household manager who attends to daily necessities so that the lord of the house might enjoy the freedom and leisure necessary to engage in philosophic thought (*MM* 1.34.1198b9-20; see *EE*8.3.1249b4-25). The difference between this account and the one given in the *Nicomachean Ethics* is instructive. Although both discussions clearly affirm the superiority of the philosophic life, in the *Ethics* moral virtue is said to be subordinate to, but never the servant of, philosophic contemplation. Whereas the latter view suggests that ethical virtue is ultimately devoid of intrinsic dignity, the argument of the *Ethics* is distinctive precisely for its insistence on an independent status for ethical virtue. Indeed, Aristotle's often-repeated assertion that moral acts are undertaken for their own sake comes as close as any single line to constituting a refrain for the entire book. In the *Ethics* Aristotle subordinates the life of ethical virtue to the philosophic way of life while at the same time retaining a sense of its importance. The life of ethical virtue, unlike the life of slavery, does result in substantial human happiness. Nevertheless, a still greater possibility exists for those who are able to take their bearings from the supremely happy activity of philosophic contemplation.

It is, I believe, a mistake to conclude that Aristotle's teaching on the best life is inconsistent. The deeper consistency that I have attempted to bring to light is reflected in his refusal to simplify the question of the best way of life. His depiction of ethical virtue is faithful to the phenomenon of ethical virtue as it appears in the lives of its best exemplars. At the same time, his account of philosophic activity preserves without emphasizing a sense of the inevitable controversy that accompanies a life of radical inquiry. Theoretical and practical matters vie for the attention of human intelligence and, given the very different and necessarily limited capacities of human beings, the full development of one can lessen appreciation for the importance of the other.[12] Aristotle consistently resists the temptation to try to reconcile completely two elevated ways of life that cannot be in every respect reconciled.

The well-known conclusion of the *Ethics* regarding the superiority of the philosophic life is shaped by a considerably less-appreciated Aristotelian concern for the character and limits of nonphilosophic readers. Although it would be wrong to conclude from an awareness of the rhetorical dimension of his arguments that Aristotle considers those arguments to be false, it would be equally misleading to identify them in an unqualified way with his own view of the subject. The rhetorical presentation of philosophy in the *Ethics* succeeds in muting, without actually denying, a fundamental tension between philosophy and politics. Careful study of the concluding book of the *Ethics* provides the reader with an example of the Aristotelian understanding of the art of rhetoric, an art that is used not to obscure the nature of philosophy but rather to reveal substantial, if incomplete, truths about it. If, as Aristotle maintains, Alcidamas's rhetorical claim that philosophy should be considered "a bulwark of the laws" is too exaggerated to be credible (***Rh. [Rhetoric]*** 3.3.1406b5-15), Aristotle's rhetorical art is calculated to win at least a partial acceptance of philosophy on the part of those who are or will be most responsible for directing the affairs of the city.

Notes

[1] The exceptions concern two of Eudoxus's arguments in support of the view that pleasure is the good. Eudoxus observes that all things seek pleasure and avoid pain and that pleasure is sought as an end in itself. Although Aristotle's subsequent clarification provides an implicit alternative to these arguments, it should also be recalled that Aristotle had himself employed comparable evidence in defense of the view now attributed to Eudoxus. The fact that all beings seek pleasure was cited by Aristotle to support the view that pleasure is the supreme good (7.13.1153b25-32). Similarly, his argument that some pleasures enjoy the status of ends was intended to demonstrate that there need not be anything better than pleasure (7.12.1153a7-11). The absence of an explicit critique for these two Eudoxian arguments might prompt attentive students to recall Aristotle's earlier endorsement of these positions.

[2] Aristotle later uses the same verb *(suzeugnumi)* to describe the relationship between prudence and moral virtue (10.8.1178a16-17). Both the dismissal of the question of pleasure (to which we will return) and subsequent argument about prudence and pleasure share the same degree of clarity as his circular exposition of the relationship between prudence and moral virtue in Book VI. Cf. 6.12.1144a20-31 and 6.13.1144b21-24.

[3] As we have had occasion to observe, Aristotle considers a similar problem in Book I; namely, that pleasure, especially sensual pleasure, appears to constitute happiness for human beings. In that context, however,

he simply disparages this view, maintaining that such a life is equally well suited to cattle (1.5.1095b14-22; see 2.9.1109b7-12).

[4] The morally debilitating effect of the example of the powerful appears to motivate Polus's attack on Socrates in the *Gorgias*. Polus maintains that everyone, including Socrates, consciously or unconsciously envies the powerful (468e; 470e-71e).

[5] Aristotle is elsewhere more forthcoming about the difference between the moral-political and contemplative ways of life. One might recall, for example, his differentiation of three ways of life at the outset of the *Ethics* (1.5.1095b14-96a5) or the discussion of prudence and wisdom and the different exemplars supplied for each (see 6.5.1140a24-b11; 6.7.1141a20-b14). His reference in the *Politics* to the dispute between those who agree that the most choiceworthy life is accompanied by virtue explicitly acknowledges the magnitude of the controversy that he plays down in the present context (see, esp. *Pol.* 7.2.1324a25-35).

[6] The kinship between excellent practical activity and contemplation is central in Kraut's interpretation of the *Ethics*. See esp. pp. 58-59, 325.

[7] I agree with Germaine Paulo's suggestion that Aristotle's account of contemplative activity in X.7-8 is to some extent a caricature of philosophic activity, although we offer different assessments of both the nature and purpose of this caricature. I disagree with her contention that these arguments are essentially ironic, although Paulo's analysis opens up the interesting possibility that Aristotle's use of rhetoric in the *Ethics* is also shaped by a concern for his philosophic audience, particularly those influenced by the teachings of Plato. "The Problematic Relation between Practical Virtue and Theoretical Virtue in the *Nicomachean Ethics*: Integration or Divergence?" Presented at the annual meeting of the Midwest Political Science Association, Chicago, 1994.

[8] Although the peak moral virtues of magnificence and magnanimity require an abundance of resources, both material and political, Aristotle includes less splendid and less political versions of these dispositions in his account of moral virtue. Generosity and a nameless virtue regarding honor require only modest resources (see esp., 4.4.1125b1-8). Whereas the former two virtues may prove to be a hindrance to contemplation, this is not clearly the case with respect to the latter.

[9] If the preceding section sketches the extent of my agreement with Hardie, Clark, and Kraut, the discussion that follows indicates something of my appreciation for the problems raised by Ackrill and Cooper.

[10] Gauthier and Jolif, *L'Éthique*, vol. 2, pp. 843-44. Cf.

Burnet, *Ethics,* pp. 437-38.

[11] Some indication of Aristotle's restraint on this point emerges in contrast to Plato's more grating formulation of the problem in the *Republic*. Socrates likens philosophic activity to dwelling among the Isles of the Blessed, in comparison to which a preoccupation with life in the polis seems to be a kind of madness (*Rep.* 496a-e).

[12] I have been influenced by Nagel's formulation of the competition between theoretical and practical reason although we emphasize different aspects of the contest. "Aristotle on *Eudaimonia*," pp. 257-58.

Bibliography of Cited Works

References to Aristotle and Plato are to the page and line numbers of the Oxford Classical Text editions.

Ackrill, J. L. "Aristotle on *Eudaimonia*." In *Essays on Aristotle's Ethics,* edited by A. Rorty. Berkeley: University of California Press, 1980.

Burnet, John, ed. *The Ethics of Aristotle.* London: Methuen, 1900.

Clark, Stephen. *Aristotle's Man: Speculations Upon Aristotelian Anthropology.* Oxford: Clarendon Press, 1975.

Cooper, John. "Contemplation and Happiness: A Reconsideration." In *Moral Philosophy: Historical and Contemporary Essays,* edited by Starr and Taylor. Milwaukee: Marquette University Press, 1989.

———. "Forms of Friendship." *Review of Metaphysics* 30 (1977): 619-48.

———. *Reason and Human Good in Aristotle.* Cambridge: Harvard University Press, 1975. Reprint, Indianapolis: Hackett Publishing Company, 1986.

Gauthier, René, and Jean Jolif, eds. *L'Éthique à Nicomaque.* 2 vols. Louvain: Publications Universitaires, 1970.

Hardie, W. F. R. "Aristotle on the Best Life for a Man." *Philosophy* 54 (1979): 35-50.

———. "Aristotle's Doctrine That Virtue Is a Mean." In *Articles on Aristotle.* Vol. 2, *Ethics and Politics,* edited by Barnes, Schofield, and Sorabji. New York: St. Martin's Press, 1978.

———. *Aristotle's Ethical Theory.* Oxford: Clarendon Press, 1968.

———. "The Final Good in Aristotle's *Ethics.*" *Philosophy* 40 (1965): 277-95.

———. "Magnanimity in Aristotle's *Ethics.*" *Phronesis* 23 (1978): 63-79.

Kraut, Richard. *Aristotle on the Human Good.* Princeton, N.J.: Princeton University Press, 1989.

Nagel, Thomas. "Aristotle on *Eudaimonia.*" In *Essays on Aristotle's Ethics,* edited by A. Rorty. Berkeley: University of California Press, 1980.

———. "Aristotle on *Eudaimonia.*" *Phronesis* 17 (1972): 252-59.

Paulo, Germaine. "The Problematic Relation between Practical Virtue and Theoretical Virtue in the *Nicomachean Ethics:* Integration or Divergence?" Paper presented at the annual meeting of the Midwest Political Science Association, Chicago, 1994.

Abbreviations

Apology	*Apo.*
Eudemian Ethics	*EE*
Gorgias	*Grg.*
Magna Moralia	*MM*
Metaphysics	*Meta.*
Nicomachean Ethics	*NE*
Politics	*Pol.*
Posterior Analytics	*Pos. An.*
Protagoras	*Protag.*
Republic	*Rep.*
Rhetoric	*Rh.*
Topics	*Top.*

FURTHER READING

Allan, D. J. "The Shape of Wisdom." In *The Philosophy of Aristotle,* second edition, pp. 70-29. London: Oxford University Press, 1970.

> Outlines the topics covered in *Metaphysics,* focusing on the nature of *being.*

Allen, Sister Prudence. "Aristotle." In *The Concept of Woman: The Aristotelian Revolution; 750 B.C.-A.D. 1250,* pp. 83-126. Grand Rapids, Mich.: William B. Eerdmans Publishing Co., 1985.

> Examines in detail the manner by which Aristotle develops, through several works including *Metaphysics,* the concept of sexual polarity.

Bambrough, Renford. "Aristotle on Justice: A Paradigm of Philosophy." In *New Essays on Plato and Aristotle,* edited by Renford Bambrough, pp. 159-74. London: Routledge & Kegan Paul, 1965.

> Examines Aristotle's response to the criticism of his usage of the term "justice" to denote, in one sense, "justice-in-general," and in another sense, "virtue-in-general."

Burnyeat, M. F. "Aristotle on Learning to Be Good." In *Essays on Aristotle's Ethics,* edited by Amélie Oksenberg Rorty, pp. 69-92. Berkeley: University of California Press, 1980.

> Attempts to "reconstruct Aristotle's picture of the good man's development over time," and studies as well the "weak-willed . . . man who knows the good but does not always achieve it in action."

Cooper, John M. "Moral Virtue and Human Flourishing." In *Reason and Human Good in Aristotle,* pp. 89-143. Cambridge, Mass.: Harvard University Press, 1975.

> Argues that Aristotle's notion of "human flourishing" was meant to be a coherent theory, even though it is often regarded as a "set of disconnected remarks." Cooper provides a detailed analysis of the subject and attempts to account for the apparent inconsistencies within the theory as presented in *Nicomachean Ethics.*

Fortenbaugh, W. W. "Aristotle on Slaves and Women," in *Articles on Aristotle: 2. Ethics and Politics,* edited by Jonathan Barnes, Malcolm Schofield, and Richard Sorabji, pp. 135-39. London: Duckworth, 1977.

> Examines Aristotle's views on the roles of women and slaves in society, as well as on the narture of their souls. Fortenbaugh demonstrates that Aristotle's political views on these subjects are supportred by his ethical and psychological theories regarding the varying abilites of women and slaves to deliberate.

Hintikka, K. Jaakko J. "Aristotle and the Ambiguity of Ambiguity." *Inquiry* 2, No. 3 (Autumn 1959): 137-51.

> Maintains that Aristotle's "notion of ambiguity is not as unambiguous as one perhaps hopes." Hintikka explains that Aristotle differentiates between two types of "multiplicity of meaning": multiplicity of applications and "mere ambiguity," or homonymy.

Homiak, Marcia. "Feminism and Aristotle's Rational Ideal." In *Feminism and Ancient Philosophy,* edited by Julie K. Ward, pp. 118-37. New York: Routledge, 1996.

Asserts that despite the reputation of Aristotle's works as being derogatory toward women, in fact his view of the rational life, the life that offers the full measure of happiness, is "neither inherently masculine nor inherently exploitive."

Jaeger, Werner. "Aristotle's Place in History." In *Aristotle, Fundamentals of the History of His Development,* translated by Richard Robinson, pp. 368-406. Oxford: Clarendon Press, 1934.

Assesses the contributions and achievements of Aristotle in the areas of analytical thinking, science, metaphysics, the analysis of man, and the development of philosophy as the "universal science."

Reale, Giovanni. "The Basic Points of Contact between Plato and Aristotle: The Truthfulness of the 'Second Voyage'," and "The Basic Differences between Aristotle and Plato." In *A History of Ancient Philosophy, Vol. II. Plato and Aristotle,* edited and translated by John R. Catan, pp. 253-58 and 259-61. Albany: State University of New York Press, 1990.

Maintains that a study of Aristotle's works must begin with an understanding of Aristotle's criticism of Plato within a historical and a philosophical perspective; summarizes the Platonic metaphysical issues which Aristotle reinterpreted and elaborated on; notes aspects of metaphysical thought newly developed by Aristotle (not found in Plato); and traces the points of metaphysical opposition between Plato and Aristotle.

Poetics

INTRODUCTION

In the *Poetics,* Aristotle presents the principles of artistic composition. While the work treats many forms of imaginative creation, including comedy, epic, dialogue, and even music and dance, it focuses most particularly on the elements of tragedy.

Textual History

Little is known about the fate of Aristotle's works after his death. It is believed by some scholars that for about two hundred years following his death, the works were either lost or hidden. They were discovered by Sulla (138-78 B.C.) and brought to Rome. According to one prominent scholar, Lane Cooper, the *Poetics* dates from some time prior to 323 B.C. Cooper comments that the *Poetics* is perhaps a version of Aristotle's lecture notes, or perhaps even a collection of notes transcribed by someone who attended Aristotle's lectures on the subject. Modern editions of Aristotle's works derive from Roman editions dating back to the late first century b.c. In the Middle Ages, Latin and Arabic translations broadened the influence of Aristotle's teachings, although, as Marvin Herrick has noted, the translations available in England during this time were often thought to be of poor quality. By the end of the fifteenth century, however, Greek versions of the text of the *Poetics* were available in Italy, and Englishmen traveled there to study it. From that point on, Aristotle's views on the poetic art gained and lost influencein various periods, but gradually became a significant force in the criticism of poetry, drama, and literature.

Critical Reception

Just as Aristotle devotes most of his attention in *Poetics* to tragedy, modern scholars dedicate much of their critical energy to evaluating Aristotle's views on tragedy. In the English translation of Aristotle's definition, tragedy is an "imitation" of a "serious and complete" action, with a "definite magnitude," or theme, that is "humanly significant." Tragedy employs "pleasing language" or "enhanced utterance;" it is characterized by action rather than narration; and it achieves "through pity and fear" what is known as "catharsis" or "purgation." A major issue of critical debate is this concept of imitation. Often, critics attempt to answer the question of what is to be imitated, and in doing so, defend the concept of dramatic imitation against the negative connotation of an imitation being less pure or noble than the original. John W. Draper has noted that while "imitation" has often been misunderstood, it should be conceived of as art's imitation of nature, where nature is understood to be the "creative force of the universe." Charles Sears Baldwin has discussed the Aristotelian concept of imitation as the representation of the character, emotions, and actions of men. Like Draper, Laurence Berns has argued that by imitation Aristotle meant the imitation of nature. Berns goes on to explain that not only is art to imitate what is "actual in nature," but the perfection that is potential in nature as well. Norman Gulley has taken a position similar to Baldwin's by maintaining that art represents human behavior and its moral aspects.

Critics also grapple with other aspects of Aristotle's definition of tragedy, especially the role of catharsis. Catherine Lord has explained that to Aristotle, tragedy was a "goal-directed system," with the goal being catharsis. G. S. Brett has examined this goal, noting that the Greek term infers purgation and purification. Brett has also stressed that Aristotle's definition of tragedy makes no reference to the effects to be experienced by spectators, and suggests that purgation is essential to tragedy without an audience to undergo the catharsis. Berns, on the other hand, maintains that the catharsis Aristotle describes is, in effect, a moral purification in which audience members or readers are taught what to fear and what to pity.

Another major source of debate among critics is Aristotle's emphasis on the primacy of plot over all other elements of tragedy. Catherine Lord has quoted the *Poetics* as stating that "without action there cannot be a tragedy; there may be without character." After noting that many critics resist this notion that character is entirely subordinate to plot, Lord has argued that in fact all issues related to character are a function of plot. Lord discusses the concept of *hamartia* as a function of plot as well, maintaining that while this word is often interpreted as the hero's tragic flaw, it is in fact a "simple mistake," not a moral frailty. Colin Hardie, however, has contended that plot and character are inseparable within the context of Aristotle's entire theory of poetics, even though parts of the *Poetics* seem to identify an antithesis between plot and character. Hardie explains that within the drama, the "facts and circumstances" through which character becomes defined are the plot. It is in an effort to "guarantee the individuality of character," Hardie maintains, that Aristotle emphasizes the significance of plot.

Aristotle's treatment of tragedy, combined with his coverage of other poetic arts, has contributed to the lasting significance of this treatise. The work has greatly influenced the development of literary criticism and continues to be regarded, in the words of Lane Cooper, as "one of the most illuminating and influential books ever produced by the sober human mind."

PRINCIPAL WORKS

*De Poetica [Poetics] (treatise)

*The date of composition for the work is unkown, but it is believed to have been written before 323 B.C.

PRINCIPAL ENGLISH TRANSLATIONS

The Works of Aristotle Translated into English [edited by J. A. Smith and W. D. Ross] 1910-52

Aristotle's Theory of Poetry and Fine Art [translated by S. H. Butcher] 1911

CRITICISM

John W. Draper (essay date 1921)

SOURCE: "Aristotelian 'Mimesis' in England," in *PMLA*, Vol. XXXVI, No. 3, September, 1921, pp. 372-400.

[In the following essay, Draper studies the way in which the understanding of "mimesis," or imitation (as discussed by Aristotle in Poetics*), changed over the course of the eighteenth century in England. Draper notes that, in general, the concept was largely misinterpreted.]*

Of the many disputed terms in the *Poetics*, [*mimēsis*] "imitation," has always been one of the most fruitful of discussion and of misconception; and these misconceptions are particularly significant because, for whole periods, they were potent in moulding creative activity not only in literature,[1] but also in painting and in music. When "imitation" is considered in the light of its technical use in Plato and in Aristotle, its real meaning emerges with some distinctness.[2] Far from the naturalistic theory of a direct and slavish copy of objects and actions, Aristotle's [*mimēsis*] is a distinctly idealistic conception, and signifies "creating according to a true idea."[3] Thus, when we are told that Art imitates Na-

ture, "Nature" is not a particular thing or act, but is the creative force of the universe.[4] With this conception, we can justify Aristotle's declaration that music is the most imitative of all the arts: it is the most fluid; and its flux is governed most completely by the universal laws of unity, proportion, and symmetry. The conception is almost Platonic; and it makes Aristotelian [*mimēsis*] appear in a sense almost diametrically opposed to the common meaning of the Latin *imitatio* and the English "imitation."

English critics of the Seventeenth Century, however, following the Italian and French Aristotelians, translated [*mimēsis*] as "imitation"; and, moreover, they argued, since Homer and Virgil give us a perfect view of "Nature methodized," let us copy them instead of Nature. Thus [*mimēsis*] was burdened with two false meanings, one making it a copy of actions and things, the other a copy of accepted masterpieces.[5] Until the latter part of the century, both these false meanings passed current in England as vulgate Aristotelianism, and indeed did some injury to the fame of their supposed author among critics of a semi-Romantic stamp. The editors of the Greek text[6] who, one might suppose, would have corrected the error, give it at least tacit support[7]; and the translators regularly render [*mimēsis*] as "copy" or "imitation." An anonymous English version through the French of Dacier,[8] which held this field alone until 1775, excepted only Bacchic songs from the general idea of copying; and the fact that music had to be made an exception, whereas Aristotle found it the most imitative of all the arts, shows how far "imitation" had wandered from its original meaning. A first-hand knowledge of Aristotle, even in translation, seems to have been exceptional: Walpole mentions him five times in his letters—usually coupled with Bossu and the "Rules"[9]; and Cowper, at the age of fifty-three, had "never in his life perused a page of Aristotle."[10] The *Poetics* were much reverenced, but little read; and the interpretation of [*mimēsis*] depended almost altogether upon secondary sources. Some writers in fact seem to have used it without any thought of an Aristotelian origin.

The dictionaries shed very little light upon the subject: even Dr. Johnson gave no meaning that approximates the Aristotelian sense.[11] Writers on rhetoric and the severer critics of poetic theory, when they had occasion to treat of "imitation" at all,[12] regularly interpreted it as copying. Bysshe urged the "superior Mind" to "generous Emulation" of Shakespeare, Milton and Dryden, and, by way of auxiliary, appended "A Collection of the Most Natural and Sublime Thoughts," codified in convenient form.[13] Constable advised imitation of the ancients;[14] and the anonymous author of the *Prolusiones,* writing with Aristotle directly in his eye, unquestionably takes *"imitatio"* to mean *"copy."*[15] As late as 1785, moreover, Owen translated *Juvenal* in order that "the young scholar" might learn to superadd his "spirit" to the "correct and graceful ease" of Horace.[16] "Imitation" in the sense of copying was the common conception that the age gleaned from its dictionaries and rhetorics, as well as from the commentators and translators of Aristotle. The rhetoricians, moreover, regularly accepted it as a copy of models, enjoined it in the school-room, and so moulded the taste and the creative production of the age. Very truly did Hurd declare: "The most universal cause, inducing *imitation* in great writers, is the force of early *discipline and education*."[17]

Many writers on æsthetic theory, moreover, especially in the earlier part of the century, advocated "imitation" in the sense of copying models. Felton's *Dissertation on the Classics,* which appeared in 1709, and passed into its fifth edition in 1753, discussed "imitation" in the sense of free translation, and then added that "more properly," it meant "proposing some excellent Writer for a Pattern, and endeavoring to copy his Perfections in the most distinguishing Parts of his Character."[18] Gildon in his *Complete Art of Poetry,* declared Aristotle to be based on "Reason, Nature, and the Practice of the Ancients;" apparently one is to imitate the ancients, and follow the rules derived from their work.[19] Lord Lansdowne actually thought that Nature might be imitated by following the rules of Mulgrave and Roscommon.[20] Even in the latter part of the century, there are examples of this point of view. Stockdale distinguished "imitation" from plagiarism,[21] by declaring that an imitation was an "improvement" of the original.[22]

But more important than the force of tradition and the influence of the schools and of the critics was the actual example of recognized authors. According to Johnson, the copying of literary models started with Oldham and Rochester, and was "Pope's favorite amusement."[23] Swift, in *The Art of Sinking in Poetry,* casts satiric shafts at the "universal genius" who "pours forth five or six epic poems with greater facility, than five or six pages can be produced by an elaborate and servile copier after nature or the ancients."[24] Most of Pope's best work, from the *Essay on Criticism* down through the *Epistles,* imitates Horace. Johnson imitated Juvenal; and the *Georgics* and *Eclogues* of Virgil furnished models for the mob of gentlemen who wrote with only too much ease. Many of the leisure class translated and paraphrased the classics for enjoyment; and many respectable clergymen and teachers did so for either pleasure or patronage. Example was further enforced by numerous *obiter dicta.* Steele advised imitation.[25] Pope praised Virgil for imitating Homer;[26] and, in the *Preface* to his own *Poems,* he says:

> All that is left us is to recommend our productions by the imitation of the Ancients: and it will be found true, that in every age, the highest character for sense and learning has been obtain'd by those who have been most indebted to them.[27]

Even Joseph Wharton, who belongs to an opposing school, allowed a place to literary imitation.[28] Mason declared that the aspiring author is "to take the best models of antiquity for his guides; and to adapt those models, as near as may be, to the manner and taste of his own times."[29]

During the earlier half of the century, [*mimēsis*] interpreted as a rather servile copy, sometimes of Nature, more frequently of approved masterpieces, largely dominated English letters. It had been ingrained by a long tradition; it had been fortified by the laxity of the lexicographers and the Aristotelian commentators, by the formalism of the rhetoricians and the schoolmasters, and by the subtle but powerful conditions of book-selling and literary patronage. But literature cannot live indefinitely upon its own vitals. Rymer and Bysshe at the very opening of the century brought the theory of imitation to the *ne plus ultra;* and Pope accomplished in practice the last refinements of literary copying. The later Neoclassicists acknowledged Pope as their master; but his very superiority obliged them to differ somewhat from the detail of his practice: thus reaction became a fact in literature not only with Thomson, Young, Gray, Beattie, Mason and the pseudo-romanticists of the mid-century, but even with men like Churchill, Colman and Lloyd, in subtle matters of diction, versification, and trope.[30]

The reaction of the theorists against "imitation" is foreshadowed even in the Seventeenth Century. Shaftesbury, in his [*To Kalon*] put Beauty on a par with the Good; he declared, moreover, that nothing was "so improving, nothing so natural, so congenial to the liberal arts, as that reigning liberty and high spirit of a people, which from the habit of judging in the highest matters for themselves, makes them freely judge of other subjects."[31] Such an æsthetic criterion has nothing in common with the copying of models; and Shaftesbury's influence was powerful for many decades.[32] Hutcheson, who popularized and attempted to systematize his work, freed himself largely from Aristotle, and declared that there were two sorts of beauty, "absolute" and "relative," the former beautiful because of the "Uniformity in the object itself," the latter, because of the "Resemblance to some Original." In the former class, he put geometrical and mathematical figures,[33] music, architecture, gardening and rural nature, with its plants and animals.[34] Only to the second type of art did he allow the applicability of "imitation."[35] Thus he limited the term, and denied its universal dominance.

Various foreign influences, moreover, especially French, contributed to the movement. Abbé du Bos made "imitation" apply only to the "artist without genius:" it might make him correct, but could not make him great.[36] Estève broke away from the imitation of models to fall into the slavish mimicking of external Nature;[37] he is, however, sentimental enough to submit all writing to "vérité du sentiment."[38] Batteaux declared: "imiter c'est copier un modèle;"[39] but the "model" turns out to be the existing world, the historic world or the fabulous world.[40] The rationalistic spirit of *l'Encyclopédie*, furthermore, manifested in the psychological investigations of the Abbé de Condillac[41] was inclined to ignore imitation; and Montesquieu[42] and Voltaire[43] agreed in making taste the result of our analysis of æsthetic impressions: the authority of Aristotle and his Renaissance commentators was being replaced by an effort at scientific investigation. The vogue of Longinus, moreover, whose treatise *On the Sublime* went through at least a dozen British editions during the century,[44] and the rise of interest in Plato and Neo-Platonism,[45] did not contribute to support any contracted and false theory of [*mimēsis*].

As early as the fourth decade of the century, writers can be found who ignored "imitation" entirely,[46] but more common are those who discuss imitation either to attack, to limit, or to re-define it. A rather large number of authors rejected "imitation" entirely in its more extreme interpretation of copying models. As early as 1713, Felton in his *Dissertation on the Classics* had advised that the aspiring author "imbibe their Sense" without "tying himself up to an Imitation of any of them; much less to copy or transcribe them."[47] Blackwall praised Theocritus for having "the Air of genteel Negligence and unforced Easiness which no Study or Imitation can reach."[48] In 1724, Welsted declared: "Imitation is the Bane of Writing, nor ever was a good Author, that entirely formed himself on the Model of another. . . . "[49] Fielding would have nothing of "the abominable rules of Aristotle."[50] Byrom pointed out the danger of imitating faults as well as good qualities; and he adds that, even when the archetypes are of the best, "Barely to imitate is not so well."[51] Lloyd ridiculed the whole process:

> While those who grasp at reputation,
> From imitating imitation,
> Shall hunt each cranny, nook and creek,
> For precious fragments from the Greek,
> And rob the spital and the waste,
> For sense and sentiment and taste.[52]

Young found two kinds of "imitation," one of nature, one of authors; and he devoted several pages to a comparison, much to the disadvantage of the latter.[53] Armstrong thought the copying of models of use only for the tyro.[54] Greene put the case at length:

> The garden of Criticism has almost constantly been over-run with the weeds of Ill-management. The earlier laborers, who have ranged its walks with a methodical exactness, have sacrificed beauty to decorum, while the finical conceits of modern refinement have turned them into an open lawn, preserving only in favorite corners some inelegant ornaments. . . . [55]

Sterne felt that the truth of imitation in both painting and poetry should, if needs must, be sacrificed to beauty.[56] *The Circle of the Sciences* declared that "the rules observed by ancient poets" do not apply;[57] and, in 1781, Cowper unequivocally stated: "Imitation even of the best models, is my aversion; it is servile and mechanical, a trick that has enabled many to usurp the name of author. . . . "[58]

The repudiation of models was intimately connected with the discussion of "imitation" as a transcript of Nature; and a large number of writers, especially in the midcentury, tried to adjust this conception to *dicta* borrowed from Sentimental or from Rationalistic sources. Dacier had opened the way by his vague definition of "imitation;" and Addison had excepted "the fairy way of writing" from all ordinary rules.[59] Trapp and Pemberton were disturbed that Aristotle had made "action" the subject of "imitation." The former extended imitation to include the copying of static objects;[60] the latter declared art to be the imitation of men, and called Aristotle "this presumed oracle of criticism."[61] Brown admitted degrees of imitation in various arts, according to their ability to give a literal transcript of life. He found tragedy more imitative than epic, and pure description the most imitative of all poetry.[62] According to Francklin, all that "Art hath called her own" is imitation:

> Great Nature only is Original.[63]

The late '50's and the early '60's are full of discussion of "imitation." Joseph Warton took a stand[64] somewhat similar to that of Trapp and Pemberton, and applied "imitation" to "the internal constitution of man," to "characters and manners and sentiments."[65] Burke, on the other hand, felt that no poetry but dramatic could be classed as "strictly imitation."[66] Hume sought the basis of good taste in the critic's delicacy of imagination.[67] Dr. Johnson's common-sense Neo-classicism disapproved entirely of anything smacking of plagiarism; he expressed doubt about the copying of models—although he indulged in it himself in *London,* and he allowed extensive borrowing.[68] Armstrong tried to conciliate "imitation" of Nature with a thoroughly sentimental theory of art: he paints the genius as a paragon of moral and æsthetic sensibility, and gives him the task of depicting the passions and emotions of Man.[69] Gerard thought that "exactness of resemblance" could "degenerate into disagreeable servility."[70] Goldsmith, in like manner, expressed the opinion: "It is the business of art to imitate nature, but not with a servile pencil."[71] Webb tried to classify the arts according to their ability to imitate, and found painting inferior to poetry and music inferior to painting.[72] Ogilvie quoted Dacier's vague definition, and referred the reader to his translation of the ***Poetics.***[73] Lord Kames distinguished at least two different sorts of imitation, epic and dramatic;[74] and Akenside, in 1763, called imitation of models only as a "secondary pleasure" in works of imagination, but seemed to consider all art a mere transcript of Nature: " . . . painting and sculpture directly copy external appearances . . . music and poetry bring them back to remembrance by signs universally established and understood."[75]

During the last third of the century, "imitation" lost ground very rapidly. Hurd found poetry "above all *other modes of imitation*," because it "conveys distinct and clear notices of this class of *moral and religious* conceptions;"[76] but he looks to "experience" as the material upon which the mind of the artist is to work. In 1772, Sir William Jones seemed to attach a certain slur to "imitation," and he tried to prove from an examination of their origins that poetry and music are not imitative arts.[77] Aikin called "imitation" "as great an air of reality as possible," and in this sense applied it especially to descriptive poetry.[78] Mason felt that "imitation" should be supplemented by "the original."[79] In 1782, the *Monthly* declared itself against copyist poets who confine themselves "like packhorses, to the same beaten track;"[80] and in the same year hedged on the application of [*mimēsis*] to comedy;[81] and by 1809 Walker classified theatrical "representations" according to "their effects upon the heart;" and, although he quoted and discussed the Abbé du Bos, he managed largely to ignore Aristotelian "imitation."[82]

During the first third of the century, "imitation" was triumphant, especially in the guise of copying models; during the second third, this interpretation gave place in most writers to "imitation" of Nature. The Aristotelian theory was sharply criticized; and numerous efforts were made to adjust it to Sentimental theories of æsthetics and to the psychological and historical contributions of the Rationalistic philosophers. Some critics, like Pemberton, limited "imitation" to the copying of certain types of things; some, like Burke, applied the term only to certain *genera* or species of art, or like Goldsmith and Lord Kames, admitted kinds or degrees of "imitation;" and some, like Gerard, felt vaguely that "imitation" could "degenerate into disagreeable servility." During the last third of the century, "imitation" became a less and less vital part of literary criticism.

The æsthetic problem, moreover, quickly made itself evident in other arts. The "Ut pictura poesis' of Horace had long united painting and poetry as imitative arts of a like nature.[83] Painting itself was looked upon as the handmaid of history;[84] and, even in making contemporary portraits and landscapes the painter strove for a copy, the closer the better, of objective reality. Even Shaftesbury accepted this view, and implied that painting is the mere adjunct of sculpture[85] or of poetry. Addison mentioned painting as one of the arts that depended for its effect on copying life.[86] Welsted objected to the copying of one painting by another; but

he leaves one to infer that he saw nothing in originals but the reproduction of external objects.[87] During the entire century, Dufresnoy's *De Arte Graphica,* translated by Dryden and others and annotated by de Piles and Sir Joshua Reynolds, was a paramount influence upon the æsthetics of painting.[88] Although he does not wish to "fetter Genius," Dufresnoy is strongly classical:

> Præcipua imprimis artisque potissima pars est,
> Nôsse quid in rebus natura creärit ad artem
> Pulchrius, idque modum juxta, mentemque
>   vetustam . . . [89]

Harte, who claims to have written independently of Dufresnoy, arrived at the same conclusion, and spoke of "a Titian or a Pope" as "The forming glory of a thousand years."[90] At last, however, this facile theory was challenged; and Hogarth wrote his *Analysis* without even mentioning "imitation" in his list of "principles" that "cooperate in the production of beauty."[91] The old opinion, nevertheless, still persisted; and John Scott spoke of painting as "mimic Being."[92] "Imitation" was applied to various things, and defended in various ways. Webb based his Romantic apology for color on a Neo-classical appeal to vivid "imitation."[93] Count Algarotti urged imitation of a general style or manner, like the poetic imitations of Horace or Virgil;[94] and Pott, in direct contradiction, lamented that the English "have contented themselves with imitating the ideas of other masters when they should have copied nature only."[95] Sir Joshua Reynolds, with the attitude of the professional creator rather than of the literary theorist, advised the artist to follow Nature, but not "at second hand;"[96] and by following Nature he did not mean servile copying; for he tells us to proceed from a model and to depart from it,[97] and his concept of the creative impulse was essentially spiritual.[98] Reynolds would doubtless have denied that his art, in such a sense, was "imitative."[99] In short, "imitation" came into painting in both senses: the copying of models and of external Nature. Hogarth, however, ignored it; and Reynolds left room for pure creation.

In music, the revolt was earlier and much more determinate; for "imitation," in either of the contemporary senses, applies to it but poorly. There seems to have been no attempt to introduce the copying of accepted masterpieces; but a number of writers—especially those whose knowledge of the art was limited—tried to make music merely an imitation of human feelings or of natural sounds. Addison attempted to justify it by the "imperfect notions" that it raises and by its power to "set the hearers in the heat and hurry of battle" or to "overcast their minds with melancholy scenes and apprehensions of deaths and funerals."[100] Armstrong declared that all music imitated the passions, and ruled out "mere Harmony" as being no more music than versification is poetry.[101] Moor also seems to apply "imitation" to music;[102] and Busby declared that music, when it tries to represent "operations of nature, art or human passion; as the rolling of thunder . . . the clashing of swords . . . and the tones of sorrow, love . . . or triumph . . .; exerts some of its sublimest energies; transports us to the very scenes it describes, or kindles the feeling of those expressions it copies."[103]

Much more commonly, however, even those writers who might have insisted on poetry and painting as "imitative," were inclined to make an exception of music. Among these may be numbered several really competent critics. Dacier admitted that "players on the Flute and Harp, play often on those Instruments, without Imitating anything."[104] Hutcheson, in interpreting Shaftesbury, likewise made allowance for absolute music.[105] Avison, who wrote with professional knowledge, declared himself opposed to copying, and called the composer "culpable" who, "for the Sake of some low and trifling *Imitation*, deserted the Beauties of Expression."[106] The Italian librettist Metastasio, whose vogue was considerable in England,[107] excepted music from among the imitative arts.[108] Harris, whose *Three Treatises* appeared in 1744, and passed into their fifth edition in 1792, tried to reconcile Aristotle to Shaftesbury: painting and poetry he called "imitative" in that they copy Nature; but of music he was obliged to make an exception.[109] Sir William Jones, also, could find no "imitation" in music;[110] but his *Treatise of the Art of Music*[111] seems to allow imitation, a stand to which the reviewer took definite exception.[112] Burney, the greatest musical critic of the age, discussed the theory of his art "unshackled by the trammels of authority,"[113] and hardly referred to imitation, even in treating of opera and oratorio.[114] The historian Hawkins, who allowed painting to be entirely imitative, and poetry largely so, ruled out music almost altogether.[115] By degrees the opinion spread from professional circles into the intellectual world at large; and, in 1778, the poet Beattie felt certain that music could not be classed as an imitative art.[116] By 1789, music was no longer looked upon necessarily as a copy of either natural sounds or human passions; and Bayly declared it the basis of poetry and oratory and the criterion by which they should be judged:[117] music had emerged from a dependent to a predominant æsthetic position.

Music as such cannot, indeed, be called imitative; but, ever since the days of Gluck and certainly since those of Wagner and Schubert, vocal and dramatic music have been thought of as the close associates, if not actual imitations, of their texts. The vocal and even the operatic settings of the early and middle Eighteenth Century are almost unrelated to the accompanying words; but a few writers, even of that period, anticipated in their theories the music of the Nineteenth Century. Most important of these was Rousseau. In his *Dictionary of Music,* which reached its second English edition in 1779, he pointed out:

La musique dramatique ou théâtricale concourt à *l'imitation,* ainsi que la poésie et la peinture: c'est à ce principe commun qui se rapportent tous les beaux-arts, comme l'a montré M. Le Batteux.[118]

And because dramatic music is "imitative," he exalts it above all music that is not.[119] At least one contemporary English writer suggested the same point of view. Webb urged that poetry be united with music in order that the latter might be truly imitative.[120] Brown tried to defend instrumental music, and declared:

Musical *Instruments* . . . are but *Imitations* of the human Voice, or of other natural Sounds, produced gradually by frequent Trial and Experiment.[121]

In the 1780's, Mason thought that "music as an imitative art" was so far inferior to poetry and painting, that it could "hardly be so termed with propriety;"[122] but he elsewhere urged that sacred music should reproduce the cadence and meaning of the text.[123] Gluck was even then struggling for instrumental recognition of libretti; but the theory was not fully accepted and developed until the Nineteenth Century, and then without any thought of Aristotle or of [*mimēsis*].

The application of Aristotle to music was, on the whole, that which gave the most trouble throughout the Eighteenth Century. The canons and fugues of Bach, the Handel and Haydn symphonies, even the opera, music that pleased by no pictorial or emotional quality but by sheer beauty of design, in short, absolute music, was characteristic of the age; and absolute music could not be justified as any form of copying. At last, a reinterpretation of Aristotle came in the light of his exaltation of music as an "imitative" art. In 1789, Twining brought out his *Aristotle's Treatise on Poetry, translated with notes, and Two Dissertations on Poetical and Musical Imitation.* He was well read in the æsthetic philosophers of the school of Shaftesbury and Rousseau.[124] He was deeply interested in music and an intimate friend of Burney.[125] He was an accomplished Grecian,[126] and had become interested in Aristotle on music as early as 1761. He seems to have started to work seriously about 1779,[127] and he published ten years later.

The Dissertation on Poetry Considered as an Imitative Art, points out that poetry by its onomatopœia and by its denotative and connotative faculties, can represent, portray, "imitate," both objective sense-impressions and subjective feelings and passions. This attitude is at once liberal and definite; and the inclusion of feeling as an object of imitation largely relieves [*mimēsis*] of the stigma of the photographic, but it gives instead a sentimental tinge, certainly not inherent in Aristotle or in the idea of creating art according to Universal Truth. The *Dissertation on Musical Imitation* is even more significant. To music, he assigned "three distinct effects:" an effect upon the ear, in "simply delighting the *sense;*" an effect upon the passions, in "raising the *emotions;*" and an effect upon the "imagination," in "raising ideas." An analysis of this first type, which he dismissed as merely sensuous, comparing it to the "smell of a rose" or the "flavor of a pineapple," might have led him to the idealistic sense that Aristotle seems to have intended;[128] but, unfortunately, he passed rapidly on to a discussion of the second category, the emotional power of music. By the third type, he understood program-music, that which copies directly sounds or motions or things; and he agreed with the large body of æsthetic critics in finding it very "imperfect."[129] It was music as an emotional force that appealed to Twining. Whereas such a writer as Bysshe represents the thorough Neo-classicizing of "imitation," Twining uses the same word largely emptied of its former meaning, emotionalized and sentimentalized in conformity with the Romantic *Zeitgeist.*

Twining's Aristotle re-appeared in 1812 and 1851; and the *Dissertations* were widely read. The *Monthly* gave it a long and enthusiastic review.[130] In the early 1790's, Mason referred to "Twining" as if the work were a recognized standard.[131] Cowper mentioned "Mr. Twining's valuable volume," and found the writer "sensible, elegant and entertaining."[132] More recent scholarship has taken cognizance of Twining.[133] Moore,[134] Sandys,[135] Bywater,[136] and Carroll[137] have recognized his importance.[138] Alison's two sorts of "imitation," that of "beautiful forms" and that of "Passions or Affections,"[139] and Hazlitt's idea of imitation applied especially to man's imagination and passions,[140] probably derive from him; but the Romantic Movement, even as early as the 1790's, was too much interested in original genius to care for Aristotle—even interpreted according to its own views.[141] The historical criticism of Warton and Ritson was not primarily interested in him; and the psychological criticism of Lord Kames and of Priestley looked to the empirical sciences for a basis of æsthetic judgment.[142] The Neo-Platonic critics,[143] moreover, and the impressionistic followers of Longinus[144] cared little about imitation. Upon creative literature, Twining's work seems to have had no more influence than upon æsthetic theorists, although Coleridge certainly knew of the book, at least through Pye's *Commentary;*[145] and it may have contributed to his early thought.[146] In Germany, Twining received some immediate recognition. C. H. Heyne, of Göttingen, to whom Tyrwhitt refers as *"vir eruditissimus,"*[147] wrote Twining a long and appreciative letter, in which he declared:

> Valde delectavit me opera a te posita in notione *imitationis* accurate constituenda. Turbavit illa vox non minus populares meos: verum nos adsciscimus aliam vocem eamque minus in fallaciam et fraudem indescentem, *Darstellung. . . .*[148]

He promised, moreover, to review the *Dissertations*[149] and to speak of them in a course of lectures; and J. T.

Buhle of Göttingen in his *Opera omnia* of Aristotle, published in 1791, made numerous references to "Twiningius" in his *Animadvertiones criticæ* of the *Poetics.*

The early Eighteenth Century is the period of the application of the theories of Renaissance scholarship to creative endeavor. The enthusiasm of the Elizabethan Age and the strained affectation of the Jacobean had at last given away before common sense and the "Rules." Neo-classicism saw the triumph of restraint, of authority, of decorum, of all-too-reasonable compromise. "Imitation" received the simplest—and most mistaken—interpretation: in poetry, it meant primarily the copying of models; in painting, the copying of old masters or of natural objects; in music, it was interpreted in any way that the ignorance or the ingenuity of the writer might suggest. There was little room for the emotional, for the ideal, or for artistic progress. But even during the triumph of Neo-classicism, the Sentimental revolt was under way; and, at an early stage, the "imitation" of emotional values was suggested as a justification of poetry and music. During the middle of the century, "imitation" was interpreted and re-interpreted, in an effort to adapt it to Sentimental and to Rationalistic thought. After the 1760's, its definition became only a minor phase of the conflict; for the discredit of "the Rules" carried with it a discredit of all Aristotelian theories. More and more of the writers ignored "imitation" entirely; and the interpretation of Twining, even had it been less timid, would probably have had little actual effect upon either the poets or the æsthetic philosophers. The semantic history of [*mimēsis*] reflects the period of authority during the first third of the century, and the period, during the middle decades, of scientific inquiry and of sentimental reaction, which later passed into the age of Romantic revolt.

Notes

[1] Saintsbury has pointed out the prevalence of literary imitation in his *History of Criticism, sub* Bysshe.

[2] It must, however, be admitted that Aristotle is not perfectly consistent—or that the scribe has not reported faithfully. On one occasion, he seems to include narrative as an "imitative" art, and, on another, to exclude it. See I. Bywater, *Aristotle on the Art of Poetry,* Oxford, 1909, 100-101.

[3] S. H. Butcher, *Aristotle's Theory of Poetry and Fine Art,* London, 1902, 153.

[4] *Ibid.,* 116.

[5] On Imitation in Seventeenth Century England, see W. G. Howard, *Ut Pictura Poesis, Publ. Mod. Lang. Assoc.,* XXIV, 44; I. Babbit, *The New Laokoon,* Boston, 1910, 12; Gregory Smith, *Elizabethan Critical Essays,* Ox-

ford, 1904, I, xxxviii; J. W. Bray, *History of English Critical Terms,* Boston, 1898, 160 ff.; and J. E. Spingarn, *Critical Essays of the Seventeenth Century,* Oxford, 1908, I, xlviii ff.

[6] For a list of these, see Schwab's *Bibliographic d'Aristotle,* Paris, 1896.

[7] Cooke's ed., Cambridge, 1785, is quite definite, iii.

[8] *Aristotle's Art of Poetry,* London, 1709.

[9] Horace Walpole, *Letters,* Toynbee ed., Oxford, 1903, IV, 398; VI, 201; VIII, 176; X, 132; XII, 359.

[10] William Cowper, *Letters,* ed. Wright, London, 1904, II, 196.

[11] Johnson's *English Dictionary,* London, 1755. He gives three senses: the "act of copying, attempt to resemble"; "that which is offered as a copy" (the quotation from Dryden shows that he means this to include literary "imitation"); and "a method of translating looser than paraphrase, in which modern examples and illustrations are used for ancient, or domestic for foreign." Later dictionaries quote Johnson.

[12] Many of them seem to have taken it so completely for granted that they ignored it. William Walker, *Rhetoriticae libri duo,* London, 1672, 162, discusses it only as a figure in oratory. Charles Butler, *Rhetoricae libro duo,* London, 1684, leaves it out entirely. So also do William Dugard, *Rhetorices Elementa,* London, 1721, 1741, etc.; and John Ward, *De Ratione Interpugendi,* London, 1739.

[13] Edward Bysshe, *The Art of English Poetry,* 4th ed., London, 1710. See title page.

[14] John Constable, *Reflections upon Accuracy of Style,* London, 1731, 81.

[15] *Prolusions Academiæ,* Oxon., 1765. The author's attitude toward imitation seems inconsistent. He seems opposed to it as contradictory to divine inspiration; but, on the other hand, he declares: "Perversa nullorum Imitatio cum chamæleonte comparatur." p. 89.

[16] Edward Owen, *The Satires of Juvenal,* London, 1785, *Preface.*

[17] Richard Hurd, *A Discourse on Poetical Imitation,* Works, II, 217. For the relation of "imitation" to the theory translation in the Eighteenth Century, see an article by the present author in the current volume of *Neophilologus.*

[18] Henry Felton, *A Dissertation on Reading the Classics and forming a Just Style,* 5th ed., London, 1753,

146. For an extended treatment of Felton, see R. S. Crane, *Imitation of Spenser and Milton in the Early Eighteenth Century: A New Document, Studies in Philology,* XV, 195 ff.

[19] Charles Gildon, *Complete Art of Poetry,* Dialogue II (1718) in Durham's *Critical Essays of the Eighteenth Century,* New Haven, 1915, I, 73 ff.

[20] Lord Lansdowne, *Essay upon Unnatural Flights in Poetry.* See Gildon's *Laws of Poetry,* London, 1721, 345.

[21] William Lauder in his *Essay on Milton's Use and Imitation of the Moderns,* London, 1750, fastened a bad sense on imitation.

[22] Percival Stockdale, *An Inquiry into the Nature and Genuine Laws of Poetry,* London, 1778, 76.

[23] Samuel Johnson, *Life of Pope, Works,* Oxford, 1825, VIII, 295.

[24] Jonathan Swift, *Works,* Edinburgh, 1814, XIII, 43.

[25] *The Guardian,* No. XII, in Durham's *Critical Essays of the Eighteenth Century,* New Haven, 1915, I, 295.

[26] Alexander Pope, *Preface* to the *Iliad, Works,* London, 1757, VI, 303.

[27] Alexander Pope, *Preface* to *Poems, Works, ed. cit.,* I, XV.

[28] Joseph Warton, *Essay on Pope,* London, 1806, II, 36.

[29] William Mason, *Works,* London, 1811, II, 180. By a stroke of irony, Mason prefixed to his *Works,* I, 2, a quotation from the Greek of Dionysius to the effect that copies can never be equal to their archetypes. See Dion. Halicar., . . . Leipzig, 1899, I, 307.

[30] See, for example, J. M. Beattie, Jr., *The Political Satires of Charles Churchill, Studies in Philology,* XVI, 303 ff. Beattie points out that Churchill forsakes the finished artfulness of Pope's versification for the more robustious, freer style of Dryden. Of course, the present paper makes no attempt to cover in any definite or detailed fashion, the actual literary imitations of the Eighteenth Century. The object is merely to note the explanations and applications of Aristotelean [*mimēsis*] and to explain somewhat the influence and vogue of each interpretation.

[31] Lord Shaftesbury, *Second Characters or the Language of Forms,* ed. B. Rand, Cambridge (Eng.), 1914, 23.

[32] For the tracing of this influence on the purely liter-

ary side, see C. A. Moore, *Shaftesbury and the Ethical Poets of England,* 1700-1760, *PMLA.,* XXXI, 264.

[33] By implication, he includes Moorish arabesques and other nonpictorial designs.

[34] Francis Hutcheson, *An Inquiry into the Original of our Ideas of Beauty and Virtue,* London, 1725, 15-37. He allows sculpture also to be an absolute art in so far as it concerns itself with proportion of parts rather than the copying of an original. Hutcheson's distinction is a sound one, although he does not always apply it accurately in matters of detail.

[35] *Ibid.,* 39-40.

[36] Abbé J. B. du Bos, *Critical Reflections on Poetry, Painting and Music,* tr. into Eng., London, 1748, II, 43-5. *Ed. princ.,* Paris, 1719, anon. For the relation of du Bos to the history of criticism, see A. Lombard, *L'Abbé du Bos, Initiateur de la Pensée moderne,* Paris, 1913. Du Bos is probably too early to have been influenced by England; but undoubtedly English example had a good deal to do with the rise of Sentimental and Rationalistic æsthetic theories in France in the second and third quarters of the Eighteenth Century. Cf. Joseph Texte, *Jean-Jacques Rousseau et les Origines du Cosmopolitisme Littéraire,* Paris, 1895, Chapter II.

[37] Pierre Estève, *Esprit des Beaux Arts,* Paris, 1753. Ch. III, 43 ff.; 92 ff.

[38] *Ibid.,* 60, 68, *etc.*

[39] Charles Batteaux, *Principes de la Littérature,* Paris, 1802, I, 16 ff. The complete edition, according to the *Brit. Mus. Cat.* appeared in 1764, and was augmented in 1774-88.

[40] Batteaux applied this theory to painting, sculpture, dancing, music and poetry. In a long note, he attacked Schlegel for excluding the dance from among the "imitative" arts. He gives no satisfactory explanation as to how music can be "imitative."

[41] Condillac's work seems to have been very influential in England. His *Origin of Human Knowledge* was translated by Thomas Nugent in 1756. The *Critical* reviewed it at great length, II, 193-219. In general, he looks at the arts from the standpoint of psychology; and he casts aside imitation, except for the imitation of the passions in music, p. 222 *et al. loc.* Cf. Léon Dewaule, *Condillac et la Psychologie Anglaise Contemporaine,* 84 ff.

[42] Montesquieu, *Œuvres Complète,* ed. Laboulaye, Paris, 1879, VII, 116. The *Essai sur le Goût* was posthumously published in *l'Encyclopédie,* ed. 1775, VII, s. v.; but it doubtless represents the views of the entire

group for many years before.

[43] Voltaire, *Œuvres Complètes,* Paris, 1879, XIX, 270 ff. This article first appeared in *l'Encyclopédie,* ed. 1757, VII, s. v.

[44] The *Brit. Mus. Cat.* lists one edition of the Greek text alone, Oxford, 1718, a translation into Latin by J. Hudson, Oxford, 1710, a "third edition" in 1730 and another at Edinburgh in 1733. Another translation into Latin by Z. Pearce appeared at least eight times in England, 1724, 1732, 1751, 1752, 1763, 1773, 1778, and at least once in Amsterdam, 1733. English translations from the French of Boileau were common; there were besides one by Welsted, 1712, 1724, and one by Smith, sec. ed., 1743, 1751, 1756, and 1770. References to Longinus are numerous in writers on æsthetic theory; and Edward Burnaby Greene incorporated *Observations on the Sublime* in his *Critical Essays,* London, 1760 [1770?]. J. Churton Collins briefly discusses the vogue in *Longinus and Greek Criticism, Studies in Poetry and Criticism,* London, 1905, 215 ff.

[45] Plato's influence on Harris' *Three Treatises* is noted by Sarah Coleridge. S. T. Coleridge's *Works,* New York, 1853, III, 391.

[46] For example, Henry Brooke, *Universal Beauty,* 1735. He seems to be under the influence of Shaftesbury and Hutcheson. See also Anselm Bayly, *Introduction to Languages.* London, 1758, 102. His work shows the influence of Longinus, and favors original genius.

[47] Henry Felton, *A Dissertation on Reading the Classics and Forming a Just Style,* 5th ed., London, 1753, 33 ff. The *ed. princ.* appeared in 1713.

[48] Anthony Blackwell, *Introduction to the Classics,* London, 1746, 21. *Ed. princ.* 1718.

[49] Leonard Welsted, *A Dissertation concerning the Perfection of the English Language,* in Durham, *op. cit.,* I, 377.

[50] Henry Fielding, *Covent-Garden Journal,* No. LXI, Aug. 29, 1752, ed. Jenson, New Haven, 1915, II, 93.

[51] John Byrom, *Epistle to a Friend on the Art of English Poetry,* in Alexander Chalmers, *English Poets,* London, 1810, XV, 213.

[52] Robert Lloyd, *The Poetry Professors* in Chalmers, *op. cit.,* XV, 79.

[53] Edward Young, *Conjectures on Original Composition,* London, 1759, 9. Cf. J. L. Kind, *Edward Young in Germany,* New York, 1906, Chapter I; and cf. M. W. Steinke, *Edward Young's "Conjectures on Original Composition" in England and Germany,* New York,

1917, 10 ff. Kind is inclined to overestimate the novelty both of Young's ideas and of his influence in Germany. Steinke corrects these impressions.

[54] Launcelot Temple, *pseud.* for John Armstrong, *Sketches,* London, 1758, 44 ff. See also *Mon. Rev.* XVIII, 580 ff.

[55] Edward Burnaby Greene, *Critical Essays,* London [1770?], i ff. As his notes show, Greene is deeply indebted to Longinus.

[56] Lawrence Sterne, *Tristram Shandy,* Vol. II, Chap. IV. He adds, however, that this is to be understood *"cum grano salis."*

[57] *The Circle of the Sciences,* London, 1776, 95.

[58] William Cowper, *Correspondence,* ed. Wright, London, 1904, I, 386.

[59] *Spectator,* No. 419.

[60] Joseph Trapp, Prof. of Poetry at Oxford, *Prælectiones Poeticae,* London, 1736, I, 26-31. The book was translated under the title, *Lectures on Poetry,* London, 1742.

[61] Henry Pemberton, *Observations on Poetry,* London, 1738, 5-7. This is a characteristically Neo-classical variation of Aristotle to conform with Pope's dictum: "The proper study of mankind is Man."

[62] John Brown, *Essays on the Characteristics,* London, 1751, 19-20. Perhaps this latter attitude together with the veneration for Aristotle, helps to explain the vogue of descriptive poetry in the Eighteenth Century.

[63] Thomas Francklin, *Translation a Poem,* London [1753], 8. He also treats of imitation as translation and copying of approved masterpieces. Francklin was Professor of Greek at Cambridge.

[64] Perhaps this implies a more conscious consideration of the subject than Warton actually gave. As a matter of fact, many of the interpretations here quoted are chance *obiter dicta,* thrown off on the spur of an occasion. They serve, however, to illustrate the general attitude toward imitation.

[65] Joseph Warton, *Essay on Pope,* London, 1756, 51.

[66] Edmund Burke, *Philosophical Inquiry into the Sublime and the Beautiful,* London, 1757, 29, 179 ff.

[67] David Hume, *Four Dissertations,* London, 1757. The *Monthly Rev.* gave it a long and rather appreciative review, XVI, 122-140.

[68] *Rambler,* No. 143. Johnson's objections to plagiarism probably arose, not from any dislike of literary imitation but from disgust at the thievery of book-sellers. Some of his *Idler* papers appear to have been stolen. See his letter of protest to the *Univ. Chron.* 1759, 149.

[69] L. Temple, *pseud., op. cit.,* 4 ff.

[70] Alexander Gerard, *Essay on Taste,* London, 1759, 49-56. The reference to Hutcheson's *Inquiry* suggests that Sentimentalism accounts for his unwillingness to subscribe to utter Neo-classical copying. Gerard's *Essay* was "very well received in London" according to Hume. Hume to Robertson, May 29, 1759, in Dugald Stewart, *Life of Robertson,* London, 1802, 252.

[71] O. Goldsmith, *Works,* N. Y., 1850, I, 275, Essay XVIII, *On the Cultivation of Taste,* et seq. This sounds like a rather liberal view of [*mimēsis*]; but the second clause turns out to mean only that the artist is to avoid the disgusting. These essays first appeared in *The Bee,* 1761-2-3.

[72] Daniel Webb, *Remarks on the Beauties of Poetry,* London, 1762, 102 n. q.

[73] John Ogilvie, *Poems,* London, 1762, vii ff. In his *Philosophical and Critical Observations on Composition,* London, 1774, I, 295-6, Ogilvie took up the matter again. He referred "imitation" either directly to sense impressions or to "such materials as are more generally supplied by reflection and experience." He seems to have had in mind a less stringent copying; but it was hardly a creative expression of the Universal.

[74] Henry Home, Lord Kames (or Kaims), *Elements of Criticism,* 2nd ed., "with additions and improvements," Edinburgh, 1763, III, 244-5. The *Preface* is dated 1761.

[75] Mark Akenside, *Pleasures of the Imagination,* London, 1884, I, 46.

[76] Richard Hurd, *On Poetical Imitation, Works,* London, 1811, II, 171-2. He says: (p. 176) "The *objects* of imitation, like the *materials* of human knowledge, are a common stock, which experience furnishes to all men. And it is in the *operations* of the mind upon them, that the glory of *poetry,* as of *science* consists." This seems like an idealistic, and almost Shelleyan, view of poetry, until one notes, from the passage quoted in the text, that to Hurd the most important of these "*operations*" of the mind" are of the didactic sort, to convey "distinct and clear notices . . . of moral and religious conceptions."

[77] Sir William Jones, *Poems,* Oxford, 1772, Essay II, *On the Arts Commonly Called Imitative,* 201-2.

[78] John Aikin, *Essays on Song-Writing,* 2nd ed.,

Warrington 1774, 7-8.

[79] William Mason, *Works,* London, 1811, I, 315-6.

[80] *Mon. Rev.,* LXVII, 262.

[81] B. Walwyn, *Essay on Comedy,* see *Mon. Rev.,* LXVI, 308-9.

[82] George Walker, *Essays,* London, 1809, 41 ff.

[83] For a tracing of this æsthetic alliance, see W. G. Howard, *Ut Pictura Poesis, Publ. Mod. Lang. Assoc.,* XXIV, 40 ff.

[84] The classicists of course looked upon historical painting as painting *par excellence.* In this way the art became subservient to a literary text actual or implied. The situation is well illustrated in T. Rowlandson's *The Historian Animating the Mind of a Young Painter,* reproduced in George Paston's *Social Caricature of the Eighteenth Century,* plate CVI.

[85] Lord Shaftesbury, *Second Characters,* ed. Rand, Cambridge (Eng.), 1914, 117, "Statuary the mother art to painting," and 167, "A painter therefore must imitate the dramatic and scenical, not the epic and merely recitative poet."

[86] *Spectator,* No. 416. The essential difficulty with this point of view is the definition the Neo-classicists gave to "life": They took little account of color and almost none of light and air.

[87] Leonard Welsted, *The State of Poetry,* in Durham, *op. cit.,* I, 377.

[88] The poem was composed at Rome between 1633 and 1653 and first published in 1668, annotated by Roger de Piles. Dryden made a translation in 1695; J. Wright, in 1728; James Willis, in 1754; and William Mason in 1781. To Mason's translation Sir Joshua Reynolds added notes. For bibliography on Dufresnoy and his influence, see Paul Vitry, *De C. A. Dufresnoy Pictoris Poemate quod "De Arte Graphica" insoribitur,* diss., U. of Paris, Paris, 1901; and see L. Gillet, *La Peinture, XVII et XVIII Siècles,* Paris, 1913, 314 ff. The influence of Pliny's *Nat. Hist., Lib.* XXX, was also important.

[89] William Mason, *Works, ed. cit.,* III, 26, ll. 37-40.

[90] Walter Harte, *Essay on Painting,* Chalmers, *op. cit.,* XVI, 320.

[91] William Hogarth, *Analysis of Beauty,* London, 1753, 12. Hogarth agreed with Welsted in objecting to the copying of masterpieces; and Thomas Bardwell in his *Practice of Painting,* London, 1756, defended both not

only in the trade but also as a pedagogical method. See *Mon. Rev.,* XV, 284 ff.

[92] John Scott, *Essay on Painting* [c. 1770?]. Chalmers calls the work Scott's "feeblest effort," *op. cit.,* XVII, 451.

[93] Daniel Webb, *Inquiry into the Beauties of Painting,* London, 1760, 1761, 1769, 1777, p. 70.

[94] Count Algarotti, *Essay on Painting,* translated into English, London, 1774, 171.

[95] J. H. Pott, *Essay on Landscape Painting,* London, 1782.

[96] *Vide* Reynolds' *Notes* to Mason's translation of Dufresnoy's *De Arte Graphica,* Mason's *Works,* III, 101 ff. For an analysis at length of Sir Joshua's point of view, see E. N. S. Thompson, *Discourses of Sir Joshua Reynolds, Publ. Mod. Lang. Assoc.,* XXXII, 339 ff.

[97] *Ibid.,* 105-6.

[98] *Ibid.,* 140.

[99] The utter decadence of stained glass in the Eighteenth Century is largely explained as part of the general distaste for Gothic. An additional reason, however, is the dominance of "imitation" over æsthetic theory. The materials and the purpose of glass-painting make Realistic portrayal of Nature ineffective if not impossible; and the copying of models intrenches the pictorial technique, proper to canvas and fresco, which has so injured the glass of the Renaissance.

[100] *Spectator,* No. 416. As Hawkins very truly pointed out, *History of Music,* London, 1776, I, v ff., Shaftesbury, Temple and Addison knew very little about music.

[101] L. Temple, pseud., *op. cit.,* 26 ff.

[102] James Moor, *Essays,* Glasgow, 1759, 3, 133 ff.

[103] Thomas Busby, *A Complete Dictionary of Music,* London [1800?], s. v.

[104] Dacier, *op. cit.,* 7. According to his view, some music, on the other hand, represents an "Action or a Passion." 6-7.

[105] Hutcheson, *op. cit.* 25.

[106] Sir Charles Avison, *Essay on Musical Expression,* London, 1752, 61, 90 etc. Watt in *Bibl. Brit.* suggests that Brown supplied the content of this work—an improbable theory in view of his attitude toward imita-

tion in his *History of Poetry.* See following.

[107] The *Brit. Mus. Cat.* lists twenty-six English editions before 1800 of various libretti by Metastasio, some set to music, some with Italian text, some with English, some with both. This includes Arne's famous setting of *Artaxerxes* which passed through at least seven editions before 1800 and four more during the fifteen years following. There is also Anna Williams' *The Uninhabited Island, 1766 (L'Isola Desabitata),* not listed in *Brit. Mus. Cat.* Hoole translated his *Works* in 1767 (another ed. 1800); some of his *Poems* appeared, Coventry, 1790, his sonnets, 1795; Burney published his *Life* in 1796 (sec. ed. ?1810). His fame extended throughout the first half of the Nineteenth Century.

[108] Pietro Metastasio, *Opere,* Florence, 1831, XIII, 37. But he called poetry "imitative" because it expresses emotions and embellishes Nature, *ibid.,* 25. *A priori* we might expect one like Metastasio who was accustomed to think of music in conjunction with words, to urge the imitating of the words by the music; but it is to be remembered that the composers of Italian *opera seria* of the Eighteenth Century, the musicians with whom Metastasio came in contact, regularly sacrificed relation of sense and sound—and even coherence of organic structure—to opportunities of vocal display for the *prima donna* and *primo uomo.*

[109] James Harris, *Three Treatises,* London, 1764, 95.

[110] Sir William Jones, *Poems,* Oxford, 1772, 201-2.

[111] W. Jones, *Treatise of the Art of Music,* London, 1786, *Preface.*

[112] *Monthly Rev.,* LXXV, 105 ff.

[113] Charles Burney, *A General History of Music,* London, 1776-89, *Preface,* I, xiii.

[114] *Ibid.,* I, 153 ff.

[115] In a long note, Hawkins gives a list—to which additions might easily be made from Haydn's *Creation* and other well-known works of the period—of musical imitations of natural sounds, scenes and events; "but these powers of imitation," he adds, " . . . constitute but a very small part of the excellence of music. Hawkins, *General History of Music,* London, 1776, *Preliminary Discourse,* I, ii-iii.

[116] James Beattie, *Essays,* London, 1778, 128. See also Sir William Forbes, *Life of Beattie,* London, 1806, 542.

[117] Anselm Bayly, *The Alliance of Music, Poetry and Oratory,* London, 1789, 2. Of course, there were still exponents of the more conservative attitude; and, in the same year, the *Monthly,* I (n. s.), 38, objected to the idea that music was "the first and immediate thought of Nature."

[118] J. J. Rousseau, *Œuvres,* Paris, 1824, XII, *Dictionnaire de la Musique,* I, 376 ff.

[119] *Ibid., Sub Harmonie,* 365.

[120] Webb, *op. cit.,* 102, n. q. Webb's *Remarks* appeared in 1762; and the *ed. princ.* of Rousseau's *Dictionary* in 1767.

[121] Brown, *History of Poetry,* Newcastle, 1764, 12. This work also antedates Rousseau. His theory seems to be that instrumental music originally arose as an imitation of the human voice. The facts of primitive life do not seem to support it.

[122] Mason, *Works,* London, 1811, III, 287. This *Essay* first appeared at York, 1795.

[123] Mason, *op. cit.,* III, 393 ff. The idea appears throughout his four *Essays* on music.

[124] His interest in Rowley, in Percy's *Reliques* and in Welsh scenery shows him abreast of the rising tide of Romanticism; the titles of two of his published sermons (see *Brit. Mus. Cat.* and *Mon. Rev.,* LXXVII, 176) show a philosophic background in Shaftesbury and Hutcheson; and he refers in his notes to the writings of Rousseau and Hutcheson, and criticises Lord Kaims, Harris, Beattie and Avison.

[125] He and Burney exchanged letters; Burney asserted that Twining's "least merit" was "being perfectly acquainted with every branch of theoretical and practical music," and, furthermore, Burney relied on him for much of the Greek and Latin material in his *History of Music.* Burney, *op. cit.,* I, xix.

[126] Dr. Parr said that his Greek scholarship was excelled by "no critic of his day." See *Recreations and Studies of a Country Gentleman,* London, 1882, 11-12. This book contains a *Memoir of Twining* and a number of letters.

[127] *Recreations and Studies,* 14, 57.

[128] Of course, such musical literature is not to be classified with the mere "flavor of a pineapple." Schopenhauer recognized this; and it was probably to absolute music that he referred when he declared that Music *was* the Will, the essence of life, whereas the other arts merely pictured it. *Die Welt als Wille und Vorstellung,* Leipzig, 1873, II, 512. Schopenhauer's view was largely anticipated by Bayly, *op. cit.,* 2: "Music, indeed, if traced to its origin, will be found the first and immediate daughter of nature, while poetry and oratory are only near relations of music, mere

imitations of nature. . . . ."

[129] He very justly remarked that a musical resemblance "cannot be seen till it is, in some sort, pointed out," and that "even when it is so, it is not very evident."

[130] *Mon. Rev.,* IV (N. S.), 383-8; VII, 121. The reviewer did not, however, pay particular attention to "imitation."

[131] William Mason, *Works,* London, 1811, III, 287. Mason brackets Twining and Harris; and he seems to fail to realize that the two are not altogether agreeable in their interpretations. Mason, in his text, seems to follow Harris.

[132] William Cowper, *Letters, op. cit.,* III, 372-3.

[133] Tyrwhitt made no mention of Twining, apparently thinking a mere translator beneath his notice. T. Tyrwhitt ed., *De Poetica Aristotelis,* London, 1794.

[134] Edward Moore, Aristoteles, . . . Oxford, 1875, *Preface.*

[135] J. E. Sandys, *Hist. of Classical Scholarship,* Cambridge, 1908, II, 420-I.

[136] I. Bywater, *Aristotle on the Art of Poetry,* Oxford, 1909, *Preface,* x.

[137] M. Carroll, reviewing Bywater in the *Am. Jour. of Philol.,* XXXII, 86.

[138] None of these writers, however, seem to appreciate the importance of Twining's work on "imitation."

[139] A. Allison, *Essays on Taste,* London, 1790. Blair, on the other hand, seems to lapse back to the idea of "imitation" as a mere copy. See *Essays on Rhetoric and Science,* Boston, 1793, 209. Knight defined "imitation" vaguely as "the faculty of improved perception." See *Principles of Taste,* London, 1805, 100. Taylor noted three sorts of imitation, corresponding to Plato's three states of the soul: divine, scientific or intellectual, and reproductive in a mere literal fashion. Which of these he conceived Aristotle to have meant, is uncertain. Indeed, he prided himself on leaving *minutiae* to the "critical vermin." See *Aristotle's Poetic,* ed. Taylor, London, 1812, II, viii ff.

[140] William Hazlitt, *On Poetry in General, Lectures,* Philadelphia, 1818, 5.

[141] E. g. George Walker, *Essays on Various Subjects,* London, 1809, II, 76-7.

[142] *Mon. Rev.* LVII, 89 ff. attributes the origination of psychological criticism to Lord Kames. Priestley in his *Lectures on Oratory and Criticism,* London, 1777, fol-lowed his lead, and tried to find a more scientific basis in Hartley's psychology.

[143] E. g. Thomas Taylor, translator of Plotinus' *Concerning the Beautiful,* London, 1787.

[144] One of the most notable of these was Thomas Robertson, Fellow of the Royal Society of Edinburgh, who, in his *Inquiry Concerning the Fine Arts,* London, 1784, called Scotch folk songs "some of the finest melodies in Europe." The *Review* sneered at them as "ploughman's language," *Mon. Rev.,* LXXIV, 191 fl.

[145] H. J. Pye, *A Commentary Illustrating the Poetic of Aristotle,* London, 1792. Sara Coleridge certainly knew Pye (see her note to *Biog. Lit.,* Coleridge's *Works,* N. Y., 1853, III, 399); and probably Coleridge drew from Pye (182-3), his *obiter dictum* on the perfection of the plot of *Tom Jones* (*Table Talk,* July 5, 1834). Pye refers constantly to Twining, praises him and quotes him especially on "imitation." See Pye, *Preface,* x-xi, 91. It is of interest to note that Pye drew heavily on Lessing's *Hamb. Dram.,* "a work not generally known." *Pref.,* XV.

[146] Of course in his later years, Coleridge went far beyond Twining, and recognized "imitation" as an exalted act of artistic creation. See for example, *Lecture* XIII, *Works,* New York, 1854, IV, 330.

[147] T. Tyrwhitt *De Poetica Aristotelis,* London, 1794, xi. Heyne was the best classical scholar of the day in Germany.

[148] *Recreations and Studies,* 252.

[149] I have been unable to find anything of this review either in C. G. Heyne, *Opuscula Academia,* Göttingen, 1785-1802, or in A. H. L. Heeren, *Christian Gottlob Heyne, Biographisch Dargestellt,* Göttingen, 1813, bibl. of Heyne's works, 489 ff. I have not had access to a complete file of the *Göttingische gelehrte Anzeigen.*

G. S. Brett (essay date 1922)

SOURCE: "Reflections on Aristotle's View of Tragedy," in *Philosophical Essays Presented to John Watson,* Queen's University, 1922, pp. 158-78.

[*In the following essay, Brett examines the concept of catharsis, or purgation, which Aristotle discusses in* Poetics. *Brett suggests that while Aristotle's definition of tragedy omits direct reference to purgation as experienced by an audience, the concept is still a significant part of his definition of tragedy.*]

I

In all literature, ancient and modern, there are a few conspicuous passages which afford the perennial charm of mystery. Each generation of students looks on them, as Desire looks on the Sphinx; and one or another is drawn by magic into the maze of explanations which are the ghosts of former efforts. Such is the passage in which Aristotle once defined Tragedy, and if this essay achieves no final solution of the riddle, it may at least deserve the grace due to any honest venture which sustains the unfinished quest.

As this is not, in the words of the academic regulations, a contribution to knowledge, I have called it a budget of reflections. It represents in fact a voyage of the mind, a voyage of exploration directed more by desire than purpose and terminated by arrival at a stopping place rather than a final goal. The beginning of the quest was in the passage which defines the nature of tragedy (**Poetics,** 1449b 24) and more particularly in the word [katharsis]. The way led naturally through a forest of explanations, all of them familiar to students of Aristotle, and left one uncertain whether this grove was not the one originally designated by the philologists as 'lucus a non lucendo.'

Thus far the journey had been uneventful and my experience seemed to coincide with the slightly pessimistic mood of Zeller. The right course seemed to be to acknowledge frankly that there was no real solution of the puzzle, or that life was too short for such quixotic campaigns. But in an age that substitutes 'becoming' for 'being' and admires process more than finality, there is no small excuse for the unambitious pilgrim who only desires to tell his story. Accordingly I will continue to explain why satisfaction was not felt, and how the quest proceeded. This will lead to a final statement that the most useful part of this study was the comparison of the different works from which material could be drawn, namely the **Politics,** the **Ethics,** the **Rhetoric,** the **Poetics.** The results can hardly claim to be novel or revolutionary, but some value may be discerned in a method which elucidates a topic by widening the scope of its significance.

II

The original topic is the idea expressed by the term [katharsis] This word has many shades of meaning, but we may follow the expositions of the editors and reduce them to three. Summarily stated these are (a) the religious, with the meaning 'lustration'; (b) the pathological, or medical sense of 'purgation'; (c) the moral, with the idea of 'purification.'

These three interpretations are clearly not exclusive; they do not form a true logical classification, because there is no single principle of classification and no way of determining the limits of each division. If, for example, religious purification is taken to include the relief of a burdened conscience, it includes one part of the medical significance: for 'purgation' is defined as

producing relief and restoring a normal state in an organism whose equilibrium depends equally on physical and psychic factors: while the third meaning is a compound of the other two, since moral purification implies the objective ritual of 'lustration' and the subjective 'purgation' of the humours which corrupt body and soul. These three interpretations, therefore, differ only in emphasis.

This rather tame conclusion is, in fact, a significant point. If the student will read through Bywater's list of translations, beginning from Paccius in 1527,[1] he will see that they are different (when there is any difference) because their authors knew that the emphasis might be put on one or other of these three phases, but had no established principle on which to base their preference. Bywater[2] claims to have shown that 'the pathological interpretation of [katharsis] was not unknown in Italy in the sixteenth and seventeenth centuries': as that was the time when the 'humours' were again made the basis for explaining character, temperament and the passions, this fact is not surprising. Bywater himself thinks this 'physiological metaphor' is the real explanation of [katharsis]. His reasons are mainly philological, that is to say he relies on the uses of the word in Aristotle. He is prepared therefore to reject Lessing's view that 'the tragic purification of the passions consists merely in the conversion of pity and fear into virtuous habits of mind.' In addition to all other reasons for doubting this interpretation there is one of supreme importance; for Lessing obviously deduces his views of [katharsis] from his view of Tragedy. To estimate the value of Lessing's view we should be compelled to discuss the whole question as to whether Lessing's idea of tragedy coincided with Aristotle's; and whether in any case the definition given in the **Poetics** states what Tragedy actually does, or gives an ideal definition of what it ought to do. But this discussion will be postponed indefinitely, because it is enough for the present purposes to recognize the profound difference which exists between a statement of actual psychological effects due to a specific art . . . and a theory of aesthetic values. Whatever means we adopt for establishing the exact sense of [katharsis], the argument must *not* take the form 'since tragedy ought to have a moral effect, therefore its elements must have a purifying effect.' On the contrary (as Bywater recognizes) we must first decide scientifically how passions are aroused and what phenomena are normal, leaving it to the 'politician' to make use of these facts if our science of poetry affords him the means to his own ends.

III

The question of means and ends introduces a new phase of the subject. Aristotle is distinguished from his master Plato by his love of system; and this is not merely a love of divisions, subdivisions and titles; it is rather a love of order and relevancy by which he is perpetually driven to make fine distinctions and limit his topics. Knowing that this is Aristotle's very nature, we must not forget its influence even where it is not expressly shown. On the contrary we may assume that context, in the wide sense, is all-important: we may assume, for example, that the field of one treatise will differ from that of another in such a way as to alter the focus of all its constituent parts. On this assumption there will be good ground for making separate investigations into the different treatises involved.

Margoliouth[3] tells us 'every one agrees that the first clue is the passage near the end of the **Politics,** where there is a reference to the **Poetics** for further light.' This statement encourages us to expect a real solution of the problem, but in fact Aristotle says: 'the word *purgation* we use at present without explanation, but when hereafter we speak of poetry, we will treat the subject with more precision'! And Jowett adds, faintly in a foot-note, 'cp. *Poet.* c. 6, though the promise is really unfulfilled'![4] Apart then from what we read *into* this passage, we have little warrant for expecting any help from it. Yet the whole passage in the **Politics** is important, for reasons now to be considered.

The general topic in the **Politics,** Book VIII (Jowett's trans.), is education. The work as a whole being a handbook for statesmen, the subject of education is treated in a manner which is strictly 'practical'. We can imagine ourselves attempting to justify our ways to an inspector who asks, What are you educating them *for*? We prepare ourselves with a list of suitable answers—the useful, virtue, knowledge—but in fact we remain a little uncertain which answer is likely to turn away wrath: perhaps the best course is to survey what tradition makes us accept, and analyse the curriculum!

Some subjects are easily placed: reading and writing, of course, for all manner of obvious advantages: gymnastic for the body: 'music, to which is sometimes added drawing.'[5] Alas! these 'extras' never seem quite well placed: the parents want them, but object to the fees: the Inspector worries about their utility: and some one in the smart set says that anyhow the flute will never do, it makes you look so funny![6] A musical genius, lacking in good taste, suggests that music is really quite valuable, something like sleep or intoxication;[7] and when this shocking remark dies away, a solemn voice is heard pointing out that God plays no instrument!

What help are we to get from this abortive attempt to conciliate the Education Department. Frankly I should expect none save for the fact that Aristotle is trying to solve a really profound problem, the last great problem of the statesman—how to educate a nation to make right use of its leisure. This is the real 'problem' of education: the busy man is a slave; he runs after things which spring up automatically before him; but leisure

is the activity which creates and creative activity has its place in civilization because a 'leisured class' appreciates it, encourages it, and may even practise it. This is the answer so far as music is concerned: we did not invent it, for it is natural: we did not make it pleasant, for it always had a curious affinity with our moods which makes us enjoy even a melancholy strain: we cannot neglect it, for people whistle and sing of their own accord, and classical music is really only the most refined way of 'playing with the rattle.'![8] The elaboration of these phases would be a 'metaphysic' of music: our present scope is politics, and all we need to prove is that the good of the community requires its citizens to be good judges of musical performances: every one must be so far acquainted with music as to know what kind of music is being played and what its value is for the audience. A normal audience is simply a 'gathering', and music is a good 'entertainment' because it provides an occupation (hearing) in which all can share. There are also parts of audiences to be considered separately—the young, the extreme temperaments, the 'vulgar crowd composed of mechanics, labourers and the like.' Here too our statesman is justified. The experts tell us that there are 'ethical melodies, melodies of action, and passionate or inspiring melodies'[9]: and all the statesman requires to know is the results which the experts give him. So Aristotle passes on to his next point, that music should be studied for the sake of many benefits—namely education, purgation, intellectual enjoyment.

This is our climax, and its character should be carefully estimated. The state must keep music in its curriculum because it will in the future need at least three types of persons: (1) those who understand its use for education and become music teachers, either as being great performers or composers or theorists (exponents of the theory of music); (2) those who understand its use as a part of the medical treatment of the pathological emotions; ((3) those who form the cultured audiences and are the genuine critics, who do not perform on instruments or practise on patients, but live the life of the just citizen made perfect.

In all this, finally, Aristotle says nothing specifically about purgation and nothing at all about tragedy: he only explains why music is to be a part of education as regulated by a state. Unlike Plato he seems to regard the question as primarily concerned with occupations. The highest occupation of man is the use of intellect, and this is shown in sound judgement. Drawing is to be studied because it produces sound judgement of the human form: and we may add that as such it will be useful in the criticism of gymnastics, for the citizen will disapprove of physical training if it tends to brutalize. Similarly music is to be studied because it produces sound judgement of melodies and rhythms, which are important because they increase and decrease passions, and so affect deeply the life of man, as being a mixed creature. It is significant that Aristotle provides 'popular' music for the masses: there are many degrees in a commonwealth and the 'animal' element in music is a sort of common denominator: it will not offend the cultured, for 'feelings such as pity and fear . . . have more or less influence over all', but they will regard it critically and judge its merits by the [logos] in themselves and the 'rule of art' which it embodies along with its 'sweetness.' Perhaps Aristotle understood obscurely why folk-songs and popular airs have been so often the essence of the greatest music: for nature creates them in the undiscovered depths of feeling and art recreates them for the mind that demands explicit rules of method . . . and intellectual enjoyment. . . .

IV

The problem of means and ends, from which we reached the required parts of the *Politics,* will also lead into the *Rhetoric.* Here we shall find another phase of the questions concerning 'pity and fear and the affections of this class': we shall find also that Aristotle is thinking about politics again from a different angle, and rises to a view of the whole situation which, as a whole, seems to comprehend the real essence or genus of which politics, rhetoric, and poetics are distinct.

The art of Rhetoric arises as a 'variation' from Logic. Logic, dialectics and rhetoric are all arts occupied in providing proofs. In a perfect world, controlled by reason, nothing would be needed except logical proof: all sequences or connexions could be logically demonstrated and all persons would accept the conclusions as rational. But the actual world is very different. If we admit a sphere of true science, necessary and demonstrative, there is also the important sphere of 'probabilities.' In fact, human affairs and human interests are generally uncertain and probable; so much so that a moral scepticism springs up and even honest people believe nothing is really quite certain. In this atmosphere the orator grows into a shallow 'pleader', trained in all the tricks by which emotions can be utilized to secure verdicts. This occupation is so profitable and so debased that 'rhetoric' scarcely means anything else. But Aristotle would distinguish the different types: beside the pleading of the law court . . . there is the 'consultative' . . . argument: and this is the true type of 'rhetoric'.

This point must be scrutinized minutely; for the word 'orator' and the idea are alike too commonplace for the purpose; and it is easy to fail in estimating what seems to us utterly familiar. Yet we know that from Aristotle to Quintilian the great orator tended more and more to be the type of ideal citizen. This is not strange if we remember that the orator, as here defined, has practical judgement combined with the power of securing and controlling popular support. He is therefore a phase of the politician, fit to rule wherever

government by persuasion is constitutional: and Pericles actually embodied the virtues which Aristotle assigns to the ideal orator. If we are to understand the teaching of Aristotle all ideas of oratory as merely an art of language must be relegated to the furthest background.

Yet of course nothing is more important than language in the equipment of the orator. Words are the means which he will employ and this class of 'sounds' will be his instrument, though we must not forget that he may write speeches not intended for delivery. For this reason Aristotle does not neglect the technical questions of oratory, questions of topic, style, rhythm and the like. But as these subjects are not important for the present discussion, no more attention will be given to them. The significant feature of Aristotle's treatise is that he considers the whole situation in which oratory has its function and realizes that speech is relative to hearing. If an argument falls on inattentive or disaffected ears, it is wasted. The orator must remember three things: (a) the logical method of proof, (b) the influence of his own presence according as his moral prestige . . . adds to or subtracts from the weight of his words, (c) the attitude of the audience who may be willing or unwilling to reinforce his arguments by a benevolent and unprejudiced attitude . . . . A convincing argument is therefore very different from a correct argument. The difference lies in the simple fact that an argument is only convincing if some one is convinced. Rhetoric as an art must combine with its formal or logical elements a psychological part, and this is the reason why the second book of the *Rhetoric* is so largely concerned with the emotions which an orator must control.

This second book of the *Rhetoric* is so important that it deserves to be analysed in detail, but as space will not permit so elaborate a treatment, the most important features must be selected as proofs of the argument here evolved. My thesis, briefly, is that Aristotle's view of the meaning of [katharsis] is to be derived from this source; that the required link between the *Politics* and the *Poetics* is here supplied: and, finally, that if we understand how far the politician is an orator, the orator an actor, and the actor both orator and politician, we shall attain a right interpretation of the whole subject. This in no way excludes any technical medical statements about 'purgation', all of which may be true; but it implies that neither politician nor orator nor poet is required to know the medical facts, any more than a person who regards a blush as a confession of guilt need also know what inner mechanism produces the visible effect.

In the *Rhetoric* the emotions discussed are all those which produce changes in persons and so affect their judgements. . . . They are all states which induce pleasure or pain, and the examples are anger, pity, fear. . . .[10] Anger is due mainly to the feeling that one is despised, and is expressed as resentment. The orator must remove this resentment by first adopting the attitude of the resentful person and then showing that the objects of his anger are 'either formidable, or worthy of high respect, or benefactors, or involuntary agents, or as excessively afflicted at what they have done.'[11] These 'topics' will induce 'gentleness' . . . and what is then said in defence of the offender will be accepted without prejudice.

Let us suppose that the orator wishes his audience to feel fear. . . . The *practical* orator will then make his audience 'think or feel that they are themselves liable to suffering: for (as you suggest) others greater than they have suffered: and you show that their equals are suffering or have suffered: and this came from such as they never expected it from: and when not expected.'

Pity is only possible to those who think they may suffer: men will not pity if they have already lost all, or deem themselves beyond the reach of all evil. . . . Here follows a long list of the reverses of fortune which excite pity, and may therefore be regarded as proper 'topics.' Moreover, Aristotle here admits an element of 'acting' . . . to 'visualize' the facts. . . . [12] This is supplemented in Book III by the treatment of style . . . or delivery. This subject has been neglected, says Aristotle; and the reason is that it came late into tragedy and rhapsody: yet declamation is an important part of rhetoric and poetic, and it is gaining more importance owing to the corrupt state of public life.

The relation between appeals to emotion by 'acting' and the 'corruption' of the commonwealth must be emphasized here. As the basis of Rhetoric is conviction . . . and this is presumably right opinion, the purest form is rational, closely akin to logic: but the practical orator always has to consider the weakness of the audience, which is also fundamentally a decline in public standards. . . . [13] Similarly in the *Poetics,* the use of appeals to emotion by extraneous arts is only justified by the weakness of the audience. . . . Thus Rhetoric and Poetic have a common basis in the presentation of a plain unvarnished tale, which by its own virtue carries conviction: but the weakness of human nature requires the use of further appeals to the senses (of hearing in the case of sounds that reproduce expressions of joy or grief, of sight in the case of actions, gestures, or even mourning attire). Though these aids are practically necessary, they are not essentials, and it is therefore a matter for regret (***Rhet.,*** iii. 1.) that the prizes are won by the actors rather than the poets, thus making the production more important than the play. All this, we can well understand, must have been very repugnant to Aristotle.

V

The preceding sections are intended to clear the ground. They show that each treatise has a specific topic and deals with a group of ideas from distinct points of view. This is to be noted carefully, for any light we may hope to get on the subject of tragedy must be derived from this fact. Our thesis is, in brief, that some, if not all, of the difficulties vanish when we remember that Aristotle limits himself in the ***Poetics*** to the analysis of a form of art. If this is the case, we can deduce at once that no question of effects produced on the spectators enters into the definition of tragedy. On general principles it seems to me almost impossible that Aristotle should include in a definition of an 'essence' anything that is extraneous or accidental: he would be far more inclined to assert that a tragedy remains a tragedy, though no one hears or sees it, just as virtue remains virtue though unrewarded, and a triangle is a triangle though embodied in no material form. But as this a priori argument will lead into many conflicts with existing views, I will present it purely as a working hypothesis.

Let us assume then that the actual definition of Tragedy involves no reference to any 'purgation' experienced by the audience, and that the purgation remains an essential part of tragedy. This view will be supported (a) by those who reject Lessing's 'moral' interpretation, (b) by Margoliouth in so far as he realizes that the passions would be excited and therefore increased rather than expelled, (c) by the shrewd comment of Bywater[14] that this treatment would be so rare and intermittent as to be worthless. Special attention may be given to Bywater's point because it is almost the only sign I have found among editors that they appreciate the false subjectivity of modern commentators. Nothing can be achieved until the reader's mind is cleared of the notion that Aristotle is speaking of a modern theatre to which people can turn for relief six days a week, if they like; or that 'psychological appeal' is to be regarded as having any place in the ancient conception of an art.

But the most potent argument for our hypothesis is the fact that it is very difficult to find in Aristotle any reference to this 'purgation' of the audience. The original definition says nothing about it; at 1450b 16 Aristotle says 'the tragic effect is quite possible without a public performance and actors': and when the audience is mentioned it seems to be regarded as having a 'weakness' which induces the writer of plays to aim at pleasure and corrupt his art (1453a 35). The 'spectacle' is excluded from the essence of tragedy, though it is a part of theatrical production (1450b 20), and Aristotle remains throughout more clear on this distinction between the play and its [*chorēgia*] than most of his commentators. In matter and in tone there is a striking parallel between these passages and the corresponding sections of the ***Rhetoric***: the good speech is also a work of art, corrupted by any appeal to emotions and made perfect by the right union of logical proof, character . . . and diction. The actual outcome of successful oratory is a conviction. Perhaps the real work of Tragedy is to produce a type of conviction suited to the transcendent nature of its topics.

I would digress a moment to ask whether even Bywater's excellent translation is not really affected by his view of the function of tragedy, and actually distorted to maintain it. To show that this is the case I will consider what Aristotle says about the 'Fable or Plot' (Bywater, p. 23 *seqq.*). The Plot is the most important thing in Tragedy: it is by nature an organism, almost: its unity is logical, an inner bond of necessity: its incidents arouse pity and fear. What then should the Poet aim at? (*ibid.*, p. 35). What are the conditions of the tragic effect? Aristotle says: '(1) A good man must not be seen passing from happiness to misery, or (2) a bad man from misery to happiness. The first situation is not fear-inspiring or piteous, but simply odious to us.' (p. 35). So runs the translation, but there is nothing in the Greek about 'to us'! So again 'The second is the most untragic that can be; . . . it does not appeal either to the human feeling in *us,* or to *our* pity or to *our* fears.' But the text has no equivalent for any of these words underlined. Is it significant that Bywater puts them in and Aristotle leaves them out? I think it is, and without citing further evidence I will explain why the translator should avoid such additions.

I think Aristotle meant [*eleeinon*] and [*phoberon*] to stand by themselves as marks of real causes, things truly pitiable and truly fearful, whether any one actually felt pity and fear or not. There might always be a Jason to say, 'What's Hecuba to me?' but Hecuba is a tragic figure [*haplōs*], not [*pros hemās*]. So in the **Ethics** we are told that the man who excused himself for killing his mother talked nonsense: there is no such excuse! But if no one feels pity and fear, what is the meaning of the remark? The answer is that Aristotle is making an analysis: the sequence of events in the drama is the point at issue. The plot is bad if the cause of fear is inadequate, because the *dramatis persona* who responds with the tragic horror is then merely ridiculous. The quality of the play depends on the just balance of action and reaction: to express fear when nothing is truly fearful is comedy: to be indifferent toward the ordinary causes of fear is merely to fail in sustaining the part.

The persons who ought to 'feel' what the situations involve are the poets (1455a 31): they must have the special gift, almost a touch of madness, to see that invisible world of thoughts and motives which will be reincarnated in the actors. The audience can be expected to feel pleasure, for there is a pleasure of tragedy (1453a 36), and it is wholly distinct from the 'pleasant ending' which is in character more comic than tragic. Tragedy requires to be serious, and therefore the pleasure it affords can hardly be a feeling of joviality: it must rather be a sense of satisfaction. If this is satisfaction with the divine order of the world, if tragedy thus 'justifies the ways of God to men,' we come back to the 'moral' view of its function. And this I think Aristotle would admit to be the actual result of the best tragic dramas, but I feel equally sure that he would not include this extraneous result in the definition of the *essence* of tragedy. In any case, the resulting satisfaction would not be a subjective mood of purified passion, but a function of judgement.

This argument can now be concluded. The definition of Tragedy is taken to be a definition of its essence: this essence consists practically in the nature of the plot, for the rest is really a matter of production in the technical sense, the 'staging': the plot of a tragedy (as distinct from comedy) is always concerned with situations which involve pity and fear: these are the two factors with which it works, and it ends in a resolution of the tension indicated by these emotions, a clearing up of the emotions which belong to its sphere. It is difficult to invent such situations, for the persons involved must be 'better than ourselves': the plane of tragedy is elevated, and a 'hero' must by necessity occupy a conspicuous position; so that the poet is easily tempted to over-reach himself and achieve that success which we call melodrama. Since the situation must be 'possible', and yet a marvel to all, Aristotle thinks the poets do well to use only the accepted subjects, such as *'The Oedipus.'* Clearly the audience was very *critical;* it might easily discount all the merits of a play by refusing to accept its plot: as Aristotle says, if a thing *has* happened, no one can dispute its possibility. The history of Greek drama certainly suggests that the audiences had no craving for novelty of subject: surprise was an element in the treatment rather than the choice of a subject. All this goes to show that the audiences must have been as a rule pretty well acquainted with the pitiable and fearful things they were to behold: and this familiarity would hardly increase the 'purgative' effect, or might even produce immunity.

As the actual 'histories' of Priam, Hecuba, Oedipus and others were well known, so the moral theme of [*hubris*] is recognized as having become the focus of tragic drama. The sin has been committed somewhere at some time: God is not mocked: there is a cosmic tribunal where the Eternal Reason by the logic of cause and effect delivers its judgements: the prisoner at the bar is not a common criminal but something greater in scope, an inheritor of crime: he has no guilty conscience, but dark forebodings rise in the soul where memory . . . slumbers fitfully: as the coming doom draws near the indefinite suspicion becomes oppressive fear: in the climax the suffering is excessive, because the individual suffers for the sins of others and pays in his person for the guilt of his race: he is 'excessively afflicted' and therefore becomes truly pitiable.

If this is a correct outline of a typical tragedy as conceived by Aristotle it will show automatically why fear and pity are the chief emotional elements. Suffering is expressly included as an essential (1452b 10.). It is also significant that Aristotle says the chorus should be regarded as actors. This opinion must be due to the fact that the chorus tends to guide and control the development of the play on its emotional side: it emphasizes in words the emotional significance which the actors can only present symbolically. To put the matter a little crudely, the actor can only die physically: the chorus must add that he dies undeservedly or justly. Out of the welter of facts and emotions there should emerge a concrete idea of life, exhibited in an ideal type, showing why things must have happened as they did and why the verdict of time is reasonable. The merit of a work of art is to be convincing and this is its [*katharsis*].

VI

By way of epilogue and conclusion I may refer to some points which otherwise might seem unduly neglected.

Considerable attention has been paid in recent times to the medical terms used by Aristotle. One of the virtues of Greek thought is the grasp which it always retains on the idea of the whole organism. Whether the corporeal elements, the 'body' as flesh, are praised, tolerated, or condemned they are at least not forgotten. The emotions, the expression of the emotions, and the whole complex of typical characters were subjects of increasing attention. The 'characters' of Theophrastus may be regarded as word-pictures of types, which actors might profitably study. But we cannot on this account quote Aristotle's medical phrases to prove that tragedy is a kind of medical treatment. For this reason the reliance placed on the technical passages in the *Problems* seems to me an error: they furnish no proof of the point at issue—namely, that Aristotle regarded the production of these physiological changes as a function of tragedy.

The relation of Aristotle to Plato is an important topic which cannot be adequately treated here. Bywater's reference to *Republic*, Book X, seems to me important for reasons other than his. Bywater[15] thinks that Plato regarded drama as harmful because it nourishes the weaker elements of our nature, the tendency to tears and laughter. This is truth but not the whole truth. The view I would suggest is that Plato and Aristotle agreed in thinking that the 'weakness' of the audience and the 'corruption of the constitutions' (quoted above) rendered the drama a source of danger. We might quote modern instances to show that a play involving a murder can inspire one of the weaker sort to commit murder. The fact is that susceptible people are affected *emotionally* and may therefore abstract from their context the emotional incidents of the play. The real justifica-

tion of a play is in the appeal which it makes to judgement, not in the incidents which present the constituent events. While Plato sees an actual danger which can only be overcome by the production of the right type of spectator, Aristotle confines his attention to the nature of tragedy itself. So far as concerns the proper end of tragedy there is no reason to suppose that Plato and Aristotle did not completely agree in regarding it as an imitation of life with significance for those who understand. All art is removed from reality and has an element of illusion: but harm only results for those who forget this and are corrupted in their judgements.

There remains the haunting fascination of Aristotle's words—'through pity and fear achieving its catharsis of such emotions.' Are these words 'pity and fear' merely symbols of emotions, chosen at random, or is there a deeper significance in their appearance here? They suggest an antithesis and challenge attention by force of the reasons which must have made them prominent in Aristotle's mind. If nothing can be set down as certain, perhaps a benevolent hearing may be granted to one more speculative reconstruction.

Plato, as it seems, looked for a profound moral reform before the drama could be an aid to the good life. Aristotle here, as always, leans to a more gradual development, achieved through existing means. The beginning of life as action is the conative impulse . . . : the end is contemplation. The young live by their feelings: years may bring the philosophic mind. The drama shows us life in a way which enables us to contemplate it: it presents a specimen of a class of lives so that it can be seen as a logical whole. In the slow movement of daily life we lose our sense of proportion: if we prosper, we think no harm can ever come to us: if we meet disaster, we think there can be no relief and justice is dead. Sometimes we forget God and are insolent: sometimes we despair and blame God. Margoliouth says that in their conduct 'every *dramatis persona* is hitting or missing an imaginary mark.' I am not sure that I understand this phrase in its context, but I will give it the meaning I should like it to have. The mark is the mean, as Aristotle describes it in the ***Ethics.*** Every actor shows us how the true mean may be hit or missed. Those who run to excess and over-reach themselves are to be reduced by fear: those who suffer are to find pity and relief in the working of 'poetic justice.' If this interpretation is narrowed and taken to refer to a single person, then the mean will consist simply in fearing what is greater and pitying what is inferior. In either case the terms 'pity and fear' may be taken to indicate the limits of passion in the two directions which are typically defect and excess: for pity corrects the tendency toward intolerance and inhuman conduct, while fear sets a limit to the ambition that o'erleaps itself. If this interpretation is accepted it indicates that Aristotle's definition was after all little more than a compact statement of the aims common to all the Greek tragedians. For the mean in human life is part of the order of the universe and the man who transgresses it will sooner or later bring into play all the forces that make for righteousness in the universe. The conflict between man's variable nature and the laws which rule him inexorably is the essence of tragedy. To present this concretely in action is to define it in terms of act and feeling, freed from all that is confusing and irrelevant. This will be the particular catharsis which tragedy achieves, and which the spectator will judge to be truth because his reason accepts what is clear and by intuition grasps the finality of the conclusion.

The reasons for the affinity between the **Politics,** the **Rhetoric** and the **Poetics** can be stated thus. In the **Politics** the question of education involves the development of character, and music has a distinct place in the 'diet' which nurtures the soul: in the **Rhetoric** the *emotions* are to be considered as the irrational factors which affect judgement, and the result desired is a definite verdict for or against a particular act or person. Here the conclusion is on a relatively lower plane, because it is 'practical' and ends in the deliberate choice of action, a direction of desire in the sphere of things mutable. In the **Poetics** there is no question of future action, no pleading for a verdict: the scene is laid in the past, the events are therefore eternal and immutable: the spectator judges 'theoretically', that is contemplatively. As an aesthetic judgement this involves only aesthetic values, and perhaps Aristotle would not have rejected the idea that after the analysis of science and the analysis of the 'practical reason' he had in fact laid the foundations for a critique of 'judgement' in the Kantian sense. I would argue that failure to recognize these fundamental changes of viewpoint has been the chief error in interpretation and has obscured the fact that a term like [*katharsis*] takes its meaning from its context.

Notes

[1] Bywater, *Aristotle on the Art of Poetry,* p. 361.

[2] *op. cit.,* p. 152.

[3] Margoliouth, *Aristotle, Poetics,* p. 56.

[4] *Aristotle's Politics, translated by Benjamin Jowett,* p. 314, 1905.

[5] *Politics,* 1337b.

[6] *Pol.,* 1341b.

[7] *Pol.,* 1339a.

[8] *Politics,* 1340b.

[9] *Pol.,* 1341b.

[10] Others are actually discussed but the details cannot be given and this epitome, as given by Aristotle, is valuable as showing how pity and fear are uniformly selected to represent the whole group.

[11] Cope, *The Rhetoric of Aristotle,* vol. II, p. 41.

[12] *Rhetoric,* ii. c. 8 §14 (Cope, vol. II, p. 105).

[13] *Rhet.,* iii. 1. 5.

[14] p. 156.

[15] Bywater, p. 153.

Lane Cooper (essay date 1923)

SOURCE: "Character, Antecedents, and General Scope of *Poetics,*" in *The Poetics of Aristotle and Its Meaning and Influence,* Cornell University Press, 1923, pp. 3-14.

[*In this brief overview, Cooper reviews such textual issues as the date of composition of* Poetics *and the possible sources on which Aristotle drew to write the treatise. Cooper also discusses the structure, function, and goal of poetry as analyzed by Aristotle.*]

The **Poetics** of Aristotle is brief, at first sight hard and dry, and yet one of the most illuminating and influential books ever produced by the sober human mind. After twenty-two centuries it remains the most stimulating and helpful of all analytical works dealing with poetry—and poetry is the most vital and lasting achievement of man. This pregnant treatise, dating from some time before the year 323 B. C., is indeed short and condensed. Castelvetro's famous 'exposition' of it (Vienna, 1570) fills 768 pages, and runs to something like 384,000 words. The **Poetics** itself contains perhaps 10,000 words. In the great Berlin edition of Aristotle (1831) it takes up only 30 columns of print, or 15 pages; in the last notable edition of the **Poetics,** that of Bywater (1909), the text occupies 45 pages out of 431. The **Poetics** makes about a hundredth part of the extant works of Aristotle.

Though never long, it doubtless once was longer; and it probably was associated with another work of Aristotle, now represented only by fragments, his dialogue **On Poets,** and with his **Homeric Problems.** In the same group of writings were the **Peplos** and the **Didascaliæ,** the latter a history or record of the Greek dramatic contests, with the names of victors and similar data. The dialogue **On Poets** seems to have been of a more literary character. At all events the **Poetics** does not now resemble the finished work of that Aristotle whose style was praised by Cicero and Quintilian. What we have of it may be the notes that served the master through various years for some part of his lectures; such notes he would expand in oral discussion, adding examples, reconciling apparent contradictions, solving difficulties with his pupils in the Peripatetic fashion. The defence of Homer toward the end of the book connects it with the *Problems,* and the last chapter, on the relative merits of epic and tragic poetry, has the look of an embryo dialogue. Or we may have in the *Poetics* the notes of some person who attended Aristotle's lectures and colloquies—a hypothesis that would explain omissions and discrepancies that troubled the last generation of modern scholars. Or, finally, the work may be the grudging abstract by some student of the Alexandrian age or later, who took the essentials from one book or section by the master, and therewith joined what seemed important or germane from one or two others. There may have been several steps in the reduction of the *Poetics* to its present state, which it had reached some time before the sixth century A. D. If so, the history of the treatise would resemble that of Greek learning as a whole in the gradual decay of scholarship and science, until in the Dark Ages the rich and detailed investigations of the Alexandrian period—in biology, for example—had dwindled to the barest epitomes. There is at least one unexpected gap in our *Poetics.* The treatise does not fulfil its own promise regarding a discussion of comedy; certain scholars have found the promise redeemed in a fragment known as the *Tractatus Coislinianus,* the merest outline, descended from a body of critical doctrine, now lost, of wider range than the extant *Poetics.*

We have no adequate knowledge about the composition of Aristotle's works in literary criticism. His *Rhetoric,* though the text is now corrupt, fared better in the Græco-Roman world than the *Poetics,* meeting the practical needs of Roman orators. We do not know when either treatise was written, yet there has been a tendency to regard the *Poetics* as the earlier. Doubtless both existed side by side during some part of Aristotle's activity as teacher, and underwent occasional revision at his hands. After his death the *Rhetoric* was included in a body of like treatises, now mostly of uncertain origin. But the *Poetics* is the only technical discussion of its subject that has come down to us from ancient Greece. For the study of Greek art, including poetic art, it is, after the masterpieces themselves, the most valuable document we have from antiquity.

In its own time, however, it was not a solitary work; and it had predecessors as well as contemporaries in its field. Here Aristotle did not, as in the *Topica,* feel that he labored as a pioneer, but had models on which to improve. In *Poetics* 8 he suggests that Homer may have worked with conscious art. If a full-fledged theory of rhetoric came from the Sicilian to the Athenian orators, why, we may ask, should not a theory of the poetic art come to the Athenian drama, if not from Sicily, then from Asia Minor—from Miletus or Smyrna—along with a body of epic tradition that furnished subject-matter for the Attic stage? The more we learn of early Ægean culture, and of its persistence at the Sicilian and Ionian fringes when the centre was swept away, the greater seems the debt of Athens to that culture for the seeds of art and science. Some notions of Homeric rules of art, accordingly, may have drifted down to the predecessors of Aristotle with the *Iliad* and the *Odyssey.* In the *Republic* Plato makes Socrates speak of the 'ancient quarrel between philosophy and poetry.' How early did the naughty Homeric tales of the gods, of Mars and Venus, become a topic of debate between moralist and literary critic? The *Poetics* notes that Xenophanes (*fl.* 530 B. C.) thought them very bad, and implicitly takes issue with the *Republic* for likewise condemning them with no appeal to standards of art.

But the foregoing are vaguer considerations. There is evidence in Plato's *Phædrus,* as in the *Poetics,* that Sophocles consciously observed dramatic laws. And, among other sayings, he declared that Æschylus 'did right without knowing why'; he himself, then, composed aright, *knowing why.* The *Poetics* records a maxim of Agathon on dramatic probability; and indeed, in acting and staging their plays, and in training the chorus and actors, the tragic poets must have reflected much on their art. That the great dramatists had a store of reflections is evinced by Aristophanes' *Frogs,* which in effect is the work of a great literary critic, and shows the poet to be familiar with tragic technique, and with stock terms and methods of criticism; his comic purpose should not blind us to his actual knowledge. Another (lost) play of Aristophanes was itself called *Poiesis,* while of his contemporaries Plato (not the philosopher) produced a *Poet* and *Poets,* and Nicochares likewise a *Poet.* These comedies were the forerunners of those with similar titles in the age of Aristotle: *Poets* and *Poetry* by Alexis, *Poiesis* by Antiphanes, and a *Poet* each by Biottus and Phœnicides.

In prose, it has been assumed that the Dialogues of Plato were background and incentive to the treatise of Aristotle; it is often held that the *Poetics* is a defence of poetry against the attacks of Socrates upon Homer and the dramatists in Books 2, 3, and 10 of the *Republic.* But the prose background was larger. The circle to which Plato belonged was a group of theorists and investigators,[1] including botanists, students of biology, of grammar, of music—of art and science in general. Among other disciples of Socrates, we find Crito, Simmias of Thebes, and Simon, who produced, according to Diogenes Laertius, works discussing poetry and fine art. Of uncertain date, but a precursor of Aristotle, was a Democritus who wrote a treatise *On Poetry* and another on *Rhythms and Harmony.* And again, of the members of the Platonic school,

Speusippus dealt with rhetoric and art, while Xenocrates wrote on oratorical and literary problems; the learned Heracleides of Pontus wrote on music, and on poetry and the poets. In the **Poetics** Aristotle himself alludes a dozen times or more to critical treatises bearing on his subject; he mentions by name the authors Protagoras, Hippias of Thasos, Eucleides, Glaucon, and Ariphrades. Their works are lost; his alone remains, if not as he might have chosen to leave it for posterity, yet in a shape by which the world has benefited, and can benefit more. We may suppose that from this body of writings he as usual eliminated the chaff, and reorganized the essentials, synthesizing, emphasizing, subordinating, filling out in a large and luminous perspective. Through him we probably owe much to his contemporaries and predecessors.

At the same time the **Poetics** must be thought an original work, based upon observation and comparison of many narrative poems, and a thousand Greek dramas of which we now have but a fraction. Our author had an ample assortment of cases for study. And though he took all knowledge for his province, neglecting perhaps no subject cultivated by the Greeks save geography, though he brought to the analysis of poetic art a mind exercised in philosophy, ethics, politics, logic, psychology, and rhetoric, we should remember that he was the son of a physician, had himself a medical training, and was, if one thing more than another, what we call a biologist. He is interested in life and the principles of life. He therefore studies poetry, a form of life, as a philosophical and also a specialized anatomist and physiologist. He considers its structure and its function. Above all is he concerned with the function and ultimate purpose of it. The common mistake of unoriginal students, in our day as in his, has been to dissect a poem—a complete organism—without regard to the meaning and purpose of the whole. It is the mistake of pedants who divide a masterpiece, and do not rejoin the parts in living union; and thus their pupils, who love life, come to hate the work—of Milton, say—that they are 'studying.' But the originality of Aristotle helps us to relive the life of Greek epic and dramatic poetry. Dry (not dull) though his treatise may at first appear, I have yet to meet the student, mature enough to grasp the outline of a narrative or a drama, whose interest can not be quickened by applying to the narrative or drama the Aristotelian principles of life and art.

The **Poetics** does not merely help us to appreciate the few Greek dramas that survive, to imagine the other Greek critical treatises from which it partly sprang, and to feel that almost every critical problem our minds conceive was broached by the Greeks; it also tells us much concerning the vast body of Greek dramas that are lost, and yields much of our information regarding Greek stage-practice. We have but 7 whole plays by Æschylus, who is said to have written from 70 to 90;

but 7 by Sophocles, who is credited with 123; and but 18 or (with the *Rhesus*) 19 by Euripides, who wrote perhaps 92. Of late, considerable fragments have been regained of an eighth play, the *Trackers,* by Sophocles. Of the 160 plays by Chœrilus, somewhat earlier than Æschylus, we know almost nothing. Of tragedy in Aristotle's own lifetime we have possibly one example, the *Rhesus,* if that is not by Euripides. Yet, including the fifty plays which his own friend Theodectes produced with conspicuous success, Aristotle could easily have read, from those of Chœrilus down, well over a thousand Greek tragedies. Most of these, when we hear of them at all, are to us little more than names; some, at best, survive in chance fragments of a few lines only. Then, in addition to the 11 plays of Aristophanes that have come down to us, Aristotle must have known the lost works of that author, not to mention other poets of the Old Comedy, such as Cratinus and Eupolis, or the mass of plays in the age succeeding—the so-called Middle Comedy, which we must mainly judge by the quotations by Athenæus.

But we should not expect too much from the **Poetics.** The treatise as its stands tells us little about Greek Comedy. And if we go to it for light on poetry as this is vaguely conceived by modern readers we shall be disappointed. Nowadays people think of poetry as versified composition about vernal flowers and the breath of 'nature.' When they meet lyrical effusions like Tennyson's *Crossing the Bar,* or Wordsworth's *Tintern Abbey,* or anything else in which they hear of the human soul being reabsorbed into the world-soul, or of 'a motion and a spirit . . . that rolls through all things'— in other words, when they meet the notion of divine immanence lyrically expressed, when they meet versified Neoplatonism—readers think they have found true poetry. For the treatise of Aristotle, however, poetry is epic poetry (as Homer is the greatest poet) or dramatic poetry (as tragedy is the noblest poetical type). Aristotle does, indeed, consider the choral odes of tragedy, but not apart from the drama. Had he chosen to examine what we call the lyric, as a separate form, he probably would have done so, not in a treatise on poetry, but in one on music; though to him, as to the Greeks in general, the activities of poet and musical composer were not far apart. In the days of Æschylus, Sophocles, and Aristophanes, a poet wrote both words and music for his drama. The author of the **Poetics,** coming later, does not boast of a very thorough musical education.

Notes

The plan of the series forbids an inclusion of systematic references in support of many statements in this volume. The works cited in the following Notes, or listed in the Bibliography, do not exhaust the account of the sources to which I am indebted for facts or opinions. Only a few salient references can be given.

[1] 'Investigators': see Hermann Usener, *Vorträge und Aufsätze* (Leipsic, 1907), p. 83. . . .

Charles Sears Baldwin (essay date 1924)

SOURCE: "The Poetic of Aristotle," in *Ancient Rhetoric and Poetic*, Peter Smith, 1959, pp. 132-66.

[*In the following essay, Baldwin offers a general overview of Aristotle's* Poetics, *discussing in particular the role of imitation in Aristotle's poetic theory.*]

Veneration of Aristotle has been impatiently classed with "other mediæval superstitions," both by those who disliked authority and by those who revolted against the inlaying and overlaying of his text with centuries of interpretations.[1] Since the Renaissance the *Poetic* has, indeed, fared in this regard somewhat as the Bible; and in both cases those deviations from the original intention are widest, perhaps, which have arisen from "private interpretation," from missionary zeal more anxious to read *into* the text than to read *in* it. What may be called on the other hand communal interpretation, the consentient application of Aristotle's ideas to the typical problems of a whole group or period, constitutes an important guide in the history of criticism. Both kinds of interpretation imply in the original an extraordinary fertility. This vitality, it is also clear, is of principles, of ideas set forth not only as classifying, but as constructive. The principles have been from time to time crystallized in rules; and some of the rules, having been found restrictive or even inhibitory, have thereupon been flung aside. But again and again a return to Aristotle's *Poetic* for orientation of practise and of criticism has vindicated it as constructive. It is not what Professor Dewey has lately called a "closed system."[2] It has exceptionally little of that mathematically abstract method which Bergson[3] found unsatisfying for survey of human activities in time. Rather its method is inductive. It examines how imaginative conceptions have been so composed and so expressed as to kindle, direct, and sustain the imagination of an audience; and its formulation is typically like what modern science calls an hypothesis, that is a generalization interpreting facts so far as they are known, and fruitful in their further investigation.

To reinterpret the *Poetic* in 1924, therefore, should be not merely to reconsider the drama and the epic of Aristotle's time, valuable as this is historically, but according to Aristotle's intention to consider what makes drama, our own as well as his, and what vitally moves it to possess an audience. Each interpretation of so fundamental a work must have its own preoccupations. The French interpretations of the seventeenth century had an emphasis different from that of the Italian of the sixteenth; and we in turn must see with our own eyes. But the correction that therefore becomes necessary, lest we make Aristotle say what we wish, lies in the text itself. Fortunately the *Poetic* is short enough to be read attentively in two hours; and its terms, though translated somewhat variously, sometimes imperfectly, now and then perversely, really demand not so much erudition as patience, attention to the context, and some acquaintance with the processes of art. The *Poetic* should be read consecutively as a whole and then scrutinized in its parts. Interrupted though it is here and there, in some few places even fragmentary, it nevertheless progresses as a whole.[4] As to its terms, the best precaution is to remember that they mean to express the processes of actual composition and the results of the actual representation of drama or of the actual recitation of epic. In this sense the book is practical. It is not, as Bywater implies,[5] the less theoretical; but it deals with the composing as well as with the thing composed.

That Aristotle's survey of human expression included a *Poetic* as well as a *Rhetoric* is our chief witness to a division[6] oftener implied in ancient criticism than stated explicitly. Rhetoric meant to the ancient world the art of instructing and moving men in their affairs; poetic the art of sharpening and expanding their vision. To borrow a French phrase,[7] the one is composition of ideas; the other, composition of images. In the one field life is discussed; in the other it is presented. The type of the one is a public address, moving us to assent and action; the type of the other is a play, showing us in action moving to an end of character. The one argues and urges; the other represents. Though both appeal to imagination, the method of rhetoric is logical; the method of poetic, as well as its detail, is imaginative. To put the contrast with broad simplicity, a speech moves by paragraphs; a play moves by scenes. A paragraph is a logical stage in a progress of ideas; a scene is an emotional stage in a progress controlled by imagination. Both rhetoric and poetic inculcate the art of progress; but the progress of poetic is distinct in kind. Its larger shaping is not controlled by considerations of *inventio* and *dispositio*,[8] nor its detail by the cadences of the period.[9] In great part, though not altogether, it has its own technic. The technic of drama in Aristotle's day was already mature and was actively developing. The technic of narrative, in epic derived from the great example of Homer, in "mime" and dialogue still experimental, was less definite. To set forth the whole technic, the principles of imaginative composition, in a single survey is the object of Aristotle's *Poetic*.

TABULAR VIEW OF THE ***POETIC*** OF ARISTOTLE[10]

The first section moves from definition of poetic in general to the mode of drama (chapters i-v.)

I. The art of poetry	Chapter

A. is one of the arts that imitate men in action

1. belonging with instrumental music and dancing   ii

a. as using rhythm and melody besides words

B. has two typical modes   iii

1. narrative
2. drama
   a. tragedy
   b. comedy

C. developed historically   iv

1. from the instincts of imitation and rhythm
2. toward
   a. idealizing what men may be
   (1) as in epic and tragedy
   b. satirizing what men are
   (1) as in lampoons and comedy
   c. differentiation of form
   (1) drama tending toward unity of plot
                                               v

   (a) through the successive improvements of Eschylus and Sophocles

   (2) but keeping variety in verse.

The second section discusses plot as the mainspring of tragedy (chapters vi-xviii)

II. In the mode of drama, tragedy

A. (definition) is an imitation of an action
                                               vi

1. serious
2. determinate
3. in language enhanced by rhythm, melody, and song
4. by action, not by narrative
5. issuing in emotional catharsis

B. is primarily plot

1. the subsidiary elements being character, diction, thought, spectacle (including make-up), and song
2. (definition) Plot is a course of action planned to move causally from a beginning through a middle to an end
                                               vii

3. Plot is thus animated
   a. not merely by one main person
                                               viii

   b. but by such consistency
   (1) as arises from truth, as distinct from facts   ix
   (2) as is opposed to the episodic
   (3) as is necessary to the catharsis

4. Plot may be complicated by reversal or recognition   x
   a. arising causally from the plot itself
                                               xi

   b. and has as a third element emotion and suffering

5. Plot is the consistent working out, in an illustrious personage, of some human error

to its issue

a. Prologue, episode, etc., are merely formal parts   xii
b. Plot is not mere reversal of fortune in a character altogether good or bad
                                               xiii

   (1) for consistency, plot should be single, not divided by reversal to make a "happy ending"
   (a) as in inferior tragedies
   (b) and in comedy
c. Plot achieves catharsis by its own consistency   xiv
   (1) not by spectacular means
   (2) for the effect of fear and pity arises from the clash of motive with circumstance
d. Plot imposes consistency also on characterization   xv
   (1) generally consistency with
   (a) goodness
   (b) the moral habit of the class
   (c) the received idea of the particular person
   (d) itself; i. e., actions must be clearly motivated
   (2) particularly consistency with the causal weaving of the plot
   (a) excluding the *deus ex machina*
e. Plot is the true measure of the various kinds of recognition   xvi
   (1) The least artistic is recognition by bodily marks
   (2) No better is mere disclosure
   (3) A third, by recollection, arises from some incident in the plot
   (4) A fourth is through the inference of the personæ
   (5) But the best of all is that which arises causally from the course of the action

6. Plot, in the actual process of playwriting
   a. demands a habit of visualizing
                                               xvii

   (1) furthered by the dramatist's acting out of his own scenes
   b. begins in the dramatist's mind with a scenario
   (1) for the amplifying incidents must be fewer than in epic
   c. is worked out as complication and solution   xviii
   (1) This is the technical point in which tragedies are similar or dissimilar
   (2) The four typical kinds of tragedy, i. e., (a) those that depend mainly on reversal and recognition, (b) on emotion, (c) on character, (d) on spectacle, show the four elements of interest which the dramatist should seek to combine

   d. precludes the extensiveness of epic

e. involves making the chorus one of the actors

(1) not a mere singer of interludes

C. The subsidiary element of thought, the rhetorical element in tragedy, includes the effects produced directly by persuasive speech, as distinct from those produced by action.   xix

D. The subsidiary element of diction, to set aside what belongs under delivery, includes letters, syllables, connectives, nouns and verbs (with their inflection), and word-combinations.   xx

1. Words may be classified as
                                                                     xxi

a. single or double

b. ordinary or extraordinary (figurative, coined, etc.)

c. masculine or feminine

2. Virtue in the choice of words consists in being clear without being colorless
                                                                    xxii

a. Though extreme or habitual deviation from ordinary use is a fault, occasional deviation is necessary to distinction

b. Though it is a great thing to use variations of diction with propriety, the greatest thing is to be master of metaphor.

The third section defines epic and compares it with tragedy (chapters xxiii-xxvi).

III. In the mode of narrative, epic
A. has some general likeness to tragedy
                                                                   xxiii

1. in that its [component] stories should be single, complete, having beginning, middle, and end

a. giving the pleasure of a living whole

b. not following the method of history

(1) as inferior poets do, but not Homer

2. in that it may be simple or complex, emphasize either character or emotion, and has some of the same elements as tragedy
                                                                   xxiv

B. differs in length and in meter
1. Its characteristic advantages are scope and variety

2. The respective meters are the result of experience in appropriateness

C. shows in Homer the superiority of making the characters reveal themselves without explanation

D. can make freer use of the marvelous
1. by vividness of description

2. from the fact that the causal sense is weaker in reading or merely listening than in witnessing stage representation

E. may be defended against the typical charges that it is impossible, improbable, corrupting, contradictory, or artistically incorrect   xxv

F. is inferior to tragedy   xxvi
1. The charge that tragedy is more vulgar and exaggerated applies not to tragedy, but to acting

2. It has fewer elements of appeal
a. lacking music and spectacle

3. It is less vivid than tragedy read [much less than tragedy acted]

4. It is less concentrated [and so less intense]
a. lacking dramatic unity

I

The principle of poetic art is imitation. Its two kinds are drama in several forms and that other kind which ranges from epic to dialogue and which has no single generic name. All its forms in both kinds—tragedy, comedy, dithyramb in the one; epic, mime, dialogue in the other—are grouped with the arts of the flute, the lyre, and the dance, and apart from those of painting and singing. Thus begins Aristotle's **Poetic** with that chapter of definition which, as in the **Rhetoric,** opens and illuminates the whole subject.

As to poetic art[11] I propose to discuss what it is in itself and in the capacity of each of its species, how plots must be organized if the poem is to succeed, furthermore the number and nature of the parts, and similarly whatever else falls within the same inquiry, beginning systematically with first principles.[12]

Epic and tragedy, comedy also and the [dramatic[13]] art of the dithyramb, and most of the art of the flute and of the lyre are all, taken together, imitations. They differ one from another in three respects: in the means of imitation, in the object, or in the mode [i. e., all are essentially imitation; in imitation they are generally alike, and in imitation they are specifically different].

For as there are those who by colors and outlines imitate various objects in their portrayals, whether by art or by practise, and others who imitate through the voice, so also in the arts mentioned above. All [these] make their imitation by rhythm, by language, and by music, whether singly or in combination. Thus only rhythm and music are used in the art of the flute, of the lyre, and in such other arts, similar in capacity, as that of the pipes. Rhythm itself, without music, [suffices for] the art of the dancers; for by ordered rhythms they imitate both character and emotion and action [i. e., dancing compasses the whole scope of representation]. Words alone, whether prose or verse of whatever kind, are used by an art which is to this day without a name. We have no common name for the mime of Sophron or Xenarchus and the Socratic dialogue. Nor should we have one if the imitation were in trimeters or elegiacs or some other kind of verse. . . . [For it is not verse, Aristotle goes on to say, that makes poetry, but imitation.]

So much for differentiation. There are some arts that use all the means mentioned above, i. e., rhythm, music, and verse, e. g., dithyrambic and nomic poetry and also both tragedy and comedy; but they differ in that the first two use all the means in combination, whereas the latter use now one, now another. Therefore I differentiate these arts by their respective means of imitation.

To proceed surely from this opening chapter, it is evidently necessary to grasp what Aristotle means first by imitation, secondly by that nameless art which uses only words, thirdly by classifying the art of poetry with that of music and that of the dance.

By imitation Aristotle means just what the word means most simply and usually, but also and more largely the following of the ways of human nature, the representation or the suggestion of men's characters, emotions, and actions.[14] At its lowest, imitation is mimicry; at its highest, creation. The latter is often implied in the Greek word *poetic.*[15] Poetic is one of the fine arts. By whatever means, in whatever forms, it is a direct showing of life, as distinct from any account of life through experiment or reasoning. The artist enhances our impressions of life by the suggestions of music or of story, the representations of dance or of drama. All these ways are called by Aristotle imitation because they follow the movements of human life. It is noteworthy that he presents imitation primarily as a constructive or progressive principle. The more obvious imitation achieved by a single phrase, a single melody, or a single dance-movement is reserved for later discussion of detail.[16] The poet is a maker, as indeed he was called by our Elizabethans as well as by the Greeks, in the sense that he is creative. Poet, poetry, poetic, all are used by Aristotle with this broad implication of creative composition,[17] of "imitating men in action."

Secondly, Aristotle specifies as kinds of the poetic art tragedy and comedy, which belong together as drama, and on the other hand epic, mime, dialogue, which also belong together, but have no common name. We lack, he says, a generic name for those forms of poetic art which, however various, are alike in having for their sole means of imitation words. The generic name that Aristotle desired to cover all prose and all metrical compositions in which the imitation is through words alone is still to seek. Yet that the genus is distinct through many varieties of form is even clearer to-day than in his time. The imitation of dancing and of all forms of drama is through representation; the imitation of music without words is through suggestion. Now so

is the imitation of words without music. True, the words in the latter case carry something besides imitation; they convey ideas; but in so far as they achieve imitation, they do so by suggestion, and it is this suggestive imitation that makes them poetic. What is needed, then, is a term to cover all composition in words that proceeds by suggestion. Perhaps the nearest term in modern English is *narrative.* Using narrative widely enough to include, as in common modern use it often does include, dialogue and description, we have the term that Aristotle desired. *Story* would serve if it were not often used of the plot of a play or of an account in a newspaper. *Narrative* usually connotes a distinct method. A distinguishing generic term is more important to-day than in the time of Aristotle. Modern authors have developed narrative in directions little explored by the ancients. We have thus a variety of narrative forms which was quite unknown to Aristotle. Still, through all this variety, runs what he discerned as a common controlling method, the method of suggestion. In this fundamental *Gulliver's Travels* and the *Sentimental Journey* and *The Lady of the Lake,* to take examples as different as possible, belong together; and together they belong apart from *Othello.*

Thirdly, what is the significance of grouping all these forms of poetic art with music and dancing? Painting, which even in Aristotle's day was a fine art, is mentioned only as an analogy from another group. Singing, or chanting, also is only mentioned for analogy, perhaps because it is not creative. Architecture may have been omitted as being primarily at that time a useful art; but sculpture was both a fine art and, perhaps most obviously of all arts, imitative. Though we need not assume that Aristotle intended here a comprehensive classification of the arts, it is clear that he intended to group poetic art with the arts of music and dancing. Nor is his principle of division far to seek. Clearly he regards poetic as one of the arts of movement in time, and as distinct from the static arts of line and color, balance, mass, and pose. True, music and dance entered largely into early Greek drama and were still present in the drama of Aristotle's time; but that fact does not explain the grouping together of "epic, tragedy, comedy, dithyramb, flute-playing, and lyre-playing," with the later inclusion of dancing. Aristotle does not say that these occur together; and the mention of epic precludes any such interpretation. He says that they are alike. He saw all poetic art, especially drama, as primarily an art of movement. What is implied here in the opening chapter is carried out consistently, in doctrine and in terms, through the whole book. No one should deny a certain fundamental likeness among all the arts; but the likeness is not in technic except among those arts which have like "means" of expression, such as "rhythm, language, and music." Modern application of terms from architecture and painting to drama and story has spread no little confusion. Aristotle will have us think along right lines; and, as in his **Rhetoric,** the first chapter is the most important of all. We are to think of poetic composition not as structure, but as movement.

[Chapter ii differentiates the epic and the tragic art, which idealize "men in action" by seeking higher types of manhood and exhibiting men's aspirations, from the comic art, which exaggerates human failings. Chapter iii differentiates the two typical modes of poetic imitation as the narrative and the dramatic. Chapters iv and v, starting from the common impulses toward imitation, toward music, and toward rhythm, summarize the history of tragedy and of comedy. The conclusion is that tragedy differs from epic not only in proceeding by representation instead of narrative, but by being focused on a short period of time, normally twenty-four hours; in a word, by being intensive. Thus we arrive at the famous analysis of the essentials and the elements of tragedy.]

A tragedy,[18] then, is an imitation of an action that is (1) serious and, (2) as to size, complete, (3) in language enhanced as may be appropriate to each part, (4) in the form of action, not of narrative, (5) through pity and fear effecting its catharsis of such emotions. . . . Every tragedy,[19] therefore, must have six constituents, according to which we estimate its quality: plot, character, diction, thought, spectacle, and music.

The greatest of these is the plan of the actions (the plot); for tragedy is an imitation not of men, but of action and life . . . and the end [for which we live] is a certain form of action, not a quality. By their characters men are what they are; but by their actions they are happy or the reverse. [In a play] therefore they do not act in order to imitate character; they include character for the sake of the actions. Hence the actions and their plot are the end of tragedy; and the end is greatest of all. Furthermore, without action there may not be tragedy; without character there may be . . . By stringing together speeches expressive of character and well made as to diction and thought you will not achieve the tragic function. Much rather is it achieved by a tragedy which, however deficient in these, has plot and plan of actions. Besides, those things by which tragedy moves us most, scenes of reversal and of discovery, are parts of the plot. A further proof is that novices in dramaturgy can put a fine point on diction and characterization before they compose deeds; and it is the same with nearly all the early dramatists. The principle and, as it were, the soul of tragedy is plot.

Second is character . . . Third[20] is thought, i. e., the ability to say what is necessary and appropriate, which in public address is the function of politics and rhetoric. . . . Characterization is what shows habit of mind . . . Thought appears in formal reasoning.

Fourth is diction, i. e., the expression of meaning in words, which is essentially the same in verse as in prose.

Of the remaining elements, melody is the greatest of enhancements; and spectacle, though moving, is [in general] the least artistic and [in particular] has the least to do with the art of the drama.

The history of criticism involved in the successive interpretations of this much discussed section and the following may be postponed, The immediate concern is the meaning of the definition and the division for dramaturgy, i. e., for the actual composition of a tragedy and for the analysis of tragedy in terms of composition. Aristotle begins with the subject-matter. The theme itself must be tragic, and is so if it is first serious and secondly complete within its own extent. A playwright considering the possibilities of such-and-such material is to ask first whether it is serious. The Greek word[21] means not solemn in the sense of sad, but such as to interest the composer and the audience by its importance. It might be rendered *humanly significant*. The question, Is there drama here? becomes, then, first of all, Is there action here that will engage emotional participation? That is the first question; for it is fundamental.

Secondly, is this action dramatically manageable as to extent? Will it finish within the time of a drama, come to its issue, focus; or is its interest such as to demand more extensive development in time; in a word, is it a drama plot or an epic plot? The epic of "much-enduring Odysseus" demands extent of time; the tragedy of Oedipus, compression of time. *Complete*[22] here means concluded, i. e., susceptible, within dramatic limits, of a conclusion emotionally satisfying. To be dramatic, the action must be self-consistent and self-determining. Tragedy is characteristically intensive.[23]

So far our tragedy has no words; it may even do without them. Nevertheless in its higher ranges it expresses itself also through suggestive language. In the third place, then, tragedy uses the whole range of "enhanced utterance," i. e., rhythm, and occasionally music and song. In conception a tragedy must be significant and complete; in expression it may be variously suggestive.

The fourth distinction of tragedy is its characteristic movement, which is acting, not narrative. The process of drama is representation; the process of story is suggestion. Drama shows men and women doing; story tells what they did. That is essentially dramatic, then, which is best brought home by actual representation. In this regard imaginative conceptions of human life differ essentially. Some are best conveyed by the indirect but abundant suggestions of narrative; others have their poignancy only through the few direct strokes of visible action.

Finally, tragedy is defined by its effect, the tragic catharsis. Tragedy "through pity and fear achieves its purgation of such emotions."[24] It is complete, then, not only in action, but in emotion. Emotion is not merely aroused; it is satisfied; it is carried through to a release. Tragedy is thus thoroughly emotional, more emotional than any other form of art. It is emotional not incidentally, but essentially; for it offers not merely emotional excitement, but emotional satisfaction. As all art enhances by imitation our impressions of life, so tragedy reveals our motives and moves us onward through vicarious experience. We yearn toward our fellows moved as we are, only more deeply; we fear in some great crisis what obscurely threatens us all day by day; and we know the inevitable end not with our minds, but with our awakened hearts.

From definition of tragedy by its essential characteristics Aristotle proceeds to enumeration of its constituents. Of these the *sine qua non* is plot. The insistence on this is so ample and so convincing as hardly to need interpretation. Characterization comes second. Third is the expression of thought, as distinct from the expression of emotion or of character. The persons of the play not only reveal their individualities; they have also occasion to expound or persuade, and here poetic leans on rhetoric. For drama, though its movement is imaginative, though it primarily expresses emotion and character, cannot dispense with logic. Fourth is diction. Here again it is noteworthy that Aristotle puts this fourth, though tyros, he says, can master it before they can manage plot. Whether the diction be verse or prose he regards as negligible at this point. With the same brevity he enumerates finally musical and scenic accompaniments. What he enlarges upon is plot and characterization, and upon plot as the essential and determining factor.

> These distinctions made, let us thereupon discuss of what sort the plan of the actions (the plot) must be, since this is both the first and the greatest [constituent] of tragedy. We have shown tragedy to be imitation of an action complete and whole which has a certain magnitude. Though there is such a thing as a whole without any appreciable magnitude, we mean by a whole that which has beginning, middle, and end. A beginning is that which does not itself follow anything by causal necessity, but after which something else naturally is or comes to be. An end, on the contrary, is that which itself naturally follows some other thing, either by causal necessity or as a rule, but has nothing following it. A middle is that which follows something as some other thing follows it. Plots that are well planned, therefore, are such as do not begin or end at haphazard, but conform to the types just described.[25]

Plot, then, is what makes a play "complete and whole"; it is a planned sequence of actions. Aristotle's terms connote, not space and structure, but time and causal

movement. The beginning is the point at which the cause is set in motion; the end is the result; the middle is the course from the one to the other. Plot is thus a significant course of action determined by permanent impulses; it imitates, not the mere surface movements of life, but its undercurrents. It is not a "slice of life," such as the experience of this day or that, but a course of life, moving from a "serious" crisis of determining emotions, through actions that carry these emotions out, to the final action in which they are seen to issue. Plot gives us what we often miss in actual experience, and consequently seek in the vicarious experience of drama, a sense of progress to completion. Experience is interrupted and complicated; drama moves steadily on a single course. Plot is the means by which dramatic art simplifies life, in order from the facts of life to extract the truth.

Furthermore, plot means technically management of a significant course of action within a practicable time. The tragedy must be long enough to show the action as progressive, yet short enough to be grasped as a single whole. "Beginning, end, middle" are thus very practical considerations. Every playwright considers every plot in this aspect. Where is he to take hold in order to make the situation clear? What final action is, for his conception, the inevitable end? What are the stages between, leading one to another, in which the action will best be seen as a progressive course? Without limiting his consideration to the time-rules of the actual dramatic competitions of his day, Aristotle seeks

> the limit determined by the very nature of the act; the greater, within the limits of clearness, the finer by its scope. To define roughly, that scope is sufficient within which the sequence of events according to probability or necessity may change from ill fortune to good, or from good to ill.[26]

What Aristotle finds necessary is time enough to make the action convincing, to carry out the dramatic consequences to their conclusion. Compressed within too short a time-lapse, the plot may remain fragmentary; stretched out too long, it may sag or trail. "Beginning, end, middle," then, constitute a formula for plot.

> A plot does not gain unity by being, as some think, all about one person. . . . . For as in the other imitative arts, the imitation is unified by being of one thing, so also the plot, since it is an imitation of an action, must be the imitation of an action which is one and entire and whose parts are so composed of acts that the transposition or omission of any part would disjoin and dislocate the whole [That, indeed is what we mean by a part]; for a thing whose presence or absence makes no visible difference is no part of the whole.

From what has now been said it is plain that the function of a poet is this, to tell not the things that have happened, but such things as may happen, things possible as being probable or necessary. The historian and the poet differ not by writing in verse or in prose. The work of Herodotus might be put into verse, and none the less it would be history, with verse or without. No, the difference is in this, that the one tells the things that have happened; the other, such things as may happen.[27]

Consistency of plot, consistency of characterization also, as Aristotle goes on to show, imply that the poet interprets. He is not merely a recorder. The acts . . . of his *personœ* are not statistics; they are parts of the consistent presentation of a single whole. Every one of them, quite differently from the acts of real life, is seen to be significant. In thus including the significant and excluding the insignificant, the poet interprets according to his conception of the springs of action. He simplifies life according to his view of causes and motives, "according to probability or necessity."

In this the poet differs from the historian more generally. Tragedy is true to life not by rehearsing what men have done, but by revealing in significant action what men do, what they must do, being the men that the dramatist shows them to be. History records a man's deeds, and reasons from this evidence; drama directly represents the doer doing what he should do "according to probability or necessity." Plot, then, implies actions shaped to a unifying consistency. It imitates life; but it imitates by creative interpretation.

> Therefore poetry is something more philosophical and more serious than history; for poetry speaks rather in universals, history in singulars. By universal I mean what such or such a man will say or do according to probability or necessity. . . . It is evident from these considerations that the *poet* must be rather a *poet* of plots than of verses. He is a *poet* by virtue of imitation; and what he imitates are actions. Even if he chance to *make*[28] history, none the less for that is he a *poet;* for nothing hinders some historical events from being just what they should be according to probability or possibility, and it is [only] in that aspect of them that he is their *poet.*[29]

That dramatic composition is thus primarily the devising of a convincing sequence is seen conversely when the sequence is defective.

> Of all plots and actions the episodic are the worst. By an episodic plot I mean one in which the sequence of the episodes is not determined by probability or necessity. Actions of this sort are composed by bad poets through their own fault, and by good ones on account of the players; for as they compose for competitive presentation, and stretch a plot beyond its capacity, they are often compelled to twist the sequence.[30]

The essential dramatic force, then, is sequence, steady onward movement to a convincing issue. Scenes merely episodic, however vivid or clever each may be in itself, weaken this essential force. The episodic fault, whether it arise from weakness in the composer or from an actor's insistence on having a "part" to suit himself rather than to suit the play, makes the worst plays because it is a fault at the source.

Finally on cogency of plot depend the tragic pity and fear. The catharsis depends on our feeling the issue to be inevitable. Unexpected to the actors it may be, and most strikingly; but it cannot be fortuitous. While it is surprising to them, it must be satisfying to us as the outcome of their action.

> Considering the imitation as not only of a complete action, but also of events arousing fear and pity, we find these too at their height when they are [at once] unexpected [by the *dramatis personœ*] and consequential. For so we shall be more struck than by what happens of itself or by chance.[31]

> ["Reversal" or "recognition," Aristotle goes on in chapters x and xi, if the plot is so far complicated, must arise from the plot itself, not be merely added.]

> Two parts of the plot, then, reversal and discovery, are such as has been shown; a third is [actual] suffering . . . action destructive or painful, such as deaths on the stage, tortures, wounds, and the like.[34]

This latter passage is tantalizingly brief. So far as the context shows, *suffering* is used here to denote single scenes of unusually violent action. Why should such a scene be called a "part of the plot"? The word [*pathos*] is used generally—and in the plural it is used repeatedly throughout the earlier chapters of this work—to mean emotion. Emotion is not a part of the plot in the sense that reversal or recognition may be a part. Rather it is a pervasive principle and an object. *Suffering,* to translate the singular noun so, may be regarded as a part of the plot in the sense that it may be an element of tragedy. So taking it, we may suppose Aristotle to countenance here such scenes of violence as were more familiar on the Elizabethan stage than on the Greek.[35] At any rate, Aristotle here inserts a chapter[36] on the formal parts (prologue, episode, exodus, etc.), before proceeding with the methods by which the plot may be worked out.

Chapter xiii insists that the vital principle of plot is causal consistency. This rules out mere reversal. A turning-point . . . is, indeed, characteristic of drama. There is usually and typically a crisis, in which the hero's fortunes turn from good to bad; but this reversal will not suffice by itself. The mere turn of fortune does not achieve the catharsis of pity and fear.

There remains, then, the [hero] between [the typically virtuous man and the typically depraved], a man neither exceptional in virtue and righteousness nor falling into adversity by vice and depravity, but by some error, a man among those who live in renown and prosperity, such as Œdipus or Thyestes or other illustrious men of such families.

The perfect [tragic] plot, therefore, must be single, not, as some say, double;[37] the change of fortune not from adversity to prosperity, but on the contrary from prosperity to adversity; not through depravity, but through great error on the part of a man either such as we have described or rather better than worse.[38]

Why this insistence on character in the midst of the discussion of plot? Why the iteration of "not through depravity, but through error"? Because, as Aristotle shows below,[39] plot implies consistency of characterization, but more fundamentally because consistency of plot has for its very beginning and mainspring the realization of a central figure like ourselves progressively winning our sympathy. The essence of plot is motivation. What moves us is never mere luck, never mere surprise, but the causation that springs from human will. Consistency of plot means clear causation; and causation in drama is the working of will. So the first consideration is the title rôle, the main "part." He or she should be illustrious because the action is thereby conspicuous and partly known in advance; but his course of action must be moved by springs that we feel in ourselves. Macbeth is a warrior of an elder day and a king; but we, though neither warriors nor kings, feel the perversion of his manhood as like enough to our own to purify us through pity and fear.

Fear and pity may, indeed, be aroused by mere spectacle, but they may also be aroused from the very plan of the actions,[40] and the latter is superior and shows a better dramatist.

This is the second consideration of consistency. First, the best tragedy springs from a great personal will gone wrong; secondly, it springs from a compelling progress of actions, from the plot itself. It depends not on the shock of this violent deed or that, but on the causal movement of the whole.

Character is discussed in chapter xv as a distinct topic, but still with reference to plot. For throughout this section, especially from chapter xiii on, the topic is consistency.[41] Consistency, though it refers primarily to plot, must also include characterization. In general, characterization must be consistent with the morality of the individual purpose, with the moral habit of the social group, with the received idea of the person, and finally with itself.[42] In particular,

it is necessary in the characters, as in the plan of the actions, to seek always the inevitable or the probable, so that the saying or doing of such-and-such things by such-and-such a person, just as the happening of this event after that, shall be inevitable or probable. Evidently, therefore, the solutions also [as well as the complications] of plots must come about from the plot itself, and not, as in the Medea . . . by the *deus ex machina*.[43]

In a word, consistency of characterization is part of the causal weaving of the plot.

Chapter xvi applies the principle of consistency to "recognitions," or "discoveries."[44]

Best discovery of all, however, is that which arises from the actions themselves, when the surprise comes as a natural result, as in the Œdipus of Sophocles and in the *Iphigenia*.[45]

Chapters xvii and xviii turn to the actual processes of dramaturgy, to the work of the playwright. This is concerned mainly with plot; but first Aristotle urges the fundamental necessity of visualizing.

One must compose plots and work them out in the "lines" by putting [the scenes] before his eyes . . . and as far as possible by acting out, even with the gestures.[46] . . . . .

His stories, whether already made or of his own making, he must first set out in general (i. e., make a scenario), then put in the incidents and carry out.[47] . . .

Every tragedy has both complication and solution, the events that precede [the opening scene] and often some of those within the play constituting the complication, and the rest the solution. By complication I mean all from the beginning to that scene which is just before the change in the hero's fortunes; by solution, all from the beginning of the change to the end [of the play].[48] . . .

It is necessary to remember what I have said often and not make a tragedy an epic system—by epic I mean aggregative—as if one should dramatize the whole story of the Iliad.[49] . . .

The chorus too should be regarded as one of the actors, be a part of the whole and share in the action, be not as in Euripides, but as in Sophocles.[50]

Visualizing actively at every stage, the playwright is to compose his plot before he works out his lines. He is to determine his play by the method of solution, to avoid the extensiveness of epic, and to make even the chorus contributory to the plot.

The bearing of the meager observations on the logical element and on diction (xix-xxii) will be clear from the tabular view.[51] They are not distinctive except in the saying "the greatest is the being metaphorical";[52] and they have surprisingly little on dramatic rhythms.

The third section of the *Poetic* (xxiii-xxvi) defines epic and compares it with tragedy.

> As to metrical narrative, its plots [severally] should have the movement of drama in focusing on an action whole and complete with beginning, middle, and end, that [each] may give its proper pleasure as an organic unity, and not be composed as history, which has to exhibit not a single action, but a single time, whatever chanced to happen in this period to one person or to more.[53]

The general likeness of epic to drama, then, is in interpretative focus, as distinct from the chronicle method of history. Story, as well as drama, selects in order to unify. Moreover (xxiv) story, too, as well as drama, has its crises, its recognitions, its emotional outbursts. The epic poet, if he have something of Homer's skill, can make his characters express themselves without intruding his explanations. These are general likenesses throughout the whole poetic field. For characteristic differences, epic has the advantages of scope and variety. It gains from the marvelous, which can generally be suggested better than it can be represented.[54] These points are as significant to-day as in the time of Aristotle. Not so the defense (xxv) of epic against certain typical objections which smack more of the schoolmaster than of the critic. To argue whether a given epic story were possible or probable or promotive of good morals was in fact one of the regular elementary exercises of the later schools. The closing exaltation of drama over epic[55] is summary, indeed; but that is natural, since the points, having been made before, are here simply reviewed comparatively. The idea of intensity through unity is a logical conclusion of the *Poetic* as a whole.

II

From Aristotle's introductory grouping of drama with music and dance, throughout his long discussion of plot, runs the idea of movement. The dramatic mode of imitation is to set human life in motion before us and to heighten our sense of living by carrying it through to a significant issue. Has this idea animated other drama than the Greek? Is its vitality shown by its permanence? Is it essential? As all art heightens our impressions of life and our sense of living, so the art of the dramatist in particular heightens and extends our sense of human life by vicarious experience. Its object is to make us feel human experience more widely and more intensely. All the technic of the stage, whether ancient or modern, whether simple or elaborate, has

for its main object this sort of creative imitation. The dramatist tries to induce and to hold the illusion of actual experience. In so far as he succeeds, we forget that we are in the theater; we imagine that we are seeing a reality more real than we can piece out of our fragmentary glimpses at men and women; and in his greatest successes we almost pass from spectators to actors. Toward this result how important is Aristotle's idea of movement, his doctrine that plot is a progressive synthesis of actions, unified but never static?

Those who have superficially thought of Greek drama as static, who may even have pictured it as statuesque, can hardly have studied the great play of Sophocles that Aristotle offers as an example, *Œdipus the King*.

> Laius, King of Thebes, and his wife Jocasta cast out their infant son Œdipus to die. But the shepherd commissioned to do away the child gave it instead to a stranger, who carried it to Corinth. There the little Œdipus, fostered by a Corinthian couple, was brought up as their son. In the strength of his manhood setting forth to make his own way, he met in a narrow pass another traveler who haughtily bade him yield passage. The dispute warmed to blows. Œdipus killed him. It was his own father Laius. Proceeding to Thebes, Œdipus found the throne vacant and the city in terror of the monster Sphinx. He silenced the Sphinx, and, hailed by the people as their deliverer, he became their king and married the widowed queen Jocasta, his own mother. But Apollo having in time sent a pestilence upon Thebes, Œdipus was besought by the people to be once more their savior. His emissary to the oracle, Creon his brother-in-law, brought back word that Thebes must put away the unclean person who had slain Laius. By searching investigation Œdipus discovered that he himself was the pollution, that he had slain his own father and married his own mother, that not only he but his children were accursed, that the outlawry which he had invoked upon the guilty fell upon his own head. Thereupon he put out his eyes in an agony of horror, after Jocasta had killed herself, and groped his way from Thebes led by his wretched daughters.

This is the legend. Its events extend over many years. Which of them shall be chosen for the stage as having most dramatic value? Which to an audience can be made most significant; and how shall these vital scenes be arranged in such continuous and progressive movement as will convey, and at the same time enhance, our sense of the movement of life? Sophocles with his own dramatic skill, but in the form typical of all the best Greek tragedy, arranged his whole action within the compass of its last poignant hours. Omitting nothing that is emotionally essential, nothing that is essential to clear understanding, he yet relegated some events to the background in order to represent fully the great crisis. He gathers together the whole visible action into an hour and a half on the stage and a half-dozen persons; and in this brief compass he unfolds that action with increasing intensity by making every scene move from the last and to the next, on to the awful close.

The Theban people, represented by the chorus supplicating their savior king, rehearses his great achievements for their deliverance. Œdipus in the strong confidence of his power and his mission stands before his palace like a god. At the end of the play he is led slowly from that palace a broken man. But the composition of the play is not mere reversal for contrast. Between the first scene and the last, action moves without haste, but without delay or interruption. The vigorous and self-reliant king chafes at the cryptic response brought from the oracle by Creon; he is indignant, then furious, at the tragic silence of the seer Tiresias. His quick intelligence scents a plot between the two. Breaking through the interposition of Jocasta, he wins from her false hopes while he gives her no less unwittingly the premonition of doom. Once suspecting, however darkly, he must know, he will know, he knows a dreadful part, he knows more, he knows all. So this great play, though it is focused on a single day, though it excludes all the past history and the development of character, is never static. It is never for a moment tableau. Because of its compression it moves not less, but more.

For that is why Aristotle insists that the dramatic action should be self-consistent, limited in scope. The object of dramatic unity is not bareness, but fulness and continuity. It is to give time for full and intense realization of what actual life merely hints interruptedly. It is to give us human life undisturbed and uninterrupted, so that we may see it clearly and whole. We are to have the illusion of actual experience, yes, but of larger and deeper experience than we can get from the mere reproduction of facts or from the cross-currents of life itself. Like every other art, drama is a simplification of life because it is an interpretation. The dramatic simplification is seen by Aristotle to consist essentially in moving from revealing crisis to revealing crisis up to a final revelation. It excludes all the accidental and the irrelevant that embarrass our actual movements; it tells what has happened through what is happening; it cuts to the quick. It takes those moments only in which a man is himself, suppressing those in which he is indistinguishable from other men. But it does not leap or halt between; it brings out our real sequences. It reveals life to us by showing the emotional connection of its great moments.

That such dramatic unity became sometimes a bondage in seventeenth-century French classical drama was due not to any defect of the Aristotelian principle, but partly to making the practise too rigidly a code, and still more to stiffening the movement into tableau. The classical French application of the principle of dramatic unity is not, as has often been pointed out, altogether Aristotelian. Least of all is it Aristotelian when it hinders dramatic movement. French classical tragedy when it is cold—and to think of it as generally cold is a prejudice—is static; it is feeble in movement. The free movement, not to say the loose movement, of Elizabethan plays, which was hailed by Hugo and other Romanticists as a deliverance from the classical code, is indeed better than tableau; but it is compatible with bad playwriting. He would be rash who should assert that Elizabethan plays are in general more effective dramatically than French classical plays. Rather, since the two traditions bring out different dramatic values, each has something to learn from the other. But it is plain that the progress of the Elizabethans in dramaturgy was in the direction of unity, of more highly organized movement. To see this we need go no farther than Shakspere. The difference between his earlier plays and *Othello* is largely a difference in unification. *Othello* by itself is sufficient proof of the value of dramatic unity for dramatic intensity. And with or without unity, with the Greek and the French focus of time or the Elizabethan lapse of years, drama demands movement from scene to scene. The value of unity is only to heighten this sense of movement.

Drama, of course, has its differences of age and of race. We are not to think that at its best it must always be Greek. One of the large differences between ancient drama and modern is, indeed, a difference of emphasis. Ancient drama relies more on plot, modern drama on characterization. The ancient playwright had above all, for his theater, to realize the emotional values of a situation by seeing that his play was well put together; the modern playwright has sometimes, in a theatre giving opportunity for facial expression, relied far more on realizing his persons, on writing what the actor calls a good part. Nevertheless, though playwriting does not always need the compactness of Greek form, many modern plays have chosen this compactness, this closely organized movement, for intensity.[56]

Undoubtedly such dramatic composition demands of the playwright definiteness of interpretation. His selection, his limiting of time and place, his leading from scene to scene, are only the technical means of realizing his emotional intention. He is trying to show us human life, not in random and interrupted glimpses, not in the jumble and discord of its surface, not in aimless and frustrated movements, but in the animating emotions of its crises. In order to represent crises, he is compelled to show us wherein they are critical; in order to give to emotion full expression, he must make it significant. Rather it is this significance which first caught his attention, which gave him the conception of his play and guided his realization. If his dramatic movement halts or lapses, the reason may lie deeper than technic in uncertainty of intention; and if on the other hand he is able to sustain it and carry it through, the fundamental reason is that his conception of its issue is strong and clear.[57]

This presumption has more than once been challenged. Why must the dramatist have an intention, a theme? Why may he not simply represent life? Represent life he not only may, but must, to the extent that he must reflect life, not reflect *on* it; but what is represented? Life in its multitudinous complexity, its unfulfilled intentions, life as it whirls past and escapes us? That is a task beyond drama. No playwright has ever represented life except as he saw it, or made his representation intelligible without interpretation. And as the dramatist has to interpret in order to compose, so the audience wishes to be led up to some issue. We desire not mere emotional excitement, but emotional release. Else the pity and fear, to use Aristotle's words, will not bring us purgation. A play shows us life in critical moments, and these are moral moments, moments of the clash of wills. Drama assumes free will, and its movement is by motives. Motivation, on which Aristotle so much insists, is to make the issue convincing. The dramatic representation of life is creative imitation largely in proportion as it thus moves to an end; and the typically dramatic end is not blind fate, but poetic justice.

Poetic justice sums up what Aristotle means by saying that "poetry is something more philosophical and more serious than history." It means the truth revealed beneath facts, the real cause and effect moving beneath the surface. An audience, desiring deeper emotional experience than it achieves through daily observation, desires especially to see how its sharper conflicts issue. It asks of the dramatist not only sight, but insight. It is not satisfied with "mere reversal." "The mere spectacle of a virtuous man brought from prosperity to adversity moves neither pity nor fear; it merely shocks us." The same criticism is implied in Stevenson's objection to Meredith's *Richard Feverel,* that it "began to end well" and then cheated us.

The convincing close, expressing the playwright's intention and resulting from the whole course of action, is thus a fair measure of what used to be called problem plays. It measures how far they are in Aristotle's sense serious, how far they are penetrative and significant, in a word how far they are tragic. Each disclosure, each critical scene of the dramatic progress, having its full emotional value separately and for itself, leads on to the next. Such planning for momentum is not only Aristotelian; it is permanently dramatic.

Creative imitation of human life, thus moving us along that course of actions which is both the means and the measure of creative power, makes drama of all the arts most poignant. Whether it is, as it has always seemed to its devotees, the highest form of poetic, at least its appeal is at once the largest and the most direct. In the very persons of men and women it speaks to us by face and gesture, by the message, the imagery, and the rhythm of words, most of all by the order of its actions. Plato, indeed, would have us draw from this the moral that our own lives should be ordered poetically, that is creatively, that we should control and direct our lives to harmonious movement.

> For we are ourselves according to our power poets of a tragedy at once fairest and best. Every social order becomes for us an artistic creation of the fairest and best life, which we say to be essentially the truest tragedy.[60]

Notes

[1] The best recent editions of the *Poetic* for English readers are: (1) S. H. Butcher, *Aristotle's Theory of Poetry and Fine Art,* text, translation, notes, essays, London, 1895, 4th edition 1911 (text with translation issued separately); (2) Ingram Bywater, *Aristotle on the Art of Poetry,* text, translation, introduction, commentary, Oxford, 1909. For other translations and for a select bibliography see Butcher. Lane Cooper has added to his "amplified version with supplementary illustrations for students of English," Boston, 1913, an essay (1923) on *Meaning and Influence.*

[2] *Reconstruction in Philosophy,* New York, 1920, chapter iii.

[3] *L'évolution créatrice,* chapter. i.

[4] I say this without forgetting that the *Poetic* as we have it is probably but a part. If a part, it is still self-consistent, as I have tried to show in the tabular view below.

[5] viii, 206, 232.

[6] See Chapter i.

[7] See page 4.

[8] See page 42.

[9] See page 27.

[10] This analysis is intended to supplement, and in some cases to emend, the outlines of Butcher and of Bywater by bringing out the significance of the parts in relation.

[11] [*poiētikēs*]. The adjective means generally active, productive, creative, *efficiens,* as commonly in Aristotle's philosophy, in Dionysius and Demetrius, and in Plotinus. Specially it means poetic, as of diction. The noun [*ne poiētikē*] . . . includes all imaginative composition in words.

[12] Bywater (page vii), protesting against too generalizing interpretations, goes to the other extreme of undue restriction. That the treatment is philosophical and intends to suggest large inferences appears from both its plan and its language. Certainly the *Poetic* is technical; but no less certainly it is theoretical.

[13] The interpretation of Bywater.

[14] . . . 1447 a, where Aristotle is speaking of dancing.

[15] See foot-note 11 above.

[16] In Chapter ix, 1451 b, Aristotle says: "It is evident from the above that the poet should be rather the poet of his plots than of his verses, inasmuch as he is a poet by virtue of his imitation, and it is actions that he imitates."

[17] Butcher (pages 110-124) in pointing out that the Greek phrase for the fine arts is *imitative arts . . .* , says that Aristotle applies it specifically only to poetry and music. In this opening chapter of the *Poetic* he evidently means to include dancing. That Aristotle had no thought of "bare imitation," of that reproductive copying which Ruskin confused with artistic truth, has been remarked also by other critics. Butcher adds suggestively, though not with strict reference to the text, that to imitate nature was for Aristotle not to evoke the mere background which romanticism has taught us to spell with a capital N, but to work in nature's ways. Nature . . . in Aristotle is not the sensible world, but "the creative force, the productive principle." So the immediate objects of poetic imitation are human characters, emotions, and actions, not as objective phenomena, but as expressions of human will. "The common original," Butcher concludes, "is human life . . . essential activity of the soul." Though this is true to the underlying idea of the *Poetic*, Aristotle does not use any single phrase corresponding to "imitation of nature."

[18] 1449 b.

[19] 1450 a.

[20] 1450 b.

[21] [*Spoudaīos*], which of persons means *earnest;* of things, what we mean by *serious* in such phrases as a *serious proposal* and *serious consideration.*

[22] Bywater makes one item, "as having magnitude, complete in itself." Butcher makes two items, "complete, *and* of a certain magnitude." The former seems closer to the Greek text and, on the whole, more consistent with the context; but both renderings give much the same meaning ultimately.

[23] The distinction has lately been pointed by Mr. Hardy's *Dynasts*. This, whatever else may be thought of it, is not "complete as to size," but indeterminate. Doubtless that is why it is styled an "epic-drama." Certainly, for all its "enhanced utterance" and occasionally striking dialogue, it is not, by any definition, a drama.

[24] Bywater, pages 152-161, has discussed this phrase amply, and in an appendix, 361-365, has compiled with their dates the successive critical translations.

[25] vii. 1450 b.

[26] 1451 a.

[27] viii-ix, 1451 a-1451 b.

[28] The verb here translated *make* corresponds to the noun *poet*. The insistence brought about by the repetition will be made clear by rendering the words italicized *creator* and *create*, or, to revive an older use, *maker* and *make*.

[29] ix. 1451 b.

[30] ix. 1451 b.

[31] ix. 1452 a. . . .

[34] xi. 1452 b.

[35] Both Butcher and Bywater so interpret; but Butcher's rendering "tragic incident" seems hardly to meet the context. Bywater's rendering "suffering" seems preferable if we may venture to interpret it as meaning, more generally than Bywater suggests, the working out of the plot to its full emotional expression. So taken, it corresponds to the climax of pity and fear, as "reversal" and "recognition" correspond to the preceding complication.

[36] xii. 1452 b. This has been challenged as an interpolation. It is at least meager and, as it were, impatient, as is the corresponding section in the *Rhetoric* (III. xiii. 1414 b) on the formal parts of an oration.

[37] . . . The context seems to show that this means *divided* in interest and issue, insufficiently focused. Aristotle does not mean that the plot should not be complicated; for at the opening of this chapter he says that the plot of the perfect tragedy is not simple, but complicated. . . . What he adds here is that the complication should not be such as to divide our sympathy. The plot should not, indeed, be simple; but it should be single.

[38] xiii. 1453 a.

[39] xv.

⁴⁰ xiv. 1453 b. . . .

⁴¹ See the tabular view, page 136.

⁴² I follow Bywater's note, pages 227-228.

⁴³ 1454 b.

⁴⁴ . . . 1454 b. "This and the next two chapters form a sort of Appendix; they discuss a series of special points and rules of construction which had been omitted in the sketch of the general theory of the [*muthos*]." Bywater, page 233. I am not convinced of an interruption here. What seems to me the bearing of this chapter and the following on the discussion of consistency from Chapter xiii on is indicated in the tabular view on page 136.

⁴⁵ 1455 a.

⁴⁶ xvii. 1455 a.

⁴⁷ xvii. 1455 b.

⁴⁸ xviii. 1455 b.

⁴⁹ xviii. 1456 a.

⁵⁰ xviii. 1456 a.

⁵¹ Page 138. As to whether xx is an interpolation, see Bywater.

⁵² xxii. 1459 a.

⁵³ xxiii. 1459 a.

⁵⁴ A most striking exemplification of this is *Paradise Lost*.

⁵⁵ Sainte-Beuve, *Étude sur Virgile*, vii. page 151, disputes the superiority of drama to epic.

⁵⁶ The most familiar instances are certain plays of Ibsen. Of plays recently on the stage, Bernstein's *Voleur*, Mirbeau's *Les affaires sont les affaires*, Besier's *Don*, Kenyon's *Kindling*, show that this type of dramatic movement is not confined to any particular school. Of plays that on the contrary dispense with this and rely mainly on characterization the most familiar to Americans is the dramatization of *Rip Van Winkle* used by Joseph Jefferson.

⁵⁷ The paragraph is adapted from the author's *College Composition*, page 248. . . .

⁶⁰ *Laws* 817 b; quoted by Bywater on Aristotle's *Poetic*, 1450 a.

Marvin Theodore Herrick (essay date 1930)

SOURCE: "The Middle Ages and the Renaissance," in *The Poetics of Aristotle in England*, Yale University Press, 1930, pp. 8-35.

[*In the following essay, Herrick traces the influence of Aristotle's* Poetics *on English literature from Roger Bacon's (c. 1214-1294) mention of the treatise in his works through the possible influence of Aristotle's ideas on Shakespeare.*]

The first Englishman to mention Aristotle's **Poetics** was Roger Bacon (*c.* 1214-1294). Like most of his learned contemporaries, Bacon pursued philosophical and scientific studies as means to the greater study of theology. While his primary aim, then, was neither philosophical, scientific (in our sense of the word), nor literary, he fully realized the need for an adequate understanding of the ancient languages and literatures, since they alone, he believed, could furnish the proper tools for more exalted labors.[1] He was convinced that up to his own day Boethius alone, in the West, had fully understood both Greek and Latin.[2] The chief reason for the prevailing ignorance of Bacon's day was the difficulty of obtaining the classical writings, not only in the long-neglected Greek, but in Latin as well. Robert Grosseteste (*c.* 1175-1253), Franciscan scholar and Bishop of Lincoln, had invited Greek teachers to England, and encouraged the study of Aristotle; but himself made little progress in Greek literature.[3] Aristotle's reputation had gone far ahead of his writings. Bacon tells us that there was little opportunity to study the great philosopher:

> Aristotle, as Tully says in the **Topics,** was known to very few. . . . In fact, slowly has any thing of Aristotle's philosophy come into use among the Latins, because his Natural Philosophy and his Metaphysics, with the commentaries of Averroes and others, have been translated in our own times, and forbidden at Paris before the year A.D. 1237 on account of the eternity of the world and of time, on account of the book on the divination of dreams, which is the third book about sleeping and waking, and on account of many other things erroneously translated. Furthermore, his logical works have been slowly received and read; for the blessed Edmund, Archbishop of Canterbury, first read the book of *Elenchi* in my time, and I have seen Master Hugo who first read the book of **Posteriors [Posterior Analytics]**, and I have examined the work. So there were but few, considering the multitude of Latins, who were of any account in Aristotle's philosophy; nay, very few indeed, and almost none up to this year of our Lord 1292, which shall be fully and conclusively shown in the following chapters. Still later was the **Ethics** of Aristotle made known, and only lately read by the masters, and then rarely. All the rest of Aristotle's philosophy, in a thousand volumes, in which he treated all the sciences, has not yet been translated or made known to the Latins.

Therefore almost nothing worthy is known of the philosophy of Aristotle, and so far there have been but three who have been able truly to judge about the few books already translated.[4]

Bacon probably was one of the three competent judges.

Bacon repeatedly complains of the poor Latin translations of Aristotle's writings, most of them prepared from Arabic texts of Moorish scholars; chief among these, Avicenna and Averroes were largely responsible for reviving the Aristotelian doctrines. Latin translations of Arabic versions, which were more than likely adapted from a Syriac version of the Greek text, were naturally unsatisfactory. Take, for example, the work of Hermannus Alemannus, who journeyed to Spain about the middle of the thirteenth century, and at Toledo in 1256 turned the Arabic version of the *Rhetoric* into Latin.[5] The *Rhetoric* he did complete. The *Poetics* was too much for him; for this he rested content with translating the Arabic commentary of Averroes. Since the German scholar apparently knew little Arabic, and the Arabic version itself was bad enough, this *Aristotelis Poetria* of Hermannus was too wretched to be of any real influence. Bacon dismisses it with contempt.[6]

There is another mention of the *Poetics* in Bacon, a specific reference in his *Greek Grammar,* where he notes that Aristotle, in his books on the art of poetry, says that syllables and conjunctions are parts of speech, but parts in themselves non-significant. The reference may be traced to *Poetics,* ch. 20, but Bacon takes it from Boethius' Commentary on Aristotle's *De Interpretatione.*[7]

The learned friar was not specially interested in either rhetoric or poetry, and like most mediæval scholars, he regarded them as parts of logic and moral philosophy.[8] Nevertheless he speaks of the need for good translations of those parts of Aristotle's logical works (*Rhetoric* and *Poetics*?) that Hermannus Alemannus has so miserably garbled.[9] Very wisely, therefore, Bacon would have none of the Arabic-Latin translations. He maintained that the efforts of Hermannus Alemannus and William the Fleming, another contemporary student of Aristotle, were worse than useless.[10] In fact, could he have had his way, all the current Latin versions of Aristotle, since their influence was merely to create error and multiply ignorance, would have been burnt.[11]

It is, indeed, hardly possible to exaggerate the ineffectiveness of these Latin versions of the Arabic Aristotle; the *Poetics,* at least, was practically worthless. A mediæval scholar, even a Moor, might arrive at some definite conception of what Aristotle was discussing in the *Rhetoric;* but to such a reader the criticism of Greek drama and epic poetry in the *Po-etics* would have been all but incomprehensible. Even the most notable scholars in the thirteenth century showed no more than a perfunctory acquaintance with the two treatises. Roger Bacon, however, was not the only man to recognize the shortcomings of the Arabic-Latin texts. Thomas Aquinas fostered the first mediæval Latin translation of Aristotle direct from the Greek. Some time before 1273 he invited William of Brabant to turn all the Aristotelian writings into Latin. Further, William accepted the invitation, and set to work, translating, among others, the *Rhetoric;*[12] but before he attempted the *Poetics* his industry failed him, or he may not have been able to lay hand on the Greek text. Perhaps it is just as well, for this William of Brabant was none other than William the Fleming whose scholarship Bacon so heartily condemned. On the other hand, William must have done something with the *Rhetoric.* Dante evidently was acquainted with a fairly accurate translation,[13] and probably used the one prepared under the direction of Thomas Aquinas.

We now begin to find a few traces of traditional Aristotelian criticism among the English writers, though the Latin translation of the Arabic commentary on the *Poetics* might just as well have been burnt by Roger Bacon.

Richard de Bury (1287-1345) coupled Aristotle's doctrine of pleasure as activity with the 'profit and delight' of Horace in the *Ars Poetica,* a practice that hundreds later were to follow; but his Aristotelian concept was not derived from the *Poetics.*[14] The morally-philosophic sense was prevalent enough, the aesthetic still dormant.

Chaucer picked up a mediæval definition of tragedy, which probably goes back ultimately to Aristotle, though it is common property in the Middle Ages. For example, one of the glosses in Chaucer's translation of *Boethius* (Book 2, Prose 2) runs as follows: 'Tragedie is to seyn, a ditee of a prosperitee for a tyme, that endeth in wrecchednesse.' There is a similar statement in the Monk's Prologue:

> Tragedie is to seyn a certayn storie,
> As olde bokes maken us memorie,
> Of him that stood in greet prosperitee
> And is y-fallen out of heigh degree
> Into miserie, and endeth wrecchedly.[15]

Chaucer could not read Greek; but could he have seen one of the mediæval Latin versions of the *Poetics*? Probably not. It is extremely doubtful if even the Clerk of Oxenford, with all his passion for Aristotle's books, could have secured a copy of the *Poetics.* It is even more doubtful that his logically trained faculties could have appreciated the book, had he secured it. He might possibly have known of the *Rhetoric;* the catalogue of

Oriel College Library lists a commentary on this treatise in 1375,[16] and Ranulf Higden, who died nine years before, mentions Aristotle's Dialogue on Poets and his Tractate on Rhetoric.[17] But the *Poetics* is missing.

Not until near the end of the fifteenth century did the Greek text of the *Poetics* come to light in Italy; in 1483 Politian owned a manuscript of the work.[18] Printing soon followed. Giorgio Valla brought out an Italian version in 1498; and ten years later appeared the Aldine *editio princeps* of the Greek text, the *Poetics* being included along with the *Rhetoric* in the well-known *Rhetores Graeci.*

Even before this time Englishmen were going to Italy to learn Greek, some of them under Politian himself. The study of the classical languages and literatures, for which Roger Bacon long ago had pleaded, was now firmly established, and the great revival of ancient learning slowly but surely made itself felt not only on the Continent but also in England, there fostered by distinguished scholars such as John Colet, William Graye, Thomas Linacre, William Grocyn, and Bishop Latimer. Perhaps both Linacre and Latimer took part in producing the great Aldine Aristotle in 1495-8.[19] To-day the only perfect set of this famous edition is the one Linacre formerly used.[20] Unfortunately, however, the Aldine Aristotle, for some reason, omitted the *Poetics,* and we have no evidence that Linacre read Politian's manuscript. In fact, it seems unlikely that the projected plan for a Latin translation of Aristotle, by Grocyn, Linacre, and Latimer, took account of the treatise; apparently the only work actually produced was Linacre's translation of the *Meteorologica.*[21]

Englishmen had now taken the first steps. They were rapidly becoming familiar with the great body of classical literature. As early as 1499 Erasmus had noted the remarkable progress of Englishmen in ancient learning. Writing to his friend Robert Fisher in Italy, he enthusiastically exclaims:

> I have met with so much kindness and so much learning, not hackneyed and trivial, but deep, accurate, ancient Latin and Greek, that but for the curiosity of seeing it, I do not now so much care for Italy. When I hear my Colet, I seem to be listening to Plato himself. In Grocyn, who does not marvel at such a perfect round of learning? What can be more acute, profound, and delicate than the judgment of Linacre? What has Nature created more sweet, more happy, than the genius of Thomas More? I need not go through the list. It is marvelous how general and abundant is the harvest of ancient learning in this country, to which you ought all the sooner to return.[22]

The study of ancient criticism was bound to follow. If Englishmen did not pick up the *Poetics* abroad, we may be sure that some of the distinguished foreign visitors soon brought it to their attention. Erasmus took part in editing the first 'complete' Greek text of Aristotle, which was printed at Basel in 1531, and included both the *Rhetoric* and *Poetics,* but he betrayed no particular interest in either of them.[23] It was otherwise, however, with the Spanish humanist Vives, who lived in England from 1523 to 1528, lecturing at Oxford, and serving as tutor to Princess Mary. During his stay he made many warm friends among the English scholars, including Sir Thomas More, who had the highest regard for this Spaniard. We can readily imagine that Vives, outside the lecture-room, exerted a very considerable influence upon the intellectual life at More's hospitable house. And Vives knew something about the *Poetics.*[24] We cannot be sure that he ever introduced the doctrines of Aristotle on poetry into familiar conversations with his English fellows, but we shall see that just such doctrines were soon to form the topic for conversation at Cambridge.

Erasmus' praise to Fisher, enthusiastic and rhetorical as it was, did not exaggerate the progress of England in the New Learning. Roger Ascham went to Cambridge about 1530. In 1542-3 he writes from the University:

> Aristotle and Plato are now read by the boys in the original language, but that has been done among us at St. John's for the last five years. Sophocles and Euripides are now more familiar to us than Plautus was when you were here. Herodotus, Thucydides, and Xenophon are more read now than Livy was then. They talk now as much of Demosthenes as they did of Cicero at that time. There are more copies of Isocrates to be met with now than there were of Terence then. Yet we do not treat the Latin writers with contempt, but we cherish the best of them who flourished in the golden age of their literature.
>
> It was Cheke who gave the first impulse towards bringing about this state of things; he twice read through Homer, Sophocles, Euripides, and Herodotus at a public lecture, and that too without taking any fee. He meant to do the same for all the Greek poets, historians, orators, and philosophers, if ill luck had not stood in the way of such a great advancement of learning. For when Cheke wished to enlarge his course of usefulness in the cause of learning by bringing back the true and ancient pronunciation of Greek, lo, the right reverend the bishop of Winchester, yielding to the requests of certain envious men, issued a decree to forbid the use of this new mode, and thus not only stopped the new pronunciation in spite of the remonstrances of almost all the university, but almost wholly extinguished all the zeal for learning which had been kindled up among us.[25]

Ascham tells us that at his first coming to Cambridge it was the custom to read the precepts of Aristotle without illustrating them from other authors, but that Cheke, Thomas Smith, Walter Haddon, John Watson, and others, had reformed the bad practice. For example:

> When Mr. Watson in St. John's College at Cambridge wrote his excellent tragedy of *Absalon,* Mr. Cheke, he, and I, for that part of true imitation, had many pleasant talks together in comparing the precepts of Aristotle and Horace *de Arte Poetica* with the examples of Euripides, Sophocles, and Seneca. Few men in writing of tragedies in our days have shot at this mark. Some in England, more in France, Germany, and Italy, also have written tragedies in our time, of the which not one, I am sure, is able to abide the true touch of Aristotle's precepts and Euripides' examples, save only two that ever I saw, Mr. Watson's *Absalon* and Georgius Buchananus' *Jepthe*.[26]

Watson's *Absalon* is lost, and Buchanan's *Jepthah* hardly bears out Ascham's statement, at least for the precepts of Aristotle; the examples of Euripides and Seneca are clearly present. Nor does Buchanan afford definite evidence that he has studied the *Poetics*.[27] Sir John Cheke, however, is a more substantial witness. The famous controversy between Cheke and Stephen Gardiner, Bishop of Winchester, over the new pronunciation of Greek at Cambridge took place during the summer of 1542.[28] In one of his letters to Gardiner, Cheke definitely refers to the remarks on the length of [o] and [ō] in Aristotle's chapters on diction in the *Poetics*.[29] As far as I can discover, there is no reference to the *Poetics* in Gardiner, or in Thomas Smith, who allied himself with Cheke in the battle. In fact, but for Ascham's account of the Aristotelian conversations at St. John's, we might reasonably doubt Cheke's knowledge of the *Poetics;* perhaps he picked up this reference in the work of some Continental grammarian. There are similar references in Theodore Beza,[30] Adolphus Mekerchus[31] (a contemporary scholar in Holland), in Stephanus,[32] and numerous allusions in Peter Ramus.[33] All these scholars, however, wrote later than Cheke, and Mekerchus avowedly follows the Englishman. Cheke might have found the reference in Aldus Manutius, who is supposed to have discussed the pronunciation of Greek vowels in a lost work called *Fragmenta*.[34] In view of Ascham's testimony and of other evidence that scholars, both on the Continent and in England, were deeply interested in Greek literature, we are fairly safe in saying that the *Poetics* was known at Cambridge by 1542, if not before.

Cheke's reference to Aristotle's brief remarks on diction, with no mention of the more important principles of poetic composition, is natural enough. English scholars in the early part of the sixteenth century were still in a preliminary stage of the revival of Greek; they had to learn to read the language before they could venture upon criticism. The friendly debates over dramatic style that Ascham recalls at Cambridge must have owed

somewhat more to the familiar *Ars Poetica* of Horace than to the 'precepts of Aristotle.' The modern assimilation of the *Poetics* has been a long process.

Very likely both Cheke and Ascham were indebted to their German friend, Johann Sturm, for an interest in Aristotle's critical treatises. Ascham openly acknowledges his debt in the Preface to the *Schoolmaster:*

> Yet, nevertheless, I myself spending gladly that little that I got at home by good Sir John Cheke, and that that I borrowed abroad of my friend Sturmius, beside somewhat that was left me in reversion by my old masters Plato, Aristotle, and Cicero, I have at last patched it up as I could, and as you see.[35]

From Sturm also—and possibly from Cheke—Ascham took his view of dramatic imitation: 'The whole doctrine of comedies and tragedies is a perfect *imitation,* or fair lively painted picture of the life of every degree of man.'[36] Here Ascham follows Horace and Plato rather than Aristotle, for he adds: 'Of this *imitation* writeth Plato at large in 3 *de Rep.,* but it doth not much belong at this time to our purpose.'[37] Though a glimpse of the Aristotelian concept of imitation was here given to English readers, Ascham's real notion was rather that of copying or emulation. The same notion was characteristic of Sturm, who, while he referred to the *Poetics,* even mentioning the six Aristotelian parts of an imitative work,[38] clearly regarded imitation as emulation.[39]

The same influence appeared about this time in another English work, *A Rich Storehouse or Treasurie for Nobilitye and Gentlemen* (1570), translated from Sturm's *Nobilitas Literata* by one 'T. B. Gent.'[40] There is in the book frequent mention of Plato and Aristotle, and of imitation . . . ;but here again is meant emulation, a copying of the patterns of the ancients.

As to dates of publication, the *Schoolmaster* was not published until 1570, two years after the author's death, while Cheke's letters were published fifteen years before Ascham's book. In 1554, an exile on his way to Italy, Cheke stopped for a time at Basel. There he lent the seven letters of the linguistic dispute to Caelius Secundus Curio, a scholar who took it upon himself to publish them at Basel, and did so in the following year, 1555. Therefore, until further evidence is brought forward, we shall have to say that 1555 marks the first reference to Aristotle's *Poetics* by an Englishman after the dubious allusion of Roger Bacon in the thirteenth century. Ascham still holds the honor of making the first reference in English to the *Poetics.*

Not long after Cheke and Ascham the allusions became more numerous, though the foreign scholars residing in England still furnished most of them. Thus Martin Bucer, the German Reformer who taught for a time at Cambridge, quoted Aristotle's . . . (reversals of fortune or of intent) in *De Honestis Ludis*,[41] a part of his *De Regno Christi* which he presented in manuscript to Edward VI as a New-Year's gift in 1551; the work was not published until 1557, when it appeared at Basel. In 1576 Robert Peterson translated Giovanni della Casa's *Galateo*, which contains an intelligent expression of the Aristotelian tragic *catharsis:*

> Men have many times more need to weep than to laugh. And for that cause, he said, these doleful tales which we call tragedies were devised at first, that when they were played in the theatres (as at that time they were wont) they might draw forth tears out of their eyes that had need to spend them. And so they were by their weeping healed of their infirmity.[42]

The quotation is of particular interest since it furnishes one of the earliest anticipations of the 'modern pathological theory' of the *catharsis*,[43] and apparently is the first allusion to it in England.

There is a passage in the *Mirror for Magistrates* (1578), that treasure-house of tragedies, which may owe something to Aristotle:

> 'Surely,' said one of the company, 'this lady hath done much to move the hearers to pity her, and hath very well knit up her tragedy according to the beginning, but I marvel much where she learned all this poetry touched in her tale, for in her days learning was not common, but a rare thing, namely in women.' 'Yes,' quod Master Ferrers, 'that might she very well learn of the Duke her husband, who was a prince so excellently learned, as the like of his degree was nowhere to be found; and not only so, but was also a patron to poets and orators, much like as Maecenas was in the time of Augustus Caesar. This Duke was founder of the Divinity-School in Oxford, whereas he caused Aristotle's works to be translated out of Greek into Latin.'[44]

There is no reason to suppose that the Duke and Duchess of Gloucester knew any thing about the *Poetics*, but perhaps the poet Ferrers did.

All three of the foregoing references—if the last be a real reference—bear upon plot, according to Aristotle the most important element in poetic composition. By the middle of the sixteenth century the Italian critics were laboring with classical structure, but the scanty allusions to Greek poetical theory in England were hardly more than echoes from the Continent. We do not expect, after all, to find many doctrines of Aristotle in the writings of romantic Tudor poets and playwrights; the school-masters were the men most seriously concerned with the New Learning.

We have seen that the masters of St. John's College applied the critical precepts of Horace and Aristotle to the ancient dramas and to contemporary imitations; but, though such practice was common enough on the Continent, it was rare in England. The deciphering of the classical texts was a slow process. As we saw in the case of Sir John Cheke, most of the English scholars had to begin with the study of grammar. Poetics in sixteenth-century England, both for the classical and the native English literature, was an evolution from the technicalities of pronunciation and grammar to versification, to figures of speech (long popular in rhetoric), and only gradually to literary criticism comparable to that contained in Aristotle's treatise. Sir John Cheke was the pioneer, and Roger Ascham his worthy successor. But with Ascham's death in 1568 many of the Cambridge traditions died. It seems that the work was not more than well-begun when the younger followers lost interest in it.

Gabriel Harvey, who went up to Cambridge some time before 1565, wrote to his friend Edmund Spenser in 1580, complaining of the growing neglect of the classics. 'Aristotle,' he says, 'is much named, but little read.'[45] Harvey himself was no Cheke, although, according to his own account, he became renowned beyond all precedent as a Lecturer on rhetoric.[46] In the lectures we find him using the conventional authorities of the Renaissance, Cicero and Quintilian,[47] without definite reference either to the **Rhetoric** or the **Poetics.** He knew something about Aristotle's theory, but apparently was content to take Peter Ramus' word that all of it was too impractical, too philosophical, for modern use. Like Ramus, Harvey was mainly interested in style and delivery, and his supreme authority was Cicero. 'I produce my folly to make you wiser. I worshiped M. T. as the God of Latinity, and would rather have been a Ciceronian than a saint.'[48]

In poetical matters. Harvey was mainly concerned with style and versification. There is sound sense in his letters to Spenser on English verse, but no definite sign of Aristotle. His neglect of the **Poetics** is strange when we consider his delight in displaying erudition. All his writings, both English and Latin, swarm with classical allusions and quotations in which Aristotle often appears— though never the **Poetics.** We should expect Harvey to know something about the treatise, however, since he aimed to know everything. In his *Marginalia* he does specifically mention the **Poetics,** when, in going over George Gascoigne's *Certayne Notes of Instruction concerning the Making of Verse or Ryme in English* (1575), he makes the following comment:

> His aptest partition had been into precepts of Invention, Elocution, and the several rules of both, to be sorted and marshaled in their proper places. He doth prettily well, but might easily have done much better, both in the one and in the other, especially by the direction of Horace's and Aristotle's *Ars Poetica*.[49]

If he knew the *Poetics,* why did he not himself make more use of it?

Harvey would have us believe, then, that Gascoigne, also a Cambridge man, neglected Aristotle, and doubtless Harvey was right. Although Gascoigne was a staunch advocate of his native English language and versification, and although modern scholars have shown that he was not so well-versed in classical literature as was once supposed—his Euripidean *Jocasta* owes nothing to Euripides, but is based on an Italian version—he could not escape the growing influence of classical criticism and practice. For example, he believed in *decorum,* and did not approve of mingling serious and comic matter in the same poem.[50] Gascoigne's friend, George Whetstone, was even more insistent upon *decorum,* objecting to the English playwrights' disregard of the Unity of Time, and their indiscreet mingling of clowns and kings in the same play.[51] Thus we see classical criticism, or an Italian version of it, penetrating the writings of men chiefly interested in their own native literature.

So far we have been mainly concerned with Cambridge, where the study of the *Poetics* doubtless began, but we may be sure that all this while Oxford, the stronghold of the 'Old Aristotle,' was not idle. It was at Oxford, let us recall, that Vives lectured. The chief interest in the critical treatises of Aristotle, however, seems to have turned to the *Rhetoric* rather than the *Poetics,* for Oxford was still more devoted to logic than to poetry.

Before 1552,[52] we find John Jewel, the Bishop, a most distinguished scholar in his day, referring to Aristotle's work on rhetoric,[53] in no very complimentary terms, to be sure, but showing that he knew something about it. John Reynolds (1549-1607), another man of prodigious learning and strict morality, lectured on the three books of the *Rhetoric.*[54] One may still examine his copy of the work (Morel's edition, Paris, 1562) in the Bodleian Library. The book is interleaved with the most copious notes, liberally sprinkled with references to Cicero and Quintilian, all written in a beautifully clear hand. As yet we have no evidence that any Oxonian labored over the *Poetics* as carefully as did Reynolds over the *Rhetoric.* Apart from a vague allusion in a Latin address *(Oratio in Laudem Poeticae)* we have no reason to suppose that even the great Reynolds studied the *Poetics.*[55] Probably the Christian piety which did not permit him to condone such immoral productions as 'stage-playes,'[56] would not have permitted him to condone Aristotle's emphasis upon the drama.

Thomas Lodge (1558-1625), also an Oxford man, was well-acquainted with many of Aristotle's writings, the logical works, the *Ethics* and the *Politics,* and many of the books on natural science. His *Defence of Poetry* (1579) is far removed from Aristotle, yet he has picked up at least one familiar doctrine: 'But (of truth) I must confess with Aristotle that men are greatly delighted with imitation.'[57] When he adds, however, that 'it were good to bring those things on stage that were altogether tending to virtue,' we see that, as usual, the Horatian influence is much the more important.

The fiery Giordano Bruno, coming to Oxford in 1583, startled orthodox scholars by attacking the sacred Aristotle. His battle was waged in the main against the 'scientific' writings, but even the *Poetics* did not escape him. In the *Eroici Furori,* printed at London in 1585, and dedicated to Sir Philip Sidney, Bruno delivers one of the first unfavorable comments on the 'rules of Aristotle':

> CICADA. To whom, then, are the rules of Aristotle useful?

> TANSILLO. To him, who unlike Homer, Hesiod, Orpheus, and others, could not sing without the rules of Aristotle, and who, having no Muse of his own, would coquette with that of Homer.[58]

The passage shows the influence of those Renaissance commentators on the *Poetics* who were the real formulators of the 'rules.' It also leads us to infer that the 'rules' were firmly enough established in England for Bruno to think it worth while to attack them.

Sir Philip Sidney, as an Oxford man, had consequently read some of Aristotle at an early age. In 1574 he wrote to his tutor, Hubert Languet, of his desire to master Greek so that he might read Aristotle in the original; the current translations struck him as inadequate.[59] At the time, he particularly wished to read the *Politics,* though in a subsequent letter he speaks of the *Ethics* as the 'beginning and foundation of all his [Aristotle's] work.'[60] In another letter he definitely referred to the *Rhetoric.*[61]

In addition to his first-hand acquaintance with Aristotle, Sidney, in his foreign travels, evidently had seen the commentaries, on the *Poetics,* of the leading Italian critics, Scaliger, Minturno, and probably Castelvetro. Therefore his *Defence of Poesie,* or *An Apologie for Poetrie,* probably written before 1583, but not published until 1595, became a typical Renaissance blend of Aristotle and Horace, with a good measure of Plato thrown in. The aim of poetry, to Sidney, was didactic; the ideal poet was more of a popular philosopher than an artist. His conception of poetic criticism, however, was the most marked advance towards the classical, and towards Aristotle, that any Englishman had yet made. Sidney was fairly well acquainted with Greek literature—with Homer, Sophocles, Euripides, Plato, and Xenophon, among others; and, with the aid of the Italians, he managed to grasp the outstanding features of Aristotle's theory of poetry. Horace was conjoined, of course.

In the *Defence of Poesie,* after the customary Renaissance eulogy of poets and their creations, Sidney offers the notion that poetry is an idealization of Nature; like all other art, it is an imitation:

> Poesy, therefore, is an art of imitation, for so Aristotle termeth it in the word *Mimesis,* that is to say, a representing, counterfeiting, or figuring forth: to speak metaphorically, a speaking picture, with this end, to teach and delight.[62]

Here we have a good Horatian view of the early passages in the *Poetics.* We may be sure, however, that Sidney has Aristotle chiefly in mind when he speaks of poetical imitation as having the 'most conveniency to nature of all other; insomuch that, as Aristotle saith, those things which in themselves are horrible, as cruel battles, unnatural monsters, are made in poetical imitation delightful.'[63]

In discussing poetry and history, Sidney goes even beyond Aristotle,[64] making out poetry to be superior not only to history but to philosophy as well:

> Truly, Aristotle himself, in his discourse of Poesy, plainly determineth this question, saying that Poetry is *Philosophoteron* and *Spoudaioteron,* that is to say, it is more philosophical and more studiously serious than History. His reason is because Poesy dealeth with *Katholou,* that is to say, with the universal consideration; and the History with *Kathekaston,* the particular, 'Now,' saith he, 'the universal weighs what is fit to be said or done, either in likelihood or necessity (which the Poesy considereth in his imposed names), and the particular only marketh whether Alcibiades did, or suffered, this or that.' Thus far Aristotle; which reason of his (as all his) is most full of reason.[65]

The best, the 'right,' poets, 'to imitate, borrow nothing of what is, hath been, or shall be; but range, only reined with learned discretion, into the divine consideration of what may be and should be.'[66]

Sidney's brief remarks on the drama are of peculiar interest to the student of Aristotle, for the *Defence of Poesie* marked the beginning of dramatic criticism in England. This beginning was essentially Aristotelian, and we shall find that for many years dramatic criticism continued to be so.

With the aid of the Italian commentators, Sidney managed to grasp many of the leading doctrines of the *Poetics;* but he could not fully comprehend the most fundamental principle, namely, that every good poem must form an organic whole. The common Renaissance interpretation of poetic unity was mechanical, not artistic in the true Greek sense; it seldom went much beyond the *decorum* that forbade indiscriminate mingling of clowns and kings and violations of the 'Uni-

ties' of Time and Place. As a result, Sidney had no definite idea of the most important classical unity, Unity of Action. In the *Defence of Poesie,* he condemns his native English drama as crude and ill-formed. The only English play, he says, that observes the rules either of 'honest civility' or 'skilful poetry' is *Gorboduc* (the first notable neo-classical tragedy in English), and even it is not without serious flaws:

> Notwithstanding as it is full of stately speeches and well-sounding phrases, climbing to the height of Seneca his style, and as full of notable morality, which it doth most delightfully teach, and so obtain the very end of poesy; yet in truth it is very defective in the circumstances, which grieves me, because it might not remain as an exact model of all tragedies. For it is faulty both in place and time, the two necessary companions of all corporeal actions. For where the stage should always represent but one place, and the uttermost time presupposed in it should be, both by Aristotle's precept and common reason, but one day; there is both many days and places inartificially imagined.[67]

Sidney does not favor the native variety of comedy that 'naughty playmakers and stage-keepers have justly made odious':

> Only thus much now is to be said, that the comedy is an imitation of the common errors of our life, which he representeth in the most ridiculous and scornful sort that may be; so as it is impossible that any beholder can be content to be such a one.[68]

The writers of comedy must beware of striving only to arouse laughter, for the 'great fault even in that point of laughter, and forbidden plainly by Aristotle, is that they stir laughter in sinful things, which are rather execrable than ridiculous, or in miserable, which are rather to be pitied than scorned.'[69] Comedy, even at its best, as in the plays of Plautus and Terence, though a worthy creation, is inferior to nobler tragedy:

> So that the right use of comedy will, I think, by nobody be blamed, and much less of the high and excellent tragedy, that openeth the greatest wounds, and showeth forth ulcers that are covered with tissue; that maketh kings fear to be tyrants, and tyrants manifest their tyrannical humors; that with stirring the effects of admiration and commiseration teacheth the uncertainty of this world, and upon how weak foundations gilden roofs are builded. . . . But how much it can move, Plutarch yieldeth a notable testimony of the abominable tyrant Alexander Phereaus, from whose eyes a tragedy, well made and represented, drew forth abundance of tears, who without all pity had murdered infinite numbers, and some of his own blood; so as he that was not ashamed to make matters for tragedies, yet could not resist the sweet violence of a tragedy.[70]

The influence, direct or indirect, of Aristotle is obvious; here Sidney has some notion of a tragic *catharsis,* the moving of pity and fear, the tears that are brought forth by the 'sweet violence of a tragedy.' Sidney's interpretation, however, is not so much 'pathological' as moral: the proper effect of a tragedy is purification of the spectator's emotions. In his conception of tragedy, a noteworthy element that does not go back to Aristotle, though it soon was to be associated with Aristotelian doctrine, is the idea of 'admiration' as one of the emotions properly aroused. The Italian Minturno added 'admiration' to the 'teaching and delight' of poetry,[71] and Sidney also has some such notion; but apparently he took 'well-raised admiration' to be a tragic emotion as well: 'The tragedies of Buchanan do justly bring forth a divine admiration.'[72] Sidney almost anticipated the seventeenth century when 'admiration' was raised to the level of Aristotle's 'pity' and 'fear.'

On the relative merits of tragedy and the epic poem, Sidney follows the Italians, and falls into the conventional Renaissance encomium of heroic poetry:

> But if anything be already said in the defense of sweet poetry, all concurreth to the maintaining the heroical, which is not only a kind, but the best and most accomplished kind, of poetry; for as the image of each action stirreth and instructeth the mind, so the lofty image of such worthies most inflameth the mind with desire to be worthy, and informs with counsel how to be worthy.[73]

Thus the *Defence of Poesie* stands out as an epitome of literary criticism in the Renaissance,[74] and the beginning in England of that Aristotelian criticism which, with varying fortunes, has persisted to the present day. The schoolmasters of early Tudor times established the study of classical literature; Sidney and his followers established a classical criticism.

In the philosophical conception of poetic art no other Elizabethan critic can compare with Sidney. The others are still worrying over rhetorical figures of speech, and quarreling about rhyme and versification; or else they are content to repeat what Sidney has already said. The problems of rhyme and versification are highly important features in the history of native English criticism, and the efforts of Gascoigne, Spenser, and Harvey materially aid the development of English poetry; but as far as Aristotelian theory goes the *Defence of Poesie* stands almost alone. When Sidney says, 'Aristotle writes the Art of Poesy,'[75] one hesitates to doubt his first-hand knowledge of the treatise. With the other Elizabethan apologists and defenders of poetry, however, the evidence usually points to second-hand information, or worse.

William Webbe's *Discourse of English Poetrie* (1586) abounds in Horatian maxims and Renaissance conventions, and there are a few dubious allusions to the *Poetics.* The vague remark that Aristotle reports no important poets in Greece before Homer has some foundation in chapter 4 of the *Poetics.*[76] Likewise, Webbe's statement that, according to Aristotle, good versification came in with Homer, may be traced to chapter 24 of the *Poetics.*[77] Nor can we unhesitatingly dismiss Webbe's comparison of Homer and Empedocles: 'Aristotle sayth of Empedocles that in his judgment he was only a natural philosopher, no poet at all, nor that he was like unto Homer in any thing but his metre or number of feet, that is, that he wrote in verse.'[78] Webbe's phrasing is clumsy, but the quotation is undeniably close to a passage in the *Poetics.* If Webbe were not a consistently unoriginal person, one might be tempted to give him the benefit of the doubt and credit him with first-hand knowledge. In any case, however, a reading of the *Discourse of English Poetrie* readily shows that the author failed to grasp a single one of the important principles in Aristotle's treatise.

The *Arte of English Poesie* (1589), by Puttenham, is a significant book in early English criticism, but not a guide-book for the student of Aristotle. Puttenham's theories of poetic imitation are entirely conventional, and more mediæval than classical. He, too, was primarily concerned with the rhetorical elements in poetry, and, with external form and versification. Perhaps it is worth noting, however, that Puttenham traced the popular *decorum* of the Latin writers to the Greek [*to prepon*], the phrase in the *Poetics.*[79]

Sir John Harington was closer to the Italian critics, and consequently to Aristotle. In the *Briefe Apologie of Poetrie* prefixed to his translation (1591) of the *Orlando Furioso,* Harington argues for the 'rules' of poetic composition. He undertakes to justify Ariosto's art by Aristotle's precepts:

> Briefly, Aristotle and the best censurers of poesy would have the Epopeia, that is the heroical poem, should ground on some history, and take some short time in the same to beautify with his poetry. So doth mine author take the story of K. Charles the Great, and doth not exceed a year or thereabout in his whole work. Secondly, they hold that nothing should be feigned utterly incredible. And sure Ariosto neither in his enchantments exceedeth credit (for who knows how strong the illusions of the devil are?), neither in the miracles that Atolfo by the power of St. John is feigned to do, since the Church holdeth that prophets both alive and dead have done mighty great miracles. Thirdly, they would have an heroical poem (as well as a tragedy) to be full of Peripetia, which I interpret an agnition of some unlooked-for fortune either good or bad, and a sudden change thereof. Of this what store there be the reader shall quickly find.[80]

To his own satisfaction, at least, Harington succeeds in proving that the *Orlando Furioso* conforms to the classical laws of epic poetry: 'As for Aristotle's rules, I take it he [Ariosto] hath followed them very strictly.'[81]

Harington's understanding of 'Aristotle's rules' is fairly typical of the Elizabethan critic; he seldom tries to discriminate between Horace and Aristotle, and usually trusts to the Italian critics for his knowledge of the latter. Poetic art, says Harington, is 'but an imitation (as Aristotle calleth it), and therefore [the poets] are allowed to feign what they list . . . —may lie, if they list, *cum privelegio*.'[82] Tragedy is free from the taint of scurrility and lewdness, since it represents 'only the cruel and lawless proceedings of princes, moving nothing but pity or detestation.'[83] Always didactic, Harington consistently prefers the Virgilian epic poem to tragedy.

At the close of the sixteenth century Aristotle was in the air. Many of the commentators were as absurd as Harington, but the literary men were growing familiar with the neo-classical theories that passed as Aristotelian. The puzzle of the tragic *catharsis,* and the problem of the dramatic unities on the modern stage, doubtless furnished rich material for the evening debates in London taverns, and occasionally a reflected light from Aristotle appeared in the plays and other poems of the time.

Spenser, educated at Cambridge, and familiar with the **Politics** and **Ethics,**[84] apparently accepted from some source Aristotle's notion of 'pity and fear.' In the *Ruines of Time* we read:

Much was I troubled in my heavie spright,
At sight of these sad spectacles forepast,
That all my senses were bereaved quight,
And I in minde remained sore agast,
Distraught twixt feare and pitie.[85]

Robert Yarington, an obscure Elizabethan playwright, probably had a similar notion. In his *Two Lamentable Tragedies* (1601), he writes:

I see your sorrows flow up to the brim,
And overflow your cheeks with brinish tears,
But though this sight bring surfeit to the eye,
Delight your ears with pleasing harmony,
That ears may countercheck your eyes, and say,
'Why shed your tears, this deed is but a play.'[86]

According to Charles Lamb, the 'whole theory of the reason of our delight in tragic representations, which has cost so many elaborate chapters of criticism, is condensed in these four last lines—Aristotle quintessentialized.'[87] Possibly so. But we must confess that the rest of the tragedy scarcely conforms to Aristotle's precepts.

The great playwright of the sixteenth century is perhaps more renowned for breaking than for following any alien rules of the drama. Yet Shakespeare would have been the last man to rebel against established traditions, if the traditions were useful. The Elizabethan debt to classical Roman drama, to Seneca, Plautus, and Terence, appears in Shakespeare as well as in less-inspired contemporaries. Shakespeare also knew the 'rules.' He was well-acquainted with the formal distinctions that orthodox criticism made between tragedy, comedy, history, and pastoral. He knew that the critics preferred the play with 'scene undividable' (thus preserving the precious 'Unity of Time') to the 'poem unlimited,'[88] and although he had little use for such barren formalities, he occasionally apologized for his violation of the established 'rules.'

Thus the Chorus in *Henry V* (Act 2) refers to the neglect of 'Unity of Place':

Linger your patience on; and well digest
The abuse of distance while we force a play.

In the *Winter's Tale* (Act 4) the Chorus speaks of violating the 'Unity of Time':

Impute it not a crime
To me or my swift passage, that I slide
O'er sixteen years, and leave the growth untried
Of that wide gap; since it is in my power
To o'erthrow laws, and in one self-born hour
To plant and o'erwhelm custom.

And finally, the Chorus in *Henry V* (Act 5) asks allowance for the general disregard of all the Unities:

I humbly pray them to admit the excuse
Of time, of numbers, and due course of things,
Which cannot, in their huge and proper life
Be here presented.

As an instance of more constructive dramatic criticism one could cite the well-known speech of Hamlet to the players. If we take Hamlet's theories as serious expressions of the author, we see that Shakespeare thought of the drama as a representative imitation of nature: the purpose of playing 'was and is, to hold, as 't were, the mirror up to nature.'[89] There may be a trace of Aristotelian theory in King Richard's lament (*Richard II* 5.1.44-8):

Tell thou the lamentable tale of me,
And send the hearers weeping to their beds;
For why, the senseless brands will sympathize
The heavy accent of thy moving tongue,
And in compassion weep the fire out.

But we must not here attempt to deduce Shakespeare's principles of dramatic composition. That he was alive to current dramatic theories, however, particularly after the year 1598, when he became acquainted with Ben Jonson, is evident. Further, he was perfectly able, and, upon at least one occasion, willing, to construct a play that conformed to the all-important 'Unities'—witness the *Tempest*. On the other hand, who can say that even the *Tempest* is Shakespeare's concession to the 'rules'? Ben Jonson, from whom Shakespeare may well have learned of the 'rules,' would probably have said that any regularity in Shakespeare's plays was pure accident.

> I tell him he needs Greek;
> I'll talk of rules and Aristotle with him,
> And if his tongue's at home he'll say to that:
> 'I have your word that Aristotle knows,
> And you mine that I don't know Aristotle.'
> He's all at odds with all the unities,
> And what's yet worse, it does n't seem to
>   matter;
> He treads along through Time's old wilderness
> As if the tramp of all the centuries
> Had left no roads—and there are none for
>   him;
> He doesn't see them, even with those eyes—
> And that's a pity, or I say it is.[90]

At the close of the century the 'rules' of Aristotle, as formulated by the Italians, arrived in England to take almost undisputed possession of the critical field, and to make serious inroads upon creative literature. Even in liberty-loving England, Aristotle the critic was destined to become almost as formidable an authority for the seventeenth and eighteenth centuries as 'the Philosopher' was for the Middle Ages. The great romantic literature of the Elizabethans was just forming when Sir Philip Sidney laid the foundations of English literary criticism with essentially classical and Aristotelian materials. For nearly two centuries English criticism was to remain classical and Aristotelian. We must bear in mind, however, that from the first these English interpretations of Aristotle's theories were hopelessly adulterated with Horatian maxims and Continental scholarship, first with Italian, then with Dutch, and finally, and most influental of all, with French. We may agree with Robinson's Ben Jonson, and regard it as unfortunate that Shakespeare, for one, could not have studied the **Poetics** at first hand, without the accretions and inflammations from men of less insight than either Aristotle or Shakespeare.

Notes

[1] Bacon's humanistic attitude is in strong contrast with that of Giraldus Cambrensis (*c.* 1146-1220) who, though he bemoans the decay of learning in England, regrets the importation of Aristotle's logical treatises from Spain; for he believes they will tend to foster heresy. See Giraldus, *Opera,* ed. by J. S. Brewer, London, 1861-91, 4. 9-10.

[2] See Bacon, in *Opera Inedita,* ed. by J. S. Brewer, London, 1859, pp. 33, 472.

[3] See Bacon, in *Opera Inedita,* p. 33. Grosseteste is said to have prepared a commentary on the *Nicomachean Ethics.* See F. S. Stevenson, *Robert Grosseteste,* London, 1899, p. 248.

[4] Bacon, *Compendium Studii Theologiae,* ed. by Rashdall, Aberdeen, 1911, pp. 33-4.

[5] See Jourdain, *Recherches Critiques sur l'Âge et l'Origine des Traductions Latines d'Aristote,* pp. 57, 149-52.

[6] See Bacon, *Opus Majus,* ed. by Bridges, Oxford, 1897, 1. 101: 'Sic docuit Aristoteles in libro suo de poetico argumento, quem non ausus fuit interpres Hermannus transferre in Latinum propter metrorum difficultatem, quam non intellexit, ut ipse dicit in prologo commentarii Averrois super illum librum.' Cf. Bacon, *Opera Inedita,* pp. 471-2.

[7] See *The Greek Grammar of Roger Bacon,* ed. by Nolan and Hirsch, Cambridge, 1902, p. 28: 'Unde Aristoteles, in libris de arte poetica, partes locucionis dicit esse sillabas et coniuncciones, sed sillabe in quantum huius nihil significant; coniuncciones vero non per se significant.'

Cf. Boethius, *Commentarii* 2. 6: 'Unde etiam ipse quoque Aristoteles in libris quos de poetica scripsit locutionis partes esse syllabas vel etiam coniunctiones tradidit, quarum syllabae in eo quod sunt syllabae nihil omnino significant, conjunctiones vero consignificare quidem possunt, per se vero nihil designant.'

[8] See Émile Charles, *Roger Bacon,* Paris, 1861, p. 122, note.

[9] See Bacon, *Opus Majus* 1. 101; *Opera Inedita,* pp. 266, 307 ff.

[10] See Bacon, *Opera Inedita,* p. 469.

[11] *Ibid.*

[12] See Jourdain, p. 71.

[13] See Dante, *Convivio,* trans. by Jackson, Oxford, 1909, p. 154. Cf. Dante, *Epistle 10,* ed. and trans. by Toynbee, Oxford, 1920.

[14] See *The Philobiblon of Richard de Bury,* ed. and trans. by E. C. Thomas, London, 1888, p. 221.

[15] Chaucer, *Canterbury Tales,* B 3163-7. Cf. *Poetics* 7. 1451ª 11-15.

Chaucer's definition is commonplace, but in the Prologue to the *Legend of Good Women* (A 511-14) he presents a puzzle to the critics:

> Wel hath she quit me myn affeccioun
> That I have to hir flour, the dayesye!
> No wonder is thogh Iove hir stellifye,
> As telleth Agaton, for hir goodnesse!

It looks as if here we had a reference to Agathon's tragedy, *Antheus,* or 'The Flower,' and the only known source for such a reference is Aristotle's *Poetics* 9.1451ᵇ21. Skeat (*Works of Chaucer* 3. xxxiii) has noted the problem. See John W. Hales, *Chaucer's 'Agaton,'* in *Modern Language Quarterly* I (1897). 5-8; George Lyman Kittredge, *Chaucer's Lollius,* in *Harvard Studies in Classical Philology* 28 (1917). 75.

[16] 'Sententie super libros Rhetoricorum Aristotelis secundo folio *omnia* per Cobildik precio.' 'Cobildik' apparently was the donor of the work. See *Collectanea* (First Series), ed. by Fletcher (Oxford Historical Society), 1885, p. 70.

[17] See *Polychronicon Ranulfi Higden,* ed. by Babington and Lumby, London, 1865-86, 3. 360.

[18] Lane Cooper, *The Poetics of Aristotle, its Meaning and Influence,* p. 100.

[19] See P. S. Allen, *Linacre and Latimer in Italy,* in the *English Historical Review* 18 (1903). 514-17.

[20] See Thomas F. Dibdin, *An Introduction to the Greek and Latin Classics* (4th ed.), London, 1827, I. 313.

[21] See Thomas More, *Opera Omnia,* Frankfort-on-Main, 1689, p. 298; Bale, *Index Britanniae Scriptorum,* ed. by Poole, Oxford, 1902, p. 126, *s.v.* 'Grocin.'

[22] Erasmus, *Epistles,* trans. by Francis M. Nichols, London, 1901, I. 226.

[23] Erasmus merely mentions the two treatises in a letter; see *Epistle 1159* in his *Opera Omnia,* Leyden, 1703.

[24] Vives, *Opera,* Basel 1555, I. 146: 'In theatris ad publicam exhilarationem exprimebatur hominum vita, velut tabella quadam vel speculo, quae res vehementer delectat propter imitationem sicut Aristoteles ait in *Arte Poetica.* Quippe imitatione, inquit, omnes capiuntur mirifice, et est homo animal maxime imitationi natum, et ea quae in natura sua nollemus cernere, expressa et assimulata nos detinent.' Cf. *Poetics* 4.1448 b 4-24.

[25] Ascham, *Works,* ed. by Giles, London, 1864-5, I. xxxvii.

[26] Ascham, *Schoolmaster,* in *Works* 3.240-1; also in Gregory Smith, *Elizabethan Critical Essays* 1.23-4. Cf. Francis Meres, *Palladis Tamia* (1598), in Gregory Smith 2.322.

[27] Of the men Ascham mentions, only Cheke and Walter Haddon show any acquaintance with Aristotelian theory. Haddon says that Ascham had introduced him to the *Rhetoric.* See his letter to Johann Sturm (December 6, 1566) in *Lucubrationes passim Collectae et Editae,* London, 1567, pp. 347-8.

[28] See Herrick, *Sir John Cheke and Aristotle's Poetics,* in *The Classical Weekly* 18 (1925). 134-5.

[29] Cheke, *De Pronuntiatione Graecae,* Basel, 1555, p. 122; also in Syvert Havercamp, *Sylloge Scriptorum,* Leyden, 1736-40, 2.286. Cf. *Poetics* 21.1458ª10-15.

[30] See Havercamp 1.333; cf. 1.306.

[31] *Ibid.* 1.110.

[32] *Ibid.* 1.459; cf. 1.391.

[33] See Ramus, *Scholae in Liberales Artes,* Basel, 1578, Book 2 of the *Scholarum Grammaticarum Libri XX.*

[34] See Bywater, *Erasmian Pronunciation of Greek and its Precursors,* Oxford, 1908.

It is perhaps worth noting that both Gardiner and Smith refer to Aristotle's remarks on diction in *De Interpretatione* (Havercamp 2.323, 483-4), just as Boethius, and after him Roger Bacon, did. The linguistic remarks in Plato's *Cratylus* and Aristotle's *De Interpretatione* and *Poetics* have often been associated. Perhaps Richard Mulcaster has the collocation in mind when he says that it is not necessary to prove his statements on the properties of words by Plato's *Cratylus* or Aristotle. (See his *Elementarie,* London, 1582, p. 168). It is impossible to determine who is mainly responsible for this association.

[35] Ascham, *Works* 3.84.

[36] Ascham, *Works* 3.213; in Gregory Smith 1.7.

[37] *Ibid.*

[38] See *Commentarii in Artem Poeticam Horatii Confecti ex Schelis Jo. Sturmii,* Strasburg, 1576.

[39] See *Ioannis Sturmii de Imitatione Oratoria Libri Tres,* Strasburg, 1574.

[40] 'T. B. Gent,' the author of the *Rich Storehouse,* is identified in the *Dictionary of National Biography* as Thomas Blundeville (*fl.* 1561).

[41] See Bucer, *Scripta Anglicana,* Basel, 1577, p. 144.

[42] Peterson, *Galateo,* ed. by H. J. Reid, 1892, p. 31.

[43] See Bywater, *Milton and the Aristotelian Definition of Tragedy,* in *Journal of Philology* 27 (1901). 274.

[44] *Mirror for Magistrates,* ed. by Joseph Haslewood, London, 1815, 2.126.

[45] Harvey, *Works,* ed. by Grosart, 1884, 1.69.

[46] *Ibid.* I. xiii.

[47] See Harvey's *Rhetor,* London, 1577, and his *Ciceronianus,* London, 1577.

[48] Harvey, *Works* I. xvii (quoted by Morley). Cf. the *Ciceronianus,* pp. 18-19, 28. Cicero was worshiped by nearly all the English men of letters in Harvey's day. Walter Haddon (*Poemata,* London, 1567, p. 67) writes:

In Marcum Tullium Ciceronem

O Deus, o splendens Romanae gloria gentis,
Virtutis specimen, vitae praeceptor honestae.
O Cicero doctos inter doctissimus omnes,
Cur tua, temporibus nostris, non iuncta
    fuerunt?

[49] Harvey, *Marginalia,* ed. by G. C. Moore Smith, Straford, 1913, p. 168.

[50] See Gascoigne, in Gregory Smith 1.48

[51] See Whetstone, Dedication of *Promos and Cassandra,* in Gregory Smith 1.59.

[52] See Thomas Fowler, *History of Corpus Chisti College,* Oxford, 1893, p. 95.

[53] See Jewel, *Works,* Cambridge, 1850, 4.1286.

[54] See Anthony à Wood, *Athenae Oxonienses,* (2nd ed.), London, 1721, 1.339.

[55] See Reynolds, *Orationes Duodecim,* London, 1619, p. 248.

[56] See Reynolds, *The Overthrow of Stage-Playes,* 1599.

[57] Lodge, in Gregory Smith 1.83.

[58] Bruno, *Heroic Enthusiasts,* trans. by L. Williams, London, 1887, 1.39; cf. 1.37-8.

[59] See Sidney, *Works,* ed. by Albert Feuillerat, Cambridge, 1922-3, 3.84.

[60] *Ibid.* 3.124.

[61] *Ibid.* 1.118. John Hoskins, in his *Figures of Rhetoric,* says that Sidney translated the two first books of Aristotle's *Rhetoric.* See *The Life of Sir Philip Sidney,* by Malcolm William Wallace, Cambridge, 1915, p. 327.

[62] Sidney, *Works* 3.9; Gregory Smith 1.158.

[63] Sidney, *Works* 3.20; Gregory Smith 1.173. Cf. *Poetics* 1448 ^{b} 8-12.

[64] See Spingarn, *Literary Criticism in the Renaissance,* p. 273.

The notion that poetry is superior to philosophy was common in England after Sidney's day. In 1674 we find Thomas Rymer, for example, attributing to Aristotle the statement that 'Tragedy more conduces to the instruction of mankind than even Philosophy itself.' See Spingarn, *Critical Essays of the Seventeenth Century* 2.164.

[65] Sidney, *Works* 3.16; Gregory Smith 1.167. Cf. *Poetics* 1451 ^{a} 36-8, 1451 ^{b} 1-11.

[66] Sidney, *Works* 3.10; Gregory Smith 1.159.

[67] Sidney, *Works* 3.38; Gregory Smith 1.196-7.

[68] Sidney, *Works* 3.23; Gregory Smith 1.176-7.

[69] Sidney, *Works* 3.41; Gregory Smith 1.200. Cf. *Poetics* 1449 ^{a} 32-7.

[70] Sidney, *Works* 3.23-4; Gregory Smith 1.177-8.

[71] See Minturno, *De Poeta,* Venice, 1559, p. 106: 'Illud autem ne te praetereat uelim, sic poetis esse dicendum, ut siue doceant, siue oblectent, siue moueant, haec singula statim admiratio legentis, audientisue consequatur.' Also p. 180: 'Uerum enim eiusmodi hoc rerum genus esse plane intelliget, qui huius poetate munus esse animaduertet, in admirationem adducere auditorem. Admiranda uero esse, quae uel afferunt miserationem, uel terrorem incutiunt.'

Cf. Scaliger, *Poetices* 3.96.

[72] Sidney, *Works* 3.41; Gregory Smith 1.201.

[73] Sidney, *Works* 3.25; Gregory Smith 1.179.

[74] See Spingarn, *Literary Criticism in the Renaissance,* p. 268.

[75] Sidney, *Works* 3.35; Gregory Smith 1.192.

[76] See Webbe, in Gregory Smith 1.235.

[77] *Ibid.* 1.248.

Aristotle's remarks on early poetic composition were fairly well known to English critics in Elizabethan times. Samuel Daniel, in his *Defence of Rhyme* (1603?), speaks of Aristotle's theory that poetic composition arises naturally and spontaneously; see Daniel, in Gregory Smith 2.360. John Florio's translation of Montaigne in 1603 contains a passage that is usually referred to chapter 24 of the *Poetics:* 'His words [Homer's] (according to Aristotle) are the only words that have motion and action; they are the only substantial words.' See *Essays,* Book 2, ch. 36. It is much more likely that Montaigne has in mind the *Rhetoric* 1411 [b] 32.

[78] Webbe, in Gregory Smith 1.236.

Cf. *Poetics* 1447 [b] 17-20. (Bywater's translation): 'Homer and Empedocles, however, have really nothing in common apart from their metre; so that, if the one is to be called a poet, the other should be termed a physicist rather than a poet.'

[79] See Puttenham, in Gregory Smith 2.174. Cf. *Poetics* 1455 [a] 25. Puttenham may have taken the phrase from Cicero's *Orator* (ch. 21): 'The Greeks call this [*prepon*], we call it *decorum.*'

[80] Harington, in Gregory Smith 2.216.

[81] Harington, in Gregory Smith 2.216.

[82] *Ibid.* 2.200-1.

[83] *Ibid.* 2.209.

[84] See W. F. De Moss, *The Influence of Aristotle's Politics and Ethics on Spenser,* Chicago, 1918.

[85] Spenser, *Ruines of Time* 575-9.

[86] See *Two Lamentable Tragedies,* in Tudor Facsimile Texts, 1913.

[87] Lamb, *Works,* ed. by MacDonald, London, 1903, 9.100, note.

[88] See *Hamlet* 2.2.401-7.

[89] See *Hamlet* 3.2.20-4. Hamlet's advice on acting, and his insistence on restraint, offer a striking parallel to Aristotle's criticism of excessive gesture (*Poetics* 1461 [b]29-35, 1462 [a]1-4).

[90] Edwin Arlington Robinson, *Ben Jonson entertains a Man from Stratford.*

Humphrey House (essay date 1956)

SOURCE: "The Relation of Character and Plot," in *Aristotle's Poetics*, Rupert Hart-Davis, 1967, pp. 68-81.

[*In the following essay, written in 1956, House maintains that Aristotle's views regarding the importance of plot in tragedy actually reveal his "attempt to guarantee the individuality of character."*]

This brings us to the famous argument by which Aristotle says that "plot" is more important than "character"; it is stated in the second half of ch. vi (pp. 36-9) and has produced a great deal of discussion. It is absurd in any language (quite apart from questions of translation) to bandy about complicated terms like "character", "plot" and "action" as if they were "fixities and definites". In this particular discussion much avoidable trouble has been caused by the assumption that the meanings of the terms "character" and "action" are self-evident, and that there is some kind of elementary opposition between them.

The essential clues to the proper interpretation of this latter half of ch. vi are present in the language that Aristotle uses in the chapter itself; but they can be understood more clearly by reference to what he says in the **Nicomachean Ethics.** And this is one of the passages which, as I said before, does presuppose some knowledge of the **Ethics** and the terminology used there.

The point to get hold of first is this: although Aristotle in the **Poetics** uses expressions which present the matter as if there were a sharp antithesis between "character" and "plot", or "character" and "action", this antithesis is not present in his whole theory, in which character and action were not opposed to each other, but inseparable. There is an interesting discussion of this in Butcher. He presents the matter as a question.

"If character and action were so intimately related in Aristotle's general theory of behaviour, why did he, in the **Poetics,** so emphatically present character as if it were in some kind of antithesis to plot? Why did he present his case in an exaggerated way?" (*Aristotle's Theory of Poetry and Fine Art,* 4th edn. 1907, esp. pp. 344-5.)

Much of what Butcher has to say on this point is very relevant. He quotes the most extreme statement of Aristotle's position, the statement which is given in Bywater's translation, ch. vi (p. 37) as:

> A tragedy is impossible without action, but there may be one without Character. . . . [50 a 23-5])

Butcher's footnote to this passage bears out much that I have been saying in these lectures and have now to say; it contains germinal ideas of which much more could have been made in his main argument:

> In the popular antithesis of the two terms "character" has not its full dramatic value, and instead of signifying "characters producing an action", it stands for an abstract impression of character left on our minds by the reading of a play. Similarly "plot" is regarded as the "story" in a play, viewed in abstraction from the special nature of the persons; and, in particular, denotes a complication exciting wonder or suspense—an idea, however, which is not necessarily present in the word [*muthos*].

What follows is a very much simplified statement of arguments in the **Nicomachean Ethics,** especially Books I and II.

Aristotle says first that we are not good or bad in character *by nature.* This is in contrast to certain physical capacities which we do have by nature. The physical senses of seeing and hearing, for instance, are in us by nature. We had the sense of sight before we even saw; the sense of hearing before we even heard: we did not acquire these senses by acts of seeing and hearing. In so far as we have by nature a capacity for action it is physical action, which is ethically neutral or indifferent, and therefore does not involve character at all.

But the virtues (and the vices) are acquired only in so far as we have acted well or badly. We learn to become good or bad by acting well or ill just as a builder learns to build by building. By repeated acts of a certain kind we acquire a habit or bent . . . of character. In this way qualities of character are legacies of past acts.

Historically in each individual, character is thus formed by action, is dependent on action for its very being, and has its qualities in virtue of the quality of the actions from which it is derived. In real life, quite apart from drama, character is subordinate to action because it is a product of action.

Secondly, he says that we are not good or bad merely in respect of *knowing* what is good or bad. Here Aristotle is partly answering the intellectualist ethics of the Platonic Socrates, so often expressed in the epigram "Virtue is Knowledge". Against this Aristotle insists (1) that the guiding principle of ethics is not the Absolute Good but a practical good, attainable as the end for man: and this end he ultimately identifies with happiness; (2) that in all ethical situations there is an element of desire which is the stimulus to decision, and the determinant of direction.

This inclusion of the element of desire is also part of Aristotle's revision of Plato's ethics. Its importance in

Aristotle's scheme is that it is the "end" which we desire. We have a desire or wish to bring about a certain state of affairs, and it is this desire for the "end" which distinguishes human ethical action from the undirected play of circumstance. Action which is ethical is a movement towards an end.[1] The "character" which, as I have said, a man acquires *by acting* is formed by the kind of "ends" which he habitually proposes to himself as desirable. In so far as this is so, character is only a tendency, and it does not become fully "actual" unless a particular end is desired and the "movement" is thus set on foot towards it.

At this point in the argument Aristotle attempted to assimilate his ethical terminology to his metaphysical terminology, where the distinction between "potentiality" and "actuality" is a fundamental one. The processes by which he did this are technical and difficult to state clearly; and they hardly concern us, even if I were competent to expound them.

I must state the matter in an over-simplified way: "character", in that it is a bent, a tendency, a legacy of past acts, is not fully "actualised" or "realised". It is only fully realised when it is "in act", as it is not, for instance, when we are asleep.

Thus, from the point of view of drama, "character" in its full and proper sense occurs only in action. The mere presentation or description of certain "qualities" of character is the presentation of something less than the fullness of character.

Thus in Aristotle's ethics, with or without reference to the drama, character may be looked upon as the arbitrarily stabilised meeting-point of two series of actions; the antecedent series which has gone to its formation, and the consequent series in which it will be actualised in future. Character in itself is not fully "real" until it is "in act", or "in action".

I might make this clearer by a comparison; but it is not to be taken as an exact analogy, for it is not. Suppose you have a training-film of athletics, and stop it in the middle so that you have a "still" of a runner in his stride; the "still" will show you certain qualities of him as a runner—his build, his muscular development, his position, his way of holding himself, his style so far as that can be seen without movement. But it will not tell you whether he has a weak heart or poor staying-power; or how fast he runs or whether he is likely to win against such-and-such an opponent under such-and-such conditions: it will not even tell you much about his style as a whole. Movement is necessary for that.

In a broad way Aristotle's view of "character" in literature may be thought of as such a "still".

And indeed the comparison with athletes is one of Aristotle's own comparisons. In the **Nicomachean Ethics,** I, 8, 1099ª3, he says (in Sir David Ross's translation, Oxford, 1925):

> And as in the Olympic Games it is not the most beautiful and the strongest that are crowned but those who compete (for it is some of these that are victorious), so those who act win, and rightly win, the noble and good things in life.

To Aristotle even happiness itself, which, when properly understood, is the ultimate end of man, is not a *state* but a form of activity. In the **Nicomachean Ethics** I, 8, 1098ᵇ 22, happiness is defined as "a sort of good life and good action". And Aristotle (b 30 ff.) goes on:

> With those who identify happiness with virtue or some one virtue our account is in harmony; for to virtue belongs virtuous activity. But it makes, perhaps, no small difference whether we place the chief good in *possession* or in *use,* in state of mind or in activity. For the state of mind may exist without producing any good result, as in a man who is asleep or in some other way quite inactive, but the activity cannot; for one who has the activity will of necessity be acting, and acting well.

You see how this elaborates the position which is very shortly stated in **Poetics,** ch. vi (p. 37):

> All human happiness or misery takes the form of action; the end for which we live is a certain kind of activity, not a quality. Character gives us qualities, but it is in our actions—what we do—that we are happy or the reverse.

It is saying something more than that we can only "know" the "characters" in a drama through what they say and do: it is saying that they only exist as characters in what they say and do. It is a truth of major importance for dramatic criticism. They exist only in their dramatic context and by their dramatic function. Much recent criticism of the drama—especially of Shakespearean drama—has been recovering this side of Aristotle's doctrine. The swing away from Bradley in Shakespearean criticism has been a swing away from the tendency to make back-inferences from the text to determine a supposed full and stable view of the "character's character", and then to project this inferred (and artificially rounded and complete) "character" back into disputable areas of the play as an instrument of interpretation. The protest against such methods can call on Aristotle for support. It has been a swing towards emphasis on plot, on the whole dramatic design and composition.

With pupils beginning the serious criticism of dramatic poetry, I find the mistake of method often takes even more extreme forms. "Characters" like Oedipus and Samson are spoken of as if they have a firm, known "character" from legend or history; and Sophocles and Milton are virtually judged according to how nearly they get them "right". Or, commoner still, the character of Oedipus in the Colonus play is judged by the character of Oedipus as he appears in *King Oedipus;* or Sophocles is blamed for treating Creon differently in two different plays. But, as these two plays were not parts of a trilogy, Sophocles has absolute freedom to create and use what "characters" he likes. We must now return to, and examine, Aristotle's most extreme and most epigrammatic statement of his position. "A tragedy is impossible without action, but there may be one without character."

Note that in Aristotle's Greek, as in English, there is an ambiguity in the use of the word for "character". I have just illustrated this in English by using the phrase "the character's character". The word is used either for "the dramatic personage" or "the ethical nature", which may be of a dramatic personage, or of a person in real life. So also Aristotle uses his word [*ethos*] sometimes for the dramatic presentation of *ēthos*, sometimes for *ēthos* or character in its ethical sense whether in a play or not. This famous epigram does not of course mean that there may be a tragedy without characters, that is, without dramatic personages; it means that there may be a tragedy without dramatic personages who exhibit what Aristotle specifically calls "character" in the ethical sense. He then proceeds, in ch. vi (pp. 38-9), to describe very shortly what he means by "character" in this sense:

> Character in a play is that which reveals the moral purpose of the agents, i.e. the sort of thing they seek or avoid, where that is not obvious—hence there is no room for Character in a speech on a purely indifferent subject.

Even taking Bywater's translation at its face value this is a rather ambiguous sentence (there are in fact problems about the correct reading of the Greek text).

In any case, it is evident that by "tragedies without character" Aristotle means plays in which personages go through a change of fortune (probably a change from happiness to misery, rather than the opposite) in which they suffer and act, but act *without showing why,* without adequately revealing the habit, bent and tendency of their characters, and without showing *their characters in act,* without showing their minds working upon the means to the actualisation of their desires. A tragedy of circumstance and event of this kind is probably capable of rousing the emotions of the audience; by self-projection into the cipher on the stage some kind of pity may be felt, and external circumstances alone may cause a kind of fear. This such plays are at least better than plays deficient in action; where there is nothing but a set of speeches describing static qualities. Aristotle says beginners can do this, "can write descriptive monologues, but fail to show action and interaction, and make their personages speak like rhetoricians".

The important positive doctrine is that "character in the play is what reveals the moral purpose in the personages". Now the word (and the related words) translated here "moral purpose" is the term for the actualising process by which we decide on an action as a means to achieve an end that we desire; this is sometimes translated "choice", and the verb of it "choose".

To explain this I quote from a paper by Mr. Colin Hardie, to whose knowledge and advice these lectures in general owe more than I can say. There is nothing unfamiliar to readers of Aristotle in what he writes, but it summarises the point clearly and suitably for our purpose:

> An action is an activity designed to bring about an "end" and it has in it both an element of trained desire and an intellectual element. We have a desire or wish for a certain state of affairs. From this we argue back by a chain of means, until we arrive at something we see to be in our power here and now. We will the end and perceive the present state of affairs, and to link these two by a chain of means is the work of deliberation. This may be impossible, but if we think it is possible to achieve the end, we choose . . . to do this act for the sake of the result it will bring about. The word [*proairesis*], usually translated "choice", is not choice between alternative ends nor choice between alternative means to one end, but simply the act of will which starts a bodily movement to put the chain of means in motion, and causes a change designed to produce the end. Now the nature of the end aimed at reveals and determines our character . . . ; if we actualise a tendency in ourselves to obtain this or that end, we are good if the end is what the good man aims at. This is not to say that the end justifies the means. On the contrary, a good act must be done *as* the good man does it. . . . If we desire what is good in itself, we may still make a mistake in calculating the means, either through ignorance of a fact or facts or through ignorance of what will bring about what (of the general rules governing conduct and of the probable or necessary consequences of any step). This calculation is the intellectual element . . . , is scientific and can be discussed. Thus any action involves both "character" and "thought". . . .

The distinction between "character" and "thought", as made in ch. vi of the *Poetics,* is thus much plainer. So far as thought is an element in the speeches of individual personages in the play relative to their particular circumstances and decisions, it covers this area of deliberation or calculation—"all they say when proving or disproving some particular point" (ch. vi, p. 39).

As character is shown in the choice of ends (we can be said to "choose" both the end and the means to it), so thought is the deliberation about means to the end.

Aristotle means the "element of thought" to be partly this internal deliberative casuistry of the individual;[2] but it need not, of course, always be internal to any one personage in the play; others may take part in the deliberation and have an influence on the decision. But "thought" in this sense is deliberation about action, whether internal or not—"whatever can be said or whatever is appropriate to the occasion" (p. 38). Here Aristotle is presupposing some knowledge of the ***Rhetoric,*** especially perhaps of Book II, chs. xxi and xxii. His mention of ***Rhetoric*** and ***Politics*** here in the context is partly a cross-reference to the earlier work. He is there speaking of the kind of arguments to be used "on such subjects as moral action is concerned with, and such things as are to be chosen or avoided with a view to action".

Discourse of this kind is said to belong in part to the art of Politics; because deliberation about "whatever is appropriate to the occasion" in any moral situation will almost certainly have to take into account social factors—something beyond the individual; for the occasion is an occasion in society, and the deliberation is about "whatever is appropriate" to it. In the more special sense, of course, it becomes "political" in typical tragedies as Aristotle knew them (and as Shakespeare wrote them) because the personages are of high position, with political influence and power, and the fate, good or ill, of many others depends on their personal decisions.

I should like to say in passing that it was one of the unfortunate consequences of the individualistic "character" criticism of the last century, that this political or social element in great tragedy was overlooked or underestimated. And I have found that even now beginners tend to underestimate it. I ask you to reflect how much there is, even in the few plays of our syllabus alone, of this deliberation about what "is to be chosen or avoided with a view to action" in a wide social and political context. In the *Oedipus at Colonus,* in the relations of Oedipus to Theseus, to Creon and, above all, to Polynices, how much depends on their views of him as a political asset, and on his views of them in their estimation and treatment of him from their own points of view! In *Samson* the matter is made almost diagrammatically clear. Samson's dialogues, especially with Manoa and Dalila, are set pieces of deliberation on what particular things to "avoid" if the half-apprehended destiny of saviour of Israel is to be fulfilled, in some future course of action not yet determined or foreseen. Manoa and Dalila present each a different possible solution of Samson's political relation to the Philistines; and by different processes of argument, both are rejected and "avoided". Equally, *Lear, Polyeucte,*

Andromaque, All for Love cannot be understood without taking into account the political element.

Next, thought is said to be shown alternatively in "enunciating some universal proposition". I fear that Bywater's verbal insensitivity has here once more done Aristotle a bad service. "Enunciating" is such a desperately awful word, a deathly word! The word means to show, to set something out so that it can be seen. The whole phrase here means, as a metaphor in literary criticism, something like "expressing some general matter", some general reflection on life or some general maxim of conduct—such as "treat your enemies as though they would become friends". Cf. *Rhetoric*, II. xxi on maxims . . . , as distinct from the particular deliberation about means to ends in the action. And this phrase covers generalised comment upon the action or growing out of it. It covers such things as the chorus in *King Oedipus:*

> All the generations of mortal man add up to
>   nothing!
> Show me the man whose happiness was
>   anything more than illusion
> Followed by disillusion.
> Here is the instance, here is Oedipus, here is
>   the reason
> Why I will call no mortal creature happy.
>   (E. F. Watling, *Theban Plays,* 1947, p. 63.)

The chorus, indeed, shows the very process of thought moving from the particular to the general.

It covers such things as Macbeth's speech:

> She should have died hereafter:
> There would have been a time for such a
>   word.—
> To-morrow, and to-morrow, and to-morrow,
> Creeps in this petty pace from day to day,
> To the last syllable of recorded time;
> And all our yesterdays have lighted fools
> The way to dusty death.
>   (V, v, 17-23.)

Another point to consider is this: Aristotle treats this element of "thought" very shortly and very drily; and it is not perhaps evident on the face of the treatise, how much he intends to include within it. He presents it first as a form of reasoning about means to ends; but this reasoning takes into account "*whatever* can be said, *whatever* is appropriate to the occasion". It is therefore reasoning *about* the emotional factors too; the speeches, the discourse, include everything relevant. It is only necessary to pick up his cross-reference to the *Rhetoric* and glance at the *Rhetoric* in even a superficial way, to see his awareness of the fact that deliberation of this kind, and persuasion (whether it is self-persuasion or the persuasion of others) involves opinion and feeling (taking all affections and hatreds into account); the emotional side of human nature provides the stuff on which the mind works.[3] Aristotle's sense of Tragedy as an artistic whole, his sense of the total design, of the end, his sense that ultimately Tragedy deals with the great theme of "success or failure in their lives" (p. 36), *does* lead him to treat some of the subordinate points cursorily. Especially on the emotional side, he is so much concerned with the major emotions of the whole design and of the end, that the emotional element in the intermediate stages seems to be pushed rather out of sight, or at least not treated in proper proportion. But still his theory includes and allows for it at the vital points: (1) in the element of "desire" for the end, which is the mainspring, the sustaining force of the action; (2) in that all through, in the detail of the episodes, thought is working upon material charged with emotion.

I used just now the word "casuistry". In Protestant countries it is liable to carry derogatory implications, about deceit and shuffling and putting cushions under the elbows of sinners, and so on. But it is in fact that part of ethics, or of moral theology, which discusses not the general rules of conduct but the application of general rules to particular *cases* and the conflict of rules. And I used the word in the context of a character in a play deliberating upon the particular means to the achievement of the end he desires. This particularity is most important; and to show how, I call your attention to a sentence at the beginning of ch. vii of Book II of the *Nicomachean Ethics:*

> Among statements about conduct those which are general apply more widely, but those which are particular are more genuine[4] . . . , since conduct has to do with individual cases, and our statements must harmonize with the facts in these cases.

Aristotle's whole treatment of ethics is concrete, definite and practical; and therefore he has very little respect for judgments about actions which take no account of the circumstances.[5] With a man in real life, you might be able to say that as the result of the accumulated experience of his past actions he had a bent or tendency towards actions of one kind or another: but you would not be able to make any very useful ethical judgment on his conduct till the particular facts and circumstances were known. So too, within a play, "character" means very little indeed until the particular facts and circumstances have been laid down through which the character declares itself. These facts and circumstances *are the Plot.*

All through the *Ethics* Aristotle is implicitly protesting against the Platonic tendency to generalise ethical judgments, to establish sweeping theories of value. And in the *Poetics* his doctrine of the pre-eminence of "plot" and "action" over "character" bears all in the same direction. It is a monstrously paradoxical fate that he should have been misunderstood as slighting and minimising the individuality of character, which it is supposed to have been the great glory of later drama (especially English Elizabethan drama) to portray. His theory provides most explicitly for its portrayal. Indeed, his theory of the importance of plot is best understood as an attempt to guarantee the individuality of character. This is in complete harmony with the particularity of method which he proposes as necessary for the poet in ch. xvii. I touched on this for a different purpose in an earlier lecture, but now we are in a better position to understand its full implications.

The poet, Aristotle says (pp. 60-1), should remember:

> (1) To put the actual scenes as far as possible before his eyes. In this way *seeing everything with the vividness of an eye-witness,* as it were, he will devise what is appropriate, and be least likely to overlook incongruities.

> (2) As far as may be, too, the poet should even act his story *with the very gestures of his personages . . .* he who feels the emotions to be described will be *the most convincing.*

This is not the language of a theorist of generality. It is most necessary to emphasise this concern of Aristotle's with particularity and individuality, to which his whole theory of action leads up, because he is so often represented, or misrepresented, as the advocate of a generalised form of drama, and of a generalised or "typical" handling of character. The source of this in the Renaissance critics is rather Horace than Aristotle.

In more modern interpreters the explanation is quite plain—that more attention is given to what Aristotle says about the difference between poetry and history than to what he says about the relation between the particular and the general *within poetry itself.*

In the comparison between poetry and history he says that poetry is more closely related to the universal than history, because of the arbitrary succession of historical events in time, in which the links between event and event cannot be easily seen to follow laws of probability or necessity. He never anywhere says that poetry does not deal with individuals and particulars at all, but that it *does* deal with individuals and particulars so related to each other that they reveal these laws of action and connection. There is nothing at all in his theory which precludes the subtlest development of character and motive, or the maximum, most concrete, poetic realisation of dramatic fact.

Notes

[1] See R. P. Hardie, "The *Poetics* of Aristotle", *Mind,*

IV (N.S. 1895), 350-64.

[2] *Hamlet* and *Macbeth* are plays in which this side of it takes a very large part, in which soliloquy on questions of means to ends is a major part of the play's doings.

[3] And still more, of course, that kind of "thought" which expresses the general matter is thought *upon* the emotional content of the play.

[4] Grant translates "more real": what about "bear more the stamp of truth"?

[5] [Cf. II, 9, 1109 b 23: Such [deviations from the mean] depend on particular facts, and the decision rests with perception. . . .

Humphrey House (essay date 1956)

SOURCE: "The Tragic Action and Character," in *Aristotle's Poetics,* Rupert Hart-Davis, 1964, pp. 82-99.

[*In the following essay, written in 1956, House analyzes the features of dramatic characters which Aristotle discusses in* Poetics. *In particular, House focuses on the tragic hero and on the concept of hamartia, noting that the understanding of hamartia as the hero's "tragic flaw" is misleading.*]

In the definition of Tragedy in ch. vi, Bywater's version makes Aristotle say that Tragedy is an imitation of an action that is "serious"; this is also Butcher's translation at that point. But in fact the Greek word here in the definition [*spoudaĩos*] is the same as that used at the beginning of ch. ii (p. 25) in the sentence:

> The objects the imitator represents are actions, with agents who are necessarily either good men [*spoudaĩos*] or bad.

The word for the good men in ch. ii is the same as the word translated "serious" in ch. vi. Is this difference justified?

Many people have argued for and defended the translation "serious" in ch. vi; and I have been among them in the past, and must now recant. The reason for wanting to defend it is obvious. If it can be made out that "serious" is right (as meaning "having importance", "being of import", "having weight", and so on), Aristotle's general theory is rescued from some of its heavier moralistic implications.

But there is no doubt that the whole range of parallel and contrasting words as they occur both in the ***Poetics*** and in the ***Ethics*** makes it unjustifiable to isolate this use of the term [*spoudaīos*] in ch. vi: it does mean "good", ethically good: and in the **Poetics** itself the clearest passage to bring in support of this view is that at the beginning of ch. xv (p. 55):

> In the Characters there are four points to aim at.
> First and foremost, that they shall be good.

The word here is not [*spoudaīos*] but a word which has an unequivocal sense of "ethically good" [*khrēstos*]. Aristotle is here speaking of "character" in the sense I explained it in the last lecture, as an ethical nature revealed only in act, in the desiring of an end and in the choosing of the means towards it. The goodness he here requires in the moral purpose is inseparably linked to the goodness of the whole action.

The word [*spoudaīos*] in ch. ii must be taken as synonymous with this word [*khrēstos*] in ch. xv; and it would be too glaring an inconsistency for [*spoudaīos*] in ch. vi to be used differently.

In ch. xv (pp. 55-8) Aristotle says that in treating dramatic "characters" (the word does not mean "personages" but characters in the sense I spoke of in the last lecture) there are four points to aim at; and every one of them raises important questions. They are:

(1) that the characters should be "good". . . .

(2) that they should be "appropriate". . . .

(3) that they should be "like reality". . . .

(4) that they should be "consistent". . . .

I shall take these four points in turn, as applying to the characters in general, referring, as necessary, to the special case of the tragic hero as I go along, and shall then discuss at the end what Aristotle says about the hero alone.

1. *"Goodness" of Character*

This predominant and main requirement of "goodness", which seems at first sight rather strange, is essential to Aristotle's whole theory because it is the foundation of that initial sympathy in spectator or reader without which the tragic emotions cannot be roused or the tragic pleasure ultimately conveyed. Aristotle assumes in his spectators a normally balanced moral attitude, by which they cannot give their sympathies to one who is "depraved" or "odious"; and sympathy is the very basis of the whole tragic pleasure. In particular, the special kind of sympathy which is pity. The bad man, Aristotle says in ch. xiii (p. 50), falling from happiness to misery arouses some kind of human feeling in us, but not pity.

Also, when he comes to details of plot, he says (ch. xiv, p. 53) that the most tragic situations arise between

friends or between blood-relations, that is between those in whom are found the affections and loyalties which characterise the good. In such situations there is the maximum possibility of pity.

But does Aristotle mean that all characters in Tragedy should be equally good, and that interplay of character as between good and bad is ruled out? He has no explicit statement about this, but his answer is by implication absolutely plain.

It is plain, both from ch. xv (p. 56) when he speaks of the badness of character of Menelaus in the *Orestes* as being "not required", and also from ch. xxv (p. 92) when, again using the example of Menelaus, he says there is "no possible apology" for "depravity of character" *when it is not necessary and no use is made of it,* that he admits that badness may be necessary in certain tragedies. In both chapters the words for badness are extreme words . . . meaning out-and-out badness, real baseness, depravity, wickedness: they are not intermediate words meaning absence of perfection or anything like that.

The action of the play as a whole should be a "good" one (i.e., it should portray efforts to bring about a "good" result), and the personages setting on foot the main action necessarily therefore are "good": but *in so far as this main action requires it,* bad characters, even depraved and wicked characters, may occur. The Creon of *Oedipus at Colonus* is not ruled out; nor is Iago.[1]

Nothing is further from Aristotle's mind than the recommendation of a negative or fugitive or cloistered virtue. Not only is his whole ethical theory a theory of activity, but the very word [*spoudaī os*] implies a zealous and energetic goodness. [This is doubtful, even if the adjective is derived from [*spoudē*], zeal.]

Some forms of Hebraic and Christian morality have emphasised negative virtue, especially in the avoidance of "sin"; but Aristotle's good man is not good unless he is desiring specific, positive, good ends and working towards their attainment.

This suggests another reason why, for Aristotle, the tragic hero was to be "not pre-eminently virtuous and just", but something less than that. The only explicit reason he gives in the **Poetics** for this decision (ch. xiii, p. 50) is that the entirely good man passing from happiness to misery "is not fear-inspiring or piteous, but simply odious to us"; he rejects such a character, in effect, because his suffering offends our sense of justice. But taking his theory as a whole it necessarily involves another reason. The perfect or nearly perfect man would be one whose desires were so trained and controlled, whose intellect also was so habituated to the right calculation of means and the making of the right practical inferences, that he would formulate to himself ends more immediately in his power. The gap between the desired end and what is in his power here and now would tend to close; right action would tend to become more and more immediate and spontaneous; the sphere of deliberation would be more and more limited; and in the ideal situation the opportunity for the dramatic display of action would disappear.

The insistence on "goodness" has no objectionably moralistic implications; it is quite free from the taint of direct didacticism. And though the word [*spoudaīos*] in ch. vi should not be *translated* "serious", it certainly involves the conception of seriousness. A tragedy is for Aristotle essentially a play in which great moral issues are involved—matters of the greatest possible importance to human life: and these cannot be made plain except in characters who are basically and mainly good. An evil man has already a bent or habit of evil; and if this kind of action altogether controls a play, it is either, if seriously treated, merely horrible, or, if not seriously treated, the play is a comedy, and we are made to laugh at his evil and not be shocked by it.

Aristotle would certainly rule out, as not being tragedies, plays of policy in which the leading character is a calculating and unscrupulous person of a Machiavellian type, plays like *The Jew of Malta* or *The Massacre at Paris,* in which there is not even any suggestion of ultimate benefit to the state to justify villainy.[2] He would scarcely have understood the phrases "the Hero as Villain" and "the Villain as Hero". The required initial sympathy would be absent.

2. *Appropriateness of Character*

The second point is that the characters should be "appropriate". . . . Bywater in his edition glosses this word by saying that there should in the individual character be "nothing at variance with that of the class to which the individual belongs". F. L. Lucas takes this even further by his rendering of the word "true to type", and he then goes on to say that "a modern dramatist would be very moderately flattered by being told that his characters were absolutely typical" (*Tragedy,* p. 111). This is making a point by overstatement, by a gradual edging further and further away from what Aristotle actually says.

There is no doubt that Lucas is edging in the direction of what many later writers took Aristotle to *mean:* and he himself quotes an extreme example of its application in Thomas Rymer's saying

> that Iago is a badly drawn character because soldiers are notoriously an honest class of men.

This is a very sensitive point in the whole interpretation of the ***Poetics;*** one about which it is easy to be intellectually dishonest. I hope that, at least, I have left

no doubt in your minds about my own bias: for I argued at very considerable length in the last chapter that Aristotle's insistence on the importance of plot is to be understood as an attempt to guarantee the individuality of character. My interest in the word "appropriate" is to clear Aristotle of the charge that he ultimately reduces all characterisation to the mere presentation of types.

There is no word in the Greek at all corresponding to "type". The word translated "appropriate" . . . is quite fairly so translated; it is an intransitive participle meaning "fitting"; it is used first absolutely with no indication of what the character is to be fitting or appropriate *to;* and that is where the scope for various interpretation begins. The first example of applying the principle is the broad and very obvious one of the difference between the sexes. I must avoid going off into a digression about the Greek view of women. But it is important to realise that what Aristotle is here talking about (where Bywater translates "a female character") is "a womanly *ēthos*",[3] not just a female personage in a play. However recent analytic psychology may have demonstrated that each sex possesses qualities of the other, which may be found more or less developed, nobody even now pretends that the psychological make-up of the sexes is identical. It may well be possible to create a woman (say like Lady Macbeth) with certain masculine characteristics; but even now it still makes sense to say that if you want to create a womanly woman it is inappropriate to make her a manly woman. We may well think that Aristotle was wrong in calling some specific things unwomanly (such as being cleverly sceptical about the popular idea of monsters, which is the point at issue in the speech that Euripides gave to Melanippe), but it does not therefore follow that there is no sense or meaning in the conception of "womanliness". Classification of human characters is, *in some sense,* not only justifiable but necessary. Rostagni agrees with Bywater that classification of characters is what Aristotle is talking about, so that we can rule out the idea that he means that characters should be "appropriate" to the traditional accounts of them. The question is, what kind of classification, and how far does he mean it to be carried? The only other example that he gives of something "inappropriate" is a rather obscure one about the "lamentation of Ulysses in the *Scylla*", a work of the dithyrambic poet Timotheus. The context is not known; but I confess it looks rather like an example which opens up the possibility that Aristotle may have been moving somewhere towards the ground I want to keep him clear of. But even there you can see that there may be some sense in the judgment. If Ulysses was made to speak some desperately sentimental drivel, it might well have been "inappropriate": but, in default of detailed knowledge, the case, I admit, seems to lie on the borderline between EITHER being inappropriate to the traditional accounts of Ulysses, as that he was "wily" or tough, OR being inappropriate to some other preconceived conception of the *sort* of person he ought to be, OR being inconsistent with what Timotheus had shown him to be elsewhere. This third possibility is ruled out by Aristotle's later discussion of "consistency", which is evidently something different from "appropriateness": and I think the reference to the traditional stories as a criterion should be ruled out here also. We are therefore left with the problem of trying to define what preconception of a "class" may have been in Aristotle's mind, such as would govern the dramatic characterisation of women and of Ulysses.

If we consider not merely the narrower context of what Aristotle says about "appropriateness", but also the wider context of the whole chapter in which it occurs, it appears that women, slaves and Ulysses are being used as examples of something of a different sort from what Iphigenia is meant to exemplify. She is being considered at a different level of dramatic individualisation.

Very tentatively indeed I wish to suggest that the controlling conception in Aristotle's mind, in what is plainly a kind of classification, may have been that of "status"—of political and social status, as that was defined by law, by custom, and by function. In Athens, of course, neither women nor slaves had the citizenship, and their position was defined and restricted in countless other ways by law. Ulysses would have a peculiar and clearly defined status in that he was a king.

In all ancient and medieval societies this concept of "status" has been fundamental. Athenian democracy itself was a democracy of adult male citizens only; the right to citizenship was jealously guarded and contested; the lesser rights of those who had not the citizenship were graded and defined by law. Aristotle himself, as a foreigner in Athens, could not be the owner of real property. In medieval Europe the feudal system, much as it varied from time to time and in different countries, was characteristically a system which perpetuated an elaborate hierarchy of status, from king to serf, each status in the hierarchy being related to a social and political function. Medieval political thought hinges on the concept of status. The first polity to be based upon the theoretical rejection of status was the Republic of the United States of America; and France followed. In England, even at the present day, you find surviving relics of status in the monarchy and the House of Lords; in certain legal privileges of hereditary peers; in the fact that a married woman living with her husband does not make an independent income tax return.

In all societies based upon status the positions of slaves, of women and of kings provide marked and extreme examples of the definition of status by law and custom.

The relation of character to status needs consideration in two aspects. Aristotle, with his insistence on practice as the source of character, would certainly have maintained that one brought up in slavery, doing the acts of a slave, would become slavelike if not, in the more pejorative sense, slavish. His theory of the genesis of character would have tended to stabilise a type of character appropriate to the status. One brought up, as he had seen Alexander brought up, as heir to a monarchy would stabilise a habit of command and authority; and so on. In this sense his feeling for "appropriateness" corresponds to the modern belief in the importance of environment. Environment would have a greater formative influence when it was clearly defined by law and daily imposed legal and social restrictions, and would tend more to the production of "types".

Secondly, when the conception of legal status was fundamental to the whole organisation of society, and there was no conception of a society in which it did not play a great part, breaches of what was "appropriate" to any status would have been breaches of the political and social order in the play. There might, of course, be a play *about* such breaches (and then the violation of appropriateness would, in Aristotle's terminology, be "necessary"), or involving a critique of the social order: but a typical Tragedy does not necessarily, for Aristotle, involve anything of that kind, but does take place within a social order which is familiar and intelligible; and the behaviour of the characters is referred to it.

If I am right in this connection of appropriateness with legal and customary status, it does tend in one way towards the typical; but in another way it tends to clarify the uniqueness and particularity of moral situations: our moral judgments "have more of the stamp of truth on them" when the circumstances are known; and the legal status of a character (e.g., bond or free) is one of the circumstances which have to be known. Also, within each status, there still remains the greatest freedom for individuality of characterisation; all women are not the same, any more than all slaves. In fact we can much better understand from this viewpoint the emphasis which should be given to that remark of Aristotle's (also in this ch. xv, pp. 55-6) which is so startlingly offensive to modern opinion:

> Such goodness is possible in every type of personage, even in a woman or a slave, though the one is perhaps an inferior, and the other a wholly worthless being.

In spite of all the accepted legal restrictions of rights, scope and power, *in spite of* the limitations of status which the whole of society takes for granted, the individual may rise above the inevitable tendency to run true to type. And this involves dramatic treatment too.

3. "Likeness" of Character

> The third is to make them like . . . which is not the
> same as their being good and appropriate, in our
> sense of the term.

This is a very difficult criterion to assess and involves
large questions of general theory; especially it is difficult in this context because Aristotle gives no example to illustrate what he means. Bywater in his
edition takes up the word as it is used farther on,
towards the end of ch. xv, in the comparison with
portrait-painters. There is no doubt that in that context the word does mean "likeness to the original".
But *here* what Aristotle actually says, in his telegraphic
style, is "Third is the being like". . . . He is master-
fully silent in answer to the question "like what?"
Bywater prejudices the matter by his addition "like
THE reality". *The* reality: *What* reality, is the point!
His note in his edition makes it plain when he says:
"the literary portrait produced by the poet should be
'like *the* original', i.e., like what the personage in
question is in history or legend". This deprives the
poet of all his creative freedom and ties him to a
quite indefinable examplar, because history and legend are themselves largely the creation of other writers. Butcher here also feels the necessity of answering in his translation the essential question "Like
what?" which Aristotle does not answer in his text;
but Butcher answers the question in what is to my
mind the much saner and more likely way by translating: "Thirdly character must be true to life." Rostagni
here in his note goes along with Butcher in saying
that he understands Aristotle to mean that the characters should be "natural".

This requirement, of likeness, must also be taken in
conjunction with the whole of ch. ii (pp. 25-7) in
which Aristotle is differentiating Tragedy from Comedy by the consideration of the types of character
shown acting in each. The analogy with portrait-painters comes in here too. He says that characters are
either better or worse than ourselves, or just like
ourselves: and at the very end of the chapter he says
that Comedy makes its personages "worse" and Tragedy makes its personages "better than the men of the
present day".

It is clear that "ourselves" and "the men of the present
day" are here to be equated. Taken together they represent what is now often summed up in the phrase "the
man in the street".

As I tried to show at length in the last lecture, it is
impossible to treat character and action, on Aristotle's
theory, as separable: they are inextricably interdepen-
dent. The action of a tragedy has, as we have also
seen, a greater coherence, a greater unity, a more clearly
defined end than a slice of real life or a slice of history. To be necessarily fitting to such an action, character also must be modified from the commonplace
norm of real life.
The question is how much and in what way is it to be
modified, and how is the modification reconcilable with
this requirement of "likeness"?

I want for the present to leave that in the form of a
question and to return to it in the final lecture, when
I shall discuss the general theory of poetry as "imitation".

4. Consistency

Very little need be said about the fourth of these requirements for character; for nobody could seriously
dispute that consistency is a basic need. The character must be seen as a whole; development must take
place according to intelligible principles. I have already discussed those principles when dealing with
probability and necessity—what such-and-such a character will probably or necessarily say or do. And
Aristotle properly provides for waywardness of all
degrees in the formula "consistently inconsistent"
(. . . homalously anomalous). This, as Twining says,
note III, p. 332 (1789); II, 145; (1812), is not concerned with momentary conflicting passions (what we
should call emotions), but with "the basis or foundation of a character", which is what I have been calling its habit, bent or tendency. Aristotle is not recommending a dead level, not a flat uniformity, but a
living coherence.

5. Hamartia

I have already mentioned two reasons why the tragic
hero cannot be perfect:

> *(a)* As Aristotle explicitly says, his misfortunes
> would be odious to us—i.e. offend our sense of
> justice.

> *(b)* By implication his whole theory requires a hero
> less than perfect in order to allow scope for action
> at all.

He does not say what kind of moral imperfections he
is thinking of: he states the matter negatively only: the
hero should be an intermediate kind of personage not
pre-eminently virtuous or just.

This brings us to the famous and vexed question of
"hamartia" . . . it is wise to use the word transliterated
into English, as "hamartia".

The first thing to grasp about this famous word is that
it is *not* a general inclusive descriptive phrase for those
moral shortcomings in which the hero, as already described, is said to fall short of being "pre-eminently

Aristotle (right) teaching his pupil Alexander the Great.

virtuous and just". It should be quite plain from the two uses of the word in ch. xiii (p. 50) that Aristotle is quite clearly and deliberately distinguishing the hamartia from these general moral failings:

> *(a)* misfortune . . . is brought upon him *not* by vice and depravity but by some error of judgment (hamartia)

and again (pp. 50-1):

> *(b)* and the cause of it must lie *not* in any depravity, but in some great error (hamartia) on his part; the man himself being either such as we have described, or better, not worse, than that.

This second passage shows the emphasis very clearly: if anything the hero is to be *better* than "the intermediate kind of personage", but still he commits this "hamartia". So little does the word concern his general moral character, that Aristotle attaches it, if anything, to the better man rather than to the worse. A further point, which Butcher feels bound to give weight to, even though it goes rather against the general drift of his argument, is that "great" or "big" . . . "is not a natural adjective to apply to a mental quality or a flaw in conduct."[4]

A clear warning is needed against the tendency of critics to use Aristotle's phrase "hamartia" as a general inclu-sive phrase to cover moral faults and failings. "Hamartia" is not a moral *state;* but a specific error which a man makes or commits.

The phrase "tragic flaw" should be treated with suspicion. I do not know when it was first used, or by whom. It is not an Aristotelian metaphor at all, and though it *might* be adopted as an accepted technical translation of "hamartia" in the strict and properly limited sense, the fact is that it *has not been* so adopted, and it is far more commonly used for a characteristic moral failing in an otherwise predominantly good man. Thus, it may be said by some writers to be the "tragic flaw" of Oedipus that he was hasty in temper; of Samson that he was sensually uxorious; of Macbeth that he was ambitious; of Othello that he was proud or jealous—and so on. These things may be true of those characters, and it may be important that they are so; but these things do not constitute the "hamartiai" of those characters in Aristotle's sense.

Bywater and Rostagni agree on this point, and I think I can safely say that all serious modern Aristotelian scholarship agrees with them, that "hamartia" means an error which is derived from "ignorance of some material fact or circumstance."[5]

The main evidence upon which this interpretation is based is to be found in two passages in the

Nicomachean Ethics, Book V, ch. viii, and Book III, ch. i. Talking of the kinds of injury in transactions between man and man, Aristotle says (V, viii) that "those done in ignorance are *mistakes* when the person acted on, the act, the instrument, or the end that will be attained, is other than the agent supposed".

Aristotle calls "acts done by reason of ignorance of fact" *non*-voluntary (III, i); a special class lying between acts which are "voluntary" and those which are "involuntary". Such acts share some characteristics of voluntary action because they are derived from a wish for an end and proceed by the processes of deliberation; but they share some characteristics of involuntary action because the ignorance of some particular fact or circumstance produces a result other than that which was expected. Such acts are regretted by the doer, and are proper objects of our pity and pardon.

It is important to realise that the ignorance involved is not ignorance of the end, or a mistake in the kind of end to be aimed at; for that means a voluntary action and a bad one.

It is also most important to realise that Aristotle does not assert or deny anything about the connection of hamartia with moral failings in the hero. He assumes as a matter of course that the hamartia is accompanied by moral imperfections; but it is not itself a moral imperfection, and in the purest tragic situation the suffering hero is not morally to blame.

Now, it is plain, when this theory is understood as involved in the "error" of the tragic hero, that it fits the play *King Oedipus* like a glove. Oedipus sets in motion voluntarily, with a good end in view, the whole train of action which aims to discover the polluted person and so release Thebes from the plague. But he is ignorant of the circumstance that he has killed his own father; and the discovery of that fact produces a result other than what he expected.

It also fits many more tragedies than its rather dry and technical statement by Aristotle might make it appear: but that does not become quite so plain till we take it in relation to Peripety and Discovery.

6. *Peripety*

The "hamartia" of the hero so understood is closely and inseparably connected with the "peripety" or reversal and the "discovery", which are the characteristic features of what Aristotle calls a "complex" as distinct from a "simple" plot (chs. x and xi, p. 46).

> The action . . . I call simple, when the change in the hero's fortunes takes place without Peripety or Discovery; and complex, when it involves one or the other, or both.

This makes it quite plain that the peripety is *not* just the general change in the hero's fortunes which is essential for all tragedy. Even the simple plot involves a radical change from good to bad fortune. "Peripeteia" must not be translated or paraphrased "Reversal of Fortune"; for a reversal of fortune may well happen without it. If it is to be paraphrased at all, the phrase which fits best is "reversal of intention". For that is what it is, from the point of view of the character involved. From the point of view of the spectator or reader it is, in the plot of the play as a whole, a reversal of the direction of the action. As Aristotle himself says at the beginning of ch. xi (p. 46):

> A Peripety is the change from one state of things within the play to its opposite of the kind described . . . in the probable or necessary sequence of events.

Aristotle nowhere says that a peripety can happen only in relation to the hero. No doubt he was thinking that in some of the best tragic plots this was so, and that the hero and others were involved in the sudden swift reversal. But it is worth noting that even in *King Oedipus* one character was not involved in the reversal. Teiresias all along knew that Oedipus was the guilty man.

Within any tragic plot a minor peripety may occur within the main course of the action, involving primarily some other character than the hero. For instance there is such a subordinate peripety in the *Oedipus at Colonus,* when Polynices comes to his father in hope of a blessing and gets a curse. The very means that he chooses produce this unexpected result. Aristotle himself gives the example of the messenger in *King Oedipus,* at the beginning of ch. xi.

In the word peripety is contained the idea of the boomerang or recoil effect of one's own actions, of being hoist with one's own petard, falling into the pit that one has dug for someone else. The action is complex because it moves on two levels, as it appears to the doer and as it really is, and because the cause of the disaster is woven in with the good intentions and right means to achieve them. Aristotle makes a technical term of what had often before been felt from Homer onwards. . . .

The whole of **Rhetoric** II, 5, should be read: the idea, though not the word "peripety", underlies much of it.

7. *Discovery*

The "discovery" is in its essence, as Aristotle quite clearly says (ch. xi, p. 47), "a change from ignorance to knowledge". The recognition of a person, or the discovery of the identity of a person, like the recognition of Orestes by Iphigenia and of Iphigenia by Orestes (mentioned by Aristotle at the end of ch. xi, p. 48), is merely one special kind of this "change from igno-rance to knowledge" which is what is meant in general by "discovery". It is rather a pity that in ch. xvi (pp. 58-60), which is entirely given up to discussing the various methods and processes of argument by which "discoveries" may be brought about, nearly all the examples should be examples of the discovery of the identity of persons. For this is merely one vivid and easily intelligible kind. The statement of the general principle in the middle of ch. xi (p. 47)—that it is a "change from ignorance to knowledge"—is of far wider significance, and Aristotle shows this, though in a rather loose way, when he says that it

> may happen in a way in reference to inanimate things, even things of a very casual kind; and it is also possible to discover whether someone has done or not done something.

Thus it is intended to include the discovery of whole areas of circumstance, whole states of affairs, about which there was previous ignorance or mistake. Such discoveries may come about, technically, through the recognition of some object or person or some trivial or minor thing; but the total implications of the discovery are not trivial or minor at all; they may include, as Aristotle in his quiet way says in passing, such terrific changes as the change from love to hate or from hate to love.

You will see at once how closely this is linked to the "hamartia" when that is properly understood. The dis-covery of the truth of the matter is the ghastly waken-ing from that state of ignorance which is the very es-sence of "hamartia".

Hamartia, peripety and discovery all hang together in this ideal schematisation of tragic plot.

The common old phrase "getting hold of the wrong end of the stick" may help as an illustration. The hama-rtia, or error of ignorance, is not to know that you have got hold of the wrong end, or not to know which is the right end or the wrong, or not to know that it is the sort of stick that has a right end and a wrong, and to hit yourself very hard with it as a result.

The "peripety" is a real reversal, a turning of the stick round the opposite way, brought about by force of circumstances or by the action of other charac-ters.

The "discovery" is the realisation of which really is the right end, ánd of the fact that you had got hold of the wrong one, and also, perhaps, of a whole train of con-sequences.

Of course such little illustrative analogies must not be pressed into details.

F. L. Lucas in one of the very best parts of his book, *Tragedy,* discusses the question (pp. 91-105) and I refer you to him in excuse of my rather summary discussion.

Notes

[1] [Later moral ideas, e.g., that goodness consists in trying to do one's duty, must not be read into Aristotle. By "good" he means the habitual possession of one or more of the separate virtues, . . . such as courage, temperance, liberality, magnificence, gentleness, truth-fulness, friendliness and even wittiness. . . . See the list in Sir David Ross, *Aristotle,* p. 203, and his discus-sion of goodness of character and the moral virtues, pp. 192-208.]

[2] Cf. U. Ellis-Fermor, *Christopher Marlowe* (London, 1927), p. 90 and notes *ad loc.*

[3] Accepting Bywater's conjecture [*gunaikeiō*] at 54 a 23.

[4] Butcher *op. cit.,* p. 319, *n.* 3.

[5] Bywater, edn. p. 215. Rostagni writes: "cioè errore proveniente da inconsapevolezza, da ignoranza di qualche fatto o di qualche circostanza: colpa *involuntaria*". 1st edn., 1927, p. 48; 2nd edn., 1945, p. 71.

Laurence Berns (essay date 1964)

SOURCE: "Aristotle's *Poetics,*" in *Ancients and Moderns: Essays on the Tradition of Political Philoso-phy in Honor of Leo Strauss,* edited by Joseph Cropsey, Basic Books Inc., Publishers, 1964, pp.

[*In the following essay, Berns reviews several aspects of Aristotle's* Poetics *which he believes have been mis-understood. He examines what Aristotle meant by the term "imitation"; the role of pity and fear in enabling purgation; and character traits of the "tragic hero."*]

Henry Jackson, the highly respected classical scholar, an editor of some texts of Aristotle, paid the following compliment to Aristotle's ***Politics.*** "It is an amazing book," he said. "It seems to me to show a Shakesperian understanding of human beings and their ways. . . . " Aristotle, the philosopher, is praised because his un-derstanding of human beings approaches or matches that of Shakespeare, the poet. The poet's understand-ing is the standard. In this remark, Jackson seems to take it for granted that the poet's understanding of human beings and their ways is somehow the most adequate and most profound understanding. This is not hard for us modern men to understand. For one thing, the poet's picture of the world preserves that wonder and mystery which seem to dissolve and disappear in the accounts of the philosophers and scientists. Furthermore, the great poet convinces us of his knowledge in a much more powerful way than bare argument and reasoning can ever do. His conceptions are constantly put to a practical test—a test of their ability or inability to move man through his emotions.

What kind of power or understanding is it that the great poet possesses? What is it that makes a great work of art so convincing and moving? It could not have been very long after men were first moved by great works of art that they began to reflect on the nature of art and the artist. This is intelligible, for great art fills us with a sense of wonder, wonder about the artist's subject and the artist himself, and, Aristotle informs us, "in wondering is the desire to learn." Today, too, the enormous amount of literature devoted to literary and artistic criticism testifies to the fact that the desire to understand and learn about great art and artists is just as strong. However, the purpose of art criticism is not only theoretical, to understand the mysterious power of great art, but practical as well, to help artists improve their works and to help us enlarge our capacities to appreciate and enjoy great art.

With such expectations in mind, we turn directly to Aristotle's *Poetics.* What we might provisionally call the fine arts are defined by Aristotle as forms of imitation. The words "creativity," "aesthetics" and "self-expression" do not occur in Aristotle's definition. "Imitation" is the key term. The idea of art as imitation immediately creates a problem for us. It seems to depreciate art. Imitations are secondary or derivative: one need only think of imitation leather, or imitation flavor. Imitations immediately refer us to those more fundamental things of which they are imitations. If art in general is imitation, what does it imitate? Nature is the traditional answer. The phrase "imitation of nature" does not occur in the *Poetics,* but I shall explain later why I think it is what Aristotle meant.

Imitation of nature is often misunderstood, because what Aristotle means by nature is often misunderstood. Imitation of nature does not mean a simple copying of what we happen to find actually existing. Natural things, according to Aristotle, possess certain capacities for development. A thing realizes its nature more, the more it fulfills these capacities, the more it approaches its own specific perfection. Nature, as Aristotle uses the term, includes what ought to be, and imitation of nature means not mere copying of things, but also the imitation of things in their perfection. The artist is enjoined by the doctrine of imitation of nature to look carefully at the real world about him, not in order to copy it, but in order to see that the ideal characters or perfections that he will portray have some basis in the real world, that they are developments of truly existing possibilities and, hence, more convincing. Santayana wrote of Aristotle's conception of human nature: "Everything ideal has a natural basis, and everything natu-

ral has an ideal development." Art imitates not only what is actual in nature, but also what is potential in nature.[1]

From this point of view, many of the arguments directed against the doctrine of imitation of nature from the point of view of creativity lose their force. The artist, according to Aristotle, certainly can and ought to portray things which have never actually been known to exist, but to be convincing as works of art, they ought to be things which we know could possibly exist.

We have an indication of what Aristotle means by nature in the brief history of tragedy which he sketches out in the *Poetics.* He speaks of how tragedy first grew out of crude, improvised imitations and slowly developed and advanced as each of the things which added to its perfection became known. Then he says: "And having gone through many changes, tragedy stopped when it attained its own nature." The perfection, or full development, of the thing is identical with its nature. This understanding of things can still be found implicit in ordinary language; for instance, one can say of a very good play, "Now that really *is* a play," meaning it contains all of what we expect from a play. And we can say of a very bad play, "Do you call that a play?" Or we have to add qualifications like "bad," saying, "That is a bad play," meaning that it lacks those qualities we expect to find in a play. It does not live up to or realize the nature of a play. It is not fully a play. If we follow this thought a bit further, we may get a clue as to why the *Poetics,* which purports at its outset to be a book about poetry in general, is largely taken up with a discussion of tragedy.[2] If the nature of a thing is seen most fully in the perfection of that thing, then the nature of poetry should be seen most fully in the most nearly perfect form of poetry. There is some indication in the *Poetics* that Aristotle regarded tragedy as the most nearly perfect form of poetry. Among the Greeks the two main contenders for the crown of poetry were evidently epic poetry and tragedy. In the final chapter of the *Poetics,* Aristotle argues that the crown should go to tragedy because it contains everything epic poetry contains and more, and, in addition, it realizes the purpose of poetry more fully.

By pursuing this line of thought even further, we see that Aristotle is concerned in the *Poetics* not with any tragedy, but with the best tragedies, those which provide the models and standards for all other tragedies. It is mostly to Sophocles, Euripides, and Shakespeare that Lessing turns when seeking models to demonstrate the truth of Aristotle's canons for tragedy.

However, things are said to be perfect in two ways, as wholes in themselves and as parts of larger wholes.[3] The latter consideration entails reflection on the function of tragedy within the larger whole of political and social life.

Although the *Poetics* begins with a discussion of poetry in general that lasts for five chapters, this discussion culminates, at the beginning of Book six, with the famous definition of tragedy. The book contains twenty-six chapters, and seventeen of these, chapters 6-22, are devoted to tragedy. The definition of tragedy reads as follows: "Tragedy is an imitation of an action that is serious and complete, and of a definite magnitude, with sweetened or pleasing language, each form of which is used separately in the parts of the tragedy. The imitation is done by means of men acting, not through narration, accomplishing through pity and fear the catharsis of such passions." Most of the rest of the book could be regarded as an analysis of that definition. The definition tells us first what tragedy is in general, namely, imitation. Imitation of what?—of a serious action and an action that is complete and of a definite size. What is the medium used to convey the imitation to its audience?—pleasing or embellished language. How or in what manner is the language presented?—through men acting, not through narration.

Up to this point Aristotle builds on his previous discussion, and discusses only the work of art in itself. But with this statement about the effect, end, function, or purpose of tragedy, something new enters the discussion. What should the tragedy do to or for its audience or readers? By means of pity and fear it should effect a purgation or purification of these kinds of emotion.

This answer is by no means as lucid as the others. Why are pity and fear selected as the key passions? What does catharsis mean? We shall take up the last question first. There is, perhaps, no subject which has divided interpreters of the *Poetics* more. This problem is not only a problem of textual interpretation, but is a reflection of a basic difference of opinion about the fundamental purpose of art and the role of the artist. To put it simply: Is it the primary function of the artist to please, move, and entertain his audience, or should he be a moral teacher?[4] We shall examine the catharsis problem with a view to this larger question.

The word catharsis in Greek means both purgation and purification. Purgation is used here primarily as a medical term in homeopathic medicine. The old theory could be characterized roughly as follows. If the body is suffering, say from an excess of acidity, the physician gives the patient, in some form or another, more acid, which, somehow, causes a reaction to acid that purges away or removes the excess. The removal of the disturbing excess and the return of the body to health are accompanied by a feeling of being lightened or relieved, which is pleasant. Let us apply the theory to tragedy. Those of us with an excess of pity and fear in our souls go to the theater. After feeling fear with and pity for the hero of the tragedy, our excessive pity and fear are drained off, and we experience pleasure from

the relief. The production of this special pleasure is said to be the end of tragedy. There are some difficulties which come to mind immediately. First, it would seem that only those who are somewhat sick, suffering from an excess of pity and fear in their souls, can fully benefit from tragedy. One could reply that the poet first arouses pity and fear before purging them away; that is, he first creates the excess so that he can provide the pleasurable relief from the purgation. Yet, as one considers how most appreciative spectators feel after seeing a great tragedy, this theory becomes more and more implausible. Such spectators are not simply drained of emotion, relieved and contented, but stirred and moved by powerful feelings somewhat different from those they came in with. The purification theory of catharsis is simpler. The artist arouses pity and fear in his audience in order to train them to fear those things which ought to be feared and to pity those things which ought to be pitied. For example, from Sophocles' *Antigone* the spectator might learn to feel that dishonor is more to be feared than death. Purification here means moral purification. As Euripides says, in Aristophanes' *Frogs,* speaking for the poets: "We make men better. . . . " Those who hold strictly to the purgation theory tend to regard the *Poetics* more as a technical treatise.[5] They would tend to argue that Aristotle, the scientist, concentrating on differences in subject matters, freed Western man's understanding of art from the preoccupation with morality which limited the vision of his predecessors, especially Plato. Those who hold to the purification theory say that in fundamentals Aristotle agreed with Plato and held a moral theory of art.[6]

It should be clear that both theories require art to be pleasant, but the status of that pleasure is what is in question. According to what we are calling the pure purgation theory, the great artist has no other aim, as artist, than making a work of art that produces that pleasure in his audience. According to the purification theory, the pleasure is subordinate to, and in the service of, moral improvement. These distinctions correspond to what has been called the difference between pure or autonomous art and didactic art. The other places in Aristotle's writings where the word catharsis occurs are not especially illuminating. In the *Politics,* in the section on music in education, catharsis is discussed in what seems to be the medical sense of purgation.[7] The word occurs only once more in the *Poetics,* and there it clearly means purification, a religious purification from sin.[8] Perhaps the best way out of the difficulty is to try to analyze the whole problem from the beginning.

The more fundamental problem we have in mind is, to repeat, What is the function and purpose of tragedy? By means of pity and fear to accomplish the catharsis of such emotions, Aristotle tells us in chapter six; and in chapter fourteen we are informed that tragedy has its own special kind of pleasure, the pleasure from pity and fear through imitation. Aristotle was not the first man to single out pity and fear as key passions in poetry. In the *Ion,* among other places, Plato touches on the subject.[9] Ion, a man who made his living by reciting epic poems, is being questioned by Socrates about how he most amazes his spectators. Socrates mentions five instances of moving passages in Homer. The first is the scene just as Odysseus is about to kill all of the panic-stricken suitors. The next is Achilles chasing Hector around the wall. Hector, the hero of Troy, is, we know, about to be killed. Our fear for his life is mixed with pity. The next three examples concern Andromache, Hector's wife; Hecuba, his mother; and Priam, his father. Each is more pitiful than the preceding. In Ion's answering speech, where he describes how moved he is himself when he moves others, the only passions mentioned are pity, terror, and fear. Fortunately, Aristotle has analyzed these passions in his *Rhetoric;* a large part of our discussion will be based on that analysis.

I believe that the order of Socrates' examples was not accidental: fear first, changing to pity. Fear and pity go together, and this is the usual order. As the revelations about Oedipus begin to unfold, we begin to fear that we will learn that he is the murderer, the cursed one. As the evidence comes in and the evil and suffering are upon him, our fear ˙changes to pity. When King Lear strips himself of all his power and puts it in the hands of his unworthy daughters, along with Kent, we fear for the evil approaching him and the country. And when that evil has arrived, the fear has transformed itself into pity for his suffering. Fear, Aristotle says, is a kind of pain or trouble from the imagination of an imminent evil, a deadly or painful evil. Fear is different from grief. We grieve when some very painful evil has already happened. A sense of urgency goes along with fear; while we still fear there is hope of escape. Perhaps the old shepherd will assure Oedipus that Laius was killed by a band of robbers, not one man and not Oedipus himself. Perhaps Lear will pay heed to Kent's warning or his Fool's prodding. Pity, according to Aristotle, is a kind of pain which comes from the occurrence of a manifest evil to someone else who does not deserve it. Or, to use the shortened formula of the *Poetics,* we feel pity for someone who suffers undeserved misfortune. As hope dies out and we see suffering coming on, our initial fear, the fear for what is about to happen to the tragic hero, transforms itself for the most part into pity.

Pity and fear are connected in another way. Fear is felt primarily for ourselves or those who are very close to us and then for those who are like ourselves. And all of those things which men fear will happen to themselves they can pity when they happen to others. This suggests that there is no pity without fear[10] though there can be fear without pity. Thus, the fear allied with pity, a more generalized fear stemming from the

entire course of action imitated by the plot, can be distinguished from the initial fear of the specific disaster approaching the tragic hero. And so we move from this initial fear to a fear of the causes of such events. Pity, here, is to be distinguished from what Aristotle calls humaneness or fellow-feeling, which is not necessarily painful and does not involve a sense of justice.[11]

What Aristotle says in the *Poetics* about fear being aroused by terrible things happening to one who is like ourselves seems to correspond to what in modern psychological terms would be called identification. The tragic hero must be sufficiently like ourselves to enable us somehow to conceive of ourselves undergoing his or a similar fate. Otherwise, we will not be able to fear the impending disaster, enjoy the suspense, and receive the full effect of the tragedy. What is implied is that in order fully to experience a great tragedy, an act of imagination is required. The spectator must be able, in a sense, to imagine himself in the tragic situation. The presentation of a drama on the stage can be more moving than the reading of the drama, for since the evil and the suffering are brought right before our eyes less imagination is required. But according to Aristotle, spectacle, though it is able to lead on the soul, is hardly a concern for the poet. The pity and fear should be built into the incidents of the plot, so that they are felt also by readers, who, with the poet's help, are able to rely on their own imaginations. In chapter twenty-six of the *Poetics,* Aristotle indicates that the great poet places a higher value on his reading audience than on his seeing audience.

The conditions of pity and fear, then, play a large role in determining the character of the tragic hero. He must not be so good that it is impossible to imagine what it would be like to be in his position nor so bad as to forfeit our active pity. He does terrible things, but not out of baseness, because we would not pity the suffering he undergoes for his errors if they stemmed from baseness. On the other hand, if he did and suffered terrible things simply from bad luck or by chance, it would be sad, but not very frightening. It becomes really frightening when the terrible things he does and suffers result from some natural cause, some flaw in his nature, a flaw that is likely to be found in all natures like his—which means in our natures too, insofar as we are like him, or would like to be like him. His flaw prevents him from foreseeing the evil consequences that will result from his actions. Or, it betrays him into becoming an instrument for evil men. That he does not intend or foresee evil is shown by the misery and remorse he undergoes when the evil is recognized by him. His sense of guilt and repentance is our sign that he was not fundamentally malicious and thus entitles him to our pity.[12] Yet his suffering is not meaningless. He is partly responsible for being the kind of man he is. It is both just and frightening that his lack of self-knowledge can be atoned for only through suffering. The tragic hero is generally a man in a very high position, not only because every fall must be from a height, and the higher the height the harder the fall, but because the fates and fortunes of many more people are involved with the errors of men in great positions; hence, the disasters they bring about are more frightening, and their sufferings and sense of guilt are usually greater. The life of every Theban is affected by Oedipus' and Antigone's doings. All England is plunged into war as a result of Lear's mistakes. Also, what happens to our betters is more frightening because, as Aristotle notes in the *Rhetoric,* those who are able to harm our betters are more able to harm us.[13]

One reason the great tragedians have concentrated on the passions of pity and fear, Aristotle's analysis suggests, is that they were aware that these two passions were better adapted for safeguarding and improving morality and religion than any others. What passion moves most men more readily than fear? What or who are those most fearful beings which, because they are able to harm and humble our betters, are more able to harm us? To speak in the vein of Greek tragedy and King Lear, the answer would be the gods. The gods are the guarantors of public morality. The epic and tragic poets, by showing how even the most lofty can be brought down by the gods, help to instill in people a proper fear of those gods. Pity tends to instill in us a sensitivity to the sufferings of others, and thus renders us less apt to harm others.

The best tragic plots, Aristotle tells us, are those wherein the sufferings are inflicted by and occur among loved ones and the hero discovers what he has done only after it is too late to remedy it. As a result of a flaw natural to his kind, the tragic hero harms and destroys those he loves most. It is those very qualities for which he is admired and honored that cause him to wreak great evils. Furthermore, the more noble the character of the tragic hero, the more dreadful is his suffering when he realizes what he has done. All of this leads to the impression that in some frightful and pitiable way human excellence and mankind's noblest aspirations are inextricably linked with evil. As this impression makes itself felt both in the tragic hero and in his audience, a certain sense of guilt naturally arises, a sense of guilt that comes close to being a sense of original sin. Tragic pity and fear might be thought of as the human roots of the sense of sin.

The connection of pity and fear in tragedy is important in still another way: the two passions tend to purify each other.[14] Terror, Aristotle tells us, casts out pity. It tends to fill us with a selfish and narrow concern for our own safety. The tragedy, by linking our fear with pity for the tragic sufferer, tends to prevent our fear from degenerating into narrow selfishness. On the other hand, the characteristic vice of pity is to degenerate into a loose or morbid sentimentality. By linking pity with things which are really frightening as well, and by inviting us to play at sitting in judgment upon his characters, the poet teaches us to pity things really worth pitying. Tragic pity is the basis of true charity.

John Milton may have had these things in mind when he recommended the study of Aristotle's *Poetics:* "This would make them [students] soon perceive what despicable creatures our common-rhymers and play-writers be; and show them what religious, what glorious and magnificent use might be made of poetry, both in divine and human things."[15] The purification and purgation interpretations of catharsis do not necessarily contradict each other. In the light of the foregoing analysis, catharsis would be fundamentally purification. But, by arousing pity and fear and by leading them toward objects worthy of them, the poet purges these passions of their unhealthy elements. Pity and fear are purified into a kind of humane reverence or awe.

Seen in this light, the *Poetics* could be regarded as the primary source for the Aristotelian analysis of piety and religion. Since religion, for Aristotle as well as Plato, is a political matter, the *Poetics* would have to be regarded as, in a sense, a political book.[16] The perfection of a tragedy then is also to be determined by how well it functions in taming the pride of the powerful and, in general, elevating the moral sense—the sense of justice—of the political community.

Although purification may be the poet's chief aim, the largest part of his audience comes mainly to be pleased or entertained. Unless the poet pleases, he will have little opportunity to purify. We are still faced by the problem of understanding tragic pleasure. The pleasure proper to tragedy, Aristotle tells us, is the pleasure from pity and fear through imitation. But pity and fear are forms of pain. If it is not contradictory, it certainly is paradoxical to speak of a pleasure from pain. What this indicates is that the pleasure appropriate to tragedy is a very complicated phenomenon. We shall try to distinguish some five constituents of that pleasure.

A Hobbesian might argue that the pleasure comes from a somewhat malicious satisfaction at being free from the miseries we see engulfing others. But this is not sufficient; it hardly does justice to the feeling of elevation that seems to be a part of the pleasure from tragedy.

Aristotle, however, speaks of the pleasure from pity and fear through imitation. Imitation is the most natural thing in the world for men. All men as children first learn how to get on in the world through imitation. There is no one who is not familiar with the pleasure from a successful imitation. We learn from imitation, and though study may be hard, the actual learning itself is naturally pleasant. Learning is most pleasant for all men according to Aristotle. In the *Poetics* and the *Rhetoric,* he says we get pleasure from something that has been well imitated, even if that which has been imitated is itself not pleasant, for it is the reasoning, the inferences connecting the imitation with the object imitated, the learning, that is pleasant.[17] Art which cannot communicate, which cannot represent or imitate, also cannot teach and cannot appeal to those things in our nature which gave rise to art in the first place.

But does not the character of the things imitated also contribute something to the pleasure? We learn through suffering, say the poets. But through the tragedies, safe in our seats, or at our desks, we learn about things which could otherwise be learned only through suffering them. By playing at suffering we learn and are, so to speak, rescued from the suffering that would normally accompany such learning. Also, is not the pleasure from tragedy more intimately involved with the great sufferers themselves? Perhaps the fact that the suffering and sufferers are great may account for the feeling of exaltation mentioned earlier. The characters, Aristotle says, should be better and usually more illustrious than we are. We experience a sense of exaltation from being admitted into a kind of intimacy with the great, and perhaps even beyond that, a feeling that we have somehow been brought nearer to the greatest powers of all, the powers controlling all human destiny, all nature.

Also, if the function of the poet is, as Aristophanes' Euripides says, to make men better, to purify and educate their passions, the pleasure from learning through playing at great suffering would also contain a certain satisfaction based on the sense of having been made better.

The last constituent of the pleasure from tragedy we should like to mention is that rooted in wonder. Tragic heroes are generally better than we are. They are usually men from whom we expect exemplary conduct—consider Othello, Coriolanus, Lear, Macbeth, Oedipus. They are, in a sense, exemplary and noble, and yet they come to do terrible things. "How all too riddling and unclear is everything you say," Oedipus says to Tiresias. "Are you not best at finding out riddles?" Tiresias answers. "Yes taunt me in those things where you will find me great," is the reply. "Indeed this very luck has destroyed you," Tiresias answers. The very things which make the tragic hero great cause him to wreak great evils and in the end destroy him. This is something not only to be feared and pitied, but also something to be wondered at. The best plots, full of suspense, arouse our wonder, and, Aristotle explains, "to wonder is pleasant for the most part, for in wondering is the desire to learn." The best plots, wondrous, though tragic, are also pleasant, because they offer a promise of and invitation to further learning.

Earlier we spoke of poetic imitation as imitation of nature, and mentioned that the phrase "imitation of nature" occurs nowhere in the *Poetics.* It does occur in other writings of Aristotle, but chiefly in reference to the useful arts. However, it is clearly implied, almost clearly stated, in what Aristotle says about a good plot or myth. The plot is the controlling element, as it were, the soul of the tragedy. The plot, he says, following Plato's *Phaedrus,* should be an organic whole. The composition or synthesis of the incidents should end up in the formation of one overall action. The plot is the direct imitation of such an action. There ought to be nothing superfluous, nothing whose absence or displacement would not change the unity of the whole. What is a whole? Aristotle's answer seems absurdly simple: that which has a beginning, a middle, and an end. It is not so simple. The beginning need not be connected with any other events by necessity; it may come about by chance. But it must be followed by events which develop *naturally* out of it. The middle comes after such events. And from the middle, events follow naturally either by necessity or for the most part leading up to the end or completion. What we have here is a three-fold classification of events which also occurs elsewhere in the works of Aristotle. Things come about either always in the same way, by necessity; or they come about usually in the same way, so that we say it will probably be or it is likely to be this way. We cannot say that events in the latter class always come about in the same way, because sometimes in this class things happen in an unusual way, contrary to what is likely. These unusual and unexpected events are chance events. The three kinds of events, then, are (1) those which occur by necessity, (2) those which are probable or occur for the most part, or usually, and (3) those which occur by chance.

Chance events, as chance events, are essentially unintelligible or irrational according to Aristotle. We can know in general why there are such things as chance events, but the chance element in the events themselves is essentially unintelligible.[18] We can have genuine knowledge only of those things which are or come to be by necessity and for the most part and those things are identified in the *Poetics* with what comes about naturally. What comes about naturally is susceptible to rational explanation. (We can make valid universal statements about what exists or comes into being by necessity, and valid general statements about what comes into being for the most part.) Chance is ruled out of the best plots, according to Aristotle. The great poet conquers chance, intellectually and imaginatively. There should be an intelligible reason for everything which happens from beginning to end. The length of the story cannot be any chance length, but one appropriate to the action. And it is necessary, Aristotle says, for the characters, as for the connection of incidents in the plot, to act in accordance with necessity or likelihood. From this we can understand Aristotle's strange remark that poetry is more philosophical than history. It is strange because Aristotle, a philosopher, is naturally concerned with the truth, and history aims at the truth, while poetry is manifestly fiction and Homer is praised for knowing how to tell lies well. The reason that poetry is more philosophical than history is that history, which deals with what actually happened, must also include what happened by chance, what happened for no intelligible reason. Poetry, by excluding chance, is more rational, more meaningful, than history. For the same reason, it is more meaningful than real life. Plots based on chance events are not convincing, they are episodic; we do not learn from them and are consequently less pleased by them.

Lessing has made a distinction between the poetic genius and the great poetic wit. Genius, he says, loves simplicity, wit complication. "Genius is only busied with events that are rooted in one another, that form a chain of cause and effect." Wit, he says, is concerned with events that just happen at the same time; it thrives on invention and shock, on throwing us so rapidly from one surprise to another, that we do not have time to consider the improbability of the whole action. But with every step taken by the personages invented by a poetic genius, "we must acknowledge that we should have taken it ourselves under the same circumstances and the same degree of passion, and hence nothing will repel us but the imperceptible approach to a goal from which our imagination shrinks, and where we suddenly find ourselves filled with a profound pity for those whom a fatal stream has carried so far, and full of terror at the consciousness that a similar stream might also thus have borne ourselves away to do deeds which in cold blood we should have regarded as far from us."[19] The irrational, then, should be excluded as much as possible from a plot, Aristotle says. However, irrationalities, which include stories about the gods and supernatural contrivances, must be introduced, sometimes out of deference to what most men assert and find convincing and sometimes in order to arouse the sense of wonder.[20] But even irrationalities or things which happen by chance will be more wondrous if they seem to be in accordance with natural human desires, if they appear to fit into some rational and providential design, like the statue of Mitys which fell upon and killed the man who was the cause of Mitys' death.

But the best way to arouse the sense of wonder is to have the events inspiring pity and fear come into being in a way that runs counter to accepted opinion and expectation, and yet in such a way that the events come about on account of one another. As Samuel Butcher put it, it is the combination of the unexpected with the inevitable.[21] In this passage, near the end of chapter nine of the **Poetics,** we can see how closely the understanding of the great poet approaches that of the philosopher. Philosophy, both Plato and Aristotle say,

begins in wonder and begins with common opinion and the awareness of its inadequacy. The great poet arouses our wonder by presenting events which run counter to common opinion and expectation. He who is willing to part company with common opinion, to look deeper and harder at those wondrous events, will be rewarded by the discovery of a marvelously lucid, though hidden, chain of natural causes.[22] It must have been such an understanding of poetry that led Plutarch to speak of poetry as a kindly and intimate friend leading young men into the presence of philosophy.[23] Tragedy exists not only as a part of political life, a part of the political whole. Its perfection is also to be determined by how it functions in relating the life of man to the larger all-comprehensive whole, to nature.[24]

It is through the turn-about or reversal of the protagonist's fortune and his recognition or discovery of who has brought on the tragedy that the fear, surprise, pity, and wonder arise, Aristotle says. The tragic effect is attained most successfully when the actions undertaken by the protagonist, which bring about his downfall and remorse, destroy or ruin those closest to him, his loved ones, his immediate family. But who can be closer to a man than himself? Oedipus has not only destroyed his father and his wife and mother, he has destroyed himself as a political man. Lear has not only brought on the destruction of his daughters, he has destroyed himself as a political man.

In the best plots, like that of the *Oedipus,* Aristotle says, and like *King Lear,* we suggest, the reversal and recognition are conceived so as to develop out of the incidents of the plot at the same time in an organic unity. That is to say, the recognition should take place at that most poignant time when the tragedy is seen to be inevitable, when that hope on which the suspense is based is decisively frustrated and the initial fear is relieved, transforming itself into pity. Oedipus' most important discovery is the discovery about himself. Lear finally learns who does and does not love him. But in order to learn that he is loved for what he is, not for what he has, he has had to strip himself of all worldly and non-worldly powers and protections. Cordelia's experience prefigured Lear's: it was only after she had been stripped of all wealth and power that the difference between the false love of Burgundy and the noble love of France could be discovered. "Gods, Gods!" France says about Cordelia, "'tis strange that from their coldest neglect my love should kindle to inflamed respect." What Aristotle says about the conjunction of reversal and discovery in the best plots points, we suggest, to what may be the highest theme of tragedy, namely, what sacrifices men must make for the sake of self-knowledge.

It could be argued that King Lear is not a very good illustration of Aristotelian poetic principles, for unity of plot is the central consideration for Aristotle, and in

Lear we have the unfolding of two related but not unified lines of action: the story of the house of Lear and the story of the house of Gloucester. The unity of the two lines of action can be seen, we suggest, in the unity of the philosophic theme underlying them. As Harry Jaffa has pointed out,[25] the Lear story illustrates the natural limits of political and legal authority. The natural force of noble love cannot be commanded or controlled by any political or conventional authority. The Gloucester story and perhaps the stories of Goneril and Regan as well illustrate exactly the other side of the coin: how the natural force of ordinary, or physical, love needs to be bounded by the law, by political authority. Edmund was conceived in adultery. Because he is illegitimate he is banished from the family circle. He is devoid of family-feeling. He is an "unnatural" son. Gloucester pays dearly for his transgression of the law.[26] The Lear story points to the tension or opposition between nature and convention; the Gloucester story points to the need for cooperation between nature and convention, how human nature has to be completed by the legislative art.

There are grounds for thinking that Sophocles himself adhered to a conception of tragedy not far from that of Aristotle.[27] Sophocles, it seems, has always been regarded as the master craftsman of plot and character formation. Yet the plot of his *Ajax* seems strangely out of joint.[28] The story builds up with great dramatic intensity to a climax with the suicide of Ajax. If considerations of dramatic effect alone were to prevail, one would expect the play to end there, but it continues for roughly one-third of the play's entire length with a large part of that time devoted to rather mean wrangling between Teucer, Ajax' brother, and Agamemnon and Menelaus about whether Ajax' corpse is to have an honorable or dishonorable burial. Odysseus, Ajax' chief enemy, persuades Agamemnon and Menelaus to allow Ajax an honorable burial. Odysseus, because of his powers of reflection, his power to generalize from the fate of Ajax, and his power to apply his generalizations successfully, rises above the hate, enmity, and pride gripping all the other characters in the play. In the first part of the play, he seems to show his superiority to the goddess Pallas Athene, the conqueror of the hero, Ajax. In the last undramatic one-third of the play, he shows his superiority to all the other human characters. The last undramatic one-third of the play would appear to indicate that Odysseus' superiority, fundamentally an intellectual superiority, is essentially untragic, essentially undramatic.[29]

Notes

[1] Cf. *Poetics* 1451[a] 37-38, 1451[b] 5, 1460[b] 34-36.

[2] Another book, or section, on comedy is said to be lost.

[3] Cf. Thomas Aquinas *Summa Theologica* II-II Q. 184, A. 1, ad. 2; A. 3; A. 4.

[4] We shall provisionally use the term "purgation theory" to refer to the former position and "purification theory" to refer to the latter.

[5] Cf. Aristotle's *Poetics,* translation and analysis by Kenneth A. Telford (Chicago: Gateway, 1961), pp. 59 ff. However, Telford's interpretation of catharsis differs from those we have sketched out in one crucial respect; see pp. 103-104, and cf. note 12 below.

[6] E.g., Jean Racine, *Phèdre,* Préface, the last paragraph.

Socrates' criticism of the poets in Book ten of the *Republic,* in our opinion, is not meant to be taken simply at face value. The best city, according to Socrates in the *Republic,* is the city according to nature. Yet in the *Republic* there is a deliberate and systematic depreciation and distortion of everything strictly private, of everything in human nature that does not directly pertain to justice or philosophy. Those distortions, it has been suggested, serve the purpose of alerting the critical reader to those aspects of human nature which will always interfere with the perfection of justice and philosophy. Just as the power and significance of family feelings are minimized in books five and seven, so are those elements in our nature which call for tragedy and comedy minimized in Book ten. These distortions would seem to compel the critical reader to try to think his way to a more adequate appreciation of what Socrates has deliberately distorted.

There is in such natures as ours, Socrates suggests to Glaucon, a certain tenderness or gentleness which from the perspective of citizen-virtue alone(. . . , 607[c] end, see also 607[a] end) has no place. Tragedy, through pity, caters to and nourishes this part of human nature. Unalloyed citizen-virtue requires a certain harshness or toughness that practice in pitying might tend to dissolve. Pity has no place in the soul of guardians and soldiers in the best city.

In going on to speak of the temptations from comedy, Socrates shifts from "we" to "you" (sing.). Glaucon is particularly susceptible to such temptations, Socrates is not. While the passions nourished by comedy are not explicitly singled out as pity is for tragedy, Glaucon's character (357[a], 372[c] 2-374[b] 3, 468[b] end-468[c] 4) and Socrates' remarks (606[d]) suggest to us that anger and lust are the chief passions here. These arguments could be interpreted as providing materials for arguments about the legitimate and proper function of tragedy and comedy within civil society.

There are certain private psychic needs whose satisfaction civil life cannot provide for, and further, which come into conflict with the requirements of civil life. Institutions are required in all states other than Socrates' Republic to gratify and to temper, civilize, or purify those parts of our souls. Tragedy's task is to soothe, civilize, and purify the gentler element, and comedy is to do primarily the same for anger and lust. Shakespeare's Angelo in *Measure for Measure* best exemplifies, insofar as we know, how anger (moral indignation) and lust can work together, feed on and reinforce each other. Comedy then should aim at making characters like Angelo impossible.

[7] 1341[b] 33 ff. See also 1339[b] 11-1340[b] 19.

[8] 1455[b] 15.

[9] 535[b], 535[c].

[10] I.e., that our pity is always associated with a fear that what happened to the one we pity could have happened or could happen to us. Cf. Sophocles *Ajax* 11. 118-133 and 1355-1373.

[11] Butcher explains his translation of [*to philanthrōpon*] (*Poetics* 1453[a]) as "moral sense." (*Aristotle's Theory of Poetry and Fine Art* [New York: Dover, 1951], note, p. 303.) Our interpretation follows Lessing, *Hambürgische Dramaturgie*, nos. 75 and 76, translated as *Dramatic Notes in Lessing's Prose Works* in the Bohn's Standard Library edition. (Reprinted as *Hamburg Dramaturgy* [New York: Dover, 1962].) According to this interpretation, literally "love (or friendship) for mankind," is a more elementary or primitive phenomenon (see *Nicomachean Ethics* 1155[a] 16 ff.), akin to the fellow-feeling of birds and beasts for members of their own species. The sense of justice presupposed by Aristotle's definition of tragic pity could exist, as tragedy itself, only in a rather highly developed from of political society. Cf. Gerald F. Else, *Aristotle's Poetics: the Argument* (Cambridge: Harvard University Press, 1957), pp. 367-371.

[12] Cf. Gerald F. Else, *op. cit.,* pp. 373, 378-383, note 54, 438-439.

[13] For the problem of the tragic hero and modern life, see William Hazlitt, *Characters of Shakespeare's Plays,* the chapter on Coriolanus; *Round Table,* "Why the Arts Are Not Progressive"; and especially Winston S. Churchill, *Thoughts and Adventures,* "Mass Effects in Modern Life."

[14] Cf. Butcher, *op. cit.,* pp. 265-266, and Lessing, *op. cit.,* no. 78.

[15] Quoted from his essay *On Education;* cf. the prologue to *Samson Agonistes* and *The Reason of Church Government Urged against Prelaty,* Introduction to Book II.

[16] This assertion would appear to be contradicted by Aristotle's statement that correctness in politics and correctness in poetry are not the same (1460[b] 14-15). The statement may mean little more than that the kind of man and action that makes for a good ruler is different from the kind of man and action that makes for a good tragic hero. This is implicit clearly in the notion of the tragic flow, among other things, and in the differences between the ends of the poetic and political arts. What we are suggesting is that in certain decisive respects the understanding that enables one man to portray a tragic hero well is the same as the understanding that enables another man to practice the art of governing well. Also, that two arts serve some ends that are different in no way prevents them from serving other ends that are the same nor from being subordinate to the same overall end. Furthermore, Aristotle, we suggest, used the word politics in more than one sense, a broad and a narrow sense. In *Politics,* 1322[b] 17, he speaks of the care of religion and of the priesthood as being a kind of office different from political offices like those of the police, judiciary, executive, and the military. Yet, he asserts, the priesthood and religion are necessary for the political community and are common concerns of the entire *polis* (1322[b] 30-32, 1328[b] 2-24, 1329[a] 27-36, 1330[a] 8 and 9). Religion and poetry are not political in the sense of being directly concerned with the everyday administration of governmental affairs. They are political in the more fundamental sense of determining the habits, ideals, and moral sense of the community, the way of life which determines the pattern of the administration of the laws, and sometimes the pattern of the laws themselves. The poets and writers are teachers of legislators. (See Plutarch's *Parallel Lives,* the lives of Lycurgus, Solon, and Alexander; and Rousseau, *The Social Contract* II, Ch. 7, the chapter on the legislator.) They are in this sense "legislative." The distinction between the political art in the narrow sense and the architectonic legislative art . . . is drawn in *Nicomachean Ethics* 1141[b] 23 ff. Cf. also *Poetics* 1450[b] 4-8. Politics and poetics differ also in that poetics deals with those things in our nature which are both beneath and beyond politics. It aims, or should aim, at civilizing politics.

(Since this writing the following texts have come to my attention: Alfarabi's *Philosophy of Plato and Aristotle,* trans. and ed. Muhsin Mahdi [New York: The Free Press of Glencoe, 1962], pp. 43-47, 92-93; and *Medieval Political Philosophy: A Sourcebook,* ed. Ralph Lerner and Muhsin Mahdi [Glencoe, Ill.: The Free Press, 1963]. In the latter volume, consider Roger Bacon's discussion on pp. 376-388.)

[17] Cf. Thomas Aquinas *Summa Theologica* I-II. Q. 27, A. 1, ad. 3. Cf. also II-II. Q. 145, A. 2, and II-II. Q.

180, A. 2, ad. 3.

[18] Cf. *Nicomachean Ethics* 1140[a] 18 ff., *Metaphysics* 1027[a] 14, 1032[a] 20-23, 1036[a] 9.

[19] Lessing, *op. cit.,* no. 32.

[20] Also cf. *Poetics* 1460[b] 33-1461[a] 1.

[21] Butcher, *op. cit.,* p. 267.

[22] At such a stage uncertainty, hope, fear, and pity would be completely purged.

[23] Cited by Butcher, *op. cit.,* pp. 217-218.

Thus the *Politics* would appear to be that book of Aristotle's which comes closest to dealing with one of the key questions of Martin Heidegger's thought: the question, stated in non-Heideggerian terms, of how fear, tragedy, and natural piety contribute to the establishment of the mood, or disposition, out of which philosophy develops.

[24] Cf. Thomas Aquinas *Summa Theologica* II-II. Q. 182, A. 2.

[25] Harry V. Jaffa, "The Limits of Politics: An Interpretation of *King Lear,* Act I, Scene I," *American Political Science Review* (June 1957), pp. 405-427.

[26] *King Lear* V. iii. 170-175

[27] See H. D. F. Kitto, *Sophocles—Dramatist and Philosopher* (London: Oxford University Press, 1958).

[28] See H. D. F. Kitto, *Greek Tragedy* (New York: Anchor, 1954), pp. 124-129, and *Form and Meaning in Drama* (New York: Barnes and Noble, 1960), Ch. 6. R. C. Jebb offers a part "historical" explanation and part apology in his Introduction to the *Ajax* (Cambridge: The University Press, 1896), pp. 28-45.

[29] Consider also Theseus in *Oedipus at Colonus.* The counterpart to Odysseus and Theseus in *King Lear* would appear to be Edgar.

Catherine Lord (essay date 1969)

SOURCE: "Tragedy without Character: *Poetics* VI.1450[a] 24," in *The Journal of Aesthetics and Art Criticism,* Vol. XXVIII, No. 1, Fall, 1969, pp. 55-62.

[In the following essay, Lord examines Aristotle's elevation of plot above all other elements of tragedy and argues that he does indeed assert that all aspects of character, including the concept of "hamartia," are a function of plot.]

I

It is commonly believed that there are two kinds of readers or spectators. There are those who read primarily for plot, story, action, narrative, and who especially enjoy spectacle—the vulgar. Then there are those, the connoisseurs of letters, the cognoscenti—ourselves—who place a greater premium on character, thought, and diction. When we find Aristotle expressly giving the pride of place to plot among the six parts of Tragedy—Plot, Character, Thought, Diction, Spectacle, and Music—we are instantly perplexed, if not outraged. Even those of us who may be sympathetic to Aristotle on some fairly general ground are strongly tempted to suppose that what Aristotle means by plot, *mythos* in some places, *logos* in others, cannot possibly be that crude thing, namely, story and action. He must mean something more subtle than that. Those of us who are not prepared to give Aristotle the benefit of the doubt will insist that he does, indeed, mean the crude thing and that he is insensitive to the finer features of the literary art.

In this essay I shall assume that Aristotle does mean that plot, story, action, the crude thing, is primary and I shall undertake to defend his thesis in regard to one point. This point has been felt to be the most vulnerable of all his assertions of the primacy of plot. Aristotle is not content to say merely that plot is the primary part of tragedy. He goes further. He says, "Without action there cannot be a tragedy; there may be without character" (1450[a] 24).[1] I shall understand this statement in its most uncompromising form; by taking it quite literally I hope to show what tragedy without character entails.

More important still, there is a general principle at work here which lies at the foundation of aesthetic inquiry. I have argued that to understand a work of art is to understand the kind of unity it possesses.[2] Here, then, is a program that requires us to show in detail how the parts of a certain type of work, in the present case a tragedy, function together to produce a unity. To discover what kind of unity a tragedy possesses one must try to separate in thought what may or may not be separable in reality in an effort to determine whether or not it is indeed actually separable in reality. If the theory of organic unity is correct, it may be supposed that such an effort at separation will prove a failure. But having questioned the doctrine of organic unity, we are prepared to accept in certain cases quite a different verdict. It is surprising that the philosopher who is especially associated with the theory of organic unity should be willing to allow for a tragedy without character. Presumably, then, Aristotle does not regard character as being, in the strict sense, organically entailed by tragedy, even though he assigns it a role second only to plot.

If we look at what Aristotle actually does in the *Poetics,* we find that his remark in VI, 1450ª 24 is by no means an isolated apercu. He is engaged in the ambitious enterprise of understanding tragedy through what can only be called a total dismantling or disassembling of tragedy into its component parts. What is being dismantled is a system (not an organism) which, in the process of being reassembled, is seen to exhibit a fairly complex kind of unity. The present essay is designed as a specific application of a more general method of aesthetic inquiry (call it systems-analysis, if you will) which can be employed in the examination of any work of art.

My discussion remains entirely within the Aristotelian framework; it does not depend on a redefinition of Tragedy, "an imitation of an action that is serious, complete, and of a certain magnitude: in language embellished with each kind of artistic ornament, the several kinds being found in separate parts of the play; . . ."[3] on a redefinition of Character, "that in virtue of which we ascribe certain qualities to agents[4] . . . that which reveals moral purpose, showing what kind of things a man chooses or avoids,"[5] nor on a redefinition of Plot, "the arrangement" or "combination of the incidents" (Aristotle uses the word *synthesis*).[6]

Those commentators who seem to respect Aristotle's emphasis on the primacy of plot usually undermine this emphasis by their modifications of it. Drawing upon Aristotle's work in ethics, they argue that since character is formed by action, tragedy is to be viewed as character-in-action. This is essentially the position of S. H. Butcher and Humphry House. House goes even further to insist that Aristotle's emphasis on the primacy of plot "is best understood as an attempt to guarantee the individuality of character."[7] Such modifications of Aristotle's thesis tend to make plot and character correlative. The fact of the matter is that Aristotle explicitly states: " . . . Tragedy is an imitation, not of men, but of an action. . . . "[8] More fully,

> Dramatic action . . . is not with a view to the representation of character; character comes in as subsidiary to actions. Hence the incidents and the plot are the end of a tragedy; and the end is the chief thing of all.[9]

For House, plot becomes subservient to character because it supplies the material conditions which individuate character.[10]

To make plot and character correlative is to ignore the individual nature of these two parts of tragedy and to misconstrue their actual relationship to each other. There is no justification for the view that all six parts of a tragedy, taken together, should exhibit organic unity: Aristotle defines organic unity in specific connection with his discussion of plot. He tells us that the plot should exhibit a unity such that if any one of the parts of the plot is "displaced or removed the whole will be disjointed and disturbed."[11] We must not identify the parts of the plot with the six parts of tragedy: the plot is one of those six parts.

Three considerations argue for the independence and the separability of at least some of the parts of a tragedy. First, Aristotle grades them in importance. Character is given second place.[12] Spectacle is said to be least important because a work can achieve the proper effect just in the hearing.[13] This means that the parts have "grades of relevance," as I have called it.[14] In particular, then, there is at least one part, spectacle, which is both separable in thought and separable in reality.

The second consideration derives from the fact that most of the parts are said to possess each its own intrinsic power. Thought can arouse "pity, fear, anger and the like."[15] Spectacle can also arouse pity and fear[16] and it has an emotional attraction of its own.[17] Music, though termed an embellishment,[18] gives especially intense pleasure (as does spectacle) and we know from the *Politics*[19] that music has the power to induce catharsis. Notice that we now have two parts, spectacle and music, which, even though they contribute to the tragic effect, cannot be taken as essential or indispensable.

Finally, Aristotle expressly maintains that there can be tragedy without character. No longer need we regard this statement as some oddity or stumbling block which must be excused in some way or dismissed as an extravagance. His statement is all of a piece with his general approach. Aristotle even entertains (for him) the more radical possibility of a plotless tragedy, or quasi-tragedy, when he says,

> . . . if you string together a set of speeches expressive of character, and well finished in point of diction and thought, you will not produce the essential tragic effect nearly so well as with a play which, however deficient in these respects, yet has a plot. . . . [20]

To sum up these results: we see that Aristotle, in his very investigation of tragedy, overhauls and dismantles it part by part. Accordingly, we find that we can have tragedy without spectacle. We can have tragedy without music. We can have tragedy without character. We may perhaps have tragedy without thought, for the incidents should speak for themselves.[21] And we can even have tragedy without plot. Let us not, however, commit the fallacy of composition and conclude that we can have tragedy without all of these parts taken collectively!

Aristotle sees tragedy as a goal-directed system. The goal is catharsis. He disassembles tragedy in order to see how each part functions to promote that goal. Precisely because each part does individually contribute to the whole, no one part is absolutely necessary. The system is overdetermined and redundant. In this respect tragedy is indeed like a living organism. It is what W. R. Ashby calls ultrastable. Damage to a part of a living organism often receives compensation from another part. For instance, one part of the brain will take over for an injured part. Leonard Meyer has pointed out that this kind of analysis in particular brings to clear sight overdetermination and redundancy, features of a living organism. Furthermore, we can now see the advantages of the functional approach which an organic theory invites. I only inveigh against what might be termed the indispensability-interdependence view of organic unity.

II

Interestingly enough, it is Humphry House, with all his concern for the importance of character, who gives the key to tragedy without character. House maintains that the famous "flaw," the *hamartia,* has nothing to do with a moral state at all. He argues that the *hamartia* should not be viewed as a flaw or a moral frailty. Rather, it should be taken to mean a mistake due to ignorance of circumstance.[22] Nearly all scholars now accept the interpretation of the *hamartia* as simple mistake. Gerald F. Else summarizes the scholarship and elaborates on the implications of this interpretation.[23] His conclusions (commended by Richmond Lattimore)[24] accord with House's thesis. Accordingly, I shall maintain without argument that *hamartia* means simple mistake. This mistake should not be construed as an error of judgment as Bywater does in his translation. An error of judgment implies a failure of practical wisdom and this, for Aristotle certainly, is a flaw in character. But anyone, anyone at all, can make a simple mistake. When Oedipus married Iocasta he made a mistake; there was no error in judgment. It may be difficult for us to accept the possibility that the tragic reversal can be brought about by an elementary error. Perhaps this is due to our traditional preoccupation with *hubris* as well as to a general fascination with flaws, preferably tragic, in ourselves and others.

Despite his interpretation of the *hamartia* as a simple mistake, House insists that Aristotle "assumes as a matter of course that the *hamartia* is accompanied by moral imperfections. . . . "[25] Does Aristotle make any such assumption? Here House is assuming, as a matter of course, the second part, Character, which seems likely to be flawed because the hero must not be "eminently" good. But to discover what tragedy without character is like we must respect Aristotle's dissociation of the *hamartia* from moral imperfection, be it vice, in the full-blown sense, or faulty judgment, a failure of practical wisdom.

Once we take the *hamartia* as a simple mistake without modification, explicit or implied, then we see that it is a function of the plot. House argues along these lines and Else urges further that the *hamartia* is complemented by the discovery.[26] The mistake is made in ignorance; the discovery involves the recognition of the mistake and is followed by or coincides with the reversal. When we see that the *hamartia* is a part of the plot together with the discovery and the reversal, then we realize that tragedy need not involve character at all.

Let us look at what Aristotle regards as the best kind of plot.

> The last case is the best, as when in the *Cresphontes* Merope is about to slay her son, but, recognising who he is, spares his life. So in the *Iphigenia,* the sister recognises the brother just in time. Again in the *Helle,* the son recognises the mother when on the point of giving her up.[27]

These plots turn on a simple mistake involving ignorance of identity. Of course the mistake is serious, but there is no vice, sin, moral frailty, or error of judgment in them. Again, as a function of the plot, the *hamartia* takes its place among those elements which Aristotle deems the most powerful in tragedy, the discovery and the reversal.[28] The *hamartia,* then, is the mistake which leads to the reversal. The discovery is the discovery of the mistake.

We are told that the best discovery involves persons closely related[29] and entails the shift from hate to love or love to hate.[30] Do these specifications of a good discovery introduce character, it could well be asked? To reply we must draw an important distinction. We must observe the difference between character and agent. Aristotle himself makes the distinction when he says,

> Character in a play is that which reveals moral purpose of the agents, i.e. the sort of thing they seek or avoid, where that is not obvious.[31]

But surely the actions of the agents imply character? After all Aristotle tells us that

> . . . the action involves agents, who must of necessity have distinctive qualities both of character and thought, since it is by these that we ascribe certain qualities to their actions . . . [32]

All agents, in so far as they are capable of deliberation and choice, possess character, the disposition to choose or avoid certain things. However, an action need not reveal the character of the agent. We should note that Aristotle says, "character in a play . . . reveals moral purpose . . . *where this is not obvious.*" All actions require agents, but an action need not reveal the char-

require agents, but an action need not reveal the character of the agent, for instance, Oedipus's action in marrying Iocasta.

At this point protest may be raised that Aristotle is concerned with serious action and serious action is bound to reveal character. Here let me make another distinction, the distinction between the serious and the moral. The moral is not always introduced through deliberation and choice. A choice may bring about tragic consequences through a simple mistake. Then it is morally neutral. Furthermore, tragedies may evolve from sheer suffering; it is obvious that Aristotle's conception of an action includes suffering as well as doing. However, the action of most tragedies is a moral matter because it involves killing, incest, adultery, as well as conflicts within and between the domestic, religious, and political domains. And, Aristotle is in fact primarily concerned with moral action. Must not moral action surely reveal character? In *Oedipus* the action is such that one might say, "If I had known so and so (of which I was ignorant at the time) I would have acted differently." Had Oedipus known that he was marrying his mother he would have acted differently. The remorse, which coincides with his discovery of the identity of Iocasta, testifies to this. Is not Oedipus's character thereby defined? No. I think we can say without any hesitation that if Al Capone were to discover that he had married his mother, he would be in a state of the greatest remorse, if remorse is not too weak a word. But knowing this about him is to know nothing. We have reached such a fundamental level that we can take certain responses for granted. This is also true of the shift from hate to love or love to hate which attends discovery, as when Merope recognizes her son, Iphigenia her brother, and the son in *Helle* recognizes his mother. I am not suggesting that *Oedipus Rex* is a play without character; I am exploring what tragedy without character is like and what it means to say that plot is primary.

It must be stressed that tragic actions involving members of the same family are so serious in themselves that they do not call for considerations of character. The fact of being an agent in a given relationship does not, in itself, reveal character. To be a mother, son, brother, or a sister does not commit the agent to a definite character. Nor does the discovery of the identity of the agent, in itself, entail character. When the discovery involves members of the same family it is sure to give rise to extreme emotions and these do not in themselves reveal character. We expect certain emotions to be aroused in members of the same family in certain situations. We have a minimal expectation, that, as a matter of course, a son will not be pleased to discover that he has married his mother. We assume Oedipus's remorse. Finally, the events are so terrible and the suffering so great in tragedy that it is meaningless to ask what the agents involved are like.

Both in literature and in life tragedy is a great leveler of character. When we hear of a widow who has lost her only two sons in a war, we do not ask (outside the seminar room, that is) whether she is a good woman or what her sons were like. Thus since tragedy, by its very nature, does not call for considerations of character, we can readily understand why, on simply hearing the plot, we "thrill with horror and melt to pity at what takes place."[33]

In the foregoing, I have tried to show how the *hamartia,* the discovery, and the reversal function together as parts of the plot in a way that enables the plot to do its work without the presence of character. The entire action of the play turns on these three parts. A mistake is made, the discovery is the discovery of the mistake, and this is followed by or coincides with the reversal of the entire action. The actions or events, which the plot orders into a total action, require agents or doers, but the character of the agents is not revealed. Aristotle demonstrates this when he gives the plot of *Iphigenia:*

> A young girl is sacrificed; she disappears mysteriously from the eyes of those who sacrificed her; she is transported to another country, where the custom is to offer up all strangers to the goddess. To this ministry she is appointed. Some time later her own brother chances to arrive. The fact that the oracle for some reason ordered him to go there, is outside the general plan of the play. However, he comes, he is seized, and when on the point of being sacrificed, reveals who he is . . . he exclaims very naturally: "So it was not my sister only, but I too, who was doomed to be sacrificed," and by that remark he is saved.[34]

Merely to read this account, knowing nothing else about the play, does indeed make us thrill with horror and melt with pity at what takes place. There is no definition of character here. There are agents certainly. There are actions. And there is suffering narrowly averted, but there is no character. In fact such an intimate exchange between brother and sister would seem to make the addition of character superfluous.

Again let us look at Aristotle's summary of the *Odyssey.*

> A certain man is absent from home for many years; he is jealously watched by Poseidon, and left desolate. Meanwhile his home is in a wretched plight—suitors are wasting his substance and plotting against his son. At length, tempest-tossed, he himself arrives; he makes certain persons acquainted with him; he attacks the suitors with his own hand, and is himself preserved while he destroys them.[35]

"This is the essence of the plot," Aristotle concludes, "the rest is episode." The likely exclamation, "The rest is episode, indeed!" invokes the distinction between story and plot. Such summaries, it may be countered, correspond to the general form or outline which Aristotle advises the poet to work out first. The "tempest tossed" corresponds to the episodes with which the poet fills out the general plan. But Aristotle, himself, makes no distinction between plot and story. He uses the terms, *mythos* and *logos,* interchangeably. For the *Iphigenia* he uses *mythos,* for the *Odyssey, logos.* Else accepts the identification of the two.[36] These summaries give the main events and give them in their proper order. Character has dropped out entirely; the wily Odysseus is simply "a certain man."

Here another point may be pressed: These summaries set forth the action so that the character of the agent is bound to drop out. To put this criticism in another way, it could be urged that one can define an action so generically as to render the delineation of character unnecessary. This is a very serious criticism. It correlates with the view that when the episodes are filled in, character emerges. Thus the details of Odysseus's journey will show him to be wily. This is House's thesis when he argues that the plot guarantees the individuality of character.

How shall we answer this objection? We can only say, "Look!" Look at the plots without prejudging the issue one way or the other. Above all let us look at the plots which Aristotle especially recommends. Take the *Iphigenia.* Without doubt, as in almost any extensive narration, the very scope of the terrain to be covered will make it very difficult to avoid some minimal sketching in of character if only to fill out the play. But it is by no means true that all plots require character to the same extent and the plots which Aristotle favors scarcely seem to require it at all. The tragic effect of the *Iphigenia* cannot occur unless we know something very important about the agents, namely, that they are brother and sister. To know this is to know nothing of their character and anything we might actually say as to their character could only contribute to the arousal and purging of pity and fear in some auxiliary way.

To these considerations it might be countered that although we can describe a play in which character has no part, a play that turns on plot, there cannot be tragedy in the fullest sense where there is no delineation of character. This is Butcher's contention.[37] We can have drama, but not a tragedy, presumably a play arousing pity and fear and achieving catharsis.

In the *Rhetoric* Aristotle defines pity as

> a feeling of pain caused by the sight of some evil, destructive or painful, which befalls one who does not deserve it, and which we might expect to befall ourselves or some friend of ours . . . [38]

He concludes later,

> Most piteous of all is it when, in such times of trial, the victims are persons of noble character; whenever they are so our pity is especially excited, because their innocence, as well as the setting of their misfortune before our eyes makes their misfortunes seem close to ourselves.[39]

The *Poetics* tells us simply that " . . . pity is aroused by unmerited misfortune, fear by the misfortune of a man like ourselves."[40] Learning that a sister has accidentally killed her brother inspires us with pity over her undeserved misfortune. Now it is indeed possible that if the sister were known to be Lucretia Borgia we might well feel that her misfortune was a case of "poetic justice." This is a negative consideration that must be acknowledged. Might some one then press that this acknowledgment concedes the case for character?

Aristotle gives two very different specifications of the character of the hero, namely, that he should be good or noble and that he should be like ourselves. These two approaches are reflected in the *Poetics* itself where we find that Aristotle sometimes requires that the hero be good and at other times requires that he be like ourselves. What is it to be like ourselves? It is not to be good. We are told in the *Rhetoric* that

> most men tend to be bad, slaves to greed, and cowards in danger . . . [and] as a rule men do wrong to others whenever they have the power to do it.[41]

Else argues that although to be like ourselves and to be good are irreconcilable, he maintains that the *homoios* should not be taken as a separate category introducing another object of imitation.[42] His argument, interesting as it is, does not respect Aristotle's observation that the poet must of necessity represent men as better, worse, or as they are.[43] The examples given are Homer who makes man better, Cleophon who makes them as they are, and Nicochares who makes men worse than they are.[44] Furthermore, Sophocles is quoted as saying that he drew men as they ought to be; Euripides as they are.[45] And we might note here that Aristotle points to Euripides as the one who is felt to be "the most tragic of the poets."[46] When Aristotle says that the hero must be good he explains summarily that the character of the hero is good if his intention is good.[47] But to arouse pity the disaster does not have to occur to a good man. It must only be undeserved. This necessary innocence is established by the fact that a mistake was made in ignorance as well as on the basis of the most general assumption as to the character of the hero. Only a monster, a Nero, deserves to kill his father and marry his mother unwittingly. In this regard, it is striking that Aristotle allows a quasi-pity for a bad man who is punished. He tells us that, although this would inspire neither pity nor fear (hence a plot concerning the downfall of an utter villain is inappropriate for tragedy), the fall of a bad man does arouse *philanthropia,*[48] "human feeling," or, more precisely, sympathy. Because the tragedies with which Aristotle is concerned occur within the context of the family, because, concommitantly, the reversal is so terrible, character is not indispensable. The tragic effect will occur without it.

Obviously a tragedy with character is better than one without character. Nobody would contest this. The best tragedy has all six parts. And character is, after all, second in importance among the parts. But, as I have pointed our before, to judge that something makes a thing better is not to hold that it is necessary.[49] This point is crucial and it is connected with the separability of the parts of tragedy. Plot does not, *ipso facto,* involve character. Furthermore, character is not rendered necessary because it makes tragedy better. This is fundamentally Aristotle's view. The good and the necessary should not be confused. The fact that character makes a work better, but is not necessary, becomes a normative principle for the construction of a good play. "Do not stake your all on character," Aristotle seems to be saying. This is especially useful instruction for a working poet, for, according to Aristotle, "Beginners succeed earlier with the Diction and Characters than with the construction of the story (Plot)."[50] Thus he advises the poet not to stake his all on character because there may be tragedy without character; there cannot be tragedy without plot.

Notes

[1] Aristotle *Poetics* VI. 1450ᵃ, trans. S. H. Butcher. Bywater reads: "Besides this, a tragedy is impossible without action, but there may be one without Character." I draw on both translations throughout.

[2] Catherine Lord, "Organic Unity Reconsidered," *JAAC* (Spring 1964) and "Unity with Impunity," *JAAC* (Fall, 1967).

[3] *Poetics* VI. 1449ᵇ 24-26.

[4] *Poetics* VI. 1450ᵇ 12.

[5] *Poetics* VI. 1450ᵇ 8.

[6] *Poetics* VI. 1450ᵃ 5.

[7] Humphry House, *Aristotle's Poetics* (London, 1961), Ch. V, p. 80.

[8] *Poetics* VI. 1450ᵃ 15.

[9] *Poetics* VI. 1450ᵃ 19.

[10] House, Ch. V, p. 79.

[11] *Poetics* Ch. VIII, 1451ᵃ 33-34.

[12] *Poetics* VI. 1450ᵃ 39.

[13] *Poetics* XIV. 1453ᵇ 5.

[14] *Unity with Impunity* (especially).

[15] *Poetics* XIX. 1456ᵇ 1.

[16] *Poetics* XIV. 1452ᵃ 39.

[17] *Poetics* VI. 1450ᵇ 18.

[18] *Poetics* VI. 1449ᵇ 29.

[19] Aristotle, *Politics,* trans. B. Jowett (Oxford), Bk. VIII, Ch. 6.

[20] *Poetics* VI. 1450ᵃ 29-31.

[21] *Poetics* XIX. 1456ᵇ 5.

[22] House, VI, 5, p. 94.

[23] Gerald F. Else, *The Argument of Aristotle's Poetics* (Harvard Univ. Press, 1963), Ch. 13, pp. 376-399.

[24] Richmond Lattimore, *Story Patterns in Greek Tragedy* (Univ. of London, 1964), Ch. I, p. 10: "Professor Else has demonstrated with I think complete and sensational success that the famous Aristotelian *hamartia* can mean neither fault, or flaw, in character, nor yet an error in judgment, but simply a mistake about the identity of a person."

[25] House, *Lecture VI,* 5, p. 95.

[26] Else, Ch. 13, p. 379.

[27] *Poetics* XIV. 1454ᵃ 5.

[28] *Poetics* VI. 1450ᵃ 13.

[29] *Poetics* XIV. 1453ᵇ 15-20.

[30] *Poetics* XI. 1452ᵃ 31.

[31] *Poetics* VI. 1450ᵇ 10-11.

[32] *Poetics* VI. 1450ᵇ 1.

[33] *Poetics* XIV. 1453ᵇ 5-6.

[34] *Poetics* XVII. 1455ᵇ 3-12.

[35] *Poetics* XVII. 1455ᵇ 16-24.

[36] Else, Ch. 6, pp. 243-244.

[37] S. H. Butcher, *Aristotle's Theory of Poetry and Fine Arts,* Ch. 9, p. 344.

[38] Aristotle *Rhetoric,* trans. W. Rhys Roberts (Oxford), BK. II, 8, 1385[b] 13-15.

[39] *Rhetoric,* Bk. II, 8, 1386[b] 5-10.

[40] *Poetics* XII. 1453[a] 5-6.

[41] *Rhetoric,* Bk. II, Ch. 5, 1382[b] 10.

[42] Else, Ch. 15, pp. 475-483.

[43] *Poetics* II. 1448[a] 1-2 and XXV, 1460[b] 9-10.

[44] *Poetics* II. 1448[a] 11-13.

[45] *Poetics* XXV. 1460[b] 35-36.

[46] *Poetics* XIII. 1453[a] 29-30.

[47] *Poetics* XV. 1454[a] 19.

[48] *Poetics* XIII. 1453[a] 2.

[49] *Unity with Impunity,* pp. 105-106.

[50] *Poetics* VI. 1450[a] 35-38.

Norman Gulley (essay date 1979)

SOURCE: "Aristotle on the Purposes of Literature," in *Articles on Aristotle: 4. Psychology and Aesthetics,* edited by Jonathan Barnes, Malcolm Schofield, and Richard Sorabji, Duckworth, 1979, pp. 166-75.

[*In the following essay, Gulley studies Aristotle's use of the term "imitation" and the relationship between that which the dramatic or literary artist represents and that which is "true."*]

In beginning this inaugural lecture I am aware that the notion of inauguration carries the notion of what is propitious. To inaugurate, in its literal Latin sense, is to take omens from the flight of birds. It has a transferred sense of consecrating a place or installing a person in office. In this sense the implication is that the ceremonial omens are favourable. Here are two modern dictionary definitions of it:[1] (i) to begin or initiate under favourable circumstances, with a good deed or omen, or with propitious exercises; (ii) to commence or enter upon, especially something beneficial.

This suggests that, in an inaugural lecture, I should say something about the beneficial nature of what I am

entering upon and indicate in what respects the omens are favourable for me. It suggests also, perhaps, since my profession is to provide students with a classical education, that I should indicate the benefits of a classical education.

But this would be too extensive a programme for the occasion. What I propose to do is to give you a sample of Greek thought. It is a piece of analysis by a Greek philosopher. The philosopher is Aristotle. The analysis is highly original. Its influence on European literary theory has been considerable. Perhaps these are good enough reasons for looking at it today. But I have a further reason for selecting this piece of analysis. Its conclusions have their place in Aristotle's views about what constitutes a truly beneficial education. In this respect they can serve to illustrate what I consider to be a distinctive feature of an education in the classics. If I say something, however briefly, about this when I have dealt with the analysis, I will be meeting in some part the strictly inaugural requirements of my lecture.

The piece of Aristotelian analysis I want to discuss is part of his analysis of what he calls the *poiêtikê technê,* the poetic art. The Greek phrase has a generic sense which gives it much wider application than the English 'poetic art'. It means the art of producing or constructing something. It embraces products such as beds and pots and temples and tables as well as literary products. Before Aristotle, there was a specific use of it to refer to literary composition in verse, and a similarly specific use of the noun *poiêtês* for the verse composer, specific uses which have largely prevailed in English since we took over the Greek words. Aristotle is not happy about this specific sense. Granting that there is a literary species of *poiêtikê technê,* why should metrical form be a distinctive quality of it? For it was clear to Aristotle that the specifically literary art he wished to analyse included instances not written in verse, for example a Socratic dialogue, and excluded others which *were* written in verse, for example Empedocles' scientific work *On Nature* (**Poet.** 1447b9-20).[2] Nor was Aristotle happy about the use of a generic term—*poiêtikê*—for a literary species. But he accepts the difficulty of finding a suitable specific term. As he points out, no one up to his time had found one (1447b9). He himself does not offer one.

We have had the same difficulty in English. Perhaps it will serve as an advance indication of the kind of literary field Aristotle wants to define if we look briefly at two English candidates for a title for this field. The first is 'literature' in the narrow modern sense which makes the more generic term do duty for the more specific. In this sense 'literature' is used chiefly, in Webster's dictionary phrase,[3] 'of writings distinguished by artistic form or emotional appeal', as opposed to those which are technical or erudite or informational or utilitarian. We sometimes add the adjective 'imaginative' when we use 'literature' in this sense. It is the sense we have principally in mind when we speak of a student of English or French or German 'literature'. We think of such students as readers of novelists and dramatists and poets rather than of historians and philosophers and scientists. This narrow use of 'literature' indicates fairly well, I think, the subject of Aristotle's analysis.

The other candidate is 'fiction' in its literary use. This is an altogether neater and more specific term. In its basic literary significance as a Latin term it comes very close to what Aristotle wants to analyse as an art. Unfortunately, modern English uses of the word make it unsatisfactory in several respects. Its most popular use excludes its application to all dramatic and most poetic literature (I use 'poetic' here in the usual English sense). Its scholarly use is much wider but still, I think, too narrow as an indication of the full range of Aristotle's *poiêtikê technê*. Scholars readily classify *Hamlet* as fiction. Most of them fight shy of the term when it comes to the *Sonnets*. And I am not sure that Aristotle would have wanted to rule out the *Sonnets*. However, despite the lack of a precise specific term, whether in Greek or English, to indicate the range of Aristotle's subject, perhaps these preliminary remarks will serve as a rough indication of it.

Let me now turn to Aristotle's analysis. He begins in his brisk, systematic way by classifying the *poiêtikê technê* as a form of imitation (*mîmêsis;* 1447a16). He specifies its medium as language. He adds that this is both a prose and a verse medium. It is not verse, he says, which distinctively marks off the literary artist from other writers. It is the imitative nature of his art (1447b15, 1451b28-29). And having made this obviously basic distinction, Aristotle rather blandly leaves us to infer, partly from examples he gives of *non*-imitative literature, what he means here by imitation.

Here are his examples (1447b16-20, 1451a38-b5). A work on medicine or natural science is non-imitative. A work on history is non-imitative. And Aristotle emphasises that putting such works into verse does not make them imitative works. So we can see that the literary artist's field of operation is non-factual and non-theoretical. At least it is not his job to give information about matters of fact or to provide a scientific explanation of what is already established in its structure. The distinction, then, between non-imitative and imitative literature (I use 'literature' here in the broad sense) is a distinction between literature which uses language descriptively to refer to what is already there to be described or explained, and literature which is the product of a *poiêtikê technê*. And in Aristotle's analysis the literary significance of the phrase *poiêtikê technê,* the art of making or constructing or creating something, entails that what the artist directly expresses in language is, in the broadest sense of the word, fic-

tional. The artist makes it up. So that there is a close connection between using language to imitate something and using it to present what is fictional. It would appear that it is only through fictions that you use language to imitate something.

Now when Aristotle uses 'imitation' as a term to describe what the artist is attempting to do he is using a term which was used readily by the Greeks in reference to literary works. Down to Aristotle's time the Greeks were accustomed not so much to the private reading of literature as to literary *performances,* whether dramatic performances or the public recitations of a rhapsode. Both the actor and the rhapsode were readily thought of as imitators (see Plato, *Rep.* 392cff.). As we ourselves might say when watching a dramatic performance: That isn't *really* Macbeth strutting about up there. It's Willie Morgan dressed up. He is dressed up to look *like* Macbeth, indeed he is attempting to behave *like* Macbeth, to represent him. It is this Willie Morgan level of imitation which made the idea of imitation in reference to literature familiar to the Greeks. But this level does not interest Aristotle. As he points out (1462a11-13; see also 1450b19-20), the dramatic poet can achieve his aim whether you watch his story enacted by Willie Morgan and company or you read it. What interests Aristotle is the usefulness of the notion of imitation, or representation as we would more naturally call it, once the Willie Morgan level is removed.

You cannot apply the Willie Morgan analogy at another level in any simple and straightforward way. You cannot say that as Willie Morgan represents Macbeth, so Macbeth represents someone else. But you can say that what Macbeth does and says, and the various events put into his life by the artist, represent something other than what is directly presented by the artist, that is, what is directly described through the conventional references of his language. As Aristotle has indicated, this direct kind of description is proper to an entirely different kind of literature. But the imitative literary artist, in presenting his fictions, is giving significance to those fictions by making them represent something else. So what are his fictions intended to represent?

Aristotle's initial answer to this is a broad specification of the field of operation for representations. He says that the field is human behaviour (1448a1, 27-8). This is a sound enough answer. Certainly it is sound as a generalisation from the Greeks' past practice in the art of literature. But it is clear that Aristotle had further grounds for specifying this field as proper for the work of the literary artist. Most importantly, he recognised that it is a field with a high degree of variability in its events (***EN [Ethica Nicomachea]*** 1094b14-19). Patterns of behaviour differ from individual to individual. And no one individual is likely to follow a perfectly regular and consistent pattern. There is *no* set pattern. Nor are there agreed rules for commending or condemning this pattern rather than that. A wide range of moral attitudes is possible. This makes the field of human behaviour the richest possible field for literary invention. It satisfies the important condition that wide freedom in *inventing* patterns of events inside it remains compatible with plausibility.

There is one more specification which Aristotle makes about the field—that it is the *moral* aspects of human behaviour which the literary artist is especially concerned with (1448a1-5). We must not take this in too narrow a sense. Aristotle's point is that the aspects of human behaviour which are fundamental for the artist's purposes are those which are capable of engaging our moral sympathy or antipathy in any way. It is essential for the artist to prompt reactions of approval or disapproval, whether with regard to what a character says or does or with regard to what happens to him. If Hamlet passes the salt, this directly serves the artist's purposes only in respect of any moral significance it has, for example if Hamlet passes the salt as salt, knowing it to be poison, to someone he intends to kill, or if he passes it as a pre-arranged signal for removing the king's head. Similarly, when Tolstoy describes Anna Karenina's abrupt death at the railway station, his intention is not to illustrate that people who throw themselves under railway trains lose their lives. As Aristotle would have said, that sort of truth belongs to non-imitative literature, perhaps a treatise on physiology. What Tolstoy and Aristotle consider to be relevant to the artist's purposes are those aspects of her death which engage our moral sympathies, for example our sense of the bad luck or the unfair treatment which brought her to suicide. It is an engagement of our emotions which is essential in what is represented, not the provision of information.

This specification of the representational field gives a broad indication of what is represented in literary art. We can be more specific if we take into account what Aristotle says about the artist's concern with the universal. He says (1451b5-10) that the literary artist tries to express what is universal rather than what is particular; he presents particular events and particular people; but he intends them to represent the kind of things which certain kinds of people say and do. It is in this respect, Aristotle says, that the literary artist's construction is 'more philosophical' than history.

This Aristotelian notion of the universalising aim of literature is now a very familiar one. Here are some simple examples. In his Preface to *Chuzzlewit* Dickens says that at the time of its composition Mrs Sarah Gamp was a fair representation of the hired attendant on the poor in sickness, and that Mrs Betsey Prig was a fair specimen of a hospital nurse. Moreover, the events making up the fictional lives of these two characters are intended by Dickens to represent certain general moral truths about the behaviour of people of this kind,

for example that it is socially undesirable that the treatment of sick people should be left to this kind of person. Similarly, Jonas Chuzzlewit is representative of a bad type of character resulting from a bad type of education. And note that Dickens says that the recoil of Jonas' vices on the old man who educated him 'is not a mere piece of poetical justice, but the extreme exposition of a direct truth'.

This last statement makes explicit that what Jonas' fictional fortunes represent can be formulated as a general moral truth. Dickens is inviting us to agree that, while in his fictional world the truth or falsity of what takes place is irrelevant, yet the fictional image can *represent* what is generally true and in that way point obliquely to what it does not express directly.

In most respects Dickens' remarks indicate well enough what Aristotle means when he says that the literary artist expresses what is universal, and that his work is more philosophical than the historian's. Aristotle is saying that the literary artist's fictions are designed to prompt generalisations. They are designed to prompt us to see that what Agamemnon, for example, is doing in this particular situation is the sort of thing which that sort of man is likely to do in that sort of situation. By this means they are designed to prompt generalisations about recurring patterns of events in human life—'pride goes before a fall' and 'he who hesitates is lost' are two very trite examples. This is the sort of thing a Greek chorus tends to talk about in order to prompt the audience to make the right inferences from what is presented to what is represented.

But in one important respect it would be misleading to take Dickens' remarks as a guide to Aristotle's meaning. Dickens claims that his fictions represent what is true. Aristotle makes no such claims for the literary artist. He claims that his work is more philosophical than the historian's. But this does not imply, nor is it intended to imply, that the literary artist has some special insight into the nature of things or that he aims in his work to represent the truth. Aristotle himself explains that it is in respect of its tendency to express what is universal rather than what is particular that he describes the literary artist's work as 'more philosophical' than the historian's. His explanation sufficiently specifies the meaning of 'more philosophical' here. To be 'more philosophical' is to have a greater propensity towards *sophia* ('wisdom') than the other man. And at the beginning of his **Metaphysics** (**Meta.** 981a25-b20) Aristotle illustrates what it means to say that one man is 'wiser' than another. He illustrates from a number of examples that one person is properly called 'wiser' than another in so far as he has a better grasp of general principles. A doctor is reckoned 'wiser' in the field of medicine than the man who just knows that he has stomach-ache. A master-builder is reckoned 'wiser' than the man who humps the stones. Similarly, a liter-

particular facts. For it is part of his job to make generalisations within his operational field of human life and behaviour.

I have given a good deal of emphasis to this point. For it is important not to read into Aristotle's mention of 'philosophical' any grandiose conception of the literary artist as a speculative thinker. Conceptions of that kind have been the source of much of the misguided idealisation of Aristotle's views on literature since the Renaissance. The kind of idealisation I have in mind is illustrated by Wordsworth, in his Preface to the second edition of the *Lyrical Ballads*. He presents Aristotle's view as the view 'that Poetry is the most philosophic of all writing'.[4] He goes on: 'It is so: its object is truth, not individual and local, but general, and operative; . . . carried alive into the heart by passion'. Aristotle would have approved of the terms 'general' and 'operative'. He would have approved of Wordsworth's link between these terms and specifically emotional effects. But he would have dissociated himself from the views that 'Poetry is the most philosophical of all writing' and that 'its object is truth'. Admittedly Wordsworth offers the first view as one which has been 'told' to him. But he really should have checked it.

One thing which is abundantly clear about Aristotle's literary universals is that it is not their truth-value which is a criterion for their validity. It is their evocative function, their value in arousing attitudes of fear and pity, surprise and admiration, amusement and indignation. When Aristotle gives his fine analysis of what is the best tragedy he is giving an analysis of the most effective means of achieving certain emotional effects. In the case of tragedy the emotions to be aroused are pity and fear (1449b27). And the artist's aim is not simply to arouse them but also to *regulate* them. Aristotle recognises that what the artist represents has not merely what I have called an evocative capacity in affecting the emotions. It has also a regulative capacity. It is this latter capacity which Aristotle's notion of *katharsis* (1449b28) or *purgation* of emotion is concerned with. Whatever else we might think of this notion as a piece of psychology, it does at least include the valuable insight that imaginative literature can regulate the quality and the intensity of particular emotions so as to achieve what are considered desirable results. It is here, according to Aristotle, that we should look for the purposes of literature. Aristotle is right. All literary art is propagandist in its aims. Accepting this, Aristotle considers it important that its emotional effects should be good effects.

In furthering this purpose the literary universals act as essential middlemen. For the artist is appealing, through his fictions, to what Aristotle calls *philanthrôpia* (1452b38, 1453a2, 1456a21), fellow-feeling, the kind of community of emotions and interests which Conrad, in his own discussion of the purposes of fiction, calls 'solidarity'.[5] Hence it is by generalising his appeal, by so constructing his fictions that they can represent the general rather than the particular, that the artist gains the emotional effects he wants. As regards the truth-value of what is represented, Aristotle's view is that it is not the artist's proper aim to try to represent what is true in his field of operation, that is, the field of moral behaviour. In this field it is the job of the *moral philosopher* to enquire into the problem of what general propositions can be established as true. And it is the aim of the moral philosopher, not the literary artist, to present the truth as he sees it, if he chooses to put his inquiries into writing. The guideline for the artist, in Aristotle's view, is not what *is,* but what *can be* (1451a36 ff.). And according to the genre he is working in he has to judge what can *plausibly* be represented, that is, he must avoid anything improbable or irrational which is likely to thwart his aim of engaging his readers' sympathies. In this field of moral behaviour, as indeed in any other, Aristotle would have thought it a curiously oblique and superfluously elaborate method, with no advantages of either clarity or precision, to employ imitative literature to achieve a presentation-of-truth aim.

There are many varied reasons for the tendency in much European criticism since the Renaissance to idealise Aristotle's views on the aims of the literary artist. One reason is that his views were often overlaid by the didactic Roman ideals of Horace's *Ars Poetica*. Another, which I have already noted, is that Aristotle's remarks about the literary artist's 'more philosophical' approach readily lent themselves to metaphysical dressing-up. It became very easy to put forward as a basically Aristotelian view the didactic notion that the poet's job was to communicate to others his vision of the truth. The literary attitudes of Johnson, in his *Preface to Shakespeare,* provide a simple illustration of this.[6] Aristotelian notions are reflected in many parts of this Preface, as they are in the Wordsworth Preface. Shakespeare's characters, says Johnson, 'are commonly species'. 'They act and speak by the influence of those general passions and principles by which all minds are agitated.' But note that Johnson asserts as a general principle, in Horatian vein, that the end of poetry is to instruct by pleasing. He does not, of course, mean instruction in any and every field. He means moral instruction, through the representation of moral truths which the artist implicitly invites his readers to accept. Indeed he raps Shakespeare's knuckles very sharply for giving more attention to pleasing than to instructing, and for 'sacrificing virtue to convenience' as he puts it. What he means by this is that Shakespeare's plays represent general views about the relation between virtue and happiness which he, Johnson, considers to be false. The poet should limit himself, he says, to what he calls 'just representations of human nature'. This will rule out 'irregular combinations of fanciful

This will rule out 'irregular combinations of fanciful invention'. The mind can only repose, Johnson says, on 'the stability of truth'.

This last remark is a particularly interesting example of the kind of metaphysical idealism grafted on to Aristotle's views on literature by English critics. Notice how readily an individual critic's moral convictions can be equated with the stability of truth and used to determine what are *just* representations and what combinations of the artist's invention are *regular*. There is no immediately obvious implausibility in this. And what goes for the critic goes for the author. In the infinitely varied field of moral behaviour and moral attitudes the author has as much freedom in claiming truth for the general views which he intends his fictions to represent as he has in constructing his fictions. And in each respect much freedom is compatible with plausibility. Thus the equation of what is represented with what is true is easy to make. It is not only easy. It is extremely tempting to make it in the case of fictional literature. It is a token of the value of the fictions. We respect the truth. And it is understandable that the frequent criticism that fictional literature presents what is false should be taken as a criticism that it is lacking in value. Hence the temptation to maintain that, while what is directly presented cannot claim to be true, yet what is *represented can* claim to be true. Indeed it is sometimes claimed as one of the strengths of a representational theory that it effectively by-passes the criticism that the first-level symbolism of fiction is false and trivial. It does so by claiming truth for its second-level symbolism.

I think it is one of the great merits of Aristotle's theory that he avoids this temptation. He was very well aware of the kind of criticism I have mentioned. In the *Poetics* he deals explicitly with a number of such criticisms (1460b6 ff.). And it is worth looking briefly at his answer to them. It will serve to make a little more precise his views on this important question of the truth-aims of the literary artist. The main criticism Aristotle had to meet was that literature was lacking in serious purpose and value because it was a tissue of false statements, of absurdities and impossibilities. This sort of criticism can take two forms. It can be argued that the fictional statements made by the literary artist are necessarily false. Or it can be argued that his statements are in fact false; they can be shown to be false by reference to what is in fact the case. Let us look at the first form. If I say that Mr Micawber was recklessly improvident, or that Mr Squeers was unpopular with his pupils, or that Mrs Gamp was ungrammatical in speech, I am saying what is true only in the trivial sense of stating correctly what Dickens portrays as being the case. It is nonsense to ask whether the statements are true in any sense which implies that Mr Micawber or Mr Squeers or Mrs Gamp at some time existed, and were, respectively, improvident, unpopular, and ungrammatical. And since it is nonsense to ask this, it might be argued that Dickens is not writing about anyone, either in these cases or in the case of his other fictional characters, and that whatever he states to be the case with regard to them is necessarily false. His imaginative fictions might on this ground be criticised as at best profitless and at worst calculated to misguide and deceive.

The other form of criticism—that the literary artist's statements are in fact false—was used in a variety of ways by Plato in the *Republic* (377B ff., 598D ff.). Here are some of Aristotle's own examples of this kind of criticism, taken from the *Poetics* (1460b18 ff.). It might be argued, he says, that the literary artist is guilty of technical inaccuracies in his work, for example in medical detail, or that he makes false theological assumptions, or that he is grossly idealistic in depicting the moral behaviour of his characters, or that he describes what is impossible or irrational, for example the behaviour of the Greeks and Trojans in standing idly by while Achilles pursues Hector, or, as we might add ourselves, Alice drinking out of the bottle and shooting up in size.

Neither Aristotle nor any other Greek, as far as I know, distinguished these two forms of criticism. But I think it likely that the frequent criticism in Greece, dating from as early as the eighth century B.C. (cf Hesiod, *Theogonia* 27-8), that poets were liars sometimes confused the two forms of criticism in its attitudes and allowed one to intensify the other. Aristotle realised the importance of meeting this criticism. His distinction between imitative and non-imitative literature enables him to do this. Non-imitative literature, as we have seen, uses its language descriptively, with reference to what is already there to be described or explained. It is the statements of this kind of literature to which truth or falsity apply as the proper standards of correctness. If the criticism that the statements of fiction are necessarily false had been made explicit in Greece, Aristotle's answer to it would rightly have been that it is not their function to be true or false; the criteria of truth and falsity do not apply to them.

This kind of answer comes out clearly when Aristotle is dealing with the second form of criticism—that the statements of fiction are in fact false. What is to be noted about this form of criticism is that, unlike the first; it can be applied not only to what is directly presented by the literary artist but also to what he implicitly *represents* through his fictions. Aristotle's answer to it applies to both these levels. His answer (1460b14 ff.) is that it is what is *artistically* correct which matters, not any other kind of correctness, not, for example, the kind of correctness we call truth. And an artist's fictions are artistically correct if their construction is such as to achieve certain emotional effects. The appropriate emotional effects will differ from one literary genre to another. But in *no* genre will the truth of what is represented be a criterion for success in evoking the emotions. The literary artist's working criterion is not truth, but plausibility.

Aristotle is shrewdly perceptive in what he says about the varying limits, from one literary genre to another, of what is artistically plausible. In tragedy you soon lose the sympathy of your audience if you introduce events which fly in the face of natural laws or if the behaviour of your characters transgresses all psychological probability. Tragedy is too close to the facts of life for that. In epic the area of plausibility is a good deal wider (1460a11ff.). Homer, says Aristotle, tells the best tall stories. He knows how to give an air of conviction to the impossible. And this, as Aristotle says in his familiar dictum, is better than failing to give conviction of what *is* possible (1460a26-27, 1461b11-12). The golden rule is to observe the limits of plausibility appropriate to the genre in which you are working. And you must be consistent in this. Oedipus cannot be transplanted to the Mad Hatter's tea party nor Mrs Gamp to *The Cherry Orchard*. Nor would we forgive Miss Austen if Mr Darcy suddenly committed hara-kiri in the hall at Petersfield.

All that Aristotle says on this score of what is artistically correct is well said. Much of it concerns the proper application of this criterion at the level of what is directly presented by the literary artist. But what makes it especially important for the literary artist to have a good eye for what he can *plausibly* present is the fact that the particularities of his fiction represent what is universal, and succeed in their aim only if these representations too have the requisite plausibility. Plausibility in detail at level one governs plausibility at level two. Such general views about human behaviour and the human situation as are *represented* by the artist need make no claim to be true. But they must have sufficient plausibility to gain the emotional effects the artist is seeking.

Perhaps you remember the man Brown in Conrad's *Lord Jim,* the 'latter-day buccaneer' as Conrad calls him, who 'sails in his rotten schooner into Jim's history, a blind accomplice of the Dark Powers'. Brown's part in Jim's history illustrates what Conrad, in a letter to Bertrand Russell, called his 'deep-seated sense of fatality governing this man-inhabited world'.[7] And there are other things which Conrad wants to represent through Jim's fictional experiences, general views about the psychology of cowardice and self-esteem and self-discipline. Conrad tells us, in his preface to *The Nigger of the Narcissus,* what purposes he thinks the literary artist serves by his representations. Much of what he says is remarkably Aristotelian in spirit, especially his distinctions between the artist and the thinker or scientist, and his thesis that the essential appeal of fiction as an art is to temperament and not, as he puts it, 'to that part of our being which is dependent on wisdom'. Yet in the end Conrad cannot resist making the claim that the artist, like the thinker or scientist, seeks the truth, and that what the artist reveals through his fictions is 'all the truth of life'. Thus Conrad provides yet another illustration of the metaphysical idealisation of the Aristotelian view of literary art. An interesting reflection of the influence of this idealising tradition is found in Webster's dictionary definition of 'imitation' (*op. cit.,* s.v.) in its aesthetic sense. It is, says Webster, 'a simulation of life or reality in art; imaginative embodiment of the ideal form of reality'. Webster adds that this is 'a use following Aristotle'. But notice the metaphysical transformation of Aristotle's notion of imitation.

I have spent a long time discussing Aristotle's view of the relation between what the literary artist represents and what is true. Yet it is a point of special importance in any consideration of literary values. In upholding the values of imaginative literature post-Renaissance European criticism has always tended to use the 'insight-into-the-truth' card as its trump-card. Aristotle's views on the values of literature are also decisively influenced by his acceptance of the value of this card. For the reason why Aristotle gives a comparatively *low* value-rating to literature is that he considers the 'insight-into-the-truth' card to be a card which the literary artist can never legitimately play.

You may ask why the lack of any such card in your hand entails that you have a comparatively poor hand. The answer lies in the end to which the playing of the card is directed. This determines the comparative value of your cards. And in the large game of human life the value of imaginative literature has to be measured against other activities or studies in relation to the end of life. That is how Aristotle measured it. Naturally and straightforwardly Aristotle, like any other Greek thinker, makes his value judgments in relation to some conception of human excellence—*aretê*—in a broad moral sense. Equally naturally he looks at human excellence functionally and starts from the notion of man as a rational animal (*EN* 1097b25 ff.) And perhaps it is equally natural again, since Aristotle is a philosopher, that he finished with a conception of human excellence in terms of what he considers to be the highest intellectual activities (*ibid.,* 1177a12 ff) This is not the occasion for considering the metaphysical and other grounds on which Aristotle bases his grading of intellectual activities. But his conclusion is that the wisdom which is the distinctive mark of human excellence is found through the pursuit of truth in high realms of theory—in physics, in mathematics, in metaphysics, and in theology (*Meta.* 982a5 ff., 1026a6-32). Literature cannot measure up to these. In Aristotle's view the proper methods and aims of literature are such that neither the practice nor the study of it calls for the exercise of high intellectual activity. It does not have the pursuit of truth as its aim. Even if it did have such an aim it does not operate in a field in which any properly scientific method is applicable. Nor is it a field which can provide objects of study with a high metaphysical grading. As Aristotle puts it, man may be the best of the animals but he is not metaphysically the best of objects (*EN* 1141a33-b2).

Now all this does not mean that for Aristotle imaginative literature is *without* value. He values it for its capacity to refine and extend our emotional sensibilities. And he values its capacity to *regulate* those sensibilities. Indeed, since literary works are artificial things, producible in an enormous range of patterns, Aristotle sees that their regulative function can be socially and politically important. In his **Politics** (1340a ff.) he recognises, more generally than in the **Poetics,** that imitations or representations, whether in music or literature, can be used in a system of education to regulate emotion and hence character to an approved pattern. In this way they can further human excellence, at the practical level of character training. And this constitutes, for Aristotle, the final purpose of imaginative literature.

We may disagree, of course, with Aristotle's hierarchy of values, a hierarchy which puts literature and music in the kitchen, logic and mathematics in the dining-room, and philosophy and theology in the drawing-room. We may think there are good grounds for adjusting these value-ratings. But any changes which may be made in the comparative value-ratings do not invalidate in any way Aristotle's ideal of the educated man as one who does not spend his time exclusively in the kitchen or the dining-room or the drawing-room but spends time in them all and recognises the relative value of each of them for the furtherance of the good life.

This is an ambitious ideal of education. Yet it must not be thought that it is in any way exceptional in the world of classical civilisation. It can fairly be said to be the standard type of ideal in Greek and Roman thought. There are, naturally enough, movements up and down in the value-rating of this or that subject of study. In respect of particular value-rating the contrast between Greek and Roman ideals is in fact a fairly sharp one. Yet the Greek educational ideal of the truly wise man remains unchanged in Rome in certain fundamental respects. It is still an ideal of human excellence in a broad moral sense. It has the same comprehensiveness in the range of studies thought to be necessary for realising the ideal and the same resistance to specialisation. And each field of study is evaluated in relation to the common moral end which it serves.

I hope I will not be thought guilty of special pleading if I say that this classical ideal of education finds its clearest and indeed most appropriate exemplification in classical studies. The student of classics studies a civilisation. He studies its languages and literature, its religion and philosophy, its history and art. I consider this to be valuable and beneficial for much the same reasons as Aristotle when he put forward his own educational ideals. I think too that there is an increasing recognition nowadays that what best educates a university student for life and leisure—and perhaps too for business—is to work in this kind of broad and varied and demanding field of study. This recognition is reflected in the curricula of some of the universities, especially the newer universities, as well as in the discussions of professional educationists. It is a trend which Aristotle and I wholeheartedly support.

Notes

[1] *Webster's New International Dictionary,* 2nd edn., s.v.

[2] Subsequent references to Aristotle's text are to the *Poetics,* unless otherwise stated.

[3] *Op. cit.,* s.v. Surprisingly omitted from the third edition.

[4] *Wordsworth's Poetical Works,* ed. de Selincourt (Oxford, 1944), Vol. 2, pp. 394-5.

[5] In his Preface to *The Nigger of the Narcissus.*

[6] Quotations from the Yale edition of Johnson's *Works,* Vol 7 (New Haven, 1968), pp. 59 ff.

[7] Quoted by Russell in his essay on Conrad in *Portraits from Memory* (London, 1956).

Mark Packer (essay date 1984)

SOURCE: "The Conditions of Aesthetic Feeling in Aristotle's *Poetics,*" in *British Journal of Aesthetics,* Vol. 24, No. 2, Spring, 1984, pp. 138-48.

[*In the following essay, Packer argues that the "formal and psychological requirements of good tragedy" outlined by Aristotle in* Poetics *cannot be thought of as a definition of tragedy. Rather, Packer maintains, Aristotle intends them as "the premises and conclusion of a demonstration" that identifies the causal relationship between the formal features of tragedy and the psychological response of the audience or reader.*]

An important question raised by Aristotle's analysis of tragic art concerns the relative significance of, and relation between, two sets of requirements for good tragedy stipulated in Chapter VI of the **Poetics.** The first, which I shall call the 'formal requirement', lists several rules of composition and form the text itself must exhibit in order to have value as tragic poetry, such as its length and the kinds of actions it must present;[1] and the second, which hereafter shall be referred to as the 'psychological requirement', specifies pity and fear as the most appropriate emotional responses the reader or spectator of good tragedy should experience. To which requirement, if either, Aristotle gives priority, and how, if at all, Aristotle believes the formal characteristics of a text can elicit these particular emotions are questions that the argument of the *Poetics* does not answer clearly or thoroughly.

One's immediate impression of *Poetics* VI is that Aristotle is providing a comprehensive and exhaustive definition of tragedy that includes among its defining elements its imitative function, the kinds of incidents tragedy must imitate, its specific magnitude, use of language, form, and finally its effects on the mind of the reader or audience.[2] Brief reflection reveals, however, that this last point, concerning the psychological experience of pity and fear, does not seem to belong to this list along with the other requirements mentioned. Pity and fear, as emotional experiences, are not species or properties of the art work, as they do not follow from the essential divisions and characteristics of art developed earlier in the *Poetics*. Some commentators, such as Golden, Telford, and Srivastava, have concluded that Aristotle does not mean that pity and fear should be experienced emotionally, but that the concepts of these feelings are formal features of tragedy that are intellectually clarified by the text.[3] Brunius and others, in contrast, have been led to the opposite view, and have argued that the formal characteristics of the text are links in a psychological chain of communication between the poet and the audience, and are therefore completely subordinate to the emotional effects tragedy should produce.[4] Skulsky and Schaper, on the other hand, have claimed that both conditions, the formal and psychological, are equally important, but their arguments in general fail to explain just how they are connected either logically or aesthetically.[5]

The origin of this confusion and disagreement can be traced, I believe, to a specific mistaken assumption about the purpose served by Aristotle's stipulation of these requirements. Most commentators seem to believe that both these conditions are intended as parts of a unified definition of tragedy that Aristotle is developing at this point in his argument, and are therefore puzzled by the fact that the formal elements of a text and psychological states of the soul do not exhibit the obvious logical connections the components of a definition should have. In this paper, I will argue that the conjunction of the formal and psychological requirements of good tragedy discussed by Aristotle in *Poetics* VI does not constitute a definition at all, but these conditions serve respectively as the premises and conclusion of a *demonstration* that establishes a causal relation between the formal defining characteristics of a text on the one hand, and the responses of its reader or audience on the other. Although it has been argued before that some causal relation holds between them,[6] I do not believe that the connection has been explicated thoroughly or accurately. I will show that it is by means of a practical syllogism reasoned by the reader or spectator that pity and fear can follow as effects from the recognition of a tragedy's formal features, but that this point is a suppressed premise in the argument of the *Poetics*, which has led so many commentators to confuse this enthymeme with a definition. Although the results of this discussion have strong bearing on the meaning of *katharsis* in Aristotle's theory of art, I regard that as a separate issue and will focus instead on how pity and fear are elicited in the first place by tragic poetry according to the thesis of the *Poetics*.

I

In a very thorough and illuminating paper on the construction of the definition of tragedy in *Poetics* VI,[7] M. Pabst Battin shows that each element in this definition is derived by a method of division developed in the *Posterior Analytics*, *diaeresis*, which requires that the essence of the object under investigation be located through the methodic differentiation of its genus. It is stated explicitly in the *Posterior Analytics* that a definition constructed by this method must conform to three specific conditions: (1) the division should admit only those elements in the definable form; (2) these elements should be arranged in the proper order; and (3) no such elements should be omitted.[8] In the *Poetics*, Aristotle employs the method of *diaeresis* to distinguish the various arts from one another by noting the essential differences in their means, objects and manner,[9] and these differences appear to be exhausted by the formal characteristics of tragedy mentioned in Chapter VI prior to the introduction of pity and fear. By attaching these psychological references to an already exhaustive classification of tragedy's defining elements, it appears that Aristotle has violated the first condition of definition by division, viz., that only those elements essential to the defining form be admitted into the construction. Battin concludes that the pity and fear clause is a mere 'tag' to the definition of tragedy, and thereby renders defective what is otherwise a well-formulated definition.

This argument is clearly correct on at least one point, that pity and fear do not figure in the definition of tragedy developed through *diaeresis*. But it does not follow from this that the pity and fear clause is either superfluous or deleterious to the thesis of *Poetics* VI. What Aristotle is establishing at this point is that some connection holds between the incidents properly presented by tragedy and the experience of pity and fear. However, because a connection is suggested here by Aristotle does not imply that it is one of differentiation or division within a defining formula. Rather, in so far as the connection is not established by *diaeresis*, the link between the formal features and psychological effects of tragedy is of some kind other than the relation among defining elements, and must therefore be exhibited by some means other than definition, which, I will show, is demonstration.

Aristotle remarks in the *Posterior Analytics*[10] that there is an important distinction between proving essential nature on the one hand, and proving the fact of a connection on the other. It is the purpose of definition, he claims, to reveal essential nature, whereas it is for demonstration to show that there is or is not an attachment between a particular attribute and a specific subject.[11] A definition, in other words, signifies a subject's essence,[12] and thus establishes a relation of numerical, specific, or generic sameness between the subject and its defining terms.[13] Aristotle concludes that if two things can be shown not to be the same in any of these three senses, they cannot be conjoined in a definition.[14] Pity and fear are affects and movements of the soul, not species or divisions of artistic imitation. The relation between these emotions and the formal characteristics of tragedy, therefore, is not one of sameness as specified above, which implies that pity and fear do not belong with the formal elements in a definition of tragic art. Whatever connection holds between the defining formula of tragedy and these passions is one that is accidental or coincidental,[15] and therefore requires a demonstration for its proof.

However, the demonstration that would establish or exhibit this relation is articulated by Aristotle neither in *Poetics* VI nor anywhere else in the text where pity and fear are discussed. There is evidence for the claim that the relation is for Aristotle causal, as there are several passages in the *Poetics* where pity and fear are mentioned as the effects tragedy has on the reader or audience.[16] The problem thus concerns the discovery of the missing premises that would explicate or complete the demonstration of a causal relation between the defining elements of tragedy and its psychological effects, which requires looking beyond the text of the *Poetics* to Aristotle's writings on psychology and ethics, where the passions of the soul and their causes are discussed in greater detail. I realize that since the publication of Else's commentary in 1957[17] many researchers have felt obliged to interpret the *Poetics* exclusively 'out of itself', but I don't believe the text is sufficient for the completion of the inquiry into this essential demonstration.

II

Roman Ingarden has observed that in the *Poetics* 'Aristotle dispenses completely with psychological terminology. Nowhere is there any mention of anything such as the experience of the author or reader, as somehow part of the work.' Aristotle thereby 'excludes, almost inadvertently and somewhat naively, the literary work from the sphere of everything psychical . . . '.[18] Though his point may be stated too strongly, Ingarden's remark does express the observation that an important omission occurs in the *Poetics* that results in difficulties for understanding the relation of the audience's emotional responses to the formal characteristics of the tragedy's text. Ingarden proceeds to fill in some of the gaps by noting two essential points: first, the 'ultimate purpose to be achieved through the realization of unity of action and other principles of composition is always the production of a greater effect on the spectator or reader';[19] and second, that some act of cognition is required for the reader to be affected by the tragedy's literary qualities.[20] Ingarden is thus suggesting that the tragedy's formal elements and its psychological effects are brought into relation with one another by the soul of the reader or spectator, who grasps the text's formal qualities through a cognitive mental act which then produces the specific emotional effects pity and fear.

There are, however, two questions left unanswered by Ingarden's analysis, which require more thorough treatment if Aristotle's demonstration is to be explicated fully. First, how for Aristotle does cognition affect the emotions? And second, what specific kind of cognition does Aristotle believe is necessary in aesthetic experience to elicit or occasion the particular feelings pity and fear? In the remainder of this section, I will be concerned only with the first question, reserving discussion of the second question for Section III.

Aristotle's writings on the nature of the soul and moral psychology leave no doubt that he believes very strongly that the intellect has a major influence on the emotions. The soul, for Aristotle, has both rational and irrational faculties: the former comprises the capacity for theoretical contemplation and practical deliberation, and the latter is rooted in the vegetative and appetitive dispositions. This distinction, however, is not exclusive, for it is Aristotle's firmest conviction that the appetitive and desiring elements of the soul can and do obey reason,[21] which is evidenced, he believes, by receiving advice, exhortation and reprimand,[22] as well as by the ability of the continent man to subject his appetites and desires to the control of reason.[23] More specifically, of the two parts of the rational soul, the contemplative and the calculative, it is the latter that has the most compelling and direct influence on the irrational faculty. In fact, the cultivation of a virtuous disposition and the very possibility of moral education depend in large measure for Aristotle on the influence exercised by reason on desire *(orexis)*.[24] It is desire that follows from opinion, rather than opinion from desire,[25] for it is only by means of perception, imagination or conception that desire can arise in the first place,[26] and is transformed into rational wish *(boulesis)* when the object of desire is judged by correct reasoning.

It is with this last point in mind that Aristotle develops his theory of practical syllogism, the purpose of which is to formulate the means by which correct judgement occasions the desire most appropriate for the realization of a particular end.[27] Although Aristotle never thoroughly schematizes the form of the practical syllogism, its construction and composition may be surmised as follows[28]: the major premise expresses a universal judgement concerning the kind of object, situation, or person that is good or valuable; the minor premise is a particular judgement expressing either that an instance of the universal rule articulated by the major premise is at hand, or else describes the means available for the realization of the good or end under consideration; and the conclusion is the desire necessary to originate the appropriate movement or action.[29] The specific movement or action need not be the actual result of the deliberating process. All that need follow as the conclusion of a practical syllogism is the *resolution* to perform the action,[30] or in other words, the appropriate wish.

The passions and desires are understood by Aristotle to be natural motions of the soul,[31] the efficient causes of which are judgements concerning the goodness or desirability of the objects to be pursued or avoided.[32] Cognition of this practical variety is seen by Aristotle as indispensable for the very possibility of choice, which he describes as 'either desiderative reason or ratiocinative desire'.[33] If the reasoning process involved in practical syllogism occurs according to the rules specified above, then one particular feeling or another will be produced, depending on the specific value or disvalue expressed in the major premise, and the information provided about particular objects and means-ends relations by the minor. When pity and fear are experienced by the reader or spectator of tragedy, a similar practical reasoning process is at work, in this case one that concerns the moral qualities displayed by the characters and their actions. But in order to understand just how pity and fear are produced by the reader's cognition of a tragedy's incidents and characters, it is first necessary to examine the specific kinds of judgement necessary to elicit them.

III

The facts of moral experience may appear to contradict Aristotle's claims concerning the production of feeling by practical judgement. It seems that emotional responses to persons or situations often occur too quickly and spontaneously to include a well-defined process of deliberation among their causes. Aristotle is perfectly aware of this fact, as is evidenced by his remarks in **De Motu Animalium** that desires and the actions they produce can arise with such spontaneity that the mind does not actively deliberate the premises.[34] This does not preclude, however, the process of judgement from the production of feeling, but indicates the facility with which the reasoning process occurs in the experienced and morally mature mind. This spontaneity is most evident in the act of perception that provides the premises of the practical syllogism. What is apprehended by sense is not merely the individual Alcibiades, but a universal content as well, such as 'man', or in the case of a moral judgement, 'magnanimous man'.[35] It is true that for Aristotle sensation by itself is of the particular, but when sensation is accompanied by knowledge, as it is in most cases, a universal is apprehended at the same time,[36] and it is only by a deliberate act of reflection that the two may be distinguished and expressed separately.

Although Aristotle never says so directly, it can be reasonably assumed that a practical syllogism will most likely be articulated explicitly only when the spontaneity conditioned by earlier training and experience somehow fails, requiring in its place conscious and deliberate consideration of the issue at hand; or when justification is demanded for a choice made or an action committed, and the agent wishes to show the choice or action to have been reasonable. When spontaneity does prevail, however, feeling is still the product of a judgement, though one that may be enthymematic or habitual.

The situation is similar in the case of aesthetic experience. Presented by tragedy are individual characters, such as Hecuba, Orestes or Antigone, but individuals who express through their speech and action several universal qualities and characteristics. In Chapter VI of the **Poetics** and the passage immediately following, Aristotle discusses in detail the general rules a good tragedy is to display, and among them are types of universal traits and characteristics that must be exhibited by the actions of the tragic personages. The characters, we are told, reveal not the particular actions performed by the historical figures after whom they are named, but the kinds of actions people of a certain character type might probably or necessarily do.[37] The statements expressed by poetry, Aristotle remarks, are therefore universal, as they show not particular facts, but possibilities.

Similarly, the moral qualities of the characters are not the traits and habits of actual persons, but reveal the features of a certain moral type Aristotle describes as 'the intermediate kind of personage', who is neither primarily just nor exclusively depraved.[38] The speech and actions of these characters must also exhibit certain universal features, such as the general rules Aristotle discusses for the construction of the Discovery and Peripeteia, and for the unification of action. A tragic poem that does not reveal these universal structures and characteristics would not be poetry at all for Aristotle, but history, the purpose of which is to describe only individuals and their deeds by means of singular statements.[39]

The reader or spectator of good tragedy is thus presented with the information necessary to formulate the major and minor premises of a practical syllogism. As in moral judgement, an individual is perceived or imagined who is an instance of a universal rule or category of moral value. In the case of tragedy, the specific personage is one who suffers great pains and losses, but one who is judged as underserving of such misfortune in virtue of the general moral type he or she represents. Both the universal and particular judgements may occur together in a single act of aesthetic perception, but the truths they express are distinguishable by reflection and can be articulated respectively as the major and minor premise of a practical syllogism. Recognition of an individual character who exhibits the general moral qualities mentioned above will be sufficient, Aristotle suggests, to occasion the experience of pity, which is caused, he claims in the ***Rhetoric*** and ***Poetics,*** by the sight of someone of this kind suffering underserved misfortune.[40] In virtue of the intermediate moral traits displayed by the tragic personage, Aristotle infers that the character will be 'one like ourselves', which he claims is sufficient to elicit the experience of fear, a feeling he describes as the expectation for oneself of some imminent pain or evil.[41]

Pity, then, is the result of a judgement concerning the possession by the tragic character of certain general moral features, and fear is conditioned by the realization that these general moral qualities are attributable to oneself as well. In both cases, the specific emotions experienced are caused by a reasoning process, no matter how subtle or spontaneous, performed by the reader or spectator that is closely similar to the deliberation by practical syllogism that occurs in moral experience. In moral as well as aesthetic reasoning, a specific person or character is judged to be an instance of a general type or rule, and a particular feeling is thereby produced as a result of this judgement. The similarity between the two is facilitated further by the fact that tragic poetry, as a species of art, is an imitation, and what is imitated by tragedy is human character and its moral capabilities.[42]

IV

The articulation of the practical syllogism reasoned by the spectator or reader of tragedy explicates the premise missing from the demonstration presupposed by ***Poetics*** VI of the causal relation connecting the text's formal characteristics and psychological effects. Pity and fear follow from the fulfilment of the formal requirements because these conditions furnish the general qualities that must be exhibited by tragic characters and their actions in order for the major premise of the practical syllogism to be thought or assumed; and visual perception of the characters displaying these qualities, or their presence to the aesthetic imagination, furnish the instantiation necessary for the minor premise. From the reader's cognition of the conjunction of these features and characteristics, all of which are specified by the formal definition of tragedy, the appropriate psychological effects follow as the conclusion conditioned by these premises.[43]

Although the similarities between the reasoning processes involved in moral and aesthetic judgement are very striking, there are some significant differences as well. Aristotle believes that if desire and purpose are to initiate action, the agent must be affected by objects apprehended either through sensation or imagination.[44] The calculative imagination may be sufficient by itself to *stimulate* desire and appetite,[45] but this faculty alone does not provide the deliberating agent with the true opinions necessary for sound moral reasoning.[46] For imagination to serve its function in moral deliberation, perception or sensation of the relevant moral facts is also required.[47]

The case of aesthetic judgement, however, is quite different. Although sensation and perception are involved when the spectator of tragedy apprehends the actions presented on stage, what is perceived is merely an imitation or representation *(mimesis)* of possible action, rather than actual persons and events. The imitative or imaginary nature of the events depicted in aesthetic presentation is what prevents action by the spectator from following as the result of his or her practical reasonings about the characters and events being perceived. Although action is not the proper effect of practical reasoning in aesthetic experience, the emotions that do occur in these circumstances are none the less similar in strength and quality to the feelings that precipitate action in moral situations.

Aristotle observes in ***De Anima*** that the soul employs images in the thinking process as though they were the contents of perception, and so judges them to be good or bad which in turn is sufficient to stimulate desire or aversion, respectively.[48] But a further judgement is obviously necessary to distinguish imaginary or aesthetic images on the one hand, from those based on actual moral facts and existing situations on the other. Without this additional judgement, the distinction between the moral and aesthetic employments of practical syllogism would be overlooked, and hence the effects proper to these separate uses of the syllogism might be confused. The result would be one of two types of madness, depending on which application of the practical reasoning process was required at the moment: either the spectator of tragedy will be moved to act by the events depicted on the stage and will thus be ushered out of the theatre for disturbing the performance; or else the moral agent, instead of performing the actions necessitated by the circumstances, will merely applaud or hiss at the events or persons constituting the moral situation in which he or she is engaged. Here too there is rarely any need for an explicit articulation of this judgement, but it is none the less assumed by every sane and rational employment of practical syllogism.

These distinctions are clarified further by Aristotle's claim in **De Motu Animalium** about the two kinds of premises a practical syllogism may express, one concerning the good, the other the possible.[49] Although either kind of premise may occur in a moral or aesthetic judgement, each employment of the practical syllogism will place a stronger emphasis on one or the other depending on whether the judgement is about an actual good to be realized in action, or one that is merely possible as an object of aesthetic imagination.[50] It is this last point that I believe ultimately measures the essential difference between moral and aesthetic judgement. Knowledge of moral values is certainly required for the cognition of a tragedy's formal characteristics, but it is the mark of practical wisdom to translate this knowledge into action.[51] It may be the case that for Aristotle, *katharsis* serves the mediating function of transforming aesthetic judgement into practical wisdom, but any such claim would at this point be merely tentative and conjectural.

A consequence of this interpretation of the **Poetics** that is even more significant concerns the stronger emphasis we now see Aristotle placing on the formal conditions and intellectual antecedents of aesthetic experience. I suspect that many reconstructions and interpretations of the theory have been motivated by the interest in diminishing this cognitive stress, either to defend Aristotle against the traditional charge of formalism, or to correct the intellectualism that many aestheticians believe constitutes the major flaw of the **Poetics.** This latter motive appears to me to have some merit, but its execution must be tempered with the appropriate caution; for Aristotle's theory of art is undoubtedly formalist to the highest degree, and this point must be preserved in exegesis and analysis of the **Poetics** regardless of the philosophic contentions one may have with its thesis.

Of course this raises once again the essential question concerning the adequacy of Aristotle's exclusive emphasis on form and intellectual cognition for the appreciation of aesthetic value. Omitted by the theory is any allowance for intuition or empathy as the source of aesthetic feeling, and in its place we find a bald reduction of the aesthetic emotions to functions of judgement and discursive reasoning. There can be no doubt that cognition and judgement make some contribution to the experience of the emotions relevant to art, especially tragedy, but one question must be raised about Aristotle's treatment of the intellect's aesthetic importance, viz., is judgement by itself *sufficient* to occasion the aesthetic emotions? Though it may be true that deliberate reflection can articulate the causes of tragic pity and fear as moral judgements, this constitutes, it

seems, a *post hoc* reconstruction and analysis of an experience that is conditioned primarily by the feeling of intuitive empathy a reader or spectator of tragedy is likely to feel for a tragic personage whose character is developed by the poet with the appropriate sensitivity and craftsmanship.[52] It is important to distinguish, here as elsewhere, a *description* of an aesthetic response from a reflective *evaluation* or *justification* of that response as appropriate or inappropriate. Intuition and empathy are frequently occasioned by a direct and immediate apprehension of character traits that appeal primarily to the emotions in unmediated spontaneity. Reflection executed subsequent to this experience may reveal that the empathy was misdirected, which may then undergo some modification or perhaps even be transformed into contempt for the character initially evaluated so sympathetically. Arguments and analyses of art works certainly can and do have these effects, but only when deliberation and reflection are required.

It may not have been Aristotle's intention to formulate a description of the spectator's spontaneous responses to the art work, but this does not imply that the distinction between description on the one hand and the canons of reflective evaluation provided by the **Poetics** on the other should not be observed. To overlook the essential differences between the two imports an intention into Aristotle's theory that is inappropriate, and thereby generates unnecessary objections and criticisms.

Notes

[1] By 'formal' characteristics of a text I understand those elements of its structure or design that are predicable universally of all pieces of tragic poetry.

[2] Here, as elsewhere, Aristotle does not distinguish a definition from a normative criterion. When he stipulates in the *Poetics* the requirements for tragedy, Aristotle is at the same time providing a standard with which to judge good instances of tragic art.

[3] Leon Golden, 'The Purgation Theory of Catharsis' in *Journal of Aesthetics and Art Criticism* 31, pp. 473-9; 'Catharsis' in *Transactions of the American Philological Association* XCIII, pp. 51-61. K. G. Srivastava, 'A New Look at the "Catharsis" Clause of Aristotle's *Poetics*' in *British Journal of Aesthetics* 12, pp. 258-75; 'How Does Tragedy Achieve Catharsis?' in ibid., 15, pp. 131-41. Kenneth Telford, *Aristotle's Poetics: Translation and Analysis* (Gateway, Chicago, 1961).

[4] Teddy Brunius, *Inspiration and Katharsis* (Acta Universitatis Upsaliensis, Upsala, 1966). See also W. Hamilton Fyfe, *Aristotle's Art of Poetry: A Greek View of Poetry and Drama* (Clarendon Press, Oxford, 1940).

[5] Harold Skulsky, 'Aristotle's *Poetics* Revisited' in *Journal of the History of Ideas* 19, pp. 147-60. Eva

Schaper, 'Aristotle's Catharsis and Aesthetic Pleasure' in *Philosophical Quarterly* 18, pp. 131-43.

6 Lane Cooper, 'Introduction' to *Aristotle on the Art of Poetry* (Ginn and Co., Boston, 1913). Telford, op. cit. Schaper, op. cit.

7 'Aristotle's Definition of Tragedy in the *Poetics,* Part I', in *Journal of Aesthetics and Art Criticism* 33, pp. 155-70; 'Part II', pp. 293-302.

8 An. Post., 97a23-25.

9 Poet., 1447a16-18.

10 90b39-91a3.

11 See An. Post., 91a9-12 for further distinctions between definition and demonstration.

12 Top., 101b39.

13 Top., I, 7.

14 Top., 102a13-16.

15 An. Post., 73b4.

16 1449b28, 1452a2, 1452b2, 1452b29, 1453a1, 1453b1, 1453b5-12, 1453b13-15, 1456a20-22, 1456a39, 1456b4.

17 *Aristotle's Poetics: The Argument* (Harvard University Press, Cambridge, Mass., 1957).

18 'A Marginal Commentary on Aristotle's *Poetics,* Part I' in *Journal of Aesthetics and Art Criticism* 20, pp. 171-2.

19 Ibid., Part II, p. 276.

20 Ibid., Part II, p. 278.

21 EN, 1102a29, 1102b30; Pol., 1260a5-8, 1333a16-25; EE, 1219b42, 1220b5-10, 1219b26-37.

22 EN, 1102b37.

23 Ibid., 1102b20; EE, 1219b42; Pol., 1260a5-8, 1333a16-25, 1334b18-24.

24 See T. H. Irwin, 'Aristotle on Reason, Desire and Virtue' in *Journal of Philosophy* 72, pp. 567-578. W. W. Fortenbaugh, *Aristotle on Emotion* (Harper and Row, New York, 1975); 'Aristotle's *Rhetoric* on Emotion' in *Archiv Für Geschichte Der Philosophie* 52, pp. 40-70.

25 Met., 1072a27-30.

26 De Mot. An., 701a35-36.

27 De An., 432b27-433a8.

28 See David Wiggins, 'Deliberation and Practical Reason' in *Essays on Aristotle's Ethics,* ed. by Amelie Oksenberg Rorty (University of California Press, Berkeley, 1980), p. 230.

29 De An., 434a16-22; De Mot. An., 701a23-24; EN, 1141b14-16.

30 See Richard Sorabji, 'Aristotle on the Role of Intellect in Virtue' in Rorty, ed., pp. 201-20.

31 An. Pr., 70b12.

32 EE, 1227a2-4.

33 EN, 1139b4, tr. by W. D. Ross in *The Basic Works of Aristotle,* ed. by Richard McKeon (Random House, New York, 1941).

34 701a25-30.

35 An. Post. 100a17-100b1.

36 Joseph Owens remarks in connection with this point: 'The universal is there, as a datum. It is observable through reflection. To find in the Aristotelian treatises an adequate account of it in terms of its causes or grounds, however, becomes a disappointing endeavor.' 'The Grounds of Universality in Aristotle' in *American Philosophical Quarterly* 3, p. 169.

37 1451b8.

38 1453a7-9.

39 1451b5-7.

40 Poet., 1453a5-6; Rhet., 1385b13-16; See also EN, 1115a8-10.

41 Rhet., 1382a20-30.

42 Poet., 1448a1-5.

43 It is difficult to articulate with any degree of precision the exact formulation of the practical syllogism relevant to aesthetic experience that would hold universally in all instances. In its most basic and general form, it would appear as something like the following:

All persons of moral type X are undeserving of great pain and misfortune.

Character A is a person of moral type X *who is suffering such pain and misfortune.*

Experience of pity.

The differences between the practical and theoretical syllogism are made apparent in this illustration by the fact that no mention of pity need be made in either of the premises as it would if some proposition about pity were being derived in a theoretical inference.

[44] De Mot. An., 701a4-6.

[45] De An., 433a20-21, 433b28-31; De Mot. An., 701b17-22.

[46] EN, 1139a23-31.

[47] De An., 427b15-25; EN, 1142a27-29, 1143b3-6.

[48] De An., 431a14-17, 431b2-5.

[49] 701a23-24.

[50] Cf. p. 144 above.

[51] EN, 1143a8-10, 1144b13, 1152a7-8.

[52] For an interpretation of Aristotle's theory of tragedy that includes 'fellow-feeling' as a condition of the tragic emotions, see D. D. Raphael, *The Paradox of Tragedy* (Bloomington, University of Indiana Press, 1960).

Stephen Halliwell (essay date 1986)

SOURCE: "Aristotle's Aesthetics 1: Art and Its Pleasure," in *Aristotle's "Poetics,"* Duckworth, 1986, pp. 42-81.

[*In the following essay, Halliwell examines Aristotle's conceptualization of "mimetic arts" and argues that the pleasure which results from experiencing a work of mimetic art is "a response to the intelligible structure imposed on his material by the artist's rational capacity."*]

There is evidence to be found in the *Poetics,* and it receives some confirmation from material elsewhere in the corpus, that Aristotle's thoughts on poetry were not formed in isolation from comparative reflections on other related activities, especially the visual arts, music and dancing—activities which it is now automatic for us to describe collectively as art'. For Aristotle the most significant common factor shared by these activites, and their products, was mimesis, and it is directly in connection with mimesis that we encounter in the *Poetics* and occasionally in other works general pronouncements covering both poetry and one or more of the arts indicated above. Such pronouncements were not without precedent, and it is possible in particular to discern some influence on Aristotle of the analogy between poetry and painting frequently drawn and exploited by Plato. But Aristotle's use of the comparison was not merely conventional, and its repeated occurrence in the *Poetics* associates it with such vital matters as artistic form and unity, the relation between action and character in the portrayal of human life, and the nature of the pleasure to be derived from works of mimesis. It is for this reason that in the present and the following two chapters I shall be concerned with the broader foundations of the Aristotelian theory of poetry: that is, with concepts and principles which are presented in the treatise as the essential framework of an understanding of poetry, but whose scope it is clear that the philosopher regarded as encompassing the other activities too which I have mentioned.

In exploring the extent and the stability of these foundations, one must at once confront the question of whether Aristotle can legitimately be said to have possessed a unitary concept of art corresponding even approximately to the now prevalent use of this term. This basic issue elicited very different responses from the two most important English works on the *Poetics* written around the turn of the nineteenth century. The title of Butcher's influential study, *Aristotle's Theory of Poetry and Fine Art,* in itself boldly declares its author's position on the matter. Butcher was in fact contributing to a tradition already well established in Germany of attempts to reveal the existence of systematic aesthetic ideas in Aristotle, comparable to, and aligned with, his metaphysical, political and ethical systems. Butcher believed, with some minor qualifications, that 'the cardinal points of Aristotle's aesthetic theory can be seized with some certainty', and much of his book rather ambitiously undertakes to give substance to the claim. Bywater, however, in the preface to his edition of the *Poetics,* countered such views with the statement that 'the very idea of a Theory of Art is modern, and . . . our present use of this term 'Art' does not go further back than the age of Winckelmann and Goethe'. Bywater conceded that there are ideas in Aristotle's work 'which we should regard as coming under Aesthetics', but he objected to the aspiration to supply a systematic elaboration of them, when Aristotle himself had never done so.[1]

While I do not accept that Aristotle's thought in this area is as fully structured or as accessibly close to our own as Butcher in his more confident flights tended to suppose, neither can I altogether share Bywater's negative approach. Not only is it virtually impossible in practice to dispense with 'art' and related terminology in discussing the *Poetics* and certain aspects of Aristotle's philosophy, but it also, and more positively, seems to me feasible and worthwhile to give to this term a faithfully Aristotelian significance which makes clear both where it coincided with, and where it diverged from, modern views of art. It will be the first task of this chapter to show that while Aristotle had a comprehensive concept (now lost) of *technê,* for which both 'craft' and 'art' in its older sense are rough but imperfect translations, he was also capable of demarcating within this larger notion a restricted group of activities for which the normal modern use of 'art' is the only simple equivalent, though 'mimetic art(s)' is perhaps a preferable description. In the later part of the chapter I shall go on to argue that it is also possible to identify an important Aristotelian theory of the pleasure properly entailed in the experience of these mimetic arts, but especially in poetry. I must emphasise at the outset that by referring to this and to other Aristotelian ideas as 'aesthetic' I do not mean to assume or appeal to any independent philosophy of art—least of all, any *aestheticist* philosophy. Except where otherwise indicated, 'aesthetic' is employed in a plain, unprejudicial sense, referring either to the properties or to the experience of those activities and works which Aristotle believed to be connected by the element of mimesis, and which most post-Enlightenment thinking takes, in its use of the term 'art', to be unified by expression or some other factor.[2] It must also be noted that since the first part of this chapter deals with the lineaments of the Aristotelian view of mimetic art, mimesis as such receives some attention here, but it is also reserved for the fuller treatment which it merits later in the book.

To elucidate Aristotle's conception of mimetic art, we must start with its foundation in the wider notion of *technê. Technê* had earlier become the standard Greek word both for a practical skill and for the systematic knowledge or experience which underlies it. The resulting range of application is extensive, covering at one end of the spectrum the activity of a carpenter, builder, smith, sculptor or similar manual craftsman, and at the other, at least from the fifth century onwards, the ability and practices of rhetoricians and sophists. It is therefore translatable in different contexts as 'craft', 'skill', 'technique', 'method', or 'art', and I mentioned in the introductory chapter the use of the term to denote a formal treatise or manual containing the exposition of the principles of an art. In the light of these linguistic facts, it is not surprising that in the classical period the word could be applied to the poet's ability, particularly if we take into account the close alignment between the range of meaning of *technê* and the usage of the term for productive activity, *poiêsis,* which had come to be employed specifically for poetry . . . . If *technê* and *poiêsis* had originally been restricted to skills directed to material results, they had at any rate developed so as to become capable of designating a much larger sphere of activity, and also so as to denote a characteristic type of disposition or procedure, or even a *theoretical* framework for procedure, as much as a particular kind of artefact. *Technê* implied method and consistency of practice; it represented a vital part of the ground of man's practical and inventive intelligence, as opposed to the forces of nature (including any uncontrollable elements in man's own nature). Hence the arguments which arose (so prominently in Plato) over whether certain activities could correctly be included in this category. Where poetry was concerned, *technê* could be set up, by Plato at least, as the antithesis of inspiration; but that is to anticipate a further issue which will receive consideration in my next chapter.

Aristotle accepts unequivocally that poetry, painting, sculpture, music and dancing are all forms of *technê.*[3] But the mere fact that the term can be readily translated as 'art'—a fact which depends historically on the persistence in English, as a secondary sense, of the original meaning of this word as derived from *ars,* the Latin equivalent of *technê*—evidently does not yield an Aristotelian concept of art in the desiderated sense, since *technê* as 'art' embraces a much larger range of activity than the mimetic arts alone. The contrast between the broad category of *technê* and the significance possessed by the standard modern use of 'art' is striking, and one element in this contrast is the fact that the distinction between art and craft which has come to seem essential to some modern aestheticians, and to be a common if not a universal assumption in general attitudes to art, had no existence for Aristotle.[4] The 'family resemblance' between the whole gamut of methodical skills and activities encompassed by *technê* was not weakened by the specific affinities which might be discerned between particular sets of *technai.* If mimesis is more in evidence, and more problematic, in the **Poetics** than *technê,* that is because the latter is actually more fundamental but also more easily assumed without explanation or explicit definition. It is therefore all the more important for the modern reader of the treatise to be sure about what presuppositions are carried by Aristotle's adherence to the belief that poetry and the other mimetic arts mentioned were *technai.*

In the case of the visual arts, with their necessary component of material craftsmanship, it hardly needs to be stressed that Aristotle's acceptance of the concept of *technê* was in conformity with widely held attitudes. But for the musico-poetic arts too (whose *performing* practitioners—actors and instrumentalists—are not in question here, though they too had their *technai: Rhet.* 1404a 23f.) the connection, at least on the superficial level, is sufficiently clear: the notion (though not the name) of poetic *technê* was at least as old as Homeric epic, it was reflected in the later adaptation of the language of 'making' *(poiêsis)* to poetry, and it was reinforced by the strongly genre-based conventions of Greek poetry, in which the poet's task was often defined partly in terms of the requirements of a social, religious or other context. Aristotle's attunement to such attitudes was, moreover, implicitly close to that strand of sophistic thinking which had asserted the cultural importance of verbal skills, *technai,* particularly rhetoric. The whole ethos of the **Poetics** is to some degree a reflection of the sophistic development of the formalised theory and exposition of linguistic skills. And if, as I suggested in the last chapter, the *Poetics* is not a teaching manual as such, it at any rate presupposes the possibility of poetic teaching grounded in the principles and procedures of the *techné:* according to Aristotle, metaphor is the *only* thing in poetry which one cannot learn from someone else (59a 6f.).

To understand what the status of poetry as a *techné* entailed for Aristotle, however, it is necessary to go beyond popular Greek ideas or the sophistic importance of formal teaching of verbal skills. For Aristotle elaborated the concept of *techné* at a deeper level within his own philosophical thinking, and it is here that we must look for the assumptions which underlie his treatment of individual arts. In the *Ethics techné* is defined as 'a productive capacity involving true reasoning' (1140a 8-10, 20f.). This may not seem to carry us far beyond what has already been said about the scope of the term in ordinary Greek, but it does laconically indicate how *techné* fits into a fundamental Aristotelian mould of thought. *Techné* involves a true alignment of the axis of potential/realisation in human productive activity: it is concerned with bringing into being, by intelligible and knowledgeable means, objects whose existence depends on their maker (1140a 10-14). An immediate point to notice—it will recur—is the necessary entailment of objective, rational standards in all *techné*. A further implication of the definition is that Aristotle, more markedly than in general Greek usage, shifts the emphasis of the concept from activity as such to the potential or ability for a certain sort of activity. *Techné* is a capacity to act in accordance with reasoned procedures so as to produce designed results: the reasoned regularity and stability of the activity means that it is possible to abstract the theory of the practice from it, and it is in this theory, which constitutes a form of knowledge, that a primary locus of the *techné* can be situated: the philosopher is, indeed, sometimes prepared to treat *techné* and knowledge as virtually synonymous.[5]

One reason for attending carefully to Aristotle's refinement of this notion is to dispel any suspicion that the idea of a poetic or other mimetic *techné* necessarily brings with it crude associations of physical craft. It is essential to observe that this is not so for Aristotle, and had probably not been so for some time before him. But there are further, and more positive, aspects to Aristotle's understanding of *techné*. Although in Book 6 of the *Ethics* from which the earlier definition was taken *techné* is distinguished from nature ('art' cannot produce thóse things which come into being naturally, 1140a 14f.), Aristotle is often at pains to assimilate them. In several works we find him stating the principle that *techné* stands in a relation of mimesis to nature, a principle which is usually but perhaps misleadingly rendered as 'art imitates nature'. What the phrase affirms is that art follows procedures analogous to nature's, and that similar patterns and relations can be discerned in the workings of each; but it is vital to insist on the proviso that the claim does not apply exclusively to the mimetic arts themselves (whose own mimetic character is a separate matter) but to the sphere of *techné* as a whole. Aristotle's position is clarified by his observation that *techné* may sometimes complete the work of nature, or supply its deficiencies, and by a number of other connections and comparisons made between the two forces.[6] From all the material bearing on this point it emerges that what *techné* and nature have in common is *teleology:* both, as Aristotle would say, control processes for bringing things into being, and both are guided, and in one sense determined, by the ends or purposes towards whose fulfilment they move.[7] It is presupposed in this theory that *techné* and nature both have a similar tendency to aim at the best, to effect the finest or most successful organisation of their material.

The most problematic feature of this philosophical thesis might well be thought to be what it predicates of nature, not its treatment of human *techné,* since the purposive procedures of the latter make at least a limited teleological definition of them readily intelligible. But even if we put on one side, as we here must, the general difficulties raised by Aristotle's natural teleology, the two spheres cannot be entirely disengaged, and there remains more to be said about the relation between nature and human productive activity. To the analogy posited between the two types of process as teleological, we need to add the conviction that, from one point of view at least, *techné* is itself a part of nature, and its ends are to be regarded as naturally given or determined. Because man is part of nature, and all *techné* involves his rational productive capacities, the teleology of 'art' is in some degree subordinate to and dependent on that of nature as a whole. The operation of this premise can be confirmed and exemplified specifically for poetry from the *Poetics* itself, and while I shall attempt a separate analysis of its implications for Aristotle's attitude to cultural tradition in my next chapter, it is apposite here to locate it in its broader context.

For my present purpose I emphasise only one passage, though there are others which are germane. In *Poetics* 4 Aristotle provides a brief account of the 'natural' causes of poetry, and in so doing advances a compound explanation of the reasons both for the production of poetry and for the pleasure taken in it. A preliminary point to be made about this passage is that, while it begins by reference to poetry, its perspective opens out, as sometimes happens elsewhere in the treatise, to include other mimetic arts, and we can therefore legitimately take Aristotle's arguments here to have a wider applicability to most forms of mimesis. The argument is, in fact, despite its characteristically plain and condensed presentation, an ambitious one, and it is crucial to the interpretation of more than one issue in Aristotle's aesthetic philosophy. Its significance for the present question lies not in the positing of natural human instincts for mimesis, but in the way in which Aristotle proceeds from this premise to sketch a theoretical view of the natural development or evolution of the major Greek literary genres. Nature enters into the sequence of thought at three stages, supplying a progressive series of reference-points: first (48b 5ff.) as the general provision of a human instinct and capacity for mimetic activity, encompassing musical and rhythmic instincts which are themselves mimetically charged (cf. n. 29 below); secondly (48b 22ff.) as the source of particular inclinations and talents shown by early poets, and hence as the motive force behind the first period of generic evolution (marked by the basic distinction between serious and base subjects); finally (49a 2-15), and most importantly, as the true process contained in the direction of cultural development, a process embodied in the gradual unfolding of the natural potential of specific poetic forms. On this last point Aristotle is most explicit in the case of tragedy (though we can fairly extrapolate for other genres), of which he says that 'it ceased to change, once it had acquired its own nature' (49a 15)—that is, its mature perfection, the fulfilment of its potential.

It is clearly implied in this last remark that the history of tragedy has to be comprehended ultimately in terms not of contingent human choices and tradition, but of natural teleology mediated through, or channelled into, acts of human discovery of what was there to be found. Aristotle's point need not be strictly deterministic, since he does not appear to believe that tragedy was bound to be invented and developed; but he does clearly affirm that once its development became a cultural possibility (once it had 'appeared' or 'been glimpsed', 49a 2) the end result was a naturally fixed goal. To return to the implications of this example for *techne* in general, we can now see that not only do human productive activities form an analogue to the generative and purposive patterns of nature, but their individual histories evolve in accordance with intrinsic seeds of natural potential. Although Aristotle seems nowhere to work the point out fully, it is corroborated by his belief that all *technai* have been repeatedly discovered and developed (and then lost) in the history of the world: this is because they are rooted in man's inescapable relation to nature.[8] Aristotle's concept of *techne*, it transpires, is a highly charged philosophical doctrine, and must therefore be differentiated both from ordinary nonphilosophical Greek notions of skill, method and practical intelligence, and also from the standard modern understanding of craft. While the Aristotelian concept shares with these applicability to a wide range of activities in which rational, controlled procedures represent a structured relationship between means and ends, purposes and products, it goes beyond them in its theoretical entailments concerning the natural foundations of these activities.

Techne represents the first layer or level in Aristotle's concept of the mimetic arts; these arts count as arts, in the first place, precisely by virtue of belonging to the category of rational, productive procedures. It is important, however, to avoid the common distortion involved in reducing this doctrine to the belief that 'all arts are crafts', since the refined notion of *techne* includes, but is not simply equivalent to, craft. Nonetheless, we must not attempt to minimise the radical discrepancy between this aspect of Aristotle's thinking and the dominant modern view of art. It would be similarly wrong to try to reduce the discrepancy by placing weight on the passage in the **Metaphysics** where Aristotle distinguishes between arts of utilitarian value and those designed to give pleasure.[9] The distinction is, for one thing, broad, and not intended (in the case of the non-utilitarian, at any rate) to offer a careful delimitation of a particular set of activities; there is no reason to suppose that the arts of pleasure would be identical with, though they would evidently include, the mimetic arts. Nor is this passage of the **Metaphysics** designed to give a proper account of the types of pleasure derivable from *techne*, for this will reflect the nature of individual activities, and we shall see later in this chapter that the theory of aesthetic pleasure sketched in the **Poetics** cannot be understood simply as the antithesis of practical usefulness. Pleasure alone, therefore, will not make Aristotle's view of the mimetic *technai* conformable to modern attitudes. The primary reason for the remaining conceptual distance between the two is that Aristotle's acceptance of the framework of *techne* for the interpretation of poetry and related practices imports an inescapably objectivist element, as well as a naturalistic teleology, which is alien to the belief in creative imagination that has grown in strength since the Renaissance, and that has dominated Romantic and later aesthetic thinking. In Aristotle's system, the mimetic artist is devoted to the realisation of aims which are determined independently of him by the natural development of his art, and by the objective principles which emerge from this development.

I shall return to this contrast at the end of this section, but it is now necessary to move on to the second and the distinctive criterion of the mimetic arts, mimesis itself. Mimesis alone, it must be stressed, is insufficient to yield a definition of the mimetic arts, since there are mimetic activities (mundane forms of imitation) which are not *technai*. The combination of both *techne* and mimesis is therefore required to give us the core of Aristotle's concept of poetry, painting, music and the rest—the concept of *art,* in other words, in the fuller sense. For without prejudicing the question of where and how this concept is consonant with, or divergent from, later ones, there need be no serious doubt that the substantial coincidence between the activities counted as mimetic *technai* by Aristotle and those usually counted as art in modern European culture (the *Beaux Arts* of the Enlightenment) provides adequate justification for referring in this way to an Aristotelian concept of art or mimetic art. The centrality of mimesis to this concept calls for the extensive treatment which I give to it in ch. IV, where many details in the interpretation of the *Poetics'* understanding of mimesis are examined. Here a more synoptic view of the subject must be offered.

If *technê* is a definition or theory of the relation between the productive artist and his product, mimesis stands for, and purports to characterise, the axis between the product and reality. That mimesis can be written as an ordinary English noun (as it has been since at least the seventeenth century) is a testimony to the persistence of mimeticist thinking and terminology in the European tradition; and the fact that the language of mimesis and *imitatio* was for so long indispensable to neo-classicism (and that it still lurks, thinly disguised, around much that is said and thought about art) may suggest that its potential belies some of the more severe rejections which it has met with in recent times. But it need hardly be said that the influence of neo-classicism has also created a specious familiarity which is an obstacle in the way of attempts to recover the original Greek context and development of the idea. Indeed, the very familiarity of the whole question and problem of the relation between art and the world makes it difficult to realise the good reasons for the faltering movement of Greek thought towards a philosophical formulation of the issues involved, or towards a concept of the shared or analogous features of poetry, the visual arts and music (to go no further). As with *technê*, so with mimesis, it is important to appreciate the basis of Aristotle's thinking on the matter in already existing attitudes and assumptions, as well as the ways in which he builds on and reshapes this basis. In the case of mimesis Aristotle worked against the background both of Plato's persistent approaches to the idea, and also of the more widely held mimeticist views which Plato himself attests.[10] The notion of mimesis as a common or defining characteristic of a variety of cultural activities and products was not the discovery of a single thinker or period. It emerged untidily from a long development in the meaning and application of mimesis language, and may not have been wholly consciously articulated before Plato. But in the act of shaping a theory or doctrine of mimesis, Plato at the same time placed a considerable philosophical and often polemical burden on the concept, and as a result he did not pass on to Aristotle a freshly honed idea, but a whole set of suggestions, issues and challenges which were superimposed on the intricacies of existing non-philosophical uses of the word. Moreover, as I shall later show, Plato's own interests in mimesis were not as cut-and-dried, nor as entirely negative, as is often be-

lieved, and he demonstrated that the idea might have a contribution to make to a large area of philosophical enquiry.

Aristotle's pronouncements on mimesis, taken collectively, reflect the scope for uncertainty and instability produced by the earlier history of the word's applications. It is possible here to give some idea of the complexity of the problems raised by his view of mimesis, but also to bring some order into the relevant material, by trying to separate two salient dimensions of mimesis and two types of theoretical question associated with them. Starting from the minimal proposition that all Greek notions of mimetic art entail a necessary subject-object distinction, and that this must in some way structure a relationship between a mimetic art or work (in whatever medium) and an aspect or level of reality, it becomes possible to identify two main ways in which such a proposition might be elaborated. The first is to define what might be called a *formal* relationship between work and object, that is a relationship between the medium or mode of the mimetic representation and the relevant features of the represented object. Such a definition requires exemplification by particular arts, though the formal relationship established for one art may be, and often was, used as a model for the understanding of another, or even of mimetic art in general. The question of formal mimetic relationships points especially towards the importance in Greek thinking of analogy between poetry and painting, an analogy which appears in the early classical period and is central to the interpretation of both Plato's and Aristotle's treatments of mimesis.[11] The formal aspect of visual mimesis is amenable to a straightforward formulation (however *simpliste* it might seem to some): colours and forms, as both philosophers would put it, correspond to, and so represent, the colours and forms of visible reality (and perhaps of more besides). There is no doubt that this formulation made it easier for the idea of poetic mimesis, and of mimetic art in general, to become acceptable. Plato can be demonstrably convicted of exploiting the elision in thought involved in taking visual as the paradigm for poetic mimesis, when he sets out to degrade artistic activity to the level of a shallow reproduction of the surfaces of the material world.[12] Despite the lack of a precise connection between poetic and visual mimesis, the analogy between painting and poetry was one which Aristotle was not prepared to surrender: it appears in the opening chapter of the *Poetics*, and repeatedly in later passages. It should be added that the visual model of mimesis was paralleled by, and in some contexts (such as acting and dancing) found in conjunction with, dramatic or enactive mimesis of human behaviour. In both cases the nature of mimesis can be intimated by noticing that it aspires, or might be held to aspire, to the condition of being indistinguishable from the original.[13] It is unclear how the same could be said of any conception of poetic mimesis, even if Plato was polemically ready to suggest this.

Aristotle was, however, undoubtedly aware of the specific issue of the formal relation between mimetic art and its objects. This is apparent in the passage from Book 8 of the **Politics** (1340a 28ff.) where he distinguishes between the true mimesis of human character which he states to be possible in music, and the weaker relationship—'symbolic', rather than properly mimetic, representation—to be found in the portrayal of character in visual media. It is regrettably common for this passage to be erroneously paraphrased as claiming that music is, *tout court,* the most mimetic of the arts, but we must correct this by observing that Aristotle refers only to the mimesis of character. Understanding of the point is obscured by our ignorance of Greek music, but it appears to be the case that what is involved is a putatively precise correspondence between the expressive movement of music and the 'kinetic' dimension of active human character.[14] If this remains an alien instance, the **Poetics** itself, with its tendency towards the idea of dramatic enactment (which is not to be confused with performance as such) as the essence of poetic mimesis, is more easily comprehensible. What underlies this thrust in Aristotle's thinking is the concern for as close a formal match as possible between poetry and its human subject matter, and this leads to the stress on enactive mimesis in which the direct speech of agents gets us as near as language can come to the nature of significant action itself. Such a degree of correspondence is, however, not consistently adhered to as a necessary criterion of mimesis, and it is perhaps possible to see why. The more that certain types of formal equivalence are pressed, the weaker becomes the unifying factor in all the mimetic activities mentioned in the first chapter of the **Poetics.** Although interested in refining the concept of mimesis analytically by his differential scheme of media, objects, and modes, outlined in the first three chapters of the treatise, Aristotle had nonetheless inherited, particularly from Plato, a general and loose concept of mimesis, and the preservation of such a concept depended on a willingness to accept a fundamental element of mimetic correspondence which cut across the divisions between the arts, and so made intelligible, for example, the kinship between poetry and painting.

The second dimension of mimesis, which is in theory independent of the first but in practice not always kept apart from it, concerns the cognitive status and value of the mimetic work and its content. However the formal relation, as I have called it, is construed for particular types of mimetic art (as direct equivalence, as a kind of symbolism, or as some more complex kind of representation), the question still remains to be asked about the truth-value of mimetic works. The question's importance can be seen in the context of Plato's discussions of mimesis, since if his polemics against art are characterised by a refusal to separate the cognitive aspect of mimesis from the formal (so that the supposed limitation of the latter to literal copying con-

demns its products to the realm of the derivative and spurious), Plato elsewhere intriguingly gestures towards a notion of philosophical mimesis which would allow its powers of signification to rise above its formal limitations (see ch. IV). Aristotle may have been influenced by this latter fact towards the development of his own doctrine that artistic mimesis is capable of representing universals or general truths, and need not be tied to the reproduction of particulars. It is far from clear, however, that Aristotle sees this capacity as belonging intrinsically to mimesis, for he continues to acknowledge cases of the mimetic representation of particulars, as well, of course, as non-mimetic ways, above all philosophy itself, in which universals can be communicated.[15] Because of this doubt, it might be legitimate to conclude that the chief refinement in Aristotle's view of mimesis pertains to its formal aspect, that is to the analysis of the various types of correspondence to reality which can be achieved in different artistic media (visual, linguistic, musical, etc.); and, as a corollary of this, to regard the claims made in **Poetics** 9 for the quasi-philosophical potential of poetry as expressing a principle of the use of mimesis, rather than its necessary attribute. But as the **Poetics** stands, such a conclusion would be tidier than is warranted by the evidence, which suggests a coalescence, as in Plato, between considerations of the formal and the cognitive issues raised by mimetic art.

This preliminary approach to Aristotle's concept of mimesis should demonstrate the difficulty of reaching a clear-cut interpretation of it; but two broad inferences, which will receive further substantiation in ch. IV, can be drawn from the preceding argument: first, that Aristotle unquestioningly accepts the existence of a distinctive group of mimetic arts, and that by so doing he commits himself to a compendious criterion of mimesis as a form of correspondence in which some aspect of reality is reconstituted in a medium as close as possible in equivalence to the object; secondly, that he is prepared to attribute to some mimetic works a cognitive significance which goes beyond particulars to the embodiment of universals. The relationship between this notion of mimesis and the underlying idea of *technê* which I earlier examined can now be clarified by a brief look at a further area of terminology— the *poiêsis* word-group—which denotes poetry itself (and perhaps some other mimetic arts too) but is also closely related to *technê* as a whole. The root meaning of the *poiêsis* word-group is 'making' or 'producing', and for Aristotle all *technê* involves *poiêsis* of some kind: the former is the rationalised, systematic capacity for the latter. But the specific application of these same terms, *poiêsis* and its cognates, to poetry was a linguistic development well established by Aristotle's time. Extracted from their philosophical context, the remarks of Diotima in Plato's *Symposium* furnish a reliable description of the phenomenon: 'You know,' she says to Socrates, 'that making *(poiêsis)* takes many forms.

something comes into being from non-being, so that the activities of all crafts and arts *(technai)* are types of *poiêsis,* and the craftsmen are all makers *(poiêtai)* . . . Nevertheless . . . some have different names, and a determinate part of the whole area of *poiêsis,* the part concerned with music and verse, is called by the name that belongs to the whole. For it is only this part that is called *poiêsis* (making/'poetry') and its practitioners *poiêtai* (makers/'poets')' (205b8-c9).

Since Aristotle himself used *poiêsis* terminology both for the definition of *technê* in general and to describe a particular type of mimetic *technê* (poetry), it is reasonable to suppose that the latter took some of its colouring from the former. In this respect we can both compare and contrast Aristotle's position with ordinary usage, since twice in the **Poetics** he adverts to the normal conception of the poet as a maker *(poiêtês)* of verses (47b 13-16, 51b 27-9). Against this Aristotle opposes his own conception of the poet as a maker of plot-structures *(muthoi),* that is unified mimetic representations of human action. An immediate point to note is that this new definition of poetic art clearly presupposes, similarly to the case of *technê* . . . , that the language of *poiêsis* has lost any unnecessary material connotations: what the poet 'makes' or produces is not a tangible object, but a mimetic construct in language (and other media) to be apprehended by the mind. It is profitable to draw a further contrast here with the passage in Plato's *Phaedo* (61b) in which Socrates describes the content of poetic composition as *muthoi,* the term adapted to his theory by Aristotle: but what Socrates has in mind is setting Aesop's fables *(muthoi)* to verse, so that the making *(poiêsis)* which is the 'poetry' would precisely be the making of verses.[16] In ch. 9 of the **Poetics,** on the other hand, Aristotle argues that, whether or not the poet's raw material is pre-existent (traditional myths being an equivalent to Socrates' Aesopic fables), his task as a poet-maker *(poiêtês)* is still to design and organise his plot-structure in such a way as to give its content the universal intelligibility of which Aristotle believes poetry to be capable.

The elements of *poiêsis* in the Aristotelian concepts of *technê* and poetry are mutually reinforcing. In neither case does the maker necessarily produce a tangible artefact, though in some *technai* he will do so. But whatever his media, the maker aims, by the application of rational method, to bring something into being, and in the case of the mimetic arts this is, if successful, a unified construction which must be comprehended as embodying a representation of a possible reality.[17] Although the **Poetics** elaborates this doctrine in relation to poetry, there is no doubt that Aristotle presupposes a comparable attitude to arts such as music and painting. Thus we can be confident that he would have said that the painter, for example, is not a maker of shapes and colours: these are his media, but they are

used to produce, to bring into being by rational art, an image of possible human reality, and an image capable of being understood, at its best, in universal rather than particular terms. Consideration of either the specific *poiêsis* of poetry or the generic *poiêsis* of all mimetic art therefore brings us back round to the question which was earlier raised about the cognitive value of mimesis in Aristotle's aesthetic thinking. The 'making' which is the procedure of the poet's or the painter's art is the imparting of design and order to his material, and this design will carry a mimetic correspondence to a conception of reality. But the Aristotelian emphasis on coherence and unity, as we find it applied to the concrete doctrine of poetic plot-structure, gives the poet a very different responsibility for his artistic product from the one assigned to him by Plato, in whose eyes the artist must be accountable for his raw material, not just for what he makes of it. Aristotelian *poiêsis* is a positive, potent force, whose implications of productive control and purpose should dispel any lingering associations of the derivative or passive from the understanding of mimesis. *Poiêsis* and mimesis are tightly interwoven strands of the thinking which lies behind the **Poetics;** and if *poiêsis* cannot solve all the problems of mimesis for us, it does at any rate help to bond together the elements of *technê* and mimesis in the Aristotelian concept of mimetic art which it is my aim to delineate.

The argument up to this point has deliberately tolerated the linguistic intricacy and cumbersomeness which are entailed in any attempt to stay close to Aristotle's own language, and so to avoid superficial assimilation of his ideas to later views of art. There is also, however, the lesser danger that the peculiar features of Aristotle's thought will be allowed to exaggerate the alien ethos of his concept of mimetic art, and to impede recognition of the affinities it may have with later attitudes. It will consequently serve a purpose to draw some provisional conclusions about Aristotle's understanding of the mimetic *technai,* and to try to relate it to some of the more characteristic modern beliefs on the subject. The basis for such a comparison, as earlier indicated, is the fact that the range of activities circumscribed by mimetic *technê* agrees approximately with the standard modern categorisation of the arts. The historical link between the two lies in the transmission of ancient notions of mimesis and imitation to the Renaissance, and the elaboration of these notions in the period of neo-classicism into the foundation for a system of fine arts whose central principle was the 'imitation of nature'.[18] But we saw earlier . . . that the origin of this principle in Aristotle is very far removed from its later use as an aesthetic slogan, since in contrast to the vagueness of the latter the Aristotelian formula stands for a philosophy of all rational productive activity, both mimetic and non-mimetic. If neo-classical imitation of nature is manipulable to various effects (including, for instance, a strong idealism) the effects (including, for instance, a strong idealism) the original analogy between *technê* and nature not only has broader scope but commits its holder to a specific teleology of mimetic art.

This teleology differs less from the orthodox neo-classical aesthetic, however, than it does from the attitudes to art which have grown up since the eighteenth century and to some extent in reaction against neo-classicism. Typical theorists of the sixteenth and seventeenth centuries might have understood Aristotle's insistence on an objective concept of art, structured by the rational relation between the artist and his work, much better than could the Romantic or his modern epigone. The shift represented by the rise of Romanticism can be located, for present purposes, in the new aesthetic centrality of the idea of creative imagination, an idea for which the eighteenth century discovered that Longinus was a much more sympathetic classical source than Aristotle or Horace. The contrast with Aristotle can be illuminated by observing that the origins of this concept of imagination are to be traced in the ascription to the artist of free, creative powers analogous to those of a God who can bring a world into being *ex nihilo.*[19] For Aristotle, on the other hand, the model for *technê,* which embraces all mimetic art, is a nature whose generative workings are regulated by the teleological realisation of form in matter. Creative imagination is inimical to tradition and sees the spring of art within the exceptional capacities of special individuals. Hence the importance in modern aesthetic attitudes of various notions of *expression,* usually centring around the idea of that which is brought forth from the mind of the artist and given new or unique form. While Aristotle can of course acknowledge the unusual abilities of certain individuals, above all Homer, and the importance of their contribution to the development of an art, this development itself is not only the essential framework within which particular achievements must be placed, but the unfolding of a *natural* potential: it constitutes a large-scale dimension of teleology to arch over the small-scale teleology of individual mimetic works. Aristotle's artist may be gifted, but his gifts are not unique or *sui generis;* they are at the objective service of his art, to be harnessed to the realisation of aims which have a potential existence that is independent of the individual (and which, as we saw, have been realised before and will be realised again). And if mimetic art can be said at all, in Aristotle's scheme of things, to be expressive, it is certainly not expressive of the artist himself. For not only is Aristotle's concept of art objectivist, but its accent falls on the universal significance to which mimesis can attain: mimesis makes art outward-facing, and locates its subject in general human reality, not in the privileged inner experiences of the artist.

A caution must be entered here. My characterisation of one of the dominant strands in modern attitudes to art

is not meant to imply that free, creative imagination is a universally accepted principle, or that aesthetic objectivism has altogether disappeared. The contrast I have drawn is a deliberately schematic one, designed to put Aristotle's views in perspective. The danger of simplification, both of Aristotle's and of later positions, becomes acute when we reach the question of the purpose of function of art. Without raising this question, and seeking an answer to it in the *Poetics* and in Aristotle's other references to mimetic art, it is difficult to feel that the concept I have so far analysed is a fully rounded one. But we here encounter a striking paradox which may serve as an appropriate introduction to the next stage of my argument. In the two broadest phases which can be demarcated in European theory and criticism of art since the Renaissance, those of neo-classicism and the Romantic reaction (with all its modern off-shoots) against neo-classicism, it is remarkable that Aristotle has been enlisted within both as a supporter of the prevailing view of the function of art. Under neo-classicism, the *Poetics* was used as a pillar of the dominant moralism, according to which art could be justified in terms of its capacity to be ethically edifying and improving. In the reaction against such views, the last two centuries have seen a growing, though hardly uniform, adherence to the belief that art's ultimate legitimation lies in some sort of self-sufficient pleasure or gratification. Such a belief does not require Aristotelian sanction, but it is nonetheless discernible that it has influenced the common reading of the *Poetics* and has led to an orthodoxy in which Aristotle's view of art is held to be essentially formalist and aestheticist: that is, one which attributes an autotelic status to poetry and the other arts, which grounds the experience of them in pleasure, which identifies the properties of works of art as purely internal attributes of form, and which entails a strong divorce between art, on the one hand, and morality, religion and politics, on the other. Thus the *Poetics,* despite the major differences from modern views of art which I have tried to locate in it, is brought into line with the aesthetic consensus which has evolved since the Enlightenment, and in which art has been freed from what is often considered to be the taint of a direct concern with, or effect on, the ideas and values belonging to the realms indicated above.

Alert to the possibility that it may be wrong to hope to adjudicate between these two antithetical views of the *Poetics,* the didactic and the formalist, in the terms in which their proponents themselves formulate the dichotomy, I want now to undertake a scrutiny of Aristotle's references to the pleasure or pleasures of mimetic art, in the expectation that it will bring to light a vital area of the treatise's philosophical foundations.

That art is pleasurable, and in its own peculiar ways, is a datum of experience which the Greeks did not need to wait for theorists or philosophers to call to their attention. The seductive pleasures even of works of art which portray exceptional suffering are attested from the beginnings of Greek poetry, and not only attested but illuminated in a number of Homeric scenes with a dramatic insight which is irreducible to prosaic paraphrase.[20] But from the philosophical point of view, there remained much scope, and much need, for the investigation of the subject. Aristotle had more than one good reason to be interested in discriminating between the types of pleasure which might enter into the experience of poetry and the other arts, not least because the need to take pleasure in the right things was a pervasive principle of his educational and ethical thought. Aristotle's own philosophical psychology posited a rich and complex range of pleasures, related to particular types of activity and the human faculties employed in them. He conceives of pleasure primarily as a level or aspect of experience which supervenes on and completes (like the 'bloom' of those in their physical prime) any activity in which man's abilities are put successfully to their natural use. Pleasure marks the fulfilment of a natural potential, and to understand how and why pleasure arises in individual cases, we must comprehend the special character of the given activities.[21] In view of the cohesiveness which we have seen his attitude to the mimetic *technai* to possess, we would reasonably expect a conception of aesthetic pleasure to be an integral element of Aristotle's thinking about mimesis.

A further factor to prompt reflection on the subject was the variety of references to pleasure in Plato's discussions of art. In the *Laws* and elsewhere Plato claimed that the ordinary man's expectation of art was that it should provide pleasure, and he alleged contemptuously that pleasure was the sole popular standard of artistic merit.[22] The Athenian at first rejects such a mentality as 'blasphemous', and later observes that the decadence of recent Greek poetry has followed from an indiscriminate belief in the audience's pleasure as the aim of art and the criterion of success. Yet Plato's spokesman himself comes round to arguing that a certain, very different kind of pleasure *is* to be desired in art: the pleasure of the educated and morally upright man. This correct and laudable species of pleasure will be the result simply of the artistic presentation of moral truth—the dramatic portrayal, for example, of virtuous men. Elsewhere, in the difficult *Philebus* (51), Plato argues that the apparent pleasures of art are actually false and synthetic, and he contrasts with the specious pleasure taken in an artistic form the true pleasure which may be derived from contemplation of intrinsically, that is geometrically, beautiful shapes, and perfect pure colours. Without venturing any further, then, into the shifting significances of Plato's treatments of this subject, we already have glimpses in these two passages alone of four different kinds of pleasure arguably relevant to art: the ordinary man's uncultured pleasure, which will involve the grati-

fication of the lower part of the soul; the good man's moral pleasure in the celebration of virtue; pleasure from the sensual forms used in mimetic works; and the pleasure of contemplating pure shapes, colours and musical tones.

In the *Poetics* too we encounter a wide range of references to pleasure. Before attempting to provide a synthesising interpretation of these, it will be as well to offer a preliminary tabulation of the types or occasions of pleasure mentioned in the treatise, roughly in the order in which they occur.

(a) Ch. 4, 48b 8ff.: *natural* pleasure taken in mimetic works *(mimêmata)*, even when these represent objects, such as corpses, which are inherently unpleasant.[23] The cause of this pleasure is that the experience entails a process of understanding and learning. I shall contend below that we have also to put in this category the pleasure which, according to ch. 24, 60a 17, derives from 'the wonderful', which is itself closely related, as ch. 9, 52a 1-11 indicates, to the arousal of pity and fear by tragic poetry.

(b) Ch. 4, 48b 17-19: pleasure due to the execution, surface or some other such aspect of a work of mimetic art; this pleasure is *independent* of the work's mimetic status.

(c) Ch. 6, 49b 25-31: 'pleasurably garnished' language is given in the definition of tragedy, and then explained as 'language with rhythm and melody'—that is, the sensual elaborations (both verbal and musical) of the lyric sections of tragic drama (called 'the greatest of the garnishings' or embellishments at 50b 16), and probably also the rhythmical dimension of the ordinary spoken parts of a play. Similarly, in ch. 26, 62a 16f., *mousikê,* which here means something close though not identical to the 'pleasurably garnished' language of ch. 6, is cited as a source of vivid pleasures which give tragedy an advantage over epic. This is evidently not meant to deny pleasurable embellishments altogether to the epic poet's art: the pleasure of epic style may be at least part of what is meant in the reference to Homer at 60b 2.

(d) Ch. 6, 50b 16f.: although denying that theatrical spectacle is strictly part of the dramatist's art, Aristotle does describe it as 'stirring' or 'seductive'. The word he uses is *psuchagôgikon,*[24] and its cognate verb is found earlier in ch. 6, 50a 33, applied to the effect of tragic reversal and recognition. This helps to establish that Aristotle is prepared to attribute a strong emotive potential to spectacle, though it is less well defined, and obviously much less valuable for him, than the potential of the complex plot-structure. Such emotional effects carry implicit pleasure with them. The point is confirmed in ch. 14, 53b 8-11, where the use of spectacle to produce the specious effect of 'the portentous' is frowned on as supplying a pleasure alien to the true tragic experience of pity and fear, for which see (g) below.

(e) Ch. 6, 50a 39- 50b 3: reference is here made to the contrasting types of pleasure afforded by the (hypothetical) painting which consists of random patches of colour, and the colourless outline sketch or drawing. The latter is said to be analogous to the plot-structure of tragedy.

(f) Ch. 9, 51b 23, 26: Aristotle here touches in passing on the pleasure of tragedy, in making the point that it is unaffected by whether the material of a play is conventional or invented. For another general reference to pleasure see 62b 1, in connection with the superiority of tragic concentration over epic diffuseness.

(g) Finally, there are four important references in the **Poetics** to the particular pleasure of tragedy (to which there are corresponding comic (53a 36) and epic (59a 21, 62b 13f.) pleasures): ch. 6, 50a 33-5; ch. 13, 53a 35f.; ch. 14, 53b 10-14; ch. 26, 62b 13f. The third of these passages, which stipulates 'the pleasure arising from pity and fear through mimesis', is the fullest, and indicates that the proper pleasure of tragedy is linked directly with the experience of its distinctive emotions, pity and fear (hence the justification for the inclusion of the first passage in the list), while resting on the basis of the generic pleasure of poetic mimesis ((a) above). The notion of pleasures proper or peculiar to individual activities appears prominently in Aristotle's mature views on the subject in **EN** Book 10.[25]

I think it is possible to advance beyond this preliminary catalogue, and to integrate most of this material into a coherent pattern, by deducing three main levels or types of aesthetic pleasure—that is, to reiterate, pleasure derivable from the mimetic arts. It would certainly be fanciful to try to forge a completely systematic theory out of this collection of passages: Aristotle draws analogies with the visual arts, but even so it is not always easy to see just how his principles could be elaborated for mimetic art in general. But the following scheme of analysis is economical, positive, and based squarely on the evidence cited above, with supplementary guidance from other relevant passages in the corpus. I shall attempt to define and analyse the three types of aesthetic pleasure in ascending order of both importance and delicateness of interpretation.

In the lowest position in the scheme comes the inessential, and potentially inappropriate, enjoyment of theatrical spectacle, *opsis,* by which Aristotle probably means chiefly the visual presentation of the actors (see Appendix 3). In this first case, there are no grounds for extrapolating from poetry to other arts; *opsis* is not even a feature of all poetry (epic lacks it: 59b 10, 60a 14), but only of dramatic poetry in performance. Fur-

thermore, in his animadversions on spectacle Aristotle does not have in mind the general visual aspect of performance, but the specific exploitation of it for emotional effect. Thus, properly used, *opsis* can contribute to the tragic effect of pity and fear (53b 1f.), and I suggested earlier that this must also be part of Aristotle's point at the end of ch. 6, when he describes the potency of spectacle with a term already applied to the elements of the complex plot-structure. It is also in this latter passage, however, that spectacle is relegated to the status of an accessory art. This severely limits Aristotle's attention to it within the theory of tragedy, but the brief acknowledgements of its capability should not be wholly forgotten. We can probably infer that the correct use of *opsis* would be regarded simply as visual reinforcement of the intrinsic dramatic effect, and the pleasure accruing from the former should therefore be categorised as a secondary manifestation of the true and proper pleasure of tragedy, to which I shall be returning. In any case, Aristotle's concern at the start of **Poetics** 14 seems to be more with the *incorrect* use of spectacle to produce a purely sensational pleasure that would distract from, or impede, the appropriate tragic emotions and their concomitant pleasure. The 'portentous' is dismissed as a spurious substitute for these emotions,[26] and whatever else one may think about Aristotle's sharp divorce between dramatic poetry and its performance, his attitude at least confirms his philosophical interest in discriminating between types of pleasure, and in evaluating their relative worth.

The devaluation of *opsis* is also a reflection of Aristotle's aim of shifting the locus of the poet's art from the realm of the sensual to that of the cognitive. But a more subtle and significant indication of this aim is provided by the distinction drawn in **Poetics** 4 between the natural pleasure derivable from mimetic works, and the sensual pleasure which may be taken in them independently of their mimetic status. It is the latter which is the second of the three main levels of aesthetic pleasure to be analysed.[27] Outside the **Poetics** there are other passages in which Aristotle differentiates between sensual and intellectual pleasures, and it is evidently in the former category that we must place the pleasure noted in item (b) in my earlier list: a pleasure which can be given by works of art entirely in respect of their sensible properties, and without any specifically cognitive or emotional element. Into this category we must also bring item (c) and the first of the types referred to in item (e). The objects of this species of pleasure are the forms, textures, patterns and sounds of art, apprehended in and for themselves and not as the medium of mimetic significance. This is the disjunction which Aristotle makes explicitly at 48b 17-19, by immediate reference to a visual example, but as part of a larger argument whose scope covers also the whole of poetic mimesis. Although condensed, this passage is sufficient to establish that sensual pleasure cannot, in Aristotle's terms, properly account for the experience of any mimetic art, though it is recognised as having a legitimate, secondary part to play. That such pleasure seems to be most readily identifiable in the case of the visual arts is suggested by the fact that in two of the three relevant passages of the *Poetics* cited above Aristotle makes his point by reference to painting (items (b) and (e)). If we ask what the applicability of the concept is to the non-visual arts, Aristotle's answer is embodied in what he has to say about the rhythmic and musical enhancements of language ((c) above): it is the most directly sensible aspects of the language of poetry, its rhythmical and melodic 'garnishings', as the philosopher regards them, which supply the closest equivalent to the sensual forms and colours of visual art.[28] But the inference is not easily to be elaborated, since Aristotle's view of the mimetic nature of music reduces the scope for the derivation of a purely sensual pleasure from it, and the evidence of both the *Poetics* and the *Rhetoric* implies that this qualification holds good even for rhythm independently of melody.[29]

It is at any rate clear that any sensual pleasure afforded by poetry cannot in Aristotle's theory be of more than secondary significance, and it is worthwhile to note that this inference has a bearing on his attitude to *performance,* since the availability of pleasure from the rhythmic and melodic aspects of poetry clearly depends on this. In the case of the rhythms of spoken verse, this condition would be satisfied by the standard practice of reading aloud (alluded to perhaps, for different purposes, at 53b 3-7),[30] but for sections of lyric poetry presumably no alternative to musically accompanied performance would be sufficient. Various lines of thought therefore converge to produce a devaluation of lyric in the *Poetics:* the conception of its distinctive features as an embellishment or 'garnishing' of tragedy (and consequently inessential); the separation of poetry proper from performance and its attendant arts; and the relegation of the sensual pleasure of poetry to the level of the subordinate. That this devaluation does indeed result in a failure on Aristotle's part to do justice to the lyric dimension of Greek tragedy is something I shall argue in greater detail in ch. VIII.

But it is not only the particular connection of sensual pleasure with performance and with lyric poetry which explains its status in the *Poetics,* for we have seen that the passage in ch. 4 where Aristotle distinguishes between a cognitive and a sensual pleasure from works of art refers directly to a visual example, and suggests that the principle ought to be applicable to mimetic art in general. If so, the reason must be sought in a larger aspect of Aristotle's philosophy. At the opening of the *Metaphysics* Aristotle makes the famous pronouncement that 'all men by nature desire knowledge', and he goes on to relate this postulate to the observation that we value the senses, regardless of utility, for the pleasure they afford us. This pleasure, however, particu-

larly that of sight, is not merely sensual; its cause is the cognitive content of our perceptions, the contribution which they make to the acquisition of knowledge to which our very nature predisposes us. Hence the supreme value of sight, for 'this is the sense which allows us to apprehend the most, and which reveals the most discriminations'.[31] This passage in fact generalises the principle which is enunciated specifically for the experience of mimetic art in *Poetics* 4, and it indicates the broader foundation on which Aristotle bases his claim that the true pleasure of this experience entails a process of understanding and learning. The negative corollary of this is that the purely sensual enjoyment of form, colour, texture, rhythm and so on, does not involve the full use of the senses' natural cognitive capacity.

It is, then, to the elucidation of the third and highest level of aesthetic pleasure posited by the *Poetics* that I must now turn. Two items from my original list are left for consideration: the natural pleasure of learning and understanding through mimesis (a), and the proper pleasure of tragedy (g), 'the pleasure arising from pity and fear through mimesis' (taking the passages in (f) to represent indefinite allusions to the latter). What I wish to argue is that these two items in fact present aspects of the same phenomenon, or, more precisely, that they are related as genus to species, so that the pleasure proper to tragedy is one example, and perhaps for Aristotle the supreme instance, of the generic concept of pleasure from mimetic works sketched in *Poetics* 4. But to establish the cogency of this position, which has not been widely adopted in interpretation of the treatise, will require some close reasoning, and in the first place a scrutiny of the crucial passage in ch. 4.[32]

It is a paradoxical part of the difficulty of dealing with *Poetics* 4 that its train of thought is ostensibly so plain and unremarkable. It is possible to carry away from a reading of it, seduced by its very simplicity, and undisturbed by consideration of how Aristotle's reasoning here must be integrated with what he offers later in the book, the impression of nothing more than the concise formulation of rudimentary and preliminary points. Nor is this impression entirely erroneous; but it is essential to dissociate the straightforwardness of the argument from the question of how far-reaching the implications of it can be seen to be.[33] The theme of the first half of the chapter is the original causes of poetry, though the progression of thought, with its general references to mimesis and its visual examples, leaves little room to doubt that the enquiry applies to all mimetic art. Aristotle suggests, with typical ingenuousness, two 'natural' causes for poetry. It is possible, I believe, to discern that these are really facets of a single explanation. The first cause or reason is the instinct in human beings from childhood onwards to engage in mimesis, for which we here need to have in mind at least the two ideas of 'imitation' and 'enactment' (static or active representation). Moreover, even early mimesis involves learning, though Aristotle makes the point so briefly that it is impossible to determine how wide a range of behaviour he means his audience to understand.[34] At any rate, we can say that alongside man as a political creature and a rational creature, we may juxtapose, in Aristotle's perspective, man as the most mimetic of creatures. Mimesis is rooted in human nature, and is implicated in distinctively human patterns of action. We recognise readily that within the naturalistic terms of Aristotelian philosophy mimesis is thus vindicated in the face of the intrinsically suspect and shallow status to which Platonic metaphysics had often condemned it, and that the mimetic *technai* now have a doubly natural grounding and sanction: first, as I earlier demonstrated, in the teleological character of *technê*, productive art, in general; secondly, in the human propensity towards mimesis. The mimetic arts consummate this propensity by developing it into various types of rational art.

Aristotle's second cause of poetry also concerns mimesis,[35] but adjusts the point of view to that of the recipient or spectator, rather than that of the agent or artist. To the universal instinct for engaging in mimesis Aristotle now adds the equally natural pleasure which is taken in the mimetic activities or works of others, and from his elaboration of the point we gather that these two factors coalesce as elements of a single phenomenon. For the underlying explanation of the pleasure taken in the apprehension of mimetic objects (which need not be *physical* objects) is the primary human pleasure in learning: learning and understanding therefore appear as the basis of both the active and the receptive interest in mimesis (48b 12f. refers back to 5-8). Moreover, the cognition involved in mimesis is equally a source of pleasure in both cases, since Aristotle's claim that there is a natural human instinct for mimesis entails, given his philosophy of pleasure, that men take a natural pleasure in exercising it as well as in appreciating its products. The two causes of poetry, then, and of mimesis in general, turn out to be aspects of a single psychological and cultural hypothesis, and one which contains the nucleus of a highly serious concept of aesthetic pleasure.

One reason for a common refusal to take that last step in my argument seems to be a sense, to which I have already referred, that ch. 4 of the *Poetics* represents a preliminary or marginal part of the treatise, and can offer no insight into the centre of Aristotle's idea of poetry or art. It is, of course, the case that this passage is initially offered by way of accounting for the *origins* or causes of poetry: it furnishes what might be regarded as the psychological and anthropological premises from which Aristotle can advance to the sketch of poetic evolution which follows in the rest of the chapter. But to infer from this that Aristotle's causes

of poetry have only a hypothetical or historical reference, and have no bearing on the developed forms of art, would simply be to overlook the fact that these causes are presented as putatively permanent, because natural, data about human engagement in mimetic activities. Origins correspond to fulfilment: in Aristotle's beginning is his end. The argument is, in fact, not properly historical at all, but philosophical—committed, that is, to the explication of underlying and universal causes. It should be remarked, moreover, that Aristotle's verbs are all in the present tense in this passage: 'mimetic activity is natural to men from childhood onwards . . . man is the most mimetic of creatures . . . we enjoy looking at pictures . . . ', and so on. Aristotle's conclusion that 'if one has not seen the object of a picture before, it will not produce pleasure *qua* work of mimesis, but by virtue of its execution etc.'[36] therefore unequivocally states a principle about the status and comprehension of mimetic works in general, though its implications remain to be drawn out. While external confirmation of this is hardly needed, it happens to be available in the fact that Aristotle makes the same point in very similar language in Book 1 of the *Rhetoric,* where he affirms, without reference to anything but *existing* forms of mimetic art, that the aesthetic pleasure derived from them contains a process of recognition and understanding implicit in the appreciation.[37]

That Aristotle should regard the basis of aesthetic pleasure to be an experience for which he finds the language of 'learning', 'comprehending' and 'reasoning' apt, is a conclusion of major import for his philosophical view of art, and particularly of poetry.[38] Yet the clarity of this position belies the problems which confront a deeper interpretation of it. Perhaps the most immediate of these problems arises from the fact that in explaining the natural human roots of poetry, Aristotle chooses, as he also does in the passage from the *Rhetoric* mentioned above, an illustration from visual art, and one, moreover, of arguably disappointing simplicity. The example of a picture, or other visual work, which portrays an identifiable (though not necessarily a real) figure, and to which the mind of the beholder may respond with the reasoning, 'this is so-and-so', might well be thought to shed little enough light on the type of cognition involved in the experience of paintings, and none at all on the understanding of poetry. Given the ambitious scope of the context—an explanation of the psychological causes of poetry, and implicitly of all mimesis—we must assume both that Aristotle gives a visual instance of something which can take non-visual forms, and also that he is deliberately citing a simple case of an experience which must have more complex varieties (in the apprehension of both visual and non-visual art).[39] In one respect the simplicity of the illustration does serve well to mark the tenor of the passage as a whole, for Aristotle is sketching a view of a large range of human activity but contending that there is a fundamental unity in the experiences which underlie it; the fact that the passage contains references to both the playing of children and the philosopher's pleasure in knowledge, is significant of the potential scope of the argument. The implicit comparison between the pleasure of mimetic art and the pleasure of philosophical knowledge recurs more pointedly in the **Parts of Animals** (645a 7-15), where we also find the example of unattractive animals— animals which, because *ex hypothesi* repellent, cannot be a source, whether in art or in life, of *sensual* pleasure. Although this passage is explicit on the reason for philosophical pleasure (the understanding of causes), it leaves that of art less than clear; but given its analogy between art and nature (a theme explored earlier in this chapter) it may not be unreasonable to infer a kind of cognition of causes in the pleasure derived from mimetic works too.

The outline of a cognitive theory of aesthetic pleasure in **Poetics** 4 accords with Aristotle's mature view that pleasure involves the natural exercise of human faculties. In the experience of mimetic works any element of purely sensual pleasure must be subordinate to the processes of recognition and learning which constitute the proper response to mimesis. Without cognitive recognition, the status of the mimetic work—the representation of a possible reality which it embodies—cannot be grasped and therefore cannot be enjoyed, though the senses may take separate pleasure in certain material aspects of the work (48b 17-19). But the use of a rudimentary visual example at **Poetics** 48b 15-17 (a general mannerism, incidentally, of Aristotle's philosophical method) seems at first sight to impede further illumination of this fundamental layer in the thought of the treatise. In order to make headway with the interpretation of Aristotle's concept of aesthetic pleasure, we need therefore to explore the possibility of implicit connections between what is said in the first part of ch. 4 and some of the work's other doctrines. Two lines of enquiry can be initially distinguished. The first is to examine the relation between the general cognitive pleasure of ch. 4 and the 'proper pleasure' of tragedy referred to elsewhere in the work. After this, it will be necessary to consider more closely the idea of comprehension or learning which Aristotle ascribes to the enjoyment and appreciation of mimesis.

An attempt to combine **Poetics** 4 with later parts of the treatise is encouraged, among other things, by the passage from Book 1 of the **Rhetoric** which I mentioned earlier. Aristotle there associates understanding with 'wonder', both of which he says are usually pleasurable: understanding, because, in short, it fulfils man's nature, and wonder, because it involves a desire to learn. Elsewhere we find Aristotle repeating what Plato had said before him, that wonder is the source or origin of philosophy itself, because it represents man's primary thirst for knowledge.[40] We have here a pointer

to one possible link between parts of the **Poetics,** for there are a number of passages in the treatise where Aristotle touches on the poet's use of 'the wonderful'. The most revealing of these occurs near the end of ch. 9, where it is proposed that pity and fear are best aroused in tragedy by events which happen 'unexpectedly but on account of one another', and that such events will produce wonder more than would chance happenings. It emerges here that there is a kinship, in tragedy, between pity and fear and 'the wonderful': the same kinds of tragic events (in the ideally complex drama, at any rate) should elicit both. Furthermore, the effect of wonder to which Aristotle here refers is explicitly related to the intelligible causation of the events of tragedy (notwithstanding the immediate impact of surprise), and that this is so is corroborated by the following remark that even chance events arouse more wonder when they appear to happen for a purpose— that is, *appear* to be part of an intelligible sequence.[41] If, then, we put this passage together with the one from **Rhetoric** 1, wonder becomes a link between the tragic emotions, on one side, and our understanding of the structure of a dramatic action, on the other. Wonder itself does not seem to be simply identifiable either with the particular emotions elicited by tragedy, or with the process of understanding: yet it has both an emotional and a cognitive significance, in that it is felt alongside—as part of the same experience as—pity and fear, and offers a challenge to the mind which, ideally, stimulates and leads on to comprehension or knowledge. Aristotle's comments on wonder in the **Poetics** and **Rhetoric** help a little to strengthen the case for trying to see the general thesis of **Poetics** 4 and the detailed analysis of tragedy later in the treatise as interrelated and mutually illuminating.

In the juxtaposition of the tragic emotions with wonder in ch. 9 of the **Poetics** we have an indication that the peculiar pleasure of tragedy, which Aristotle defines in ch. 14 as 'the pleasure arising from pity and fear through mimesis', should be regarded as one species of the generic aesthetic pleasure whose elements are sketched in ch. 4. Such a claim gives some illustration of the need to seek out associations which our text of the treatise omits to make explicit, and which Aristotle may either have taken for granted or else have drawn out orally in his philosophical teaching. The cogency of such claims depends on the possibility of discerning multiple signs of underlying relations between superficially discrete ideas or doctrines, and this can, I believe, be plausibly achieved for my argument that the peculiar pleasure of tragedy represents in one specific form, adapted to the particular characteristics of the genre, Aristotle's essential or primary concept of aesthetic pleasure, in which cognition and emotion are integrated. In **Poetics** 6 Aristotle picks out the components of the complex plot as the most potent of the resources of tragedy, a remark which can only be understood in terms of the distinctive tragic emotions of his own definition. This observation is borne out by the later concentration on the complex plot in the prescriptions for the ideal tragedy. Recognition and reversal are the focus of the finest tragic plot-structure, and so the focus of the emotions aroused by it. In the passage from ch. 9 to which I have already drawn attention it can reasonably be inferred that Aristotle has these aspects of the complex plot, perhaps particularly reversal, in mind: for he says that pity and fear will be best produced by events which happen 'unexpectedly but on account of one another', and this can be taken virtually as a definition of reversal (peripeteia). It is, therefore, telling that in **Rhetoric** 1 Aristotle singles out precisely sudden and unforeseeable reversals of fortune (peripeteiai) as a source of wonder (1371b 10): they both surprise us and arouse our minds to look for an underlying explanation of the ostensibly inexplicable. Once again we see a convergence of ideas, the sign of a nexus of associations between the complex plot, the tragic emotions, and wonder, with the latter's implications for learning. To this we must add the crucial fact, which can only be stated here but will be discussed in detail in ch. VI, that Aristotle's conception of the emotions, pity and fear, itself rests on a cognitive basis: properly educated, at any rate, these emotions are not arbitrary or irrationally impulsive, but are aligned with the recognition and understanding of certain types and patterns of suffering or misfortune.

The provisional conclusion can therefore be drawn that the peculiar pleasure of tragedy is not a wholly autonomous phenomenon, a self-sufficient category of experience. It is, in the first place, a species of the genus of aesthetic pleasure, the pleasure taken in mimesis, which Aristotle defines in ch. 4 as entailing a necessary process of recognition, learning or understanding. The particular tragic species of aesthetic pleasure involves distinctive emotions, but these emotions are themselves only fully intelligible and justifiable in terms of the cognitive apprehension of certain kinds of human actions and their consequences. The proper tragic pleasure not only shows the relevance of Aristotle's general comments on aesthetic pleasure, by providing an instance of their embodiment in the theory of an individual genre, but also gives some idea of the ways in which we can expect the elementary model of ch. 4—the identification of a subject in visual art—to be complicated and made more sophisticated by internal factors of a genre. Most obviously, the example used in ch. 4 posits a case of simple recognition without an emotional dimension, whereas Aristotle's whole theory of tragedy assumes an interplay and integration of the intellect and the emotions. Furthermore, the illustration in **Poetics** 4 involves particulars ('the man in the picture is so-and-so') while Aristotle's theory of poetry assigns to the art the potential to deal with universals: the cognitive experience of such art needs correspondingly to be framed in far richer terms than those used in ch. 4's outline of Aristotle's position.[42]

If my argument so far has attempted to orient us in the direction in which the interpretation of Aristotelian aesthetic pleasure ought to lie, it also could be said to force us back to consider the notions of learning, understanding and reasoning of which both **Poetics** 4 and the passage from **Rhetoric** 1 speak in connection with mimesis. Since it is doubtful whether a scrutiny of Aristotle's terms will in itself allow us to make much progress on this point, for their range of meaning is too broad, we need to look for other clues to the elucidation of the type of cognitive experience which he takes to be implicit in the proper appreciation of mimetic works. One such clue may be furnished by a further detail which the passages from the **Poetics** and **Rhetoric** have in common. In the latter, Aristotle describes wisdom, which is virtually synonymous with philosophy, as 'the knowledge of many wonders', thus reinforcing his observations in the **Metaphysics** on the status of wonder as the motive of philosophising.[43] Philosophy is also mentioned in **Poetics** 4, where it is said that 'learning is highly pleasurable not only to philosophers but likewise, if to a lesser degree, to all other men'. While this reference to philosophy sharpens the paradoxical simplicity of the instance of cognition which Aristotle goes on to give, it should not be lightly underestimated; I cited earlier the passage from the **Parts of Animals** where the experiences of philosophy and of mimesis are also connected. It ought to be stressed that *any* direct comparison between philosophy and the mimetic arts, however seemingly casual and qualified, could hardly fail to strike someone familiar with the Platonic background as bold; and the comparison was not one which most philosophers would have easily accepted.[44] That Aristotle should have drawn it in several of his works is evidently significant. It intimates that the cognition involved in the appreciation of mimesis is not wholly different in kind, though it may be in degree, from philosophical thought, and the **Parts of Animals** passage suggests that the understanding of causes can play a part in both. We have, therefore, corroboration for the interpretation of **Poetics** 4 as of fundamental importance for the assessment of Aristotle's view of art and the experience of art, and we also have a prompting to draw into the enquiry the other passage in the **Poetics** where philosophy is mentioned.

'Poetry is more philosophical and more serious than history' (51b 5f.). If we look to this famous sentence from ch. 9 for further light on Aristotle's idea of the comprehension implicit in the experience of mimesis, we can notice at once that ch. 9 as a whole offers a more refined notion of intellectual activity than the one suggested by ch. 4's example from the visual arts. Part of the dissatisfyingly *simpliste* impression given by that earlier illustration lies in its apparent equation of understanding with factual knowledge, so that it remains uninstructive just what the value is of being able to recognise that a picture of, say, Achilles in his tent is just that. Part of the importance of *Poetics* 9 is that it helps to rectify this impression, by providing a more elaborate account of the kind of cognition which poetic mimesis calls for, as well as a more detailed placing of poetry in relation to other intellectual activities. *Poetics* 9 represents a broadening out into general poetic principles of the particular prescriptions given in the preceding chapters (6-8) for the structure and unity of tragic plot. Unity of plot, as I shall argue in ch. III, is not for Aristotle a purely formal matter, for the essential reason that plot itself, *muthos,* is not an exclusively formal concept, but a concept of significant (because mimetic) form. The criterion of unity on which so much emphasis is laid is that of 'necessity or probability', which is a principle of the logical and causal relations between actions or events. For poetry to conform to this criterion is for it to produce plots—mimetic structures of human action—which embody generalised patterns of universals, as opposed to the random particulars of history. Such universals are meant to be intelligible precisely as such: that is, the mind which contemplates poetic mimesis can perceive it and understand it as the dramatic communication of universals. This notion of poetic significance is so far from the impression given by *Poetics* 4 that, if we were to take the latter's example of visual mimesis at face-value, and infer from it a poetic equivalent, the result would be closer to ch. 9's view of *history,* with its alleged restriction to the particular, than to its claims for a quasi-philosophical art of poetry.[45] But this is an argument not for ignoring the general implications of ch. 4, but for adjusting our interpretation of it, and particularly of the status of its illustration from visual mimesis, in the light of what is to be learnt about poetic mimesis later in the treatise.

Thus *Poetics* 9 serves to carry Aristotle's view of the cognitive experience of mimesis beyond the limitations of the earlier formulation. As a further reason for treating ch. 4 as a simple statement of a principle capable of much more complex elaboration for particular arts and genres, we can now add the overall tendency of Aristotle's handling of mimesis, which I shall be returning to in ch. IV. Given that Aristotle repudiates the need for mimetic works to involve a one-to-one correspondence with reality, the simplicity of the visual example in ch. 4 is best regarded as a deliberately minimal and uncontroversial process of cognition, but one which would clearly be insufficient where the nature of the mimetic work is richer. Once this qualification on the argument of ch. 4 is accepted, it follows that further enlightenment on Aristotle's concept of aesthetic pleasure can only be pursued within the context of the study of his treatment of individual genres. I have already argued that the proper pleasure of tragedy is to be taken as a species of the generic type indicated in *Poetics* 4; the pleasure provided by the genre matches the distinctive emotional experience of it, and this emotional experience is itself integrated

with the understanding of the structure and causation of human action dramatised in the tragic plot. It therefore becomes impossible to specify more closely the nature of the proper pleasure of tragedy other than by investigating the *Poetics'* theory of tragedy as a whole, and by attempting to ascertain whether the treatise allows us to identify a particular area of universals in the apprehension of which the particular cognitive-cum-aesthetic pleasure of tragedy resides. This investigation will be undertaken in later chapters of this book.

The interpretation of aesthetic pleasure in the *Poetics* is, then, not readily to be brought to a definitive conclusion. The brevity of Aristotle's explicit remarks on the subject stands in the way of a complete exposition of his views. But it must also be said that if the line of argument I have followed is correct, then it is not altogether surprising or objectionable that Aristotle should have failed to supply a full statement of his concept of aesthetic pleasure, since the hints that we are given gesture in the direction of a theory which does not separate off aesthetic experience as discrete and self-contained, but relates it both to natural human instincts and to the 'higher' intellectual activity of philosophy. While we may regret that Aristotle did not examine these relations in more detail, he says enough to establish the fundamentally cognitive character of the experience of mimesis, and so to imply the kind of framework within which the rest of his discussion of poetry must be placed. And if we associate, as I have contended, the particular pleasure of tragedy with this underlying notion of aesthetic pleasure, then we are now in a position to see why it is so misleading, as I suggested in my introductory chapter, to attribute to Aristotle, without the necessary qualifications, the belief that the aim of poetry is pleasure:[46] misleading, principally because such a formulation of his position is likely to import an idea of aestheticism, in which the autonomy of works of art is linked with the autonomous character of our enjoyment of them. The central role of pleasure in Aristotle's aesthetics needs to be understood, as I have tried to show, in close conjunction both with the broad indications given in the treatise of the essentially cognitive experience of mimetic works, and with the particular content of the theory of tragedy. Seen in this way, aesthetic pleasure complements the analysis of the Aristotelian concept of art which I offered earlier in the chapter, for the pleasure of those who experience mimetic works is a response to the intelligible structure imposed on his material by the artist's rational capacity. And these two things, the maker's art and the recipient's pleasure, are a reflection of the natural status of mimesis and of the framework within which its individual types evolve: successful mimesis is of significance in Aristotle's eyes, and can be vindicated against Platonic condemnation, because it fulfils man's natural potential to understand reality by reconstituting it in some of the materials over which he has rational control.

Notes

[1] See Butcher viii (though cf. 113f. for reservations) and Bywater vii. For judicious criticism of Bywater see H. Lloyd-Jones, *Blood for the Ghosts* (London 1982) 18 (where the quotation shows that Bywater to some extent confused conceptualisation with terminology: on this point cf. R. Wollheim, *Art and its Objects* 2nd edn. (Cambridge 1980) 103f.). Perhaps the most ambitious attempt to find an aesthetic system in Ar. is that of Teichmüller vol. 2; for a sketch of other nineteenth-century works see Svoboda 5-9, whose own book provides flat paraphrase of some of the relevant material.

[2] On 'aesthetic' cf. also n. 27 below and p. 229 with n. 37. I limit the term in this way for the sake of historical, not philosophical, clarity: for a possible distinction between 'aesthetic' and 'artistic' see D. Best, *Philosophy* 57 (1982) 357-72 (revised as ch. 11 in his *Feeling and Reason in the Arts* (London 1985)).

[3] For *technê* in the *Poetics* see Kassel 75, *Index Graecus*. It is used of music and dance at 47a 21-8, and of the visual arts at 47a 20, as at *PA* 640a 32, 645a 12, *EN* 1141a 9-12, 1175a 24, *Pol.* 1281b 12-15. Outside Ar. *technê* is used of poetry especially by Aristophanes (see ch. I n. 16); Plato sometimes but not always denies *technê* to poetry: see Appendix 2 under 47a 20f. For the visual arts compare e.g. Emped. fr. 23.2, Plato *Gorg.* 450c 9f., *Diss.Log.* 3.10, 17, and see A. Burford, *Craftsmen in Greek and Roman Society* (London 1972) 198-217.

[4] See e.g. Collingwood 15-41 (developing a Crocean aesthetic), whose statement of the concept of *technê* (esp. 18f.) is, however, not always reliable: for necessary reservations on this and other points see S. H. Rosen, *Phronesis* 4 (1959) 135-48. On *technê* in general cf. Pollitt 32-7.

[5] *Technê* and knowledge *(epistêmê)* are carefully distinguished in *EN* 6.3-4, 1139b 14ff., but elsewhere they are often assimilated: e.g. *An.Pr.* 46a 22, *Met.* 981al-b9, *EN* 1097a 4-8, *Rhet.* 1355b 32, 1362b 26, 1392a 25f. For the use of the two terms cf. Bonitz 759, s.v. *technê*. On the relation of the *Poetics* to Ar.'s wider concept of *technê* see Olson (1965) 175-86, and on the latter alone cf. K. Bartels, 'Der Begriff Techne bei Aristoteles', in *Synusia: Festgabe für Wolfgang Schadewaldt,* edd. H. Flashar and K. Gaiser (Pfullingen 1965) 275-86. For Ar.'s abstraction of theoretical *technê* from practice note esp. *Met.* 981a 30-b 6.

[6] 'Art imitates nature': *Phys.* 194a 21f., 199a 16f., *Meteor.* 381b 6; cf. *Protr.* B13, 14, 23 Düring (1961) (with his comments on p. 187), and ps.-Ar. *Mund.* 396b 12. Other analogies: *Phys.* 194a 21ff., 199a 8-20, b 1-4, 26-32, *PA* 639b 16ff., 640a 26ff., 645a 8, *GA* 730b

7, 743a 26, *Met.* 1032a 12ff., 1034a 33ff., *EN* 1099b 21-3, 1175a 23f., *Pol.* 1333a 22-4, 1337a 1-3, *Protr.* B47 Düring (1961). For the essentially shared teleology of mind and nature see *De An.* 415b 16f. On both Ar. and others see A. J. Close, 'Philosophical Theories of Art & Nature in Classical Antiquity', *JHI* 32 (1971) 163-84.

[7] See esp. *Phys.* 194a 27ff., *GA* 762a 16f., 767a 17, 775a 20-22, *Met.* 1032a 12-14, 1070a 6-8, *EN* 1140a 10-16, *Protr.* B11-15 Düring (1961).

[8] *Met.* 1074b 10-12, *Pol.* 1329b 25ff. It is clear in both these passages that the doctrine does not apply only to arts which cater for necessities.

[9] *Met.* 981b 17ff.; for the dichotomy cf. e.g. *Pol.* 1329b 27-9 and Isoc. 4.14. We must take account of the fact that non-utilitarian pleasures can be encompassed by Ar.'s concept of *diagôgê*—cultured leisure related to happiness: *Pol.* 1338a 1-34.

[10] Esp. *Laws* 668b 9ff., where the speakers agree that everyone would accept that all products of *mousikê* (which here includes poetry, music and visual art) are 'mimesis and image-making'. Ar.'s acceptance of mimesis as a general view of art is seen most obviously at *Poet.* 47a 13-22 and *Rhet.* 1371b 4-8.

[11] For various comparisons between poetry and visual art see: Simonides *apud* Plutarch 346f, Ion of Chios fr. 8, *Diss.Log.* 3.10, Plato e.g. *Rep.* 377e, 596ff. (cf. Appendix 2 under 47a 18ff.), Isoc. 9.73-5, Ar. *Poet.* 47a 18-20, 48a 5f., 48b 9-19, 50a 26-9, 39ff., 54b 9-11, 60b 8f., 17ff., 31f., 61b 12f., *Rhet.* 1371b 6f.

[12] On this flaw (or polemical tendentiousness) in *Rep.* 10 see Annas's article, and cf. more generally Keuls 33-47.

[13] For this idea see e.g. *Hom.Hymn Apollo* 163f., Plato *Rep.* 598c, *Soph.* 234b (but note *Crat.* 432b-c for a logical qualification), and the famous story about Zeuxis and Parrhasius at Pliny *NH* 35.65. Note also the idea of visual works like *living* things, à la Daedalus: Pind. *Ol.* 7.52, Eurip. fr. 372, Plato *Phdr.* 275d. On artistic 'deception' cf. ch. I n.20.

[14] See ch. IV p. 125 and n.29.

[15] *Poet.* 48b 15-19 clearly cites a visual instance of the mimesis of particulars (though the *implications* are wider: see pp. 73ff.) and 51b 14f. refers to the equivalent in iambic poetry: 48b 33f. shows, I believe, that *pace* Janko e.g. 61 iambus probably does count as poetry for Ar., though certainly of an inferior and negligible kind. The remarks in *Poetics* 9 show the strongly normative thrust of Ar.'s theory (cf. pp. 38f.): he is here attempting to define the nature of the best

poetry (an important part of any *technê: Pol.* 1288b 10-21) and generalises from this position without quite trying to deny (as 51b 14f. intimates) that *some* poetry may deal with particulars. On iambus cf. ch. IX n. 36.

[16] It is true that Socrates thinks of setting already existing fables as a *pis aller,* since he cannot invent his own. This still does not bridge the gap between Plato's and Ar.'s positions.

The original sense of *muthos* was anything said or told: an utterance, speech, story, report, etc. It later acquires the idea of something intrinsically false: a myth, fable, fiction, etc. Cf. LSJ s.v. II 1-4. References to *muthoi* in poetry before Plato (e.g. Hom. *Od.* 11.368, Pind. *Ol.* 1.29, *Nem.* 7.23) simply reflect the ordinary meanings of the term. Plato, exploiting the connotations of falsehood (as well as associations with idle tales and the like), treats *muthologia* (story-telling) as the essence of poetry: e.g. *Phaedo* 61b 4f., e2, 70b 6, *Rep.* 377d ff., 380c 2, 392d 2, 394b 9f., *Laws* 941b-c.

Outside the *Poetics,* Ar.'s use of *muthos* and cognates almost invariably carries implications of falsehood, though not always as disparagingly as at *Met.* 995a 4f., 'fictional *(muthôdê)* and childish'. He applies the words chiefly to: myth and legend (*Phys.* 218b 24, *Cael.* 284a 18ff., *HA* 580a 17, *MA* 699a 27ff., *Met.* 982b 18f., *EN* 1100a 8, *Pol.* 1257b 16, 1269b 28, 1284a 22, 1341b 3), poetic theology (*Met.* 1000a 18, 1074a 38ff., 1091b 9), fable (*Meteor.* 356b 11-17, *HA* 578b 25, 579b 4, 609b 10, 617a 5, *PA* 641a 21). Although there are some general references to poetic *mutholgia* (e.g. *EE* 1230a 3), I cannot find the *Poetics'* special sense of *muthos* anywhere else in the corpus. What this means is that Ar. has taken a term with the senses of story-fable-legend-myth, and without erasing these altogether (they can be seen within the *Poetics* itself at 51b 24, 53a 18, 37, 53b 22) he has given the word a new critical edge and significance. We must observe in particular the subtle movement away from the associations of *traditional* myths: a poetic *muthos* need not be traditional (51b 23ff.), and it may even borrow from history (ibid. 30-2). But whatever the source of material, it must be made afresh—i.e. shaped into a coherent design—by the maker-poet, and the true *muthos* is the result, not the original material, of this act (esp. 51b 27-9). See also ch. I pp. 22f.

[17] Ar.'s underlying notion of *technê* puts the stress on the maker-product axis, but this should not be formulated as a focus on the art rather than its products, as it is by Else (1957) 6, 9, 12, 237, 279f. etc. To take just one detail, note how 'thought' *(dianoia)* is defined at 50b 4-12 as *both* a poetic capacity *and* a property of poems.

[18] On the emergence of this system see Kristeller, but in pressing the lack of an ancient version of eighteenth-century aesthetics too hard (166-74) he gives an inadequate account of the place of mimesis in Ar.'s theory (171f., with some *naïveté* regarding Plato too). The general comparison of ancient and modern views of art by W. Tatarkiewicz, *JHI* 24 (1963) 231-40, is also marred by a neglect of mimesis and a misunderstanding of Ar.'s concept of it (233).

[19] See ch. III n.1.

[20] In particular *Il.* 3.125ff. (Helen's embroidery), 9.186ff. (Achilles' song), *Od.* 1.325ff. and 8.499ff. (Phemius' and Demodocus' songs of the Trojan War). For sensitive comment on such material see Macleod 6-12.

[21] Ar.'s most extensive discussions of pleasure are in *EN* Book 7, chs. 11-14, 1152b 1ff., Book 10, chs. 1-5, 1172a 16ff., and (less subtly) *Rhet.* Book 1, ch. 11, 1369b 33ff. For a recent and full discussion see J. C. B. Gosling & C. C. W. Taylor, *The Greeks on Pleasure* (Oxford 1982) chs. 11, 14-15. On the relation of pleasure to virtue cf. ch. VI n. 39.

[22] See the whole of *Laws* 655c-660e, and later 667b ff., 700e, 802c-d; cf. *Hipp.Maj.* 297e-8a, *Gorg.* 501d-2d, *Rep.* 607a.

[23] Note the implicit relevance of this example to tragedy and the paradox of tragic pleasure; similarly in the parallel passage at *Rhet.* 1371b 4-10, and compare the pleasurable memory of things not pleasant at the time, *Rhet.* 1370b 1-7.

[24] *Psuchagôgein* (and cognates), originally meaning 'to conjure souls', became used in various ways of the captivating power of language, particularly poetry and rhetoric, and also of the visual arts (*contra* Pollitt 101 n.34): see esp. Aristoph. *Birds* 1555 (a pun?), Xen. *Mem.* 3.10.6, Plato *Phdr.* 261a, 271c, Isoc. 2.49, 9.10, Timocles fr. 6.6 (echoing Ar. himself? cf. Appendix 5 §2), and LSJ with Suppl. s.v. for later passages (to which add Marc.Aur. *Med.* 3.2 and 11.6). This metaphorical development was probably influenced by Gorgias's theory of the magical and bewitching powers of language, *Helen* (fr. 11) 10-14, which itself is a development of the archetypal Homeric idea of poetry as enchantment: on this and related points see ch. VI pp. 188ff. and nn. 26-8.

[25] *EN* 1175a 22ff.: the phrase 'peculiar pleasure' *(oikeia hêdonê)* occurs at 1175a 31, b 14, 21, 27 etc. It was also used by Plato, but to denote pure, 'true' pleasures: *Phileb.* 51d, 63e, *Rep.* 586e, 587b. The attempt of Else (1938) to connect Plato and Ar. on this point is misguided, and involves him in the claim (194) that the proper or peculiar pleasure of the *Poetics* is not specific to individual genres: this will not stand up to scrutiny.

[26] The basis of the portentous, as *GA* 770b 8ff. helps us to see, would be unnatural phenomena (grotesque horrors), which means that they would flout necessity or probability: hence their spuriousness, in contrast to the intelligibility of events which cause pity and fear. For the possibility of a reference to Aeschylus at 53b 9 see ch. III n.20.

[27] The use of 'aesthetic' by Lucas (1968) on 48b 13 and 17 to refer *only* to this type is question-begging, and is rightly criticised as such by M. Hubbard, *CR* 20 (1970) 177. On the distinction between purely sensual and cognitive pleasure, parallel to *Poet.* 48b 10-19, see *PA* 645a 7-15, and cf. e.g. *EN* 1175a 26f., 1176a 2f. This distinction is related to that between the sensible and the knowable, e.g. *De An.* 431b 21ff.

[28] For the translation 'garnishings' see ch. VIII n.3. The comparison of characterisation to colour at 50a 39ff. ((e) in the text), which effectively reiterates the emphasis of 48b 15-19, does not, of course, imply that character is sensually apprehended, only that it needs the formal framework of plot-structure to have its proper significance.

[29] For general references to musical pleasure see *EN* 1173b 30f., 1175a 13f., 34f., *EE* 1230b 27f., *Pol.* 1339b 20f., 1340b 16f. The mimetic nature of music is indicated at *Poet.* 47a 14-16, 23-6, *Pol.* 1340a 28ff. (and cf. 1340a 13f. with Susemihl's emendation: see Anderson 126, 186-8). The equestion arises how far Ar. allowed a sensual pleasure to musical tones *independently* of their mimetic significance, as Plato does at *Phileb.* 51d. *Poet.* 47a 15 implies that some music is not mimetic, but the adverb 'most vividly' at 62a 17 implies a mimetic force (cf. the same word at 55a 24). The general impression left by *Politics* 8 is of music as a naturally mimetic art. The point affects rhythm too, for which some degree of intrinsically mimetic or expressive value is posited at *Poet.* 49a 21ff., 59b 31ff., 60a 4, *Pol.* 1340a 19ff., b 8ff., 1341b 19-27, *Rhet.* 1408b 21-9a 23: compare e.g. Plato *Laws* 669c, 798d (but note 669e on the difficulty of understanding rhythm and music *without words*). Isocrates 9.10-11 appears to treat the pleasure of rhythm as autonomous. Finally, *Pol.* 1341a 14f. distinguishes between the 'common' and evidently sensual pleasure of music and rhythm (available even to some animals) and the sensibility to enjoy 'beautiful melodies and rhythms', which probably entails a mimetic significance.

[30] Ar. also refers to *epic* recitation at 59b 30. Note that Plato describes poetry as the form of mimesis which operates through our *hearing* at *Rep.* 603b 6f. On the Greek practice of reading aloud see B. Knox, *GRBS* 9 (1968) 421-35.

[31] *Met.* 980a 21-7. On the general love of knowledge cf. *Protr.* B17, 72-7, 97-102 Düring (1961).

[32] Ross 280 calls ch. 4's explanation of the mimesis-instinct 'too intellectualistic' and misses its significance. Lord (1982) 90f. talks of a 'purely intellectual' understanding of mimesis, and Else (1957) 128-30 finds the 'emphasis on the intellect' a sign of a marginal addition (cf. ch. I n. 51 above). These judgements all seem to me to misconstrue the implications of the passage. The essential import is that the basic cognitive pleasure takes particular forms, such as that from tragedy, in which it is engaged with emotion and other factors. For a recent philosophical attempt to use *Poetics* 4 as a starting-point for an aesthetic thesis see A. Savile, *The Test of Time* (Oxford 1982) ch. 5, esp. 86f., 95f.

[33] It is specifically the simplicity of the passage which has led scholars such as Twining 186-91, Butcher 201f., Rostagni (1945) LXIV, and Lord (1982) 90-2 into underestimating its importance: against Rostagni and Lord it is particularly pertinent to observe that the educative effect of poetry on the passions (for which they rightly argue: cf. ch. VI n. 40) cannot be divorced from the cognitive experience of the mimetic structure of a poem (see esp. 53b 12 for an indication of this).

[34] The obvious parallel is *Pol.* 1336a 32-4, where children's games are said to be imitations or enactments of adult activities and to 'prepare the way for their later occupations'. See Plato *Rep.* 395d 1f., and cf. ps.-Ar. *Probl.* 956a 14.

[35] There has been much disagreement on this point (and the issue is old: cf. Weinberg 462). I take *mimeisthai* at 48b 20 to refer to *both* causes, and the instinct for melody and rhythm to be an additional but *closely related* factor (a point usually overlooked) in view of Ar.'s understanding of these things as naturally mimetic (n.29 above).

[36] That this latter, purely sensual pleasure could be for Ar. 'the true pleasure', as Gomme 64f. suggests, makes nonsense of the treatise and flatly contradicts the reference to mimesis in the definition of tragic pleasure at 53b 11-13. *Pol.* 1340a 25-8 provides an important parallel: there the form *(morphê)* is an attribute of the human subject of the image (cf. *Poet.* 54b 10), and the pleasure derived from it is cognitive (the recognition of physical strength, athletic beauty, etc.) and dependent on mimesis; the reference to 'another reason' is parallel to *Poet.* 48b 18f. The difficult passage, *Mem.* 450b 21ff., is also germane: for the interpretation see R. Sorabji, *Aristotle on Memory* (London 1972) 84. It confirms that the proper appreciation of visual mimesis involves treating a work as an image of a possible reality (for an image, *eikôn,* is precisely the product of mimesis: *Top.* 140a 14f.). It might be possible to discern allusions to cognitive and non-cognitive pleasure in visual art at, respectively, *EE* 1230b 31-4, *EN* 1118a 3f.

[37] *Rhet.* 1371b 4ff.: the relevance of the passage is correctly indicated by Hubbard 134 (though the word 'just' does not belong in the translation), in line with her brief but exemplary explanation of the theory of aesthetic pleasure on pp. 86f. Cf. also Tracy's article, Redfield 52-66, and Goldschmidt (1982) 212-17. Closely related passages are those on metaphor (*Poet.* 59a 7f., *Rhet.* 1410b 10-26), on 'wit', including types of metaphor (*Rhet.* 1412a 17-b 23), and on other kinds of comparison (*Rhet.* 1394a 5). It is regrettable that an emphasis on the importance of *Poetics* 4's explanation of aesthetic pleasure has been confused with the issue of *katharsis* in Golden (1962) and later articles: see Appendix 5 §5(a).

[38] *Manthanein* leads to knowledge: e.g. *De An.* 417b 12f., *Rhet.* 1362a 30f., 1363b 31f. For *sullogizesthai* cf. *Poet.* 55a 7, 10f., 61b 2, *Rhet.* 1371b 9. Although this latter term should not everywhere be pressed in its technical logical sense (cf. Appendix 1 p. 326), the language of *Poet.* 48b 16 allows for a process in which new understanding may be reached (cf. e.g. Plato *Euthyd.* 277e-8a). See n. 42 below.

[39] The point is reinforced by the reference to non-philosophers at 48b 13f.: the following example is intentionally rudimentary, with the implication that more sophisticated forms are possible. Cf. the parallel drawn between the study of art (dramatic performances) and philosophical study at *Protr.* B44 Düring (1961).

[40] *Rhet.* 1371a-b, cf. 1404b 12, *Met.* 982b 12ff., 983a 12ff., Plato *Theaet.* 155d. Ar.'s 'wonder' all too easily became *admiratio*, hence admiration, for neo-classical readers of the *Poetics*: cf. ch. X n.21. Ar.'s and Plato's views on wonder deserve closer study. For a sensitive general essay on the subject see R. Hepburn, *Wonder and Other Essays* (Edinburgh 1984) 131-54.

[41] It is true that at 60a 11ff. 'the wonderful' is related to the irrational, which is undesirable in poetry. Although there may be something of a tension here, it is reasonable to infer that there are degrees of wonder, which lies on the boundary of the explicable and the inexplicable, and so can slip into the latter (and hence become the irrational) or, properly used, may stimulate and challenge understanding, as at 52a 4ff. Cf. Else (1957) 624f., and ch. VII n. 16.

[42] In the full understanding of universals in poetry it is not easy to know what would correspond to the pre-existing knowledge of *Poet.* 48b 17. Certainly not factual acquaintance with myths: see 51b 21-6. Perhaps knowledge (which for Ar. is not true knowledge) of particulars, from which we are led to a grasp of the universals embodied in the poetry: cf. *Top.* 108b 10-12 for the movement from particulars to universals through 'likenesses'. For the movement from existing to new knowledge in a different context see *An.Post.* 71a 1ff.

[43] *Met.* 982b 12ff., *Rhet.* 1371b 27f.

[44] It does not seem to have been accepted, for instance, by Ar.'s successor, Theophrastus: see fr. 65, translated in Russell 203f. On Plato's comparisons between poetry and philosophy see Appendix 2 under 51a 5f.

[45] Else (1957) 131f. can hardly be right to see a reference to universals in the visual example of ch. 4, but this is tied up with his belief (128) that the point concerns scientific models and diagrams, a belief refuted by *Poet.* 48b 17-19 and the parallel passage, *Rhet.* 1371b 4ff. (On Ar.'s independent use of diagrams cf. ch. VII p. 218 and n. 23.)

[46] E.g. Twining 399-401, Butcher ch. 4, Gudeman 99, Allan (1970) 155, Schadewaldt 225, 228f. Cf. ch. I p.6. For the comparison between poetry and philosophy there is an analogue in the affinities allowed at *Rhet.* 1356a 20-7 between rhetoric and dialectic (and *politikê*), and at *Rhet.* 1359b 8-12, *An.Post.* 71a 9-11 between rhetoric and logic, ethics, and dialectic.

Abbreviations

1. Aristotelian works

An.Post.	*Posterior Analytics*
An.Pr.	*Prior Analytics*
Cael.	*De Caelo*
Cat.	*Categories*
De An.	*De Anima*
EE	*Eudemian Ethics*
EN	*Nicomachean Ethics*
GA	*De Generatione Animalium*
GC	*De Generatione et Corruptione*
HA	*De Historia Animalium*
Int.	*De Interpretatione*
MA	*De Motu Animalium*
Mem.	*De Memoria*
Met.	*Metaphysics*
Meteor.	*Meteorologica*
PA	*De Partibus Animalium*

Phys.	*Physics*
Poet.	*Poetics*
Pol.	*Politics*
Protr.	*Protrepticus*
Rhet.	*Rhetoric*
SE	*Sophistici Elenchi*
Top.	*Topics*

2. Pseudo-Aristotelian works (prefaced by ps.-Ar.)

Aud.	*De Audibilibus*
MM	*Magna Moralia*
Mund.	*De Mundo*
Probl.	*Problemata*
Rh.Alex.	*Rhetorica ad Alexandrum*

3. Journals

CJ	*Classical Journal*
CL	*Comparative Literature*
CP	*Classical Philology*
CQ	*Classical Quarterly*
CR	*Classical Review*
CW	*Classical World*
G & R	*Greece & Rome*
GRBS	*Greek Roman and Byzantine Studies*
HSCP	*Harvard Studies in Classical Philology*
JAAC	*Journal of Aesthetics and Art Criticism*
JEGP	*Journal of English and Germanic Philology*
JHI	*Journal of the History of Ideas*
JHS	*Journal of Hellenic Studies*
JP	*Journal of Philology*

MH	*Museum Helveticum*
MLR	*Modern Language Review*
Mnem.	*Mnemosyne*
MP	*Modern Philology*
PCPS	*Proceedings of the Cambridge Philological Society*
Philol.	*Philologus*
SP	*Studies in Philology*
SR	*Studies in the Renaissance*
TAPA	*Transactions of the American Philological Association*

Deborah H. Roberts (essay date 1992)

SOURCE: "Outside the Drama: The Limits of Tragedy in Aristotle's *Poetics*," in *Essays on Aristotle's 'Poetics'*, edited by Amelie Oksenberg Rorty, Princeton University Press, 1992, pp. 133-49.

[*In the following essay, Roberts contends that in discussing the natural limit of plot length, Aristotle conceived of some action as taking place "outside" of the drama's plot. Roberts analyzes what types of action might fall into this category and the methods by which events taking place outside of the play's action could be conveyed to the audience.*]

In Chapter 7 of the **Poetics** (1450b26-31). Aristotle notes that the action of which a play is an imitation must be whole, that is, must have a beginning, a middle, and an end; a beginning, he goes on to say, is that which does not follow naturally or necessarily from anything else, and an end is that from which nothing else follows. This claim often strikes readers at first as obvious and then as untrue. What Aristotle says seems obvious in the sense that a play's action has in fact a duration limited in time; it starts and it stops. It seems untrue in the sense that there appears to be a great deal that precedes the actual beginning of many Greek tragedies, and that tragedies often end with some indication that there is more to come; furthermore, what precedes is often causally connected with the events of the play itself, and what follows often constitutes the later ramifications of an outcome only partially revealed on stage.

It is, of course, precisely the fact that the plot of any literary work implies continuing action which takes place before and after the events narrated that makes Aristotle's claim subtler than at first appears. Recall Henry James's often-quoted remarks in the Preface to *Roderick Hudson:* "Really, universally, relations stop nowhere, and the exquisite problem of the artist is eternally but to draw, by a geometry of his own, the circle in which they shall happily appear to do so."[1] Recent work on closure has complicated our ideas about this geometry, that is, about how literature achieves what Frank Kermode calls "the sense of an ending."[2] The problem of creating beginnings and endings that seem genuinely to begin and to end is particularly prominent in the case of Greek tragedy, which like much of ancient literature took its plots primarily from a body of stories that were continuous with each other and to some extent known to audience or reader.[3]

Aristotle's account in the *Poetics* recognizes that any given work is selective and therefore limited in relation to the larger myth—indeed, insists that it must be so. An action (epic or tragic) with a proper beginning, middle, and end will in Aristotle's terms be a whole. But Aristotle makes clear that an action that is itself a whole may also be selected from a larger whole, in keeping with requirements of unity and of size. An epic or tragic plot must have unity, and cannot therefore include (for example) all the events of an individual's life (8.1451a16-30); the natural limit of a plot's length (for both tragedy and epic) is one that allows that plot to be clearly grasped (7.1451a3-6, 23.1459a32-34, 24.1459b18-20). Where even epic is limited in what it can actually include, tragedy—both shorter and more compact—is more radically so.[4]

Aristotle further recognizes the limits of tragedy by several times noting that there are events that occur outside: outside the drama, outside the tragedy, outside the story or plot. In these passages, Aristotle is not speaking of the world outside the drama, that is, the world of the audience, the nonfictive world, but rather of some part of the larger story from which the play draws its plot.[5]

For some scholars, the limits Aristotle puts on the tragic plot by relegating certain events to "outside" point to other limits Aristotle imposes on the subject matter of tragedy and ultimately to the limits—or limitations—of Aristotle's imagination as a critic tragedy, limits based in his profound rationalism.[6] But Aristotle's rationalism, properly appreciated, is itself at times as revelatory as any leap of the imagination, and it may be rewarding to consider the implications even of some of his less fully developed ideas. His concept of what is outside the drama has implications for our understanding of the nature of dramatic limits and of audience response.

I

Aristotle refers to what is in some sense "outside" in six passages in the *Poetics.* Of these, three are concerned with the action of the play, one with the audience's knowledge, and two with the presence in the play of the irrational or inexplicable.

A. *Action*

(1) In a discussion of actions that arouse pity and fear (14.1453b29-34), Aristotle gives as an example the Sophoclean Oedipus' unknowing murder of his father, but notes that this is in fact outside the drama *(exō tou dramatos).*

(2) In his discussion of the way to set out a plot in general terms before the addition of names and episodes (17.1455b2-15), Aristotle gives as his first example an outline of an *Iphigenia* which is in all essentials Euripides' *Iphigenia in Tauris;* the divine command and the purpose that lie behind the arrival of the central character's brother (Orestes) are said to be outside the plot or story *(exō tou muthou)* (1455b6-9).[7]

(3) In his account of plot-complication *(desis)* and denouement *(lusis),* Aristotle notes that the plot-complication of a tragedy includes the things outside *(exō then)* and some of the things within (18.1455b23-26). It seems safe here to take "outside" as the equivalent of "outside the tragedy," since tragedy has just been mentioned. The example given is a lost play (the *Lynceus* of Theodectes) and Aristotle specifies no events in that play as outside, merely alluding to the things that have occurred beforehand *(ta propepragmena).*

B. *Knowledge*

(4) After commenting that the denouement should come from the plot itself, Aristotle notes (15.1454a37-1454b6) that the *deus ex machina (apo mēchanēs)* should not be used, as in Euripides' *Medea,* to bring about a play's resolution, but only for "the things outside the drama" *(ta exō tou dramatos),* that is, for things which happened either before or after the play, are inaccessible to human knowledge, and must therefore be revealed by a god.[8]

C. *The irrational*

(5) Aristotle adds to his remarks on the *deus ex machina* that there should be nothing irrational *(alogon)* in the play's events, or if there is, it should be outside the tragedy *(exō tēs tragoidias),* as in Sophocles' *Oedipus* (15.1454b6-9). This allusion will be explained only later, in Chapter 24. That "outside the tragedy" is here equivalent to "outside the drama" is made clear both by the identification elsewhere of the two terms and by the wording in Chapter 14, which contrasts a play in

which something happens outside the drama with two in which the same thing happens in the tragedy itself.

(6) In stressing the importance of plausibility (24.1460a27-32), Aristotle again (as in Chapter 15) consigns what is irrational (alogon) to outside, here exō tou mutheumatos.[9] What mutheuma seems to mean is the plot as enacted or represented—essentially the equivalent of the drama. This interpretation is supported by the opposition in this passage between what is outside the mutheuma and what is in the drama; mutheuma is used here in place of drama because Aristotle is speaking of epic as well as of drama.[10] He here clarifies his earlier reference to something alogon in the Oedipus: it is Oedipus' ignorance of how his predecessor died that is both outside and hard to account for.

Of these references to what is outside some poetic boundary, all but one (the example of Orestes from Chapter 17) are stated in terms that seem in this context to be equivalent: something is outside the drama, the tragedy, or the story as represented. All Aristotle's examples of things outside are things that have actually been mentioned inside the drama; he does not cite any events that might have been known to the audience from other sources but are not mentioned in the play.[11] None of Aristotle's instances of what is outside the drama involves a report of something that is supposed to have occurred in the course of the play, rather than before or after. Nor does he include in his category allusions to stories that are parallel to the play's story, the sort of mythic exempla usually found in choral odes. What is outside the drama, then, appears to be anything continuous with the action of the play that occurs before or after the play as staged and is mentioned in it.

But the example from Chapter 17 complicates matters. If muthos here (like mutheuma in Chapter 24) refers to the plot as represented and is thus also essentially the equivalent of "drama," then not all reported events that precede the play's beginning count for Aristotle as outside the drama. For here he appears to include in the plot Iphigenia's past history but not Orestes'; yet neither is enacted within the play, and both must presumably be recounted.[12] Unless there is some other reason for the different treatment of the two, muthos must then be distinct from (and more inclusive than) drama.[13] The past history of Iphigenia is part of the muthos, that is, of the plot in a larger sense (and thus included in the general outline), but not part of the drama. The background of Orestes' arrival is less essential to the muthos in this sense, since he could presumably have been made to arrive for some other reason; it is therefore outside both drama and plot.

It is hard to be confident of a reading based on a particular understanding of muthos, given the great variety of ways in which Aristotle uses the word.[14] But such a distinction is consistent with our other passages. What is outside the drama may count as among the play's events in some sense (en tois pragmasin, 15.145b6-7), and may in fact be a crucial antecedent to the play, as is Oedipus' killing of his father (14.1453b30-32). The claim in Chapter 18 that a play's actual plot-complication will normally include things outside the drama makes it explicit that something may be essential to the plot's construction and development and still be considered outside the tragedy. The beginning of the plot and the beginning of the play are not necessarily the same.

What is outside the drama, then, precedes or follows the play's action and is reported in the play, but something outside the drama may be (though it need not be) a part of the plot or story. This view has an intuitive appeal; most readers think of Oedipus' killing of his father (for example) as in some sense a part of the plot of the Oedipus Tyrannus. It is also in keeping with the dominant approach in current narrative theory, for which everything connected with the story line that is actually mentioned is part of a play's story (its events, what it tells) and is simply given in a different order in the discourse or narrative that is the play itself.[15]

II

But if what is outside the drama may be part of the plot, which is after all the soul of tragedy, why does Aristotle continue to invoke an apparently secondary distinction between what is inside and what is outside the drama?[16]

Taken together, the passages that refer to this distinction reflect the general importance of boundedness and selection for Aristotle, in the **Poetics** as elsewhere in his writings.[17] The unity of the plot is his central concern, but the drama as staged has its own limits, and these are marked in part by what is excluded.

The passages in which the issue is action outside the drama suggest, as it were, the limitations of the drama's limits and the subordination of staged drama to plot. That is, it is by noting that an action central to the plot may be outside the drama (14.1453b29-34), and that the plot-complication will normally include events outside the drama (18.1455b23-26) that Aristotle makes the point (albeit in passing) that the staged drama and the plot are not the same thing and that the latter crosses the bounds of the former.

Since some events crucial to the plot (as well as much ancillary information) will be outside the drama, these must be made known to the audience in some way other than by enactment; the passage in which the issue is knowledge of what is outside the drama points to one such way. Aristotle's comment (in his critique of the *deus ex machina,* 15.1454a37-1454b6) that the gods provide knowledge of earlier or later events inaccessible to humans suggests that divine prologues and epilogues serve the function which in an epic (or a novel) is often served by a narrator, the function of providing knowledge that the audience must have in order to understand the story, and that only a god (or a narrator) could have.

Such knowledge of what is outside the drama itself helps constitute the limits of the drama, since it tells where both plot and play begin and end and thus helps the audience grasp the work as a whole.[18] Aristotle makes a related point in the **Rhetoric** (3.14.1415a17-33), noting that as in speeches and epics the exordium lets the hearers know something of the subject in advance, so tragic poets make clear what a play is about—either immediately, like Euripides, or at some point in the prologue, like Sophocles.[19] Such knowledge is critical because "what is unbounded/undefined *(aoristos)* leads one astray" (3.14.1415a14).[20]

III

So far I have been considering what is "outside the drama" from the perspective of the boundary it defines. But what is outside the drama may also be said to constitute a region or area, and that there is something distinctive about this region is suggested by the passages (15.1454b6-9, 24.1460a27-32) in which Aristotle relegates to outside the drama an otherwise undesirable element he calls the *alogon,* variously rendered as the inexplicable, the improbable, or (most often) the irrational.

Even when, in the later chapters of the **Poetics,** Aristotle's initial exclusion of the *alogon* (15.1454b6-7). is qualified, the presumption remains that the irrational is best done without. Epic is more likely than tragedy to accept the irrational, which is the chief element in the amazing, because in epic we do not actually see the events in question (24.1460a11-17; Aristotle's example here is the surprising restraint of the other Greeks during Achilles' pursuit of Hector at *Iliad* XXII.205-7). But even in epic the irrational is undesirable; as a general rule, a story *(logos)* should not be made up of irrational *(aloga)* parts. It should contain nothing irrational, but if it does, the place for it is outside the represented story (24.1460a27-37). Again, one may defend the irrational against critics (25.1461b14-25) either by appealing to "what people say" or by arguing that it is likely that unlikely things should sometimes happen; nonetheless, one should not unnecessarily introduce something irrational for no purpose.[21] Why does Aristotle tell us that there should as a rule be nothing irrational in the story or events, and that if there is, it should be outside the drama or story as represented?

IV

Does this exclusion of the irrational, as some have thought, spring primarily from a more basic wish to exclude the divine or supernatural?[22] On such a view, the critique of the use of the *deus ex machina* in Chapter 15 is a rejection of any significant involvement of the gods in the dramatic action itself,[23] and the description of the god's (Apollo's) sending of Orestes in the *Iphigenia in Tauris* as "outside the plot" (Chapter 17) similarly reflects a rejection of divine agency.[24]

In fact, Aristotle has little to say about the role of the gods in tragedy, and this omission has often disturbed readers.[25] But it is not to the use of the gods *per se* that Aristotle objects in Chapter 15. Medea's appearance in her divine chariot at the end of Euripides' play is a surprise, and most modern readers would see it as a typical and successful instance of Euripides' playing with the audience's expectations. But it is a surprise for which the drama hardly prepares us, and it is for this reason that Aristotle disapproves of it. There are other instances of divine intervention in tragedy whose abruptness would be likely to meet with Aristotle's disapproval, most notably the sudden arrival of Apollo in Euripides' *Orestes* to solve what appears on the human level to be a hopeless conflict. But there seems to be no reason in Aristotelian terms why the gods may not be used in the action when their arrival is called for by a plot in which they have previously had some involvement (Hermes in Aeschylus' *Prometheus* or Artemis in Euripides' *Hippolytus*) or when they are fully involved in the action throughout (Apollo and Athena in Aeschylus' *Eumenides* or Dionysus in Euripides' *Bacchae*). Nor does the fact that Aristotle cites "a standard mode of involvement of a deity in the action of the *Iliad*"[26] necessarily suggest that he is critical of all divine involvement; Athena's intervention in *Iliad* II, like the intervention of some gods *ex machina,* is a case of divine interference in something that would otherwise have gone in an entirely different direction; without her, the Greeks would have returned home "contary to fate."[27] What Aristotle objects to, in tragedy or in epic, is divine action that is inadequately prepared for and inadequately connected with the rest of the action.[28]

Nor is the exclusion from the plot of Orestes' reason for coming to the land of the Taurians (Chapter 17) a rejection of the divine. It is difficult to be certain of Aristotle's grounds for this exclusion, but it can be plausibly argued that he sees Orestes' arrival but not the reason for it as integral to what is essentially Iphigenia's story. Halliwell rejects the view that what lies behind Orestes' arrival is excluded simply as inessential to the plot, arguing that if that were so, his arrival would appear to constitute just the sort of "unintelligible coincidence" to which Aristotle objects elsewhere.[29] But the omission of Orestes' motive at this stage does not mean that the play in its final form would lack such a motive (any more than the omission of names means the characters would lack names); it means simply that the particular motive given in Euripides' version is not essential to the plot as outlined. The mention of Polyidus' version of the recognition makes it plain that although this general outline is based on Euripides' play, it is not identical with it, and one can easily conceive of a play in which Orestes comes for quite other reasons.[30]

Furthermore, although there is no mention of the god's playing an active role in the story of Iphigenia as given here,[31] the comment that she disappeared in a manner mysterious *(adēlōs)* to those who had sacrificed her suggests an action that cannot be explained in human terms and that is nonetheless counted as part of the story or plot as outlined. It is therefore difficult to make the presence or absence of the supernatural the feature that distinguishes Iphigenia's arrival (inside the plot) from Orestes' arrival (outside the plot). Finally, in the outline of the *Odyssey* that follows Aristotle seems to have no problem with the role of Poseidon.

Under certain conditions Aristotle even welcomes the presence in tragedy of action inexplicable in human terms. At 9.1452a1-12 he singles out for praise events which cause amazement because they occur contrary to expectation but in a causal sequence *(para tēn doxan di' allēla)*. As an example (taken not from tragedy but from life) he cites the statue of Mitys, which killed Mitys' killer by falling on him. Such events, says Aristotle, do not seem to come about by chance. Note, then, that here is something which is praiseworthy in part because it follows in likely sequence (or at least in the semblance of likely sequence) even though it cannot be explained in purely human terms.[32] Unexpected but fitting events in tragedy may well involve the divine, for example in the form of the unexpectedly fulfilled oracle. Compare Aristotle's acceptance of such events—magical but nonetheless logical—with his rejection of Medea's magical but unmotivated departure in a chariot or of Oedipus' ordinary but unlikely ignorance about his predecessor's death; such a comparison serves to support the view that Aristotle really objects not to the supernatural *per se* but to the unmotivated or unlikely, whether divine or human in origin.[33]

In tragedy itself the more magical aspects of divine activity are usually located outside the central action and offstage; such aspects of the divine seem to play a secondary role in tragedy for the tragedians themselves. If, then, Aristotle has some special difficulty with irrational *divine* action (as opposed to the irrational in general), he may simply be reflecting an exclusion already dominant in tragedy, rather than excluding out of an obstinate secularism what is really central to the genre, that is, the mysterious but somehow ordered role of the gods in the way things are.

But Aristotle does not even seem to have any such special difficulty with the irrational involvement of the gods. Indeed, with the possible exception of Medea's departure *ex machina,* all the examples Aristotle actually gives of the objectionable *alogon* have to do with instances of human rather than divine behavior. It is *alogon* that Oedipus does not know how his predecessor died (Chapters 15, 24), and that Aegeus suddenly appears in Corinth in Euripides' *Medea* (Chapter 25),[34] but in neither case does Aristotle suggest the involvement of the gods. Aristotle's two remaining examples of dramatic *aloga* (Chapter 24) are harder to interpret, but no one has suggested that there is anything supernatural about either of them. The reporting of the Pythian games in the *Electra* is variously read as constituting an anachronism or as entailing an unlikely delay in the news. The case of the man who comes without speaking from Tegea to Mysia seems irrational because of the unlikelihood of someone making such a journey in silence. Nor do the two examples from epic (24.1460a11-16, 35-36) have any clear connection with divine activity: the gods are not involved either in Achilles' unassisted pursuit of Hector or in the putting ashore of Odysseus on Ithaca in *Odyssey* XIII, presumably an *alogon* because he fails to wake up when the Phaeacians leave him there.[35]

That Aristotle's own views of the divine are quite different from those of epic and tragedy is no problem; he evidently considers it appropriate to speak of the gods in various ways to suit various contexts. The **Rhetoric,** for example, reflects traditional views of the gods where other works call them into question.[36] And surely poetry can use tradition as rhetoric does; in Chapter 25, Aristotle offers the response "that's what people say" as a defense against those who object to stories about the gods in epic. Indeed, Aristotle uses a traditional view of the gods to justify his explicit approval of one form of divine involvement: the *deus ex machina* should be used to provide knowledge of past and future, "for we attribute to the gods the capacity to see all things" (15.1454b3-6).[37]

Chapter 25 provides further evidence for Aristotle's willingness to retain the traditional divine framework in the world of poetry. He twice mentions a way of rationalizing divine activity, but in neither case does the rationalization entail an explanation in human terms: although the gods drink no wine, Ganymede may be said to pour wine for Zeus if we understand this metaphorically (1461a29-31); if we change the accent of a verb, it was the dream of Zeus sent to Agamemnon in *Iliad* II that lied, not Zeus himself (1461a22).[38] These corrections demand not that the gods be explained away but that the world of the gods make sense in itself; as we know, the gods drink nectar, and what Zeus says should be valid.[39] The fragmentary evidence for the lost *Homeric Problems* presents a similar picture.[40] Aristotle is here concerned with apparent contradictions, factual difficulties, and implausible behavior in the Homeric poems; those problems that have to do with the gods are almost all problems of consistency or probability within the poem or the tradition, not problems with the divine presence *per se*. Most striking is Aristotle's treatment of one of the relatively rare instances in Greek literature in which a portent involves not merely a significant natural event (two eagles chase a pregnant hare, an eagle carries off and drops a snake) but an event which is supernatural; at *Iliad* II.308-319 Odysseus recalls an omen in which a snake eats eight nestlings and their mother and then is turned to stone by Zeus. What troubles Aristotle about this passage is not any implausibility in the magical transformation itself, but rather Calchas' failure to interpret that transformation, apparently the most portentous feature of the omen.[41]

Aristotle, then, does not actually treat the role of the gods as central to tragedy (or epic) in his own account, but neither does his account require a rejection of their role. Discourse about the gods is for Greek tragedy and Greek culture generally the language in which human experience and human action are expressed; Aristotle can allow tragedy to continue speaking that language while himself analyzing experience and action in his own terms.

V

What then is the significance of the irrational or *alogon*? Aristotle's examples suggest for the most part either a kind of commonsense implausibility (the unlikely ignorance of Oedipus, the surprising behavior of the other Greeks during the pursuit of Hector) or a lack of dramatic connectedness (the coincidental arrival of Aegeus, the unprepared for departure of Medea).[42]

Whatever we make of the *alogon,* however, we must ask the further question: why does it make sense in Aristotle's view for the poet to locate what is irrational outside the drama? Part of the explanation is suggested by the contrast between epic and drama at **Poetics** 24.1460a11-17, where epic is said to admit the irrational more readily than drama because in epic we do not actually see the action; the restraint of the other Greeks as Achilles chases Hector would be ridiculous if the action were actually performed on stage, but its absurdity escapes notice in epic. Compare the importance given to the visual in tragedy at 17.1455a2-29, where it is said that in constructing plots the playwright must be careful to place what is happening before his eyes; otherwise he may find himself introducing into the action contradictions that would escape the notice of someone who did not *see* them but will bother an audience when actually staged.

In both passages, some problem goes undetected (the verb is *lanthanein*) by one who does not actually see

the action staged. Aristotle is here stressing not our diminished emotional response to the merely heard, but our weakened apprehension of it. We are not only less bothered by oddities in action we do not see; since such action is less striking, we actually fail to notice what is odd about it.

Something irrational or inexplicable may then affect us more strongly when we actually see it, and will therefore be more acceptable if it is ouside the drama and thus (as in epic) only heard.[43] But this explanation does not work equally well for all cases of the *alogon*. The pursuit of Hector and the landing of Odysseus might well be more implausible on a stage. It is harder to see how Aegeus' arrival in the *Medea* (whether it is understood as coincidental and thus unmotivated by the plot, or as absurdly off-course and thus offensive to common sense) would be less implausible if not seen. And consider Aristotle's main example of something irrational outside the drama, that is, Oedipus' ignorance of how Laius died. Why would the general implausibility of this ignorance—is it likely that a man would accept a recently vacated throne without asking how his predecessor died?—be more or less striking depending on whether or not the audience saw presented the failure to seek information? And what exactly would it mean to *see* such a failure?

What is important in this case is not so much the difference between what is seen and what is merely heard *per se* as the related difference (one Aristotle stresses in Chapter 3) between what is enacted and what is merely narrated. The crucial feature of that difference for our purposes is this: what is narrated can be more selective than what is enacted, and therefore omissions in narrative may be less noticeable. This comment may at first seem surprising, since in some sense tragedy is more selective than epic, constrained by limitations of size and staging. Once one has chosen to enact an event, however, that enactment cannot be elliptical in the way that narrative can.[44] If Oedipus tells us he never knew how Laius died, he need say nothing about the context that reveals this surprising lack. But if Sophocles had actually portrayed a Theban delegation offering the throne to Oedipus and explaining that their own king had recently died, the absence of an important question between the offer and the acceptance would be more apparent.

Indeed, since throughout the **Poetics** Aristotle stresses the fact that it is the structure of events in likely or necessary sequence that is chiefly productive of audience response, the difference between the fully enacted and the merely narrated should be as important for audience response as the difference between what is seen and what is heard. If what is seen is more striking than what is heard, and therefore commands our powers of attention more fully, what is enacted is less selective than what is narrated, and therefore makes a greater demand on our powers of connection.

But several times in the **Poetics** Aristotle seeks to diminish the importance for tragedy of what we see, that is of staging or enactment. He tells us in Chapter 6 that the effect *(dunamis)* of tragedy may be achieved without staging (1450b18-20); later he comments that in the work of the best poets, pity and fear result from the plot and not from the spectacle (14.1453b1-7), and that if the plot is well constructed we should be able to experience pity and fear, even without seeing the play, by hearing of its events. Finally, although spectacle may make our pleasures especially vivid, that very vividness can be achieved by a reading as well as by enactment (26.1460a15-18). What is important, then, for audience response is not the difference between what is enacted and what is narrated, but the difference between what is *written to be enacted* and what is narrated or written to be narrated. Such an account receives support especially from the passage in Chapter 26, in which the spectacle seems to create an effect that is somehow present even when the play is only read.

Even this distinction, however, is not without difficulties in the context of the **Poetics** as a whole. Epic is a narrative genre, yet Aristotle makes it clear that epic has almost as strong an effect on the audience as tragedy, and that its events too must be connected; in epic too the irrational is undesirable, even if it is more acceptable there than in tragedy.

What is implicit here is that the more closely narrative approximates to drama (a desideratum suggested by Aristotle's praise of Homer in Chapter 24 for being more mimetic in the dramatic sense than other epic poets), that is, the more vivid and more detailed its narration, the more it will evoke the same response as drama, and the less freely it will admit of the marvellous and the irrational or absurd. If the audience heard Oedipus (or a narrator) telling the story of his taking the throne as fully as he tells the story of his encounter with Laius, it might well have as much difficulty with the narration as with an enacted version. Perhaps, then, the crucial limitation on what is outside, the limitation that makes it an appropriate home for the irrational, is not *that* it is narrated so much as *how* it is narrated.

The view that an audience is similarly affected by what is actually seen, what is made vivid, and what is narrated in a complete way gains support from Aristotle's **Rhetoric**.[45] In **Rhetoric** II.8.1386a34 Aristotle describes speakers who arouse pity by using gesture, voice, and dress to place events before the hearers' eyes either as just having happened or as about to happen. Here, clearly, the greater effect is due to a kind of dramatic enactment, and the events described are placed before the eyes in a sense only once removed from the literal.

Elsewhere in the treatise, however, Aristotle suggests that a certain kind of verbal presentation alone may have the same effect; in III.11.1411b24, he explains that things may be placed before the eyes by expressions that signify actuality—in particular by metaphors that animate what they describe. Here, the bringing before the eyes, itself metaphorical, results from vivid narration rather than from dramatic mimesis. That what is important is not so much *that* something is narrated as *how* it is narrated is further supported by a third passage from the **Rhetoric**. In III.16.1417a12-16, in the course of a discussion of narrative in oratory, Aristotle recommends that one should relate past events as having happened *(pepragmena)* unless their being described as happening *(prattomena)* will effect either pity or fear.[46] As an example, he cites the long story Odysseus tells to Alcinous in *Odyssey* IX-XII, which as told to Penelope in *Odyssey* XXIII takes only sixty lines; the point is the contrast between the first version, told at length as happening, and the second, told in summary form as having happened. Aristotle supplies two more examples which are instances of the summary ("having happened") form; one of these is the unknown Phayllus' treatment of the epic cycle (presumably an epitome), the other, tellingly for our purposes, the prologue to an *Oeneus* plausibly identified as Euripides'.[47] A story told as happening has a considerably different effect from one told as completed, and it is the former that elicits the traditional tragic response.

Aristotle's location of the *alogon* outside the drama, then, has to do not with his supposed discomfort with traditional beliefs but with the much more fundamental issue of audience response, and suggests that an audience will understand and react differently to what is outside the drama for reasons that have to do with its mode of narration.

Let me sum up what has been argued so far: (1) By "things outside the drama" Aristotle means events that precede or follow the drama and are reported in it. He does not count all such events as outside the plot; indeed, he makes it explicit that although what is outside the drama may be merely background, it may also be a part of the plot. It seems likely that something with a strong causal connection to the staged action (such as the murder of Laius by Oedipus) is outside the drama but inside the plot, whereas something that Aristotle takes to be incidental to the central praxis (the command that brings Orestes to the land of the Taurians) is outside the plot as well. (2) The identification of certain things as outside derives partly from a general concern in the **Poetics** with boundedness and selection. (3) This identification also reflects an interest in the different effect on the audience of what is outside the drama. Partly because it is reported and not seen, and partly because it is less fully represented than events that are enacted, what is outside the drama not only affects the audience less strongly[48] but (we may conclude from Aristotle's treatment of the *alogon*) elicits its critical attention less fully than the drama itself. Since, however, vivid and detailed narration (a story told "as happening") may approximate the effect of dramatic enactment, it seems possible that Aristotle would not identify as outside the drama something so recounted.

VI

Tragedy must frequently refer to earlier or later events without staging them, and some of these events are crucial to the plot. The tragedians exploit this generic constraints as they do others, developing the relationship of staged drama to larger myth in a variety of ways. Aristotle's scattered remarks on what is outside the drama reflect the basic fact of tragedy's reference to past and future events but do not constitute anything like a theory of this rich feature of tragic narrative; they are neither comprehensive nor analytic. Nevertheless, his outside/inside distinction both takes account of a central problem for the tragedians and reflects a significant variation in the way they deal with events not staged, a variation which has implications for audience response.

Consider the range of references in extant tragedy to action before or after the events staged. In the parados of Aeschylus' *Agamemnon*, the chorus recount events from ten years before the play with a declared confidence in the nearly magical efficacy of their own singing. They are selective in the manner characteristic of Greek lyric, but can surely be said to bring what they tell before our eyes. Here is how they tell the sacrifice of Iphigenia:

> Her supplications and her cries of father
> were nothing, nor the child's lamentation
> to kings passioned for battle.
> The father prayed, called to his men to lift her
> with strength of hand swept in her robes aloft
> and prone above the altar, as you might lift
> a goat for sacrifice, with guards
> against the lips' sweet edge, to check
> the curse cried on the house of Atreus
> by force of bit and speech drowned in
>   strength.
>
> Pouring then to the ground her saffron mantle
> she struck the sacrificers with
> the eyes' arrows of pity,
> lovely as in a painted scene, and striving
> to speak—as many times
> at the kind festive table of her father
> she had sung, and in the clear voice of a
>   stainless maiden
> with love had graced the song
> of worship when the third cup was poured
>
>   (227-247).[49]

Such vivid and detailed treatment of past events may be found in Sophocles and Euripides as well, but is less common. More typical of Euripides are the explanatory prologue and the parting speech by a *deus ex machina*, where what is told tends to take the form not of detailed descriptive narrative but of summary. Such summary rarely has the rhetorical effect of placing something before our eyes, confining itself to giving us the facts as facts, though not necessarily without emotion. Here again is the sacrifice of Iphigenia, this time from the *Iphigenia in Tauris*, narrated in the opening speech by Iphigenia herself:

> I came to Aulis, wretched I. I was caught and
>   held
> above the death-pyre, and the sword was ready
>   to kill.
> But Artemis stole me away, and gave to the
>   Achaians
> a fawn in my place, and carried me through
>   the bright air
> to this land of the Taurians, and settled me
>   here
>
>   (26-30).[50]

Such prologue speeches seem clear instances of what Aristotle calls in the **Rhetoric** presenting things as having happened (*pepragmena*) rather than as happening (*prattomena*); recall that one of the examples given there was in fact a prologue, probably from a Euripidean play. The flatness and sameness of such speeches was an object of mockery already in antiquity; witness Aristophanes' parody in the *Frogs* (1198-1247).

A third mode of reference to past and future is particularly characteristic of Sophocles. What preceded the action of the play is introduced gradually and piecemeal, in the form of references to the past by various characters rather than full-scale accounts; the future too is more often alluded to that narrated in full. References to past and future are often so conditioned by a given character's perspective and by the particular discursive context that our sense of past and future is incomplete. In Sophocles' *Electra* the story of Iphigenia's sacrifice is told in typically Sophoclean fashion, introduced by characters as a briefly told part of their versions of events. Thus, Clytemnestra, defending her killing of Agamemnon as just, says:

> This father of yours, your constant
>   lamentation,
> Alone of all the Greeks was bold enough
> To sacrifice your sister to the gods.
> The pain he suffered over her was not the
>   same
> As mine—he only sowed, while *I* gave birth
>
>   (530 ff.).[51]

Electra's response tells more of the background to the sacrifice (558-574), but still as part of an argument, and the sacrifice itself is mentioned as briefly as possible (573); again, as with the Euripidean example above, the events are clearly related as having happened, not as happening.

In contrast with Aeschylus, then, both Euripides and Sophocles—although in different ways, indeed almost opposite ways—frame what is beyond the play as being distinctively outside. So it is not surprising that Aristotle's examples of what is outside include the Euripidean and the Sophoclean modes but not the Aeschylean. This may be because in general Aristotle pays less attention to Aeschylus than to the other two tragedians, but it may also have to do with the way in which Aeschylus presents the material in question. His more visually detailed accounts of preceding events seem likely to evoke the sort of audience response evoked by dramatic action; they bear as well some resemblance to messenger speeches, which Aristotle nowhere treats as instances of what is outside. Where Aristotle does count as outside the drama an event told with some detail and vividness, namely Oedipus' killing of his father,[52] he excludes this event from the drama almost as an afterthought (14.1454a29-32); his treatment displays ambivalence about the place of this deed in the tragedy, an ambivalence that has to do not only with its centrality in the plot but also with the dramatic force with which it is narrated.

Varied modes of narration make events seem to varying degrees a part of the drama, and evoke varying responses from the audience. A tragedian may exploit the possibility of variation in order to evoke different responses from the audience; Aeschylus' treatment of Iphigenia's sacrifice will again serve as an example.

In the *Agamemnon,* the sacrifice of Iphigenia is recounted in detailed and vivid terms up until the moment when the chorus can no longer bear to describe what happened; there are a number of further references to Iphigenia in the text (1415-1418, 1432, 1525-1529, 1555-1559) and she is kept carefully on our mind by Clytemnestra's words. In the next play of the trilogy, however, the *Choephori,* Iphigenia is never mentioned by name; the clearest reference to her and to her story occurs in line 242, when Electra, explaining to Orestes that she feels for him all the love she might have given the rest of her family speaks of her "sister who was pitilessly sacrificed." The story is here, in epitome, and so is a judgment on the story. But there is no effort to concentrate the audience's attention on that story, to make the audience understand it as part of a sequence of events, or to bring it vividly before their eyes. The sacrifice which was in all but staging a part of the drama of the *Agamemnon* is here clearly outside the drama.

Iphigenia's presence is still further diminished in the last play of the trilogy; her sacrifice is not mentioned at all, and seems to be quite outside the plot. Of course, given that the three plays form a trilogy, to be seen together, the audience will recall the events (seen and narrated) of the earlier plays while watching the later. But each of the plays has a unity of its own, with a beginning, a middle, and an end, and the fact that we obviously retain knowledge from the earlier plays only makes more interesting the fact that the shift in treatment of the Iphigenia story changes the degree to which we respond to it as part of the play we are currently watching. What is important is not so much what we know or even how recently we thought of it as the way that knowledge is structured and called to mind. The play itself shows us what we are to treat, by a selective act of attention, as truly part of the play.

A final question: to what extent do the extant tragedies follow Aristotle's rule that the *alogon* should if possible be kept outside the drama?[53] Are there many examples of irrational or absurd events in what is merely narrated? In fact, and perhaps this is Aristotle's point, I have not noticed many—except the ones that Euripides shows us. For although it is true that Euripides does to some extent seem to locate the irrational or unlikely outside the drama (in prologue, in epilogue, or in choral reminiscence) he seems positively to call our attention to it, deliberately arousing the skepticism, discomfort or laughter that Aristotle implies would naturally be weakest in us at such times. "Seems" is too mild; sometimes Euripides explicitly draws our attention to implausibilities in the background story: could a woman be born from an egg, or the sun go backwards in response to human wrong?[54] Nor is it only in what is outside the drama that Euripides reveals and questions the *alogon;* the case that most seems to fit Aristotle's description of the irrational is virtually flung in our face by Euripides in his famous parody of the Aeschylean scene in which Electra becomes aware of Orestes' presence by a series of unlikely signs.[55] But this may only be to say that Euripides is the most important pre-Aristotelian critic of tragedy.[56]

VII

I conclude by setting these comments about the limits or boundaries of drama in a larger context—outside the drama in quite another sense. It is a commonplace of contemporary narratology that we seek to give narrative structures to our lives as well as to our fictions, and that our desire for bounded narratives is in part a way of dealing with our inability to be fully aware of either our own beginning or our own end, let alone what precedes and follows.[57] Greek culture generally, and tragedy in particular, show a concern both with escaping the boundedness of the human perspective (consider the role of oracles) and with establishing boundaries (consider the role of oracles). And the wisdom of Herodotus' Solon, that we may call no one happy until death, suggests that we require to know the boundaries within which we are to judge the worth of human life.[58]

In *Nicomachean Ethics* I.11, in the context of his discussion of happiness, Aristotle turns to a discussion of Solon's view, and asks whether happiness can be affected by things that happen after death. After noting that we are in any case variously affected by different things that happen to us, he concludes that the happiness of the dead may be affected by the experiences of their descendants, but not very much, and makes the following comparison: it makes more difference whether suffering happens to the living or the dead than whether terrible events are presupposed by the drama or presented onstage (1101a32 ff.).

This analogy suggests the way in which we give varying qualities of attention and significance to what is within and without boundaries, and points not only to Aristotle's own concern with boundaries but to our human preoccupation with boundaries in literature and in life. I am not suggesting that these connections are explicit either here or in the *Poetics,* but that here as elsewhere Aristotle's eye for similitude—the eye not only of the philosopher, but of the dream interpreter and the maker of metaphors[59]—points us beyond the connection he sees to connections that perhaps for him remain outside the range of vision.[60]

Notes

[1] Preface to *Roderick Hudson,* rpt. in *The Art of the Novel,* ed. R. P. Blackmur (1907; New York, 1962), 6. D. W. Lucas (comm., *Aristotle's Poetics,* Oxford, 1968) cites James ad 1450b24. The text of the *Poetics* used here is R. Kassel's Oxford Classical Text (Oxford, 1965).

[2] F. Kermode, *The Sense of an Ending* (Oxford, 1966). See also B. H. Smith, *Poetic Closure* (Chicago, 1968), D. P. Fowler, "First Thoughts on Closure: Problems and Prospects," *Materiali e discussioni per l'analisi dei testi classici* 22 (1989) 75-122, and bibliography cited in Fowler.

[3] Cf. Lucas, *Aristotle's Poetics* (ad 1451b26). It is unclear exactly how well known the stories were. Aristotle himself suggests that the main lines of the narrative must be respected (14.1453b22-26) but notes also that one need not base tragedies only on traditional stories, since "even what is familiar is familiar only to a few but pleases everyone" (9.1451b25-26). Audience knowledge probably varied considerably, with the basic facts of certain central stories known to most though not all.

[4] Cf. also 9.1451b37-39 on playwrights who stretch the plot by adding episodes. In the course of the *Poetics*

Aristotle discusses size from three different perspectives: the length of time a work takes in performance (7.1451a6-9), the length of the play or epic itself on what might now be called the level of discourse (passages cited here and 7.1451a9-15), and the length of the story the play or epic tells (5.1449b12-16, 7.1451a11-15). Epic is said in Chapter 5 to be, like early tragedy, unlimited in time; given the comparison with tragedy and what is said later, this clearly refers only to the duration of the story, that is, of the events narrated. On the relation of these different levels see esp. R. Dupont-Roc and J. Lallot, trans. and comm., *Aristote, La Poétique* (Paris, 1980) ad. loc.

[5] Recent developments in narrative theory have led to heightened interest in the narratological aspects of the *Poetics.* See for example E. Downing, "Hoion Psychê: An Essay on Aristotle's Muthos,"‧*Classical Antiquity* 3 (1984) 164-178; Dupont-Roc and Lallot, *Aristote, La Poétique;* S. Halliwell, *Aristotle's Poetics* (London and Chapel Hill, 1986); S. Halliwell, trans. and comm., *The Poetics of Aristotle* (London and Chapel Hill, 1987); P. Ricoeur, *Time and Narrative,* Vol. 1, trans. K. McLaughlin and D. Pellauer (Chicago and London, 1984), trans. of *Temps et Récit,* Vol. 1 (Paris, 1983). Halliwell's treatment of Aristotle's "outside the drama" is the most thorough to date.

[6] See esp. Halliwell, *Aristotle's Poetics,* and *The Poetics of Aristotle.*

[7] The variation in terminology is rendered doubly problematic by textual debate. Kassel's text gives the manuscript reading, and brackets (following W. von Christ) the words most frequently left out *(dia tina aitian exō tou katholou).* If we accept this emendation, we read that the fact that the god commanded the brother to come, and the purpose of his doing so, are outside the plot or story *(exō tou muthou);* if we leave the text unemended (so most recently R. Janko, *Aristotle, Poetics I with the Tractatus Coislinianus);* (Indianapolis, 1987) and Dupont-Roc and Lallot, *Aristote, La Poétique),* we learn in addition that the god gave his command for some reason outside the general sketch *(exō tou katholou).* Depending on our choice, either the general background of Orestes' arrival is outside the *muthos,* or that general background is outside the *muthos* and contains an element which is outside the general outline as well. Those who try to distinguish the *katholou* from the *muthos* run into difficulties not so much because of theoretical problems as because it is difficult to see the cause of the oracle as having a different status from the oracle itself and the purpose of the god in sending Orestes. The duplication of "outside" in one speech is awkward, even for the *Poetics;* stranger still is that the "outside" apparently more relevant to the subject here under discussion—"outside the general outline"—is the one in-

troduced parenthetically. See Dupont-Roc and Lallot and Janko ad loc. for the most interesting attempts at interpreting the ms. text.

[8] This section of Chapter 15 appears to deal with some concerns of plot that intrude briefly on a larger discussion of character; on the problem of the passage's relation to what proceeds see the various commentators ad loc. Aristotle is here using the term *apo mēchanēs* (literally, "from the crane") in an extended sense, to cover other sorts of (sudden) divine intervention as well (see Lucas, *Aristotle's Poetics* ad loc., and cf. Else, *Aristotle's Poetics* (Ann Arbor, MI, 1967), 470-473 for a different view).

[9] The topic here is ostensibly epic, but the constraint seems to apply to either genre, and Aristotle's examples are mostly drawn from tragedy, in which he thinks the presence of the *alogon* is more problematic.

[10] See on this point esp. Janko, *Aristotle Poetics I* and Dupont-Roc and Lallot, *Aristote, La Poétique.* The term *mutheuma* occurs nowhere else in the *Poetics,* and all the other examples of its use seem to be considerably later. The word is sometimes taken (by Lucas, *Aristotle's Poetics,* for example, ad loc.) as the equivalent of *muthos* (see E. Downing), "Hoion Psyche: An Essay on Aristotle's Muthos," *Classical Antiquity* 3 (1984) 164-178).

[11] E.g. Laius' rape of Pelops' son Chrysippus, long before the events of Sophocles' *Oedipus Tyrannus,* or Heracles' fatal second marriage, to Deianeira, after the events of Euripides' *Heracles.*

[12] See Euripides' play, 1-66, 77-93; even if we envision a somewhat different play, the way Aristotle speaks of Iphigenia's past suggests that it is not actually enacted.

[13] O. B. Hardison (*Aristotle's Poetics,* trans. L. Golden, 2nd edn (Tallahassee, FL 1981), ad loc.), takes *logos* (1455a34, rendered as "argument") as the larger, more inclusive term, and *muthos* as the less inclusive; his discussion is interesting but not altogether convincing. For a different reason for Aristotle's exclusion of Orestes' past, see below on Else, *Aristotle: Poetics* and Halliwell, *Aristotle's Poetics.*

[14] Again, see Downing, "Hoion Psychê."

[15] See (for example) G. Genette, *Narrative Discourse: An Essay in Method,* trans. J. E. Lewin (Ithaca, 1980), trans. of "Discours du récit," *Figures III* (Paris, 1972), and T. Todorov, "Les catégories du récit littéraire," *Communications* 8 (1966) 125-151. For a helpful general account of issues and terminology in narrative theory, see S. Chatman, *Story and Discourse: Narrative Structure in Fiction and Film* (Ithaca, 1978).

[16] Cf. Halliwell, *The Poetics of Aristotle,* ad Ch. 18; he sees Aristotle's distinction as even more problematic than I have suggested here. On his response to this question, see below.

[17] Dupont-Roc and Lallot, *Aristote, La Poétique* (ad 1450b37) cite *Politics* VII, 1326a33 ff. and its limitations on the best city-state, *Metaphysics* 1078a36 on the beauty of mathematical entities in virtue of order, symmetry and limitation *(to horismenon).* Cf. also Aristotle on *exō tou pragmatos* in the *Rhetoric* and his complex and interesting discussion of what is *exō tou ouranou* in *De Caelo* I, 9.

[18] Cf. 24.1459b18-20. When Iphigenia speaks the prologue to Euripides' *Iphigenia in Tauris,* she tells us, among other things, both where the plot begins (with her sacrifice, according to Aristotle's outline in Ch. 17) and where the play begins (many years later, the morning after her dream about Orestes).

[19] What is made known may be the general topic (as in the epic examples given), but it may also be information from the past, as in Sophocles' "my father was Polybus" (Sophocles' *Oedipus Tyrannus* 774, not the prologue in any usual sense).

[20] Cf. also *Poetics* 23.1459a17-21 on the importance of wholeness and unity for the production of the proper pleasure *(oikeia hēdonē)* of a work.

[21] There is one further reference to the *alogon* at 25.1461a35-1461b9, a description of critics who unreasonably make assumptions about what an author means and then criticize him for it; this passage may serve as a caution to Aristotle's own critics.

[22] See esp. Else (*Aristotle: Poetics,* ad Chs. 15, 17; cf. also 306), Halliwell, *Aristotle's Poetics* (231-234 and Ch. 7 *passim*), and Halliwell, *The Poetics of Aristotle* (11-15 and *passim*); cf. also Dupont-Roc and Lallot, *Aristote, La Poétique* (ad 15.1454b8). Halliwell gives a particular prominence to the association between the inside/outside distinction and the *alogon;* in fact, for him this association points to the orientation that explains Aristotle's insistence on a separation between outside and inside. Aristotle's emphasis on tragedy's connectedness in terms of purely human action means that he cannot accept the irrational elements that are a part of the role of the divine in tragedy. Halliwell's wording is telling: Aristotle "deliberately reinterprets the possibilities of tragic drama so as to make the religious ideas of myth *marginal* [my italics] to its purpose" (*The Poetics of Aristotle,* 12).

[23] For Halliwell it is the inclusion of an example from epic that "indicates what we might anyway infer from

the repeated insistence on the principles of coherent plot-construction: that Aristotle's ideal of dramatic action does not readily permit the intervention of divine agency in any form, except "outside the plot"—which is where, we note, the "irrational" in general belongs" (*Aristotle's Poetics* 231, and cf. *The Poetics of Aristotle,* ad loc.). Else, *Aristotle: Poetics* (463-475) reads *Aulidi* for *Iliadi,* thus replacing a reference to epic with another to Euripides, but he too reads the passage as "a warning that the gods are not to be tolerated in the tragic action in any organic capacity" (475).

[24] Halliwell, *Aristotles Poetics,* 232 and cf. his comm., *The Poetics of Aristotle* ad loc.; Else, *Aristotle: Poetics* ad loc., 507-508.

[25] See Halliwell, *Aristotle's Poetics,* p. 233 n. 42 for bibliography on this issue.

[26] Halliwell, *Aristotle's Poetics,* p. 231.

[27] *Iliad* II.155. Athena wrenches the story back to its required and traditional sequence much as Apollo does in Euripides' *Orestes* or Heracles in Sophocles' *Philoctetes.* Aristotle seems to have commented on this intervention in his *Homeric Problems* (see V. Rose, *Aristotelis Qui Ferebantur Librorum Fragmenta* (Leipzig, 1886), fr. 142) but it is not altogether clear how much of the discussion in this fragment and its larger context is Aristotle's own; see n. 41 below.

[28] Cf. Hardison, *Aristotle's Poetics,* ad loc.

[29] That is, it would be an *alogon* like the arrival of Aegeus in the *Medea* (25.1461b21); Halliwell, *Aristotle's Poetics* 232.

[30] Cf. Janko. *Aristotle, Poetics* I., ad loc.; cf. also Else, *Aristotle: Poetics,* ad loc. (508) on the significance of understanding "the priestess's brother" here rather than "Orestes."

[31] Aristotle mentions the custom of sacrificing strangers to the (unnamed) goddess. Halliwell notes the absence from this outline of Athena's concluding intervention (*Aristotle's Poetics,* 232).

[32] Halliwell (*The Poetics of Aristotle,* ad Ch. 9, 111) sees the sort of thing described here as still falling short of the "deep and final inscrutability" tragedy in fact involves. But although Aristotle shows no particular interest in the deep and inscrutable action of the gods we also have no clear evidence that he objects to such action.

[33] Cf. Hardison, *Aristotle's Poetics,* ad Ch. 15, 209-210.

[34] This is apparently what Aristotle has in mind when he says "as Euripides uses Aegeus."

[35] Some scholars (cf. Hardison, *Aristotle's Poetics;* Else, *Aristotle: Poetics;* and Lucas, *Aristotle's Poetics,* ad loc.) suggest that the irrational elements in the casting ashore include the Phaeacian's magical boat and Poseidon's turning that boat to stone. But the former is not at all stressed in the actual putting ashore (the Phaeacians row in), and the latter is a separate matter.

[36] Compare (for example) *Rhetoric* II.22.7-8 and *NE* I.12.3 on praising the gods; cf. also *Rhetoric* II.5.21 and II.17.6.

[37] For Halliwell's view of the necessary limitations on Aristotle's acceptance of traditional religion in poetry, see Halliwell, *Aristotle's Poetics,* 233.

[38] See Lucas, *Aristotle: Poetics,* ad loc. on this interpretation of Aristotle's highly elliptical remark.

[39] The gods are not of course consistent truth-tellers in Greek tradition but there is at least as strong a stress on the force of Zeus' word as on divine deception.

[40] See Rose, *Aristotelis qui Ferebantur Librorum Fragmenta* (Leipzig, 1886), frs. 142-179.

[41] Fr. 145; cf. frs. 142, 149, 153, 163, 170, 171, 172, 174, 175, 178. Fr. 175 is the sole example of allegorical treatment; the rationalization Janko (*Aristotle: Poetics I,* ad 1454b2) cites as part of fr. 142 (not actually included in Rose's fragment, but drawn from its context) may or may not be Aristotle's; see W. Dindorf, *Scholia Graeca in Homeri Iliadem,* Vol. 3 (Oxford, 1877), 91-92, and H. Schrader, *Porphyrii Quaestionum Homericarum ad Iliadem Pertinentium Reliquias* (Leipzig, 1880), 24-25.

[42] It is sometimes hard to tell into which category a particular example falls: some commentators think that Aegeus' arrival is an *alogon* because it is not motivated within the plot, others that it is simply unlikely that a man should return from Delphi to Athens by way of Corinth.

[43] Cf. (somewhat differently) Dupont-Roc and Lallot, *Aristote, La Poétique,* ad 15.1454b8.

[44] Cf. S. Chatman on the difference between novel and film narrative (*Story and Discourse: Narrative Structure in Fiction and Film* (Ithaca, 1978)).

[45] In the relevant passages from the *Rhetoric* Aristotle stresses the emotional response, but it is clear that he is also talking about the degree to which (and the way in which) the audience really takes in what is heard.

[46] See the Cope and Sandys edition for this interpretation. The proper translation of this passage is much debated; I have seen no version that makes better sense than Cope's (E. M. Cope and J. E. Sandys, *The Rhetoric of Aristotle,* 3 vols (Cambridge, 1877)).

[47] On these examples see Cope and Sandys, *The Rhetoric of Aristotle,* and M. Dufour and A. Wartelle, *Aristote, Rhétorique,* Vol. 3, (Paris, 1973) ad loc.

[48] See Lucas, *Aristotle's Poetics,* ad 1454b7.

[49] Trans. R. Lattimore, *The Complete Greek Tragedies,* eds. D. Grene and R. Lattimore, Vol. 1 (Chicago, 1953).

[50] Trans. R. Lattimore, *Euripides, Iphigenia in Tauris* (London, 1974).

[51] Trans. W. Sale, *Electra by Sophocles* (Englewood Cliffs, NJ, 1973).

[52] Sophocles' *Oedipus Tyrannus* 800-813; the terrifying restraint of the narration gives this factual account its own vividness.

[53] Modern scholars share Aristotle's concern with the inexplicable or irrational as a problem in the drama itself—witness the endless articles on the double burial in the Antigone, and other such matters—but often suggest (the opposite of Aristotle's view) that it is precisely when such irrational actions *are* staged that an audience is least likely to notice such problems; what is peculiar will go unnoticed as the drama holds our attention.

[54] See *Helen* 257-259, 17-21, *Electra* 737-745; cf. also *Bacchae* 286-297.

[55] *Electra* 518-544.

[56] Euripides allows his characters to be more critical of unlikely divine action than Aristotle is; he often problematizes these criticisms at the same time, as for example in the *Heracles,* where the hero expresses at 1340-1346 disbelief in the sort of divine misbehavior which is part of this very play's background, calling the tales of such misbehavior "wretched stories of the poets."

[57] See for example P. Brooks, *Reading for the Plot* (New York, 1984), esp. his discussion (in Chs. 1, 4) of W. Benjamin's "The Storyteller [Der Erzähler]," *Illuminations,* trans. H. Zohn (New York, 1969). Cf. also Kermode, *The Sense of an Ending.*

[58] Herodotus, *Histories* I.32.

[59] See *Poetics* 22.1459a5-8, *On Divination in Sleep* 464b6-7.

[60] This paper is based on one presented at the Princeton Colloquium on Classical Philosophy in December 1989; earlier versions of small parts of it were presented at the Comparative Drama Conference at the University of Florida at Gainesville and at an NEH Summer Institute on Language in the Greek Enlightenment. I am grateful to Mark Griffith, my commentator at Princeton, and to the other participants in these occasions for their comments and questions.

FURTHER READING

Bibliography

Herrick, Marvin T. "A Supplement to Cooper and Gudeman's Bibliography of the Poetics of Aristotle." *The American Journal of Philology* LII, No. 2 (April, May, June 1931): 168-74.

> Introduces new titles and includes titles that were omitted from Lane Cooper and Alfred Gudeman's 1928 *A Bibliography of the Poetics of Aristotle.*

Criticism

Adkins, Arthur W. H. "Aristotle and the Best Kind of Tragedy." *The Classical Quarterly* New Series, Vol. XVI, No. 1 (May 1966): 78-102.

> Examines Aristotle's qualifications for the appropriate subject matter of tragedy and the relevancy of such requirements to extant Greek tragedy. Also considers why Aristotle considered some types of experience unsuitable for tragedy.

Belfiore, Elizabeth. "Aristotle's Concept of *Praxis* in the *Poetics.*" *The Classical Journal* 79, No. 2 (Dec.-Jan. 1983-1984): 110-24.

> Studies Aristotle's use of the term *praxis,* or "action" in the *Poetics* and argues that contrary to what critics often maintain, *praxis* as it is used in the *Poetics* does not refer to an action qualified as moral or ethical; rather, *praxis* refers simply to an event.

Boggess, William F. "Aristotle's *Poetics* in the Fourteenth Century." *Studies in Philology* LXVII, No. 3 (July 1970): 278-94.

> Investigates the usage of one of the two Latin versions of the *Poetics* available in the fourteenth century in western Europe.

Bremer, J. M. "The History of the Interpretation of Hamartia." In *Hamartia: Tragic Error in the Poetics of Aristotle and in Greek Tragedy,* pp. 65-98. Amsterdam: Adolf M. Hakkert, 1969.

> Surveys the interpretation of the concept of "hamartia" as discussed in Aristotle's *Poetics* from the middle ages through the twentieth century. Bremer notes that by the twentieth century, two types of interpretations

have evolved: hamartia is viewed either as a moral flaw or as an error. The majority of critics, Bremer states, reject the moralistic interpretation of hamartia and view it as an error.

Cooper, Lane. "Fundamental Demands of Aristotle." In an Introduction to *An Aristotelian Theory of Comedy with an Adaptation of the* Poetics *and a Translation of the "Tractatus Coislinianus,"* pp. 45-53. Oxford: Basil Blackwell, 1924.

In this section of Cooper's introduction, he examines the *Poetics* in order to understand Aristotle's requirements for a comedy to be considered "a perfect work of art."

Davis, Michael. *Aristotle's* Poetics: *The Poetry of Philosophy.* Lanham, Md.: Rowman & Littlefield Publishers, 1992, 183p.

Analyzes the *Poetics* as both a discussion of poetry with the emphasis on tragedy and, on another level, a discussion of reason focusing on human action.

Hutton, James. Introduction to *Aristotle's* Poetics, pp. 1-41. New York: W. W. Norton & Co., 1982.

Offers an overview of the *Poetics,* discussing its content, method, and its influence.

Kitto, H. D. F. "Catharsis." In *The Classical Tradition,* edited by Luitpold Wallach, pp. 133-47. Ithaca, N.Y.: Cornell University Press, 1966.

Provides a detailed analysis of Aristotle's usage of the term catharsis in the *Poetics* as well as in the *Politics,* arguing that because Aristotle devotes only a few words to catharsis in the *Poetics,* one must gain an understanding of the doctrine from the paragraph regarding catharsis found in the *Politics.* Kitto suggests that catharsis may be understood as the purification "of painful incidents effected by the mimesis."

Lucas, F. L. *Tragedy: Serious Drama in Relation to Aristotle's Poetics.* London: The Hogarth Press, 1957, 188p.

Examines the elements of tragedy as discussed by Aristotle in the *Poetics,* including the definition of tragedy, its emotional effect, plot, character, diction and spectacle, and the three unities.

Rees, B. R. *"Pathos* in the *Poetics* of Aristotle." *Greece and Rome,* Second Series, Vol. XIX, No. 1 (April 1972): 1-11.

Reviews the deficiencies in critical analyses of pathos and examines passages in the *Poetics* in order to determine a more concrete understanding of the term as it applies to tragedy.

Sastri, P. S. "Aristotle's Theory of Imitation." In *Aristotle's Theory of Poetry and Drama,* pp. 15-21. Delhi, India: Kitab Mahal (W. D.) Pvt. Ltd., 1963.

Analyzes Aristotle's theory of imitation as presented in the *Poetics* as a reply to Plato about the nature and purpose of literature. Sastri notes the influence of Plato on Aristotle's thinking.

Rhetoric

INTRODUCTION

Major Works

Most critics agree that *Rhetoric* was composed during Aristotle's second residency in Athens, which occurred between 335 and 322 B.C. The composition date has been placed from 336 to 330 B.C. Although there is little agreement regarding Aristotle's intention in this work, in general *Rhetoric* discusses methods of persuasion, logical and ethical proofs, and the style and arrangement of rhetorical arguments.

It is believed that in addition to his *Rhetoric,* Aristotle wrote a number of other rhetorical works which have since been lost. John Henry Freese has noted that Diogenes Laertus, in his *Life of Aristotle,* listed six such works, among them the dialogue *Gryllus.* Critical attention has focused on the extant fragments of this text and on references to it in other texts. The son of Xenophon, Gryllus died in battle in 362 B.C. After his death, elaborate eulogies were prepared for him, and some critics believe that Aristotle's *Gryllus* was one such commemoration. Others, including Anton-Hermann Chroust, have argued that the dialogue is actually a polemic against this obsequious style of rhetoric.

Textual History

Scholars believe that Aristotle revised the work over a number of years following its composition. Some have conjectured that *Rhetoric* was used by Aristotle as a set of lecture notes. Keith V. Erickson has noted that despite stories regarding the loss and recovery of the text, it apparently was preserved by the Lyceum (the school in Athens at which Aristotle taught). The work may have seemed to disappear, Erickson has suggested, simply because it was not taught for many years. Although Cicero (143-06 B.C.) frequently mentioned *Rhetoric* in his works, there is little to indicate the extent to which the text was studied for the next approximately six hundred years. Erickson has noted that it was the last of Aristotle's works to be recovered in the Middle Ages. The text was translated into Arabic, and then into Latin from Arabic in 1256. Around 1475, the first published analysis of *Rhetoric* appeared, prepared by George of Trebizond. The sixteenth and seventeenth centuries saw the publication of numerous translations and commentaries on the work. After a century of little interest in the work, *Rhetoric* enjoyed a nineteenth-century revival, which has continued into the twentieth century and has resulted in its publication in many languages.

Critical Reception

Modern critical analyses of *Rhetoric* have focused on the construction of the work, on the psychological concepts Aristotle discusses, and whether or not Aristotle proves the legitimacy of rhetorical discourse. Charles Sears Baldwin has studied the way in which Aristotle distinguishes logic from rhetoric. Baldwin has pointed out that while both rhetoric and logic are methods of "bringing out truth, of making people see what is true and fitting," rhetoric seeks to have this truth "embraced" by the people. Gerard A. Hauser has examined the two "instruments of logical proof" used by Aristotle in *Rhetoric:* the enthymeme* and the example. Hauser has noted that Aristotle seems to present example first as an independent method of proof (in Book 1) and then as subordinate to the enthymeme (in Book 2). By exploring the logical relationship between induction and example in Aristotle's other writings, Hauser has concluded that Aristotle presents a single doctrine with regard to example, but one which is bifurcated. Theresa M. Crem has offered a similarly technical analysis of *Rhetoric,* stating that Aristotle approaches the subject as a logician. Crem has reviewed portions of the work as "a scientific presentation of the rhetorical method."

The psychology of *Rhetoric* is also a source of commentary among critics. William J. Jordan has argued that by studying the context of Aristotle's statements in *Rhetoric* concerning the use of metaphor, it becomes apparent that Aristotle regarded the metaphor as a psychological tool. Aristotle's conception of metaphor, Jordan has stated, identifies "semantic and structural characteristics" designed to affect the behavior of listeners or readers. Alan Brinton has also taken up the issue of the psychology explored in *Rhetoric.* Brinton maintains that the psychological concepts present in the text are not the type which become dated, since they are not psychological theories "in the social-scientific sense."

Critics have also addressed the issue that was hotly debated during Aristotle's life—the question of whether rhetoric is legitimate, rational discourse or whether it is sophistry, a method of verbal manipulation with a disregard for the soundness of argumentation. Larry Arnhart has explained that because rhetorical arguments

220

generally lack the strict exactness of scientific knowledge, Aristotle faced the challenge of demonstrating that such arguments were still rational. Arnhart maintains that Aristotle used the concept of enthymeme in order to distinguish rhetoric from both science and sophistry, and that Aristotle successfully demonstrated the rationality of rhetorical discourse. Similarly, Mary Margaret McCabe has studied the objections to rhetoric raised by Aristotle's contemporaries, as well as his responses in *Rhetoric* to such objections. McCabe has concluded that Aristotle avoids both extremes: Plato's complete condemnation of rhetoric and Isocrates's absolute endorsement of it. She maintains that Aristotle demonstrates that rhetoric is truly an art that can be practiced legitimately.

A syllogism is an argument, or proof, used in logic, in which the conclusion of the argument is supported by two premises. An enthymeme is a syllogism in which one of the two premises is unexpressed.

PRINCIPAL WORKS

Gryllus (dialogue) c. 360 B.C.

Rhetorical [*Rhetoric*] (treatise) c. 336 B.C.

PRINCIPAL ENGLISH TRANSLATIONS

The Rhetoric of Aristotle [translated by Sir Richard Claverhouse Jebb] 1909

The Rhetoric of Aristotle [translated by Lane Cooper] 1932

The Art of Rhetoric [translated by H. C. Lawson-Tancred] 1991

On Rhetoric: A Theory of Civic Discourse [translated by George A. Kennedy] 1991

CRITICISM

Charles Sears Baldwin (essay date 1924)

SOURCE: "The *Rhetoric* of Aristotle," in *Ancient Rhetoric and Poetic*, Peter Smith, 1959, pp. 6-21.

[*In the following excerpt from a work originally published in 1924, Baldwin examines both the construction and content of Books 1 and 2 of* Rhetoric. *He*

maintains that in this work, which should be regarded as a philosophical survey rather than a manual, Aristotle demonstrates "the full reach of his intelligence."]

The only art of composition that concerns the mass of mankind, and is therefore universal in both educational practise and critical theory, is the art of effective communication by speaking and writing. This is what the ancients and most moderns call rhetoric. More ample and exact definition, though unnecessary for elementary practise, is demanded for fruitful theory; and the theory of rhetoric has always concerned so many more people than the theory of any other art as to be part of every pedagogy. Here the practise of education not only may be guided by philosophy; it must be. For any coherence in its teaching, rhetoric must be comprehended not only in its immediate functions, but in its pervasive relations to other studies. It is at once the constant in educational schemes and the art among sciences. How we are in a given time and place to learn or teach rhetoric depends on how we understand its function and scope in specific relations.

The importance of a theory of rhetoric in this aspect was discerned by the greatest philosopher of antiquity. In Aristotle's comprehensive survey of thought and action rhetoric is not merely included; it has substantive place. Aristotle's **Rhetoric,**[1] though professedly more analytical than constructive, has a consecutive development. Neither his ethics nor his politics receives more scrutiny or shows more penetration and grasp. As if he dared not slight it, he shows in this work, comparatively brief though it is, the full reach of his intelligence. In detail it has been questioned; but in conception and plan, in direction of thought and order of presentation, it has remained fruitful.

Book I

Book I *surveys by definition and division the opportunity of the public speaker.* (i) Rhetoric is the complement of logic (dialectic). It is the art of persuasion formulated by investigating the methods of successful address; and its object is to promote a habit of discerning what in any given case is essentially persuasive. Proof as contemplated by rhetoric proceeds by such means as may be used in public address. Instead of the syllogism, which is proper to abstract logic, rhetoric typically uses the enthymeme, that approximate syllogism which is proper and necessary to the actual concrete discussion of public questions. Thus rhetoric serves as a general public means (1) of maintaining truth and justice against falsehood and wrong, (2) of advancing public discussion where absolute proof is impossible, (3) of cultivating the habit of seeing both sides and of exposing sophistries and fallacies, and (4) of self-defense. (ii) The means of persuasion outside of rhetoric . . . are witnesses, documents, and other evidence; the means within the art of rhetoric . . . are the moral force of the speaker, his adaptation to the disposition of the audience, and his arguments. (iii) The three fields of rhetoric are: (1) deliberative address to a popular assembly, discussing the expediency of a proposal for the future; (2) forensic address to a court, discussing the justice of a deed in the past; and (3) panegyric, commemorating the significance of a present occasion. The eleven remaining chapters of this book analyze each of these fields in its main aspects, or fundamental topics, *e. g.,* wealth, happiness, government, crime, virtue, etc.[2]

The bare digest will show that Aristotle's **Rhetoric** is hardly a manual. In fact, it is rather less a manual than is his **Poetic.** It is a philosophical survey. The scope of rhetoric is measured not by any scheme of education, but by the relations of knowledge to conduct and affairs. To be comprehended, this great work should be read consecutively, for it is not merely systematic; in spite of parts undeveloped, it is progressive, and its chief significance, perhaps, is from its total development. The following discussion presupposes a fresh and consecutive reading.

About rhetoric Aristotle would first of all have right thinking, conceptions large enough to be suggestive and distinct enough to be true. So the definition in his first chapter is slowly inductive. First we are to distinguish rhetoric from logic.[3] As modes of thought the two are alike general, both applicable universally, neither having its own subject-matter. As modes of utterance they differ typically in that while logic is abstract, rhetoric is concrete; while the one is analytic, the other is synthetic; while the one is a method of study, the other is a method of communication.

Rhetoric, no less than logic, has subject-matter in every given case. Only its perverters teach it as merely an art of dealing with persons, of reaching an audience. No less than logic, it is a means of bringing out truth, of making people see what is true and fitting. But rhetoric contemplates having truth embraced. It is the application of proof to people. Its distinction from logic is here, in the typical mode of proof. The type in logic is the syllogism; the type in rhetoric Aristotle calls the enthymeme.[4] By this he means concrete proof, proof applicable to human affairs, such argument as is actually available in current discussion. The enthymeme is not inferior to the syllogism; it is merely different. Actually, public address on current public questions cannot be carried on by syllogisms or by final inductions. That by which it can be carried on, the strongest proof possible to actual discussion, Aristotle calls enthymeme.

From this typical mode of rhetoric Aristotle gathers its fourfold function: first and foremost, to make truth prevail by presenting it effectively in the conditions of actual communication, to move; second, to advance

inquiry by such methods as are open to men generally, to teach; third, to cultivate the habit of seeing both sides and of analyzing sophistries and fallacies, to debate; and finally to defend oneself and one's cause. That truth does not always prevail shows the need of effective presentation. The first function, then, of rhetoric is to make truth prevail among men as they are. Truth cannot be learned by the mass of men through scientific investigation; for that demands special training. A second direction, then, of rhetoric is to make the results of investigation generally available, to teach truth in general human terms. Debate, Aristotle's third item, which is one whole field of rhetoric, may indeed be mere logical fence, using terms and propositions as mere counters; but real skill in debate, the habit of seeing both sides and of analyzing sophistries and fallacies, tends to make truth emerge from current discussion. The fourth use of rhetoric, for self-defense, seems added merely for completeness and to rebut the common objection that rhetoric is abused. That, says Aristotle, is no argument against it.[5]

The definition implied and sketched in Chapter I and formulated in Chapter II, may be summed up in the word persuasion, if we are careful to speak of persuasion not as achievement, but as method. Just as we ask of medicine, not that it shall infallibly heal—a degree of achievement impossible in human affairs—but that it shall discern and use all the means of healing available in the given case, so the true end of rhetoric is to induce such habitual skill as shall *discern in any given case the available means of persuasion.*[6]

As means of persuasion we must include both those that are extrinsic and those that are intrinsic,[7] those that lie outside the art of rhetoric in the domains of subject-matter and those that lie within, the facts of the case and the technic of making them tell. For rhetoric has to include subject-matter, the forces of knowledge. Though this is extrinsic in the sense of lying outside the art of rhetoric, it is essential. Rhetoric is an art, as Aristotle is careful to show; but it differs from other arts in the degree of importance it must always attach to its subject-matter. The division here into extrinsic means and intrinsic means as both necessary to persuasion is not merely the obvious one into matter and manner, substance and style; it is a division of the springs of composition, the sources of effectiveness, into those that lie outside and those that lie inside of utterance, or presentation. It frankly accepts rhetoric as more than artistic, as never self-sufficient and absolute, as always relating presentation to investigation.

Equally philosophical is the following division[8] of the intrinsic means of persuasion into: (1) those inherent in the character or moral potentiality . . . of the speaker, (2) those inherent in his actual moving of the audience, and (3) those inherent in the form and phrase of the speech itself. That the three are not mutually exclusive is evident and must have been deliberate. Aristotle is telling us that rhetoric as an art is to be approached from these three directions and in this order. The division is comprehensive not only as being satisfying psychologically, but as constituting an outline for the whole work, the headings of the development in three books: first, the speaker himself; secondly, the audience; and finally, in the light of these two, and as the bringing of the one to bear on the other, the speech. Book I deals with the speaker as himself the prime means of persuasion. Rhetoric, Aristotle implies, is necessarily ethical in that everything consecutively imparted or communicated, as distinct from the abstractions of geometry or logic, is subjective. Moreover, in making the speaker the point of departure Aristotle admits that other trend of classical pedagogy which made rhetoric a cultivation of personality. Book II, proceeding to the second item of the division above, deals with the audience, with knowledge of human nature, especially of typical habits of mind; for rhetoric in this aspect too is ethical. It deals with the interaction of moral forces in speaker and audience, and also with the direct arousing of emotion. The speech itself, the final utterance, which is the subject of Book III, has thus been approached as the art of adjusting the subject-matter of a given case through the intelligence and emotion of the speaker to the intelligence and emotion of the audience. This is the only book of very specific technic; and it comes last psychologically.

Aristotle's division and its order are the division and the order not merely of analysis, but of much the same synthesis as underlies the actual processes of composition. I begin with myself; for the subject-matter else is dead, remaining abstract. It begins to live, to become persuasive, when it becomes my message. Then only have I really a subject for presentation. A subject, for purposes of address as distinct from purposes of investigation, must include the speaker. It is mine if it arouses me. I consider next the audience, not for concession or compromise, but for adaptation. What is mine must become theirs. Therefore I must know them. . . . My address becomes concrete through my effort to bring it home. The truth must prevail-through what? Against what? Not only through or against reasoning, but through or against complexes of general moral habit and the emotions of the occasion. I must establish sympathy, win openness of mind, instruct in such wise as to please and awaken, rouse to action. My speech is for these people now. Only thus am I ready to consider composition; for only thus can I know what arguments are available, or what order will be effective, or what style will tell.

This is the philosophy of presentation. What is its practise? Rhetoric ranges for subject-matter most often in the fields of social ethics and politics, tempting its professors, Aristotle adds acutely, to assume the mask of politics.[9] It deals with "the ordinary and recognized subjects of deliberation,"[10] with matters still in dispute and doubt. Thus dealing with social and political conduct, it can neither proceed, as logic does, by absolute propositions nor arrive at logical demonstration. Its premises are not universals, but generally accepted probabilities. That is, to resume his previous distinction, the mode of rhetoric is not the syllogism or induction proper to logical formulation, but the enthymeme or instances proper to actual presentation. The mode of scientific induction emerges to-day in the "gas laws" or the formula of the velocity of light; the mode of rhetoric emerges in Huxley's "Piece of Chalk." Abstract deduction is summed up in the syllogism;[11] concrete deduction, in the enthymeme. By enthymeme, as Aristotle has now made fully clear, is meant a "rhetorical syllogism" in the sense of a deduction available concretely for presentation, as distinct from a deduction formulated abstractly for analysis. His enthymeme is deductive method used constructively. It is not mere popular reasoning, logic modified for popular consumption, but public reasoning, such reasoning as is available with the public for building up public opinion and policy.

Therefore the headings, or "topics," of rhetoric are not peculiar to a particular field of investigation, but general or "common topics" such as justice or expediency, which express common human relations. To deviate from these into the method peculiar to a given subject-matter, physics for example, is to pass[12] from rhetorical method for presentation over to scientific method for analysis; and this, of course, the speaker must do to the extent of mastering his subject-matter before he presents it. Though he must not forget that his ultimate task is to present to an audience and therefore concretely, neither can he forget that what is to be presented must be acquired. In so far as he investigates he will follow scientific method, the analysis proper to the field, the "special topics." Thus for his education he needs some study of the "special topics" of those sciences that furnish most of his subject-matter, the "special topics" of ethics and politics. Of these he must have, as part of his equipment, a practical or working knowledge, the orator's equipment for considering each case within its own field as well as in its general relations to human nature. Aristotle's distinction here between general and special "topics" coincides with his earlier division (page 10) of the means of persuasion into intrinsic and extrinsic. The extrinsic means are knowledge, to be got by the methods of getting; the intrinsic means are utterance, to be given by the methods of giving.

At this point, the opening of Chapter iii,[13] Aristotle makes his scientific division of rhetoric by its fields. The three fields of rhetoric are: (1) the *deliberative,* persuasion in public assemblies as to matters of current discussion, looking to the future, urging expedi-

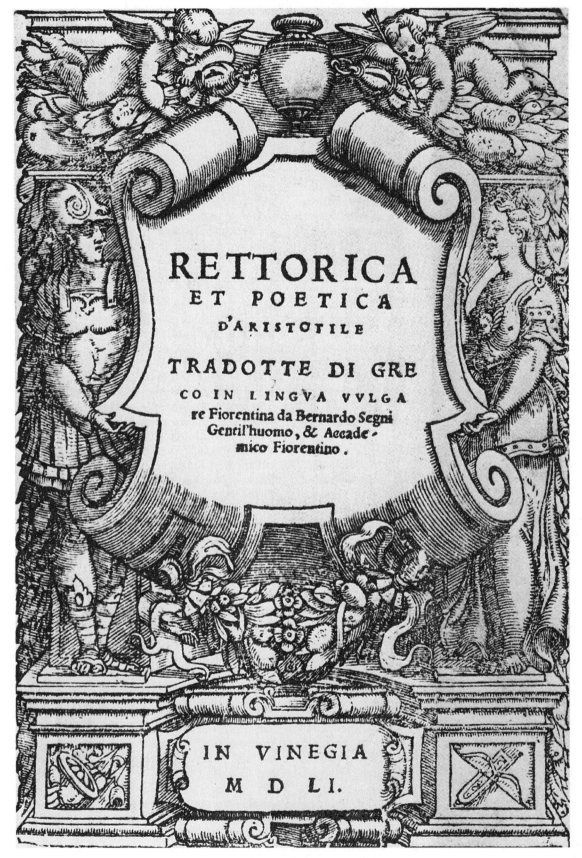

RETTORICA
ET POETICA
D'ARISTOTILE

TRADOTTE DI GRE
CO IN LINGVA VVLGA
re Fiorentina da Bernardo Segni
Gentil'huomo, & Accade-
mico Fiorentino.

IN VINEGIA
M D LI.

Frontispiece to the 1551 edition of the Rhetoric.

ency; (2) the *forensic,* accusation and defense in courts, looking to the past, urging justice; and (3) the *occasional,*[14] praise or blame, looking to the present, urging honor. The underlying, general, or "final topics" of rhetoric, as distinct from the special topics that it uses from other studies, are thus seen to be expediency (including practicability), justice, honor, and their opposites; and the special topics drawn by rhetoric from philosophy, ethics, and politics may be grouped in a speaker's compend of these studies according as they apply to the deliberative, the forensic, or the occasional field.

In deliberative oratory[15] the speaker deals with good and bad, not in the abstract as the philosopher contemplates virtue or happiness, but in concrete matters of doubt and dispute. So his topic of possibility is not abstract, as in mathematics, but concrete, in relation to human will. So in general Aristotle disclaims for his classification of the ordinary subjects of deliberative oratory any attempt at scientific division or scientific method of investigation. Those he follows in his other works; here the analysis that he provides is avowedly practical. Since in politics,[16] for example, the public speaker needs to know something of finance, war, commerce, legislation, Aristotle gives him a suggestive summary of what he should learn. In our modern educational systems such a summary has far less importance; but the correlation remains vital. Pedagogically as well as philosophically, deliberative oratory must be correlated with its natural subject-matter. So to-day college courses in rhetoric demand correlation with college courses in history, sociology, economics, and politics. The professors of these subjects train for investigation, teaching the scientific method proper to each; the professor of rhetoric trains for presentation, teaching general methods, Aristotle's general or "final topics," for handling all such material. But unless each method of training can make use of the other, both will suffer. Rhetoric must lean upon such real knowledge of a given subject-matter as is furnished by the studies dealing with that subject-matter scientifically, i. e., by its "special topics." Meantime Aristotle's summary is intended not to explore these special topics, but to show what they are.

Similarly the student of deliberative oratory needs such a survey of philosophy[17] as will acquaint him with current ideas concerning happiness, whether of rank, offspring, wealth, honor, health, beauty, or strength, and concerning a good old age, friendship, fortune, and virtue. Therefore Aristotle, summarizing these conceptions, supplies[18] a cursory examination of good in general and of goods, or good things, in particular, proceeding[19] both by definition and by comparison, and not limiting his discussion to the deliberative field. To the latter, and to politics, he reverts in the concluding chapter[20] of this section by enumerating briefly the

common forms of polity: democracy, oligarchy, aristocracy, and monarchy.

Since occasional oratory[21] demands an equipment primarily ethical, Aristotle provides a summary of moral nobility[22] by definition and comparison. This is applied more specifically than the preceding section to rhetorical method, in this case to the method of enhancing or heightening and to the method of comparison.

For forensic oratory[23] Aristotle provides as a speaker's compend of philosophy a survey of the objects and conditions of crime. He makes no specific mention of what we now call criminal tendencies; and his division of "extrinsic proofs," i. e., of legal evidence (laws, witnesses, contracts, tortures, the oath) is for the modern lawyer neither scientific nor significant.

Book II

As Book I is the book of the speaker, Book II is the book of the audience. The audience is not merely discussed; it furnishes the point of view. As Book I considers the necessities and opportunities of the speaker, so Book II considers the attitude of the audience. Book I is rhetoric as conceived; Book II is rhetoric as received.

> Since rhetoric is for judgment-for even deliberative speeches are judged, and forensic is [concerned entirely with] judgment-we must see to it not only that the speech shall be convincing and persuasive, but also that the judge shall be in the right frame of mind. For it makes a great difference to persuasion, especially in deliberative speeches, but also in forensic, how the speaker strikes the audience—both how the hearers think he regards them, and in addition how they are disposed toward him. How the speaker strikes the audience is of more practical concern for deliberative speeches; how the hearer is disposed, for forensic. The effect is not the same on a friendly audience as on a hostile one, on the angry as on the tranquil, but either different altogether or different in degree. . . . Three [impressions] constitute persuasiveness—three, that is, outside of the arguments used: wisdom, virtue, and good will [i.e., a speaker's persuasiveness, in the sense of his personal effect on his hearers, depends on their believing him to be wise, upright, and interested in them]. . . . From what sources [in moral habits. . .], then, the speaker may strike his hearers as wise and earnest we must gather from the analysis of the virtues, whether his immediate purpose be to make his audience feel thus and so or to appear thus and so himself; but good will and affection we must discuss now under the head of the emotions. . . . By emotions I mean any changes, attended by pain or pleasure, that make a difference to men's judgment [of a speech]; e.g., anger, pity, fear, etc., and their opposites. The consideration of each emotion—anger, for instance—must have a threeford division: (1)how people are angry, (2)

what they are angry at, and (3) why; for if we should know only one or two of these, not all three, it would be impossible to excite anger, and so with the other emotions.[24]

In this way Aristotle proceeds to analyze, in Chapters ii-xi, the common emotions: anger, love, fear, shame, benevolence, pity, envy, emulation, and their opposites. The relation of these to the formation of character leads to six chapters on character in youth, in age, in the prime of life, and on the typical dominant traits of character seen respectively in persons of social rank, of wealth, of power, and of good fortune.[25] The classicifaction here will be more satisfying as psychology if we remember that it analyzes the common types of character and emotion in a crowd. Aristotle is attempting neither an analysis of mental operations nor a science of human nature, but such a practical classification as may inculcate the habit of adaptation to the feelings of an audience.

The psychological analysis of the audience concluded with Chapter xvii, Aristotle turns to rhetoric in our ordinary sense at Chapter xviii with a recapitulation.[26] "The use of persuasive discourse," he says, resuming the language of the opening of this book, "is for judgment," or decision; i. e., persuasion connotes an audience to be persuaded. After showing that this is true in all cases, and summarizing briefly the main aspects of Books I and II, he concludes his transition by saying: "it remains for us to go with the common topics."[27] With these he actually goes on, not merely extending the treatment of them in Book I. . . , but considering them now as to their availability, their effect upon hearers. More explicit statement, however, of this distinction might well have made the bearing of these latter chapters clearer. The topic of possibility implies the range of the argument from antecedent probability (*a priori*). Example includes analogy, both from history and from fiction, with specific mention of fables. In this wide sense, including mere illustration, it means little more than vividness of presentation through the concrete and specific; but that its persuasive value far exceeds its logical cogency no one doubts who knows audiences. This is the angle, too, from which Aristotle discusses maxims. "They have great service for speeches because audiences are commonplace. People are pleased when a speaker hits on a wide general statement of opinions that they hold in some partial or fragmentary form."[32] The same point of view controls the further discussion of enthymemes,[33] which includes a hint of something like Mill's Canon of Concomitant Variations,[34] directions for logical exclusion, for analysis demanding particulars, for dilemma, and for *reductio ad absurdum*. Remarking the popularity of the refutative, or destructive enthymeme over the constructive, and touching the fallacies of *petitio principii post hoc*, the book concludes[35] with methods of refutation. . . .

Notes

[1] *Text*, edited with notes, commentary, and index, Cope, E. M., and Sandys, J. E., 3 volumes, Cambridge, 1877.
  Translations (the best recent ones in English), Welldon, J. E. C., with analysis and critical notes, London, 1886; Jebb, R. C., edited with introduction and supplementary notes by Sandys, J. E., Cambridge, 1909. Welldon's tabular view is valuable. Jebb's rendering of technical terms is generally more discerning.
  Criticism. Aristotle having engaged the attention of nearly every important writer on rhetoric—for over two thousand years, a list of the commentaries and criticisms would be endless and bewildering. Nor would any addition here to the bibliographies already available be especially suggestive. The history of Aristotle's *Rhetoric* will emerge incidentally throughout this work. The best single exegesis in English, especially of the relations of the *Rhetoric* to the Aristotelian philosophy, remains E. M. Cope's *Introduction to Aristotle's Rhetoric*, London, 1867.

[2] Quoted from the author's article on Aristotle in the *Cyclopedia of Education.*

[3] 1354 a.

[4] 1355 a.

[5] 1355 b.

[6] 1355 b. . . .

[7] . . . Cope, *Introduction*, page 150, translates "unscientific and scientific"; Welldon, "inartistic or artistic"; Jebb, "inartificial or artificial." None of these translations is satisfactory in connotation. *Scientific*, or *artistic*, or *artificial* suggests associations not borne out by the context and ultimately misleading. Aristotle says simply "means that lie outside of the art and means that lie within it." The means that lie within are hardly, in fact or in his intention, *scientific*. They are *artistic* in the broadest sense of being attainable by art, not in the narrower sense of belonging to fine art, nor in the colloquial sense of being pretty. *Artifical* they are not at all, except when they are misapplied.

[8] 1356 a.

[9] 1356 a.

[10] 1357 a.

[11] 1356 a.

[12] 1358 a.

[13] 1358 b.

[14] Of the various translations of Aristotle's [XXXXX], "demonstrative" is flatly a mistranslation, "oratory of display" is quite too narrow a translation, and "epideictic" is not a translation at all. The nearest word in current use is "*panegyric*," which is right as far as it goes. But English use, though it lacks a single equivalent word, is none the less familiar with the thing. The kind of oratory that Aristotle means is the oratory of the Gettysburg Address, of most other commemorative addresses, and *of many sermons. The French equivalent is* discours de circonstance.

[15] Chapter iv. 1359 a.

[16] 1359 b-1360 a.

[17] 1360 b-1361 b.

[18] Chapter vi. 1362 a-1363 b.

[19] Chapter vii. 1363 b.

[20] Chapter viii. 1366 a.

[21] Chapter ix. 1366 a-1368a.

[22] [*to kalon*], treated again in Book II from the point of view of the audience.

[23] Chapters x-xv. 1368 b-1377 b.

[24] Chapter i. 1377 b. "In regard to [XXXXX] and [XXXXXX], which move juries, the most important part is to know how these emotions are aroused and allayed. This alone, judging that it is none of their business, the rhetors have not borrowed from Aristotle, though they have borrowed everything else." Philodemus, *Rhetorica*, trans. Hubbell, Transactions of the Connecticut Academy, vol. 23 (September, 1920), page 338.

[25] "The import of these 'characters,' as of the [XXXXX] in I. 8. 6, and the use to which they are to be applied, may be thus expressed in other words. Certain ages and conditions of men are marked by different and peculiar characteristics. A speaker is always liable to be confronted with an audience in which one or the other of these classes forms the preponderating element. In order to make a favorable impression upon them, he must necessarily adapt his tone and language [Aristotle means rather his method and arguments] to the sentiments and habits of thought prevailing amongst them, and the feelings and motives by which they are usually influenced. And for this purpose he must study their characters, and make himself acquainted with their ordinary motives and feelings and opinions. And the following analysis will supply him with topics for this purpose." Cope, *Introduction*, foot-note to page 248.

[26] Certain difficulties here in the text, with the principal emendations proposed, are discussed by Cope in his *Introduction*, and more largely in the Cope and Sandys edition. Vahlen was so convinced of an error in transmission that he proposed to restore what he considered the original order by transposing bodily Chapters xviii-end and Chapters i-xvii. But in spite of difficulties of detail, the present order shows sufficiently clear progress if we remember that these latter chapters (xviii-end) are written, as all the rest of the book is written, from the point of view of the audience. So viewed, what has seemed repetition and expansion of Book I is seen to be distinct, and not merely additional, but progressive.

[27] 1391 b. . . .

[32] 1395 b.

[33] Chapters xxii-xxiv.

[34] Opening of Chapter xxiii.

[35] Chapters xxv-xxvi. . . .

Anton-Hermann Chroust (essay date 1973)

SOURCE: "Aristotle's First Literary Effort: The *Gryullus*—A Work on the Nature of Rhetoric" in *Aristotle: New Light on His Life and on Some of His Lost Works*, Vol. II, University of Notre Dame Press, 1973, pp. 29-42.

[*In the following essay, Chroust argues that, based on the extant fragments of and references to Aristotle's* Gryllus, *the work appears to be an attack on certain types of rhetoric, as well as a defense of "proper" rhetoric, and is similar in content to passages in Plato's* Gorgias.]

In their respective 'catalogues' of Aristotle's writings, Diogenes Lacrtius,[1] Hesychius of Smyrna (the author of the *Vita Aristotelis Hesychii*)[2] and Ptolemy (-cl-Garib)[3] include a composition entitled ***Concerning Rhetoric or Gryllus*** (generally cited as *Gryllus* or *Grylus*). With the exception of a few relatively insignificant fragments, excerpts or references, this *Gryllus*[4] has been completely lost in the course of time, as were most of the other carliest . . . works of Aristotle. Assuming that they actually relate to the lost *Gryllus,* these few extant fragments, however, enable us to draw certain significant conclusions concerning the original form, nature and content of this composition.

When recording the various arguments made by people who denied that rhetoric is an art . . . ; Quintilian observes that 'Aristotle, as was his habit, advanced some tentative arguments of his own in the ***Gryllus*** which are indicative of his mental subtleness and inge-nuity.'⁵ And Diogenes Laertius relates: '[In his *Gryllus*] Aristotle maintains that there are innumerable authors of epitaphs and eulogies upon Gryllus [the son of Xenophon] who wrote, in part at least, for the purpose of ingratiating themselves to his father.'⁶ These two fragments or reports, to which we might add some passages from Quintilian, *Institutio Oratoria* II. 17. 1-14, are apparently the only ancient literary remnants that make direct or indirect reference to the Aristote-lian *Gryllus.*

From the brief remarks found in Quintilian and Diogenes Laertius, it might be reasonably supposed that Aristotle composed a work on rhetoric (in one book) which he apparently entitled *Gryllus.*⁷ In this composition, it seems, he insisted that not every form or manner of rhetoric is an art. . . . Moreover, the remarks by Quintilian and Diogenes Laertius plainly imply that the *Gryllus* was also a polemic (or critical) work. According to Diogenes Laertius, Gryllus (or Grylus), who fought on the side of Sparta against Thebes, fell in a cavalry skirmish which preceded the battle of Mantinea in the summer (June?) of 362 B.C.⁸ In the words of Diogenes Laertius, when Aristotle composed the *Gryllus,* 'a great many epitaphs and eulogies upon Gryllus' already had been written in memory of him. Several years, therefore, must have passed between the death of Gryllus and composition of the Aristotelian dialogue.⁹ Hence, it might be sur-mised that the *Gryllus* was written about 360 B.C., or perhaps, a little later.¹⁰ It may also be assumed that the *Gryllus* is probably the first 'published' or major com-position which can safely be credited to Aristotle, and the existence of which can still be ascertained. In sum, the *Gryllus* was probably written during Aristotle's eighth or ninth year of study with Plato in the Acad-emy, that is, when Aristotle was approximately twenty-five or twenty-six years old.¹¹ It is interesting to note that in what appears to be Aristotle's first major work, the young man takes to task and castigates some of the most prominent and most renowned rhetoricians of his time.

It is commonly though by no means universally¹² held that Aristotle's *Gryllus* was composed in dialogue form, although it is practically impossible to determine whether it was, in W. Jaeger's terminology, a 'dia-logue of discussion' or an 'obstetric dialogue' fash-ioned after the earliest (Socratic) dialogues of Plato. As will be shown presently, in its content it seems to have been written in fairly close imitation of those passages in Plato's *Gorgias* which denounce certain prevailing types of rhetoric. Hence, it might be ex-pected that the *Gryllus* would also imitate, at least to some extent, the external form of the Platonic *Gorgias.* Moreover, tradition has it that the earliest composi-tions of Aristotle, as they have been recorded and listed by Diogenes Laertius, the *Vita Aristotelis Hesychii,* and

by Ptolemy (-cl-Garib), were all dialogues¹³—in a cer-tain sense, 'Platonic' dialogues.¹⁴ Finally, the very title of this work likewise suggests that it was a dialogue. For this unusual title—unusual for Aristotle—seems to be an imitation of Plato's manner of entitling his own dialogues.¹⁵ . . . [As] W. Jaeger has convincingly pointed out, the Aristotelian dialogues, even the earliest ones, appear to have been primarily 'expository' rather than 'dramatic' works—dramatic' in the sense of Plato's early ('obstetric') dialogues.¹⁶

What, then, might be the connection between the title of this work, *Gryllus,* and its ostensible subject, rheto-ric? E. Heitz,¹⁷ among others, advances the thesis that, as is the case with Aristotle's lost dialogue, *Eudemus or On the Soul,*¹⁸ where the title is purely dedicatory, Aristotle chose the title *Gryllus* primarily in order to commemorate and honor one of his personal friends. Just as the *Eudemus,* composed shortly (?) after 354-53 B.C.,¹⁹ commemorates Aristotle's close friendship with Eudemus of Cyprus (who fell in battle trying to liberate Syracuse), Heitz argues, the *Gryllus* was occa-sioned by the death of Gryllus in 362 B.C., and written shortly thereafter in memory of a dear friend Hence, it would also be a sort of *consolatio mortis* or memorial. To justify the title *(Gryllus)* for a work on rhetoric, Heitz concludes that Gryllus himself must have been one of the discussants, and perhaps the main discus-sant, in the dialogue bearing his name.²⁰ P. Thillet points out, however, that Heitz's thesis is highly conjectural, not to say improbable.²¹ Moreover, there is no evi-dence whatever that Aristotle and Gryllus ever were personal friends, or that Aristotle wished to honor the memory of Gryllus in a special dialogue. It is even doubtful that the two men knew each other. Thus, the connection between Gryllus and a discussion of the nature of rhetoric, between the young hero and the dialogue named after him, would seem to be purely accidental.

P. Thillet and F. Solmsen, on the other hand, have suggested what seems to be a more plausible and prob-ably the only plausible explanation of this unusual combination of Gryllus' name and the subject of rheto-ric. On the strength of Quintilian's remark that 'Aristotle . . . advances some tentative arguments of his own in his *Gryllus,* which are indicative of his mental subtle-ness and ingenuity,'²² Thillet and Solmsen arrive at the persuasive conclusion that the *Gryllus* is primarily a polemic piece rather than a constructive or doctrinal work.²³ It is most certainly not a simple memorial, for it would be most unbefitting to turn a memorial or a *consolatio mortis* into a polemic. This seems to follow, Thillet and Solmsen maintain, from the fact that Quintilian refers to the Aristotelian *Gryllus* in the context of his lengthy discussion of 'whether rhetoric is an art.' Quintilian recalls that neither the past teach-ers of rhetoric nor the rhetoricians themselves ever questioned the categorization of rhetoric as an art, and that they were supported in this by many philosophers, among them the majority of the Stoics and Peripatetics.[24] As regards those philosophers who hold the opposite view—who insist that rhetoric is not an art—Quintilian continues, it must always be borne in mind that these particular philosophers, among them presumably Aristotle, did not truly affirm what they actually believed. They merely disputed involved and difficult issues in order to display their ingenuity of reasoning as well as their cristic talents.[25] Of the several arguments advanced in support of the thesis that rhetoric is not an art, Quintilian remembers those which maintained that rhetoric was a 'natural gift';[26] those which insisted that 'nothing that is based upon art can have existed before the art in question existed, whereas from time immemorial men have always spoken in their own defense or in the denunciation of others,' and long before the art or the teaching of rhetoric was invented;[27] and those which claimed that that which a man does or can do without having first formally learned or studied it cannot belong to any art—and all men are capable of speaking, even those who have never (in a technical or formal sense) learned how to speak.[28]

Some of these statements or arguments, it is believed, originally appeared in the Aristotelian *Gryllus*. According to this 'fragment,' Aristotle must have alleged that proper rhetoric, and not every form of rhetoric, has always been considered an art, and not merely a natural faculty or talent; that no one had ever seriously disputed this; and that the several arguments which attempted to deny that true rhetoric was an art, despite their acumen, may not be taken seriously in that they were purely dialectical performances or devices without any real merit—an intellectual veneer invented to enliven and dramatize the whole discussion.[29] In this the young Aristotle still seems to adhere to Plato's early 'obstetric' method of discussion as it becomes manifest, for instance, in the Platonic *Gorgias* or the *Phaedrus*. As a disciple and admirer of Plato, Aristotle probably believed that under the circumstances this particular form of eristic dialogue constituted the established and hence the only proper vehicle for adequately expressing a philosophic thought or for effectively arguing a disputed issue.

Quintilian further notes that although in his *Gryllus* Aristotle offers 'some tentative arguments of his own'[30] against the argument that rhetoric is an art, the Stagirite 'also wrote three books on the art of rhetoric. In the first book he not only admits that rhetoric is an art, but also treats it as a department of politics and of dialectics (or logic).'[31] From this remark Thillet and Solmson conclude that Aristotle's *Gryllus* must have denied that rhetoric, or at least certain types of rhetoric, constitutes an art . . . in Plato's terms. They further assume that at the time he wrote the *Gryllus*, Aristotle was a Platonist and, as such, under the spell of the Platonic *Gorgias* and *Phaedrus*. In view of the change of position which becomes manifest in the first book of the Aristotelian **Rhetoric,** Quintilian apparently considers the *Gryllus* primarily a polemic not against rhetoric in general, but against a certain type of rhetoric as well as against certain rhetoricians or teachers of rhetoric who were prominent during Aristotle's time. Hence, Quintilian also implies that the *Gryllus* is not a doctrinal work or treatise. With this in mind we might better appreciate Diogenes Laertius' observation that 'Aristotle insisted that a great many people had composed epitaphs, eulogies or encomia upon Gryllus, largely for the purpose of ingratiating themselves . . . to his father [Xenophon].'[32] The expression [*tekhnē*] is frequently used by Plato to characterize the servility or obsequiousness of certain sophists and rhetoricians who indulged in abject flattery.[33] Hence, from the fact that Aristotle calls the eulogists of Gryllus (or Xenophon) 'obsequious' . . . , we may also infer that he was hostile towards these rhetoricians, and that in the *Gryllus* he gave vent to this hostility. The *Gryllus,* therefore, must be considered primarily a polemic work aimed at certain rhetoricians and teachers of rhetoric who in their performances had debased rhetoric and, hence, had aroused Aristotle's displeasure as well as provoked his scathing criticism. At the same time, it is probably also a defense of rhetoric—the proper (Platonic) rhetoric as it had been expounded in Plato's *Gorgias* and *Phaedrus*—and, in all likelihood, a lengthy statement as to what constitutes proper rhetoric.

If all this be true, then the remark of Diogenes Laertius (II. 55) can be fully harmonized with the observations made by Quintilian. The realization, that the *Gryllus* is primarily a polemic against certain rhetoricians would also explain the otherwise puzzling title of this dialogue: the *Gryllus* was not written, as some scholars insist, to honor the memory of Gryllus, but to chastise those rhetoricians who, in a spirit of abject flattery, had composed many epitaphs and eulogies commemorating the heroic Gryllus.[34] The death of Gryllus became the occasion for a plethora of obsequious eulogies. These eulogies drew the ire of Aristotle and induced him to attack their composers and the kind of rhetoric they were employing.[35] This is the only possible connection between the title of this dialogue and its real subject matter—between *Gryllus* and rhetoric. Had the Aristotelian *Gryllus* actually been an epitaph or eulogy upon Gryllus, this work would have implied a serious contradiction: flattering Gryllus (or Xenophon) while condemning Gryllus' flatterers.

In sum, when composing the *Gryllus,* Aristotle was motivated not perchance by a personal admiration for Gryllus or Xenophon, but rather by his determined disapproval of the large number of eulogies upon Gryllus and the fawning tenor of these eulogies. Aristotle's ire was probably even more aroused[36] by the participation of some of the most prominent rhetoricians of the day, among them the renowned Isocrates, in the obsequious praise of Gryllus.[37] There can be little doubt that some of these eulogies were abject in tone and over-ingratiating in sentiment. On the strength of the surviving, though extremely scanty, evidence it could even be maintained that the Aristotelian *Gryllus,* as shall be shown presently, is a fierce polemic aimed at Isocrates in particular.[38] If this be so, then the *Gryllus* is also part of that anti-Isocratic literature which originated with Plato and the Academy. In particular, it is the beginning of Aristotle's protracted literary controversy with Isocrates. This controversy, it is commonly believed, was continued in Aristotle's *Protrepticus*[39] and possibly in Aristotle's *Politicus.*[40] Isocrates, in turn, seems to have answered these charges and denunciations in his *Antidosis* which, according to some scholars, preceded (and provoked) the *Protrepticus,* while according to others, it constituted Isocrates' reply to the *Protrepticus.* The *Against Aristotle,* composed about 360 B.C. or shortly thereafter by Cephisodorus, a pupil of Isocrates, among other issues also contained a defense of Isocrates against the attacks made by Aristotle in the *Gryllus;*[41] and the *Ad Demonicum,* authored by an unknown disciple of Isocrates, in turn might have been a rebuttal of the *Protrepticus.*

The excessive number of prominent eulogies and the many obsequious praises which they heaped on Gryllus (and his father) implied, at least to Aristotle and the members of the Academy, that certain rhetoricians regarded rhetoric simply as a convenient means of arousing emotions and passions. Through the deliberate efforts of certain eulogists, in order to achieve purely emotional reactions, rhetoric apparently had been degraded to an emotional appeal to the irrational part of the soul.[42] Hence, it is not surprising that Aristotle, who as a disciple of Plato was conversant with the Platonic *Gorgias*(and *Phaedrus*), should violently object to such contemptible practices, denounce the ultimate philosophic outlook underlying them, and chastise the men who engaged in and countenanced such practices. In rejecting and denouncing this type of rhetoric, Aristotle acts in full accordance with the spirit and tenets of Plato's basic teachings as regards rhetoric and philosophy in general.

Moreover, in refuting these eulogists Aristotle also wishes to reestablish the undisputed supremacy of reason over passion, the primacy of intellectual integrity (in the Platonic sense) over worldly success,[43] and perhaps the superiority of the Academy over the school of Isocrates. In short, he attempts to restore and reaffirm the supremacy of the theoretic life over the practical and pragmatic life advocated by Isocrates, a supremacy which had seriously been threatened by Isocrates and his followers. Furthermore, it is likely that Aristotle, in formulating his attacks upon the eulogists and upon Isocrates in particular, availed himself of the invectives with which Plato had chastised the sophists and rhetoricians in his *Gorgias.*[44] As a matter of fact, it would be reasonable to surmise that the *Gryllus* reiterates in substance—perhaps in a more 'expository' and 'methodical' manner—certain anti-sophistic and anti-rhetorical arguments and utterances found in the Platonic *Gorgias.* Hence, in order to reconstruct the essential tenor of the *Gryllus,* it might be appropriate to turn to this Platonic work. When comparing the *Gryllus* and the Platonic *Gorgias,* we must keep in mind, however, that in the *Gryllus,* Aristotle probably does not engage in eristic duels of verbal thrusts and counter-thrusts so characteristic of Plato's early dialogues. Rather, he might have restricted himself to more prosaic discussions and demonstrations. It was probably in this context that Aristotle, in the words of Quintilian, displayed 'his usual mental subtleness and acumen.' In this respect, the dialogues of Aristotle always differ from those of Plato.

In the *Gorgias,* Plato maintains that rhetoric 'is not an art . . . at all . . . [but] something which, as I was lately reading in a work of yours [*scil.,* Polus'], you claim having turned into an art. . . . [Rhetoric] is a sort of experience . . . producing a kind of emotional delight and gratification. . . . The whole, of which rhetoric is but a part, is not an art at all, but the habit of a ready and bold wit which knows how to manipulate men. And this habit I sum up under the heading of "flattery". . . .'[45] Because true art, that is, Platonic [*tekhnē*] is exclusively concerned with that intellectual activity which always gives a rational account of empirical facts by relating them to ultimate principles and causes, rhetoric, as practiced or promulgated by certain sophists and rhetoricians, including Isocrates, in the opinion of Plato cannot possibly be a [*tekhnē*]. Therefore, Plato insists, rhetoric, like flattery, is actually something ignoble . . . because it aims at pleasure without giving any thought to what is "best." An art I do not call it,' Plato concludes, 'but only an emotional experience, because it is unable to explain or to offer a reason for the nature of its own application. And I do not call an irrational (unprincipled) thing a [*tekhnē*].'[46]

It is quite likely that in his *Gryllus* Aristotle uses similar arguments. However, we must not assume that Aristotle merely restates the basic theses advanced in the Platonic *Gorgias.* From Quintilian's observation that in the *Gryllus* Aristotle 'produces some tentative arguments of his own [that is, not those of Plato?] which are indicative of his mental subtleness and ingenuity,'[47] it might be inferred that in the *Gryllus* Aristotle not only adopts the basic position held by Plato, but also devises some original ideas and arguments of his own, as well as a certain original and distinct method of argument. In so doing, he apparently displays considerable acumen, ingenuity and originality.[48] It is possible, as Thillet points out,[49] that Quintilian actually quotes, some of Aristotle's own arguments, such as the statement that 'all arts have their own subject matter . . . whereas rhetoric has none';[50] that 'no art will acquiesce in false opinions, because a true art must be based on immediate perceptions . . . whereas rhetoric gives its assent to false conclusions';[51] that 'every art has some definite and proper end towards which it directs its efforts, whereas rhetoric, as a rule, has no such end, even though at times it claims to have such an end without, however, succeeding in fulfilling its promise';[52] that 'the arts know when they have attained their proper end, whereas rhetoric does not';[53] that 'rhetoric does things which no art does, namely, makes use of vices that serve its ends, inasmuch as it proclaims falsehoods and excites passions';[54] that 'rhetoricians speak indifferently on either side of an argument . . . and [whereas] no true art is self-contradictory, rhetoric does contradict itself, and whereas no true art attempts to demolish what it itself has built up, this does happen in the operations of rhetoric';[55] and that because 'rhetoric teaches either what ought to be said or what ought not to be said, it is not an art, inasmuch as it teaches also what ought not to be said, or because while it teaches what ought to be said, it also teaches precisely the opposite.'[56] These arguments, some of which are remarkably acute and subtle, could very well have been advanced or developed in Aristotle's *Gryllus* independently, though probably under the general influence of Plato's *Gorgias,* and used in support of Aristotle's contention that rhetoric—or a certain type of rhetoric—is not a [*tekhnē*]. Hence, it may also be maintained that Quintilian's *Institutio Oratoria* II. 17. 14-30, contains substantial 'fragments' of the lost Aristotelian *Gryllus.*[57] But it will be noted that many of these arguments can also be found in Plato's *Phaedrus, Gorgias* and elsewhere.[58]

It has already been pointed out that in all likelihood the Aristotelian *Gryllus* is a polemic directed at contemporary rhetoricians in general (or at least at those orators who appealed to emotions and passions through flattering memorials and obsequious eulogies), and at Isocrates in particular. This latter statement requires additional substantiation. We know from Diogenes Laertius that 'Isocrates likewise wrote an encomium of Gryllus.'[59] The fact that Diogenes Laertius mentions this valuable bit of information in the context of his report that 'a great many people composed epitaphs and eulogies on Gryllus,' and that Aristotle denounced these people for doing this, seems to indicate that Aristotle, in the *Gryllus,* not only refers to Isocrates by name, but probably also chastises him for his obsequious abuse of rhetoric.[60] It would plainly be unthinkable for Aristotle to take issue with these rhetoricians without engaging Isocrates, the most outstanding and most renowned orator of the time, who likewise composed an obsequious encomium on Gryllus (and who was the much detested rival of the Academy).

Quintilian relates that Isocrates was the most distinguished pupil of Gorgias of Leontini.[61] If this was the case, Isocrates' rhetorical style and standards were probably patterned after those of his renowned teacher. Gorgias, it will be remembered, was savagely denounced in Plato's *Protagoras* and *Gorgias.* As has been argued, Aristotle probably had Plato in mind when he patterned some of his own invectives against the rhetoricians (and against Isocrates) in the *Gryllus.*[62] This would lend additional support to the thesis that the *Gryllus* is under the influence of Plato's *Gorgias.*

The surmise that the *Gryllus* contains a sustained criticism of and attack upon Isocrates and the type of rhetoric he advocated also seems to be supported by Philodemus, *De Rhetorica,* col. XLXVIII, 36-col. LV, 44. This lengthy and vitriolic passage, aimed at Aristotle, seems to contain some 'fragments' of the *Gryllus* which so far have been either overlooked or simply ignored: [Aristotle] advanced a number of reasons for engaging in politics [political rhetoric?], namely, first, that one who is not familiar with political events [and with political oratory] is frequently of the opinion that he is surrounded by general unfriendliness. Second, that philosophy will make considerable progress in a city that is well governed; and, third, that he was disappointed in most of the contemporary politicians [and political orators] who were constantly embroiled in petty party politics.'[63] It is not unreasonable to assume that Philodemus quotes here from some arguments which Aristotle used in the *Gryllus* in support of his theses as to what constitutes proper rhetoric or political rhetoric. The above three arguments are refuted by Philodemus in the following manner: 'Of the [three] reasons why he [*scil.,* Aristotle] advocates [in the *Gryllus?*] that one who has the ability to engage in politics [in political oratory?] should actually do so, the first argument applies to himself rather than to a man who takes no active interest in communal affairs. For if he was of the opinion that a man who took no part in current political events would have no [political?] friends, the plain truth is that he himself had no friends, or if he had a friend he could not keep him for any length of time. . . . Philosophy [here Philodemus takes issue with the second reason, *note by the present author*] was not prevented from making considerable progress, just as it did not prevent Aristotle. But even if it had been prevented by someone from making progress, philosophy would never have been brought into general contempt, because philosophy is independent and needs no assistance from any man. . . . He also stated [here Philodemus takes issue with the third reason, *note by the present author*] that he was dissatisfied with present conditions. But we cannot now, as in the golden age, expect sudden improvements, and if we do refer to the golden age of which the poets speak, we would deal with non-existing things and hunt the dreams of the ancients.'[64] All these statements of Philodemus, although in a badly garbled form, might contain allusions to what Aristotle had said in the *Gryllus* about Isocrates and the special kind of rhetoric Isocrates had recommended.

Philodemus continues: 'One who wants to make himself a popular figure among the people who despise the gifts which philosophy so graciously bestows, and who exalt rhetoric as their true benefactor . . . such a person for a short time might have a number of pupils until he returns to philosophy proper. . . . '[65] Aristotle 'did not behave like a true philosopher [when he attacked Isocrates]. . . . For, if the rhetoric of Isocrates was of no use, the proper thing for Aristotle was to let Isocrates go on with it. If, on the other hand, it was useful [for Aristotle to speak out against Isocrates], Aristotle should have done so irrespective of whether or not Isocrates existed. If, however, it was neither of the two, Aristotle should not have devoted himself to rhetoric in order that he might not seem incompetent in the eyes of certain people or to be acting from sheer envy. . . . '[66] When denouncing Isocrates, Aristotle 'most certainly did not understand the true purpose of rhetoric. . . . '[67] For when attacking Isocrates, Aristotle 'was certainly less noble than the teachers of rhetoric [than Isocrates?], for they attempt to impart a certain technique and try to hand down the principles of rhetoric, not merely for the sake of one's peace of mind, but also for the health of the body, except of course those few orators who practice rhetoric for its own sake and delight in denouncing certain theses. . . . '[68] 'If, on the other hand, he [*scil.,* Aristotle] was searching for the truth . . . why did he choose the rhetoric of Isocrates—which he denounced in various ways—rather than political oratory which he considered to be different from that of Isocrates?'[69] Moreover, Aristotle 'had some strange reasons for urging young men to concentrate on political oratory: first, if they acquired practical experience and would immediately take up a practical (political) career, they would be prevented from pursuing some disinterested studies and, hence, would appear lacking the proper philosophic training. If, on the other hand, they would have no practical experience, they could not be effective statesmen unless they would study for a very long time. . . . '[70]

It is fairly reasonable to assume that Philodemus refers here to some arguments which had been made by Aristotle in the *Gryllus* against Isocrates and the kind of rhetoric that had been advocated and practiced by the latter. Hence, this part of Philodemus' *De Rhetorica,* with some reservations and alterations, may be included among the genuine fragments of the lost Aristotelian *Gryllus.* It must always be borne in mind, however, that Philodemus, the Epicurean and persistent detractor of Aristotle, quotes from the *Gryllus* in an essentially confusing manner, trying to discredit the Stagirite in the traditional Epicurean fashion. Hence, it is safe to surmise that he intentionally distorts some statements made by Aristotle. Moreover, in this lengthy and informative passage Philodemus also alludes to what Aristotle probably had said in his course of lectures on rhetoric, which he offered in the Academy between *c.* 360 and 355 B.C.[71] In any event, what is of paramount importance to us is Philodemus' report that Aristotle criticized and chastised Isocrates for the kind of rhetoric the latter had been advocating. And this is exactly what Aristotle seems to have done in the *Gryllus.*

The assumption that in his *Gryllus* Aristotle also denounces Isocrates finds further support in the fact that Cephisodorus, a disciple of Isocrates, at one time attacked Aristotle. In his *Against Aristotle,* probably published between 360 and 355 B.C.,[72] this Cephisodorus reproaches Aristotle for having criticized and wholly misunderstood Isocrates' method, educational policy and general philosophic outlook:[73] 'Cephisodorus, when he saw his master and teacher Isocrates being attacked by Aristotle . . . waged war on Aristotle.'[74] This, in turn, impels the conclusion that in the *Gryllus* Aristotle had denounced Isocrates and the kind of rhetoric or philosophy he propagated. Thus, Aristotle's denial of rhetoric's categorization as an art would seem to be aimed directly at Isocrates.[75] If this be the case, then Aristotle seems to attach to Isocrates, reputedly the greatest orator of his day, the label of dilettante and falsifier. Moreover, in Aristotle's judgment, Isocrates' brand of rhetoric is emphatically not a [*tekhne*]..[76]

The question might now be raised as to what the particular issues were which prompted Aristotle's attack upon Isocrates. It is known that Plato had made the radical claim that henceforth all true *paideia,* including true rhetoric and true intellectual culture, must be founded exclusively on the rational knowledge of imperishable values or absolute principles and on the exclusive use of *phronesis.* In short, he recommended the purely 'theoretic life' without compromise. However; the educational and cultural ideas of the sophists, despite Plato's savage denunciations in the *Protagoras* and in the *Gorgias,* succeeded in retaining a prominent place in the educational, intellectual and cultural life of Greece.[77] This was due in no small degree to the efforts of Isocrates, who pronounced rhetoric—his brand of rhetoric—the sound foundation of all higher education or educational philosophy. More than that: Isocrates severely criticized and ridiculed not only the almost mythical importance which Plato and the Platonists attached to *phronesis,* but also the apparently exaggerated Platonic intellectualism, which held up pure intellectual knowledge as the panacea for all the ills of this world.[78] Isocrates, on the other hand, attempted to find practical solutions to man's almost infinite problems—solutions which could reasonably and effectively be translated into concrete action and, at the same time, retain some moral meaning.[79] Thus, whenever Isocrates refers to philosophy, he has in mind something radically different from what Plato would call philosophy: to Isocrates, philosophy meant nothing more, and nothing less, than a general intellectual and humanistic *paideia.*[80] Isocrates, in fact, became the founder of a literary humanism which in its general outlook was centered on the concrete conditions of life, while Plato fervently advocated a purely philosophic, theoretic and essentially abstract attitude towards man. The clash between these two basic intellectual positions constitutes one of the main events in Greek intellectual history during the fourth century b.c. Much to Plato's annoyance, Isocrates persuasively and effectively advocated his realistic approach to life, arguing it in his orations and writings, as well as teaching it in his school, which about the year 360 B.C. had acquired a considerable reputation (and an impressive enrollment) not only throughout Greece, but also beyond the Hellenic orbit. A fierce denunciation of Isocrates and of the views he expressed in the *Nicocles, Ad Evagoram* and in the *Ad Nicoclem* may, for instance, be found in Plato's *Republic:* 'The harsh feelings which many people entertain towards philosophy originates with certain pretenders [*scil.,* Isocrates], who rush in uninvited and are always abusing those, and find fault with those, who [*scil.,* like Plato] make persons instead of things the theme of their philosophic discussions.'[81]

One is led, therefore, to assume further that in the *Gryllus* Aristotle discusses and criticizes the very principles (or lack of principles) which Isocrates proposed in his rhetoric and, indeed, in his whole philosophy of life.[82] It is here that Aristotle for the first time openly confronts and violently opposes Isocrates' philosophic and educational ideals.[83] The attacks which Aristotle launches against Isocrates and his whole school also reveal something about the intellectual outlook of the young Aristotle, who around 360 B.C. still professed most enthusiastically the intellectual ideals so eloquently propagated by his teacher and mentor Plato, as he would for several years to come. As a faithful and, one might assume, ambitious student of Plato, he was fully convinced that Plato's lofty ideals of the 'theoretic life' were infinitely superior to the intellectual and cultural (humanistic) notions advocated by Isocrates, the most successful and, at the same time, the most dangerous rival of Plato and the Platonic Academy in the Greek orbit.

Finally, Isocrates' eulogy of Gryllus (and Xenophon) probably presented a unique opportunity for Aristotle to participate actively in the 'great conflict of ideas' which separated the school of Plato from that of Isocrates—to take part in the crucial contemporary 'dialogue' between the two most outstanding men of the time on problems touching upon the ultimate foundations, the final significance and the very heart of the truly intellectual life.[84] Moreover, this was also a splendid opportunity to 'strike a telling blow' for the cause of the Academy and thereby earn the attention, and perhaps the admiration and gratitude, of his teacher Plato and the entire Academy. By championing in his *Gryllus* the Platonic-Academic views in the bitter and prolonged debate with Isocrates over the constitution of the truly intellectual and philosophic life, Aristotle

probably displayed all the uncompromising enthusiasm characteristic of youth. At the same time he employed, in the words of Quintilian, all the dialectical acumen, intellectual subtleness and mental ingenuity he could possibly muster, making it a brilliant display of his philosophic (and dialectical) talents. With the sense that he was supporting and furthering the work of his teacher and of his associates in the Academy, Aristotle could not but condemn the cultural and intellectual ideals advocated by Isocrates.

This clash between Aristotle (who here completely subscribes to Plato's philosophic standpoint) and Isocrates—a clash which in all likelihood constituted the main theme of the *Gryllus*—might be reduced to a conflict between an uncompromisingly 'principled philosophy' and a less principled 'practical and result-oriented philosophy of life' which, in a humanistic flair, takes into account worldly success, practical effectiveness and the general human condition within an existential rather than ideal (Platonic) world.

It also appears that the *Gryllus* produced certain practical or tangible results—rewards for which Aristotle had perhaps hoped when composing this polemic. As a consequence of, or reward for, his *Gryllus,* Aristotle was permitted—perhaps even urged—to offer a course of lectures on rhetoric in the Academy. Certainly, this signal honor can at least partially be attributed to this demonstration of his qualification as a teacher and advocate of Platonic rhetoric, and to his loyalty to the Academy in standing up to the mighty Isocrates, a man much condemned and much disliked (and maligned) by Plato and the Academy.[85]

In summation,[86] it may be maintained that Aristotle's *Gryllus* was not perchance a 'memorial' honoring Gryllus, but rather a composition on the nature of rhetoric; that its title, *Gryllus,* is purely incidental; that it was probably written in dialogue form; that it was composed shortly after the death of Gryllus, presumably about 360 B.C. or shortly thereafter; that it adhered in substance to the rhetorical and philosophic standards which Plato had established in the *Protagoras* and *Gorgias* (and in the *Phaedrus*); that it contained a sustained and, presumably, violent attack upon certain contemporary rhetoricians and, especially, on Isocrates; that it denounced Isocrates' alleged indifference or opposition to true—Platonic—philosophy and its attendant rigoristic educational ideals; that it made a strong and impressive case in support of a rhetoric (and philosophy) based upon a comprehensive grasp of ultimate and absolute moral as well as intellectual (theoretic) values; that in the *Gryllus* the youthful Aristotle already displayed the logical, dialectic and eristic acumen for which he later gained much renown; and that in consequence of the *Gryllus,* Aristotle was judged qualified to offer a course of lectures on rhetoric in the Academy.

Notes

[1] . . . See P. Moraux, *Les Listes Anciennes des Ouvrages d'Aristote* (Louvain, 1951), *passim.*

[2] . . . See P. Moraux, *op. cit.,* pp. 195 ff.

[3] . . . See P. Moraux, *loc. cit.*

[4] See J. Bernays, *Die Dialoge des Aristoteles* (Berlin, 1863), p. 62; V. Rose, *Aristoteles Pseudepigraphus* (Leipzig, 1863), pp. 76 ff.; E. Heitz, *Die verlorenen Schriften des Aristoteles* (Leipzig, 1865), pp. 189 ff. In keeping with his general though wholly erroneous thesis that all of the so-called 'exoteric' works credited to Aristotle are spurious, Rose denies that the Stagirite ever authored a *Gryllus.* He ascribes the *Gryllus* to Theophrastus. Rose's theses were refuted by E. Heitz.

[5] Quintilian, *Institutio Oratoria* II. 17. 14 (frag. 69, Rose; frag. 2, Ross).

[6] DL II. 55 (frag. 68, Rose; frag. 1, Ross).

[7] It seems probable that in his earliest works Aristotle followed the Platonic model and, hence, used one-word titles, often naming these dialogues after some personage. See Diogenes Laertius V. 22 (*Nerinthus, Menexenus, Eudemus* and *Alexander;* or *Sophistes, Eroticus, Symposium* and *Protrepticus*). It might be conjectured that the 'sub-title,' *On Rhetoric,* is a later addition.

[8] DL II. 54-5. See also Pausanias I. 3. 4.

[9] While most scholars (see p. 30) are of the opinion that the *Gryllus* was composed shortly after the death of Gryllus in 362 B.C., F. Solmsen, *Die Entwicklung der aristotelischen Logik und Rhetorik* (Berlin, 1929), p. 200, insists that it must have been written several years after 362, because it apparently refers to many eulogies on Gryllus. See also P. Moraux, *op. cit.,* pp. 33, 323 ff.; P. Thillet, 'Note sur le *Gryllos,* ouvrage de jeunesse d'Aristote,' *Revue Philosophique de la France et de l'Étranger,* vol. 147 (1957), pp. 352 ff; O. Gigon, 'Interpretationen zu den antiken Aristoteles-Viten,' *Museum Helveticum,* vol. 15 (1958), pp. 169 ff., and note 42.

[10] See A.-H. Chroust, 'The probable dates of some of Aristotle's lost works,' *Rivista Critica di Storia della Filosofia,* vol. 22, fasc. 1 (1967), pp. 3-23, especially pp. 3 ff., and Chapter I.

[11] Aristotle was born in 384 B.C., and according to tradition, entered the Academy in 367 B.C.

[12] See P. Thillet (note 9), pp. 353 ff.

[13] The fact that Aristotle's earliest compositions were dialogues is attested to by Ammonius, *Commentarius in Aristotelis Categorias, CIAG,* vol. IV, part 4 (ed. A. Busse, Berlin, 1887), p. 6, lines 25 ff.; Simplicius, *Commentaria in Aristotelis de Caelo, CIAG,* vol. VII (ed. J. Heiberg, Berlin, 1894), p. 288, lines 31 ff.; Simplicius, *Commentaria in Aristotelis Physicorum Libros Quattuor Priores, CIAG,* vol. IX (ed. H. Diels, Berlin, 1882), p. 8, lines 16 ff.; Olympiodorus, *Prolegomena et in Aristotelis Categorias Commentarium, CIAG,* vol. XII, part 1 (ed. A. Busse, Berlin, 1902), p. 7, lines 5 ff.; Philoponus (*olim* Ammonius), *Commentarium in Aristotelis Categorias, CIAG,* vol. XIII, part 1 (ed. A. Busse, Berlin, 1898), p. 3, lines 16 ff.; Elias (*olim* David), *Commentarii in Porphyrii Isagogen et in Aristotelis Categorias, CIAG,* vol. XVIII, part 1 (ed. A. Busse, Berlin, 1900), p. 114, lines 15 ff. and lines 22 ff.; p. 115, lines 3 ff.; p. 124, lines 3 ff. See also Plutarch, *Adversus Coloten* 14 (*Moralia* 1115BC); Dio Chrysostom, *Oratio* LIII. 1; St Basil, *Epistola* 135.

[14] Plutarch, *Adversus Coloten* 14 (*Moralia* 1115BC) and 20 (1118C), calls the early writings of Aristotle 'Aristotle's Platonic works,' implying that in their literary form as well as in their philosophic content these writings were very similar to Plato's dialogues. See also Cicero, *Ad Atticum* IV. 16. 2 and XIII. 19. 4; Cicero, *De Oratore* III. 21. 80; Cicero, *Ad Familiares* I. 9. 23; Ammonius (see note 13), p. 6, lines 25 ff.; Elias (see note 13), p. 114, lines 15 ff.; p. 115, lines 3 ff.; p. 124, lines 3 ff.; Simplicius, *Commentarius in Aristotelis Categorias, CIAG,* vol. VIII (ed. C. Kalbfleisch, Berlin, 1907), p. 4, lines 20 ff. See Eusebius, *Praeparatio Evangelica* XIV. 6. 9: 'Cephisodorus . . . thought that Aristotle was a follower of Plato. Hence he denounced Aristotle, but he was really attacking Plato.'

[15] See note 7. Cicero, who read some of Aristotle's earliest dialogues, attests that they were composed in a clear and incisive style; that they were remarkable for their literary form; and that they were replete with logical acumen. See Cicero, *De Oratore* I. 11. 49; Cicero, *Academica Priora* II. 38. 119; Cicero, *De Inventione* II. 2. 6; Cicero, *De Finibus Bonorum et Malorum* I. 5. 14; Cicero, *Topica* I. 3; Cicero, *Brutus* XXXI. 120-1; Cicero, *Lucullus* XXXVIII. 119; Cicero, *Ad Atticum* II. 1. 1. The Ciceronian testimony substantiates the remark of Quintilian, *Institutio Oratoria* II. 17. 14 (see note 5) and X. 1. 83. See also Themistius, *Oratio* XXIII. 319C.

[16] See W. Jaeger, *Aristoteles: Grundlegung einer Geschichte seiner Entwicklung* (Berlin, 1923), pp. 29 ff. (*Aristotle: Fundamentals of the History of his Development,* Oxford, 1948, pp. 28 ff.). All subsequent references to Jaeger are from the translation of 1948. It will be noted that in his later dialogues, Plato changes

from a 'dramatic' literary style to a more 'expository' treatment of his subject. W. Jaeger, *loc. cit.,* also credits Aristotle with having originated a type of dialogue which is tantamount to a 'scientific discussion.'

[17] E. Heitz (see note 4), p. 167.

[18] See A.-H. Chroust, '*Eudemus or On the Soul:* a lost Aristotelian dialogue on the immortality of the soul,' *Mnemosyne,* vol. 19 (series 4), fasc. 1 (1966), pp. 17-30, and Chapter IV.

[19] See A.-H. Chroust (note 18), pp. 19 ff.; A.-H. Chroust (see note 10), pp. 3 ff. See also Chapter IV.

[20] E. Heitz, *loc. cit.*

[21] P. Thillet (see note 9), pp. 353 ff. Thillet argues that the *Gryllus* is a work on rhetoric, which might be referred to as *Gryllus,* but which should really be called *On Rhetoric.* He correctly assigns great importance to the fact that the proper and full title of this dialogue is apparently *On Rhetoric or Gryllus* (and not merely *Gryllus*). To Thillet this particular order or sequence within the title is highly significant.

[22] See note 5.

[23] F. Solmsen (see note 9), pp. 196 ff.; P. Thillet, *op. cit.,* p. 353. See also E. Berti, *La Filosofia del Primo Aristotele* (Università di Padova, Pubblicazioni della Facoltà di Lettere e Filosofia, vol. 38, Padua, 1962), pp. 162 ff.

[24] Quintilian, *op. cit.,* II. 17. 1. See frag. 69, Rose; frag. 2, Ross.

[25] *Ibid.,* II. 17. 4.

[26] *Ibid.,* II. 17. 5.

[27] *Ibid.,* II. 17. 7.

[28] *Ibid.,* II. 17. 11.

[29] See, for instance, *ibid.,* II. 17. 14.

[30] See note 5. Quintilian remarks that Aristotle displays 'his usual mental subtleness and acumen,' when he devised 'some tentative arguments of his own.' Quintilian, *op. cit.,* II. 17. 14.

[31] Quintilian, *op. cit.,* II. 17. 14.

[32] See note 6.

[33] See Plato, *Gorgias* 462C; 463B; 502E; 513D. See also F. Solmsen, *op. cit.,* pp. 196 ff.

[34] See F. Solmsen, *op. cit.,* pp. 196 ff.

[35] That Xenophon was not exactly a friend of Plato is attested by DL II. 57: 'He [*scil.,* Xenophon] and Plato were jealous of each other. . . . ' See also *ibid.,* III. 34: 'And it appears that Xenophon was not on good terms with him [*scil.,* with Plato]. At any rate, they have written similar accounts as if out of rivalry with each other. . . . And in the *Laws* [694C] Plato declares that the story of Cyrus' education [as reported in Xenophon's *Cyropaedia*] was a mere fiction. . . . ' There can be little doubt that Aristotle, who was at the time a member of the Academy and a pupil of Plato, probably shared Plato's dislike of Xenophon.

[36] It is entirely possible that Plato himself should have urged his pupil Aristotle to take these flatterers to task, especially since Isocrates, Plato's old rival, had also composed an epitaph or eulogy on Gryllus. Obsequious eulogies certainly violated the canons of rhetoric laid down by Plato in the *Gorgias* and more recently in the *Phaedrus.*

[37] DL II. 55, on the authority of Hermippus, *The Life of Theophrastus,* reports that Isocrates, the most prominent and best known rhetorician of the mid-fourth century B.C., had likewise composed an encomium on Gryllus. It is quite possible that Isocrates (or perhaps Gorgias, the teacher of Isocrates) was the originator of this type of eulogy. This may be gathered from certain passages in Plato's *Gorgias,* which seem to be directed also against Isocrates. It will be noted that Plato, too, discusses the good man and father who 'had the misfortune of losing his son.' The good man, Plato insists, will bear the loss with greater equanimity than the bad man.

> He . . . will be moderate in his sorrow. . . . For there is a principle and dictate of reason in him, which commands him to resist [the temptation to give vent to his emotions]. . . . This principle would tell him to display patience in his sufferings and not to give way to impatience, as there is no way of knowing whether such things are good or evil. . . . He would take counsel about what has happened . . . and . . . not like children . . . waste his time in setting up a howl, but always accustom his soul forthwith to apply a remedy, raising up that which is sickly and fallen, banishing the cry of sorrow by the healing art [*scil.,* philosophy]. . . . This is the true way of meeting the incidents of fate. (Plato, *Republic* 603E ff.)

[38] See P. Thillet, *op. cit.,* p. 353. F. Solmsen, *op. cit.,* p. 198, note I, suggests that the *Gryllus* contained three distinct parts: (1) a critique of the traditional epitaphs and eulogies; (2) a critique of contemporary rhetoric in general; and (3) a critique of Isocrates in particular. See also some of the remarks in P. Merlan, 'Isocrates, Aristotle and Alexander the Great,' *Historia,* vol. 3

(1954), pp. 60-81.

[39] See, among others, A.-H. Chroust (note 10), especially pp. 13-17, and Chapter I.

[40] See A.-H. Chroust (note 10), pp. 17-18 and Chapter I.

[41] See notes 72-5 and the corresponding text.

[42] Undoubtedly, at that time Aristotle still adhered to Plato's doctrine of the tri-partite soul. Hence, rhetoric, as exemplified in some of these eulogies, would appeal exclusively to the appetitive—irrational—part of the soul, which, in the Platonic system, constitutes the lowliest part of the soul.

[43] Plato, it will be remembered, entertained a purely intellectual notion of [tekhne]. To him [tekhne] is that disciplined objective activity of the intellect which gives account of the true facts and of true reality by relating these facts to their ultimate cause or causes—the Ideas. See here É. des Places, *Lexique de la Langue Philosophique . . . de Platon* (Paris, 1964), *s.v.*, and p. xiii.

[44] This is not the place to discuss in detail the extent to which the *Gryllus* was influenced by Plato's *Phaedrus*. The *Phaedrus,* it will be noted, sheds new light on Plato's later views about the nature of rhetoric (and also on his relationship with Isocrates?). Modern scholarship insists that the main theme of the *Phaedrus* is the connection between philosophy and rhetoric. See A. Diès, *Autour de Platon* (Paris, 1927), vol. III, p. 418. In the *Phaedrus,* Plato maintains that any form of rhetoric which merely attempts to mislead the listeners is most certainly not a [tekhne]. See Plato, *Phaedrus* 260E ff. But there exists another kind of rhetoric which is founded on an understanding of truth and of the one true reality from which it derives its arguments and methods. This kind of rhetoric may be called a [tekhne]. *Ibid.,* 263B ff. But if rhetoric is the art of persuading the soul in order to make it virtuous, then the orator must know something about the nature of the soul. He

> must learn the differences of human souls, for there are so many souls . . . and from them come the differences between man and man. . . . [He] will next divide speeches into their different categories: 'Such and such persons,' he will say, 'are affected by this or that kind of speech in this or that way,' and he will tell you why. The pupil must have a good theoretical notion of them first, and then he must have experience of them in actual life and be able to follow them with all his senses about him, or he will never get beyond the precepts of his masters and teachers. But when he understands what persons are persuaded by what arguments, and sees the person about whom he was speaking in the absstract actually before him, and knows that it is

> he, and can say to himself, 'This is the man or this is the character who ought to have a certain argument applied to him in rder to convince him of a certain opinion' —he who knows all this and knows also when he should speak and when he should keep silent, and when he should use pithy sayings, pathetic appeals, sensational effects and all the other modes of speech which he has learned—when, I repeat, he knows the times and seasons of all these things, then, and not till then, is he a perfect master of his art. . . .

Ibid., 271E ff. Different scholars disagree as to whether Artistotle was acquainted with the Platonic *Phaedrus* at the time he composed the *Gryllus*. Jaeger's thesis, however, seems highly conjectural. The *Phaedrus,* it is widely held, was sritten about 370-69, or shortly thereafter, while the *Gryllus* is usually dated about 360 or shortly thereafter. It would have been rather unusual for Aristotle, 'the great reader,' not to have known the *Phaedrus* by 360 or, as seems even more unlikely, simply to have ignored it. But since the Platonic *Gorgias* which, judging from Aristotle's lost *Nerinthus*, made such an impression on Aristotle (see Themistius, *Oratio* XXIII, 295CD), denounces without exception the sophists and orators as well as their peculiar rhetoric, the *Gorgias* rather than the more conciliatory *Phaedrus* supplied Aristotle with the kind of materials and the form of argument he needed for his *Gryllus*. This might explain why Aristotle apparetnly did not make much use of the *Phaedrus* when composing the *Gryllus*. It must also be admitted that in the *Phaedrus* Plato discusses a type of rhetoric that is fundamentally different from the kind of rhetoric which he had condmewned in *Gorgias*. Hence, Plato could very well call rhetoric a [tekhne] in the *Phaedrus*, whereas in the *Gorgias* he denies its categorization as a [tekhne]. Finally, it should also be observed that in the *Gryllus* Aristotle attacks only obsequious rhetoric, that is, those orators who attempted to arouse emotions and passions. Here he denies that theirs is a [tekhne], but he does not denounce rhetoric in principle which can, after all, still be a [tekhne], provided it complies with certain rational principles. See also P. Kucharski, 'La rhetorique dans le *Gorgias* et le *Phedre*,' *Revue des Etudes Grecques,* vol. 74 (1961), pp. 371 ff.

[45] Plato, *Gorgias* 462 R ff.

[46] *Ibid.,* 465A.

[47] See notes 5 and 30.

[48] See also F. Solmsen, *op. cit.,* pp. 198 ff.

[49] P. Thillet, *op. cit.,* pp. 353 ff. See also F. Solmsen, *op. cit.,* pp. 201 ff.

[50] Quintilian, *op. cit.,* II. 17.17.

[51] *Ibid.,* II.17.18. It will be remembered that in the *Phaedrus, Theatetus* and *Sophist* Plato warns us not to rely on deceptive opinions.

[52] Quintilian, *op. cit.,* II. 17.22.

[53] *Ibid.,* II. 17.26.

[54] *Ibid.*

[55] *Ibid.,* II. 17.30. This could possibly be a reference to Isocrates, who in his younger days was a forensic orator or *logographer* taking on clients and arguing 'on both sides of a case' before the heliastic courts of Athens.

[56] *Ibid.*

[57] It is possible, however, that some of these arguments might also have been advanced by Athenodorus of Rhodes, Critolaus, Carneades, Diogenes of Babylonia, Clitomachus, Epicurus and others, all of whom were opposed to the rhetoricians and, hence, criticized their methods. See Quintilian, *op. cit.,* II. 17; Sextus Empiricus, *Adversus Rhetoricos, passim*; Cicero, *De Oratore, passim*; Philodemus, *Volumina Rhetorica, passim*; etc.

[58] This fact alone would lend support to the contention that Quintillian, *Institutio Oratoria* II. 17. 14-30, contains fragments of the *Gryllus.*

[59] DL II.55. This information is apprently derived from Hermippus' *Life of Theophrastus. Ibid.*

[60] See P. Thillet, *op. cit.,* pp. 353 ff.: P. Moraux (see note 1), p. 31; F. Solmsen, *op. cit.,* p. 204.

[61] Quintilian, *op. cit.* III. I. 13. Quintilian continues: 'Our authorities are not in agreement as to who was his [*scil.,* Isocrates'] teacher. I, however, accept the statement of Aristotle on this subject [namely, that Gorgias was the teacher of Isocrates] . . . ' Frag. 139, Rose; frag. 3, Ross. V. Rose lists this passage from Quintilian among the fragments . . . , but W. D. Ross lists it among the fragments of the *Gryllus.* J. Bernays (see note 4), p. 157, already conjectured that this fragment belonged to the *Gryllus.* In any event, it is quite likely that Quintilian derived his information directly from Aristotle's *Gryllus.* Hence, it may also be assumed that in the *Gryllus,* Aristotle refers to Isocrates as the (most renowned?) disciple of Gorgias.

[62] See also A.-H. Chroust, 'Aristotle's earliest course of lectures on rhetoric,' *Antiquite Classique,* vol. 33, fasc. I (1964), pp. 58-72, especially, pp. 69 ff.; vol. I, Chapter VIII.

[63] Philodemus, *De Rhetorica,* in *Volumina Rhetorica,*

col. XLVIII, 36-7 (vol. II, pp. 50-1, ed. S. Sudhaus, Leipzig, 1896).

[64] *Ibid.,* col. LV, 43-4 (pp. 60-1, ed. S. Sudhaus), and col. LVI, 45-col. LVII, 46 (p. 62, ed. S. Sudhaus).

[65] *Ibid.,* col. XLVIII, 37-col. XLIX, 37 (pp. 51-2, ed. S. Sudhaus).

[66] *Ibid.,* col. LI, 40 (p. 55, ed. S. Sudhaus).

[67] *Ibid.,* col. LII, 41 (pp.. 56-7, ed. S. Sudhaus).

[68] *Ibid.,* col. LIII, 42-col. LIV, 42 (p. 58, ed. S. Sudhaus).

[69] *Ibid.,* col. LIV, 42 (p. 59, ed. S. Sudhaus).

[70] *Ibid.,* col. LIV, 43-4 (pp. 60-1, ed. S. Sudhaus).

[71] See A.-H. Chroust (see note 62), and Vol. I, Chapter VIII.

[72] See, for instance, Athenaeus, *Deipnosophistae* II. 60 DE; III. 122B; VII 354B; Dionysius of Halicarnassus, *De Isocrate* 18; Themistius, *Oratio* XXIII. 285AB (p. 345, ed. L. Dindorf); Eusebius, *Praeparatio Evangelica* XIV. 6. 9-10: Dionysius of Halicarnassus, *Epistola ad Cn. Pompeium* I. The *Against Aristotle* consisted of four books.

[73] F. Blass, *Attische Beredsamkeit,* vol. II (Leipzig, 1892), pp. 451 ff., holds that Cephisodorus' *Against Aristotle* was written after the death of Isocrates (338. B.C.); E. Bignone, *L'Aristotele Perduto e la Formazione Filosofica di Epicuro,* vol. II (Florence, 1936), pp. 58 ff., maintains that the *Against Aristotle* was a rejoinder to Aristotle's *Protrepticus* (written about 350 B.C.) which, in turn, was a rebuttal of Isocrates' *Antidosis*; and I. During, *Aristotle in the Ancient Biographical Tradition* (Goteborg, 1957), pp. 389 ff., on the strength of the evidence found in Dionysius of Halicarnassus, *Epistola ad CN. Pompeium* I, assumes that Cephisodorus' *Against Aristotle* was intended primarily to 'set the record straight.' During also insists that the *Against Aristotle* was composed about 360 B.C, or shortly thereafter. Should During's thesis prove to be correct, then the *Against Aristotle* could have been 'provoked' by the Aristotelian *Gryllus.* This would also lend support to the thesis that in the *Gryllus* Aristotle criticized Isocrates and his methods.

[74] Eusebius, *op. cit.,* XIV. 6.9.

[75] Quintilian, *op. cit.,* II. 17. 14.

[76] Aristotle, *Rhetoric* 1354 a II ff., it will be noted, contains a pointed attack on Isocrates, although in the main Aristotle's *Rhetoric* seems to take a more friendly

attitude towards Isocrates.

[77] See H. von Arnim, *Leben und Werke des Dion von Prusa* (Berlin, 1896), pp. 4 ff; W. Jaeger, *Paideia,* vol. III (New York-Oxford, 1944), *passim.*

[78] Isocrartes, *Against the Sophists* 20 ff. The *Against the Sophists* seems also to be directed against the 'Socratics,' including Plato and his school.

[79] It was probably this particlar point of view which became the main target of Aristotle's (and Plato's) attacks: Isocrates' willingness to come to terms with existential reality, with the concrete human condition and with what is reasonably practical—a position which, in the eyes of Plato and the young Aristotle, was unforgivable 'heresy.'

[80] See Isocrates, *Against the Sophists* I; W. Jaeger (see note 77), pp. 83 ff. See also Isocrates, *Helen* I and 2-7; Isocrates, *Panegyricus* 47-9; Isocrates, *Nicocles* 8-9; Isocrates, *Ad Nicoclem* 35.

[81] Plato, *Republic* 500B.

[82] Judging from Quintilian, *op. cit.,* II. 17. 30, Aristotle's *Gryllus* also contained the information that in his earlier days Isocrates had been a *logographer* or forensic orator—not always a reputable profession—in order to make money. See note 55; Dionysius of Halicarnassus, *De Isocrate* 18; Cicero, *Brutus* 28. In later years Isocrates was most reluctant to mention this period of his life. In his *Gryllus* Aristotle probably brought to light these early activities of Isocrates, noting also that many of Isocrates' old forensic speeches could still be found in Athenian book shops. Dionysius of Halicarnassus, *loc. cit.*

[83] The *Antidosis* of Isocrates, published in 353-52 B.C. might well be a 'rebuttal' of Aristotle's *Gryllus*. In the *Protrepticus*, published about 350 B.C., Aristotle also takes issue with the *Antidosis*. See A.-H. Chroust, *Aristotle: Protrepticus—A Reconstruction* (Notre Dame, 1964), p. xiv. Thus it appears that the Aristotle-Isocrates feud went on for some time. See notes 39-41 and the corresponding text.

[84] In the light of all this, the report of Quintilian becomes comprehensible, namely, *op. cit.* III. I. 14: '[Aristotle]. . . [in the form of a travesty] quoted the well-known line from [Euripides'] *Philoctetes* as follows: "Isocrates still speaks, hence it would be a shameful thing should I remain silent."' The name of Isocrates is substituted for the original term 'barbarians' in the *Philoctetes*. See Euripides, *Philoctetes,* frg. 785, Dindorf; frag. 796, Nauck. See also DL V. 3, where Aristotle is credited with having remarked: 'It would be a base thing to keep silent and let Xenocrates speak out.' This, too, is a travesty of Euripides' line. Some scholars suggest that Xenocrates is but a corruption of Isocrates. See also Cicero, *De Oratore* III. 35. 141; Synesius, *Scholia in Hermogenem* II. 59. 21 ff. (ed. H. Rabe); Philodemus (see note 63), col. XLVIII, 36 (vol. II, p. 50, ed. S. Sudhaus).

[85] A.-H. Chroust (see note 62), and Vol. I, Chapter VIII.

[86] E. Berti (see note 23), pp. 115-16; pp. 159-66; pp. 174-5; p. 520; p. 522.

Theresa M. Crem (essay date 1974)

SOURCE: "The Definition of Rhetoric According to Aristotle," in *Aristotle:The Classical Heritage of Rhetoric,* edited by Keith V. Erickson, The Scarecrow Press, Inc., 1974, pp. 52-71.

[*In the following essay, Crem examines the first chapter and the beginning of the second chapter of Book 1 of Aristotle's* Rhetoric, *arguing that he offers a scientific treatment of the subject in that he approaches rhetoric not as a rhetorician but as a logician.*]

Introduction

Aristotle's treatise on rhetoric is unique, in that it is a properly scientific consideration of the subject. This characteristic becomes manifest, when we compare it with other rhetorical treatises, such as those of Cicero. The works of this great rhetorician are of high value because of his wide experience in the field; nevertheless, they do not methodically treat of the nature of rhetoric. Rather, they are handbooks of practical advice on public speaking and on the formation of the rhetorician.

On the other hand, Aristotle speaks not as an experienced rhetorician, but as a logician. Rhetoric is a part of logic understood in the broad sense, i.e., taken to include all disciplines which direct the act of reason. In the order of logical treatises, the ***Rhetoric*** is placed immediately after the ***Topics,*** which is concerned with dialectic. Hence, because he is proceeding from a logical point of view, and since these two parts of logic have a great deal in common, Aristotle very aptly begins his consideration of rhetoric by comparing it to dialectic.

Aristotle's aim in writing this work is a scientific presentation of the rhetorical method. Thus, besides setting down its nature in the first two chapters, he also discusses the many things which the rhetorician must know in order to practice his art successfully. Hence, in the remainder of Book I he divides rhetoric into three genera: deliberative, forensic, and epideictic; and gives the characteristics and special topics proper to each. In Book II he discusses passions, human character, virtues and vices; for without some knowledge of these, the rhetorician would be incapable of constructing a speech proportionate to his audience, and of arousing their passions. After this, he treats of common topics, which are applicable to rhetoric in general. Book III is principally devoted to style and arrangement which, though secondary, obviously must be included in any complete study of rhetoric. It is evident, then, that although Aristotle was not himself a rhetorician, still he was far from lacking experience in this domain. For besides possessing the universality proper to a scientific treatise, his work contains a wealth of concrete detail.

The commentary which is to follow, however, is limited to the first and the beginning of the second chapter of Book I, which is the most important part of the treatise, for it contains a definition of rhetoric and an explanation of the rhetorical method. Aristotle's text has been incorporated herein, therefore we do not think it necessary to quote it apart. This article is a literal commentary, based on the principle that the sole function of a commentator is to be an intermediary between the master and the reader, by making the master's thought more explicit and hence more easily understood. In order to assure greater fidelity, we have compared various translations[1] of the Greek original.

I. Common Considerations on the Nature of Rhetoric

This first section has four divisions: a *quid nominis* of *rhetorica utens*, the *an est* of *rhetorica docens*, a common consideration of what should constitute the rhetorical method, and a résumé.

1) *A "Quid Nominis" of "Rhetorica Utens"*

Here Aristotle does three things: he compares rhetoric to dialectic, gives the reason for this comparison, and substantiates this reason by examples drawn from common experience.

a) *A Comparison of Rhetoric and Dialectic*

Aristotle states that rhetoric is the antistrophe of dialectic. This is an instance of the *locutio exemplaris,* i.e., the use of a word having a sole, concrete signification to manifest something else. There is no new imposition as is the case in analogy; nor is the word given an improper or figurative sense as in the metaphor.[2]

Aristotle draws his example from the Greeks' everyday life, using something with which all were familiar, the choral odes. The antistrophe is that part of the choral ode which alternates with and answers the strophe. Thus, what is meant by this *locutio exemplaris* is that there is a special relation between dialectic and rhetoric. Just as the strophe and antistrophe are similar in that they are corresponding parts of the choral ode, so too, dialectic and rhetoric have certain characteristics in common. In the same way, just as the strophe and antistrophe are distinct from one another and ordered in a particular way, inasmuch as the antistrophe is always consequent upon the strophe; so also, rhetoric is distinct from dialectic, and is in a way consequent upon it. Hence, it is clear that by means of this *locutio exemplaris* any Greek familiar with dialectic would immediately acquire a fundamental, though common notion of the nature of rhetoric.

It is unfortunate that in English translation, "antistrophe" is usually rendered by another term, such as "counterpart"; for by this departure from the precision of Aristotle's terminology, the principle of manifestation which he intended is lost.

b) *The Reason for This Comparison*

Aristotle does not now consider the aspects in which rhetoric and dialectic differ, for this presupposes more distinct knowledge. However, he immediately states what they have in common: both dialectic and rhetoric are concerned with matters which are in some way known by all men, and which are proper to no definite science. These two characteristics are closely related, being effects of the same cause. Such matter does not belong to any particular science because it is common; i.e., it extends to many things, but in a superficial way. For this same reason, it falls within the comprehension of all men. On the contrary, the subject proper to a given science is known only to the initiated in that science, and unknown to the majority of men. This is obvious from the fact that the multitude cannot understand scientific reasoning. But dialectic and rhetoric are not limited to any determinate genus of being. They treat of any subject whatever, arguing not from principles proper to a given thing, but from certain common principles familiar to all.

There are other similarities between rhetoric and dialectic; in fact, they are so closely related that distinct knowledge of rhetoric implies knowledge of the **Topics.** However, we are now concerned only with a confused and common knowledge, a *quid nominis* which will lead us to distinct knowledge. Therefore, Aristotle restricts himself to mentioning a similarity which is most manifest, one which can be understood even by those having no knowledge of rhetoric.

c) *Aristotle Substantiates this Reason*

A proof that the matter of rhetoric and dialectic is such things as are known by all men is the fact that all make use of these faculties to some extent: dialectic, when they criticize opinions or seek to uphold them; rhetoric, when they defend themselves or accuse others.

2) *The "An Est" of "Rhetorica Docens"*

These faculties can be used in two ways, either by chance or by acquired habit. In either way success is possible; therefore we can inquire as to the reason for this success. Once this cause has been found, we can set up principles which will enable the intellect to proceed in a determinate fashion. Such an inquiry obviously is the function of a method, for the very word "method" means "a short way."[3]

This rhetorical method is *rhetorica docens . . .*, which must not be confused with *rhetorica utens. . . .* To clarify this point it may be useful to manifest the same distinction as applied to dialectic. *Dialectica docens*, the doctrine contained in the **Topics,** is the speculative art concerned with directing probable argument. It proceeds demonstratively, and so is a science in the strict sense. *Dialectica utens* is the application of *dialectica docens* in actual argument. This use of dialectic declines from the mode of science because its matter is only probable.[4] Thus, when Aristotle describes rhetoric as the antistrophe of dialectic, possessed by all and having common matter, he is referring to both rhetoric and dialectic under the aspect of *utens*. For the matter of *dialectica* and *rhetorica docens,* like that of all the other sciences, is not common but proper; it is not possessed by all, but must be acquired.

By proceeding in this fashion, Aristotle also manifests the priority in time or generation of *rhetorica utens* over *rhetorica docens*. The same doctrine is taught by Cicero: "But to my thinking the virtue in all the rules is, not that orators by following them have won a reputation for eloquence, but that certain persons have noted and collected the doings of men who were naturally eloquent: thus eloquence is not the offspring of the art, but the art of eloquence. . . . "[5]

3) *In What the Rhetorical Method Should Consist*

Aristotle proceeds to develop the *quid,* first by a negative treatment, then by a positive consideration. He does three things: manifests the errors in the treatises written by his predecessors, shows by a positive approach what should constitute the method, and states the utility of such a method.

a) *A Negative Treatment:*

The Errors of Aristotle's Predecessors

Aristotle begins with a history of the method in order better to manifest the *quid*. This is an example of using history to illuminate a question of properly doctrinal import. He says that those who have written treatises on rhetoric have constructed only a small part of the method. For proofs are the only true constituents of the method; all else is merely accessory. Now these au-

thors say nothing about enthymemes, which are the substance of rhetorical persuasion, but deal principally with non-essentials. The arousing of prejudice, pity, anger, and other passions has nothing to do with the essential facts, but is merely a personal appeal to those judging the case. A sign of the irrelevance of such procedure is that it is forbidden by law in well-governed states. If these laws were applied everywhere, such writers would be left with nothing to say. Yet this is sound law and custom, and all men agree that it should be so. For it is wrong to prevert the judge by moving him to anger, envy, or pity. Aristotle likens this to warping a carpenter's rule before using it. This is an apt comparison, because the judge is as a rule of justice.[6] Now since passion can impede reason, it is possible to influence him in favor of one side or another by arousing his passions; but this is to put an obstacle in the way of the exercise of his function.

That passion can be detrimental is easily shown; for example, in anger there is a certain use of reason insofar as the angry man reasons that he must avenge an injury, yet his reasoning is imperfect, lacking determination and order. Because of the velocity of its movement, anger excludes deliberation.[7] In the **Ethics,**[8] Aristotle compares the angry man to hasty servants who start out on an errand before they have heard the entire command, and therefore make mistakes; and to dogs which bark as soon as they hear a knock at the door, before knowing whether it is friend or foe.

However, passion can either precede or follow judgment. If it precedes, it is an obstacle because it impedes deliberation, which is necessary for the formation of the judgment. But it passion occurs after the judgment has been formed, it is a help rather than a hindrance. Such passion is a sign of the motion of the will, which in its intensity, overflows into the inferior appetite. It can also be an instrument aiding execution by enabling one to act more promptly and easily.[9] For this reason, passion should not precede discourse, but rather, should be its effect. Hence, Aristotle says that once the rhetorician has clearly stated the facts and evaluated them, then he must arouse the passions of the audience.[10]

The rôle of the litigant is merely to show whether or not a fact is so, whether it has or has not happened. As to whether a thing is important or unimportant, just or unjust, the judge must not take advice from the litigants, but it is his duty to decide for himself all points which the law does not already specifically define for him.

It is of great importance that good laws should themselves determine as many points as possible and leave very few to the decision of the judges; and this for three reasons. First, because law-making is restricted to one or to a few public personages having the whole people under their care,[11] and it is easier to find one or a few men who are wise and capable of legislating, than it is to find the large number which would be necessary to judge each particular case.

Secondly, laws are made after long deliberation, whereas court decisions must be given on short notice, a fact which makes it difficult for the judge to satisfy the claims of justice and expediency.

The third and most important reason is that the judgment of the legislator is not particular but universal and concerning future events; whereas the judge must decide actual, particular cases. Laws are universal propositions of the practical reason which are ordered to operation. They hold the same position with respect to operations as propositions of the speculative reason hold with respect to conclusions.[12] Any precept in regard to some particular work is devoid of the nature of law except insofar as it regards the common good.[13]

Since law bears not on the particular, but on the universal and future, it is free from passion. Because men's acts and choices are concerned with singulars, the appetite is affected in relation to the singular. Therefore, from the very fact that the sensitive appetite is a particular power, it has great influence in disposing man so that something seems to him desirable or undesirable in particular cases. For example, that which seems good to a man when angry no longer seems good to him when he is calm. Thus, the intellect is moved to judge in accordance with appetite, for according as a man is, such does the end seem to him.[14] Consequently, reason is said to govern the sensitive appetite with a political rule as opposed to a despotic rule, for the irascible and concupiscible powers can resist the commands of reason, just as free men can act counter to the commands of their ruler.[15] From this we can conclude that the more reason is liberated from passion, the more easily can it judge rightly.

Hence in law courts, where particular and actual issues are under consideration, the judges are often so influenced by feelings of friendship, hatred, or personal interest that they are no longer capable of discerning the truth adequately, and their judgment is obscured by personal pleasure or displeasure. For this reason, the judge should be allowed to decide as few things as possible only those particular facts which cannot be foreseen by the legislator, as for example, whether something has or has not happened.

If all this is true, it is evident that those who make rules about such matters, as what must be the contents of the introduction, or the narration, or any of the other divisions of a speech, are treating non-essentials as if they pertained to the method. For they are concerned not with proof, but only with putting the judge into a favorable frame of mind, and they completely ignore what is proper to the rhetorician, namely, the construction of enthymemes.

Consequently, although the method of deliberative and forensic rhetoric is the same, and although the former, being more directly concerned with the common good, is nobler and more befitting a statesman than the latter, which is limited to transactions between private individuals, these authors say nothing about deliberative rhetoric, but all devote themselves to writing treatises on how to plead in court. The reason for this is that in deliberative rhetoric there is less inducement to talk about non-essentials, because since it treats of issues which are of more general interest, there is less opportunity for unscrupulous practices. In a political debate, the man who forms a judgment makes a decision about his own vital interests the good at stake, being a common good, belongs to him also. Thus, there is no need to prove anything except that the facts are in reality what the supporter of a measure maintains them to be. The fact that Aristotle's predecessors neglected this nobler branch of rhetoric, in which there is little chance of moving the judge, is a sign that their method consisted principally in a consideration of the passions, with moving the judge as the end in view.

On the contrary, in forensic rhetoric merely upholding the facts does not suffice; it is very useful to win over the listeners. For here it is other people's affairs that are to be decided; therefore, the judges, intent on their own satisfaction and listening with partiality, give in to the disputants instead of judging between them. Hence, as we have seen, in many states irrelevant speaking is forbidden in the law courts; but in the public assembly, those who have to form a judgment are themselves able to guard against it.

b) *Positive Consideration*

Aristotle then manifests in a common way in what the rhetorical method (*rhetorica docens*) should consist; a proper treatment is reserved for Chapter II. He states that it is now clear that this method, in its strict sense, is concerned with the modes of persuasion, i.e., with proofs. Here it is important to note that rhetorical persuasion is not convertible with persuasion in all its amplitude, but is restricted to persuasion in view of action of the common good. For rhetoric deals with political things,[16] and is therefore subordinated to politics,[17] which is concerned with the highest common good operable by man.[18]

Now it is evident that persuasion is a kind of demonstration, since we are most completely persuaded when we consider a thing to have been demonstrated. Here, by "demonstration" Aristotle does not mean the *ratio propria* as given in the **Posterior Analytics,** which is verified only in demonstration *propter quid,* but the *ratio communis* taken to include all kinds of proofs.

Rhetorical demonstration consists principally in the enthymeme which is, in general, the most effective of the modes of persuasion. The term "enthymeme" . . . is derived from [the Greek word] which means "to keep in mind," "to consider"; and a rhetorical syllogism is so-called from the fact that only one of its propositions is expressed, whereas the other is merely understood or kept in the mind.

Hence, the enthymeme is nominally defined as "an argument consisting of only two propositions, an antecedent and its consequent; a syllogism with one premiss omitted."[19]

Thus, the enthymeme is a kind of syllogism, and the consideration of every kind of syllogism pertains to logic—either to logic as a whole, or to one of its parts. Since the end of logic is to direct the act of reason, so that man may be able to proceed with order, facility, and without error,[20] it is concerned with the act of reason as with its proper matter.[21] But the syllogism, being a kind of discourse from the known to the unknown, is proper to the third operation of the mind; consequently, it is evident that logic must treat of every kind of syllogism. Aristotle distinguishes between "logic as a whole" and "one of its parts," because the syllogism can be considered either as to form alone, or as to both matter and form. The study of the syllogism as to form, prescinding from determinate matter, pertains to a part of logic, namely, to the **Prior Analytics.** Since the principles laid down in this treatise apply to all syllogisms regardless of their determinate matter, this part of logic can be said to consider every kind of syllogism.[22] If, however, we consider also the matter of the syllogism, then different parts of logic are devoted to different kinds: the **Posterior Analytics,** to the demonstrative syllogism having necessary matter; the **Topics** and the **Sophistics,** to the dialectical syllogism, which has probable matter; and the **Rhetoric,** to the enthymeme. Thus, if we consider the syllogism as to both matter and form, the study of every kind of syllogism pertains to the whole of logic.

It is to be noted that both "syllogism" and "logic" are understood in a broad sense. "Syllogism" is not restricted to the true syllogism, i.e., to one having perfect syllogistic form, but is taken to include the enthymeme, which is imperfect, and which therefore can be called a syllogism only *secundum quid.* In the same way, "logic" is taken to include all disciplines which direct the act of reason, and therefore also *rhetorica docens,* whose function it is to direct the act of reason in forming enthymemes.[23]

Some thought that even logic in the broad sense was concerned only with the true syllogism, thus determining the common subject of logic from the principal subject. This position is untenable because logic, being the mode of all science, must have a subject equally applicable to them all. But the true syllogism requires a universal, and therefore cannot always be used, as is the case in *rhetorica utens.*[24]

By comparing the enthymeme to the syllogism, Aristotle relates the method of rhetoric fundamentally to logic. He who possesses logic and is proficient in constructing syllogisms will also be skillful in forming enthymemes, once he has learned what the subject of the enthymeme is, and how the enthymeme differs from the logical syllogism. Furthermore, although it is principally ordered to science, logic must also consider probable knowledge, for the true and the apparently true are apprehended by the same faculty. Men have a certain natural capacity for truth, and therefore usually do attain it.[25] This applies to the probable also, for the same power which enables us to arrive at truth, also enables one to recognize the probable.

c) *The Utility of the Rhetorical Method*

Next, Aristotle gives four reasons why such a method is useful:

1) The true and the just have a natural tendency to prevail over their opposites; therefore, if decisions are not what they should be, the defect must be due to the speakers themselves. *Rhetorica docens* can remedy this.

2) In dealing with some audiences, not even the possession of the most distinct knowledge will make it easy for us to persuade them. For argument based on such knowledge implies instruction, and there are people whom one cannot instruct. In fact, under such circumstances, the use of distinct or scientific knowledge would actually impede persuasion. For although man is by nature proportionate to truth in a common way, this does not extend to particulars. Consequently, confused knowledge is more certain than distinct knowledge, because its object is common, and therefore more proportionate to our intellect, which proceeds from potency to act. Because our intellect must operate in this fashion, we first know things in a general way and under a certain confusion before knowing them distinctly; for confused knowledge is intermediate between pure potency and perfect act. It is important to note that confusion is opposed not to certitude, but to distinctness. For example, we can know with certitude that man is animal, but this is confused rather than distinct knowledge, for it is not a complete knowledge of man up to his ultimate difference, since "animal" contains "rational" only in potency.[26]

Hence, the rhetorician must use as modes of persuasion and argument, notions already possessed by all; as Aristotle states also in the **Topics,**[27] where he speaks of the utility of dialect for handling a popular audience: "[Dialectic] is useful because when we have considered the opinions held by most people, we shall meet them on the ground not of other people's convictions, but of their own, while we shift the ground of any argument that they appear to us to state unsoundly."

3) We must be able to employ persuasion, just as strict reasoning can be employed, on opposite sides of a question, not in order that we may in practice employ it in both ways (for we must not make people believe what is wrong), but in order that we may see clearly what the facts are, and that if another person argues unfairly, we on our part may be able to refute him. Of the arts, only *rhetorica* and *dialectica utens* draw opposite conclusions. In commenting on Aristotle's ***Topics,*** St. Albert states that because *dialectica docens* enables us to find common appearances, it enables us to argue probably about any problem with ease from either side of a contradiction.[28]

Both of these arts draw opposite conclusions impartially; yet the facts do not lend themselves equally well to the contrary views. Rather, things that are true and things that are better are, by their very nature, almost always easier to prove and easier to believe.

4) It is absurd to hold that a man should be ashamed of being unable to defend himself by physical strength, but not of being unable to defend himself by speech and reason, when the use of speech is more proper to man than the use of his limbs.

If it is argued that one who uses such power of speech unjustly may do great harm, this is an objection which applies equally to all good things except virtue (for virtue, understood in its primary sense, i.e., moral virtue, by its very definition implies a perfectioning of the agent and an assurance of good operation),[29] especially to those things which are most useful, such as strength, health, wealth, or military power. For as a man can confer the greatest benefit by using these properly, so can he inflict the greatest injuries by abusing them.

4) *Résumé*

It is clear then, that *rhetorica utens* does not deal with a particular genus of things, but that like *dialectica utens,* it is universal. It is also evident that it is useful. Furthermore, its function is not simply to succeed in persuading, but rather, to discover the means of persuasion available in each particular case.

The rhetorician does not always succeed in persuading, for there are three possible impediments: a bad case, perverse judges, and weakness of argument due to the contingency of the matter. Yet, if he operates well according to the principles of his art, we say that he has sufficiently attained his end, even should he fail to persuade.[30] For in any discipline we cannot seek more than its principles warrant.[31] In this, *rhetorica*

utens resembles all the other arts. For example, the function of medicine is not simply to restore the patient to health, but to promote this end as far as possible; for even those who will never recover can be given proper treatment.

Moreover, it is evident that it pertains to rhetoric to discover the real and the apparent means of persuasion, just as it is the function of dialectic to discern the real and the apparent syllogism. This does not make the dialectician a sophist, for the sophist is defined not by his knowledge, but by his moral purpose—he is morally perverse. An argument can be sophistic without its proponent's being a sophist. Dialectic is ordered to truth; bad intention is completely extrinsic to it. Thus a man is a dialectician because of his knowledge or faculty; he is a sophist because of his evil intention.[32] However, in rhetoric there is no such distinction, for the rhetorician may be denominated either from his faculty, or from his intention.

Aristotle brings his first chapter to a close with a statement of what is to follow in the next chapter. He says that we shall now treat of the rhetorical method itself to see how we can attain our goal. But first, we must make a fresh start, and before going further, define rhetoric anew.

In this chapter, Aristotle began with a *quid nominis* of *rhetorica utens,* which gave us only a vague notion of its nature. Next he proceeded to the *an est* of *rhetorica docens,* and finally, by means of first a negative and then a positive approach, he enabled us to acquire further insight into what rhetoric is—principally, that the substance of the method consists in proofs. However, this does not as yet give us the distinct *quid;* it is still confused and common knowledge.

In Chapter II, Aristotle will incorporate our newly acquired knowledge into a new definition, thus furnishing us a fresh point of departure. From there, he will continue in a proper way the positive treatment of the rhetorical method.

II. *A Proper Treatment of the Rhetorical Method*

This section has two divisions: the *quid rei* of *rhetorica utens,* and a consideration of the end of rhetoric.

1) *The "Quid Rei" of "Rhetorica Utens"*

Aristotle begins by defining rhetoric as the faculty of discovering, in any given case, the available means of persuasion. Rhetoric is a faculty, because it has no determinate subject. For every art and science can instruct or persuade about its own particular subject: for instance, medicine deals with health and sickness; geometry, with the properties of magnitudes; and arithmetic, with numbers. But rhetoric is the power of observing the means of persuasion on any subject which presents itself, and this is why we say that it is not concerned with any particular or definite genus of things.

2) *The End of Rhetoric: Persuasion*

This definition makes it clear that *rhetorica utens* aims at effecting persuasion.[33] Now, persuasion implies the presentation of an object as an *operable good*.[34] But the good is said in relation to appetite,[35] and furthermore, it is envisioned by the rhetorician as *operable*. Therefore, persuasion is not a purely speculative assent, but it also involves appetite, and is ordered to moving the will.[36]

Because of this, it is of capital importance that the rhetorician should consider the dispositions of his audience; for according as men are differently disposed, so will different things seem good to them. Since the passions play an essential rôle in disposing man, St. Thomas holds that rhetoric, unlike demonstration, is not restricted to the domain of reason; but that in order to attain its end, it must also arouse the passions of the audience.[37] It is evident then, that persuasion involves two elements, one which is appetitive, and the other which is properly rational.[38] The latter consists in a partial inclination to reason to one side of a contradiction which is known as suspicion.[39]

Suspicion can be said to be a mean between doubt and opinion. It is opposed to doubt and resembles opinion, in that it involves inclination to one side of a contradiction. Yet, it differs from opinion, inasmuch as this inclination is not total, and is therefore not a true adherence.[40] To make these differences more explicit: in doubt, the intellect is completely undetermined; for there is no greater inclination to one side of a contradiction rather than to the other. Opinion involves a total inclination, or a true adherence to one side of a contradiction which, however, does not result in complete assent; for there remains a fear that the other side may be true.[41] This adherence constitutes a determination of reason, albeit incomplete, inasmuch as the inclination is totally to one side.[42] But in suspicion, the inclination of reason is only predominantly, and not totally to one side of a contradiction.[43]

Thus, we can assign two reasons for the necessity of arousing the passions in rhetoric: the weakness of rhetorical argumentation, which renders it incapable of effecting a true assent of reason, and the fact that mere presentation of truth is insufficient to move men to action. St. Augustine very aptly explains the latter aspect:

> Verum quoniam plerumque stulti homines ad ea quae suadentur recte, utiliter et honeste, non ipsam sincerissimam quam rarus animus videt veritatem,

> sed proprios sensus consuetudinemque sectantur, oportebat eos non doceri solum quantum queunt sed saepe et maxime commoveri. Hanc suam partem quae id ageret, necessitatis pleniorem quam puritatis, refertissimo gremio deliciarum, quas populo spargat, ut ad utilitatem suam dignetur adduci, vocavit rhetoricam.[44]

A further insight into the rôle played by the dispositions of the audience can be had by examining the words of Cicero:

> This indeed is the reason why, when setting about a hazardous and important case, in order to explore the feelings of the tribunal, I engage wholeheartedly in a consideration so careful, that I scent out with all possible keenness their thoughts, judgments, anticipations and wishes, and the direction in which they seem likely to be led away most easily by eloquence. . . . If however an arbitrator is neutral and free from predisposition, my task is harder, since everything has to be called forth by my speech, with no help from the listener's character. But so potent is that Eloquence, rightly styled by an excellent poet, "soulbending sovereign of all things," that she can not only support the sinking and bend the upstanding, but, like a good and brave commander, can even make prisoner a resisting antagonist.[45]

Is this contrary, then, to the position maintained by Aristotle when he criticizes his predecessors? Not at all, for his criticism is aimed at those who give no thought to argumentation, but make rhetoric consist entirely or principally in moving the passions. That Aristotle does not underestimate the importance of the dispositions of the audience is evident from the fact that he devotes the greater part of Book II to a study of the various passions and types of human character. Also, of the three modes of persuasion, only the third is based on argumentative proof. The difference lies in that Aristotle holds argumentation to be essential: "enthymemes . . . are the substance of rhetorical persuasion";[46] arousing the passions, though necessary, is only secondary. Hence, they are not to be aroused at the outset, when they could impede judgment, but only in the epilogue. "Next, when the facts and their importance are clearly understood, you must excite your hearers' emotions."[47] By then, the rhetorician has proceeded as far as possible in the line of argumentation, i.e., he has aroused suspicion. But because the matter is too contingent to merit assent, he must bridge the gap by an appeal to the emotions.[48] Thus, the foundation of judgment is laid by means of an exposition of the facts of the case, but judgment is completed and assured through movement of the passions.

Once it has been understood that rhetoric is ordered to persuasion, we have the key to the entire rhetorical method: For the end is the cause of causes,[49] inasmuch as all else is intended for the sake of the end, and must therefore be proportionate to it.

Notes

[1] *Rhetoric,* trans. W. Rhys Roberts, ed. Solmsen, N. Y., Random House, 1954; *The Art of Rhetoric,* trans. John Henry Freese, The Loeb Classical Library, Cambridge, Mass., Harvard University Press, 1939; *Art Rhétorique,* trans. Jean Voilquin et Jean Capelle, Paris, Librairie Garnier, 1944.

[2] The *locutio exemplaris* and the metaphor resemble each other and are opposed to analogy inasmuch as they are not new impositions of a word. However, they differ in that the metaphor implies a new and figurative sense, whereas the *locutio exemplaris* does not. In constructing a metaphor, a word which properly signifies a certain object is applied to something else bearing some resemblance to that object. But despite this resemblance, the word cannot properly signify the new object; therefore, it must do so only in a figurative or improper sense. This figurative sense then becomes the principle of manifesting a characteristic of the new object. Thus, the metaphor is a kind of discourse notable for its brevity, for in one word it signifies a thing and that to which the thing is compared. In the *locutio exemplaris,* however, there is no question of a new and improper sense, for it is not the application of a name to a new object. Rather, it is merely the comparison of an object relatively unknown, to another which is better known, in order to attain a more complete knowledge of the former. The principle of manifestation lies in the proper sense of the words used.

[3] "Est autem quod dicimus *methodum metaphorice:* dicitur enim *methodus* brevis via, quae via est compendii, et vulgariter vocatur summa. Per similitudinem ergo transfertur ad istam scientiam proprie et artem: quia cum speculabilia et operabilia multa offerantur, sua multitudine et longitudine, distantiae quidem ipsorum dispendere faciunt, nisi per formam scientiae et artis ad compendium redigantur: et ab hae similitudine nomen methodi ad artem et scientiam transfertur" (St. Albert, in I *Topicorum,* Prooemium, cap. 2).

[4] "Dialectica enim potest considerari secundum quod est docens, et secundum quod est utens. Secundum quidem quod est docens, habet considerationem de istis intentionibus, instituens modum, quo per eas procedi possit ad conclusiones in singulis scientiis probabiliter ostendendas; et hoc demonstrative facit, et secundum hoc est scientia. Utens vero est secundum quod modo adiuncto utitur ad concludendum aliquid probabiliter in singulis scientiis; et sic recedit a modo scientiae" (St. Thomas, in IV *Metaphysicorum,* lect. 4, edit. Marietti, n. 576). Cf. also St. Albert, in I *Topicorum,* Prooemium, cap. 1.

[5] *De Oratore,* I, cap. 32, n. 146; trans. E. W. Sutton, The Loeb Classical Library, Cambridge, Mass., Harvard Univ. Press, 1942.

[6] " . . . Sic cum debemus uti judice tanquam regula rectitudinis, non debemus illum ad hanc vel illam partem inflectere, excitando in eo iram, misericordiam, invidiam, etc. . . . " (Sylvester Maurus, in I *Rhetoricorum,* cap. 1, a.2, n.5).

[7] St. Thomas, in III *Ethicorum,* lect. 5, edit. Marietti, n.442.

[8] VII, chap. 6, 1149 a 25-31.

[9] St. Thomas, *Q.D. de Veritate,* q. 26, a. 7, c. and ad 3; in IV *Ethicorum,* lect. 8, n.805.

[10] *Rhetoric,* III, chap. 19, 1419 b 24.

[11] St. Thomas, *Ia IIae,* q. 90, a.3.

[12] *Ibid.,* a.1, ad 2.

[13] *Ibid.,* a.2.

[14] St. Thomas, *Ia IIae,* q. 9, a.2, c. and ad 2.

[15] "Invenitur enim inter partes hominis quod anima dominatur corpori, sed hoc est despotico principatu in quo servus in nullo potest resistere domino . . . et hoc videmus in membris corporis, scilicet manibus et pedibus quod statim sine contradictione ad imperium animae applicantur ad opus. Invenimus etiam quod intellectus seu ratio dominatur appetitui, sed principatu politico et ragali qui est ad liberos, unde possunt in aliquibus contradicere: et similiter appetitus aliquando non sequitur rationem. Et hujusmodi diversitatis ratio est, quia corpus non potest moveri nisi ab anima, et ideo totaliter subjicitur ei; sed appetitus potest moveri non solum a ratione, sed etiam a sensu; et ideo non totaliter subjicitur rationi" (St. Thomas, in I *Politicorum,* lect. 3, Laval Univ. Edit., p. 22). Cf. also *Ia IIae,* q. 9, a.2, ad 3; Ia *Pars,* q. 81, a.3, ad 2.

[16] St. Thomas, in I *Ethicorum,* lect. 3, n. 36.

[17] *Ibid.,* lect. 2, n.28.

[18] "Tertio possumus accipere dignitatem et ordinem politicae ad omnes alias scientias practices. Est enim civitas principalissimum eorum quae humana ratione constitui possunt. Nam ad ipsam omnes communitates humanae referuntur. Rursumque omnia tota quae per artes mechanicas constituuntur ex rebus in usum hominum venientibus, ad homines ordinantur, sicut ad finem. Si igitur principalior scientia est quae est de nobiliori et perfectiori, necesse est politicam inter omnes scientias practicas esse principaliorem et

architectionicam omnium aliarum, utpote considerans ultimum et perfectum bonum in rebus humanis. Et propter hoc Philosophus dicit in fine decimi *Ethicorum* quod ad politica perficitur philosophia, quae est circa res humanas" (St. Thomas, in I *Politicorum,* Prologus).

[19] Webster's *New International Dictionary of the English Language,* the word "enthymeme."

[20] St. Thomas, in I *Posteriorum Analyticorum,* Prooemium, edit. Marietti, n.1.

[21] *Ibid.,* n.2.

[22] " . . . Vel per dialecticam totam vel per aliquam ejus partem, puta per illam, quae traditur in libris Priorum, habemus facultatem conficiendi syllogismos universim et varias species syllogismorum. . . . " (Sylvester Maurus, in I *Rhetoricorum,* cap. 1, a.3, n.10). Here "dialectic" means "logic": " . . . Nomine dialecticae intelligendo non solum Topicam, sed logicam universam, quae agit de omni syllogismo" (*Ibid.*).

"Secundum autem quod simpliciter dicitur simplex formale a sua acceptum simplicitate formali, non tractat de syllogismo simpliciter tota logica, sed determinatur in uno librorum ejus. . . . " (St. Albert, in I *Priorum Analyticorum,* tract. 1, cap. 1).

[23] " . . . Logica generaliter dicta totum comprehendit trivium vel quatrivium secundum Aristotelem. . . . Haec ergo comprehendit . . . rhetoricam. . . . " (St. Albert, in I *Topicorum,* tract. 4, cap. 2).

[24] "Inter species autem argumentationis praecipua est syllogismus. Propter quod quidam dixerunt quod logica tota est de syllogismo et partibus syllogismi: determinantes commune subjectum logicae secundum id quod est subjectum principale. Non enim de omnibus fides esse poterit per syllogismum, propter hoc quod discursus syllogisticus non est nisi ab universali universaliter accepto: quod in multis scientiis esse non poterit, ut in rhetoricis. Propterea quod in illis praecipue locales habitudines attenduntur, a quibus per enthymemata concluditur id quod quaesitum est. Cum igitur logica, ut dicit Aristoteles, det omni scientiae modum disserendi, et inveniendi, et dijudicandi quod quaesitum est: oportet quod de tali sit ut de subjecto, quod omnibus in omni aequaliter applicabile est. . . . Propter quod syllogismus commune subjectum logicae esse non potest" (St. Albert, *De Praedicabilibus,* tract. 1, cap. 4).

[25] This statement must not be taken in an absolute way, for as regards proper, scientific knowledge man is usually in error. (Aristotle, *On the Soul,* III, chap. 3, 427 b 1; St. Thomas, in *III de Anima,* lect. 4, edit. Marietti, n.624). It must be understood in its context, taking into consideration that this is a rhetorical trea-tise. Now, the matter of rhetoric is common and concerned with civil things, and as regards such *communia* man usually does arrive at truth. That rhetorical matter is proportionate to the masses may be seen from the fact that a rhetorical proposition is called an opinion held by the common people: "In tertio autem ordine est propositio opinabilis opinione plurimum non sapientum: et argumentatio ex his composita vocatur ratio vel argumentatio rhetorica" (St. Albert, in I *Posteriorum Analyticorum,* tract. 1, cap. 2).

[26] St. Thomas, in I *Physicorum,* lect. 1, edit. Marietti, n.7; in II *Metaphysicorum,* lect. 1, nn. 282, 285; Ia *Pars,* q. 85, a.3.

[27] I, chap. 2, 101 a 30-34; trans. W. A. Pickard-Cambridge, ed. McKeon, N. Y., Random House, 1941.

[28] " . . . Hanc methodum . . . (quae docet communia invenire) . . . conferens ad facile de proposito arguendum de utraque parte contradictionis, valet ad exercitationes . . ." (in I *Topicorum* tract. 1, cap. 5).

[29] " . . . Virtutes sunt principia actionum quae non transeunt in exteriorem materiam, sed manet in ipsis agentibus. Unde tales actiones sunt perfectiones agentium. Et ideo bonum harum actionum in ipsis agentibus consistit" (St. Thomas, in II *Ethic.,* lect. 4, n.282).

" . . . Omnis virtus subiectum cuius est, facit bene habere, et opus eius bene se habens . . . secundum virtutem propriam unaquaeque res et bona sit, et bene operetur" (*Ibid.,* lect, 6, nn. 307-308).

" . . . Per virtutem aliquis non solum potest bene operari, sed etiam bene operans: quia virtus inclinat ad bonam operationem, sicut et natura" (*Ibid.,* n.316).

" . . . Virtus, ex ipsa ratione nominis, importat quamdam perfectionem potentiae . . ." (St. Thomas, *Ia IIae,* q. 55, a.2).

" . . . Virtus humana, quae est habitus operativus, est bonus habitus, et boni operativus . . ." (*Ibid.,* a.3).

"Virtus autem humana . . . secundum perfectam rationem virtutis dicitur, quae requirit rectitudinem appetitus; huiusmodi enim virtus non solum facit facultatem bene agendi, sed ipsum etiam usum boni operis causat. . . . Constat autem quod perfectum est principalius imperfecto. Et ideo virtutes quae continent rectitudinem appetitus, dicuntur principales. Huiusmodi autem sunt virtutes morales . . ." (*Ibid.,* q. 61, a. 1).

[30] "Neque enim rhetoricus advocatus omnino et universaliter persuadebit, impedimento triplici impeditus: malitia causae, perversitate judicis, et debilitate allegationis suae. . . . Sed si unusquisque . . .

ex contingentibus secundum suae artis facultatem nihil omiserit, dicemus disciplinam et disciplinabilem finem habere sufficenter secundum artis contingentiam, quamvis non semper habeat finem sufficenter in alio secundum effectum persuasionis . . ." (St. Albert, in I *Topicorum,* tract. 1, cap. 5).

[31] " . . . Nemo quaerat in scientia quod ex principiis ejusdem non poterat" (*Ibid.*).

[32] "A sophista vero differt philosophus 'prohaeresi,' idest electione vel voluptate, idest desiderio vitae. Ad aliud enim ordinat vitam suam et actiones philosophus et sophista. Philosophus quidem ad sciendum veritatem; sophista vero ad hoc quod videature scire quamvis nesciat" (St. Thomas, in IV Metaph., lect. 4, n. 575).

[33] " . . . Per rhetoricam, quae componit ad persuadendum, ut sc. supra dixit, quod non fuit intentionis quod sua praedicatio niteretur philosophicis rationibus; ita nunc dicit non fuisse suae intentionis niti rhetoricis persuasionibus" (St. Thomas, in I *ad Corinthios,* lect. 4, cap. 2).

[34] "Per modum quidem persuasionis, sicut cum proponitur aliquid virtuti cognoscitivae ut bonum" (St. Thomas, *Q. D. de Malo,* q. 3, a. 4).

"Nulla igitur substantia creata potest movere voluntatem nisi mediante bono intellecto. Hoc autem est inquantum manifestat ei aliquid esse bonum ad agendum: quod est *persuadere.* Nulla igitur substantia creata potest agere in voluntatem, vel esse causa electionis nostrae, nisi per modum persuadentis" (St. Thomas, *Summa Contra Gentiles,* III, cap. 88).

"Tertio modo, ille qui persuadet objectum propositum habere rationem boni: quia et hic aliqualiter proponit proprium objectum voluntati, quod est rationis bonum vel apparens" (St. Thomas, *Ia IIae,* q. 80, a. 1).

[35] "Ex parte quidem obiecti, movet voluntatem et ipsum bonum quod est voluntatis obiectum, sicut appetibile movet appetitum; et ille qui demonstrat obiectum, puta qui demonstrat aliquid esse bonum. Sed sicut supra dictum est, alia quidem bona aliqualiter inclinant voluntatem; sed nihil sufficienter movet voluntatem, nisi bonum universale quod est Deus. . . . Angelus ergo non sufficienter movet voluntatem neque ut obiectum, neque ut ostendens obiectum. Sed inclinat eam, ut amabile quoddam, et ut manifestans aliqua bona creata ordinata in Dei bonitatem. Et per hoc inclinare potest ad amorem creaturae vel Dei, per modum suadentis" (St. Thomas, Ia *Pars,* q. 106, a. 2).

[36] " . . . Voluntas ad aliquid inclinari dicitur dupliciter: uno modo ab exteriori; alio modo ab interiori. Ab exteriori quidem, sicut ab obiecto apprehenso; nam bonum apprehensum movere dicitur voluntatem; et per

hunc modum dicitur movere consilians vel suadens, in quantum scilicet facit apparere aliquod esse bonum. . . . . Obiectum non ex necessitate movet voluntatem; et ideo nulla persuasio ex necessitate movet hominem ad agendum" (St. Thomas, *De Malo,* q. 3, a. 3).

"Et mediante hoc obiecto potest aliqua creatura inclinare aliquatenus voluntatem, non tamen necessario immutare; sicut patet cum aliquis persuadet alicui aliquid faciendum propenendo ei eius utilitatem et honestatem; tamen in potestate voluntatis est ut illud acceptet vel non acceptet, eo quod non est naturaliter determinata ad id" (St. Thomas, *Q. D. de Veritate,* q. 22, a. 9).

[37] "Cuius ratio est, quia consideratio huius libi directe ordinatur ad scientiam demonstrativam, in qua animus hominis per rationem inducitur ad consentiendum vero ex his quae sunt propria rei; et ideo demonstrator non utitur ad suum finem nisi enunciativis orationibus, significantibus res secundum quod earum veritas est in anima. Sed rhetor et poeta inducunt ad assentiendum ei quod intendunt, non solum per ea quae sunt propria rei, sed etiam per dispositiones audientis. Unde rhetores et poeta plerumque movere auditores nituntur provocando eos ad aliquas passiones, ut Philosophus dicit in sua Rhetorica" (St. Thomas, in I *Peri Hermeneias,* lect. 7, edit. Marietti, n. 87).

[38] "Unde secundum quod aliquis est causa quod aliquid apprehendatur ut bonum ad appetendum, secundum hoc movet voluntatem. Et sic solus Deus efficaciter potest movere voluntatem; angelus autem et homo per modum suadentis, ut supra dictum est. Sed praeter hunc modum, etiam aliter movetur in hominibus voluntas ab exteriori, scilicet ex passione existente circa appetitum sensitivum; sicut ex concupiscentia vel ira inclinatur voluntas ad aliquid volendum. Et sic etiam angeli, inquantum possunt concitare huiusmodi passiones, possunt voluntatem movere. Non tamen ex necessitate quia voluntas semper remanet libera ad consentiendum vel resistendum passioni" (St. Thomas, *Ia Pars,* q. 111, a. 2, c).

"Dicitur tamen diabolus incensor cogitationum, inquantum incitat ad cogitandum, vel ad appetendum cogitata, per modum persuadentis, vel passionem concitantis" (*Ibid.,* ad 2).

[39] We have thought it best to use the English word "suspicion" to translate the Latin *suspicio*. However, a few precisions must be made to clarify its meaning in this context. The first meaning of "suspicion" is " . . . imagination or apprehension of something wrong or hurtful, without proof, or on slight evidence. . . . " (Webster's *New International Dictionary of the English Language,* the word "suspicion"). But suspicion, as an effect produced by rhetorical argumentation, does not necessarily imply "something wrong or hurtful." Rather, it should be understood in the sense in which

it is synonymous with "surmise" and "conjecture." The second meaning given for "surmise" is "suspicion"; the third meaning is "a thought or idea based on scanty evidence; a conjecture; a random conclusion . . ." (*Ibid.,* the word "surmise"). "Conjecture" is defined as " . . . to form opinions concerning, on grounds confessedly insufficient to certain conclusion"; and "suspect" is given as a synonym (*Ibid.,* the word "conjecture").

[40] "Quandoque vero, non fit complete fides vel opinio, sed suspicio quaedam, quia non totaliter declinatur ad unam partem contradictionis, licet magis inclinetur in hanc quam in illam. Et ad hoc ordinatur *Rhetorica*" (St. Thomas, in I *Posteriorum Analyticorum,* Prooemium, edit. Marietti, n. 6).

[41] "Quandoque vero intellectus inclinatur magis ad unum quam ad alterum; sed tamen illud inclinans non sufficienter movet intellectum ad hoc quod determinet ipsum in unam partium totaliter; unde accipit quidem unam partem, tamen semper dubitat de opposita. Et haec est dispositio opinantis, qui accipit unam partem contradictionis cum formidine alterius" (St. Thomas, *De Veritate,* q. 14, a. 1).

[42] " . . . Quandoque quidem etsi non fiat scientia, fit tamen fides vel opinio propter probabilitatem propositionum, ex quibus proceditur; quia ratio totaliter declinat in unam partem contradictionis, licet cum formidine alterius, et ad hoc ordinatur *Topica* sive *Dialectica*" (St. Thomas, in I *Post. Anal.,* Prooemium, n. 6).

"Licet opinans non sit certus, tamen iam determinavit se ad unum . . ." (St. Thomas, in VI *Ethicorum,* lect. 8, edit. Marietti, n. 1221).

"Et dicit, quod omne illud de quo habetur opinio, iam est determinatum quantum ad opinantem, licet non sit determinatum quantum ad rei veritatem" (*Ibid.,* n. 1226).

[43] "Quidam vero actus intellectus habent quidem cogitationem informem absque firma assensione: sive in neutram partem declinent, sicut accidit dubitanti; sive in unam partem magis declinent sed tenentur aliquo levi signo, sicut accidit suspicanti; sive uni parti adhaereant, tamen cum formidine alteris, quod accidit opinanti" (St. Thomas, IIa IIae, q. 2, a. 1).

[44] *De Ordine,* II, cap. 13, n. 38: *Oeuires de saint Augustin,* éd. Bénédictine, Paris Desclée de Brouwer, 1948, Vol. IV.

[45] *Orator,* II, cap. 44, n. 186; trans. H. M. Hubbell, The Loeb Classical Library, Cambridge, Mass., Harvard Univ. Press, 1939.

[46] *Rhetoric,* I, chap. 1, 1354 a 14.

[47] Aristotle, *Rhetoric,* III, chap. 18, 1419 b 24, trans. W. Rhys Roberts, ed. Solmsen, N. Y., Random House, 1954.

[48] "The emotions are all those feelings that so change men as to affect their judgments, and that are also attended by pain or pleasure" (*Ibid.,* II, chap. 1, 1378 a 20).

[49] St. Thomas, in V. *Metaphysicorum,* lect. 3, n. 782.

William J. Jordan (essay date 1974)

SOURCE: "Aristotle's Concept of Metaphor in *Rhetoric*," in *Aristotle: The Classical Heritage of Rhetoric,* edited by Keith V. Erickson, The Scarecrow Press, Inc., 1974, pp. 235-50.

[*In the following essay, Jordan studies Aristotle's use of metaphor in* Rhetoric, *asserting that the context of Aristotle's statements about metaphor indicates that his conception of metaphor was psychological in nature. Aristotle, Jordan notes, identifies "semantic and structural characteristics which affect reader and listener behavior."*]

Unlike much of Aristotle's rhetorical theory, his concept of metaphor has received relatively little attention from contemporary rhetorical theorists. Traditionally, rhetoricians have either overlooked or have not been concerned with Aristotle's psychological aspects of metaphor, as Kennedy observes that "none of the later Greek or Roman accounts seem to share Aristotle's philosophical concern with the psychological bases of figures of speech."[1] Osborn's recent discussion of metaphor likewise denies a psychological consideration of Aristotle's concept of metaphor. According to Osborn:

> The emphasis in Aristotle remains primarily upon the linguistic character of metaphor, and the reasons for this emphasis again lie both in the natural tendency of early theory to stress the most obvious characteristics of the figure, and in the conceptual framework which placed the figure under the canon of Style. Moreover, there is no explicit acknowledgment in these observations that the psychological dimension of metaphor is an integral component of its occurrence, an essential part of its being. Certainly the Aristotelian definition does not at all suggest such an essentiality.[2]

While the Aristotelian definition, alone, may not suggest a psychological orientation to metaphor, the context of his statements concerning metaphor in both the **Rhetoric** and **Poetics** provides support for the thesis that Aristotle's concept of metaphor is essentially psychological in that it identifies semantic and structural characteristics which affect reader and listener behavior. The following analysis seeks to reconstruct Aristotle's concept of metaphor, identifying his particular emphases on the psychological elements of the rhetorical metaphor.

Characteristics of Metaphor

Aristotle's statements which indicate his concern with semantic characteristics of metaphor consider the relationship between words and meanings. While the term *word . . .* is quite common in Aristotle's writings, and refers to meaningful speech sounds or their written counterparts, his term for *meaning* varies.[3] In addition to using the term *meaning,* Aristotle refers to "mental experience" or "images in the thinking soul." Aristotle argues that words denote meanings when he refers to spoken words as "the symbols of mental experience and written words are the symbols of spoken words. Just as all men have not the same writing, so all men have not the same speech sounds, but the mental experiences, which these directly symbolize, are the same for all, as also are those things of which our experiences are the images."[4] That is, for the speakers of a language, most words will be used to refer to a specific set of things, objects, concepts or referents.[5] The common meaning accompanying the generally accepted usage of a word may be considered its denotation. What the word names is its referent. The meaning, however, according to Aristotle, is neither the denotation nor the referent but the mental experience which the word evokes in a listener. From this basis Aristotle's statements concerning metaphor may be considered as part of a semantic construct.

Aristotle's statements which indicate his concern with structural characteristics consider relationships between words. Aristotle makes comparisons between words and groups of words in terms of their frequency of occurrence in the language and their length. These statements provide a basis for considering the structural characteristics of metaphor. After establishing the distinction in Aristotle's writings between semantic and structural characteristics of words, this discussion considers the specific characteristics which distinguish metaphor from literal language.

Buckley sees a distinction in Aristotle's writings between two classifications of word characteristics, a semantic class and a structural class. Each class may be subdivided into two species of words. . . .

These classifications may be diagrammed as discrete categories.

Semantic Class

literal words, [*loikeia*]
metaphors, [*metaphorai*]

Structural Class

words in general use, [*kuria*]
unfamiliar words, [*glōttai*]

This distinction explains Aristotle's identification of "the regular . . . and proper . . . terms for things," by emphasizing that words have both semantic and structural aspects.[7]

This distinction has been ignored by Cope who says that [*kuria*] and [*oikeia*] are virtually the same.[8] Welldon concurs: "There seems to be practically no difference in meaning between 'proper' and 'special' names; they are the names employed in ordinary speech."[9] Gillies, however, seems to support Buckley's distinction: "[*kuria*] are words ordinary and appropriate, in opposition to [*glōttai*] and [*pepoi hemena*], foreign and new coined words: [*oikeia*] are proper words, in opposition to metaphors."[10] Aristotle's use of [*kuria*], which Roberts translates in the following context as "Clearness is secured by using the words (nouns and verbs alike) that are current and ordinary," also suggests that Aristotle was concerned with a distinct structural element.[11]

It should be noted that these two classifications are not mutually exclusive. A literal word may be either familiar (in general use) or unfamiliar. Likewise, a metaphor may be composed or either familiar or unfamiliar words. This interrelationship of the semantic with the structural aspects of metaphor is central to Aristotle's concept of the effective metaphor.

Semantic Characteristics

Semantically, metaphor differs from literal language in that it denotes a new or unique meaning. According to Aristotle, "ordinary words convey only what we know already; it is from metaphor that we can best get hold of something fresh."[12] Aristotle provides the following example of metaphor denoting new meaning. "When the poet calls old age 'a withered stalk,' he conveys a new idea, a new fact, to us by means of the general notion of 'lost bloom,' which is common to both things."[13] This basic semantic nature of metaphor, the denotation of new meaning, can be attributed to the semantic characteristics which distinguish metaphor from literal language.

Semantically, metaphor differs from literal language in terms of its conceptual denotation and in some cases its sensory denotation. These may be thought of as cognitive discrepancies in that they are based on both the listener's and the speaker's knowledge of how things and ideas are related.

Conceptually, for Aristotle, "metaphor consists in giving the thing a name that belongs to something else; the transference being either from genus to species, or from species to genus, or from species to species, or on grounds of analogy."[14] Words used as metaphor denote either a) a specific meaning instead of a more general literal meaning (genus to species), b) a general meaning instead of a more specific literal meaning (species to genus), c) a different specific meaning instead of a literal specific meaning (species to species), or d) an analogous meaning instead of a literal meaning.[15] In all of these cases, the cognitive discrepancy grows out of the metaphor's denotation of a meaning which is different from the literal or ordinary meaning of the words used as metaphor.

The second type of cognitive discrepancy described by Aristotle as being potentially denoted by metaphor is sensory discrepancy. According to Aristotle, metaphor has a discrepant sensory denotation when the words used as metaphor denote a referent capable of expending energy. At the outset, it must be noted that sensory denotation, as a semantic characteristic, is ancillary to metaphor. It is not inherent in all metaphor, nor is it unique to metaphor; other words may also have this characteristic. Sensory discrepancy is considered here because Aristotle explicitly emphasizes this characteristic when treating metaphor.

What Aristotle means by sensory denotation or activity . . . is best illustrated in his examples. Activity is expenditure of energy.

> So with Homer's common practice of giving metaphorical life to lifeless things: all such passages are distinguished by the effect of activity they convey. Thus,
>
> Downward anon to the valley rebounded the boulder *remorseless;*
> and
> The (bitter) arrow *flew;*
>
> and
> Flying on *eagerly;*
> and
> Stuck in the earth, still *panting* to feed on the flesh of heroes;
> and
> And the point of the spear *in its fury* drove full through his breastbone.
> In all these examples the things have the effect of being active because they are made into living beings; shameless behavior and fury and so on are all forms of activity.[16]

English translations read [*energeia*] as either "activity" or "actuality" (except Buckley, who translates this as "personification"). This suggests that a metaphor which has a sensory denotation is not limited strictly to visual referents as some translations seem to suggest.

Apparently activity has been selected by some translators because Aristotle relates metaphorical activity and physical vision in his introduction to his discussion of the sensory metaphor.

> By making them "see things" I mean using expressions that represent things as in a state of activity. Thus, to say that a good man is 'four-square' is certainly a metaphor; both the good man and the square are perfect; but the metaphor does not suggest activity. On the other hand, in the expression 'with his vigor in full bloom' there is a notion of activity; and so in 'But you must roam as free as a sacred victim'; and in
>
> Threat up sprang the Hellenes to their feet, where 'up sprang' gives us activity as well as metaphor, for it at once suggests swiftness.[17]

Freese translates the first sentence of the preceding passage as "I mean that things are set before the eyes by words that signify actuality."[18] . . . Roberts explains activity as setting things "before the eyes" of the listener. As a result of this interpretation, Roberts calls the active metaphor a "graphic metaphor," implying that the metaphor is limited to representing *visually* active referents.[19] As the examples provided by Aristotle suggest, the active or sensory metaphor is not limited to denoting visual activity. Thus, "remorseless," "eagerly," "panting," and "in its fury" as examples of the sensory metaphor are understood better as metaphors which denote expenditure of energy, rather than graphic metaphors. Aristotle even notes that things not in motion may be thought of as capable of expending energy.[20] The example, "with his vigor in full bloom," is not a movement but a state of being which can be sensed. Therefore, the concept of sensory denotation seems to encompass all of the possibilities suggested by such terms as graphic, active, representing actuality. . . .

In describing metaphor, Aristotle suggests that metaphor differs from literal language in its evaluative or affective denotation. This discrepancy is considered affective because it concerns the evaluations which the speaker or listener places upon the referent. According to Aristotle, when the speaker uses metaphor and gives the thing a name that belongs to something else, he necessarily denotes meaning which is more favorable or less favorable than would be denoted by literal language. Aristotle argues that two different words denote different evaluations. "Two different words will represent a thing in two different lights; so on this ground also one term must be held fairer or fouler than another. For both of two terms will indicate what *is* fair, or what *is* foul, but not simply their fairness or their foulness, or if so, at any rate not in an equal degree."[21] On this point Aristotle's translators are in agreement. Metaphor and the word it replaces meet the criterion of two different words, for if they were the same in their denotation, then one could not be metaphor.

According to Aristotle, all possible words whose meanings can be denoted by other words will differ in the evaluative meaning which they denote. Aristotle explains that "it is like having to ask ourselves what dress will suit an old man; certainly not the crimson cloak that suits a young man. And if you wish to pay a compliment, you must take your metaphor from something better in the same line; if to disparage, from something worse."[22] For example, "Somebody calls actors 'hangers-on of Dionysus,' but they call themselves 'artists': each of these terms is a metaphor, the one intended to throw dirt at the actor, the other to dignify him. And pirates now call themselves 'purveyors.' We can thus call a crime a mistake, or a mistake a crime."[23] Semantically metaphor is more than a word substitution technique. It is the selection of a word for the purpose of changing the evaluative relationship which exists between the referent and the word which names it. All metaphors are evaluative.

Structural Characteristics

Aristotle's concept of metaphor concerns the occurrence of words within a language and the norms which are descriptive of their occurrence. In the ***Rhetoric***, Aristotle's treatment of structural phenomena is inexact and unsystematic. On the basis of his observations, Aristotle identifies two structural characteristics relevant to metaphor. These characteristics are the frequency of occurrence of the words which compose the metaphor and the length of the metaphor.

Aristotle's concern with the frequency of occurrence of words in speech is evident in his linguistic classification of words into two subgroups. The first consists of ordinary words, . . . which Aristotle defines as those "in general use in a country."[24] Due to their general use, these words would have a relatively high frequency of occurrence. The second group of words consists of strange words, or words "in use elsewhere,". . . . Frequency of occurrence distinguishes [ordinary words] from [strange words]. According to Aristotle, "the same word may obviously be at once strange and ordinary, though not in reference to the same people; [*sigunon*], for instance, is an ordinary word in Cyprus, and a strange word with us."[25] Strange words are, necessarily, words with a low or no frequency of occurrence in the language. Other words which have a low frequency of occurrence and which Aristotle includes in the category of [strange words] are compound words, invented words, lengthened words, curtailed words, and words altered in form, for all of these deviate from normal speech.[26]

The ***Rhetoric*** recommends that metaphor be constructed from high frequency words. According to Aristotle,

the speech of ordinary life, or high frequency words, are of two kinds. "In the language of prose, besides the regular and proper terms for things, metaphorical terms only can be used with advantage. This we gather from the fact that these two classes of terms, the proper or regular and the metaphorical—these and no others—are used by everybody in conversation."[27] Because they are used by everybody in conversation, words used metaphorically can be identified as high frequency words. In addition, Aristotle says that "metaphor . . . gives style clearness . . . as nothing else can."[28] And clearness is obtained by using high frequency words. Aristotle says that "style to be good must be clear, as is proved by the fact that speech which fails to convey a plain meaning will fail to do just what speech has to do. . . . Clearness is secured by using the words (nouns and verbs alike) that are current and ordinary."[29] Because metaphor gives style clearness, and clearness is also obtained from words of high frequency, Aristotle asserts that the effective metaphor will be composed of high frequency words.

Limitations

In developing limitations to the invention of metaphor, Aristotle explicitly states that knowing the characteristics which compose metaphor does not guarantee the successful construction of metaphor. Specifically, Aristotle states that "their actual invention can only come through natural talent or long practice; but this treatise may indicate the way it is done."[30] The invention of metaphor, or the way it is done, is accomplished by combining the necessary semantic and structural characteristics in selecting words for discourse. The basic limitation imposed by Aristotle upon the selection process is that the words be appropriate to rhetorical discourse.

By appropriate, Aristotle means that metaphor should denote discrepant meaning which, while differing from literal meaning, also is related to the literal language which the speaker would normally use in the same situation. According to Aristotle, "metaphor must be drawn, as has been stated already, from things that are related to the original thing, and yet not obviously so related."[31] But Aristotle warns against constructing a metaphor which is too discrepant. "Metaphors must not be far-fetched," and "we must draw them not from remote but from kindred and similar things."[32]

Aristotle provides examples of metaphor that are too "far-fetched," or too discrepant. According to Aristotle: "Others [metaphors] are too grand and theatrical; and these, if they are far-fetched, may also be obscure. For instance, Gorgias talks of 'events that are green and full of sap,' and says 'foul was the deed you sowed and evil the harvest you reaped.' That is too much like poetry. Alcidamas, again, called philosophy 'a fortress that threatens the power of law,' and the *Odyssey* 'a goodly looking-glass of human life,' and talked about 'offering no such toy to poetry.'"[33] While Aristotle's translators seem to object to these metaphors because they are too much like poetry, the point Aristotle seems to be making is that the potential meanings of the words used as metaphor in these instances were either too discrepant from or too similar to the literal words which would describe the same referents.[34] Ideally, then, metaphor should obtain some optimal mean of discrepancy although that mean is unidentified in Aristotle's concept of metaphor.

Effects of Metaphor

Whereas the preceding discussion has focused on the specific characteristics of metaphor, this discussion explains how Aristotle sees those characteristics contributing to a rhetorically functional metaphor, one which is potentially advantageous in discourse. Aristotle's concept points to three potential rhetorical advantages evolving from metaphor: liveliness, appetence and pleasure. These advantages evolve from the characteristics which Aristotle attributes to metaphor. These advantages, in conjunction with the characteristics previously described, constitute a composite explication of Aristotle's concept of the rhetorically functional metaphor.

Metaphor and Liveliness Effects

Aristotle identifies metaphor as evoking new meaning rapidly and with little effort for the listener. Although Aristotle develops this point with a concept of liveliness, this rhetorical advantage may be described more precisely in terms of the listener's efficiency of response.

Aristotle explicitly relates rapid evocation of new meaning to liveliness when he says "both speech and reasoning are lively in proportion as they make us seize a new idea promptly."[35] Stated somewhat differently, words which require little mental effort to understand utilize a characteristic of liveliness which allows the listener "to get hold of new ideas easily."[36] The Greek term for "lively" is [asteia], which is defined as "of the town, urbane, courteous, polite, witty, elegant, neat, and pretty."[37] Translations of [asteia] read "smart and popular, clever and popular, urbanities, and lively, pointed, sprightly, witty, facetious, clever, and popular sayings."[38] Aristotle's metaphorical use of [asteia] is not clarified by his translators. From what Aristotle says about liveliness in the **Rhetoric,** however, "efficiency" seems to be the better term to describe how metaphor evokes new meaning. While liveliness rather ambiguously describes a characteristic of language, efficiency is more descriptive of a behavioral response.

Aristotle identifies metaphor as an efficient symbol when he states that "liveliness is specially conveyed by metaphor."[39] According to what Aristotle says concerning liveliness, a word may be more efficient when it is semantically discrepant with the listener's expectations, when it evokes sensory denotations, and when it is linguistically or structurally frequent and brief.

Metaphor may create the potential advantage of efficiency because it is discrepant with the expectations of the listener. In Aristotle's terminology "liveliness is specially conveyed by metaphor, and by the further power of surprising the hearer; because the hearer expected something different, his acquisition of the new idea impresses him all the more."[40] Aristotle's implication here is that the listener expects literal language. That is, he expects words to be used in consistent ways. Because it is cognitively and affectively different from literal language, any specific metaphor should be unexpected. As a result, when the listener perceives a metaphor, he is either aware of being "deceived" or "surprised," depending upon translators, because metaphorical meaning is unexpected.

Metaphor may be more efficient than other symbols when it has sensory denotations. Although the **Rhetoric** does not provide a detailed analysis of how the active or sensory metaphor evokes new meaning efficiently, it does suggest that sensory metaphors are more efficient.

According to Aristotle, "liveliness is got by . . . using expressions that represent things as in a state of activity," and "activity is movement."[41] The psychological implications of this premise are explained, in part, by Aristotle in his psychological treatise **On the Soul.** In Aristotle's concept of the physical world of perceivers and referents (as opposed to the verbal world of listeners and words), of all things capable of being perceived, man most readily perceives movement. This is because all states of an object's existence are, according to Aristotle, states of movement. "The objects which we perceive incidentally through this or that special sense, . . . we perceive by movement, e.g., magnitude by movement, and therefore also figure (for figure is a species of magnitude), what is at rest by absence of movement."[42] Because movement or its absence is more readily perceived, Aristotle seems to attribute efficiency to metaphors which represent things as moving or capable of moving.

In addition to semantic characteristics, Aristotle suggests that structural characteristics may also contribute to metaphor's potential efficiency.

According to Aristotle, literal words are inefficient in evoking new meaning rapidly and easily. This assumption applies to both infrequent and frequent words when used literally. A structurally infrequent or strange word is not generally understood by a listener, and a frequent or ordinary word is one whose literal meaning is not new to the listener. According to Aristotle, "strange words simply puzzle us; ordinary words convey only what we know already."[43] Neither of these structural units, when used literally, evokes new meaning easily or efficiently.

Metaphor, however, may be an efficient source of new meaning, particularly when constructed of structurally frequent words. According to Aristotle, "it is from metaphor that we best get hold of something fresh."[44] Two alternatives exist for metaphor. It can be either an infrequent word used uniquely or a frequent word used uniquely. Since infrequent words usually have no literal meaning for the listener, he cannot perceive that the word is being used metaphorically and no new meaning is evoked. This implies that what may be metaphor for a speaker may not be metaphor for a listener. When such a situation occurs, Aristotle would suggest that the meaning is unclear.

To achieve efficiency and still insure clarity, Aristotle recommends using high frequency words in unique ways. According to Aristotle, "clearness is secured by using the words (nouns and verbs alike) that are current and ordinary."[45] At the same time clearness is obtained, the essential discrepant nature of metaphor also may be obtained by using words uniquely. This is apparently what Aristotle means when he states that metaphor gives style "clearness" and "distinction" at the same time.

Related to frequency is the structural characteristic of length. The shorter the metaphor, the more efficient it should be in evoking new meaning. Specifically Aristotle states that "the more briefly . . . such sayings [metaphors] can be expressed, the more taking they are, . . . brevity [impresses the new idea] more quickly"; or "conciseness gives knowledge more rapidly."[46] Aristotle is not concerned here with absolute length of words, but rather with relative lengths of alternative words, whether it be a shorter word in place of a longer word, or a shorter passage in place of a longer passage. As a case in point, Aristotle's major criticism of the simile is that it is unnecessarily long: "The simile, as we have said, is a metaphor differing only by the addition of a word, wherefore it is less pleasant because it is longer."[47] The essence of Aristotle's argument seems to be that words which do not contribute to new meaning impede the efficiency of the other words which are being used to evoke new meaning. Thus, by eliminating the unnecessary words within the metaphor, the length is shortened, and the shortened metaphor may be more efficient.

Metaphor and Appetence Effects

In Aristotle's concept, metaphor potentially has an effect on the motivational states of the listener. In terms of a rhetorical advantage, metaphor associates meaning with the desire of the listener to avoid or pursue the referent of the meaning to a greater degree than literal symbols. While Aristotle does not use the term motivation, he does talk about appetence, that faculty "of which desire, passion, and wish are the species."[48] In Shute's analysis of Aristotle's concept, motivation follows perception in that "the presence of sensation always arouses some kind of desire, for what is sensed causes pleasure or pain, and desire is a craving for what is pleasant."[49] As Aristotle would explain motivation theory, "when the object is pleasant or painful, the soul makes a quasi-affirmation or negation, and pursues or avoids the object."[50] Aristotle illustrates how the motives of a person may filter what he perceives in the process of associating meaning and values.

> The faculty of thinking then thinks the forms in images, and . . . what is to be pursued or avoided is marked out for it. . . . E.g. perceiving by sense that the beacon is fire, it recognizes in virtue of the general faculty of sense that it signifies an enemy, because it sees it moving; but sometimes by means of the images or thoughts which are within the soul, just as if it were seeing, it calculates and deliberates what is to come by reference to what is present; and when it makes a pronouncement, as in the case of sensation, it pronounces the object to be pleasant or painful, in this case it avoids or pursues; and so generally in cases of action.[51]

The listener may not make a simple yes-no type of evaluation. Instead, as Shute explains Aristotle's concept of motivation, the process of associating referents with values may be very complex.

> This process of deliberation may be immensely complicated. It may lead to considerations which nullify the claims of the goal. But if it reaches its end, that conclusion is the conclusion of the individual, for the mind is the organism thinking, rather than something apart from it. Thus the conclusion of this mental activity is identical with the actualizing or energizing of the individual in relation to his object, and the overt activity is in progress.[52]

Because of this complexity of the intervening considerations, metaphor is qualified as "potentially" affecting motivation.

Metaphor potentially may affect motivation because it evaluates its referent. As discussed previously, Aristotle states that no two words used to denote the same meaning will evoke the same meaning. The meanings will differ at least in evaluation. Stated another way, metaphor evokes a different evaluation of a referent than does the literal word. The purpose of the evaluation, according to Aristotle, is to identify the referent as being either more or less pleasant or more or less painful. Aristotle provides examples of these possibilities.

When metaphor evaluates a referent as pleasant, it identifies it as an object of pursuit for the listener. Of course there may be relative degrees of pleasantness. When the referent is evaluated as more pleasant than the listener's evaluation, the referent potentially becomes an object of increased pursuit. When the referent is evaluated as less pleasant than the listener's evaluation, the referent potentially becomes an object of decreased pursuit. Aristotle's example of two terms for a religious title illustrates this. "So Iphicrates called Callias a 'mendicant priest' instead of a 'torchbearer,' and Callias replied that Iphicrates must be uninitiated or he would have called him not a 'mendicant priest' but a 'torchbearer.' Both are religious titles, but one is honourable and the other is not."[53] The religious position of Callias, a potential object of pursuit, is evaluated as an object of greater pursuit by the metaphor "torchbearer," and as an object of lesser pursuit by the metaphor "mendicant priest." Again, it should be emphasized that any possible evaluation only potentially affects the listener. He may accept the evaluation or reject it. If he accepts the evaluation, according to Aristotle's explanation of motivation, he should act accordingly. To the extent that metaphor may be held responsible for associating the meaning with the pursuit motives of the listener, it may be considered a persuasive stimulus.

When metaphor evaluates a referent as painful, it is identified as an object for the listener to avoid. The evaluation may suggest greater or lesser avoidance of the referent. Evaluation which identifies the referent as an object of greater avoidance is evidenced, says Aristotle, when we call actors "hangers-on of Dionysus," or say that a thief "plundered his victim," or that Orestes is a "mother-slayer."[54] Evaluation which identifies the referent as an object of lesser avoidance is evidenced when begging is described as "praying," when pirates call themselves "purveyors," when a crime is called a "mistake," when a thief is said to "take" a thing, or when Orestes is called his "father's avenger."[55] All of these examples, according to Aristotle, attempt to change the evaluative meaning of the referent through metaphorical transfer which identifies the referent as an object to avoid. To the extent that the listener accepts the evaluation and avoids the referent, the metaphor may be considered persuasive.

Metaphor and Pleasure Effects

In addition to describing metaphor as a motivational element, Aristotle suggests that metaphor creates pleasure. In Aristotle's philosophy, pleasure is a normal or natural state of man which results from human activity or movement. In *Metaphysics,* Aristotle states that "pleasure in its highest form of speculative philosophical pleasure, is identical with the highest happiness . . . [and] is represented as the pleasure of the Supreme Being; and because this is the nature of pleasure, all

states of activity, waking, sensation, thinking give the highest pleasure; and to one of these all other pleasure, as those of anticipation and recollection are due."[56] Ross concludes from this definition that pleasure "cannot be a movement. . . . But it is in fact something complete in itself."[57] Pleasure, then, is a resulting condition or state. Cope prefers this to the definition found in the **Rhetoric** which he dismisses as being sufficient enough for the rhetorician, but "both virtually and actually contradicted" in Aristotle's other writings.[58] In the **Rhetoric,** Aristotle defines pleasure as both the activity leading up to and the final effect of the listener's achieving a normal state of being: "We may lay it down that Pleasure is a movement, a movement by which the soul as a whole is consciously brought into its normal state of being."[59] When viewed as a natural state rather than a movement or process, pleasure may be studied more profitably from a rhetorical viewpoint as a potential effect of metaphor rather than a process.

Metaphor potentially creates a pleasurable state in the listener because it causes the activity of learning to occur. Aristotle uses the term "learning" to describe a pleasurable experience when he states that "learning things and wondering at things are also pleasant as a rule; wondering implies the desire of learning, so that the object of wonder is an object of desire; while in learning one is brought into one's natural condition."[60] Acts of imitation also cause learning because "the spectator draws inferences ('That is a so-and-so') and thus learns something fresh."[61] In almost identical terms Aristotle talks about the pleasure derived from metaphor. "Easy learning is naturally pleasant to all, and words mean something, so that all words which make us learn something are most pleasant. . . . It is metaphor, therefore, that above all produces this effect."[62] And again, "Well-constructed riddles are pleasant for the same reason—the solution is an act of learning; and they are expressed metaphorically, too."[63] Metaphor causes the listener to learn, and to Aristotle this is a pleasurable experience. The pleasure which can be created by metaphor exists as a potential rhetorical advantage in Aristotle's concept.

Conclusion

Whereas all symbols may function to evoke new meaning, Aristotle distinguishes metaphor from all other evocative symbols. Aristotle's essentially psychological concept of metaphor suggests that the listener potentially responds to metaphor by constructing new meaning more efficiently than if the new meaning were evoked by literal language, by changing his evaluation of the metaphor's referent, and by deriving pleasure from the metaphor. Both semantic and structural characteristics appear to account for these effects. This interpretation of Aristotle's concept of metaphor is pertinent to modern studies of style. Aristotle's essentially psychological emphasis provides a deeply traditional basis for a behavioral study of the rhetorical effects of metaphor. Not only does Aristotle's concept identify those effects, it also identifies stimulus characteristics pertinent to any behavioral study of metaphor.

Notes

1 George Kennedy, *The Art of Persuasion in Greece* (Princeton: Princeton University Press, 1963), p. 111.

2 Michael M. Osborn, "The Function and Significance of Metaphor in Rhetorical Discourse," (unpublished Ph.D. dissertation, The University of Florida, 1963), p. 21.

3 *Categories* 1a. Unless indicated, all subsequent quotations from Aristotle's works are from the Oxford edition, *The Works of Aristotle,* 2 Vols., ed. by W. D. Ross, in *Great Books of the Western World,* Vols. 8-9, ed. by Robert Maynard Hutchins (54 vols.; Chicago: Encyclopaedia Britannica, Inc., 1952). In addition to the Rhys Roberts translation of the *Rhetoric* in the Oxford edition, additional texts and translations of the *Rhetoric* have been consulted. These are: *Aristotle's Rhetoric* (London: Printed by T. B. for Randall Taylor near Stationers-Hall, 1686); Theodore Buckley, *Aristotle's Treatise on Rhetoric and the Poetic of Aristotle* (fourth edition, London: George Bell and Sons, 1906); Lane Cooper, *The Rhetoric of Aristotle* (New York: Appleton-Century Crofts, Inc., 1932); Edward Meredith Cope, *The Rhetoric of Aristotle,* ed. by John Edwin Sandys, (3 vols.; Cambridge: University Press, 1877); Daniel Michael Crimmin, *A Dissertation on Rhetoric, translated from the Greek of Aristotle* (second edition, London: J. J. Stockdale, 1812); J. H. Freese, *Art of Rhetoric* (Cambridge, Mass.: Harvard University Press, 1926); John Gillies, *A New Translation of Aristotle's Rhetoric* (London: T. Cadell, 1823); Richard Claverhouse Jebb, *The Rhetoric of Aristotle,* ed. by John Edwin Sandys (Cambridge: University Press, 1909); J. E. C. Welldon, *The Rhetoric of Aristotle* (London: MacMillan and Company, 1886); and G. M. A. Grube, *On Poetry and Style: Aristotle* (Indianapolis: Bobbs-Merrill Company, Inc., 1958).

4 *On Interpretation* 16a.

5 As used by Ogden and Richards, "referent" seems to be the most all inclusive term. C. K. Ogden and I. A. Richards, *The Meaning of Meaning* (New York: Harcourt, Brace and World, Inc., 1923), pp. 9-12.

6 Buckley, *Aristotle's Treatise,* p. 209.

7 *Rhetoric* 1404b.

8 E. M. Cope, *An Introduction to Aristotle's Rhetoric* (London: Macmillan and Company, 1867), pp. 282ff.

9 Welldon, *The Rhetoric,* p. 230.

10 Gillies, *A New Translation,* p. 368.

11 *Rhetoric* 1404b.

12 *Ibid.* 1410b.

13 *Ibid.*

14 *Poetics* 1457b. In *Posterior Analytics* 96b ff., Aristotle treats genus and species as categories of thought. As such, these may be viewed as inventive "places" from which the speaker develops metaphor. While Osborn recognizes this kind of inventive system in Peacham's *The Garden of Eloquence,* he overlooks this interpretation of Aristotle's definition; see Michael M. Osborn, "The Evolution of the Theory of Metaphor in Rhetoric," *Western Speech,* XXXI (Spring, 1967), 123-26. When genus and species are viewed as categories of thought, Aristotle's definition of metaphor does point to an essential psychological dimension.

15 Aristotle's definition of metaphor concerns the generic concept rather than the specific trope Metaphor found in most modern treatments of style. According to Welldon, "the Aristotelian use of [*metaphora*] is considerably wider than that of 'metaphor' in English. Any transference of a word from its proper or ordinary application to another would be a [*metaphora*] whether it involved a comparison or not," *The Rhetoric,* pp. 232-33.

16 *Rhetoric* 1411b-1412a.

17 *Ibid.* 1411b.

18 Freese, *Art of Rhetoric,* p. 405.

19 *Rhetoric* 1411b.

20 *On the Soul* 425a.

21 *Rhetoric* 1405b.

22 *Ibid.* 1405a.

23 *Ibid.*

24 *Poetics* 1457b.

25 *Ibid.*

26 *Rhetoric* 1404b. In *Poetics,* Aristotle classifies metaphor with deviate forms. "On the other hand the diction becomes distinguished and non-prosaic by the use of unfamiliar terms, i.e. strange words, metaphors, lengthened forms, and everything that deviates from the ordinary modes of speech." *Poetics* 1458a. This is

contradicted in the *Rhetoric.* "These two classes of terms, the proper or regular and the metaphorical—these and no others—are used by everybody in conversation." *Rhetoric* 1404b. Metaphor, in rhetoric, is a semantic deviation, a deviation from norms of word usage, while at the same time not deviating from word frequency norms. Perhaps a difference between the poetic metaphor and the rhetorical metaphor is that the rhetorical metaphor attempts to clarify meaning and the poetic metaphor attempts to obscure meaning.

[27] *Rhetoric* 1404b.

[28] *Ibid.* 1405a.

[29] *Ibid.* 1404b.

[30] *Ibid.* 1410b.

[31] *Ibid.* 1413a.

[32] *Ibid.* 1410b; 1413a.

[33] *Ibid.* 1406b.

[34] According to Grube, "We should agree with Aristotle that Gorgias' reference to Philomela, who in legend was changed into a swallow, is frigid. We should also condemn most of his other examples, but the *Odyssey* as a mirror of human life rather appeals to us, except that by this time it is a cliché." Grube, On *Poetry,* p. 75.

[35] *Rhetoric* 1410b.

[36] *Ibid.*

[37] See Henry George Liddell and Robert Scott, *The Classic Greek Dictionary* (Chicago: Follett Publishing Company, 1927), p. 109.

[38] *Rhetoric* 1412a.

[39] *Ibid.*

[40] *Ibid.*

[41] *Ibid.* 1411b; 1412a.

[42] *On the Soul* 425a.

[43] *Rhetoric* 1410b.

[44] *Ibid.*

[45] *Ibid.*

[46] *Ibid.* 1412b; Freese, *Art of Rhetoric,* p. 413.

[47] *Rhetoric* 1410b.

[48] *On the Soul* 414b.

[49] Clarence Shute, *The Psychology of Aristotle* (Morningside Heights, New York: Columbia University Press, 1941), p. 85. This is Shute's summary of the concepts found in *On the Soul* 413b, 414b, and 431a.

[50] *On the Soul* 431a.

[51] *Ibid.* 431b.

[52] Shute, *The Psychology,* pp. 82-3.

[53] *Rhetoric* 1405a.

[54] *Ibid.* 1405a, 1405b.

[55] *Ibid.*

[56] This is Cope's interpretation of *Metaphysics* 1072b in *An Introduction,* pp. 238-39.

[57] W. D. Ross, *Aristotle* (fifth edition, London: Methuen and and Company, 1949), p. 228.

[58] Cope, *An Introduction,* p. 235.

[59] *Rhetoric* 1370a.

[60] *Ibid.* 1371b.

[61] *Ibid.*

[62] Freese, *Art of Rhetoric,* pp. 395, 397.

[63] Cooper, *The Rhetoric,* p. 312.

Keith V. Erickson (essay date 1975)

SOURCE: "A Brief History of Aristotle's *Rhetoric,*" in *Aristotle's "Rhetoric": Five Centuries of Philological Research,* The Scarecrow Press, Inc., 1975, pp. 1-20.

[*In the following essay, Erickson traces 2,300 years of the history of* Rhetoric, *from its probable composition date, the myths regarding the loss and recovery of the text, early translations and publications, and into the twentieth century.*]

Tracing the history of Aristotle's **Rhetoric** logically begins with its "completion" or "publication" date. Although numerous scholars have attempted to date the **Rhetoric** there is little conclusive evidence to confirm a particular date. Edward M. Cope, a century ago, summarized research concerning the **Rhetoric**'s completion or publication date: "As is usual in these cases the result is meagre and unsatisfactory: no certainty is attainable; we have to content ourselves with sufficiently vague and indefinite conjecture as to the time and mode of the composition of the work."[1] Cope's remarks are echoed by contemporary investigators such as Paul D. Brandes,[2] who concludes that the **Rhetoric**'s exact completion date remains unknown. There are several reasons for the confusion.

Book publishing as we know it, of course, did not exist in ancient Greece. To "publish" a work held a quite different meaning for Aristotle and his counterparts. One of the principal differences lay in the audience to which scholarly works were addressed. Students enrolled in the Academy, Lyceum, Isocrates' school and the general circle of enlightened scholars at Athens made up the major audience for scholarly works in ancient Greece. Beyond these and similar schools a market for such works did not exist. Many of the philosophers, "perhaps the majority of them, never can be said to have published a philosophical work in any sense other than that in which a lecturer publishes his thoughts to his audience."[3] Shute, for example, believes the extant Aristotelian works were in lecture or notebook form during the Stagirite's lifetime, and as such, were never published formally. He notes that, "moreover . . . those works which have come down to us . . . are clearly neither prepared nor designed for a large circle of readers. I think, then, we safely may conclude that there was no publication in any sense of these works during Aristotle's lifetime."[4]

The best evidence indicates that Aristotle completed the "final" draft of the **Rhetoric** during his second residency at Athens. Cope believes 336 B.C. to be the work's earliest possible completion date, as Spengel[5] has identified a passage referring to Phillip's embassy to Thebes in 338 B.C. and an alliance with Alexander in 336 B.C. The **Rhetoric,** though, as is generally agreed, was an evolving manuscript, revised and edited over a number of years. There is substantial research indicating that it developed genetically rather than systematically; that it was not written in one inspired seizure but developed over a period of several years. Although we need not fully examine the arguments here, Solmsen, Jaeger, and Hill are of the opinion that the **Rhetoric**'s internal evidence indicates that it was revised many times. The **Rhetoric**'s irregular organization, lack of internal consistency, contradictions, and repetitions support this thesis; no other explanation accounts for these internal faults. Brandes summarizes our point by suggesting: "The clear thrust of internal evidence and scholarly speculation is toward the view that the **Rhetoric** is not a 'book' in the usual sense but is a set of lecture notes subjected to a series of revisions, not always systematic."[6] To summarize, the final draft of the **Rhetoric,** if indeed Aristotle even considered it a

completed work, can be attributed reasonably to the second residency.

Loss and Recovery of the Rhetoric

The difficulty of dating the **Rhetoric** is equaled by the difficulty of reconstructing its history. There are numerous accounts of how the **Rhetoric** survived antiquity. The topic must be approached with caution, as we are ignorant of much of this period and of the men associated with the work.

The principal ancients advancing an account of the loss and recovery of Aristotle's works are Strabo[7] and Athenaeus.[8] By comparing their explanations with modern interpretations a probable account of the **Rhetoric**'s history can be reconstructed. Our story begins with the death of Aristotle in 322 B.C. Theophrastus assumed the Lyceum's leadership, previously held by Aristotle. During the later years of his directorship Theophrastus confronted dissension within the Lyceum; there arose what appears to have been doctrinal as well as personal in-fighting. As old age approached, Theophrastus wished the conservative Neleus of Scepsis to be his successor. Neleus seemed a plausible choice and Theophrastus envisioned little difficulty in having him appointed as *scholarchate*. Thus, as was the tradition, he willed the Lyceum's library, containing his own as well as Aristotle's works, to Neleus. Due, perhaps, to the conflict existing within the school, the "elders" elected Strato of Lampsacus over Neleus—undoubtedly a surprise to Neleus. He decided, perhaps in light of this, to return to Scepsis, taking with him his newly inherited library. It is at this point that our story takes some interesting turns.

Strabo's intriguing account relates that upon Neleus' death, his collection passed to his family. Said to have been illiterate and generally unaware of the priceless nature of the books, they stored or buried them in a cellar. Strabo suggests they feared that Eumenes II, a neighboring King of Pergamum (who was a noted collector of manuscripts and books), would attempt to recover the collection by force. With time the books and manuscripts deteriorated badly; nearly one hundred and fifty years passed until the library's value was recognized by one of the descendants. The collection was recovered and sold to Apellicon of Teos, reputedly for a huge sum of money. About 100 B.C. the library was transported to Athens, whereupon Apellicon began the difficult task of correcting and publishing Aristotle's works. He was in no sense of the term a philosopher, a handicap which severely hindered his attempt to render faithful copies of the works. No trace of his edition remains. Sixteen years later the library of Apellicon was taken as booty by L. C. Sulla, who defeated Athens in 86 B.C., and returned to Rome. In 78 B.C. Faustus Sulla acquired the library and after twenty-three years of disinterest sold it by auction to

Tyrannion of Amisos, a grammarian. One would think Tyrannion suited to edit Aristotle's work. But, like Apellicon before him, he provided an inadequate edition: "Tyrannion apparently not only mishandled the severely damaged texts, but also incorrectly filled in the many and often lacunae."[9] Strabo also laments at certain manuscript copyists or booksellers who acquired Aristotelian manuscripts from Sulla's auction and later mass-produced copies for sale. These copies are said to have been grossly inadequate and riddled with textual inaccuracies.

Strabo's account of the recovery of Aristotle's works, however, cannot be taken at face value. Strabo tells us, for instance, of the elation of the Peripatetics at having acquired, through the hand of Apellicon, authentic works of Aristotle. He suggests the Peripatetics had been without the majority of Aristotle's works for many years: "The statement at first blush seems so absurd and impossible that one cannot wonder that many editors have rejected it as utterly false."[10] It seems illogical that Theophrastus would not have allowed his school access to the library's manuscripts and books. The Lyceum was his very life, no less upon his death. Likewise, it is not logical that Neleus, irrespective of his disappointment at not having been appointed *scholarchate,* would have taken the library without allowing his colleagues the opportunity to make copies. Moreover, would the members of the Lyceum have so easily given up their tools—the very life-blood of the institution? "If the books were already in any sense published, there would have been no difficulty about this; if they were not, we must remember that Neleus himself was a Peripatetic, and is hardly likely to have refused his fellow disciples so simple a boon as the right to copy these precious volumes, a boon which involved no loss to himself, but an inestimable advantage to those to whom it was granted."[11]

Chroust agrees in essence with Shute. He considers Strabo's story, that upon the death of Theophrastus no esoteric copies remained (except those possessed by Neleus), to be untrue—a fantastic myth: "This myth, it might be contended, was probably invented for the purpose of explaining (and incidentally, of excusing) why after the death of Theophrastus the majority of the Peripatetics 'deviated' to a considerable degree from the teaching of both Aristotle and Theophrastus. Also, this would explain why apparently during the second century B. C. the philosophical achievements of the Peripatus, on the whole were negligible. Left without any authoritative guides and materials, the post-Theophrastian Peripatetics simply floundered about badly."[12] The citation of the supposedly lost works by post-Theophrastian authors, however, plainly refutes Strabo's story.[13] Also, there is little doubt that the immediate disciples of Aristotle possessed copies of his works and that later Peripatetics relied heavily upon them. These notes and copies were used as the basis

for their lectures and various investigations: "It is safe to surmise, therefore, that during the period Aristotle's works were located in Scepsis (or essential parts of them) they were still known (and used) through fairly accurate copies that were to be found in the possession of some Peripatetics."[14]

We have yet to address ourselves to Athenaeus' account of the *corpus.* He tells us that the Ptolemys bought Aristotle's works from both Theophrastus and Neleus in order to enrich the Alexandrian library. There is little question that Alexandria was a great center and storehouse of Aristotelian writings. Ptolemy Philadelphus, for instance, is said to have possessed more than a thousand pieces of *Aristotelica.* There was in general great respect for Aristotle, even to the extent of Aristotelian "clubs" being formed. But Athenaeus' story is marred by a contradiction. In his description of later Athenian history he relates essentially Strabo's account of Apellicon having secured the Aristotelian library at Scepsis. Shute resolves this conflict by suggesting that Ptolemy Philadelphus could not have bought all the books from Neleus; that very likely Theophrastus sold him only those previously published works, such as the historical works and dialogues, and that Neleus sold him books of assembled notes.

What then can be said of the account of Strabo and Athenaeus concerning the disposition of Aristotle's library? Unlike Shute and Vleeschauwer,[15] Chroust suggests Strabo's story to be at best pure fiction. Chroust's reasoning is based upon, in addition to the evidence already cited, Plutarch's[16] mention of Andronicus of Rhodes and Strabo's indirect reaction to him. Plutarch claimed Andronicus saved the *corpus Aristotelicum* from becoming a textual catastrophe.

Andronicus was schooled at Rhodes, which for many years had reflected the Peripatetic tradition. Here he was steeped in Aristotelian philosophy and quite likely had occasion to examine many *Aristotelica* dating to Eudemus. Hence, Andronicus possessed a strong background in Aristotelian studies as preserved at Rhodes and taught by the Rhodian Peripatus. Chroust argues that it is not unlikely that Andronicus traveled to Rome for the express purpose of examining Tyrannion's source materials. Once there, he somehow acquired these materials and soon realized their immense value. He was able to compare his knowledge of Rhodian *Aristotelica* with Tyrannion's, recognizing as he did, that many unique items were among this collection. This presented a spectacular opportunity for an otherwise undistinguished scholar. Here was his chance to refresh the dwindling intellectual storehouse of the Peripatus through the restoration of Aristotle's works. Such an effort, he believed, would restore the Peripatus to a leading position among schools throughout the Hellenistic-Roman world. Beyond that: "If he could successfully convince people that he was in possession of a very large part of Aristotle's writings and that his collection was the only 'authentic' collection in existence of Aristotle's own manuscripts, he would become the undisputed head and leader of the whole revived Peripatetic movement."[17] It is at this point that Andronicus submitted his claim to be the new *scholarchate*.

Strabo must surely have been aware of Andronicus' claims. He does not mention him by name, however, which suggests ill feeling between them. Strabo, however, does refer to booksellers of Rome who employed poor copyists—a remark apparently directed at Andronicus. Strabo and other Peripatetics, it appears, were putting up strong resistance to Andronicus' claim of possessing the only authentic Aristotelian works. Quite naturally they felt that if anyone was heir to the Aristotelian tradition, it should be a Greek not a Rhodian. In the words of Chroust: "In order to discredit Andronicus and especially his claim that he was in the sole possession of the original manuscripts of Aristotle (and of the only authoritative and 'orthodox' materials dating back to the very founders of the school), these antagonists, who were simply competitors of Andronicus, in all likelihood alleged that if he actually did gain possession of Aristotle's own writings—something which in their opinion was by no means certain; and if these writings had been buried in a damp cellar for so many years, they must be severely damaged and hence, for all practical purposes virtually useless."[18] Extending this reasoning they suggested that both the works of Tyrannion and Andronicus were inferior to those versions already possessed by the Peripatetics. To support their claim they had only to point to the shoddy editing by Apellicon and Tyrannion and to indicate that incompetent Roman copyists and booksellers produced the texts. Chroust concludes that both the Scepsis burial story and any preliminary attempts by Apellicon and Tyrannion to edit Aristotle's works are highly doubtful. Perhaps, suggests Chroust, Apellicon and Tyrannion attempted initial editing but soon found the work exceeding their capabilities. Andronicus, since it cannot be denied that he published an edition of Aristotle's works, at best consulted these earlier efforts while editing his version. This conclusion in many respects runs counter to those of Shute and Vleeschauwer but appears the more logical version.

We have sketched a history of the *corpus Aristotelicum* without specific mention of the **Rhetoric**. Apparently, regardless of the authenticity of the Scepsis story, the **Rhetoric** was never lost but was preserved by members of the Lyceum either before or upon Aristotle's death. Shute believes the work was "continually extant and continually subject to alteration in the whole period between Aristotle and Andronicus."[19] This hypothesis would be in keeping with the thesis of both Shute and Chroust that the lectures continued without interruption. To be sure, as the years passed, men of lesser abilities assumed teaching positions and, with a changing philosophy in the school, the **Rhetoric** may well have slipped in stature, doomed to gather dust on the shelves of the school. Disuse, therefore, may account for the "disappearance" of the work.

Cicero was familiar with a number of Aristotle's works (all of which, with the exception of the **Rhetoric**, were in dialogue form). Moreover, he makes frequent mention of the **Rhetoric**, reflecting his familiarity with the work.[20] In comparing his understanding of the **Rhetoric** with our copy we find them to be remarkably similar: "That Cicero's **Rhetoric** of Aristotle is substantially the same as ours no one can doubt, nor I think, can any reasonable person dispute that this book at least he read firsthand."[21] In addition, the *Synagôgê technôn* is mentioned by Cicero[22] in *De orator* where he speaks of a history of orators, and in the *Brutus* where he relates incidents of Tisias, Theodorus, and Gorgias which could only have been taken from this source.

After Cicero we have little evidence as to either the use or study of the **Rhetoric** for at least a century. Oddly, while Rome was now the center of Aristotelian study the **Rhetoric** enjoyed little popularity. Ciceronian rhetoric, of course, far exceeded any impression the **Rhetoric** made; nor had the latter an effect upon Greek oratory of this later period. In this period Dionysius of Halicarnassus is one of the few commentators on the rhetorical influence of Aristotle. "We notice that his citations from the **Rhetoric** are not only roughly but actually the same as the text which we now have."[23]

The **Rhetoric** now appears temporarily to have run its course. The early medieval ages were to overlook the work. Lee Hultzen,[24] however, identified two rhetorics of this period which were possibly influenced by or familiar with the **Rhetoric**. Aquilas Romanus' *Aquilae Romani de Figuris sententiarum,* written in the later part of the third century, cites the **Rhetoric** as its only reference. Also, Victorinus' commentary upon the *De inventione* makes references to *pistis* and arrangement which seem Aristotelian. Since these citations are not found in Cicero's books Victorinus may have had firsthand knowledge of the **Rhetoric**. Hultzen, though, summarizes the **Rhetoric's** influence during this period by noting that "there is in the principal medieval rhetorics no evidence of the use of Aristotle's **Rhetoric**, nothing later than the fourth century."[25]

There is nearly a six hundred year gap in our history during which little is known of the **Rhetoric's** fate; it was among the last of Aristotle's works to emerge in the Middle Ages. During the Middle Ages the Aristotelian tradition was at its lowest ebb in Western Europe, with only the **Organon** attracting scholastic interest. Edgar Lobel, for example, "assigned on palaeographical evidence"[26] a Greek manuscript of the tenth century which would constitute the first extant manuscript of Aristotle's *Rhetoric* [although it is a superior Greek manuscript the copyist is unknown]. There was, however, a strong Arabic tradition. Syrian scholars, who acquired their copies of Aristotle's works from early Syriac versions, are probably to be credited with preserving these works. The extent of Syriac acquaintance with the *Rhetoric* and its influence on Syrian scholarship is unknown. Severus Sebokht (A.D. 667), a little-known author in an unknown work, reportedly discussed select passages of the *Rhetoric*.[27] The *Fihrist* of al-Nadīm[28] (an encyclopedia of early Arabic scholarship) identifies several Arabic scholars who were familiar with the *Rhetoric* but makes no mention of a Syriac version. Syrian translations were passed on to Arabic copyists, though, for according to F. E. Peters the colophon to Ishāq ibn Hunayn's translation (to be discussed shortly) indicates Ibn al-Samh had access to a Syriac version of the *Rhetoric*. Likewise, in an abridgment by al-Kindi (an Arabic scholar) it appears a Syriac version existed at least a generation before Ishāq.

A few Arabic works on poetry and criticism are hypothesized to have been acquainted with the *Rhetoric*. Tāhā Husayn,[28] in a much referred to study, suggests that Book III of the *Rhetoric* influenced Qudāma's *Criticism of Poetry* and the anonymous (wrongly ascribed to Qudāma[29]) *Naqd an-Nathr (The Criticism of Prose)*.

Ishāq translated the *Rhetoric* into Arabic [Paris MS BN 2346] and Abū 'Ali ibn al-Samh (m. A.D. 1027) incorporated it in his edition. S. M. Stern notes that the colophon to Book III carries the following cryptic remark: "This book is not very useful and has not been studied, therefore one does not find a correct copy or a person interested in its correction."[30] Another scholar, Ibrāhīm ibn 'Abdallāh, translated Ishāq's work, but for some unknown reason burned it shortly before his death. Trabulsi[31] suggests that Ishāq's translation also spurred Ibn al-Mu 'Tazz to write his *Book of the Ornate Style*. "Trabulsi's theory is ingenious, but at the same time difficult to accept, for the figures of speech which are the main subject of Ibn al-Mu 'Tazz's book are treated in Aristotle's *Rhetoric* only in passing and in a manner quite different from that of Ibn al-Mu 'Tazz."[32]

Chief among the early Arabic commentators of Ishāq's translation, however, was the tenth-century scholar, Al-Fārābi.[33] An avid Aristotelian, he is said to have had a special fondness for the *Rhetoric*, having read it two hundred times and written seventy books on it. Alfārābi's *didascalion* or "gloss" and a partial translation interspersed with his own comments survives. Approximately three hundred years later, the German scholar Hermannus Alemannus translated portions of the commentary into Latin. [This *Declaratio* (Paris, MS BN *lat.* 16097) was edited by Lancilotus Zerlis

and published at Venice in 1481.] Until approximately 150 years ago it was assumed that Hermannus Alemannus had not translated the *Rhetoric*. This issue generated much debate. "The most reputable authorities, relying primarily on the translator's prologues . . . after brief and infrequent forays into the no man's land of translations themselves, brought back reports so varied and contradictory that one might wonder if they had seen the same thing or were even serving on the same front."[34] In an excellent study comparing primary text materials William F. Boggess (see note 34) conclusively proves that Hermannus did execute a translation of the *Rhetoric*. Boggess demonstrates that a comparison of Hermannus' translation and the Greek *Rhetoric* shows them to be remarkably similar. Hermannus translated the *Rhetoric* into Latin from Arabic at Toledo in 1256 A.D. "Whatever the nature or worth of Hermannus Alemannus' translation . . . it does not appear to have made much of an impression except to draw the censure of Roger Bacon."[35] Bacon severely chided the German scholar for his lack of precision and apparent inability to render Arabic into Latin. He thought Hermannus' translations were virtually impossible to understand.

The Arabic books of Aristotle were brought to Spain following the Mohammedan invasion. "It was here that the *Rhetoric* first re-appeared in Western Europe."[36] The Spanish philosopher Averröes composed a *Middle Commentary* and a paraphrase of the *Rhetoric*, sections of which were also translated by Hermannus. Aristotelian texts continued to attract Eastern scholars, however. Herrick indicates that Eustathius, Bishop of Thessalonica in the last half of the twelfth century, refers to the *Rhetoric* in his extended commentary upon the *Iliad*.[37]

Two translations of the *Rhetoric* into Latin from Greek occurred in the thirteenth century. Of their existence we have the surest proof—extant copies. The *translatio vetus*, approximately 1250 A.D., may have ties with the Hermannus Alemannus debate. Its origin and translator, though, are unknown. Spengel believes it a translation of Bartholomaeus of Messina, while Mandonnet[38] attributes it to Hermannus (which is unlikely). Only three copies of this manuscript exist; it was little used in schools and less consulted by scholars familiar with its existence. The reason for its lack of popularity is not known, although Murphy suggests that William of Moerbeke's translation, *translatio Guillelmi*, may have overshadowed it.[39]

Moerbeke, a Flemish Dominican of the thirteenth century, translated many of the works of Aristotle. Ninety-six manuscripts of his translation of the *Rhetoric* survive, the most frequently consulted being *Parisiensus lat.* 7695. The work, like Hermannus' translations of Al-Fārābī's and Averröes' glosses, received the censure of Roger Bacon, who termed it unimaginative.

Sandys,[40] though, thinks the baldness of Moerbeke's knowledge of Greek contributed to the work's literal translation. In any event, Moerbeke's translation was well received. Without doubt, Thomas Aquinas, who sponsored the translation, lent heavily to its credibility. The work appears to have been completed about 1270 (a second manuscript, *Parisiensus lat.* 14696, bears the date 1281), at the height of Aristotelian interest in Paris. Its popularity far exceeded that of any other version. Curiously, we have no knowledge of the Greek manuscript consulted by Moerbeke. Moreover, "there is no reason to believe that Moerbeke even consulted previous renditions; in any case his independent version so completely dominates schools and libraries that for all practical purposes it may be regarded as the typical medieval Latin version."[41]

At the close of the thirteenth century at least twenty-two manuscripts of the *Rhetoric* had been prepared. The fourteenth century produced fifty-seven manuscripts, the fifteenth century, seventeen. We would assume that extensive scholastic interest accounted for this number of manuscripts; likewise, we would suspect rhetorical training and contemporary rhetorics to reflect the work. The opposite appears to have been the case. Murphy's investigation of the *Rhetoric*'s influence during this period found it to be minimal. He suggests, based in part upon the commentary of Aegidius Romanus,[42] that the *Rhetoric* was not thought of as a rhetorical or dialectical work but one allied with political science and ethics. Close examination of manuscript pairings bears out this judgment, for of the seventy-nine instances of the *Rhetoric* paired with one or more works, sixty-nine include the *Politica* or *Ethica:* "In any event, the history of Aristotle's *Rhetoric* in the Middle Ages indicates quite clearly that even though it did not serve its original purpose directly as a textbook on oral and written discourse, it did find a significant place in European culture, particularly in the areas of ethics, morality and politics."[43]

The Invention of Printing

Our history of the *Rhetoric* essentially concludes with Gutenberg's invention of the printing press. This new found art of book manufacturing was to be a boon to European scholarship. While movable type would arrive too late to affect the Italian Renaissance (Bolgar concludes that the "novelty" of the printing press contributed little to the rise of Greek letters[44]), it was nonetheless seized upon for its capacity to reproduce rare manuscripts in quantity. Men of both learning and finance (who soon recognized the commercial possibilities of printing) established presses in centers of learning. All across Europe presses were built and the task of resurrecting the classics from the hand of scribes began. The copyists' monumental efforts to reproduce texts by hand were erased almost overnight. Venice alone licensed between 200 and 268 printing houses

by the end of the fifteenth century.[45] The impact of movable type upon the printing of classical literature was staggering; most of the Latin *editiones principes* appeared between 1465 and 1475, most of the Greek between 1493 and 1518.[46]

The first published analysis of Aristotle's *Rhetoric* was prepared by George of Trebizond, published in Paris by Petrus Caesaris and Johannes Stol. Trapezuntius was an avid, if somewhat lackluster, student of Aristotle. As a professor of Greek and rhetoric at Rome and Venice he was perhaps a suitable choice, however, to bring the *Rhetoric* to the house of Caesaris and Stol. The book's catalogue title runs: *Aristotelis Rhetoricorum liber III, ex interpretatione Georgii Trapezuntii.* The book does not carry a publication date and as a result many estimates have been made of its entrance into print. I accept the *Gesamtkatalog der Wiegendrucke*'s ascribed date of 1475.[47]

Other incunabula of the fifteenth century present only minor bibliographical problems in comparison with George of Trebizond's. In 1481 Lancilotus Zerlis, whom we have already mentioned, published his edited compendium of Hermannus Alemannus' translations. In 1485 Francesco Filelfo's translation was published, three years following his death—his only translation of an Aristotelian work. Excerpts or paraphrases of the *Rhetoric* were printed by T. Ferrariis in 1493; portions of the *Poetics* were included as well. The famed Aristotelian *Opera Omnia,* printed from 1495 to 1498 by the Aldine Press under Aldus Manutius[48] (a scholar and exacting printer), excluded the *Rhetoric.* Some suggest that Aldus Manutius was unable to secure an acceptable manuscript of the *Rhetoric,* an unlikely hypothesis since nearly one hundred manuscripts were extant at this time. Ten years later, however, with the editorial assistance of Demetrius Ducas,[49] Manutius included the *Rhetoric* in the *Rhetores Graeci* (an exceptionally important collection of Greek treatises on rhetoric). Manutius probably foreplanned the *Rhetores Graeci* and thought that work a more suitable vehicle for the work's presentation. Georgius Dottanius' assistance on the Moerbeke translation, printed by Jakob Thanner at Leipzig in 1499, concludes our discussion of the fifteenth century.

Numerous paraphrases, commentaries and translations of the *Rhetoric* emerged from sixteenth century publishers. Counting reprints and revised editions, well over eighty volumes were produced. The twentieth century, by comparison, has less than twenty commentaries or translations in perhaps twice the number of languages. It is neither our intention nor purpose to describe each of these editions or indicate their influence upon Greek letters or rhetorical theory. Suffice it to say that numerous scholars turned their attention to the explication and correction of the *Rhetoric.* These men include Pietro Vettori (perhaps the greatest Italian

Greek scholar), Desiderius Erasmus, Alessandro Piccolomini, Antonio Riccoboni, Bernardo Segni, Carolo Sigonio, Annibale Caro, Robert Estienne, Antonio Majoragio and Isaac Casaubon. The works of George of Trebizond, Ermalao Barbaro, Antonio Majoragio, Alessandro Piccolomini, Antonio Riccoboni and Pietro Vettori appear (judging by the variety and number of reprints) to have enjoyed the greatest popularity. Nearly all the major centers of book production included the **Rhetoric** among their lists; no English translation or commentary had yet been attempted, however.

Scholars of the seventeenth century likewise translated and commented upon the **Rhetoric.** The frenzied publication exhibited by the sixteenth century is not characteristic of the seventeenth, however; still, over twenty scholars investigated it. This list includes Francois Cassandre, Christopher Schrader and Emmanuel Tesauro. Of interest to the reader of English is Thomas Hobbes' London edition: *A brief art of the rhetorique containing in substance all that Aristotel hath written in his three bookes of that subject, except only what is not applicable to the English tongue.* The best evidence suggests it was published in 1637. The first translation of the **Rhetoric** in England, however, was Theodore Goulston's Greek and Latin version. It was published under the imprint of Eduard Griffin in 1619.

Just as suddenly the eighteenth century, apparently satiated with able editions of the **Rhetoric,** turned its critical attention elsewhere. Only three new translations were published during this century, although there were reprintings of Caro, Du Val and Hobbes' translations from earlier periods and a spattering of essays and abridgments. The nineteenth century, however, saw a strong revival in the study of Aristotelian rhetoric.

Great interest in classical philology marked European universities (especially German) during the nineteenth century. The whole spectrum of classical literature was investigated with great vigor. Each member of the Aristotelian *corpus* was studied with careful adherence to establishing critically correct texts. The issuance of periodical journals aided these efforts immeasurably. Now, as never before, scholars shared with the whole of the academic community various philological emendations; prior to this, such research had to be privately circulated. No less than twenty scholars published either translations or commentaries of the **Rhetoric,** while authors of essays and monographs well exceed one hundred. Thomas Gaisford published the first modern critical edition by comparing five Parisian manuscripts. Immanuel Bekker, using 105 manuscripts, also published a critical edition. Leonhard von Spengel, in addition to a translation, devoted (perhaps more than

any other man of the nineteenth century) exacting detail to philological and historical considerations; his interest in the work would span his entire lifetime. Likewise, our understanding of the **Rhetoric** owes much to the work of Johannes Vahlen and Adolph Roemer. Theodore Buckley published an English translation and analysis imprinted under the popular Bohn series of classical works. The foremost English translator and commentator of the **Rhetoric** was Edward Meredith Cope. His commentary, published in 1867, and the three-volume translation and interlinear commentary (posthumously edited by John E. Sandys in 1877) remain today standard reference works. It is difficult, in our brief sketch, to assess adequately the contributions of the nineteenth century, for to illuminate the contributions of one scholar necessitates an examination of another.

The twentieth century is not without its contributors. The work of Lane Cooper, Rhys Roberts, Sir W. David Ross, Médéric Dufour, Paul Gohlke, Ignacio Granero, Friedrich Solmsen, Wilhelm Kroll, Richard C. Jebb, Antonio Russo and Armando Plebe long will be felt. The **Rhetoric** also found its way into new languages during the past seventy-five years. Readers of the Hindi, Japanese, and Polish languages now benefit from the text's availability.

We have briefly traced the course of Aristotelian rhetoric across 2,300 years. While we have noted the **Rhetoric**'s published history, we have done so only briefly. It remains for other studies to explore this area, and we hope that this bibliography, which was compiled with the intent of spurring additional investigations of a critical and historical bent, will contribute to this end.

Notes

[1] Edward M. Cope, *An Introduction to Aristotle's Rhetoric; with Analysis Notes and Appendices* (London, 1867), 37.

[2] Paul D. Brandes, "The Composition and Preservation of Aristotle's *Rhetoric,*" *Speech Monographs,* 35 (1968), 482-91.

[3] Richard Shute, *On the History of the Process by which the Aristotelian Writings Arrived at Their Present Form* (Oxford: Oxford at Clarendon Press, 1888), 1.

[4] Shute, 1888, 3.

[5] Leonhard von Spengel, *Specimen Commentariorum in Aristotelis Libros de Arte Rhetorica* (München: Libraria Scholarum Regia, 1839).

[6] Brandes, 1968, 487.

[7] Strabo, *Geography,* trans. by H. L. Jones (New York, 1929), VI.

[8] Athenaeus, *The Deipnosophists,* trans. by C. B. Galich (New York, 1927), 1.

[9] Anton-Hermann Chroust, "The Miraculous Disappearance and Recovery of the *corpus Aristotelicum,*" *Classica et Mediaevalia,* 23 (1962), 53.

[10] Shute, 1888, 29.

[11] Shute, 1888, 30.

[12] Chroust, 1962, 56.

[13] Eduard Zeller, "Aristotle, Die Rhetorik," in *Die Philosophie der Greichen in ihrer geschichtlichen Entwicklung* (Leipzig: Fuece Verlag [R. Reisland], 1879, 147-52.

[14] Chroust, 1962, 62.

[15] Herman Jean de Vleeschauwer, *L'Odyssée de la Bibliothèque d'Aristote et ses Répercussions Philosophiques* (Pretoria, 1957).

[16] Plutarch, "Sulla," in *Plutarch's Lives,* trans. by Bernadotte Perrin (London, 1914-16), 407.

[17] Chroust, 1962, 63.

[18] Chroust, 1962, 64.

[19] Shute, 1888, 100.

[20] Cicero, *De orator,* iii, 47, 182-183.

[21] Shute, 1888, 49.

[22] Cicero, *De orator,* ii, 38, 160.

[23] Shute, 1888, 67.

[24] Lee S. Hultzén, "Aristotle's *Rhetoric* in England to 1600." (Unpublished Ph.D. dissertation, Cornell University, 1932), 21-23.

[25] Hultzén, 1932, 23.

[26] Edgar Lobel, *The Greek Manuscripts of Aristotle's Poetics* (Oxford: Oxford University Press, 1933), 6.

[27] F. E. Peters, *Aristotles Arabus. The Oriental Translations and Commentaries on The Aristotelian Corpus.* Leiden: E. J. Brill, 1968. 26.

[28] Tāhā Husayn, "Le rapport entre la rhétorique arabe et la rhétorique grecque." Paper presented at the Congress of Orientalists in Leiden, 1931. The paper is summarized in *Actes du XVIIIᵉ congrès international des orientalistes* (Leiden, 1931), 241-42.

[29] S. A. Bonebakker, "Aspects of the History of Literary Rhetoric and Poetics in Arabic Literature," *Viator,* 1 (1970), 89.

[30] S. M. Stern, "Ibn al-Samh," *JRAS,* (1956), 42.

[31] A. Trabulsi, *La critique poétique des Arabes jusqu' au Vᵉ siècle de l'hégire.* Damascus, 1956.

[32] Bonebakker, 1970, 90.

[33] Aimable Jourdain, *Recherches Critiques sur l'age et sur des commentaires Grecs ou Arabes employés par les docteurs scolastiques* (Paris, 1843), 139-41.

[34] William F. Boggess, "Hermannus Alemannus's Rhetorical Translations," *Viator,* 2 (1971), 227.

[35] Hultzén, 1932, 39.

[36] Marvin T. Herrick, "The Early History of Aristotle's *Rhetoric* in England," *Philological Quarterly,* 5 (1926), 243.

[37] Herrick, 1926, 243.

[38] Pierre Mandonnet, *Siger de Brabant et l'Averroïse Latin au XIIIme Siecle* (Louvain, 1911), I, 14.

[39] James J. Murphy, "Aristotle's *Rhetoric* in the Middle Ages," *Quarterly Journal of Speech,* 52 (1966), 110-111.

[40] John E. Sandys, *A History of Classical Scholarship* (Cambridge, 1896), Vol. I, 564.

[41] Murphy, 1966, 111.

[42] James J. Murphy, "The Scholastic Condemnation of Rhetoric in the Commentary of Giles of Rome on the *Rhetoric* of Aristotle," *Arts libéraux et Philosophie au moyen age* (Montreal, 1969), 833-41.

[43] Murphy, 1966, 115.

[44] R. R. Bolgar, *The Classical Heritage* (New York: Harper Torchbooks, 1964), 280.

[45] H. Brown, *The Venetian Printing Press* (London, 1891), 50.

[46] Bolgar, 1964, 281.

[47] In addition to the *Rhetoric* of Aristotle, Trapezuntius published in 1470 his own *Rhetoric* based, in part,

upon the theories of Hermogenes. Bunker, *A Bibliographical Study of the Greek Works and Translations published in France During the Renaissance: The Decade 1540-1550* (New York: Columbia University Press, 1939), p. 3, confusing these editions, advances 1470 as the first edition date. She cites the edition as printed by the Sorbonne Press under Gaguin, Fichet, and Heynlin. No such work appears to have been published; I, at least, have no tangible grounds for belief in its existence. Her authority, Gustav Gröber, *Geschichte der mittelfranzosischen Literatur,* II (Berlin and Leipzig: Zweite Auflage, Bearbeitet von Stefan Hofer, 1933), pp. 235-37, for example, cites the date 1474. However, Bunker may have misread Gröber's citation of an edition of Cicero's published in 1470 for the *Rhetoric.* Gröber's date of 1474 is in itself puzzling as no catalogue or holding of this edition is cited. Marie Pellechet, *Catalogue g_n_ral des incunables des bibliotheques publiques de France, par M. Pellechet* (Paris: A Picard et fils, 1897), no. 1189, cites the work but gives no date. Likewise the *Bibliotheque Nationale* does not fix a date. The *Gesamtkatalog der Wiegendrucke,* which cross-references Pellechet, dates the edition at 1475 and describes the edition in much detail.

[48] A. Firmin-Didot, *Alde Munce et l'hellenisme a Venise* (Paris, 1875); E. Goldsmith, *A Biographical Sketch of the Aldine Press at Venice* (Edinburgh, 1887); F. J. Norton, *Italian Printers* 1501-1520 (London, 1958); E. Robertson, "Aldus Manutius, The Scholar-Printer," *Bulletin of the John Rylands Library,* 33 (1950).

[49] Deno John Geanakoplos, *Greek Scholars in Venice* (Cambridge, Mass.: Harvard University Press, 1962), 227.

Larry Arnhart (essay date 1981)

SOURCE: "The Rationality of Political Speech: An Interpretion of Aristotle's *Rhetoric,*" in *Interpretation: A Journal of Political Philosophy,* Vol. 9, Nos. 2 & 3, September, 1981, pp. 141-54.

[*In the following essay, Arnhart maintains that Aristotle uses the concept of enthymeme (a logical argument, or syllogism, in which one of two conclusion-supporting premises is unexpressed) to defend the legitimacy of rhetorical discourse and to distinguish rhetoric from both science and sophistry.*]

I

Is rhetoric some form of rational discourse about the intelligible reality of politics? Or is it merely a means for verbally manipulating men through fallacious arguments and appeals to irrational impulses? In short, can rhetoric be distinguished from sophistry?

One might say that the rhetorician—by his use of public speech to interpret, evaluate, and deliberate about political action—maintains somehow the rule of reason in political affairs. Does not rhetoric require political men to *talk* about and thereby to *think* about what they have done, are doing, or will do? Does not rhetoric thus elevate politics by bringing thought to bear upon action? "We weigh what we undertake and apprehend it perfectly in our minds," Pericles declared in his funeral oration, "not accounting words for a hindrance of action but that it is rather a hindrance to action to come to it without instruction of words before" (Thucydides, *Peloponnesian War* II 40).

But rhetoric also has a darker side. Does not the rhetorician sometimes employ emotional appeals and deceptive arguments to move his listeners to whatever position he wishes? Indeed, does not rhetoric consist of techniques that can be used as easily for the *wrong* as for the *right* side of any issue? In other words, there surely is some justification for the ancient criticism of rhetoric as permitting speakers to make the weaker argument appear to be the stronger. As Gorgias boasted, "Many are the men who shape a false argument and persuade and have persuaded many men about many things" (*Helen* 11).

So the problem is that, while rhetoric seems in some respects to be the means by which reason guides political action; it often seems to be an art of deception that hinders rational deliberation. Furthermore, to the extent that rhetoric is the primary mode of political reasoning, how one decides this question as to whether or not rhetoric is a genuine form of reasoning will determine the place of reason in political life.

The rationality of rhetoric becomes especially dubious if scientific demonstration is taken to be the sole model of valid reasoning. For it is obvious that rhetorical argument cannot attain the exactness and certainty that is possible in scientific inquiry. And therefore if only scientific demonstration is truly rational, rhetoric must be irrational. As a result, rhetoric becomes virtually indistinguishable from sophistry. For since there are no rational standards for political discourse, the power of rhetoric must depend upon manipulation through verbal deception and not upon any pervasive intelligibility of the speech itself. As a further consequence, the political itself becomes irrational. Since the ordinary discourse of citizens about political things has little to do with scientifically demonstrable knowledge, the political life of men must be understood to be guided by opinions with little foundation in reason.

But could one save the rationality of political speech—and of the political realm as a whole—by viewing rhetoric as occupying some middle ground between science and sophistry? This could be done if one could show that the realm of reason extends beyond the confines of scientific demonstration, and therefore that rhetorical argument can be in some sense truly rational even though it lacks the certainty and exactness of scientific knowledge. In this way one would restore the meaning of rhetoric as rational discourse.

And in fact this would seem to be the project that Aristotle sets for himself in the **Rhetoric.** For he criticizes the sophistical rhetoricians, whose common practice is to use purely emotional appeals to distract their listeners from the subject at hand, for failing to see that the true art of rhetoric is essentially a mode of *reasoning,* although without the rigor of apodictic proof. He explains rhetorical reasoning as reasoning through enthymemes, and it is in his conception of the enthymeme that his theory of rhetoric is most fully embodied. My claim, therefore, in this essay, is that Aristotle's rhetorical theory is an account of the rationality of political speech. To fully substantiate this interpretation of the **Rhetoric** would require a much more extensive commentary on the text than is possible here.[1] But I can at least state some of the major points.

How Aristotle uses his theory of the enthymeme to differentiate rhetoric from science on the one hand and from sophistry on the other, becomes clearer in the light of four tripartite distinctions. First, *persuasion,* which is the aim of the enthymeme, differs, both from *instruction* and from *compulsion.* Second, *opinion,* which provides premises for the enthymeme, does not conform to absolute *truth,* but neither is it absolute *falsehood.* Third, the *probability* characteristic of most enthymematic inferences falls somewhere between *necessity* and mere randomness or *chance.* Finally, the *enthymeme* itself differs from a strict *demonstration* but without being a sophistical *fallacy.* I shall comment briefly on each of these points.

II

That men are by nature both rational and political is manifest in the natural human capacity for speech. Men are naturally more political than gregarious animals, Aristotle says in the **Politics** (1253a15-18), because human community rests upon a union in discourse and thought. Other animals may signify to one another with their voices their sensations of pleasure and pain but men through rational speech . . . can share with one another their concepts of expediency, justice, and goodness. Human beings achieve a more intimate community among themselves than is possible for other creatures, because only human beings can found their association on mutual understanding through speech.

One might conclude from this that rhetoric—the artful practice of public speech—is the fundamental activity of politics, and that politics expresses the rational nature of men insofar as political activity is founded upon rhetoric. But does rhetoric encompass the whole of politics? Or is it perhaps important for only a limited realm of political life? That Aristotle does not simply identify politics with rhetoric is clear from his remarks at the end of the **Nicomachean Ethics.** Speeches or arguments . . . , he explains, are not sufficient to make men virtuous (1179b4-1180b28). At best they are effective with youths who because of some natural endowment or good moral training have a love of the noble. Most men, especially in their youth, live by passion and the pleasures of the body, and hence they can be controlled by force but not by arguments. For these people it is necessary that the laws coercively habituate them from their youth to do those virtuous things that they would never choose to do on their own. Thus the moral training of a community requires that the legislator apply legal compulsion where moral persuasion would be futile.

It is at this point that Aristotle criticizes the sophists for showing their ignorance of politics by making it the same as, or lower than, rhetoric (**Nicomachean Ethics** 1181a12-16).[2] This is often taken to indicate that Aristotle thought the sophistical view of politics to be too cynical, but from the context one might infer something quite different: the sophistical assumption that the art of persuasion can govern all political activity manifests a naive blindness to the true harshness of political life. Rhetorical reasoning displays the nobler side of politics, that area of political activity governed by persuasion through speeches. But most men respond not to persuasion but to force, and therefore the greater part of politics must be concerned with compelling men, and through repetition habituating them, to do without thought what they could never be persuaded to do. The success of rhetoric, Aristotle implies, presupposes the formation by the laws of an *ethos* in the community that makes people open to persuasion. The taming of the most irrational impulses demands force rather than argument; but once the lowest part of the soul has been subdued, the rhetorician can appeal to that part of the soul that can be persuaded by reason. Rhetoric is therefore subordinate to politics since the multitude of men would never be amenable to rhetorical reasoning unless they were first properly habituated by the laws.

Hence rhetoric introduces the rule of reason into human affairs since it moves men by persuasion rather than by force. And yet Aristotle makes it clear that rhetoric fails to attain the highest level of reasoning insofar as rhetorical *persuasion* falls short of scientific or philosophic *instruction* (**R** 1355a22-29). The exact knowledge and complex demonstrations necessary for scientific instruction are rarely effective in political speeches. To be persuasive, the rhetorician must draw the premises of his enthymemes not from the first principles of the particular sciences, but from the common opinions of his audience. And he must simplify and abbreviate his line of reasoning so that ordinary citizens can grasp it quickly and easily (*R* 1357a8-23, 1395b24-30, 1419a18-19). Thus the good rhetorician can persuade, but he cannot instruct.

Since the premises of the enthymeme are derived from common opinions, and since opinion surely differs from truth, it might seem that the enthymeme is a false form of reasoning, and therefore that all rhetoric is sophistical. But in fact Aristotle regards the common opinions that enter the enthymeme as being for the most part neither completely true nor completely false but at least partially true (*R* 1357b21-25, 1361a25-27; *NE* 1098b26-30, 1145b1-7; *EE* 1216b28-35). Therefore, although this reliance on opinions does impose certain limits on enthymematic argumentation, this does not prevent the enthymeme from being a valid form of reasoning. Although the "reputable opinions" . . . on any particular subject are usually confused and even apparently contradictory, Aristotle assumes that in most cases they manifest at least a partial grasp of the truth and therefore that any serious inquiry into moral or political subjects must start from them. So while Aristotle treats certain subjects differently in the *Rhetoric* than he does in the *Politics* or in his ethical treatises, since rhetoric involves opinions in their original state without the refinements of philosophic examination, his expositions in the *Rhetoric* still reflect in some fundamental manner those in his other works. For example, the account of "happiness" . . . in the *Rhetoric* clearly reflects, even if somewhat dimly, the philosophic understanding of "happiness" set forth in the *Nicomachean Ethics* (compare *R* 1360b15-19 with *NE* 1097b7-21, 1176b4-7; see also *P* 1323b21-1324a4, 1325b14-31).

Furthermore, in its dependence on common opinions, rhetoric is distinguished both from science and from sophistry. Each science begins not with common opinions, but with the primary truths that are fundamental to the science (*R* 1358a17-27, *PoA* 71b18-72a6, *SR* 172a12-172b4). (But as I shall indicate later, even these scientific truths depend ultimately on some commonsense understanding of things.) And sophistry consists either of arguing from what *appear* to be common opinions but are not, or of making something *appear* to follow necessarily from common opinions when it does not (*SR* 165a37-165b12, 176b29-177a8). Moreover, the fact that sophistical arguments cannot be truly derived from common opinions confirms the epistemological solidity of these opinions.

One of the limitations of common opinions, however, is that they usually hold for the most part but not in every case. Therefore, enthymemes have probable but not necessary validity, since the conclusions are true in most cases but not in all. Enthymemes, then, rarely achieve the necessity of scientific demonstrations. The one exception noted by Aristotle is the enthymeme founded on a "necessary sign" . . . (*R* 1357a24-34).

That enthymematic reasoning usually involves probability rather than necessity does not make the reasoning invalid. For, according to Aristotle, both the things that happen always or by necessity and those that happen as a rule or for the most part, can be objects of knowledge. Probability must be distinguished from chance, because unlike probable things those things that happen only rarely or by chance cannot be known (*PoA* 87b19-28). That rhetoric should rest upon probabilities is consistent with the Aristotelian principle that one should demand only that degree of certitude that is appropriate to the subject matter. For like ethics and politics the subject of rhetoric is human action, and the regularities of human action can be known with probability but not with absolute certainty (*R* 1356a14-17, 24-33, 1402b21-37).

Since the enthymeme rests upon opinion rather than absolute truth, since its premises and conclusion are probable rather than necessary, and since its final aim is persuasion rather than instruction, enthymematic reasoning lacks the rigor of scientific demonstration. And yet rhetorical argument is still a valid form of reasoning, and therefore it provides an alternative to sophistry. Popular opinions manifest a commonsense grasp of reality that cannot be dismissed as simply false. Probabilities are fit objects of reason because they presuppose regularities in things, which are not random or by chance. And, finally, the persuasion for which the rhetorician strives requires an appeal to reason rather than force.

But to support the claim that Aristotle's *Rhetoric* is a theory of rhetoric as truly rational discourse, one must answer the serious objections that can be made to this interpretation. In particular, the following four points deserve attention. (1) It could be argued that enthymemes cannot be valid because Aristotle defines them as incomplete or otherwise defective syllogisms. (2) Furthermore, even if the enthymeme were a genuine syllogism, it could still be argued that Aristotle's discussions of persuasion through the character of the speaker and through the passions of the audience would show the reliance of rhetoric on irrational appeals. (3) Also, since Aristotle insists that rhetoric includes *apparent* as well as genuine "proofs," and since he describes it as a neutral instrument that may be used on either side of any issue, one might infer that he does not clearly distinguish rhetoric from sophistry. (4) Finally, Aristotle's remarks in Book Three of the *Rhetoric* on the style and arrangement of speeches seem to be further evidence that he does not view rhetoric as founded on rational argument. I shall reply to each of these objections.

III

Aristotle's enthymeme is a true syllogism; and therefore it is not, as has been commonly assumed, an incomplete syllogism. For if the enthymeme were an invalid or incomplete syllogism—to cite only one argument from the text—why would Aristotle distinguish between apparent and true enthymemes and declare that apparent enthymemes "are not enthymemes since they are not syllogisms" (*R* 1397a3)?

Aristotle refers to the enthymeme as "a sort of syllogism" . . . (*R* 1355a9-10), and some readers have taken this use of [*tis*] as implying that the enthymeme is not a true or complete syllogism. But the falsity of this interpretation is made evident by a passage in the *Prior Analytics* (24a10-16, 25b26-31). Here Aristotle explains that his theory of the syllogism in the *Prior Analytics* is more general than his theory of "demonstration" . . . in the *Posterior Analytics:* "for demonstration is a kind of syllogism . . . , but not every syllogism is a demonstration." Since there is no reason to believe that a "demonstration" is anything less than a true syllogism, it is clear that the phrase [*sullogismos tis*] is intended only to indicate that a "demonstration" is *one kind* of syllogism to be differentiated from other kinds (see also *Poetics* 1450a18). Likewise, the enthymeme can be one distinctive type of syllogism without being syllogistically defective, which is born out by Aristotle's repeated references to the syllogistic character of the enthymeme (see, for example, *R* 1362b29-30, 1394a9-11, 1400b25-33; *PrA* 68b8-14; *PoA* 71a1-11). Since the premises and therefore the conclusion of the enthymeme are founded on common opinions and are probable but not absolutely certain, the enthymeme differs from the scientific syllogism; and since the enthymeme must be simple enough to be understood by the ordinary man, it differs from the dialectical syllogism. But neither of these points entails that the enthymeme be an invalid or incomplete syllogism.

Enthymematic reasoning is popular because by providing listeners with "quick learning," it satisfies their natural desire for learning (*R* 1400b25-33, 1410b6-35). For this reason, the enthymeme should be neither too superficial and obvious nor too long and complex. It should be simple enough to be quickly grasped, but at the same time it should give the listeners the pleasure of learning something new: it should be informative without being esoteric.

One of the ways to make the enthymeme an instrument of "quick learning" is to abbreviate it by leaving unstated whatever the listeners can be expected to add on their own (*R* 1356a19, 1357a17-23). But this practical rule is not part of the definition of the enthymeme; and furthermore, even when it is abbreviated, the enthymeme is a complete syllogism as stated in *thought* despite its incompleteness as stated *verbally* (*PoA* 76b23-28). Even in the most rigorously demonstrative reasoning, Aristotle suggests, premises that are clear or well known need not be explicitly stated (*PoA* 76b1-23). Moreover, the abbreviation of enthymemes is a tribute to the love of learning found in the audience. For when a speaker leaves unstated those steps in the reasoning that the listeners can easily supply themselves, he allows them to help construct the very arguments by which they are persuaded; and thus he gives them the satisfaction of thinking through the reasoning on their own.

IV

Aristotle begins the *Rhetoric* by condemning those sophistical rhetoricians who rely exclusively on exciting the passions of their listeners and thereby preventing them from making a rational judgment about the issues at hand. These speakers ignore the enthymeme, which is "the body of proof" for rhetoric. But when Aristotle sets out the three "proofs" . . . [3] of rhetoric, he includes appeals based on "character" . . . (that is, the "character" of the speaker) and "passion" . . . as supplementary to persuasion through the "speech" or "argument" itself . . . ; and in Book Two he carefully delineates the passions with which the rhetorician must deal. Thus Aristotle seems to throw into doubt the rationality of rhetorical argument by introducing the same techniques for moving audiences through their passions that he initially condemns.

A closer examination, however, will show that Aristotle's emphasis on the enthymeme is consonant with his treatment of the passions, because the enthymeme combines reason and passion. Since it is "the body of proof," the enthymeme is the vehicle not just for one of the three "proofs" . . . but for all three . . . (*R* 1354a12-16, 1354b20-21, 1396b28-1397a6, 1403a34-1403b1). Enthymemes may be used not only to establish a conclusion as a probable truth, but also to alter the emotions of the listeners or to develop their confidence in the character of the speaker. Aristotle denounces the sophistical rhetoricians not because they appeal to the passions of the audience, but because they do this in a defective manner. Their solicitation of the passions would be acceptable if it were an integral part of an enthymematic argument pertinent to the subject under examination, but their exclusive reliance on the passions with no connection to any form of argument only distracts the listeners with things irrelevant to the matter at hand (*R* 1354a13-15, 1354b18-22, 1356a9-19). The sophist excites the passions to divert his listeners from rational deliberation, but the Aristotelian speaker controls the passions of his listeners by reasoning with them.

Aristotle assumes that the passions are in some sense rational, and that a rhetorician can talk an audience into or out of a passion by convincing them that the passion is or is not a reasonable response to the circumstances at hand (*R* 1378a20-31, 1380b30-33, 1382a16-18, 1385a29-35, 1387b18-21, 1403a34-1403b1). Since a passion is always *about* something, since it always refers to some object, it is reasonable if it represents its object correctly or unreasonable if it does not. Men's passions are not always reasonable, but they must always *believe* that they are: they have reasons for their passions although their reasons are not always good ones. The passions may often arise from false judgments about reality, but the mere fact that passions require judgments, whether true or false, suffices to show the rational character of the passions. And a rhetorician who understands this can learn to change the passions of his listeners by changing their minds.

It is the rationality of the passions that distinguishes them from purely bodily sensations and appetites. It would be ridiculous to judge an itch or a pang of hunger as true or false, reasonable or unreasonable; and it would be equally absurd to argue with a man who felt an itch or a sensation of hunger in order to convince him that his feelings were unjustified. But it is not ridiculous to judge a man's anger as reasonable or unreasonable or to try to argue with him when his anger is unjustified. A man's anger depends upon his belief that anger is a proper response to something that has occurred, but a man's sensations or physical appetites do not require that he believe this or that (*NE* 1149a25-1149b3).

The passions are rational in that they are founded on judgments of what the world is like, but they are less than perfectly reasonable to the extent that they are founded on shortsighted, partial, biased, or hastily formulated judgments. Yet the fact that the passions often depend on defective reasoning should not obscure the fact that they do require some sort of reasoning, and it is this element of reasoning that gives the rhetorician a lever for controlling the passions.

That enthymemes are often directed to the emotions of the listeners indicates again the difference between enthymematic and demonstrative reasoning. Emotions are irrelevant to scientific demonstration; but since enthymematic argumentation is a *practical* form of reasoning, its aim is to move men not just to *think,* but also to *act;* and argument cannot move men to action unless it somehow elicits the motivational power of emotion.

V

The interpretation of the enthymeme that I have advanced here suggests that Aristotle considered rhetorical argument to be governed by definite epistemological standards. But his treatment of enthymemes includes a study of "apparent enthymemes"—that is, fallacious arguments—and there are other examples of the care with which Aristotle instructs the rhetorician in the techniques of verbal deception. Indeed, the art of rhetoric is said to provide the power to be persuasive on the

opposite sides of every question. So what is to prevent this art from being used to advance falsehood and injustice rather than their opposites? In other words, what is to keep the **Rhetoric** from being a handbook for sophists?

First of all, it may be answered that Aristotle recognizes that if the rhetorician is to be well armed, he must know all the tricks of sophistry so that he can properly defend himself. The Aristotelian rhetorician might even have to employ such tricks himself in those cases where otherwise bad means are justified by their advancement of good ends (*R* 1355a29-34, 1407a32-1407b7). Presumably, Aristotle would have the rhetorician follow the example of the dialectician: although he prefers to speak only with those who maintain discussion at a high level, the dialectician is able to defend himself in debates with unscrupulous opponents by using their own sophistical weapons against them, even to the point of showing himself more skillful with their weapons than they are themselves (*T* 108a33-37, 164b8-15; *SR* 175a32-175b3; compare *R* 1407a32-1407b7).[4]

In some cases, Aristotle does instruct the rhetorician in arguing opposite sides of an issue depending upon which side is most favorable to his position at the moment. But this is not a sophistical exercise, because in each case there *is* something valid to be said on both sides. In practical matters there is sometimes equally strong support for opposing arguments, and the prudent man must recognize this (see, for example, *R* 1375a25-1376b31).

It should also be said that, although the rhetorical art in itself is a morally and epistemologically neutral instrument, rhetoric tends to serve the true and the just. Even though there are no ends intrinsic to the art itself, ends are prescribed by the rhetorical situation—the speaker, the subject matter, and the audience. Since speakers who display good character are more persuasive, the noble rhetorician has an advantage over the sophist, who must attempt to hide his bad character (*R* 1356a6-13, 1378a6-19). Also, the sophistical speaker is restrained by the nature of the subject matter and by the opinions of the audience. With respect to the subject matter, it is generally the case that the true and the just are naturally more easily argued and more persuasive; and the opinions of the audience generally display this same tendency (*R* 1354a21-26, 1355a12-23, 36-38, 1371b5-11, 1373b3-13, 1396a4-1396b19, 1409a35-1409b12, 1410b9-35). Thus, in most cases, a speaker who has something to hide is more vulnerable than one who has not (*R* 1397b23-25, 1402a23-28, 1419a13-17). It is difficult to give a good speech for a bad cause (see Thucydides, *Peloponnesian War* III 36-48). This is not to deny, however, that sometimes the weaker argument can be made to appear the stronger. But—and this seems to be Aristotle's point—is it not usually easier to make the stronger argument appear to be the stronger, especially when it is skillfully presented?

VI

Matters of style and composition seem extraneous to the rational content of rhetoric since they seem unnecessary for the substantive argument of issues. Indeed, when Aristotle takes up these matters in Book Three, he begins by complaining that a concern with such things is only a concession to corrupt audiences (*R* 1403b15-1404a12, 1415a5-1416a2).

But in his treatment of these elements of rhetoric, Aristotle stresses the extent to which they contribute to rational argument. For Aristotle good style is not merely ornamentation, since the goodness of style is determined by how well it satisfies the natural desire of listeners for learning through reasoning (*R* 1404b1-13, 1408b22-29, 1409a23-1409b12, 1410a18-22, 1412b21-32, 1414a21-28). Metaphor, for example, the most important instrument of rhetorical style, provides listeners, in a manner similar to the enthymeme, with "quick learning" (*R* 1405a5-12, 33-37, 1410b6-35, 1412b9-12, 18-28). And Aristotle insists that the best arrangement for a speech is that which presents the substantive argument as clearly and directly as possible: a speaker should first state his case and then prove it (*R* 1414a30-1414b18). The Aristotelian rhetorician strives for the same end in his style and composition as he does in his enthymematic reasoning—to be clear but not commonplace and informative but not recondite.

VII

I have argued that Aristotle views rhetoric as rational discourse, and that he wishes to show that rhetoric is a form of reasoning to be distinguished from sophistry, even though rhetorical reasoning is less exact and less certain than scientific demonstration. Measured by the standards of strict, demonstrative logic, the political argumentation of citizens does not usually qualify as genuine reasoning at all. But such argumentation can be seen to be quite rational if it is judged according to the logical criteria of rhetoric. Aristotle's theory of rhetoric rests on the assumption that one should evaluate political arguments according to their degrees of plausibility without demanding absolute certainty or exactitude. Thus Aristotle's theory conforms to the logical practice of citizens, who are able to judge the plausibility of arguments despite the fundamental uncertainty of all practical reasoning.

But what would the modern political scientist say about all this? He might protest that rhetoric is surely not a valid form of reasoning since it violates even the most elementary rules of scientific rationality.[5] The funda-

mental problem, he might explain, is that the rhetorician's arguments can be only as reliable as the commonsense political opinions from which he draws his premises, but common opinions are at best uncertain and inexact reflections of political reality and at worst unexamined prejudices with no claim to truth. In contrast to the rhetorician's dependence on the vague and deceptive impressions of common sense, the contemporary political scientist might appeal to the epistemological criteria of a scientific methodology for precise standards of political knowledge. But does the modern scientific method provide a better starting point for political inquiry than does rhetoric?

This question was first clearly posed by Thomas Hobbes. For he rejected Aristotelian political science and applied the scientific method to political study, and in doing so he became the founder of modern political science. Now Hobbes did admire Aristotle's **Rhetoric** for its psychological insights; but he certainly denied Aristotle's claim, which is essential for his rhetorical theory, that common opinions can be the foundation of political reasoning. Classical political philosophers such as Aristotle could never lead us to genuine political knowledge, Hobbes argued, because "in their writings and discourse they take for principles those opinions which are vulgarly received, whether true or false; being for the most part false."[6] Instead of starting with political opinions, Hobbes's political science would start with exact definitions and axioms; and from these principles one would deduce a theoretical framework that would provide the certainty and precision of geometry. Thus did Hobbes initiate the project to which many political scientists today have devoted themselves.[7]

Is there anything to be said in favor of Aristotle's reliance on common political opinions as the foundation of political knowledge? On the one hand, Aristotle's theory of rhetoric as a valid form of political reasoning depends on the assumption that common opinions reflect a rational grasp of political life. But, on the other hand, Aristotle presents those opinions as often offering a confused, crude, and distorted view of political reality, thus falling short of the rigor, refinement, and comprehensiveness necessary for political philosophy. It seems that political opinions are the starting point for the Aristotelian political scientist, but they are *only* the starting point. That is to say, the respect that he gives to those opinions does not require an uncritical acceptance. Since the political theorist seeks to move from opinion to knowledge, he will not completely accept the answers given in political speech. And yet even in his movement beyond the common political opinions, he will be guided by the questions to which those opinions point: he will try to give an *adequate* answer to the questions that political opinions answer only *inadequately*.[8]

But if Aristotle finds common opinions so defective that he has to transcend them, why does he not reject them from the start in order to reason from scientific principles in the manner advocated by Hobbes? Aristotle might answer with two types of arguments. First, the phenomena studied by the political scientist differ from those studied by the natural scientist in ways that justify a difference in method. Second, all reasoning, even that of the natural scientist, depends ultimately upon the truth of our commonsense understanding of things.

Because political phenomena are contingent rather than necessary, and because they are essentially cognitive rather than physical, the political scientist, Aristotle might argue, must rely on commonsense opinions in a manner that would be inappropriate for the natural scientist. Political reality is contingent because it depends upon human choices that change from time to time and from one situation to another. The nature of political life will vary, for example, depending upon the type of regime in existence: oligarchic politics differs from democratic politics. A regime is a product of certain choices as to the organization and the goals of political rule. To understand these choices, the political scientist must study them as they are manifested in common opinions. And it would be a mistake to try to examine these things as if they were as unchangeable as the Pythagorean theorem or the motion of the planets. Moreover, political things are not physical objects that can be studied through sense perception. A political scientist who restricted himself to sense data would never see anything political. For political phenomena come into view only when one pays attention to what people *think* about politics as indicated by what they *say* about it. Thus, again, an appeal to political opinions is unavoidable.

But in the most fundamental respect, *all* reasoning—not just that of political science—depends upon commonsense opinions. This is so because all reasoning rests upon presuppositions drawn from our commonsense awareness of things. The rules of logic govern the deduction of conclusions from premises, but these rules cannot determine the truth or falsity of the first premises. Reasoning is grounded upon fundamental assumptions that cannot be proven because they are the source of all proofs. A conclusion is demonstrated when it is shown to follow from certain premises. And the premises may themselves be shown to follow as conclusions from other premises. But eventually one must reach principles that are taken as true without proof, these being the starting points of reasoning. Indeed, are not the rules of logic themselves assumptions that cannot be proven logically?

Even the most rigorous empirical science cannot avoid reliance on unprovable assumptions. Scientific induction, for example, rests on the presupposition that one may generalize from particular cases, which depends in turn on the broader assumption that nature falls into recurrent patterns: one must assume that the universe is governed by laws, and that these laws do not change arbitrarily from one moment to another.[9] Thus does scientific knowledge presuppose a prescientific knowledge of things. This is what Aristotle means when he says that to examine the first principles of any science, one must appeal to the "common opinions" . . . that are the source of the principles (*T* 100a18-100b22, 101a37-101b4). Werner Heisenberg, the great twentieth-century physicist, seems to make the same point when he observes: "the concepts of natural language, vaguely defined as they are, seem to be more stable in the expansion of knowledge than the precise terms of scientific language, derived as an idealization from only limited groups of phenomena." This is the case because, on the one hand, "the concepts of natural language are formed by the immediate connection with reality"; but, on the other hand, scientific concepts require idealization and precise definition through which "the immediate connection with reality is lost." So Heisenberg concludes: "We know that any understanding must be based finally upon the natural language because it is only there that we can be certain to touch reality, and hence we must be skeptical about any skepticism with regard to this natural language and its essential concepts."[10] A similar line of thought is found in the writings of Alfred North Whitehead. For although he helped to formulate modern mathematical logic, he insisted: "Logic, conceived as an adequate analysis of the advance of thought, is a fake. It is a superb instrument, but it requires a background of common sense."[11]

Our commonsense awareness of reality is more reliable than any epistemological theory could ever be. In fact, the truth of any epistemological theory will depend upon how well it accounts for our reliance on common sense.[12] The Hobbesian political scientist may think he can acquire political knowledge through a formal method that is totally abstracted from commonsense experience. But in practice his choice of assumptions will always be guided, even if unintentionally, by his own natural grasp of political reality. How could he even begin looking for political phenomena if he did not already somehow know what politics was like? As with Lewis Carroll's Alice, he must learn that if he is completely lost, he will never find his way; for if he does not know where he wants to get to, it does not matter which way he goes. But the Hobbesian political scientist knows more than he will admit. For like any sensible human being, he begins with a natural awareness of political things that directs his scientific inquiry. He is not *completely* lost after all. He knows at the start, even if only vaguely, where he wants to go; so it is not surprising that he usually finds a way to get there.

To fully understand the fundamental importance of commonsense experience for political reasoning, one must see the limits of the Hobbesian method, and one must recover the Aristotelian tradition of political science. Aristotle's **Rhetoric** is an essential part of that tradition. More clearly than any other Aristotelian text, it brings into view the common political opinions of human beings as the primary ground of political knowledge. Although the political scientist must eventually go beyond those opinions through a process of philosophical refinement, he must always look to them for guidance. For only by continually turning his attention to the political questions found in ordinary political speech, can the student of politics understand political things as they are in themselves.

Notes

1 Here I can only sketch the outline of an argument that I have developed in detail in *Aristotle on Political Reasoning: A Commentary on the "Rhetoric"* (DeKalb: Northern Illinois University Press, 1981). I have applied Aristotle's rhetorical theory to American rhetoric in an unpublished paper, "*The Federalist* as Aristotelian Rhetoric" (presented at the 1979 Annual Meeting of the Midwest Political Science Association, Chicago, April 18-21).

2 Henceforth I shall abbreviate my references to Aristotle's works as follows: *Eudemian Ethics (EE), Nicomachean Ethics (NE), Politics (P), Posterior Analytics (PoA), Prior Analytics (PrA), Rhetoric (R), Sophistical Refutations (SR), Topics (T).*

3 Since [*pistis*] can be translated as "belief" or "trust," Aristotle's use of this word in connection with rhetoric has been interpreted by some commentators as suggesting the weakness of rhetorical reasoning. But in fact Aristotle employs the term to refer to any belief that arises from a syllogism or from induction (see *PrA* 72a26-72b4; *T* 100b18-22; *SR* 165b3; *NE* 1139b32-34, 1142a18-21; *P* 1323a34-1323b7).

4 Does Aristotle discuss the tricks of the base to instruct good men and thus to dispel the smug assumption of bad men that good men must be naive? See *R* 1355a29-34; compare *R* 1373a3 with Xenophon, *Anabasis* II.vi.24-26; see also *P* 1313a34-1315b39.

5 From the perspective of the contemporary political scientist, rhetoric may appear to be nothing more than the manipulation of irrational symbols that do not reflect empirical reality. See, for example, Murray Edelman, *The Symbolic Uses of Politics* (Urbana: University of Illinois Press, 1964), pp. 18-21, 29-35, 41-42, 96-98, 115-17, 121, 124-25, 161, 172-73, 179-81; Edelman, *Politics as Symbolic Action* (New York: Academic Press, 1971), pp. 1-2.

6 *Elements of Law,* 1.13.3. See John W. Danford, *Wittgenstein and Political Philosophy* (Chicago: University of Chicago Press, 1978), pp. 16-42.

7 See, for example, Harold Lasswell and Abraham Kaplan, *Power and Society: A Framework for Political Inquiry* (New Haven: Yale University Press, 1950).

8 Here and elsewhere in these concluding remarks I have drawn ideas from Leo Strauss, "An Epilogue," in *Essays on the Scientic Study of Politics,* edited by Herbert J. Storing (New York: Holt, Rinehart and Winston, 1962), pp. 307-27; Wilhelm Hennis, *Politik und praktische Philosophie* (Berlin: Luchterhand, 1963), pp. 89-115; and Eugene F. Miller, "Primary Questions in Politics," *The Review of Politics,* 39 (July, 1977), 298-331.

9 On the assumptions necessary for modern science, see A. D'Abro, *The Rise of the New Physics,* 2 vols. (New York: Dover, 1951), I, 14-27. See also my article, "Language and Nature in Wittgenstein's *Philosophical Investigations,*" *Journal of Thought,* 10 (July, 1975), 194-99.

10 *Physics and Philosophy* (New York: Harper & Row, 1958), pp. 200-202.

11 "Immortality," in *The Philosophy of Alfred North Whitehead,* edited by Paul Arthur Schilpp, 2nd ed. (La Salle, Ill.: Open Court, 1951), p. 700. The importance of "common sense" for mathematics is a theme of my unpublished paper, "Mathematics and the Problem of Intelligibility."

12 One should keep in mind here the long rhetorical tradition of speculation about the nature of "common sense." See, for example, Thomas Reid, *Essays on the Intellectual Powers of Man* (Cambridge: M.I.T. Press, 1969), pp. 556-68; and Hans-Georg Gadamer, *Truth and Method* (New York: The Seabury Press, 1975), pp. 19-29.

Alan Brinton (essay date 1990)

SOURCE: "The Outmoded Psychology of Aristotle's *Rhetoric,*" in *Western Journal of Speech Communication,* Vol. 54, No. 2, 1990, pp. 204-18.

[*In the following essay, Brinton examines the canonical status of* Rhetoric, *defending it against those who would reject the text as dated due to the "emergence of the social-scientific study of communication in the twentieth century." Brinton argues that the psychological conceptions found in* Rhetoric *are, unlike some psychological theories, "not the kind which perish . . ." and that the text remains relevant to students of rhetorical theory.*]

However rhetoric ought to be defined, the great rhetorics of the past have, whatever their defects, at least some claim to the name. They may also deserve respect as relics of the past. But how importantly, if at all, ought they to figure in the education of students of rhetorical theory? And to what extent, if any, is it appropriate for contemporary rhetorical theorists to work from, say, Aristotle's **Rhetoric** as a basic text, to address questions in rhetorical theory for modern readers in its terms? However (and whether or not) rhetoric ought to be defined in conceptual terms, during any given period certain texts help to define it for the student and for the scholar, if not always for the practitioner. That is to say, there is for students and scholars, for good or ill, a sort of *de facto* canon of texts, however loosely identified, in whose terms they conceive the rhetorical. In times of theoretical unrest, the canonical status of particular works is one of the things which comes into question. In times of extreme theoretical unrest, such as the present, the very notion that ancient texts ought to be definitional at all is at least questioned and perhaps supplanted by a tendency to think in terms of a rolling canon, or a loose canon, or no canon at all (even, conceivably, to the point of canonizing anti-canonical texts). It is not my intention in this essay to justify the *de facto* practice of defining rhetoric in terms of particular texts, nor even to argue in favor of the perpetual canonical status of particular classical texts. My concern is rather with the tendency to *reject* certain texts, to expel them from the *de facto* canon, on the grounds that they are outmoded. If works such as the **Rhetoric** tend to evoke reverential attitudes from some (as they surely do) simply on the basis of their antiquity, they also tend, on the same basis, to evoke dismissive attitudes, if not contempt, from others. "Aristotle's Rhetoric," writes Gary Cronkhite in a recent article,

> contains little of value for the contemporary technical student interested in communication, or for students of any other practical persuasion. The kindest evaluation is that it is one of Aristotle's weakest works. Were it not for the fact that it was produced by one of the western world's greatest intellectuals . . . , and were it not for the desperate search for legitimacy conducted by the founders of our discipline, it would have been recognized long since as the historical curiosity which it is. Some of its prescriptions are useful only in the cultural context in which it was written, others are obvious to any casual contemporary observer, and the rest are ill advised.[1]

Cronkhite has a number of bones to pick with the **Rhetoric,** not all of which relate to its antiquity. But some of his complaints do have to do with just that. The "pernicious trisection of proof into 'logos,' 'pathos,' and 'ethos,'" for example, he sees as undermined by recent social-scientifically oriented work on "the *functions* of sources in communication in terms of the myriad ways in which they facilitate listeners' goal-achievement in specific situations" (p. 287). Cronkhite's critique of the **Rhetoric** as outmoded grows increasingly vociferous over its few pages:

> Need I make embarrassing comparisons between Aristotle's discussion of the constituents of happiness and some of the more contemporary treatments cited in public speaking textbooks, a notable example being Maslow's hierarchy of primary and secondary needs? Must I point out what mental gymnastics are required to wrest the treatment of laws, witnesses, contracts, tortures, and oaths out of ancient Greek culture and apply it in any meaningful way to twentieth century American politics and jurisprudence? (p. 288).

Cronkhite ends his piece by commending to students the **Nicomachean Ethics,** on the other hand, as a work "of more than historical interest" (p. 289).

There are some substantive theoretical objections which Cronkhite raises in this article and in others against some of the theoretical conceptions of the **Rhetoric.** However, what concerns us at the moment is this other aspect of his critique, the implication that on account of its being a product of ancient Greek culture, and on account of the emergence of the social-scientific study of communication in the twentieth century, Aristotle's **Rhetoric** is of little importance to contemporary students of rhetoric, that it is merely an historical artifact.

In a more subtle and influential critique of Aristotelian conceptions, published some years earlier, Edwin Black also complained about the "misplaced antiquarianism" of relying upon ancient rhetorical principles:

> . . . we can hardly expect the principles of rhetoric formulated two thousand years ago to be uniformly germane today. The nature of political institutions and the modes of communication have drastically changed in twenty centuries. It would be naive to suppose that there would not be concomitant changes in the character of rhetorical discourse. . . . The world changes, and the uses of language with it.[2]

Aristotelian rhetoric, Black also charged, and neo-Aristotelian criticism, are "founded upon a restricted view of human behavior . . ." (p. 131). In a more general criticism of classical rhetorics in the influential first issue of *Philosophy and Rhetoric,* Douglas Ehninger complained that, "hampered by the primitive psychology and epistemology with which they worked, as a group the classical writers tended either to scant or to present a patently naive account of the relation between the speech act and the mind of the listener."[3] Major deficiencies of the classical rhetorics were corrected, Ehninger went on to observe, by the "new" rhetorics of the eighteenth century, but these too, grounded as they were in faculty and associationist psychologies, are "now largely dated" (p. 52).[4]

There is little reason to think that Black or Ehninger (or even, perhaps, Cronkhite) meant to suggest that the careful study of older rhetorics in general, or of Aristotle's *Rhetoric* in particular, is a waste of time for contemporary students. But their comments do tend to encourage a dismissive attitude toward the rhetorical "classics" and lend themselves to the view that ignorance about works such as Aristotle's *Rhetoric,* Cicero's *De Inventione,* and Quintilian's *Institutio Oratoria* on the part of contemporary rhetorical theorists is at least excusable.

The serious issue is not the one which Cronkhite's article ostensibly addresses, whether Aristotle's *Rhetoric* ought to be used as a textbook in introductory courses. The question is whether serious study of such works is essential to rhetorical education and scholarship. But the narrower question which I wish to examine is whether what might appear to be grounds for taking the *Rhetoric* lightly really are so. And, in fact, there are two prongs to this aspect of the indictment of the *Rhetoric* which might seem to allow us to circumvent the need for even pausing to refute it. One is the notion that because of its antiquity, because it was written by an ancient Greek for ancient Greeks, it cannot be applicable for, or of much interest to, modern American rhetoricians. The other is the notion that Aristotle's rhetorical conceptions are outmoded on account of being grounded in outmoded psychological conceptions. This latter observation (like the former) we can make without ever reading a line of the *Rhetoric.* And we can safely assume, it would seem, without bothering to look at *any* of Aristotle's works, that his psychological conceptions are hopelessly antiquated. Psychology as a social science, with real theories, was not even invented until more than two millennia after Aristotle. In what follows, I want to comment briefly on the first of these prongs and then to deal with the second at somewhat greater length.

II

It is of course undeniable that Aristotle's *Rhetoric* is the product of a time and culture whose rhetorical situations were remarkably different from our own. Indeed, it would be unreasonable to expect it or other works from antiquity to be "uniformly germane today." Aristotle's *Rhetoric,* that is to say, is a product of, and a response to, its own rhetorical situation. It is, in fact, patently, even paradigmatically (if not perfectly) so. The same is true for Gorgias's *Helen,* for Cicero's *De Inventione,* and for a variety of other works which have been, or which according to some historians of rhetoric deserve to have been, of enduring interest to students and historians of rhetoric. Strange though it might seem at first glance, though, it is the very "datedness"

of such works which makes them of enduring importance. The point is this: Any reasonable attempt to understand what rhetoric is requires attention to rhetorical acts and rhetorical situations, and any reasonable attempt to develop a meaningful understanding of what rhetorical *theory* is requires attention to theoretical constructs of the appropriate kind, as well as attention to the contexts in which they arose. Late twentieth century rhetorical theorists (to say nothing of their students) are in an extraordinarily weak position with respect to assessing the great theoretical rhetorical constructs of our time in relation to the rhetorical situations to which these constructs are a response. We stand to learn more about the nature of rhetoric and rhetorical theory by studying works such as Aristotle's *Rhetoric,* that is to say, than by studying any particular theoretical artifacts produced by our contemporaries. We can be surer in our identification of the great works of the past, and (according to no meaner authorities than Aristotle's critics) those works were the products of a much simpler culture, responses to a much simpler rhetorical situation. This is one reason, I take it, why scholars such as Black and Ehninger take Aristotle's *Rhetoric* seriously, even if they inadvertently (by making disparaging remarks) encourage their readers to do otherwise.

III

A second possible reason for relegating older rhetorics to the status of historical relics is that at least some of them seem to be grounded in other sorts of theories, in particular in *psychological* theories, whose outdatedness and whose inadequacy as theories of their type are well established. Rhetorical theories have from the beginning had important connections with other kinds of theoretical frameworks—most conspicuously with psychological and ethical theories. Such connections are required for a true art of rhetoric, according to Plato's *Gorgias.* And it seems clear that Aristotle and his successors were consciously concerned to trace out and establish such connections or dependencies. But some kinds of theories seem to be more susceptible to becoming outmoded than others. Let us call those theoretical frameworks which are especially susceptible to becoming obsolete *endangered* theories. An endangered theory, then, is the sort of theory which is susceptible to theoretical extinction.

Ethical theories have almost never been regarded, at least by serious ethical theorists, as "endangered" in this sense, except in those instances in which they have been grounded in an "endangering way" in other theories which are.[5] *Psychological* theories, on the other hand, have typically been so regarded by psychological theorists.[6] The *Nicomachean Ethics,* for example, is still, in a sense, a "serious contender" in 20th Century moral philosophy; but *De Anima* is not, for contemporary psychologists, even in the ratings.[7]

Now, what are we to say of the great rhetorics of the past? Should we think of them as moral philosophers (and even Professor Cronkhite) think of the *Nicomachean Ethics,* or should we have the sort of attitude toward them that psychologists have toward *De Anima*? Is it simply anachronistic for a twentieth century rhetorical theorist to make use of the *Rhetoric* in the ways in which contemporary philosophers continue to make use of Aristotle's ethics, to work with its conceptions and to sometimes begin their inquiries by asking what Aristotle had to say on a subject? The question is not whether Aristotle's rhetorical conceptions are mistaken or inadequate, but whether they are inevitably so on account of being grounded in a psychological point of view which is inadequate by the standards of contemporary psychological theory.

Aristotle himself seems consciously to have accepted and responded to the demand of Plato's *Gorgias* that a true art of rhetoric requires "knowledge of the soul." That is to say, Aristotle's rhetoric *is* in some sense grounded in his psychology. But Aristotle's theory of the soul is, let us grant, outmoded from the point of view of psychological theory. The question we have to face, then, is whether it follows that his rhetorical theory is also outmoded.

The view that the conceptions of Aristotle's rhetoric and of other "classics" in the rhetorical tradition are outmoded on account of their grounding in outdated psychological conceptions was vigorously advanced in a series of articles published by Charles H. Woolbert early in this century. A main target in Woolbert's assault was the conviction-persuasion dichotomy, a well-worn distinction in classical rhetoric, one presupposed by Aristotle's classification of rhetorical proofs into *logos, ethos,* and *pathos,* as well as by Cicero's classification of "ends" of rhetoric. The thesis of Woolbert's 1917 article, "Conviction and Persuasion: Some Considerations of Theory," is that "any division of appeal and speech into conviction and persuasion is unsound from the point of view of psychology and unnecessary from the point of view of rhetorical theory."[8] As to whether conviction and persuasion ought to be regarded as two things or one, Woolbert's claim was that we cannot expect an answer from rhetoricians. Since this is a question which has to do with influencing the minds of others (so to speak), its answer "is to be found in psychology alone" (p. 253). If what psychologists tell us on the matter seems to conflict with ordinary usage, so much the worse for ordinary usage: "once we submit our problems to the court of psychology, we must abide by the decisions and the laws of evidence enforced in that court" (p. 255).[9] The main thrust of Woolbert's attack relies on the concept of *action.* The offending duality and its related concepts involve a bifurcation of belief and action; but for psychologists, claims Woolbert, "there is only one concept that describes what hap-

pens when an organism is stimulated in any and all possible ways, and that concept is expressed in the term *action,* or its synonyms, *activity* and *reaction*— as the psychologist uses them-all mean fundamentally the same thing" (pp. 253-254). "The psychologist," he goes on to say, "cannot today make any distinction between 'physical' action and 'mental' action; to him it is one and the same thing" (p. 255). The theorist of communication, then, ought to defer to psychological theory and accept the fact that the distinction between *proving* and *moving,* between convincing and persuading, is no longer viable.

These moves are, of course, part of a larger agenda. The details of psychological theory with which we find Woolbert to be enamored are precisely the kinds of details which become dated, and we find not only that he regarded classical rhetorical theory as grounded in outmoded psychological theory, but that he also meant to recommend adopting the conceptions of *current* psychological theory as the basis for understanding rhetorical phenomena. The larger agenda was to turn speech theory away from classical rhetoric and toward the social sciences (as conceived in recent times), turning to them for the justification, clarification, and elaboration of basic rhetorical concepts and assumptions. The observation that this is a turn which has been taken by many in the decades following the publication of Woolbert's "Conviction and Persuasion" and related articles does need to be documented.[10]

Our question is not about the legitimacy of the social-scientific study of rhetorical phenomena, however, but about whether the terms in which Aristotle addressed the questions which he was concerned to investigate (and which many of us are still concerned to investigate) are linked in an endangering way to endangered (and now defunct) psychological conceptions. A related question is about the *appropriateness* of the kinds of conceptions whose character is such as to "endanger," about their appropriateness for the kinds of inquiry in which classical rhetorical theorists have been engaged.

IV

What is it which endangers conceptions? Or, better yet, what is it that preserves conceptions from endangerment? Why and how is it, for instance, that the conceptions of ethical theory (of Aristotle's *Nicomachean Ethics,* for example) are so much less likely ever to come to be regarded as obsolete by moral philosophers? Why are they not "dated" in the way in which the doctrines and conceptions of *De Anima* are for psychologists? The answer relates partly to fundamental differences between subject-matters. Aristotle's explicit comments about the subject-matter and method of ethical studies are helpful in this context. "Precision," he says in Chapter 3 of Book I of the *Ethics,* "is not to be sought for alike in all discussions." But "fine and just actions," which he identifies as the subject-matter of ethical studies, "admit of much variety and fluctuation of opinion." We must, as a result, be satisfied, he says, "in speaking about things which are only for the most part true, and with such premises, to reach conclusions which are no better."[11]

His own method involves working from common conceptions and ordinary manners of speaking, attempting to develop a theoretical framework which in a sense begins from ordinary ethical experience and in the end has to square with it. His sketch of the "good" in Book I of the *Nicomachean Ethics,* for example, begins with observations about the different sorts of lives people actually lead and about their conceptions of the good. Then he says, after completing the sketch, that it must be evaluated "in the light not only of our conclusions and our premises, but also of what is commonly said" (1098b). The point is that ethical conceptions themselves have their origin in moral experience. Whatever refinements might be suggested, and whatever the attempt might be to ground them in some more technical or artificial theoretical framework, the discussion of ethical theory itself is conducted by Aristotle, as by Plato and nearly every other important moral philosopher, in terms of ordinary moral conceptions such as *virtue, goodness, obligation, responsibility, right* and *wrong*—and also in terms of ordinary *non*-moral conceptions such as *action, passion, voluntariness, habit, the will, reason,* and the like. Unless and until there are radical changes in the character of moral experience, much more radical changes than there have been from Aristotle's time to our own, the main conceptions of the *Nicomachean Ethics* are not in danger of becoming outmoded. There have, no doubt, been very great changes in ways of thinking and feeling about morality, but the persistence of the basic terms of inquiry testifies to how firmly entrenched these conceptions are in human experience.

Now some of the non-moral conceptions in question are psychological ones, but they are again conceptions which arise fairly directly out of ordinary experience. Psychologists may declare, perhaps with good reason, that there are no parts to the soul, or that there is no such faculty of mind as the Will. But ordinary people and moral philosophers will continue, with even better reason, to worry about conflicts between reason and emotion and to be troubled about weakness of the will. The terms of ordinary discourse, which are essentially the terms in which moral inquiry is conducted, are not the terms of psychological theory. Nor are the conceptions of ordinary discourse and of moral philosophy *in competition* with those of psychological theory—not any more than *physiological* descriptions of human behavior are in competition with psychological descriptions of the same behavior.[12] The one may in some

respects inform the other, may suggest insights and whatnot, but this is (to exaggerate just a little) as far as it goes.

When Aristotle says, for example, that virtue has to do with actions and passions, with how people *act* and with how they are *acted upon,* his thought may very well be inspired by the more general dichotomy in his metaphysics between actuality and potentiality; but serious students of the *Ethics* have not been tempted as a result to think that Aristotle's ethical views stand or fall with the doctrines of the *Metaphysics* or the *Physics.*[13] They have not been so tempted because it is a straightforward fact about human existence that we act and are acted upon, and because the concepts of agency and patiency, of acting and being acted upon, seem essential to moral theory.

Ethical theory (or "meta-ethics," as it is sometimes called) is an examination of ethical conceptions, of the conceptions of ethical practice and evaluation. If an ethical theorist were to start out by suggesting that there are really no such things as agents or actions, or that the conception of moral responsibility or of a person's character is outmoded, it is hard to conceive of what would come next. If the Epicureans, for example, having declared that reality consists in nothing more than atoms, the swerve, and the void, insisted on carrying out their ethical discussions in those terms, what would have remained to be said? Of course they did not; they carried on their ethical discussions in terms of human actions and passions and beliefs. In the same way, the language of stimulus and response, which could conceivably be adequate for the purposes of psychological theory (not to suggest that it is), could never suffice for ethical theory. Moreover, the strangeness and radical inappropriateness of the language of stimulus-response for ethical theory has nothing to do with inadequacies in either behaviorism or ethical theory; it has to do with differences in, to use Gilbert Ryle's terminology, "conceptual territory."

There is a good deal of psychology in the *Nicomachean Ethics;* but that it is of a different character from the more technical discussions of *De Anima,* the *Metaphysics,* and certain other of Aristotle's works is in effect acknowledged when he says that the student of ethics "must know *somehow* the facts about soul"— that is, as he says, "to the extent [and in the *way,* we might add] which is sufficient for the questions we are discussing" (*EN* 1102a). On the question of parts of the soul, for instance, he goes on to say in the same passage that

> Some things are said about it, adequately enough, even in the discussions outside our school, and we must use these, e.g. that one element in the soul is irrational and one has a rational principle. Whether these are separated as the parts of the body or of

anything divisible are, or are distinct by definition but by nature inseparable, like convex and concave in the circumference of a circle, does not affect the present question.

The *Nicomachean Ethics* is not in danger of becoming obsolete on account of its psychological conceptions, because its psychological conceptions are not the conceptions of psychological theory.[14]

The nature of "moral psychology," that is, is quite different from the nature of psychology as conducted (quite rightly) by the psychologist as social scientist, even if and when there is to some extent shared terminology. Terms and distinctions which are adequate for either one may be inadequate for the other. In particular, conceptions that become outmoded for the social scientist may be alive and well for the moral philosopher, and may in fact be indispensible. This is why it is not *nonsense* (though it may be open to debate) for a contemporary moral philosopher to make the claim that students will learn more about ethics by reading Aristotle than by reading any particular book written in the twentieth century. In the same way, I want to suggest, it is not ludicrous to say that students are likely to learn more about rhetoric from Aristotle's *Rhetoric* than from any particular book written in the twentieth century.

V

I have already, without saying much of anything about rhetoric, given my reason for rejecting the notion that rhetorical theories die with their psychological conceptions: their psychological conceptions are not the *kind* which perish along with dying psychological theories. At least this is true of rhetorical theory as practiced in the great classics of the rhetorical tradition, though it may not be true of the field of communication studies, conceived and practiced as a social science. The problem, as it appears in the Woolbertian assault on the conceptions of classical rhetoric, lies in the tendency to conceive of the kind of inquiry which goes on in the works of classical rhetorical theorists and that which goes on in the new social science of communication as competitors, as if both are up to the same things, with the former suffering under the disadvantage of being equipped with outmoded psychological conceptions. Woolbert's assault is particularly interesting, because of his influence in the early development of communication as a discipline, and because he so boldly confuses categories. The nature of the confusion is most apparent in a final collapsing of psychological distinctions on *physiological* grounds. This move is repeated in his later attack on the distinction between the rational and the nonrational in "The Place of Logic in a System of Persuasion," on the grounds that "Inferences, judgments, logical connections, are made in neuro-muscular patterns" (p. 39), and on the grounds that the

neuro-muscular patterns underlying so-called "nonrational" thinking are governed by the same physiological laws and are just as lawlike as those which underlie socalled "rational" thinking. "Ten propositions," he writes in a later article, "mean ten sets of movements."[15]

I draw attention to the physiological aspects of Woolbert's reduction in order to portray more graphically the *kind* of confusion which I believe also characterizes his reduction of rhetorical theory to psychological (or "social-scientific") theory. Rhetorical theory is, at least in part, *an examination of the conceptions of rhetorical practice and evaluation.* In this respect it is akin to ethical theory. With respect to the ethical or moral, there is a kind of theoretical inquiry about human values and attitudes, a kind of empirical inquiry, which is categorically different from the kind of inquiry which goes on in the *Nicomachean Ethics* or in other works in moral philosophy. The empirical kind of inquiry about values is rightly pursued as a kind of social science. Some of its products attain the status of "findings," and may be appropriately appealed to as such. These "findings" are, however, subject to disconfirmation. They, and the technical conceptions and distinctions in terms of which they are formulated and promulgated, are *endangered* in the sense we referred to earlier. What suits them for social-scientific inquiry is precisely what endangers them. But moral philosophy is an inquiry of a radically different kind. In the same way, there is a kind of inquiry about matters rhetorical which is categorically different from the social-scientific study of rhetorical phenomena. Aristotle, Isocrates, Cicero, Quintilian, and others among the great classical rhetorical theorists are generally concerned with the practice of public persuasion and with the evaluation of rhetors and rhetorical acts. Conceptions which are adequate for the purposes of that kind of inquiry may not be (and should not be expected to be) at all adequate for social-scientific inquiry—and vice-versa.

But still, Aristotle's rhetoric, like his ethics, does involve psychological conceptions, and the question whether the conceptions of Aristotle's *Rhetoric* are adequate for discussing its problems in rhetorical theory is in a way a question about the adequacy of the psychology of that work. But what exactly *is* the psychology of the *Rhetoric,* this psychology which is supposed to be adequate for a theoretical discussion of rhetorical practice and rhetorical evaluation?

VI

There are three identifiable components to the psychology of Aristotle's *Rhetoric,* and they constitute nothing like a psychological theory in the social-scientific sense. The first component is developed in Chapters 5-7 of Bk.I. "Every individual man," Aristotle says, "and all men in common aim at a certain end which determines what they choose and what they avoid. This end, to sum it up briefly, is happiness (*eudaimonia*) and its constituents."[16] Aristotle is interested here, of course, in what *motivates* people, in what they identify as goods to be pursued, since the orator will need to make reference to these goods (and to corresponding evils). But what Aristotle offers us in this part of the **Rhetoric** is nothing like a psychologist's theory of motivation. It is more akin to the discussion of the good in Book I of the **Nicomachean Ethics,** except that here he is more exclusively concerned with what are *perceived* as goods by the likely members of audiences. The "goods" he identifies are things like health, wealth, friends, fame, power, and virtue, goods which people do in fact seek and which they are likely always to seek.

The second component of the psychology of the **Rhetoric** is the treatment of the passions (*pathe*) in Chapters 2-11 of Bk.II. This is the closest we come to real psychological theorizing in the **Rhetoric.** Aristotle has what we would now call a "cognitive" view of the emotions. He examines a variety of particular emotions or passions in terms of (1) the state of mind of the person who experiences the emotion, (2) the sorts of persons or objects toward which it is felt, and (3) the *grounds* on which it is felt. Now, if the cognitive view of the emotions taken in the **Rhetoric** is the closest Aristotle comes in the work to proposing a psychological theory, it is also the aspect of the psychology of the work which is most likely to be of enduring interest to psychological theory.[17] That is, however, a matter mainly of Aristotle's having observed and taken note of one feature of emotional life which is of critical importance in the development of psychological theories of emotion, namely the fact that emotional experience typically involves cognition and often follows it. However, the main concern in this part of the **Rhetoric** is with how, and under what circumstances, and in the light of what beliefs, and in what sorts of persons, particular emotions are aroused. The details of this part of the **Rhetoric** are more a matter of astute observations by a careful observer of human nature than either entailments of or empirical supports for a psychological theory of human emotion. Aristotle agrees with Plato that the orator must have a knowledge of sorts about the soul; but what we are told about the soul here, as well as elsewhere in the **Rhetoric,** gives us no reason to believe that Aristotle thinks that the orator requires a metaphysical or "scientific" knowledge of the soul.

The third component of the **Rhetoric**'s psychology is the discussion of types of characters in Chapters 12-17 of Bk. II. This consists in "character sketches," more or less akin to what we find later worked out in more detail in the *Characters* of Theophrastus and in similar works written in the 17th and 18th centuries. In other words, Aristotle's main concern in these chapters is to make practical observations about how differences in age, for example, or social position, affect people with respect to the other two components of the psychology of the **Rhetoric.** Again, there is nothing like a psychological theory, in the psychologist's sense, in this part of the **Rhetoric.** In fact, all three aspects of the psychology of the work present us with relatively uncontroversial *data* of which psychological theory must take account. Moreover, in the **Rhetoric,** even more clearly than in the **Ethics,** there is no dependence upon the doctrines of the soul which are developed in Aristotle's "scientific" works. Whether the soul is a *substance,* for example, or whether it literally has parts, has no bearing on the discussions of the **Rhetoric.**

Maybe a more theoretical psychology than is provided in the **Rhetoric** is desirable for the grounding of the kind of theoretical activity which goes on in that work. But if this is so, this more theoretical psychology will be of a piece, I suggest, with the *moral psychology* of the **Ethics;** it will consist, that is, in an analysis and synthesis of ordinary psychological conceptions. We ourselves will find more of it, in the 20th Century, in the *Proceedings of the Aristotelian Society* than in the proceedings of the American Psychological Association.

VII

In closing, let me make some more general observations about the relevance of the classics in rhetorical theory to modern students and scholars. Narrowly technical fields of study, whose ends are narrowly practical, engineering for example, do just fine without a historical component. The well-rounded person who happens to be an engineer will probably have some knowledge of the history of the subject, but familiarity with the written works of the masters of bygone eras of engineering is absolutely not required for good engineering. An engineer who insisted on engineering on the basis of the *De Architectura* of Vitruvius or the pseudo-Aristotelian *Mechanica* would be some kind of a crank. The study of old engineering "classics" would be at best an especially fitting hobby for an engineer. Technical rhetoric (the *practice* of rhetoric, that is), very narrowly conceived, is not quite like engineering in this respect, however, for two reasons. One reason is that the rhetorical treatises of Aristotle, say, or of Cicero, are themselves rhetorical artifacts, of a most unusual and interesting kind, rhetorical artifacts produced in response to rhetorically loaded, self-consciously rhetorical situations. Another reason is that at least some of them are written by unusually astute and perceptive observers of human nature; as a result, some of these treatises (Aristotle's **Rhetoric,** for example) abound (to a much greater extent, some would argue, than do contemporary communication textbooks) in particular observations and insights which are directly relevant to rhetorical practice.

Most communication teachers and scholars are, of course, loath to think of their discipline in such narrow technological terms. On the other hand, there is some inclination to think in social-scientific terms. The tendency to think of works like Aristotle's **Rhetoric** as historical artifacts and the tendency to think of the history of rhetoric as a separate field of study are manifestations, I believe, of a too narrowly social-scientific way of thinking about the study of rhetoric and of rhetorical theory. But even the social scientist who wants to think clearly about the nature of social-scientific theory, and who wants to see currently accepted views for what they are, needs to pay some attention to their antecedents, even to antecedents which may be very justly said to be outdated or antiquated. The education of a university level psychologist or sociologist who is uninformed about the history of psychology or sociology may with equal justice be said to be incomplete. There is a significant hole in such a scholar's competence. Such a scholar has an incomplete understanding of the character of his or her subject matter. Such a scholar simply inherits whatever theoretical constructs are passed along with assurances that these constructs supercede those which came before. The hole is not adequately filled by a few observations about foreshadowings or inadequacies in the works of antiquity.

But for the rhetorical theorist, as opposed to the mere (or pure) social scientist of communication, matters are still more complicated. Even the reflective social-scientist is aware that there are questions about the social sciences which are not themselves social-scientific questions, that some of them are philosophical, and that the language in which these questions are addressed is in some sense a different language from the language in which the "findings" of social-scientific research are reported and interpreted. But for the rhetorical theorist, concerns which are clearly not social-scientific are more immediate and harder to relegate to some other field of inquiry. The language which is adequate for addressing these concerns is not the language of social science. The language and conceptual apparatus of psychology as a social science, for example, are inadequate for exactly those aspects of rhetorical theory which make the rhetorical treatises of an Aristotle or a Cicero or a Quintilian of enduring interest. It is, therefore, as inappropriate for the rhetorical theorist to submit conceptions to the court of psychology as it would be for the psychologist to send conceptual problems in psychology to the biology department for adjudication. (This is not to say that an understanding of Aristotle's scientific works has no relevance to the interpretation of his **Rhetoric**.[18]) In particular, an adequate conceptual apparatus for rhetorical theory must provide for critical judgments about

rhetorical acts. In this respect rhetorical theory is akin to logical theory, ethical theory, and aesthetic theory. One of the demands on rhetorical theory is, moreover, that it should provide for some account of relationships among the rhetorical, the logical, the ethical, and the aesthetic. This could not be done by a theory whose most fundamental conceptions were social-scientific. What sorts of discussions can we expect from theorists armed only with the concepts of social science on topics such as the ends of rhetoric, the character of the orator, or the legitimacy of appeals to authority or of the arousing of the passions of an audience? It is with respect to questions such as these that the conceptual framework of Aristotle's **Rhetoric** is alive and well. And it is on account of their ongoing relevance to these sorts of questions, and not simply on account of their degree of influence on later theorists, that certain works stand out as especially worthy of study by the historian of rhetoric, the same sorts of works which the contemporary rhetorical theorist cannot afford to neglect.[19]

Notes

[1] Gary Cronkhite, "Aristotle's Rhetoric as an Historical Artifact, Being a Response to the Suggestion it be Used as a Textbook," *Communication Education* 36 (1987): 286.

[2] Edwin Black, *Rhetorical Criticism: A Study in Method* (1965; Madison: U of Wisconsin P, 1978) 125, 124.

[3] Douglas Ehninger, "On Systems of Rhetoric," *Philosophy and Rhetoric* 1 (1968): 131-144. Rpt. in *Contemporary Rhetoric: A Reader's Coursebook,* ed. Douglas Ehninger (Glenview, IL: Scott, Foresman, 1972) 51.

[4] Compare Stephen W. Littlejohn's comment in *Theories of Human Communication,* 2nd ed. (Belmont, CA: Wadsworth, 1983):

> Aristotelian theory probably was effective in its day. Its problems result primarily from modern-day applications. Because the theory employs a linear model in which a strong distinction is made between rhetor (source) and audience (receiver), it leaves little room for interaction among communicators. As such it neglects the process nature of communication. . . .

> Aristotelian theory has also been criticized because of its three-fold analysis of ethos, pathos, and logos. In actual practice separating information into these categories is difficult. Any argument or appeal may, and probably does, involve a combination of personal regard, feelings, and logic. Aristotle presents these three elements as descriptors of message parts, but they probably more accurately relate to dimensions of perception that do not

correspond perfectly with specific message appeals (136).

Notice the imposition of modern-day jargon on Aristotle: "linear model," "source-receiver," "descriptors of message parts." Also, notice that the second criticism is not well-grounded in the text of the *Rhetoric;* Aristotle does not in fact sort out ethos, pathos, and logos in terms of message parts, either in his treatments of the three modes of proof in Bks. 1-II, or in his discussion of the parts of a speech in Bk. III. See, also, Kenneth E. Andersen's *Persuasion: Theory and Practice* (Boston: Allyn and Bacon, 1971): "Aristotle typifies the approach in which a person analyzes communication and then sets forth his estimation of the key factors without empirical verification" (220).

[5] Ethical theories which have been seriously built upon the foundations of endangered theories typically have not stood the test of time. Herbert Spencer's "evolutionary" ethical theory (See his *Principles of Ethics,* 2 vols. (London: 1892-93)) is a clear case of this, even though evolutionary theory is alive and well among biologists. The point is that Spencer's ethics is adjudged to involve a kind of confusion, and thus not really to be a theory of the type it is supposed to be. In other words, what is wrong with it, from the moral philosopher's point of view, is not that the evolutionary theoretical framework is deficient as a theory of *its* type, but that there is a confusion of types. For a brief but incisive critique of Spencer's theory, see John Hospers, *Human Conduct: An Introduction to the Problems of Ethics* (New York: Harcourt, Brace and World, 1961).

[6] Though not by Aristotle, who devotes the second chapter of *De Anima* to a review of the views of his predecessors, "in order that we may profit by whatever is sound in their suggestions and avoid their errors," trans. J. A. Smith (Oxford: Clarendon, 1956) 403b.

[7] I oversimplify, of course, by referring just to *De Anima.* Also, I should make it clear that it is psychologists to whom I am referring. Certain aspects of Aristotle's psychology are still taken quite seriously by philosophers, especially by moral philosophers.

[8] Charles H. Woolbert, "Conviction and Persuasion: Some Considerations of theory," *The Quarterly Journal of Public Speaking* 3 (1917): 249.

[9] See also Mary Yost's "Argument from the Point-of-View of Sociology," *Quarterly Journal of Public Speaking* 3 (1917): 109-127: "The generally accepted theory of argument as expressed in the text-books . . . is based on a psychology not in harmony with the modern ideas of the way the mind works. . . . Almost all of the textbooks state that an argument effects its end by means of *conviction* and *persuasion.* . . . Now this explana-

tion of the terms *conviction* and *persuasion* was formulated when the belief held sway that the mind was divided into three compartments, the reason, the emotions, the will—roughly the assumptions of the old faculty psychology. Today, however, the leading psychologists have found these assumptions inadequate to explain the phenomena of the mind" (110-111).

[10] Other important related articles by Woolbert in *The Quarterly Journal of Speech* include "The Place of Logic in a System of Persuasion," 4 (1918): 19-39; "Persuasion Principles and Method," 5 (1919): Part I, "Underlying Principles," 12-25; Part II, "Analysis," 101-119; and Part III, "Synthesis," 212-238. On the significance of Woolbert's attack on the Aristotelian framework, see Carroll C. Arnold and Kenneth D. Frandsen, "Conceptions of Rhetoric and Communication," in *Handbook of Rhetorical and Communication Theory* (Boston: Allyn and Bacon, 1984) 10. For more recent expression of the Woolbertian view, see Gerald R. Miller's "On Being Persuaded: Some Basic Distinctions," *Persuasion: New Directions in Theory and Research,* Michael E. Roloff and G. R. Miller, eds. (Beverly Hills: Sage 1980):

> . . . some writers . . . have explored the wisdom of distinguishing between convincing and persuading— the so-called *conviction-persuasion duality.* . . . While this distinction has unquestionably influenced some of the research carried out by contemporary persuasion researchers . . ., its utility seems dubious at best. Attempts to crisply conceptualize and operationalize distinctions between logical and emotional appeals have been fraught with difficulty. . . . Faced with these considerations, it seems more useful to conceive of persuasive discourse as an amalgam of logic and emotion. . . . Furthermore, the motivation for distinguishing between conviction and persuasion rests largely on value concerns for the way influence ought to be accomplished. . . . (14-15).

See Cronkhite on the conviction-persuasion dichotomy as well (1987, 287). Miller goes on to make, however, the very point whose converse I want to emphasize in defending the conceptions of the *Rhetoric:* " . . . conceptual distinctions that make for sound ethical analysis may sometimes make for unsound scientific practice . . ." (1980, 15). See also Andersen's comment in *Persuasion: Theory and Practice:* "The separation between persuasion and conviction or emotional appeal and logical appeal has lost ground among contemporary persuasion theorists. This division has been *discarded* on the grounds that psychological theory no longer supports a "faculty" concept, and, further, the separation *has been difficult to operationalize* . . ." (1971, 221; emphasis mine).

[11] *The Nicomachean Ethics of Aristotle,* trans. D. Ross (Oxford: Clarendon, 1925) 1094b. Further reference

will be to *"EN."*

[12] The classic discussion of this matter is to be found in Gilbert Ryle's *Dilemmas* (London: Cambridge U P, 1954). See especially Ch. V, "The World of Science and the Everyday World," and Ch. VI, "Technical and Untechnical Concepts."

[13] I bring the *Metaphysics* into the picture here since it is in its metaphysical aspects, in part, that the endangeredness of Aristotle's psychology seems to lie. On the action-passion dichotomy, its metaphysical connections, and its significance in Aristotle's ethics, see L. A. Kosman, "Being Properly Affected: Virtues and Feelings in Aristotle's Ethics," in A. O. Rorty, ed., *Essays in Aristotle's Ethics* (Berkeley: U of California P, 1980) 103-116.

[14] This is another oversimplification. There are some aspects of the *Nicomachean Ethics* which *do* seem to be "endangeringly" grounded in psychological theory, most conspicuously the discussion of "the good for man" in Chapter 7 of Bk. I.

[15] Woolbert, "Underlying Principles" 17. The upshot is that there is no special appeal to *logos,* from which other kinds of rhetorical appeals can be distinguished. However, propositions are *logical,* not *physiological* phenomena; the theoretical activity of a logician who had to submit conceptions and distinctions to the "court of the physiologist" would be stopped short. The language and the conceptions of the physiologist are no more adequate for logical or rhetorical theory than they are for ethical theory. The physiologist can never provide us, for example, with a conception of *reasons* for action or belief (as opposed to in some sense providing us with an account of their *causes*).

[16] *The Rhetoric and Poetics of Aristotle,* trans. W. Rhys Roberts, with an introduction by Edward P. J. Corbett (New York: Random House, 1984) 1360b.

[17] For a discussion of Aristotle's theory of the emotions and its relevance to modern discussions, see William Lyons's *Emotion* (Cambridge: Cambridge U P, 1980) especially Chs. 2-4. See also W. W. Fortenbaugh's *Aristotle on Emotion: A Contribution to Philosophy, Psychology, Rhetoric, Poetics, Politics, and Ethics* (London: Duckworth, 1975).

[18] Ray D. Dearin makes a good case for the relevance of *De Anima* to the interpretation of the *Rhetoric,* in "Aristotle on Psychology and Rhetoric," *Central States Speech Journal* 17 (1966): 277-282. The one informs the other. But Dearin puts it too strongly when he says in conclusion that "the theory of persuasion enunciated in the *Rhetoric* rests firmly upon the psychological foundations of *De Anima*" (282). Dearin also unfortunately illustrates the tendency of some contemporary communication theorists to adopt the social-scientific mode of inquiry and expression in the ways in which he appeals to the work of other scholars, as evidenced in the use of forms of expression such as the following: " . . . since Werner Jaeger and others have shown that . . . ," "Thonssen has shown that . . . ," " . . . according to Griffin . . . ," and the like. A comparative rhetoric of appeals to authority would make an interesting study. The social-scientific mind appeals to "findings": so-and-so has been established and now defines the parameters of our inquiry; we may proceed without much concern about how these conclusions (now assumptions of inquiry) were established, without attention to the arguments. This mode of appeal seems odd, at least, when carried over into other kinds of inquiry and argument (into ethical discourse, for example).

[19] I am grateful to Carole Blair and to Michael Leff, as well as to two anonymous referees, for very helpful comments and suggestions on an earlier draft.

Mary Margaret McCabe (essay date 1990)

SOURCE: "Arguments in Context: Aristotle's Defense of Rhetoric," in *Aristotle's "Rhetoric,"* edited by David J. Fuley and Alexander Nehamas, Princeton University Press, 1990, pp. 129-66.

[*In the following essay, McCabe defends the structure and the content of* Rhetoric, *arguing that both support Aristotle's view that rhetoric is indeed an art and that it can be practiced in a legitimate manner.*]

Is the opening of Aristotle's **Rhetoric** a muddle, an agglomeration of two versions of the text, haphazardly assembled? Or is there a coherent strategy to be found here? It has been persuasively suggested that two different strands of argument within the **Rhetoric** correspond to two stages in the development in Aristotle's logic (an earlier, **Topics**-based stage, and a later one that uses the theory of the syllogism put forward in the **Prior Analytics**).[1] But I shall argue that the **Rhetoric** is not ill-knit after all. For the appearance of fracture derives from Aristotle's standard practice of considering the views of the many and the wise to arrive at a coherent theory of his own. In this case, I claim, Aristotle explicitly confronts the opposed theories of his predecessors: Plato, who denied that there could be an art of rhetoric, and the tradition of the rhetors and sophists which maintained that rhetoric is the overarching science because the practice of rhetoric is all-pervasive. This debate about the status of rhetoric turns on two issues: The first is theoretical: is the art of rhetoric properly systematic—is rhetoric a *technē*? The second is ethical (and political): is the practice of rhetoric legitimate or disgraceful? Aristotle, by showing how the first question can be answered in the affirmative, gives an account of how rhetoric may legitimately be practiced. In the process he avoids both Plato's absolute condemnation of the rhetors and Isocrates' wholehearted endorsement of their art. The result is a subtle theory of rhetoric which is complex but not incoherent.[2]

Plato's Challenge

Notoriously Plato had argued that the art of rhetoric is either no art form at all (because the practice of rhetoric is merely flattery, like cooking) or turns out to be philosophy. He makes the case for the first in the *Gorgias* and for the second in the *Phaedrus;* but the grounds for both are the same and threefold. He has an epistemological argument, an ethical argument, and a political one; the three are closely tied together.

Because it aims to persuade, ordinary rhetoric is fake and insincere. It puts on the clothing of something else[3] and pretends to be a real skill, concerned to confer real benefit. In fact, however, it is mere hedonist flattery, an irrational knack, not a proper art (*technē, Grg.* 464b ff.). Why is rhetoric not a *technē*? Because the rhetor is the jack of all trades (as Gorgias boasts); he is able to persuade anyone about anything, but he lacks a subject matter of his own (*Grg.* 458e ff.). He has no real understanding (*Grg.* 465a); instead his objective is to make himself plausible (*pithanōteros, Grg.* 459a; cf. *Phdr.* 272d) in order to convince the ignorant, not to teach the truth (*Grg.* 459a, cf. *Phdr.* 272e) nor to improve the souls of his audience, as the politician should (*Grg.* 464c). After all, rhetoric does whatever it can to win its point, because it has itself no moral position to take (cf., e.g., *Grg.* 460e; and witness Gorgias' vacillations on whether or not rhetoric is just). So rhetors are nothing but Sophists, who care only for the correctness of words and never get to grips with "things" (*ta pragmata, Euthd.* 278b). And if the practice of rhetoric is flattery, an unsystematic knack, then a fortiori there can be no theory of rhetoric, no *ars rhetorica*. In that case, those who claim to teach rhetoric in fact do no such thing: the sophists are charlatans.

Plato's first objection to rhetoric, then, is an *epistemological* one. Philosophy aspires to absolute and objective standards (e.g., at *Rep.* 511b); and once those standards are achieved, they provide a systematic science. But neither the practice of rhetoric nor its theory can lay claim to objective knowledge: and for that reason neither can lay claim to the title of a *technē*.

His second objection is an *ethical* one. Gorgias and his colleagues are interested in winning their cases in court, in persuading the assembly, in impressing their audience. Their activities aim at power and success. Socrates, on the other hand, denies that this is power at all; and he cares only for the inquiry into truth, which he conducts by a meticulous examination of his interlocutors one by one. Now the contrast between Socrates and the Sophists is not just a matter of good intentions; rather, Plato argues that the methods of rhetoric are fundamentally misguided, lacking as they do the proper ethical focus.

We may see this in two connected ways: i) in the argument of the *Gorgias* about power; and ii) in the Socratic method itself.

i) The art of rhetoric, the rhetors say, gives you power—over juries, over friends and enemies, over cities (*Grg.* 466b ff.). This kind of power is bound to be a good thing, because it lets you have whatever you want and do as you will (*Grg.* 466CI). Socrates disagrees: this is not power at all. For the tyrant may do what he thinks is best; but he does not do what he wants, because what he wants is what really turns out to be the best. So unless he knows what he is doing (*Grg.* 466d10), he will end up getting only what he thinks is best—and then he will be wrong, disappointed, and not powerful at all.[4]

Power, on Socrates' account, is about knowledge and getting things right. He contrasts two different levels of belief— "shallow" belief (what we think we want; what we are persuaded to want, what the orators convince us of) and "deep" belief (the deep structure of our beliefs and desires[5]). These two levels of belief (Socrates suggests) are usually at odds with each other; but only deep belief corresponds to what is true and objectively valuable (what we really want). Getting at our deep beliefs, therefore, is in our interests; disguising them with shallow ones is disastrous. So philosophy turns out to be a good thing, and rhetoric a bad one. If philosophy is power over ourselves, then rhetoric gives others power over us, without allowing them power over themselves either (because they don't know what they are doing, are not experts in anything, as Gorgias admitted). Power over ourselves is something we get from our own intellectual activity, and not something we can achieve either by manipulating others, or by being manipulated by them, or by manipulating ourselves. The only thing that matters, then, is the active philosophical life,[6] the true life of the soul.

ii) The methods of rhetoric compare unfavorably with the Socratic method of elenchus.[7] A collection of premises is made (from various sources) which includes some proposition under scrutiny; an argument is mounted to investigate the coherence of the premise set; and in the end the premise set is shown to be inconsistent. The method is quite general, not (or not legitimately) to derive the contradictory of the hypothesis directly but rather to evaluate the coherence of the entire set of propositions. So the logical focus of the elenchus is consistency, which characterizes a collection of beliefs.

An elenchus also demands that the interlocutor "say what he believes."[8] Thus, for example, Socrates encourages Charmides to discover hypotheses about self-control from introspection—because Charmides is "obviously" self-controlled (*Chrm.* 159a). Or Callicles needs to reflect on what he really believes, in order to engage in argument with Socrates (*Grg.* 482). The investigation into what he really believes, Socrates suggests, will itself produce inconsistency with what he appears to believe—and hence he will arrive at impasse, *aporia*. Now *aporia* is not a thesis in an argument, it is a state of mind.[9] Unlike ignorance, *aporia* is highly self-conscious—it has all kinds of trappings of embarrassment and shamefacedness, but it is not a condition that its patient can ignore. Socrates' position on this is famous, featured as it is in his self-defense—we are better off, he claims, being *aware* that we are ignorant, than wrongly thinking we know (*Ap.* 21b ff.). Someone whose premises have been shown inconsistent clearly does not know what to think; and in this respect he is aware of his own ignorance—so he is better off than he was at the beginning of the argument. And this positive result of the elenchus would be impossible if the interlocutor were insincere—because it would not be his views that ended up in difficulties.

What is the connection between the consistency of the belief-set and the sincerity with which those beliefs are held? In the elenchus, inconsistency is a bad fit of beliefs *held by a particular person;* and a person can only reveal what his or her beliefs are by meeting the sincerity condition. But then this same person will feel the discomfort of inconsistency; and the need for consistency then turns out to be a condition of the self, a disposition of the soul.

Hence recurs a theme of the Platonic Socrates' attack on the Sophists and their denial that consistency matters. "Who will you become if you are taught by Sophists?" Socrates asks (*Prt.* 311b-c). "I need to know myself," he insists; "I need to make sure I do not contradict myself."[10] Why does it matter whether I contradict myself or not? First of all, Socrates suggests that I care about consistency because finding myself inconsistent affects my personal integrity (compare *Grg.* 482a ff., *Euthd.* 283c ff., 287b ff.). This is why *aporia* is so unsettling—because I seem then to be in conflict with myself—and why I aspire always to eliminate inconsistency from my belief set. But this aspiration is not, on Plato's view, merely an attitude to the logical relations of my beliefs. On the contrary, the drive toward inconsistency is fundamentally ethical. For without psychological integrity, not only can I have no coherent life-plan, but even the "I" who is central to my having a life-plan at all is impaired.[11] Indeed, questions of power and success are trivial in comparison to this central ethical matter, of the harmony of my soul. So (Plato develops this point from Socrates, *Rep.* 436b

ff.) to be psychologically harmonious is just what it is to be happy; and for this the consistency of my beliefs is a necessary condition. Indeed, if the only fully consistent set of beliefs is the set of true beliefs—and if those beliefs are only explicitly held when reason rules in the soul—then consistency is not only a necessary condition for a proper ethical life; it is also a sufficient condition for a happy one.[12]

This radical acount of the relation between the logical matter of consistency and the ethical matter of happiness is, I suggest, fundamental to Plato's rejection of the practice of rhetoric (and thus of its art). For rhetorical persuasion can only mask the proper relations between my beliefs and interfere with the consistency of my soul. By contrast the elenchus (as would any other legitimate philosophical method) uncovers those relations and allows me to aspire toward a unified consciousness. And that—on Plato's thoroughgoing intellectualist account—is all that matters.

All this would be true for any rhetoric that is not based on knowledge. On the other hand, we might imagine a "real" rhetoric based on knowledge (*Phdr.* 270ff.). This, both in theory and in practice, would be a genuine science, free of the shenanigans of the Sophists. And in such a case rhetoric would turn out to be philosophy. So the "real" rhetor would be, we may suppose, a philosopher-king; his task would be to understand the soul of the persons to whom he speaks (*Phdr.* 270e) and to tailor his speeches to each soul "explaining what each soul is like and showing by what speeches and for what reason one is necessarily persuaded, the other not" (*Phdr.* 271b). Has Plato changed his mind about rhetoric? I think not. The *Phaedrus* shows what kind of epistemic claims the Sophist would have to make in order to defend himself against the criticisms launched in the *Gorgias*. If, Socrates here suggests, the rhetor *really* knew what he was doing, then he would really ("necessarily") persuade his audience. But such knowledge, Socrates insists, must be concerned first and foremost with the soul; it is in this deep understanding of psychology that the ordinary orator totally fails.[13]

This account of what ideal rhetoric might be points to Plato's third, *political* objection to the rhetors. Philosophers care for their souls; philosopher-kings care for the souls of their subjects. This means that the proper relations between the philosopher-king (the "real" rhetor) and the citizens in the state he rules should be uncontaminated by persuasion, unmuddied by the confusions of rhetoric. Instead they should be, as it were, soul to soul. Just as the elenchus demands of me that I be honest about my own beliefs, so "real" rhetoric demands that I be honest with everyone else. Contrariwise, if I fail to face the truth I am not merely mistaken; I am actively a corrupting influence on the state in which I live.

And for that reason rhetoric turns out to be morally reprobate and philosophy to be good for us, because philosophy cares for the soul while rhetoric doesn't mind what you (or anyone else) *really* believe, just so long as you are persuaded. Socrates worries most of all about deep psychological health. But the Sophists fail to concern themselves with sincerity and consistency because they are just interested in what goes on at the surface—they are just interested in winning. That superficiality, that misdirection is why rhetoric and sophistry are fatally misguided—on, to recapitulate, three grounds: epistemological (rhetoric is based on no objective truth), ethical (rhetoric is self-deceiving and thus bad for its practitioners), and political (rhetoric deceives others and damages the interests of those it addresses). Anyone who would rescue rhetoric needs to answer all three charges.

The Rhetors' Challenge

Plato did not, however, have the last word. He claimed that the professional rhetors had nothing to teach, because rhetoric is a non-subject. The professionals, on the other hand, both teachers of rhetoric and Sophists, claimed that, so far from philosophy excluding rhetoric, rhetoric encompasses philosophy. Philosophy is no special discipline; instead, philosophy as rhetoric takes over the world.

Alcidamas (e.g., *On Sophists* 3[14]) attacks people who write their speeches. Instead we should speak extempore, because that is not only a sign of the highest intellect, but useful, too. For speaking off the cuff, we can seize the rhetorical "moment" (*kairos*) and defend ourselves against any point that happens to come up. The extempore speech is alive (*On Sophists* 27) and has a mind of its own; a written speech, which lacks that spontaneity, is not real at all.[15]

Isocrates offers a deeper, but connected, defense of rhetoric. Rhetoric is not a fixed set of rules (*Against the Sophists* 12) but an ability. It is the power[16] to innovate, to be flexible in the face of the immediate circumstance, to seize the rhetorical moment. This is philosophy. Philosophy trains souls (*Antidosis* 181ff.), in a way complementary (*antistrophos*) to the skills of the gymnastic trainer. For after all, *logos* ("speech; argument") rules (*Antid.* 257)—it is the power (*dunamis*) by which we can secure the greatest goods. How? By conveying the truth as we can understand it (*Antid.* 271). What does that mean? Isocrates suggests that human truth is to be found in *nomos* (*Antid.* 82ff., 254ff.) not in nature. For that reason, the art of speaking which presents and discovers what is true by *nomos* is bound to be of fundamental importance and power.

The Sophists were held in contempt by Plato and Isocrates equally.[17] Sophists care only for winning—they will use any kind of argument, any sleight of tongue to achieve that end.[18] In the extreme cases they claim that whatever the opponent says they can tie him in knots; they can even argue that whatever they say must be true, whatever anyone else says cannot contradict them (Plato, *Euthd.* 283ff.). Thus they could be associated with a radical theory of truth: everything is true and contradiction is impossible (Plato, *Tht.* 151ff.); with an extreme logic: consistency does not matter (Plato, *Euthd.* 285); and with a moral nihilism that suggested that people are not to blame for anything they do (Gorgias, *Helen*).

Sophists like this are radical relativists. What of Isocrates? His job description commits him, it might appear, to the primacy of language: speech shapes our understanding of what there is.[19] Perhaps this comes from cultural relativism—everything we think or do is mediated by ideology.[20] Or perhaps Isocrates offers a theory of truth: what is true is exactly what is interpreted by us. Or perhaps Alcidamas and Isocrates were talking about art: what we invent or create matters at least as much as what happens to us; art and creativity alone allow us to escape the determined world of causes and effects. Any of those claims might appeal to someone practicing forensic or deliberative oratory, or to an epideictic rhetor. In court, for example, maybe the facts of the matter are determined (rather than discovered) by the judge; up to that point, there are only points of view, represented by the opposing parties.[21] That need not be out-and-out subjectivism; nor need it underpin a sophistic approach to forensic and political debate ("I'll do anything so long as I win my case"), which supposes that the end (winning) justifies any rhetorical means. On the contrary, the moral relativist like Isocrates may indeed be of unimpeachable character, only not convinced of the Platonic view that there are real, natural values unmediated by human thought. In that case, his claim to a skill or a science cannot be based on his access to objective truths; but then the sheer universality of rhetoric for someone like Isocrates might justify his claim that there are rules and principles to underpin his art of rhetoric. It is not, after all, true that a scientist cannot also be a relativist.

This view of rhetoric (which for brevity I shall call "Isocratean") might well be correct. First, maybe ideology does determine everything we say and do. Second, maybe the imagination is autonomous and thus an important manifestation of what it is to be human. Third (and perhaps consequently) value and virtue may indeed depend on the humans who employ them. Isocratean rhetoric, then, might turn out to be humanism and a thoroughly good thing; it may thus not be vulnerable to either the ethical or the political objections launched by Plato.

The Sophist and the Isocratean rhetor have one fundamental tenet in common: rhetoric is all-pervasive, nothing is free from rhetorical shape, nothing can be expressed without language, so language comes first. Rhetoric is communication—a relation between the rhetor and his audience. But in that case, the audience is an essential part of its definition. While Plato pays attention to truth and argument in souls, Isocrates thinks about the *social context*—the actual persons who give the speeches and the persons who hear them. Rhetoric is constituted by the interpersonal context in which it appears. And thus for Isocrates the Platonic distinction betwen real truth and the lying manipulation of the rhetors is misplaced—for there is only the truth that comes mediated by language. This may, indeed, be demonstrated pragmatically—by showing how there are always opposed arguments on any subject, by showing how people do disagree, with no serious hope of a decisive resolution. It is rhetoric itself that shows that no truth is unvarnished.

Isocrates, therefore, makes two points against Plato. Where Plato insists—almost solipsistically—on the integrity of persons, Isocrates insists on the social context of rhetoric, on the fact that rhetoric is communication between persons. So his first point, we might say, is sociological, a counter to Plato's ethical and political objections. His second point is about the nature of language and it counters Plato's epistemological objection that rhetorical practice is unsystematic. Where Plato insists that rhetoric is limited to the blandishments of dishonest speakers, Isocrates argues instead that rhetoric is all-pervasive: there is no speech (no meaningful speech) that is not communication. Rhetoric, that is, is just language: and it is therefore both systematic and a suitable object of a *technē*.

The Strategy of Aristotle's Rhetoric

These opposed views on the status of rhetoric suggest that we either go for all of it, or not at all. Given that rhetoric is a phenomenon of the marketplace, the debate about whether it can be systematically studied and whether it can be justified is clearly important. The contrast between the Platonic view and the Isocratean one is extreme, as I have characterized them, but no less compelling for that. Such, moreover, is clearly Aristotle's view, because he uses this debate as the opening gambit of the **Rhetoric;** and, as I shall argue, he hangs the theory of the work as a whole on the resolution of these opposed arguments.

It might be objected, of course, that the accounts I have given of Plato and Isocrates are mere thumbnail sketches, hardly doing justice to the real views of the men themselves. If Aristotle attacks this Plato and this Isocrates, he is tilting at historical windmills and his whole enterprise is thereby rendered ridiculous. But to that objection there are two retorts:

First, as a matter of evidence, Aristotle himself sets up the dispute between Plato and the rhetorical tradition to which Isocrates was heir. For the opening of the **Rhetoric** invokes directly the imagery and the arguments of both these parties to the rhetorical debate, as I shall argue. So in what follows I shall treat this Plato and this Isocrates as theoretical constructs, part of the apparatus of Aristotle's developing argument.

Second, as a matter of method, think of Aristotle's standard procedure, dominated by two maxims: "save the phenomena" and "start with the *endoxa.*"[22] Now people do rhetoric all the time—in the street and in the schoolroom, in the agora and in court; here are the phenomena. But then the question arises how we are to *explain* the phenomena. When it comes to explanation, we should look first to the *endoxa,* the opinions of the many and the wise—especially so that we may find ourselves a good puzzle, one where the opposed opinions are clearly set out but still unresolved (**Metaph.** 3.1, 995a28ff.). On rhetoric, then, Aristotle should perhaps turn first to Plato and Isocrates, his concern not so much historical fidelity (he is no doxographer) but the setting out of a good puzzle—and between the positions of Plato and Isocrates, as I have presented them, there is just that sort of puzzle.

But if Aristotle starts with the appearances, he cannot simply reject the appearance that there are both rhetoric and philosophy, each separate from the other but both practiced (whether by the many or by the few) in a systematic way. Instead, he must negotiate the middle ground between his wise predecessors to arrive at a solution; the solution must fully explain why Plato and Isocrates disagreed, and how the appearances can be saved after all. The resolution is not just a matter of picking one side or the other; instead, progress consists in the discovery of a new approach or new understanding—not just adjudicating between the old. The test of Aristotle's success in this balancing act is whether we can see how the new explanation does indeed supplant the old, and resolve the opposed arguments on the way.

Aristotle first invokes his predecessors by echoing their language. He starts his account of rhetoric with a challenge, "Rhetoric is *antistrophos* to dialectic." This gauntlet is not merely thrown at the feet of Plato,[23] who wants to say that rhetoric is the counterpart of cookery, and so not a proper *technē* at all (*Grg.* 465d7-e1). Isocrates too had claimed that rhetoric (philosophy) has a counterpart, the proper training of the body (*Antid.* 181-82). Isocrates and Plato both use analogy (rhetoric is *antistrophos* to something else) to show either that rhetoric is nothing at all (as is cookery) or that it is in fact proper philosophy (just as gymnastic is proper physical training). Aristotle, however, tries to turn the tables on both men, by offering not an analogy between rhetoric and some unrelated skill but instead a formal comparison between the argumentative techniques of rhetoric and those of dialectic. So there are both philosophy and rhetoric, similar and yet formally distinct. Aristotle must establish that distinction against both Plato and Isocrates.

"Enthymeme is the body of conviction" (**Rhet.** 1.1.3, 1354a15). This is Aristotle's claim for the argumentative core of rhetoric, and it exploits both Platonic imagery and a complex analogy offered by Alcidamas. For Plato, the comparison between rhetoric in its contemporary form and true philosophy is the contrast between the flattering clothes and cosmetics that disguise the reality, and the real beauty of the naked truth (*Grg.* 464c ff.). But when rhetoric is transmuted into philosophy (*Phdr.* 276a ff.), it has a body that can act on its own and defend its own ideas; it comes alive.[24] For Alcidamas, proper rhetoric—the immediate activity of improvisation—is alive, it is a real creature with a mind of its own; but the written word is just a fake, an image of reality. For Aristotle, enthymematic argument is the body of conviction, real or apparent, able to come to the defense of the truth (**Rhet.** 1.1.12, 1355a39). We may think it wears the clothes of politics (**Rhet.** 1.2.7, 1356a27); but true rhetoric is the body within (compare **Rhet.** 3.14.8, 1415b8-9), a part and the image of dialectic (**Rhet.** 1.2.7, 1356a31).

Aristotle's deployment of his precedessors' imagery reflects the play of his argument, where he resolves this dispute between the philosophers and the rhetors; and he appropriates their language for his own account of rhetoric. The argument of the opening chapters has the same character. The opening chapters of the *Rhetoric* may seem to vacillate between different points of view,[25] but once Aristotle's use of the endoxic method is remembered and once his deployment of rhetorical devices to invoke his opposed arguments is noticed, the apparent vacillation begins to look like a coherent argument. Consider the argument of the opening chapters in stages.

1. Is rhetoric a *technē*? Plato says it is not; Aristotle says it is, but a general one, about common principles. The truth of this is obvious from the fact that people employ rhetoric both automatically and as a result of deliberate practice. So there must be a technical procedure.[26] And yet current writers on rhetoric (Isocrates and co.?) miss the technical center of rhetoric; they write, instead, about the "clothes" of rhetoric. They fail to see that the enthymeme is the "body of conviction"; instead they occupy themselves with peripheral matters, such as how to affect the jurors. This must be wrong; well-run states forbid speaking "outside the matter." Only if rhetoric is centered on argument is it morally correct; to try to affect the emotions of the judge is like trying to make a straight ruler crooked.[27] So the disputants have no other task than to prove the case *(to pragma)*—did it happen or did it not? The decision whether it was done well or badly, justly or

otherwise is a matter that should be left to the judge (**Rhet.** 1.1. 1-6, 1354a1-31).

This opening salvo opposes the "body" of rhetoric to its clothes, rhetorical argument (the enthymeme) to improper attempts to sway the emotions of the jurors. So against Plato Aristotle first claims that rhetoric has a technical core, namely its arguments; against Isocrates that some rhetoric is illicit (whatever is outside the subject).

2. Aristotle goes on to consider the role of the judge (or the assembly). His opening gambit might have suggested that there is no need for a judge or an assembly (because the orator should properly discuss only the facts of the matter). But even the best-constituted states need judges—after all, the laws are general, and the job of the jury is to judge the particular. So the jury is needed to decide the facts of the matter in the particular case, but nothing further. And for this reason the rhetors' discussion of emotion is outside the subject, for this is about affecting the juror in a particular way; the rhetors should have discussed the technical convictions (*entechnai pisteis*) that make someone enthymematic (**Rhet.** 1.1.7-9, 1354a31-b22).

Here Areistotle repudiates both the actual activities of contemporary rhetors and Isocrates' theoretical claim that rhetoric is all-pervasive and thus morally neutral—on the contrary, rhetors should not manipulate their audience. Like Plato, Aristotle wants to prescribe "true" rhetoric—as the non-manipulative presentation of a case to a judging audience. Unlike Plato, Aristotle allows the activities of ordinary judges (not ideal or Socratic ones) to be important and legitimate.

3. He returns to the attack on the technical writers. They concentrate on forensic oratory, because it provides a better opportunity for manipulating the audience, with the result that the jurors "surrender a decision," they do not judge. This is why some states prohibit speaking "outside the subject." Why are juries easily manipulated? Assemblies are deliberating about their own interests while juries are judging what does not concern them. The very detachment of juries from the case—Aristotle suggests—makes them easily swayed when the orator does introduce their interests (and when by doing so he embarks on what is outside the case; **Rhet.** 1.1.10, 1354b22-55a3)

4. Rhetoric is about conviction (*pistis*); and conviction is demonstration of a kind—for we are convinced most of all when we accept that the point has been demonstrated.[28] This is achieved by the enthymeme, which is the rhetorical equivalent of a dialectical argument and is the most authoritative of the convictions. So just as there are rules for dialectical arguments, there are rules for enthymematic argument; therefore there is a technique of rhetoric—

namely the capacity to see "the truth and what is like it" (that is, for rhetoric no less than for dialectic, experts are able to see when the arguments have followed the rules).[29] And after all, we are naturally inclined toward the truth—so the same person can make a stab at[30] the truth and at the *endoxa*.[31] (***Rhet.*** 1.1. 11, 1355a3-18).

Here Aristotle claims that rhetoric has at its center a series of argumentative (logical) rules; so, he concludes, there can be experts in rhetoric (which Plato denies), provided they concentrate on what rhetoric is really about—argument (which Isocrates and co. ignore). At this stage, he has turned the other way again, to repudiate the Platonic view that there is no subject matter for rhetoric; the theory of the enthymeme is designed to respond to exactly that difficulty.

5. Aristotle returns to the problem of the technical writers. Clearly they do write about what is outside the subject (that follows from the centrality of the enthymeme). But rhetoric is useful just because we are naturally predisposed in favor of the truth. Rhetoric allows the truth clear expression, without which it might shamefully be defeated. It substitutes for scientific demonstration in cases where the people in the audience are so appalling[32] that no manner of scientific knowledge could convince them; and its ability to argue on both sides does not commit us to acting inconsistently but enables us to understand and resist the view of the opposition (***Rhet.*** 1.1.12, 1355a19-33).

Now rhetoric is persuasion, justified by the natural moral priority of the truth. Here, then, Aristotle seems to prefer Isocratean rhetoric to the austerity of Plato. In order to persuade, rhetors need to know how to argue on both sides of the case. Plato's objection was that thus the rhetor could persuade his audience of anything, whatever the truth of the matter. But Aristotle returns, to rebut this, to his comparison with dialectic. Rhetoric and dialectic are alone in being able to argue on both sides of a case. But this does not imply that each side is indifferent to the truth; rather, what is naturally true and what is naturally better are more easily argued and more convincing. So rhetoric allows us to defend ourselves verbally as well as physically. That it may be used for immoral ends is true; but it is a common feature of many things, that used properly they are of great benefit, while used improperly they do great harm (***Rhet.*** 1.1.12-13, 1355a33-b7).

6. This is the first move in Aristotle's case against the view that rhetoric is manipulative and morally unsound. On the contrary, he argues, rhetoric is the means to protect the natural rightness of truth; the fact that it may be exploited for bad ends is no reason to throw out the whole of the persuasive art. So, Aristotle concludes, it is clear that rhetoric is a general *technē* like dialectic. What is more, it is valuable, not trivial nor

manipulative, because it is there to discover the available possibilities in each case. So rhetoric is interested in what is actually plausible and what appears so,[33] just as dialectic is concerned with syllogisms and apparent syllogisms. Rhetoric differs from sophistic in its intention, not its capacity. (***Rhet.*** 1.1.14, 1355b8-21).

7. In the second chapter Aristotle embarks on a more detailed analysis of the "convictions" and offers his tripartite analysis of the subject matter of rhetoric—the arguments, the speaker, and the audience. He opens with a new definition: "Rhetoric is the power of considering the possible plausibility in each case." For rhetoric differs from the other arts and skills, each of which both teach and persuade about their particular subject matter. Rhetoric, on the contrary, has as its subject matter what is plausible about any topic whatever—and thus it spans the subject matter of all the particular arts (***Rhet.*** 1.2.1, 1355b25-34).

8. Aristotle returns to the notion of "technical convictions," which are to be contrasted with the convictions that are ready to hand (witnesses and tortures etc.). The technical convictions are the ones we supply or discover for ourselves, and they are three: the character of the speaker; the disposition of the audience; and the demonstration, or apparent demonstration, of the case. Of these, the conviction through the character of the speaker is the most authoritative, in those cases where the character of the speaker comes across through the speech itself—for in cases like that our moral inclination to believe the speaker speeds up the process of persuasion. The conviction that comes from the audience occurs when the audience is affected by something in the speech (after all, our reactions are different when we hate or love, are happy or sad); and this is the preoccupation of the technical writers. Convictions produced by the arguments are evidenced when we show a truth or an apparent truth from what is plausible in each case (***Rhet.*** 1.2.2-6, 1355b25-56a20).

9. If rhetoric has indeed this tripartite structure, then it is the task of the rhetor to consider arguments *and* character *and* affections, so that rhetoric is an offshoot of dialectic and politics. It puts on the clothing of politics—but it is in fact a part and an analogue of dialectic, not having any particular subject matter other than argument itself (***Rhet.*** 1.2.7, 1356a20-33).

Aristotle returns here to the language of Plato to reinforce the position of ***Rhetoric*** 1.1, occupying the middle ground between Plato and Isocrates. The universal nature of rhetoric ensures that the subject matter of the art of rhetoric is argument, not politics—it has a political appearance because these arguments are presented *by speakers, to an audience*. Rhetorical arguments are *contextualized* in the political arena. Yet Aristotle continues to suggest that argument, not politics, is the distinguishing mark of rhetoric, and to press the similarity between rhetoric and dialectic as he draws a parallel between the enthymeme and the syllogism, the example and induction: these alone are the means to produce conviction through argument. These arguments are *plausible* (**Rhet.** 1.2.8-10, 1356a34-b27).

Plausible, however, means plausible *to someone* whether directly or mediated by some argument. But if rhetoric is to be a *technē,* then like dialectic it must concern itself with the general, not the particular—with what people believe, not what appeals to Socrates or to Callias. Yet rhetoric and dialectic differ in their subject matter—dialectic is about what needs explaining, rhetoric about what needs deciding. So rhetoric is about what could be otherwise, what we can affect—and it takes place especially before audiences that cannot cope with long chains of reasoning (**Rhet.** 1.2.11-12, 1356b28-57a7).

The course of Aristotle's argument in these two chapters is hardly straightforward (so that it is tempting to blame it all on a muddle in the text). In the first chapter Aristotle works by contrasting opposed views of the definientia of rhetoric. There is (my section 1) a difference between rhetorical *arguments* (the most authoritative persuasions) and the manipulation of the emotions of the audience (by the devices of the technical writers—prologue etc.). Then (2-3) there is a contrast between the proper reaction of the people in the *audience* (a proper judgment) and their "surrendering" to the orator; this corresponds to cases where their interests have been left untouched, and those where they have been illicitly involved. And finally (4-6) there is the opposition of the moral and the immoral use of rhetorical technique by the *speaker,* where what is moral sides with the truth, what is immoral with the reverse. All of these contrasts work against the background of a play-off between Plato and Isocrates, as Aristotle gradually refines his position away from either extreme. He argues, that is, that the art of rhetoric is not to be collapsed into dialectic nor allowed to take over all speech. Instead he grants the practice of rhetoric a quite precise description (the enthymeme is its body) and a specific task (to defend the truth against fabricators). In that case, the practice of rhetoric can be formalized—there can be an art of rhetoric (this meets Plato's epistemological objection). At the same time, Aristotle fends off the Isocratean view (that rhetoric is all-pervasive) by showing that the manipulative part of rhetoric (what is off the point) is not a proper part of it; nonetheless, it does have a persuasive aspect (rather than a purely argumentative one) because the circumstances prohibit pure argument in many cases; and our duty to defend the truth positively urges us to use rhetorical techniques in its defense (this meets Plato's ethical objection).

In the second chapter (my 7-9), Aristotle seems to change direction. He continues to press the idea that

rhetoric is the counterpart of dialectic because it is about the common features of speech. But his emphasis has altered. While the first chapter talked about argument, the second focuses instead on the business of persuasion (and it is here, no doubt, that the lines of fracture between two versions of the **Rhetoric** may appear). Indeed, the text as we have it seems to contain a direct inconsistency. In **Rhetoric** 1.1 the "most authoritative of the convictions" was the enthymeme; in 1.2 it is the character of the speaker; and the program of 1.2 is picked up in the rest of the work, which discusses not only the formality of the enthymeme, but also (with just as heavy emphasis) the character of the speaker and the emotions of the audience (not to mention the analysis of rhetorical or literary style offered in the final book). We may be forced to conclude that the interplay between Plato and Isocrates was a feature of the first chapter alone—while the rest of the work reflects a more workmanlike treatment of the rhetorical practices of Aristotle's time—Aristotle's own *ars rhetorica* purified of Platonic influence.

That, perhaps, is a counsel of despair; particularly because from a Platonic perspective Aristotle's own theory is vulnerable to criticism. Plato's objection to rhetoric was that since, both in theory and in practice, it fails the test for a *technē* it also fails the ethical (political) test for the proper care for the soul (of its practitioner or its audience or its pupil). Aristotle's first defense against Plato is to reinstate the technical status of rhetoric by giving it a subject matter (rhetorical arguments, especially enthymemes). But he elaborates this position by suggesting, first, that rhetoric also has an ethical function (the defense of the truth) and second that it has (what I have called) political status as well, because it is concerned both with the character of the speaker and the emotions of the audience.[34] How far, Plato might ask, are these different aspects of rhetoric unified into a single *technē*? He might object, first, that while his arguments in favor of philosophy provide a *necessary* connection between knowledge and happiness (or virtue), Aristotle has merely taken for granted the connection between enthymematic arguments and the natural value of the truth. Plato might complain, second, that unless there is some rigorous account to be given of the relation between rhetorical arguments and the virtue of the speaker then rhetoric is still open to abuse and vulnerable to the charge that if the orators are merely interested in winning the argument, the art of rhetoric just cares for showing them how to do it. Isocrates may argue the opposite case. If rhetoric as it appears in the market place is a relation between persons, and Aristotle insists that it is a system of formalized argument, has he saved the phenomena at all?

We may put this point a different way. As a result of the opposed arguments of Plato and Isocrates, Aristotle has isolated two aspects of the art of rhetoric: the argumentative one, in which it resembles dialectic, and the "persuasive" or sociological one, in which it resembles the activities of the technical writers. How far are these aspects of Aristotelian rhetoric properly connected? On the one hand, Aristotle may (disappointingly) simply have declared that these are two aspects of the same thing (rather than two quite separate and different notions of rhetoric); he saves the phenomena, then, by fiat and not by argument—and is himself the victim of the opposed arguments. On the other hand, he may be arguing that rhetoric is an organic unity, which displays these two aspects, and that both Plato and Isocrates were wrong, one-sided in their views. Persuasion and argument, in this view, are naturally one thing. But then he badly needs to explain what that unity would be. Unless Aristotle can show that there is some *essential* connection between rhetorical arguments, the character of the speaker, and the emotions of the audience, then his theory of rhetoric may just be a gluing together of his predecessors' views (just as the text itself may be badly joined) without any proper theoretical unity of its own. And this, of course, is exactly the challenge that Aristotle has set himself, by his strategy of presenting the opposed arguments of the wise.

In *Rhet.* 1.1 Aristotle moved from the point about rhetoric being a *technē*, through the charge that it is manipulative, to conclude that the method of enthymeme is thoroughly respectable. At each stage he resisted both the Platonic and the Isocratean account, because he insisted on a clear differentiation between rhetoric and dialectic; and at each stage he suggested that the proper ("inside the matter") methods employed by the orator are technical and susceptible to analysis. His distinction between "inside" and "outside" the matter is clearly crucial to his position; this allows him to reject the view that all communication is legitimate rhetoric, while continuing to assert that there is a technical core. The problem arises when we try to determine how much more than argument proper lies "inside" the subject of rhetoric. After all, the remainder of the *Rhetoric* deals not only with rhetorical argument forms, but also with the character of the speaker and the affection of the audience—if Aristotle's own work exemplifies his own definition of rhetoric, we should expect the definition to contain all three aspects. So from the outset, he needs to show that the *context* of rhetorical argument is as much one of its definientia as the arguments themselves. And he must explain then how rhetoric turns out to be a unified whole, rather than an accidental association of argument and context, and consequently how his own theory of rhetoric is not merely an uncomfortable amalgam of Plato with Isocrates, but a coherent unity.

He might begin with the old Platonic metaphor. Suppose our rhetor is standing up in a (well-constituted) court and hoping to persuade the jury of the innocence of his client. Over and over again Aristotle points out that the enthymeme alone is not enough to do that; and often he concedes that the enthymeme is indeed unsuitable for such a task. What then determines what is legitimate in such cases? The answer to that still must be "the enthymeme itself" because it is the *body* of conviction. Suppose that the rhetor's argument can be understood in terms of an enthymeme (or a paradeigma)—even if it is not fully expressed that way—then what he says may be counted legitimate. If, on the other hand, there is no central argument holding his speech together, then what he says should be ruled out of court. If there is an argument beneath what he says, than anything that *represents that argument* to the audience is licit; whatever is not organically related *to that argument* is to be discounted as sheer manipulation. The metaphor of a body and its clothes is fundamental—enthymeme is the body of conviction; the reasonable use of *ēthos* and *pathos* will be genuine natural parts of the rhetorical episode, cohering by virtue of their relation to its body. Conversely, manipulative appeals to the emotions will be separable from the argumentative body, the clothes it can take off and do without. So what is licit and what is not are determined simply by whether they are related to, naturally connected with, or relevant to the enthymeme that lies at the heart of the episode (even if, as may happen in cases of particularly inadequate audiences, the enthymeme is not formally expressed). The enthymeme, then, is what holds the whole thing together, the formal (formalizable) argument at the heart of the speech. The context (the dispositions or whatever of the persons involved) is whatever is necessary to and inseparable from the central argument—all the rest is superfluous cosmetics and should be illegal.

Can this metaphor be supported by argument? I shall suggest that it can, for Aristotle's account of the enthymeme is such as to locate it firmly in the context, first of value (the interests of the various parties) and then in the twin issues of character and emotion; this takes up the discussion of the first two books of the **Rhetoric.**

Rhetorical Arguments

Aristotle's first defense of rhetoric against Plato is that there are rhetorical arguments that can be formalized; this then legitimates both the practice and the art of rhetoric. Rhetoric's arguments are enthymemes.

Now Aristotle's solution to the Platonic problem must meet two conditions: First, he must show that rhetoric's arguments are indeed specific to rhetoric (and not dialectic in disguise) but still general (so that rhetoric does not collapse into, say, physics). Second, he must demonstrate that their specific features are an intrinsic feature of the arguments themselves (an argumentative or logical feature), rather than part of the way they are presented. After all, if the enthymeme is just a dialectical argument *presented in a persuasive way,* there would after all be no special subject matter for rhetoric, only a special attitude to the subject matter of dialectic. So Aristotle needs an account of the enthymeme that is logical or epistemological, not psychological or rhetorical.

Accordingly, Aristotle contrasts two modes of argument—the arguments with which dialectic deals, and enthymemes. The former are about what is generally true; the latter are about *pisteis* (e.g., **Rhet.** 1.1, 1354a13,15,b21; 1355a3,4,5,7,28; 1.2, 1356a1,b6); about what is *pithanon* (e.g., 1.1, 1355a38; 1.2, 1355b11,15, 26, 32; 1356a20); what is *endoxon* (e.g., 1.1, 1355a17; 1.2, 1356b33); what is *endechomenon* (e.g., 1.2, 1355b13, 26; 1357a14, 24); what is *eikos* (e.g., 1.2, 1357a34). Several of these expressions are common to earlier discussions of rhetoric (e.g., *pithanon, Grg.* 456c, *Phdr.* 269c; *eikos, Phdr.* 267a ff.); but in those contexts they emphasize *persuasion*—as indeed do the translations we are inclined to use—"conviction," "plausible," "generally believed," "likely" (*endechomenon* is an important exception, "contingent"). How can persuasion be a condition for formal argument in the Aristotelian mode?

Consider the phenomena once again. Rhetoric happens in two special places, the court and the assembly. There what is at stake is not the eternal verities (as is true of scientific knowledge) but *either* individual matters of fact ("did he do it?") *or* general matters of practical policy ("should we exact a poll tax?"). Aristotle recognizes both these special features of rhetoric (cf., e.g., the problems of corruption in a jury trial, **Rhet.** 1.1.10, 1354b23ff.).

First, he argues that the reason for having judges and juries is that particular matters of fact cannot be decided by the legislator, who deals only in generalities. In the ideal situation, therefore, the judge is concerned with deciding (as little as possible, but) whether it happened or not, is or is not the case, will or will not be a consequence (**Rhet.** 1.1.7, 1354a31-b16). Now these decisions are not taken at random, but with thought; but because they involve particular premises ("this is the man whose fingerprints are on the blunt instrument"), they are not susceptible to demonstration in the full sense of the word—they are not amenable to scientific understanding (whatever the state of the fingerprinting art).

Second, enthymemes are not about what is necessary, but about what is "for the most part," or what could be otherwise (e.g., **Rhet.** 1.2.14, 1357a22ff.). Why? Aristotle makes the same point about the subject matter of ethics.[35] If we are going to decide what to do, there is no point in deciding to do something that cannot be affected by us (**Rhet.** 1.2.12, 1357a4). Practical reasoning is not about the shape of the earth, but about

how to get to the marketplace and why. Political reasoning is about practical reasoning, generally understood—so it is about what we can effect as a matter of general policy (poll tax for everyone, free school milk, regular symposia).[36] The conclusions of such reasoning will be general, but not necessary (some people may refuse to pay their poll tax, the last child in the queue may not get any milk, the symposia may be ruthlessly terminated). That they are "capable of being otherwise" does not make them irrational, but it does make them improper subjects for scientific reasoning (the rhetor's subject matter of rhetoric differs from the physicist's, insofar as physics is about the general rules that may have exceptions; rhetoric is especially about the things that could be otherwise—cf. **Rhet.** 1.4.1-3, 1359a35ff.).

If rhetoric is what happens in the lawcourts and in the assembly,[37] then rhetoric always involves either what is particular or what is general but could be otherwise (compare the discussion of equity at **Rhet.** 1.13.13, 1374a29ff.). How far are either of those two matters amenable to formal argument?

Particular matters of fact, we might easily concede, are objective, they happened, and the propositions describing them are objectively and straightforwardly true. They can be assimilated to argument in one of two ways—either by existential quantification, or by treatment as examples of a general law—and thus they can figure either as propositions in a deductive argument or as steps in an induction. But in neither case do they provide a very sound basis for any general claim (Aristotle dismisses their contribution to argument at **Rhet.** 1.2.18, 1357b13); they cannot found a necessary proposition[38]—at worst a contingent one (the existential quantification), at best a "for the most part" (a general law derived from induction). Individually, they are not enough for either induction or deduction proper; instead, they partake of the rhetorical forms enthymeme and example (**Rhet.** 1.2.10, 1356b21ff.)

General issues of policy may not fit easily into argumentative form for a quite different reason—here arguments contain not only matters of fact but matters of opinion and evaluations of their use or general desirability. That, at any rate, may be our view of value judgments—and it may also have been Isocrates'. But Aristotle's view, it seems, was rather different. His analysis of value (the good) in the **Nicomachean Ethics**[39] starts from a metaphysical point about essence and function, and a linguistic point about the performance of the word *good* (it is syncategorematic). Value, in Aristotle's view, is an expression of the essence or form of something; it is defined in terms of good functioning and not determined by the eye of the beholder or the view of the valuer.[40] In that case, it is perfectly possible to have general, objective value judgments operating as the premises in an argument (compare the discussion of natural justice, ***Rhet.*** 1.13.2-3, 1373b4ff.).

Yet, because value reflects what we pursue and avoid, such judgments must represent things we can choose to pursue or avoid; so even if they are general, they cannot be necessary, for otherwise there would be no point in deliberating about them at all (but that is what rhetoric must do, ***Rhet.*** 1.2.12, 1357a1). Moreover, value is a matter of dispute (as Plato had observed, *Euthyphro* 4eff. and as Aristotle agrees—compare the decision procedures offered in ***Rhetoric*** 1.7). Hence deliberative rhetoric, because it is about value, may well be disputatious (***Rhet.*** 1.3.5-6, 1358b20ff.); this may be the source of disagreement and opposed arguments (cf. ***Rhet.*** 1.6.17, 1362b29ff.). That value is a matter of dispute may lead us to suppose that it is in some sense relative; but this does not make value merely subjective. Consider two sorts of evaluative relativity: i) Helen may be beautiful relative to Quasimodo, ugly in comparison to Aphrodite; nonetheless, Helen's beauty may still be an intrinsic, natural feature of Helen, not something bestowed upon her by the onlooker. Relativity of value does not imply subjectivity. ii) Seawater may be good for fishes and poisonous for humans. This does not imply that its goodness is in the eye of the fish and so subjective, but rather that its goodness is relative to creatures with gills: value may be objective and still relative.

Can these two different sorts of proposition—the statement of particular fact and the value judgment—be incorporated into rhetorical logic? Aristotle seems to think so (***Rhet.*** 1.2.14-15, 1357a30-b3 and a more systematic view at 1.9.40, 1368a25ff.; cf. 2.25.8-10, 1402b13ff.)

The particular statement is a "sign," a *sēmeion;* the general (but not necessary) proposition is a "likelihood," an *eikos*. Both may figure as the premises of enthymemes (***Rhet.*** 2.25.8, 1402b13ff.); and that seems to be the distinctive feature of enthymematic argument (***Rhet.*** 1.3.7, 1359a6-10). Some of these arguments could, perhaps, be formalized and set out in the same way as is the syllogism (cf. ***Rhet.*** 1.2.13, 1357a15).[41] However, the modality of the propositions in rhetoric must be different from the modality of demonstration. For the propositions in demonstration are necessary, while rhetoric needs a modality of possibility or contingency (***Rhet.*** 1.3.8, 1359a11ff.), *to endechomenon*[42] (***Rhet.*** 1.12.2, 1372a9ff., where this figures in the calculations of the criminal; 2.18.3, 1391b27ff.).

Now contingency and possibility are defined not in subjective terms (as what is plausible to someone or other) but in objective terms (what can happen but may not; what does follow but may not, 1.2.18, 1357b19; 1.4.1, 1359a31ff. "Did he do it?" "Is this law worth the paper it's written on?" "Can I get away with it?" "probably"; "probably not.").[43] In that case, the logic of rhetoric is about propositions that are likely (*eikos, **Rhet.*** 1.2.15, 1357a34)—that is, likely to be true objectively.

Has Aristotle shown that the art of rhetoric is a *technē* in its own right, not to be collapsed into any other, whether general or specific? Rhetoric concerns ethics, politics, and jurisprudence; but the art of rhetoric is none of them, because it is *about* argument, not directly about value or justice or expediency. In that way it is general, like dialectic (and like nothing else). But dialectic is about things that need explaining, rhetoric is about things that need deciding.[44] So its generality is determined by its modality—what is contingent, possible, or even probable.[45] Rhetoric's treatment of contingency, however, differs from the way in which physics, for example, deals with the exceptions to the rules (what happens "for the most part").[46] In physics the exceptions are incorporated into the rules; they are explained by virtue of what happens generally, regularly, as a matter of natural course. In ethics, however, and so in rhetoric, "for the most part" points to the way in which the world can be affected by our action (cf, e.g., ***Rhet.*** 1.4.3, 1359a35ff.; 2.21.2, 1394a25ff.). In ethics possibility is about what could be otherwise; in physics things could be otherwise, but they occur according to natural regularities that are not otherwise. So while dialectic may deal with propositions that are universal or accidental, rhetoric deals with what is contingent per se.[47]

"Rhetoric is *antistrophos* to dialectic"—Aristotle's programmatic remark should not be taken lightly. On the contrary, his opposition to the Platonic view of rhetoric (*antistrophos* to cookery) reflects his view of the real world. Rhetoric happens, so it cannot be denied; and it does have an argumentative center, governed by the modality of contingency. If any sense can be made of the modality of contingency or of Aristotle's version of it, then Aristotle can argue that the practice of rhetoric can be systematized into a *technē*; and he has his first point against Plato. What is more, his account of natural value allows him to suppose, against Isocrates, that the evaluative fabric of the world exists independently of us, prior to speech and understanding. In that case there is a difference between the objective core of rhetoric and communication in general; and Aristotle may deny that rhetoric is all-pervasive. On both grounds he is entitled to claim that there is after all an art of rhetoric.

Souls and Enthymemes

So Aristotle may resist an Isocratean account of rhetoric as (any) communication by insisting on an austere description of the logic of the enthymeme. He may also resist Plato's denial that the practice of rhetoric is systematic. But in the process he may lay himself open to Plato's ethical complaints—in a rather unexpected way.

For Plato, I suggested, arguments take place in souls (logic and ethics are thus inextricably linked). Aristotle, by contrast, has a thoroughly austere view of argument (*Top.* 1. 1, 100a25ff). Arguments are collections of propositions,[48] where the premises are causally related to the conclusion. Different sorts of premise generate different sorts of conclusion—the premises may be quantified differently, or modally qualified. But all arguments are significantly similar in one important respect—that the premises *generate* the conclusion.[49] Why?

Take the primary case—of scientific understanding. Here the premises generate the conclusion because they explain why the conclusion is true. What is more, in grasping the argument we understand why the conclusion is so. The explanation, as Aristotle puts it, *makes* the understanding (*A Po.* 1.2, 71b20-25). To cite causes is to explain, to get an explanation is to understand.[50] But causal relations are real relations in the world; so understanding comes from real states of affairs in the world (especially from essential features of the world). If *p* explains *q,* the reason is that the state of affairs that *p* describes is a "cause" (in the special Aristotelian sense, a "because") of *q*. Our understanding of that is a *direct consequence* of the argument that represents the facts of the matter—so the cognitive state (understanding) follows from the real state of affairs.[51] Let us say that arguments are *transitive*—the facts are transmitted through the arguments to the mind that receives them.[52]

On this view of the metaphysics of understanding, the mind's role is largely a passive one. Aristotle's account of the logical relations between propositions confirms this impression. His syllogistic system is based on the insight that validity can be determined *by inspection* in the paradigm cases.[53] An apodeictic syllogism in Barbara is *obviously* valid, because of the structure of the syllogism and the operators on the propositions it contains. But if validity is (sometimes) obvious, then validity is one of the phenomena that Aristotle is committed to save. It is an actual, objective relation between propositions—not something that we impose on argument or make up as we go along. Validity is a matter of logical fact, not a hypothesis of theory—and certainly not a piece of ideology.

Aristotle makes mileage from that. For if validity (a relation between propositions of particular types) is obvious, then formalization of arguments is possible; our systematic understanding may then (if argument is transitive) follow. But to understand arguments is then a very different thing from inventing them. Arguments just are valid; we see them as valid because they are

so, not the other way about; and so we also see logical system because it is actually there—system is not imposed by the minds of those who understand it. Once again, then, and for logical reasons, arguments cause understanding; and the understander plays a relatively passive role. The same psychological account may be true for the enthymeme. Thus we are convinced when we take something to have been demonstrated (*Rhet.* 1.1. 1355a5); so we are primarily convinced by argument (not by the character of the speaker or by our own emotions). Conviction follows from demonstration[54]—rhetorical arguments are transitive.[55]

In that case, conviction is something that *happens* to us in the face of a rhetorical argument—we directly receive the argument itself (we perceive it, cf. *Rhet.* 2.23. 30, 1400b30ff.) Being convinced, on that view, is not like being persuaded ("Will I?" "Won't I?"); for being convinced does not reflect some decision procedure on our part. Nor is being convinced like feeling an emotion—for it is not a feeling at all but would better be understood as a purely cognitive mental event. Hence "conviction is a demonstration" (*Rhet.* 1.1.11, 1355a5), produced by the two sorts of rhetorical argument, *paradeigma* and enthymeme (1.2.8, 1356b6). So what happens—if rhetorical arguments are indeed transitive in this way—is that an argument about possibility can then be described as *plausible* to its audience. Thus rhetoric deals with what is possible *and* what is plausible (*to pithanon*). Plausibility turns up both as a general possibility (1.2.1, 1355b26) and as a particular issue (1.2.6, 1356a20); but in either case, what is genuinely plausible (cf. 3.1.3, 1403b19) should be distinguished from what merely appears so (1.1.14, 1355b15).[56] So the job of rhetoric is to "see the existing plausibilities in each case" (1.1.14, 1355b10)—just as in ordinary logic validity is a formal feature of the argument itself.[57]

But still what is plausible is plausible *to someone* (*Rhet.* 1.2.11, 1356b28). If we understand Aristotle's account of argument in the austere way I have described (arguments are transitive), then both the speaker of a rhetorical argument and its audience will be insignificant in the definition of what rhetoric is. The delivery of rhetorical arguments will be a series of bare events that happen to both speaker and hearer—and there will be nothing left to the rhetor's insistence that rhetoric is about communication between persons. There will be no agents in rhetoric, and no acts—merely events and things.[58] Plausibility will collapse into objective possibility, and persuasion will simply be the result of a rhetorical argument's happening to its audience.

If that were Aristotle's position, it would be an uncomfortable one. First of all, it would be hard to understand how, or why, arguments from contingency would be constructed at all. Unlike pure syllogisms, they cannot be purely formal, because they are embedded in the possibilities *that interest us*. So while a dialectician may care about formality for argument's sake, our interest in contingency comes from the hope, or the fear, that things may indeed turn out that way. Enthymemes, that is, cannot be formalised away from their context in the easy way that syllogisms can. To give a Platonic objection: Aristotle has, if he offers a theory of bare argument to explain rhetoric, ignored the ethical dimension of Plato's charge against the rhetors and the sophists.

Second, if the audience of an enthymeme, by hearing it, simply suffers it then Aristotle's account of the art of rhetoric will be vulnerable to Plato's charge that rhetoric exercises force majeure over its audience. And yet this conclusion is clearly one that Aristotle wants to avoid—consider, for example, the way he contrasts the passivity of a manipulated jury (they "surrender a verdict") with the activity of proper judgment.

Third, I have suggested that Aristotle treats plausibility as equivalent to possibility. But that—given his insistence that what is plausible is plausible to someone—surely will not do. Possibility may be construed (and formalized) in terms of actual and possible events in the world. Plausibility, however, is about how events or things or persons or arguments appear to us; plausibility must have an audience. Bare enthymemes (again on the transitive view of argument) have no audience—only a recipient, and any recipient would be as good as another. If rhetoric is genuinely about what is plausible, there must be some real role for the audience to play. Isocrates was not so far wrong.

The opening of the **Rhetoric** makes some play with the judicial proprieties. The technical writers go wrong because they allow what is beside the point, while what is needed in court is a proper judgment, not a surrendered verdict. It is the notion of "judgment" that bears the weight of Aristotle's defense against Plato's ethical objection; and it allows him to distinguish, against Isocrates, between cases where the people in the audience are properly involved in rhetorical argument and cases where they are manipulated.

Consider three examples of "judgment" from outside the **Rhetoric**.

1. The defense of the law of noncontradiction (**Metaphysics** 4.3-8). One sophistic strategy to demonstrate that truth is radically relative is the use of opposed arguments: whatever we say, we end up contradicting ourselves. For an extreme relativist of this sort, the "opposed arguments" manoeuvre shows not only that truth is radically relative, but also that consistency does not matter and that contradictions may both be true. This person might be Protagoras—and it could also be an extreme Isocratean, who goes for cultural relativism. Against Protagoras Aristotle insists that the physi-

cal world out there "comes first"; that it is stable, real and accessible to us.[59] But the dispute is not (as Aristotle himself realizes) easily resolved—because neither party concedes the basis of the other's argument. Aristotle's strategy is to demonstrate his position (that the law of noncontradiction holds) by refutation of his opponent (let him only "signify something" and he is done for). But his own position remains vulnerable to a relativist complaint: even if the real world out there is ever-present and stable, how is it ever-present *to us?* How is it that we have reliable access to what is real or true and are not at the mercy of relativism anyway, whatever the facts of the matter may be? Here Aristotle appeals to a different notion—the "proper judge," the need to find a *correct judge* for any question (**Metaph.** 4.6, 1011a5-6). If consistency matters, and the law of noncontradiction is true, the reason is that there are facts of the matter (things); another reason is that the determinate nature of the world is reflected in what we say and think. There must be some way of resolving what we say and think in favor of the facts of the matter; and that resolution is a matter of *judgment*. Now this account repudiates hopeless relativism (and its cousin subjectivism) by continuing to insist on the primacy of objective truth; but it reassures us also that there is some active part to be played by the judge.

2. Dialectical progress. At **Metaphysics** 3.1, 995b3 we resolve opposed arguments by judging between the opponents. The imagery of the passage emphasizes first of all the *effect* the opposed arguments have on the judge. He starts out tied and trapped by the opposed arguments; only familiarity and practice allow him to untie the knot and escape; to begin with, the arguments are in control. Once again, arguments are thought of as obvious—so the dialectician deals with his perplexity by *seeing* all the difficulties; only then is the terminus of his search *obvious* to him. Similar metaphors of perception turn up throughout the **Rhetoric** to describe the activities of the judge (e.g., 1.1.7, 1354b10-11) who is, of course, also a spectator (1.3.1, 1358b1-2; 2.1.1, 1377b20ff.; 2.18.1, 1391b10). And yet the release of the *aporia* in the **Metaphysics** describes a process of gaining control over opposed arguments—the judge (not the arguments) are winning by the time the knot is untied. Once again, the notion of *judgment* shows how the audience is crucial to the argument, and an active participant in the process.

3. Meno's paradox. Compare the way Aristotle handles some old epistemological chestnuts in the last chapter of the **Posterior Analytics** (2.19, 99b17ff.). How does the mind ever move from knowing nothing (no universal) to knowing something? Does it have ideas all along? Or does it acquire them somehow—if so, how? Plato said we remember from before—Aristotle says we perceive now. The universal is established in the mind when sense-impressions are retained in the memory and reinforced by repetition. So the mind is

affected by the world, and universals are thereby acquired. Is the mind then totally passive? Not quite, Aristotle suggests, for it can *judge*. Judgment is the *capacity* of the mind to think universals (to identify one and discriminate it from another). Once again, the judge is in control.

Aristotle dovetails his metaphor of judgment elsewhere with the theory of the ***Rhetoric***. Judgment is something that is done by the receptive mind; it is something that people in an audience can produce when the argument is properly presented to them, and they are dispassionately disposed. In the ideal case, therefore, the formal arguments of rhetoric must be contextualized *by being assessed by the audience*. Now this does not mean that any audience will do; on the contrary, Aristotle distinguishes between cases when there has been proper judgment and those where the audience has been improperly manipulated; and thus he resists the temptations of a universal Isocratean rhetoric. We might understand this in judicial terms—Aristotle wants to limit as far as possible the discretion of a judge or jury. In the ideal case, they should be concerned solely with what did or did not happen, is or is not true, will or will not occur. Judges should decide particular areas of factual doubt, then, but nothing else. So to judge the truth is to grasp or to have access to the facts. Judging is to be rid of extraneous influence; otherwise it is not judgment at all—but just handing over a verdict (***Rhet.*** 1.1.10, 1354b34-55a1). And in the latter case, the judge has been unwarrantably affected by the art of persuasion.

How far does this respond to the *ethical* objection Plato launched against rhetoric (as opposed, say, to some objection taken from the philosophy of mind)? Recall that opposed arguments may seem to be in equipoise—but in fact the balance is tipped in favor of natural truth (***Rhet.*** 1.1.12, 1355a37). So practice in dealing with opposed arguments is a way of coming to see clearly what is true and what is false (***Top.*** 1.2, 101a35). And to defend the truth, of course, is something to which we are naturally fitted (***Rhet.*** 1.1.11-12, 1355a3-33)—and thus something that it is appropriate for us to do.

Aristotle introduces his long discussion of *ēthos* and *pathos* thus: "Since the art of rhetoric is for the sake of judgment—for people judge deliberative matters and judicial proceedings are a judgment—we should not only look to the argument, how it can best be demonstrative and trustworthy, but also that the speaker appears in a particular way, and the judge is affected in a particular way" (***Rhet.*** 2.1.2, 1377b20-24). Here he shifts from the formal view of rhetorical arguments to pay attention to the act of judgment, and thus to the disposition of the audience and the character of the speaker. Judgment is now not only about argument, because it also concerns the appearances.[60] That is, it

concerns how things appear *to us*—what is plausible is plausible to us. Even if rhetorical arguments can be formalized, they are arguments spoken by someone to someone else; they are contextualized. Always? Yes—the formalization of dialectical arguments can be context-free, but the discussion of what we can change, what we can avoid or pursue, what actually happened on a particular dark night always carries a reference to persons and context; the discussion of _thos and *pathos* brings that personal feature to the fore.

Arguments, if purely formal, would be transitive and their audiences passively affected by them. But judgments involve the active participation of the hearer—and hence the importance of the metaphor of judgment in other metaphysical or epistemological contexts. The proper exercise of rhetoric is constrained by the proper mental disposition of its audience. So the definition of rhetoric is not context-free: instead it demands the proper cognitive disposition of its audience. And that disposition is naturally inclined toward the truth. So proper judgment and ethical propriety go hand in hand.

Arguments in Context

The ***Rhetoric*** contains long discussions of the social context in which rhetorical arguments may appear. Thus Book 2 discusses at length the way in which the character of the speaker can influence the audience, or how the audience's emotions can be exploited for persuasive ends. And Book 3 shifts to a handbook of rhetorical technique: how to adopt a weighty style, how to use metaphor, how to avoid (or exploit) prejudice. With reference to the work as a whole, then, it is hard to argue that Aristotle completely replaces the phenomena of rhetoric with his formal analysis of rhetorical argument. Instead, he integrates the enthymeme into its context without relying merely on the metaphor "the enthymeme is the body of conviction." In justifying the claim that rhetorical arguments are essentially contextualized, he meets Plato's political objection against rhetorical practice (that it is only superficially interpersonal, never "soul-to-soul"); at the same time he makes some concessions to Isocrates' sociological account without conceding that rhetoric is all-pervasive.

Aristotle argues in three stages: first, he elaborates on the evaluative features of the enthymeme; second, he explains how these features are inextricably bound up with the disposition of the audience; and third, he shows that because emotions are attitudes toward persons, then the character of the speaker is an essential feature of the rhetorical occasion. The development of the claim that rhetorical arguments are contextualized by their very nature takes up the first two books of the work. But it depends on the initial characterization of the enthymeme—so that the ***Rhetoric*** turns out to be well-formed after all.

The art of rhetoric concerns itself with what is possible just because the practice of rhetoric is about actions and decisions; other sorts of possibilities hold no interest for us. In court, for example, we may wonder whether he did bash his wife with a blunt instrument; in the agora we may debate the question whether we should pull down all the theatres to make way for schools of philosophy. In either case we are talking about actions to be pursued or avoided—in either case we are interested in *value*. So the possibilities discussed in enthymemes are not dull (could this stone crack before it is worn away?) but interesting ones (could we have caviar and champagne for supper?). And if these possibilities are interesting, they are interesting *to someone*.

Aristotle outlines his theory of rhetoric in *Rhetoric* 1. 1-3 and then turns to the detailed discussion of deliberative rhetoric (which is, after all, the central feature of rhetoric in classical Athens). He starts with a complex discussion of "the good and bad things" with which the deliberative rhetor is concerned—these are limited to things over which we may have some control (*Rhet.* 1.4.1, 1359a30ff.). They are specified—they are "those things which by nature can be referred to us and which have the beginning of their generation in us" (*Rhet.* 1.4.3, 1359a38-39; compare a similar point in *EN* 3.3.7, 1112a30). Value, that is, is interesting because it is interesting *to us*. Hence in the case of practical reasoning I deliberate with myself about what is up to me; and I act when what is good or apparently good for me seems to be possible. The case of public deliberation is analogous; this is a matter of what is possible and what is interesting *to the persons concerned*. So the entire discussion of value in *Rhetoric* 1.4-9, including the discussion of virtue and vice (*Rhet.* 1.9.1-34), is predicated on the view that these values are relative to persons and that the rhetor aims to discuss what is valuable to the particular persons in front of him: "Speaking generally, there is a target both for individuals and for men acting together; this is what they aim at when they decide what to choose or avoid; and this, briefly, is *eudaimonia* and its parts. So for the sake of an example let us grasp what *eudaimonia* is, and what are its parts composed of; for all exhortation and dissuasion are about this and the things which conduce to it and their opposites" (*Rhet.* 1.5.2, 1360b4ff.).

But then the discussion of value and the discussion of what is possible are inextricably linked (*Rhet.* 1.4.1-4, 1359a30ff.). Enthymemes, therefore, are not bare arguments at all; instead they have an ethical component all along, because they concern value, and value is relative to persons (to reemphasize the point, this does not imply that they are subjective; Aristotle does not fall into the sophistic trap here).

Where people have an interest, their interest is affected by their emotions. For example, "people choose to do the things just mentioned, and they choose to do bad things to their enemies and good things to their friends where they can" (*Rhet.* 1.6.26, 1363a20-21). Emotions are first of all dispositions toward our interests. Anger, for example, may be caused by an insult. If someone says to me, "You fool!" my pride, my amour propre or my *timē* (if I am a Greek) is affected and my interests have been damaged. Likewise anger may prompt me to action: "And some pleasure goes along with all anger, namely the anticipation of revenge; for it is pleasant to think that one may reach what one aims at, while no-one aims at what appears impossible, and the angry man aims at what is possible to him" (*Rhet.* 2.2.2, 1378b1ff.). So if the enthymeme is necessarily about what interests me (and is possible), it will be about what *affects* me; in that case it will only be effective if I am properly disposed—and that is a matter of the proper arrangement of my emotions. So not all emotion is provoked by force majeure—not all cases of emotion are cases where we are "swayed by our emotions." For example, we may be moved to pity by some apparently deserving person—and then change our minds when it is explained to us that he is in fact a thoroughly bad lot and worth no pity at all (*Rhet.* 2.9.16, 1387b16ff.).[61] Second, and most important, emotions do not preclude active judgment; Aristotle denies the audience of the rhetor must be mere patients of his rhetoric, even if their emotions are involved. "The emotions are the things through which people change their judgments, and which are accompanied by pleasure and pain" (*Rhet.* 2.1.8, 1378a19ff.)—this does not mean that any decision that is made in a state of emotion is a faulty decision. But the function of the people in the audience, as he insists from the begining of the work, is to judge, to come to a decision—in this manner, Aristotle argues, they are actively involved and (to meet the Platonic objection) suitable moral agents.

Emotions are determined by three factors: the disposition, for example, of being angry; the occasions for anger; and the persons at whom the anger is directed (*Rhet.* 2.1.8, 1378a19ff.). Throughout *Rhetoric* 2.1-11 Aristotle makes it clear that emotion is an interpersonal affair—the emotions we feel, even in a legitimate way, to the proper degree and without undue pressure from a clever speaker, by their very nature involve us with others—we feel pity toward a victim, anger toward a criminal, fear toward an enemy, goodwill toward a friend. But then if the emotions are what relate us to others, not only are the emotions central to establishing the *context* of a rhetorical occasion; they are also fundamental to creating what I have called the political element in rhetoric—the element that shows that we are genuinely involved here with the others who share our community with us. So the discussion of the emotions is the complement of the discussion of the virtues of character, just because emotions are felt toward others as we perceive them; so how they represent themselves to us provokes our emotions, either properly or otherwise.

Plato, it will be recalled, claimed that only "real" rhetoric was clearly interested in the souls of the audience; for only rhetoric based on the high standards of objective knowledge he demanded could satisfactorily interact with the souls of others—only "real" rhetoric met the ideal demands of the political situation. But Aristotle has established against Plato that there is some system to the everyday practice of rhetoric (and thus some possibility of an art of rhetoric); and he has shown (I have argued) that the audiences of, say, the deliberative rhetor are not mere pawns in his nasty sophistic game but active moral agents to be taken with due seriousness. This aspect of the audience has its counterpart in the discussions of the character of the speaker himself. For the discussion of the rhetor's character (initiated in the discussion of value and virtue in **Rhetoric** 1.9) is developed in Aristotle's account of how the people in the audience believe the rhetor to be well-disposed.[62]

> Since rhetoric is about judgment . . . we should look not only to the argument and how that may be demonstrative and convincing, but also to how the speaker himself may be presented as of a particular character and how the judge may be disposed. For it makes a great difference when it comes to conviction, and particularly in deliberative rhetoric . . . that the speaker should seem to be of a particlar character and that the audience should suppose him to be disposed in a certain way towards them. (**Rhet.** 2.1.3, 1377b20-27)

This condition on rhetoric is elaborated in the detailed account of the virtues of character (1.9; 2.12-17). For first of all the apparent character of the rhetor is persuasive—if we are confronted with someone who appears to be of goodwill, we are likely to trust this person's recommendations as being genuinely in our interests. Correspondingly, we should expect the true rhetor actually to be a man of goodwill, genuinely offering advice that will benefit his audience. On the whole, the characters are described as they would appear to an audience; but Aristotle's point is not so much a contrast between appearance and reality (that is what Plato latches on to). Instead Aristotle wants to insist on the intrinsic relations between the values that rhetorical argument concerns itself with, the emotions of the audience, and the character of the speaker (cf. **Rhet.** 1.9.1, 1366a23ff.). And his account of this last feature suggests that virtue and character are to be understood not absolutely but relatively to others; after all, it is by virtue of character "that we can make both ourselves and others trustworthy in respect of virtue" (**Rhet.** 1.9.1, 1366a27-28). The character of the speaker is therefore the third feature of the context in which rhetorical arguments appear; and it is a feature determined by the other two.

Rhetorical arguments, therefore, necessarily appear in a social context; and Plato's political objection to rhetoric, Aristotle can argue, fails. The rhetor has a system of arguments to practice, and these arguments are about possibility and value. If they are about value, they are relative to the beneficiaries of the value; if they are relative to the beneficiaries, then they also reflect the benefactors. All rhetoric, then, is contextual. But is, then, all contextualized speech rhetoric? Has Aristotle defeated Plato only to fall prey to Isocrates' all-pervasive rhetoric? Once again, he resists the relativist view. For, as the program of the opening of the **Rhetoric** makes clear, true rhetoric, the rhetoric that is "inside the matter," is focused on the enthymeme; arguments that lack that cohesive feature are not arguments at all but mere attempts at manipulation. But arguments focused on the enthymeme are not therefore devoid of ethical or political content. On the contrary, both the systematic nature and the subject matter of the enthymeme ensure first that these arguments are naturally best suited to presenting the truth, and second that the character of the speaker and the emotional disposition of the audience matter. In this way, Plato's objections to rhetoric are finally silenced, and Aristotle resists the Isocratean takeover.

So both Plato (who denied that Isocratean rhetoric was anything at all) and Isocrates (who said that rhetoric was all-pervasive) are wrong; or (to put the matter in an Aristotelian manner) they are in some ways right and in some ways wrong. Now one view might be that this compromise is effected by ambiguity. We might generalize and say that rhetoric is about "what is likely." Aristotle has shown that rhetorical arguments are about contingency, about what is in fact likely; so they concern *to eikos* in the sense of "what happens for the most part" (**Rhet.** 1.2.15, 1357a34). He has also argued that rhetorical devices are about persuasion, about what seems likely to the audience; so they concern *to eikos* in the sense of "what seems plausible" (whatever the facts of the matter may be) (e.g., **Rhet.** 1.15.17, 1376a17ff.). Rhetorical arguments aim at *ta endoxa,* the opinions of the many and the wise which are inclined toward natural truth (**Rhet.** 1.1.11, 1355a14ff.). Rhetorical devices exploit what people commonly believe—*ta endoxa* (e.g., **Rhet.** 2.25.2-3, 1402a34ff.)—or even what they find paradoxical (**Rhet.** 2.23.22, 1400a5ff.). We are convinced by rhetorical arguments because they are (in a loose sense) demonstrative (**Rhet.** 1.1.11, 1355a5ff.). We are convinced by rhetorical devices because they exploit *ēthos* and *pathos* (**Rhet.** 1.2.4, 1356a4ff.). So "what is likely" may represent "what is possible" or "what is plausible to someone"— but the two senses are not necessarily connected. Is this ambiguity between possibility and plausibility hopeless?

Surely not. As so often elsewhere, Aristotle explains the wide scope of a word (or a collection of ideas) in terms of a central core of meaning. At the center of rhetoric is the formal account of argument understood without a context.[63] But this formal rhetoric both establishes and delimits its own context, in such a way that Aristotle can include the ordinary phenomena of rhetoric in his account of rhetorical arguments. Licit rhetoric is held together by the way in which the context is always focused on the argument,[64] so that the art of rhetoric is, after all, really about argument.[65] And the truth that lies at the center of the arguments has itself a natural priority, which explains the natural coherence of the body of rhetoric and its parts. Argument is the body of rhetoric because it is about things, it is objective (cf. *Metaph.* 4.4, 1006b11). This is where rhetoric is parallel to dialectic, the enthymeme to the syllogism. So opposed arguments can be resolved by objective logical standards—they are neither indeterminate (no answer) nor subjective (answered by the whim or the preferences of the speaker). But the audience of formal rhetorical argument—in parallel with Plato's emphasis on the psychological dimension of argument-is actively engaged in judgment. What is more, rhetorical arguments are contextualized: rhetorical arguments are essentially communicated. So in the ordinary business of forensic or deliberative rhetoric, *people* make decisions; they are influenced by the character of the *speaker* and swayed by their own emotions. To understand this aspect of rhetoric, we must understand *ēthos* and *pathos* as well as pure *logos*. Together they form a natural whole that allows for a genuine *technē* of rhetoric.

To reach this conclusion, Aristotle has rejected both the Platonic view of rhetoric (objectivity or bust) and the Isocratean one (rhetoric is all-pervasive). Instead, he argues, we need *both* a formal account of argument (so that rhetoric may be a *techne*) *and* a contextual one (to save the phenomena), arranged and unified by the central account of rhetorical argument. So the encounter in the first chapters between Plato and the rhetoricians is a model for the balancing act of the whole work. Aristotle then deploys the method of *endoxa*—treating the opposed arguments of the wise—to extricate us from the puzzle and provide us with a new account of rhetoric. Rhetoric is a natural whole, whose body is the arguments modally suited to the arena of rhetoric—arguments about what is possible. It is those arguments that organize the art of rhetoric: here Aristotle deploys imagery from nature suitable to his afternoon lectures. In the morning, perhaps, he would have told us about focal meaning.

Notes

[1] By F. Solmsen, *Die Entwicklung der Aristotelischen Logik und Rhetorik* (Neue Philologische Untersuchungen), Berlin: Wiedmann, 1929. ch. 3; then by J. Barnes, "Proof and the Syllogism" in Berti, E., ed., *Aristotle on Science: the Posterior Analytics* (8th Symposium Aristotelicum), Padova: Antenore, 1981, pp. 51ff.

[2] As I now think: in my original paper to the Symposium I gave a harsher verdict on Aristotle. My thanks to the other members of the symposium for their comments on my first version of this paper—and in particular to Aryeh Kosman, Geoffrey Lloyd, Michael Frede, John Cooper, Mario Mignucci, and David Charles; my thanks also to the editors and to an anonymous commentator, who sent me back to the drawing board.

[3] . . . *Grg.* 464c ff., picked up at *Rhet.* 1.2.7, 1356a27.

[4] Well, he might, anyway—there is a question here about whether Plato is suggesting that the tyrant will not invariably get what he does want; or whether, because he is ignorant, he will always get what he does not want.

[5] Compare his point on what people really believe about justice at 474b.

[6] Plato takes the notion of the *active* philosophical life seriously. Philosophy is what you do, not what you suffer; but we are helpless in the face of rhetoric's force majeure. In the *Theaetetus* Socrates insists that his method of philosophy brings the truth out of the souls of his interlocutors, rather than imposing it on them from without (*Tht.* 150b ff.); and that is why he denies the charge of teaching the young (anything at all—as at *Ap.* 24c ff.). Philosophy is done *by* minds (whether they be conceived as wax tablets or aviaries or scribes or painters), not done *to* them; and it is for that reason that the method of dialectic is understood as "soul-leading" . . . , *Phdr.* 261a, cf. *Rep.* 523a ff.). It is souls who think and understand; so argument happens in souls (*Sph.* 263e), judgments are made by souls (*Tht.* 185d ff.). This factor in Plato's account of the philosophical life is significant when we come to consider Aristotle's account of judgment.

[7] See G. Vlastos, "The Socratic Elenchus." *Oxford Studies in Ancient Philosophy* I (1983), 27-58.

[8] Vlastos p. 35.

[9] Compare, e.g., the discussion of [*alogia*] in the *Meno* (80a ff.), where the watershed of the experiment with the slave-boy is the moment at which he realizes that he does not know the answer to Socrates' question. Cf. Mackenzie, "The Virtues of Socratic Ignorance," *Classical Quarterly* 1988, pp. 331ff.

[10] Cf., e.g., Socrates' dispute with the "other" Socrates, *Hp.Ma.* 293b, 304c; or his investigation of "know thyself" at *Chrm.* 166d.

[11] I discuss Plato's account of the unity of persons in detail in *Plato's Individuals* (Princeton, forthcoming) ch. 9. It is an oddity of Plato's account of personal integrity (which contains both metaphysical and ethical components) that he can think of personal unity as something to which we aspire—being "one" is honorific.

[12] Cf Mackenzie, *Plato on Punishment* (Berkeley: 1981), ch. 10.

[13] Some suppose (e.g., G. R. F. Ferrari, *Listening to the Cicadas, A Study of Plato's Phaedrus,* Cambridge: Cambridge University Press, 1987; C. Rowe, "The Argument and Structure of Plato's *Phaedrus,*" *Proceedings of the Cambridge Philological Society* 1986) that the *Phaedrus* represents a modification of the *Gorgias* account of rhetoric—Plato has changed his mind. Consequently for my present purposes, there is no single "Platonic" view on rhetoric for Aristotle to consider. Against this complaint I offer three considerations: i) The strategy of Plato in the *Phaedrus* seems to be to appropriate rhetoric's terms of art ("rhetoric," "persuasion") for the legitimate activities of philosophy or dialectic—he is *not* making concessions to ordinary rhetoric; ii) even when he does this, he subverts his own conclusions (turns everything upside down, 272b) to show that nothing of what he says may be taken at face value, cf. Mackenzie, "Paradox in Plato's *Phaedrus,*" *Proceedings of the Cambridge Philological Society* 1982, 64-76; and iii) as far as Aristotle's treatment of Plato is concerned, the view represented in the *Gorgias* is the Plato he takes on—there is no commitment in the method of [*endoxa*] to reflect with fidelity any changes of mind by the wise.

[14] Text in L. Radermacher, *Artium Magistri et Scriptores—Reste der voraristotelischen Rhetorik.* Wien: Osterreichische Akademie der Wissenschaften, 1951, p. 135ff.

[15] There is of course an echo—or a twist—of this point in the *Phaedrus* (264c, 275d ff.). Not only Plato but Aristotle too picks up Alcidamas' imagery, as I shall suggest.

[16] Cf. . . . *Antid.* passim, e.g., 271-and compare the discussion of rhetoric as power in Plato's *Gorgias.*

[17] Compare *Grg.* e.g., 459b ff., or *Sph.* 234a ff. with Isoc. *Soph.* 1ff.; *Antid.* 148.

[18] Compare here Isocrates' complaint . . . *Soph.* 7.

[19] Grimaldi appears—implausibly—to attribute this thesis to Aristotle, to explain the purpose of the *Rhetoric,* in *Studies in the philosophy of Aristotle's Rhetoric* (Hermes Einzelschriften 25). Wiesbaden: Franz Steiner Verlag, 1972, pp. 5ff.

[20] By "ideology" here I mean the collection of inherited assumptions and norms that constitute the society and that, as such, remained unquestioned by it. For a discussion of the influence of ideology on Aristotle (a major issue when it comes to considering his endoxic method), see M. Schofield, "Ideology in Aristotle's Politics," in Patzig, G., ed., *Aristotle's Politics* (11th Symposium Aristotelicum), Berlin, 1990.

[21] This, you might say, is a "mouthpiece" theory of legal counsel, where the advocate acts, not as judge of his client's case but as his client's mouthpiece. That view is essential to a thorough answer to the question, "Can you defend anyone you know to be guilty?" Guilt is a matter for the judge and is a fact only after the judgment takes place. . . . Here the connection between epistemological relativism and its ethical counterpart is very clear.

[22] Cf., of course, G. E. L. Owen, *"Tithenai ta phainomena,"* in his *Logic, Science and Dialectic,* London: Duckworth, 1986, pp. 239-51; and then, e.g., J. Barnes, "Aristotle and the Methods of Ethics," *Revue Internationale de Philosophie,* 133-34 (1980), 490-511.; M. C. Nussbaum, "Saving Aristotle's Appearances," in Schofield, M., and Nussbaum, M. C., eds., *Language and Logos,* Cambridge: Cambridge University Press, 1982; but now a much more complex account of Aristotle's approach to the business of philosophy, T. Irwin, *Aristotle's First Principles,* Oxford: Clarendon Press, 1989, pp.30ff.

[23] Plato is not mentioned by name, but the allusions are obvious; compare here W. Rhys Roberts, "References to Plato in Aristotle's *Rhetoric.*" *Classical Quarterly* 18 (1924), 344-45.

[24] Compare *Rhet.* 1.1.12, 1355a38 with Plato's complaint about the helplessness of the written word, *Phdr.* 276.

[25] Cf. W. W. Fortenbaugh, "Aristotle's Platonic Attitude toward Delivery," *Philosophy and Rhetoric* 19 (1986), 242-54.

[26] Is the technical procedure one for doing rhetoric or for studying it (cf. Brunschwig, this volume)? At times Aristotle concentrates on the teachers of rhetoric and at times on the practicing rhetor. Fair enough—Plato's attack is both on the teachers of rhetoric, for failing to teach anything at all, and on its practitioners, for their lack of system and their moral decrepitude. I have suggested, however, that for Plato the two points are connected; Aristotle's defense of rhetoric correspondingly copes with both.

[27] Compare Aristotle's remarks, *EN* 5.10, 1137b29ff. on the use of a flexible rule in ethics (and building). Is there a gruesome joke lurking here? Aristotle talks about

making a ruler crooked, . . . cf., e.g., Ar. *Clouds* 620, Antiphon 5.32.

[28] Cf. Burnyeat, this volume, on this passage.

[29] This comment, *Rhet.* 1.1.11, 1355a14-15, seems to make the point about what sort of skill an enthumematic person would have; it is comparable, I take it, to the skilled logician's being able to *see* validity. On this more below.

[30] . . . Cf.—*Grg.* 465a2; for Plato this word is pejorative-but Aristotle's usage seems to point rather to the contingent nature of the subject matter of rhetoric; this need not make rhetoric the disaster Plato takes it to be. Cf. here Cooper, this volume, and compare *Rhet.* 1.5.1, 1360b5 with *EN* 6.1, 1138b22ff.

[31] İ shall return to the sense of [*endoxa*] below.

[32] We should be a little wary here—does Aristotle mean "stupid" or "reprobate"? If the issue is whether they can understand argument, the emphasis ought to be on the former, and on their character only insofar as they fail to perform proper human functions (i.e., to be sensible, not stupid). Compare here *Top.* 1.2, 101a30; and *Rhet.* 3.14.8, 1415b5-6, where Aristotle's complaint is that we have to deal with a lousy auditor (someone who is bad *at hearing*)—not a lousy person (someone who is bad at being a moral agent). Compare his own strictures against Plato, *EN* 1.6, 1096a19ff.

[33] The contrast between the plausible and the apparently plausible seems, by the analogy with the syllogism, to be a logical contrast between valid and invalid arguments, not a psychological one between what actually persuades and what merely appears to do so (indeed, it is hard to see what the latter would mean).

[34] Note, however, the reservation, "Rhetoric wears the clothes of politics." But "politics" may be said in many ways: as I have construed Plato's objection, rhetoric should be "self-to-self" and interpersonal, so political in that sense. This sort of "politics" is exactly what Aristotle goes on to elaborate in his account of what I describe as the "context" of rhetorical argument.

[35] Cf. *EN* 1.3, 1094b11ff; 3.3, 1112a18ff.; 6.1, 1139a12ff.

[36] See Aristotle's recommendation that the deliberative orator should know about economics, military strategy, foreign policy, etc., *Rhet* 1.4.7, 1359b19ff.

[37] Epideictic rhetoric seems not to be of prime interest to Aristotle—see, e.g., *Rhet.* 1.1.5, 1354a22ff. Perhaps this is true because [*epideiseis*] often take the form of either forensic or deliberative speeches—compare, e.g., Gorgias' *Helen,* Isocrates' *Antidosis,* and *Rhet.* 1.9.35,

1367b37. Or perhaps Aristotle's lack of interest in epideictic may be a part of his emphasis on what is real as opposed to what is invented, and thus part of his stance against Isocratean rhetoric. In what follows my main focus of attention will be deliberative rhetoric—in keeping with the main target of Plato's criticisms.

[38] At least only insofar as past propositions are necessary, cf., e.g., *Rhet.* 1.3. 8, 1359a11ff.; 3.17.5, 1418a5; they do not have the necessity of general statements of essence.

[39] Aristotle argues against the Platonic view that value is uniform, but goes along along with Plato in the assumption that value is natural or objective; cf. *EN* 1.6-7.

[40] E.g., *EN* 1.7,1097a32, what is good is sought *in itself.* Aristotle's naturalism about the good does not, of course, preclude his taking the view that goods are relative to persons or circumstances; hence the discussion of the mean, *EN* 2.6, 1106a26ff. Compare here also the suggestion that the judge should *recognize* . . . the justice or otherwise of a case, *Rhet.* 1.1.6, 1354a29ff. The metaphors of light and darkness at 1.1.7, 1354b10-11 imply that, though personal interest may affect a judge's decision, both interest and truth are nonetheless real features (of the world), not inventions or subjective views of the judge himself.

[41] While I hope I shall have shown that the project of the *Rhetoric* is coherent, this allows for the possibility that the syllogistic framework is a later incorporation into the original series of afternoon lectures.

[42] Cf above, n. 30. Plato rejected the stochastic approach, *Grg.* 463a, 465a. [*To endekhomenon*] inevitably is said in many ways, *A Pr.* 1.3, 25a37ff.; and compare the problems of the conversion of contingent propositions at *Int.* 12 and 13, 21a34ff. Cf. here W. and M. Kneale, *The Development of Logic,* Oxford: Clarendon Press, 1962, pp. 83ff.

[43] Cf., e.g., *Int.* 12, 21b10; and compare the discussion of possibility and actuality in *Metaph.* 9, esp. the comparison with natural actuality, e.g., 9.8, 1049b8. Possibility is treated as a rhetorical, [*topos*] at *Rhet.* 2.19.1, 1392a8ff.

[44] There will still be [*topoi*] common to rhetoric and dialectic; cf. *Rhet.* 1.2.21, 1358a10ff.; 1.3.8-9, 1359a16ff., put into practice at 1.7.1, 1363b5ff.; 2.18.2, 1391b22ff.

[45] Cf. . . . *Rhet.* 2.19.1, 1392a8ff.

[46] Notice the reference to *A Pr.* 1.8, 29b29ff.; 1.13, 32a15ff. at *Rhet.* 1.2.14, 1357a29.

[47] Look here at *Rhet.* 1.4.3, 1359a35ff. or at the discussion of chance at 1.10.12, 1369a32ff; or the contrast between habit, nature, and accident at 1.11.3, 1370a6.

[48] The notion of "syllogism" that appears in this passage in the *Topics* need only mean "argument," even of so rigorous a type that the conclusion follows "from necessity"; we need not be dealing with the canonical three-proposition syllogism of the *Prior Analytics.* Cf. . . . *Rhet.* 1.2.7, 1356a22 to describe enthymematic arguing. Cf. Burnyeat, this volume.

[49] Cf. here, e.g., *A Pr.* 1.1, 24b18ff.

[50] E.g., *Ph.* 2.3, 194b17ff.

[51] Cf. here M. F. Burnyeat, "Aristotle on Understanding Knowledge," in Berti, E., ed., *Aristotle on Science: The Posterior Analytics* (8th Symposium Aristotelicum). Padova: Antenore, 1981, 97-139.

[52] Compare the way the mind *receives* sense-data and form, *De An.* 3.4, 429a10ff.

[53] Look, e.g., at *A Pr.* 1.6, 28a36; 28b30 etc. etc. and cf. J. Lear, *Aristotle, the Desire to Understand,* Cambridge: Cambridge University Press, 1989, 211ff.

[54] Of a sort, cf. Burnyeat, this volume.

[55] Cf. here the idiom of sight to describe how the judge sees, or fails to see, the truth, e.g. at *Rhet.* 1.1.7, 1354b10-11; 1.1.11, 1355a10, 15, etc.

[56] Thus enthymemes are presented as real arguments by contrast with apparent enthymemes, which are fallacious (and thus deceitful), *Rhet.* 2.24.1, 1400b34-01a1.

[57] Some enthymematic kinds of argument (maxims) offer *obvious explanations, Rhet.* 2.21.6, 1394b21; cf. 2.23.30, 1400b30ff.

[58] In what follows I shall not be suggesting that Aristotle' anticipated Austin or Searle; but see J. L. Austin, *How to Do Things with Words.* Oxford: Oxford University Press, 1976, e.g., p. 52 on the context of an utterance.

[59] Inevitably this argument is hugely controversial; see most recently Irwin pp. 179ff.

[60] Notice the emphatic use of [*phainesthai*] from *Rhet.* 2.1.3, 1377b26 onward.

[61] This will generate a cognitivist account of emotion. Compare M. C. Nussbaum, *The Fragility of Goodness* Cambridge: Cambridge University Press, 1986 with Lear, "Katharsis," *Phronesis* 1988, 297-326.

[62] See Cooper, this volume.

[63] "It is first by nature," *Rhet.* 3.1.3, 1403b18-19.

[64] Compare *Metaph.* 4.2, 1003a33; 7.4, 1030a17, where the metaphysics of this strategy is announced. Cf. Owen, "Logic and Metaphysics in Some Earlier Works of Aristotle," in *Logic, Science and Dialectic,* pp. 180-99. Of course Aristotle could have deployed the strategy of focal meaning without having enunciated it (that is, the *Rhetoric* need not postdate the late books of the *Metaphysics*); and he could have used it in his afternoon lectures without subjecting his audience to the rigors of metaphysical argument.

[65] Argument is the most authoritative of the convictions, . . . *Rhet.* 1.1.11, 1355a7; cf. here, e.g., *Metaph.* 5.4, 1015a14; 8.6, 1045a36; *De An.* 2.1, 412b9; *EN* 6.13, 1144b3ff. . . . .

Bibliography

Austin, J. L. *How to Do Things with Words.* Oxford: Oxford University Press, 1976.

Barnes, J. "Proof and the Syllogism." In Berti, 17-59.

———. "Aristotle and the Methods of Ethics." *Revue Internationale de Philosophie* 133-34 (1980), 490-511.

Berti, E. *Aristotle on Science: The Posterior Analytics* (8th Symposium Aristotelicum). Padova: Antenore, 1981.

Burnyeat, M. F. "Aristotle on Understanding Knowledge." In Berti, 97-139.

Ferrari, G. R. F. *Listening to the Cicadas, A Study of Plato's Phaedrus.* Cambridge: Cambridge University Press, 1987.

Fortenbaugh, W. W. "Aristotle's Platonic Attitude toward Delivery." *Philosophy and Rhetoric* 19 (1986), 242-54.

Grimaldi, W. M. A., *Studies in the Philosophy of Aristotle's Rhetoric* (Hermes Einzelschriften 25). Wiesbaden: Franz Steiner Verlag, 1972.

Irwin, T. *Aristotle's First Principles.* Oxford: Clarendon Press, 1989.

Kneale, W., and M. Kneale. *The Development of Logic.* Oxford: Clarendon Press, 1962.

Lear, J. "Katharsis." *Phronesis* 1988, 297-326.

———. *Aristotle, the Desire to Understand.* Cambridge: Cambridge University Press, 1989.

Mackenzie, M. M. (McCabe). *Plato on Punishment.* Berkeley: University of California Press, 1981.

——"Paradox in Plato's *Phaedrus.*" *Proceedings of the Cambridge Philological Society* 1982, 64-76.

——"The Virtues of Socratic Ignorance." *Classical Quarterly,* 1988, 331-50.

McCabe, M. M. (Mackenzie). *Plato's Individuals.* Princeton: Princeton University Press (forthcoming).

Nussbaum, M. C. "Saving Aristotle's Appearances." In Schofield, M., and Nussbaum, M. C., eds., *Language and Logos.* Cambridge: Cambridge University Press, 1982.

——*The Fragility of Goodness.* Cambridge: Cambridge University Press, 1986.

Owen, G. E. L. *"Tithenai ta phainomena."* In his *Logic, Science and Dialectic.* London: Duckworth, 1986, pp. 239-51.

——"Logic and Metaphysics in Some Earlier Works of Aristotle." In *Logic, Science and Dialectic,* pp. 180-99.

Radermacher, L. *Artium Magistri et Scriptores—Reste der voraristotelischen Rhetorik.* Wien: Osterreichische Akademie der Wissenschaften, 1951.

Rowe, C. "The Argument and Structure of Plato's *Phaedrus*" *Proceedings of the Cambridge Philological Society,* 1986, pp. 106-25.

Rhys Roberts, W. "References to Plato in Aristotle's *Rhetoric.*" *Classical Quarterly* 18 (1924), 344-45.

Schofield, M. "Ideology in Aristotle's Politics." In Patzig, G., ed., *Aristotle's Politics* (11th Symposium Aristotelicum). Berlin: de Gruyter, 1990

Solmsen, F. *Die Entwicklung der Aristotelischen Logik und Rhetorik* (Neue Philologische Untersuchungen). Berlin: Wiedmann, 1929.

Vlastos, G. "The Socratic Elenchus." *Oxford Studies in Ancient Philosophy* 1 (1983), 27-58.

FURTHER READING

Benoit, William Lyon. "Aristotle's Example: The Rhetorical Induction." *The Quarterly Journal of Speech* 66, No. 2 (April 1980): 182-92.

Responds to critical interpretations of Aristotle's use

of example offered by Gerard Hauser and Scott Consigny and provides a different interpretation and explanation.

Brandes, Paul D. *A History of Aristotle's* Rhetoric *with a Bibliography of Early Printings.* Metuchen, N.J.: The Scarecrow Press, 1989, 222p.

Traces the composition, preservation, and manuscript history of *Rhetoric* through the twentieth century.

Consigny, Scott. "Transparency and Displacement: Aristotle's Concept of Rhetorical Clarity." *Rhetoric Society Quarterly* XVII, No. 4 (Fall 1987): 413-19.

Examines Aristotle's statements regarding rhetorical clarity found in Book 3 of *Rhetoric,* demonstrating that while many understand Aristotle to be advocating clarity as "a virtue, and indeed a criterion of the accurate, undistorted transmission" of ideas, Aristotle actually goes on to state that such clarity is "achieved through artifice."

Cooper, Lane, trans. Introduction to *The Rhetoric of Aristotle.* New York: D. Appleton-Century Company, Inc., 1932, 259p.

Introduces the text of *Rhetoric* by placing it within the context of Aristotle's other writings, defining special terms used in the text, and using Lincoln's "Gettysburg Address" as an example which illustrates the methodology described by Aristotle. Cooper describes *Rhetoric* as "a practical psychology."

Freese, John Henry. An introduction to *Aristotle: The "Art" of Rhetoric,* pp. vii-xxvii. Cambridge: Harvard University Press, 1939.

Provides a brief history of classical rhetoric and Aristotle place in it.

Garver, Eugene. "Aristotle's *Rhetoric:* Between Craft and Practical Wisdom." In *Aristotle's* Rhetoric: *An Art of Character,* pp. 18-51. Chicago: University of Chicago Press, 1994.

Explores the apparent conflict between the "professional art of rhetoric" as described by Aristotle and the notion of the civic good, concluding that while both rhetoric and virtue "have internal ends," the one should not attempt to assimilate the two.

Grimaldi, William M. A. *Studies in the Philosophy of Aristotle's Rhetoric. Hermes: Zeitschrift fur Klassiche Philologie,* Wiesbaden: Franz Stiener Verlag GMBH, 1972, 151p.

Examines the unity and development of the text of *Rhetoric,* as well as Aristotle's focus on the enthymeme and its function as a mode of rhetorical argumentation.

Hauser, Gerard A. "The Example of Aristotle's Rhetoric: Bifurcation or Contradiction?" *Philosophy and Rhetoric* 1, No. 2 (Spring, 1968): 78-90.

Discusses Aristotle's two "seemingly disparate" doctrines regarding example and finds them not to be contradictory, but meant in two different senses.

Hill, Forbes. "The Amorality of Aristotle's *Rhetoric.*" *Greek, Roman, and Byzantine Studies* 22, No. 2 (Summer 1981): 133-47.

> Responds to critics who suggest that *Rhetoric* contains a moral component, stating that the implication is that without moral content "the work would lack seriousness." Hill contests this idea, siding with critics who regard *Rhetoric* as both a serious work and a morally neutral one.

Lawson-Tancred, H. C., trans. Introduction to *The Art of Rhetoric,* by Aristotle. London, Penguin Books, Ltd., 1991, 291 p.

> Provides a detailed introduction in which the author discusses the state of ancient rhetoric at the time Aristotle lived; the historical background of *Rhetoric; Rhetoric* as *technē,* or within the realm of practical reasoning; the psychological aspects of the text; *Rhetoric*'s style and composition; and the influence of *Rhetoric* on other thinkers, writers, and disciplines.

Lord, Carnes. "The Intention of Aristotle's 'Rhetoric.'" *Hermes: Zeitschrift fur Klassiche Philologie,* pp. 326-39. Wiesbaden: Franz Stiener Verlag GMBH, 1981.

> Argues that *Rhetoric* is a unified and coherent doctrine informed by Aristotle's desire to "effect a transformation of contemporary attitudes toward rhetoric."

Olian, J. Robert. "The Intended Uses of Aristotle's *Rhetoric.*" *Speech Monographs* XXXV, No. 2 (June 1968): 137-48.

> Maintains that Aristotle's views on "who should speak and who should listen" are factors which pertain to Aristotle's ethical position in *Rhetoric* and which make this position "elusive."

Science

INTRODUCTION

Major Works

Aristotle's works on logic were collected into the *Organon (Instrument, Tool)*, which is comprised of several treatises, including *Categories, On Interpretation, Prior* and *Posterior Analytics,* and *Topics. Categories* is concerned with the structure of language, and the classification of the various elements that constitute the nature of any entity. *On Interpretation* also focuses on the structure of language, as well as on the nature of truth. Often considered the more significant treatises of the *Organon,* the two *Analytics* treat scientific knowledge and formal logic. In *Topics* Aristotle discusses the proper analysis of a proposition.

While Aristotle wrote numerous treatises on animals, concerned with their history, parts, and motion, the most frequently discussed of the biological treatises appears to be *On the Generation of Animals*. This work deals with the contributions of males and females to the creation of new life and also explores the means by which the soul is transmitted to the new individual.

Although *On the Generation of Animals,* like many of Aristotle's works in other fields, touches in some respect on the soul, *De Anima* is devoted to this topic. In this treatise, Aristotle formulates his theory of the soul. The work concentrates on sensation, thought, imagination, and reason, and is considered to be the first definitive work on the topic of psychology.

Physics treats what Aristotle referred to as "natural philosophy," and examines such topics as nature, cause, and motion. In this work, Aristotle explicates his doctrine regarding the four causes of physical change.

Textual History

Little is known about the fate of Aristotle's works after his death. It is believed by some scholars that for about two hundred years the works were either lost or hidden. They were discovered by Sulla (178-38 B.C.) and brought to Rome. Modern editions of Aristotle's works derive from Roman editions dating back to the late first century B.C. In the Middle Ages, Latin and Arabic translations broadened the influence of Aristotle's teachings; his philosophy was studied by St. Thomas Aquinas (c. 1225-74) and later by Francis Bacon (1561-

1626), who adopted Aristotle's doctrine of the four causes. As relatively few of Aristotle's writings can be dated with any degree of accuracy, the focus of nineteenth- and twentieth-century scholars has been on determining the chronological development of the works.

Critical Reception

Michael V. Wedin opens his discussion of Aristotle's doctrine of the soul with an observation on Aristotle's contribution to logic, noting that he provided "the first virtually complete system of certain kinds of logical inference. It is for this reason that we rank him as the inventor of the *science* of logic." It seems that few critics dispute this point; rather, they attempt to illuminate Aristotle's logical theories. J. M. E. Moravcsik focused on Aristotle's theory of categories, examining in particular the relationship between language and reality. Moravcsik has argued that while Aristotle did not regard the structure of language as parallel to the structure of reality, he did believe that the correlation between specific items of language and reality revealed a significant link between the two. Similarly, G. E. R. Lloyd has explored the doctrine of categories, as well as the syllogism, and the concept of scientific knowledge. Lloyd praises Aristotle's work on logic as "particularly comprehensive, very largely original, and for the most part eminently lucid." Compared to Moravcsik and Lloyd, Michael T. Ferejohn has offered a decidedly more technical approach in his analysis of Aristotle's doctrine of logical priority and how this doctrine developed from Aristotle's approach to the concept of necessary truth.

Many modern critics approach Aristotle's biological and psychological works from a similar angle: they probe what appears to be revealed in *The Generation of Animals* and *On the Soul* as Aristotle's distinctly misogynistic or sexist views. Lynda Lange has argued that Aristotle characterizes women as inferior, particularly as demonstrated in Aristotle's description of the respective contributions of man and woman to the generation of new life. Yet Lange maintains that despite this "unacceptable" characterization, Aristotle nevertheless offers an explanation consistent with his biological theories. Daryl McGowan Tress, on the other hand, has defended Aristotle against such criticism, presenting Aristotle's assertion that the male and female together are the "principles of generation." Tress emphasizes that any seeming inequality between the sexes in Aristotle's theories is a product of Aristotle's attempt to address certain philosophic problems, and does not arise from any sexism or misogyny on his part. Aristotle's treatment of the human soul is similarly dissected. Christine M. Senack has examined Aristotle's division of the soul into rational and irrational parts, as well as his claim that the rational part of the woman's soul does not have authority over the irrational part, thereby making her socially inferior to the man. Senack has concluded that as Aristotle's views on this matter are a product either of inaccurate data produced by the scientific community of his era, or of the cultural bias against women in ancient Greece, he is not to be considered a misogynist. Michael V. Wedin has offered a different approach to Aristotle's doctrine of the soul, providing a technical analysis that focuses on the soul as a functional and cognitive system.

One of the main critical issues regarding Aristotle's *Physics* focuses on the doctrine of the four causes. After examining the modern resistance to Aristotle's philosophical, non-mathematical approach to physics, Joe Sachs has discussed the content of the treatise, including Aristotle's views on motion and the four causes. The four causes of motion include material, form, the "external source of motion" (which Sachs notes is sometimes inaccurately termed "efficient cause"), and final cause. Sachs briefly touches on the relation of purpose to final cause, a topic to which David Bolotin has devoted much attention. Bolotin has identified final cause as "the end or purpose for which something comes into being or for which it exists." In his analysis of Aristotle's notion of final causality, Bolotin has also called attention to problem areas in Aristotle's treatment of "natural purpose."

---

*PRINCIPAL WORKS

Logic

Analytica Posteriora [*Posterior Analytics*] (treatise)

Analytica Prioria [*Prior Analytics*] (treatise)

Categoriae [*Categories*] (treatise)

De Interpretatione [*On Interpretation*] (treatise)

Topica [*Topics*] (treatise)

Biological Works

De Generatione Animalium [*On the Generation of Animals*] (treatise)

De Incessu Animalium [*On the Progression of Ani-*

mals] (treatise)

De Motu Animalium [*On the Motion of Animals*] (treatise)

De Partibus Animalium [*On the Parts of Animals*] (treatise)

Historia Animalium [*History of Animals*] (treatise)

Psychological Works

De Anima [*On the Soul*] (treatise)

De Divinatione per Somnum [*On Prophesying through Dreams*] (treatise)

De Longitudine et Brevitate Vitae [*On the Length and Brevity of Life*] (treatise)

De Memoria et Reminiscentia [*On Memory*] (treatise)

De Sensu et Sensibili [*On Sensation*] (treatise)

De Somniis [*On Dreams*] (treatise)

De Somno [*On Sleep*] (treatise)

De Vita et Morte [*On Life and Death*] (treatise)

Physics

Physica [*Physics*] (treatise)

*Since the dates of Aristotle's treatises are unknown, his works are listed here in alphabetical order.

PRINCIPAL ENGLISH TRANSLATIONS

De Anima [translated by R. D. Hicks] 1907

The Works of Aristotle Translated into English [edited by J. A. Smith and W. D. Ross] 1910-52

CRITICISM

LOGIC

J. M. E. Moravcsik (essay date 1967)

SOURCE: "Aristotle's Theory of Categories," in *Aristotle: A Collection of Critical Essays,* edited by J.

M. E. Moravcsik, Doubleday & Company, Inc., 1967, pp. 125-48.

[In the following essay, Moravcsik examines the categories devised by Aristotle and offers an explanation regarding their role in Aristotle's theories. Moravcsik maintains that the nature of the list of categories demonstrates Aristotle's views regarding the structure of language and regarding the relationship between the structure of language and the structure of reality.]

In several of his writings Aristotle presents what came to be known as a "list of categories." The presentation of a list, by itself, is not a philosophic theory. This paper attempts a few modest steps toward an understanding of the theory or theories in which the list of categories is embedded. To arrive at such understanding we shall have to deal with the following questions: What classes of expressions designate items each of which falls under only one category? What is the list a list of? and What gives it unity? To show this to be a worthwhile enterprise, let us consider a few passages in which the list of categories is introduced or mentioned.

In *Topics* 103b20 ff. the list is introduced as containing certain kinds *(gené)* within which one can find the accidents, genus, properties, and definition of anything. Thus apparently all (simple?) elements of the nature of any entity are to be found in one of the categories. In *Metaphysics* 1028a10 ff. we are told that 'is' has as many senses as there are categories. Thus we see that Aristotle analyzes the ambiguity of 'is' with the list of categories as an assumed background. What he takes to be the systematic ambiguity of 'is' provides one of the cornerstones of his metaphysical speculations. In *Physics* 225b5 ff. Aristotle analyzes the concept of *kinésis* and concludes that instances of this can be found in three of the categories.

Each of these passages presents problems; some of these will be taken up later in this paper. This brief preliminary survey is intended only to show that the list of categories plays an important role in several of Aristotle's theories, and thus it is reasonable to assume that the list has constitutive principles and unity.

I

Which parts of language designate an item in one of the categories? In *Categories* 1b25 ff. the list of categories is introduced as containing the kinds (e.g. quality, quantity) of those items (e.g. white, grammatical, three cubits long) which are signified by "things said without any combination" (Ackrill's translation, contained in this volume). Chapters 2 and 4 of the *Categories* taken together make it quite clear that the "things" in question are linguistic items. Our first task is to determine which parts of language Aristotle is referring to in the passage under consideration. Ear-

lier, in 1a16 ff. we read that "Of things that are said, some involve combination while others are said without combination. Examples of those involving combination are 'man runs', 'man wins'; and of those without combination 'man', 'ox', 'runs', 'wins'."[1] In view of the meagerness of the examples, the key term in this account is "combination." As Ackrill,[2] and a century ago Trendelenburg,[3] pointed out, the Greek term *sumploké* used here by Aristotle had been previously used by Plato to refer not to mere conjunction or juxtaposition, but rather to the interweaving of words and phrases into sentences.[4] This would suggest that the uncombined elements are parts of language from which sentences can be formed. This is confirmed by 2a4 ff., where Aristotle says that the combination of these items produces a true or false sentence. (Aristotle regards sentences as the bearers of truth-value.) There is an interesting parallel to this passage in *Topics* 101b26-28, according to which the key elements in a statement are property, genus, definition, and accident, and it is emphasized that none of these by themselves make up a statement. Thus as a reasonable first approximation we can say that Aristotle is interested in potential elements of sentences that are true or false, or definitions. One is tempted to add the qualification: "sentences of subject-predicate form," for neither in the examples given nor in the subsequent discussions are sentences expressing identity or existence treated. Their inclusion in the discussion would raise some interesting questions about the extent to which these types of sentence could be regarded as "interweaving," and about the senses of 'is' involved. The addition of this qualification would be in harmony with Trendelenburg's remark that Aristotle in this context seems to have in mind what Kant called judgments,[5] (a notion which carries similar limitations).

Having specified the relevant class of sentences, we should investigate whether the Aristotelian theory entails that every element of such a sentence designates an item, and whether every element that designates is supposed to designate an item falling into only one of the categories. An affirmative answer to either question would place the theory in jeopardy. There is, however, evidence that:

(i) Aristotle does not think that every word or phrase which could be part of a sentence of subject-predicate form has the function of designating an entity.

As both Steinthal and Trendelenburg remarked,[6] Aristotle does not ascribe the same type of significance to every word within a sentence, and he does not think that every word has a designative role. In *Poetics* 1456b38 ff. he separates from nouns and verbs (to which he also assimilates adjectives) the so-called connectors or auxiliary expressions. These are said to include particles and prepositions, but in order to complement the theory of categories they ought to include a great deal more: logical constants, articles, and the ordinary language equivalents of quantifiers must also be members of this class. There is evidence to support the view that Aristotle intended the connectors to include a great deal more than he explicitly mentions. For one thing, what he says about them applies to a much larger group than his examples would suggest, for he says that these expressions (a) do not designate and (b) do not contribute to the content of a new (larger) linguistic unit, i.e. the sentence. these criteria are interesting, for they show that Aristotle did not mark off the connectors on purely syntactic grounds. The criteria can be taken as foreshadowing the characterization of what were later called the syncategorematic expressions. In any case, these conditions would allow all the above-mentioned types of expression to qualify. It is impossible to say how many of these Aristotle had in mind when he wrote the *Poetics,* but the fluidity of the classification is witnessed by *Rhetoric* III 5 where— as Steinthal saw—Aristotle blends articles, pronouns, and conjunctives into one class. Steinthal's interpretation of what Aristotle thought of as the main parts of speech is of further relevance here, for it is claimed that apart from nouns and verbs Aristotle recognized only one more class, i.e. the connectors.[7] None of this is direct evidence, but taken all together it renders plausible the interpretation of the class of connectors on the suggested broad basis.

With this we have narrowed down the candidates for the "uncombined elements" to the members of the class of designative expressions which can be elements of those sentences that are definitions or are of subject-predicate form. Still, further restrictions are obviously needed. Fortunately there is evidence to support additional qualifications.

(ii) Aristotle does not think that every noun or verb designates an item in one of the categories.

In *De Interpretatione* 16a13 ff. Aristotle lists as a necessary condition for the production of what is true or false the combination of verb and noun, and in this context treats "being" as a verb. We see, however, from his treatment of being in the *Categories* and the *Metaphysics* (see the reference in the beginning of this paper) that he does not construe being as falling into only one of the categories. His claim that being is not a genus, and the argument backing up this claim,[8] are sufficient ground on which to base the interpretation that 'being'—and similar terms like 'same', 'one', etc.—have either no designative role or a divided designative role.

Before we consider further qualifications, let us look briefly at the interesting status that definitions had for Aristotle. It is not clear whether he regarded definitions as true or false, and whether they counted as instances of combination. The passage quoted from the *Topics* above casts doubt on their counting as combinations. Now in *De Interpretatione,* chapters 4 and 5, he argues that what is true or false must contain such interweaving or combination. Again in *Poetics* 1457a25 ff. Aristotle says that, though definitions are sentences, they need not contain a verb. This passage, however, can be construed as saying only that no verb need appear explicitly in a definition; the same is true in Greek for many other types of sentences. Again in *De Anima* III 6 it is pointed out that a definition does not involve a mental task of synthesis as an assertion does. All of this together supports the interpretation according to which Aristotle did not regard definitions as true or false or as produced by combination. Nevertheless, we must assume that he thought of parts of definitions as falling under one category.

(iii) There are some noun- or verb-phrases (other than words like 'being', etc.) that designate items falling under more than one category.

An obvious example of a phrase designating a complex that spans two categories is the expression 'incontinent man'. In order to rule out such cases we have to introduce further qualifications. The restriction to be put forward here is not backed by direct textual evidence, but it is supported by what we took to be the significance of *sumploké* and the proposed broad delineation of the class of connectors: it is to rule out as not completely uncombined all those phrases which the mere addition of connectors can transform into a sentence. For though 'red colored' and 'incontinent man' are not sentences, they can be expanded into the sentences 'all red things are colored' and 'some men are incontinent' by the mere addition of connectors. Here one can see the importance of our previous qualification that only sentences of subject-predicate form are under consideration. Without it our current restriction would turn out to be so strict as to leave no word in the "uncombined" class, since the addition of "there are some . . . things" will render 'white' or 'heavy' into sentences; yet 'white' and 'heavy' are known to be expressions which Aristotle regards as "in no way combined."

Throughout this discussion we have taken the notion of a sentence for granted. It is time to see what Aristotle has to say on this topic. But his account of a sentence as significant sound, some part of which is significant in separation as an expression (*De Interpretatione* 16b26 ff. and *Poetics* 1457a23 ff.), is obviously inadequate since it fails even to separate sentences from clauses. The reason for this seems to be that Aristotle finds himself in a curious predicament. He cannot accept the Platonic account of a sentence as the interweaving of noun and verb since he recognizes counterexamples to it. On the other hand, he knows that he cannot use the theory of categories to explain a sentence as an intercategorial connection, since he knows that a sentence like 'all men are animals' does not combine elements from different categories. Thus he lacks a conceptual framework that would enable him to give an adequate account of what a sentence is. In view of this, we shall have to continue in this discussion to take the notion of a sentence for granted.

We are not yet finished with the required restrictions, for we must admit the following:

(iv) Not all relevantly simple nouns and verbs designate items falling into only one category.

As Aristotle saw, one can simply define a word x as 'incontinent man' and thereby create a word which our previous restrictions allow as uncombined but which designates something that spans two categories. What is clearly needed is a further restriction that would rule out expressions like x as somehow ill-formed. There is evidence that Aristotle did have such a qualification in mind, for in *De Interpretatione,* chapters 8 and 11, he discusses the problem of the extent to which a predicate expression may or may not designate a "genuine unity." The discussions are sketchy and no adequate interpretations of them have so far been offered. Thus Ackrill wrote[9] that the difficulty of deciding what Aristotle regards as a genuine unity "corresponds" to the difficulty of deciding which simple phrases are supposed to designate items falling into only one category. Ackrill is quite correct in emphasizing the magnitude of the task facing the interpreter, but this should not keep us from seeing that the notion of a genuine unity could still be invoked by Aristotle in an account of the "uncombined" elements of language. For as 18a18 ff. shows, there are certain predicates, e.g. that which is the equivalent of 'horse and man', which designate items falling into one category only, which nevertheless Aristotle would not regard as having genuine unity. Thus whatever the correct account of genuine unity is, the passage under consideration shows that it does not presuppose the correlation between uncombined elements and the list of categories, and thus it could be invoked without circularity to place further restriction on what is to count as an uncombined element.

In view of these considerations it is not unreasonable to suppose that Aristotle could describe x defined as 'incontinent man' as an expression not designating a genuine unity; that he could do so without assuming anything about its correlation with any of the categories, and that he could on this ground rule that it is not one of the legitimate uncombined elements. This final restriction leaves us with the following formulation of Aristotle's view:

(v) Those elements of sentences of subject-predicate form, or definitions, which (a) are not connectors; (b) are not, like 'being', otherwise non-designative in nature; (c) cannot be turned into sentences of subject-predicate form, by the mere addition of connectors; and (d) designate genuine unities, are "uncombined elements" of language, and designate items falling into one and only one category.

Intuitively restated, Aristotle's principle says that by what we would call semantic and syntactic analysis[10] we can discover certain basic units among the elements of sentences of subject-predicate form, and that these turn out to designate those simple elements of reality which fall into only one category. Thus the designative link between these simple parts of language and the simple parts of reality which fall into only one category is, according to Aristotle, the key link between the structure of language and the structure of reality.

This account is not without difficulties. The main problem is the as yet unexplained doctrine of genuine unity. Another problem is the fact that the restriction ascribed to Aristotle that rests on the possibility of expanding certain phrases into sentences with the help of connectors is not supported by direct evidence. But it is not a weakness of the interpretation that it seeks to connect what is said in the *Categories* with some of what is said in the *Poetics* and the *Rhetorics.* On the contrary, to show that under a certain interpretation these passages complement the views of the passages in the *Categories* is to give that interpretation added plausibility.

Given the difficulties, we might cast around for alternative interpretations. In this connection it is worth noting that both the possible solutions listed by Ackrill,[11] and perceptively criticized by him, turn out to be inferior to the account presented in this paper. One of these solutions takes "without combination" to mean "designates an item falling into only one category." The main difficulty with this view is that—as Ackrill observes—it construes the statement introducing the list of categories in chapter 4 as analytic. If the statement that the elements which are in no way combined designate items falling into only one category is analytic, it is deceptively so; for this would imply that there is no way of sorting out the uncombined elements of a sentence except by observing whether their designata fall into only one category. Thus the beginning of chapter 4 could just as well have started: "some sentential elements designate . . . and we regard these as being without any combination." Furthermore, according to this interpretation what Aristotle says about the combined and uncombined parts of language rests entirely on metaphysical grounds and thus cannot be connected with what he says elsewhere about the structure of language.

The other possible solution fares hardly better, since according to it the distinction between what is and what is not combined is identical with the distinction between simple words and more complex sentential elements. In order to accept this view we would have to assume that in chapter 4 of the *Categories* Aristotle forgets about the possibility of simple terms with complex meanings. However, we saw above that this possibility is discussed in *De Interpretatione,* and to suppose that Aristotle is not aware of this issue in a context in which it is vital is to accuse him of too gross a mistake. Moreover, this version suggests that Aristotle's distinction among different parts of language rests on purely superficial features, whereas the passages quoted from the *Topics* and the *Poetics* assure us that this is not so.

To sum up, if we can regard the evidence presented in support of the interpretation argued for in this section as adequate, the interpretation recommends itself on the following grounds: it links Aristotle's metaphysical speculation with his view on the structure of language; it relates the *Categories* to what is said in other works on language; it helps to explore Aristotle's views on language, which turn out to be far from simple-minded; and it sketches the structure of an explanation that Aristotle would be likely to give as justification of the claim that there are certain "uncombined" elements in language with a—to him—vital designative role.

II

The unity and completeness of the list of categories. In the beginning of chapter 4 of the *Categories* we find a list of ten categories. The labels given to them are oddly heterogeneous. Some are philosophical constructs, some are ordinary questions, and some are lifted out of simple singular sentences of subject-predicate form.[12] Thus at first glance it is not clear whether the list is supposed to yield an ontological classification or an analysis of the structure of propositions. Some interpreters have gone as far as accusing Aristotle of having failed to give the list sufficient unity. Perhaps the most famous of these critics is Kant,[13] who assumes that Aristotle was interested in the same task that he was—i.e. to give a set of necessary conditions under which judgments are possible—and then concludes that Aristotle failed in this task. A comparison of Kant's categories with those of Aristotle, however, suggests the not too surprising alternative that Kant and Aristotle designed their categories with different purposes in mind. Many of Kant's categories must be construed as properties of judgments or ideas (e.g. universality or singularity). Aristotle's list, on the other hand, cannot be so construed. His items are either very general properties of objects or not properties at all. There is no reason why the two lists should coincide, and once the difference in their aims has been discerned, the two need not be regarded as conflicting.[14]

One way of explaining the heterogeneity of the labels is to assume that Aristotle is concerned primarily with the types to be designated, and not with the manner of designation. As we shall see, the adoption of this assumption is rewarding. We must note at this point, however, that it leads us to reject a claim like that made by Trendelenburg, according to which the list of categories is derived from grammatical considerations.[15]

Let us begin by considering one commonly accepted characterization of the categories, the one that describes them as the "highest predicables."[16] In order for this view to be even initially plausible, we must construe 'predicable' in a technical sense. For not only is the first category ambiguous between primary and secondary substance, but some of the examples given for the other categories, e.g. 'in the Lyceum' and 'yesterday', cannot be regarded as predicables in the ordinary sense of the term. What this technical sense of 'predicable' wide enough to embrace everything falling under each of the ten categories could be is far from clear. But even if such a sense could be found, further difficulties arise in connection with the term 'highest'. There are two ways in which the metaphorical value of this term could be captured by logical analysis. On one interpretation predicate p^I is higher than predicate p^{II} if and only if all members of the class which makes up the range of application of p^{II} are also members of the class which makes up the range of application of p^I but not the other way around. In this sense *animal* is higher than *man*. The other interpretation takes p^I as higher than p^{II} if and only if p^I is an attribute of p^{II}. In this sense *category* would be a higher predicate than *quality* or *quantity,* and *colour, quality, category* would constitute a hierarchy. It is clear, however, that Aristotle does not want such a pyramid. He denies the ontological reality of the higher strata here indicated. Not to do so would leave him far closer to Platonism than he would find comfortable. Thus the sense in which the categories would have to be "higher" is the former sense—as Cook Wilson noted.[17] That is to say, as we go to wider and wider genera, the particulars contained in any one genera are on the same level as the particulars contained in the wider genera. Given this characterization of the categories, one is confronted with the question: where must one stop? Why call the categories the "highest" (actually the "widest") genera? The only plausible Aristotelian reply is: "because by some principle the genera that would have even wider comprehensions are not genuine genera; i.e. they have no ontological status." Such a reply takes us back to a metaphysical principle, and it is the explication of that principle, rather than the phrase "highest predicables," that will shed light on the nature of the categories.

Another current interpretation could be characterized as the "linguistic view." Among its advocates are Ryle[18] and Anscombe.[19] According to this view Aristotle uses the list of categories to mark off the different kinds of fairly simple things that can be said about a substance. As such, the list could not be regarded as final or complete, since there may be an indeterminate number of ways in which one can raise questions about substances. The most important achievement of the list turns out to be—according to this interpretation—the anticipation of the concept of semantic category and the notion of a "category-mistake," a confusion which supposedly underlies a type of semantically deviant sentence. (E.g. an answer in terms of food to a question about the size of a substance allegedly does not make sense, even though the sentence expressing the answer is—on the surface at least—syntactically well formed.)

This is not the place to hold autopsy over the notion of a category-mistake as used by recent analytic philosophers. To show that this could not be the correct interpretation of Aristotle's theory will have to suffice. Three considerations prove fatal to this account. First, according to this view once the significance of the list is properly understood, questions about completeness could not arise. But, as some of the passages quoted at the beginning of this paper show, Aristotle committed himself to claims which entail that the list should contain mutually exclusive categories which are jointly exhaustive of reality. (More on this point below.) Thus either this interpretation is incorrect, or we must suppose that Aristotle himself completely misunderstood the significance of his own theory. Such an assumption should be adopted by a historian only as a last resort. Secondly, the only basis for the individuation of the categories would be the linguistic intuition which allows us to detect category-mistakes. It is clear, however, that Aristotle does not leave the individuation of his categories to intuitions, linguistic or otherwise. He states their differentiating characteristics quite explicitly: e.g. quality is that in virtue of which things can be said to be similar; quantity is that which can be said to be equal or unequal.[20] These characteristics do not depend on the notion of semantic anomaly. Finally, it is difficult to suppose that had Aristotle been concerned with semantic anomaly, he would have missed the glaring fact that to describe a shape as red or blue is semantically odd, even though both shape and colour belong to the same Aristotelian category, i.e. that of quality. Thus the linguistic interpretation can be safely rejected.

Let us proceed to the consideration of the interpretation put forward by Professor Ackrill.[21] According to this view Aristotle arrived at the list of categories in two ways. One of these is the sorting out of the different types of question that can be asked about substances. The other is to start by asking what any given thing is and to continue by repeating that question with reference to whatever the previous answer revealed. Both these approaches are supposed to come to an end when irreducible genera are reached. Ackrill thinks that the two ways are exemplified in *Topics* I 9. He does not find it surprising that they should result in the same list, with the exception that only the second brings particulars into the classification. He leaves open the question of completeness, since he does not think that Aristotle had any grounds, in the form of a general argument or principle, on which he could have concluded that his list includes all and only irreducibly different genera.

This summary shows that Ackrill's account has an element in common with the "linguistic view." Both interpretations assume that the list of categories is arrived at by the consideration of questions, or classes of properties, concerning substances. The only evidence in favour of this assumption is the fact that Aristotle's examples seem to be about a substance, i.e. man. We must remember, however, that Aristotle employed the category-structure in his attempt to show substances to be prior to all else. Thus if we accept this hypothesis, we must attribute to him the grand design of outlining a set of categories by classifying questions about substances, and then using this structure to show that substances are prior to all entities collected under the other categories. Such an outrageously question-begging procedure should not be attributed to any philosopher except in the face of overwhelming evidence. After all, the use of a pattern such as the one under consideration would make proofs of ontological priority surprisingly easy. For example, one could collect all the questions which can be raised about shadows, classify the relevant predicates gathered through the answers to these questions, and conclude that the items in the categories thus formed are posterior to shadows since they are specifications of shadows. As long as Aristotle's general account of his list and his characterizations of the several categories lend themselves to alternative accounts, which avoid such question-begging, these alternatives should be explored.

This objection leads to the observation that it would be surprising indeed if the two approaches described by Ackrill were to yield the same list. Why should the classification of the aspects of one kind of entity, e.g. substance, coincide with an exhaustive classification of the essences of all entities that make up reality? Would this be true also of other types of entity, such as events, qualities, numbers, etc.? Such a correlation will not hold unless one views everything as a modification or relational accident of the type of entity preferred. These ways of viewing things are trivial.

Ackrill's second way of arriving at the list of categories also contains an inherent weakness. For there are an indeterminate number of ways in which we can classify things by the repeated asking of the question: What is it? Furthermore, how could one decide whether the highest genera have been reached? Intuitions, as we saw, are not enough. To take one of Aristotle's examples, why should one not arrive at change *(kinésis)* as one of the categories? It certainly answers a "what is it?" question. Yet, as we know, Aristotle does not think that this is one of the categories; on the contrary, he thinks that the list of categories must be presupposed by the adequate analysis of this concept which shows it to be cutting across three categories.

It does not, therefore, seem likely that Aristotle arrived at his list in either of the ways that Ackrill suggests. In view of this we should take a look at the passage in the *Topics* (103b22 ff.)—mentioned above—which Ackrill construes as containing the second way of arriving at the list. It states, among other things, that the essence of anything will be found in one of the categories. This statement does not entail Ackrill's second approach, but only that the categories make up such an exhaustive classification of reality that no real essence will cut across categories. Thus it is consistent with the possible claim that there are irreducible ultimate genera within the categories, or that the categories could be reduced in number. Most importantly, the statement is only a necessary condition for the correct list of categories; in itself it does not provide a procedure for arriving at the list. Nor does it give a principle of unity for the list of categories.

In turning to the more constructive task of spelling out a plausible alternative interpretation, let us begin by noting—partly on the basis of the negative discussion above—some necessary conditions for any adequate interpretation. These conditions arise out of the ways in which Aristotle employs the list of categories in his philosophizing.[22] The passages quoted previously from the *Topics, Physics,* and *Metaphysics,* together with *Metaphysics* 1017a, show that Aristotle uses the list in his analyses of key concepts such as being and change, and also in his claiming priority for substances. Thus the list has to be complete in the following ways: (i) It must be exhaustive of all that Aristotle takes to be existing. (ii) No reduction of the number of categories should be possible without violating the principle upon which the list is constructed. (iii) No further subdivision of the categories should be possible without violating the constitutive principle. Without these conditions Aristotle could not claim that *kinésis* can be found in exactly three categories, or that by saying that 'is' has as many senses as there are categories he is giving a significant characterization of being.

These conditions help in resolving the question whether the categories include only universals, or particulars as well. Underlying this issue is the debate whether there are particulars and universals in each category, or only universals in all but the first.[23] It is difficult to conceive of each category as containing universals; for example, what universal would correspond to 'in the Lyceum'? On the other hand, it is equally difficult to conceive of particulars falling under each category. What particulars would we find under the category of relation? The conditions laid down above do not entail that each category must contain both universals and particulars; they entail rather, that the categories jointly must contain all the universals and particulars that Aristotle would acknowledge as existing. This leaves open the possibility that in some categories there may be only universals, in some only particulars, and in some both. In any case, events, processes, and abstract entities such as numbers must be contained within the categories. The analysis of *kinésis,* and the explanation of the category of quantity reveals how Aristotle conceived of this inclusion.

The constitutive principle which we seek is likely to be one that shows how the categories make up classes of predicates (in a very wide sense of 'predicate') to each of which some type of entity must be related. Apart from the issue of question-begging, our conditions of completeness guarantee that the type in question cannot be that of substance; for in order to be a sensible substance an entity must have both shape and weight, and these two properties fall under the same Aristotelian category of quality. Thus if the categories are those classes of predicates of which substances must partake, then the list as we have it would have to be subdivided to put weight and shape into different categories, a violation of the completeness conditions.

A more adequate interpretation can be given, based partly on Bonitz's suggestion[24] that Aristotle's list yields a survey of what is given in sense experience, and that each entity thus given must be related to some item in each of the categories. According to this interpretation the constitutive principle of the list of categories is that they constitute those classes of items to each of which any sensible particular—substantial or otherwise—must be related. Any sensible particular, substance, event, sound, etc. must be related to some substance; it must have some quality and quantity; it must have relational properties, it must be related to times and places; and it is placed within a network of causal chains and laws, thus being related to the categories of affecting and being affected. The only categories of the complete list of ten that cause difficulties for this interpretation are those of "having" and of "being-in-a-position." In this connection the following should be noted. First, these two categories are not always included in the list Aristotle gives. Secondly, 'have' is taken by Aristotle—as chapter 15 of the *Categories* shows—in a variety of senses, one of which is the sense of "having" parts. Given this construction, all sensible particulars relate to that category. The category of "position" is an obscure one, and it causes difficulties for any interpretation, including the ones surveyed critically above.

This proposed interpretation meets the completeness conditions stated above. Neither a reduction nor a further subdivision would leave the list as definitive of that to which sensible particulars must be related. The account also meets the exhaustiveness condition, at least as far as Aristotle is concerned. For the Stagirite believed that all properties, including the second-order ones, are ultimately related to what is presented by our senses. Finally, this account construes the list of categories as the proper background for Aristotle's investigations of being, change, and priority relations. If it is question-begging, it is so only in the same way that one might construe Aristotle's general preference for what is presented to the senses—a preference never defended—as question-begging. Thus this interpretation fulfills the promise made at the beginning of this paper; we have shown how the list of categories can be construed as part of a theory and how this in turn serves as a background for other Aristotelian theories.

Conclusion. The theory of categories is partly a theory about language and partly a theory about reality. With regard to language it states that certain elements of a language have key-designating roles, the full understanding of which requires that we understand the designata as falling within those classes which jointly form the set definitive of that to which a sensible particular must be related. We can see from this that Aristotle did not think of the structure of language as mirroring the structure of reality. But he did believe that there are specific items of language and reality the correlation of which forms the crucial link between the two.

Notes

[1] J. L. Ackrill's translation here is far superior to the old Oxford version, which renders the first part of this passage as: "Forms of speech are either simple or composite." This suggests, wrongly, that Aristotle is saying something about all forms of speech, and, equally wrongly, that the distinction to be drawn is a surface distinction between what is syntactically simple or analyzable.

[2] J. L. Ackrill, *Aristotle's Categories and De Interpretatione* (Oxford, 1963), p. 73. (See earlier in this volume p. 102.)

[3] A. Trendelenburg, *Geschichte der Kategorienlehre* (Hildesheim: Olms, 1846 [1963]), p. 11.

[4] On Plato's views on this see J. M. Moravcsik, "Sumploké Eidoon," *Archiv für die Geschichte der Philosophie,* XLII (1960) 117-29; also "Being and Meaning in the *Sophist,*" *Acta Philosophica Fennica,* XIV (1962), especially pp. 61-65.

[5] Trendelenburg, op. cit., p. 12.

[6] Trendelenburg, op. cit., pp. 24 ff. and H. Steinthal, *Geschichte der Sprachwissenschaft* (Hildesheim: Olms, 1890 [1961]), Vol. I, pp. 263 ff.

[7] Steinthal, op. cit., pp. 260 ff.

[8] The most profound discussion of this argument is to be found in John Cook Wilson's paper "Categories in Aristotle and in Kant," *Statement and Inference,* Vol. II, pp. 696-706 [above, pp. 75-89].

[9] Ackrill, op. cit., p. 126.

[10] Aristotle, like Plato, did not distinguish between these.

[11] Ackrill, op. cit., pp. 73-74 [pp. 102-103 above].

[12] Ackrill, op. cit., p. 73 and Trendelenburg, op. cit., p. 13.

[13] *Critique of Pure Reason* B 105-107.

[14] For a different view of the relation between Aristotle and Kant see H. W. B. Joseph, *An Introduction to Logic* (Oxford, 1916), pp. 63-65. Also Cook Wilson, op, cit,, p. 704 [p. 85].

[15] Trendelenburg, op. cit., p. 33.

[16] As remarked but not endorsed by W. D. Ross in *Aristotle,* pp. 27-28. According to Joseph, op. cit., pp. 48-49, the Greek word for category . . . means 'predicate,' but for counterexamples see H. Bonitz, *Über die Kategorien des Aristoteles* (Vienna, 1853), pp. 30-31.

[17] Cook Wilson, op. cit., pp. 696 and 705 [pp. 75 and 86].

[18] G. Ryle, "Categories," *Logic and Language,* second ser., ed. A. Flew (Oxford, 1955), pp. 65-81. Ryle—like Kant—thinks that Aristotle was really interested in what he, Ryle, is interested in doing but that he did not do it so well. I find deeply depressing this tendency of philosophers to think that the great men of the past tried to do what they are doing but that they did not do it so well.

[19] G. E. Anscombe, in *Three Philosophers* (Oxford, 1961), pp. 14-15.

[20] *Categories* 11a15-20 and 6a26.

[21] Ackrill, op. cit., pp. 78-81 [pp. 109-12].

[22] "Da endlich jede Lehre erst in ihren Folgen ihre Stärke und Schwäche offenbart, so wird es wichtig sein, die Kategorien in der Anwendung zu beobachten." Trendelenburg, op. cit., p. 11.

[23] See Ross. op. cit., p. 28, n. 20.

[24] Bonitz, op. cit., pp. 18, 35, and 55.

G. E. R. Lloyd (essay date 1968)

SOURCE: "Logic and Metaphysics," in *Aristotle: The Growth and Structure of His Thought,* Cambridge at the University Press, 1968, pp. 111-32.

[*In the following excerpt, Lloyd discusses Aristotle's doctrine of categories, the syllogism, and the idea of scientific knowledge. In studying the works in which these topics are presented, Lloyd stresses the comprehensive, original, and lucid nature of Aristotle's writings on the subject of logic.*]

The first part of this study has been devoted to giving the outlines of Aristotle's intellectual development. In the second I shall take the main branches of his work in turn and attempt to describe and elucidate the fundamentals of his thought, locating his principal ideas in the context of the philosophical and scientific discussions of the time, and assessing their value and importance. The first general field I shall consider is logic. Here his work is particularly comprehensive, very largely original and for the most part eminently lucid. It is, moreover, highly professional, and the specialist will find a great deal that is of interest in the logical treatises apart from those sections of them that contain what still remains an excellent introduction to the study of elementary logic. For the sake of illustrating his work in this field, however, it will be enough to select three topics for particular comment, his doctrine of categories, his syllogistic and his conception of so-called 'scientific' knowledge.

The logical treatises, known collectively as the Organon or 'tool' of thought, begin with two short works, the *Categories* and the *de Interpretatione,* dealing with terms and with propositions respectively. The first chapter of the *Categories,* for example, begins by drawing distinctions between things named (1) 'homonymously', (2) 'synonymously' and (3) 'paronymously'. Things are named 'homonymously', first, when they have only the name in common and the definition corresponding to the name is different in each case. In English, 'box' is the name of both a container and a shrub, but the definition corresponding to the name is different in each case. Secondly, things are named 'synonymously' when both name and the corresponding definition are the same. A man and an ox are both said to be 'animals', and the definition corresponding to the term 'animal' is the same in both cases. Thirdly, a thing is named 'paronymously' when it derives its name from some other word, as a grammarian derives his name from grammar.

In the *de Interpretatione,* ch. 4, for example, he distinguishes between a sentence and a statement or proposition. A sentence is any significant combination of words. A proposition is a sentence that affirms or denies something—a predicate—of something else—the sub-

ject. Propositions are either true or false, but this is not true of every sentence. A prayer, for instance, is a sentence but is neither true nor false (*Int.* 17 a 4 f.). And later in the same work, ch. 10, 19 b 5 ff., he discusses various pairs of affirmations and negations, where he points out, for example, that the contradictory of 'every man is just' is not 'every man is not-just', but rather 'not every man is just'.

These are all simple distinctions that seem obvious enough to us, but it is worth bearing in mind that for the most part they had not been stated clearly and explicitly before Aristotle. The doctrine of the categories itself is at once better known and more obscure than these useful but elementary logical points. In ch. 4 of the *Categories* he classifies the things that are signified by simple expressions under ten heads, giving examples of each:

> substance (man, horse)
> quantity (two cubits long, three cubits long)
> quality (white, grammatical)
> relation (double, half, greater)
> place (in the Lyceum, in the market)
> time (yesterday, last year)
> position (lies, sits)
> state (has shoes on, has armour on)
> action (cuts, burns)
> affection (is cut, is burnt).

Elsewhere there are slightly different classifications, and the number of categories mentioned varies. In the *Topics* (1, ch. 9) there are again ten, although when the list is introduced at 103b22 the first category is referred to as 'what it is', . . . rather than as . . . substance or being. In other passages there are shorter lists, of eight or six or five categories, but substance, quantity and quality are always included. Such differences are not particularly important, but we should beware of assuming that Aristotle intended any of his lists to be definitive and exhaustive.

The first question that might be raised is whether the classification is one of things or of terms, an ontological, or a logical, classification. To this the answer must be that the categories are primarily intended as a classification of reality, of the things signified by terms, rather than of the signifying terms themselves. This, at least, is how the classification is introduced at the beginning of ch. 4 (1b25ff.): 'of things said without combination, *each signifies* either substance or quantity . . . ' Yet he evidently arrived at his classification mainly from a consideration of linguistic facts, that is of what kinds of things may be said, and of what kinds of questions may be asked, about anything, and this is natural enough, for he assumes that the logical distinctions that these data suggest will reflect and reveal the real distinctions between the things signified in which he is interested. The original logical meaning of the word [*katēgoria*] 'predicate', although in the first category primary substances, that is individuals such as Callias or Socrates, are not logical predicates, but subjects of which other things are predicated: the term for subject is . . . what underlies, the same term that he uses in a different context for the 'substratum'. In part, the categories may be derived from considering what may be predicated of a subject and examining what sorts of things these predicates signify. Callias is six foot tall, white, larger than Socrates and so on. If we ask what whiteness, for example, is, we shall answer first that it is a colour, but then we can ask the same question about colour, answering in turn that it is a quality: when we arrive at the category, the process stops.

The categories are the ultimate classes into which whatever exists or is real may be said to fall. But what is the use or value of this doctrine? When in ch. 5 he develops the distinction between 'primary' and 'secondary' substance, he is evidently combatting Plato. For Aristotle, 'what is called a substance most strictly, primarily and most of all' is the individual man, the individual horse and so on (2a11ff.). The species and genera—man, horse, animal—are secondary substances. Even though the Platonic Forms are not mentioned, he is clearly joining issue, in this passage, with Plato's view that the Forms are ontologically prior to the particulars. Against the Platonic doctrine Aristotle argues that individuals are substances in the strictest sense, for they are the subjects for all other things, and all other things are either predicated of them or are in them (2b15ff., 37ff.). If the primary substances did not exist, he says at 2b5f., it would be impossible for any of the other things to exist: qualities, for example, cannot exist by themselves, that is apart from the individual substances that have the qualities.

The distinction between primary and secondary substance, and the doctrine that the other categories presuppose substance, are important points that Aristotle brings out in the course of developing his doctrine. But in general he does not spell out in the **Categories** itself how his doctrine is to be used. Its usefulness and value only become apparent when we turn to passages in other treatises where Aristotle puts the doctrine to work to draw distinctions either between classes of things or between the meanings of terms. Thus in the **Physics** (1, chh. 7 and 8 and v, chh. 1 and 2) and in the **de Generatione et Corruptione** (1, ch. 3) he points out that change differs according to the category in which the change takes place, and this is particularly relevant to earlier physical speculation, since it helps him to emphasise that to deny that there is unqualified coming-to-be in the category of substance is not to deny that other types of change may take place, for example locomotion in the category of place. To deny that anything can come to be from what is totally non-existent is not to deny that a hot thing may become

cold, or that a young animal may grow into a mature one, or that an arrow may be shot from a bow. Again at several points in the **Metaphysics,** for example at 1017a22ff., he brings the doctrine of categories to bear on the vexed question of the ambiguities of the verb 'to be', and in the **Topics,** 107a3ff., he recommends examining the categories in which a predicate is used as a general method of detecting ambiguities in reasoning.

The syllogism

By far the best known, and the most typical, product of Aristotle's work in logic is the theory of the syllogism. In its usual form the syllogism consists of two premisses and a conclusion. Very occasionally the conclusion is stated in the form of an *inference: A* belongs to all *B; B* belongs to all *C; therefore A* belongs to all *C.* But as a general rule the syllogism is expressed as a form of *implication: if A* belongs to all *B,* and *B* belongs to all *C, then A* belongs to all *C.*

The premisses and conclusions of syllogisms are differentiated according to three criteria, quantity, quality and modality. Under quantity, first, he distinguishes universal, particular and indefinite statements. In a universal statement something is said to belong to all or none of *X,* and in a particular one something is said to belong, or not to belong, to some of *X.* These are usually illustrated by such examples as 'all men are animals' and 'some men are wise', but Aristotle's premisses are generally stated in a slightly different form, which is rather less natural in English, thus: 'animal belongs to, . . . , or is predicated of, . . . , every man'; wisdom belongs to some men'. Finally an indefinite statement says that something belongs or does not belong to *X* without specifying whether it is to all or to some of it: one of Aristotle's examples is 'pleasure is not good'.

Secondly under quality he distinguishes affirmative and negative statements. If we leave aside indefinite statements, these first two differentiae may be combined to give a fourfold division of statements:

> universal affirmative: *A* belongs to all *B*
> universal negative: *A* belongs to no *B*
> particular affirmative: *A* belongs to some *B*
> particular negative: *A* does not belong to some
>   B.

These four types, which form the traditional schedule of propositions, are referred to, for the sake of convenience, by the letters *A, E, I* and *O* respectively, these letters being derived from the vowels in the two verbs *affirmo* and n*ego.*

Thirdly under modality he distinguishes between the three types of statements (i) '*A* belongs to *B*', (ii) '*A* necessarily belongs to *B*' and (iii) '*A* may belong to *B*', or put more simply (i) '*B* is *A*', (ii) '*B* must be *A*' and (iii) '*B* may be *A*'. These three kinds are generally referred to as 'assertoric', 'apodeictic' and 'problematic' statements respectively.

Passing from his consideration of different types of premiss in the opening chapters of the first book of the **Prior Analytics** Aristotle turns in ch. 4 to examine how syllogisms are produced, for not every combination of a pair of premisses enables a conclusion to be drawn. Here he distinguishes between three different *figures* of the syllogism according to the relationships between the terms in the premisses. These terms themselves are known as major, middle and minor. Take the stock Aristotelian example, 'if *A* belongs to all *B*, and *B* belongs to all *C*, then *A* belongs to all *C*'. The *middle term* is that which appears in both premisses—*B*. The *major term* is that which is predicated of something else in the conclusion—*A*. And the *minor term* is that of which something else is predicated in the conclusion—*C*. The major and minor terms each appear in only one of the two premisses, and the premiss in which each appears is named after it. Thus the *major premiss* is the one in which the major term appears—'*A* belongs to all *B*' in my example—and the *minor premiss* is that in which the minor term appears—'*B* belongs to all *C*'.

Syllogisms in the first figure may be described as those in which something is predicated of the middle term in the major premiss, and the middle term is predicated of something else in the minor premiss. The stock example is the one I have been using: 'if *A* belongs to all *B*, and *B* belongs to all *C*, then *A* belongs to all *C*'.

Syllogisms in the second figure are those in which the middle term is predicated of something else in both the major and the minor premiss, as in 'if *M* belongs to no *N*, and *M* belongs to all *O*, then *N* belongs to no *O*'.

Syllogisms in the third figure are those in which something is predicated of the middle term in both the major and the minor premiss, as in 'if *P* belongs to all *S*, and *R* belongs to all *S*, then *P* belongs to some *R*'.

The three figures are, as it were, the genera of the syllogism that Aristotle recognises. But in each figure there are different *moods*, depending on the quantity and the quality of the premisses. Take syllogisms in the first figure. In the stock example, 'if *A* belongs to all *B*, and *B* belongs to all *C*, then *A* belongs to all *C*', both premisses are universal affirmatives. But a combination of a universal affirmative major premiss and a particular affirmative minor one also yields a syllogism, this time with a particular affirmative conclusion: for if *A* belongs to all *B*, and *B* belongs to some *C*, then *A* belongs to some *C*. On the other hand, if one combines a universal affirmative major premiss with a

particular negative minor one no conclusion follows: if we are given that animal is predicated of all men, and that man is not predicated of some white things, this does not allow us to establish any relation between animals and white things. Equally in the second and third figures there are various valid moods besides the examples I have already given. At *APr.* 27a36ff., for instance, Aristotle shows that a combination of a universal affirmative major premiss and a particular negative minor one, which was found to produce no syllogism in the first figure, yields a particular negative conclusion in the second: if *M* belongs to all *N*, and *M* does not belong to some *O*, then *N* does not belong to some *O*.

Book I of the **Prior Analytics** contains a detailed exposition of the three figures of the syllogism not only with 'assertoric', but also with 'apodeictic' and 'problematic' premisses and with the various combinations of these, such as one assertoric with one apodeictic and so on. In the course of his discussion he draws some general conclusions, as for example that it is only in the first figure, and only in one mood of that figure, that a universal affirmative conclusion can be established: this alone yields what he calls 'perfect' syllogisms, and all the other valid moods of the syllogism can be reduced to universal syllogisms in the first figure. Again in the second figure only negative conclusions can be established, and in the third only particular ones. He gives general rules for syllogisms in any figure, pointing out that a syllogism contains three and only three terms, for even if intermediate terms are introduced, there is still only one term that acts as a middle term in each syllogism. And for a syllogism to be formed one or other premiss must be universal, and one or other premiss must be affirmative.

The most remarkable feature of the theory as a whole is undoubtedly its originality. Concrete arguments that have a syllogistic form are occasionally found in earlier texts, and there are several passages in fifth and fourth century writers where the logic of individual arguments is challenged. Moreover Plato drew attention to several important general points connected with different types of argument, as for instance when he emphasised the distinction between demonstrative and merely probable arguments in passages in the *Phaedo* (92cd) and *Theaetetus* (162e). But none of this alters the fact that it was Aristotle who conducted the first systematic analysis of the forms of argument as such. It was he who took the important step of introducing the use of symbols that can stand for *any* term, and he was the first to investigate the conditions of the validity of arguments and to draw up rules of implication.

His theory of the syllogism is, as far as it goes, admirably lucid, thorough and economical. But as is hardly surprising when we remember that it was Aristotle himself who invented the science of formal logic, it does not go far enough, and he was mistaken in his claim that all other forms of reasoning can be reduced to the syllogism. That he did not recognise the so-called fourth figure of the syllogism is a point of small importance. The fourth figure is that in which the middle term is the predicate in the major premiss and has something else predicated of it in the minor, reversing the positions it has in these premisses in the first figure, but most of the syllogisms that occur in the fourth figure are more naturally dealt with under the other three, and indeed he implicitly recognises each of the valid moods of this figure during the course of his discussion. But a more serious criticism of his syllogistic is that while his discussion of the four types of propositions, *A, E, I* and *O,* is very full, there are other types that he discusses much less fully or indeed scarcely at all. In his analysis of syllogistic argument he is chiefly interested in propositions that express relations of class-inclusion and class-exclusion between two terms. But he only rarely mentions, and certainly never deals systematically with, propositions expressing such transitive relations as, for example, 'greater than', 'equal to' or 'simultaneous with', although these too form syllogisms, such as 'if *A* is greater than *B* and *B* is greater than *C,* then *A* is greater than *C*'. And while he introduced symbols to stand for *terms,* he failed to appreciate the value of employing symbols to stand for *propositions*. Had he done so, he might have drawn attention to other relations of inference and types of implication besides those that have a pure syllogistic form, as for instance compound arguments formed from the combination of a composite premiss and a simple one such as the following: either *p* or *q; not p;* therefore *q* (where *p* and *q* stand for propositions). Or again: not both *p* and *q; q;* therefore not *p*. As it is, while he uses certain arguments of these forms in practice quite often, he does not analyse them systematically, and it was left to later logicians to classify their types.

'Scientific' knowledge

Having given his theory of the syllogism in the ***Prior Analytics,*** Aristotle turns in the ***Posterior Analytics*** to discuss demonstration, for demonstration, he says, is a form of syllogism, specifically a syllogism that is capable of producing [*epistēmē*]. [*Epistēmē*] itself is defined as the sort of knowledge 'when we know the cause on which the fact depends as the cause of the fact, and that the fact could not be otherwise' (*APo.* 71b10ff.). This knowledge comes from a demonstration that has a syllogistic, that is deductive, form. But being syllogistic, demonstration must proceed from premisses. These premisses must have certain intrinsic characteristics. They must be true, and they must be primary, indemonstrable and immediate, in the sense that the predicate attaches to the subject directly, not through a middle term. Aristotle denies both that all propositions are demonstrable, and that no proposition

is demonstrable, maintaining that certain conclusions can be demonstrated from premisses that are themselves indemonstrable but known to be true. The premisses must, moreover, contain the causes of the conclusions, for it is only when we know the cause that we have [*epistēmē*].

All teaching and learning that take place by means of reasoning proceed, Aristotle says, from already existing knowledge, and he distinguishes three kinds of starting-points or primary premisses that 'scientific' demonstration requires, namely (1) 'axioms', (2) 'definitions' and (3) 'hypotheses'. The 'axioms' are the principles without which no reasoning is possible, as for example the law of excluded middle that states that any predicate must be either truly affirmed or truly denied of any subject, provided, of course, that neither the subject nor the predicate is used equivocally. 'Definitions' are the assumptions of the meanings of terms, 'hypotheses' the assumptions of the existence of certain things corresponding to the terms: the geometer, in one of Aristotle's examples, assumes both the meaning and the existence of points and lines.

'Scientific' knowledge is of things that cannot be otherwise than they are. It demonstrates connections that are 'universal', [*epistēmē*] in a special sense that Aristotle elucidates in ***Posterior Analytics*** 1, ch. 4 (73b26ff.). First the attribute must belong to every instance of the subject without exception. Secondly it must belong to the subject *per se,* that is it must be essentially, not merely accidentally, true of it. Thirdly it must belong to the subject precisely *qua* itself. There is, then, a 'universal' connection between subject and attribute when (1) the attribute is proved true of any instance of the subject, and (2) the subject is the widest class of which it is proved true. Thus possession of angles equal to two right angles is a universal attribute of 'triangle', but not of 'figure', nor of 'isosceles triangle'. It is not a universal attribute of figure, obviously, since while it can be proved true of some figures, it cannot be proved true of any chance figure. But it is not a universal attribute of 'isosceles triangle' either, for although it satisfies the first requirement, it does not satisfy the second. It can be proved true of all isosceles triangles, but it is true of them not *qua* isosceles, but *qua* triangle, and 'triangle' is in fact the widest class of which the attribute is proved true.

The ***Posterior Analytics*** is a detailed investigation of the conditions of certain knowledge and proof. In the strict sense of the terms, knowledge and demonstration are concerned with necessary, eternal, 'universal' connections, and almost all of Aristotle's examples in the first book are drawn either from mathematics itself or from such mathematical sciences as optics, harmonics and astronomy. Yet while the mathematical sciences serve as his chief model throughout the ***Posterior Analytics,*** his study is not solely directed to mathematics and to the deductive element in proof. In the second book, where he discusses definition and other related topics, a broader selection of examples is used, including several drawn from the biological sciences. Thus in II, ch. 17, 99a23ff., he uses as an example of a strict demonstration a syllogism in which the conclusion is that all broad-leaved trees are deciduous. It is clear that while mathematics provides the paradigm of knowledge throughout the treatise, he believes that his analysis of the conditions of knowledge applies in other fields as well.

Induction

Moreover while most of his attention is devoted to the deductive element in demonstration, he also recognises the importance of induction. In particular it is by induction that we get to know the universal, and it is again by induction that we apprehend the immediate primary premises—axioms, definitions and hypotheses—on which demonstrations are based. It is true that this is only discussed at length in a single chapter (II, ch. 19) of the *Posterior Analytics,* and his scattered remarks on induction elsewhere in the Organon are in several respects unsatisfactory. Thus in the *Prior Analytics* (II, ch. 23) he attempts to reduce induction to a deductive form, primarily, one suspects, in order to establish the priority and superiority of his favourite type of argument, the syllogism. He shows that when the induction is perfect or complete, that is when all the particulars of a class are passed under review, an inductive argument can be expressed in the form of a syllogism. His example is: if man, horse, mule, etc. *(C)* are long-lived *(A),* and man, horse, mule, etc. *(C)* are bileless *(B),* then—provided *B* is no wider than *C*—it follows that all bileless animals *(B)* are long-lived *(A).*

His remarks on induction in the *Posterior Analytics* indicate that it has a much more important role than the analysis in *APr.* II, ch. 23 would lead us to expect, but at the same time they leave unresolved certain questions about its nature. Thus he stresses that we cannot *know* the particular, only the universal: this is stated explicitly at 81b6f., for instance, and again in the *Metaphysics,* for example at B, ch. 4, 999a26ff. And yet he also recognises on four separate occasions that we arrive at knowledge of the universal only from an examination of particulars. Thus at *APo.* 81b2ff. he says that it is impossible to get a view of . . . universals except by induction, and that this is true even when the universals are abstractions: an example might be when a student learns from inspecting a diagram that a mathematical figure has certain properties. At 88a4f. he says that the universal becomes clear from the several particulars. At 97b7ff. he suggests that in defining we must start by trying to see what is common to a set of similars, that is the similar individuals. And finally in II, ch. 19 he considers how we know the primary premisses of demonstrations, and he argues that this knowl-

edge is not innate but acquired by means of induction. He does not justify this process, but merely describes its origin and development. Typically he traces its ultimate origin to a faculty that is common to both men and animals, namely sense-perception. But only a few animals have memory, the power of retaining what they have perceived. From memory comes experience, and from experience in turn both . . . 'art', and . . . 'scientific knowledge'.

The *Posterior Analytics* investigates the conditions of knowledge and proof as exhibited particularly in mathematics. But while most of Aristotle's discussion is devoted to deductive reasoning, his brief remarks on induction make it clear that it plays a fundamental role in his theory of knowledge, since it is by induction that we know universals and the primary premises on which demonstrations are based. He has, however, little to contribute on that favourite problem of later philosophy, the validity of induction, for he does not attempt to justify the process whereby we come to know the universal, but merely asserts and assumes, as well he may, that it does take place. . . .

Michael T. Ferejohn (essay date 1981)

SOURCE: "Aristotle on Necessary Truth and Logical Priority," in *American Philosophical Quarterly,* Vol. 18, No. 4, October, 1981, pp. 285-93.

[*In the following essay, Ferejohn traces Aristotle's effort to provide an accurate account of a specific kind of necessary truth which pertains to the "'definitional' features" of sentences. Ferejohn argues that Aristotle's work in this field led him to the development of the doctrine of logical, or definitional, priority—a doctrine which Aristotle later applied as an analytical tool in other types of philosophical endeavors.*]

Aristotle was not the first to worry about necessary truth; the peculiarly Greek insistence that the objects of knowledge "cannot be otherwise" seems to have had as much a formative effect on the Platonic epistemology as it did on the theory of demonstrative science set out in the *Analytics.*[1] Nor was Aristotle the first to see a close connection between necessary truth and such properties of sentences as may be roughly termed *analyticity,* or *definitional truth.* At least a rudimentary appreciation of this connection is undoubtedly reflected in the distinction between inter-Form and Form/particular participation in the *Sophist.*[2] Yet it is perhaps a reflection of their respective philosophical temperaments that where this latter observation held little more than a passing and incidental interest for Plato, it evidently struck his successor as of such tremendous importance that he returned to it again and again throughout his philosophical writings. In fact, there is a group of passages representing diverse parts of the **Corpus,** which, viewed as a whole, constitute a plain record of his increasingly more sophisticated attempts to give a correct account of a certain type of necessary truth in terms of certain "definitional" features of the sentences to which it applies. My aim here is to chart Aristotle's course through two successive stages of this long-standing project, and then explain how his efforts to produce an explanation of necessary truth presented him with the doctrine of logical (or definitional) priority (which he eventually came to regard as a valuable analytical tool in treating other philosophical problems).

I

This account begins, naturally enough, with **Categories.**[3]

To speak quite generally (and somewhat crudely), there are two very basic ways one might go about constructing theories to explain the manifest fact that among the true sentences of his language there are some whose truth is a matter of necessity. One of these ways is what I'll call the *semantical* approach. This project consists in explaining necessary truth in terms of some extralinguistic structure associated with the language under study. A common form of this approach proceeds by identifying (or perhaps positing) some extralinguistic entities (e.g. individuals, properties, sets, propositions, possible worlds, etc.), connecting these to parts of the language by means of some *semantical* relations, and then giving conditions for truth and necessary truth in terms of relations among these entities. The other way of proceeding is what I'll call *syntactic* (or *proof-theoretic*). As the name suggests, the idea here is to construct a theory out of facts about the sentences in question themselves, as distinct from something they or their parts are supposed to "stand for." One identifies a number of operations upon sentences (such as rules of inference) and then seeks to characterize necessary truth using such notions as provability, i.e. in terms of certain pre-designated outcomes of repeated applications of these operations.

These two types of approach are not actually so far apart as they might seem, and this for a couple of reasons. There are, to begin with, theories which I put into the syntactic group even though some of the operations they employ are not *purely syntactic* because they depend blatantly on semantical considerations. Examples of such operations are rules for substitution of co-referential terms, or of definitional equivalents. In addition, the two approaches are not incompatible alternatives, but often go hand-in-hand. In fact, if modern logical systems are thought of as *(inter alia)* formal theories about relevant classes of necessarily true (i.e. valid) sentences of artificial languages, then the typical way of presenting them (outside of the Polish school), by elucidating their proof theory *and* provid-

ing them with formal semantics, provides a clear example of how the two types of approach can be used to complement one another.

Aristotle never tried to give a theory of the *tautologies* (i.e., those valid, complex sentences of his language whose truth is wholly due to the way their component sentences are put together with truth-functional connectives). And while the **Prior Analytics** does contain a pair of theories which can be construed as pertaining to two other classes of logically true complex sentences (viz. those conditionals which express modal and non-modal syllogisms[4] and conversions), these theories are both exclusively *syntactic* on the above distinction. But if I have him right, Aristotle employed both types of approach in the first few chapters of **Categories** to mark off within the class of simple, affirmative, declarative, subject-predicate sentences a special sort which have subsequently been characterized as necessarily, though not logically, true. I have reference here to such categorical statements as,

(1) Man (is) animal[5]

whose truth has traditionally been regarded as precipitated by the relations obtaining between the meanings of (or concepts signified by) the terms they contain. Let's now consider how Aristotle theorized about such sentences in **Categories.**

The fact that [*tōn ontōn*] at 1 a 20 is such an obvious contrast with [*tōn legomenōn*] at 1 a 16 gives strong reasons for believing that the tetrachotomous division given in the lines following (1 a 20-b 8):

> Of things there are: (a) some are *said of* a subject but are not *in* any subject . . . (b) some are *in* a subject but are not *said* of any subject, . . . (c) some are both *said of* a subject and *in* a subject . . . (d) some are neither *in* a subject nor *said of* a subject.

is a division of *things* . . . and not of *linguistic expressions.* . . . This means of course that the two relations which jointly constitute the principle of this division . . . and the *inherence* relation . . . are themselves supposed to take as terms [*onta*] and not [*legomena*]. This much is uncontroversial. What has not been generally appreciated, though, is that Aristotle's real interest in this chapter is not in classificatory metaphysics for its own sake. For when the tetrachotomy passage is put beside the opening lines of Chapter 2,

> Of things that are said, some involve combination while others are said without combination. [1 a 16-20]

and these are considered with Chapter 4, where Aristotle first introduces the categories,

Of things said without any combination, each signifies either [Here Aristotle lists the categories]. . . . None of the above is said just by itself in any affirmation, but by the combination of these with one another an affirmation is produced. For every affirmation, it seems, is either true or false, but of things said without any combination, none is either true or false. [1 b 25-2 a 10]

there emerges the view that the said-of/inherence distinction plays a central role in a wider project of Aristotle's to provide an informal semantics for indefinitely quantified, affirmative, subject-predicate sentences (or *atomic* sentences for short).[6]

This view is prompted by the otherwise mysterious intertwining in the two chapters of ontological doctrines (viz. the tetrachotomy and the theory of categories) with meta-linguistic remarks about such things as truth, falsity, and signification. We are told at 1 a 16 that "things said" . . . , or at least a subclass of them, come in two distinct varieties: those "said with combination", and those "said without combination." Aristotle's examples in Chapter 2 indicate that the former are invariably constructed out of precisely two of the latter (which I shall therefore call sentential *elements*) by the process of "combination" . . . which is apparently just concatenation, since the copula is dispensable in Greek. Now according to 2 a 4-10 it is only things said *with* combination that give rise to (express?) affirmations . . . and hence these are the exclusive bearers of truth and falsity. Each sentential element, on the other hand, is said at 1 b 25-2 a 4 to *signify* . . . some entity [*on*] in one or other of the categories, and these [*onta*] according to 1 a 20-b 9, supply the terms for the said-of and inherence relations. It is not difficult to distill from these remarks the following array of semantical principles.

(S1) Simple indefinitely quantified, affirmative subject-predicate (atomic) sentences are either true or false. [2 a 6-8]

(S2) Atomic sentences are constructed by combination out of two uncombined expressions (sentential elements). [1 a 15-20, 2 a 4-6]

(S3) Each element signifies some entity in one or other of the categories. [1 b 25-2 a 4]

(S4) Some pairs of these signified entities stand in the said-of relation, and others stand in the inherence relation. [1 a 20 b-10]

All that is needed to make this into a fully explicit semantical theory for atomic sentences is a principle which makes the truth of atomic sentences depend on the two relations mentioned in (S4). No such principle is given in *Categories*, but Montgomery Furth[7] has supplied one in the form of the following truth definition.

(S5) "B is A" is true *iff* (i) A is said-of B, or (ii) A inheres in B. (where "A" signifies A and "B" signifies B)

With this addition, we have before us now an Aristotelian semantical system (call it (S)) which draws a sharp distinction between analytic, and non-analytic atomic truths. For Aristotle's examples in Chapter 2 make it evident that such "definitional" truths as

(1) Man (is) animal

will be accorded truth by (S) because the significata of its elements stand in the said-of relation, whereas such "accidental" truths as

(2) Socrates (is) bald

are given truth as their values because their significata-pairs stand in the inherence relation.

Besides this semantical treatment, *Categories* also contains a partial *syntactic* account of analyticity in the form of some remarks about the distinctive logical behavior of said-of predications. More specifically, Aristotle formulated two conditions which he took to be characteristic of this type of predication but not of the other.

One of these is given in Chapter 3 at 1 b 9 and is fairly straightforward. It is simply that where "A is B" is a (true) said-of predication, then for any predicate "C," if "B is C" is true, so is "A is C." This principle is easily mistaken for one asserting the transitivity of the said-of relation, but in fact it neither entails nor is entailed by it. For this principle has application even where "B is C" is an inherence predication, and it does not require that where "B is C" is a said-of predication, then so is "A is C." For obvious reasons, I'll call this the condition of *vicarious predication*.

The other condition, which is a bit more difficult to understand, is expressed in Chapter 5 at 2 a 19 ff.

. . . if something is said of a subject both its name and its logos are necessarily predicated of the subject . . . But as for things which are in a subject, in most cases neither the name or the logos is predicated of the subject.[8]

Following Aristotle's own way of referring to this condition in *The Topics*,

The definition of *participation* is the admitting of

the logos of that which is partaken. [121 a 11-12]

we may call this the *participation* condition.

In order to see precisely what the participation condition amounts to, it must be first noted that both of these conditions are meant to apply to the *colloquial* atomic sentences whose truth is explicated by (S) (i.e., such "things said with combination" as "man wins," and "man (is) animal"), and *not* to the more perspicuous *canonical* expressions which inhabit instantiations of the right side of (S5). Now the participation condition can be seen to be essentially grammatical. For while the canonical counterparts to said-of *and* inherence predications are all formed by joining together pairs of nominal (or substantive) expressions by means of the technical locutions "is said-of" . . . and "inheres in" . . . , there is a significant lack of parallel between the *surface grammar* of the two types of sentence. The predicate part of a said-of predication, e.g.

(1) Man (is) animal

is typically a nominal form (or, as *we* might specify further, a *sortal* expression, though of course this classification is not so obvious when you don't have an indefinite article in your language). Inherence predications, on the other hand, generally have as *their* predicate parts adjectival or verbal forms. No doubt the absence of "placeholding" or "dummy" sortals (such as "thing" in English) in his language made this grammatical account of the said-of/inherence distinction all the more attractive to Aristotle because it made it impossible for him to formulate such apparent counter-examples as,

(3) Socrates is a sitting thing

Why did Aristotle choose to express this grammatical distinction by means of the participation condition given at 2 a 19? I think the answer to this lies in the fact that in the **Organon** at least, only nominal forms . . . are what may be replaced by defining logoi.[9] This is apparently a consequence of Aristotle's tendency to define *things* instead of expressions. Now in the case of a said-of predication, the predicate is already a nominal form, and therefore the applicability of the logos of what is signified by the predicate will follow unproblematically from Aristotle's oft-repeated insistence that an adequate definitory logos is always substitutable for the name of what it defines.

But now consider the case of an inherence predication, for instance,

(4) Socrates (is) generous

Here things are not quite so simple. If substitutivity of definitional equivalents were allowable for adjectival

expressions as well as [*onomata*], then this sentence would satisfy the participation condition on the grounds that the logos definitionally equivalent to "(is) generous" (which might be "has the propensity to give freely to himself") is true of Socrates if (4) is true. But this is not Aristotelian. For him the fact that the expression, "(is) generous" is adjectival means that there is no definitory logos definitionally equivalent to it. What *can* be defined is the *entity* signified by "(is) generous" (namely, generosity), and *its* logos (say, "the propensity to give freely of oneself") is itself a nominal form and is intersubstitutable with . . . "generosity," though not with its adjectival paronym "generous." Thus, Aristotle's point in saying (at 2 a 28) that in such predications as (4), "neither the name or the logos predicated of the subject," is that both

(5) Socrates (is) generosity and (6) Socrates (is) the propensity to give freely of oneself

are false or worse.[10]

II

It appears that when Aristotle came again to consider the distinction between necessary and contingent truth in the **Posterior Analytics** (with an eye towards isolating those necessary predications suitable for use in demonstrations) he found a number of reasons to be unhappy with the said-of/inherence distinction of **Categories,** and that his general reaction was to formulate the complex doctrine of *per se* and *per accidens* predication. My present aim is to show that Aristotle's specific reaction to two of these perceived inadequacies was to introduce and explicate two distinct types of *per se* predication,[11] and that these divisions together with a corresponding residual classification of *per accidens* predications constituted a major refinement on his **Categories** attempts to mark off the distinction between definitional and non-definitional truth.[12] These explications are introduced at **Posterior Analytics** 73 a 35-b 5:

one thing belongs *per se* [to another] if (1) it is in the what-is-it [of the other] . . . , i.e., belongs in the *logos* which expresses the *what-is-it* [of the other] . . . or (2) it is an attribute in the *logos* of whose *what-is-it* its subject belongs . . . Such things as belong *per se* in neither of these ways I call *per accidens*.

Some minor surgery on the passage will make its sense more evident. This will involve slightly reformulating the explication for the sake of perspicuity, using free variables in place of cumbersome pronominal expressions, and attaching subscripts for purposes of disambiguation:

x belongs *per se*1 to y if x is in the logos of the

what-is-it of *y* . . . , *x* belongs *per se*2 to *y* if *y* is in the *what-is-it* of *x* . . . , *x* belongs *per accidens* to *y* if *x* belongs to *y* but x belongs neither *per se*[1] nor *per se*[2] to *y*.

In this and the following section, it will be demonstrated how the emergence of each of these two types of *per se* predication can be viewed as a reaction to some deficiency in theory (S).

One of these deficiencies stems from the fact that (S) is informative only insofar as it is possible to make sense out of the two relations which form its explanatory basis. However, it appears that Aristotle did not find the "said-of"/"inherence" terminology in ordinary Greek, but simply invented them as technical locutions for his own special purposes in *Categories.* Moreover, in keeping with the terse and somewhat cryptic style of the work, the exact nature of the relations stood for by these expressions is never specified. Furth[13] has eased this difficulty to some extent by extracting some necessary categorial conditions on each of these relations from the examples given in the tetrachotomy passage. These may be expressed by a pair of auxiliary principles to (S):

(S6) If *A* is said-of *B*, then *A* and *B* are in the same category (i.e. are *homocategorial*) (S7) If *A* inheres in *B*, then *B* is in Substance, and *A* and *B* are in different categories (i.e. are *heterocategorial*).

Now these principles do provide *some* information about the two relations in terms of the categories . . . and to that extent they enhance the intelligibility of (S). But notice that (S6) and (S7) are both conditionals whose respective biconditional strengthenings are false. Hence, inasmuch as the said-of and inherence relations are technical inventions which have no meaning independent of what they are given in *Categories,* we have not yet been provided at this point with sufficient conditions for the truth of either of these sorts of predication.

Aristotle apparently never had much more to say about inherence predications beyond his essentially negative remarks at *Categories* I a 24-25, nor is there any reason to suppose that he thought much more *could* be said in view of his belief that many instances of this type owe their truth to the operations of *chance* . . . . [14] On the other hand, I want to suggest that Aristotle was able to move considerably beyond his *Categories* treatment of said-of predications in the *Posterior Analytics.*

The problem again is that the doctrine of the categories, as it is presented in *Categories* 4, simply does not make fine enough distinctions to provide sufficient conditions for the truth of said-of predications. This is because the homocategoriality condition given in (S6) is satisfied by a great many false predications, e.g.

(7) Socrates (is a) horse.
(8) Man (is) Socrates.
(9) Black (is) white.

The problem behind this problem is that for all that is said in *Categories* 4, the categories might be nothing more than a set of aggregatory groupings into which [*onta*] were to be pitched willy-nilly. However, Ackrill[15] has given cogent arguments that Aristotle thought of the categories in this way only part of the time. At other times he apparently thought of them as strict hierarchical structures composed of all the particulars, species and genera which fell under their respective heads, and ordered by the member-species and species-genus relations.

Now it's clear that this hierarchical conception of the categories is submerged in *Categories* 4, and therein lies the source of the inability of (S) to provide sufficient conditions for the truth of said-of predications. For it is to just the finer, intra-categorial distinctions contained in this conception that Aristotle needed to appeal in order to distinguish true from false homocategorial predications. This is one respect in which the doctrine of *per se* predication can be plausibly viewed as marking a significant advance over the characterization of necessary truth given in *Categories.* It is my contention that Aristotle was able to overcome this difficulty by exploiting the hierarchical conception of the categories in explicating the first sense of *"per se"* at 73 a 35-38.

One thing belongs *per se* [to another] if it is in the-*what-is-it* . . . [of that other] . . . i.e. belongs in the logos which expresses the *what is it* [of the other].

The key phrase in this explication is [*to ti esti*], which is just a simple nominalization of the question . . . ("What is it?"). Now since on Ackrill's account[16] the hierarchical categorial structures are built up from the level of particulars by repeated askings of the question. "What is it?", it is plausible to regard the "*what-is-it* of *x*" in the above explication as including all the *species and genera which include or contain x.*[17] In other words, the relation, *x* is in the *what is it* of *y,* is precisely the relation which gives to the contents of each category a strict hierarchical ordering. Moreover, if we consider the logos of a thing's *what-is-it* as containing a complete (though perhaps abbreviated[18]) designation of the species and genera it falls under, then (by resolving a minor use-mention confusion) we can interpret this metalinguistic explication of *per se*[1] predication at a 38

x belongs *per se*1 to *y iff* [the name of] *x* occurs in the (unabbreviated) *logos* of *y*'s *what-is-it.*

as stating both necessary and sufficient condition for the truth of homocategorial predications.

III

The second very general reason why *(S)* is inadequate to the purpose of characterizing those necessary categorical truths capable of serving in Aristotelian science is that there are a number of types of sentence that do not fall neatly into the crude said-of/inherence dichotomy. Among these misfits are true sentences having elements signifying differentiae . . . , such as

(10) Man (is) two legged.

There are actually two distinct, though closely related, problems occasioned by the existence of such sentences. One is the *semantical* problem of providing an adequate explanation of their truth conditions. The other, whose solution will evidently have a direct bearing on the first, is the *ontological* problem of saying where differentiae fit into the classificatory metaphysical scheme given in *Categories* 4.

It is not hard to guess how Aristotle could have found himself in the midst of these difficulties. In *The Topics* and elsewhere, his favorite means of definition is *per genus et differentia*. Moreover, inasmuch as this style of definition is the heart of the method of Division practiced by Plato in the *Sophist,* it must surely be counted as part of the baggage Aristotle carried away from the Academy.[19] But it often happens that there is a price attached to Aristotle's acceptance of Platonic doctrines. In this case, it is that he thereby committed himself to recognizing such sentences like (10) and such "things" as *two-leggedness*. Thus, in order not to sacrifice the generality of the *Categories* program, he had to find a place for both of these items in that framework. So what we have here in effect is an instance where what Aritstotle took over from Plato came into conflict with his own, independently developed, doctrines. I shall now show that despite Aristotle's confident statements to the contrary, this conflict is not resolved in *Categories.*

It is true that in *Categories* 5 (3 a 21-28) we find the pronouncement that differentiae are said-of the species they differentiate (and this, by (S6), would entail that differentiae are homocategorial with those species). Furthermore, there is no mystery, given what we already know about the purpose of theory (S), why Aristotle should have wanted this to be so. Since differentiae are as much a part of the definition as the genus (according to the Platonic legacy) then surely differentiae-predications should be accorded a treatment that respects their status as definitional (and necessary) truths and does not dump them unceremoniously into the class of scientifically disreputable inherence predications.

But for all this, there are also reasons why Aristotle was not free to treat differentiae-predications as said-

of predications. Chief among these is that they do not satisfy the participation condition. Now Aristotle did quite a bit of pushing and pulling trying to get such sentences to pass this test, but in the end (as Ackrill argues[20]) his efforts must be regarded either as self-deceptive or as so much desperate cosmetics. Very briefly, his trick was to test for satisfaction of this condition *only after* first putting the differentia-predication through a regimentation so that it came out containing only nominal forms. And certainly, in this form such predications do satisfy the participation condition. But this maneuver is only open to him at the cost of having to dispense with the participation condition altogether. For there is nothing to prevent the same move in the case of a paradigmatic inherence predication. One could use virtually the same form of reasoning displayed above, for instance, to show that the inherence-sentence

(4) Socrates (is) generous

satisfies the participation condition by first throwing it into the regimented form,

(4') Generosity is predicated of Socrates

and then arguing that the logos of generosity is substitutable for its name in (4') without loss of truth-value). At base, the difficulty is this: since differentia-predications are like inherence-predications (and unlike said-of predications) in the respect that their predicates are typically not sortals, then Aristotle's contortions notwithstanding, the fact is that differentia-predications will satisfy the participation condition only if inherence predications satisfy it also. Hence, insofar as Aristotle was unwilling to give up the participation condition as a means of distinguishing the two types of sentence treated by (S), he could not legitimately treat differentia-predications as expressing the said-of relation.

Evidently, Aristotle was more successful in dealing with differentiae in the *Posterior Analytics*. In fact, his explication of *per se*[2] predication at 73 a 38—b 4 can plausibly be interpreted as such a passage. This passage doesn't contain anything more about the relation between a differentia and the species it differentiates, but it does specify the relation which holds between the differentia and the *genus* whose subordinate species it differentiates.

Aristotle specified this relation by invoking a belief he had about differentiae that has been largely misunderstood. It is the belief expressed at *Top.* [D.] 6 128 a 26, where it is stated that differentiae (more accurately, terms that stand for differentiae) always signify a "qualification of a genus" . . . This point is illustrated by the observation that a person who uses the expression "footed," which signifies a differentia, thereby signifies "some qualification" . . . of the genus *animal.*

Because of the occurrence of the expression [*poion*] . . . here, and the fact that this is the same expression used in **Categories** to designate the Category of Quality, this passage has understandably led some to the mistaken view that Aristotle put all differentiae into that category.[21]

But despite this unfortunate choice of terminology, Aristotle's point here has nothing to do with his theory of categories. It is simply an observation of a pretheoretical fact about language, that expressions signifying differentiae are always equivalent to expressions of the form, "a qualification of [*F*]" where [*F*] stands for the name of the genus whose subspecies the differentia in question differentiates.

It appears that in his explication of *per se*[2] predication, Aristotle incorporated this observation into his conception of definitional truth by expanding the notion of a *what-is-it* for differentiae. This expansion comes quite naturally if one thinks of the *what-is-it* of *x* quite generally as the set of things that will be referred to in giving an exhaustive answer to the question, "What is *x*?". For while, on this general understanding, the *what-is-it* of a particular species or genus will contain everything of which it is a member or a subset (e.g. Socrates is a man, and is an animal, and so on), the what-is-it of a differentia, on the other hand, will contain just the genus which it divides. For instance, if one asked, "What is footedness?" the complete answer, "A qualification of *animal*" would make reference to just a single entity, the genus *animal*. Of course, one *could* ask further "What is animal?", but in so doing he would, strictly speaking, have moved away from the question, "What is footedness?", and taken up the *new* question: "What is it of which footedness is a qualification?". Furthermore, because the *what-is-it* of a differentia is always single-membered in the way just described, its logos will always contain just one name: that of the genus of which the differentia is a qualification.

We are now in position to comprehend Aristotle's treatment of differentiae in the **Posterior Analytics.** The problem in **Categories** again was that differentiae-predications did not fall cleanly on either side of the said of/ inherence dichotomoy. He wanted to regard them as definitional (and necessary) truths, but they failed to satisfy an essential condition of the only intensional relation countenanced by (S). In **Posterior Analytics,** Aristotle repudiated that dichotomy by making room for another intensional relation besides the said-of (per se[1]) relation; one that holds between a differentia and the genus it divides. That he was able to describe these relations in a way that made them *appear* to be the inverses of one another, and so to give the doctrine of

per se predication the semblance of having more unity than it actually has, can be credited to a combination of luck and ingenuity.

It might well be interjected at this point that this "solution" is no solution at all. For while Aristotle was able to say *something* about *some* differentia-predications (viz. genus-differentia predications) in this passage, he left untouched both the semantical problem of explaining the truth of species-differentia predications and the ontological problem of fitting differentiae into the categorial scheme of things.

This complaint is well-founded. I do not think that Aristotle's ultimate solution to these problems is contained in the passage we have been discussing. That solution, which is implicit in the doctrine of the unity of definition, came with his recognition that the ontological problem is not a genuine problem because differentiae do not *need* a place in the hierarchical structure of the categories. That is, it came with the recognition that differentiae-terms do not signify a distinct class of [*onta*] which may be divided into genera and species. They simply denote the *ways in which* genera are divisible into species (that is, in the language of **Top.** 128 a 26, they denote "qualification of genera"). As such, differentiae are not themselves subject to categorial classification; they are simply the principles by which this classification is accomplished.

Along with this dissolution of the ontological problem comes a way of dealing with such species-differentiae predications as

(10) Man (is) two-legged.

Since differentiae are the principles by which specific division proceeds, there is obviously a one-to-one correspondence between species and differentiae. This point is recognized by Aristotle at **Metaphysics** 1038 a 17. From there it is but a small step to saying that each differentiae-term somehow "specifies" (not to say signifies) the species it differentiates, and in fact Aristotle apparently equated species and differentiae in this way at 1038 a 19. On this understanding, a sentence like (10) would be thought of as a notational variant of

(11) Man (is) man

and so as necessarily true.

In any case, I am not so much interested here in Aristotle's final solution to the problem of differentiae as with discerning how his attempts to deal with it influenced his characterization of definitional truth in the **Posterior Analytics.** The explications of *per se* predication at 73 a 35-b 4, expressed as they are in both the material and the formal mode, can be represented as containing refinements of the semantical *and* syntactic treatments of definitional truth in *Categories.* For we may, to begin with, now replace truth definition (S5) in (S) with a more sophisticated version which recognizes *three* distinct types of configuration which might underlie a true predication,

(S5') "*B* is *A*" is true *iff* (i) *A* is in the what-is-it of *B*, or

(ii) *B* is in the what-is-it of *A*, or

(iii) *A* inheres in *B*.

(where *"A"* signifies *A,* and *"B"* signifies *B*).

Syntactically, the distinction between definitional *(per se)* and non-definitional *(per accidens)* truth can be characterized by the *logos-inclusion* condition: *A* (true) sentence, "*B* is *A*." is a *per se* predication iff either the name of *A* occurs in the logos of the what-is-it of *B* or the name of *B* occurs in the logos of the what-is-it of *A*.

Let's now consider how and why Aristotle fashioned his doctrine of logical priority out of the notion of logos-inclusion.

The expression "prior" . . . , like so much Aristotelian terminology, was thought by him to be ambiguous, or, in his own words, "said in many ways." It is therefore not surprising, in light of the fact that he counted the disambiguation of key philosophical terms as one of his most valuable analytical techniques, that there are a number of passages where different meanings of this term are separated. It appears, moreover, that Aristotle's views on the number and identity of these meaning underwent developmental changes.

Four distinct types of priority are listed at *Categories* 14 a 26 ff. These are *temporal priority* (whose nature is obvious), priority of an *irreversible sequence* (as a number is prior to its successors), *priority with respect to some ordering* (which is apparently just a catch-all category), and *natural priority* (which turns out to be *importance*). To this list is then added, in rather tentative terms, another type which is also called *natural priority*. This type, which might as well be called *ontological priority*, is the type which *x* has over *y* when the existence of *y* entails the existence of *x* but not vice-versa.

Throughout the *Corpus* Aristotle was quite settled in his belief that a genus is prior *in some way* to its species, and at 15 a 5 he took up the issue of deciding in which of the five senses of "prior" this is so. His decision, no doubt arrived at by default, was that a genus is *ontologically prior* to its species. Although the biological example given in support of this is based on an obsolete taxonomy, its point can be seen in an updated version. The genus *animal* is prior to the species *man* in the sense that the existence of men would necessitate the existence of animals, even though it is possible for there to be only non-human animals.

It would be easy (though not correct) to think of this view as at odds with Aristotle's general anti-Platonic tendencies, and even as inconsistent with his observation at *Metaphysics* 1038 a 6 that "the genus absolutely does not exist apart from its species," and perhaps it was difficulties such as these which caused him to have second thoughts on this subject.[22]

Whatever the reason, he evidently became open to the possibility that there are better ways to characterize the priority of genera over species. As early as the *Physics* (227 a 19, 265 a 22) we find included in his enumerations of the types of priority a new member, that which he called "priority with respect to logos," or *logical priority*. This type of priority is given its first explication in terms of logos-inclusion at *Metaphysics* 1035 b 5, "Such things as are parts of the logos, and into which the logos may be divided are prior," and again at 1077 b 3, "Such things are logically prior from whose logoi (other) logoi are composed." That these two characterizations are equivalent follows from Aristotle's view that a name and its corresponding logos are interchangeable (*De Int.* 21 a 29, *An. Pr.* 49 b 5, *Top.* 101 b 39-102 a 1, 130 a 39, 142 b 3). I'll represent this doctrine by the following biconditional: *x* is logically prior to *y* iff the name (or logos) of *x* is in the logos of *y*, but not vice-versa.

Metaphysics 1038 b 33 makes it evident that logical priority is supposed to supercede ontological priority as the specification of the priority of genera:

> I mean that neither animals nor any other element in the logos can exist apart from the species.

For the point of this remark is precisely that while the genus is *logically* prior to the species, the species is nevertheless *ontologically* prior to the genus.

Notes

[1] Cf. *Posterior Analytics,* Book A, chs. 1-14 (and esp. ch. A6, 74 b 5-13).

[2] *Sophist* 252B-258C.

[3] I am assuming here that at least the first five chapters of *Categories* are authentic and rather early compositions, and more generally that the orthodox ordering of the *Corpus* (given in the introduction to the Loeb Library edition of *The Physics,* pp. xci-xciv) is substantially correct. I do not, however, think my central contentions herein would be seriously affected if these assumptions proved false, so long as it is granted that *Categories* presents Aristotle's system of thought. (But cf. note 12, *infra*).

[4] I am persuaded by the textual arguments in J. Lukasiewicz, *Aristotle's Syllogistic From the Standpoint of Modern Logic,* 2nd ed. (Oxford 1957), to the effect that Aristotelian valid syllogisms are given in the *Prior Analytics* as logically true conditional sentences, rather than as deductive argument forms.

[5] Though (1) is a quite literal translation of a typical Aristotelian formula (cf. e.g., *Cats.* I, 1 a 8-10), it makes for stilted and somewhat obscure English. However, Aristotle's treatment of these sentences depends essentially on their grammar, which makes literalness indispensable. If it were not, the sense of (1) might be more perspicuously expressed by

The species *man* is an animal-species.

Thus, (1) should be construed here as entailing, but not entailed by

Necessarily, all men are animals.

Unless otherwise specified, I am responsible for the translations given here. I have borrowed freely from both the Oxford and Loeb Library translations when they seemed impossible to improve upon.

[6] That this early Aristotelian semantics is limited to the analysis of what I call *atomic* sentences is evidenced by the choice of examples of "combined expressions" at 1 a 18: "Man runs." . . . and "Man wins." . . . At 2 a 6-7 is found the admission that "denials" . . . as well as "affirmations" can be formed by means of "combination", but Aristotle was apparently not concerned with analyzing sentences involving negation in *Categories.* In *De Interpretatione,* chs. 10 and 11, however, he can be seen extending this rudimentary semantical analysis to sentences involving negation in various ways, as well as to what we now categorize as quantified sentences.

[7] Montgomery Furth, "Cross- and Intra-categorial Predication in Aristotle's Categories" (unpublished ms., *circa* 1972).

[8] The multi-purpose Greek expression [*logos*] will be used here to signify any string of words which could be used to explicate the nature of some entity. The term also has a number of separate Aristotelian meanings (e.g. "speech," *Generation of Animals* E7, 786 b 21; "rational faculty," *Metaphysics* [*Theta*] 1, 1046 b 2; "argument," *Metaphysics* K6, 1063 b 10-11; "mathematical ratio," *Metaphysics* A9, 991 b 13, 17) which may be disregarded here.

[9] *Prior Analytics* 21 a 26, 49 b 5, *Topics* 101 b 39-102 a 1, 130 a 39, 142 b 2-6, 147 b 13-15, 149 a 1-2, b 3-5.

[10] This is followed immediately (2 a 28-34) by the observation that there are some special cases, e.g. that of whiteness, where the name of an inherent is applicable to what it inheres in, but even in those cases the definition fails to apply. This, as Furth *(op. cit.)* and others have noticed, records Aristotle's apprseciation of the linguistic happenstance that the adjectival form . . . ("white") performed extra duty in Greek by occasionally standing in for the noun-form . . . ("whiteness") as the name of whiteness.

[11] There are two other senses of *"per se"* and *"per accidens"* introduced in *Posterior Analytics* A4 (73 b 5-16), but they are not pertinent to this study.

[12] I wish to avoid strict commitment to the historical thesis that *Categories* represents a relatively immature stage of Aristotle's thought, while the *Analytics* were composed at a later stage of his philosophical development. The view I am proposing is simply that, for whatever reason, the *Analytics* reflect a more sophisticated semantical system than what is presented in *Categories.* I take this to be roughly consistent both with the "juvenalia" view of the *Calegories,* and with what may be called the "primer" view, according to which the treatise was intended as a sort of propadeutic, written with full awareness of Aristotle's mature philosophy. However, it should also be pointed out that my contention in section III that there are serious and unresolved conceptual difficulties reflected in the treatment of differentiae in *Categories,* seems to cast some doubt on the "primer" interpretation.

[13] Furth, *op. cit.*

[14] Actually, Aristotle did not give up entirely on the project of providing further explication of the inherence relation. It appears that the fourth type of *per se* predication discussed in *Posterior Analytics* A4 (73 b 8-16), which he characterized as "true for the most part" . . . , were not thought by him to be purely fortuitous, so that they could perhaps be given systematic treatment in terms of statistical regularity.

[15] J. L. Ackrill, *Aristotle's Categories and De Interpretatione* (Oxford 1963), pp. 78-80.

[16] *ibid.*

[17] It is something of a puzzle that even though passages in other works (*Metaphysics* [*D*] 18, 1022 a 25-30, *Topics* A9, 103 b 20-31) clearly put the genera and species to which a thing belongs into its what-is-it, the actual geometrical examples of type I *per se* predications given at 73 a 35-38 (*viz.* "*line* belongs to *triangle*", and "*point* belongs to *line*") do not themselves seem to involve predication of species or genera. This suggests that the notion of a what-is-it is not pegged to definition *per genus et differentia,* and can be taken

generally to contain any item mentioned in a defining logos. It remains a subject for further study to determine precisely how Aristotle thought geometrical species like *triangle* were to be defined, if not *per genus et differentia*. Cf. J. Barnes, *Aristotle's Posterior Analytics* (Oxford 1975), p. 114. In any case, it appears certain that where definition *per genus et differentia is* appropriate, a thing's what-is-it will contain its superordinate genera and species.

[18] *Metaphysics* Z12, 1038 a 9-33.

[19] For Aristotle's characterization of the method of division as definition *per genus et differentia,* cf. *Posterior Analytics* B5 (with, e.g., Plato's *Sophist* 219 ff); for his endorsement of the method, cf. *Posterior Analytics* B13 (esp. 96 b 15-97 a 23), *Topics* Z4 141 b 26-7; and for his views about its limitations, cf. *Prior Analytics* A31, and *Posterior Analytics* B5, 91 b 12-28.

[20] Ackrill, *op. cit.,* pp. 85-7.

[21] J. Kung, "Aristotle on Essence and Explanation" *Philosophical Studies,* vol. 31 (1977), pp. 361-383; and Russell Dancy, "On Some of Aristotle's First Thoughts About Substances" *The Philosophical Review,* vol. 84 (1975), pp. 338-373.

[22] Actually, this difficulty is circumnavigable (although there is no reason to believe that Aristotle saw the way around it). There is no inconsistency between saying (i) that each animal-species, taken separately, is ontologically dependent on the genus *animal* (for there could be animals if there were no men, but not vice-versa), and (ii) that the continued existence (i.e. exemplification) of the genus depends on its having *at least one* non-empty species.

BIOLOGICAL WORKS

Lynda Lange (essay date 1983)

SOURCE: "Woman Is Not a Rational Animal: On Aristotle's Biology of Reproduction," in *Discovering Reality,* edited by Sandra Harding and Merrill B. Hintikka, D. Reidel Publishing Company, 1983, pp. 1-16.

[*In the following essay, Lange argues that while Aristotle's conception of woman as a "privation of man" may be "unacceptable," Aristotle does, however, provide a thorough explanation of this notion within the context of his own thought and theories.*]

> Aristotle . . . pretends that women are but monsters. Who would not believe it, upon the authority of so renowned a personage? To say, it is an impertinence;

would be, to choak his supposition too openly.

> If a woman, (how learned soever she might be), had wrote as much of men, she would have lost all her credit; and men would have imagined it sufficient, to have refuted such a foppery; by answering, that it must be a woman, or a fool, that had said so.

From *De l'égalité des deux sexes* (Paris, 1673) François Poulain de la Barre (1647-1723), anonymously translated into English as *The Woman as Good as the Man* (London, 1677).

The conservatism of Aristotle has long been a subject of discussion among philosophers. His belief in the superiority of the male sex, however, while it has not entirely escaped their notice,[1] has not thus far been carefully examined. In a path-breaking article,[2] Christine Garside-Allen brought to our attention the possibility that the work of Aristotle is in fact the study of the male human, rather than the human species, and pointed to the possibility that this may be true of most influential philosophers. This task of hers was an explicit necessity because in most cases philosophers' ideas about sex difference are not now widely known. In what are known as the "main" theories of various political or moral philosophers, distinctions of sex are not often mentioned, or they are alluded to briefly in a way that makes them appear inessential to the theory. I want to suggest that the reason for this is not that their views of sexual differences are incidental to the theory but that in almost every case they are considered to be a question which is prior to general ethical or political issues. This may be the case regardless of whether or not these views are actually discussed in any detail. For most of these thinkers, however, there will be found a treatise of some sort on the subject. It has been the practice of twentieth-century scholars and educators in the face of the greater equality of women, simply to disregard these works, which they view as minor or peripheral, or perhaps crankish, like Berkeley's late essays on the value of tar water. Unfortunately, this policy is not soundly based on the actual role of these views in most political and social philosophy. I believe that in the case of Aristotle, these views are more than an "analogy between the biological and ethical relations of man and woman", as Garside-Allen suggested.[3] According to her, Aristotle draws this analogy but does not explain *why* a woman is, as he claims, a privation of man.[4] I want to argue that, however unacceptable his characterization of women may be, within the framework of his own thought he actually does explain it to perfection, in terms of the four types of cause. In fact, judging by the number of references to the question, Aristotle considered the existence and nature of women to be one of the features of life that most compellingly called for an explanation. To Aristotle, it was obvious, as we shall see, that women are inferior, and did not actualize the unique human potential of self-governance by reason. In terms of final causes, there was for him a question as to why they existed at all as separate individuals, rather than there being one type of human capable of reproducing itself in a hermaphroditic fashion.

Aristotle's biological writings as a whole, and not only what he writes about women, have also been treated by many as dispensible for the study of his philosophy, a fact which tends to aid and abet the practice of ignoring his sexism. It has been traditional to approach Aristotle through the logical and metaphysical writings, yet there is evidence that Aristotle himself considered the biological works of great importance. According to J. H. Randall, "his most characteristic distinctions and emphases grow naturally out of the intellectual demands of the subject matter of living processes."[5] This is a controversial claim, but regardless of whether or not it is true, the fact remains that the important Aristotelian distinctions between "form" and "matter", "mover" and "moved", "actuality" and "potentiality", are all used by Aristotle to distinguish male and female. His theory of sex difference is at the very least interwoven in a consistent manner into the fabric of his philosophy, and it is not at all clear that it can simply be cut away without any reflection on the status of the rest of the philosophy.

In this paper, I shall first present Aristotle's theories of generation and sex distinction, and then proceed to a philosophical examination of their basis and their implications. The outline of the more empiricist skeleton of "the biology" helps to clarify the discussion of the issues, although it must be borne in mind that this is a gross modernization of the concept of biology. The unified Aristotelian view of science, however, ought to emerge in the subsequent section on Aristotle's methods and assumptions.

The Biology

Aristotle's initial definition of "male" and "female" in **De Generatione Animalium** is the following: "For by a male animal we mean that which generates in another, and by a female animal that which generates in itself". (716 a 13) To Aristotle this indicates not only a difference of anatomical parts but a difference in their "ability or faculty". (716 a 18) "The distinction of sex", he writes, "is first principle". (716 b 10) As such, it has many other differences consequent upon it.

The Aristotelian theory of generation must have been developed in a milieu of considerable biological speculation, judging by the amount of discussion of rival theories. The question of whether or not both male and female produce semen, where semen is loosely conceived of as "whatever-it-is" that initiates the movement of growth of a new living individual, appears to

have been a major controversy. The central question of generation for Aristotle is the explanation of the transfer or creation of soul to give life to the material of flesh and blood, for, as he puts it, a hand is not a hand in a true sense if it has no soul. (726 b 25)

Another question was whether or not "semen" (in the sense in which Aristotle was using the term) comes from the whole of the body of the parent, or only from some part. Aristotle poses both of these questions and states that if "semen" does not come from the whole of the body, then "it is reasonable to suppose that it does not come from both parents either". (721 b 8) It is apparent that this does not follow rigorously, a fact which the translator attempts to explain by saying that Aristotle wishes to reject the Hippocratic view which combined two distinct theories, and appears to assume that oversetting one of them affords a presumption against the other. However, I think this is a somewhat naive underestimate of Aristotle's dialectical discussion, for reasons which will appear below. After numerous arguments against the view that semen comes from the whole body of the parent(s)[6] Aristotle reiterates, "if it does not come from all the male it is not unreasonable to suppose that it does not come from the female", (724 a 8) to which the translator observes in a note "I do not follow this argument"! Indeed, it seems the reverse position is just as plausible: that if the "semen" *does* come from the whole of the body, it would need to do so from only one parent to create a new individual. Conversely, if it comes from a specialized part, both parents might make a contribution. The latter view would be consistent with modern biology, according to which half the genetic endowment is from the male in the sperm and half from the female in the ovum. The problem of explaining why offspring are sometimes female and sometimes male remains with all of these views, and is dealt with by Aristotle separately. What *does* follow from the view that the "semen" does not come from all the body, is that it is *possible,* from a strictly logical point of view, that it does not come from both parents. If it is a specialized function of some part to begin with, there is no *logical* reason why both parents would have to have the same function, or share aspects of the function between them. Aristotle chooses to proceed on the hypothesis that it does not come from both parents, and encounters nothing to contradict this view. He then addresses himself to the question of what "semen" is.

In Aristotelian terms, "semen" must be either the material from which the offspring is made, or the form which acts upon something else, or both at once. (724 b 5) Since semen "contributes to natural growth" it must be a secretion of useful nutriment, rather than a waste product or other excretion. Aristotle reasons that semen is a secretion of the blood, because all other parts of the body are from the blood when "concocted and somehow divided up". (726 b 5) It is the last and finest concoction of the blood because it is produced best by healthy individuals in the prime of life, and absent or infertile in the old and sick. In the case of children he reasons that they use up all their nutriment for growth before this stage of concoction is reached. Further proof that semen is highly refined and concentrated nutriment, says Aristotle, is the fact that the emission of even a small quantity of semen is exhausting, like the loss of nutriment as a result of bleeding! (725 b 6) The view that "semen" is a concoction of the blood was also used to explain resemblance, since the "semen" is a sort of quintessence of the blood which comes from all parts of the parent's body. Thus the "semen" "is already the hand or face or whole animal" potentially, either "in virtue of its own mass" or because it has a certain power. (726 b 13)

Aristotle argues that the catamenia (menses) in females are analogous to "semen" in males. His argument here is based on several principles of biology that he terms "necessary", which all involve the concept of vital, or soul, heat. According to Aristotle: (1) "the weaker animal should have a secretion greater in quantity and less concocted"; (2) "that which Nature endows with a smaller portion of heat is weaker"; and, (3) woman has less vital heat than man. (726 b 30) It follows from these principles that the catamenia are this secretion, and the fact that their presence is associated with generation in women further supports the conclusion. It is clear that if the catamenia are a less thorough concoction of the blood than "semen", on account of lesser heat, the female cannot have "semen" also. (727 a 27) From this Aristotle concludes that "the female contributes the material for generation and this is in the substance of the catamenia". (727 b 31) The fact that a woman may conceive without the sensation of pleasure in intercourse is for Aristotle further proof that she has no "semen". (727 b 8) The suppressed premise, of course, is that the emission of "semen" is accompanied by pleasure, which is one of the more superficial examples of male bias in Aristotle's biology. The ovum of the female would in fact be "semen" in the sense in which Aristotle is using the term, but of course its release is not usually accompanied by any sensation at all.

Since the female contributes the material of the new individual, it cannot be the case that she also has the power to infuse soul into it, for then she could reproduce herself without a male. However, there are males, and according to Aristotle, "Nature does nothing in vain". Aristotle therefore concludes by a process of elimination that the male must impart the motion and the form, and the male semen is the means of doing it, analogous to a craftsman's tool. The form of the child exists potentially in the male soul, and the semen, as the tool, possesses "motion in actuality". (730 b 21) What causes the semen to be productive is vital heat. It is interesting to note that the observations of Aristotle

could not possibly have suggested any role for the male except the mere addition of material in the form of semen, so that he has assigned the male a reproductive function for which, by definition, there could be no observation-base, namely the transmission of the form of the soul. Had he set out consciously to formulate a theory of male superiority that would be difficult to disprove, given the intellectual milieu of his age, he could scarcely have done better than he did.

As to the existence of separate sexes, there are two distinct questions. The first is: why are there males and females of a species, rather than individuals with the faculty of self-generation? Second, what causes a particular individual to be male or female?

The first question concerns final causes, and the determination of why it is better that there be two separate sexes. Aristotle's explanation for this is succinct:

> . . . as the first efficient or moving cause, to which belong the definition and the form, is better and more divine in its nature than the material on which it works, it is better that the superior principle should be separated from the inferior. Therefore, wherever it is possible, and so far as it is possible, the male is separated from the female. (732 a 6)

The separation of the sexes is not required for generation itself, since as Aristotle knew, there are hermaphroditic animals. These, however, are all lower forms of life, a fact that is not without significance.

The question of why a particular individual is female or male concerns efficient causes. According to Aristotle, the material secretion of the female contains, potentially, all the parts of the animal, including the parts of both male and female that differentiate them from each other. The sexual parts of both are included, since the male, by Aristotle's analogy with the craftsman, contributes no material from his body to the offspring. (737 a 25) The material of the offspring prior to conception is therefore potentially either male or female. The essential distinction between male and female is the capacity or incapacity to concoct semen containing vital heat. According to Aristotle, the male, who can do this, is hotter than the female, and therefore the cause of maleness must be greater vital heat. The amount of vital heat a copulating male has varies with his nature, his age, his state of health, and the weather! Semen is said to be less well concocted if there is greater moisture, hence if a moist south wind is blowing at the time of copulation, the offspring are more likely to be female. (766 b 34)

The female has some effect on the sex of the embryo. The catamenia as well may be better or worse concocted, and, not surprisingly, "If the generative secretion in the catamenia is properly concocted, the movement imparted by the male will make the embryo in the likeness of itself". (767 b 17)

According to Aristotle, the determination of sex occurs at the very beginning of embryonic development, at which time nature gives both the faculties and the organs of the sexes at the same time.

There is a further refinement of the theory of generation in connection with the rational soul. This is necessary because the theory of generation concerns all animals, and only humans have a share in reason. The rational soul, according to Aristotle, may exist without body, "for no bodily activity has any connexion with the activity of reason". (736 b 29) The nutritive and sensitive souls, however, are not entities, but "the actuality of something that possesses a potentiality of being besouled". (*De Anima,* 414 a 28) In other words, they are the living organization of matter. Since they do not exist without matter, they cannot logically be transferred without the transference of matter, which the craftsman-father does not do. Aristotle resolves the difficulty by concluding that these souls are present potentially in the female. "It remains then", he writes, "for the reason alone so to enter and alone to be divine." (736 b 29) The rational soul, of course, is the type of soul that is distinctive of human personhood.

The Archai of Generation

Aristotle's notion of science includes not only a collection of "the facts", but also "the reasons why" the facts are as they are observed to be. These reasons why consist in each case of formal and/or final causes. The full explanation usually also includes some principles, which may be either metaphysical or generalizations of a more or less empirical nature. Each subject matter has its own "starting points", among which are the distinctive *archai,* or "principles", which guide the investigation, and according to J. H. Randall, "always function very much as what we should today call 'hypotheses'".[7] The *archai* themselves are arrived at by a process which is a form of induction. However, this process, as it appears in Aristotle, is undeniably weighed down by familiar epistemological problems in the philosophy of science that are associated with the analysis of induction. It raises at least as many questions as it answers. The process appears to be a form of reflection on the observation of phenomena that is meant to result in "understanding" it. According to Randall "those *archai* themselves are established and validated, not by reasoning and demonstration, but by *noûs:* by "seeing" that it is so, that this is the way in which the facts can be understood".[8] These *archai* lead to the determination of causes which ought to form the premises from which the "observed facts" can be demonstrated as a conclusion. According to Aristotle, the *archai* of the sciences are determined by the rational order of the world.

Considered as a description of the *practice* of science this view is one that many would consider today to be basically correct, as far as it goes, with respect to hypothesis formation and the relation of general hypotheses to causal laws and observation. This is largely because hypothesis formation is still considered essentially unexplained. The "causes", in modern terms, are of course always "efficient", i.e., physicalist. The observation of a contradiction between the *archai* and "the facts" counted for Aristotle as disconfirmation of the *archai,* and the logic of this too is essentially the same as that of the modern practice. It is just that Aristotle did not devote most of his energy to looking for disconfirmation, which we now consider it the obligation of a scientist to do.

In view of the stature and influence of Aristotle as a philosopher of science, and scientist, it is of some interest to feminist scholarship to determine how, in the use of his method, Aristotle arrived at the views he did, especially since, as a practitioner of it, Aristotle is not held to be among the worst.[9] It is not enough to say that Aristotle was limited by the lack of a microscope, or, what Aristotle himself would have considered much more relevant, a thermometer. With all the hardware of modern science, the differences in higher "nature", if any, between female and male, are still virtually unknown, and who can say what it is we currently lack that limits our vision? Nor is it sufficient, I think, to brush the theory aside as obviously inferior, unless we are willing to be equally cavalier about other aspects of the history of science and philosophy. Aristotle's theory of generation went largely unchallenged for about as long as his logic.[10] And the intuitions which appear to have given rise to, and been reinforced by, the theory, especially in its ethical and political implications for women, are by no means dead yet. It is useful, therefore, to attempt to identify precisely at least some of the points in Aristotle's pursuit of biology where specific bias is introduced.

The initial task for Aristotle was to identify the subject matter as to kind. This identification is what Hintikka calls in Aristotle a "generic premise", which is a definition of immediate terms which "consists in an indemonstrable assumption of what they are". (*Posterior Analytics,* II, 94 a 9)[11] Of kinds of things, there are, for example, the living and the non-living. Among the living, there are plants and animals, in a graded series as to amount of vital heat, the lowest having the least. Aristotle writes in *Historia Animalium,* "So throughout the entire animal scale there is a graduated differentiation in amount of vitality". (588 b 21) Within species there is female and male. Aristotle's initial identification of the female as being the kind of thing "which generates in itself" seems unobjectionable. Even this, however, is immediately followed by the observation that this must be why the poets call the earth Mother, and the sun and heaven (i.e., the gods) Father!

This poetic analogy is unimportant, however, compared with other characterizations of the female that appear later on in the discussion. These have serious implications, but they seem to be for Aristotle equally a matter of simple identification of the type, rather than the outcome of rational discourse.

It appears that Aristotle does something with the study of humans that in general terms survives as a controversy in our own day. He takes a scientific method that works well for the study of the natural world and applies it to the study of human nature (and, by implication, social relations), expecting it to work equally well there. Yet, like his modern colleagues, he ends with questionable and controversial results. Why does this occur in Aristotle's biology? The "generic premises", according to Hintikka, are supposed to be an account of how a term should be defined in view of an exhaustive knowledge of the relevant facts.[12] Although this approach works well with fish (Aristotle's classification of fish still stands), it may be observed that with reference to people this approach is inevitably biased in favour of what is the case at the time the analysis is made. Furthermore, since Aristotle's view of soul (i.e., life) was teleological, he saw the nature of living things in terms of function or purpose. For example, if the eye were an animal its soul would be sight. Thus the type of soul of such social groups as women or slaves, according to Aristotle, fitted them, not surprisingly, for the functtion which they happened to be fulfilling. Aristotle's method does not draw attention to the differences between a biological function and a social function. For example, if it is a matter of fact that gestation occurs in a (socially) inferior being, this method makes it natural to assume that gestation is itself an inferior function to impregnation.

As we have seen, at the end of his critical examination of existing opinions as to whether or not the female contributes any "semen" to generation, Aristotle introduces a set of assertions which enable him to resolve the question. Among these are the general statement that what "Nature endows with a smaller portion of heat is weaker", and "it has already been stated that such is the character of the female". (726 b 32) This prior statement concerning women is not in the *De Generatione Animalium* itself, and appears to be a reference to *De Partibus Animalium.* In the discussion of blood, Aristotle writes that "Noblest of all are those whose blood is hot", and that in these respects the male is superior to the female. (648 a 10-15)

While the amount of heat in the blood appears to be considered a matter of fact by Aristotle, its greater warmth is an indication of greater faculties of soul, and it is these gradations of faculties, rather than the amount of heat *per se,* that perform the actual job of explanation. Given this scheme, the superiority of maleness is naturally said to have the form of an incre-

ment of faculties. The female is therefore quite literally a privation of the male, or as Aristotle puts it:

> The woman is as it were an impotent male, for it is through a certain incapacity that the female is female, being incapable of concocting the nutriment in its last stage into semen. (728 a 18)

In the *De Generatione Animalium* the assertions concerning the weakness and lesser heat of women are listed along with another "fact" of observation. He writes that the weaker animal will have a reproductive secretion greater in quantity and less concocted, and being less concocted, it will be more like blood. This the female has. Since Aristotle ranked animals according to amount of vital heat, the female was identified at the start as a notch below the male in the graduated differentiation of animals. The alleged inferiority of the female, therefore, is for Aristotle one of the "starting points" of science, based on a feature of experience which it is the task of natural philosophy to make intelligible, and not the outcome of rational discourse.

Hintikka uses a phrase which neatly captures the nature of a principle such as the one that women have less vital heat than men. It is a "discussion-stopper". Thus a brief questioning of an Aristotelian about the status of women might run as follows:

"Every woman is (and ought to be) a non-citizen."

"Why?"

"Because every woman is inferior to every male citizen."

"Why?"

"Because every woman is devoid of the highest form of human reason."

"Why?"

"Because every woman has inadequate vital heat for the exercise of the highest form of human reason."

"Why?"

Discussion-stopper: "Because having less vital heat than the male is what a woman *is*."

or "That is how "woman" ought to be defined."

According to Hintikka, "the finitude of the elements in question is according to Aristotle a consequence of the knowability of essences."[13] Since the world is rationally ordered the nature of things must be rationally determinable. As we have seen, however, an approach which has done yeoman service in the history of natural science is full of pitfalls when it comes to the study of human nature and social relations.

There is another, equally consequential, source of bias. According to Aristotle, the forms of soul are distributed in a sort of pyramid structure, the lowest (nutritive soul), being common to all living things. Each form of soul has its function, the functions of the nutritive being the use of food and reproduction. For living things, after eating, "the most natural act is the production of another like itself". (415 a 28) For this there is a final cause, for the sake of which all animals do whatever their nature makes possible. They seek to "partake in the eternal and the divine". Since as perishable living things they cannot be eternal as individuals, they seek to reproduce another like themselves, so as to be members of an eternal species. (415 b 1-8) Their final cause is to perpetuate their species because "soul is better than body, and the living, having soul, is better than the lifeless which has none, and being is better than not being, living than not living." (731 b 29) These *archai* of generation are meant to explain, at the most basic level, why there is "that which generates" and "that from which it generates", regardless of how these principles might be manifested. These final causes have a direct application to the efficient causes of maleness and femaleness. Since the reproduction of the same type of individual is the goal of reproduction, Aristotle operates in **De Generatione Animalium** on the hypothesis that *exact* reproduction of the parent in the offspring is the most "natural". The existence of such a norm which is "always a perfected activity", is said to be characteristic of Aristotle's practice of science.[14]

Aristotle refers loosely to mother and father as parents, but the real parent is clearly the male, since it is he who contributes the human soul. Also, as we have seen, the most perfect functioning of the reproductive process is said to produce a child "like the father and not like the mother" in non-sexual characteristics as well as sexual. Any departure from the likeness of the father is a deficiency in terms of this norm. (767 b 23) A further characterization of the nature of the female emerges when Aristotle writes:

> Even he who does not resemble his parents is already in a certain sense a monstrosity; for in these cases Nature has in a way departed from the type. The first departure indeed is that the offspring should become female instead of male; (. . .) And the monstrosity, though not necessary in regard of a final cause and an end yet is necessary accidentally. (767 b 5ff)

We have the paradox that although the most natural act for an animal is said to be the reproduction of another like itself, the most perfect functioning of the female is said to be to produce a male like her partner. What

does this mean? While the production of males by the male is a sign of superiority, *vide* "Hercules, who among all his two and seventy children is said to have begotten but one girl", (585 b 23), the production of females by the female is not, being caused by "improper" concoction of the catamenia. On the other hand, the production of *males* by a female is no woman's glory either, because of Aristotle's notion of conflict between the male and female elements in the determination of sex, whereby her femaleness is "prevailed over" if she produces a male. The unavoidable implication is that her most perfect functioning involves creating the conditions for the male element to prevail.[15]

It is apparent that the logic of the reproductive norm only holds for the male. The individuals who seek to partake in the eternal and the divine by reproducing themselves are by implication only the males. *Her* partaking is quite different. She is instrumental to species eternity, and potentially rather than actually human. The actuality of her human potential is the incubation of a male child.

Aristotle regarded the "monstrosity" of the female as an accidental necessity *of the species,* the norm of which species is obviously male. This position is very different from that wherein maleness and femaleness are considered as accidents of individuals. The latter view makes it possible to assign full human ends to all individuals, whereas Aristotle's view does not. Final causes he found operant only in relation to the whole species, male and female, or in relation to the male alone. The final cause of the female individual, *qua* deficient human, was quite literally outside herself, and was that of being instrumental to the reproduction of male humans. Given the function of the female, and the sense in which Aristotle thought of the organs of the body as "instruments" of the unified person, the female has been defined as virtually an organ of the male body. The organs of the body are matter set in motion by and for the soul of the unified person, for the ends of the species. These organs, or parts, are "material causes" of animals, and it may be noted that the female is no more than a material cause of the animal. Reading 'male' for 'person', what else are women but "matter set in motion by and for the soul of the unified male, for the ends of the (male) species"?

Conclusion

According to Randall, Aristotle did not look to knowledge—not even to what a modern would call scientific knowledge—to *do* anything other than give understanding. Randall writes "we can say that for Aristotle the highest power a man can exercise over the world is to understand it—to do, because he sees why it must be done, what others do because they cannot help themselves."

Aristotle's political philosophy, in which he includes what are called the ethics, is meant to tell us how to be good, rather than how to be free, although it is in the nature of his concept of virtue that its mainspring must be within the individual, and not imposed externally. It requires autonomy because its basis is the having of certain dispositions or habits. Insofar as freedom was a concern of Aristotle's, I think he can be interpreted as believing that human freedom of action is only authentic if based upon a solid understanding of the ends and the limitations that arise out of the nature of humankind and the rest of the living and non-living world.

Since virtue for a woman must also be founded on the understanding of the causes (of all sorts) that explain her nature, the biology of Aristotle has an obvious relation to his ethical and political views concerning women. This relation may be regarded as foundational or it may be that the "starting points" of the biology and the politics have in common the "fact" of the inferiority of women. The woman herself, of course, could not have knowledge of this, but only true opinion, based on the acceptance of male authority. Given this scheme, it would be an act of positive virtue for a man to attempt to dominate a woman and compel her to be obedient to him. Conversely, a man who treated a woman as an equal would be acting in a shameful manner.

The best support for the relevance of the biology to the ethics and politics comes from Aristotle himself. In the **Eudemian Ethics** he writes:

> . . . we should not think even in political philosophy that the sort of consideration which not only makes the nature of the thing evident but also its cause is superfluous, for such consideration is in every enquiry the truly philosophic method. (Book I, Ch. 6)

According to Randall, "What is often felt as the "conservatism" of Aristotelian spirit and temper is the conservatism inherent in trust in experience, in facts long encountered".[15] Randall finds Aristotle willing to build on the observations and opinions of others, and suggests that this is because Aristotle viewed science as a gradual accretion of knowledge to which successive thinkers could add. I think this may be misleading, since Aristotle does not merely build on previously acquired "knowledge". In the biology, he invariably opens the discussion of each issue by refuting the theories of other thinkers, before proceeding to argue for his own theory. It *is* true, however, that Aristotle seldom challenges an observation of "facts" because he did not regard their determination as involving any difficulty, other than the practical. Science was not for him the discovery of "facts". According to Marjorie Grene,

Natural science, as (Aristotle) understands it, remains within the framework of everyday perception and makes more precise, within that framework, our formulation and understanding of the essential natures of quite ordinarily accessible entities.[16]

It is quite consistent with this approach to science that Aristotle simply accepted the "observation" of his time and place that women are inferior, although he did not accept the explanations for it that had thus far been developed.

For many people today the inferiority of women is a "fact long encountered". However, since the advent of the concept of theory-laden observational data and "facts", even those who vehemently disapprove of the concept have been forced to be more self-conscious about whether or not they dress their "facts" in the costumes of a particular theory. Some people believe there are unadorned facts (known as "brute" or "raw" facts), and some believe there is really no such thing as a fact at all: there is only the "conceptual framework", a sort of theoretical clotheshorse. Aristotle's facts, it seems clear, come dressed in the full regalia of Greek philosophy and social practices. Thus he explains all, but challenges nothing, and all heaven and earth is marshalled in interlocking hierarchies patterned after the structure of Greek society.

My purpose is not to malign Aristotle as an individual. What is called, with deserved contempt, the phallocentric world view (i.e., the conflation of "male" and "human"), is, however, still very much alive, and there is a presumption that knowing the history of an idea is always useful in attaining full command of it, or, effectively opposing it.[17]

Notes

All references to Aristotle are to *The Works of Aristotle*, ed. by J. A. Smith and W. D. Ross (Oxford University Press: Oxford, 1908-1952).

[1] In his preface to the 1910 translation of *De Generatione Animalium*, Arthur Platt remarks on the "curious depreciation of the female sex."

[2] Garside-Allen, Christine, 'Can a Woman be Good in the Same Way as a Man?', *Dialogue* 10 (1971), 534-544.

[3] Garside-Allen, p. 536.

[4] Garside-Allen, p. 537.

[5] Randall, J. H., *Aristotle* (New York, 1960), pp. 220, 242.

[6] Aristotle makes, for example, the ingenious argument

that this does not in fact explain ressemblance, which it was intended to do, for "if really flesh and bones are composed of fire and the like elements, the semen would come rather from the elements than anything else, for how can it come from their composition? Yet without this composition there would be no resemblance. If again something creates this composition later, it would be *this* that would be the cause of the ressemblance, not the coming of the semen from every part of the body." (722 a 34)

[7] Randall, p. 41.

[8] Randall, p. 46.

[9] Darwin wrote "Linnaeus and Cuvier have been my two gods, though in very different ways, but they were mere schoolboys to old Aristotle" (*Life and Letters,* vol. iii, p. 252.)

[10] Even Randall, writing in 1960, remarks on Aristotle's errors in connexion with spontaneous generation, and refers to his "generally correct" theory!

[11] Hintikka, Jaakko, 'On the Ingredients of an Aristotelian Science", *Noûs* 6, 55-69 MR 72.

[12] Hintikka, p. 59.

[13] Hintikka, p. 58.

[14] "The object of investigation is always an end, or function of the subject matter: what that kind of thing does, how it operates. And the problems of that science are how everything in the subject matter, all the facts there displayed, are related to and involved in that function. The inquiry thus seeks to analyze the factors involved in a certain function. Hence it is important at the outset to establish norms: in the *De Anima,* knowing; in the *Ethics,* the "prudent" or intelligent man. The norm is always a perfected activity, . . ." Randall, p. 52.

[15] Should it be doubted that such a concept reflects any significant tendency, consider the admiration of Nietzsche for Greek civilization, where "Woman had no other mission than to produce beautiful, strong, bodies, in which the father's character lived on as unbrokenly as possible". "Human All Too Human', in *The Complete Works of Nietzsche,* trans. O. Levy (New York, 1964), p. 238, #259.

[15] Randall, p. 52.

[16] Grene, Marjorie, 'Aristotle and Modern Biology', *Journal of the History of Ideas* 33, 395-424.

[17] It has been objected to me that this entire paper is a mistake, on the ground that terms like "active" and "passive", "masculine" and "feminine", and even "inferior" and "superior", are mere metaphysical terms, and have nothing to do with actual inferiority and superiority. In this connection, it may be noticed that the translator, Arthur Platt, remarks that throughout *De Generatione Animalium* "the male" and "the female" are in *the neuter,* and their force cannot be conveyed precisely in English. These tortured ideas are the basis of the notion that Aristotle is not really a sexist, and that he meant only that "the female" (in the neuter, of course) was not a bearer of the highest form of rationality, and not necessarily that actual females (in the female) were such. Whatever this may mean, it's supposed to be a good thing for women. But if this were the case, why does Aristotle go ahead and conclude that women are in fact inferior, and ought to have an inferior position in society? Perhaps it is only "the female" or "the female principle" he meant to exclude from political life. If so, actual women have nothing to worry about. Leaving their "principles" at home, they may presumably involve themselves in politics as men do!

G. E. R. Lloyd (essay date 1987)

SOURCE: "Empirical Research in Aristotle's Biology," in *Philosophical Issues in Aristotle's Biology,* edited by Allan Gotthelf and James G. Lennox, Cambridge University Press, 1987, pp. 53-64.

[*In the following essay, Lloyd surveys the sources and types of empirical data Aristotle used in developing his biological treatises. Lloyd notes that while Aristotle does not always adhere to his methodology, he at least states his methodological principles. In conclusion, Lloyd emphasizes that despite the limitations of Aristotle's work, one should not undervalue the vast scope of his achievements in the area of biological inquiry.*]

The range of Aristotle's investigations in zoology is such that a discussion of his use of empirical methods has to be drastically selective. Yet the need to come to some assessment of his performance in this field is all the more pressing in that it has been subject to such divergent judgments. Some of the most extravagant praise, but also some of the most damning criticisms, have been directed at his empirical researches in zoology.[1]

The massive array of information set out in the main zoological treatises[2] can hardly fail to impress at the very least as a formidable piece of organization. But both Aristotle's sources and his principles of selection raise problems. As we have already noted in connection with his use of dissection, it is often impossible to distinguish Aristotle's personal investigations from those of his assistants, although, given the collaborative nature of the work of the Lyceum, that point is not a fundamental one. It is abundantly clear from repeated references in the text that he and his helpers consulted hunters, fishermen, horse-rearers, pig-breeders, bee-keepers, eel-breeders, doctors, veterinary surgeons, midwives and many others with specialized knowledge of animals.[3] But a second major source of information is what he has read, ranging from Homer and other poets, through Ctesias and Herodotus to many of the Hippocratic authors.[4] In general he is cautious in his evaluations of all this secondary evidence. He points out, for example, that hunters and fishermen do not observe animals from motives of research and that this should be borne in mind.[5] He recognizes, too, the need for experience—a trained eye will spot things that a layman will miss[6]—though even experts make mistakes.[7] He frequently expresses doubts about the reports he has received, emphasizing that some stories have yet to be verified,[8] or flatly rejecting them as fictions[9]—though understandably there are tall stories that he fails to identify as such[10]—and on some occasions the different degrees of acceptance exhibited in different texts may suggest some vacillation on his part.[11] He is particularly critical of some of his literary sources, describing Ctesias as untrustworthy[12] and Herodotus as a 'mythologist'.[13] Yet he sometimes records baldly as 'what has been seen' something for which his principal or even his only evidence may be literary. Thus when at *HA* [*History of Animals* or, *Historia Animalium*] III. 516a19-20 we read that an instance 'has been seen' of a man's skull with no suture, his (unacknowledged) source may be the famous description of such a case on the battlefield of Plataea in Herodotus (IX 83). When we are told that lions are found in Europe only in the strip of land between the rivers Achelous and Nessus[14] the authority for this may again be a passage in Herodotus (VII 126) which makes a similar suggestion, though the river Nessus appears by its alternative name Nes*t*us.

Aristotle's use of these sources and of his own personal researches is, naturally, guided throughout by his theoretical interests and preoccupations. The very thoroughness with which he tackles the task of the description of animals reflects his declared aim to assemble the 'appearances' (*phainomena*), the differentiae of animals and their properties, before proceeding to state their causes.[15] As we have noted, this very program obliges Aristotle to be comprehensive in his account, and certain features of the way he implements it stand out. His stated preference for the formal and final causes, rather than the material, dictates greater attention being paid to the functions of the organic and inorganic parts than to their material composition, although the latter is also discussed, indeed sometimes, as in the case of blood,[16] at some length. More importantly, the form of the living creature is its *psuchē*, life or soul, and his psychological doctrines influence his investigations not only in insuring a detailed discus-

sion of, for example, the presence or absence of particular senses in different species of animals in the *De Sensu,* of the different modes of locomotion in the *De Motu* and *De Incessu,* and of the fundamental problem of reproduction in the *De Generatione Animalium,* [*GA*] but also by providing the general framework for his description of the internal and external parts of animals in the *Historia.*

Thus at *PA* [*Parts of Animals*] 11.655b29ff. and *Juv.* 468a13ff. he identifies the three main essential parts of animals as (1) that by which food is taken in, (2) that by which residues are discharged, and (3) what is intermediate between them—where the *archē* or controlling principle is located: in addition animals capable of locomotion also have organs for that purpose, and in the corresponding passage in *HA* 1.2 and 3 he further adds reproductive organs where male and female are distinguished.[17] In his detailed account of the internal and external parts of the four main groups of bloodless animals (cephalopods, crustacea, testacea and insects) in *HA* IV.1-7 he evidently works quite closely to this broad and simple schema. Thus he regularly considers such questions as the position of the mouth, the presence or absence of teeth and tongue or analogous organs, the position and nature of the stomach and gut and of the vent for residue, as also the reproductive organs and differences between males and females. A series of passages shows that he actively considered whether or not certain lower groups produced residue and attempted to identify and trace the excretory vent.[18] But while the whole course of the alimentary canal is thoroughly discussed in connection with each of the bloodless groups,[19] he has little or nothing to say about the brain[20] or about the respiratory (or as he would say refrigeratory) system.[21] Again while the external organs of locomotion are carefully identified and classified, the internal musculature is ignored throughout.[22] It would certainly be excessive to suggest that his observations are everywhere determined by his preconceived schema: yet the influence that that schema exercised on his discussion is manifest.

In other cases too it is not hard to trace the influence of his theoretical preoccupations and preconceptions on his observational work, not only—naturally enough—on the questions he asked, but also—more seriously—on the answers he gave, that is on what he represents as the results of his research. His search for final causes is an often cited example though it is not so much his general assumption of function and finality in biological organisms as some of his rather crude particular suggestions, that are open to criticism: moreover he is clear that not everything in the animal serves a purpose[23] and that it is not only the final cause that needs to be considered. But many slipshod or plainly mistaken observations (or what purport to be such) relate to cases where we can detect certain underlying value judgments at work. The assumption of the superiority of right to left is one example that has been mentioned before.[24] His repeated references to the differences between man and other animals, and between males and females, are two other areas where errors and hasty generalizations are especially frequent. Man is not only marked out from the other animals by being erect—by having his parts, as Aristotle puts it, in their natural positions[25]—and by possessing the largest brain for his size, hands and a tongue adapted for speech:[26] Aristotle also claims, more doubtfully, that man's blood is the finest and purest,[27] that his flesh is softest,[28] and that the male human emits more seed, and the female more menses, in proportion to their size.[29]

While his general distinction between male and female animals relates to a capacity or incapacity to concoct the blood,[30] he records largely or totally imaginary differences in the sutures of the skull,[31] in the number of teeth,[32] in the size of the brain,[33] and in the temperature,[34] of men and women. His view that in general males are better equipped with offensive and defensive weapons than females[35] is one factor that leads him to the conclusion that the worker bees are male.[36] To be sure, he sometimes notes exceptions to his general rules, as when he remarks that although males are usually bigger and stronger than females in the non-oviparous blooded animals the reverse is true in most oviparous quadrupeds, fish and insects,[37] and while he goes along with the common belief that male embryos usually move first on the right-hand side of the womb, females on the left, he remarks that this is not an exact statement since there are many exceptions.[38] But although there are certainly inaccuracies in his reported observations besides those that occur where an *a priori* assumption is at work, those where that is the case form a considerable group.[39]

We can document the influence of his over-arching theories on what he reports he has seen: but there are other occasions when the theories themselves appear to depend on, and may in some cases even be derived from, one or more observations (however accurate or inaccurate) which accordingly take on a particular significance for his argument. Undoubtedly the most striking example of this[40] is his often repeated statement that the heart is the first part of the embryo to develop. This is introduced at *Fuv.* 468b28ff. as something that is 'clear from what we have observed in those cases where it is possible to see them as they come to be'. At *PA* III. 666A18ff. he says that the primacy of the heart is clear not only according to argument, but also according to perception,[41] and in reporting his investigation of the growth of hen's eggs in particular he remarks that after about three days the heart first appears as a blood spot that 'palpitates and moves as though endowed with life'.[42] The circumstantial detail of this and other accounts show that they are based on first-hand inspection, although the conclusion Aristotle

arrived at is not entirely correct: as Ogle put it, 'the heart is not actually the first structure that appears in the embryo, but it is the first part to enter actively into its functions'.[43] However the consequences of Aristotle's observation were momentous. This provides the crucial empirical support for his doctrine that it is the heart—rather than say the brain—that is the principle of life, the seat not just of the nutritive soul, but also of the faculty of locomotion and of the common sensorium. As in the physical treatises, so too in his biology, Aristotle often constructs a general theory largely by extrapolation from a slight—and sometimes insufficiently secure—empirical foundation.

Destructively, however, his deployment of observations to refute opposing theories is often highly effective. This can be illustrated first with some fairly straightforward examples. (1) The idea that drink passes to the lungs is one that we know to have been widely held,[44] although it is attacked by the author of the Hippocratic treatise *On Diseases* IV.[45] At *PA* III. 664b6ff. Aristotle dismisses it primarily on the simple anatomical grounds that there is no communicating link between the lungs and the stomach (as there is between the stomach and the mouth, namely the esophagus), and the confidence with which he rebuts the theory is clearly seen in his concluding remarks: 'but it is perhaps silly to be excessively particular in examining silly statements'.[46] (2) At *GA* II. 746a19ff. he refutes the view that human embryos are nourished in the womb by sucking a piece of flesh: if that were true, the same would happen in other animals, but it does not, as is easy to observe by means of dissection. And while that remark is quite general,[47] he follows it with a specific reference to the membranes separating the embryo from the uterus itself.[48] Dissection again provides the evidence to refute (3) those who held that the sex of the embryo is determined by the side of the womb it is on,[49] and (4) the view that some birds copulate through their mouths.[50]

In such instances an appeal to easily verifiable points of anatomy was enough to undermine the theory. But more often no such direct refutation was possible, and Aristotle deploys a combination of empirical and dialectical arguments to attack his opponents' positions. One final example of this is his extended discussion, in *GA* I. 17 and 18, of the doctrine that later came to be known as pangenesis, that is the view that the seed is drawn from the whole of the body.[51] Here most of what passed as empirical evidence was agreed on both sides, and the strengths of Aristotle's discussion lie in his acute exploration first of the coherence of his opponents' doctrine, and secondly of the inferences that could legitimately be drawn from the available data.

One of the principal arguments he mounts against pangenesis poses a dilemma:[52] the seed must be drawn either (1) from all the uniform parts (such as flesh, bone, sinew) or (2) from all the non-uniform parts (such as hand, face) or (3) from both. Against (1) he objects that the resemblances that children bear to their parents lie rather in such features as their faces and hands, than in their flesh and bones as such. But if the resemblances in the non-uniform parts are not due to the seed being drawn from *them,* why must the resemblances in the uniform parts be explained in that way? Against (2) he points out that the non-uniform parts are composed of the uniform ones: a hand consists of flesh, bone, blood and so on. Moreover this option would suggest that the seed is not drawn from *all* the parts. He tackles (3) too by considering what must be said about the non-uniform parts. Resemblances in these must be due either to the material—but that is simply the uniform parts—or to the way in which the material is arranged or combined. But on that view, nothing can be said to be drawn from the *arrangements* to the seed, since the arrangement is not itself a material factor. Indeed a similar argument can be applied to the uniform parts themselves, since they consist of the simple bodies combined in a particular way. Yet the resemblance in the parts is due to their arrangement or combination, and has therefore to be explained in terms of what brings this about,[53] and not by the seed being drawn from the whole body.

A series of further arguments follow, for example that the seed cannot be drawn from the reproductive organs at least, because the offspring has only male or female organs, not both (*GA* I. 722b3ff.), and again that the seed cannot be drawn from all the parts of both parents, for then we should have two animals (b6ff.). At *GA* I. 722b3off. he considers how the uniform and non-uniform parts are to be defined, namely in terms of certain qualities and functions respectively. Thus unless a substance has certain qualities it cannot be called 'flesh'. But it is plain that we cannot call what comes from the parent *flesh,* and we must agree that that comes from something which is not flesh.[54] But there is no reason not to agree that other substances may do the same, so again the idea that all the substances in the body are represented in the seed fails.

At the same time it is notable that he not only challenges the scope and significance of the evidence his opponents cite, but also shows some ingenuity in collecting other data that pose difficulties for them. One of the main arguments they used depended on the supposed fact that mutilated parents produce mutilated offspring, and among the evidences *(marturia)* they cited was that of children born with scars where their parents were scarred, and a case at Chalcedon of a child of a branded father born with a faint brand mark: it was claimed, as Aristotle puts it, that children resemble their parents in respect not only of congenital characteristics *(ta sumphuta)* but also of acquired ones *(ta epikt ta).*[55] But this he counters simply by pointing out that not all the offspring of mutilated parents are themselves mutilated, just as not all children resemble their parents.[56] Among the evidence he brings against pangenesis he cites (1) that many plants lack certain parts (they can be torn off, and yet the seed thereafter produces a new plant that is identical with the old, *GA* I. 722a11ff.) and (2) that plant cuttings bear seed—from which he says it is clear that even when the cutting belonged to the original plant the seed it bore did not come from the *whole* of that plant (*GA* I. 723b16ff.).

But the most important consideration, in his view, is (3) what he claims to have observed in insects (*GA* I. 723b19ff.). In most cases, during copulation the female insect inserts a part into the male, rather than the male into the female. This by itself looks quite inconclusive, but Aristotle believes that in such cases it is not semen, but simply the heat and the *dunamis* (capacity) of the male that brings about generation by 'concocting' the fetation.[57] He remarks quite cautiously that not enough observations have been carried out in such cases to enable him to classify them by kinds, and his remark that the males do not have seminal passages is introduced with *phainetai* in the tentative sense, 'appears' rather than 'it is evident'.[58] Yet this erroneous observation is not only his 'strongest evidence'[59] against pangenesis, but also one of the crucial pieces of 'factual' support that he cites for his own view that the role of the male in reproduction is to supply the efficient cause, not to contribute directly to the material of the offspring.[60] In the main the arguments mounted against pangenesis are telling ones, and they draw on well known, and some not so well known, data to good effect: even so, the chief point that derives from Aristotle's personal researches in these chapters is one where, under the influence, no doubt, of his general theories, he assumed too readily that his observations yielded a conclusion that supported them.

It is apparent that much of Aristotle's biology—like his physics—does not live up to his own high ideals. His drawing attention to the inadequacy of certain of the information available to him and to the need to survey all the relevant *huparchonta* ('data'),[61] does not prevent him from being less than persistent in his research in some areas, nor deter him from some highly speculative theories in others. Where he remarks on other writers' inexperience of internal anatomy, for example,[62] or charges them with not taking what is familiar as the starting-point of their inquiries,[63] with generalizing from a few cases or otherwise jumping to conclusions on inadequate evidence,[64] or with guessing what the result of a test would be and assuming what would happen before actually seeing it,[65] in each case similar criticisms could be leveled at him to some—if not the same—extent.

Nevertheless two simple but fundamental points remain. First, if he does not always live up to his own methodological principles, at least they are stated as the principles to follow. The end is defined in terms of giving the causes and resolving the difficulties in the common assumptions: he is no fact-collector for the sake of fact-collecting. But as means to his ends the appeal to the evidence of the senses is allotted its distinct role, alongside the reference to generally accepted opinions and the use of reasoned argument, and he makes it clear that in certain contexts at least it is the first of these that is to be preferred. Moreover his is the first *generalized* program of inquiry into natural science: his doctrine of causes identifies the kind of questions to be asked, and he provides an explicit protreptic to the study of each branch of natural science as far as each is possible.[66]

Secondly the limitations of his observational work should not lead us to ignore the extrordinary scope of what he did achieve in the various departments of the inquiry concerning nature. An analysis of what he says he has observed and of how he uses this to support his theories sometimes reveals the superficiality of his empirical research. Yet as the first systematic study of animals, the zoological treatises represent a formidable achievement, not only in the individual discoveries that are recorded, but also in the patient and painstaking amassing of a vast amount of data concerning many different species and in the ingenious interplay of data and arguments in his assault on such obscure problems as those connected with reproduction.

Notes

This selection is excerpted from Lloyd 1979: ch. 3, 'The development of empirical research', pp. 211-20.

[1] Contrast the evaluations in, for example, Bourgey 1955 and Lewes 1864.

[2] The authenticity of some of the later books of *HA* (VII, VIII and IX) is open to doubt, but I shall treat the whole (with the exception of X, which most scholars treat as un-Aristotelian) as evidence for work organized and planned by Aristotle, if not carried out by him. Recently D. M. Balme has argued for the authenticity of I-IX, as a whole (Introduction to Balme forthcoming, and ch. I above, 16-17) and, as an earlier work not part of *HA*, of X (Balme 1985).

[3] There is a convenient analysis of Aristotle's principal sources in Manquat 1932: 31ff., 49ff., 59ff. Cf. also Lones 1912, Le Blond 1939:223ff., Bourgey 1955:73ff., 83ff., Louis 1964-9:xxxiv ff., Preus 1975:21ff., Byl 1980.

[4] See Manquat 1932: chs. 4 and 5, and cf. the analyses of the relationship between Aristotle and the Hippocratic treatises in Poschenrieder 1887 and Byl 1980.

[5] See, e.g., *GA* III. 756a33.

[6] See, e.g., *HA* VI. 566a6-8 (outside the breeding season, the sperm-ducts of cartilaginous fish are not obvious to the inexperienced), 573a11ff., 574b15ff.

[7] E.g. *GA* III. 756b3ff.

[8] E.g. *HA* I. 493b14ff., VI. 580a19-22. That further research is necessary is a point repeatedly made in other contexts as well.

[9] E.g. *HA* VI. 579b2ff., VIII. 579a32ff. *PA* III. 673a10-31 is a careful discussion of stories about men laughing when wounded in the midriff: he rejects as impossible the idea that a head, severed from the body, could speak (since voice depends on the windpipe) but accepts that movement of the trunk may occur after decapitation.

[10] E.g. *HA* V. 552b15ff. on the salamander extinguishing fire.

[11] As in the notable case of his reports on the phenomenon now known as the hectocotylization of one of the tentacles of the octopus, recorded without endorsement at *HA* V. 541b8ff., cf. 544a12ff., and apparently accepted at IV. 524a5ff., but rejected at *GA* I. 720b32ff. Such divergences may, of course, indicate not a change of mind, but inauthentic material in, or plural authorship of, the zoological works.

[12] *HA* IX. 606a8.

[13] The context suggests that the term *muthologos,* used of Herodotus at *GA* III. 756b6ff., there carries pejorative undertones.

[14] *HA* VI. 579b5ff., cf. VIII. 606b14ff.

[15] See *PA* I. 639b8ff., 640a14-15, *HA* I. 491a9ff. especially.

[16] E.g. *PA* II.4 and cf. the subsequent chapters on fat, marrow, brain, flesh and bone. *PA* II.2 discusses the problems posed by the ambiguity of hot and cold and stresses the difficulty of determining which substances are hot and which cold.

[17] *HA* I. 488b29ff., especially 489a8ff., and cf. also *PA* II. 650a2ff.

[18] See *HA* IV. 530a2ff., 531a12ff., b8ff.

[19] *HA* IV. 527b1ff. concludes that the stomach, esophagus and gut alone are common to bloodless and blooded groups (the passage is considered suspect by some editors, but it sums up Aristotle's position well enough). In the strictest sense in which the term *splanchnon* is reserved for red-blooded organs, the bloodless animals have no viscera at all, but only what is analogous to

them: *HA* IV. 532b7ff., *PA* III. 665a28ff., IV. 678a26ff.

[20] In *HA* IV. 1-7 the brain is mentioned only at 524b4 and in a probably corrupt passage, 524b32. Cf. *HA* I. 494b27ff., and *PA* II. 652b23ff.

[21] In *Resp.* 475b7ff., however, he says that the crustacea and octopuses need little refrigeration and at 476b30ff. that the cephalopods and crustacea effect this by admitting water, which the crustacea expel through certain opercula, that is the gills (cf. also *HA* IV. 524b21ff.).

[22] This point can be extended also to his descriptions of the blooded animals. Although his account of the external organs of locomotion in *IA* is, on the whole, quite detailed, he has almost nothing to say of the disposition and functioning of the muscles. Similarly his osteology (with the exception of his description of the limbs) is in general crude: even though he writes in praise of the hand, remarking on the importance of the opposition of thumb and fingers for prehension (see *PA* IV. 687a7ff., b2ff., 690a30ff.) he limits his account of its bones to remarks on the number of fingers and toes in the forelimbs of different species.

[23] There is an explicit statement to this effect at *PA* IV. 677a15ff., for example.

[24] The main examples of anatomical doctrines influenced by his beliefs that right is superior to left, up to down, and front to back, are collected in Lloyd 1973.

[25] E.g. *PA* II. 656a10ff., *IA* 706a19-20, b9-10.

[26] See, e.g., *PA* II. 653a27ff., IV. 687b2ff., II. 660a17ff. and Lloyd 1983: 26ff.

[27] See *HA* III. 521a2ff., cf. *PA* II. 648a9ff., *Resp.* 477a20-1.

[28] *PA* II. 660a11, cf. *GA* V. 781b21-2.

[29] See *HA* III. 521a26-7, *HA* VII. 582b28ff., 583a4ff., *GA* I. 728b14ff.

[30] See *GA* I. 728a18ff., IV. 765b8ff. and Lloyd 1983: 94ff.

[31] See *HA* I. 491b2ff., *HA* III. 516a18ff., *PA* II. 653b1.

[32] See *HA* II. 501b19ff.

[33] See *PA* II. 653a28ff. (on which see Ogle 1882: 167).

[34] E.g. *GA* IV. 765b16-17, 775a5ff.

[35] E.g. *HA* IV. 538b15ff., *PA* III. 661b28ff.

[36] See *GA* III. 759b2ff.

[37] *HA* IV. 538a22ff., V. 540b15-16, *GA* I. 721a17ff.

[38] See *HA* VII. 583b2ff., and 5ff., and cf. further below, p. 59, on *GA* IV. 764a33ff. Cf. also *HA* VII. 584a12ff. on exceptions to the rule that women have easier pregnancies with male children.

[39] Another important group of mistakes relates to exotic species (for which parts of *HA* especially show some predilection) where he was, no doubt, relying more on secondary sources or hearsay. Thus many of his statements about the lion are erroneous (see Ogle 1882:236). See also the mistakes mentioned by Bourgey 1955:84-5 (there are inaccuracies in those listed by Lewes 1864:164ff.).

[40] Two others would be (1) his claim to have verified that the brain is cold to *touch*, *PA* II. 652a34-5 (not true of a recently dead warm-blooded animal)—which was no doubt a major factor in contributing to his theory that the primary function of the brain is to counterbalance the heat of the heart and (2) his reported observation that a bull that had just been castrated was able to impregnate a cow (*GA* I. 717b3ff., cf. *HA* III. 510b2ff.)—which presumably influenced his doctrine that the testes are mere appendages, not integral to the seminal passages (e.g. *GA* I. 717a34ff.).

[41] Again at *GA* II. 740a3ff. he says that not only perception but also argument shows that the heart is the first part to become distinct in actuality. Cf. also *PA* III. 666a8ff., *GA* II. 740a17-18, 741b15-16.

[42] *HA* VI. 561a6ff., 11-12, *PA* III. 665a33ff.

[43] Ogle 1897: 110 n. 24, and cf. 1882: 193.

[44] This we know from *Morb.* IV ch. 56, Littré VII 608.17ff. The view is found in Plato, *Ti.* 70c, is attributed to Philistion by Plutarch (*Quaest. Conv.* VII I, 698A ff., at 699C) and after Aristotle was the subject of an attempted experimental demonstration in *Cord.* ch. 2, Littré IX 80.9ff.

[45] The nine proofs, *historia,* that this author adduces are a very mixed bag: they include not only a reference to the epiglottis and its function (VII 608.23ff.) but also arguments that if drink went to the lungs, one would not be able to breathe or speak when full, that another consequence would be that dry food would not be so easily digested, that eating garlic makes the urine smell, and other often inconclusive or question-begging considerations, see VII 606.7ff.

[46] *PA* III. 664b18-19.

[47] Some of Aristotle's general appeals to what would

be shown by dissection are clearly hypothetical and were not followed up: thus at *PA* IV. 677a5ff. he dismisses the view of Anaxagoras' followers that the gall-bladder causes acute diseases with the claim that those who suffer from such diseases mostly have no gall-bladder and 'this would be clear if they were dissected'.

[48] *GA* II. 746a23ff. says that this is true for all embryos in animals that fly, swim and walk.

[49] *GA* IV. 764a33ff., cf. 765a16ff.; yet he is prepared to allow that males often move first on the right-hand side (*HA* VII. 583b2ff.; cf. b5ff.), and also that, given that the right-hand side of the body is hotter than the left, and that hotter semen is more concocted, seed from the right side is more likely to produce males (*GA* IV. 765a34ff., but cf. b4ff.).

[50] *GA* III. 756b16ff., especially 27ff.

[51] Our principal original sources for the pangenesis doctrine are the Hippocratic treatises, *Genit., Nat. Puer.* and *Morb.* IV. See Lesky 1951: 70ff and Lonie 1981.

[52] *GA* I. 722a16-b3.

[53] The semen has just such a function, as supplying the efficient cause, in Aristotle's own theory.

[54] He is led from this to consider Anaxagoras' theory that none of the uniform substances comes into being.

[55] *GA* I. 721b17ff., and 28ff.

[56] *GA* I. 724a3ff., cf. *HA* VII. 585b35ff.

[57] See especially *GA* I. 729b21-33, and cf. other references to species that do not emit seed in copulation, 731a14ff., II. 733b16ff.

[58] See *GA* I. 721a12, 14ff.

[59] *GA* I. 723b19.

[60] See *GA* I. 729b8-9 and 21-2, where in both cases there is a contrast between *logos* and *erga*. Cf. also b33ff. with some equally doubtful evidence such as the supposed fact that a hen bird trodden twice will have eggs that resemble the second cock.

[61] Apart from *PA* I. 639b8ff., 640a14ff., *HA* I. 491a9ff., see also, e.g., *GA* II. 735b7-8, 748a14ff.

[62] See, e.g., *Resp.* 470b8-9, 471b23ff.

[63] E.g. *GA* II. 747b5-6, 748a8-9, IV. 765b4-5.

[64] E.g. *PA* IV. 676b33ff., *GA* III. 756a2ff., b16ff., V. 788b11ff., 17ff.

[65] *GA* IV. 765a25-9.

[66] *PA* 1.5 644b22ff.: the study of the heavenly bodies and of animals each has its own attractions.

Daryl McGowan Tress (essay date 1992)

SOURCE: "The Metaphysical Science of Aristotle's *Generation of Animals* and Its Feminist Critics," in *The Review of Metaphysics: A Philosophical Quarterly,* Vol. 46, No. 2, December, 1992, pp. 307-42.

[*In the following essay, Tress defends Aristotle's* Generation of Animals *against comments voiced by feminist critics, stressing that Aristotle observes that both male and female are the "principles of generation." Tress further maintains that the apparent inequality of the sexes in Aristotle's theories stems not from misogynistic or sexist views, but from specific philosophical problems that Aristotle treats.*]

I

How does life begin? How is it and why is it that a child comes into being? To answer these questions about life and its origins requires a system of presuppositions about a great many metaphysical matters, such as causation and its modes of operation, relations of identity and difference, and, perhaps above all, the transition from not-being to actualized existence. In his treatise, ***Generation of Animals (GA),*** Aristotle takes up the theme of the origins of animal and human life. His treatment of the subject is both empirical, offering descriptions of how the process occurs in nature, and metaphysical, pursuing the deeper how and answering questions about why it is that offspring are generated and how this phenomenon is meaningfully connected to the cosmos as a whole.

In recent years, feminist critics of the history of philosophy have been severe in their condemnation of Aristotle as a chief spokesman, if not founder, of sexism in the philosophical tradition: "We have become accustomed to regarding Aristotle as the fountainhead of one long tradition of western misogyny."[1] The theory proposed in *GA,* which in outline reads that in generation the male parent contributes the form and the female parent contributes the matter, is adduced by some of Aristotle's critics to show that he regards females as inferior to males in the process of reproduction and that this view of female inferiority can be seen to be carried into other, if not all, areas of his philosophizing.[2]

Despite Aristotle's current status as *défectueux* from a feminist point of view, his treatise is worthy of renewed exposition for several reasons. First, his path to understanding how and why life begins—his very ability to ask how and why together—is richer and more fruitful than our modern view of reproduction, which is constructed for the most part on materialistic presuppositions. It is largely a modern materialist view of reproduction that feminism has inherited. From the start, the phenomenon Aristotle is studying is generation rather than reproduction, and the method he adopts for apprehending this expanded phenomenon is empirical-metaphysical rather than strictly mechanical or medical. Aristotle's ability to integrate metaphysical considerations with scientific ones offers modern readers a model for a rationally enlarged conception of generation.[3] In anticipation, we may say at this point that the results of his analysis show generation to be entwined with multiple dimensions of the natural world, not merely the sexual partners who are the parents of the offspring.[4]

Second, one reason that the feminist critics fail to appreciate the virtues of Aristotle's metaphysical science of generation has to do with the differing aims of classical metaphysics and modern feminism. Aristotle's intentions in taking up generation are metaphysical; he asks, What is generation? and looks to see how the phenomenon accords with the principles he has laid down in the *Metaphysics* and the *Physics.* The feminist, on the other hand, asks about reproduction, Who controls it? That is, the question is one of power and the aim is political: the altering of perceived unfair power relations. Because feminism is centrally concerned with power and politics, it tends to have little use for metaphysics and little patience with it. This impatience is apparent in the methodology of some feminist criticism of Aristotle, in the quoting of offensive sentences out of their context as evidence in the sexism case against him. This practice neglects the overall form and much of the content of Aristotle's treatises, and inevitably leads to misreadings of these complex and difficult texts, in particular to misconstruals of the very gender issues to which Aristotle's feminist critics wish to draw attention.

Third, when reading Aristotle's offensive comments without the benefit of a knowledge of his historical context, his feminist critics generally have failed to notice the ways in which Aristotle's theory of generation has the effect of elevating the female role in generation, when compared to another view that prevailed in his day. "Preformation," according to which the mother does not significantly contribute to generation, had wide currency in Aristotle's time (and was still holding its own into the nineteenth century). Aristotle argues against this approach on metaphysical grounds and states emphatically from the beginning of *GA* that male and female together are the principles of generation. In this respect, his treatise is worthy of our attention because it represents an advance in biology and, contrary to the usual feminist interpretation, an advance also in the appreciation of the maternal contribution to

generation. As this exposition of *GA* proceeds, the three foregoing points will be shown in greater detail.

This is not to say, however, that the feminist criticism is simply to be dismissed. To begin with, there appears to be a long history of the use of Aristotle's treatise against women.[5] The text is complex and is liable to be misunderstood and misused. In *GA* Aristotle devotes greater attention to the male contribution to generation, and it may appear to modern readers that the female contribution is less active and important than that of the male. The association of the male contribution with the superior "form" and the female contribution with "matter," along with the appearance of a preponderance of causal power in the male, is what feminists have noticed and is what has led, in part, to their objections against Aristotle's unfairness. A feminist critic, whose aim is to avoid any devaluation of the maternal contribution to reproduction, might insist that Aristotle be judged by a standard which at the very least makes the female and male equally active, and which guarantees that their contributions are of equal value by seeing them as the same in kind.[6] This implict or explicit demand is, however, another instance of feminism's inattention to Aristotle's metaphysical aims. In fact, what imbalance there is in his treatment arises not from misogyny or sexism, but from particular philosophical problems Aristotle is addressing in the treatise.[7]

Examination of the philosophical problems involved in the subject of generation is what is required to move beyond accusation toward understanding the extent and the source of the perceived sexual imbalance that develops in this work. Let us now consider what those philosophical problems are and how they emerge within the original thinking that Aristotle brings to bear on the phenomenon of generation.

II

The work whose title is translated *Generation of Animals* is in the Greek *peri zōiōn geneseōs,* "on the coming into being of living creatures." *Genese s,* from the verb *gignomai,* is used primarily to refer to the "origin" or "source" or "beginning" of a natural entity. The root *gen-* concerns family, offspring, creation, birth, descent. What should be noted from the outset is the contrast between modern concepts of "reproduction," leaning on metaphors of production and manufacture of artifacts, and the ancient focus on procreation and begetting of living things as a process which occurs in a larger natural nexus.[8]

The expanded meaning available in the Greek title serves as a reminder that Aristotle raises his scientific questions regarding generation in a philosophical context; that is, his scientific questions are metaphysically informed and they are raised within a long lineage of attempts at understanding *genesis,* the transition from not-being to being.

It is worth paying particular attention to the opening of *GA* to determine what Aristotle's own aims are in this treatise. The subject, announced in the title, is the generation of animals. But how does this subject itself arise? The very first lines of the treatise answer this question. Aristotle explains that with one exception, he has already spoken of all the parts of animals, and of the various causes of these parts. Thus, in respect to generation of animals, a part remains to be described and a cause explained. He does not make it plain why this subject was saved for a separate work. It is, however, the final, culminating treatise of his zoological works. This is a series of books which, according to traditional dating, begins with *History of Animals*— Aristotle's general observations and descriptions of animal life—and proceeds thence to consider, first, the material parts and functions *(Parts of Animals),* and then those parts and functions which involve both matter and *psyche* (*Movement of Animals, Progression of Animals,* and ultimately *Generation of Animals*).[9] The progression of this series of investigations follows Aristotle's general principle of learning: We first study that which is closest or most available in our experience (thus, in this case, the initial record of observations of nature and inquiries into the material parts) and work from there toward that which is first in the order of being. So at the start of *GA* we have with Aristotle, as it were, already gone through virtually every other part and principle of these creatures as preparation for the investigation of generation. Those studies lead to the present one, that is, back to the source of the "coming to be" of animal life.

From the first lines of the treatise Aristotle speaks of causes, indicating that generation, governed by causes, is an ordered, intelligible process. By contrast, generation is not to be viewed as mere effluence, nor as a mere rearrangement of parts, nor as a divine dispensation. That is, generation is not to be understood poetically, or artistically, or religiously. He delineates the four basic causes: (1) the final cause, "'that for the sake of which' a thing exists, considered as its 'end'"; (2) the formal cause, "the *logos* of the thing's essence" (715a4-5). Together, the final and formal causes determine a distinctively metaphysical trajectory for the discussion of generation, involving universal characterization of nature's mode of operation and a vision of nature working not only in accord with the forces of necessity but also for the good.[10] (3) The material cause is "the matter for the thing" (715a6). As Aristotle says in the *Physics,* it is "material for the generating process to start from" (194b24). In *GA,* the female parent provides the material cause. (4) The moving cause is "that from which comes the principle of the thing's movement" (715a6). In speaking of the moving cause in the *Physics* he says, "There must be something to

initiate the process of the change or its cessation" (194b30). In *GA* Aristotle singles out the moving cause as most germane to the phenomenon of generation; he is particularly interested in determining how life or the principle of motion arises.

The inclusion of formal and final causes in a scheme explaining the origination of an organism presents a chief point of difference between classical and modern scientific outlooks. Eliminating formal and final causes from scientific explanation proper was an explicit goal of some early modern empiricist philosophers, such as Francis Bacon and John Locke.[11] In their battle with the Aristotelian outlook, they insisted that only the material and moving causes be used as instruments of scientific investigation. They intended, ultimately, to eliminate Aristotle's concept of substance altogether from scientific analysis and thereby, from their point of view, eliminate subjective elements from scientific study.

For different reasons, but with some similar results, contemporary feminists have targeted essentialism—in the relevant sense, the position that human beings possess an original nature which determines or structures development in significant ways prior to social conditions—as a concept which must be eradicated. Feminist theorists oppose above all essentialism's deterministic consequences. For example, feminist critics might point to some passages in *GA* itself as evidence of the way in which Aristotle conceives of a woman's nature as biologically determined and hence unchangeable, inescapable. It is true that in *GA* Aristotle defines female and male biologically, in terms of their differing generative roles. He says, "By a 'male' animal we mean one which generates in another, by 'female' one which generates in itself" (716a14-15). Beyond this simple statement of fact, however, Aristotle presently does not venture. His essentialism has no necessary consequences here for differing valuations of the female and male roles in generation. Indeed, Aristotle makes the important declaration that "the male and the female are the principles of generation" (716a5-7).[12] Aristotle's statement at the opening of the treatise that male and female are the *archai* of generation functions as the principle thesis in his theory of generation. The remainder of his discussion is intended to display both how male and female function as *archai* and the physical and metaphysical considerations that derive from this basic thesis. Aristotle not only does not depart from this basic commitment, but the entirety of *GA* should be regarded as the working out, scientifically and philosophically, of the basic observation that male and female together are the principles of generation.[13]

As evidence that female and male are both principles of generation, Aristotle mentions that they both secrete *sperma,* generative fluid.[14] Even when, several lines later, he asserts that female and male differ with respect to their *logos*, "in that the power or faculty possessed by the one differs from that possessed by the other" (716a18), Aristotle's explanation of the differing powers concerns, once again, the differing generative functions of the female and male and only those: the power to give rise to offspring either within oneself or within another. Clarifying further his understanding of the two sexes he states, "Male and female are indeed used as epithets of the whole of the animal, [but] it is not male or female in respect of the whole of itself, but only in respect of a particular faculty and a particular part" (716a28-31). That is, male and female do not differ substantially, but differ only with respect to their separate capacities to give rise to young, and with respect to the parts of their bodies which serve this function.[15]

Essentialism need not be a source of gender problems, as many feminist critics contend. Rather, conceived along Aristotle's lines it can provide the outline of a solution to a variety of practical and theoretical difficulties relating to the two sexes. As we will see in detail, Aristotle's understanding of the four causes permits the distinctions in female and male anatomy and physiology to be acknowledged as far as they go, and allows for him to retain a way of indicating the dimensions, both physical and metaphysical, in which female and male are the same.

For the remainder of *GA* 1.1, Aristotle directs his attention to the phenomenon of two sexes. He observes, to begin with, that all the kinds of animals which possess two sexes come into being from the union of male and female. There is a regularity to the generative process which is productive of further regularity. After acknowledging the exceptions—such as some bloodless animals which originate not from a union of the sexes but from rotting earth and excrement, and whose offspring are neither male nor female (so that sexual generation is impossible)—Aristotle again observes that all animals produced by union of the male and female themselves generate offspring of their own kind. Animals that arise from decaying matter, in contrast, "generate, indeed, but produce another kind and the product is neither male nor female" (715b5). But production of another kind, generation after generation of different kinds, would amount to irregularity ad infinitum, and, Aristotle insists, "nature flies from the unbounded; the unbounded is imperfect and nature always seeks an end" (715b14-16). The way of infinite variation and novelty, as in a modern evolutionary model, a materialist view, is not nature's way, according to him. What is striking and important to Aristotle is the ability of almost all animals almost all of the time to generate creatures of the same kind as themselves. This regularity among animal species has its sources in the *archai* of generation, namely, male and female.[16]

Natural regularity will serve as a generalized theme throughout the rest of the treatise, first as a phenomenon which itself requires an account (*GA* 1.2-*GA* 2), and then as a basis for and background against which Aristotle will investigate related matters: the regular development of the embryo, along with the species variations in embryonic development which are also apparent (*GA* 2.6-3.11). Aristotle then returns (in *GA* 4) to a further consideration of male and female, this time inquiring into the origination of these two regulating principles of genesis themselves, including in later sections of book 4 a discussion of various irregularities in generation (for example, the occurrence of monstrosities, superfetation, and miscarriage). He ends book 4 with brief discussions of some regular features of reproduction (for example, lactation and normal gestational periods). Book 5, which closes the treatise, examines regular natural variations (for example, eye and skin color, hair color and its changes over time) and their causes. In the closing lines of *GA* Aristotle speaks again about causes, just as he did at the opening of the treatise, reminding his readers once again of the physical and metaphysical lawfulness of generation. *GA* as a whole is an expression of Aristotle's philosophical concern with nature's regularity and order, that is, with intelligibility, and the physical and metaphysical lines of explanation that are required to make sense of this. He displays an open-minded awareness of the numerous variations and exceptions that nature produces as he moves back and forth between discussion of things that are so for the most part and things that are so only exceptionally. In Aristotle's vision of nature, regularity is supreme, but it is productive of degrees of difference—indeed, it requires sexual differentiation in order that productive sexual union can take place.

In *GA* 1, male and female are coprinciples of generation and therefore stand as the principles of the orderly unfolding of nature. Aristotle supports this initial thesis first with descriptions of the generative anatomical parts of the two sexes in a variety of species, followed by a discussion of the more controversial subject, the generative fluids. So in *GA* 1.3-16 Aristotle examines the arrangement of the testicles or seminal ducts in fishes and serpents, lizards and tortoises, birds and dolphins and man; as well as the placement of the uterus or uterus-like organs in crustacea and cephalopods, insects and octopuses. He develops ideas, regarding the variations in generative anatomy of different species of animals, which rest on nature's operating principles: what happens does so because it is necessary or because it is better. The anatomical forms serve the functions of copulation and of gestation, either because copulation and gestation must take place in a particular way for a class of animals, or because it is better that it occur that way.[17] Then, having described those anatomical parts that serve generation (that is, having shown that female and male are both principles of generation in this respect), in *GA* 1.17 Aristotle leaves behind the anatomy (or the "instrumental parts") and begins his discussion of the generative fluids, the *spermata*. The discussion of *sperma* bears crucially on the correct understanding of Aristotle's view of the role of female and male in generation.

III

Somewhat surprisingly, the question that first occupies Aristotle regarding *sperma* is, Is *sperma* drawn from the whole body? Two different theories had currency in his time: Hippocratic "pangenesis," the notion that *sperma* comes from all parts of the body and thereby provides the parts of the body for the offspring; and the "preformationist" or "homunculus" theory, that the *sperma* contains an animalcule or a little human already formed and waiting simply to grow.[18] Aristotle is trying to contend with these on his way to establishing his own claims about the nature of the generative fluids. He presents a variety of reasons for objecting to pangenesis and preformation.[19] All of his reasons argue against what he regards as the real problem: the materialistic reduction and oversimplification that those two theories represent. Both theories fail to explain what principle organizes the many parts of the body. Generation, after all, produces a substantial entity, a unified and coherent creature. In the case of pangenesis it would be absurd, of course, to suppose that the many parts of the body come together in their ordered, regular way merely by chance; nor can it be imagined that the parts actively arrange themselves. Something above and beyond the parts alone must be operative in order to explain the regular generation of animals. For Aristotle, this something is *psychē*, soul, "the first actuality of a natural body which potentially has life."[20] In his view, body is aimed at soul from the very beginning. This is a principle which the materialisms, pangenesis and preformationism, do not comprehend. His conclusion to the problem at hand, then, is that pangenesis must be rejected; *sperma* is not drawn *from* all parts of the body but rather goes *to* all parts of the body. In this way, he emphasizes final causality over what he regards as ultimately unworkable mechanical explanations (725a23).[21]

Aristotle will have more arguments to offer in book 2 against preformationism, the view that an animalcule or homunculus is transferred from the father and planted in the mother's body, with her functions being strictly incubation and feeding.[22] His mention of it at this point (722b5), however, permits us to note that preformationism had been employed in Greek cultural life to deny women any role in generation, and consequently to deny them any significant connection with their children and any connection of their children with

them. A stunning example of this can be found in Aeschylus's *Eumenides,* when Apollo defends Orestes' murder of his mother in this way:

> The mother of what is called her child is no parent of it, but nurse only of the young life that is sown in her. The parent is the male, and she but a stranger, a friend, who, if fate spares his plant, preserves it till it puts forth.[23]

Aristotle's opposition to preformationism is not founded on the grounds that it demeans women's part in generation. Rather, it fails to make sense on its own terms because it cannot explain how female offspring could be produced: how could the female generative parts arise from a male body? (see also his arguments at 734a11-12). Against this historical background, Aristotle's alternative theory, by establishing the female as a principle of generation, represents an important elevation of the woman's role in generation. Furthermore, political assumptions and considerations are notably absent in Aristotle's treatment of this subject. That is, his aims at this point, in distinction from the feminist critique which itself is already directed toward the politicization of sexuality, do not include the demotion or the elevation of women and their role in the process of generation. Instead, arguments are assessed by him one by one, on theoretical grounds or on observational grounds or on both, and conclusions are drawn about the phenomenon itself.

Some of Aristotle's feminist critics have misread him on this fundamental issue, mistaking Aristotle's theory for a version of preformationism, and hence they have assigned to him the sexist consequences of that theory. The claim frequently made is that Aristotle reproduces and enlarges a model in which the female body serves only passively in generation as a source of warmth and nourishment for the growing embryo whose source is strictly the male parent.[24] But his effort in book 1 of *GA,* as we have begun to see, is to reject preformationism, which these critics confuse with Aristotle's own view, and to establish the validity of his own initial thesis that male and female are both *archai* of generation.[25]

Other feminists criticize Aristotle's theory as inferior to the other of his rival theories, pangenesis.[26] Pangenesis, in Empedocles' version, holds that male and female both make contributions of the same sort,[27] and so this theory appears more acceptable by general feminist criteria. But proponents of pangenesis fail to take seriously Aristotle's stated objections to Empedocles' theory, namely, that the parts torn apart from each other (in the female and male parents, prior to being fitted together) would be in such an incomplete and imperfect state that they could not stay alive and healthy. On the other hand, if each separate part of the body had a vital principle of its own to maintain its life and health, then it would remain to be shown what organizes or coordinates all these separate vital principles and how they merge to form one unified organism. Aristotle's objections to Empedocles here (and explicitly later in *GA* 764a1-765a4) are in keeping with the other arguments he has made against excessively materialistic theories of generation: these theories, Empedocles' included, which rely for their explanations exclusively on a thing's material constituents, simply cannot account fully for the regularity and ordered nature of generation. Thus, Aristotle's rejection of Empedocles' approach is not motivated by an unwillingness to allow the female a fuller share in generation, as these feminist critics believe. His end here is to establish a metaphysical point: the necessary inclusion of nonmaterial explanatory principles (in this case, the soul or form of the body as organized, and the whole, unified, mature animal as the *telos* or final cause of the process, along with the action of the eternal and divine).

Returning to the progress of the discussion in *GA,* we can, in fact, make some sense of why Aristotle's discussion of the generative fluids should begin as it does, with what sounds like a subordinate and somewhat technical question about whether or not *sperma* derives from the body as a whole. This question allows him at the outset to display the current rival theories of generation and to critique them in terms of their reliance on limited materialist presuppositions. Having explained the insufficiency of these approaches and stated in a preliminary way his own alternative—that is, a generative theory which fully includes physical causal components as well as nonmaterial organizing and directing principles whose aims and mode of operation differ from material causal principles—Aristotle can pursue his examination of the working of both physical (material and moving) causes and the metaphysical (formal and final) ones, along with the ways in which these causes cohere.

We might note, then, the way in which Aristotle's discussion is shaped by rival theories against which he defines his own. His determination to establish the metaphysical dimension of generation against both the Presocratic materialists and the Hippocratic medical establishment leads to special highlighting of form over matter in books 1 and 2, perhaps in part to make form more readily evident to his opponents. In the treatise, the special attention to form, later to be identified as the male's contribution to generation, may seem to some modern readers to be one more instance of Aristotle's concentration on the male at the expense of the female. Read in its historical context, however, we see that the chief point of difference between Aristotle's theory and other theories concerned the concept of form, and so it naturally required fuller explication. On the other hand, another rival theory which remains within Aristotle's range of vision is Plato's, in which eternal Forms remain at some removal from material things. Aristotle

wants to be sure that no mistake is made in this direction either. In his own theory, form is united with matter fundamentally to produce substantial entities. It is this very union which Aristotle is challenged to demonstrate in *GA.*

Next Aristotle examines the general nature of *sperma* and says, "Now the aim of *Sperma* is to be, in its nature, the sort of stuff from which the things that take their rise in the realm of Nature are originally formed" (724a17). Analyzing the meaning of the "from which" in his definition of *sperma,* he shows that the two senses of "from which" that are relevant for generation are the matter from which and the movement from which a living creature derives. The question whether *sperma* is one or the other, or perhaps both material and moving cause, is raised and then temporarily set aside while a more precise determination of *sperma* and its derivation is pursued. Aristotle concludes that *sperma* is derived from a healthy residue, what remains from the body's useful nourishment (725a11). He then raises a crucial question:

> Does the female discharge *sperma* as the male does, which would mean that the object formed is a single mixture produced from two *spermations;* or is there no discharge of *sperma* from the female? And if there is none, then does the female contribute nothing whatever to generation, merely providing a place where generation may happen; or does it contribute something else, and if so, how and in what manner does it do so? (726a31-32)

The question reveals why Aristotle is concerned about the claim that the female discharges *sperma* as the male does. If the female's *sperma* is the same as the male's, the fetation resulting from copulation might appear to be (merely) a mixture; that is, each of the two parents would contribute the very same thing, and then somehow when they are added together a living creature comes into being. On such a view, the appearance of a new substance would depend entirely on the accumulation of a sufficient quantity of material being. According to Aristotle, however, such a "mixture" view leads to impossible results. Primarily, if the contribution to generation by the male and the female were identical, there would be nothing to prevent each from generating on its own, without the other, or for that matter for females to generate together by mixing menstrual blood, or for males to mix their fluids to produce offspring.[28] But this is manifestly not the way nature operates. Male and female, together, constitute the *archai* of generation, as Aristotle has already established. Their separate insufficiency indicates, for him, that their contributions must be of different kinds.[29] Furthermore, Aristotle's dissatisfaction with a strictly materialist reading of generation reveals why he would be unwilling to accept a "mixture" theory of the phenomenon, a view to which he would be committed if the female fluid were the same *sperma* as the male's. Either (a) there is no organizing principle, which is inadequate; or (b) there are two organizing principles, which is one principle too many. If (a), the material mixture has no organizing principle, then there is no possible explanation for how a unified, coherent, highly complex and directed creature is formed or forms itself from the body's residual food. But if (b), the male and female *sperma* are identical and so both contain organizing principles, one is then left with the daunting task of explaining how these independent principles could unite, as they must, to create a single principle to direct the unified development of the particular creature.

Here is what Aristotle decides on the question: menstrual fluid is a residue of healthy nourishment and it is "the analogous thing" in females to the male fluid. (The generative fluids of both male and female are blood or are derived from blood.) He demonstrates the status of menstrual blood as healthy (it is not a colliquescence, he explains), as a residue (which has been distilled from the body's nourishment, as has semen), and above all as generative or spermatic, that is, as playing a causative role in generation. In Aristotle's scheme, menstrual blood is not a waste product, nor is a woman's body regarded as simply a warm environment for the growth of the fetation. Despite the feminist claim that for Aristotle the female makes little, if any, genuine contribution and functions only as a container for the developing embryo, his determination that the menstrual fluid is spermatic is exactly what we would expect, since it is perfectly consistent with the initial thesis that male and female are both *archai* of generation.

Aristotle must now, for the reasons mentioned above, find a way of differentiating menstrual fluid from semen. Thus to his original question, Does the female discharge *sperma* as the male does? the answer must be yes and no. The female contributes *sperma* but not as the male does; she does not contribute semen. Her contribution is less fully heated or concocted than the male's semen. Misogyny does not direct Aristotle's analysis and lead to his yes and no conclusion. On the contrary, Aristotle here is rejecting the identification of generative fluid with the male semen, and establishing instead a fuller conception of *sperma* that includes both male and female contributions, contributions that do differ in kind. Each is unique; both are necessary.[30]

What we have here, then, is the outcome of his continuing endeavor to accomplish two aims: (1) to take the evidence seriously, in this case, that male and female are both involved most basically in generation, that they do differ anatomically, that the fluids produced by each do in fact have different features, and that separately each sex is insufficient to generate offspring; and (2) to develop a philosophical scheme that

will permit the metaphysical dimensions of the phenomenon of generation to be exhibited.

From the opening of the treatise this scheme is being prepared, as Aristotle reminds his readers of the basic four causes. Two of these causes, the material and the moving, are components of causality physically understood; and the other two, the formal and the final, are components of causality metaphysically understood. Having established in *GA* 1, both by way of empirical scrutiny and theoretical considerations, that male and female are coprinciples of generation and that they differ with respect to their contributions to generation, Aristotle begins to assign causal efficacy to the male and female parents according to his scheme of the four causes.

Aristotle makes his first assignment seem easy. The menstrual blood, the *katamenia,* being heavier and bulkier, looks like a material contribution. Aristotle could also draw upon the evidence that during gestation the developing fetus must be nourished; the female parent can generally be said to be the source of nourishment for growth, so the association with material might seem obvious on these grounds as well. So Aristotle declares that "the contribution which the female makes to generation is the matter used therein" (727b30); the *katamenia,* then, is the material cause of the offspring. There is, of course, nothing commonplace about the material the female parent provides; rather, it is specialized and highly refined for generation. Unlike ordinary material, it contains all the parts of a body, potentially (737a23). Furthermore, it is specialized for generating just the kind of animal the female parent is. Aristotle soon takes an opportunity to make his second and third assignments on his list of philosophical causes: "The male provides the 'form' as well as the 'principle of movement'," that is, the male provides the moving and formal causes (729a10). The analogy he offers to justify associating both the moving and the formal principles with the male is the coagulation of milk when rennet is added to it. Just as the rennet initiates a reaction in the milk such that the fluid is set in motion and begins to coalesce, so the semen imparts a motion to the generative material of the female which causes it to set.

However unsatisfactory this analogy is, since animals and human beings decidedly do not begin simply by being "set" like cheese or custard—and Aristotle himself would reject any materialistic explanation of substantial generation by means of chemical or other strictly physical reaction—the analogy is illuminating in at least one way. After having assigned the first sort of physical principle, the matter, to the female, Aristotle looks to assign the second kind of physical principle, the moving cause, to the male. This he will do (with a good deal of the explanation of how still to come in book 2), thereby providing full *physical* accountability, via female and male, for the generation of the offspring. But the physical dimension, while distinguishable, is not separable from the metaphysical one, as Aristotle's example about the rennet setting the milk shows. When the rennet and milk react, setting up a motion in the milk, the motion is not arbitrary, but is already ordered; it is motion toward the form. It might better be said that the motion *is* the forming. (Additionally, we can observe that the fully actualized form functions as that for the sake of which, that is, as the final cause.) With this analogy of rennet and milk which he calls upon several times in *GA* (739b21-34, and at 772a22-25, where he notes the disanalogy), Aristotle indicates the linkage between physical and metaphysical levels of explanation, and why it is in his system that the moving and material causes of the physical level are especially bound to the metaphysical. Living motion is always directed, always ordered, and its order and direction can be properly understood only in terms of form and *telos*.[31]

In elaborating his ideas about semen and its causal powers, Aristotle moves as far as possible away from the materialisms of pangenesis and preformation. His idea is that the semen does not contribute in any way to generation by its material (729b1-22), but rather produces a specific effect by way of "some disposition, and some principle of movement" (726b21). Aristotle is emphatic that the male's contribution is nonmaterial; instead, he says, the semen is a tool which Nature uses to impart motion (730b19).

Aristotle certainly makes his point against the materialist philosophers and physicians by regarding semen in this way. He also furthers his own philosophical mapping of generation by way of the four causes; in terms of physical causality, he now has the two necessary components, matter and motion, which together in his scheme are adequate to provide a physical explanation of the phenomenon of generation. But he has yet to explain how the semen, a material fluid, could convey form or soul.[32] This is a philosophical problem, to which Aristotle develops a startling answer in book 2. But in book 2, the linkage of moving cause with the male, and material cause with the female, as it is developed in terms of act and potency, has furnished further evidence in the sexism case, and this also needs to be examined.

IV

Aristotle's move from the level of physical causality to that of metaphysical causality is apparent immediately at the start of *GA* 2. If we were to express the central question of book 1 as, How does generation occur? and see Aristotle's answer to be that generation occurs through the *archai*, male and female, then his metaphysical deepening of that initial question is presented at the beginning of book 2: How are these *archai* them-

selves generated? Aristotle takes note of the route of physical explanation available for answering the question about the source of the sources, but he postpones that exploration (until book 4) and instead offers a commentary on how the two *archai* arise: not out of the forces of necessity but because of "what is better [*to beltion*], that is, on account of the final cause [the cause 'for the sake of which']" (731b23). Aristotle declares that, viewed in this metaphysical way, the determining principle of generation has its source in the upper cosmos. He seems to realize that his readers might wonder about such a statement, and he explains that there are some things which are eternal and divine, other things that admit both of being and nonbeing. The things that are eternal and divine reside in the upper cosmos and they act "as a cause which produces that which is better in the things that admit of it" (731b26-27). As he explains in the *Metaphysics,* the final cause "causes motion as being an object of love" (1072b4). Living creatures like ourselves, who come into being and pass away, are acted upon by the divine and the beautiful to the extent that we are capable of being affected.[33] The divine and beautiful give rise in us (by means of final causality) to that which it is better to have or be: it is better to be ensouled than to be only a body; it is better to be than not to be; it is better to be alive than dead. This is the metaphysical "why" of the generation of animals: generation occurs for the sake of actualizing a good. The good is not actualized absolutely in this way, since it is impossible for individual creatures to exist eternally; but it is accomplished specifically, Aristotle says, that is, by way of the eternal perpetuation of the species.[34] Thus, male and female *as such* serve generation, and generation serves the end of actualizing the good (eternal, beautiful, divine being) that resides in the most elevated domain of the cosmos.

In his thoroughness Aristotle wishes to give not only the metaphysical explanation for the existence of male and female but to explain as well the fact that these two principles for the most part are separate in the animal world. He states that because that which possesses the form is better and more divine than that which possesses the matter, "it is better also that the superior one should be separate from the inferior one" (732a5). In this instance, as in some others in *GA*, we have evidence of the infusion of Aristotle's commonplace views into his more careful philosophical thinking. There is, after all, no reason he has given to hold that those whose generative fluid transmits form are superior as a kind or class to those whose generative fluid transmits matter. It is true, of course, that within Aristotle's metaphysics form has preeminence over matter, but neither Aristotle nor his reader is entitled, on the basis of what has been established so far in *GA*, to conclude that this preeminence accrues to male creatures *qua* male. Recall from book 1 that organisms are male or female not as a whole but only with respect to their generative roles; he establishes further that both male and female are fully members of the same species, one implication of which is that both male and female individuals possess the same "substantial formula" of matter and form (see 730b34-5, for example; and *Metaphysics* 10.9). There is no philosophical justification, then, for this remark about the superiority of the male.

Returning to the progress of the discussion in book 2, Aristotle's next task is an embryological classification of animals. The metaphysical outlook of the opening of book 2 can be seen to dominate here as well when Aristotle makes the "perfection of the young" the basis for his classificatory system. That is, offspring are perfect in this case when they are brought forth, not as eggs or larvae, but as "similar to" the parents. Viviparous animals whose offspring are born in this state are themselves more perfect than oviparous or larvae-producing creatures. It appears to be more demanding for nature to produce young viviparously; animals that do so possess a more highly developed capacity for respiration and are able to generate a higher degree of needed body heat. Using the criteria of breath and vital heat, Aristotle describes the regular arrangement with which nature brings about generation in various classes of animals (733a35-b16). At the top of this series is man and then the other mammals, followed by birds, scaly fishes, and so forth. Near the bottom of the scale are those animals which begin as larvae.[35] Finally there are those, too, which do not arise from *sperma* and the union of the male and female *archai*.

Mention of these exceptional nonspermatic animals leads Aristotle's attention back to *sperma*. It is "no small puzzle," he states, to determine how any animal is formed out of the *sperma*. He analyzes the process of forming into three components: (a) out of something, (b) by something, and (c) into something. The "out of something" is the "material out of which," supplied by the mother.[36] But the question Aristotle says he is interested in pursuing at this point is not, Out of what? but, By what? This "by what" is analyzed as something either external or internal to the fetation. He acknowledges that he is confronted with a problem: it is hard to see how something external could be in a position to act to form the fetation, for what is in close enough contact with it to form it? On the other hand, if there is something in the fetation from the start that forms it, Aristotle is then dangerously close to the pangenesis and preformation theories which hold that the miniaturized creature or the parts of the creature are already in the generative fluid. Aristotle opts for a more subtle dichotomy than internal-external, and switches to the concepts of "actual" and "potential" to solve the dilemma.[37] The "something" by which the fetation is formed is declared to be soul; this must be so since the fetus is living and growing, and all living things possess soul, the first actualization (or perfection, *entelechia*) of a living body (*De anima* 2.1). Aristotle takes the opportunity to repeat that none of the physical properties alone can explain the *logos* or the highly organized nature of the organism (734b32-33).[38] The *logos* derives from the parent who imparts movement. This parent is in actuality (that is, a living animal of a specific kind) what the offspring is potentially.[39] With the conjunction of material and moving causes, the newly formed organism has separate identity, and one part develops which can direct the rest of the new animal's growth. As Aristotle puts it, "Nothing generates itself, though as soon as it has been formed a thing makes itself grow" (735a14).

What are we to understand happens here? The generation of a new creature is, within Aristotle's conceptual scheme, the actualizing of a potential. The two specialized potentialities contributed by the female and male *archai* actualize in conjunction with one another. The offspring is the actualization of the union of the two potentials. His theory has been read by feminist critics and other commentators as maintaining that in the act of generation the passive, potential female matter is bestowed with life by the actualized and soul-bearing form of the male. This, however, is not Aristotle's view. Rather, the dynamic of generation which he develops in *GA* is subtle and at the same time is perfectly consistent with principles he lays down in both the *Physics* and *Metaphysics* regarding potency and act. Instead of associating the female and her contribution with passive potentiality and the male and his contribution with activating actuality, Aristotle sees both adult parents as actualities, both female and male fluids as potentialities, and the offspring resulting from their conjunction as an actuality.[40] Even though the male parent's *sperma* bears the form which, in Aristotle's system, has preeminence over matter, that preeminence is minimized by virtue of the potential status of both the female and male *sperma* and the actual status of the female and male parents. Thus male and female continue to be regarded by him as coprinciples of generation.

Aristotle's discussion of act and potency in connection with movement in *Physics* 3.3 is illuminating in this regard. There he explains that the two potentialities, mover and moved, actualize together, and that the result is singular: "The actualizing of the two potentialities coincides" (*Physics* 202a19). In the passage in the *Physics* mover and moved together give rise to motion.[41] Correspondingly, in *GA* the conjunction of mover (male fluid) and moved (female fluid) gives rise to generation. Moreover, because in the generation of animals the moving cause is also bearing the formal and final causes (that is, the structure for and aim of the animal's development), once the conjunction of the material and moving causes occurs all four causes are really at work and the necessary and sufficient conditions have been met for (the beginning of) the realization of the new offspring. Everything it needs is available. So, Aristotle states, "Nothing generates itself, though as soon as it has been formed it makes itself grow" (735a14); and he repeats and develops this conclusion (735a16-17) that once a creature is formed—in the coactualization of the female and male principles—it must grow. The parallel case of motion is again pertinent since, for Aristotle, nothing moves itself, just as nothing generates itself. But having been generated, being a natural creature now possessing its own internal principle of motion, it must move, or, biologically speaking, it must grow.

At the start of *GA* 2.2 Aristotle returns to the topic of *sperma* and of semen in particular. It being the work of semen to contribute motion, and in some way *logos* and soul, from an actual adult parent to matter which is an animal potentially—and in an active state of desire for form and what it offers (see *Physics* 1.9)—he undertakes a close examination of semen which will try to answer the question of how this transmission takes place. Based on descriptions of its physical properties, especially its foaminess, and its behavior, Aristotle determines that semen is composed of water and *pneuma,* heated air. Now Aristotle has already committed himself to the notion that the male's semen does not provide material input of any kind into the fetation. So two questions arise for him: (1) What becomes, then, of the material stuff of which the semen is composed?; and the more crucial question, (2) Is soul in the semen and/or in the fetus to begin with? (736a27-28). He first addresses the second of these questions and decides as far as nutritive soul is concerned, the basic faculty of self-growth by which a living thing persists, that *spermata* (of the male and female parents) and fetations possess this aspect of soul potentially. He continues by saying that sentient soul, the perceptive dimension of soul unique to animals, is possessed potentially by semen. The most elevated dimension of soul, reason, possessed only by human beings, cannot, however, arise from some potential in the stuff of the semen or menstrual fluid or the developing body of the fetation: "Reason alone enters in, as an additional factor, from outside, and . . . it alone is divine, because physical activity has nothing whatever to do with the activity of reason" (736b28-29). Reason is divine, but all soul, Aristotle continues, has a connection with a physical substance "which is different from the so-called 'elements' and more divine than they are" (736b30-33). In other words, for Aristotle, soul is naturalized or physicalized to some basic degree (in distinction from Plato), but its material is highly rarefied and unique (in distinction from the physicians and the Presocratic materialists). There is a scale of substances, he says, concerned with levels of psychic transmission. In all cases, semen contains *pneuma,* and the *pneuma* contains enclosed within itself a substance that "is analogous to the element which belongs to the stars" (736b37). This element, unnamed in the text but evidently aether, Aristotle sometimes calls "the first of the elements." It

Aristotle, painted by Raphael.

is the material of which the stars are made and is unlike the four earthly elements—earth, air, fire, and water—in that it is eternally existent, indestructible, and divine, moving forever in a circular motion in the celestial domain. It is never found naturally in this earthly region.[42]

Aristotle immediately emphasizes that the vital heat which supports this "complex" by means of which soul is transmitted has nothing to do with fire (that is, a common, earthly element favored in the theories of some early naturalists) and should not be confused with it. Rather, the heat for the *pneuma,* which in turn is the source of the movement imparted by the male generative fluid to the female generative fluid, which in turn is the source of life for the new fetation—this heat has its own original source, not in the father's body or in some element occurring naturally in the environment, but in the region of the stars (see also 777b30-31). Aristotle does not say how this sublime element, this link between body and soul, between earth and stars, between the physical and the metaphysical, establishes itself in both these worlds. The absence of an explanation of the link may indicate that for him no explanation is required. Nature itself is a coherent whole; no fundamental division exists in nature which would be in need of philosophical repair.

Having, so it seems, answered the question about how semen provides motion, soul, and *logos* for the menstrual material, Aristotle returns to the more mundane level of his two earlier questions, that is, What becomes of the stuff of the semen after it has done its job? An explanation is required here to meet the suspicions of the partisans of pangenesis and preformation. That the semen cannot all be recovered after copulation is taken by them as evidence that the substance of the semen has been used up materially in the creation of the fetation. Now Aristotle can make short work of this question. He states as a general rule that the soul principle for which the semen is a vehicle is partly separable from physical matter (especially in those animals which possess a divine element) and partly inseparable from it. Here, once again, Aristotle stakes out his own position, distinct from the materialists and from Plato. The physical part of the semen, as fluid, "dissolves and evaporates." Semen has conveyed something indispensable to the fetation, but this something is the soul principle, neither an animalcule nor unassembled anatomical parts, as Aristotle's rival theorists contend. He closes these questions by reiterating his position that *spermata* and fetations have soul potentially but not in actuality (737a17-18).

The semen is a residue, and, Aristotle says,

> The female's contribution, of course, is a residue too, just as the male's is, and contains all the parts of the body potentially, though none in actuality; and "all" includes those parts which distinguish the two sexes. Just as it sometimes happens that deformed [*pepērōmenōn*] offspring are produced by deformed parents, and sometimes not, so the offspring produced by a female are sometimes female, sometimes not, but male. The reason is that the female is as it were a deformed male; and the menstrual blood is *sperma,* though in an impure condition; i.e. it lacks one constituent, and one only, the principle of soul. (737a22-30)

Aristotle's comment that the female is "as it were a deformed male" is no doubt the one most frequently quoted by his feminist opponents. It is on the face of it a disturbing remark. We find, however, in the immediate context of the comment, confirmation that Aristotle regards both semen and menstrual fluid as *spermatic* residues. We also have seen through the course of this discussion that in order to maintain that both are truly generative and to avoid simultaneously a materialistic theory of generation, Aristotle has had to differentiate the two fluids, and the differentiation turns on the conveyance of sentient soul by the semen. His unfortunate comment about the female as a deformed male is prompted in this passage by a specific difficulty encountered earlier: to the extent that Aristotle's theory of generation includes a material component, and to the extent that is associated exclusively with the female, he must explain how it is that the material for the formation of a male body is available in a physical female body which does not possess

male anatomical parts. Recall that he rejected preformationism on just such grounds: How could the father's body supply the sex-specific body parts for female offspring? His comment here about deformity is intended to anticipate and counter an objection to his theory; his crude-sounding analogy is meant to show that females can and do produce male offspring because they do possess (potentially) the "extra" male organs. But they themselves, as females, do not manifest them and so might be said, in this way only, to be like those who are deformed or underdeveloped in that they possess parts which are of no use to them.[43] Aristotle is not in this passage offering a philosophy of woman as a deformity of nature or as an underdeveloped human but rather he is trying to solve some technical difficulties facing his theory. He overcomes them by positing an extended potentiality to this generative material of the female, potential to generate what the female herself does not exhibit.

Aristotle really has had two problems to overcome, one relating to each sex, in this portion of his discussion in book 2. The first, regarding how semen could be a vehicle of soul, he has tried to solve by way of the potentiality of the sublime, celestially connected element. The second, regarding the capacity of the female body to produce offspring which differ from her, has led Aristotle once again to a widened potential of the menstrual fluid, widened beyond the body features specific to females—and widened again, we might say, beyond the potential attributed to it within preformationism or other contemporary theories.

Apropos of Aristotle's penchant for expansion, if we return for a moment to book 1, we find that in attributing the material cause to the female, Aristotle makes the following remark: "The natural substance of the menstrual fluid is to be classed as prime matter" (730a32). Prime matter comes up for discussion in the *Metaphysics* and in the *Physics*. He explains there that "prime" means "primary in general," that is, that out of which the four elements arise, the most fundamental stuff of the cosmos, and also "primary in relation to the thing," the very first material of a particular entity (*Metaphysics* 1015a8-9). It has been suggested that the remark about menstrual fluid as prime matter should be interpreted as "primary in relation to the thing."[44] But considering Aristotle's comment now in connection with his celestial move in book 2 where he tells of the tie between semen and the element of the stars, aether, there is reason to suppose that Aristotle has in mind both the particular and the cosmic meaning of "primary." What he posits in his remark that the menstrual fluid is prime matter, therefore, is that it serves as a highly specialized basic material out of which the new entity will arise, and also that there exists a tie between the generated creature and the most primordial stratum of the natural world. What is produced, then, in the first two books of *GA* is an "axis" that stretches from the bottom to the top edges of the universe, along which the appearance of the new creature must be understood. The primordial, preelemental power that inheres in prime matter expresses itself (as potentiality) in the adult female's generative material. The active, moving power that is unique to the heavens expresses itself (as potentiality) in the male generative material. Viewed on a cosmic scale, then, the generated offspring is the outcome of the meeting of a vast scale of forces as these are embodied in the *archai* of generation, the female and male.[45]

Aristotle turns his attention next to the different patterns of embryological development found among the creatures in his classificatory scale (the scale of *GA* 2.1 based on the creatures' perfection). Consideration of this topic and the others he studies later in the treatise is beyond the scope of this paper. In assessing the course of the discussion in book 2 up to this point, however, it is evident that Aristotle has provided a deepened and more thorough metaphysical analysis of generation and its sources in the female and male. This is precisely what he indicates he will do in the first lines of book 2:

> I have already said that the female and male are *archai* of generation and I have also said what is their *dynamis* and the *logos* of their essence. As for the reason why one comes to be formed and is female and another male, . . . insofar as this occurs on account of what is *better,* i.e. on account of the final cause [the cause "for the sake of which"], the principle is derived from the upper cosmos [*anōthen echei tēn archēn*]. (731b18-24)[46]

In these lines Aristotle offers the thesis developed in the discussion that follows: the principles of generation, the female and male *archai,* are themselves generated according to the direction of the better, that is, final causality as it affects nature as a whole. This direction has its ties to the upper cosmos, he says, the system of concentric spheres whose movement is continuous and eternal.[47] After explaining the working of this causality, that things are affected by the noble and eternal to the extent that they are able to be, Aristotle moves immediately to the classification of animals in the natural world. Having supplied the details of the distinctions among the animal kinds in his hierarchy he observes, "We should notice how well nature brings generation about in its several forms: they are arranged in a regular series" (733a35-b1). We are now in a position to see that Aristotle regards the female and male as the means for this orderly unfolding of nature's series according to the direction of the better. This is what it means in his system to be a *principle* of generation, rather than a tool or machine. The principles of generation are themselves tied to all four aspects of causality as it operates from the particular individual case to the universal. The female and male *archai*

generate particular offspring, and they stand at the head of the ordering of the animal species. At the same time they themselves stand on an extended axis of cosmic causal influence, actualizing more remote potentialities.

It is evident now why Aristotle's discussion turns to potency and act in book 2 (734b). It is not, as sometimes supposed, that he turns to these concepts because there is no other solution available to the *aporia* about the formation of the fetation by an internal or external agent. A solution is needed for this technical problem, to be sure; but by introducing potency and act Aristotle shows, first, that the process of generating offspring requires the application of the same physical and metaphysical concepts as other phenomena require in order to be understood. The action involved in giving rise to offspring is consistent with the way nature moves and changes always and in all respects (the potency of the *spermata* becoming actualized), and thus generation is an intelligible process. He also shows, second, that generation, understood on the full natural scale, beyond the capacities and activities of the individual parents, is itself the actualization, insofar as it is possible, of nature's ultimate aims.[48]

V

In book 1 Aristotle accomplishes his aim of demonstrating that male and female are both principles of generation. He shows there that they are both, clearly, anatomically fitted for the work of generating offspring, and he also establishes the more controversial point that both contribute generative fluids so that male and female must both be regarded as causally efficacious in generation. He studies their coeffectiveness, however, primarily at the level on which material and motive causality operates, that is, the physical level where necessity is the dominant factor. In book 2 Aristotle deepens his reflections on metaphysical causality in generation in his effort to give a full reckoning of generation in terms of all four causes stated at the outset of the treatise. He does this, as we have seen, both with respect to generation of individual offspring and to generation understood as the coming into being of nature itself as an ordered whole directed by final causality.

In our examination of these sections of books 1 and 2 we have seen Aristotle's complex philosophical elaboration of his initial thesis that female and male are both *archai* of generation. Contrary to the feminist claim, then, that in his system only the male parent effects generation, it is now clear that for Aristotle both are causally effective. In establishing his thesis Aristotle critiques rival theories, demonstrating that among their shortcomings, they become unworkable because of the sexual imbalance upon which they are premised. Indeed, it is Aristotle's theory in which the female and her distinctive contribution is recognized and integrated. Methodologically, the necessity for a full and detailed reading of Aristotle's text has become evident; excerpted sentences or passages can neither convey the intellectual context within and against which he worked nor represent accurately the intricacies of his thinking on this subject. Above all, a close reading of the text provides us with a glimpse of a theory quite unlike the reproduction theory bequeathed by modern science: Aristotle's metaphysical science of generation ties the offspring meaningfully to the parents, and the parents and offspring together to the whole of nature.[49]

Notes

[1] Eve Browning Cole, in a review of Page DuBois, *Sowing the Body,* in *American Philosophical Association Newsletter on Philosophy and Feminism* 89 (Fall 1989): 88-9.

[2] As evidence of Aristotle's sexism, Mary Mahowald offers, without comment, passages from *Generation of Animals* in her book, *The Philosophy of Woman* (Indianapolis: Hackett Publishing Company, 1983), 266-72. Caroline Whitbeck speaks of Aristotle's "flowerpot" theory of pregnancy in her article, "Theories of Sex Difference," in *Women and Philosophy,* ed. Carol C. Gould and Marx W. Wartofsky (New York: G. P. Putnam's Sons, 1976), 54-80. Lynda Lange holds that Aristotle's sexist views on sex difference are not separable from his general philosophical thought, that they are interwoven with and may, she proposes, be the basis for ideas he develops in his political, metaphysical, and logical writings; see her "Woman is Not a Rational Animal: On Aristotle's Biology of Reproduction," in *Discovering Reality,* ed. Sandra Harding and Merrill B. Hintikka (Boston: D. Reidel Publishing Company, 1983), 1-15. Prudence Allen's thesis in her book, *The Concept of Woman: the Aristotelian Revolution 750 B.C.-1250 A.D.* (Montreal: Eden Press, 1985), is that Aristotle systematically devalues women, with long term effects both for women and for the history of philosophy. Page DuBois offers a similar assessment of Aristotle in her book, *Sowing the Body* (Chicago: University of Chicago Press, 1988). "Aristotle's Views on Women," by Rhoda Kotzin (in *American Philosophical Association Newsletter on Philosophy and Feminism* 88 (1989): 21-5) lists Aristotle's offensive assertions in the biological and political treatises. Kotzin believes not only that "it is beyond dispute that Aristotle was wrong about women" (p. 21), but also that Aristotle is not entitled to make the claims that he does and that they are inconsistent with other elements of his philosophy.

[3] The promotion of fertility goddess worship, for example, by some feminist writers must be regarded at best as an attempt to imaginatively infuse a desiccated modern notion of conception and pregnancy with some meaning.

[4] As Peck remarks in the Preface to his translation of *Generation of Animals:* " . . . for in reproduction, as understood by Aristotle, not only the individual is concerned but the cosmos at large: it is a business in which the powers of the universe are concentrated and united."; (Aristotle, *Generation of Animals,* translation and introduction by A. L. Peck (Boston: Harvard University Press, 1979), p. v. Translations of *Generation of Animals* in this article are for the most part those of Peck, although occasionally I make modifications.

[5] See Maryanne Cline Horowitz, "Aristotle and Woman," *Journal of the History of Biology* 9 (1976): 183-213.

[6] The demand that male and female contributions be the same in kind follows along the lines of ancient theories such as those of Empedocles and Hippocrates (as will be seen later in this essay), as well as of modern genetic views of reproduction. In both the ancient theories cited and the modern scientific one, strong materialist assumptions are at work. Feminist critics (for example, Allen) who endorse this criterion of acceptability may, wittingly or not, adopt a materialist framework along with it.

[7] Other commentators have responded to the apparent sexism in *GA.* Johannes Morsink sees Aristotle not as a sexist but as a scientist involved in a battle of scientific theory with Hippocrates and his school; see his "Was Aristotle's Biology Sexist?" *Journal of the History of Biology* 12 (1979): 87-8. Anthony Preus sees Aristotle making the mistake of linking matter and form exclusively with female and male respectively; see his "Science and Philosophy in Aristotle's *Generation of Animals.*" *Journal of the History of Biology* 3 (1970): 4. Montgomery Furth sees the source of the sexism in Aristotle's reluctance to divide form; see his *Substance, Form and Psyche: An Aristotelian Metaphysics,* (New York: Cambridge University Press, 1988), 137-41.

[8] Aristotle explains the distinction between natural generation *(genesis)* and artificial production *(poiesis)* in *Metaphysics* 7.7. He distinguishes nature and things natural from art and things humanly produced in *Physics* 2.1.

[9] Peck, *Generation of Animals,* p. vii.

[10] This line of thought is termed "metaphysical" here because in the *Physics* Aristotle declares that the formal cause and its nature is the work of first philosophy, or metaphysics, to determine (192a34-36). In the *Metaphysics* he says that the form is a cause because "the question 'why' is ultimately reduced to the *logos,* and the primary 'why' is cause and principle" (983a28-29). Thus, the formal cause and the ultimate meaning

of an entity should be regarded as metaphysical—or should be regarded metaphysically. Joseph Owens cites both of the above passages; see his *The Doctrine of Being in the Aristotelian Metaphysics* (Toronto: Pontifical Institute of Mediaeval Studies, 1978): 176-7.

[11] See Hans Jonas, *The Phenomenon of Life* (New York: Dell Publishing Co., 1966): 33-4.

[12] See also the preliminary justification at 716a11-12. See also 716b10-12, 731b18, 732a1-3; and at 732a12: "Thus things are alive in virtue of having in them a share of the male and the female." We may note that in the *Metaphysics* too, in defining *archē* as a source from which come motion and change, Aristotle adds "as the child comes from the father and mother" (1013a8-9).

[13] On this particular sort of structuring of the argumentation in Aristotle, where the thesis is stated first and the remainder of the discussion in a given Book secures that thesis, see Helen Lang, "Aristotelian Physics: Teleological Procedure in Aristotle, Thomas, and Buridan," *Review of Metaphysics* 42 (1989): 569-91. Lang demonstrates the teleological structure of argumentation in the *Physics,* where Aristotle posits his thesis at the start, and the discussion that follows in that book supports rather than extends or alters the initial thesis. Also see Joseph Owens' observation, regarding the first sentence of the *Metaphysics,* "All men by nature desire to learn." Owens writes, "This one short sentence, as will be seen . . . , contains the whole *motif* of the Aristotelian *Metaphysics*"; Owens, *The Doctrine of Being,* 158, n. 5. On the philosophical importance of Aristotle's form of presentation see also Werner Jaeger, *Aristotle* (Oxford: Clarendon Press, 1948), 6; and Owens, *The Doctrine of Being,* 72.

[14] In the translation of *GA* by Peck in the Loeb edition, *sperma* is routinely translated as "semen." Platt also translates *sperma* as "semen" in the Oxford edition; A. Platt, *Generation of Animals,* in *The Complete Works of Aristotle,* vol. 1, ed. Jonathan Barnes (Princeton: Princeton University Press, 1984). Translating *sperma* in this way gives the wrong impression that Aristotle regards only the male discharge as authentically generative, and completely obscures an important question raised in *GA* 1: whether the female parent contributes *sperma,* that is, generative fluid, to the process. It can be noted in advance that Aristotle's answer is that the female does contribute *sperma,* although it differs from that of the male parent, that is, it is not semen. Sexism here has its sources, not in Aristotle, but in his nineteenth- and early twentieth-century translators. In my discussion I will simply transliterate *sperma* when it appears in the text, rather than follow Peck's translation of the term.

[15] See *Metaphysics* 10.9, where Aristotle states that male and female do not differ substantially. They possess the same human form and their differences are only with respect to matter. Also see *GA* 730b34-35, where he states that male and female "are identical in species"; and *GA* 741a6: "Granted that the female possesses the same soul [as the male] . . ."

Aristotle's view of female and male difference is not, however, a simple functionalist one. He recognizes the ways in which the generative parts have complex ties to other aspects of an entity's life. The extensiveness of these ties is what leads Aristotle to regard femaleness and maleness as each a "principle," rather than a natural variation on the order of hair or eye color. That is, he notes that in general it is when a principle changes, even in a small way, that numerous other dependent things are affected. He has observed, for example, that castrated animals undergo extensive changes after the generative organ alone has been destroyed. He concludes, based on the frequency of this observation, that femaleness and maleness are on the order of "principles."

[16] For Aristotle's discussion of the regularity of nature see *Physics* 1. In *Physics* 2.5 he explains that things which always happen in the same way or do so for the most part cannot come about by chance. See also his comments in *Parts of Animals* 641b27-28: "For a given seed does not give rise to any chance living being, nor spring from any chance one; but each springs from a definite parent"; *Parts of Animals,* trans. W. Ogle, in *The Complete Works of Aristotle,* vol. 1.

[17] For an example of the necessary anatomy-better anatomy distinction see 717a16-17.

[18] Of interest on the subject of ancient embryological theories is chapter 1 of Joseph Needham, *A History of Embryology* (New York: Abelard-Schuman, 1959) (although Needham is not always a careful reader of Aristotle). Also see Preus, "Science and Philosophy," 5-7.

[19] See the extended discussion which begins at 721b12.

[20] *De anima* 412a27.

[21] See Preus, "Science and Philosophy," 7. Also of interest is the Hippocratic treatise, "The Seed," in *Hippocratic Writings,* ed. G. E. R. Lloyd (New York: Penguin Books, 1978), 317-23; and Needham's comments on Hippocrates' "mechanical approach" to viewing generation in Needham, *A History of Embryology,* 33.

[22] See Peck, *Generation of Animals,* 372-3, n. *a;* and Preus, "Science and Philosophy," 6, n. 6. Needham discusses "Denials of Maternity and Paternity," in Needham, *A History of Embryology,* 43-6.

[23] *Eumenides* 658-9; quoted from Needham, *A History of Embryology,* 43. (Peck and Preus also cite this passage from *Eumenides.*)

[24] Caroline Whitbeck, describing Aristotle's view as "the flower pot theory" of pregnancy, believes that Aristotle holds that "the woman supplies the container and the earth which nourishes the seed but the seed is solely the man's"; Whitbeck, "Theories of Sex Difference," 55. Page DuBois writes, "The great scientific work of Aristotle, read and accepted as truth for centuries, takes up the metaphorical system . . . that the female body is a container, like an oven, to be filled up with the semen, which provides soul and form to the material container"; DuBois, *Sowing the Body,* 126. Maryanne Cline Horowitz regards Aristotle's theory as "an extreme position in the process of the masculinization of procreation"; Horowitz "Aristotle and Woman," 186. She states, "Unlike the medical school of Hippocrates, Aristotle taught that *sperma,* in its narrow sense as the seed from which an embryo grows, is secreted only by males" (p. 192). Prudence Allen says, "Borrowing the use of hot and cold from Empedocles and Hippocrates, Aristotle developed a theory of sex identity that argued that the female provided no seed in generation because she was by nature colder than the male"; Allen, *The Concept of Woman,* 34.

[25] At 728a25, near the close of these considerations, he states, "Hence, plainly it is reasonable to hold that generation takes place from this process: for, as we see, the menstrual fluid is *sperma,* not indeed *sperma* in a pure condition, but needing still to be acted upon." In addition, at 730a35 he says, "The male and female both deposit together what they have to contribute in the female." Preus's careful reading of the text leads him, too, to the conclusion that for Aristotle the menstrual contribution of the female is *spermatic:* "Given Aristotle's notion that the 'menstrual fluid' is the female *sperma* of the mammalia . . ."; Preus, "Science and Philosophy," 8. And also, "The menstrual fluid should be that spermatic contribution which serves as matter for generation" (p. 9).

Among Aristotle's feminist critics, the misinterpretation seems to arise from a failure to appreciate the importance of the material cause in Aristotle's metaphysics, and from reading "matter" in a post-seventeenth-century sense. This might be particularly the case in Whitbeck's criticism ("Theories of Sex Difference," 55-7). Horowitz, in "Aristotle and Woman," notices that Aristotle calls both semen and menstrual blood *sperma,* but she does not notice or find it significant that he also calls them both the principles of generation. Her attention is directed exclusively at the higher degree of concoction of the semen, and this leads her to exaggerate the subordination of the material principle in Aristotle's scheme, making that principle almost worthless.

Other commentators on *GA* have read the text in this way as well. John M. Cooper writes, "The menstrual fluid is also a 'seminal residue' *(spermatikon perittoma),* less concocted and less pure than sperm, and so not capable of generating anything, i.e. not capable of coming alive by itself or making anything else come alive (I.20.728a18, 26 [sic.]; II.3.737a27-30; II.7.746b26-9)"; John M. Cooper, "Metaphysics in Aristotle's Biology," in *Biologie, Logique et Métaphysique Chez Aristote,* ed. Daniel Devereux and Pierre Pellegrin (Paris: Éditions du CNRS, 1990), 57. Nothing, for Aristotle, comes alive by itself ("nothing generates itself"; 735a14), so this is not a legitimate criterion for determining the spermatic status of menstrual fluid. The capacity "to make something come alive," which as a way of describing generation sounds a bit magical rather than Aristotelian, is a potential that can only be exercised in concert with specialized material which itself has a potential capacity to be formed as a particular kind of creature. See also Cooper's note on symmetry, where he explicitly denies that "there is any kind of interaction between the two factors, in the sense of a joint working together by two independent but proportionately coordinated agents with a view to a common product" (p. 59, n. 6). What Cooper eloquently denies is very much the same thesis that Aristotle is developing in *GA.*

[26] Allen, *The Concept of Woman,* 33-4, 84-6.

[27] Note that these contributions may not, in his theory, be equal ones. See 722b12-13, where Aristotle says that Empedocles postulates a tally, that is, broken pieces of a whole. The broken pieces fit together but need not be of the same size.

In a different vein, we might notice Empedocles' use of the word *symbolon,* "symbol," as Aristotle quotes him, and its connection with modern genetic theory which relies upon the interpretation of symbolic or coded information.

[28] For Aristotle, the puzzle appears not so much to be generation out of the union of the same sexes, but independent generation by the female: "Why does not the female accomplish generation all by itself and from itself?"; 741a4-5. Note that his first answer to this question depends on what he has already argued: that the fetation will be alive only on acquiring sentient soul, and this is what the male contributes. But, almost recognizing that this answer begs the question, he pursues the puzzle to arrive at a metaphysical explanation, in keeping with the tenor of book 2. His explanation relies on the concept of *telos:* "The female [by herself] is unable to generate offspring and bring it to completion; if it could the existence of the male would have no purpose, and nature does nothing which lacks purpose"; 741b3-4.

[29] It is useful to recall that the egg cell was not discovered until 1827. The principles for the discovery of the unique character of the germ cells (egg and sperm), each possessing only one half the ordinary complement of genetic material in readiness for fertilization, was not established until the middle of the nineteenth century. See Anthony Preus, "Science and Philosophy," 8, n. 11.

Aristotle's theory of generation resembles modern genetics and reproductive science in that he, too, sees the necessity for the union of two complementary components, which he believes to be matter and form rather than egg and sperm or—in the case of human beings—*X* and *Y* chromosomes. Scientifically, his is an advance over ancient "double seed" theories in which the female and male contributions are identical. Even if, in genetic engineering, it is possible to produce offspring without the union of the male and female cells, cloning of this sort is replication and not generation in Aristotle's sense: the production of a new and unique substantial creature.

[30] It appears to have been Hippocrates' theory, sometimes termed the "double seed theory," that both male and female contribute semen. Aristotle may have Hippocrates in mind when he argues against the suggestion that both female and male contribute semen to generation; see "The Seed," and Morsink's discussion of *GA* in relation to it in Morsink, "Was Aristotle's Biology Sexist?" Aristotle's argument at 727a26-30 is that no one animal produces two spermatic fluids, and since the female contributes the menstrual fluid, she does not contribute semen *(gonē)* as the male does.

There is a difficulty with the Greek terms which undoubtedly has aided the misunderstanding of Aristotle's intentions. He does not restrict the designation *sperma* to semen, as has been shown, but often enough when referring to semen he simply uses the broader term *sperma*. Sometimes it is plain from the context and his description which of the two *spermata* he has in mind; sometimes he seems to distinguish "generative fluid" from "semen" by use of *sperma* and *gonē* respectively, but this usage is far from consistent (for example at 729a21-23: "The foregoing discussion will have made it clear that the female, though it does not contribute any semen [*gonē*], yet contributes something, namely, the substance constituting the menstrual fluid"). While the lack of clear and consistent terminology easily can lead to confusion and support the sexism charges against Aristotle, it is plausible that the difficulty he has maintaining a clear distinction in the text by means of the language then available is, on the contrary, evidence of the conceptual advance that he is attempting in regarding both fluids as spermatic.

[31] Matter is always "formed," too, to some extent (see Furth, *Substance, Form, and Psyche,* 84-7: matter is

that which is capable of further formation, and so it too is linked to the metaphysical dimension). See also Peck's note on prime matter and on matter at its highest degree of formation being equivalent to form; Peck, *Generation of Animals,* 110-11, n. *e.*

[32] At 730b56 he offers a preliminary analogy to house building to help explain this at 730b5-6.

[33] See also his statement in *Parts of Animals* 1.5: "Absence of the haphazard and conduciveness of everything to an end are to be found in nature's works in the highest degree, and the end for which those works are put together and produced is a form of the beautiful"; 645a23-25.

[34] See also *De anima* 415a25-26.

[35] Aristotle's higher animal types almost always correspond to Darwin's "later" types.

[36] Notice again that the material contribution is considered within the topic of the working of *sperma,* indicating once more that Aristotle regards the maternal fluid as generative.

[37] For Aristotle's fuller exposition of these concepts see *Physics* 3.3.

[38] See also 735a13: "The cause of this process of formation is not any part of the body."

[39] This holds true, of course, for the mother as well. She is in actuality what the offspring is only potentially.

[40] Regarding the maternal contribution, he speaks of ". . . the generating parent, who is in actuality what the material out of which the offspring formed is potentially"; 734b35. Regarding the paternal contribution he says, "It is clear that *sperma* [in context, "semen"] possesses soul, and that it is soul, potentially"; 735a9; see also 734b18-19. In *Metaphysics* 9.7 he says, "We must, however, distinguish when a particular thing exists potentially and when it does not . . . , e.g. is earth potentially a man? No, but rather when it has already become *sperma,* and perhaps not even then"; 1048b37-1049a5. In *Parts of Animals* he says, "Moreover, the seed is potentially something, and the relation of potentiality to actuality we know"; 641b36. In *De anima* he says, "So seed [*sperma*] and fruit are potentially bodies [which have the capacity to live]"; 412b26.

[41] With respect to the mutuality posited in this interpretation, Aristotle, speaking of body and soul, makes the following comment in *De anima:* "For it is by this association [*koinonian*] that the one acts and the other is acted upon, that the one moves and the other is

moved; and no such mutual relation is found in hap-hazard combinations"; 407b18-20. The partnership of matter and form is emphasized, the partnership whereby the one *can* move and the other *can* be moved.

Regarding Aristotle's theory of the initiation of move-ment, as Frederick Woodbridge explains, "Motion strictly is not a transfer of movement from one body to another, but the change from rest to movement or the change from what can happen into an actual happen-ing"; Frederick Woodbridge, *Aristotle's Vision of Na-ture* (New York: Dell Publishing, 1965), 13-14. There must be contact between the two bodies; but according to Aristotle, movement cannot be grasped as a me-chanical collision. Some of Aristotle's commentators seem to assume a mechanical model when considering his explanation of the moving cause in generation—a model characteristic of modern science rather than Aristotle's physics. It is the modern model which in-volves one body in motion and one inertly at rest. For Aristotle, on the other hand, matter actively desires form, as he says in *Physics* 1.9; its potentiality is its orientation toward form. Thus, matter is not just the passive recipient of an external, haphazardly arising force.

On this subject Helen Lang writes, commenting on *Physics* 1.9: "Here we reach a key issue: før Aristotle, to be moved does not imply a passive principle. Matter (or potential), which is moved by form (or actuality), is moved precisely because it is never neutral to its mover: matter is aimed at—it runs after—form. Be-cause of the active orientation of the moved towards its mover, no third cause is required to combine matter and form. They go together naturally: form constitutes a thing as natural and matter is aimed at form"; Helen Lang, *Aristotle's Physics and Its Medieval Varieties* (Albany: State University of New York Press, 1992), 26.

42 See Peck, *Generation of Animals,* 170-1, n. 1; and Friedrich Solmsen, "The Vital Heat, the Inborn *Pneuma* and the Aether," *Journal of Hellenic Studies* 77 (1957): 119.

43 Peck offers "underdeveloped" as an alternate trans-lation for *peperomenon:* "underdeveloped," then, rela-tive to the full range that is available to the female. See, too, Aristotle's statement that "the female's con-tribution . . . contains all the parts of the body poten-tially, though none in actuality; and 'all' includes those parts which distinguish the two sexes"; 737a24-25. Compare this with the comment in the Hippocratic treatise, "The Seed": "The children of deformed par-ents are usually sound. This is because although an animal may be deformed, it still has exactly the same *components* as what is sound"; *Hippocratic Writings,* 323. This comment can be read in keeping with the interpretation of Aristotle offered here, that is, that

Aristotle holds that the female parent has all the ana-tomical components (male as well as female) poten-tially, even though she herself does not exhibit them. She is not, therefore, a deformity; it is only the prin-ciple that applies analogically. It is possible that the Hippocratic passage influenced Aristotle's statements, but Aristotle does not mention Hippocrates by name in *GA.*

44 Preus, "Science and Philosophy," 9, n. 14.

45 At the start of the treatise, just after Aristotle has stated his thesis that the female and male are the *archai* of generation, he makes this remark about cosmology: "This is why in cosmology too they speak of the nature of the Earth as something female and call it 'mother', while they give to the heaven and the sun and anything else of that kind the title of 'generator' and 'father'"; 716a15. Aristotle does not himself subscribe to this mythic way of speaking, but it is suggestive, perhaps, that he thinks of earth and heaven directly after estab-lishing his thesis.

46 In the Greek, Aristotle mentions "the female" before "the male" twice in this passage, although both Peck and Platt render these lines with "the male" first. The adjustment in Peck's translation above is mine. Platt translates the last phrase as follows: "That they exist because it is better and on account of the final cause, takes us back to a principle still further remote"; Platt, *The Generation of Animals,* 1135-6.

47 Peck, *Generation of Animals,* 568.

48 As one immediate indication that in book 2 Aristotle's interest has expanded beyond that of book 1 and the working of generation in the case of particular male and female mates, to the consideration of generation with regard to classes of animals, see his statements at 732a1-2. He explains that since "the better" cannot be brought about in and for each individual creature, "there is always a class of men, of animals, of plants; and since the principle of these is 'the male' and 'the fe-male' . . ." That is, Aristotle now takes up male and female as the principles of the classes, not just of the offspring of individual acts of generation.

49 I would like to thank Helen Lang for her helpful comments on earlier drafts of this paper.

PSYCHOLOGICAL WORKS

D. A. Rees (essay date 1960)

SOURCE: "Theories of the Soul in the Early Aristotle," in *Aristotle and Plato in the Mid-Fourth Century,* edtied by L. Düring and G. E. L. Owen, Göteborg, 1960, pp. 191-200.

*[In the following essay, Rees studies the relationship between Aristotle's conception of the soul and Plato's views on moral psychology. Rees stresses that the three works by Aristotle which discuss the nature of the soul (*Eudemus, Protrepticus, *and* De Philosophia) *should not be analyzed as exhibiting the development of Aristotle's views on the soul, since they focus on distinct aspects of the soul.]*

In this paper I shall be concerned with three, and three only, of Aristotle's earlier works, all of them literary productions, the **Eudemus, Protrepticus** and **De Philosophia.**

Aristotle's **Eudemus,** it is known, cannot have been composed before 354 B. C., but it was probably composed either in that year or soon after.[1] At the same time it is clear that it was a reminiscence of the *Phaedo,* both in the fact that the one commemorated the death of Socrates, the other that of Eudemus, and also to a large extent in content. Now we shall probably not be far wrong if we date the *Phaedo* about 380 B.C.—it is clearly earlier than the *Republic,* and has affinities with the *Symposium*—and thus we find Aristotle modelling himself on a dialogue written perhaps some twenty-five to thirty years earlier, when he was no more than a small child, and this in spite of the intense philosophical activity which had occupied Plato in the meantime, and of the mass of philosophical discussion which had agitated the members of the Academy, and in the midst of which Aristotle had found himself when he had arrived as long ago as 368/7.[2]

The significance of these differences in date is not always, I think, taken fully into consideration, and, if I am right in so thinking, I wish to suggest that the relation of the *Phaedo* to the **Eudemus** is only to be seen in its proper light if the function of the **Eudemus** is carefully differentiated from those of the **Protrepticus** and **De Philosophia.** There is a temptation to see the series **Eudemus-Protrepticus-De Philosophia** as representing successive stages in Aristotle's conception of the soul, all, of course, prior to the formulation of his own characteristic philosophy, of which the psychological side is represented, above all, in the **De Anima.** Now there is a certain amount of truth in this general scheme, but it may be helpful to develop, even if only briefly, some points where it requires modification. In doing so I must not be taken to imply that any one has held precisely the position I have just outlined, though I think that an insufficiently careful reader of Jaeger might be tempted to think along these lines, and that in his elaborate work Nuyens does in fact put forward something not far from it.[3] Further, there is a danger that a disproportionate emphasis on the generally accepted, and indeed most probable, chronological relations of these three early works may appear to support conclusions about the function of Aristotle's ethical treatises, their relation to the rest of his trea-

tises and their place in the chronology of his philosophical output which are insufficiently grounded and in some respects probably erroneous.[4]

One possible way of dealing with the **Eudemus,** which is to some extent attractive, is not strictly consonant with the suggestion that it represents the initial point in a straightforward line of development. It rests on the emphasis of two factors, the first the occasion of its composition and the motive of personal affection which to a large extent inspired it, and the second the apparent reversion to a philosophical position which Plato had occupied twenty-five to thirty years previously, and consists in regarding the **Eudemus** less as a piece of philosophical argumentation than as the expression of a sentiment which found its natural embodiment in a regression to a stage of philosophy which was already a thing of the past but which answered Aristotle's emotional aspirations. It may be added that Bignone, rightly or wrongly, thought the **Eudemus** more religious and mystical, and less strictly rational, than the *Phaedo.*[5] If this is a true picture, the problem of relating the doctrines of the **Eudemus** to those of the **Protrepticus** and **De Philosophia** will not arise, still less of exhibiting the three as successive stages in a single line of development. But in any case, as I have already suggested, there is some place for a reexamination of the purpose and function of the three works in question, supported by some consideration of the different strands in Plato's treatment of the soul.

In the first place, then, we have to face a question exceedingly difficult to answer, namely how far Plato would, in his later years, have continued to endorse what he had written about the soul in the *Phaedo.* It is a question rendered more complex by the connexions of the psychology of that dialogue with its ethics and theory of pleasure, and also with its epistemology and doctrine of Forms. Clearly there were changes: the moral psychology of *Republic* IV is a better tool than anything to be found in the *Phaedo;* the treatment of pleasure is crude by the standards of *Republic* IX and (especially) the *Philebus;* and, whatever the true solution of the controversies over the *Parmenides* and the later logical dialogues in general, there is at least reason to think that Plato would not in his later years have endorsed without qualification the theory of Forms as it appears in the *Phaedo.*[6] Nevertheless, the essential points for us are that Plato at no point ceased to believe in the immortality of the rational element in the soul, which was in his eyes the real soul or real self,[7] and that he never abandoned his conviction, which shines through the *Symposium, Phaedo, Republic, Phaedrus* and *Timaeus,* of the supreme value of the theoretical life. If the *Laws* seems at first sight an exception, it is concerned rather with different issues, and not those of the ideal life;[8] nor must one forget the intellectualistic overtones of the *Epinomis,* whoever it was who actually wrote it.[9] In any case, the changes away from the *Phaedo* which one encounters are, with important exceptions, largely changes of emphasis and (above all) of interest; just as the treatment of the soul as the source of motion in the *Phaedrus* and other dialogues does not mean the abandonment of anything Plato had held previously. In spite of the connexion of the self-movement of the soul with eternity of motion and the soul's immortality, that issue was essentially one of cosmological significance, and it was the transcendence of the rational soul that Aristotle in the *Eudemus,* like Plato in the *Phaedo,* was above all concerned to stress, its superiority to the world of nature rather than its connexions with it.[10] (What I shall be saying in general in this paper on the early Aristotle will be largely an application to his early literary productions of what would be a matter of general agreement in the case of the similar literary output of Plato.) As for the theory of the soul as self-moved and as the source of motion, that was common property in the Academy,[11] and it is perfectly possible that it was mentioned in the *Eudemus,* though the extant fragments do not enable us to say.

One may note at this point that Themistius[12] was clearly correct when he asserted that the conclusion reached by the *Phaedo,* when it argued for the immortality of the soul, was substantially identical with that reached by the *Eudemus,* when it argued for that of the intellect: it was intellect that was, for Plato, the real soul.[13] What change there is consists simply in giving greater precision to the earlier position, in the light of the differentiation of faculties in the soul. In view of the general character of the *Eudemus* and the Platonic antecedents, the line of distinction indicated by the term [*nous*] would seem to be that which produced first the tripartition of the soul into the rational element, the spirited and the appetitive, and secondly the bipartition into the rational element and the irrational, rather than, or at least as much as, that by which Aristotle in the *De Anima* distinguished [*nous*] from [*psukhē*]—though Plato himself could, in a very different context from those of the *Phaedo* or the *Eudemus,* distinguish these from each other,[14] and though epistemological considerations as well as ethico-metaphysical are to be found in the *Eudemus,*[15] where, however, the line of thought involved is much less developed than that of the *De Anima,*[16] epistemologically the *Phaedo* places the senses, by contrast with thinking, in the realm of the body and the passions.[17]

In the *Phaedo* the ethical aspects are both inseparable from the metaphysical and strongly emphasized in themselves. In the *Eudemus* they appear in the myth of Silenus,[18] but it does not appear from our slender evidence that they were as strongly marked as in the *Phaedo,* difficult though it is to be sure. In the *Protrepticus,* however, ethical considerations preponderate, and to that composition we may now turn.

The moral thesis of the *Protrepticus* has two aspects; it both recommends the intellectual life (i. e. the life of philosophy) for its own sake, and prescribes it as the true guide for practice, not only in the life of the individual but also in the affairs of state. It alone enjoys perfection of exactitude in its vision and in the objects it contemplates, and thus provides alone a satisfactory criterion for action.[19] On the psychological side, this moral prescription rests on an analysis of the soul into two parts, a rational and an irrational,[20] which foreshadows the treatment of the soul running through the *Eudemian* and *Nicomachean Ethics,*[21] employed from time to time in the *Politics,*[22] and consonant with the central conceptions of the *Rhetoric*[23]. . . .

If the *Protrepticus* is to be interpreted aright, one must see it in connexion less with the *Eudemus* than with the tradition of Plato's moral psychology. Plato's tripartition of the soul has its classical and most elaborate exposition in the *Republic,* in connexion with the tripartition of the ideal state. It appears also in the *Phaedrus*[24] and the *Timaeus.*[25] On the other hand, there are also traces in Plato of a tendency towards a bipartition of the soul, distinguishing one element which is rational and immortal and another which is irrational and mortal.[26] It is clear in *Republic* X 608 d ff. that the rational element alone is the real and immortal self, while the spirited and appetitive have their existence simply in virtue of our temporary bodily attachment, and the same point is reinforced in the *Timaeus,* which is careful to distinguish that part of the soul which is immortal from those which are mortal, making this indeed the most important division.[27] The very same distinction occurs also at *Politicus* 309 c,[28] while the *Laws* carefully avoids committing itself definitely either to a bipartition or to a tripartition, the crucial passage being IX 863 b, . . . the moral psychology of the dialogue being interpretable either in a bipartite sense or in a tripartite.[29] It is likely enough that a bipartition of the soul had come into favour in the ethical discussions of the Academy—a point for which the fragments of the *Protrepticus* could be adduced as part of the evidence—and that Plato did not, at this date, attach any great importance to the difference between the two conceptual frameworks (either could be used, as best suited the context), now that he was no longer concerned to advocate a three-class state on the basis of a three-part soul.

The relevance of this to the *Protrepticus* is obvious; Aristotle was there propounding a characteristically Academic moral thesis on the basis of a moral psychology equally characteristic of the Academy. This psychology in no way conflicts with the *Eudemus,* at any rate as far as we can tell; while again on the other hand it must not be treated as comparable to, and such as to be supplanted by, the scientific psychology found in the *De Anima.* The *Nicomachean Ethics,* like the *Eudemian,* retains the bipartition of the soul, while insisting that it has no claim to be treated as a scientific psychology constructed for theoretical purposes and adequate to the rigorous standards these imply.[30] We have not, then, in the strict sense a case of the supersession of one psychology by another,[31] though it is perfectly true that when Aristotle wrote the **Protrepticus,** not having as yet envisaged his later scientific psychology, he would not have felt the need to delimit as rigorously as he did later the sphere within which the soul was to be treated as bipartite;[32] that such an absence of delimitation holds for Plato is shown by the place the tripartition of the soul occupies not simply in his ethics but also in the (admittedly teleological) cosmology of the *Timaeus.*[33]

The special function of this moral psychology in Aristotle's treatises is shown by the fact that, outside the **Eudemian** and **Nicomachean Ethics,** it is most noticeable in the **Politics,** while, though it scarcely comes to the actual surface in the **Rhetoric,** the plan of that work, and the place it occupies in Aristotle's classification of knowledge, are alike consonant with it. On the score of adequacy for theoretical purposes, on the other hand, the bipartition of the soul is, like the old tripartition, explicitly attacked in **De Anima** III. 9. 432 a 24-26.[34] That bipartition is, once again, to be distinguished from that other psychology which it is the great and permanent merit of Nuyens to have uncovered and analysed (though he identified it with the moral), namely that phase of the scientific psychology which is earlier than the **De Anima,** which, like that of the **De Anima,** has no parallel in the early literary productions, and which, locating the soul in the heart, sees it as the efficient cause of the movements of the body, in what may be called a 'vital force' theory;[35] this is to be found in at least parts (Ross thinks the whole) of the *Parva Naturalia,* in **De Partibus Animalium** II-IV and in the **De Motu Animalium.**)[36] Nuyens is, of course, right in his identification to the extent that there are affinities between this earlier scientific psychology and the moral, that both envisage the soul as an entity controlling the body, and that, but for the familiarity of this conception in moral and (generally) nonscientific contexts, it would probably not have occurred also in scientific. (For the matter of that, the later scientific psychology bears directly on moral issues in introducing an account of pleasure and action which is, and is inevitably, of moral relevance).[37]

That, when we leave the **Protrepticus** for the **De Philosophia,** we find yet a different treatment of the soul, does not mean that Aristotle had left the former work definitely behind him. This would not follow even if the moral treatises did not lie ahead to disprove it. Once again we find ourselves among a different range of problems, this time the cosmological, where Aristotle is interested in the soul as a source of motion, and any theory of a single line of development must find the fragments of the **De Philosophia** an awkward stum-

bling-block. The tradition is that of the *Phaedrus, Timaeus, Laws* and *Epinomis,* with their successive elaborations of this theory, and while on the one hand it connects with **Physics** VII-VIII and the **De Caelo,** and points forward to **Metaphysics** [L], in another sense, as exhibiting the soul as a cause of the phenomena of movement, it foreshadows the earlier scientific psychology mentioned in the preceding paragraph. The soul is certainly immortal, as in the **Eudemus,** but Aristotle is concerned here not so much with its transcendence of nature as with the part it plays in nature's movements: the eternity of the soul, while no doubt contrasted with the transience of individual things in the physical world, is made the basis of the eternity of motion in that world.[38] This is true whatever be the precise degree of reliability to be accorded to Cicero's account of the manner in which the nature of the soul was conceived.[39]

The close association of each of the theories I have been discussing with the particular problem, or set of problems, it set out to cope with may be illustrated if we recall that in the *Phaedrus* Plato had introduced both the theory of soul as the source of motion[40] and the moral psychology of the human soul as tripartite,[41] without any thoroughgoing attempt to connect them, and that, as already noted, the cosmological treatment of the soul in *Laws* X is largely distinct from the moral psychology of that dialogue. But such an accommodation of different elements, if it were genuinely to hold, would of course only be possible if no flagrant contradiction occurred between the results reached from each standpoint, such as would have occurred if the **De Philosophia** had held the rational soul not to be immortal. Cicero, indeed, reports the rational soul as being material in the **De Philosophia,**[42] whereas it is clearly immaterial in the **Eudemus;** if the report is correct, what answer Aristotle would have given if pressed on the discrepancy we have no means of knowing. We can only say that neither of these positions was to satisfy him permanently.

Notes

[1] *Fr.* 1, Walzer and Ross.

[2] Diog. Laert. V. 9; cf. I. Düring, *Aristotle in the Ancient Biographical Tradition* (Göteborg, 1957), esp. pp. 249-55.

[3] F. Nuyens, *L'Évolution de la psychologie d'Aristote* (Dutch edition, *Ontwikkelingsmomenten in de zielkunde van Aristoteles.* Amsterdam, 1939; French translation, Louvain-The Hague-Paris 1948), ch. ii.

[4] See, besides Nuyens, *op. cit.,* esp. ch. iv, P. Moraux, *Les listes anciennes des ouvrages d'Aristote* (Louvain, 1951), ch. vii (esp. pp. 317 and 320) and Appendix; id., *À la recherche de l'Aristote perdu: Le dialogue*

'Sur la justice' (Louvain-Paris, 1957), pp. 41-48; Aristote, *L'Éthique à Nicomaque,* tr. R.-A. Gauthier et J.-Y. Jolif, tome i (Louvain-Paris, 1958), esp. pp. 35-36; R.-A. Gauthier, *La morale d'Aristote* (Paris, 1958), ch. i.

[5] E. Bignone, *L'Aristotele perduto e la formazione filosofica di Epicuro* (Florence, 1936), vol. i, p. 71.

[6] Cf. esp. F. M. Cornford, *Plato and Parmenides* (1939).

[7] *Rep.* X. 608 d ff., *Phdr.* 245 c-246 a, *Tim.* 41 d-42 e; cf. also *Rep.* IX. 588 d ff.

[8] Cf. esp. J. P. A. Gould, *The Development of Plato's Ethics* (Cambridge, 1955).

[9] Esp. *Epin.* 988 e ff.

[10] It will be seen that I find it difficult to accept in its entirety Professor I. Düring's interpretation of this period of Aristotle's philosophy: see, e. g., his 'Aristotle and Plato in the Mid-Fourth Century' (*Eranos,* 54 (1956), pp. 109-20). I doubt, however, if the points of difference greatly affect the main lines of my present argument.

[11] Aristotle mentions it at *Top.* VI. 140 b 3, and elsewhere in that work: cf. IV. 127 b 15.

[12] *In De An.* 106. 29-107. 5 Heinze = Arist. *Eud. fr.* 2 W and R.

[13] Cf. n. 3 p. 193, and also *Eud. fr.* 8, from Simplicius, *In De An.* 221. 20-33 Hayduck.

[14] *Soph.* 248 e-249 c; cf. . . . *Rep.* VII. 533 d, and also (whether by Plato or not) *Alc. I* 133 b ff.

[15] *Eud. fr.* 5 W and R.

[16] *De An.* III. 5. 430 a 22-25, 7. 431 a 16-17.

[17] 66 b-67 b.

[18] *Eud. fr.* 6 W and R, from Plut. *Cons. ad Apoll.* 115 b-e.

[19] *Protr. frs.* 5, 13, 14 W and R.

[20] *Eud. fr.* 6, W and R.

[21] *E. E.* II. 1. 1219 b 26-1220 a 2 (with 1219 b 20-24), and also II. 2. 1220 b 5-6, II. 4. 1221 b 27-34 and VIII. 1. 1246 a 26-b 36 (a very corrupt passage); in *E. N.* see esp. I. 13. 1102 a 23-1103 a 10; also V. 15. 1138 b 5-13; VI. 1. 1138 b 35-1139 a 17; 12. 1143 b 14-17; 13. 1144 a 1-13; 1145 a 11; IX. 8. 1168 b 19-1169 a 6.

[22] *Pol.* I. 1254 a 24 ff., III. 1277 a 5-10, VII. 1332 a 38 ff., 1333 a 16-30.

[23] Cf. e. g. *Rhet.* I. 1368 b 37 ff., 1370 a 18 ff.

[24] 246 a ff.

[25] 69 c-71 a.

[26] Plato, *Statesman,* tr. J. B. Skemp (London, 1952), p. 229, n. 1; p. 239; D. A. Rees, 'Bipartition of the soul in the Early Academy', *Journal of Hellenic Studies,* 77 (1957), pp. 112-18.

[27] *Tim.* 65 a, 72 d. It is true that on the other hand the assignment of each of the three parts of the soul to a separate bodily organ (44 d-45 a, 69 c-71 a, with 71 a-e) reinforces the tripartition.

[28] See Professor Skemp *ad loc.*

[29] D. A. Rees, loc. cit. The cosmological treatment of soul in Book X is, significantly enough, something largely distinct, as belonging to a different tradition.

[30] Cf. esp. *E. N.* I 13. 1102 a 23-26; J. Burnet, *The Ethics of Aristotle* (London, 1900), pp. 63-65; H. H. Joachim, *Aristotle, The Nicomachean Ethics; A Commentary* (Oxford 1951), pp. 62-63. The parallel passage in *E. E.* (II. 1. 1219 b 26-1220 a 4) has nothing corresponding to 1102 a 23-26.

[31] D. A. Rees, review of Nuyens, *op. cit., Mind,* 60 (1951), pp. 412-14.

[32] As a further change, which is at the same time an instance of cross-fertilization from the scientific psychology to the moral, it may be noted that both in the *Eudemian Ethics* and in the *Nicomachean* Aristotle mentions the nutritive soul, though only to dismiss it as irrelevant to ethics: *E. E.* II. 1. 1219 b 20-24, *E. N.* I. 13. 1102 a 32-b 12, b 28-31, VI. 13. 1144 a 9-11; cf. I 6. 1097 b 33-1098 a 1.

[33] I have said nothing of the dialogue *On Justice,* which was of a substantial length, comprising four books. The usually recognized fragments (as in the collection of Ross) contain nothing directly psychological, but Professor Moraux (P. Moraux, *A la recherche de l'Aristote perdu: Le dialogue 'Sur la justice'* (Louvain, 1957), esp. pp. 41-47, 91-93) has argued that the regular psychology of the moral tradition, with its bipartition of the soul, characterized it also. That must in any case be highly probable—more probable than any reversion to the tripartition of the *Republic*—whether Aristotle actually expounded this psychology or merely presupposed it.

[34] . . . Nuyens' discussion, distinguishing correctly the

psychology of the *De Anima* from that of the *Eudemian* and *Nicomachean Ethics,* but taking insufficient account of their differences in function, leads him to conclusions about the dates of these ethical works (as of the *Politics* and *Rhetoric*) for which these data provide inadequate support, viz. that they must belong to a middle period, earlier than the *De Anima* and roughly contemporaneous with the earlier group of biological treatises mentioned below. For scholars who have followed him, see n. 2 p. 192. Ross ('The Development of Aristotle's Thought'), while giving the work of Nuyens its full importance, does not follow his conclusions about the ethical treatises and the *Politics.*

[35] I prefer this term to Nuyens' 'instrumentisme mécaniste'; the adjective 'mécaniste' has difficult associations, and the term fails to make a distinction between a moral theory of the relation of the body as a whole to the soul and a psycho-physiological theory which assigns the position of superiority and of control to one particular part of the body, namely the heart, locating the soul in it.

[36] See, besides Nuyens, loc. cit., the introductions to Dr. H. J. Drossaart Lulofs' edition of the *De Insomniis* and *De Divinatione per Somnum* (Leiden, 1947) and to Sir David Ross's edition of the *Parva Naturalia* (Oxford, 1955) (esp. pp. 11-18).

[37] *De An.* III. 9-11. The same is true at an earlier stage of the *De Motu Animalium* (esp. chs. 6, 7 and 11).

[38] *De Phil. frs.* 21 and 26 W and R.

[39] *De Phil. frs.* 21, 26 and 27 W and R. See A. Mansion, 'L'immortalité de l'âme et de l'intellect d'après Aristote', (*Rev. philos. de Louvain,* 51 (1953), pp. 444-72).

[40] 245 c-246 a.

[41] 246 a ff.

[42] *De Phil. fr.* 27 W and R: Cic. *Acad.* I. 7. 26; *Tusc.* I. 10. 22.

Michael V. Wedin (essay date 1988)

SOURCE: "Aristotle on the Science of the Soul," in *Mind and Imagination in Aristotle,* Yale University press, 1988, pp. 1-22.

[*In the following essay, Wedin maintains that in* De Anima, *Aristotle provides a general theory of the soul which he extends and develops in other works. Wedin goes on to explore the relationship between psychology and physics, and analyzes the "form and function" of the soul according to Aristotle, arguing that*

Aristotle's conception of the soul is as a functional, cognitive system.]

It is a commonplace that Aristotle invented logic—not that he invented logical inference, nor even that he was the first to treat inferences in explicitly logical terms, but rather that he gave us the first virtually complete system of certain kinds of logical inference. It is for this reason that we rank him as the inventor of the *science* of logic. As with logic, so with the soul. From his predecessors Aristotle inherited a wealth of insight and speculation on the nature of the soul, but it was left to him to invent its science. In a series of related works, we are given for the first time a surprisingly systematic account of the nature and interconnection of a wide variety of psychological capacities, processes, and activities. The centerpiece is unquestionably **De Anima.** It contains what might be called Aristotle's general theory of the soul because, while he is cautious about calling it a definition, **De Anima** does attempt a fully general formulation of the soul and an equally broad account of the nature and number of its principal faculties and operations. Subsequent works, principally those that have been collected as the **Parva Naturalia,** apply the general theory to a broad array of psychological phenomena from memory and recollection to dreaming, sleeping, and waking.[1]

The systematic nature of his account, however, is not the only reason that Aristotle qualifies as the founder of psychology. Another concerns its style. It will be instructive to approach this from a more contemporary standpoint—in order to illuminate, not assimilate, the ancient account. Nowadays, it is fairly common to require of a psychological theory that it relate the ordinary commonsense behavior of a person to underlying physiological states and processes.[2] Typically, we think of persons as things that, for example, possess beliefs and desires, experience pains and pleasures, and initiate actions. This is part of our commonsense notion of a person. Although arguably the most deeply imbedded, it is still only one way of describing the person. In effect, we are describing a system of a certain kind, namely, a system with beliefs, desires, and a host of other intentional attitudes. It has, thus, become standard to speak of such descriptions as capturing the person at the intentional level and so of regarding the person as an *intentional system.*[3] I shall sometimes adopt that idiom here. But the person can also be regarded in strictly physiological terms. Thus, we can speak of descriptions at the physiological or physical level or, alternatively, we can regard the person as a *physical system.* From this perspective the task of a psychological theory will be to relate descriptions at the intentional level to descriptions at the physiological level or, more dramatically, to explain how one and the same thing can be both an intentional and a physical system.[4]

According to one view, favored by physiologically minded psychologists, a successful theory will provide more or less direct correlations between types of intentional-level behavior and types of processes or states at the physiological level. Here there is no intervening level of explanation. For cognitively minded psychologists, on the other hand, there is an explanatory gap between the intentional and the physiological levels. Between public behavior and physical process there is room for the question of how an entity is to be organized or designed in order to recognize faces, prove geometric theorems, play chess, and so on. The explanation is said to be cognitivistic because the target ability or performance is explained by appeal to various internal capacities and operations that are themselves cognitively endowed. An explanatory circle is avoided because the intentional-level performance, say, recognizing a face, is broken down into a number of simpler performances, none of which by itself counts as face recognition but all of which together manage the operation. We are to think of these performances as subroutines that go on at a lower level of the system. Each of these can, in turn, be further decomposed until, ideally, we reach a system description capable of direct realization in some kind of hardware.

For the cognitivist what is crucial is explaining how a system is designed or organized to accomplish tasks of a given sort, and this is usually held to be independent of whatever material realizes the design—be it gray matter or silicon and chips. I shall have relatively little to say here concerning Aristotle's opinion on the latitude permitted the material realization of a given form. Although he is certainly sensitive to the question—he says, for example, that saws must be of relatively inert material and that the eye need only be realized in matter that subserves and so preserves the function (*De Sensu* 438b6-9)—there simply is no clear way to decide how far he would be willing to go in the direction of alternative realizations. Whatever his attitude here, it is, I think, at least clear that Aristotle shares with the cognitivist the view that what is essential to the soul is its design or organization and that this is to be characterized at a fairly abstract level.

If we take the psychological works as a whole, *De Sensu's* distinctly physiological emphasis suggests that the difference between *De Anima* and the *Parva Naturalia* consists in the fact that the former shows little interest in physiological details. It would, however, be misleading to see the two works simply as offering introductory and detailed treatments, respectively. What needs to be appreciated is the fact that the theory of *De Anima* is formulated at a surprisingly abstract level. Although it discusses the relation of the soul and its parts to physical structures, it does so in terms that are entirely general and that display scant interest in the specific nature of these structures. In short, the question of what sort of material the soul is realized in does not appear to play a central role in *De Anima.* What does play such a role, I will argue, is the notion of the soul as a functional or cognitive system. Certainly, this turns out to be the case for that part of the soul in virtue of which the person thinks.

On the interpretation I shall be exploring, a governing assumption of Aristotle's psychology is that there is an important explanatory gap between the intentional and physiological levels. This is already evident in Aristotle's discussion of psychology as a branch of physics. That discussion also makes clear that Aristotle has doubts about closing the gap simply by explaining psychological phenomena in strictly physical terms and that one task of the psychological works is to show how to close it in a satisfactory manner. Thus, he appears to eschew explanatory reductionism and to leave room for cognitive structures to play a role in psychological explanation.

1. *Psychology as a Branch of Physics*

So let us begin with some remarks on Aristotle's classification of the sciences. In *Metaphysica* VI. 1 Aristotle identifies three theoretical sciences and individuates them in terms of three kinds of objects. Theology studies what is separate and changeless, physics what is separate but not changeless, and mathematics what is changeless but not separate. Since by "separate" Aristotle here means what can exist on its own, not what can exist apart from matter, both physics and theology study substances, the one sensible substances such as plants and animals, the other insensible substances such as the unmoved mover. Mathematics, on the other hand, does not study either kind of substance, at least not in any straightforward way, but rather focuses on certain properties of sensible substances, for example, straightness, triangularity, or oddness. Such properties neither exist separately nor are in fact changeless, for an object's shape or volume may change or vary and there may be no actual straight lines. The mathematician simply eliminates such unwanted features of actual objects and so regards them as perfectly exemplifying the properties he is investigating. In effect, he treats them *as if* they were changeless and separate . . . with respect to the property of interest. He does this by separating them in thought or, as some prefer to say, by abstracting from change and matter.[5] From Aristotle's point of view this procedure is entirely legitimate because, although surfaces, volumes, lines, and points are always found in physical substances, the mathematician does not study them as the limits *of* the physical bodies they characterize. Such ontological facts do not affect the correctness or scope of his explanations. The account of straightness, concavity, and so on, proceeds smoothly precisely because it does not require mention of matter.

When we turn to physics, on the other hand, the situation is rather different. Unlike theology its objects are subject to change and, hence, they must be material. Aristotle is not just insisting on the ontological point that what falls under an account suitable for physics *be* something that is material. The same could be said for objects of mathematics. Yet here, as Aristotle says at *Physica* II. 2, 193b34-35, "it makes no difference nor does any falsity result" if the objects are separated in thought from change . . . or, we may presume, from matter. Not so in the case of physics, however, because the material nature of what the student of physics investigates is somehow essential to the adequacy of his account. So mathematics and physics agree on an ontological point but diverge on a point about what counts as an adequate explanation. From the ontological perspective—that is, from the perspective of separateness from matter—the objects of mathematics are no more separate than those of physics. Nonetheless, the mathematician, but not the physicist, can separate his objects in thought. Since Aristotle has just insisted that such objects are not actually separate, separability in thought concerns explanatory adequacy. For the case of mathematics, then, Aristotle can be seen as giving us ontological reduction without explanatory reduction. Explanations in mathematics are autonomous with respect to the objects that instantiate mathematical properties, yet, unlike the case in Platonism, this does not require the existence of separate mathematical objects.[6]

Why exactly is the physicist barred from abstracting his objects, and, in particular, does this mean that the physicist is free to provide reductionist explanations? We can approach these points by recalling that Aristotle is fond of reminding his reader that the physicist must investigate his objects as one would investigate the essence of snubness. What stands behind this rather curious recommendation is not simply the recognition that the physicist studies the world qua material object. The connection is more intimate, and Aristotle stresses this by invoking what is almost a semantic point to make a point about worldly objects. To understand "snub" or "snubness" is ipso facto to understand that one is talking about noses. But the term applies to a nose not because the nose has the determinate property of snubness but because it has the property of concavity. For snubness *is* concavity in a nose or, to use the more explanatory idiom, snubness is a characteristic of noses that develop in a concave fashion.[7] Concavity itself, on the other hand, is not an essentially realized property or, in Aristotle's terms, an essentially realized form. Virtually anything can be or become concave. This reflects the fact that the definition of concavity places no constraints on what material the property can be realized in. So concavity, as opposed to snubness, can be separated in thought and, hence, is suited for study by the mathematician. Not so snubness. Thus, it parades as a clear model of how the objects and properties of physics are to be studied.

Like the snub, the very accounts of natural objects essentially involve reference to matter. One cannot say, at least not scientifically, what a given natural object is without saying something about its material structure. In *Physica* II. 1-2 the point is expressed in the canonical idiom of form and matter. What the physicist studies, primarily, are the principles and causes of natural things, that is, the principles and causes of their changing into and remaining what they essentially are. Although "nature" itself has two chief senses, form and matter, the physicist focuses on the form because it is a thing's form that governs and explains its natural behavior. Form is primary in the sense that the identity of a natural process depends on specifying its end and this requires mention of form. Suppose, for example, that [F] is the process that takes an acorn into an oak. Aristotle's point appears to be that one cannot say what kind of a process [F] is without mentioning oakhood, the form that is realized at the final stage of the process. But explaining how form governs a natural process or constitutes the essence of a natural object requires saying what kind of matter this is, or could be, realized in. Every natural process or object has certain material conditions and these are determined by the form. Hence, mention of matter can be omitted only at the cost of explanatory adequacy.

We might, then, say that the physicist is interested in forms that are *essentially realized* in some matter or other. This holds even when the object under investigation is the soul. As *Metaphysica* VI. 1 goes on to say, "it is clear also that it falls to the student of physics . . . to investigate a certain sort of soul, namely, whatever is not without matter . . . (1026a5-6). This passage leaves the point without comment, but it is clear how it is to be developed. When Aristotle introduces us to his official view of the soul in *De Anima* II, it appears as the form of a natural body with the potentiality for life. Since definitions are always accounts of a thing's form, to define the soul is to give a certain kind of account of one kind of essentially realized form—on the assumption, of course, that psychology is a part of physics. This assumption, which remains tacit in the *Metaphysica* passage, is explicitly endorsed in *De Anima* I. 1 where it plays a major role in shaping the overall strategy of the book. And, of course, it is *De Anima* that is of principal interest to us. So let us move to that work.

De Anima opens by advertising the value of its investigations not just to truth generally but especially to the understanding of nature. The discussion that immediately concerns us begins at 403a2-4 where Aristotle asks whether all properties of the soul. . . are common also to the body or whether some of them are peculiar . . . to the soul? A property will be peculiar to the soul if, and only if, it applies to the soul and to the soul only. If at least one property is peculiar, then it is possible for the soul to be separated. Let us defer for the moment full discussion of this notion of separation.[8] The only point we need to understand now is that were a part of the soul separable, presumably from matter, it would not fall within the study of physics. The best candidate, says Aristotle, would seem to be thinking . . . , although even it will depend on the body should it turn out to involve imagination. So the question is whether there are any essentially mental or nonphysical predicates, that is, predicates whose subjects neither are nor depend on entities, states, or processes that themselves take physical predicates.

Although discussion of thought is deferred until the third book of *De Anima,* Aristotle continues in *De Anima* I. 1 by immediately entertaining the proposition that all affections of the soul involve the body . . . and, thus, that "it is clear that the affections are principles involving matter. . . . Hence, their definitions are like: Anger is a particular movement of a body of such and such a kind . . . , or a part or potentiality of it, resulting from this thing and for the sake of that" (403a25-27). We have here one paradigm governing the relation between mental or psychological properties and the body. If the example is to be generalized, a definition of a given affection of the soul must mention at least three things: a physical process, a cause, and an end. The student of nature is said to define anger in terms of its physiological manifestation, say, the boiling of blood around the heart. For the dialectician, on the other hand, anger is desire for retaliation on account of an unjustifiable harm. Here both end and cause are mentioned. Whereas the first gives only the matter, the dialectician gives only the form and principle. . . . But this student of nature, mentioned at 403a31-b1, is presumably untutored in light of Aristotle's final view at the end of the chapter where he is charged with knowing both form and matter. For an account to be complete both are needed because in order for something to serve as a principle of this sort it must be in a certain sort of matter . . . .[9]

The forms that figure in psychological explanations are, then, essentially relized forms, and thus psychology falls under the science of physics: "the physicist is concerned with everything that is a function or affection of a certain sort of body or a certain sort of matter . . ." (403b11-12). As *De Anima*'s first chapter closes, then, we are left with the distinct possibility that all properties and functions of the soul fall within the purview of physics—unless, of course, there are some that are peculiar . . . to the soul. At this stage of the investigation, however, this caveat may simply reflect Aristotle's unusual prudence. In any case, when he finally turns to thinking . . . , the most likely candidate, what we get are a series of chapters (III.4-8) that sketch, or attempt to sketch, a naturalistic account of thinking.[10]

Although the physicist may be concerned with the same form as the dialectician, at least for certain cases such as anger, he is not concerned with the form in the same way nor for the same reasons. After all, his domain is still the material world. Thus, at the end of *Physica* II.2 Aristotle asks to what extent the physicist must know the form or essence. The doctor, says Aristotle at 194b9-11, needs to know the form in order to understand the purpose of the physical processes he is investigating. Thus, suppose for a given subject of investigation, say S1, that we have a physical process, P1, and a correlated form, F1. The physicist wants to tell us what goes on at the physical level when S1 occurs. The objection to omitting mention of F1 is not just that it leaves the physicist's account incomplete. Rather, it leaves the physicist with no account at all because the identity of P1 depends on F1. Without mention of the form there is no way of determining or significantly individuating physical processes, no way of even picking out a proper subject of inquiry.[11]

As Aristotle puts the point in *Physica* II.2, while accounts of physical phenomena cannot omit matter, neither can they proceed simply in terms of matter . . . at 194a14-15]. We can take the first to warn against the dangers of separating the objects of physics even in thought. We can also read this as asserting a version of reductionism. For it would amount to claiming only that, as far as physics is concerned, what really exist are material objects and processes involving material objects. It does not follow from this, however, that explanations can be reduced to descriptions of material bodies, their properties, positions, and the like. In short, explanatory reduction fails. Thus, even if embracing one sort of reductionism for physics, it appears that Aristotle will reject another.[12] We shall return to the topic of reductionism later. For the moment, however, there is still some scene setting to be done.

2. *Form and Function in the Aristotelian Soul*

Aristotle's classification of psychology under physics reflects more than the fact that psychological phenomena cannot exist apart from matter. Part of the point is that explanations of psychological activities and processes must mention matter. Consequently, we ought to expect Aristotle to deploy principles and techniques proper to physics in his explanations of the soul's characteristics and capacities. This, in fact, turns out to be the case, and we shall encounter a number of such instances in the course of this investigation. But psychological explanation does not simply amount to application of principles of Aristotelian physics in a new domain. Because they need to explain, for example, a system's ability to represent objects, psychological explanations are a distinctively cognitivist brand of naturalist explanation. To better see this we need to take a somewhat wider approach to the issue by looking at the general framework within which Aristotle locates the soul and its operations.

Book I of *De Anima* retails and criticizes a number of views of Aristotle's predecessors. The practice is familiar to his readers. But the book also contains a number of remarks, principally methodological, that he appears to endorse. These contain the first indications of Aristotle's attitude toward psychological theory. At the outset he announces that we should first determine the nature . . . and essence . . . of the soul and then turn to consider its properties. . . . Of the latter some might be thought to be peculiar to the soul . . . whereas others belong also to the body. For the moment let us put aside this last distinction and concentrate on that between the essence of the soul and its properties. By the first Aristotle points to the definition of the soul as the form of a body with the potentiality for life. This is the definition that inaugurates his own positive account of the soul in *De Anima* II.1-3. The balance of *De Anima* amounts to an investigation of the various properties of the soul. To get an idea of what this is supposed to look like we can begin with 403a3ff.'s examples of such properties . . . : being angry, wanting, perceiving, and thinking. These are immediately glossed in slightly more exact terms as functions or affections of the soul. . . . Thus, for simplicity, we may adopt this terminology and speak, intuitively, of the soul as the form of systems that function in certain ways.

If the system is a person, then it is tempting to speak of the soul as performing the various functions that are characteristic of persons. Thus, we might say that the soul is grieved, or rejoices, or perceives, or thinks. But there is a danger here. To say this, says Aristotle, would be like saying that the soul weaves or builds. Rather,

> it is surely better to say not that the soul pities or learns or thinks but rather that the person does so in virtue of the soul . . . and (one should say this) not because the movement takes place in the soul but because sometimes the movement reaches as far as the soul and sometimes starts from it. Thus, perception starts from particular objects . . . while recollection starts from it [. . . the soul] and extends to movements or states in the sense organs. . . . (408b13-18)

Several things about this passage merit comment. If we think of the person as a psychological system consisting of a soul and certain physical structures, then Aristotle is recommending that a function or property of the system as a whole be explained in terms of one of its parts or subsystems. Aristotle's admonition against saying that the soul perceives is not a plea for linguistic reform. The idiom is natural enough but will not do when speaking strictly. The point, rather, is that attributing to a part of the system what is properly a function or property of the system as a whole involves mixing of levels.[13] This is true even when the part in question is the one in virtue of which the system as a

whole manages the function in question. This is because it is not required that the property or function occur in that part or subsystem (what Aristotle means in requiring that the movement does not take place in the soul) but only that the part figure in a causal explanation of how the system as a whole perceives or recollects, to take the cases at hand. We are urged, in effect, to see the soul as part of the causal structure of the system as a whole.

If we put the matter this way, we can see the connection with Aristotle's doctrine of causes [*aitiai*]. It is common now to speak of Aristotelian [*aitiai*] less as causes than as "becauses," that is, as the proper factors to be mentioned in genuine scientific explanations. Thus, Moravcsik (1975) reads the so-called efficient cause as the source, the material cause as the constituent, the formal cause as the structure, and the end, or final cause as the function. In any given system or phenomenon one or more of these factors may play a role and a fully adequate explanation will be that giving the complete set of causes for the case at hand. Mathematics, for instance, has no place for the source as an explanatory factor, whereas all would figure in explaining what a person is and does. Of these four factors the form or structure is central in the sense that it specifies the essential nature of the system or entity under scrutiny. The function, or end cause specifies what the system does. Thus, to explain what a person is will involve spelling out how it operates (its form) in order to accomplish what it does (its function, or end). And, of course, for Aristotle this involves appeal to the soul as the form of the person's body. Thus, we can think of the soul as what explains how a person is able to exercise a wide variety of intentional functions. And, as we have seen, this amounts to treating the soul as a certain kind of causal structure.[14]

To explain function by form is, so far as we have gone, tantamount to treating the soul as a "black box." If, that is, we simply say that Ortcutt, for example, sees in virtue of his soul, the soul is left as an unanalyzed, internal capacity. There may be nothing wrong with this but it leaves us without a satisfactory explanation of seeing because the same explanation will be given for hearing, wanting, thinking, and the rest. So Aristotle moves to a new level of analysis. Just as the person, as a system, was decomposed, cognitively speaking, into soul and physical structure so now the soul itself is broken down into finer cognitive units—into the so-called . . . faculties of the soul. To explain, in other words, how the soul manages thinking involves, in this model, appeal to some part of the soul in virtue of which it does this. Or, paralleling the remarks two paragraphs back, rather than saying that the soul thinks, we ought to say that it thinks in virtue of one of its parts, namely the [*noētikon*] or that which thinks. But since we know that it is the system as a whole that thinks, the correct thing to say is that the person thinks *in virtue of* the faculty of thought. This is because the soul is a complex of related capacities and not something additional. From this point of view one might think of *De Anima* as a whole as pursuing a top-down strategy familiar to cognitivists: Book II.1-3 simultaneously introduces us to and cautions us against a general definition of the soul. The following chapters then consider more narrowly defined capacities such as touch, seeing, hearing, thinking, desiring, and acting.[15]

Two passages, in particular, support this line of interpretation. The first occurs at 402b9-16, as one of the methodological guidelines of the work. After remarking that there are not many souls but only parts of the soul, Aristotle says that it is difficult to decide which of them are really different from each other. . . . He links this to the methodological question of whether the parts . . . are to be investigated first or rather their functions. . . . And this in turn is linked to the question of whether one should first investigate the corresponding objects of the function. . . . Should one, for example, investigate the object of perception before that which can perceive . . . and the object of thought before the mind . . . .

Now it might appear that Aristotle is raising nothing more than a methodological question concerning the best way to do psychology. But in raising the problem of deciding which parts of the soul are different Aristotle is raising a point about the identity or individuation of the various parts or faculties of the soul. This is quite clear from the parallel passage at the beginning of *De Anima* II.4:

> If we are to say what each of them is [. . . each of the faculties], i.e., what that which thinks is or that which perceives or that which nourishes, we must first say what thinking . . . and perceiving . . . are; for activities . . . and actions . . . are prior in definition . . . to faculties. . . . And, if this is so and if yet prior to them their correlate objects should have been investigated, then for the same reason . . . we must first make a determination about these. . . . (415a16-22)

This is more than a mere methodological recommendation. In order to say *what* each faculty is we need to specify its function and this in turn requires saying toward what objects the function is directed. So this passage makes it clear that faculties are to be *individuated and identified* in terms of functions and, ultimately, objects.[16] I shall call this condition the FFO (faculty/ function/object) condition. It is important to bear in mind that the FFO condition is not extensional. An object thought of may be desired as well and what is now remembered was once perceived. What counts as an object of thought, desire, and so on, thus, depends on how the object is described. In effect, FFO pro-

poses that we determine a function by providing a description such that any object satisfying the description counts as an object of the corresponding faculty. So FFO imposes something like a formal object requirement on faculties.[17] The general picture here is that a faculty of the soul is a capacity to (cognitively) receive objects. The exercise or functioning of the faculty is simply the receiving of the object. So it is hardly surprising that Aristotle requires that faculties be individuated in terms of their objects. As he says, they are prior to both faculty and function.[18]

If 402b9-16 couches the FFO condition in the more neutral language of a *part* of the soul, 415a16-22 employs the canonical idiom of a capacity or potentiality. . . . But the picture of a faculty as a capacity is too simple.[19] Already in *De Anima* II.1, at the outset of his positive account, Aristotle had distinguished two kinds of actuality or actualization . . . , likening one to knowledge . . . and the other to contemplation. . . . The soul is an actuality of the first sort and, thus, is defined as the first actuality of a natural body with the capacity for life. . . . But this account is by its nature introductory. In *De Anima* II.5, Aristotle moves to deepen the account.

The passage of immediate interest,[20] 417a21-b16, I call the Framework Passage because it contains a model of a faculty and its function that provides a framework for a good deal of the psychology. Here is what (part of) the passage says:

> We must make some distinctions concerning potentiality and actuality . . . , for currently we are speaking of them without qualification. . . . For, in the first place, something is a knower . . . in the sense that we say a man is a knower because man is one of the things that is a knower and has knowledge; in the second place, something is a knower in the sense that we say that someone who already has knowledge of grammar is a knower. (Each of these is a potential knower . . . albeit not in the same sense—rather the first is a potential knower because his matter and kind is of this sort . . . the other because he can contemplate, if he wishes . . . , so long as nothing external prevents him.) In the third place, there is the man who is already contemplating . . . who is actually and in the strongest sense . . . knowing this A. . . .

The announced aim of this passage is to distinguish, in some detail, different sorts of potentiality and actuality, and it proposes to accomplish this by distinguishing three grades of knower:

> K1. S is a knower[1] / S is the sort of thing that is capable[1] of developing into a knower[2]
> (S belongs to the appropriate species, and so on);
> K2. S is a knower[2] / S is capable[2] of knowing[3]
> (S has actualized[1] its capability[1] to know[2]);

K3. S is a knower[3] / S is contemplating a particular object of thought

(S has actualized[2] its capacity[2] to know[3] or S is exercising its knowledge[2]).

In *De Anima* II.1 Aristotle merely asserted what he here explains, namely, that the soul is actuality in the way that knowledge is. By K2 this would mean that the soul is a capacity to *do* something. The trouble with this, as we have already seen, is that there is no one thing that counts as the soul's operation. Rather, what the soul does is a function of what its various faculties do. The faculties themselves may be described as actualizations of certain initially given capacities or as developed capacities for seeing, thinking, and the like. The latter, as the soul's proper activity, are a higher sort of actualization of the soul (an actualization[2]). But this does not constitute the soul's essence; otherwise the sleeping man would cease to be a man. Thus, for Aristotle, a faculty is a certain kind of actualization[1] or a capacity[2] to perform certain (cognitive) functions and the soul is to be regarded as a complex of such actual capacities. As what is here true for the soul as a whole is true for its various faculties so also what is true for a faculty generally is true for its various employments. Thus, in *De Anima* II.5 the accomplished mathematician has actualized[1] his mathematical capacity[1] and this is to say that he has acquired a new capacity—the capacity[2] to exercise or actualize[2] various bits of his knowledge.

Notice that the Framework Passage heeds the FFO condition. For a knower[2] is defined in terms of the knower[3] and so, ultimately, in terms of the notion of an object of knowledge.[21] Notice, also, that the notions of potentiality and actuality cannot, at least not here, be simply assimilated to the matter-form distinction. For at 412a9-11 Aristotle remarks that "matter is potentiality but form is actuality and this in two ways, on the one hand, as knowledge is and, on the other hand, as contemplation is." Matter does not figure centrally in FFO and the Framework Passage. Thus, room is left open for a somewhat abstract notion of form insofar as they call for characterizations of psychological entities that need not mention matter. The idea would be that while we can, perhaps, say *what* a given faculty is, we cannot explain *how* it does what it does without bringing matter into the account.[22] There is, in short, more to psychological explanation than definition and this is pretty much the message of the Framework Passage. Something like this may also be at work in *Metaphysica* VII. 11, 1036b1ff.'s remark that the material parts in which the form of man is realized are not, properly speaking, parts of the form and the formula.[23] So the essentially realized nature of psychological forms does not, then, conflict with the fact that Aristotle's faculties are conceived of as quite abstract structures.[24] Thus, so far from being material, the soul or, better, its faculties are the *forms*

of certain material structures and this in an appropriately abstract manner.

In the Framework Passage form and function are brought very close together. This is unsurprising if the form of a system is defined in terms of its function. We can put the point in a slightly more Aristotelian setting with the help of the following diagram:

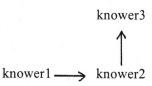

The transition, represented by the horizontal arrow, between a knower[1] and a knower[2] concerns development over time of the faculty in virtue of which S thinks, knows, or whatever.[25] The vertical arrow marks the exercise of the developed faculty. So it is in the switch from knower[2] to knower[3] that the intimacy of form and function is located. The knower[3] is, says Aristotle, "the man who is actually and in the strongest sense knowing this particular A . . . (417a28-29), and the transition to this state is rather different from the developmental process required for moving from knower[1] to knower[2] because, in moving to knower[3], a knower[2] simply "passes from having arithmetical or grammatical knowledge but not exercising it to its exercise . . . , in a different way" (417a32-b1), "for what has knowledge comes to contemplate . . ." (417b5-6). However, the switch is "into itself and into actuality . . ." (417b6-7) because "the person who reasons is not altered whenever he reasons . . . nor the builder when he builds" (417b8-9).

Form and function enjoy an especially close relation precisely because the actual functioning of a system is the highest manifestation of what it is equipped to do— that is, of its essence or form. It is, to use the Aristotelian idiom, the system's end. This much is clear from the model contained in the Framework Passage. What we do not get there is an account of the causal factors that are involved in a system's changing from actualization[1] to actualization[2]. There are two kinds of factors to consider. One is what causes the transition to the actual[2] state and the other is how the system is able to accomplish what is demanded by a given actual[2] state.[26] The first requires that we place the faculty in question in a causal context involving the object of the faculty's function. Sometimes the object will be external, as in the case of perception, sometimes internal, as in the case of thought. But in all cases it appears that what causes the faculty's actual functioning is the object of the function. We shall have more to say about this later. The second factor concerns what internal structure we need to attribute to the system in order to explain how it can accomplish perceiving, remembering, thinking, and the like. For Aristotle, central to this is the question of how the system can [re]present[27] the objects of its various intentional acts. It is here that the cognitivist side of Aristotle's psychology emerges and in the course of this investigation we shall be primarily concerned with this feature of the theory. In particular, it is the [re]presentational role of images . . . that gives the account its cognitivist flavor. In the next chapter we turn to imagination . . . proper and its role in [re]presentation. First, however, something more needs to be said about attribution of cognitivism to Aristotle.

3. *On Cognitivism in the Aristotelian Soul*

The thesis that there are cognitivist strains in Aristotle's thought is intended as a modest proposal. It would, for example, be implausible to hold out for the "essential identity" of the theory of *De Anima* with one or another modern version of cognitivism. Nonetheless, some commentators (Wilkes [1978] is a case in point)[28] have courageously argued as much for the case of functionalism. But essential identity is a strong notion. Although Wilkes does not characterize it in precise terms, presumably something like the following is involved. *T1* and *T2* are essentially identical if, and only if, *T1* and *T2* are isomorphic with respect to their essential features. The trouble lies in deciding just what counts as an essential feature. If, for example, a rigorous notion of computability is deemed essential to functionalism, then it is implausible to insist on its essential identity with Aristotle's theory. If, on the other hand, what is essential is that some kind of internal interpretation be countenanced, then, on this point at least, the isomorphism might hold up. But it would be incautious to insist that *this* supports the essential identity of the ancient and modern theories.

A less ambitious strategy is called for. Thus, let *T1* be Aristotle's theory and *T2* a modern, perhaps, functionalist theory. Suppose that we also have a more general theory *T** that is gotten by abstraction from *T1* or, perhaps, from *T1* and *T2*. The idea is that both of the specific theories satisfy the constraints of the higher level theory *T** and, thus, that they *are* identical *at that level*. Notice that even were *T** gotten from *T1* alone, the effect of the procedure, at least in the case at hand, is to strip Aristotle's theory of doctrines that no longer ring true to the contemporary ear. These, however, are precisely what makes *T1* Aristotle's theory. Still, it will be replied, the fact that *T** can be abstracted from *T1* tells us something about Aristotle's theory and, hence, about the shared basis with the contemporary theory *T2*. In the immediate case, this appears to be an impressive result because it promises us grounds for asserting the essential identity of some part of the specific theoretical bases of the ancient and modern functionalist theories. But in this case appearances promise too much. The trouble is that a host of other, unintended, theories may satisfy *T** equally well. So far as we know, nothing guarantees that *T** does not

have a dizzying array of unintended models, some of which will bear little, if any, intuitive similarity to Aristotle's theory. Thus, it is premature to begin interpretation by imposing such an apparatus of abstraction.[29]

So if we are interested in the form of Aristotle's theory, there is no substitute for deliberate and detailed attention to what he says. This does not exclude, but it does constrain the use of, contemporary frameworks. They best serve as methodological guideposts by delineating a clear picture of what the theory might look like. Actual degree of fit will depend on a detailed showing of what the ancient text can accommodate. It is in this spirit that I deploy contemporary idioms. In particular, I am interested only in exploring the extent to which Aristotle's views on imagination and thought embody two general cognitivist constraints on psychological explanation: (1) psychological systems have internal systems of [re]presentation that explain how the system's internal states (beliefs, desires, and so on) can be about the world and, thus, play a causal role in explaining the system's behavior; and (2) psychological systems have parts or subsystems that interpret these [re]presentations.

But before moving, finally, to the details of Aristotle's account, we should address a recently raised objection to the very possibility of an interpretation along the lines we are proposing. Ironically, it comes from a recent and, perhaps, overly enthusiastic use of what I have called the apparatus of abstraction. Satisfied that Aristotle is essentially a functionalist in the modern sense of the term, Wilkes (1978) is forced to deny [re]presentation any role at all in Aristotle's psychology. In short, she asserts

> W1. Functionalism implies that no internal [re]presentational devices are relevant to the formal account of cognitive activity.

and attributes it to Aristotle because "Aristotle seems to have been immune to either temptation, (i.e.) never reifying mental events nor talking of *acts* or occasions of thinking or remembering" (1978, 123).

But what is Wilkes's evidence for Aristotle's immunity on this score? It amounts to asserting or, better, borrowing an assertion to the effect that Aristotle never countenances entities such as sense data or sense impressions and then extending this point to strictly intentional modalities such as thought and desire. The assertion, recently used by Rorty to the same effect (1979, 47ff.), looks like this:

> The difficulty is in finding a Greek equivalent for "sensation" in the sense philosophers make it bear. It is true that in translation of *De Anima* one finds "sensation" and "perception" used freely where

Aristotle has *aisthesis*. But this is seldom right. *Aisthesis* means "sense" ("the five senses"), or "sensing" (a generic term for cases of seeing, hearing, etc., individually or collectively taken . . .).

. . . the comparatively rare formation *aisthema,* "that which is the consequence of the activity in *aisthesis,*" occurs in Aristotle's writings some ten times, and in three of these cases it is natural and perhaps inevitable to translate it by "sensation," "sense impression," or even "sense datum." All of them, though, occur in the treatise **On Dreams** (460b2, 461a19, 461b22), and the spooky context, the need for a word to designate a floating image not ascribable to sense perception, explains the usage. (Matson, 1966, 101)

Wilkes immediately extends Matson's point as folows:

Nor does Aristotle want to discuss occasions of thinking or desiring, or of individual memory-episodes—we no more find an ontology of the propositional attitudes than we do of sensations. Always the primary concern is with the ability to think, to desire, or to remember, rather than with specific instances of such abilities being exercised; hence, he has no reason to reify any such instances into "mental events." (1978, 124)

I shall comment first on Wilkes's use of Matson's claim and then on her extension of it. Notice that the passage says, in effect, that Aristotle refers to *aisthemata* . . . at least ten times and that on three occasions he *must* be understood to refer to something like sense data or sensory impressions. To my mind this is granting the war before the battle has begun. In fact, however, the three occurrences in question do not *demand* a nonphysicalist reading, what I take to be the upshot of a sense data-based theory, simply because Aristotle does not say in any of the cited passages that the *aisthema* itself is the free-floating image Matson refers to. Rather, as a certain activity remaining in the perceptual system, it is part of the explanation of such images in cases of deception or in dream phenomena. Whether the activity continues in the absence of the object or [*aisthēton*] that caused it, as at 460b2, or whether it comes about by a nonstandard cause, as at 461a19, there is no reason here to award [*aisthēmata*] or perceptual states, nonphysical status. Deception ensues not because the [*aisthēmata*] are nonphysical, but because the process, presumably physical, in which they figure occurs in a nonstandard context.[30]

It is important to notice that this suggests only that Aristotle does not operate with two different kinds of [*aisthēmata*]. It does not suggest that [*aisthēmata*] are nothing but physical or functional states of the subject. So far, then, it remains an open question, particularly when construed as a question about the need for [re]presentational devices. To keep the question open,

for the moment at least, we need to look at Wilkes's extension of Matson's claim. For if Aristotle is interested only in one's ability to perceive, think, and so on, then he may be committed to a dispositional analysis that leaves little room for the whole notion of [re]presentational devices. So if, as Wilkes urges, Aristotle simply has no interest in episodes of thinking, the cognitivist interpretation may be wrongheaded from the start.

For a number of reasons this conclusion should be resisted. First, Wilkes appears to endorse the principle that a theory can address episodes or occasions of thought, desire, and the like only by countenancing an ontology of propositional attitudes. This is anything but obvious. For although such a theory will, of course, invoke mechanisms involved in episodes of thought and although this will involve reflection on structure and functional organization, it need not involve an ontology of propositional attitudes. Second, although Aristotle is primarily concerned, as Wilkes indicates, with the ability to think, this concern *must* take account of the actual exercise of the ability. After all, to define a faculty as a capacity[2] is to define it as a capacity to actually[2] have an object in a certain way. But these havings just are episodes of thought, desire, and the like. So it is misleading in the extreme to suggest that Aristotle does not need to attend to episodes of thought. This is precisely what his faculty is a faculty for. Third, it is simply false to say that he never talks of occasions of thinking. Indeed, as we shall see in later chapters, a central thesis in his account of thought is the thesis that the mind *in activity* is the same as the object of thought. This is clearly a thesis about episodes of thinking. Indeed, it is part of the explanation of how persons can grasp distinct objects in acts of thought. Analogous forms of the thesis hold for perceptual faculties, so it appears that to drop occasions or episodes from Aristotle's theory of the soul is to drop a general and crucial feature of the theory.

The considerations raised in the past two paragraphs suggest, then, that Aristotle does not hold W1 as Wilkes would urge. To the extent that she agrees with commentators such as Robinson (1978) on the centrality of W1 to anything that goes by the name of functionalism, her attempt to make Aristotle a functionalist of modern stripe threatens to defeat itself. So far as I can tell the only way to avoid this situation without descending into dualist or sense-data talk in the manner of Robinson (1978) is to view Aristotle as committed to internal [re]presentations.

We can best appreciate this point by recalling that Aristotelian faculties are capacities that explain how a system is able to grasp or receive something as the object of an intentional act.[31] This appears to commit Aristotle to some version of what is sometimes called "Brentano's problem." This is the problem of giving an adequate, yet materialistically faithful, account of belief, desire, thought, and the other intentional attitudes. From the point of view of psychology as physics we can assume that Aristotle is a materialist of some description. We also take it that Aristotle held that persons do exhibit beliefs, desires, thoughts, and the like. Together these two propositions imply that Brentano's problem can be solved. But how? Again, a recent suggestion will prove instructive. Field (1978) has argued that the solution to Brentano's problem requires a system of internal [re]presentations that enables a person to have desires, beliefs, and thoughts about objects and situations in the world. Although Field thinks that something like sentence tokens are called for, Aristotle, we shall see, appears to opt for a rather different style of [re]presentation. But, even if it ultimately tells against Aristotle's theory, this difference is slight in comparison to the shared vision. For Aristotle, too, sees exactly that [re]presentations are required to explain how a physical system is capable of actual[2] operations of an intentional sort. This, at any rate, is what I intend to argue in the following chapters.

A key part of this will be providing him with a general theory of [re]presentational devices that play an essential role in the account of cognitive faculties and intentional acts.[32] In the next chapter I propose that imagination . . . plays the central role by arguing that, rather than a standard or complete faculty in its own right, imagination is best thought of as a quite general [re]presentational capability that subserves the operations of standard faculties.

Notes

[1] The lead essay of the *Parva Naturalia, De Sensu,* deals with perception and so should perhaps be seen less as an application of the theory of *De Anima* than as an extension of its remarks on perception.

[2] This oversimplifies. Behaviorists, for example, would claim that psychology has available only empirically derived correlations between behavior and external circumstances. Behaviorists, thus, reject the possibility that much can be said about how internal states play a causal role in behavior. But this is not a view that Aristotle has much sympathy for, so we shall merely mention it here.

[3] See, for example, Dennett (1978a). I give references by author's name and date. Full citations are in the References.

[4] Psychologists are, of course, interested in organisms other than persons. In the interests of simplicity and because the case of persons is the one that is relevant here, I shall, for the most part, treat the notion of a psychological system as coextensive with that of a person.

[5] One must be careful here. The separation is connected with Aristotle's notion of abstraction, but historically this has been given more than one reading. On the one hand, it has been seen as abstracting from or eliminating matter, on the other hand, as simply eliminating those of an object's properties that are irrelevant to its role as a mathematical object. The first view, favored by Philoponus (1887) and Simplicius (1882a), promotes the opinion that Aristotle's mathematical objects are properties such as diagonality and triangularity. The second, and more pleasing, view treats them as physical objects regarded in a certain way, namely, as exemplifying specific mathematical properties. (For more on this, see the helpful account in Mueller [1970]).

It is, further, a matter of some discussion whether, as Mueller (1970) and Annas (1976) urge, Aristotle denies that physical objects perfectly instantiate mathematical properties. (See, for instance, Lear's (1982) countervailing argument.) For our purposes the issue need not be decided. Indeed, the mathematician need not concern himself with the question at all, for in either case he may regard objects as perfect exemplars and this is sufficient for his mathematics. It is an additional question whether his abstraction agrees with reality or is an operation on it. It is worth noting, in this connection, that Aristotle stresses that the separation is separation *from change,* and, hence, separation from matter appears to enter only as a consequence of this. Thus, his singling out change as the focus of abstraction may be directed mainly at the fact that mathematical knowledge consists of *eternal* truths.

[6] This is admittedly a simplification of what is only one kind of interpretation of Aristotle's views on mathematics. See, for more, Mueller (1970) and Annas (1976) and, for a different account, Lear (1982).

[7] Because *snub* is defined as concave nose, talk of a snub nose would, strictly speaking, be talk of a concave nose nose. Aristotle adds (the text is *Metaphysica* VII. 5, 1030b28-1031a1) that if one then also holds that snub nose = concave nose, it follows that concave nose nose = snub nose nose and with that an infinite regress ensues. For, by the definition of *snub,* snub nose nose = concave nose nose nose. Thus, snubness cannot apply to a nose as a determinate property in the way that concavity applies. (I reserve comment on the argument's cogency.)

[8] This is discussed further in chapters 5 and 6.

[9] Thus, *Metaphysica* VIII.4, 1044b15ff., urges, in the case of sleep, inclusion of the process . . . with the formula. To say that sleep is immobility but not to say with respect to what processes the immobility is occasioned, is to fall short in point of explanatory adequacy. So, as 1044b12-13 suggests, we could have a formal

definition . . . and yet leave matters unclear . . . if we fail to indicate the (presumably, efficient) cause along with the formula . . . As *Metaphysica* VII.10-13 makes abundantly clear, it is a difficult question whether the efficient cause supplements or is part of the formal definition.

[10] This, at least, is what I argue in later chapters, especially 5 and 6.

[11] The text, *Physica* II.2, 194b10-13, says that knowing the purpose of certain physical structures requires that the physicist be concerned with things insofar as they are in matter but separable in form. . . . This is obscured by Hardie and Gaye's Oxford translation which reads "the physicist is concerned only with things whose forms are separable indeed, but [which] do not exist apart from matter." This is an odd reading of the Greek and, in any case, fails to give us a distinction between the physicist and the mathematician—the announced point of the entire chapter.

[12] The account in *Physica* III.1-3 and V.1-4 of a process . . . is itself reductionist to the extent that it denies that processes are part of the world's ultimate ontological furniture. Rather, as the actualization or actuality (to reflect the two lines of interpretation on the issue) of the potential qua potential, a process is analyzed in terms of "more basic" ontological categories such as substance and potentiality. Because the potentiality in question will be the potentiality of a thing to be something else, that is, something actual, the end of a process is essential to its specification and so this reduction will not give us an account that is . . . purely material.

[13] See Dennett (1978a) for more on this from a contemporary point of view. I have noted that Woodger (1952, 290ff.) contains an elegant warning against the mistake.

[14] See Cartwright and Mendell (1984) for some excellent remarks on formal causes and explanatory structure.

[15] Because the definitions of these capabilities will be of the form " . . . is such and such capacity of the soul," they appear to qualify as per se attributes . . . of the soul. For *Analytica Posteriora* I.4 defines two different per se relations, the second of which applies to the case at hand: (a) A belongs per se[1] to B   A occurs in the definition of B; (b) A belongs per se[2] to B = B occurs in the definition of A. (For more on this, see Wedin, 1973.) These are also the sort of attributes that figure in demonstrative science (see Tiles, 1983). So when, as we saw three paragraphs back, Aristotle promises that *De Anima* will investigate the essence and the properties . . . of the soul, he clearly means to include the soul's per se attributes. It is interesting to note,

further, that this is entirely in line with his recommendation to investigate natural objects as one would investigate the snub. For, while *De Anima* understandably stresses the ontological point that the forms physics investigates are essentially realized, elsewhere the snub is used to illustrate the logical point made in *Analytica Posteriora* I.4. In *Metaphysica* VII.5, for example, snub is coupled with odd, which is the star case of a per se[2] item in the *Analytica Posteriora* passage. They occur as examples of things that must be defined "by addition" . . . namely, snub nose and odd number. Their definitions are definitions "by addition" because they are expressions in which the same thing is said twice (1031a4-5). "Snub" already contains, as it were, "nose" and, hence, to say "snub nose" is tantamount to saying "nose" twice over.

[16] The point appears to be echoed at *Categoriae* 7b23ff., where the object of knowledge . . . is said to be prior to knowledge . . . and the object of perception . . . to perception. . . .

[17] The notion of a formal object is quite tricky. Here I am content to follow Kenny's characterization (1963, 189ff.).

[18] In *Categoriae* 7 Aristotle puts the point by saying that although faculty and object are relatives, they are not simultaneous by nature. Rather, as he says, the existence of the object of knowledge and perception is independent, respectively, of knowledge and perception themselves.

[19] At least for cognitive abilities. Perhaps the nutritive part of the soul satisfies a simpler account.

[20] Other parts of *De Anima* II.5 will figure prominently in later chapters. We shall also have occasion to make further use of the present passage.

[21] For that matter, so is the knower[1].

[22] The provisional account of *De Anima* I.1, 403a25-27, mentioned above, should be read in light of this point.

[23] *De Anima* II.1-2, on the other hand, appears to draw matter into the definition. But this may simply be reflected in Aristotle's uncertainty about calling the result a definition.

[24] Indeed, to take Aristotle's favorite case, because a nose is itself a functionally characterized entity, the dependence on it of snub already operates at a first level of abstraction from matter.

[25] The horizontal arrow should not be taken to suggest that one could develop into a knower[2] without performing actual noetic acts. It simply represents the tran-

sition to such a state, a transition that is different in kind from that represented by the vertical arrow but one whose fine structure will doubtless include performances of noetic acts. This appears to mean either that such performances are not genuine exercises of a faculty or that they somehow coincide with the acquisition of certain kinds of knowledge[2]. The first alternative harks back to *Ethica Nicomachea* II.4's distinction between acting in accordance with virtue and acting virtuously because only the second entails that one has acquired virtue. If this makes perfectly good sense where one is considering acquisition of the very faculty itself, the second alternative would appear to cover the acquisition of particular bits of knowledge, and the like, by an already able knower[2].

[26] I do not mean to imply that Aristotle has or here employs a technical notion of a system state (see Penner, 1970, who argues that Aristotle does not have any such notion). At this point I am using the word rather loosely, allowing it to cover functions, activities, or almost anything involved, internally, in explaining what a system actually *does*.

[27] I apologize for the somewhat clumsy use of brackets here. Its point is to alert the reader to the fact that I am not foisting on Aristotle the view that we do not actually perceive objects but only make inferences to them from Hume-like images.

[28] See, especially, chapter 7, "Mind Undermined."

[29] This seems to me to be the procedure followed by Wilkes (1978, chap. 7), and by David Charles when he urges (1984, chap. 1) that Aristotle's theory of action is a worthy alternative to contemporary theories. For the latter is asserted only for Aristotle's theory construed at an abstract level.

[30] For more on the topic of this paragraph, see the next chapter.

[31] Although Aristotle usually employs the idiom of function and affection, in *De Partibus Animalium* 1.5 he talks freely of practices as well. So talk of intentional *acts* is not entirely out of place.

[32] Field also argues that a system of internal [re]presentation can be made part of psychological theory without cost to the theory's functionalist credentials. If so, then Robinson (1978) (and, perhaps, Wilkes, 1978) cannot be correct to hold that functionalism is *incompatible* with the notion of internal [re]presentations.

Christine M. Senack (essay date 1994)

SOURCE: "Aristotle on the Woman's Soul," in *Engendering Origins: Critical Feminist Readings in Plato and Aristotle,* edited by Bat-Ami Bar On, State University of New York Press, 1995, pp. 1-30.

[*In the following essay, written in 1994, Senack investigates Aristotle's theories regarding the soul in order to determine his views on the differences between male and female souls. Senack finds that Aristotle conceived of the woman's rational soul as lacking authority over its irrational part, thus making woman man's social inferior. Attributing Aristotle's conclusion either to inaccurate data (resulting from an undeveloped state of scientific discovery) or the Greek cultural bias against women, Senack concludes that Aristotle was not a "classic misogynist."*]

The Approach

There is no doubt that Aristotle's theories on women are wrong. As his views are presented in what follows here, all one needs is general knowledge in areas such as biology, sociology and psychology to offer evidence against and successfully refute Aristotle's ideas about what sort of creatures women are. For example, it is not necessary to have studied gynecology to know that a woman's menstrual discharge is not an impure form of male semen as Aristotle contended. Criticizing Aristotle's views on women, once they have been made known, is an easy task. However, as with the analysis of any author's work (and especially the analysis of an author's work posthumously) it is not completely clear what are Aristotle's theories about women. It is particularly challenging because it involves piecing together sections of a number of his works. Thus the difficult task of the analysis of Aristotle's theories on women is the same task with which this paper is mainly concerned. That is, the development of a complete and coherent theory about women which can be in some manner attributed to Aristotle.

Because he is known to take an "anatomy is destiny" approach to living organisms, it is intuitively logical to begin with Aristotle's theories about the biology of women.[1] But even if this way of proceeding is correct, it might be problematic because Aristotle's "objective" scientific discoveries could be culturally biased. Recently feminist philosophers and philosophers of science have explored the influence exerted by culture and society on scientific study. They have revealed that the objectivity of science is often (if not always) limited by societal biases and that these biases are not acknowledged. The denial of these biases in science are likely not only to have an effect on the conclusions that the scientists defend but also the biases are likely to have an effect on how we interpret scientific results. In her article, "Science, Fact and Feminism." Ruth Hubbard explores the alleged objectivity in a number of the sciences, but her discussion of natural sciences is especially relevant to Aristotle's case:

Natural scientists attain their objectivity by looking upon nature (including other people) in small chunks and as isolated objects. They usually deny, or at least do not acknowledge, their relationship to the "objects" they study . . . When I report a discovery, I do not write, "One sunny Monday after a restful weekend, I came into the laboratory, set up my experiment and shortly noticed that . . ." No; proper style dictates, "It has been observed that . . ." This removes relevance of time and place, and implies that the observation did not originate in the head of a human observer . . . [2]

Nowhere in Aristotle's biological treatises or in works thought to be his notebooks is there reference to his position as an observer. Because all science is biased in the way that Hubbard describes, it is fair to assume that somehow Aristotle's scientific discoveries, including those concerning women, are biased. However, it is impossible to determine the depth of bias or the type of bias that is present in Aristotle's theories. Given this, it is best to avoid beginning with Aristotle's biological theories about women.

Where should this discussion begin? The same kind of bias that Aristotle as a natural scientist suffered can be attributed to Aristotle as a sociologist or as a psychologist. Thus if the point of least bias is the correct place to begin, no aspect of his views is any better of a starting line than the other aspects. Aristotle himself tells us where to begin with the analysis of living organisms. In *De Anima* it becomes apparent that he believes that a sound position on living organisms begins with a discussion of the soul:

> The knowledge of the soul admittedly contributes greatly to the advance of truth in general, and, above all, to our understanding of Nature, for the soul is in some sense the principle of animal life.[3]

Thus a sound understanding of the human soul will give one insight to the other aspects of human life. Because women are, of course, human beings, it is sensible to begin the development of his theories on women with an account of his view of the woman's soul. If Aristotle is correct about understanding the soul, once his view of the soul is comprehendible, this should illuminate other areas of his views on women.

One particular area that will be examined here is his argument regarding women's social inferiority. After reviewing the argument and some special Aristotelian concerns, the discussion here will comment on the areas of Aristotelian views on women that are not illuminated by the discussion of the soul, but might become visible from a different perspective.

The Human Soul

For Aristotle, though the soul is not the same in each living creature, everything living has a soul because the soul is that which causes life.[4] Although he pictures the soul as a functioning whole he notices the different functions of the soul and as a result he divides the soul into parts or faculties which correspond to these different functions. Throughout Aristotle's works the soul is divided on two levels. The first division creates a bipartite soul and the second is a division of one of the two parts of the first division.

The first division is presented in the *Nicomachean Ethics* during a discussion of the necessity of understanding the soul in other disciplines. Aristotle states " . . . one element in the soul is irrational and one has a rational principle."[5] This distinction is reiterated in a similar discussion of the soul in *De Anima.*[6] The rational part of the soul is perhaps the most sophisticated and is found only in humans. This part of the soul is divine and separated from the physical activity of the body, and because of this it is the immortal part of the soul.[7] It is this part of the soul which contains the "thinking power."

The irrational part of the soul is divided into further parts. I am interpreting these to be the locomotive, sentient, nutritive, and the appetitive.[8] The locomotive faculty of the soul is present only in some animals and it is that which causes movement in the animal. It is not discussed when the differences between men and women are addressed. I believe this was because it does not differ between them. The three faculties of the irrational soul which are relevant to the discussion of Aristotle's view of the woman's and man's soul are the sentient, nutritive, and the appetitive.

The sentient faculty is present in all animals. It becomes important in the discussion of the soul of men and woman because it is the faculty of the soul that the male contributes to the generation of a new human. In fact the contribution of the sentient soul by the male is the necessary condition to form a new human being.[9]

The nutritive faculty of the soul is yet another key when comparing and contrasting the souls of women and men. This faculty is contained in all living creatures, both plants and animals. Within the discussion of the woman's and man's soul, Aristotle speaks of it mainly in terms of the woman's soul. The female contributes this faculty of the soul to the embryo:

> Of the rational element one division seem to be widely distributed, and vegetative in its nature, I mean that which causes nutrition and growth; for it is this kind of power of the soul that one must assign to all nurslings and to embryos, and this same power to full grown creatures. . . . [10]

Although Aristotle does not directly speak of it with regard to men, I believe it must exist in men because men grow, need nutrition, and are living creatures, too.

However, it is not present to the same extent in man as compared to woman for it is in the woman's fetation but not in the man's sperm.[11]

The final faculty of the irrational soul is the appetitive. This is present in all animals. It is perhaps the most important aspect of the irrational part of the soul with regard to the discussion of man and woman, yet it is also the most unusual aspect of the irrational part of the soul. I classify it as belonging under the irrational part of the soul here because I am following Aristotle's classification of it.[12] However, it is actually a combination of the irrational and the rational parts of the soul. Unlike the nutritive faculty of the irrational part of the soul, the appetitive faculty "shares" in the rational part of the soul. This faculty is classified as irrational because it does not do the deliberation or reasoning, but it is responsive to reason. It is the faculty of the irrational part of the soul which is normally persuaded by the rational part of the soul.

Woman's vs. Man's Soul

The distinction between the rational and the irrational parts of the soul serves as a premise in an Aristotelian argument designed to prove that the scientific differences between woman and man are significant enough to support different attitudes toward the two sexes. The argument links physical and natural differences between the sexes to social ones in an effort to prove that physical sex polarity is socially relevant.

The clearest formulation of this argument is in the **Politics** 1260a where the argument appears in the context of a discussion of household management. Aristotle says:

> Here the very constitution of the soul has shown us the way; in it one part naturally rules, and the other is subject, and the virtue of the ruler we maintain to be different from that of the subject;—the one being the virtue of the rational and the other of the irrational part. Now, it is obvious that the same principle applies generally, and therefore almost all things rule and are ruled according to nature. But the kind of rule differs;—the freeman rules over the slave after another manner from that in which the male rules over the female, or the man over the child; although the parts of the soul are present in all of them, they are present in different degrees. For the slave has no deliberative faculty at all; the woman has, but it is without authority, and the child has, but it is immature.[13]

In this passage it becomes clear that Aristotle believes that the social relationships are determined by natural constraints. Nature not only determines certain dispositions people have and which ones of these are better than others, but nature, through these dispositions, also determines the place of people with certain dispositions in society. It should be made clear here that

Aristotle is not completely condemning women, children and slaves as subject to the domination of men because he concludes that all can be virtuous in their own ways and that "half of the free persons in a state are women."[14] What Aristotle's formal argument here accomplishes is proving that there are important sociological differences between man and woman.

The argument can be represented as follows:

Premise 1)	In every set of opposites there is one natural ruler.
Premise 2)	Man and woman are opposites.
Conclusion 1)	Therefore, in the relationship between man and woman, there must be a natural ruler.
Premise 3)	By nature man has a fully rational soul and woman has a rational soul without authority (akuron).
Premise 4)	The rational soul rules the irrational in the soul by nature.
Conclusion 2)	The fully rational male is naturally suited to rule over the female.[15]

The argument here has two parts. The first is a biological argument with a conclusion that states that of man and woman, one of them must be a "born ruler." The second argument adds a psychological basis for the conclusion about the social status of women. However, the argument is not without its problems. The investigation of concerns about premise two and premise three will present a clearer interpretation of the argument and perhaps a better understanding of Aristotle's views of women.

Opposition and Privation

There is little doubt that man and woman differ, but to call them opposites in Aristotle's terms means much more than what is currently meant when one uses the word. This renders the second premise ambiguous. For Aristotle, the concept of opposites is inherently intertwined with the concept of privation discussed in the **Metaphysics:**

> Privation has several senses; for it means (1) that which has not a certain quality and (2) that which might naturally have it but has not it, either (a) in general or (b) when it might naturally have it, and either [A] in some particular way, e.g., when it has not completely, or [B] when it has not it at all.[16]

For Aristotle privation is the inability of one opposite to become its other because of its lacking qualities. Aristotle uses the Greek word *steresis* for "privation." This word is the root word for "sterility" which implies emptiness, infertility and the like. In other words, when woman is termed as the privation of man, she is described in terms of what she is lacking to be a man, not in terms of what she has or lacks independently of man.[17]

This concept of opposition as privation is of particular importance in Aristotle's theory because woman lacks those characteristics which make man "better and more divine."[18] A good example of the view of woman as privation of man is seen in Aristotle's discussion of woman as a deformed male:

> Just as it sometimes happens that deformed offspring are produced by deformed parents, and sometimes not, so the offspring produced by the female are sometimes female, sometimes not, but male. The reason is that the female is as it were a deformed male; and the menstrual discharge is semen, though in an impure condition; i.e., it lacks one constituent, and one only, the principle of [the sentient] soul.[19]

Although the passage above is focused on woman's deformity with regard to reproduction, woman is not simply deformed in this sense but also throughout life. The assertion that woman is deformed throughout life assists Aristotle in his proof that biological and psychological differences justify social biases:

> [I]n women, for still within the mother, the female takes longer to develop than the male does; though once birth has taken place everything reaches its perfection sooner in females than in males—e.g., puberty, maturity, old age—because females are weaker and colder in their nature; and we should look upon the female state as being as it were a deformity, though on which occurs in the ordinary course of nature.[20]

Here, Aristotle discusses deformity of male fetuses as, birth defects. It is not clear that when he moved from the discussion of the deformity of male to female fetuses that he was using the word "deformity" in the same manner. Deformity in males is the result of their activeness in the womb, whereas deformity in females is almost seen as normal. However, at least what one can interpret from this and Aristotle's other discussions on this topic is that the deformity of woman is seen in the sense that woman is privation of the man.

When Aristotle, then, uses 'opposites' in the argument in **Politics,** 1260a his use should be understood in light of what he said in **Metaphysics.** To him woman and man are more than mere opposites, specifically woman is privation of man, and that which she lacks is impor-

tant and vital to being treated as an equal on the sociological level. Thus not only does the view of woman as privation of the male prove that they are opposites, but it also lends itself towards providing evidence to prove the superiority and inferiority of man and woman, respectively.

Woman's Rational Soul as Akuron

I think that the third premise of the argument in **Politics** 1260a which states that by nature man has a fully rational soul and woman has a rational soul "without authority" or *akuron* needs a more thorough explanation. The idea of a deliberative faculty as *akuron* can be interpreted in two different ways. The first is that the woman has the rational soul but instead of the rational soul ruling the irrational soul the rational soul is overruled by the irrational soul. A second interpretation is that woman has a rational soul but it is overruled in society. In other words, woman has the same powers of rationality as man, but it is a mere sociological power relationship between woman and man that makes her inferior.

One theorist who believes that Aristotle's view of the woman's soul is of a natural deterministic point of view is W. W. Fortenbaugh. Fortenbaugh claims that when Aristotle makes a reference to the deliberative faculty of the woman's soul, he is not drawing a conclusion from the role of women in society, but rather he is explaining why women have the role that they do. "[I]n the case of women a reference to their psychological make-up combined with their bodily condition explains their role in the household . . ."[21] Fortenbaugh believes that Aristotle argues that their bodily condition is weaker than that of the male, and he concludes that the deliberative faculty is *akuron* because it too is weak and is easily overruled by her emotions.

However, Fortenbaugh is quick to point out that just because a woman's deliberative faculty is *akuron,* Aristotle does not mean to say that women cannot think about things and give a well-reasoned answer. "His [Aristotle's] point is not that women deliberate only in some vague and illogical way, but that their deliberations and reflections are likely not to control their emotions."[22]

Fortenbaugh uses an example for Euripides' *Medea* to illustrate his point. Medea's anger (resulting from her husband leaving her for another woman), which tells her to kill their children, overrules her rational thought which concludes that murdering the children is an excessive action and is not in her own best interest. The result is that she acts from her emotions, but there has been some calculation within that scheme also for she knew that the killing of her children in the manner she was planning in fact would hurt Jason.

In the example above, Medea understands that she is going to act in a terrible manner, but this does not deter her from acting according to her emotions. Her reasoning is fine but it is either ignored or overpowered in light of her emotions. The conflict in Medea is intrapersonal. Fortenbaugh believes the rational soul's lack of authority functions in a similar manner in Aristotle theories; it can be contributed to an intrapersonal relationship within the soul of woman. Clearly women have reasoning powers, but the irrational and mainly appetitive part of the soul is that which rules.

The other manner in which "without authority" can be interpreted is shown by F. Sparshott. Rather than taking Aristotle to mean that the rational soul is *akuron* intrapersonally, he believes that Aristotle is referring to the soul as without authority in interpersonal or social relationships. Sparshott attempts to show that no Aristotelian texts support the view that women are ruled by their emotions, thus clearing the ground for his own argument. However, one passage in the **History of Animals** clearly shows that any attempt Sparshott does make to dismiss the idea that women are ruled by their emotions will be countered:

> [W]oman is more compassionate than man, more easily moved to tears, . . . more jealous, more querulous, more apt to scold and to strike. The female is also more despondent and despairing than the male, more shameless and more given to falsehood, more easily deceived and of more retentive memory. She is also more wakeful and more shrinking. And in general the female is less quick to take action and needs less food.[23]

Sparshott does address this passage in his paper, but the interpretation of it there seems somewhat confused. Sparshott believes that this passage supports his statement that Aristotle does not find females "to be flightier or more emotional than males."[24] In fact Sparshott states that the rendition of Aristotle as saying that woman is more emotional than man is an illusion of style. "In not one case is the contradictory or the contrary of a trait that is said to characterize women any less emotional, or any more intellectual or rational than its converse."[25] What is of interest here stylistically is not the passage of Aristotle, but the passage of Sparshott. Sparshott is quite correct in stating that Aristotle does not characterize man as less emotional than woman. However, this passage from Aristotle clearly states that woman is more emotional than man. And Sparshott also is quite right in stating that Aristotle is not putting forth the thesis that man is more rational than woman. What is at issue here is whether or not woman is less rational than man. Sparshott has turned the problem around backwards, in a certain sense. Instead of proving that females are not flightier and less rational than males interpersonally, Sparshott has proven something

that is not being questioned, that man is not less emotional and more rational than woman, if he has proven anything at all.

What else might be said against this interpretation of a woman's rational souls as *akuron?* Looking at the context of the **Politics** passage, it is obvious that what Aristotle has set forth is that between man and woman there is naturally a ruler, but what is a "natural ruler?" Aristotle defines the word "nature" in the following way in the part of the **Metaphysics** known as his philosophical lexicon:

> 'Nature' means (1) the genesis of growing things. . . . (2) That immanent part of a growing thing, from which its first growth proceeds. (3) The source from which the primary movement in each natural object is present in it in virtue of its own essence. . . . (4) 'Nature' means the primary material of which any natural object consists or out of which it is made. . . . (5) 'Nature' means the *essence* of natural objects. . . . (6) By an extension of meaning from this sense of 'nature' [definition 5] every essence in general has come to be called a 'nature.'[26]

What is shown by his definitions of "nature" is that it connotes things of a scientific basis, physical characteristics about the essence of organisms. Thus "nature" for Aristotle begins with view of what the organism is in and of itself, not what a society is or even what an organism's function in society is. Therefore, the lack of authority within a woman's rational soul is a conflict within the woman and not within society.

The View from a Different Perspective

So far two things have been accomplished here. The first thing is that an Aristotelian argument for the social inferiority of women has been presented. The second is that a deeper understanding of aspects of that theory has been acquired through the exploration of some concepts particular to Aristotelians. It seems that the two accomplishments are related in a manner not discussed as of yet.

Not only do the discussions of woman as privation of man and the woman's rational soul as *akuron* strengthen the argument Aristotle provides for women's socially inferior status, but they show us that perhaps the theories Aristotle develops on women are not intentionally biased. This argument seems to be well founded given his scientific findings.

It is fair to speculate that Aristotle, as a scientist, attempted to be as objective as is humanly possible. A good deal of his biology for the animal and plant kingdoms is still in use today. There is probably little chance that he would have advanced science so rapidly if he had set out on a course to create data for that which he wanted to prove correct. Also he would not have been so close to what many currently believe are correct views and objectives of science.

However, current scientific practices do have the problem mentioned at the beginning of this paper. They lack the acknowledgment of an unriddable point of view, the fact that observations are the perceptions of an individual who is also a social creature. Not only does individual experience have an effect on the objectivity of science, but also societal experiences limit the scientist's objective point of perception.

Just as scientists today are not immune from societal forces, neither was Aristotle. In the *Generation of Animals,* there is one gross mistake that Aristotle makes that exhibits the influence that outside forces had on his "objective" scientific research. During a discussion explaining the life of bees, he dismisses a (what we now know as) correct conclusion about bees because it does not fit with the conceptions he has about nature:

> The generation of bees is a great puzzle. . . . [It is not] reasonable to hold that "bees" are female and drones male; because Nature does not assign defensive weapons to any female creature; yet while drones are without a sting, all "bees" have one. Nor is the converse view reasonable, that "bees" are male and drones female, because no male creatures make a habit of taking trouble over their young whereas in fact "bees" do. . . . [I]t is impossible that some of the "bees themselves" should be male and some female, since in all kinds of animals the male and female are different.[27]

The Bee Puzzle for Aristotle is this: what appears to be scientifically correct about bees contradicts his knowledge gained through research of animals as biological and social beings. Aristotle is perhaps unintentionally biasing his research on bees based on previous scientific discoveries. Abstracting this from the particular context, Aristotle's scientific theories are built upon each other. Perhaps this does not seem so wrong at first, but think of the implication of one mistake in this chain reaction approach to science. If it is made at the beginning and considered a scientific truth, ever subsequent research project which relies on it carries that flaw.

For Aristotle's Bee Puzzle, he starts with the truths of his past biological research. From the passage it is obvious that these were at the least: 1) Nature does not give the female creatures any defense weapons and 2) Male creatures do not care intensively for their offspring. So because Aristotle did not deny either one of these truths or state that they did not apply to the case of bees, his conclusion on the generation of bees reflects these biases which are falsehoods.[28]

What can be learned from the Bee Puzzle? Take Aristotle's approach which was abstracted above and apply it to the issue of this chapter. Aristotle uses what he already has proven to further his research or philosophical theories. In the case of women, once he has developed his physical or natural theories about woman based on scientific evidence, there are social and philosophical views of women which follow by necessity. However, because they do follow by necessity, they will perpetuate any flaws present from that which they are derived.

In the case of women's social inferiority, it is based on the "truths" of Aristotle's physical findings on women which showed women to be naturally inferior beings. Maybe these "truths" were merely incorrect data due to the unadvanced state of scientific discovery, or maybe the culture in which Aristotle lived influenced the manner in which he completed his scientific research on women. However, this is not evidence that Aristotle hated women. Neither one of these possible occurrences permits the interpretation of Aristotle as the "classic misogynist" as is found in some feminist interpretations of his works.

What Aristotle said in *De Anima* is true; knowledge of the woman's soul did assist in the understanding of his theories on women. For it is not only her "principle of life," her essence and her nature, but it is also that factor that determines the world in which she lives. However, the light shed on Aristotelian views of woman through the knowledge of the soul leaves darkened corners where perceptions are incomplete. A different perspective, one of investigating and understanding the culture in which Aristotle worked, might help to perceive despite that darkness. Our light source is limited; we cannot illuminate the corners of the picture. But the darkness does not mean that we must resort to ignorance. The way of seeing can be changed. Through this alteration more of the picture can be seen and understood.

Notes

[1] The "anatomy is destiny" approach to living organisms is a deterministic theory which defends the belief that physical configuration including advantages and limitations decide the way an organism is going to live.

[2] Ruth Hubbard, "Science, Fact and Feminism," *Hypatia,* spring 1988, pp. 5-18. Also see Thomas Kuhn's *The Structure of Scientific Revolutions,* Chicago University Press, 1970, for a fairly advanced view of this. And for a very brief and anecdotal presentation of the philosophical question at issue here, see Harold J. Morowitz's *Mayonnaise and the Origin of Life,* Charles Scribner's Sons, 1985; the essay "The Paradox of Paradoxes" addresses scientific objectivity specifically, and some of the other essays indirectly pose this question.

[3] Aristotle, *De Anima* (402a 5-8).

[4] *De Anima* (415b 9) & Aristotle, *Generation of Animals* (738b 26).

[5] Aristotle, *Nicomachean Ethics* (1102a 29).

[6] *De anima* (414a 29-418a 6).

[7] Aristotle, *Generation of Animals* (736b 25-28). This statement is somewhat dubious. Aristotle mentioned the concept of immortality in his works, but he offered no well-developed proof of it.

[8] I am uncertain about the divisions of the soul as I have listed them here. Aristotle creates a bipartite division in some works and in others he develops a variety of other divisions. What I have presented here is my attempt to create a coherent view of Aristotle's parts and faculties of the soul.

[9] *Generation of Animals* (741b 7).

[10] *Nicomachean Ethics* (1102a 33).

[11] *Generation of Animals* (736a 25-736).

[12] *Nicomachean Ethics* (1102b 30).

[13] Aristotle, *Politics* (1260a 4-16).

[14] *Politics* (1260b 19).

[15] Premises 1,2 & 3 and conclusion 1 & 2 *Politics* (1260a); Premise 4 *Politics* (1102b 14-21); conclusion 2, see also *Politics* (1254b 9-20).

[16] Aristotle, *Metaphysics* (1022b 23) & (1046a 32-36).

[17] This point has been derived here from Prudence Allen, *The Concept of Woman: The Aristotelian Revolution* 750 BC-1250 AD, Eden Press, 1985. However, it is considered common knowledge among many feminist philosophers.

[18] *Generation of Animals* (732a 5-10).

[19] Ibid., (787a 26-30).

[20] Ibid., (775a 12-16).

[21] W. W. Fortenbaugh, "Aristotle on Slaves and Women," in *Articles on Aristotle,* vol. 2, p.138.

[22] Fortenbaugh, p. 139.

[23] *History of Animals* (608b 8-15).

[24] F. Sparshott, "Aristotle on Women," *Philosophical Inquiry,* vol. vii, no. 3-4, 1985, p. 183.

[25] Sparshott, p. 183-84

[26] *Metaphysics,* (1014b 16-1015a 12)

[27] *Generation of Animals* (759a 8-759b 17).

[28] Among his conclusions are that there are King bees rather than Queen bees, that "bees" are hermaphroditic and generate other drones, that King bees generate other King bees and "bees," and that drones are not capable of any reproduction.

PHYSICS

Joe Sachs (essay date 1995)

SOURCE: An introduction to *Aristotle's "Physics": A Guided Study,* Rutgers University Press, 1995, pp. 31-52.

[*In the following essay, Sachs introduces Aristotle's* Physics *by discussing its relevance to modern physics, by exploring the modern resistance to Aristotle's philosophic examination of physics, and by reviewing the content of the books of* Physics. *Sachs notes that the central themes of* Physics *include nature, cause, and motion.*]

> *Socrates: In those days, when people were not wise like you young people, they were content to listen to a tree or a rock in simple openness, just as long as it spoke the truth, but to you, perhaps, it makes a difference who is speaking and where he comes from, for you do not concentrate on this alone: is that the way things are, or not?*

> *Phaedrus: You are right to rebuke me.*

Philosophic Writing

The activity we call *science* is dependent upon and embedded within a prior activity known as *philosophy.* Any scientific understanding presupposes opinions about the way things are. Those fundamental opinions, which must be the foundations of any science, are the direct topics of reflection in thinking that is philosophic. Philosophy is a permanent human possibility, and it must have arisen in all places and times when anyone paused in the business of life to wonder about things, but it was among the ancient Greeks that it was named and described and began to be reflected in written texts. It was two thinkers who wrote during the fourth century B.C., Plato and Aristotle, who showed the world for all time the clearest examples of philosophic thinking. Plato's dialogues display the inescapable beginnings of philosophy in all questions that touch on how a human being should live, and they show that such questions must open up for examination all the comfortable assumptions we make about the world. Aristotle's writings trace an immense labor of the intellect, striving to push the power of thinking to its limits.

Reading Aristotle, to be sure, is not at all like reading Plato. The dialogues are beautiful in style, sensitive in the depiction of living and breathing people, and altogether polished works meant for the widest public. The writings of Aristotle that we possess as wholes are school texts that, with the possible exception of the **Nicomachean Ethics,** seem never to have been meant for publication. The title that we have with the **Physics** describes it as a "course of listening." The likeliest conjecture is that these works originated as oral discourses by Aristotle, written down by students, corrected by Aristotle, and eventually assembled into longer connected arguments. They presuppose acquaintance with arguments that are referred to without being made (such as the "third man") and with examples that are never spelled out (such as the incommensurability of the diagonal). They are demanding texts to follow, and they are less interested in beauty of composition than in exactness of statement. But in the most important respect, the writings of Plato and Aristotle are more like each other than either is like anything else. Both authors knew how to breathe philosophic life into dead words on a page.

In Plato's dialogues, it is the figure of Socrates, always questioning, always disclaiming knowledge, always pointing to what is not yet understood, who keeps the tension of live thinking present. Despite the efforts of misguided commentators, one need only read any dialogue to see that there is no dogma there to be carried off, but only work to be done, work of thinking, into which Plato draws us. It may appear that Aristotle rejects this Platonic path, giving his thought the closure of answers and doctrine, turning philosophy into "science," but this is a distortion produced by transmission through a long tradition and by bad translations. The tradition speaks of physics, metaphysics, ethics, and so on as sciences in the sense of conclusions deduced from first principles, but the books written by Aristotle that bear those names contain no such "sciences." What they all contain is dialectical reasoning, argument that does not start with the highest knowledge in hand, but goes in quest of it, beginning with whatever opinions seem worth examining. Exactly like Plato's dialogues, Aristotle's writings lead the reader on from untested opinions toward more reliable ones. Unlike the author of the dialogues, Aristotle records his best efforts to get beyond trial and error to trustworthy conclusions. What keeps those conclusions from becoming items of dogma? The available translations hide the fact, but Aristotle devises a philosophic vocabulary that is incapable of dogmatic use.

This claim will come as a surprise to anyone familiar with the lore of substances and accidents, categories, essences, per se individuals, and so forth, but if Aristotle were somehow to reappear among us he would be even more surprised to find such a thicket of impenetrable verbiage attributed to him. Aristotle made his students work hard, but he gave them materials they could work *with,* words and phrases taken from the simplest contents of everyday speech, the kind of language that is richest in meaning and most firmly embedded in experience and imagination. The only trouble with ordinary speech, for the purposes of philosophy, is that it carries too much meaning; we are so accustomed to its use that it automatically carries along all sorts of assumptions about things, that we make without being aware of them. Aristotle's genius consists in putting together the most ordinary words in unaccustomed combinations. Since the combinations are jarring, our thinking always has to be at work, right now, afresh as we are reading, but since the words combined are so readily understood by everyone, our thinking always has something to work with. The meanings of the words in Aristotle's philosophic vocabulary are so straightforward and inescapable that two results are assured: we will be thinking about *something,* and not stringing together empty formulas, and we will be reliably in communication with Aristotle, thinking about the very things he intended.

We need to illustrate both the sort of thing that Aristotle wrote and the way the translations we have destroy its effect. Consider the word essence. It is an English word, and we all know more or less how to use it. Perfumes have essences, beef stock can be boiled down to its essence, and the most important part of anything can be called its essence. It seems to have some connection with necessity, since we occasionally dismiss something as not essential. By the testimony of usage, that is just about the whole of the word's meaning. Essense is a relatively vague English word. If we know Latin, the word begins to have some resonance, but none of that has crossed over into English. So what do we do when we find a translation of Aristotle full of the word *essence*? We have to turn to expert help. Ordinary dictionaries will probably not be sufficient; we will need philosophic dictionaries, commentaries on Aristole, textbooks on philosophy, or trained lecturers who possess the appropriate degrees. In short, we need to be initiated into a special club; it may make us feel superior to the ordinary run of human beings, and it will at least make us think that philosophy is not for people in general, but only for specialists. Medical doctors, for example, seek just those effects for their area of expert knowledge by never using an ordinary, understandable name for anything, but only a Latin derivative with many syllables. But did Aristotle want such a result? If not, writing in such a style can hardly be presented as a translation of Aristotle.

What did Aristotle write where the translators put the word *essence*? In some places he wrote "the what" something is, or "the being" of it. In most places he wrote "what something keeps on being in order to be at all," or "what it is for something to be." These phrases bring us to a stop, not because we cannot attach meaning to them, but because it takes some work to get hold of what they mean. Since Aristotle chose to write that way, is it not reasonable to assume that he would want us to do just that? In the poet Gerard Manley Hopkins's line "Though worlds of wanwood leafmeal lie," everything in his words is readily accessible even though the pieces are combined in unusual ways. We recognize this sort of word-play as a standard device of poetry, which works on us through the ear, the visual imagination, and our feelings. The poet makes us experience a fresh act of imagining and feeling, at his direction. (Think of all that would be lost if he had written "Notwithstanding the fact that an immeasurable acreage of deciduous forest manifests the state of affairs characteristic of its incipiently dormant condition.") Aristotle's phrases in the present example do something that is exactly analogous to the poet's word-play, but it is directed only at the intellect and understanding. Other words and phrases of his do carry imaginative content, but are subordinated to the intellect and understanding. Aristotle is not a poet, but a philosophic writer, one who, like a poet, loosened and recombined the most vivid parts of ordinary speech to make the reader see and think afresh. Many philosophers have written books, but few have worked as carefully and deliberately to make the word be suited to the philosophic deed.

Translation and Tradition

A long stretch of centuries stands between Aristotle and us. The usual translations of his writings stand as the end-product of all the history that befell them in those centuries. For about five centuries up to 1600 they were the source of the dominant teachings of the European universities; for about four centuries since then they have been reviled as the source of a rigid and empty dogmatism that stifled any genuine pursuit of knowledge. One has to be very learned indeed to uncover all that history, but fortunately for those of us who are interested only in understanding the writings themselves, no such historical background is of any use. In fact, it takes us far away from anything Aristotle wrote or meant. By chance, when Aristotle's books dominated the centers of European learning, the common language of higher learning was Latin. When in turn later thinkers rebelled against the tyranny of the established schools, it was a Latinized version of Aristotle that they attacked. They wrote in the various modern European languages, but the words and phrases of Aristotle that they argued with and about came into those languages with the smallest possible departures from the Latin.

Thomas Hobbes, for example, writing in 1651 (in the next to last chapter of the last part of *Leviathan*), makes a common complaint in a memorable way:

> I beleeve that scarce any thing can be more absurdly said in naturall Philosophy, than that which is now called Aristoteles Metaphysiques. . . . And since the Authority of Aristotle is onely current [in the universities], that study is not properly Philosophy, (the nature whereof dependeth not on Authors,) but Aristotelity. . . . To know now upon what grounds they say there be Essences Abstract, or Substantiall Formes, wee are to consider what those words do properly signifie. . . . But what then would become of these Terms, of Entity, Essence, Essentiall, essentiality, that . . . are . . . no Names of Things. . . . [T]his doctrine of Separated Essences, built on the Vain Philosophy of Aristotle, would fright [men] . . . with empty names as men fright Birds from the Corn with an empty doublet, a hat, and a crooked stick.

The usual translations of Aristotle are concerned most of all with preserving a continuity of tradition back through these early modern critics of Aristotle. Richard McKeon, in a note to a philosophic glossary, defends this practice:

> The tendency recently in translations from Greek and Latin philosophers, has been to seek out Anglo-Saxon terms, and to avoid Latin derivatives. Words as clear and as definitely fixed in a long tradition of usage as privation, accident, and even substance, have been replaced by barbarous compound terms, which awaken no echo in the mind of one familiar with the tradition, and afford no entrance into the tradition to one unfamiliar with it. In the translations above an attempt has been made to return to the terminology of the . . . English philosophers of the seventeenth century. Most of the Latin derivatives which are used . . . have justification in the works of Hobbes, Kenelm Digby, Cudworth, Culverwell, even Bacon, and scores of writers contemporary with them. . . . [T]he mass of commentary on Aristotle will be rendered more difficult, if not impossible, of understanding if the terms of the discussion are changed arbitrarily after two thousand years. (*Selections from Medieval Philosophers,* Vol. 2, New York: Scribner's, 1930, pp. 422-23)

The tendency deplored by McKeon has not made its way into any translations of the writings of Aristotle known to this writer. There was some hope of it when Hippocrates Apostle, announcing a new series of translations, included the following among its principles: "The terms should be familiar, that is, commonly used and with their usual meanings. If such terms are available, the use of strange terms, whether in English or in some other language, adds nothing scientific to the translation but unnecessarily strains the reader's thought and often clouds or misleads it" *(Aristotle's Metaphys-*

ics, Bloomington: Indiana University Press, 1966, p. x). This sentiment is worth endorsing, but Apostle respects it only to the minor extent of avoiding such pretentious phrases as *ceteris paribus* (Latin for "other things being equal"), and nothing in his translations would disturb McKeon. But if Apostle's general claim is correct, and if in addition Aristotle himself never used technical jargon, then surely to use such language to translate him is to confuse Aristotle's writings with a tradition that adapted them to purposes that were not his. And if that Latin tradition distorted Aristotle's meaning and was untrue to his philosophic spirit, until all that remained was the straw man so easily ridiculed by Hobbes and every other lively thinker of his time, then to insist on keeping Aristotle within the confines of that caricature is perverse.

No text can be translated from one language to another with complete accuracy, and an author who takes liberties with common usage in his or her own language is especially difficult to translate. But in this case there is one simple rule that is easy to follow and always tends in a good direction: avoid all the conventional technical words that have been routinely used for Aristotle's central vocabulary. In fact, virtually all those words are poor translations of the Greek they mean to stand for. The word *privation,* for instance, is not found in this translation for the simple reason that its meaning cannot be expected to be known to all educated readers of English. Commentaries on Aristotle use the word extensively, but if the Greek word it refers to has been adequately translated in the first place, you will not need commentaries to tell you what it means. Here that Greek word is translated sometimes as *deprivation,* sometimes as *lack,* according as one or the other fits more comfortably into its context. What matters is not whether Latin or Anglo-Saxon derivatives are used, but whether an understandable English word translates an understandable Greek one. *Accident* is a perfectly good English word, but not in the sense in which it appears in commentaries on Aristotle; the Greek word it replaces has a broad sense that corresponds to our word *attribute,* and a narrower one that can be conveyed by the phrase "incidental attribute." In this case again, Latin derivatives are available that carry clear and appropriate meanings in English, since one does not need to know any Latin to ferret them out. It is true that one sense of *ad-cadere* could have given rise to the meanings we attach to the words *incidental* and *attribute,* but it did not in fact transmit that meaning to its English derivatives. There is some pedantic pleasure in pointing out those connections, but to use the word *accident* in that sense is to write a forced Latin masquerading as English, guaranteed to confuse the non-specialist reader, where Aristotle used the simplest possible language in a way that keeps the focus off the words and on the things meant by them.

But to undo the mischief caused by McKeon's third example, substance, stronger medicine is required. Joseph Owens records the way this word became established in the tradition *(The Doctrine of Being in the Aristotelian 'Metaphysics,'* Toronto: Pontifical Institute of Mediaeval Studies, 1951, pp. 140-43). It is a comedy of errors in which Christian scruples were imposed upon a non-Biblical theology, and a disagreement with Aristotle was read back into his words as a translation of them. This translator ignores the contortions of the tradition and without apology uses the barbarous Anglo-Saxon compound *thinghood.* Though it occurs only a few times in the *Physics,* it is a central notion in the *Metaphysics* and in all Aristotle's thought, and the word *substance* does nothing but obscure its meaning. Lively arguments about substance go on today in the secondary literature, but a choice must be made, and the primary texts of Aristotle are clearer, richer, deeper, easier to absorb, and more worth pursuing than the commentaries on them. As it stands in the usual translations, the word substance is little more than an unkown *x* for which meaning has to be deduced by a kind of algebra, while Aristotle shows (*Metaphysics* 1028b, 2-7) that just asking what the thinghood of things consists in, and what is responsible for it, unlocks the highest inquiry of which philosophy is capable. For the promise of such a return, it is worth risking a little barbarity. The barbarism of a word like thinghood is just the fact that it falls far outside common usage in our language, and not in a direction that needs any historical or technical special knowledge to capture it, but in one that invites the same flexibility that poets ask of us. We cannot read such a word passively but must take responsibility for its meaning. This in itself, in moderation and in well-judged places, is something good and is an imitation of what Aristotle does with Greek.

It has already been remarked that the present translation does not always use the same English word for the same Greek one. This is partly because no English word ever has the same full range of meaning as any Greek word, so that such a range has to be conveyed, or unwanted connotations suppressed, by the use of a variety of near-synonyms. It is partly because a Greek word may have two or more distinct uses that differ according to context; in this way, the word for thinghood will often be translated as "an independent thing." It is also partly because Aristotle always paid attention to the fact that important words are meant in more than one way. For him that was not a fault of language, but one of the ways in which it is truthful. A word often has a primary meaning and a variety of derivative ones, as a reflection of causal relations in the world. A diet can be healthy only because, in a different and more governing sense, an animal can be healthy, and there can be a medical knife only because there is a medical skill. This array of difference within sameness usually cannot be lifted over from Greek to

English, and has to be gotten at indirectly. For example, in the *Physics* every kind of change is spoken of as a motion, though the word for motion is gradually and successively limited until it refers strictly only to change of place. This progression determines the main structure of the inquiry, but in English the path would not be as clearly indicated by transitions of meaning within a single word. Finally, some words have many translations that are equally good in their different ways. In such cases, this translation rejoices in variety; this again is an imitation of Aristotle's general practice. Where the traditional translations are marked by rigid, formulaic repetitions, Aristotle loves to combine overlapping meanings, or separate intertwined meanings, to point to things his language had no precise word for. It is the living, natural, flexible character of thinking that breathes through Aristotle's use of language, and not the artificial, machine-like fixity one finds in the translations.

This last point should be taken not as a promise of smooth English but rather of the reverse. Idiomatic expressions and familiar ways of putting words together conceal unthinking assumptions of just the kind that philosophy tries to get beyond. The reader will need a willingness to follow sentences to places where meaning would be lost if it were forced into well-worn grooves, and will need to follow trains of thought that would not be the same if they did not preserve Aristotle's own ways of connecting them. As far as possible, this translation follows the syntax of Aristotle's text. Montgomery Furth followed this same procedure in a translation of part of the *Metaphysics,* and he apologizes that the result is neither English nor Greek, but Eek *(Aristotle, Metaphysics, Books VII-X,* Indianapolis: Hackett, 1985, p. vi). Furth translated this way in order to follow Aristotle's logic faithfully, but he retained all the usual Latinized vocabulary of Ross's Oxford translation, so that the resulting language might better be called Leek. The present translation goes farther, in vocabulary and syntax, beyond the Latin and toward the Greek, and could be called Gringlish, but for this as well it comes before you without apology. Furth's translation violates English sensibilities for the special purposes of graduate students and professional scholars; this translation violates them for the common human purposes of joining Aristotle in thinking that breaks through the habitual and into the philosophic.

A Philosophic Physics?

It may seem odd to combine philosophic aims with the topic of physics. It may seem that Aristotle had to speculate philosophically about the natural world because he did not have the benefit of the secure knowledge we have about it. In the current secondary literature one sees that at least some scholars think they might learn something about thinking from *De Anima*

or about being from the *Metaphysics,* but articles on the *Physics* seem at most to pat Aristotle on the head for having come to some conclusion not utterly in conflict with present-day doctrines. This kind of smugness is a predictable result of the way the sciences have been taught to us. Conjectures and assumptions, because they have been part of authoritative opinion for a few centuries, are presented to us as stories, or as facts, without recourse to evidence or argument. Particular doctrines, even when they stand on theoretical structures as complex and fragile as a house of cards, or even when they presuppose a picture of things that is flatly in contradiction with itself, tend to be prefaced with the words "we know. . . . " All the rhetoric that surrounds the physics of our time tells us that philosophic inquiry need not enter its territory, that here the philosophizing is over and done, that the best minds agree about everything, and that, in any case, nonexperts cannot hope to understand enough to assess the evidence. Strangely, the physics of the twentieth century is surrounded by the same air of dogmatic authority as was the school Aristotelianism of the sixteenth century.

But there are two kinds of support for the present-day physics that seem to lift it above dogmatism. One is a long history of experiment and successful technology, and the other is the greatest possible reliance on mathematics. These are both authorities that cannot be swayed by human preferences, and cannot lie. Their testimony, however, can be misunderstood, and can be incorporated into a picture of the world that fails in other ways. But even if the current physics contains nothing untrue, one might wish to understand it down to its roots, to unearth the fundamental claims about things on which it rests, which have been lost sight of in the onrush of theoretical and practical progress. To do this one has to stand back from it, to see its founding claims as alternatives to other ways of looking at the world, chosen for reasons. The earliest advocates of the "new physics" did just that, and the alternatives they rejected all stem from Aristotle's *Physics.* Martin Heidegger said that "Aristotle's *Physics* is the hidden, and therefore never adequately studied, foundational book of Western philosophy" ("On the Being and Conception of *Phusis* in Aristotle's *Physics* B, 1," in *Man and World,* 9, No. 3, (1976), p. 224). The physics of our times is inescapably philosophic, if only in the original choices, preserved in it, to follow certain paths of thought to the exclusion of others. To see that physics adequately and whole, we too need to be philosophic, to lift our gaze to a level at which it can be seen to be one possibility among many. Only then can we rationally and responsibly decide whether to adopt its opinions as our own.

But there is a second respect in which twentieth-century physics has opened its doors to philosophy and will not be able to close them. The physics that came of age in the seventeenth century, and seemed to have answered all the large questions by the nineteenth, is limping toward the end of the twentieth century in some confusion. Mathematics and technology have coped with all the crises of this century, but the picture of the world that underlay them has fallen apart. It was demonstrated conclusively that light is a wave, except when it shines on anything; then it arrives as particles. It is shown with equal certainty that the electron is a particle, except when it bounces off a crystal surface; then it must be a wave, interacting with the surface everywhere at once. Just when atomic physics seemed ready to uncover the details of the truth underlying all appearances, it began to undercut all its own assumptions. A wave-mechanics that held out an initial promise of reducing all appearances of particles to the behavior of waves failed to do so, and degenerated into a computational device for predicting probabilities. The most far-seeing physicists of the century have shown that particles and waves are equally necessary, mutually incompatible aspects of every atomic event, and that physics, at what was supposed to be the ultimate explanatory level, must abandon its claim to objectivity. The physicist is always describing, in part, his or her own decisions to interfere with things in one way rather than another; this brings along, as a causally necessary conclusion, the collapse of the belief in causal determinism. When Hobbes laughed at Aristotle, he was certain that he knew what a *body* is. Today all bets are off.

But some physicists have been unwilling to give up their dogmatic habits without a fight. Even Einstein, after he had taught the world to give up the rigid Newtonian ideas of time, space, and mass, was unable to suspend his unquestioned assumption that bodies have sharply defined places and cannot interact except by contact or by radiation. Niels Bohr and Werner Heisenberg had announced the most radical of revolutions, requiring physicists to ask what knowledge is, and no longer to answer by pointing to what they do. In a famous 1935 collaboration ("Can Quantum-Mechanical Description of Reality Be Considered Complete?" *Physical Review* 47, pp. 777-80), Einstein tried to hold off this final revolution, saying in effect "I know enough about the fundamental structure of the world to be certain that some things cannot happen." But experiments have revealed that those very things do happen, that the state of one particle is provably dependent on whether a measurement is performed on a distant second particle, from which no signal could have radiated.

A new and opposite tactic permits some physicists to embrace this or any other seeming impossibility without admitting the need for any philosophic re-thinking of the way things are. Listen to these words of Richard Feynman: "We always have had a great deal of difficulty in understanding the world view that quantum physics represents. At least I do, because I'm an old enough man that I haven't got to the point that this stuff is obvious to me. . . . You know how it always is, every new idea, it takes a generation or two until it becomes obvious that there's no real problem" (quoted by N. David Mermin in *The Great Ideas Today,* 1988, p. 52). So if the discoveries of quantum physics make you feel an urgent need to re-examine the presuppositions of physics, just repress that feeling for a generation or two, and it will go away.

Perhaps the strongest motive for the resistance to opening physics to philosophic examination is the plain fact that there is no need for physics to do anything differently. Whatever happens can be described mathematically, and new discoveries are readily incorporated into some mathematical scheme, and then predicted. Technology advances no less rapidly in areas in which the explanatory ground has been cut from under our feet than in those in which its workings are intelligible. But the new physics arose out of a desire to know, and it has undeniably become a highly questionable kind of knowing. Indeed, the very fact that its picture of the world can collapse while its mathematical description and practical applications are left intact is a powerful stimulus to wonder. While wishing physics well in all its uses, some of us may simply want to understand what it is and what it is not. But we cannot see how the various strands of physics have separated without understanding what it was to begin with, so again we are thrown back to the choices by which it came into being, and thus in turn to the picture of the world that it rejected. From this standpoint, though, such investigation is more than a quest to uncover something past and superseded. It entails the risk of being convinced that the original decisions of the seventeenth-century physicists are not all worthy of our own acceptance. It is possible that parts of Aristotle's understanding of the world might help heal our own dilemmas and confusions.

The Things That Are

Where should an understanding of the things around us begin? It might seem that there are plain facts that could serve as uncontroversial starting points. What are some of the plainest ones? The stars circle us at night, the sun by day. Rocks fall to earth, but flames leap toward the sky. Bodies that are thrown or pushed slow down continually until they stop moving. Animals and plants belong to distinct kinds, which are preserved from generation to generation. The visible whole is a sphere, with the earth motionless at its center. These are facts of experience, so obvious that the only way to be unaware of them is by not paying attention. If you disbelieve any of them it is not because of observation, but because you were persuaded not to trust your senses. No physics begins by looking at the things it studies; those things must always be assigned to some larger context in which they can be interpreted. Aristotle states this in the first sentence of his **Physics** by saying that we do not know anything until we know its causes. Nothing stands on its own, without connections, and no event happens in isolation; there must be some comprehensive order of things in which things are what they are and do what they do. Physics seeks to understand only a part of this whole, but it cannot begin to do so without some picture of the whole.

But it has been noted earlier that none of Aristotle's inquiries begins with the knowledge that most governs the things it studies. We never start where the truth of things starts, but must find our way there. But although we must be ready to modify our views as the inquiry proceeds, we cannot dispense with some preliminary picture of things. What is Aristotle's preliminary picture of the whole of things? It is one that permits the plainest facts of experience to be just the way they appear to us. We live at the center of a spherical cosmos as one species of living thing among many, in a world in which some motions are natural and some forced, but all require causes actively at work and cease when those causes cease to act. The natural motions are those by which animals and plants live and renew their kinds, the stars circle in unchanging orbits, and the parts of the cosmos—earth, water, air, and fire—are transformed into one another by heat and cold, move to their proper places up or down, and maintain an ever-renewing equilibrium. This picture is confirmed and fleshed out by Aristotle's inquiries in writings other than the **Physics,** but since Aristotle never writes "scientifically," that is, deductively, there is no necessary or right order in which they should be read. All those inquiries stand in a mutual relation of enriching and casting light upon one another, and the **Physics** is in an especially close relation with the **Metaphysics.**

The **Physics** assumes not only a picture of the whole, but also a comprehensive understanding of the way things are. In the **Metaphysics,** this comprehensive understanding is not assumed but is arrived at by argument, through the sustained pursuit of the question, What is being? Since being is meant in many ways, Aristotle looks for the primary sense of it, being as such or in its own right, on which the other kinds of being are dependent. That primary sense of being is first identified as thinghood and then discovered to be the sort of being that belongs only to animals, plants, and the cosmos as a whole. For these pre-eminent beings, being is being-at-work, since each of them is a whole that maintains itself by its own activity. For any other sort of being, what it is for it to be is not only something less than that, but it is in every case dependent on and derived from those highest beings, as a quality, quantity, or action of one, a relation between two or more, a chance product of the interaction between two or more, or an artificial product deliberately made from materials borrowed from one or more of

them. Life is not a strange by-product of things, but the source of things, and the non-living side of nature has being in a way strictly analogous to life: as an organized whole that maintains itself by continual activity.

In the central books of the **Metaphysics,** Aristotle captures the heart of the meaning of being in a cluster of words and phrases that are the most powerful expressions of his thinking. The usual translations of them not only fall flat but miss the central point: that the thinghood *(ousia)* of a thing is what it keeps on being in order to be at all *(to ti ēn einai),* and must be a being-at-work *(energeia)* so that it may achieve and sustain its being-at-work-staying-itself *(entelecheia).* In the standard translations of those words and phrases, that rich and powerful thought turns into the following mush: the substance of a thing is its essence, and it must be an actuality, so that it may achieve and sustain its actuality.

Once Aristotle's central thinking has been grasped, one can see that the physics that emerged in the seventeenth century adopted, in the principle of inertia, an understanding of being exactly opposite to that of Aristotle. The primary beings are what they are passively, by being hard enough to resist all change, and they do nothing but bump and move off blindly in straight lines. The picture of the world assumed by this physics is of atoms in a void, so there can be no cosmos, but only infinite emptiness; no life, but only accidental rearrangements of matter; and no activity at all, except for motion in space. This is an ancient idea, which goes back long before Aristotle's time. Some centuries later Lucretius found it appealing as a doctrine that teaches us that, while there is little to hope for in life except freedom from pain, there is little to fear either, since a soul made of atoms will dissolve, but cannot suffer eternal torment. There are reasons of two other kinds that make this picture of things attractive to the new physics. First, it makes it unnecessary to look for causes. Just because everything is taken to be reducible to atoms and the void, every possible event is pre-explained. Mechanical necessity takes over as the only explanation of anything, so the labor of explanation is finished at one stroke. And second, this picture makes every attribute of anything and every possible event entirely describable by mathematics. The glory of the new physics is the power it gains from mathematics. The world that is present to the senses is set aside as "secondary," and the mathematical imagination takes over as our way of access to the true world behind the appearances. The only experience that is allowed to count is the controlled experiment, designed in the imagination, with a limited array of possible outcomes that are all interpreted in advance.

From its beginnings, mathematical physics moves from success to success, but almost from the beginning its mechanistic picture of things fails. Newton begins his *Principia* with the assumption that all bodies are inert, but in the course of it he shows that every body is the seat of a mysterious power of attraction. Is this simply a new discovery to be added to our picture of the world? Shall we say that there are atoms, void, and a force of gravitation? But the whole purpose of the new world-picture was to avoid occult qualities. And where do we put this strange force of attraction? There is no intelligible way that inert matter can be conceived as causing an urge in a distant body. Shall we say that the force resides in a field? A field of what? The *Principia* shows that the spaces through which the planets move are void of matter. How can a point in empty nothing be the bearer of a quantity of energy? This new discovery can be described mathematically, but it does not fit into the world-picture that led to it, and cannot be understood as something added to it. Something similar happens with light, which was discovered by Maxwell to be describable as an electromagnetic wave. But a wave is a material conception: a disturbance in a string, or a body of water, or some such carrier, moves from one place to another while the parts of the body stay where they were. So when it was shown that a light-bearing aether would need to have contradictory properties, electromagnetic radiation was left as a well-described wave motion taking place in nothing whatever.

In the twentieth century the mechanist picture underlying mathematical physics has broken down even more radically, in ways that have been mentioned above. Popularizations of physics usually tell us that the ideas of Newton and Maxwell failed when they were applied on an astronomic or atomic scale, but remain perfectly good approximations to the phenomena of the middle-sized world. But in what sized world can matter be inert and not inert, and space empty and not empty? And the middle-sized world is characterized more than anything else by the presence of living things, which the atoms-and-void picture never had any hope of explaining, but only of explaining away. Shall we at least say, though, that we have learned that the world is not a cosmos? Let us listen to David Bohm:

> The theory of relativity was the first significant indication in physics of the need to question the mechanist order. . . . [I]t implied that no coherent concept of an independently existent particle is possible. . . . The quantum theory presents, however, a much more serious challenge to this mechanist order . . . so that the entire universe has to be thought of as an unbroken whole. In this whole, each element that we can abstract in thought shows basic properties (wave or particle, etc.) that depend on its overall environment, in a way that is much more reminiscent of how the organs constituting living beings are related, than it is of how parts of a machine interact. . . . [T]he basic concepts of relativity and quantum theory directly contradict each other. . . . [W]hat they have basically in common . . . is undivided wholeness. Though each comes to such wholeness in a different way, it is clear that it is this to which they are both fundamentally pointing. (*Wholeness and the Implicate Order,* London: Ark, 1983, pp. 173-76)

According to Bohm, it is only prejudice and habit that keep the evidence of the wholeness of things from being taken seriously. The contrary view is not just an opinion, but one of those fundamental ways of looking, thinking, and interpreting that permit us to have opinions at all and to decide what is and what is not a fact. To abandon the ground beneath our feet feels like violence, especially when no new authority is at hand to assure us that there is somewhere else for us to land. We tend to prefer to live with unreconciled dualities. Descartes notoriously makes the relation of mind and body a "problem." Newton speaks in the General Scholium to the *Principia* as though gravitation were incapable of explanation by physics, a supernatural element in the world. Leibniz speaks of two kingdoms, one of souls and one of bodies, as harmoniously superimposed (as in *Monadology* 79). Kant tells us that we are free, except insofar as our actions are part of the empirical world. We sometimes speak of biology as something unconnected with physics, as though what is at work in a tree or a cat is not nature in its most proper sense. We have had the habit so long that we consider it *natural* to regard ourselves, with our feeling, perception, and understanding, as an inexplicable eruption out of a nature that has nothing in common with us. Might a more coherent way be found to put together our experience? Perhaps it would be worthwhile to suspend, at least for a while, our notions of what can be and what it is for something to be, to try out some other way of looking.

A Non-Mathematical Physics

The world as envisioned in Aristotle's **Physics** is more diverse than the world described by mathematical physics, and we must accustom ourselves to a correspondingly richer vocabulary in order to read the **Physics.** *Motion* means one thing to us, but irreducibly many kinds of thing when Aristotle speaks of it, and the same is true of *cause.* We tend to use *nature* as an umbrella-word, a collective name for the sum of things, while Aristotle means it to apply to whatever governs the distinct pattern of activity of each kind of being. Different English words could be used for these three ideas, to bring out what is distinctive in Aristotle's meaning, but here it seems best to keep the familiar words and push their limits beyond their prevalent current meanings. Nature, cause, and motion are the central topics of the **Physics,** and they first come to sight as questions; it is important to see that Aristotle and the later mathematical physicists were ultimately asking about the same things. Nature is mathematized not as an interesting game, or to abadon a harder task in favor of an easier one, but in order that the truth of it may be found.

In the *Assayer,* Galileo makes the famous claim that "this grand book, the universe, . . . is written in the language of mathematics." Later in the same book, in a discussion of heat, he explains why:

> I suspect that people in general have a concept of this which is very remote from the truth. For they believe that heat is a real phenomenon, or property, or quality, which actually resides in the material by which we feel ourselves warmed. . . . Without the senses as our guides, reason or imagination unaided would probably never arrive at qualities like these. Hence I think that tastes, odors, colors, and so on are no more than mere names so far as the object in which we place them is concerned, and that they reside only in the consciousness. Hence if the living creature were removed, all these qualities would be wiped away and annihilated. (*Discoveries and Opinions of Galileo,* New York: Anchor, 1957, pp. 237-38)

But shapes, sizes, positions, numbers, and such things are not mere names, imposed on objects by the consciousness of the living creature, because "from these conditions, I cannot separate [a material or corporeal] substance by any stretch of my imagination" (p. 274). The direct experience of the world has the taint of subjectivity, but the mathematical imagination captures the object just as it is. Sadder but wiser physicists today no longer try to read themselves out of physics; they know that they too are living creatures, interpreting the experience of a consciousness, with all the risk and uncertainty that accompanies such an activity. But our use of language may betray our second thoughts, and pull us back to Galileo's point of view.

What is motion? Do you think of something like a geometrical point changing position? What about a child moving into adolescence? Warmth moving into your limbs? Blossoms moving out of the buds on a tree? A ripening tomato, moving to a dark red? Are these other examples motions in only a metaphorical sense, while the first is correctly so called? Are the other examples really nothing but complex instances of the first, with small-scale changes of position adding up to large-scale illusions of qualitative change? For Aristotle, the differences among the kinds of motion determine the overall structure of the *Physics,* but they first of all belong together as one kind of experience. The kinds of becoming correspond to the ways being belongs to anything, and being-somewhere is only one aspect of being. A thing can also be of a certain size or of a certain sort or quality, and it can undergo motion in these respects by coming to be of another size or of a different quality by some gradual transition. It can even undergo a motion with respect to its thinghood. One

thinks first of birth and death, but eating displays the same kind of motion. A cow chomps grass, and the grass is no longer part of the life of a plant, and is soon assimilated into the body of the cow. This is no mere change of quality, since no whole being persists through it to have first one, then some other quality belonging to it. Something persists, but first in one, then in another, kind of thinghood.

In any encounter with the natural world, it is the kinds of change other than change of place that are most prominent and most productive of wonder. Mathematical physics must erase them all and argue that they were never anything but deceptive appearances of something else, changing in some other way. Why? Because those merely local changes of merely inert bodies can be described mathematically. But if the testimony of the senses has a claim to "objectivity," and to be taken seriously, that is at least equal to that of the mathematical imagination, such a reduction is not necessary. And in fact the reduction of kinds of motion that is required is not just from four to one, but to less than one. Aristotle has considerable interest in change of place, but such a thing is possible only if there are places. Motion as mathematically conceived happens in space, and in space there are no places. Underneath the idea of motion that is prevalent today lurks this other idea, unexamined and taken on faith, that there is such a thing as space.

Aristotle twice argues that the idea of space, or empty extension, results only from the misuse of mathematics. His argument is the exact counterargument to Galileo's claim that ordinary people project their non-mathematical ideas onto the world. Aristotle says that the mathematician separates in thought the extension that belongs to extended bodies. (This is sometimes called "abstraction," but the word Aristotle uses is the ordinary word for subtraction.) There is nothing wrong with this falsification of things, which makes it easier to study what has been isolated artificially, so long as one does not forget that the original falsification took place. But some people do just that, reading this extension, which they have subtracted from bodies, back into the world as though the world were empty and somehow existed on its own prior to bodies. Once one has done so, one can, in the imagination, examine this "space" and determine all sorts of things about it. It is of infinite extent, for example, and since it is entirely empty, no part of it can have any characteristic by which it could differ from any other part. If our impulse, when thinking about motion, is automatically to give it a mathematical image, that is because we have presupposed that the ultimate structure of the world is space. But this supposition is laden with consequences and ought not to be adopted blindly. Aristotle says that one of the reasons physics cannot be mathematical is that the mathematician abolishes motion. Physics is the study of beings that move, and motion is a rich and complex topic, but within the constraints of "space" every form of motion disappears, except for one that is diminished out of recognition. If it is in space that our examination begins, nature will be nowhere to be found (but will survive as a mere name) because space is, from the beginning, a de-natured realm.

Conversely, without the imposition of the idea of space, nature can be understood as part of the true constitution of things, because motion in all its variety can be present. But since motion is not reduced to the pre-explained realm of mathematics, it is necessary to understand what it is. Aristotle says that, so long as we are ignorant of motion, we are ignorant of nature as well. But how can one give a rational account of motion? To assign it to some other genus would seem to make it a species of non-motion. In fact, two of Aristotle's predecessors, Parmenides and Zeno, had argued that motion is completely illusory. Parmenides argued that any attempt to say that there is motion must claim that what is-not also is. And Zeno, in four famous paradoxes preserved by Aristotle, tried to show that any description of motion involves self-contradiction of some kind. It would seem that motion has to be accepted as a brute fact of experience, from which explanations can begin, but which cannot itself be explained. But Aristotle, for the first and perhaps only time ever, did give motion a place not only in the world but in a rational account of the world, explaining it in terms of ideas that go deeper. The Parmenidean challenge is met by Aristotle primarily in the **Metaphysics,** where he shows that being must be meant in more than one way. His response to Zeno's challenge spreads over the whole of the **Physics,** and it is concentrated in his definition of motion.

Aristotle defines motion in terms of potency and being-at-work. In the first book of the **Physics** a preliminary analysis of change discovers that the ultimate explanatory notions available to the inquiry are form, material, and the deprivation of form. Material is described as that which, by its own nature, inherently yearns for and stretches out toward form. This should never be called matter, by which we mean something that stands on its own with a determinate set of properties (has weight, occupies space, preserves its state of motion in a straight line). What Aristotle means by material, on the contrary, is (1) not inert, (2) not necessarily tangible, (3) relative to its form, which may in turn be material for some other form, (4) not possessed of any definite properties, and (5) ultimately a purely "ideal" being, incapable of existing in separation, which would be rejected by any "materialist." Form, in turn, does not mean shape or arrangement, but some definite way of being-at-work. This is evident in Book II of the **Physics** and is arrived at by argument principally in the **Metaphysics,** VIII, 2. Every being consists of material and form, that is, of an inner striving spilling over into an outward activity. Potency and being-at-work are the ways of being of material and form.

The usual translations render *potency* as *potentiality,* which might suggest mere indeterminacy or logical possibility, which is never the sense in which Aristotle uses it. What is worse, though, is the rendering of *being-at-work,* and the stronger form of it used in the definition, *being-at-work-staying-itself,* as *actuality.* This has some reference, by way of Latin, to activity, but is a useless word that makes it completely impossible to get anything resembling Aristotle's meaning out of the definition. "The actuality of the potentiality as a potentiality" becomes a seventeenth-century joke, the ultimate example of the destruction of healthy common sense by pretentious gobbledygook. Does it refer to the actuality that belonged to the potential thing before it changed? That is not a motion, but something that precedes one. Does it refer to the actuality that exactly corresponds to the pre-existent potentiality? That is not a motion either, but something left when the motion ends. Does it mean, though it would have to be tortured to give this sense, the gradual transformation of a potentiality into an actuality? That at least could refer to a motion, but only by saying that a motion is a certain kind of motion. Perhaps it means that motion is the actuality of a potentiality to be in motion. This is surely the silliest version of them all, but respected scholars have defended it with straight faces. An intelligent misinterpretation of the definition was put forward by Thomas Aquinas, who took it to mean that the special condition of a thing in motion is to be partly actual while partly potential, and directed toward greater actuality of that same potentiality. But this account would not distinguish motion from a state of balanced equilibrium, such as that of a rock caught in a hand, still straining downward but prevented from falling any farther. Thomas's interpretation is subject to this ambiguity because it focuses on an instantaneous condition, a snapshot of a thing in motion, which is what an actuality is, but by no means what a being-at-work is.

What Aristotle said was that motion is the being-at-work-staying-itself of a potency, just as a potency. When an ongoing yearning and striving for form is not inner and latent, but present in the world just as itself, as a yearning and striving, there is motion. That is because, when motion is present, the potency of some material has the very same structure that form has, forming the being as something holding-on in just that particular motion. This does not mean that every motion is the unfolding of some being into its mature form; every such unfolding can fall short, overshoot, encounter some obstacle, or interact in some incidental way with some other being. It does mean that no motion of any kind would take place if it were not for those potencies that emerge of their own accord from beings. Motion depends on the organization of beings into kinds, with inner natures that are always straining to spill into activity. Only this dynamic structure of being, with material straining toward form and form staying at work upon material, makes room for motion that is not just an inexplicable departure from the way things are, but a necessary and intrinsic part of the way things are.

For example, consider the most uninteresting motion you can think of, say the falling of a pencil from the edge of a desk onto the floor. What is the potency that is at work, and to what being does it belong? The potency is *not* that of being at that spot on the floor, and the being that has it is not the pencil at all, since it is no genuine being. The potency at work here is that of earth to be down, or of the cosmos to sustain itself with earth at the center. No motive power belongs to the pencil as such, but it can move on its own because there is present in it a potency of earth, set free to be at work as itself when the obstacle of the desk is removed. And the motion is not defined by the position or state in which the pencil happens to end up, but by the activity that governs its course; the former is an actuality, but is not a being-at-work. Just as Newton's laws give a set of rules for analyzing any motion, Aristotle's definition directs us in a different way to bring the structure of any motion into focus: first, find the being, and then find the potency of it that the motion displays, or to which the particular motion is incidental. No motion, however random or incidental, gains entrance into the world except through the primary beings that constitute the world.

Aristotle sometimes argues about a body A that moves from B to C. Our first impulse may be to let A be represented by a point, the motion by a line, and B and C by positions. But Aristotle always has in mind an A with some nature, and a motion that may be from one condition to another rather than one place to another. Even if a motion from place to place is in question, those places would not be neutral and indifferent positions, but regions of the cosmos, which might or might not be appropriate surroundings for body A. The argument might be about something like continuity, so general that the particular B and C need not be specified, but it makes all the difference in the world that they represent motion in its fullest sense, as spelled out in the definition. The mathematized sort of motion, which can be fully depicted on a blackboard, is vulnerable to the kinds of attack present in Zeno's paradoxes. Motion as Aristotle understands it, constituted by potency and being-at-work, deriving its wholeness and continuity from a deeper source, overcomes those paradoxes. (The particular arguments will be looked at in the commentaries on the text.)

It is evident from this account of motion that material and form are understood as causes. The usual examples given for material and formal causes, an inert lump of bronze and a static blueprint, miss the point, namely,

that material meets form half-way and that form is always at work. And material and form cause not only motions, but everything that endures. We tend to speak of causes as events that lead to other events, since that is the only kind of causality that remains possible in a mathematically-reduced world, but Aristotle understands everything that is the case as resulting from causes, and every origin of responsibility as a cause. Something called the "efficient" cause has been grafted onto Aristotle's account; it means the proximate cause of motion, like the bumping of billiard balls. Efficient cause is sometimes even used as a translation of one of Aristotle's four kinds of cause, but not correctly. Aristotle speaks of the external source of motion as one kind of cause, the *first* thing from which the motion proceeds. The incidental and intermediate links, which merely pass motions around without originating them, are not causes at all except in a derivative sense. All of Aristotle's causes stem from beings, and they are found not by looking backward in time, but upward in a chain of responsibility.

A fourth kind of cause, in most cases the most important one of all, is the final cause. It is often equated with purpose, but purpose is only one kind of final cause, and not the most general. A deliberate action of an intelligent being cannot be understood except in terms of its purpose, since only in achieving that purpose does the action become complete. The claim that final causes belong to non-human nature becomes ludicrous if it is thought that something must in some analogous way have purposes. What Aristotle in fact means is that every natural being is a whole, and every natural activity leads to or sustains that wholeness. His phrase for this kind of cause is "that for the sake of which" something does what it does or is what it is. Does rain fall for the sake of the crops that humans grow? No, but it does fall for the sake of the equilibrium of the cosmos, in which evaporation is counterbalanced by precipitation in a cycle of ever-renewed wholeness. That wholeness provides a stable condition for the flourishing of plants and of humans in lives and acts that come to completion in their own ways. Aristotle's "teleology" is just his claim that nothing in nature is a fragment or a chance accumulation of parts. To grasp the final cause of anything is to see how it fits into the ultimate structure of things.

But surely there are fragmentary things and chance combinations to be found around us. Aristotle finds it as strange that some thinkers deny chance altogether, as it is that others think chance governs everything. But from Aristotle's standpoint, even chance always points back to that which acts for the sake of something, since it results from the interference of two or more such things. Chance therefore represents not an absence of final causes, but an overabundance of them, a failure of final cause resulting from a conflict among final causes.

Because such incidental interactions lead to innumerable unpredictable chance results, nature is not a realm of necessity, but neither is it a realm of randomness, since the forms of natural beings govern all that happens. Aristotle speaks of the patterns of nature as present not always but "for the most part." His way of understanding the causes of things does not do violence either to the stability or to the variability of the world, but affirms the unfailing newness-within-sameness that we observe in the return of the seasons and the generations of living things. It offers an example of a physics that interprets causality without recourse to mechanical necessity or mathematical law. Both the collision of billiard balls and the covariation of the two sides of an algebraic equation are too random in their beginnings and too rigid in their consequences to be adequate images of the natures we know.

The Shape of the Inquiry

It was mentioned above that all Aristotle's inquiries are dialectical. His writings have structures that are not rigid but organic, with parts that are whole in themselves but arranged so that they build up larger wholes. In the first book of most of his works he reviews what has been said by his predecessors. In Book I of the *Physics* that review is combined with a preliminary analysis of change, which concludes that change always implies the presence of some material that can possess or be deprived of form. This first analysis of everything changeable into form and material is then available as a starting point to approach any later question. Next comes the heart of the *Physics,* in Book II and the beginning of Book III, of which an account was given in the last section of this introduction. It begins with a definition of nature that has all the characteristics Aristotle attributes in I, 1 to proper beginnings: the discussion starts from what is familiar to us, it is clear in its reference but unclear in its meaning, and it takes its topic as a whole and in general, without separating out its parts or their particular instances. Since it defines nature as an inner cause of motion, the first task is to explore the meanings of cause and motion, not as words or logical classes, but through disciplined reflection on our experience. The result is a sharpened and deepened understanding of a way of encountering and interpreting the world. This is a more sustained use of the kind of analysis that took place in Book I, an analysis that dwells on a topic to unfold into clarity what was already present in an implicit and confused way.

A second kind of analytic reasoning begins after motion has been defined, a successive examination of conditions presupposed by the presence of motion in the world. This occupies the rest of Books III and IV. Zeno had taught everyone that motion presupposes infinity, and Aristotle turns first to this. He finds a non-contradictory way to understand the infinite divisibility of motion, but his conclusion that there is no infinite extended body is incomplete as it stands. It depends upon the claim that things have natural places, and so the topic of place must be explored next. Place is understood as a relation to the parts of the cosmos, but this topic in turn depends on the next topic, the void, since the exclusive array of places in the world results from the impossibility of void. The exploration of the idea of void completes this sequence, since the arguments against it stand independently. But motion also entails time, to which Aristotle turns next, finding that it is not in fact a presupposition but a consequence of motion. Time is found to result from a comparison of motions to one another, a comparison that can be carried out only by a perceiving soul. Like place, time is not a preexisting container and is not graspable by the mathematical imagination. Each of them is an intimate relation among beings, intelligible only when the particularity of this world is taken into account.

The last four books of the *Physics* take up the kind of cause and the kind of motion that are least central in Book II. The formal, material, and final causes of a living thing are internal to it and constitute its nature, and it has parents that are external sources of its motions of birth, development, and growth. But as Aristotle mentions at the end of II, 2, both other human beings and the sun beget a human being. All life is dependent upon conditions supplied by the cosmos, which seems to maintain itself primarily through cycles of local motion. Books V through VIII trace a complex argument up to the source of all change of place in the world. In its broadest outline, that argument is reminiscent of the structure of the *Metaphysics.* Though the *Metaphysics* is put together out of a large number of independent pieces, it has perhaps the clearest line of unifying structure of any of Aristotle's works. The meaning of being is pursued through four most general senses, to an eight-fold array of kinds of non-incidental predications, to its primary sense of thinghood, to the source of thinghood as form, to the meaning of form as being-at-work, to the source of all being-at-work in the divine intellect. It thus culminates in the discovery of the primary being that is the source of all being, and it gets there from the innocent question, Which of the meanings of being is primary?

A similar progressive narrowing of the meanings of motion takes place in the *Physics.* In Book III motion is said to be of four kinds: change of thinghood, alteration of quality, increase and decrease, and change of place. In Book V it is argued that motion properly understood is from one contrary to another, passing through intermediate states or conditions. But coming-into-being and destruction should be understood strictly as changes not to a contrary but to a contradictory condition, abrupt changes that have no intermediate conditions to pass through. Thus in a strict sense there are only three kinds of motion. But in Book VI it is argued that there is a certain discontinuity in every qualitative change. If something black turns white, it goes through a spectrum of intermediate shades, but it can be regarded as still being black until sometime in the course of the motion. In a change of quantity or place, once the thing is in motion it has departed from its initial condition, however much one might try to divide the beginning of the motion. So in the still stricter sense of being unqualifiedly continuous, there are only two kinds of motion. Finally, it is pointed out in Book VII that quantitative change must be caused by something that comes to be present where the changing thing is, so that it depends always upon a change of place prior to it, and it is argued in Book VIII that change of place is the primary kind of motion in every sense in which anything can be primary. The analysis goes one more step, to the primary motion within the primary kind, which is circular rotation. This is the most continuous of motions, so much so that it alone can be considered a simply unchanging motion.

Though the definition of motion in Book III applies to all motions, its application is most straightforward in the case of those motions most opposed to the primary kind, those that involve the greatest amount of change. Birth, development, and growth obviously unfold out of potencies that are present beforehand, and these changes point most directly to the inner natures of things that operate as formal, final, and material causes. But at the opposite extreme of the spectrum of change there is changeless circular motion. Because it moves without changing, it can be in contact with a completely unvarying cause. The last step of the inquiry in the ***Physics*** is the uncovering of a motionless first mover, acting on the cosmos at its outermost sphere. It is a source of local motion that not only holds the cosmos together, but contributes to the conditions of life by descending through the lower spheres, including that of the sun, to maintain the stable alternation of the seasons. Nature is thus seen as twofold, originating in sources of two kinds, the inner natures of living things and the cause holding together the cosmos as the outer condition of life. This is reflected in a bipolar relation of motion and change, in which ascending scale of motions (leading to the first external mover) is also the descending scale of changes (starting from the coming-into-being of new beings). The two-directionality of the scale is all-important. Aristotle does not reduce change to change of place, but rather traces it back, along one line of causes, to change of place. But the primacy of local motion in the cosmos does not abolish the primacy of the opposite kind of change, spilling over out of potency, which guarantees that even changes of place will be wholes, not vulnerable to the attacks of Zeno. The ***Physics*** has a double conclusion. In its final and deepest refutation of Zeno, it demonstrates the continuity rooted in potency as present in the limit of mere change of place, and this demonstration becomes one of the last steps in the argument that uncovers the motionless cause of motion. . . .

David Bolotin (essay date 1998)

SOURCE: "The Question of Teleology," in *An Approach to Aristotle's "Physics": With Particular Attention to the Role of His Manner of Writing*, State University of New York Press, 1998, pp. 31-52.

[*In the following essay, Bolotin explores the teleological nature of Aristotle's* Physics, *examining in particular Aristotle's notion of final causality. Bolotin highlights some of the difficulties within Aristotle's arguments regarding natural purpose.*]

One of the complaints most often heard about Aristotle's physics is that it is teleological, i.e., based on the assumption that there are ends or purposes in nature, and that this assumption has been refuted by modern science. And yet even though this criticism has been widely accepted, the fact remains that modern science has not refuted teleology: it has not shown that there are no ends or purposes in nature, and, indeed, it has not even attempted to do so. What it has done, rather, is systematically to disregard the possibility that they might exist. As Jacques Monod, a Nobel Prize-winning biologist, has written in his work *Chance and Necessity,*

> The cornerstone of the scientific method is the postulate that nature is objective. In other words, the *systematic* denial that "true" knowledge can be got at by interpreting phenomena in terms of final causes—that is to say, of "purpose." An exact date may be given for the discovery of this canon. The formulation by Galileo and Descartes of the principle of inertia laid the groundwork not only for mechanics but for the epistemology of modern science, by abolishing Aristotelian physics and cosmology. . . . [S]cience as we understand it today . . . required the unbending stricture implicit in the postulate of objectivity—ironclad, pure, forever undemonstrable. For it is obviously impossible to imagine an experiment which could prove the *nonexistence* anywhere in nature of a purpose, of a pursued end.

> But the postulate of objectivity is consubstantial with science; it has guided the whole of its prodigious development for three centuries. There is no way to be rid of it, even tentatively or in a limited area, without departure from the domain of science itself.[1]

I will not bother to quarrel here with Monod's contention that the systematic denial of purposes in nature is a requirement of science. What is important, rather, is his clear awareness that this denial is merely a postulate of modern science, not the assertion of an evident truth. And Monod's statement to this effect, far from being the unmasking of a hitherto unseen limitation of modern science, is only the restatement of a thought that was well understood by its originators.

Indeed, some of the founders of modern science appear personally to have believed in purposes in nature, even as they excluded all reference to them from their strictly scientific work. As Descartes put it in his fourth *Meditation,* in addressing the question whether it is for the better that God made him subject to error,

> it occurs to me in the first place that I should not be astonished if my intelligence is not capable of comprehending why God acts as he does; . . . knowing that my nature is extremely feeble and limited, and that the nature of God is on the contrary immense, incomprehensible, and infinite, I have no further difficulty in recognizing that there is an infinitude of matters in His power, the causes of which transcend my knowledge; and this reason suffices to convince me that the species of cause termed final finds no useful employment in physical [or natural] things; for it does not appear to me that I can without temerity seek to investigate the [inscrutable] ends of God.[2]

Now questions have been raised about whether Descartes's professions of piety are wholly sincere. But at all events, his *argument* against the attempt to explain natural things in terms of ends or purposes is compatible—to say the least—with there being such purposes in fact. Or to take another example, Newton himself, whose account of the motions in the solar system remains one of the greatest achievements of modern science, claimed that the solar system was originally put together by an intelligent God acting for a purpose. For although the planets and the comets, he wrote,

> may, indeed, continue in their orbits by the mere laws of gravity, yet they could by no means have first derived the regular position of the orbits themselves from those laws . . . This most beautiful system of the sun, planets, and comets, could only proceed from the counsel and dominion of an intelligent and powerful Being.[3]

Newton's claim, however, about the origin of the solar system appears only in a General Scholium that he appended to his *Principia* twenty-six years after its first publication. And these theological reflections play no role in the body of the work, just as they have played no role in the subsequent history of modern physics.

More generally, modern science from the beginning has sidestepped the question of ends or purposes in nature, while encouraging people to take less and less

seriously the possibility of their existence, by trying to formulate laws that would encompass as many phenomena as possible without any reference to such ends. But it has not succeeded, of course, in encompassing all phenomena, at least not yet. And even in the case of those phenomena that it does encompass, the claim that it has understood them adequately is dubious. For its laws are mathematical idealizations, idealizations, moreover, with no immediate basis in experience and with no evident connection to the ultimate causes of the natural world. For instance, Newton's first law of motion (the law of inertia) requires us first to imagine a body that is always at rest or else moving aimlessly in a straight line at a constant speed, even though we never see such a body, and even though according to his own theory of universal gravitation it is impossible that there can be one. This fundamental law, then, which begins with a claim about what would happen in a situation that never exists, carries no conviction except insofar as it helps to predict observable events. Thus, despite the amazing success of Newton's laws in predicting the observed positions of the planets and other bodies, Einstein and Infeld are correct to say, in *The Evolution of Physics,* that "we can well imagine that another system, based on different assumptions, might work just as well." Einstein and Infeld go on to assert that "physical concepts are free creations of the human mind, and are not, however it may seem, uniquely determined by the external world." To illustrate what they mean by this assertion, they compare the modern scientist to a man trying to understand the mechanism of a closed watch. If he is ingenious, they acknowledge, this man "may form some picture of a mechanism which could be responsible for all the things he observes." But they add that he "may never be quite sure his picture is the only one which could explain his observations. He will never be able to compare his picture with the real mechanism and he cannot even imagine the possibility or the meaning of such a comparison."[4] In other words, modern science cannot claim, and it will never be able to claim, that it has the definitive understanding of any natural phenomenon. And accordingly, we should not allow ourselves to be so dazzled by it as to suppose that it has refuted Aristotle's teaching about natural ends.

Let me turn, therefore, to an examination of that teaching itself, to try to see whether in fact it makes sense. I begin with a brief summary of Aristotle's doctrine of the four causes, among which the end or final cause is included. In trying to explain anything, or to answer the question Why? about it, there are four ways, according to Aristotle, that we can respond. These four kinds of responses, these four ways of saying "because," are each a kind of cause of the matter in question. In one sense, we speak of the cause of something as the constituent or constituents from which it comes into being and of which it is composed. Thus, for instance, we call the bronze in a statue a cause of it, because the statue could not exist without the bronze that it is made of.[5] In another and more important sense, however, we say that the cause of something is its form, since it is the form, rather than the constituent material, that explains why the being is what it is. Thus the bronze constitutes a statue because it has the form of a statue, not because it is bronze. And by the "form" of a being we do not mean its visible shape alone, but rather its whole character—a character that we may not be able to articulate clearly at first, but that we must already understand to a considerable degree simply to identify the being as what it is. To take our example again, we call a statue a statue because of its form, by which we do not mean its shape alone but, more importantly, its being the sculpted image of some other being, such as a man or a god. Similarly, we call a human being a human being because of its form, by which we mean above all that we are animals with the power of reason. Now in addition to the constituent cause and the formal cause, a third kind of cause, which helps to explain coming into being as well as all other changes or motions, is the source from which a given change begins. Hence, for example, the sculptor is a cause of the statue's coming into being, and therefore also, in a sense, of the statue itself, as the parent is a cause of the birth of its offspring and the wind is a cause of rustling in the leaves. This principle of change, which Aristotle sometimes calls the moving cause, can also, however, be a cause of a state of rest, as when a man decides to stop running and to remain still. Finally, a fourth kind of cause is the end or purpose for which something comes into being or for which it exists. Thus health, for instance, can be a cause of walking by being the purpose for the sake of which someone might take walks. Or to return to our first example, giving honor to a god or perhaps pleasure to the human beholders might be the end—or the final cause, as it is also called—for the sake of which the sculptor produced the statue.

To focus specifically now on final causality, the examples I have just given suggest a definite manner in which the end of a motion operates as a cause. First, it is present in thought to the agent who begins the motion, and it is thought of as being good, and as being attainable by his own efforts. And as a consequence, the agent proceeds to try to realize in deed the end that he originally had in mind. In these cases, then, the final cause is itself a factor, together with what we have called the moving cause, in initiating the motion that leads up to it as an end. And most people would agree, I think, that this is a true account of such motions as that of a statue being sculpted, for it is the craftsman's anticipation of the completed work that directs his hands and tools. But Aristotle says explicitly that the end is a cause of natural motions, such as the growth and reproduction of living beings, and not only of motions initiated by human art.[6] Indeed, he justifies his use of analogies from the arts in the expla-

nation of natural processes by claiming that art imitates nature; and he means by this not merely that some arts are representational but, more broadly, that all the arts derive their own directedness toward ends from that already to be found in nature.[7] He even goes so far as to speak of Nature herself as a kind of artisan who makes all things for a purpose and nothing in vain.[8] Yet we have no clear evidence to suggest that nature is an intelligent being; and since to act for a purpose would seem to presuppose intelligent forethought, it is hard to understand how nature could act in this manner, or how natural motions could be for the sake of any ends.[9] So couldn't it be, instead, the result of accident that natural processes often turn out in a manner that seems to suggest motion for the sake of an end? Now this is not, as it might appear, a question that only we in the post-Darwinian age can ask, but in fact a central question that Aristotle explicitly confronts throughout his account of purposes in nature. To see how he responds to it, let us look more closely at the text of the *Physics* itself.

Aristotle discusses accidental causation immediately after his account of the four causes, and he indicates the tremendous scope of the question about it by noting that some men had attributed the existence of this world, and indeed of all ordered worlds, to chance. Now by "this world" Aristotle means, not the hypothetically expanding universe of contemporary science, but rather this perceptible world, the world in which we live, along with other animals and plants, upon the earth and under the heaven. The beauty and grandeur of this world have always aroused in men a sense of wonder, and many have felt, as Newton did, that it must be the product of intelligent forethought.[10] Yet according to some of the early philosophers, this world of ours came into being, as did many other worlds, merely by chance. Now in response to these philosophers, Aristotle begins by saying that their claim is worthy of wonder. For those, he says, who attribute the world and the most divine of the manifest beings (i.e., the stars) to chance do not speak of animals and plants as coming into being by mere luck, but rather by nature or mind or some other such cause, on the grounds that each kind of seed typically produces some definite kind of result. And on precisely these grounds, he continues, what they say about the world as a whole is especially strange, since we see nothing in the heaven coming into being by chance, whereas we see many things resulting from luck among the perishable beings here on earth.[11] Now at this point, it would certainly be possible for us moderns to raise objections to Aristotle's argument. But I would suggest that we defer our objections and consider instead that Aristotle has not said, at least not yet, that those who attribute the world to chance are wrong, but merely that their assertion is wonderful and strange—as I venture to say it is. And he adds that if what they say is true, this very fact deserves careful attention, as indeed it does. Rather than assume, then, that Aristotle has already rejected the view in question about the origin of the world—whether on adequate or on inadequate grounds—we would do better to follow him as he goes further into the matter by investigating more generally what chance is and what its relation is to nature.

Aristotle begins his account of chance by first discussing what he calls luck and by observing that we speak of luck, not as a cause of those things that come into being always or for the most part in the same way, but rather as a cause of those that come about contrary to any such necessary or usual patterns. Yet it is not simply the unusualness of an occurrence that makes it a case of luck. It is also necessary that it be the kind of occurrence that *might* have been brought about for the sake of something and from intelligent choice. Such a result, when it comes about, however, merely by concomitance, is what is properly said to be from luck. Aristotle offers an example to help clarify what he means in saying that luck is a cause of its results by mere concomitance. A certain man, he says, would have gone to the marketplace to recover the money he was owed if only he had known that his debtor was there. But he did not know, and so he did not go to the market for that purpose; it was merely a concomitant of his going for some other reason that his trip served the purpose of recovering his debt. Thus, the result came about from luck, and the man is said to have gone to the marketplace from luck. If, however, he had chosen to go to the market for this purpose, or if he went there always or for the most part when collecting on his debts, neither his going nor its result would be from luck. To speak of luck as a cause, then, is not to deny that there must always be some definite, particular cause of a lucky result. Indeed, in keeping with the fact that luck is responsible only for the kinds of outcomes that might have resulted from intelligent choice, only rational agents, who alone are capable of such choice, can be said to act from luck. But we attribute the result to luck when the agent's action merely happens to serve a purpose without his having intended it to do so.

After preparing the way with this account of luck, which has the merit of being immediately intelligible, Aristotle turns to the discussion of chance, or spontaneity, as we might also translate the Greek term. Chance is a broader class that includes luck as a subclass. Like luck in particular, chance in general belongs to the overall category of moving causes.[12] And it too is a cause of something that, while it is the kind of thing that might have been brought about for a purpose, does not in fact occur for the sake of what results. The greater extension of the term *chance* is due largely to the fact that the particular cause of what we call a chance outcome need not be an agent capable of intelligent choice, as it must in the case of luck, but can be any being, whether animate or even inanimate. Yet Aristotle sug-

gests more of a difference between chance in the wider sense and luck in particular than this. He also suggests that chance results need not be of such a kind as even *normally* to require an intelligent agent, but that in some cases they are ones that might have been brought about by nature, where nature is understood as a power, distinct from intelligence, that nevertheless also acts for a purpose.[13] This suggestion, however, is a difficult one. For as I have already mentioned, it is hard to see what it can mean to act for a purpose if not to act from intelligent forethought, and so it is hard to understand what that nature could be that Aristotle is contrasting with chance. The examples, moreover, that he gives as illustrations of chance serve to highlight this difficulty. Let me mention only one of these examples, in which the difficulty becomes explicit. Aristotle says that a stone fell by chance when it hit a man who was passing by below; and the reason he gives for attributing its fall to chance is that it might have fallen through someone's agency, and for the sake of striking the man, although in fact it did not. In other words, to explain what he means by a chance event, he contrasts it, not with one that might have come about from nature, but with one that might have been chosen by an intelligent, if in this case an unfriendly, being.[14]

Now Aristotle is aware that his examples do not fulfill our expectation that chance results are sometimes to be contrasted with what nature, as distinct from intelligence, might have brought forth. And so he adds that chance in the wider sense is most distinct from luck in the sphere of natural generation, when an animal or plant comes into being contrary to nature, that is, maimed or with some deformity. In such cases, he says, we do not speak of luck, but rather of chance—and this not merely, it seems, because these beings are not produced by an agency capable of intelligent choice, but also because the nature that might have produced them, and done so for a purpose, is itself not an intelligence. Aristotle adds, on the basis of a consideration that I will return to later, that these impairments and deformities are not precisely even from chance. Nevertheless, his reference to them serves to support the suggestion that chance, as distinct from luck, can be a cause of what might have arisen from the purposive action of nature.

The question remains, however, of what it can mean for nature to act for a purpose. And Aristotle again calls our attention to this difficulty, in the course of a renewed attempt to answer the question about the cause of the world. What he says is this: since chance and luck are causes by mere concomitance of what either mind or nature might have caused, they cannot be prior to mind and nature themselves; so that even if chance is responsible for the world, mind and nature are necessarily prior causes, both of many other things and of this whole.[15] Now it is not immediately clear, of course, how Aristotle arrives at this conclusion or how it is to be understood. But what I would first like to emphasize is his claim that *both* mind *and* nature must be prior to chance, even on the assumption that chance is responsible for the world. That he makes this claim about mind, in particular, comes as a surprise. For the assumption about a chance origin of the world can refer, and almost certainly does refer, to chance in the wider sense, as distinct from luck. After all, the philosophic position to which Aristotle is responding claims that our world came into being through the blind interaction of the elements, not from the lucky or unlucky actions of an intelligent being. Yet if we assume that chance in this sense is responsible for the world, one might have supposed, perhaps, that nature is a still prior cause, on the grounds that chance is a cause of what might have been produced by nature, which must, therefore, already be at work. But what Aristotle says, to repeat, is that nature *and* mind must *both* be prior causes of the world. And if mind, as well as nature, must already exist for there to be chance in the wider sense, this would seem to imply that nature is not capable of acting for the sake of ends—those ends that are presupposed whenever we speak of chance—unless it is somehow accompanied by mind. And however much this view of nature might help us to understand how nature can act for a purpose, it is at odds with Aristotle's earlier suggestion that it can do so on its own.

And yet perhaps this new suggestion, that nature depends on mind in order to do its work, is an intentional modification of the earlier one; and in fact, the very next chapter tends to support this modified view of nature. Aristotle says there that a natural being has two sorts of moving causes, one of which is not natural itself, since it is wholly unmoved. He then identifies this unmoved mover with the being's end, or final cause, and also with its form; but the form he is referring to cannot be the form as it exists in perishable beings, since we have already been told that these forms are perishable themselves, and hence not entirely unmoved.[16] The reference must therefore be to some other kind of form, and the only other kind that Aristotle believes to exist is the form as it exists in thought, whether in human thought or divine thought. If natural change, then, is to be initiated in part by final causes that are also unchanging forms, it seems that these forms must be present in a divine mind, a mind that somehow solicits natural beings to move toward the perfection of their exemplars.[17] And indeed, Aristotle has already suggested something like this earlier in the **Physics,** where he said that the two highest principles of nature include one that is divine and good and aimed for and another that naturally aims for and reaches toward the first one.[18] And there are quite a few passages scattered throughout Aristotle's works that speak of a divine mind as the Prime Mover and ultimate source of all life and nature.[19]

And yet despite the attractiveness of this suggestion about the subordination of nature to a divine mind, it does not yet allow us to see how natural motion as such can be for a purpose. For purposive motion, at least as we understand it, presupposes more than the mere existence in some mind of the form that is to be aimed for as its end. It also presupposes that this mind be that of an agent which can set itself in motion with a view to that end. Thus, for instance, if the heavenly spheres are intelligent, living beings, as Aristotle says they are, it is at least conceivable that they might set themselves in motion in order to approximate the perfection of the divine forms.[20] But unless even the seeds of natural beings here on earth are self-moving, intelligent agents, or unless they are tools in the hands of some other such agent, the assumption that the forms exist in a divine mind does not yet make it intelligible how natural growth, for instance, can be purposive. Perhaps, then, the claim that led us to these speculations about the divine mind, the claim that *both* mind *and* nature must necessarily be prior to chance, allows for another interpretation. In particular, in saying that *mind* must be prior to chance, even if chance is responsible for our world, Aristotle may be trying, not to help us to see how *nature* could act for a purpose, that is, in conjunction with mind, but rather to indicate something about mind and chance in themselves.

And in fact, there is such a way of interpreting the claim about mind being prior to chance. For according to Aristotle, there are different senses of the term *priority.* In particular, if knowledge of one thing is presupposed by that of another, the former is said to be prior in terms of knowledge, without necessarily being prior in other senses, such as that of existing earlier in time.[21] Thus, if we assume, as Aristotle invites us to do, that the world emerged through chance, it might still be true, as he claims, that mind must be a prior cause of it; but perhaps this is only because of priority in terms of knowledge. At all events, Aristotle would have good grounds for saying that mind is prior to chance in this sense, for chance results are defined as those that might have been brought about for a purpose, and we understand purpose as that for the sake of which an intelligent being would act. Knowledge of chance, then, presupposes a prior knowledge of mind, or, more precisely, of ensouled minds, since it is these that are capable of action for the sake of ends.[22] Moreover, if being in the paramount sense is what is true, or what is truly understood by some mind—and Aristotle makes this claim in the **Metaphysics**—then this priority of mind to chance in terms of knowledge also implies a certain priority in terms of being.[23] Chance would not be fully what it is if it were not understood—understood, that is, in its relation to the ends pursued by intelligent beings. And this is true even of the chance, on the hypothesis that it is chance, that was first responsible for the coming into being of our world.

In trying to account for the priority of mind to chance, I said that the definition of chance contains the notion of purpose and that purpose is understood as that for the sake of which an intelligent being would act. And yet we cannot forget Aristotle's earlier suggestion that what is for a purpose is what might have been done *either* from intelligence *or else* from nature.[24] Thus, it seems that I have been overhasty in claiming that we need to understand intelligence, as distinct from nature, in order to understand chance. However, the difficulty of even conceiving what it can mean for nature to act for a purpose has been our chief puzzle all along. And so let me suggest that natural ends themselves, like the ends that just happen to result from chance, can not be understood without a prior understanding of those ends that are pursued by intelligent agents. Now it is true that when Aristotle first speaks of purpose in the **Physics,** he makes no explicit reference to intelligence. What he says, rather, is that "nature," by which he means the form of a natural being, "is an end and [that] for the sake of which; for in the case of those beings whose motion is continuous and has some end, this last stage is also that for the sake of which."[25] And yet he has to add immediately that not just *any* last stage of a being's continuous motion is a true end or purpose; after all, he observes, it was ridiculous of the poet—presumably a comic poet—to say that death was the purpose for which a certain man had been born. Aristotle goes on to explain that only the best kind of last stage wishes to be an end; and he speaks repeatedly of ends or purposes as being, or as wishing to be, what is better or best.[26] But to be better or best presupposes a range of alternatives as well as some being with the intelligence to compare these alternatives and to judge among them. Accordingly, all knowledge of what it is to be an end, including a natural end, depends on knowledge of the features of intelligent choice.

My argument has now shown, I think, how Aristotle could justify his claim that even on the hypothesis that our world emerged through chance, mind would still be prior in causality to chance. But it has not made sense of the other half of Aristotle's claim, namely, that nature would also, on this hypothesis, be prior to chance. For I have not relied on the assumption that nature, as distinct from mind, acts for the sake of ends. But unless nature does act in this way, it is not even clear how it differs from chance, let alone how it must be prior to it. After all, chance happenings themselves are of such a kind that they *might* have come about for the sake of ends. Now there is at least one difference between nature and chance, which I alluded to earlier, when I said that congenital impairments and deformities in natural beings are not precisely from chance. For Aristotle's definition of chance included a criterion that I have not yet mentioned, namely, that the causes of chance results must be external.[27] Congenital impairments and deformities, by contrast, are said to have an internal cause. And it is not only such defor-

mities in natural beings that can be distinguished from chance results on the basis of this criterion. Their normal development is also said to originate from a cause within themselves.[28] Thus, the normal growth of living beings is said to be from nature rather than from chance, since it begins from a parental seed, which has within itself, as the parent did already, the power to initiate those motions that lead to a mature animal or plant. On the other hand, Aristotle thinks, rightly or wrongly, that in some species of living beings the usual mode of generation is spontaneous, i.e., from chance. Such generation comes about, he says, because the material, such as putrefying slime, from which these animals or plants begin their development can be moved by itself with the kind of motion that more typically must be caused in maternal residue by a paternal seed.[29] In generation from chance, then, the original source of motion is something other than the kind of being that results from it; and in general, we can distinguish nature, as an internal source of change, from all external causes such as chance. Still, however, this criterion by itself does not suffice to explain why natural motion is said to be for a purpose. And neither does it allow us to understand Aristotle's claim that nature must be prior to chance. Indeed, the view that nature is only an internal cause of motion adds an additional reason for doubt on this score. After all, the survival, growth, and reproduction of natural beings are dependent on a great many external conditions. Accordingly, nature, or at least the nature of each kind of perishable being that we know of here on earth, must depend for its very existence on something else—either on some higher principle of order or else on chance.[30] And on the hypothesis that our world as a whole emerged through chance, chance would seem to be prior to nature, rather than the other way around.

If, moreover, one holds that the world as a whole emerged through chance, it becomes all the harder to see how there could be a purpose behind the internal development of particular natural beings. And some of Aristotle's philosophic predecessors had in fact argued that there was none. Aristotle recasts their argument in the form of a perplexity, as follows. Zeus does not cause rain, the argument begins, in order to make the crops grow, any more than it rains in order to damage the crops on some poor farmer's threshing-floor; rather, the rain falls by necessity as the evaporated moisture rises and then cools, and it just happens to be advantageous or harmful for human beings. And if such blind causality is the truth behind the apparently benevolent order of the world as a whole, what prevents there being the same kind of causality at work in the formation of particular natural beings? This argument acknowledges that the parts of organic beings are suitably arranged for the activities through which they survive and reproduce. But it claims that these arrangements first originated from blind necessity, as did many others, and that it merely turned out that these were serviceable, as the others were not, for survival and reproduction. The animals and plants that we see around us continue to survive because their parts turned out *as if* they had been organized for a purpose; but they were not organized for any purpose in fact.

Aristotle admits that one might be perplexed by this attempt to explain the apparent purposiveness in the structure of organic beings, but he denies that things could have happened in the way that it suggests. He offers in rebuttal a whole series of arguments that nature is truly a cause for the sake of something. And the first of these arguments at least suggests that natural purposiveness is not limited to the internal structure of organic beings. For instead of granting the premise that the causes of rain are indifferent to good and bad, and arguing that the parts of living beings are nevertheless arranged for a purpose, Aristotle lays down premises which imply that even the rain—or at least its seasonal patterns—is for the sake of something.[31] To this extent, then, he proceeds as if he assumed that it does not make sense to think of nature as acting purposefully even within a limited realm unless the world as a whole is ordered for the sake of ends.

Unfortunately, however, this first in Aristotle's series of arguments for natural purpose is extremely problematic. And yet partly for this very reason, it is of such importance that I wish to go through it in detail. Aristotle begins by saying that "these things, and indeed all things that are by nature, come into being either always or for the most part in the same way," but that "nothing that is from luck or from chance does so." In support of this assertion about luck and chance, he adds that "it is not believed to be from luck or from coincidence"—which latter term appears to be a synonym for chance—"when there are frequent rains in winter, but [only] if they come during the dog days [i.e., in summer]." Similarly, he says, "heat during the dog days is not [believed to be from luck or from coincidence], but [only] if [it happens] in winter."[32] Now it is noteworthy that the explicit basis for Aristotle's claim that normal weather patterns are not from coincidence is what is commonly believed. For those who make the argument against him, and who speak of a chance origin of the various species of living beings, would object that common opinion has too limited a time frame, and that the patterns whose regularity it is struck by exist only for a short time, in the light of eternity, as does our world itself.[33] They would say that even if the persistence of these regular patterns is not merely coincidental, but a necessary consequence of the elements in their juxtaposition, the whole order within which these patterns exist is the temporary and unintended aftereffect of an original coincidence. And yet despite the obvious fact that this is a possible objection, Aristotle does not even attempt here to justify his reliance on the common perspective regarding the permanence of our world; and by being explicit about this reliance, he calls attention to the question of whether that perspective is adequate.

Aristotle continues his argument as follows: "If, then, [things] are believed [to be] either from coincidence or for the sake of something, and if it is not possible for these things to be either from coincidence or from chance, they would be for the sake of something."[34] Now this conclusion follows, of course, if its premises are sound. But the premise that things must be either from coincidence or else for the sake of something is open to doubt. For what about the bad things that happen always or for the most part? In particular, what about the death that comes inevitably to all living beings here on earth? The fact that birth is followed by death is no mere coincidence, if anything is not, and yet it is hard to see a purpose for it. Aristotle helps us, moreover, to see the dubiousness of the claim that being from coincidence or else being for a purpose is an exhaustive alternative by explicitly basing this premise too on common opinion. And a further sign that he is aware of its weakness is that he does not go on to claim that *everything* by nature is for a purpose, even though he had begun his argument by asserting that everything by nature comes about always or for the most part in the same way. For if nothing that happens with such regularity can be from coincidence, as he asserts, and if being from coincidence and being for a purpose are indeed the only alternatives, it would follow that everything by nature—including rainfall in winter, as I mentioned earlier—*is* for a purpose. And yet, to repeat, Aristotle does not even claim that this is true.[35] What he says, rather, is that if the particular things in question, that is, the arrangement of parts in living beings, cannot be from coincidence or from chance, then *these* things would be for a purpose. By thus retreating from the full implications of his argument, Aristotle suggests that this more limited conclusion, regarding the parts of organic beings, is not meant to rely wholly on the reasons that have been made explicit. Finally, Aristotle concludes his overall argument by observing that all such things are by nature, so that there is purpose, or "the for the sake of something," among the beings that come into being and that are by nature. But this final conclusion, since it is based on the previous one, can also not be justified by the explicit argument alone.

The disregard, in Aristotle's explicit argument, of the problem of natural evils is closely related to its other difficulty, its failure to respond to his adversaries' contention about the origin of the world. For whatever weaknesses there may be in the doctrine that our world order, and in particular its species of living beings, emerged through chance and necessity alone, this view is the one most obviously compatible with a clear account of death and other natural evils. And so by pointing to his awareness that he has failed to acknowledge these evils in his own argument, Aristotle calls still further attention to his having left it open, at least for now, that his adversaries might be right about the question of ultimate origins. Moreover, in a subsequent argument against the claim that natural processes take place simply from necessity, he says that the earlier stages of such development do not lead necessarily to its culmination, but that the necessity in these cases is merely hypothetical, in the sense that there must be the appropriate preconditions if a being with a given nature is going to exist. He suggests, in other words, that there is no unqualified necessity, either from material causes or otherwise, for the existence of any natural being, and thus he again calls attention to the possibility that the world as a whole might owe its existence to chance.[36]

But what, then, is the basis for Aristotle's emphatic assertion, throughout this whole series of arguments and elsewhere, that the end or purpose is a cause of natural development? For if there is no evidence that such development results from the forethought of a self-moving agent, and if the possibility must even remain open that life itself first emerged through chance, how can he speak with such confidence of purposes or ends in nature? Now to answer this question, we must begin by noting that whatever the origin of life, if it had an origin, and whatever the more immediate moving causes of natural development may be, it remains true that this motion issues regularly, throughout human experience, in living beings whose parts work wonderfully well together in carrying out their life activities. These activities, such as nutrition, reproduction, perception, locomotion, and thought, are the manifestations of the form, or soul, of the being in question; and this form cannot be understood in the light of its material conditions alone. Rather, it is only in the light of the form that the material conditions can be seen as what they are. The bodily organs of a living being must be seen as instruments for performing its characteristic activities, activities without some of which, at least, the body itself would cease to exist; and even the more ultimate conditions of life must be understood, at least in part, in the light of their contribution to this end.[37] Accordingly, even if the term of natural development is not in general anticipated by its moving cause, as it would have to be if it were a purpose in the strict sense, the notion of purpose, or of what something is good for, remains central to the proper understanding of natural beings. And since living beings become what they most truly are by attaining their mature form, their typical growth toward maturity must also be seen in the light of this end. This is not to deny that mature development may indeed result from the same kind of blind necessity, given certain conditions, as does deformity or premature death, given certain others. But as words like *deformity, mature,* and *premature* themselves already suggest, we nonetheless see these outcomes either as successes or as failures of a tendency toward a natural

goal. We can disregard, or pretend not to notice, this privileged status of the mature form; but it remains an inescapable fact of the world as it presents itself to our experience.

Now these conclusions, to repeat, are independent of the question whether the world as a whole emerged through chance. And thus the centrality of form to the understanding of natural beings also allows us to make sense of the claim that even if the world did emerge through chance, nature would still be a prior cause of it. For the world consists primarily of natural beings, and of living beings in particular, which are properly seen as what they are in the light of their forms. Hence knowledge of these natural forms, and of these forms as the normal ends of growth, is presupposed by the very question of whether the beings they characterize, or even the world as a whole, first originated through chance. Nature as form and as the end of motion is necessarily prior to chance, at least in the sense that chance can not be understood without a prior knowledge of this nature, just as we saw earlier that it could not be understood without a prior knowledge of the features of intelligent choice.[38]

This notion of the mature form as the end of natural development is a far cry, of course, from the strict sense of purpose, according to which the end is anticipated by thought and thus helps to initiate the motions that lead up to its realization. And although my account of natural ends has the advantage of being compatible—as is the bulk of the *Physics*—with the possibility that our world emerged through chance, the fact remains that the final book of the *Physics* and the first book of *On the Heaven* contain elaborate arguments for its being eternal. Since Aristotle also claims, moreover, that the highest principle of the world is a divine mind, he still seems to hold out the hope that natural motion is somehow also activity for a purpose in the strict sense of the word. Yet as I suggested earlier, I do not think that Aristotle himself could have given credence to the notion that anything other than a self-moving, intelligent agent—which the divine mind of his theology is not—can act for a purpose.[39] Accordingly, I contend, his apparent openness to the view that natural motion in general has purposes in the strict sense is a deliberate accommodation to popular views.

Notes

[1] Jacques Monod, *Chance and Necessity,* trans. Austin Wainhouse (New York: Vintage Books, 1972), 21. The claim made in this passage is significantly qualified on p. 41 (which should be read in connection with p. 104, along with the slightly more tentative remarks on pp. 112-13). The original claim is restored, however, on pp. 176-77. Note also the quotation marks around the word "true" on pp. 21 and 176.

2 *The Philosophical Works of Descartes,* trans. Elizabeth Haldane and G. R. T. Ross, vol. 1 (London: Cambridge University Press, 1972), 173; contrast, however, p. 194.

3 *Principia,* vol. 2, *The System of the World,* Motte's translation revised by Florian Cajori (Berkeley and Los Angeles: University of California Press, 1934), 543-44. Compare p. 546 and pp. 668-70.

4 Albert Einstein and Leopold Infeld, *The Evolution of Physics* (New York: Touchstone Books, 1966), 31.

5 The fact that in the case of *natural* beings the cause from which they come into being does not persist as a constituent of the beings themselves is irrelevant to this discussion of final causality. Cf. pp. 20, 22.

6 See, for instance, *On the Soul* 415a22-b21; *On the Parts of Animals* 641b23-33; *On the Generation of Animals* 730b8-32; *Physics* 199a20-b14.

7 *Physics* 194a21-22, 199a15-17.

8 *On the Parts of Animals* 641b10-12; *On the Heaven* 291b13-14, 271a33; *Politics* 1256b20-22; *Posterior Analytics* 94b36.

9 I will sometimes use the term *intelligent* in a wide enough sense so as not to exclude the intelligence of the irrational animals, since they all appear to be capable of self-motion for the sake of ends which they sense, imagine, or even somehow understand (*Physics* 199a20-23; cf. *On the Motion of Animals* 700b15-701b1). However, Aristotle clearly limits the capacity for choice to rational animals, and so I will speak of intelligent *choice* only in reference to them.

10 See *On the Parts of Animals* 641b10-23; compare Plato, *Philebus* 30a9-c8; *Laws* 885e7-886a4.

11 *Physics* 196a24-b5.

12 *Physics* 198a2-4.

13 *Physics* 196b21-22, 198a3-6; cf. 197a5-6 and 197b18-22.

14 Cf. *Aristotle's* Physics, *Books I and II,* trans. W. Charlton (Oxford: Oxford University Press, Clarendon Press, 1970), 109-10.

15 *Physics* 198a5-12.

16 *Physics* 192a34-b1; cf. 198b1-4 (but contrast 224b5-6).

17 *Physics* 194b26; Compare Charles H. Kahn, "The Place of the Prime Mover in Aristotle's Teleology," in *Aristotle on Nature and Living Things: Philosophical and Historical Studies Presented to David M. Balme,* ed. A. Gotthelf (Pittsburgh: Mathesis Publications, 1985), 182-205. See also Thomas Aquinas, *Summa Theologica* 1, Q.2, A.3; 1-2, Q.40, A.3.

18 *Physics* 192a16-19.

19 See, for instance, *Metaphysics* 1072b13-14; *On the Heaven* 279a22-30.

20 *On the Heaven* 292a14-22, 285a29-30; *On the Motion of Animals* 700b25-32; *Metaphysics* 1072a19-b4, 1073a22-b1.

21 Compare *Metaphysics* 1018b14-37; *Categories* 14a26-b8.

22 Compare Wolfgang Wieland, *Die aristotelische Physik: Untersuchungen über die Grundlegung der Naturwissenschaft und die sprachlichen Bedingungen der Prinzipienforschung bei Aristoteles,* 2nd ed. (Göttingen: Vandenhoeck and Ruprecht, 1970), 259-60.

23 Contrast *Metaphysics* 1051a34-b6 with 1027b18-1028a6. See also *On the Soul* 426a15-26, 430a19-22, 431a1-4; and compare *Physics* 223a16-29. In the light of this need for mind if there is to be being in the fullest sense, one can also interpret the claim that mind would be a prior cause of this whole, even on the hypothesis that it first came to be from chance, as a claim that what is responsible for the completeness of this world is a more important cause than that of its mere beginnings.

24 *Physics* 196b21-22; cf. n. 13.

25 *Physics* 194a28-30ff.

26 *Physics* 194a32-33, 195a23-26, 198b8-9, 198b16-17.

27 *Physics* 197b18-22, 197b35-37; cf. 196b34-197a2.

28 *Physics* 192b8-32, 199b14-17; and contrast 197a1-2.

29 *Metaphysics* 1034b4-7; cf. 1032a25-32; *On the Generation of Animals* 715b25-30, 762a8-763b16; *History of Animals* 539a21-25, 547b18-23.

30 Consider *Posterior Analytics* 95a3-6.

31 Cf. David Furley, "The Rainfall Example in *Physics* ii 8," in *Aristotle on Nature and Living Things: Philosophical and Historical Studies Presented to David M. Balme,* ed. A. Gotthelf (Pittsburgh: Mathesis Publications, 1985), 177-82.

32 *Physics* 198b34-199a3.

[33] John M. Cooper claims that Aristotle's argument is based on the premise of the eternity of our world. See his "Hypothetical Necessity and Natural Teleology," in *Philosophical Issues in Aristotle's Biology,* ed. A. Gotthelf and J. Lennox (Cambridge: Cambridge University Press, 1986), 243-74, esp. 246-53. Compare, however, *Meteorology* 347a5-6, where Aristotle himself says that the seasonal cycle of the rains merely *"wishes* to be perpetual in its order" (emphasis mine).

[34] *Physics* 199a3-5.

[35] Cf. *On the Parts of Animals* 676b16-677a19. This discussion (of the cause of bile) in *On the Parts of Animals* makes it clear that merely to be a necessary consequence of something good is not yet to be for the sake of something, at least not in Aristotle's view. Thus, for instance, the mere fact that death comes of necessity to living beings, and to intelligent living beings in particular, does not mean that it is for the sake of something (such as the existence of those beings).

[36] *Physics* 199b34-200a32. See also 199b5-7.

[37] Cf. *On the Parts of Animals* 646a8-647a3.

[38] See above, pp. 41-42, and also consider n. 23.

[39] See above, pp. 40-41. Cf. Maimonides, *The Guide of the Perplexed,* trans. Shlomo Pines (Chicago: University of Chicago Press, 1963), pt. 2, chap. 20, 313-14.

FURTHER READING

Brennan, Sheilah O'Flynn. "The Meaning of 'Nature' in the Aristotelian Philosophy of Nature." In *The Dignity of Science,* edited by James A. Weisheipl, pp. 247-65. The Thomist Press, 1961.

> Investigates the various meanings of the word "nature" in order to determine how it is used in both Aristotelian and Thomistic natural philosophy and maintains that the meaning of "nature" is "continually modified within the science of nature."

Cook, Kathleen C. "Sexual Inequality in Aristotle's Theories of Reproduction and Inheritance." In *Feminism and Ancient Philosophy,* edited by Julie K. Ward, pp. 51-67. New York: Routledge, 1996.

> Examines Aristotle's biological theories of reproduction and inheritance, articulated in *Generation of Animals,* in order to determine the extent to which Aristotle asserts the inferiority of females, and to which Aristotle influenced later philosophical and scientific thinking on these issues.

Gotthelf, Allan and James G. Lennox, eds. *Philosophical Issues in Aristotle's Biology.* Cambridge: Cambridge University Press, 1987, 462p.

> Collection of essays which examines such topics as the role of biology in Aristotle's philosophy; Aristotle's conception of the "biological universe"; his use of definition, demonstration, and scientific methodology; the issue of teleology and how it applies to Aristotle's conception of nature; and the relationship between Aristotle's metaphysical views and biological theories.

Hardie, W. F. R. "Aristotle's Treatment of the Relation Between the Soul and the Body." *The Philosophical Quarterly* 14, No. 54 (January 1964): 53-72.

> Maintains that Aristotle does not put forth—in his surviving works excluding the dialogue fragments—two mutually inconsistent doctrines regarding the nature of the soul and its relationship to the human body.

Judson, Lindsay, ed. *Aristotle's* Physics: *A Collection of Essays.* Oxford: Clarendon Press, 1991, 286p.

> Collection of essays treating such topics as Aristotle's methodology in the field of natural science; the issue of teleological causation in *Physics;* Aristotle's treatment of time; and his views on "self-motion."

Lang, Helen S, ed. *Aristotle's* Physics *and Its Medieval Varieties.* Albany: State University of New York Press, 1992, 322p.

> Collection of essays dealing with *Physics,* including coverage of Aristotle's definition of nature and his conception of motion, as well as various medieval interpretations of Aristotle's theories.

Machamer, Peter K. "Aristotle on Natural Place and Natural Motion." *ISIS* 69, No. 248 (1979): 377-87.

> Argues that, contrary to what some critics have suggested, Aristotle's conception of "natural place" cannot be viewed as any sort of cause that influences the movement of a body toward its "natural place" or toward its form.

McKirahan, Richard D., Jr. *Principles and Proofs: Aristotle's Theory of Demonstrative Science.* Princeton: Princeton University Press, 1992, 340p.

> Examines Aristotle's theory of demonstration, including the requirements for making such demonstrations, and the use and role of axioms, definitions, and scientific "essences."

Owens, Joseph. "The Aristotelian Conception of the Pure and Applied Sciences." In *Science and Philosophy in Classical Greece,* edited by Alan C. Bowen, pp. 31-42. New York: Garland Publishing, Inc., 1991.

> Reviews Aristotle's division of science into three groups: theoretical, practical, and productive science, and argues that while it may seem as though

Aristotle's theoretical science corresponds to the modern realm of "pure science" and that practical and productive sciences correspond to the modern realm of "applied science," such a correlation must be modified when the issue is examined with greater care.

Poste, Edward. Introduction to *The Logic of Science: A Translation of the Posterior Analytics of Aristotle,* pp. 1-36. Oxford: Francis Macpherson, 1850.

Discusses the content of the *Organon,* the collection of Aristotle's works on logic, and its influence on and interpretation by later thinkers, including Mill and Kant. Reviews the construction of logical arguments as presented by Aristotle.

Preus, Anthony. "Science and Philosophy in Aristotle's *Generation of Animals.*" *Journal of the History of Biology* 3, No. 1 (Spring 1970): 1-52.

Analyzes the relationship of Aristotle's metaphysical views to his biological theories as presented in *Generation of Animals.*

Van Fraasen, Bas C. "A Re-Examination of Aristotle's Philosophy of Science." *Dialogue* XIX, No. 1 (March 1980): 20-45.

Studies Aristotle's account of science in order to determine what "philosophically controversial theses" would be implicit with the acceptance of Aristotelian science.

Additional coverage of Aristotle's life and career is contained in the following source published by Gale Re-search: *Dictionary of Literary Biography, Vol. 176: Ancient Greek Authors.*

CLASSICAL
AND MEDIEVAL
LITERATURE
CRITICISM

INDEXES

Literary Criticism Series
Cumulative Author Index

Literary Criticism Series
Cumulative Topic Index

CMLC Cumulative Nationality Index

CMLC Cumulative Title Index

CMLC Cumulative Critic Index

How to Use This Index

Calvino, Italo
1923–1985 .... CLC 5, 8, 11, 22, 33, 39,
73; SSC 3

list all author entries in the following Gale Literary Criticism series:

BLC = *Black Literature Criticism*
CLC = *Contemporary Literary Criticism*
CLR = *Children's Literature Review*
CMLC = *Classical and Medieval Literature Criticism*
DA = *DISCovering Authors*
DAB = *DISCovering Authors: British*
DAC = *DISCovering Authors: Canadian*
DAM = *DISCovering Authors: Modules*
    DRAM: *Dramatists Module*; *MST*: *Most-Studied Authors Module*;
    MULT: *Multicultural Authors Module*; *NOV*: *Novelists Module*;
    POET: *Poets Module*; *POP*: *Popular Fiction and Genre Authors Module*
DC = *Drama Criticism*
HLC = *Hispanic Literature Criticism*
LC = *Literature Criticism from 1400 to 1800*
NCLC = *Nineteenth-Century Literature Criticism*
PC = *Poetry Criticism*
SSC = *Short Story Criticism*
TCLC = *Twentieth-Century Literary Criticism*
WLC = *World Literature Criticism, 1500 to the Present*

The cross-references

See also CANR 23; CA 85-88;
   obituary CA116

list all author entries in the following Gale biographical and literary sources:

AAYA = *Authors & Artists for Young Adults*
AITN = *Authors in the News*
BEST = *Bestsellers*
BW = *Black Writers*
CA = *Contemporary Authors*
CAAS = *Contemporary Authors Autobiography Series*
CABS = *Contemporary Authors Bibliographical Series*
CANR = *Contemporary Authors New Revision Series*
CAP = *Contemporary Authors Permanent Series*
CDALB = *Concise Dictionary of American Literary Biography*
CDBLB = *Concise Dictionary of British Literary Biography*
DLB = *Dictionary of Literary Biography*
DLBD = *Dictionary of Literary Biography Documentary Series*
DLBY = *Dictionary of Literary Biography Yearbook*
HW = *Hispanic Writers*
JRDA = *Junior DISCovering Authors*
MAICYA = *Major Authors and Illustrators for Children and Young Adults*
MTCW = *Major 20th-Century Writers*
NNAL = *Native North American Literature*
SAAS = *Something about the Author Autobiography Series*
SATA = *Something about the Author*
YABC = *Yesterday's Authors of Books for Children*

See Blish, James (Benjamin)

Atherton, Gertrude (Franklin Horn) 1857-1948 **TCLC 2**
See also CA 104; 155; DLB 9, 78, 186

Atherton, Lucius
See Masters, Edgar Lee

Atkins, Jack
See Harris, Mark

Atkinson, Kate **CLC 99**
See also CA 166

Attaway, William (Alexander) 1911-1986 **CLC 92; BLC 1; DAM MULT**
See also BW 2; CA 143; DLB 76

Atticus
See Fleming, Ian (Lancaster); Wilson, (Thomas) Woodrow

Atwood, Margaret (Eleanor) 1939- **CLC 2, 3, 4, 8, 13, 15, 25, 44, 84; DA; DAB; DAC; DAM MST, NOV, POET; PC 8; SSC 2; WLC**
See also AAYA 12; BEST 89:2; CA 49-52; CANR 3, 24, 33, 59; DLB 53; INT CANR-24; MTCW 1; SATA 50

Aubigny, Pierre d'
See Mencken, H(enry) L(ouis)

Aubin, Penelope 1685-1731(?) **LC 9**
See also DLB 39

Auchincloss, Louis (Stanton) 1917- **CLC 4, 6, 9, 18, 45; DAM NOV; SSC 22**
See also CA 1-4R; CANR 6, 29, 55; DLB 2; DLBY 80; INT CANR-29; MTCW 1

Auden, W(ystan) H(ugh) 1907-1973 **CLC 1, 2, 3, 4, 6, 9, 11, 14, 43; DA; DAB; DAC; DAM DRAM, MST, POET; PC 1; WLC**
See also AAYA 18; CA 9-12R; 45-48; CANR 5, 61; CDBLB 1914-1945; DLB 10, 20; MTCW 1

Audiberti, Jacques 1900-1965 **CLC 38; DAM DRAM**
See also CA 25-28R

Audubon, John James 1785-1851 **NCLC 47**

Auel, Jean M(arie) 1936- **CLC 31, 107; DAM POP**
See also AAYA 7; BEST 90:4; CA 103; CANR 21, 64; INT CANR-21; SATA 91

Auerbach, Erich 1892-1957 **TCLC 43**
See also CA 118; 155

Augier, Emile 1820-1889 **NCLC 31**
See also DLB 192

August, John
See De Voto, Bernard (Augustine)

Augustine, St. 354-430 **CMLC 6; DAB**

Aurelius
See Bourne, Randolph S(illiman)

Aurobindo, Sri
See Ghose, Aurabinda

Austen, Jane 1775-1817 **NCLC 1, 13, 19, 33, 51; DA; DAB; DAC; DAM MST, NOV; WLC**
See also AAYA 19; CDBLB 1789-1832; DLB 116

Auster, Paul 1947- **CLC 47**
See also CA 69-72; CANR 23, 52

Austin, Frank
See Faust, Frederick (Schiller)

Austin, Mary (Hunter) 1868-1934 **TCLC 25**
See also CA 109; DLB 9, 78

Autran Dourado, Waldomiro
See Dourado, (Waldomiro Freitas) Autran

Averroes 1126-1198 **CMLC 7**
See also DLB 115

Avicenna 980-1037 **CMLC 16**
See also DLB 115

Avison, Margaret 1918- **CLC 2, 4, 97; DAC; DAM POET**
See also CA 17-20R; DLB 53; MTCW 1

Axton, David
See Koontz, Dean R(ay)

Ayckbourn, Alan 1939- **CLC 5, 8, 18, 33, 74; DAB; DAM DRAM**
See also CA 21-24R; CANR 31, 59; DLB 13; MTCW 1

Aydy, Catherine
See Tennant, Emma (Christina)

Ayme, Marcel (Andre) 1902-1967 **CLC 11**
See also CA 89-92; CANR 67; CLR 25; DLB 72; SATA 91

Ayrton, Michael 1921-1975 **CLC 7**
See also CA 5-8R; 61-64; CANR 9, 21

Azorin **CLC 11**
See also Martinez Ruiz, Jose

Azuela, Mariano 1873-1952 **TCLC 3; DAM MULT; HLC**
See also CA 104; 131; HW; MTCW 1

Baastad, Babbis Friis
See Friis-Baastad, Babbis Ellinor

Bab
See Gilbert, W(illiam) S(chwenck)

Babbis, Eleanor
See Friis-Baastad, Babbis Ellinor

Babel, Isaac
See Babel, Isaak (Emmanuilovich)

Babel, Isaak (Emmanuilovich) 1894-1941(?) **TCLC 2, 13; SSC 16**
See also CA 104; 155

Babits, Mihaly 1883-1941 **TCLC 14**
See also CA 114

Babur 1483-1530 **LC 18**

Bacchelli, Riccardo 1891-1985 **CLC 19**
See also CA 29-32R; 117

Bach, Richard (David) 1936- **CLC 14; DAM NOV, POP**
See also AITN 1; BEST 89:2; CA 9-12R; CANR 18; MTCW 1; SATA 13

Bachman, Richard
See King, Stephen (Edwin)

Bachmann, Ingeborg 1926-1973 **CLC 69**
See also CA 93-96; 45-48; CANR 69; DLB 85

Bacon, Francis 1561-1626 **LC 18, 32**
See also CDBLB Before 1660; DLB 151

Bacon, Roger 1214(?)-1292 **CMLC 14**
See also DLB 115

Bacovia, George **TCLC 24**
See also Vasiliu, Gheorghe

Badanes, Jerome 1937- **CLC 59**

Bagehot, Walter 1826-1877 **NCLC 10**
See also DLB 55

Bagnold, Enid 1889-1981 **CLC 25; DAM DRAM**
See also CA 5-8R; 103; CANR 5, 40; DLB 13, 160, 191; MAICYA; SATA 1, 25

Bagritsky, Eduard 1895-1934 **TCLC 60**

Bagrjana, Elisaveta
See Belcheva, Elisaveta

Bagryana, Elisaveta **CLC 10**
See also Belcheva, Elisaveta
See also DLB 147

Bailey, Paul 1937- **CLC 45**
See also CA 21-24R; CANR 16, 62; DLB 14

Baillie, Joanna 1762-1851 **NCLC 71**
See also DLB 93

Bainbridge, Beryl (Margaret) 1933- **CLC 4, 5, 8, 10, 14, 18, 22, 62; DAM NOV**
See also CA 21-24R; CANR 24, 55; DLB 14; MTCW 1

Baker, Elliott 1922- **CLC 8**

See also CA 45-48; CANR 2, 63

Baker, Jean H. **TCLC 3, 10**
See also Russell, George William

Baker, Nicholson 1957- **CLC 61; DAM POP**
See also CA 135; CANR 63

Baker, Ray Stannard 1870-1946 **TCLC 47**
See also CA 118

Baker, Russell (Wayne) 1925- **CLC 31**
See also BEST 89:4; CA 57-60; CANR 11, 41, 59; MTCW 1

Bakhtin, M.
See Bakhtin, Mikhail Mikhailovich

Bakhtin, M. M.
See Bakhtin, Mikhail Mikhailovich

Bakhtin, Mikhail
See Bakhtin, Mikhail Mikhailovich

Bakhtin, Mikhail Mikhailovich 1895-1975 **CLC 83**
See also CA 128; 113

Bakshi, Ralph 1938(?)- **CLC 26**
See also CA 112; 138

Bakunin, Mikhail (Alexandrovich) 1814-1876 **NCLC 25, 58**

Baldwin, James (Arthur) 1924-1987 **CLC 1, 2, 3, 4, 5, 8, 13, 15, 17, 42, 50, 67, 90; BLC 1; DA; DAB; DAC; DAM MST, MULT, NOV, POP; DC 1; SSC 10; WLC**
See also AAYA 4; BW 1; CA 1-4R; 124; CABS 1; CANR 3, 24; CDALB 1941-1968; DLB 2, 7, 33; DLBY 87; MTCW 1; SATA 9; SATA-Obit 54

Ballard, J(ames) G(raham) 1930- **CLC 3, 6, 14, 36; DAM NOV, POP; SSC 1**
See also AAYA 3; CA 5-8R; CANR 15, 39, 65; DLB 14; MTCW 1; SATA 93

Balmont, Konstantin (Dmitriyevich) 1867-1943 **TCLC 11**
See also CA 109; 155

Balzac, Honore de 1799-1850 **NCLC 5, 35, 53; DA; DAB; DAC; DAM MST, NOV; SSC 5; WLC**
See also DLB 119

Bambara, Toni Cade 1939-1995 **CLC 19, 88; BLC 1; DA; DAC; DAM MST, MULT; WLCS**
See also AAYA 5; BW 2; CA 29-32R; 150; CANR 24, 49; DLB 38; MTCW 1

Bamdad, A.
See Shamlu, Ahmad

Banat, D. R.
See Bradbury, Ray (Douglas)

Bancroft, Laura
See Baum, L(yman) Frank

Banim, John 1798-1842 **NCLC 13**
See also DLB 116, 158, 159

Banim, Michael 1796-1874 **NCLC 13**
See also DLB 158, 159

Banjo, The
See Paterson, A(ndrew) B(arton)

Banks, Iain
See Banks, Iain M(enzies)

Banks, Iain M(enzies) 1954- **CLC 34**
See also CA 123; 128; CANR 61; DLB 194; INT 128

Banks, Lynne Reid **CLC 23**
See also Reid Banks, Lynne
See also AAYA 6

Banks, Russell 1940- **CLC 37, 72**
See also CA 65-68; CAAS 15; CANR 19, 52, 73; DLB 130

Banville, John 1945- **CLC 46**
See also CA 117; 128; DLB 14; INT 128

Banville, Theodore (Faullain) de 1832-1891

NCLC 9

Baraka, Amiri 1934-**CLC 1, 2, 3, 5, 10, 14, 33, 115; BLC 1; DA; DAC; DAM MST, MULT, POET, POP; DC 6; PC 4; WLCS**
See also Jones, LeRoi
See also BW 2; CA 21-24R; CABS 3; CANR 27, 38, 61; CDALB 1941-1968; DLB 5, 7, 16, 38; DLBD 8; MTCW 1

Barbauld, Anna Laetitia 1743-1825**NCLC 50**
See also DLB 107, 109, 142, 158

Barbellion, W. N. P.   **TCLC 24**
See also Cummings, Bruce F(rederick)

Barbera, Jack (Vincent) 1945-   **CLC 44**
See also CA 110; CANR 45

Barbey d'Aurevilly, Jules Amedee 1808-1889
NCLC 1; SSC 17
See also DLB 119

Barbusse, Henri 1873-1935   **TCLC 5**
See also CA 105; 154; DLB 65

Barclay, Bill
See Moorcock, Michael (John)

Barclay, William Ewert
See Moorcock, Michael (John)

Barea, Arturo 1897-1957   **TCLC 14**
See also CA 111

Barfoot, Joan 1946-   **CLC 18**
See also CA 105

Baring, Maurice 1874-1945   **TCLC 8**
See also CA 105; 168; DLB 34

Baring-Gould, Sabine 1834-1924   **TCLC 88**
See also DLB 156, 190

Barker, Clive 1952-   **CLC 52; DAM POP**
See also AAYA 10; BEST 90:3; CA 121; 129; CANR 71; INT 129; MTCW 1

Barker, George Granville 1913-1991 **CLC 8, 48; DAM POET**
See also CA 9-12R; 135; CANR 7, 38; DLB 20; MTCW 1

Barker, Harley Granville
See Granville-Barker, Harley
See also DLB 10

Barker, Howard 1946-   **CLC 37**
See also CA 102; DLB 13

Barker, Jane 1652-1732   **LC 42**

Barker, Pat(ricia) 1943-   **CLC 32, 94**
See also CA 117; 122; CANR 50; INT 122

Barlach, Ernst 1870-1938   **TCLC 84**
See also DLB 56, 118

Barlow, Joel 1754-1812   **NCLC 23**
See also DLB 37

Barnard, Mary (Ethel) 1909-   **CLC 48**
See also CA 21-22; CAP 2

Barnes, Djuna 1892-1982**CLC 3, 4, 8, 11, 29; SSC 3**
See also CA 9-12R; 107; CANR 16, 55; DLB 4, 9, 45; MTCW 1

Barnes, Julian (Patrick) 1946- **CLC 42; DAB**
See also CA 102; CANR 19, 54; DLB 194; DLBY 93

Barnes, Peter 1931-   **CLC 5, 56**
See also CA 65-68; CAAS 12; CANR 33, 34, 64; DLB 13; MTCW 1

Baroja (y Nessi), Pio 1872-1956**TCLC 8; HLC**
See also CA 104

Baron, David
See Pinter, Harold

Baron Corvo
See Rolfe, Frederick (William Serafino Austin Lewis Mary)

Barondess, Sue K(aufman) 1926-1977 **CLC 8**
See also Kaufman, Sue
See also CA 1-4R; 69-72; CANR 1

Baron de Teive

See Pessoa, Fernando (Antonio Nogueira)
Baroness Von S.
See Zangwill, Israel

Barres, (Auguste-) Maurice 1862-1923**TCLC 47**
See also CA 164; DLB 123

Barreto, Afonso Henrique de Lima
See Lima Barreto, Afonso Henrique de

Barrett, (Roger) Syd 1946-   **CLC 35**

Barrett, William (Christopher) 1913-1992
CLC 27
See also CA 13-16R; 139; CANR 11, 67; INT CANR-11

Barrie, J(ames) M(atthew) 1860-1937 **TCLC 2; DAB; DAM DRAM**
See also CA 104; 136; CDBLB 1890-1914; CLR 16; DLB 10, 141, 156; MAICYA; SATA 100; YABC 1

Barrington, Michael
See Moorcock, Michael (John)

Barrol, Grady
See Bograd, Larry

Barry, Mike
See Malzberg, Barry N(athaniel)

Barry, Philip 1896-1949   **TCLC 11**
See also CA 109; DLB 7

Bart, Andre Schwarz
See Schwarz-Bart, Andre

Barth, John (Simmons) 1930-**CLC 1, 2, 3, 5, 7, 9, 10, 14, 27, 51, 89; DAM NOV; SSC 10**
See also AITN 1, 2; CA 1-4R; CABS 1; CANR 5, 23, 49, 64; DLB 2; MTCW 1

Barthelme, Donald 1931-1989**CLC 1, 2, 3, 5, 6, 8, 13, 23, 46, 59, 115; DAM NOV; SSC 2**
See also CA 21-24R; 129; CANR 20, 58; DLB 2; DLBY 80, 89; MTCW 1; SATA 7; SATA-Obit 62

Barthelme, Frederick 1943-   **CLC 36, 117**
See also CA 114; 122; DLBY 85; INT 122

Barthes, Roland (Gerard) 1915-1980**CLC 24, 83**
See also CA 130; 97-100; CANR 66; MTCW 1

Barzun, Jacques (Martin) 1907-   **CLC 51**
See also CA 61-64; CANR 22

Bashevis, Isaac
See Singer, Isaac Bashevis

Bashkirtseff, Marie 1859-1884   **NCLC 27**
Basho
See Matsuo Basho

Bass, Kingsley B., Jr.
See Bullins, Ed

Bass, Rick 1958-   **CLC 79**
See also CA 126; CANR 53

Bassani, Giorgio 1916-   **CLC 9**
See also CA 65-68; CANR 33; DLB 128, 177; MTCW 1

Bastos, Augusto (Antonio) Roa
See Roa Bastos, Augusto (Antonio)

Bataille, Georges 1897-1962   **CLC 29**
See also CA 101; 89-92

Bates, H(erbert) E(rnest) 1905-1974**CLC 46; DAB; DAM POP; SSC 10**
See also CA 93-96; 45-48; CANR 34; DLB 162, 191; MTCW 1

Bauchart
See Camus, Albert

Baudelaire, Charles 1821-1867 **NCLC 6, 29, 55; DA; DAB; DAC; DAM MST, POET; PC 1; SSC 18; WLC**

Baudrillard, Jean 1929-   **CLC 60**

Baum, L(yman) Frank 1856-1919   **TCLC 7**
See also CA 108; 133; CLR 15; DLB 22; JRDA; MAICYA; MTCW 1; SATA 18, 100

Baum, Louis F.
See Baum, L(yman) Frank

Baumbach, Jonathan 1933-   **CLC 6, 23**
See also CA 13-16R; CAAS 5; CANR 12, 66; DLBY 80; INT CANR-12; MTCW 1

Bausch, Richard (Carl) 1945-   **CLC 51**
See also CA 101; CAAS 14; CANR 43, 61; DLB 130

Baxter, Charles (Morley) 1947- **CLC 45, 78; DAM POP**
See also CA 57-60; CANR 40, 64; DLB 130

Baxter, George Owen
See Faust, Frederick (Schiller)

Baxter, James K(eir) 1926-1972   **CLC 14**
See also CA 77-80

Baxter, John
See Hunt, E(verette) Howard, (Jr.)

Bayer, Sylvia
See Glassco, John

Baynton, Barbara 1857-1929   **TCLC 57**

Beagle, Peter S(oyer) 1939-   **CLC 7, 104**
See also CA 9-12R; CANR 4, 51, 73; DLBY 80; INT CANR-4; SATA 60

Bean, Normal
See Burroughs, Edgar Rice

Beard, Charles A(ustin) 1874-1948 **TCLC 15**
See also CA 115; DLB 17; SATA 18

Beardsley, Aubrey 1872-1898   **NCLC 6**

Beattie, Ann 1947-**CLC 8, 13, 18, 40, 63; DAM NOV, POP; SSC 11**
See also BEST 90:2; CA 81-84; CANR 53, 73; DLBY 82; MTCW 1

Beattie, James 1735-1803   **NCLC 25**
See also DLB 109

Beauchamp, Kathleen Mansfield 1888-1923
See Mansfield, Katherine
See also CA 104; 134; DA; DAC; DAM MST

Beaumarchais, Pierre-Augustin Caron de 1732-1799   **DC 4**
See also DAM DRAM

Beaumont, Francis 1584(?)-1616**LC 33; DC 6**
See also CDBLB Before 1660; DLB 58, 121

Beauvoir, Simone (Lucie Ernestine Marie Bertrand) de 1908-1986**CLC 1, 2, 4, 8, 14, 31, 44, 50, 71; DA; DAB; DAC; DAM MST, NOV; WLC**
See also CA 9-12R; 118; CANR 28, 61; DLB 72; DLBY 86; MTCW 1

Becker, Carl (Lotus) 1873-1945   **TCLC 63**
See also CA 157; DLB 17

Becker, Jurek 1937-1997   **CLC 7, 19**
See also CA 85-88; 157; CANR 60; DLB 75

Becker, Walter 1950-   **CLC 26**

Beckett, Samuel (Barclay) 1906-1989 **CLC 1, 2, 3, 4, 6, 9, 10, 11, 14, 18, 29, 57, 59, 83; DA; DAB; DAC; DAM DRAM, MST, NOV; SSC 16; WLC**
See also CA 5-8R; 130; CANR 33, 61; CDBLB 1945-1960; DLB 13, 15; DLBY 90; MTCW 1

Beckford, William 1760-1844   **NCLC 16**
See also DLB 39

Beckman, Gunnel 1910-   **CLC 26**
See also CA 33-36R; CANR 15; CLR 25; MAICYA; SAAS 9; SATA 6

Becque, Henri 1837-1899   **NCLC 3**
See also DLB 192

Beddoes, Thomas Lovell 1803-1849 **NCLC 3**
See also DLB 96

Bede c. 673-735   **CMLC 20**
See also DLB 146

Bedford, Donald F.
See Fearing, Kenneth (Flexner)

Beecher, Catharine Esther 1800-1878 **N C L C 30**
See also DLB 1

Beecher, John 1904-1980 **CLC 6**
See also AITN 1; CA 5-8R; 105; CANR 8

Beer, Johann 1655-1700 **LC 5**
See also DLB 168

Beer, Patricia 1924- **CLC 58**
See also CA 61-64; CANR 13, 46; DLB 40

Beerbohm, Max
See Beerbohm, (Henry) Max(imilian)

Beerbohm, (Henry) Max(imilian) 1872-1956 **TCLC 1, 24**
See also CA 104; 154; DLB 34, 100

Beer-Hofmann, Richard 1866-1945 **TCLC 60**
See also CA 160; DLB 81

Begiebing, Robert J(ohn) 1946- **CLC 70**
See also CA 122; CANR 40

Behan, Brendan 1923-1964 **CLC 1, 8, 11, 15, 79; DAM DRAM**
See also CA 73-76; CANR 33; CDBLB 1945-1960; DLB 13; MTCW 1

Behn, Aphra 1640(?)-1689 **LC 1, 30, 42; DA; DAB; DAC; DAM DRAM, MST, NOV, POET; DC 4; PC 13; WLC**
See also DLB 39, 80, 131

Behrman, S(amuel) N(athaniel) 1893-1973 **CLC 40**
See also CA 13-16; 45-48; CAP 1; DLB 7, 44

Belasco, David 1853-1931 **TCLC 3**
See also CA 104; 168; DLB 7

Belcheva, Elisaveta 1893- **CLC 10**
See also Bagryana, Elisaveta

Beldone, Phil "Cheech"
See Ellison, Harlan (Jay)

Beleno
See Azuela, Mariano

Belinski, Vissarion Grigoryevich 1811-1848 **NCLC 5**
See also DLB 198

Belitt, Ben 1911- **CLC 22**
See also CA 13-16R; CAAS 4; CANR 7; DLB 5

Bell, Gertrude (Margaret Lowthian) 1868-1926 **TCLC 67**
See also CA 167; DLB 174

Bell, J. Freeman
See Zangwill, Israel

Bell, James Madison 1826-1902 **TCLC 43; BLC 1; DAM MULT**
See also BW 1; CA 122; 124; DLB 50

Bell, Madison Smartt 1957- **CLC 41, 102**
See also CA 111; CANR 28, 54, 73

Bell, Marvin (Hartley) 1937- **CLC 8, 31; DAM POET**
See also CA 21-24R; CAAS 14; CANR 59; DLB 5; MTCW 1

Bell, W. L. D.
See Mencken, H(enry) L(ouis)

Bellamy, Atwood C.
See Mencken, H(enry) L(ouis)

Bellamy, Edward 1850-1898 **NCLC 4**
See also DLB 12

Bellin, Edward J.
See Kuttner, Henry

Belloc, (Joseph) Hilaire (Pierre Sebastien Rene Swanton) 1870-1953 **TCLC 7, 18; DAM POET; PC 24**
See also CA 106; 152; DLB 19, 100, 141, 174; YABC 1

Belloc, Joseph Peter Rene Hilaire
See Belloc, (Joseph) Hilaire (Pierre Sebastien Rene Swanton)

Belloc, Joseph Pierre Hilaire
See Belloc, (Joseph) Hilaire (Pierre Sebastien Rene Swanton)

Belloc, M. A.
See Lowndes, Marie Adelaide (Belloc)

Bellow, Saul 1915- **CLC 1, 2, 3, 6, 8, 10, 13, 15, 25, 33, 34, 63, 79; DA; DAB; DAC; DAM MST, NOV, POP; SSC 14; WLC**
See also AITN 2; BEST 89:3; CA 5-8R; CABS 1; CANR 29, 53; CDALB 1941-1968; DLB 2, 28; DLBD 3; DLBY 82; MTCW 1

Belser, Reimond Karel Maria de 1929-
See Ruyslinck, Ward
See also CA 152

Bely, Andrey **TCLC 7; PC 11**
See also Bugayev, Boris Nikolayevich

Belyi, Andrei
See Bugayev, Boris Nikolayevich

Benary, Margot
See Benary-Isbert, Margot

Benary-Isbert, Margot 1889-1979 **CLC 12**
See also CA 5-8R; 89-92; CANR 4, 72; CLR 12; MAICYA; SATA 2; SATA-Obit 21

Benavente (y Martinez), Jacinto 1866-1954 **TCLC 3; DAM DRAM, MULT**
See also CA 106; 131; HW; MTCW 1

Benchley, Peter (Bradford) 1940- **CLC 4, 8; DAM NOV, POP**
See also AAYA 14; AITN 2; CA 17-20R; CANR 12, 35, 66; MTCW 1; SATA 3, 89

Benchley, Robert (Charles) 1889-1945 **TCLC 1, 55**
See also CA 105; 153; DLB 11

Benda, Julien 1867-1956 **TCLC 60**
See also CA 120; 154

Benedict, Ruth (Fulton) 1887-1948 **TCLC 60**
See also CA 158

Benedict, Saint c. 480-c. 547 **CMLC 29**

Benedikt, Michael 1935- **CLC 4, 14**
See also CA 13-16R; CANR 7; DLB 5

Benet, Juan 1927- **CLC 28**
See also CA 143

Benet, Stephen Vincent 1898-1943 **TCLC 7; DAM POET; SSC 10**
See also CA 104; 152; DLB 4, 48, 102; DLBY 97; YABC 1

Benet, William Rose 1886-1950 **TCLC 28; DAM POET**
See also CA 118; 152; DLB 45

Benford, Gregory (Albert) 1941- **CLC 52**
See also CA 69-72; CAAS 27; CANR 12, 24, 49; DLBY 82

Bengtsson, Frans (Gunnar) 1894-1954 **TCLC 48**
See also CA 170

Benjamin, David
See Slavitt, David R(ytman)

Benjamin, Lois
See Gould, Lois

Benjamin, Walter 1892-1940 **TCLC 39**
See also CA 164

Benn, Gottfried 1886-1956 **TCLC 3**
See also CA 106; 153; DLB 56

Bennett, Alan 1934- **CLC 45, 77; DAB; DAM MST**
See also CA 103; CANR 35, 55; MTCW 1

Bennett, (Enoch) Arnold 1867-1931 **TCLC 5, 20**
See also CA 106; 155; CDBLB 1890-1914; DLB 10, 34, 98, 135

Bennett, Elizabeth
See Mitchell, Margaret (Munnerlyn)

Bennett, George Harold 1930-
See Bennett, Hal
See also BW 1; CA 97-100

Bennett, Hal **CLC 5**
See also Bennett, George Harold
See also DLB 33

Bennett, Jay 1912- **CLC 35**
See also AAYA 10; CA 69-72; CANR 11, 42; JRDA; SAAS 4; SATA 41, 87; SATA-Brief 27

Bennett, Louise (Simone) 1919- **CLC 28; BLC 1; DAM MULT**
See also BW 2; CA 151; DLB 117

Benson, E(dward) F(rederic) 1867-1940 **TCLC 27**
See also CA 114; 157; DLB 135, 153

Benson, Jackson J. 1930- **CLC 34**
See also CA 25-28R; DLB 111

Benson, Sally 1900-1972 **CLC 17**
See also CA 19-20; 37-40R; CAP 1; SATA 1, 35; SATA-Obit 27

Benson, Stella 1892-1933 **TCLC 17**
See also CA 117; 155; DLB 36, 162

Bentham, Jeremy 1748-1832 **NCLC 38**
See also DLB 107, 158

Bentley, E(dmund) C(lerihew) 1875-1956 **TCLC 12**
See also CA 108; DLB 70

Bentley, Eric (Russell) 1916- **CLC 24**
See also CA 5-8R; CANR 6, 67; INT CANR-6

Beranger, Pierre Jean de 1780-1857 **NCLC 34**

Berdyaev, Nicolas
See Berdyaev, Nikolai (Aleksandrovich)

Berdyaev, Nikolai (Aleksandrovich) 1874-1948 **TCLC 67**
See also CA 120; 157

Berdyayev, Nikolai (Aleksandrovich)
See Berdyaev, Nikolai (Aleksandrovich)

Berendt, John (Lawrence) 1939- **CLC 86**
See also CA 146

Beresford, J(ohn) D(avys) 1873-1947 **TCLC 81**
See also CA 112; 155; DLB 162, 178, 197

Bergelson, David 1884-1952 **TCLC 81**

Berger, Colonel
See Malraux, (Georges-)Andre

Berger, John (Peter) 1926- **CLC 2, 19**
See also CA 81-84; CANR 51; DLB 14

Berger, Melvin H. 1927- **CLC 12**
See also CA 5-8R; CANR 4; CLR 32; SAAS 2; SATA 5, 88

Berger, Thomas (Louis) 1924- **CLC 3, 5, 8, 11, 18, 38; DAM NOV**
See also CA 1-4R; CANR 5, 28, 51; DLB 2; DLBY 80; INT CANR-28; MTCW 1

Bergman, (Ernst) Ingmar 1918- **CLC 16, 72**
See also CA 81-84; CANR 33, 70

Bergson, Henri(-Louis) 1859-1941 **TCLC 32**
See also CA 164

Bergstein, Eleanor 1938- **CLC 4**
See also CA 53-56; CANR 5

Berkoff, Steven 1937- **CLC 56**
See also CA 104; CANR 72

Bermant, Chaim (Icyk) 1929- **CLC 40**
See also CA 57-60; CANR 6, 31, 57

Bern, Victoria
See Fisher, M(ary) F(rances) K(ennedy)

Bernanos, (Paul Louis) Georges 1888-1948 **TCLC 3**
See also CA 104; 130; DLB 72

Bernard, April 1956- **CLC 59**
See also CA 131

Berne, Victoria
See Fisher, M(ary) F(rances) K(ennedy)

Bly, Robert (Elwood) 1926-CLC 1, 2, 5, 10, 15, 38; DAM POET
See also CA 5-8R; CANR 41, 73; DLB 5; MTCW 1

Boas, Franz 1858-1942   TCLC 56
See also CA 115

Bobette
See Simenon, Georges (Jacques Christian)

Boccaccio, Giovanni 1313-1375   CMLC 13; SSC 10

Bochco, Steven 1943-   CLC 35
See also AAYA 11; CA 124; 138

Bodel, Jean 1167(?)-1210   CMLC 28

Bodenheim, Maxwell 1892-1954   TCLC 44
See also CA 110; DLB 9, 45

Bodker, Cecil 1927-   CLC 21
See also CA 73-76; CANR 13, 44; CLR 23; MAICYA; SATA 14

Boell, Heinrich (Theodor) 1917-1985 CLC 2, 3, 6, 9, 11, 15, 27, 32, 72; DA; DAB; DAC; DAM MST, NOV; SSC 23; WLC
See also CA 21-24R; 116; CANR 24; DLB 69; DLBY 85; MTCW 1

Boerne, Alfred
See Doeblin, Alfred

Boethius 480(?)-524(?)   CMLC 15
See also DLB 115

Bogan, Louise 1897-1970 CLC 4, 39, 46, 93; DAM POET; PC 12
See also CA 73-76; 25-28R; CANR 33; DLB 45, 169; MTCW 1

Bogarde, Dirk   CLC 19
See also Van Den Bogarde, Derek Jules Gaspard Ulric Niven
See also DLB 14

Bogosian, Eric 1953-   CLC 45
See also CA 138

Bograd, Larry 1953-   CLC 35
See also CA 93-96; CANR 57; SAAS 21; SATA 33, 89

Boiardo, Matteo Maria 1441-1494   LC 6

Boileau-Despreaux, Nicolas 1636-1711 LC 3

Bojer, Johan 1872-1959   TCLC 64

Boland, Eavan (Aisling) 1944-   CLC 40, 67, 113; DAM POET
See also CA 143; CANR 61; DLB 40

Boll, Heinrich
See Boell, Heinrich (Theodor)

Bolt, Lee
See Faust, Frederick (Schiller)

Bolt, Robert (Oxton) 1924-1995CLC 14; DAM DRAM
See also CA 17-20R; 147; CANR 35, 67; DLB 13; MTCW 1

Bombet, Louis-Alexandre-Cesar
See Stendhal

Bomkauf
See Kaufman, Bob (Garnell)

Bonaventura   NCLC 35
See also DLB 90

Bond, Edward 1934- CLC 4, 6, 13, 23; DAM DRAM
See also CA 25-28R; CANR 38, 67; DLB 13; MTCW 1

Bonham, Frank 1914-1989   CLC 12
See also AAYA 1; CA 9-12R; CANR 4, 36; JRDA; MAICYA; SAAS 3; SATA 1, 49; SATA-Obit 62

Bonnefoy, Yves 1923-   CLC 9, 15, 58; DAM MST, POET
See also CA 85-88; CANR 33; MTCW 1

Bontemps, Arna(ud Wendell) 1902-1973C L C 1, 18; BLC 1; DAM MULT, NOV, POET

See also BW 1; CA 1-4R; 41-44R; CANR 4, 35; CLR 6; DLB 48, 51; JRDA; MAICYA; MTCW 1; SATA 2, 44; SATA-Obit 24

Booth, Martin 1944-   CLC 13
See also CA 93-96; CAAS 2

Booth, Philip 1925-   CLC 23
See also CA 5-8R; CANR 5; DLBY 82

Booth, Wayne C(layson) 1921-   CLC 24
See also CA 1-4R; CAAS 5; CANR 3, 43; DLB 67

Borchert, Wolfgang 1921-1947   TCLC 5
See also CA 104; DLB 69, 124

Borel, Petrus 1809-1859   NCLC 41

Borges, Jorge Luis 1899-1986CLC 1, 2, 3, 4, 6, 8, 9, 10, 13, 19, 44, 48, 83; DA; DAB; DAC; DAM MST, MULT; HLC; PC 22; SSC 4; WLC
See also AAYA 26; CA 21-24R; CANR 19, 33; DLB 113; DLBY 86; HW; MTCW 1

Borowski, Tadeusz 1922-1951   TCLC 9
See also CA 106; 154

Borrow, George (Henry) 1803-1881 NCLC 9
See also DLB 21, 55, 166

Bosman, Herman Charles 1905-1951 T C L C 49
See also Malan, Herman
See also CA 160

Bosschere, Jean de 1878(?)-1953   TCLC 19
See also CA 115

Boswell, James 1740-1795 LC 4; DA; DAB; DAC; DAM MST; WLC
See also CDBLB 1660-1789; DLB 104, 142

Bottoms, David 1949-   CLC 53
See also CA 105; CANR 22; DLB 120; DLBY 83

Boucicault, Dion 1820-1890   NCLC 41

Boucolon, Maryse 1937(?)-
See Conde, Maryse
See also CA 110; CANR 30, 53

Bourget, Paul (Charles Joseph) 1852-1935 TCLC 12
See also CA 107; DLB 123

Bourjaily, Vance (Nye) 1922-   CLC 8, 62
See also CA 1-4R; CAAS 1; CANR 2, 72; DLB 2, 143

Bourne, Randolph S(illiman) 1886-1918 TCLC 16
See also CA 117; 155; DLB 63

Bova, Ben(jamin William) 1932-   CLC 45
See also AAYA 16; CA 5-8R; CAAS 18; CANR 11, 56; CLR 3; DLBY 81; INT CANR-11; MAICYA; MTCW 1; SATA 6, 68

Bowen, Elizabeth (Dorothea Cole) 1899-1973 CLC 1, 3, 6, 11, 15, 22; DAM NOV; SSC 3, 28
See also CA 17-18; 41-44R; CANR 35; CAP 2; CDBLB 1945-1960; DLB 15, 162; MTCW 1

Bowering, George 1935-   CLC 15, 47
See also CA 21-24R; CAAS 16; CANR 10; DLB 53

Bowering, Marilyn R(uthe) 1949-   CLC 32
See also CA 101; CANR 49

Bowers, Edgar 1924-   CLC 9
See also CA 5-8R; CANR 24; DLB 5

Bowie, David   CLC 17
See also Jones, David Robert

Bowles, Jane (Sydney) 1917-1973 CLC 3, 68
See also CA 19-20; 41-44R; CAP 2

Bowles, Paul (Frederick) 1910-1986CLC 1, 2, 19, 53; SSC 3
See also CA 1-4R; CAAS 1; CANR 1, 19, 50; DLB 5, 6; MTCW 1

Box, Edgar
See Vidal, Gore

Boyd, Nancy
See Millay, Edna St. Vincent

Boyd, William 1952-   CLC 28, 53, 70
See also CA 114; 120; CANR 51, 71

Boyle, Kay 1902-1992CLC 1, 5, 19, 58; SSC 5
See also CA 13-16R; 140; CAAS 1; CANR 29, 61; DLB 4, 9, 48, 86; DLBY 93; MTCW 1

Boyle, Mark
See Kienzle, William X(avier)

Boyle, Patrick 1905-1982   CLC 19
See also CA 127

Boyle, T. C. 1948-
See Boyle, T(homas) Coraghessan

Boyle, T(homas) Coraghessan 1948-CLC 36, 55, 90; DAM POP; SSC 16
See also BEST 90:4; CA 120; CANR 44; DLBY 86

Boz
See Dickens, Charles (John Huffam)

Brackenridge, Hugh Henry 1748-1816N C L C 7
See also DLB 11, 37

Bradbury, Edward P.
See Moorcock, Michael (John)

Bradbury, Malcolm (Stanley) 1932- CLC 32, 61; DAM NOV
See also CA 1-4R; CANR 1, 33; DLB 14; MTCW 1

Bradbury, Ray (Douglas) 1920-CLC 1, 3, 10, 15, 42, 98; DA; DAB; DAC; DAM MST, NOV, POP; SSC 29; WLC
See also AAYA 15; AITN 1, 2; CA 1-4R; CANR 2, 30; CDALB 1968-1988; DLB 2, 8; MTCW 1; SATA 11, 64

Bradford, Gamaliel 1863-1932   TCLC 36
See also CA 160; DLB 17

Bradley, David (Henry, Jr.) 1950-   CLC 23; BLC 1; DAM MULT
See also BW 1; CA 104; CANR 26; DLB 33

Bradley, John Ed(mund, Jr.) 1958- CLC 55
See also CA 139

Bradley, Marion Zimmer 1930-CLC 30; DAM POP
See also AAYA 9; CA 57-60; CAAS 10; CANR 7, 31, 51; DLB 8; MTCW 1; SATA 90

Bradstreet, Anne 1612(?)-1672LC 4, 30; DA; DAC; DAM MST, POET; PC 10
See also CDALB 1640-1865; DLB 24

Brady, Joan 1939-   CLC 86
See also CA 141

Bragg, Melvyn 1939-   CLC 10
See also BEST 89:3; CA 57-60; CANR 10, 48; DLB 14

Brahe, Tycho 1546-1601   LC 45

Braine, John (Gerard) 1922-1986CLC 1, 3, 41
See also CA 1-4R; 120; CANR 1, 33; CDBLB 1945-1960; DLB 15; DLBY 86; MTCW 1

Bramah, Ernest 1868-1942   TCLC 72
See also CA 156; DLB 70

Brammer, William 1930(?)-1978   CLC 31
See also CA 77-80

Brancati, Vitaliano 1907-1954   TCLC 12
See also CA 109

Brancato, Robin F(idler) 1936-   CLC 35
See also AAYA 9; CA 69-72; CANR 11, 45; CLR 32; JRDA; SAAS 9; SATA 97

Brand, Max
See Faust, Frederick (Schiller)

Brand, Millen 1906-1980   CLC 7
See also CA 21-24R; 97-100; CANR 72

Branden, Barbara   CLC 44

BLC 1; DAM MULT; DC 1
See also DLB 3, 50

Browne, (Clyde) Jackson 1948(?)-   **CLC 21**
See also CA 120

Browning, Elizabeth Barrett 1806-1861
NCLC 1, 16, 61, 66; DA; DAB; DAC; DAM
MST, POET; PC 6; WLC
See also CDBLB 1832-1890; DLB 32, 199

Browning, Robert 1812-1889 NCLC 19; DA;
DAB; DAC; DAM MST, POET; PC 2;
WLCS
See also CDBLB 1832-1890; DLB 32, 163;
YABC 1

Browning, Tod 1882-1962   **CLC 16**
See also CA 141; 117

Brownson, Orestes Augustus 1803-1876
NCLC 50
See also DLB 1, 59, 73

Bruccoli, Matthew J(oseph) 1931-   **CLC 34**
See also CA 9-12R; CANR 7; DLB 103

Bruce, Lenny   **CLC 21**
See also Schneider, Leonard Alfred

Bruin, John
See Brutus, Dennis

Brulard, Henri
See Stendhal

Brulls, Christian
See Simenon, Georges (Jacques Christian)

Brunner, John (Kilian Houston) 1934-1995
CLC 8, 10; DAM POP
See also CA 1-4R; 149; CAAS 8; CANR 2, 37;
MTCW 1

Bruno, Giordano 1548-1600   **LC 27**

Brutus, Dennis 1924- CLC 43; BLC 1; DAM
MULT, POET; PC 24
See also BW 2; CA 49-52; CAAS 14; CANR 2,
27, 42; DLB 117

Bryan, C(ourtlandt) D(ixon) B(arnes) 1936-
CLC 29
See also CA 73-76; CANR 13, 68; DLB 185;
INT CANR-13

Bryan, Michael
See Moore, Brian

Bryant, William Cullen 1794-1878 NCLC 6,
46; DA; DAB; DAC; DAM MST, POET;
PC 20
See also CDALB 1640-1865; DLB 3, 43, 59,
189

Bryusov, Valery Yakovlevich 1873-1924
TCLC 10
See also CA 107; 155

Buchan, John 1875-1940   **TCLC 41; DAB;
DAM POP**
See also CA 108; 145; DLB 34, 70, 156; YABC
2

Buchanan, George 1506-1582   **LC 4**
See also DLB 152

Buchheim, Lothar-Guenther 1918-   **CLC 6**
See also CA 85-88

Buchner, (Karl) Georg 1813-1837 NCLC 26

Buchwald, Art(hur) 1925-   **CLC 33**
See also AITN 1; CA 5-8R; CANR 21, 67;
MTCW 1; SATA 10

Buck, Pearl S(ydenstricker) 1892-1973 CLC 7,
11, 18; DA; DAB; DAC; DAM MST, NOV
See also AITN 1; CA 1-4R; 41-44R; CANR 1,
34; DLB 9, 102; MTCW 1; SATA 1, 25

Buckler, Ernest 1908-1984   **CLC 13; DAC;
DAM MST**
See also CA 11-12; 114; CAP 1; DLB 68; SATA
47

Buckley, Vincent (Thomas) 1925-1988 CLC 57
See also CA 101

Buckley, William F(rank), Jr. 1925-CLC 7, 18,
37; DAM POP
See also AITN 1; CA 1-4R; CANR 1, 24, 53;
DLB 137; DLBY 80; INT CANR-24; MTCW
1

Buechner, (Carl) Frederick 1926-CLC 2, 4, 6,
9; DAM NOV
See also CA 13-16R; CANR 11, 39, 64; DLBY
80; INT CANR-11; MTCW 1

Buell, John (Edward) 1927-   **CLC 10**
See also CA 1-4R; CANR 71; DLB 53

Buero Vallejo, Antonio 1916-   **CLC 15, 46**
See also CA 106; CANR 24, 49; HW; MTCW
1

Bufalino, Gesualdo 1920(?)-   **CLC 74**
See also DLB 196

Bugayev, Boris Nikolayevich 1880-1934
TCLC 7; PC 11
See also Bely, Andrey
See also CA 104; 165

Bukowski, Charles 1920-1994 CLC 2, 5, 9, 41,
82, 108; DAM NOV, POET; PC 18
See also CA 17-20R; 144; CANR 40, 62; DLB
5, 130, 169; MTCW 1

Bulgakov, Mikhail (Afanas'evich) 1891-1940
TCLC 2, 16; DAM DRAM, NOV; SSC 18
See also CA 105; 152

Bulgya, Alexander Alexandrovich 1901-1956
TCLC 53
See also Fadeyev, Alexander
See also CA 117

Bullins, Ed 1935- CLC 1, 5, 7; BLC 1; DAM
DRAM, MULT; DC 6
See also BW 2; CA 49-52; CAAS 16; CANR
24, 46, 73; DLB 7, 38; MTCW 1

Bulwer-Lytton, Edward (George Earle Lytton)
1803-1873   **NCLC 1, 45**
See also DLB 21

Bunin, Ivan Alexeyevich 1870-1953 TCLC 6;
SSC 5
See also CA 104

Bunting, Basil 1900-1985   **CLC 10, 39, 47;
DAM POET**
See also CA 53-56; 115; CANR 7; DLB 20

Bunuel, Luis 1900-1983   **CLC 16, 80; DAM
MULT; HLC**
See also CA 101; 110; CANR 32; HW

Bunyan, John 1628-1688   **LC 4; DA; DAB;
DAC; DAM MST; WLC**
See also CDBLB 1660-1789; DLB 39

Burckhardt, Jacob (Christoph) 1818-1897
NCLC 49

Burford, Eleanor
See Hibbert, Eleanor Alice Burford

Burgess, Anthony CLC 1, 2, 4, 5, 8, 10, 13, 15,
22, 40, 62, 81, 94; DAB
See also Wilson, John (Anthony) Burgess
See also AAYA 25; AITN 1; CDBLB 1960 to
Present; DLB 14, 194

Burke, Edmund 1729(?)-1797 LC 7, 36; DA;
DAB; DAC; DAM MST; WLC
See also DLB 104

Burke, Kenneth (Duva) 1897-1993 CLC 2, 24
See also CA 5-8R; 143; CANR 39, 74; DLB
45, 63; MTCW 1

Burke, Leda
See Garnett, David

Burke, Ralph
See Silverberg, Robert

Burke, Thomas 1886-1945   **TCLC 63**
See also CA 113; 155; DLB 197

Burney, Fanny 1752-1840   **NCLC 12, 54**
See also DLB 39

Burns, Robert 1759-1796   **PC 6**
See also CDBLB 1789-1832; DA; DAB; DAC;
DAM MST, POET; DLB 109; WLC

Burns, Tex
See L'Amour, Louis (Dearborn)

Burnshaw, Stanley 1906-   **CLC 3, 13, 44**
See also CA 9-12R; DLB 48; DLBY 97

Burr, Anne 1937-   **CLC 6**
See also CA 25-28R

Burroughs, Edgar Rice 1875-1950 **TCLC 2,
32; DAM NOV**
See also AAYA 11; CA 104; 132; DLB 8;
MTCW 1; SATA 41

Burroughs, William S(eward) 1914-1997CLC
1, 2, 5, 15, 22, 42, 75, 109; DA; DAB; DAC;
DAM MST, NOV, POP; WLC
See also AITN 2; CA 9-12R; 160; CANR 20,
52; DLB 2, 8, 16, 152; DLBY 81, 97; MTCW
1

Burton, Richard F. 1821-1890   **NCLC 42**
See also DLB 55, 184

Busch, Frederick 1941-   **CLC 7, 10, 18, 47**
See also CA 33-36R; CAAS 1; CANR 45, 73;
DLB 6

Bush, Ronald 1946-   **CLC 34**
See also CA 136

Bustos, F(rancisco)
See Borges, Jorge Luis

Bustos Domecq, H(onorio)
See Bioy Casares, Adolfo; Borges, Jorge Luis

Butler, Octavia E(stelle) 1947-CLC 38; BLCS;
DAM MULT, POP
See also AAYA 18; BW 2; CA 73-76; CANR
12, 24, 38, 73; DLB 33; MTCW 1; SATA 84

Butler, Robert Olen (Jr.) 1945-CLC 81; DAM
POP
See also CA 112; CANR 66; DLB 173; INT 112

Butler, Samuel 1612-1680   **LC 16, 43**
See also DLB 101, 126

Butler, Samuel 1835-1902   **TCLC 1, 33; DA;
DAB; DAC; DAM MST, NOV; WLC**
See also CA 143; CDBLB 1890-1914; DLB 18,
57, 174

Butler, Walter C.
See Faust, Frederick (Schiller)

Butor, Michel (Marie Francois) 1926-CLC 1,
3, 8, 11, 15
See also CA 9-12R; CANR 33, 66; DLB 83;
MTCW 1

Butts, Mary 1892(?)-1937   **TCLC 77**
See also CA 148

Buzo, Alexander (John) 1944-   **CLC 61**
See also CA 97-100; CANR 17, 39, 69

Buzzati, Dino 1906-1972   **CLC 36**
See also CA 160; 33-36R; DLB 177

Byars, Betsy (Cromer) 1928-   **CLC 35**
See also AAYA 19; CA 33-36R; CANR 18, 36,
57; CLR 1, 16; DLB 52; INT CANR-18;
JRDA; MAICYA; MTCW 1; SAAS 1; SATA
4, 46, 80

Byatt, A(ntonia) S(usan Drabble) 1936- C L C
19, 65; DAM NOV, POP
See also CA 13-16R; CANR 13, 33, 50; DLB
14, 194; MTCW 1

Byrne, David 1952-   **CLC 26**
See also CA 127

Byrne, John Keyes 1926-
See Leonard, Hugh
See also CA 102; INT 102

Byron, George Gordon (Noel) 1788-1824
NCLC 2, 12; DA; DAB; DAC; DAM MST,
POET; PC 16; WLC
See also CDBLB 1789-1832; DLB 96, 110

Byron, Robert 1905-1941   **TCLC 67**
See also CA 160; DLB 195
C. 3. 3.
See Wilde, Oscar (Fingal O'Flahertie Wills)
Caballero, Fernan 1796-1877   **NCLC 10**
Cabell, Branch
See Cabell, James Branch
Cabell, James Branch 1879-1958   **TCLC 6**
See also CA 105; 152; DLB 9, 78
Cable, George Washington 1844-1925 **TCLC 4; SSC 4**
See also CA 104; 155; DLB 12, 74; DLBD 13
Cabral de Melo Neto, Joao 1920-   **CLC 76; DAM MULT**
See also CA 151
Cabrera Infante, G(uillermo) 1929-CLC **5, 25, 45; DAM MULT; HLC**
See also CA 85-88; CANR 29, 65; DLB 113; HW; MTCW 1
Cade, Toni
See Bambara, Toni Cade
Cadmus and Harmonia
See Buchan, John
Caedmon fl. 658-680   **CMLC 7**
See also DLB 146
Caeiro, Alberto
See Pessoa, Fernando (Antonio Nogueira)
Cage, John (Milton, Jr.) 1912-1992   **CLC 41**
See also CA 13-16R; 169; CANR 9; DLB 193; INT CANR-9
Cahan, Abraham 1860-1951   **TCLC 71**
See also CA 108; 154; DLB 9, 25, 28
Cain, G.
See Cabrera Infante, G(uillermo)
Cain, Guillermo
See Cabrera Infante, G(uillermo)
Cain, James M(allahan) 1892-1977CLC **3, 11, 28**
See also AITN 1; CA 17-20R; 73-76; CANR 8, 34, 61; MTCW 1
Caine, Mark
See Raphael, Frederic (Michael)
Calasso, Roberto 1941-   **CLC 81**
See also CA 143
Calderon de la Barca, Pedro 1600-1681   **LC 23; DC 3**
Caldwell, Erskine (Preston) 1903-1987CLC **1, 8, 14, 50, 60; DAM NOV; SSC 19**
See also AITN 1; CA 1-4R; 121; CAAS 1; CANR 2, 33; DLB 9, 86; MTCW 1
Caldwell, (Janet Miriam) Taylor (Holland) 1900-1985CLC **2, 28, 39; DAM NOV, POP**
See also CA 5-8R; 116; CANR 5; DLBD 17
Calhoun, John Caldwell 1782-1850NCLC **15**
See also DLB 3
Calisher, Hortense 1911-CLC **2, 4, 8, 38; DAM NOV; SSC 15**
See also CA 1-4R; CANR 1, 22, 67; DLB 2; INT CANR-22; MTCW 1
Callaghan, Morley Edward 1903-1990CLC **3, 14, 41, 65; DAC; DAM MST**
See also CA 9-12R; 132; CANR 33, 73; DLB 68; MTCW 1
Callimachus c. 305B.C.-c. 240B.C. **CMLC 18**
See also DLB 176
Calvin, John 1509-1564   **LC 37**
Calvino, Italo 1923-1985CLC **5, 8, 11, 22, 33, 39, 73; DAM NOV; SSC 3**
See also CA 85-88; 116; CANR 23, 61; DLB 196; MTCW 1
Cameron, Carey 1952-   **CLC 59**
See also CA 135
Cameron, Peter 1959-   **CLC 44**

See also CA 125; CANR 50
Campana, Dino 1885-1932   **TCLC 20**
See also CA 117; DLB 114
Campanella, Tommaso 1568-1639   **LC 32**
Campbell, John W(ood, Jr.) 1910-1971 **C L C 32**
See also CA 21-22; 29-32R; CANR 34; CAP 2; DLB 8; MTCW 1
Campbell, Joseph 1904-1987   **CLC 69**
See also AAYA 3; BEST 89:2; CA 1-4R; 124; CANR 3, 28, 61; MTCW 1
Campbell, Maria 1940-   **CLC 85; DAC**
See also CA 102; CANR 54; NNAL
Campbell, (John) Ramsey 1946-CLC **42; SSC 19**
See also CA 57-60; CANR 7; INT CANR-7
Campbell, (Ignatius) Roy (Dunnachie) 1901-1957   **TCLC 5**
See also CA 104; 155; DLB 20
Campbell, Thomas 1777-1844   **NCLC 19**
See also DLB 93; 144
Campbell, Wilfred   **TCLC 9**
See also Campbell, William
Campbell, William 1858(?)-1918
See Campbell, Wilfred
See also CA 106; DLB 92
Campion, Jane   **CLC 95**
See also CA 138
Campos, Alvaro de
See Pessoa, Fernando (Antonio Nogueira)
Camus, Albert 1913-1960CLC **1, 2, 4, 9, 11, 14, 32, 63, 69; DA; DAB; DAC; DAM DRAM, MST, NOV; DC 2; SSC 9; WLC**
See also CA 89-92; DLB 72; MTCW 1
Canby, Vincent 1924-   **CLC 13**
See also CA 81-84
Cancale
See Desnos, Robert
Canetti, Elias 1905-1994CLC **3, 14, 25, 75, 86**
See also CA 21-24R; 146; CANR 23, 61; DLB 85, 124; MTCW 1
Canfield, Dorothea F.
See Fisher, Dorothy (Frances) Canfield
Canfield, Dorothea Frances
See Fisher, Dorothy (Frances) Canfield
Canfield, Dorothy
See Fisher, Dorothy (Frances) Canfield
Canin, Ethan 1960-   **CLC 55**
See also CA 131; 135
Cannon, Curt
See Hunter, Evan
Cao, Lan 1961-   **CLC 109**
See also CA 165
Cape, Judith
See Page, P(atricia) K(athleen)
Capek, Karel 1890-1938   **TCLC 6, 37; DA; DAB; DAC; DAM DRAM, MST, NOV; DC 1; WLC**
See also CA 104; 140
Capote, Truman 1924-1984CLC **1, 3, 8, 13, 19, 34, 38, 58; DA; DAB; DAC; DAM MST, NOV, POP; SSC 2; WLC**
See also CA 5-8R; 113; CANR 18, 62; CDALB 1941-1968; DLB 2, 185; DLBY 80, 84; MTCW 1; SATA 91
Capra, Frank 1897-1991   **CLC 16**
See also CA 61-64; 135
Caputo, Philip 1941-   **CLC 32**
See also CA 73-76; CANR 40
Caragiale, Ion Luca 1852-1912   **TCLC 76**
See also CA 157
Card, Orson Scott 1951-CLC **44, 47, 50; DAM POP**

See also AAYA 11; CA 102; CANR 27, 47, 73; INT CANR-27; MTCW 1; SATA 83
Cardenal, Ernesto 1925-   **CLC 31; DAM MULT, POET; HLC; PC 22**
See also CA 49-52; CANR 2, 32, 66; HW; MTCW 1
Cardozo, Benjamin N(athan) 1870-1938 **TCLC 65**
See also CA 117; 164
Carducci, Giosue (Alessandro Giuseppe) 1835-1907   **TCLC 32**
See also CA 163
Carew, Thomas 1595(?)-1640   **LC 13**
See also DLB 126
Carey, Ernestine Gilbreth 1908-   **CLC 17**
See also CA 5-8R; CANR 71; SATA 2
Carey, Peter 1943-   **CLC 40, 55, 96**
See also CA 123; 127; CANR 53; INT 127; MTCW 1; SATA 94
Carleton, William 1794-1869   **NCLC 3**
See also DLB 159
Carlisle, Henry (Coffin) 1926-   **CLC 33**
See also CA 13-16R; CANR 15
Carlsen, Chris
See Holdstock, Robert P.
Carlson, Ron(ald F.) 1947-   **CLC 54**
See also CA 105; CANR 27
Carlyle, Thomas 1795-1881   **NCLC 70; DA; DAB; DAC; DAM MST**
See also CDBLB 1789-1832; DLB 55; 144
Carman, (William) Bliss 1861-1929 **TCLC 7; DAC**
See also CA 104; 152; DLB 92
Carnegie, Dale 1888-1955   **TCLC 53**
Carossa, Hans 1878-1956   **TCLC 48**
See also CA 170; DLB 66
Carpenter, Don(ald Richard) 1931-1995**C L C 41**
See also CA 45-48; 149; CANR 1, 71
Carpenter, Edward 1844-1929   **TCLC 88**
See also CA 163
Carpentier (y Valmont), Alejo 1904-1980CLC **8, 11, 38, 110; DAM MULT; HLC**
See also CA 65-68; 97-100; CANR 11, 70; DLB 113; HW
Carr, Caleb 1955(?)-   **CLC 86**
See also CA 147; CANR 73
Carr, Emily 1871-1945   **TCLC 32**
See also CA 159; DLB 68
Carr, John Dickson 1906-1977   **CLC 3**
See also Fairbairn, Roger
See also CA 49-52; 69-72; CANR 3, 33, 60; MTCW 1
Carr, Philippa
See Hibbert, Eleanor Alice Burford
Carr, Virginia Spencer 1929-   **CLC 34**
See also CA 61-64; DLB 111
Carrere, Emmanuel 1957-   **CLC 89**
Carrier, Roch 1937-CLC **13, 78; DAC; DAM MST**
See also CA 130; CANR 61; DLB 53
Carroll, James P. 1943(?)-   **CLC 38**
See also CA 81-84; CANR 73
Carroll, Jim 1951-   **CLC 35**
See also AAYA 17; CA 45-48; CANR 42
Carroll, Lewis   **NCLC 2, 53; PC 18; WLC**
See also Dodgson, Charles Lutwidge
See also CDBLB 1832-1890; CLR 2, 18; DLB 18, 163, 178; JRDA
Carroll, Paul Vincent 1900-1968   **CLC 10**
See also CA 9-12R; 25-28R; DLB 10
Carruth, Hayden 1921- CLC **4, 7, 10, 18, 84; PC 10**

Davys, Mary 1674-1732 **LC 1, 46**
See also DLB 39
Dawson, Fielding 1930- **CLC 6**
See also CA 85-88; DLB 130
Dawson, Peter
See Faust, Frederick (Schiller)
Day, Clarence (Shepard, Jr.) 1874-1935
TCLC 25
See also CA 108; DLB 11
Day, Thomas 1748-1789 **LC 1**
See also DLB 39; YABC 1
Day Lewis, C(ecil) 1904-1972 **CLC 1, 6, 10;**
DAM POET; PC 11
See also Blake, Nicholas
See also CA 13-16; 33-36R; CANR 34; CAP 1;
DLB 15, 20; MTCW 1
Dazai Osamu 1909-1948 **TCLC 11**
See also Tsushima, Shuji
See also CA 164; DLB 182
de Andrade, Carlos Drummond
See Drummond de Andrade, Carlos
Deane, Norman
See Creasey, John
de Beauvoir, Simone (Lucie Ernestine Marie
Bertrand)
See Beauvoir, Simone (Lucie Ernestine Marie
Bertrand) de
de Beer, P.
See Bosman, Herman Charles
de Brissac, Malcolm
See Dickinson, Peter (Malcolm)
de Chardin, Pierre Teilhard
See Teilhard de Chardin, (Marie Joseph) Pierre
Dee, John 1527-1608 **LC 20**
Deer, Sandra 1940- **CLC 45**
De Ferrari, Gabriella 1941- **CLC 65**
See also CA 146
Defoe, Daniel 1660(?)-1731 **LC 1, 42; DA;**
DAB; DAC; DAM MST, NOV; WLC
See also AAYA 27; CDBLB 1660-1789; DLB
39, 95, 101; JRDA; MAICYA; SATA 22
de Gourmont, Remy(-Marie-Charles)
See Gourmont, Remy (-Marie-Charles) de
de Hartog, Jan 1914- **CLC 19**
See also CA 1-4R; CANR 1
de Hostos, E. M.
See Hostos (y Bonilla), Eugenio Maria de
de Hostos, Eugenio M.
See Hostos (y Bonilla), Eugenio Maria de
Deighton, Len **CLC 4, 7, 22, 46**
See also Deighton, Leonard Cyril
See also AAYA 6; BEST 89:2; CDBLB 1960 to
Present; DLB 87
Deighton, Leonard Cyril 1929-
See Deighton, Len
See also CA 9-12R; CANR 19, 33, 68; DAM
NOV, POP; MTCW 1
Dekker, Thomas 1572(?)-1632 **LC 22; DAM**
DRAM
See also CDBLB Before 1660; DLB 62, 172
Delafield, E. M. 1890-1943 **TCLC 61**
See also Dashwood, Edmee Elizabeth Monica
de la Pasture
See also DLB 34
de la Mare, Walter (John) 1873-1956**TCLC 4,**
53; DAB; DAC; DAM MST, POET; SSC
14; WLC
See also CA 163; CDBLB 1914-1945; CLR 23;
DLB 162; SATA 16
Delaney, Franey
See O'Hara, John (Henry)
Delaney, Shelagh 1939-**CLC 29; DAM DRAM**
See also CA 17-20R; CANR 30, 67; CDBLB

1960 to Present; DLB 13; MTCW 1
Delany, Mary (Granville Pendarves) 1700-1788
LC 12
Delany, Samuel R(ay, Jr.) 1942-**CLC 8, 14, 38;**
BLC 1; DAM MULT
See also AAYA 24; BW 2; CA 81-84; CANR
27, 43; DLB 8, 33; MTCW 1
De La Ramee, (Marie) Louise 1839-1908
See Ouida
See also SATA 20
de la Roche, Mazo 1879-1961 **CLC 14**
See also CA 85-88; CANR 30; DLB 68; SATA
64
De La Salle, Innocent
See Hartmann, Sadakichi
Delbanco, Nicholas (Franklin) 1942- **CLC 6,**
13
See also CA 17-20R; CAAS 2; CANR 29, 55;
DLB 6
del Castillo, Michel 1933- **CLC 38**
See also CA 109
Deledda, Grazia (Cosima) 1875(?)-1936
TCLC 23
See also CA 123
Delibes, Miguel **CLC 8, 18**
See also Delibes Setien, Miguel
Delibes Setien, Miguel 1920-
See Delibes, Miguel
See also CA 45-48; CANR 1, 32; HW; MTCW
1
DeLillo, Don 1936- **CLC 8, 10, 13, 27, 39, 54,**
76; DAM NOV, POP
See also BEST 89:1; CA 81-84; CANR 21; DLB
6, 173; MTCW 1
de Lisser, H. G.
See De Lisser, H(erbert) G(eorge)
See also DLB 117
De Lisser, H(erbert) G(eorge) 1878-1944
TCLC 12
See also de Lisser, H. G.
See also BW 2; CA 109; 152
Deloney, Thomas 1560(?)-1600 **LC 41**
See also DLB 167
Deloria, Vine (Victor), Jr. 1933- **CLC 21;**
DAM MULT
See also CA 53-56; CANR 5, 20, 48; DLB 175;
MTCW 1; NNAL; SATA 21
Del Vecchio, John M(ichael) 1947- **CLC 29**
See also CA 110; DLBD 9
de Man, Paul (Adolph Michel) 1919-1983
CLC 55
See also CA 128; 111; CANR 61; DLB 67;
MTCW 1
De Marinis, Rick 1934- **CLC 54**
See also CA 57-60; CAAS 24; CANR 9, 25, 50
Dembry, R. Emmet
See Murfree, Mary Noailles
Demby, William 1922-**CLC 53; BLC 1; DAM**
MULT
See also BW 1; CA 81-84; DLB 33
de Menton, Francisco
See Chin, Frank (Chew, Jr.)
Demijohn, Thom
See Disch, Thomas M(ichael)
de Montherlant, Henry (Milon)
See Montherlant, Henry (Milon) de
Demosthenes 384B.C.-322B.C. **CMLC 13**
See also DLB 176
de Natale, Francine
See Malzberg, Barry N(athaniel)
Denby, Edwin (Orr) 1903-1983 **CLC 48**
See also CA 138; 110
Denis, Julio

See Cortazar, Julio
Denmark, Harrison
See Zelazny, Roger (Joseph)
Dennis, John 1658-1734 **LC 11**
See also DLB 101
Dennis, Nigel (Forbes) 1912-1989 **CLC 8**
See also CA 25-28R; 129; DLB 13, 15; MTCW
1
Dent, Lester 1904(?)-1959 **TCLC 72**
See also CA 112; 161
De Palma, Brian (Russell) 1940- **CLC 20**
See also CA 109
De Quincey, Thomas 1785-1859 **NCLC 4**
See also CDBLB 1789-1832; DLB 110; 144
Deren, Eleanora 1908(?)-1961
See Deren, Maya
See also CA 111
Deren, Maya 1917-1961 **CLC 16, 102**
See also Deren, Eleanora
Derleth, August (William) 1909-1971**CLC 31**
See also CA 1-4R; 29-32R; CANR 4; DLB 9;
DLBD 17; SATA 5
Der Nister 1884-1950 **TCLC 56**
de Routisie, Albert
See Aragon, Louis
Derrida, Jacques 1930- **CLC 24, 87**
See also CA 124; 127
Derry Down Derry
See Lear, Edward
Dersonnes, Jacques
See Simenon, Georges (Jacques Christian)
Desai, Anita 1937-**CLC 19, 37, 97; DAB; DAM**
NOV
See also CA 81-84; CANR 33, 53; MTCW 1;
SATA 63
de Saint-Luc, Jean
See Glassco, John
de Saint Roman, Arnaud
See Aragon, Louis
Descartes, Rene 1596-1650 **LC 20, 35**
De Sica, Vittorio 1901(?)-1974 **CLC 20**
See also CA 117
Desnos, Robert 1900-1945 **TCLC 22**
See also CA 121; 151
Destouches, Louis-Ferdinand 1894-1961**CLC**
9, 15
See also Celine, Louis-Ferdinand
See also CA 85-88; CANR 28; MTCW 1
de Tolignac, Gaston
See Griffith, D(avid Lewelyn) W(ark)
Deutsch, Babette 1895-1982 **CLC 18**
See also CA 1-4R; 108; CANR 4; DLB 45;
SATA 1; SATA-Obit 33
Devenant, William 1606-1649 **LC 13**
Devkota, Laxmiprasad 1909-1959 **TCLC 23**
See also CA 123
De Voto, Bernard (Augustine) 1897-1955
TCLC 29
See also CA 113; 160; DLB 9
De Vries, Peter 1910-1993 **CLC 1, 2, 3, 7, 10,**
28, 46; DAM NOV
See also CA 17-20R; 142; CANR 41; DLB 6;
DLBY 82; MTCW 1
Dexter, John
See Bradley, Marion Zimmer
Dexter, Martin
See Faust, Frederick (Schiller)
Dexter, Pete 1943- **CLC 34, 55; DAM POP**
See also BEST 89:2; CA 127; 131; INT 131;
MTCW 1
Diamano, Silmang
See Senghor, Leopold Sedar
Diamond, Neil 1941- **CLC 30**

See also CA 108

Diaz del Castillo, Bernal 1496-1584   **LC 31**

di Bassetto, Corno
See Shaw, George Bernard

Dick, Philip K(indred) 1928-1982 **CLC 10, 30, 72; DAM NOV, POP**
See also AAYA 24; CA 49-52; 106; CANR 2, 16; DLB 8; MTCW 1

Dickens, Charles (John Huffam) 1812-1870 **NCLC 3, 8, 18, 26, 37, 50; DA; DAB; DAC; DAM MST, NOV; SSC 17; WLC**
See also AAYA 23; CDBLB 1832-1890; DLB 21, 55, 70, 159, 166; JRDA; MAICYA; SATA 15

Dickey, James (Lafayette) 1923-1997 **CLC 1, 2, 4, 7, 10, 15, 47, 109; DAM NOV, POET, POP**
See also AITN 1, 2; CA 9-12R; 156; CABS 2; CANR 10, 48, 61; CDALB 1968-1988; DLB 5, 193; DLBD 7; DLBY 82, 93, 96, 97; INT CANR-10; MTCW 1

Dickey, William 1928-1994   **CLC 3, 28**
See also CA 9-12R; 145; CANR 24; DLB 5

Dickinson, Charles 1951-   **CLC 49**
See also CA 128

Dickinson, Emily (Elizabeth) 1830-1886 **NCLC 21; DA; DAB; DAC; DAM MST, POET; PC 1; WLC**
See also AAYA 22; CDALB 1865-1917; DLB 1; SATA 29

Dickinson, Peter (Malcolm) 1927- **CLC 12, 35**
See also AAYA 9; CA 41-44R; CANR 31, 58; CLR 29; DLB 87, 161; JRDA; MAICYA; SATA 5, 62, 95

Dickson, Carr
See Carr, John Dickson

Dickson, Carter
See Carr, John Dickson

Diderot, Denis 1713-1784   **LC 26**

Didion, Joan 1934- **CLC 1, 3, 8, 14, 32; DAM NOV**
See also AITN 1; CA 5-8R; CANR 14, 52; CDALB 1968-1988; DLB 2, 173, 185; DLBY 81, 86; MTCW 1

Dietrich, Robert
See Hunt, E(verette) Howard, (Jr.)

Difusa, Pati
See Almodovar, Pedro

Dillard, Annie 1945- **CLC 9, 60, 115; DAM NOV**
See also AAYA 6; CA 49-52; CANR 3, 43, 62; DLBY 80; MTCW 1; SATA 10

Dillard, R(ichard) H(enry) W(ilde) 1937- **CLC 5**
See also CA 21-24R; CAAS 7; CANR 10; DLB 5

Dillon, Eilis 1920-1994   **CLC 17**
See also CA 9-12R; 147; CAAS 3; CANR 4, 38; CLR 26; MAICYA; SATA 2, 74; SATA-Obit 83

Dimont, Penelope
See Mortimer, Penelope (Ruth)

Dinesen, Isak   **CLC 10, 29, 95; SSC 7**
See also Blixen, Karen (Christentze Dinesen)

Ding Ling   **CLC 68**
See also Chiang, Pin-chin

Diphusa, Patty
See Almodovar, Pedro

Disch, Thomas M(ichael) 1940-   **CLC 7, 36**
See also AAYA 17; CA 21-24R; CAAS 4; CANR 17, 36, 54; CLR 18; DLB 8; MAICYA; MTCW 1; SAAS 15; SATA 92

Disch, Tom

See Disch, Thomas M(ichael)

d'Isly, Georges
See Simenon, Georges (Jacques Christian)

Disraeli, Benjamin 1804-1881   **NCLC 2, 39**
See also DLB 21, 55

Ditcum, Steve
See Crumb, R(obert)

Dixon, Paige
See Corcoran, Barbara

Dixon, Stephen 1936-   **CLC 52; SSC 16**
See also CA 89-92; CANR 17, 40, 54; DLB 130

Doak, Annie
See Dillard, Annie

Dobell, Sydney Thompson 1824-1874 **NCLC 43**
See also DLB 32

Doblin, Alfred   **TCLC 13**
See also Doeblin, Alfred

Dobrolyubov, Nikolai Alexandrovich 1836-1861 **NCLC 5**

Dobson, Austin 1840-1921   **TCLC 79**
See also DLB 35; 144

Dobyns, Stephen 1941-   **CLC 37**
See also CA 45-48; CANR 2, 18

Doctorow, E(dgar) L(aurence) 1931- **CLC 6, 11, 15, 18, 37, 44, 65, 113; DAM NOV, POP**
See also AAYA 22; AITN 2; BEST 89:3; CA 45-48; CANR 2, 33, 51; CDALB 1968-1988; DLB 2, 28, 173; DLBY 80; MTCW 1

Dodgson, Charles Lutwidge 1832-1898
See Carroll, Lewis
See also CLR 2; DA; DAB; DAC; DAM MST, NOV, POET; MAICYA; SATA 100; YABC 2

Dodson, Owen (Vincent) 1914-1983 **CLC 79; BLC 1; DAM MULT**
See also BW 1; CA 65-68; 110; CANR 24; DLB 76

Doeblin, Alfred 1878-1957   **TCLC 13**
See also Doblin, Alfred
See also CA 110; 141; DLB 66

Doerr, Harriet 1910-   **CLC 34**
See also CA 117; 122; CANR 47; INT 122

Domecq, H(onorio) Bustos
See Bioy Casares, Adolfo; Borges, Jorge Luis

Domini, Rey
See Lorde, Audre (Geraldine)

Dominique
See Proust, (Valentin-Louis-George-Eugene-) Marcel

Don, A
See Stephen, SirLeslie

Donaldson, Stephen R. 1947- **CLC 46; DAM POP**
See also CA 89-92; CANR 13, 55; INT CANR-13

Donleavy, J(ames) P(atrick) 1926- **CLC 1, 4, 6, 10, 45**
See also AITN 2; CA 9-12R; CANR 24, 49, 62; DLB 6, 173; INT CANR-24; MTCW 1

Donne, John 1572-1631 **LC 10, 24; DA; DAB; DAC; DAM MST, POET; PC 1**
See also CDBLB Before 1660; DLB 121, 151

Donnell, David 1939(?)-   **CLC 34**

Donoghue, P. S.
See Hunt, E(verette) Howard, (Jr.)

Donoso (Yanez), Jose 1924-1996 **CLC 4, 8, 11, 32, 99; DAM MULT; HLC**
See also CA 81-84; 155; CANR 32, 73; DLB 113; HW; MTCW 1

Donovan, John 1928-1992   **CLC 35**
See also AAYA 20; CA 97-100; 137; CLR 3; MAICYA; SATA 72; SATA-Brief 29

Don Roberto

See Cunninghame Graham, R(obert) B(ontine)

Doolittle, Hilda 1886-1961 **CLC 3, 8, 14, 31, 34, 73; DA; DAC; DAM MST, POET; PC 5; WLC**
See also H. D.
See also CA 97-100; CANR 35; DLB 4, 45; MTCW 1

Dorfman, Ariel 1942-   **CLC 48, 77; DAM MULT; HLC**
See also CA 124; 130; CANR 67, 70; HW; INT 130

Dorn, Edward (Merton) 1929- **CLC 10, 18**
See also CA 93-96; CANR 42; DLB 5; INT 93-96

Dorris, Michael (Anthony) 1945-1997 **CLC 109; DAM MULT, NOV**
See also AAYA 20; BEST 90:1; CA 102; 157; CANR 19, 46; DLB 175; NNAL; SATA 75; SATA-Obit 94

Dorris, Michael A.
See Dorris, Michael (Anthony)

Dorsan, Luc
See Simenon, Georges (Jacques Christian)

Dorsange, Jean
See Simenon, Georges (Jacques Christian)

Dos Passos, John (Roderigo) 1896-1970 **CLC 1, 4, 8, 11, 15, 25, 34, 82; DA; DAB; DAC; DAM MST, NOV; WLC**
See also CA 1-4R; 29-32R; CANR 3; CDALB 1929-1941; DLB 4, 9; DLBD 1, 15; DLBY 96; MTCW 1

Dossage, Jean
See Simenon, Georges (Jacques Christian)

Dostoevsky, Fedor Mikhailovich 1821-1881 **NCLC 2, 7, 21, 33, 43; DA; DAB; DAC; DAM MST, NOV; SSC 2; WLC**

Doughty, Charles M(ontagu) 1843-1926 **TCLC 27**
See also CA 115; DLB 19, 57, 174

Douglas, Ellen   **CLC 73**
See also Haxton, Josephine Ayres; Williamson, Ellen Douglas

Douglas, Gavin 1475(?)-1522   **LC 20**
See also DLB 132

Douglas, George
See Brown, George Douglas

Douglas, Keith (Castellain) 1920-1944 **TCLC 40**
See also CA 160; DLB 27

Douglas, Leonard
See Bradbury, Ray (Douglas)

Douglas, Michael
See Crichton, (John) Michael

Douglas, (George) Norman 1868-1952 **TCLC 68**
See also CA 119; 157; DLB 34, 195

Douglas, William
See Brown, George Douglas

Douglass, Frederick 1817(?)-1895 **NCLC 7, 55; BLC 1; DA; DAC; DAM MST, MULT; WLC**
See also CDALB 1640-1865; DLB 1, 43, 50, 79; SATA 29

Dourado, (Waldomiro Freitas) Autran 1926- **CLC 23, 60**
See also CA 25-28R; CANR 34

Dourado, Waldomiro Autran
See Dourado, (Waldomiro Freitas) Autran

Dove, Rita (Frances) 1952- **CLC 50, 81; BLCS; DAM MULT, POET; PC 6**
See also BW 2; CA 109; CAAS 19; CANR 27, 42, 68; DLB 120

Doveglion

See Villa, Jose Garcia

Dowell, Coleman 1925-1985   **CLC 60**
See also CA 25-28R; 117; CANR 10; DLB 130

Dowson, Ernest (Christopher) 1867-1900
TCLC 4
See also CA 105; 150; DLB 19, 135

Doyle, A. Conan
See Doyle, Arthur Conan

Doyle, Arthur Conan 1859-1930**TCLC 7; DA;
DAB; DAC; DAM MST, NOV; SSC 12;
WLC**
See also AAYA 14; CA 104; 122; CDBLB 1890-
1914; DLB 18, 70, 156, 178; MTCW 1;
SATA 24

Doyle, Conan
See Doyle, Arthur Conan

Doyle, John
See Graves, Robert (von Ranke)

Doyle, Roddy 1958(?)-   **CLC 81**
See also AAYA 14; CA 143; CANR 73; DLB
194

Doyle, Sir A. Conan
See Doyle, Arthur Conan

Doyle, Sir Arthur Conan
See Doyle, Arthur Conan

Dr. A
See Asimov, Isaac; Silverstein, Alvin

Drabble, Margaret 1939-**CLC 2, 3, 5, 8, 10, 22,
53; DAB; DAC; DAM MST, NOV, POP**
See also CA 13-16R; CANR 18, 35, 63; CDBLB
1960 to Present; DLB 14, 155; MTCW 1;
SATA 48

Drapier, M. B.
See Swift, Jonathan

Drayham, James
See Mencken, H(enry) L(ouis)

Drayton, Michael 1563-1631   **LC 8; DAM
POET**
See also DLB 121

Dreadstone, Carl
See Campbell, (John) Ramsey

Dreiser, Theodore (Herman Albert) 1871-1945
**TCLC 10, 18, 35, 83; DA; DAC; DAM
MST, NOV; SSC 30; WLC**
See also CA 106; 132; CDALB 1865-1917;
DLB 9, 12, 102, 137; DLBD 1; MTCW 1

Drexler, Rosalyn 1926-   **CLC 2, 6**
See also CA 81-84; CANR 68

Dreyer, Carl Theodor 1889-1968   **CLC 16**
See also CA 116

Drieu la Rochelle, Pierre(-Eugene) 1893-1945
TCLC 21
See also CA 117; DLB 72

Drinkwater, John 1882-1937   **TCLC 57**
See also CA 109; 149; DLB 10, 19, 149

Drop Shot
See Cable, George Washington

Droste-Hulshoff, Annette Freiin von 1797-1848
NCLC 3
See also DLB 133

Drummond, Walter
See Silverberg, Robert

Drummond, William Henry 1854-1907**TCLC
25**
See also CA 160; DLB 92

Drummond de Andrade, Carlos 1902-1987
CLC 18
See also Andrade, Carlos Drummond de
See also CA 132; 123

Drury, Allen (Stuart) 1918-1998   **CLC 37**
See also CA 57-60; 170; CANR 18, 52; INT
CANR-18

Dryden, John 1631-1700**LC 3, 21; DA; DAB;**

**DAC; DAM DRAM, MST, POET; DC 3;
WLC**
See also CDBLB 1660-1789; DLB 80, 101, 131

Duberman, Martin (Bauml) 1930-   **CLC 8**
See also CA 1-4R; CANR 2, 63

Dubie, Norman (Evans) 1945-   **CLC 36**
See also CA 69-72; CANR 12; DLB 120

Du Bois, W(illiam) E(dward) B(urghardt) 1868-
1963   **CLC 1, 2, 13, 64, 96; BLC 1; DA;
DAC; DAM MST, MULT, NOV; WLC**
See also BW 1; CA 85-88; CANR 34; CDALB
1865-1917; DLB 47, 50, 91; MTCW 1; SATA
42

Dubus, Andre 1936- **CLC 13, 36, 97; SSC 15**
See also CA 21-24R; CANR 17; DLB 130; INT
CANR-17

Duca Minimo
See D'Annunzio, Gabriele

Ducharme, Rejean 1941-   **CLC 74**
See also CA 165; DLB 60

Duclos, Charles Pinot 1704-1772   **LC 1**

Dudek, Louis 1918-   **CLC 11, 19**
See also CA 45-48; CAAS 14; CANR 1; DLB
88

Duerrenmatt, Friedrich 1921-1990 **CLC 1, 4,
8, 11, 15, 43, 102; DAM DRAM**
See also CA 17-20R; CANR 33; DLB 69, 124;
MTCW 1

Duffy, Bruce (?)-   **CLC 50**

Duffy, Maureen 1933-   **CLC 37**
See also CA 25-28R; CANR 33, 68; DLB 14;
MTCW 1

Dugan, Alan 1923-   **CLC 2, 6**
See also CA 81-84; DLB 5

du Gard, Roger Martin
See Martin du Gard, Roger

Duhamel, Georges 1884-1966   **CLC 8**
See also CA 81-84; 25-28R; CANR 35; DLB
65; MTCW 1

Dujardin, Edouard (Emile Louis) 1861-1949
TCLC 13
See also CA 109; DLB 123

Dulles, John Foster 1888-1959   **TCLC 72**
See also CA 115; 149

Dumas, Alexandre (pere)
See Dumas, Alexandre (Davy de la Pailleterie)

Dumas, Alexandre (Davy de la Pailleterie)
1802-1870   **NCLC 11; DA; DAB; DAC;
DAM MST, NOV; WLC**
See also DLB 119, 192; SATA 18

Dumas, Alexandre (fils) 1824-1895**NCLC 71;
DC 1**
See also AAYA 22; DLB 192

Dumas, Claudine
See Malzberg, Barry N(athaniel)

Dumas, Henry L. 1934-1968   **CLC 6, 62**
See also BW 1; CA 85-88; DLB 41

du Maurier, Daphne 1907-1989**CLC 6, 11, 59;
DAB; DAC; DAM MST, POP; SSC 18**
See also CA 5-8R; 128; CANR 6, 55; DLB 191;
MTCW 1; SATA 27; SATA-Obit 60

Dunbar, Paul Laurence 1872-1906 **TCLC 2,
12; BLC 1; DA; DAC; DAM MST, MULT,
POET; PC 5; SSC 8; WLC**
See also BW 1; CA 104; 124; CDALB 1865-
1917; DLB 50, 54, 78; SATA 34

Dunbar, William 1460(?)-1530(?)   **LC 20**
See also DLB 132, 146

Duncan, Dora Angela
See Duncan, Isadora

Duncan, Isadora 1877(?)-1927   **TCLC 68**
See also CA 118; 149

Duncan, Lois 1934-   **CLC 26**

See also AAYA 4; CA 1-4R; CANR 2, 23, 36;
CLR 29; JRDA; MAICYA; SAAS 2; SATA
1, 36, 75

Duncan, Robert (Edward) 1919-1988 **CLC 1,
2, 4, 7, 15, 41, 55; DAM POET; PC 2**
See also CA 9-12R; 124; CANR 28, 62; DLB
5, 16, 193; MTCW 1

Duncan, Sara Jeannette 1861-1922 **TCLC 60**
See also CA 157; DLB 92

Dunlap, William 1766-1839   **NCLC 2**
See also DLB 30, 37, 59

Dunn, Douglas (Eaglesham) 1942- **CLC 6, 40**
See also CA 45-48; CANR 2, 33; DLB 40;
MTCW 1

Dunn, Katherine (Karen) 1945-   **CLC 71**
See also CA 33-36R; CANR 72

Dunn, Stephen 1939-   **CLC 36**
See also CA 33-36R; CANR 12, 48, 53; DLB
105

Dunne, Finley Peter 1867-1936   **TCLC 28**
See also CA 108; DLB 11, 23

Dunne, John Gregory 1932-   **CLC 28**
See also CA 25-28R; CANR 14, 50; DLBY 80

Dunsany, Edward John Moreton Drax Plunkett
1878-1957
See Dunsany, Lord
See also CA 104; 148; DLB 10

Dunsany, Lord   **TCLC 2, 59**
See also Dunsany, Edward John Moreton Drax
Plunkett
See also DLB 77, 153, 156

du Perry, Jean
See Simenon, Georges (Jacques Christian)

Durang, Christopher (Ferdinand) 1949-**C L C
27, 38**
See also CA 105; CANR 50

Duras, Marguerite 1914-1996**CLC 3, 6, 11, 20,
34, 40, 68, 100**
See also CA 25-28R; 151; CANR 50; DLB 83;
MTCW 1

Durban, (Rosa) Pam 1947-   **CLC 39**
See also CA 123

Durcan, Paul 1944-**CLC 43, 70; DAM POET**
See also CA 134

Durkheim, Emile 1858-1917   **TCLC 55**

Durrell, Lawrence (George) 1912-1990 **C L C
1, 4, 6, 8, 13, 27, 41; DAM NOV**
See also CA 9-12R; 132; CANR 40; CDBLB
1945-1960; DLB 15, 27; DLBY 90; MTCW
1

Durrenmatt, Friedrich
See Duerrenmatt, Friedrich

Dutt, Toru 1856-1877   **NCLC 29**

Dwight, Timothy 1752-1817   **NCLC 13**
See also DLB 37

Dworkin, Andrea 1946-   **CLC 43**
See also CA 77-80; CAAS 21; CANR 16, 39;
INT CANR-16; MTCW 1

Dwyer, Deanna
See Koontz, Dean R(ay)

Dwyer, K. R.
See Koontz, Dean R(ay)

Dwyer, Thomas A. 1923-   **CLC 114**
See also CA 115

Dye, Richard
See De Voto, Bernard (Augustine)

Dylan, Bob 1941-   **CLC 3, 4, 6, 12, 77**
See also CA 41-44R; DLB 16

Eagleton, Terence (Francis) 1943-
See Eagleton, Terry
See also CA 57-60; CANR 7, 23, 68; MTCW 1

Eagleton, Terry   **CLC 63**
See also Eagleton, Terence (Francis)

Early, Jack
See Scoppettone, Sandra

East, Michael
See West, Morris L(anglo)

Eastaway, Edward
See Thomas, (Philip) Edward

Eastlake, William (Derry) 1917-1997 **CLC 8**
See also CA 5-8R; 158; CAAS 1; CANR 5, 63;
DLB 6; INT CANR-5

Eastman, Charles A(lexander) 1858-1939
TCLC 55; DAM MULT
See also DLB 175; NNAL; YABC 1

Eberhart, Richard (Ghormley) 1904- **CLC 3, 11, 19, 56; DAM POET**
See also CA 1-4R; CANR 2; CDALB 1941-1968; DLB 48; MTCW 1

Eberstadt, Fernanda 1960- **CLC 39**
See also CA 136; CANR 69

Echegaray (y Eizaguirre), Jose (Maria Waldo)
1832-1916 **TCLC 4**
See also CA 104; CANR 32; HW; MTCW 1

Echeverria, (Jose) Esteban (Antonino) 1805-1851 **NCLC 18**

Echo
See Proust, (Valentin-Louis-George-Eugene-)
Marcel

Eckert, Allan W. 1931- **CLC 17**
See also AAYA 18; CA 13-16R; CANR 14, 45;
INT CANR-14; SAAS 21; SATA 29, 91;
SATA-Brief 27

Eckhart, Meister 1260(?)-1328(?) **CMLC 9**
See also DLB 115

Eckmar, F. R.
See de Hartog, Jan

Eco, Umberto 1932- **CLC 28, 60; DAM NOV, POP**
See also BEST 90:1; CA 77-80; CANR 12, 33,
55; DLB 196; MTCW 1

Eddison, E(ric) R(ucker) 1882-1945 **TCLC 15**
See also CA 109; 156

Eddy, Mary (Morse) Baker 1821-1910 **TCLC 71**
See also CA 113

Edel, (Joseph) Leon 1907-1997 **CLC 29, 34**
See also CA 1-4R; 161; CANR 1, 22; DLB 103;
INT CANR-22

Eden, Emily 1797-1869 **NCLC 10**

Edgar, David 1948- **CLC 42; DAM DRAM**
See also CA 57-60; CANR 12, 61; DLB 13;
MTCW 1

Edgerton, Clyde (Carlyle) 1944- **CLC 39**
See also AAYA 17; CA 118; 134; CANR 64;
INT 134

Edgeworth, Maria 1768-1849 **NCLC 1, 51**
See also DLB 116, 159, 163; SATA 21

Edmonds, Paul
See Kuttner, Henry

Edmonds, Walter D(umaux) 1903-1998 **CLC 35**
See also CA 5-8R; CANR 2; DLB 9; MAICYA;
SAAS 4; SATA 1, 27; SATA-Obit 99

Edmondson, Wallace
See Ellison, Harlan (Jay)

Edson, Russell **CLC 13**
See also CA 33-36R

Edwards, Bronwen Elizabeth
See Rose, Wendy

Edwards, G(erald) B(asil) 1899-1976 **CLC 25**
See also CA 110

Edwards, Gus 1939- **CLC 43**
See also CA 108; INT 108

Edwards, Jonathan 1703-1758 **LC 7; DA; DAC; DAM MST**

See also DLB 24

Efron, Marina Ivanovna Tsvetaeva
See Tsvetaeva (Efron), Marina (Ivanovna)

Ehle, John (Marsden, Jr.) 1925- **CLC 27**
See also CA 9-12R

Ehrenbourg, Ilya (Grigoryevich)
See Ehrenburg, Ilya (Grigoryevich)

Ehrenburg, Ilya (Grigoryevich) 1891-1967
CLC 18, 34, 62
See also CA 102; 25-28R

Ehrenburg, Ilyo (Grigoryevich)
See Ehrenburg, Ilya (Grigoryevich)

Ehrenreich, Barbara 1941- **CLC 110**
See also BEST 90:4; CA 73-76; CANR 16, 37,
62; MTCW 1

Eich, Guenter 1907-1972 **CLC 15**
See also CA 111; 93-96; DLB 69, 124

Eichendorff, Joseph Freiherr von 1788-1857
NCLC 8
See also DLB 90

Eigner, Larry **CLC 9**
See Eigner, Laurence (Joel)
See also CAAS 23; DLB 5

Eigner, Laurence (Joel) 1927-1996
See Eigner, Larry
See also CA 9-12R; 151; CANR 6; DLB 193

Einstein, Albert 1879-1955 **TCLC 65**
See also CA 121; 133; MTCW 1

Eiseley, Loren Corey 1907-1977 **CLC 7**
See also AAYA 5; CA 1-4R; 73-76; CANR 6;
DLBD 17

Eisenstadt, Jill 1963- **CLC 50**
See also CA 140

Eisenstein, Sergei (Mikhailovich) 1898-1948
TCLC 57
See also CA 114; 149

Eisner, Simon
See Kornbluth, C(yril) M.

Ekeloef, (Bengt) Gunnar 1907-1968 **CLC 27;
DAM POET; PC 23**
See also CA 123; 25-28R

Ekelof, (Bengt) Gunnar
See Ekeloef, (Bengt) Gunnar

Ekelund, Vilhelm 1880-1949 **TCLC 75**

Ekwensi, C. O. D.
See Ekwensi, Cyprian (Odiatu Duaka)

Ekwensi, Cyprian (Odiatu Duaka) 1921- **CLC 4; BLC 1; DAM MULT**
See also BW 2; CA 29-32R; CANR 18, 42, 74;
DLB 117; MTCW 1; SATA 66

Elaine **TCLC 18**
See also Leverson, Ada

El Crummo
See Crumb, R(obert)

Elder, Lonne III 1931-1996 **DC 8**
See also BLC 1; BW 1; CA 81-84; 152; CANR
25; DAM MULT; DLB 7, 38, 44

Elia
See Lamb, Charles

Eliade, Mircea 1907-1986 **CLC 19**
See also CA 65-68; 119; CANR 30, 62; MTCW
1

Eliot, A. D.
See Jewett, (Theodora) Sarah Orne

Eliot, Alice
See Jewett, (Theodora) Sarah Orne

Eliot, Dan
See Silverberg, Robert

Eliot, George 1819-1880 **NCLC 4, 13, 23, 41, 49; DA; DAB; DAC; DAM MST, NOV; PC 20; WLC**
See also CDBLB 1832-1890; DLB 21, 35, 55

Eliot, John 1604-1690 **LC 5**

See also DLB 24

Eliot, T(homas) S(tearns) 1888-1965 **CLC 1, 2, 3, 6, 9, 10, 13, 15, 24, 34, 41, 55, 57, 113; DA; DAB; DAC; DAM DRAM, MST, POET; PC 5; WLC**
See also CA 5-8R; 25-28R; CANR 41; CDALB
1929-1941; DLB 7, 10, 45, 63; DLBY 88;
MTCW 1

Elizabeth 1866-1941 **TCLC 41**

Elkin, Stanley L(awrence) 1930-1995 **CLC 4, 6, 9, 14, 27, 51, 91; DAM NOV, POP; SSC 12**
See also CA 9-12R; 148; CANR 8, 46; DLB 2,
28; DLBY 80; INT CANR-8; MTCW 1

Elledge, Scott **CLC 34**

Elliot, Don
See Silverberg, Robert

Elliott, Don
See Silverberg, Robert

Elliott, George P(aul) 1918-1980 **CLC 2**
See also CA 1-4R; 97-100; CANR 2

Elliott, Janice 1931- **CLC 47**
See also CA 13-16R; CANR 8, 29; DLB 14

Elliott, Sumner Locke 1917-1991 **CLC 38**
See also CA 5-8R; 134; CANR 2, 21

Elliott, William
See Bradbury, Ray (Douglas)

Ellis, A. E. **CLC 7**

Ellis, Alice Thomas **CLC 40**
See also Haycraft, Anna
See also DLB 194

Ellis, Bret Easton 1964- **CLC 39, 71, 117; DAM POP**
See also AAYA 2; CA 118; 123; CANR 51, 74;
INT 123

Ellis, (Henry) Havelock 1859-1939 **TCLC 14**
See also CA 109; 169; DLB 190

Ellis, Landon
See Ellison, Harlan (Jay)

Ellis, Trey 1962- **CLC 55**
See also CA 146

Ellison, Harlan (Jay) 1934- **CLC 1, 13, 42; DAM POP; SSC 14**
See also CA 5-8R; CANR 5, 46; DLB 8; INT
CANR-5; MTCW 1

Ellison, Ralph (Waldo) 1914-1994 **CLC 1, 3, 11, 54, 86, 114; BLC 1; DA; DAB; DAC; DAM MST, MULT, NOV; SSC 26; WLC**
See also AAYA 19; BW 1; CA 9-12R; 145;
CANR 24, 53; CDALB 1941-1968; DLB 2,
76; DLBY 94; MTCW 1

Ellmann, Lucy (Elizabeth) 1956- **CLC 61**
See also CA 128

Ellmann, Richard (David) 1918-1987 **CLC 50**
See also BEST 89:2; CA 1-4R; 122; CANR 2,
28, 61; DLB 103; DLBY 87; MTCW 1

Elman, Richard (Martin) 1934-1997 **CLC 19**
See also CA 17-20R; 163; CAAS 3; CANR 47

Elron
See Hubbard, L(afayette) Ron(ald)

Eluard, Paul **TCLC 7, 41**
See also Grindel, Eugene

Elyot, Sir Thomas 1490(?)-1546 **LC 11**

Elytis, Odysseus 1911-1996 **CLC 15, 49, 100; DAM POET; PC 21**
See also CA 102; 151; MTCW 1

Emecheta, (Florence Onye) Buchi 1944- **CLC 14, 48; BLC 2; DAM MULT**
See also BW 2; CA 81-84; CANR 27; DLB 117;
MTCW 1; SATA 66

Emerson, Mary Moody 1774-1863 **NCLC 66**

Emerson, Ralph Waldo 1803-1882 **NCLC 1, 38; DA; DAB; DAC; DAM MST, POET;**

PC 18; WLC
See also CDALB 1640-1865; DLB 1, 59, 73
Eminescu, Mihail 1850-1889   **NCLC 33**
Empson, William 1906-1984**CLC 3, 8, 19, 33, 34**
  See also CA 17-20R; 112; CANR 31, 61; DLB 20; MTCW 1
Enchi, Fumiko (Ueda) 1905-1986   **CLC 31**
  See also CA 129; 121
Ende, Michael (Andreas Helmuth) 1929-1995 **CLC 31**
  See also CA 118; 124; 149; CANR 36; CLR 14; DLB 75; MAICYA; SATA 61; SATA-Brief 42; SATA-Obit 86
Endo, Shusaku 1923-1996 **CLC 7, 14, 19, 54, 99; DAM NOV**
  See also CA 29-32R; 153; CANR 21, 54; DLB 182; MTCW 1
Engel, Marian 1933-1985   **CLC 36**
  See also CA 25-28R; CANR 12; DLB 53; INT CANR-12
Engelhardt, Frederick
  See Hubbard, L(afayette) Ron(ald)
Enright, D(ennis) J(oseph) 1920-**CLC 4, 8, 31**
  See also CA 1-4R; CANR 1, 42; DLB 27; SATA 25
Enzensberger, Hans Magnus 1929- **CLC 43**
  See also CA 116; 119
Ephron, Nora 1941-   **CLC 17, 31**
  See also AITN 2; CA 65-68; CANR 12, 39
Epicurus 341B.C.-270B.C.   **CMLC 21**
  See also DLB 176
Epsilon
  See Betjeman, John
Epstein, Daniel Mark 1948-   **CLC 7**
  See also CA 49-52; CANR 2, 53
Epstein, Jacob 1956-   **CLC 19**
  See also CA 114
Epstein, Joseph 1937-   **CLC 39**
  See also CA 112; 119; CANR 50, 65
Epstein, Leslie 1938-   **CLC 27**
  See also CA 73-76; CAAS 12; CANR 23, 69
Equiano, Olaudah 1745(?)-1797 **LC 16; BLC 2; DAM MULT**
  See also DLB 37, 50
ER   **TCLC 33**
  See also CA 160; DLB 85
Erasmus, Desiderius 1469(?)-1536   **LC 16**
Erdman, Paul E(mil) 1932-   **CLC 25**
  See also AITN 1; CA 61-64; CANR 13, 43
Erdrich, Louise 1954-   **CLC 39, 54; DAM MULT, NOV, POP**
  See also AAYA 10; BEST 89:1; CA 114; CANR 41, 62; DLB 152, 175; MTCW 1; NNAL; SATA 94
Erenburg, Ilya (Grigoryevich)
  See Ehrenburg, Ilya (Grigoryevich)
Erickson, Stephen Michael 1950-
  See Erickson, Steve
  See also CA 129
Erickson, Steve 1950-   **CLC 64**
  See also Erickson, Stephen Michael
  See also CANR 60, 68
Ericson, Walter
  See Fast, Howard (Melvin)
Eriksson, Buntel
  See Bergman, (Ernst) Ingmar
Ernaux, Annie 1940-   **CLC 88**
  See also CA 147
Erskine, John 1879-1951   **TCLC 84**
  See also CA 112; 159; DLB 9, 102
Eschenbach, Wolfram von
  See Wolfram von Eschenbach

Eseki, Bruno
  See Mphahlele, Ezekiel
Esenin, Sergei (Alexandrovich) 1895-1925 **TCLC 4**
  See also CA 104
Eshleman, Clayton 1935-   **CLC 7**
  See also CA 33-36R; CAAS 6; DLB 5
Espriella, Don Manuel Alvarez
  See Southey, Robert
Espriu, Salvador 1913-1985   **CLC 9**
  See also CA 154; 115; DLB 134
Espronceda, Jose de 1808-1842   **NCLC 39**
Esse, James
  See Stephens, James
Esterbrook, Tom
  See Hubbard, L(afayette) Ron(ald)
Estleman, Loren D. 1952-**CLC 48; DAM NOV, POP**
  See also AAYA 27; CA 85-88; CANR 27, 74; INT CANR-27; MTCW 1
Euclid 306B.C.-283B.C.   **CMLC 25**
Eugenides, Jeffrey 1960(?)-   **CLC 81**
  See also CA 144
Euripides c. 485B.C.-406B.C.**CMLC 23; DA; DAB; DAC; DAM DRAM, MST; DC 4; WLCS**
  See also DLB 176
Evan, Evin
  See Faust, Frederick (Schiller)
Evans, Caradoc 1878-1945   **TCLC 85**
Evans, Evan
  See Faust, Frederick (Schiller)
Evans, Marian
  See Eliot, George
Evans, Mary Ann
  See Eliot, George
Evarts, Esther
  See Benson, Sally
Everett, Percival L. 1956-   **CLC 57**
  See also BW 2; CA 129
Everson, R(onald) G(ilmour) 1903- **CLC 27**
  See also CA 17-20R; DLB 88
Everson, William (Oliver) 1912-1994 **CLC 1, 5, 14**
  See also CA 9-12R; 145; CANR 20; DLB 5, 16; MTCW 1
Evtushenko, Evgenii Aleksandrovich
  See Yevtushenko, Yevgeny (Alexandrovich)
Ewart, Gavin (Buchanan) 1916-1995**CLC 13, 46**
  See also CA 89-92; 150; CANR 17, 46; DLB 40; MTCW 1
Ewers, Hanns Heinz 1871-1943   **TCLC 12**
  See also CA 109; 149
Ewing, Frederick R.
  See Sturgeon, Theodore (Hamilton)
Exley, Frederick (Earl) 1929-1992 **CLC 6, 11**
  See also AITN 2; CA 81-84; 138; DLB 143; DLBY 81
Eynhardt, Guillermo
  See Quiroga, Horacio (Sylvestre)
Ezekiel, Nissim 1924-   **CLC 61**
  See also CA 61-64
Ezekiel, Tish O'Dowd 1943-   **CLC 34**
  See also CA 129
Fadeyev, A.
  See Bulgya, Alexander Alexandrovich
Fadeyev, Alexander   **TCLC 53**
  See also Bulgya, Alexander Alexandrovich
Fagen, Donald 1948-   **CLC 26**
Fainzilberg, Ilya Arnoldovich 1897-1937
  See Ilf, Ilya
  See also CA 120; 165

Fair, Ronald L. 1932-   **CLC 18**
  See also BW 1; CA 69-72; CANR 25; DLB 33
Fairbairn, Roger
  See Carr, John Dickson
Fairbairns, Zoe (Ann) 1948-   **CLC 32**
  See also CA 103; CANR 21
Falco, Gian
  See Papini, Giovanni
Falconer, James
  See Kirkup, James
Falconer, Kenneth
  See Kornbluth, C(yril) M.
Falkland, Samuel
  See Heijermans, Herman
Fallaci, Oriana 1930-   **CLC 11, 110**
  See also CA 77-80; CANR 15, 58; MTCW 1
Faludy, George 1913-   **CLC 42**
  See also CA 21-24R
Faludy, Gyoergy
  See Faludy, George
Fanon, Frantz 1925-1961   **CLC 74; BLC 2; DAM MULT**
  See also BW 1; CA 116; 89-92
Fanshawe, Ann 1625-1680   **LC 11**
Fante, John (Thomas) 1911-1983   **CLC 60**
  See also CA 69-72; 109; CANR 23; DLB 130; DLBY 83
Farah, Nuruddin 1945-**CLC 53; BLC 2; DAM MULT**
  See also BW 2; CA 106; DLB 125
Fargue, Leon-Paul 1876(?)-1947   **TCLC 11**
  See also CA 109
Farigoule, Louis
  See Romains, Jules
Farina, Richard 1936(?)-1966   **CLC 9**
  See also CA 81-84; 25-28R
Farley, Walter (Lorimer) 1915-1989 **CLC 17**
  See also CA 17-20R; CANR 8, 29; DLB 22; JRDA; MAICYA; SATA 2, 43
Farmer, Philip Jose 1918-   **CLC 1, 19**
  See also CA 1-4R; CANR 4, 35; DLB 8; MTCW 1; SATA 93
Farquhar, George 1677-1707   **LC 21; DAM DRAM**
  See also DLB 84
Farrell, J(ames) G(ordon) 1935-1979 **CLC 6**
  See also CA 73-76; 89-92; CANR 36; DLB 14; MTCW 1
Farrell, James T(homas) 1904-1979**CLC 1, 4, 8, 11, 66; SSC 28**
  See also CA 5-8R; 89-92; CANR 9, 61; DLB 4, 9, 86; DLBD 2; MTCW 1
Farren, Richard J.
  See Betjeman, John
Farren, Richard M.
  See Betjeman, John
Fassbinder, Rainer Werner 1946-1982**CLC 20**
  See also CA 93-96; 106; CANR 31
Fast, Howard (Melvin) 1914- **CLC 23; DAM NOV**
  See also AAYA 16; CA 1-4R; CAAS 18; CANR 1, 33, 54; DLB 9; INT CANR-33; SATA 7
Faulcon, Robert
  See Holdstock, Robert P.
Faulkner, William (Cuthbert) 1897-1962**CLC 1, 3, 6, 8, 9, 11, 14, 18, 28, 52, 68; DA; DAB; DAC; DAM MST, NOV; SSC 1; WLC**
  See also AAYA 7; CA 81-84; CANR 33; CDALB 1929-1941; DLB 9, 11, 44, 102; DLBD 2; DLBY 86, 97; MTCW 1
Fauset, Jessie Redmon 1884(?)-1961 **CLC 19, 54; BLC 2; DAM MULT**
  See also BW 1; CA 109; DLB 51

DLB 9, 26, 28; DLBY 93

Fuchs, Daniel 1934- **CLC 34**
 See also CA 37-40R; CANR 14, 48

Fuentes, Carlos 1928-**CLC 3, 8, 10, 13, 22, 41, 60, 113; DA; DAB; DAC; DAM MST, MULT, NOV; HLC; SSC 24; WLC**
 See also AAYA 4; AITN 2; CA 69-72; CANR 10, 32, 68; DLB 113; HW; MTCW 1

Fuentes, Gregorio Lopez y
 See Lopez y Fuentes, Gregorio

Fugard, (Harold) Athol 1932-**CLC 5, 9, 14, 25, 40, 80; DAM DRAM; DC 3**
 See also AAYA 17; CA 85-88; CANR 32, 54; MTCW 1

Fugard, Sheila 1932- **CLC 48**
 See also CA 125

Fuller, Charles (H., Jr.) 1939-**CLC 25; BLC 2; DAM DRAM, MULT; DC 1**
 See also BW 2; CA 108; 112; DLB 38; INT 112; MTCW 1

Fuller, John (Leopold) 1937- **CLC 62**
 See also CA 21-24R; CANR 9, 44; DLB 40

Fuller, Margaret **NCLC 5, 50**
 See also Ossoli, Sarah Margaret (Fuller marchesa d')

Fuller, Roy (Broadbent) 1912-1991**CLC 4, 28**
 See also CA 5-8R; 135; CAAS 10; CANR 53; DLB 15, 20; SATA 87

Fulton, Alice 1952- **CLC 52**
 See also CA 116; CANR 57; DLB 193

Furphy, Joseph 1843-1912 **TCLC 25**
 See also CA 163

Fussell, Paul 1924- **CLC 74**
 See also BEST 90:1; CA 17-20R; CANR 8, 21, 35, 69; INT CANR-21; MTCW 1

Futabatei, Shimei 1864-1909 **TCLC 44**
 See also CA 162; DLB 180

Futrelle, Jacques 1875-1912 **TCLC 19**
 See also CA 113; 155

Gaboriau, Emile 1835-1873 **NCLC 14**

Gadda, Carlo Emilio 1893-1973 **CLC 11**
 See also CA 89-92; DLB 177

Gaddis, William 1922- **CLC 1, 3, 6, 8, 10, 19, 43, 86**
 See also CA 17-20R; CANR 21, 48; DLB 2; MTCW 1

Gage, Walter
 See Inge, William (Motter)

Gaines, Ernest J(ames) 1933- **CLC 3, 11, 18, 86; BLC 2; DAM MULT**
 See also AAYA 18; AITN 1; BW 2; CA 9-12R; CANR 6, 24, 42; CDALB 1968-1988; DLB 2, 33, 152; DLBY 80; MTCW 1; SATA 86

Gaitskill, Mary 1954- **CLC 69**
 See also CA 128; CANR 61

Galdos, Benito Perez
 See Perez Galdos, Benito

Gale, Zona 1874-1938**TCLC 7; DAM DRAM**
 See also CA 105; 153; DLB 9, 78

Galeano, Eduardo (Hughes) 1940- **CLC 72**
 See also CA 29-32R; CANR 13, 32; HW

Galiano, Juan Valera y Alcala
 See Valera y Alcala-Galiano, Juan

Galilei, Galileo 1546-1642 **LC 45**

Gallagher, Tess 1943- **CLC 18, 63; DAM POET; PC 9**
 See also CA 106; DLB 120

Gallant, Mavis 1922- **CLC 7, 18, 38; DAC; DAM MST; SSC 5**
 See also CA 69-72; CANR 29, 69; DLB 53; MTCW 1

Gallant, Roy A(rthur) 1924- **CLC 17**
 See also CA 5-8R; CANR 4, 29, 54; CLR 30;

MAICYA; SATA 4, 68

Gallico, Paul (William) 1897-1976 **CLC 2**
 See also AITN 1; CA 5-8R; 69-72; CANR 23; DLB 9, 171; MAICYA; SATA 13

Gallo, Max Louis 1932- **CLC 95**
 See also CA 85-88

Gallois, Lucien
 See Desnos, Robert

Gallup, Ralph
 See Whitemore, Hugh (John)

Galsworthy, John 1867-1933**TCLC 1, 45; DA; DAB; DAC; DAM DRAM, MST, NOV; SSC 22; WLC 2**
 See also CA 104; 141; CDBLB 1890-1914; DLB 10, 34, 98, 162; DLBD 16

Galt, John 1779-1839 **NCLC 1**
 See also DLB 99, 116, 159

Galvin, James 1951- **CLC 38**
 See also CA 108; CANR 26

Gamboa, Federico 1864-1939 **TCLC 36**
 See also CA 167

Gandhi, M. K.
 See Gandhi, Mohandas Karamchand

Gandhi, Mahatma
 See Gandhi, Mohandas Karamchand

Gandhi, Mohandas Karamchand 1869-1948
 TCLC 59; DAM MULT
 See also CA 121; 132; MTCW 1

Gann, Ernest Kellogg 1910-1991 **CLC 23**
 See also AITN 1; CA 1-4R; 136; CANR 1

Garcia, Cristina 1958- **CLC 76**
 See also CA 141; CANR 73

Garcia Lorca, Federico 1898-1936**TCLC 1, 7, 49; DA; DAB; DAC; DAM DRAM, MST, MULT, POET; DC 2; HLC; PC 3; WLC**
 See also CA 104; 131; DLB 108; HW; MTCW 1

Garcia Marquez, Gabriel (Jose) 1928-**CLC 2, 3, 8, 10, 15, 27, 47, 55, 68; DA; DAB; DAC; DAM MST, MULT, NOV, POP; HLC; SSC 8; WLC**
 See also AAYA 3; BEST 89:1, 90:4; CA 33-36R; CANR 10, 28, 50; DLB 113; HW; MTCW 1

Gard, Janice
 See Latham, Jean Lee

Gard, Roger Martin du
 See Martin du Gard, Roger

Gardam, Jane 1928- **CLC 43**
 See also CA 49-52; CANR 2, 18, 33, 54; CLR 12; DLB 14, 161; MAICYA; MTCW 1; SAAS 9; SATA 39, 76; SATA-Brief 28

Gardner, Herb(ert) 1934- **CLC 44**
 See also CA 149

Gardner, John (Champlin), Jr. 1933-1982
 CLC 2, 3, 5, 7, 8, 10, 18, 28, 34; DAM NOV, POP; SSC 7
 See also AITN 1; CA 65-68; 107; CANR 33, 73; DLB 2; DLBY 82; MTCW 1; SATA 40; SATA-Obit 31

Gardner, John (Edmund) 1926-**CLC 30; DAM POP**
 See also CA 103; CANR 15, 69; MTCW 1

Gardner, Miriam
 See Bradley, Marion Zimmer

Gardner, Noel
 See Kuttner, Henry

Gardons, S. S.
 See Snodgrass, W(illiam) D(e Witt)

Garfield, Leon 1921-1996 **CLC 12**
 See also AAYA 8; CA 17-20R; 152; CANR 38, 41; CLR 21; DLB 161; JRDA; MAICYA; SATA 1, 32, 76; SATA-Obit 90

Garland, (Hannibal) Hamlin 1860-1940
 TCLC 3; SSC 18
 See also CA 104; DLB 12, 71, 78, 186

Garneau, (Hector de) Saint-Denys 1912-1943
 TCLC 13
 See also CA 111; DLB 88

Garner, Alan 1934-**CLC 17; DAB; DAM POP**
 See also AAYA 18; CA 73-76; CANR 15, 64; CLR 20; DLB 161; MAICYA; MTCW 1; SATA 18, 69

Garner, Hugh 1913-1979 **CLC 13**
 See also CA 69-72; CANR 31; DLB 68

Garnett, David 1892-1981 **CLC 3**
 See also CA 5-8R; 103; CANR 17; DLB 34

Garos, Stephanie
 See Katz, Steve

Garrett, George (Palmer) 1929-**CLC 3, 11, 51; SSC 30**
 See also CA 1-4R; CAAS 5; CANR 1, 42, 67; DLB 2, 5, 130, 152; DLBY 83

Garrick, David 1717-1779 **LC 15; DAM DRAM**
 See also DLB 84

Garrigue, Jean 1914-1972 **CLC 2, 8**
 See also CA 5-8R; 37-40R; CANR 20

Garrison, Frederick
 See Sinclair, Upton (Beall)

Garth, Will
 See Hamilton, Edmond; Kuttner, Henry

Garvey, Marcus (Moziah, Jr.) 1887-1940
 TCLC 41; BLC 2; DAM MULT
 See also BW 1; CA 120; 124

Gary, Romain **CLC 25**
 See also Kacew, Romain
 See also DLB 83

Gascar, Pierre **CLC 11**
 See also Fournier, Pierre

Gascoyne, David (Emery) 1916- **CLC 45**
 See also CA 65-68; CANR 10, 28, 54; DLB 20; MTCW 1

Gaskell, Elizabeth Cleghorn 1810-1865**NCLC 70; DAB; DAM MST; SSC 25**
 See also CDBLB 1832-1890; DLB 21, 144, 159

Gass, William H(oward) 1924-**CLC 1, 2, 8, 11, 15, 39; SSC 12**
 See also CA 17-20R; CANR 30, 71; DLB 2; MTCW 1

Gasset, Jose Ortega y
 See Ortega y Gasset, Jose

Gates, Henry Louis, Jr. 1950-**CLC 65; BLCS; DAM MULT**
 See also BW 2; CA 109; CANR 25, 53; DLB 67

Gautier, Theophile 1811-1872 **NCLC 1, 59; DAM POET; PC 18; SSC 20**
 See also DLB 119

Gawsworth, John
 See Bates, H(erbert) E(rnest)

Gay, Oliver
 See Gogarty, Oliver St. John

Gaye, Marvin (Penze) 1939-1984 **CLC 26**
 See also CA 112

Gebler, Carlo (Ernest) 1954- **CLC 39**
 See also CA 119; 133

Gee, Maggie (Mary) 1948- **CLC 57**
 See also CA 130

Gee, Maurice (Gough) 1931- **CLC 29**
 See also CA 97-100; CANR 67; SATA 46, 101

Gelbart, Larry (Simon) 1923- **CLC 21, 61**
 See also CA 73-76; CANR 45

Gelber, Jack 1932- **CLC 1, 6, 14, 79**
 See also CA 1-4R; CANR 2; DLB 7

Gellhorn, Martha (Ellis) 1908-1998 **CLC 14,**

60
See also CA 77-80; 164; CANR 44; DLBY 82

Genet, Jean 1910-1986 CLC 1, 2, 5, 10, 14, 44, 46; **DAM DRAM**
See also CA 13-16R; CANR 18; DLB 72; DLBY 86; MTCW 1

Gent, Peter 1942- **CLC 29**
See also AITN 1; CA 89-92; DLBY 82

Gentlewoman in New England, A
See Bradstreet, Anne

Gentlewoman in Those Parts, A
See Bradstreet, Anne

George, Jean Craighead 1919- **CLC 35**
See also AAYA 8; CA 5-8R; CANR 25; CLR 1; DLB 52; JRDA; MAICYA; SATA 2, 68

George, Stefan (Anton) 1868-1933 TCLC 2, 14
See also CA 104

Georges, Georges Martin
See Simenon, Georges (Jacques Christian)

Gerhardi, William Alexander
See Gerhardie, William Alexander

Gerhardie, William Alexander 1895-1977 **CLC 5**
See also CA 25-28R; 73-76; CANR 18; DLB 36

Gerstler, Amy 1956- **CLC 70**
See also CA 146

Gertler, T. **CLC 34**
See also CA 116; 121; INT 121

Ghalib **NCLC 39**
See also Ghalib, Hsadullah Khan

Ghalib, Hsadullah Khan 1797-1869
See Ghalib
See also DAM POET

Ghelderode, Michel de 1898-1962 CLC 6, 11; **DAM DRAM**
See also CA 85-88; CANR 40

Ghiselin, Brewster 1903- **CLC 23**
See also CA 13-16R; CAAS 10; CANR 13

Ghose, Aurabinda 1872-1950 **TCLC 63**
See also CA 163

Ghose, Zulfikar 1935- **CLC 42**
See also CA 65-68; CANR 67

Ghosh, Amitav 1956- **CLC 44**
See also CA 147

Giacosa, Giuseppe 1847-1906 **TCLC 7**
See also CA 104

Gibb, Lee
See Waterhouse, Keith (Spencer)

Gibbon, Lewis Grassic **TCLC 4**
See also Mitchell, James Leslie

Gibbons, Kaye 1960- CLC 50, 88; **DAM POP**
See also CA 151

Gibran, Kahlil 1883-1931 **TCLC 1, 9; DAM POET, POP; PC 9**
See also CA 104; 150

Gibran, Khalil
See Gibran, Kahlil

Gibson, William 1914- **CLC 23; DA; DAB; DAC; DAM DRAM, MST**
See also CA 9-12R; CANR 9, 42; DLB 7; SATA 66

Gibson, William (Ford) 1948- **CLC 39, 63; DAM POP**
See also AAYA 12; CA 126; 133; CANR 52

Gide, Andre (Paul Guillaume) 1869-1951 **TCLC 5, 12, 36; DA; DAB; DAC; DAM MST, NOV; SSC 13; WLC**
See also CA 104; 124; DLB 65; MTCW 1

Gifford, Barry (Colby) 1946- **CLC 34**
See also CA 65-68; CANR 9, 30, 40

Gilbert, Frank
See De Voto, Bernard (Augustine)

Gilbert, W(illiam) S(chwenck) 1836-1911 **TCLC 3; DAM DRAM, POET**
See also CA 104; SATA 36

Gilbreth, Frank B., Jr. 1911- **CLC 17**
See also CA 9-12R; SATA 2

Gilchrist, Ellen 1935- CLC 34, 48; **DAM POP; SSC 14**
See also CA 113; 116; CANR 41, 61; DLB 130; MTCW 1

Giles, Molly 1942- **CLC 39**
See also CA 126

Gill, Eric 1882-1940 **TCLC 85**

Gill, Patrick
See Creasey, John

Gilliam, Terry (Vance) 1940- **CLC 21**
See also Monty Python
See also AAYA 19; CA 108; 113; CANR 35; INT 113

Gillian, Jerry
See Gilliam, Terry (Vance)

Gilliatt, Penelope (Ann Douglass) 1932-1993 **CLC 2, 10, 13, 53**
See also AITN 2; CA 13-16R; 141; CANR 49; DLB 14

Gilman, Charlotte (Anna) Perkins (Stetson) 1860-1935 **TCLC 9, 37; SSC 13**
See also CA 106; 150

Gilmour, David 1949- **CLC 35**
See also CA 138; 147

Gilpin, William 1724-1804 **NCLC 30**

Gilray, J. D.
See Mencken, H(enry) L(ouis)

Gilroy, Frank D(aniel) 1925- **CLC 2**
See also CA 81-84; CANR 32, 64; DLB 7

Gilstrap, John 1957(?)- **CLC 99**
See also CA 160

Ginsberg, Allen 1926-1997 CLC 1, 2, 3, 4, 6, 13, 36, 69, 109; **DA; DAB; DAC; DAM MST, POET; PC 4; WLC 3**
See also AITN 1; CA 1-4R; 157; CANR 2, 41, 63; CDALB 1941-1968; DLB 5, 16, 169; MTCW 1

Ginzburg, Natalia 1916-1991 CLC 5, 11, 54, 70
See also CA 85-88; 135; CANR 33; DLB 177; MTCW 1

Giono, Jean 1895-1970 **CLC 4, 11**
See also CA 45-48; 29-32R; CANR 2, 35; DLB 72; MTCW 1

Giovanni, Nikki 1943- CLC 2, 4, 19, 64, 117; **BLC 2; DA; DAB; DAC; DAM MST, MULT, POET; PC 19; WLCS**
See also AAYA 22; AITN 1; BW 2; CA 29-32R; CAAS 6; CANR 18, 41, 60; CLR 6; DLB 5, 41; INT CANR-18; MAICYA; MTCW 1; SATA 24

Giovene, Andrea 1904- **CLC 7**
See also CA 85-88

Gippius, Zinaida (Nikolayevna) 1869-1945
See Hippius, Zinaida
See also CA 106

Giraudoux, (Hippolyte) Jean 1882-1944 **TCLC 2, 7; DAM DRAM**
See also CA 104; DLB 65

Gironella, Jose Maria 1917- **CLC 11**
See also CA 101

Gissing, George (Robert) 1857-1903 TCLC 3, 24, 47
See also CA 105; 167; DLB 18, 135, 184

Giurlani, Aldo
See Palazzeschi, Aldo

Gladkov, Fyodor (Vasilyevich) 1883-1958 **TCLC 27**
See also CA 170

Glanville, Brian (Lester) 1931- **CLC 6**
See also CA 5-8R; CAAS 9; CANR 3, 70; DLB 15, 139; SATA 42

Glasgow, Ellen (Anderson Gholson) 1873-1945 **TCLC 2, 7**
See also CA 104; 164; DLB 9, 12

Glaspell, Susan 1882(?)-1948 **TCLC 55**
See also CA 110; 154; DLB 7, 9, 78; YABC 2

Glassco, John 1909-1981 **CLC 9**
See also CA 13-16R; 102; CANR 15; DLB 68

Glasscock, Amnesia
See Steinbeck, John (Ernst)

Glasser, Ronald J. 1940(?)- **CLC 37**

Glassman, Joyce
See Johnson, Joyce

Glendinning, Victoria 1937- **CLC 50**
See also CA 120; 127; CANR 59; DLB 155

Glissant, Edouard 1928- CLC 10, 68; **DAM MULT**
See also CA 153

Gloag, Julian 1930- **CLC 40**
See also AITN 1; CA 65-68; CANR 10, 70

Glowacki, Aleksander
See Prus, Boleslaw

Gluck, Louise (Elisabeth) 1943- CLC 7, 22, 44, 81; **DAM POET; PC 16**
See also CA 33-36R; CANR 40, 69; DLB 5

Glyn, Elinor 1864-1943 **TCLC 72**
See also DLB 153

Gobineau, Joseph Arthur (Comte) de 1816-1882 **NCLC 17**
See also DLB 123

Godard, Jean-Luc 1930- **CLC 20**
See also CA 93-96

Godden, (Margaret) Rumer 1907- **CLC 53**
See also AAYA 6; CA 5-8R; CANR 4, 27, 36, 55; CLR 20; DLB 161; MAICYA; SAAS 12; SATA 3, 36

Godoy Alcayaga, Lucila 1889-1957
See Mistral, Gabriela
See also BW 2; CA 104; 131; DAM MULT; HW; MTCW 1

Godwin, Gail (Kathleen) 1937- CLC 5, 8, 22, 31, 69; **DAM POP**
See also CA 29-32R; CANR 15, 43, 69; DLB 6; INT CANR-15; MTCW 1

Godwin, William 1756-1836 **NCLC 14**
See also CDBLB 1789-1832; DLB 39, 104, 142, 158, 163

Goebbels, Josef
See Goebbels, (Paul) Joseph

Goebbels, (Paul) Joseph 1897-1945 TCLC 68
See also CA 115; 148

Goebbels, Joseph Paul
See Goebbels, (Paul) Joseph

Goethe, Johann Wolfgang von 1749-1832 **NCLC 4, 22, 34; DA; DAB; DAC; DAM DRAM, MST, POET; PC 5; WLC 3**
See also DLB 94

Gogarty, Oliver St. John 1878-1957 TCLC 15
See also CA 109; 150; DLB 15, 19

Gogol, Nikolai (Vasilyevich) 1809-1852 NCLC 5, 15, 31; **DA; DAB; DAC; DAM DRAM, MST; DC 1; SSC 4, 29; WLC**
See also DLB 198

Goines, Donald 1937(?)-1974 CLC 80; **BLC 2; DAM MULT, POP**
See also AITN 1; BW 1; CA 124; 114; DLB 33

Gold, Herbert 1924- **CLC 4, 7, 14, 42**
See also CA 9-12R; CANR 17, 45; DLB 2; DLBY 81

Goldbarth, Albert 1948- **CLC 5, 38**
See also CA 53-56; CANR 6, 40; DLB 120

H. D.   CLC 3, 8, 14, 31, 34, 73; PC 5
See also Doolittle, Hilda
H. de V.
See Buchan, John
Haavikko, Paavo Juhani 1931-   CLC 18, 34
See also CA 106
Habbema, Koos
See Heijermans, Herman
Habermas, Juergen 1929-   CLC 104
See also CA 109
Habermas, Jurgen
See Habermas, Juergen
Hacker, Marilyn 1942- CLC 5, 9, 23, 72, 91;
    DAM POET
See also CA 77-80; CANR 68; DLB 120
Haeckel, Ernst Heinrich (Philipp August) 1834-
    1919   TCLC 83
See also CA 157
Haggard, H(enry) Rider 1856-1925TCLC 11
See also CA 108; 148; DLB 70, 156, 174, 178;
    SATA 16
Hagiosy, L.
See Larbaud, Valery (Nicolas)
Hagiwara Sakutaro 1886-1942 TCLC 60; PC
    18
Haig, Fenil
See Ford, Ford Madox
Haig-Brown, Roderick (Langmere) 1908-1976
    CLC 21
See also CA 5-8R; 69-72; CANR 4, 38; CLR
    31; DLB 88; MAICYA; SATA 12
Hailey, Arthur 1920-CLC 5; DAM NOV, POP
See also AITN 2; BEST 90:3; CA 1-4R; CANR
    2, 36; DLB 88; DLBY 82; MTCW 1
Hailey, Elizabeth Forsythe 1938-   CLC 40
See also CA 93-96; CAAS 1; CANR 15, 48;
    INT CANR-15
Haines, John (Meade) 1924-   CLC 58
See also CA 17-20R; CANR 13, 34; DLB 5
Hakluyt, Richard 1552-1616   LC 31
Haldeman, Joe (William) 1943-   CLC 61
See also CA 53-56; CAAS 25; CANR 6, 70,
    72; DLB 8; INT CANR-6
Haley, Alex(ander Murray Palmer) 1921-1992
    CLC 8, 12, 76; BLC 2; DA; DAB; DAC;
    DAM MST, MULT, POP
See also AAYA 26; BW 2; CA 77-80; 136;
    CANR 61; DLB 38; MTCW 1
Haliburton, Thomas Chandler 1796-1865
    NCLC 15
See also DLB 11, 99
Hall, Donald (Andrew, Jr.) 1928- CLC 1, 13,
    37, 59; DAM POET
See also CA 5-8R; CAAS 7; CANR 2, 44, 64;
    DLB 5; SATA 23, 97
Hall, Frederic Sauser
See Sauser-Hall, Frederic
Hall, James
See Kuttner, Henry
Hall, James Norman 1887-1951   TCLC 23
See also CA 123; SATA 21
Hall, Radclyffe
See Hall, (Marguerite) Radclyffe
Hall, (Marguerite) Radclyffe 1886-1943
    TCLC 12
See also CA 110; 150; DLB 191
Hall, Rodney 1935-   CLC 51
See also CA 109; CANR 69
Halleck, Fitz-Greene 1790-1867   NCLC 47
See also DLB 3
Halliday, Michael
See Creasey, John
Halpern, Daniel 1945-   CLC 14

See also CA 33-36R
Hamburger, Michael (Peter Leopold) 1924-
    CLC 5, 14
See also CA 5-8R; CAAS 4; CANR 2, 47; DLB
    27
Hamill, Pete 1935-   CLC 10
See also CA 25-28R; CANR 18, 71
Hamilton, Alexander 1755(?)-1804 NCLC 49
See also DLB 37
Hamilton, Clive
See Lewis, C(live) S(taples)
Hamilton, Edmond 1904-1977   CLC 1
See also CA 1-4R; CANR 3; DLB 8
Hamilton, Eugene (Jacob) Lee
See Lee-Hamilton, Eugene (Jacob)
Hamilton, Franklin
See Silverberg, Robert
Hamilton, Gail
See Corcoran, Barbara
Hamilton, Mollie
See Kaye, M(ary) M(argaret)
Hamilton, (Anthony Walter) Patrick 1904-1962
    CLC 51
See also CA 113; DLB 10
Hamilton, Virginia 1936-   CLC 26; DAM
    MULT
See also AAYA 2, 21; BW 2; CA 25-28R;
    CANR 20, 37, 73; CLR 1, 11, 40; DLB 33,
    52; INT CANR-20; JRDA; MAICYA;
    MTCW 1; SATA 4, 56, 79
Hammett, (Samuel) Dashiell 1894-1961 C L C
    3, 5, 10, 19, 47; SSC 17
See also AITN 1; CA 81-84; CANR 42; CDALB
    1929-1941; DLBD 6; DLBY 96; MTCW 1
Hammon, Jupiter 1711(?)-1800(?)   NCLC 5;
    BLC 2; DAM MULT, POET; PC 16
See also DLB 31, 50
Hammond, Keith
See Kuttner, Henry
Hamner, Earl (Henry), Jr. 1923-   CLC 12
See also AITN 2; CA 73-76; DLB 6
Hampton, Christopher (James) 1946- CLC 4
See also CA 25-28R; DLB 13; MTCW 1
Hamsun, Knut   TCLC 2, 14, 49
See also Pedersen, Knut
Handke, Peter 1942-CLC 5, 8, 10, 15, 38; DAM
    DRAM, NOV
See also CA 77-80; CANR 33; DLB 85, 124;
    MTCW 1
Hanley, James 1901-1985   CLC 3, 5, 8, 13
See also CA 73-76; 117; CANR 36; DLB 191;
    MTCW 1
Hannah, Barry 1942-   CLC 23, 38, 90
See also CA 108; 110; CANR 43, 68; DLB 6;
    INT 110; MTCW 1
Hannon, Ezra
See Hunter, Evan
Hansberry, Lorraine (Vivian) 1930-1965CLC
    17, 62; BLC 2; DA; DAB; DAC; DAM
    DRAM, MST, MULT; DC 2
See also AAYA 25; BW 1; CA 109; 25-28R;
    CABS 3; CANR 58; CDALB 1941-1968;
    DLB 7, 38; MTCW 1
Hansen, Joseph 1923-   CLC 38
See also CA 29-32R; CAAS 17; CANR 16, 44,
    66; INT CANR-16
Hansen, Martin A(lfred) 1909-1955TCLC 32
See also CA 167
Hanson, Kenneth O(stlin) 1922-   CLC 13
See also CA 53-56; CANR 7
Hardwick, Elizabeth (Bruce) 1916- CLC 13;
    DAM NOV
See also CA 5-8R; CANR 3, 32, 70; DLB 6;

MTCW 1
Hardy, Thomas 1840-1928TCLC 4, 10, 18, 32,
    48, 53, 72; DA; DAB; DAC; DAM MST,
    NOV, POET; PC 8; SSC 2; WLC
See also CA 104; 123; CDBLB 1890-1914;
    DLB 18, 19, 135; MTCW 1
Hare, David 1947-   CLC 29, 58
See also CA 97-100; CANR 39; DLB 13;
    MTCW 1
Harewood, John
See Van Druten, John (William)
Harford, Henry
See Hudson, W(illiam) H(enry)
Hargrave, Leonie
See Disch, Thomas M(ichael)
Harjo, Joy 1951-   CLC 83; DAM MULT
See also CA 114; CANR 35, 67; DLB 120, 175;
    NNAL
Harlan, Louis R(udolph) 1922-   CLC 34
See also CA 21-24R; CANR 25, 55
Harling, Robert 1951(?)-   CLC 53
See also CA 147
Harmon, William (Ruth) 1938-   CLC 38
See also CA 33-36R; CANR 14, 32, 35; SATA
    65
Harper, F. E. W.
See Harper, Frances Ellen Watkins
Harper, Frances E. W.
See Harper, Frances Ellen Watkins
Harper, Frances E. Watkins
See Harper, Frances Ellen Watkins
Harper, Frances Ellen
See Harper, Frances Ellen Watkins
Harper, Frances Ellen Watkins 1825-1911
    TCLC 14; BLC 2; DAM MULT, POET;
    PC 21
See also BW 1; CA 111; 125; DLB 50
Harper, Michael S(teven) 1938-   CLC 7, 22
See also BW 1; CA 33-36R; CANR 24; DLB
    41
Harper, Mrs. F. E. W.
See Harper, Frances Ellen Watkins
Harris, Christie (Lucy) Irwin 1907- CLC 12
See also CA 5-8R; CANR 6; CLR 47; DLB 88;
    JRDA; MAICYA; SAAS 10; SATA 6, 74
Harris, Frank 1856-1931   TCLC 24
See also CA 109; 150; DLB 156, 197
Harris, George Washington 1814-1869NCLC
    23
See also DLB 3, 11
Harris, Joel Chandler 1848-1908   TCLC 2;
    SSC 19
See also CA 104; 137; CLR 49; DLB 11, 23,
    42, 78, 91; MAICYA; SATA 100; YABC 1
Harris, John (Wyndham Parkes Lucas) Beynon
    1903-1969
See Wyndham, John
See also CA 102; 89-92
Harris, MacDonald   CLC 9
See also Heiney, Donald (William)
Harris, Mark 1922-   CLC 19
See also CA 5-8R; CAAS 3; CANR 2, 55; DLB
    2; DLBY 80
Harris, (Theodore) Wilson 1921-   CLC 25
See also BW 2; CA 65-68; CAAS 16; CANR
    11, 27, 69; DLB 117; MTCW 1
Harrison, Elizabeth Cavanna 1909-
See Cavanna, Betty
See also CA 9-12R; CANR 6, 27
Harrison, Harry (Max) 1925-   CLC 42
See also CA 1-4R; CANR 5, 21; DLB 8; SATA
    4
Harrison, James (Thomas) 1937- CLC 6, 14,

33, 66; SSC 19
See also CA 13-16R; CANR 8, 51; DLBY 82; INT CANR-8
Harrison, Jim
See Harrison, James (Thomas)
Harrison, Kathryn 1961-   **CLC 70**
See also CA 144; CANR 68
Harrison, Tony 1937-   **CLC 43**
See also CA 65-68; CANR 44; DLB 40; MTCW 1
Harriss, Will(ard Irvin) 1922-   **CLC 34**
See also CA 111
Harson, Sley
See Ellison, Harlan (Jay)
Hart, Ellis
See Ellison, Harlan (Jay)
Hart, Josephine 1942(?)- **CLC 70; DAM POP**
See also CA 138; CANR 70
Hart, Moss 1904-1961 **CLC 66; DAM DRAM**
See also CA 109; 89-92; DLB 7
Harte, (Francis) Bret(t) 1836(?)-1902 **TCLC 1, 25; DA; DAC; DAM MST; SSC 8; WLC**
See also CA 104; 140; CDALB 1865-1917; DLB 12, 64, 74, 79, 186; SATA 26
Hartley, L(eslie) P(oles) 1895-1972 **CLC 2, 22**
See also CA 45-48; 37-40R; CANR 33; DLB 15, 139; MTCW 1
Hartman, Geoffrey H. 1929-   **CLC 27**
See also CA 117; 125; DLB 67
Hartmann, Sadakichi 1867-1944   **TCLC 73**
See also CA 157; DLB 54
Hartmann von Aue c. 1160-c. 1205 **CMLC 15**
See also DLB 138
Hartmann von Aue 1170-1210   **CMLC 15**
Haruf, Kent 1943-   **CLC 34**
See also CA 149
Harwood, Ronald 1934-   **CLC 32; DAM DRAM, MST**
See also CA 1-4R; CANR 4, 55; DLB 13
Hasegawa Tatsunosuke
See Futabatei, Shimei
Hasek, Jaroslav (Matej Frantisek) 1883-1923 **TCLC 4**
See also CA 104; 129; MTCW 1
Hass, Robert 1941-   **CLC 18, 39, 99; PC 16**
See also CA 111; CANR 30, 50, 71; DLB 105; SATA 94
Hastings, Hudson
See Kuttner, Henry
Hastings, Selina   **CLC 44**
Hathorne, John 1641-1717   **LC 38**
Hatteras, Amelia
See Mencken, H(enry) L(ouis)
Hatteras, Owen   **TCLC 18**
See also Mencken, H(enry) L(ouis); Nathan, George Jean
Hauptmann, Gerhart (Johann Robert) 1862-1946 **TCLC 4; DAM DRAM**
See also CA 104; 153; DLB 66, 118
Havel, Vaclav 1936-   **CLC 25, 58, 65; DAM DRAM; DC 6**
See also CA 104; CANR 36, 63; MTCW 1
Haviaras, Stratis   **CLC 33**
See also Chaviaras, Strates
Hawes, Stephen 1475(?)-1523(?)   **LC 17**
See also DLB 132
Hawkes, John (Clendennin Burne, Jr.) 1925-1998 **CLC 1, 2, 3, 4, 7, 9, 14, 15, 27, 49**
See also CA 1-4R; 167; CANR 2, 47, 64; DLB 2, 7; DLBY 80; MTCW 1
Hawking, S. W.
See Hawking, Stephen W(illiam)
Hawking, Stephen W(illiam) 1942- **CLC 63,**
105
See also AAYA 13; BEST 89:1; CA 126; 129; CANR 48
Hawkins, Anthony Hope
See Hope, Anthony
Hawthorne, Julian 1846-1934   **TCLC 25**
See also CA 165
Hawthorne, Nathaniel 1804-1864 **NCLC 39; DA; DAB; DAC; DAM MST, NOV; SSC 3, 29; WLC**
See also AAYA 18; CDALB 1640-1865; DLB 1, 74; YABC 2
Haxton, Josephine Ayres 1921-
See Douglas, Ellen
See also CA 115; CANR 41
Hayaseca y Eizaguirre, Jorge
See Echegaray (y Eizaguirre), Jose (Maria Waldo)
Hayashi, Fumiko 1904-1951   **TCLC 27**
See also CA 161; DLB 180
Haycraft, Anna
See Ellis, Alice Thomas
See also CA 122
Hayden, Robert E(arl) 1913-1980 **CLC 5, 9, 14, 37; BLC 2; DA; DAC; DAM MST, MULT, POET; PC 6**
See also BW 1; CA 69-72; 97-100; CABS 2; CANR 24; CDALB 1941-1968; DLB 5, 76; MTCW 1; SATA 19; SATA-Obit 26
Hayford, J(oseph) E(phraim) Casely
See Casely-Hayford, J(oseph) E(phraim)
Hayman, Ronald 1932-   **CLC 44**
See also CA 25-28R; CANR 18, 50; DLB 155
Haywood, Eliza 1693(?)-1756   **LC 44**
See also DLB 39
Haywood, Eliza (Fowler) 1693(?)-1756 **LC 1, 44**
Hazlitt, William 1778-1830   **NCLC 29**
See also DLB 110, 158
Hazzard, Shirley 1931-   **CLC 18**
See also CA 9-12R; CANR 4, 70; DLBY 82; MTCW 1
Head, Bessie 1937-1986 **CLC 25, 67; BLC 2; DAM MULT**
See also BW 2; CA 29-32R; 119; CANR 25; DLB 117; MTCW 1
Headon, (Nicky) Topper 1956(?)-   **CLC 30**
Heaney, Seamus (Justin) 1939- **CLC 5, 7, 14, 25, 37, 74, 91; DAB; DAM POET; PC 18; WLCS**
See also CA 85-88; CANR 25, 48; CDBLB 1960 to Present; DLB 40; DLBY 95; MTCW 1
Hearn, (Patricio) Lafcadio (Tessima Carlos) 1850-1904   **TCLC 9**
See also CA 105; 166; DLB 12, 78, 189
Hearne, Vicki 1946-   **CLC 56**
See also CA 139
Hearon, Shelby 1931-   **CLC 63**
See also AITN 2; CA 25-28R; CANR 18, 48
Heat-Moon, William Least   **CLC 29**
See also Trogdon, William (Lewis)
See also AAYA 9
Hebbel, Friedrich 1813-1863 **NCLC 43; DAM DRAM**
See also DLB 129
Hebert, Anne 1916- **CLC 4, 13, 29; DAC; DAM MST, POET**
See also CA 85-88; CANR 69; DLB 68; MTCW 1
Hecht, Anthony (Evan) 1923- **CLC 8, 13, 19; DAM POET**
See also CA 9-12R; CANR 6; DLB 5, 169

Hecht, Ben 1894-1964   **CLC 8**
See also CA 85-88; DLB 7, 9, 25, 26, 28, 86
Hedayat, Sadeq 1903-1951   **TCLC 21**
See also CA 120
Hegel, Georg Wilhelm Friedrich 1770-1831 **NCLC 46**
See also DLB 90
Heidegger, Martin 1889-1976   **CLC 24**
See also CA 81-84; 65-68; CANR 34; MTCW 1
Heidenstam, (Carl Gustaf) Verner von 1859-1940   **TCLC 5**
See also CA 104
Heifner, Jack 1946-   **CLC 11**
See also CA 105; CANR 47
Heijermans, Herman 1864-1924   **TCLC 24**
See also CA 123
Heilbrun, Carolyn G(old) 1926-   **CLC 25**
See also CA 45-48; CANR 1, 28, 58
Heine, Heinrich 1797-1856   **NCLC 4, 54**
See also DLB 90
Heinemann, Larry (Curtiss) 1944-   **CLC 50**
See also CA 110; CAAS 21; CANR 31; DLBD 9; INT CANR-31
Heiney, Donald (William) 1921-1993
See Harris, MacDonald
See also CA 1-4R; 142; CANR 3, 58
Heinlein, Robert A(nson) 1907-1988 **CLC 1, 3, 8, 14, 26, 55; DAM POP**
See also AAYA 17; CA 1-4R; 125; CANR 1, 20, 53; DLB 8; JRDA; MAICYA; MTCW 1; SATA 9, 69; SATA-Obit 56
Helforth, John
See Doolittle, Hilda
Hellenhofferu, Vojtech Kapristian z
See Hasek, Jaroslav (Matej Frantisek)
Heller, Joseph 1923- **CLC 1, 3, 5, 8, 11, 36, 63; DA; DAB; DAC; DAM MST, NOV, POP; WLC**
See also AAYA 24; AITN 1; CA 5-8R; CABS 1; CANR 8, 42, 66; DLB 2, 28; DLBY 80; INT CANR-8; MTCW 1
Hellman, Lillian (Florence) 1906-1984 **CLC 2, 4, 8, 14, 18, 34, 44, 52; DAM DRAM; DC 1**
See also AITN 1, 2; CA 13-16R; 112; CANR 33; DLB 7; DLBY 84; MTCW 1
Helprin, Mark 1947- **CLC 7, 10, 22, 32; DAM NOV, POP**
See also CA 81-84; CANR 47, 64; DLBY 85; MTCW 1
Helvetius, Claude-Adrien 1715-1771   **LC 26**
Helyar, Jane Penelope Josephine 1933-
See Poole, Josephine
See also CA 21-24R; CANR 10, 26; SATA 82
Hemans, Felicia 1793-1835   **NCLC 71**
See also DLB 96
Hemingway, Ernest (Miller) 1899-1961 **C L C 1, 3, 6, 8, 10, 13, 19, 30, 34, 39, 41, 44, 50, 61, 80; DA; DAB; DAC; DAM MST, NOV; SSC 1, 25; WLC**
See also AAYA 19; CA 77-80; CANR 34; CDALB 1917-1929; DLB 4, 9, 102; DLBD 1, 15, 16; DLBY 81, 87, 96; MTCW 1
Hempel, Amy 1951-   **CLC 39**
See also CA 118; 137; CANR 70
Henderson, F. C.
See Mencken, H(enry) L(ouis)
Henderson, Sylvia
See Ashton-Warner, Sylvia (Constance)
Henderson, Zenna (Chlarson) 1917-1983 **SSC 29**
See also CA 1-4R; 133; CANR 1; DLB 8; SATA 5

Henley, Beth CLC 23; DC 6
See also Henley, Elizabeth Becker
See also CABS 3; DLBY 86

Henley, Elizabeth Becker 1952-
See Henley, Beth
See also CA 107; CANR 32, 73; DAM DRAM,
MST; MTCW 1

Henley, William Ernest 1849-1903 TCLC 8
See also CA 105; DLB 19

Hennissart, Martha
See Lathen, Emma
See also CA 85-88; CANR 64

Henry, O. TCLC 1, 19; SSC 5; WLC
See also Porter, William Sydney

Henry, Patrick 1736-1799 LC 25

Henryson, Robert 1430(?)-1506(?) LC 20
See also DLB 146

Henry VIII 1491-1547 LC 10

Henschke, Alfred
See Klabund

Hentoff, Nat(han Irving) 1925- CLC 26
See also AAYA 4; CA 1-4R; CAAS 6; CANR
5, 25; CLR 1, 52; INT CANR-25; JRDA;
MAICYA; SATA 42, 69; SATA-Brief 27

Heppenstall, (John) Rayner 1911-1981 C L C
10
See also CA 1-4R; 103; CANR 29

Heraclitus c. 540B.C.-c. 450B.C. CMLC 22
See also DLB 176

Herbert, Frank (Patrick) 1920-1986 CLC 12,
23, 35, 44, 85; DAM POP
See also AAYA 21; CA 53-56; 118; CANR 5,
43; DLB 8; INT CANR-5; MTCW 1; SATA
9, 37; SATA-Obit 47

Herbert, George 1593-1633 LC 24; DAB;
DAM POET; PC 4
See also CDBLB Before 1660; DLB 126

Herbert, Zbigniew 1924-1998 CLC 9, 43;
DAM POET
See also CA 89-92; 169; CANR 36, 74; MTCW
1

Herbst, Josephine (Frey) 1897-1969 CLC 34
See also CA 5-8R; 25-28R; DLB 9

Hergesheimer, Joseph 1880-1954 TCLC 11
See also CA 109; DLB 102, 9

Herlihy, James Leo 1927-1993 CLC 6
See also CA 1-4R; 143; CANR 2

Hermogenes fl. c. 175- CMLC 6

Hernandez, Jose 1834-1886 NCLC 17

Herodotus c. 484B.C.-429B.C. CMLC 17
See also DLB 176

Herrick, Robert 1591-1674LC 13; DA; DAB;
DAC; DAM MST, POP; PC 9
See also DLB 126

Herring, Guilles
See Somerville, Edith

Herriot, James 1916-1995CLC 12; DAM POP
See also Wight, James Alfred
See also AAYA 1; CA 148; CANR 40; SATA
86

Herrmann, Dorothy 1941- CLC 44
See also CA 107

Herrmann, Taffy
See Herrmann, Dorothy

Hersey, John (Richard) 1914-1993CLC 1, 2, 7,
9, 40, 81, 97; DAM POP
See also CA 17-20R; 140; CANR 33; DLB 6,
185; MTCW 1; SATA 25; SATA-Obit 76

Herzen, Aleksandr Ivanovich 1812-1870
NCLC 10, 61

Herzl, Theodor 1860-1904 TCLC 36
See also CA 168

Herzog, Werner 1942- CLC 16

See also CA 89-92

Hesiod c. 8th cent. B.C.- CMLC 5
See also DLB 176

Hesse, Hermann 1877-1962CLC 1, 2, 3, 6, 11,
17, 25, 69; DA; DAB; DAC; DAM MST,
NOV; SSC 9; WLC
See also CA 17-18; CAP 2; DLB 66; MTCW 1;
SATA 50

Hewes, Cady
See De Voto, Bernard (Augustine)

Heyen, William 1940- CLC 13, 18
See also CA 33-36R; CAAS 9; DLB 5

Heyerdahl, Thor 1914- CLC 26
See also CA 5-8R; CANR 5, 22, 66, 73; MTCW
1; SATA 2, 52

Heym, Georg (Theodor Franz Arthur) 1887-
1912 TCLC 9
See also CA 106

Heym, Stefan 1913- CLC 41
See also CA 9-12R; CANR 4; DLB 69

Heyse, Paul (Johann Ludwig von) 1830-1914
TCLC 8
See also CA 104; DLB 129

Heyward, (Edwin) DuBose 1885-1940 T C L C
59
See also CA 108; 157; DLB 7, 9, 45; SATA 21

Hibbert, Eleanor Alice Burford 1906-1993
CLC 7; DAM POP
See also BEST 90:4; CA 17-20R; 140; CANR
9, 28, 59; SATA 2; SATA-Obit 74

Hichens, Robert (Smythe) 1864-1950 T C L C
64
See also CA 162; DLB 153

Higgins, George V(incent) 1939-CLC 4, 7, 10,
18
See also CA 77-80; CAAS 5; CANR 17, 51;
DLB 2; DLBY 81; INT CANR-17; MTCW
1

Higginson, Thomas Wentworth 1823-1911
TCLC 36
See also CA 162; DLB 1, 64

Highet, Helen
See MacInnes, Helen (Clark)

Highsmith, (Mary) Patricia 1921-1995CLC 2,
4, 14, 42, 102; DAM NOV, POP
See also CA 1-4R; 147; CANR 1, 20, 48, 62;
MTCW 1

Highwater, Jamake (Mamake) 1942(?)- C L C
12
See also AAYA 7; CA 65-68; CAAS 7; CANR
10, 34; CLR 17; DLB 52; DLBY 85; JRDA;
MAICYA; SATA 32, 69; SATA-Brief 30

Highway, Tomson 1951-CLC 92; DAC; DAM
MULT
See also CA 151; NNAL

Higuchi, Ichiyo 1872-1896 NCLC 49

Hijuelos, Oscar 1951- CLC 65; DAM MULT,
POP; HLC
See also AAYA 25; BEST 90:1; CA 123; CANR
50; DLB 145; HW

Hikmet, Nazim 1902(?)-1963 CLC 40
See also CA 141; 93-96

Hildegard von Bingen 1098-1179 CMLC 20
See also DLB 148

Hildesheimer, Wolfgang 1916-1991 CLC 49
See also CA 101; 135; DLB 69, 124

Hill, Geoffrey (William) 1932- CLC 5, 8, 18,
45; DAM POET
See also CA 81-84; CANR 21; CDBLB 1960
to Present; DLB 40; MTCW 1

Hill, George Roy 1921- CLC 26
See also CA 110; 122

Hill, John

See Koontz, Dean R(ay)

Hill, Susan (Elizabeth) 1942- CLC 4, 113;
DAB; DAM MST, NOV
See also CA 33-36R; CANR 29, 69; DLB 14,
139; MTCW 1

Hillerman, Tony 1925- CLC 62; DAM POP
See also AAYA 6; BEST 89:1; CA 29-32R;
CANR 21, 42, 65; SATA 6

Hillesum, Etty 1914-1943 TCLC 49
See also CA 137

Hilliard, Noel (Harvey) 1929- CLC 15
See also CA 9-12R; CANR 7, 69

Hillis, Rick 1956- CLC 66
See also CA 134

Hilton, James 1900-1954 TCLC 21
See also CA 108; 169; DLB 34, 77; SATA 34

Himes, Chester (Bomar) 1909-1984CLC 2, 4,
7, 18, 58, 108; BLC 2; DAM MULT
See also BW 2; CA 25-28R; 114; CANR 22;
DLB 2, 76, 143; MTCW 1

Hinde, Thomas CLC 6, 11
See also Chitty, Thomas Willes

Hindin, Nathan
See Bloch, Robert (Albert)

Hine, (William) Daryl 1936- CLC 15
See also CA 1-4R; CAAS 15; CANR 1, 20; DLB
60

Hinkson, Katharine Tynan
See Tynan, Katharine

Hinton, S(usan) E(loise) 1950- CLC 30, 111;
DA; DAB; DAC; DAM MST, NOV
See also AAYA 2; CA 81-84; CANR 32, 62;
CLR 3, 23; JRDA; MAICYA; MTCW 1;
SATA 19, 58

Hippius, Zinaida TCLC 9
See also Gippius, Zinaida (Nikolayevna)

Hiraoka, Kimitake 1925-1970
See Mishima, Yukio
See also CA 97-100; 29-32R; DAM DRAM;
MTCW 1

Hirsch, E(ric) D(onald), Jr. 1928- CLC 79
See also CA 25-28R; CANR 27, 51; DLB 67;
INT CANR-27; MTCW 1

Hirsch, Edward 1950- CLC 31, 50
See also CA 104; CANR 20, 42; DLB 120

Hitchcock, Alfred (Joseph) 1899-1980CLC 16
See also AAYA 22; CA 159; 97-100; SATA 27;
SATA-Obit 24

Hitler, Adolf 1889-1945 TCLC 53
See also CA 117; 147

Hoagland, Edward 1932- CLC 28
See also CA 1-4R; CANR 2, 31, 57; DLB 6;
SATA 51

Hoban, Russell (Conwell) 1925- CLC 7, 25;
DAM NOV
See also CA 5-8R; CANR 23, 37, 66; CLR 3;
DLB 52; MAICYA; MTCW 1; SATA 1, 40,
78

Hobbes, Thomas 1588-1679 LC 36
See also DLB 151

Hobbs, Perry
See Blackmur, R(ichard) P(almer)

Hobson, Laura Z(ametkin) 1900-1986CLC 7,
25
See also CA 17-20R; 118; CANR 55; DLB 28;
SATA 52

Hochhuth, Rolf 1931- CLC 4, 11, 18; DAM
DRAM
See also CA 5-8R; CANR 33; DLB 124; MTCW
1

Hochman, Sandra 1936- CLC 3, 8
See also CA 5-8R; DLB 5

Hochwaelder, Fritz 1911-1986CLC 36; DAM

Ishikawa, Hakuhin
See Ishikawa, Takuboku
Ishikawa, Takuboku 1886(?)-1912 **TCLC 15;**
DAM POET; PC 10
See also CA 113; 153
Iskander, Fazil 1929- **CLC 47**
See also CA 102
Isler, Alan (David) 1934- **CLC 91**
See also CA 156
Ivan IV 1530-1584 **LC 17**
Ivanov, Vyacheslav Ivanovich 1866-1949
TCLC 33
See also CA 122
Ivask, Ivar Vidrik 1927-1992 **CLC 14**
See also CA 37-40R; 139; CANR 24
Ives, Morgan
See Bradley, Marion Zimmer
J. R. S.
See Gogarty, Oliver St. John
Jabran, Kahlil
See Gibran, Kahlil
Jabran, Khalil
See Gibran, Kahlil
Jackson, Daniel
See Wingrove, David (John)
Jackson, Jesse 1908-1983 **CLC 12**
See also BW 1; CA 25-28R; 109; CANR 27;
CLR 28; MAICYA; SATA 2, 29; SATA-Obit
48
Jackson, Laura (Riding) 1901-1991
See Riding, Laura
See also CA 65-68; 135; CANR 28; DLB 48
Jackson, Sam
See Trumbo, Dalton
Jackson, Sara
See Wingrove, David (John)
Jackson, Shirley 1919-1965 **CLC 11, 60, 87;**
DA; DAC; DAM MST; SSC 9; WLC
See also AAYA 9; CA 1-4R; 25-28R; CANR 4,
52; CDALB 1941-1968; DLB 6; SATA 2
Jacob, (Cyprien-)Max 1876-1944 **TCLC 6**
See also CA 104
Jacobs, Harriet A(nn) 1813(?)-1897 **NCLC 67**
Jacobs, Jim 1942- **CLC 12**
See also CA 97-100; INT 97-100
Jacobs, W(illiam) W(ymark) 1863-1943
TCLC 22
See also CA 121; 167; DLB 135
Jacobsen, Jens Peter 1847-1885 **NCLC 34**
Jacobsen, Josephine 1908- **CLC 48, 102**
See also CA 33-36R; CAAS 18; CANR 23, 48
Jacobson, Dan 1929- **CLC 4, 14**
See also CA 1-4R; CANR 2, 25, 66; DLB 14;
MTCW 1
Jacqueline
See Carpentier (y Valmont), Alejo
Jagger, Mick 1944- **CLC 17**
Jahiz, Al- c. 776-869 **CMLC 25**
Jahiz, al- c. 780-c. 869 **CMLC 25**
Jakes, John (William) 1932- **CLC 29; DAM**
NOV, POP
See also BEST 89:4; CA 57-60; CANR 10, 43,
66; DLBY 83; INT CANR-10; MTCW 1;
SATA 62
James, Andrew
See Kirkup, James
James, C(yril) L(ionel) R(obert) 1901-1989
CLC 33; BLCS
See also BW 2; CA 117; 125; 128; CANR 62;
DLB 125; MTCW 1
James, Daniel (Lewis) 1911-1988
See Santiago, Danny
See also CA 125

James, Dynely
See Mayne, William (James Carter)
James, Henry Sr. 1811-1882 **NCLC 53**
James, Henry 1843-1916 **TCLC 2, 11, 24, 40,**
47, 64; DA; DAB; DAC; DAM MST, NOV;
SSC 8, 32; WLC
See also CA 104; 132; CDALB 1865-1917;
DLB 12, 71, 74, 189; DLBD 13; MTCW 1
James, M. R.
See James, Montague (Rhodes)
See also DLB 156
James, Montague (Rhodes) 1862-1936 **T C L C**
6; SSC 16
See also CA 104; DLB 201
James, P. D. 1920- **CLC 18, 46**
See also White, Phyllis Dorothy James
See also BEST 90:2; CDBLB 1960 to Present;
DLB 87; DLBD 17
James, Philip
See Moorcock, Michael (John)
James, William 1842-1910 **TCLC 15, 32**
See also CA 109
James I 1394-1437 **LC 20**
Jameson, Anna 1794-1860 **NCLC 43**
See also DLB 99, 166
Jami, Nur al-Din 'Abd al-Rahman 1414-1492
LC 9
Jammes, Francis 1868-1938 **TCLC 75**
Jandl, Ernst 1925- **CLC 34**
Janowitz, Tama 1957- **CLC 43; DAM POP**
See also CA 106; CANR 52
Japrisot, Sebastien 1931- **CLC 90**
Jarrell, Randall 1914-1965 **CLC 1, 2, 6, 9, 13,**
49; DAM POET
See also CA 5-8R; 25-28R; CABS 2; CANR 6,
34; CDALB 1941-1968; CLR 6; DLB 48, 52;
MAICYA; MTCW 1; SATA 7
Jarry, Alfred 1873-1907 **TCLC 2, 14; DAM**
DRAM; SSC 20
See also CA 104; 153; DLB 192
Jarvis, E. K.
See Bloch, Robert (Albert); Ellison, Harlan
(Jay); Silverberg, Robert
Jeake, Samuel, Jr.
See Aiken, Conrad (Potter)
Jean Paul 1763-1825 **NCLC 7**
Jefferies, (John) Richard 1848-1887 **NCLC 47**
See also DLB 98, 141; SATA 16
Jeffers, (John) Robinson 1887-1962 **CLC 2, 3,**
11, 15, 54; DA; DAC; DAM MST, POET;
PC 17; WLC
See also CA 85-88; CANR 35; CDALB 1917-
1929; DLB 45; MTCW 1
Jefferson, Janet
See Mencken, H(enry) L(ouis)
Jefferson, Thomas 1743-1826 **NCLC 11**
See also CDALB 1640-1865; DLB 31
Jeffrey, Francis 1773-1850 **NCLC 33**
See also DLB 107
Jelakowitch, Ivan
See Heijermans, Herman
Jellicoe, (Patricia) Ann 1927- **CLC 27**
See also CA 85-88; DLB 13
Jen, Gish **CLC 70**
See also Jen, Lillian
Jen, Lillian 1956(?)-
See Jen, Gish
See also CA 135
Jenkins, (John) Robin 1912- **CLC 52**
See also CA 1-4R; CANR 1; DLB 14
Jennings, Elizabeth (Joan) 1926- **CLC 5, 14**
See also CA 61-64; CAAS 5; CANR 8, 39, 66;
DLB 27; MTCW 1; SATA 66

Jennings, Waylon 1937- **CLC 21**
Jensen, Johannes V. 1873-1950 **TCLC 41**
See also CA 170
Jensen, Laura (Linnea) 1948- **CLC 37**
See also CA 103
Jerome, Jerome K(lapka) 1859-1927 **TCLC 23**
See also CA 119; DLB 10, 34, 135
Jerrold, Douglas William 1803-1857 **NCLC 2**
See also DLB 158, 159
Jewett, (Theodora) Sarah Orne 1849-1909
TCLC 1, 22; SSC 6
See also CA 108; 127; CANR 71; DLB 12, 74;
SATA 15
Jewsbury, Geraldine (Endsor) 1812-1880
NCLC 22
See also DLB 21
Jhabvala, Ruth Prawer 1927- **CLC 4, 8, 29, 94;**
DAB; DAM NOV
See also CA 1-4R; CANR 2, 29, 51, 74; DLB
139, 194; INT CANR-29; MTCW 1
Jibran, Kahlil
See Gibran, Kahlil
Jibran, Khalil
See Gibran, Kahlil
Jiles, Paulette 1943- **CLC 13, 58**
See also CA 101; CANR 70
Jimenez (Mantecon), Juan Ramon 1881-1958
TCLC 4; DAM MULT, POET; HLC; PC
7
See also CA 104; 131; CANR 74; DLB 134;
HW; MTCW 1
Jimenez, Ramon
See Jimenez (Mantecon), Juan Ramon
Jimenez Mantecon, Juan
See Jimenez (Mantecon), Juan Ramon
Jin, Ha 1956- **CLC 109**
See also CA 152
Joel, Billy **CLC 26**
See also Joel, William Martin
Joel, William Martin 1949-
See Joel, Billy
See also CA 108
John, Saint 7th cent. - **CMLC 27**
John of the Cross, St. 1542-1591 **LC 18**
Johnson, B(ryan) S(tanley William) 1933-1973
CLC 6, 9
See also CA 9-12R; 53-56; CANR 9; DLB 14,
40
Johnson, Benj. F. of Boo
See Riley, James Whitcomb
Johnson, Benjamin F. of Boo
See Riley, James Whitcomb
Johnson, Charles (Richard) 1948- **CLC 7, 51,**
65; BLC 2; DAM MULT
See also BW 2; CA 116; CAAS 18; CANR 42,
66; DLB 33
Johnson, Denis 1949- **CLC 52**
See also CA 117; 121; CANR 71; DLB 120
Johnson, Diane 1934- **CLC 5, 13, 48**
See also CA 41-44R; CANR 17, 40, 62; DLBY
80; INT CANR-17; MTCW 1
Johnson, Eyvind (Olof Verner) 1900-1976
CLC 14
See also CA 73-76; 69-72; CANR 34
Johnson, J. R.
See James, C(yril) L(ionel) R(obert)
Johnson, James Weldon 1871-1938 **TCLC 3,**
19; BLC 2; DAM MULT, POET; PC 24
See also BW 1; CA 104; 125; CDALB 1917-
1929; CLR 32; DLB 51; MTCW 1; SATA 31
Johnson, Joyce 1935- **CLC 58**
See also CA 125; 129
Johnson, Lionel (Pigot) 1867-1902 **TCLC 19**

See also CA 117; DLB 19

Johnson, Marguerite (Annie)
See Angelou, Maya

Johnson, Mel
See Malzberg, Barry N(athaniel)

Johnson, Pamela Hansford 1912-1981**CLC 1, 7, 27**
See also CA 1-4R; 104; CANR 2, 28; DLB 15; MTCW 1

Johnson, Robert 1911(?)-1938 **TCLC 69**

Johnson, Samuel 1709-1784**LC 15; DA; DAB; DAC; DAM MST; WLC**
See also CDBLB 1660-1789; DLB 39, 95, 104, 142

Johnson, Uwe 1934-1984 **CLC 5, 10, 15, 40**
See also CA 1-4R; 112; CANR 1, 39; DLB 75; MTCW 1

Johnston, George (Benson) 1913- **CLC 51**
See also CA 1-4R; CANR 5, 20; DLB 88

Johnston, Jennifer 1930- **CLC 7**
See also CA 85-88; DLB 14

Jolley, (Monica) Elizabeth 1923-**CLC 46; SSC 19**
See also CA 127; CAAS 13; CANR 59

Jones, Arthur Llewellyn 1863-1947
See Machen, Arthur
See also CA 104

Jones, D(ouglas) G(ordon) 1929- **CLC 10**
See also CA 29-32R; CANR 13; DLB 53

Jones, David (Michael) 1895-1974**CLC 2, 4, 7, 13, 42**
See also CA 9-12R; 53-56; CANR 28; CDBLB 1945-1960; DLB 20, 100; MTCW 1

Jones, David Robert 1947-
See Bowie, David
See also CA 103

Jones, Diana Wynne 1934- **CLC 26**
See also AAYA 12; CA 49-52; CANR 4, 26, 56; CLR 23; DLB 161; JRDA; MAICYA; SAAS 7; SATA 9, 70

Jones, Edward P. 1950- **CLC 76**
See also BW 2; CA 142

Jones, Gayl 1949- **CLC 6, 9; BLC 2; DAM MULT**
See also BW 2; CA 77-80; CANR 27, 66; DLB 33; MTCW 1

Jones, James 1921-1977 **CLC 1, 3, 10, 39**
See also AITN 1, 2; CA 1-4R; 69-72; CANR 6; DLB 2, 143; DLBD 17; MTCW 1

Jones, John J.
See Lovecraft, H(oward) P(hillips)

Jones, LeRoi **CLC 1, 2, 3, 5, 10, 14**
See also Baraka, Amiri

Jones, Louis B. 1953- **CLC 65**
See also CA 141; CANR 73

Jones, Madison (Percy, Jr.) 1925- **CLC 4**
See also CA 13-16R; CAAS 11; CANR 7, 54; DLB 152

Jones, Mervyn 1922- **CLC 10, 52**
See also CA 45-48; CAAS 5; CANR 1; MTCW 1

Jones, Mick 1956(?)- **CLC 30**

Jones, Nettie (Pearl) 1941- **CLC 34**
See also BW 2; CA 137; CAAS 20

Jones, Preston 1936-1979 **CLC 10**
See also CA 73-76; 89-92; DLB 7

Jones, Robert F(rancis) 1934- **CLC 7**
See also CA 49-52; CANR 2, 61

Jones, Rod 1953- **CLC 50**
See also CA 128

Jones, Terence Graham Parry 1942- **CLC 21**
See also Jones, Terry; Monty Python
See also CA 112; 116; CANR 35; INT 116

Jones, Terry
See Jones, Terence Graham Parry
See also SATA 67; SATA-Brief 51

Jones, Thom 1945(?)- **CLC 81**
See also CA 157

Jong, Erica 1942- **CLC 4, 6, 8, 18, 83; DAM NOV, POP**
See also AITN 1; BEST 90:2; CA 73-76; CANR 26, 52; DLB 2, 5, 28, 152; INT CANR-26; MTCW 1

Jonson, Ben(jamin) 1572(?)-1637 **LC 6, 33; DA; DAB; DAC; DAM DRAM, MST, POET; DC 4; PC 17; WLC**
See also CDBLB Before 1660; DLB 62, 121

Jordan, June 1936-**CLC 5, 11, 23, 114; BLCS; DAM MULT, POET**
See also AAYA 2; BW 2; CA 33-36R; CANR 25, 70; CLR 10; DLB 38; MAICYA; MTCW 1; SATA 4

Jordan, Neil (Patrick) 1950- **CLC 110**
See also CA 124; 130; CANR 54; INT 130

Jordan, Pat(rick M.) 1941- **CLC 37**
See also CA 33-36R

Jorgensen, Ivar
See Ellison, Harlan (Jay)

Jorgenson, Ivar
See Silverberg, Robert

Josephus, Flavius c. 37-100 **CMLC 13**

Josipovici, Gabriel 1940- **CLC 6, 43**
See also CA 37-40R; CAAS 8; CANR 47; DLB 14

Joubert, Joseph 1754-1824 **NCLC 9**

Jouve, Pierre Jean 1887-1976 **CLC 47**
See also CA 65-68

Jovine, Francesco 1902-1950 **TCLC 79**

Joyce, James (Augustine Aloysius) 1882-1941 **TCLC 3, 8, 16, 35, 52; DA; DAB; DAC; DAM MST, NOV, POET; PC 22; SSC 3, 26; WLC**
See also CA 104; 126; CDBLB 1914-1945; DLB 10, 19, 36, 162; MTCW 1

Jozsef, Attila 1905-1937 **TCLC 22**
See also CA 116

Juana Ines de la Cruz 1651(?)-1695**LC 5; PC 24**

Judd, Cyril
See Kornbluth, C(yril) M.; Pohl, Frederik

Julian of Norwich 1342(?)-1416(?) **LC 6**
See also DLB 146

Junger, Sebastian 1962- **CLC 109**
See also CA 165

Juniper, Alex
See Hospital, Janette Turner

Junius
See Luxemburg, Rosa

Just, Ward (Swift) 1935- **CLC 4, 27**
See also CA 25-28R; CANR 32; INT CANR-32

Justice, Donald (Rodney) 1925- **CLC 6, 19, 102; DAM POET**
See also CA 5-8R; CANR 26, 54, 74; DLBY 83; INT CANR-26

Juvenal **CMLC 8**
See also Juvenalis, Decimus Junius

Juvenalis, Decimus Junius 55(?)-c. 127(?)
See Juvenal

Juvenis
See Bourne, Randolph S(illiman)

Kacew, Romain 1914-1980
See Gary, Romain
See also CA 108; 102

Kadare, Ismail 1936- **CLC 52**
See also CA 161

Kadohata, Cynthia **CLC 59**
See also CA 140

Kafka, Franz 1883-1924**TCLC 2, 6, 13, 29, 47, 53; DA; DAB; DAC; DAM MST, NOV; SSC 5, 29; WLC**
See also CA 105; 126; DLB 81; MTCW 1

Kahanovitsch, Pinkhes
See Der Nister

Kahn, Roger 1927- **CLC 30**
See also CA 25-28R; CANR 44, 69; DLB 171; SATA 37

Kain, Saul
See Sassoon, Siegfried (Lorraine)

Kaiser, Georg 1878-1945 **TCLC 9**
See also CA 106; DLB 124

Kaletski, Alexander 1946- **CLC 39**
See also CA 118; 143

Kalidasa fl. c. 400- **CMLC 9; PC 22**

Kallman, Chester (Simon) 1921-1975 **CLC 2**
See also CA 45-48; 53-56; CANR 3

Kaminsky, Melvin 1926-
See Brooks, Mel
See also CA 65-68; CANR 16

Kaminsky, Stuart M(elvin) 1934- **CLC 59**
See also CA 73-76; CANR 29, 53

Kane, Francis
See Robbins, Harold

Kane, Paul
See Simon, Paul (Frederick)

Kane, Wilson
See Bloch, Robert (Albert)

Kanin, Garson 1912- **CLC 22**
See also AITN 1; CA 5-8R; CANR 7; DLB 7

Kaniuk, Yoram 1930- **CLC 19**
See also CA 134

Kant, Immanuel 1724-1804 **NCLC 27, 67**
See also DLB 94

Kantor, MacKinlay 1904-1977 **CLC 7**
See also CA 61-64; 73-76; CANR 60, 63; DLB 9, 102

Kaplan, David Michael 1946- **CLC 50**

Kaplan, James 1951- **CLC 59**
See also CA 135

Karageorge, Michael
See Anderson, Poul (William)

Karamzin, Nikolai Mikhailovich 1766-1826 **NCLC 3**
See also DLB 150

Karapanou, Margarita 1946- **CLC 13**
See also CA 101

Karinthy, Frigyes 1887-1938 **TCLC 47**
See also CA 170

Karl, Frederick R(obert) 1927- **CLC 34**
See also CA 5-8R; CANR 3, 44

Kastel, Warren
See Silverberg, Robert

Kataev, Evgeny Petrovich 1903-1942
See Petrov, Evgeny
See also CA 120

Kataphusin
See Ruskin, John

Katz, Steve 1935- **CLC 47**
See also CA 25-28R; CAAS 14, 64; CANR 12; DLBY 83

Kauffman, Janet 1945- **CLC 42**
See also CA 117; CANR 43; DLBY 86

Kaufman, Bob (Garnell) 1925-1986 **CLC 49**
See also BW 1; CA 41-44R; 118; CANR 22; DLB 16, 41

Kaufman, George S. 1889-1961**CLC 38; DAM DRAM**
See also CA 108; 93-96; DLB 7; INT 108

Kaufman, Sue **CLC 3, 8**

See also Barondess, Sue K(aufman)
Kavafis, Konstantinos Petrou 1863-1933
　See Cavafy, C(onstantine) P(eter)
　See also CA 104
Kavan, Anna 1901-1968　**CLC 5, 13, 82**
　See also CA 5-8R; CANR 6, 57; MTCW 1
Kavanagh, Dan
　See Barnes, Julian (Patrick)
Kavanagh, Patrick (Joseph) 1904-1967 **C L C 22**
　See also CA 123; 25-28R; DLB 15, 20; MTCW 1
Kawabata, Yasunari 1899-1972 **CLC 2, 5, 9, 18, 107; DAM MULT; SSC 17**
　See also CA 93-96; 33-36R; DLB 180
Kaye, M(ary) M(argaret) 1909-　**CLC 28**
　See also CA 89-92; CANR 24, 60; MTCW 1; SATA 62
Kaye, Mollie
　See Kaye, M(ary) M(argaret)
Kaye-Smith, Sheila 1887-1956　**TCLC 20**
　See also CA 118; DLB 36
Kaymor, Patrice Maguilene
　See Senghor, Leopold Sedar
Kazan, Elia 1909-　**CLC 6, 16, 63**
　See also CA 21-24R; CANR 32
Kazantzakis, Nikos 1883(?)-1957 **TCLC 2, 5, 33**
　See also CA 105; 132; MTCW 1
Kazin, Alfred 1915-　**CLC 34, 38**
　See also CA 1-4R; CAAS 7; CANR 1, 45; DLB 67
Keane, Mary Nesta (Skrine) 1904-1996
　See Keane, Molly
　See also CA 108; 114; 151
Keane, Molly　**CLC 31**
　See Keane, Mary Nesta (Skrine)
　See also INT 114
Keates, Jonathan 1946(?)-　**CLC 34**
　See also CA 163
Keaton, Buster 1895-1966　**CLC 20**
Keats, John 1795-1821**NCLC 8, 73; DA; DAB; DAC; DAM MST, POET; PC 1; WLC**
　See also CDBLB 1789-1832; DLB 96, 110
Keene, Donald 1922-　**CLC 34**
　See also CA 1-4R; CANR 5
Keillor, Garrison　**CLC 40, 115**
　See also Keillor, Gary (Edward)
　See also AAYA 2; BEST 89:3; DLBY 87; SATA 58
Keillor, Gary (Edward) 1942-
　See Keillor, Garrison
　See also CA 111; 117; CANR 36, 59; DAM POP; MTCW 1
Keith, Michael
　See Hubbard, L(afayette) Ron(ald)
Keller, Gottfried 1819-1890 **NCLC 2; SSC 26**
　See also DLB 129
Keller, Nora Okja　**CLC 109**
Kellerman, Jonathan 1949-　**CLC 44; DAM POP**
　See also BEST 90:1; CA 106; CANR 29, 51; INT CANR-29
Kelley, William Melvin 1937-　**CLC 22**
　See also BW 1; CA 77-80; CANR 27; DLB 33
Kellogg, Marjorie 1922-　**CLC 2**
　See also CA 81-84
Kellow, Kathleen
　See Hibbert, Eleanor Alice Burford
Kelly, M(ilton) T(erry) 1947-　**CLC 55**
　See also CA 97-100; CAAS 22; CANR 19, 43
Kelman, James 1946-　**CLC 58, 86**
　See also CA 148; DLB 194

Kemal, Yashar 1923-　**CLC 14, 29**
　See also CA 89-92; CANR 44
Kemble, Fanny 1809-1893　**NCLC 18**
　See also DLB 32
Kemelman, Harry 1908-1996　**CLC 2**
　See also AITN 1; CA 9-12R; 155; CANR 6, 71; DLB 28
Kempe, Margery 1373(?)-1440(?)　**LC 6**
　See also DLB 146
Kempis, Thomas a 1380-1471　**LC 11**
Kendall, Henry 1839-1882　**NCLC 12**
Keneally, Thomas (Michael) 1935- **CLC 5, 8, 10, 14, 19, 27, 43, 117; DAM NOV**
　See also CA 85-88; CANR 10, 50, 74; MTCW 1
Kennedy, Adrienne (Lita) 1931-**CLC 66; BLC 2; DAM MULT; DC 5**
　See also BW 2; CA 103; CAAS 20; CABS 3; CANR 26, 53; DLB 38
Kennedy, John Pendleton 1795-1870**NCLC 2**
　See also DLB 3
Kennedy, Joseph Charles 1929-
　See Kennedy, X. J.
　See also CA 1-4R; CANR 4, 30, 40; SATA 14, 86
Kennedy, William 1928-　**CLC 6, 28, 34, 53; DAM NOV**
　See also AAYA 1; CA 85-88; CANR 14, 31; DLB 143; DLBY 85; INT CANR-31; MTCW 1; SATA 57
Kennedy, X. J.　**CLC 8, 42**
　See also Kennedy, Joseph Charles
　See also CAAS 9; CLR 27; DLB 5; SAAS 22
Kenny, Maurice (Francis) 1929-　**CLC 87; DAM MULT**
　See also CA 144; CAAS 22; DLB 175; NNAL
Kent, Kelvin
　See Kuttner, Henry
Kenton, Maxwell
　See Southern, Terry
Kenyon, Robert O.
　See Kuttner, Henry
Kepler, Johannes 1571-1630　**LC 45**
Kerouac, Jack　**CLC 1, 2, 3, 5, 14, 29, 61**
　See also Kerouac, Jean-Louis Lebris de
　See also AAYA 25; CDALB 1941-1968; DLB 2, 16; DLBD 3; DLBY 95
Kerouac, Jean-Louis Lebris de 1922-1969
　See Kerouac, Jack
　See also AITN 1; CA 5-8R; 25-28R; CANR 26, 54; DA; DAB; DAC; DAM MST, NOV, POET, POP; MTCW 1; WLC
Kerr, Jean 1923-　**CLC 22**
　See also CA 5-8R; CANR 7; INT CANR-7
Kerr, M. E.　**CLC 12, 35**
　See also Meaker, Marijane (Agnes)
　See also AAYA 2, 23; CLR 29; SAAS 1
Kerr, Robert　**CLC 55**
Kerrigan, (Thomas) Anthony 1918-**CLC 4, 6**
　See also CA 49-52; CAAS 11; CANR 4
Kerry, Lois
　See Duncan, Lois
Kesey, Ken (Elton) 1935- **CLC 1, 3, 6, 11, 46, 64; DA; DAB; DAC; DAM MST, NOV, POP; WLC**
　See also AAYA 25; CA 1-4R; CANR 22, 38, 66; CDALB 1968-1988; DLB 2, 16; MTCW 1; SATA 66
Kesselring, Joseph (Otto) 1902-1967**CLC 45; DAM DRAM, MST**
　See also CA 150
Kessler, Jascha (Frederick) 1929-　**CLC 4**
　See also CA 17-20R; CANR 8, 48

Kettelkamp, Larry (Dale) 1933-　**CLC 12**
　See also CA 29-32R; CANR 16; SAAS 3; SATA 2
Key, Ellen 1849-1926　**TCLC 65**
Keyber, Conny
　See Fielding, Henry
Keyes, Daniel 1927-**CLC 80; DA; DAC; DAM MST, NOV**
　See also AAYA 23; CA 17-20R; CANR 10, 26, 54, 74; SATA 37
Keynes, John Maynard 1883-1946 **TCLC 64**
　See also CA 114; 162, 163; DLBD 10
Khanshendel, Chiron
　See Rose, Wendy
Khayyam, Omar 1048-1131 **CMLC 11; DAM POET; PC 8**
Kherdian, David 1931-　**CLC 6, 9**
　See also CA 21-24R; CAAS 2; CANR 39; CLR 24; JRDA; MAICYA; SATA 16, 74
Khlebnikov, Velimir　**TCLC 20**
　See also Khlebnikov, Viktor Vladimirovich
Khlebnikov, Viktor Vladimirovich 1885-1922
　See Khlebnikov, Velimir
　See also CA 117
Khodasevich, Vladislav (Felitsianovich) 1886-1939　**TCLC 15**
　See also CA 115
Kielland, Alexander Lange 1849-1906 **T C L C 5**
　See also CA 104
Kiely, Benedict 1919-　**CLC 23, 43**
　See also CA 1-4R; CANR 2; DLB 15
Kienzle, William X(avier) 1928-　**CLC 25; DAM POP**
　See also CA 93-96; CAAS 1; CANR 9, 31, 59; INT CANR-31; MTCW 1
Kierkegaard, Soren 1813-1855　**NCLC 34**
Killens, John Oliver 1916-1987　**CLC 10**
　See also BW 2; CA 77-80; 123; CAAS 2; CANR 26; DLB 33
Killigrew, Anne 1660-1685　**LC 4**
　See also DLB 131
Kim
　See Simenon, Georges (Jacques Christian)
Kincaid, Jamaica 1949- **CLC 43, 68; BLC 2; DAM MULT, NOV**
　See also AAYA 13; BW 2; CA 125; CANR 47, 59; DLB 157
King, Francis (Henry) 1923-**CLC 8, 53; DAM NOV**
　See also CA 1-4R; CANR 1, 33; DLB 15, 139; MTCW 1
King, Kennedy
　See Brown, George Douglas
King, Martin Luther, Jr. 1929-1968 **CLC 83; BLC 2; DA; DAB; DAC; DAM MST, MULT; WLCS**
　See also BW 2; CA 25-28; CANR 27, 44; CAP 2; MTCW 1; SATA 14
King, Stephen (Edwin) 1947-**CLC 12, 26, 37, 61, 113; DAM NOV, POP; SSC 17**
　See also AAYA 1, 17; BEST 90:1; CA 61-64; CANR 1, 30, 52; DLB 143; DLBY 80; JRDA; MTCW 1; SATA 9, 55
King, Steve
　See King, Stephen (Edwin)
King, Thomas 1943-　**CLC 89; DAC; DAM MULT**
　See also CA 144; DLB 175; NNAL; SATA 96
Kingman, Lee　**CLC 17**
　See also Natti, (Mary) Lee
　See also SAAS 3; SATA 1, 67
Kingsley, Charles 1819-1875　**NCLC 35**

Lynn, Kenneth S(chuyler) 1923-   **CLC 50**
See also CA 1-4R; CANR 3, 27, 65
Lynx
See West, Rebecca
Lyons, Marcus
See Blish, James (Benjamin)
Lyre, Pinchbeck
See Sassoon, Siegfried (Lorraine)
Lytle, Andrew (Nelson) 1902-1995   **CLC 22**
See also CA 9-12R; 150; CANR 70; DLB 6;
DLBY 95
Lyttelton, George 1709-1773   **LC 10**
Maas, Peter 1929-   **CLC 29**
See also CA 93-96; INT 93-96
Macaulay, Rose 1881-1958   **TCLC 7, 44**
See also CA 104; DLB 36
Macaulay, Thomas Babington 1800-1859
NCLC 42
See also CDBLB 1832-1890; DLB 32, 55
MacBeth, George (Mann) 1932-1992 **CLC 2, 5, 9**
See also CA 25-28R; 136; CANR 61, 66; DLB
40; MTCW 1; SATA 4; SATA-Obit 70
MacCaig, Norman (Alexander) 1910- **CLC 36; DAB; DAM POET**
See also CA 9-12R; CANR 3, 34; DLB 27
MacCarthy, Sir(Charles Otto) Desmond 1877-
1952   **TCLC 36**
See also CA 167
MacDiarmid, Hugh CLC 2, 4, 11, 19, 63; PC 9
See also Grieve, C(hristopher) M(urray)
See also CDBLB 1945-1960; DLB 20
MacDonald, Anson
See Heinlein, Robert A(nson)
Macdonald, Cynthia 1928-   **CLC 13, 19**
See also CA 49-52; CANR 4, 44; DLB 105
MacDonald, George 1824-1905   **TCLC 9**
See also CA 106; 137; DLB 18, 163, 178;
MAICYA; SATA 33, 100
Macdonald, John
See Millar, Kenneth
MacDonald, John D(ann) 1916-1986   **CLC 3, 27, 44; DAM NOV, POP**
See also CA 1-4R; 121; CANR 1, 19, 60; DLB
8; DLBY 86; MTCW 1
Macdonald, John Ross
See Millar, Kenneth
Macdonald, Ross   **CLC 1, 2, 3, 14, 34, 41**
See also Millar, Kenneth
See also DLBD 6
MacDougal, John
See Blish, James (Benjamin)
MacEwen, Gwendolyn (Margaret) 1941-1987
CLC 13, 55
See also CA 9-12R; 124; CANR 7, 22; DLB
53; SATA 50; SATA-Obit 55
Macha, Karel Hynek 1810-1846   **NCLC 46**
Machado (y Ruiz), Antonio 1875-1939 **T C L C 3**
See also CA 104; DLB 108
Machado de Assis, Joaquim Maria 1839-1908
TCLC 10; BLC 2; SSC 24
See also CA 107; 153
Machen, Arthur   **TCLC 4; SSC 20**
See also Jones, Arthur Llewellyn
See also DLB 36, 156, 178
Machiavelli, Niccolo 1469-1527 **LC 8, 36; DA; DAB; DAC; DAM MST; WLCS**
MacInnes, Colin 1914-1976   **CLC 4, 23**
See also CA 69-72; 65-68; CANR 21; DLB 14;
MTCW 1
MacInnes, Helen (Clark) 1907-1985 **CLC 27, 39; DAM POP**

See also CA 1-4R; 117; CANR 1, 28, 58; DLB
87; MTCW 1; SATA 22; SATA-Obit 44
Mackay, Mary 1855-1924
See Corelli, Marie
See also CA 118
Mackenzie, Compton (Edward Montague)
1883-1972   **CLC 18**
See also CA 21-22; 37-40R; CAP 2; DLB 34,
100
Mackenzie, Henry 1745-1831   **NCLC 41**
See also DLB 39
Mackintosh, Elizabeth 1896(?)-1952
See Tey, Josephine
See also CA 110
MacLaren, James
See Grieve, C(hristopher) M(urray)
Mac Laverty, Bernard 1942-   **CLC 31**
See also CA 116; 118; CANR 43; INT 118
MacLean, Alistair (Stuart) 1922(?)-1987 **C L C 3, 13, 50, 63; DAM POP**
See also CA 57-60; 121; CANR 28, 61; MTCW
1; SATA 23; SATA-Obit 50
Maclean, Norman (Fitzroy) 1902-1990   **C L C 78; DAM POP; SSC 13**
See also CA 102; 132; CANR 49
MacLeish, Archibald 1892-1982 **CLC 3, 8, 14, 68; DAM POET**
See also CA 9-12R; 106; CANR 33, 63; DLB
4, 7, 45; DLBY 82; MTCW 1
MacLennan, (John) Hugh 1907-1990   **CLC 2, 14, 92; DAC; DAM MST**
See also CA 5-8R; 142; CANR 33; DLB 68;
MTCW 1
MacLeod, Alistair 1936- **CLC 56; DAC; DAM MST**
See also CA 123; DLB 60
Macleod, Fiona
See Sharp, William
MacNeice, (Frederick) Louis 1907-1963 **C L C 1, 4, 10, 53; DAB; DAM POET**
See also CA 85-88; CANR 61; DLB 10, 20;
MTCW 1
MacNeill, Dand
See Fraser, George MacDonald
Macpherson, James 1736-1796   **LC 29**
See also Ossian
See also DLB 109
Macpherson, (Jean) Jay 1931-   **CLC 14**
See also CA 5-8R; DLB 53
MacShane, Frank 1927-   **CLC 39**
See also CA 9-12R; CANR 3, 33; DLB 111
Macumber, Mari
See Sandoz, Mari(e Susette)
Madach, Imre 1823-1864   **NCLC 19**
Madden, (Jerry) David 1933-   **CLC 5, 15**
See also CA 1-4R; CAAS 3; CANR 4, 45; DLB
6; MTCW 1
Maddern, Al(an)
See Ellison, Harlan (Jay)
Madhubuti, Haki R. 1942- **CLC 6, 73; BLC 2; DAM MULT, POET; PC 5**
See also Lee, Don L.
See also BW 2; CA 73-76; CANR 24, 51, 73;
DLB 5, 41; DLBD 8
Maepenn, Hugh
See Kuttner, Henry
Maepenn, K. H.
See Kuttner, Henry
Maeterlinck, Maurice 1862-1949   **TCLC 3; DAM DRAM**
See also CA 104; 136; DLB 192; SATA 66
Maginn, William 1794-1842   **NCLC 8**
See also DLB 110, 159

Mahapatra, Jayanta 1928-   **CLC 33; DAM MULT**
See also CA 73-76; CAAS 9; CANR 15, 33, 66
Mahfouz, Naguib (Abdel Aziz Al-Sabilgi)
1911(?)-
See Mahfuz, Najib
See also BEST 89:2; CA 128; CANR 55; DAM
NOV; MTCW 1
Mahfuz, Najib   **CLC 52, 55**
See also Mahfouz, Naguib (Abdel Aziz Al-
Sabilgi)
See also DLBY 88
Mahon, Derek 1941-   **CLC 27**
See also CA 113; 128; DLB 40
Mailer, Norman 1923- **CLC 1, 2, 3, 4, 5, 8, 11, 14, 28, 39, 74, 111; DA; DAB; DAC; DAM MST, NOV, POP**
See also AITN 2; CA 9-12R; CABS 1; CANR
28, 74; CDALB 1968-1988; DLB 2, 16, 28,
185; DLBD 3; DLBY 80, 83; MTCW 1
Maillet, Antonine 1929-   **CLC 54; DAC**
See also CA 115; 120; CANR 46, 74; DLB 60;
INT 120
Mais, Roger 1905-1955   **TCLC 8**
See also BW 1; CA 105; 124; DLB 125; MTCW
1
Maistre, Joseph de 1753-1821   **NCLC 37**
Maitland, Frederic 1850-1906   **TCLC 65**
Maitland, Sara (Louise) 1950-   **CLC 49**
See also CA 69-72; CANR 13, 59
Major, Clarence 1936- **CLC 3, 19, 48; BLC 2; DAM MULT**
See also BW 2; CA 21-24R; CAAS 6; CANR
13, 25, 53; DLB 33
Major, Kevin (Gerald) 1949-   **CLC 26; DAC**
See also AAYA 16; CA 97-100; CANR 21, 38;
CLR 11; DLB 60; INT CANR-21; JRDA;
MAICYA; SATA 32, 82
Maki, James
See Ozu, Yasujiro
Malabaila, Damiano
See Levi, Primo
Malamud, Bernard 1914-1986 **CLC 1, 2, 3, 5, 8, 9, 11, 18, 27, 44, 78, 85; DA; DAB; DAC; DAM MST, NOV, POP; SSC 15; WLC**
See also AAYA 16; CA 5-8R; 118; CABS 1;
CANR 28, 62; CDALB 1941-1968; DLB 2,
28, 152; DLBY 80, 86; MTCW 1
Malan, Herman
See Bosman, Herman Charles; Bosman, Herman
Charles
Malaparte, Curzio 1898-1957   **TCLC 52**
Malcolm, Dan
See Silverberg, Robert
Malcolm X   **CLC 82, 117; BLC 2; WLCS**
See also Little, Malcolm
Malherbe, Francois de 1555-1628   **LC 5**
Mallarme, Stephane 1842-1898 **NCLC 4, 41; DAM POET; PC 4**
Mallet-Joris, Francoise 1930-   **CLC 11**
See also CA 65-68; CANR 17; DLB 83
Malley, Ern
See McAuley, James Phillip
Mallowan, Agatha Christie
See Christie, Agatha (Mary Clarissa)
Maloff, Saul 1922-   **CLC 5**
See also CA 33-36R
Malone, Louis
See MacNeice, (Frederick) Louis
Malone, Michael (Christopher) 1942- **CLC 43**
See also CA 77-80; CANR 14, 32, 57
Malory, (Sir) Thomas 1410(?)-1471(?) **LC 11; DA; DAB; DAC; DAM MST; WLCS**

See also CDBLB Before 1660; DLB 146; SATA
59; SATA-Brief 33
Malouf, (George Joseph) David 1934-**CLC 28,
86**
See also CA 124; CANR 50
Malraux, (Georges-)Andre 1901-1976**CLC 1,
4, 9, 13, 15, 57; DAM NOV**
See also CA 21-22; 69-72; CANR 34, 58; CAP
2; DLB 72; MTCW 1
Malzberg, Barry N(athaniel) 1939-   **CLC 7**
See also CA 61-64; CAAS 4; CANR 16; DLB 8
Mamet, David (Alan) 1947-**CLC 9, 15, 34, 46,
91; DAM DRAM; DC 4**
See also AAYA 3; CA 81-84; CABS 3; CANR
15, 41, 67, 72; DLB 7; MTCW 1
Mamoulian, Rouben (Zachary) 1897-1987
CLC 16
See also CA 25-28R; 124
Mandelstam, Osip (Emilievich) 1891(?)-1938(?)
TCLC 2, 6; PC 14
See also CA 104; 150
Mander, (Mary) Jane 1877-1949   **TCLC 31**
See also CA 162
Mandeville, John fl. 1350-   **CMLC 19**
See also DLB 146
Mandiargues, Andre Pieyre de   **CLC 41**
See also Pieyre de Mandiargues, Andre
See also DLB 83
Mandrake, Ethel Belle
See Thurman, Wallace (Henry)
Mangan, James Clarence 1803-1849**NCLC 27**
Maniere, J.-E.
See Giraudoux, (Hippolyte) Jean
Mankiewicz, Herman (Jacob) 1897-1953
TCLC 85
See also CA 120; 169; DLB 26
Manley, (Mary) Delariviere 1672(?)-1724 **L C
1, 42**
See also DLB 39, 80
Mann, Abel
See Creasey, John
Mann, Emily 1952-   **DC 7**
See also CA 130; CANR 55
Mann, (Luiz) Heinrich 1871-1950   **TCLC 9**
See also CA 106; 164; DLB 66
Mann, (Paul) Thomas 1875-1955 **TCLC 2, 8,
14, 21, 35, 44, 60; DA; DAB; DAC; DAM
MST, NOV; SSC 5; WLC**
See also CA 104; 128; DLB 66; MTCW 1
Mannheim, Karl 1893-1947   **TCLC 65**
Manning, David
See Faust, Frederick (Schiller)
Manning, Frederic 1887(?)-1935   **TCLC 25**
See also CA 124
Manning, Olivia 1915-1980   **CLC 5, 19**
See also CA 5-8R; 101; CANR 29; MTCW 1
Mano, D. Keith 1942-   **CLC 2, 10**
See also CA 25-28R; CAAS 6; CANR 26, 57;
DLB 6
Mansfield, KatherineTCLC 2, 8, 39; DAB; SSC
9, 23; WLC
See also Beauchamp, Kathleen Mansfield
See also DLB 162
Manso, Peter 1940-   **CLC 39**
See also CA 29-32R; CANR 44
Mantecon, Juan Jimenez
See Jimenez (Mantecon), Juan Ramon
Manton, Peter
See Creasey, John
Man Without a Spleen, A
See Chekhov, Anton (Pavlovich)
Manzoni, Alessandro 1785-1873   **NCLC 29**
Mapu, Abraham (ben Jekutiel) 1808-1867

NCLC 18
Mara, Sally
See Queneau, Raymond
Marat, Jean Paul 1743-1793   **LC 10**
Marcel, Gabriel Honore 1889-1973   **CLC 15**
See also CA 102; 45-48; MTCW 1
Marchbanks, Samuel
See Davies, (William) Robertson
Marchi, Giacomo
See Bassani, Giorgio
Margulies, Donald   **CLC 76**
Marie de France c. 12th cent. -   **CMLC 8; PC
22**
Marie de l'Incarnation 1599-1672   **LC 10**
Marier, Captain Victor
See Griffith, D(avid Lewelyn) W(ark)
Mariner, Scott
See Pohl, Frederik
Marinetti, Filippo Tommaso 1876-1944**TCLC
10**
See also CA 107; DLB 114
Marivaux, Pierre Carlet de Chamblain de 1688-
1763   **LC 4; DC 7**
Markandaya, Kamala   **CLC 8, 38**
See also Taylor, Kamala (Purnaiya)
Markfield, Wallace 1926-   **CLC 8**
See also CA 69-72; CAAS 3; DLB 2, 28
Markham, Edwin 1852-1940   **TCLC 47**
See also CA 160; DLB 54, 186
Markham, Robert
See Amis, Kingsley (William)
Marks, J
See Highwater, Jamake (Mamake)
Marks-Highwater, J
See Highwater, Jamake (Mamake)
Markson, David M(errill) 1927-   **CLC 67**
See also CA 49-52; CANR 1
Marley, Bob   **CLC 17**
See also Marley, Robert Nesta
Marley, Robert Nesta 1945-1981
See Marley, Bob
See also CA 107; 103
Marlowe, Christopher 1564-1593 **LC 22, 47;
DA; DAB; DAC; DAM DRAM, MST; DC
1; WLC**
See also CDBLB Before 1660; DLB 62
Marlowe, Stephen 1928-
See Queen, Ellery
See also CA 13-16R; CANR 6, 55
Marmontel, Jean-Francois 1723-1799   **LC 2**
Marquand, John P(hillips) 1893-1960**CLC 2,
10**
See also CA 85-88; CANR 73; DLB 9, 102
Marques, Rene 1919-1979   **CLC 96; DAM
MULT; HLC**
See also CA 97-100; 85-88; DLB 113; HW
Marquez, Gabriel (Jose) Garcia
See Garcia Marquez, Gabriel (Jose)
Marquis, Don(ald Robert Perry) 1878-1937
TCLC 7
See also CA 104; 166; DLB 11, 25
Marric, J. J.
See Creasey, John
Marryat, Frederick 1792-1848   ·NCLC 3
See also DLB 21, 163
Marsden, James
See Creasey, John
Marsh, (Edith) Ngaio 1899-1982 **CLC 7, 53;
DAM POP**
See also CA 9-12R; CANR 6, 58; DLB 77;
MTCW 1
Marshall, Garry 1934-   **CLC 17**
See also AAYA 3; CA 111; SATA 60

Marshall, Paule 1929-   **CLC 27, 72; BLC 3;
DAM MULT; SSC 3**
See also BW 2; CA 77-80; CANR 25, 73; DLB
157; MTCW 1
Marshallik
See Zangwill, Israel
Marsten, Richard
See Hunter, Evan
Marston, John 1576-1634**LC 33; DAM DRAM**
See also DLB 58, 172
Martha, Henry
See Harris, Mark
Marti, Jose 1853-1895**NCLC 63; DAM MULT;
HLC**
Martial c. 40-c. 104   **PC 10**
Martin, Ken
See Hubbard, L(afayette) Ron(ald)
Martin, Richard
See Creasey, John
Martin, Steve 1945-   **CLC 30**
See also CA 97-100; CANR 30; MTCW 1
Martin, Valerie 1948-   **CLC 89**
See also BEST 90:2; CA 85-88; CANR 49
Martin, Violet Florence 1862-1915 **TCLC 51**
Martin, Webber
See Silverberg, Robert
Martindale, Patrick Victor
See White, Patrick (Victor Martindale)
Martin du Gard, Roger 1881-1958 **TCLC 24**
See also CA 118; DLB 65
Martineau, Harriet 1802-1876   **NCLC 26**
See also DLB 21, 55, 159, 163, 166, 190; YABC
2
Martines, Julia
See O'Faolain, Julia
Martinez, Enrique Gonzalez
See Gonzalez Martinez, Enrique
Martinez, Jacinto Benavente y
See Benavente (y Martinez), Jacinto
Martinez Ruiz, Jose 1873-1967
See Azorin; Ruiz, Jose Martinez
See also CA 93-96; HW
Martinez Sierra, Gregorio 1881-1947**TCLC 6**
See also CA 115
Martinez Sierra, Maria (de la O'LeJarraga)
1874-1974   **TCLC 6**
See also CA 115
Martinsen, Martin
See Follett, Ken(neth Martin)
Martinson, Harry (Edmund) 1904-1978**C L C
14**
See also CA 77-80; CANR 34
Marut, Ret
See Traven, B.
Marut, Robert
See Traven, B.
Marvell, Andrew 1621-1678   **LC 4, 43; DA;
DAB; DAC; DAM MST, POET; PC 10;
WLC**
See also CDBLB 1660-1789; DLB 131
Marx, Karl (Heinrich) 1818-1883 **NCLC 17**
See also DLB 129
Masaoka Shiki   **TCLC 18**
See also Masaoka Tsunenori
Masaoka Tsunenori 1867-1902
See Masaoka Shiki
See also CA 117
Masefield, John (Edward) 1878-1967**CLC 11,
47; DAM POET**
See also CA 19-20; 25-28R; CANR 33; CAP 2;
CDBLB 1890-1914; DLB 10, 19, 153, 160;
MTCW 1; SATA 19
Maso, Carole 19(?)-   **CLC 44**

See also CA 170

Mason, Bobbie Ann 1940-CLC **28, 43, 82; SSC 4**
See also AAYA 5; CA 53-56; CANR 11, 31, 58; DLB 173; DLBY 87; INT CANR-31; MTCW 1

Mason, Ernst
See Pohl, Frederik

Mason, Lee W.
See Malzberg, Barry N(athaniel)

Mason, Nick 1945-   **CLC 35**

Mason, Tally
See Derleth, August (William)

Mass, William
See Gibson, William

Master Lao
See Lao Tzu

Masters, Edgar Lee 1868-1950 **TCLC 2, 25; DA; DAC; DAM MST, POET; PC 1; WLCS**
See also CA 104; 133; CDALB 1865-1917; DLB 54; MTCW 1

Masters, Hilary 1928-   **CLC 48**
See also CA 25-28R; CANR 13, 47

Mastrosimone, William 19(?)-   **CLC 36**

Mathe, Albert
See Camus, Albert

Mather, Cotton 1663-1728   **LC 38**
See also CDALB 1640-1865; DLB 24, 30, 140

Mather, Increase 1639-1723   **LC 38**
See also DLB 24

Matheson, Richard Burton 1926-   **CLC 37**
See also CA 97-100; DLB 8, 44; INT 97-100

Mathews, Harry 1930-   **CLC 6, 52**
See also CA 21-24R; CAAS 6; CANR 18, 40

Mathews, John Joseph 1894-1979 **CLC 84; DAM MULT**
See also CA 19-20; 142; CANR 45; CAP 2; DLB 175; NNAL

Mathias, Roland (Glyn) 1915-   **CLC 45**
See also CA 97-100; CANR 19, 41; DLB 27

Matsuo Basho 1644-1694   **PC 3**
See also DAM POET

Mattheson, Rodney
See Creasey, John

Matthews, Greg 1949-   **CLC 45**
See also CA 135

Matthews, William (Procter, III) 1942-1997 **CLC 40**
See also CA 29-32R; 162; CAAS 18; CANR 12, 57; DLB 5

Matthias, John (Edward) 1941-   **CLC 9**
See also CA 33-36R; CANR 56

Matthiessen, Peter 1927-CLC **5, 7, 11, 32, 64; DAM NOV**
See also AAYA 6; BEST 90:4; CA 9-12R; CANR 21, 50, 73; DLB 6, 173; MTCW 1; SATA 27

Maturin, Charles Robert 1780(?)-1824 N C L C 6
See also DLB 178

Matute (Ausejo), Ana Maria 1925-   **CLC 11**
See also CA 89-92; MTCW 1

Maugham, W. S.
See Maugham, W(illiam) Somerset

Maugham, W(illiam) Somerset 1874-1965 **CLC 1, 11, 15, 67, 93; DA; DAB; DAC; DAM DRAM, MST, NOV; SSC 8; WLC**
See also CA 5-8R; 25-28R; CANR 40; CDBLB 1914-1945; DLB 10, 36, 77, 100, 162, 195; MTCW 1; SATA 54

Maugham, William Somerset
See Maugham, W(illiam) Somerset

Maupassant, (Henri Rene Albert) Guy de 1850-1893NCLC **1, 42; DA; DAB; DAC; DAM MST; SSC 1; WLC**

Maupin, Armistead 1944-CLC **95; DAM POP**
See also CA 125; 130; CANR 58; INT 130

Maurhut, Richard
See Traven, B.

Mauriac, Claude 1914-1996   **CLC 9**
See also CA 89-92; 152; DLB 83

Mauriac, Francois (Charles) 1885-1970 **C L C 4, 9, 56; SSC 24**
See also CA 25-28; CAP 2; DLB 65; MTCW 1

Mavor, Osborne Henry 1888-1951
See Bridie, James
See also CA 104

Maxwell, William (Keepers, Jr.) 1908-CLC **19**
See also CA 93-96; CANR 54; DLBY 80; INT 93-96

May, Elaine 1932-   **CLC 16**
See also CA 124; 142; DLB 44

Mayakovski, Vladimir (Vladimirovich) 1893-1930   **TCLC 4, 18**
See also CA 104; 158

Mayhew, Henry 1812-1887   **NCLC 31**
See also DLB 18, 55, 190

Mayle, Peter 1939(?)-   **CLC 89**
See also CA 139; CANR 64

Maynard, Joyce 1953-   **CLC 23**
See also CA 111; 129; CANR 64

Mayne, William (James Carter) 1928-CLC **12**
See also AAYA 20; CA 9-12R; CANR 37; CLR 25; JRDA; MAICYA; SAAS 11; SATA 6, 68

Mayo, Jim
See L'Amour, Louis (Dearborn)

Maysles, Albert 1926-   **CLC 16**
See also CA 29-32R

Maysles, David 1932-   **CLC 16**

Mazer, Norma Fox 1931-   **CLC 26**
See also AAYA 5; CA 69-72; CANR 12, 32, 66; CLR 23; JRDA; MAICYA; SAAS 1; SATA 24, 67

Mazzini, Guiseppe 1805-1872   **NCLC 34**

McAuley, James Phillip 1917-1976 **CLC 45**
See also CA 97-100

McBain, Ed
See Hunter, Evan

McBrien, William Augustine 1930-   **CLC 44**
See also CA 107

McCaffrey, Anne (Inez) 1926-CLC **17; DAM NOV, POP**
See also AAYA 6; AITN 2; BEST 89:2; CA 25-28R; CANR 15, 35, 55; CLR 49; DLB 8; JRDA; MAICYA; MTCW 1; SAAS 11; SATA 8, 70

McCall, Nathan 1955(?)-   **CLC 86**
See also CA 146

McCann, Arthur
See Campbell, John W(ood, Jr.)

McCann, Edson
See Pohl, Frederik

McCarthy, Charles, Jr. 1933-
See McCarthy, Cormac
See also CANR 42, 69; DAM POP

McCarthy, Cormac 1933- CLC **4, 57, 59, 101**
See also McCarthy, Charles, Jr.
See also DLB 6, 143

McCarthy, Mary (Therese) 1912-1989CLC **1, 3, 5, 14, 24, 39, 59; SSC 24**
See also CA 5-8R; 129; CANR 16, 50, 64; DLB 2; DLBY 81; INT CANR-16; MTCW 1

McCartney, (James) Paul 1942- CLC **12, 35**
See also CA 146

McCauley, Stephen (D.) 1955-   **CLC 50**
See also CA 141

McClure, Michael (Thomas) 1932-CLC **6, 10**
See also CA 21-24R; CANR 17, 46; DLB 16

McCorkle, Jill (Collins) 1958-   **CLC 51**
See also CA 121; DLBY 87

McCourt, Frank 1930-   **CLC 109**
See also CA 157

McCourt, James 1941-   **CLC 5**
See also CA 57-60

McCoy, Horace (Stanley) 1897-1955TCLC **28**
See also CA 108; 155; DLB 9

McCrae, John 1872-1918   **TCLC 12**
See also CA 109; DLB 92

McCreigh, James
See Pohl, Frederik

McCullers, (Lula) Carson (Smith) 1917-1967 **CLC 1, 4, 10, 12, 48, 100; DA; DAB; DAC; DAM MST, NOV; SSC 9, 24; WLC**
See also AAYA 21; CA 5-8R; 25-28R; CABS 1, 3; CANR 18; CDALB 1941-1968; DLB 2, 7, 173; MTCW 1; SATA 27

McCulloch, John Tyler
See Burroughs, Edgar Rice

McCullough, Colleen 1938(?)- CLC **27, 107; DAM NOV, POP**
See also CA 81-84; CANR 17, 46, 67; MTCW 1

McDermott, Alice 1953-   **CLC 90**
See also CA 109; CANR 40

McElroy, Joseph 1930-   **CLC 5, 47**
See also CA 17-20R

McEwan, Ian (Russell) 1948-   CLC **13, 66; DAM NOV**
See also BEST 90:4; CA 61-64; CANR 14, 41, 69; DLB 14, 194; MTCW 1

McFadden, David 1940-   **CLC 48**
See also CA 104; DLB 60; INT 104

McFarland, Dennis 1950-   **CLC 65**
See also CA 165

McGahern, John 1934- CLC **5, 9, 48; SSC 17**
See also CA 17-20R; CANR 29, 68; DLB 14; MTCW 1

McGinley, Patrick (Anthony) 1937- CLC **41**
See also CA 120; 127; CANR 56; INT 127

McGinley, Phyllis 1905-1978   **CLC 14**
See also CA 9-12R; 77-80; CANR 19; DLB 11, 48; SATA 2, 44; SATA-Obit 24

McGinniss, Joe 1942-   **CLC 32**
See also AITN 2; BEST 89:2; CA 25-28R; CANR 26, 70; DLB 185; INT CANR-26

McGivern, Maureen Daly
See Daly, Maureen

McGrath, Patrick 1950-   **CLC 55**
See also CA 136; CANR 65

McGrath, Thomas (Matthew) 1916-1990CLC **28, 59; DAM POET**
See also CA 9-12R; 132; CANR 6, 33; MTCW 1; SATA 41; SATA-Obit 66

McGuane, Thomas (Francis III) 1939-CLC **3, 7, 18, 45**
See also AITN 2; CA 49-52; CANR 5, 24, 49; DLB 2; DLBY 80; INT CANR-24; MTCW 1

McGuckian, Medbh 1950-   **CLC 48; DAM POET**
See also CA 143; DLB 40

McHale, Tom 1942(?)-1982   **CLC 3, 5**
See also AITN 1; CA 77-80; 106

McIlvanney, William 1936-   **CLC 42**
See also CA 25-28R; CANR 61; DLB 14

McIlwraith, Maureen Mollie Hunter
See Hunter, Mollie

3; CANR 2, 30, 54; CDALB 1941-1968;
DLB 7; MTCW 1

Miller, Henry (Valentine) 1891-1980**CLC 1, 2, 4, 9, 14, 43, 84; DA; DAB; DAC; DAM MST, NOV; WLC**
See also CA 9-12R; 97-100; CANR 33, 64; CDALB 1929-1941; DLB 4, 9; DLBY 80; MTCW 1

Miller, Jason 1939(?)- **CLC 2**
See also AITN 1; CA 73-76; DLB 7

Miller, Sue 1943- **CLC 44; DAM POP**
See also BEST 90:3; CA 139; CANR 59; DLB 143

Miller, Walter M(ichael, Jr.) 1923-**CLC 4, 30**
See also CA 85-88; DLB 8

Millett, Kate 1934- **CLC 67**
See also AITN 1; CA 73-76; CANR 32, 53; MTCW 1

Millhauser, Steven (Lewis) 1943-**CLC 21, 54, 109**
See also CA 110; 111; CANR 63; DLB 2; INT 111

Millin, Sarah Gertrude 1889-1968 **CLC 49**
See also CA 102; 93-96

Milne, A(lan) A(lexander) 1882-1956**TCLC 6, 88; DAB; DAC; DAM MST**
See also CA 104; 133; CLR 1, 26; DLB 10, 77, 100, 160; MAICYA; MTCW 1; SATA 100; YABC 1

Milner, Ron(ald) 1938-**CLC 56; BLC 3; DAM MULT**
See also AITN 1; BW 1; CA 73-76; CANR 24; DLB 38; MTCW 1

Milnes, Richard Monckton 1809-1885 **NCLC 61**
See also DLB 32, 184

Milosz, Czeslaw 1911- **CLC 5, 11, 22, 31, 56, 82; DAM MST, POET; PC 8; WLCS**
See also CA 81-84; CANR 23, 51; MTCW 1

Milton, John 1608-1674 **LC 9, 43; DA; DAB; DAC; DAM MST, POET; PC 19; WLC**
See also CDBLB 1660-1789; DLB 131, 151

Min, Anchee 1957- **CLC 86**
See also CA 146

Minehaha, Cornelius
See Wedekind, (Benjamin) Frank(lin)

Miner, Valerie 1947- **CLC 40**
See also CA 97-100; CANR 59

Minimo, Duca
See D'Annunzio, Gabriele

Minot, Susan 1956- **CLC 44**
See also CA 134

Minus, Ed 1938- **CLC 39**

Miranda, Javier
See Bioy Casares, Adolfo

Mirbeau, Octave 1848-1917 **TCLC 55**
See also DLB 123, 192

Miro (Ferrer), Gabriel (Francisco Victor) 1879-1930 **TCLC 5**
See also CA 104

Mishima, Yukio 1925-1970**CLC 2, 4, 6, 9, 27; DC 1; SSC 4**
See also Hiraoka, Kimitake
See also DLB 182

Mistral, Frederic 1830-1914 **TCLC 51**
See also CA 122

Mistral, Gabriela **TCLC 2; HLC**
See also Godoy Alcayaga, Lucila

Mistry, Rohinton 1952- **CLC 71; DAC**
See also CA 141

Mitchell, Clyde
See Ellison, Harlan (Jay); Silverberg, Robert

Mitchell, James Leslie 1901-1935

See Gibbon, Lewis Grassic
See also CA 104; DLB 15

Mitchell, Joni 1943- **CLC 12**
See also CA 112

Mitchell, Joseph (Quincy) 1908-1996**CLC 98**
See also CA 77-80; 152; CANR 69; DLB 185; DLBY 96

Mitchell, Margaret (Munnerlyn) 1900-1949 **TCLC 11; DAM NOV, POP**
See also AAYA 23; CA 109; 125; CANR 55; DLB 9; MTCW 1

Mitchell, Peggy
See Mitchell, Margaret (Munnerlyn)

Mitchell, S(ilas) Weir 1829-1914 **TCLC 36**
See also CA 165; DLB 202

Mitchell, W(illiam) O(rmond) 1914-1998**CLC 25; DAC; DAM MST**
See also CA 77-80; 165; CANR 15, 43; DLB 88

Mitchell, William 1879-1936 **TCLC 81**

Mitford, Mary Russell 1787-1855 **NCLC 4**
See also DLB 110, 116

Mitford, Nancy 1904-1973 **CLC 44**
See also CA 9-12R; DLB 191

Miyamoto, Yuriko 1899-1951 **TCLC 37**
See also CA 170; DLB 180

Miyazawa, Kenji 1896-1933 **TCLC 76**
See also CA 157

Mizoguchi, Kenji 1898-1956 **TCLC 72**
See also CA 167

Mo, Timothy (Peter) 1950(?)- **CLC 46**
See also CA 117; DLB 194; MTCW 1

Modarressi, Taghi (M.) 1931- **CLC 44**
See also CA 121; 134; INT 134

Modiano, Patrick (Jean) 1945- **CLC 18**
See also CA 85-88; CANR 17, 40; DLB 83

Moerck, Paal
See Roelvaag, O(le) E(dvart)

Mofolo, Thomas (Mokopu) 1875(?)-1948 **TCLC 22; BLC 3; DAM MULT**
See also CA 121; 153

Mohr, Nicholasa 1938-**CLC 12; DAM MULT; HLC**
See also AAYA 8; CA 49-52; CANR 1, 32, 64; CLR 22; DLB 145; HW; JRDA; SAAS 8; SATA 8, 97

Mojtabai, A(nn) G(race) 1938- **CLC 5, 9, 15, 29**
See also CA 85-88

Moliere 1622-1673**LC 10, 28; DA; DAB; DAC; DAM DRAM, MST; WLC**

Molin, Charles
See Mayne, William (James Carter)

Molnar, Ferenc 1878-1952 **TCLC 20; DAM DRAM**
See also CA 109; 153

Momaday, N(avarre) Scott 1934- **CLC 2, 19, 85, 95; DA; DAB; DAC; DAM MST, MULT, NOV, POP; WLCS**
See also AAYA 11; CA 25-28R; CANR 14, 34, 68; DLB 143, 175; INT CANR-14; MTCW 1; NNAL; SATA 48; SATA-Brief 30

Monette, Paul 1945-1995 **CLC 82**
See also CA 139; 147

Monroe, Harriet 1860-1936 **TCLC 12**
See also CA 109; DLB 54, 91

Monroe, Lyle
See Heinlein, Robert A(nson)

Montagu, Elizabeth 1720-1800 **NCLC 7**

Montagu, Mary (Pierrepont) Wortley 1689-1762 **LC 9; PC 16**
See also DLB 95, 101

Montagu, W. H.

See Coleridge, Samuel Taylor

Montague, John (Patrick) 1929- **CLC 13, 46**
See also CA 9-12R; CANR 9, 69; DLB 40; MTCW 1

Montaigne, Michel (Eyquem) de 1533-1592 **LC 8; DA; DAB; DAC; DAM MST; WLC**

Montale, Eugenio 1896-1981**CLC 7, 9, 18; PC 13**
See also CA 17-20R; 104; CANR 30; DLB 114; MTCW 1

Montesquieu, Charles-Louis de Secondat 1689-1755 **LC 7**

Montgomery, (Robert) Bruce 1921-1978
See Crispin, Edmund
See also CA 104

Montgomery, L(ucy) M(aud) 1874-1942 **TCLC 51; DAC; DAM MST**
See also AAYA 12; CA 108; 137; CLR 8; DLB 92; DLBD 14; JRDA; MAICYA; SATA 100; YABC 1

Montgomery, Marion H., Jr. 1925- **CLC 7**
See also AITN 1; CA 1-4R; CANR 3, 48; DLB 6

Montgomery, Max
See Davenport, Guy (Mattison, Jr.)

Montherlant, Henry (Milon) de 1896-1972 **CLC 8, 19; DAM DRAM**
See also CA 85-88; 37-40R; DLB 72; MTCW 1

Monty Python
See Chapman, Graham; Cleese, John (Marwood); Gilliam, Terry (Vance); Idle, Eric; Jones, Terence Graham Parry; Palin, Michael (Edward)
See also AAYA 7

Moodie, Susanna (Strickland) 1803-1885 **NCLC 14**
See also DLB 99

Mooney, Edward 1951-
See Mooney, Ted
See also CA 130

Mooney, Ted **CLC 25**
See also Mooney, Edward

Moorcock, Michael (John) 1939-**CLC 5, 27, 58**
See also AAYA 26; CA 45-48; CAAS 5; CANR 2, 17, 38, 64; DLB 14; MTCW 1; SATA 93

Moore, Brian 1921- **CLC 1, 3, 5, 7, 8, 19, 32, 90; DAB; DAC; DAM MST**
See also CA 1-4R; CANR 1, 25, 42, 63; MTCW 1

Moore, Edward
See Muir, Edwin

Moore, George Augustus 1852-1933**TCLC 7; SSC 19**
See also CA 104; DLB 10, 18, 57, 135

Moore, Lorrie **CLC 39, 45, 68**
See also Moore, Marie Lorena

Moore, Marianne (Craig) 1887-1972**CLC 1, 2, 4, 8, 10, 13, 19, 47; DA; DAB; DAC; DAM MST, POET; PC 4; WLCS**
See also CA 1-4R; 33-36R; CANR 3, 61; CDALB 1929-1941; DLB 45; DLBD 7; MTCW 1; SATA 20

Moore, Marie Lorena 1957-
See Moore, Lorrie
See also CA 116; CANR 39

Moore, Thomas 1779-1852 **NCLC 6**
See also DLB 96, 144

Morand, Paul 1888-1976 **CLC 41; SSC 22**
See also CA 69-72; DLB 65

Morante, Elsa 1918-1985 **CLC 8, 47**
See also CA 85-88; 117; CANR 35; DLB 177; MTCW 1

See Chekhov, Anton (Pavlovich)
Myers, L(eopold) H(amilton) 1881-1944
    TCLC 59
    See also CA 157; DLB 15
Myers, Walter Dean 1937- **CLC 35; BLC 3;**
    DAM MULT, NOV
    See also AAYA 4, 23; BW 2; CA 33-36R;
    CANR 20, 42, 67; CLR 4, 16, 35; DLB 33;
    INT CANR-20; JRDA; MAICYA; SAAS 2;
    SATA 41, 71; SATA-Brief 27
Myers, Walter M.
    See Myers, Walter Dean
Myles, Symon
    See Follett, Ken(neth Martin)
Nabokov, Vladimir (Vladimirovich) 1899-1977
    CLC 1, 2, 3, 6, 8, 11, 15, 23, 44, 46, 64;
    DA; DAB; DAC; DAM MST, NOV; SSC
    11; WLC
    See also CA 5-8R; 69-72; CANR 20; CDALB
    1941-1968; DLB 2; DLBD 3; DLBY 80, 91;
    MTCW 1
Nagai Kafu 1879-1959   **TCLC 51**
    See also Nagai Sokichi
    See also DLB 180
Nagai Sokichi 1879-1959
    See Nagai Kafu
    See also CA 117
Nagy, Laszlo 1925-1978   **CLC 7**
    See also CA 129; 112
Naidu, Sarojini 1879-1943   **TCLC 80**
Naipaul, Shiva(dhar Srinivasa) 1945-1985
    CLC 32, 39; DAM NOV
    See also CA 110; 112; 116; CANR 33; DLB
    157; DLBY 85; MTCW 1
Naipaul, V(idiadhar) S(urajprasad) 1932-
    CLC 4, 7, 9, 13, 18, 37, 105; DAB; DAC;
    DAM MST, NOV
    See also CA 1-4R; CANR 1, 33, 51; CDBLB
    1960 to Present; DLB 125; DLBY 85;
    MTCW 1
Nakos, Lilika 1899(?)-   **CLC 29**
Narayan, R(asipuram) K(rishnaswami) 1906-
    CLC 7, 28, 47; DAM NOV; SSC 25
    See also CA 81-84; CANR 33, 61; MTCW 1;
    SATA 62
Nash, (Frediric) Ogden 1902-1971   **CLC 23;**
    DAM POET; PC 21
    See also CA 13-14; 29-32R; CANR 34, 61; CAP
    1; DLB 11; MAICYA; MTCW 1; SATA 2,
    46
Nashe, Thomas 1567-1601(?)   **LC 41**
    See also DLB 167
Nashe, Thomas 1567-1601   **LC 41**
Nathan, Daniel
    See Dannay, Frederic
Nathan, George Jean 1882-1958   **TCLC 18**
    See also Hatteras, Owen
    See also CA 114; 169; DLB 137
Natsume, Kinnosuke 1867-1916
    See Natsume, Soseki
    See also CA 104
Natsume, Soseki 1867-1916   **TCLC 2, 10**
    See also Natsume, Kinnosuke
    See also DLB 180
Natti, (Mary) Lee 1919-
    See Kingman, Lee
    See also CA 5-8R; CANR 2
Naylor, Gloria 1950- CLC 28, 52; BLC 3; DA;
    DAC; DAM MST, MULT, NOV, POP;
    WLCS
    See also AAYA 6; BW 2; CA 107; CANR 27,
    51, 74; DLB 173; MTCW 1
Neihardt, John Gneisenau 1881-1973 CLC 32

See also CA 13-14; CANR 65; CAP 1; DLB 9,
    54
Nekrasov, Nikolai Alekseevich 1821-1878
    NCLC 11
Nelligan, Emile 1879-1941   **TCLC 14**
    See also CA 114; DLB 92
Nelson, Willie 1933-   **CLC 17**
    See also CA 107
Nemerov, Howard (Stanley) 1920-1991 CLC 2,
    6, 9, 36; DAM POET; PC 24
    See also CA 1-4R; 134; CABS 2; CANR 1, 27,
    53; DLB 5, 6; DLBY 83; INT CANR-27;
    MTCW 1
Neruda, Pablo 1904-1973 CLC 1, 2, 5, 7, 9, 28,
    62; DA; DAB; DAC; DAM MST, MULT,
    POET; HLC; PC 4; WLC
    See also CA 19-20; 45-48; CAP 2; HW; MTCW
    1
Nerval, Gerard de 1808-1855 NCLC 1, 67; PC
    13; SSC 18
Nervo, (Jose) Amado (Ruiz de) 1870-1919
    TCLC 11
    See also CA 109; 131; HW
Nessi, Pio Baroja y
    See Baroja (y Nessi), Pio
Nestroy, Johann 1801-1862   **NCLC 42**
    See also DLB 133
Netterville, Luke
    See O'Grady, Standish (James)
Neufeld, John (Arthur) 1938-   **CLC 17**
    See also AAYA 11; CA 25-28R; CANR 11, 37,
    56; CLR 52; MAICYA; SAAS 3; SATA 6,
    81
Neville, Emily Cheney 1919-   **CLC 12**
    See also CA 5-8R; CANR 3, 37; JRDA;
    MAICYA; SAAS 2; SATA 1
Newbound, Bernard Slade 1930-
    See Slade, Bernard
    See also CA 81-84; CANR 49; DAM DRAM
Newby, P(ercy) H(oward) 1918-1997 CLC 2,
    13; DAM NOV
    See also CA 5-8R; 161; CANR 32, 67; DLB
    15; MTCW 1
Newlove, Donald 1928-   **CLC 6**
    See also CA 29-32R; CANR 25
Newlove, John (Herbert) 1938-   **CLC 14**
    See also CA 21-24R; CANR 9, 25
Newman, Charles 1938-   **CLC 2, 8**
    See also CA 21-24R
Newman, Edwin (Harold) 1919-   **CLC 14**
    See also AITN 1; CA 69-72; CANR 5
Newman, John Henry 1801-1890   **NCLC 38**
    See also DLB 18, 32, 55
Newton, (Sir) Isaac 1642-1727   **LC 35**
Newton, Suzanne 1936-   **CLC 35**
    See also CA 41-44R; CANR 14; JRDA; SATA
    5, 77
Nexo, Martin Andersen 1869-1954 TCLC 43
Nezval, Vitezslav 1900-1958   **TCLC 44**
    See also CA 123
Ng, Fae Myenne 1957(?)-   **CLC 81**
    See also CA 146
Ngema, Mbongeni 1955-   **CLC 57**
    See also BW 2; CA 143
Ngugi, James T(hiong'o)   CLC 3, 7, 13
    See also Ngugi wa Thiong'o
Ngugi wa Thiong'o 1938-   **CLC 36; BLC 3;**
    DAM MULT, NOV
    See also Ngugi, James T(hiong'o)
    See also BW 2; CA 81-84; CANR 27, 58; DLB
    125; MTCW 1
Nichol, B(arrie) P(hillip) 1944-1988   **CLC 18**
    See also CA 53-56; DLB 53; SATA 66

Nichols, John (Treadwell) 1940-   **CLC 38**
    See also CA 9-12R; CAAS 2; CANR 6, 70;
    DLBY 82
Nichols, Leigh
    See Koontz, Dean R(ay)
Nichols, Peter (Richard) 1927- CLC 5, 36, 65
    See also CA 104; CANR 33; DLB 13; MTCW
    1
Nicolas, F. R. E.
    See Freeling, Nicolas
Niedecker, Lorine 1903-1970   **CLC 10, 42;**
    DAM POET
    See also CA 25-28; CAP 2; DLB 48
Nietzsche, Friedrich (Wilhelm) 1844-1900
    TCLC 10, 18, 55
    See also CA 107; 121; DLB 129
Nievo, Ippolito 1831-1861   **NCLC 22**
Nightingale, Anne Redmon 1943-
    See Redmon, Anne
    See also CA 103
Nightingale, Florence 1820-1910   **TCLC 85**
    See also DLB 166
Nik. T. O.
    See Annensky, Innokenty (Fyodorovich)
Nin, Anais 1903-1977 CLC 1, 4, 8, 11, 14, 60;
    DAM NOV, POP; SSC 10
    See also AITN 2; CA 13-16R; 69-72; CANR
    22, 53; DLB 2, 4, 152; MTCW 1
Nishida, Kitaro 1870-1945   **TCLC 83**
Nishiwaki, Junzaburo 1894-1982   **PC 15**
    See also CA 107
Nissenson, Hugh 1933-   **CLC 4, 9**
    See also CA 17-20R; CANR 27; DLB 28
Niven, Larry   **CLC 8**
    See also Niven, Laurence Van Cott
    See also AAYA 27; DLB 8
Niven, Laurence Van Cott 1938-
    See Niven, Larry
    See also CA 21-24R; CAAS 12; CANR 14, 44,
    66; DAM POP; MTCW 1; SATA 95
Nixon, Agnes Eckhardt 1927-   **CLC 21**
    See also CA 110
Nizan, Paul 1905-1940   **TCLC 40**
    See also CA 161; DLB 72
Nkosi, Lewis 1936-   **CLC 45; BLC 3; DAM**
    MULT
    See also BW 1; CA 65-68; CANR 27; DLB 157
Nodier, (Jean) Charles (Emmanuel) 1780-1844
    NCLC 19
    See also DLB 119
Noguchi, Yone 1875-1947   **TCLC 80**
Nolan, Christopher 1965-   **CLC 58**
    See also CA 111
Noon, Jeff 1957-   **CLC 91**
    See also CA 148
Norden, Charles
    See Durrell, Lawrence (George)
Nordhoff, Charles (Bernard) 1887-1947
    TCLC 23
    See also CA 108; DLB 9; SATA 23
Norfolk, Lawrence 1963-   **CLC 76**
    See also CA 144
Norman, Marsha 1947- CLC 28; DAM DRAM;
    DC 8
    See also CA 105; CABS 3; CANR 41; DLBY
    84
Normyx
    See Douglas, (George) Norman
Norris, Frank 1870-1902   **SSC 28**
    See also Norris, (Benjamin) Frank(lin, Jr.)
    See also CDALB 1865-1917; DLB 12, 71, 186
Norris, (Benjamin) Frank(lin, Jr.) 1870-1902
    TCLC 24

TCLC 45
See also CA 111; DLB 70
Opuls, Max
See Ophuls, Max
Origen c. 185-c. 254 **CMLC 19**
Orlovitz, Gil 1918-1973 **CLC 22**
See also CA 77-80; 45-48; DLB 2, 5
Orris
See Ingelow, Jean
Ortega y Gasset, Jose 1883-1955 **TCLC 9;**
DAM MULT; HLC
See also CA 106; 130; HW; MTCW 1
Ortese, Anna Maria 1914- **CLC 89**
See also DLB 177
Ortiz, Simon J(oseph) 1941- **CLC 45; DAM**
MULT, POET; PC 17
See also CA 134; CANR 69; DLB 120, 175;
NNAL
Orton, Joe **CLC 4, 13, 43; DC 3**
See also Orton, John Kingsley
See also CDBLB 1960 to Present; DLB 13
Orton, John Kingsley 1933-1967
See Orton, Joe
See also CA 85-88; CANR 35, 66; DAM
DRAM; MTCW 1
Orwell, George **TCLC 2, 6, 15, 31, 51; DAB;**
WLC
See also Blair, Eric (Arthur)
See also CDBLB 1945-1960; DLB 15, 98, 195
Osborne, David
See Silverberg, Robert
Osborne, George
See Silverberg, Robert
Osborne, John (James) 1929-1994**CLC 1, 2, 5,**
11, 45; DA; DAB; DAC; DAM DRAM,
MST; WLC
See also CA 13-16R; 147; CANR 21, 56;
CDBLB 1945-1960; DLB 13; MTCW 1
Osborne, Lawrence 1958- **CLC 50**
Oshima, Nagisa 1932- **CLC 20**
See also CA 116; 121
Oskison, John Milton 1874-1947 **TCLC 35;**
DAM MULT
See also CA 144; DLB 175; NNAL
Ossian c. 3rd cent. - **CMLC 28**
See also Macpherson, James
Ossoli, Sarah Margaret (Fuller marchesa d')
1810-1850
See Fuller, Margaret
See also SATA 25
Ostrovsky, Alexander 1823-1886**NCLC 30, 57**
Otero, Blas de 1916-1979 **CLC 11**
See also CA 89-92; DLB 134
Otto, Rudolf 1869-1937 **TCLC 85**
Otto, Whitney 1955- **CLC 70**
See also CA 140
Ouida **TCLC 43**
See also De La Ramee, (Marie) Louise
See also DLB 18, 156
Ousmane, Sembene 1923- **CLC 66; BLC 3**
See also BW 1; CA 117; 125; MTCW 1
Ovid 43B.C.-18(?)**CMLC 7; DAM POET; PC**
2
Owen, Hugh
See Faust, Frederick (Schiller)
Owen, Wilfred (Edward Salter) 1893-1918
TCLC 5, 27; DA; DAB; DAC; DAM MST,
POET; PC 19; WLC
See also CA 104; 141; CDBLB 1914-1945;
DLB 20
Owens, Rochelle 1936- **CLC 8**
See also CA 17-20R; CAAS 2; CANR 39
Oz, Amos 1939-**CLC 5, 8, 11, 27, 33, 54; DAM**

NOV
See also CA 53-56; CANR 27, 47, 65; MTCW
1
Ozick, Cynthia 1928- **CLC 3, 7, 28, 62; DAM**
NOV, POP; SSC 15
See also BEST 90:1; CA 17-20R; CANR 23,
58; DLB 28, 152; DLBY 82; INT CANR-
23; MTCW 1
Ozu, Yasujiro 1903-1963 **CLC 16**
See also CA 112
Pacheco, C.
See Pessoa, Fernando (Antonio Nogueira)
Pa Chin **CLC 18**
See also Li Fei-kan
Pack, Robert 1929- **CLC 13**
See also CA 1-4R; CANR 3, 44; DLB 5
Padgett, Lewis
See Kuttner, Henry
Padilla (Lorenzo), Heberto 1932- **CLC 38**
See also AITN 1; CA 123; 131; HW
Page, Jimmy 1944- **CLC 12**
Page, Louise 1955- **CLC 40**
See also CA 140
Page, P(atricia) K(athleen) 1916- CLC **7, 18;**
DAC; DAM MST; PC 12
See also CA 53-56; CANR 4, 22, 65; DLB 68;
MTCW 1
Page, Thomas Nelson 1853-1922 **SSC 23**
See also CA 118; DLB 12, 78; DLBD 13
Pagels, Elaine Hiesey 1943- **CLC 104**
See also CA 45-48; CANR 2, 24, 51
Paget, Violet 1856-1935
See Lee, Vernon
See also CA 104; 166
Paget-Lowe, Henry
See Lovecraft, H(oward) P(hillips)
Paglia, Camille (Anna) 1947- **CLC 68**
See also CA 140; CANR 72
Paige, Richard
See Koontz, Dean R(ay)
Paine, Thomas 1737-1809 **NCLC 62**
See also CDALB 1640-1865; DLB 31, 43, 73,
158
Pakenham, Antonia
See Fraser, (Lady) Antonia (Pakenham)
Palamas, Kostes 1859-1943 **TCLC 5**
See also CA 105
Palazzeschi, Aldo 1885-1974 **CLC 11**
See also CA 89-92; 53-56; DLB 114
Paley, Grace 1922- **CLC 4, 6, 37; DAM POP;**
SSC 8
See also CA 25-28R; CANR 13, 46, 74; DLB
28; INT CANR-13; MTCW 1
Palin, Michael (Edward) 1943- **CLC 21**
See also Monty Python
See also CA 107; CANR 35; SATA 67
Palliser, Charles 1947- **CLC 65**
See also CA 136
Palma, Ricardo 1833-1919 **TCLC 29**
See also CA 168
Pancake, Breece Dexter 1952-1979
See Pancake, Breece D'J
See also CA 123; 109
Pancake, Breece D'J **CLC 29**
See also Pancake, Breece Dexter
See also DLB 130
Panko, Rudy
See Gogol, Nikolai (Vasilyevich)
Papadiamantis, Alexandros 1851-1911**TCLC**
29
See also CA 168
Papadiamantopoulos, Johannes 1856-1910
See Moreas, Jean

See also CA 117
Papini, Giovanni 1881-1956 **TCLC 22**
See also CA 121
Paracelsus 1493-1541 **LC 14**
See also DLB 179
Parasol, Peter
See Stevens, Wallace
Pardo Bazan, Emilia 1851-1921 **SSC 30**
Pareto, Vilfredo 1848-1923 **TCLC 69**
Parfenie, Maria
See Codrescu, Andrei
Parini, Jay (Lee) 1948- **CLC 54**
See also CA 97-100; CAAS 16; CANR 32
Park, Jordan
See Kornbluth, C(yril) M.; Pohl, Frederik
Park, Robert E(zra) 1864-1944 **TCLC 73**
See also CA 122; 165
Parker, Bert
See Ellison, Harlan (Jay)
Parker, Dorothy (Rothschild) 1893-1967**CLC**
15, 68; DAM POET; SSC 2
See also CA 19-20; 25-28R; CAP 2; DLB 11,
45, 86; MTCW 1
Parker, Robert B(rown) 1932-**CLC 27; DAM**
NOV, POP
See also BEST 89:4; CA 49-52; CANR 1, 26,
52; INT CANR-26; MTCW 1
Parkin, Frank 1940- **CLC 43**
See also CA 147
Parkman, Francis, Jr. 1823-1893 **NCLC 12**
See also DLB 1, 30, 186
Parks, Gordon (Alexander Buchanan) 1912-
CLC 1, 16; BLC 3; DAM MULT
See also AITN 2; BW 2; CA 41-44R; CANR
26, 66; DLB 33; SATA 8
Parmenides c. 515B.C.-c. 450B.C. **CMLC 22**
See also DLB 176
Parnell, Thomas 1679-1718 **LC 3**
See also DLB 94
Parra, Nicanor 1914- **CLC 2, 102; DAM**
MULT; HLC
See also CA 85-88; CANR 32; HW; MTCW 1
Parrish, Mary Frances
See Fisher, M(ary) F(rances) K(ennedy)
Parson
See Coleridge, Samuel Taylor
Parson Lot
See Kingsley, Charles
Partridge, Anthony
See Oppenheim, E(dward) Phillips
Pascal, Blaise 1623-1662 **LC 35**
Pascoli, Giovanni 1855-1912 **TCLC 45**
See also CA 170
Pasolini, Pier Paolo 1922-1975 **CLC 20, 37,**
106; PC 17
See also CA 93-96; 61-64; CANR 63; DLB 128,
177; MTCW 1
Pasquini
See Silone, Ignazio
Pastan, Linda (Olenik) 1932- **CLC 27; DAM**
POET
See also CA 61-64; CANR 18, 40, 61; DLB 5
Pasternak, Boris (Leonidovich) 1890-1960
CLC 7, 10, 18, 63; DA; DAB; DAC; DAM
MST, NOV, POET; PC 6; SSC 31; WLC
See also CA 127; 116; MTCW 1
Patchen, Kenneth 1911-1972 **CLC 1, 2, 18;**
DAM POET
See also CA 1-4R; 33-36R; CANR 3, 35; DLB
16, 48; MTCW 1
Pater, Walter (Horatio) 1839-1894 **NCLC 7**
See also CDBLB 1832-1890; DLB 57, 156
Paterson, A(ndrew) B(arton) 1864-1941

Pineda, Cecile 1942-   **CLC 39**
See also CA 118
Pinero, Arthur Wing 1855-1934   **TCLC 32;**
DAM DRAM
See also CA 110; 153; DLB 10
Pinero, Miguel (Antonio Gomez) 1946-1988
CLC 4, 55
See also CA 61-64; 125; CANR 29; HW
Pinget, Robert 1919-1997   **CLC 7, 13, 37**
See also CA 85-88; 160; DLB 83
Pink Floyd
See Barrett, (Roger) Syd; Gilmour, David; Mason, Nick; Waters, Roger; Wright, Rick
Pinkney, Edward 1802-1828   **NCLC 31**
Pinkwater, Daniel Manus 1941-   **CLC 35**
See also Pinkwater, Manus
See also AAYA 1; CA 29-32R; CANR 12, 38;
CLR 4; JRDA; MAICYA; SAAS 3; SATA 46,
76
Pinkwater, Manus
See Pinkwater, Daniel Manus
See also SATA 8
Pinsky, Robert 1940-**CLC 9, 19, 38, 94; DAM**
POET
See also CA 29-32R; CAAS 4; CANR 58;
DLBY 82
Pinta, Harold
See Pinter, Harold
Pinter, Harold 1930-**CLC 1, 3, 6, 9, 11, 15, 27,**
58, 73; DA; DAB; DAC; DAM DRAM,
MST; WLC
See also CA 5-8R; CANR 33, 65; CDBLB 1960
to Present; DLB 13; MTCW 1
Piozzi, Hester Lynch (Thrale) 1741-1821
NCLC 57
See also DLB 104, 142
Pirandello, Luigi 1867-1936**TCLC 4, 29; DA;**
DAB; DAC; DAM DRAM, MST; DC 5;
SSC 22; WLC
See also CA 104; 153
Pirsig, Robert M(aynard) 1928-**CLC 4, 6, 73;**
DAM POP
See also CA 53-56; CANR 42, 74; MTCW 1;
SATA 39
Pisarev, Dmitry Ivanovich 1840-1868 **NCLC**
25
Pix, Mary (Griffith) 1666-1709   **LC 8**
See also DLB 80
Pixerecourt, (Rene Charles) Guilbert de 1773-
1844   **NCLC 39**
See also DLB 192
Plaatje, Sol(omon) T(shekisho) 1876-1932
TCLC 73; BLCS
See also BW 2; CA 141
Plaidy, Jean
See Hibbert, Eleanor Alice Burford
Planche, James Robinson 1796-1880**NCLC 42**
Plant, Robert 1948-   **CLC 12**
Plante, David (Robert) 1940-   **CLC 7, 23, 38;**
DAM NOV
See also CA 37-40R; CANR 12, 36, 58; DLBY
83; INT CANR-12; MTCW 1
Plath, Sylvia 1932-1963 **CLC 1, 2, 3, 5, 9, 11,**
14, 17, 50, 51, 62, 111; DA; DAB; DAC;
DAM MST, POET; PC 1; WLC
See also AAYA 13; CA 19-20; CANR 34; CAP
2; CDALB 1941-1968; DLB 5, 6, 152;
MTCW 1; SATA 96
Plato 428(?)B.C.-348(?)B.C.   **CMLC 8; DA;**
DAB; DAC; DAM MST; WLCS
See also DLB 176
Platonov, Andrei   **TCLC 14**
See also Klimentov, Andrei Platonovich

Platt, Kin 1911-   **CLC 26**
See also AAYA 11; CA 17-20R; CANR 11;
JRDA; SAAS 17; SATA 21, 86
Plautus c. 251B.C.-184B.C. **CMLC 24; DC 6**
Plick et Plock
See Simenon, Georges (Jacques Christian)
Plimpton, George (Ames) 1927-   **CLC 36**
See also AITN 1; CA 21-24R; CANR 32, 70;
DLB 185; MTCW 1; SATA 10
Pliny the Elder c. 23-79   **CMLC 23**
Plomer, William Charles Franklin 1903-1973
CLC 4, 8
See also CA 21-22; CANR 34; CAP 2; DLB
20, 162, 191; MTCW 1; SATA 24
Plowman, Piers
See Kavanagh, Patrick (Joseph)
Plum, J.
See Wodehouse, P(elham) G(renville)
Plumly, Stanley (Ross) 1939-   **CLC 33**
See also CA 108; 110; DLB 5, 193; INT 110
Plumpe, Friedrich Wilhelm 1888-1931**TCLC**
53
See also CA 112
Po Chu-i 772-846   **CMLC 24**
Poe, Edgar Allan 1809-1849 **NCLC 1, 16, 55;**
DA; DAB; DAC; DAM MST, POET; PC
1; SSC 1, 22; WLC
See also AAYA 14; CDALB 1640-1865; DLB
3, 59, 73, 74; SATA 23
Poet of Titchfield Street, The
See Pound, Ezra (Weston Loomis)
Pohl, Frederik 1919-   **CLC 18; SSC 25**
See also AAYA 24; CA 61-64; CAAS 1; CANR
11, 37; DLB 8; INT CANR-11; MTCW 1;
SATA 24
Poirier, Louis 1910-
See Gracq, Julien
See also CA 122; 126
Poitier, Sidney 1927-   **CLC 26**
See also BW 1; CA 117
Polanski, Roman 1933-   **CLC 16**
See also CA 77-80
Poliakoff, Stephen 1952-   **CLC 38**
See also CA 106; DLB 13
Police, The
See Copeland, Stewart (Armstrong); Summers,
Andrew James; Sumner, Gordon Matthew
Polidori, John William 1795-1821 **NCLC 51**
See also DLB 116
Pollitt, Katha 1949-   **CLC 28**
See also CA 120; 122; CANR 66; MTCW 1
Pollock, (Mary) Sharon 1936-**CLC 50; DAC;**
DAM DRAM, MST
See also CA 141; DLB 60
Polo, Marco 1254-1324   **CMLC 15**
Polonsky, Abraham (Lincoln) 1910- **CLC 92**
See also CA 104; DLB 26; INT 104
Polybius c. 200B.C.-c. 118B.C.   **CMLC 17**
See also DLB 176
Pomerance, Bernard 1940-   **CLC 13; DAM**
DRAM
See also CA 101; CANR 49
Ponge, Francis (Jean Gaston Alfred) 1899-1988
CLC 6, 18; DAM POET
See also CA 85-88; 126; CANR 40
Pontoppidan, Henrik 1857-1943   **TCLC 29**
See also CA 170
Poole, Josephine   **CLC 17**
See also Helyar, Jane Penelope Josephine
See also SAAS 2; SATA 5
Popa, Vasko 1922-1991   **CLC 19**
See also CA 112; 148; DLB 181
Pope, Alexander 1688-1744 **LC 3; DA; DAB;**

DAC; DAM MST, POET; WLC
See also CDBLB 1660-1789; DLB 95, 101
Porter, Connie (Rose) 1959(?)-   **CLC 70**
See also BW 2; CA 142; SATA 81
Porter, Gene(va Grace) Stratton 1863(?)-1924
TCLC 21
See also CA 112
Porter, Katherine Anne 1890-1980**CLC 1, 3, 7,**
10, 13, 15, 27, 101; DA; DAB; DAC; DAM
MST, NOV; SSC 4, 31
See also AITN 2; CA 1-4R; 101; CANR 1, 65;
DLB 4, 9, 102; DLBD 12; DLBY 80; MTCW
1; SATA 39; SATA-Obit 23
Porter, Peter (Neville Frederick) 1929-**CLC 5,**
13, 33
See also CA 85-88; DLB 40
Porter, William Sydney 1862-1910
See Henry, O.
See also CA 104; 131; CDALB 1865-1917; DA;
DAB; DAC; DAM MST; DLB 12, 78, 79;
MTCW 1; YABC 2
Portillo (y Pacheco), Jose Lopez
See Lopez Portillo (y Pacheco), Jose
Post, Melville Davisson 1869-1930 **TCLC 39**
See also CA 110
Potok, Chaim 1929-   **CLC 2, 7, 14, 26, 112;**
DAM NOV
See also AAYA 15; AITN 1, 2; CA 17-20R;
CANR 19, 35, 64; DLB 28, 152; INT CANR-
19; MTCW 1; SATA 33
Potter, (Helen) Beatrix 1866-1943
See Webb, (Martha) Beatrice (Potter)
See also MAICYA
Potter, Dennis (Christopher George) 1935-1994
CLC 58, 86
See also CA 107; 145; CANR 33, 61; MTCW 1
Pound, Ezra (Weston Loomis) 1885-1972**CLC**
1, 2, 3, 4, 5, 7, 10, 13, 18, 34, 48, 50, 112;
DA; DAB; DAC; DAM MST, POET; PC
4; WLC
See also CA 5-8R; 37-40R; CANR 40; CDALB
1917-1929; DLB 4, 45, 63; DLBD 15;
MTCW 1
Povod, Reinaldo 1959-1994   **CLC 44**
See also CA 136; 146
Powell, Adam Clayton, Jr. 1908-1972**CLC 89;**
BLC 3; DAM MULT
See also BW 1; CA 102; 33-36R
Powell, Anthony (Dymoke) 1905-**CLC 1, 3, 7,**
9, 10, 31
See also CA 1-4R; CANR 1, 32, 62; CDBLB
1945-1960; DLB 15; MTCW 1
Powell, Dawn 1897-1965   **CLC 66**
See also CA 5-8R; DLBY 97
Powell, Padgett 1952-   **CLC 34**
See also CA 126; CANR 63
Power, Susan 1961-   **CLC 91**
Powers, J(ames) F(arl) 1917-**CLC 1, 4, 8, 57;**
SSC 4
See also CA 1-4R; CANR 2, 61; DLB 130;
MTCW 1
Powers, John J(ames) 1945-
See Powers, John R.
See also CA 69-72
Powers, John R.   **CLC 66**
See also Powers, John J(ames)
Powers, Richard (S.) 1957-   **CLC 93**
See also CA 148
Pownall, David 1938-   **CLC 10**
See also CA 89-92; CAAS 18; CANR 49; DLB
14
Powys, John Cowper 1872-1963**CLC 7, 9, 15,**
46

Author Index

Rakosi, Carl 1903-   CLC 47
    See also Rawley, Callman
    See also CAAS 5; DLB 193
Raleigh, Richard
    See Lovecraft, H(oward) P(hillips)
Raleigh, Sir Walter 1554(?)-1618 LC 31, 39
    See also CDBLB Before 1660; DLB 172
Rallentando, H. P.
    See Sayers, Dorothy L(eigh)
Ramal, Walter
    See de la Mare, Walter (John)
Ramana Maharshi 1879-1950   TCLC 84
Ramon, Juan
    See Jimenez (Mantecon), Juan Ramon
Ramos, Graciliano 1892-1953   TCLC 32
    See also CA 167
Rampersad, Arnold 1941-   CLC 44
    See also BW 2; CA 127; 133; DLB 111; INT
        133
Rampling, Anne
    See Rice, Anne
Ramsay, Allan 1684(?)-1758   LC 29
    See also DLB 95
Ramuz, Charles-Ferdinand 1878-1947TCLC
    33
    See also CA 165
Rand, Ayn 1905-1982CLC 3, 30, 44, 79; DA;
    DAC; DAM MST, NOV, POP; WLC
    See also AAYA 10; CA 13-16R; 105; CANR
        27, 73; MTCW 1
Randall, Dudley (Felker) 1914-CLC 1; BLC 3;
    DAM MULT
    See also BW 1; CA 25-28R; CANR 23; DLB
        41
Randall, Robert
    See Silverberg, Robert
Ranger, Ken
    See Creasey, John
Ransom, John Crowe 1888-1974 CLC 2, 4, 5,
    11, 24; DAM POET
    See also CA 5-8R; 49-52; CANR 6, 34; DLB
        45, 63; MTCW 1
Rao, Raja 1909-   CLC 25, 56; DAM NOV
    See also CA 73-76; CANR 51; MTCW 1
Raphael, Frederic (Michael) 1931-CLC 2, 14
    See also CA 1-4R; CANR 1; DLB 14
Ratcliffe, James P.
    See Mencken, H(enry) L(ouis)
Rathbone, Julian 1935-   CLC 41
    See also CA 101; CANR 34, 73
Rattigan, Terence (Mervyn) 1911-1977CLC 7;
    DAM DRAM
    See also CA 85-88; 73-76; CDBLB 1945-1960;
        DLB 13; MTCW 1
Ratushinskaya, Irina 1954-   CLC 54
    See also CA 129; CANR 68
Raven, Simon (Arthur Noel) 1927-   CLC 14
    See also CA 81-84
Ravenna, Michael
    See Welty, Eudora
Rawley, Callman 1903-
    See Rakosi, Carl
    See also CA 21-24R; CANR 12, 32
Rawlings, Marjorie Kinnan 1896-1953TCLC
    4
    See also AAYA 20; CA 104; 137; DLB 9, 22,
        102; DLBD 17; JRDA; MAICYA; SATA 100;
        YABC 1
Ray, Satyajit 1921-1992 CLC 16, 76; DAM
    MULT
    See also CA 114; 137
Read, Herbert Edward 1893-1968   CLC 4
    See also CA 85-88; 25-28R; DLB 20, 149

Read, Piers Paul 1941-   CLC 4, 10, 25
    See also CA 21-24R; CANR 38; DLB 14; SATA
        21
Reade, Charles 1814-1884   NCLC 2, 74
    See also DLB 21
Reade, Hamish
    See Gray, Simon (James Holliday)
Reading, Peter 1946-   CLC 47
    See also CA 103; CANR 46; DLB 40
Reaney, James 1926-   CLC 13; DAC; DAM
    MST
    See also CA 41-44R; CAAS 15; CANR 42; DLB
        68; SATA 43
Rebreanu, Liviu 1885-1944   TCLC 28
    See also CA 165
Rechy, John (Francisco) 1934- CLC 1, 7, 14,
    18, 107; DAM MULT; HLC
    See also CA 5-8R; CAAS 4; CANR 6, 32, 64;
        DLB 122; DLBY 82; HW; INT CANR-6
Redcam, Tom 1870-1933   TCLC 25
Reddin, Keith   CLC 67
Redgrove, Peter (William) 1932- CLC 6, 41
    See also CA 1-4R; CANR 3, 39; DLB 40
Redmon, Anne   CLC 22
    See also Nightingale, Anne Redmon
    See also DLBY 86
Reed, Eliot
    See Ambler, Eric
Reed, Ishmael 1938-CLC 2, 3, 5, 6, 13, 32, 60;
    BLC 3; DAM MULT
    See also BW 2; CA 21-24R; CANR 25, 48, 74;
        DLB 2, 5, 33, 169; DLBD 8; MTCW 1
Reed, John (Silas) 1887-1920   TCLC 9
    See also CA 106
Reed, Lou   CLC 21
    See also Firbank, Louis
Reeve, Clara 1729-1807   NCLC 19
    See also DLB 39
Reich, Wilhelm 1897-1957   TCLC 57
Reid, Christopher (John) 1949-   CLC 33
    See also CA 140; DLB 40
Reid, Desmond
    See Moorcock, Michael (John)
Reid Banks, Lynne 1929-
    See Banks, Lynne Reid
    See also CA 1-4R; CANR 6, 22, 38; CLR 24;
        JRDA; MAICYA; SATA 22, 75
Reilly, William K.
    See Creasey, John
Reiner, Max
    See Caldwell, (Janet Miriam) Taylor (Holland)
Reis, Ricardo
    See Pessoa, Fernando (Antonio Nogueira)
Remarque, Erich Maria 1898-1970 CLC 21;
    DA; DAB; DAC; DAM MST, NOV
    See also AAYA 27; CA 77-80; 29-32R; DLB
        56; MTCW 1
Remizov, A.
    See Remizov, Aleksei (Mikhailovich)
Remizov, A. M.
    See Remizov, Aleksei (Mikhailovich)
Remizov, Aleksei (Mikhailovich) 1877-1957
    TCLC 27
    See also CA 125; 133
Renan, Joseph Ernest 1823-1892   NCLC 26
Renard, Jules 1864-1910   TCLC 17
    See also CA 117
Renault, Mary   CLC 3, 11, 17
    See also Challans, Mary
    See also DLBY 83
Rendell, Ruth (Barbara) 1930- CLC 28, 48;
    DAM POP
    See also Vine, Barbara

    See also CA 109; CANR 32, 52, 74; DLB 87;
        INT CANR-32; MTCW 1
Renoir, Jean 1894-1979   CLC 20
    See also CA 129; 85-88
Resnais, Alain 1922-   CLC 16
Reverdy, Pierre 1889-1960   CLC 53
    See also CA 97-100; 89-92
Rexroth, Kenneth 1905-1982 CLC 1, 2, 6, 11,
    22, 49, 112; DAM POET; PC 20
    See also CA 5-8R; 107; CANR 14, 34, 63;
        CDALB 1941-1968; DLB 16, 48, 165;
        DLBY 82; INT CANR-14; MTCW 1
Reyes, Alfonso 1889-1959   TCLC 33
    See also CA 131; HW
Reyes y Basoalto, Ricardo Eliecer Neftali
    See Neruda, Pablo
Reymont, Wladyslaw (Stanislaw) 1868(?)-1925
    TCLC 5
    See also CA 104
Reynolds, Jonathan 1942-   CLC 6, 38
    See also CA 65-68; CANR 28
Reynolds, Joshua 1723-1792   LC 15
    See also DLB 104
Reynolds, Michael Shane 1937-   CLC 44
    See also CA 65-68; CANR 9
Reznikoff, Charles 1894-1976   CLC 9
    See also CA 33-36; 61-64; CAP 2; DLB 28, 45
Rezzori (d'Arezzo), Gregor von 1914-1998
    CLC 25
    See also CA 122; 136; 167
Rhine, Richard
    See Silverstein, Alvin
Rhodes, Eugene Manlove 1869-1934TCLC 53
Rhodius, Apollonius c. 3rd cent. B.C.- C M L C
    28
    See also DLB 176
R'hoone
    See Balzac, Honore de
Rhys, Jean 1890(?)-1979 CLC 2, 4, 6, 14, 19,
    51; DAM NOV; SSC 21
    See also CA 25-28R; 85-88; CANR 35, 62;
        CDBLB 1945-1960; DLB 36, 117, 162;
        MTCW 1
Ribeiro, Darcy 1922-1997   CLC 34
    See also CA 33-36R; 156
Ribeiro, Joao Ubaldo (Osorio Pimentel) 1941-
    CLC 10, 67
    See also CA 81-84
Ribman, Ronald (Burt) 1932-   CLC 7
    See also CA 21-24R; CANR 46
Ricci, Nino 1959-   CLC 70
    See also CA 137
Rice, Anne 1941-   CLC 41; DAM POP
    See also AAYA 9; BEST 89:2; CA 65-68; CANR
        12, 36, 53, 74
Rice, Elmer (Leopold) 1892-1967 CLC 7, 49;
    DAM DRAM
    See also CA 21-22; 25-28R; CAP 2; DLB 4, 7;
        MTCW 1
Rice, Tim(othy Miles Bindon) 1944- CLC 21
    See also CA 103; CANR 46
Rich, Adrienne (Cecile) 1929-CLC 3, 6, 7, 11,
    18, 36, 73, 76; DAM POET; PC 5
    See also CA 9-12R; CANR 20, 53, 74; DLB 5,
        67; MTCW 1
Rich, Barbara
    See Graves, Robert (von Ranke)
Rich, Robert
    See Trumbo, Dalton
Richard, Keith   CLC 17
    See also Richards, Keith
Richards, David Adams 1950- CLC 59; DAC
    See also CA 93-96; CANR 60; DLB 53

Roquelaure, A. N.
See Rice, Anne
Rosa, Joao Guimaraes 1908-1967   **CLC 23**
See also CA 89-92; DLB 113
Rose, Wendy 1948-**CLC 85; DAM MULT; PC 13**
See also CA 53-56; CANR 5, 51; DLB 175; NNAL; SATA 12
Rosen, R. D.
See Rosen, Richard (Dean)
Rosen, Richard (Dean) 1949-   **CLC 39**
See also CA 77-80; CANR 62; INT CANR-30
Rosenberg, Isaac 1890-1918   **TCLC 12**
See also CA 107; DLB 20
Rosenblatt, Joe   **CLC 15**
See also Rosenblatt, Joseph
Rosenblatt, Joseph 1933-
See Rosenblatt, Joe
See also CA 89-92; INT 89-92
Rosenfeld, Samuel
See Tzara, Tristan
Rosenstock, Sami
See Tzara, Tristan
Rosenstock, Samuel
See Tzara, Tristan
Rosenthal, M(acha) L(ouis) 1917-1996 **C L C 28**
See also CA 1-4R; 152; CAAS 6; CANR 4, 51; DLB 5; SATA 59
Ross, Barnaby
See Dannay, Frederic
Ross, Bernard L.
See Follett, Ken(neth Martin)
Ross, J. H.
See Lawrence, T(homas) E(dward)
Ross, John Hume
See Lawrence, T(homas) E(dward)
Ross, Martin
See Martin, Violet Florence
See also DLB 135
Ross, (James) Sinclair 1908- **CLC 13; DAC; DAM MST; SSC 24**
See also CA 73-76; DLB 88
Rossetti, Christina (Georgina) 1830-1894 **NCLC 2, 50, 66; DA; DAB; DAC; DAM MST, POET; PC 7; WLC**
See also DLB 35, 163; MAICYA; SATA 20
Rossetti, Dante Gabriel 1828-1882 **NCLC 4; DA; DAB; DAC; DAM MST, POET; WLC**
See also CDBLB 1832-1890; DLB 35
Rossner, Judith (Perelman) 1935-**CLC 6, 9, 29**
See also AITN 2; BEST 90:3; CA 17-20R; CANR 18, 51, 73; DLB 6; INT CANR-18; MTCW 1
Rostand, Edmond (Eugene Alexis) 1868-1918 **TCLC 6, 37; DA; DAB; DAC; DAM DRAM, MST**
See also CA 104; 126; DLB 192; MTCW 1
Roth, Henry 1906-1995   **CLC 2, 6, 11, 104**
See also CA 11-12; 149; CANR 38, 63; CAP 1; DLB 28; MTCW 1
Roth, Philip (Milton) 1933-**CLC 1, 2, 3, 4, 6, 9, 15, 22, 31, 47, 66, 86; DA; DAB; DAC; DAM MST, NOV, POP; SSC 26; WLC**
See also BEST 90:3; CA 1-4R; CANR 1, 22, 36, 55; CDALB 1968-1988; DLB 2, 28, 173; DLBY 82; MTCW 1
Rothenberg, Jerome 1931-   **CLC 6, 57**
See also CA 45-48; CANR 1; DLB 5, 193
Roumain, Jacques (Jean Baptiste) 1907-1944 **TCLC 19; BLC 3; DAM MULT**
See also BW 1; CA 117; 125
Rourke, Constance (Mayfield) 1885-1941

TCLC 12
See also CA 107; YABC 1
Rousseau, Jean-Baptiste 1671-1741   **LC 9**
Rousseau, Jean-Jacques 1712-1778**LC 14, 36; DA; DAB; DAC; DAM MST; WLC**
Roussel, Raymond 1877-1933   **TCLC 20**
See also CA 117
Rovit, Earl (Herbert) 1927-   **CLC 7**
See also CA 5-8R; CANR 12
Rowe, Elizabeth Singer 1674-1737   **LC 44**
See also DLB 39, 95
Rowe, Nicholas 1674-1718   **LC 8**
See also DLB 84
Rowley, Ames Dorrance
See Lovecraft, H(oward) P(hillips)
Rowson, Susanna Haswell 1762(?)-1824 **NCLC 5, 69**
See also DLB 37, 200
Roy, Arundhati 1960(?)-   **CLC 109**
See also CA 163; DLBY 97
Roy, Gabrielle 1909-1983 **CLC 10, 14; DAB; DAC; DAM MST**
See also CA 53-56; 110; CANR 5, 61; DLB 68; MTCW 1
Royko, Mike 1932-1997   **CLC 109**
See also CA 89-92; 157; CANR 26
Rozewicz, Tadeusz 1921-   **CLC 9, 23; DAM POET**
See also CA 108; CANR 36, 66; MTCW 1
Ruark, Gibbons 1941-   **CLC 3**
See also CA 33-36R; CAAS 23; CANR 14, 31, 57; DLB 120
Rubens, Bernice (Ruth) 1923-   **CLC 19, 31**
See also CA 25-28R; CANR 33, 65; DLB 14; MTCW 1
Rubin, Harold
See Robbins, Harold
Rudkin, (James) David 1936-   **CLC 14**
See also CA 89-92; DLB 13
Rudnik, Raphael 1933-   **CLC 7**
See also CA 29-32R
Ruffian, M.
See Hasek, Jaroslav (Matej Frantisek)
Ruiz, Jose Martinez   **CLC 11**
See also Martinez Ruiz, Jose
Rukeyser, Muriel 1913-1980**CLC 6, 10, 15, 27; DAM POET; PC 12**
See also CA 5-8R; 93-96; CANR 26, 60; DLB 48; MTCW 1; SATA-Obit 22
Rule, Jane (Vance) 1931-   **CLC 27**
See also CA 25-28R; CAAS 18; CANR 12; DLB 60
Rulfo, Juan 1918-1986   **CLC 8, 80; DAM MULT; HLC; SSC 25**
See also CA 85-88; 118; CANR 26; DLB 113; HW; MTCW 1
Rumi, Jalal al-Din 1297-1373   **CMLC 20**
Runeberg, Johan 1804-1877   **NCLC 41**
Runyon, (Alfred) Damon 1884(?)-1946**T C L C 10**
See also CA 107; 165; DLB 11, 86, 171
Rush, Norman 1933-   **CLC 44**
See also CA 121; 126; INT 126
Rushdie, (Ahmed) Salman 1947- **CLC 23, 31, 55, 100; DAB; DAC; DAM MST, NOV, POP; WLCS**
See also BEST 89:3; CA 108; 111; CANR 33, 56; DLB 194; INT 111; MTCW 1
Rushforth, Peter (Scott) 1945-   **CLC 19**
See also CA 101
Ruskin, John 1819-1900   **TCLC 63**
See also CA 114; 129; CDBLB 1832-1890; DLB 55, 163, 190; SATA 24

Russ, Joanna 1937-   **CLC 15**
See also CANR 11, 31, 65; DLB 8; MTCW 1
Russell, George William 1867-1935
See Baker, Jean H.
See also CA 104; 153; CDBLB 1890-1914; DAM POET
Russell, (Henry) Ken(neth Alfred) 1927-**C L C 16**
See also CA 105
Russell, William Martin 1947-   **CLC 60**
See also CA 164
Rutherford, Mark   **TCLC 25**
See also White, William Hale
See also DLB 18
Ruyslinck, Ward 1929-   **CLC 14**
See also Belser, Reimond Karel Maria de
Ryan, Cornelius (John) 1920-1974   **CLC 7**
See also CA 69-72; 53-56; CANR 38
Ryan, Michael 1946-   **CLC 65**
See also CA 49-52; DLBY 82
Ryan, Tim
See Dent, Lester
Rybakov, Anatoli (Naumovich) 1911-**CLC 23, 53**
See also CA 126; 135; SATA 79
Ryder, Jonathan
See Ludlum, Robert
Ryga, George 1932-1987**CLC 14; DAC; DAM MST**
See also CA 101; 124; CANR 43; DLB 60
S. H.
See Hartmann, Sadakichi
S. S.
See Sassoon, Siegfried (Lorraine)
Saba, Umberto 1883-1957   **TCLC 33**
See also CA 144; DLB 114
Sabatini, Rafael 1875-1950   **TCLC 47**
See also CA 162
Sabato, Ernesto (R.) 1911-**CLC 10, 23; DAM MULT; HLC**
See also CA 97-100; CANR 32, 65; DLB 145; HW; MTCW 1
Sa-Carniero, Mario de 1890-1916 **TCLC 83**
Sacastru, Martin
See Bioy Casares, Adolfo
Sacher-Masoch, Leopold von 1836(?)-1895 **NCLC 31**
Sachs, Marilyn (Stickle) 1927-   **CLC 35**
See also AAYA 2; CA 17-20R; CANR 13, 47; CLR 2; JRDA; MAICYA; SAAS 2; SATA 3, 68
Sachs, Nelly 1891-1970   **CLC 14, 98**
See also CA 17-18; 25-28R; CAP 2
Sackler, Howard (Oliver) 1929-1982 **CLC 14**
See also CA 61-64; 108; CANR 30; DLB 7
Sacks, Oliver (Wolf) 1933-   **CLC 67**
See also CA 53-56; CANR 28, 50; INT CANR-28; MTCW 1
Sadakichi
See Hartmann, Sadakichi
Sade, Donatien Alphonse Francois, Comte de 1740-1814   **NCLC 47**
Sadoff, Ira 1945-   **CLC 9**
See also CA 53-56; CANR 5, 21; DLB 120
Saetone
See Camus, Albert
Safire, William 1929-   **CLC 10**
See also CA 17-20R; CANR 31, 54
Sagan, Carl (Edward) 1934-1996**CLC 30, 112**
See also AAYA 2; CA 25-28R; 155; CANR 11, 36, 74; MTCW 1; SATA 58; SATA-Obit 94
Sagan, Francoise   **CLC 3, 6, 9, 17, 36**
See also Quoirez, Francoise

See also DLB 94

Schlegel, Friedrich 1772-1829 **NCLC 45**
See also DLB 90

Schlegel, Johann Elias (von) 1719(?)-1749 **L C 5**

Schlesinger, Arthur M(eier), Jr. 1917- **CLC 84**
See also AITN 1; CA 1-4R; CANR 1, 28, 58; DLB 17; INT CANR-28; MTCW 1; SATA 61

Schmidt, Arno (Otto) 1914-1979 **CLC 56**
See also CA 128; 109; DLB 69

Schmitz, Aron Hector 1861-1928
See Svevo, Italo
See also CA 104; 122; MTCW 1

Schnackenberg, Gjertrud 1953- **CLC 40**
See also CA 116; DLB 120

Schneider, Leonard Alfred 1925-1966
See Bruce, Lenny
See also CA 89-92

Schnitzler, Arthur 1862-1931 **TCLC 4; SSC 15**
See also CA 104; DLB 81, 118

Schoenberg, Arnold 1874-1951 **TCLC 75**
See also CA 109

Schonberg, Arnold
See Schoenberg, Arnold

Schopenhauer, Arthur 1788-1860 **NCLC 51**
See also DLB 90

Schor, Sandra (M.) 1932(?)-1990 **CLC 65**
See also CA 132

Schorer, Mark 1908-1977 **CLC 9**
See also CA 5-8R; 73-76; CANR 7; DLB 103

Schrader, Paul (Joseph) 1946- **CLC 26**
See also CA 37-40R; CANR 41; DLB 44

Schreiner, Olive (Emilie Albertina) 1855-1920 **TCLC 9**
See also CA 105; 154; DLB 18, 156, 190

Schulberg, Budd (Wilson) 1914- **CLC 7, 48**
See also CA 25-28R; CANR 19; DLB 6, 26, 28; DLBY 81

Schulz, Bruno 1892-1942 **TCLC 5, 51; SSC 13**
See also CA 115; 123

Schulz, Charles M(onroe) 1922- **CLC 12**
See also CA 9-12R; CANR 6; INT CANR-6; SATA 10

Schumacher, E(rnst) F(riedrich) 1911-1977 **CLC 80**
See also CA 81-84; 73-76; CANR 34

Schuyler, James Marcus 1923-1991 **CLC 5, 23; DAM POET**
See also CA 101; 134; DLB 5, 169; INT 101

Schwartz, Delmore (David) 1913-1966 **CLC 2, 4, 10, 45, 87; PC 8**
See also CA 17-18; 25-28R; CANR 35; CAP 2; DLB 28, 48; MTCW 1

Schwartz, Ernst
See Ozu, Yasujiro

Schwartz, John Burnham 1965- **CLC 59**
See also CA 132

Schwartz, Lynne Sharon 1939- **CLC 31**
See also CA 103; CANR 44

Schwartz, Muriel A.
See Eliot, T(homas) S(tearns)

Schwarz-Bart, Andre 1928- **CLC 2, 4**
See also CA 89-92

Schwarz-Bart, Simone 1938- **CLC 7; BLCS**
See also BW 2; CA 97-100

Schwob, Marcel (Mayer Andre) 1867-1905 **TCLC 20**
See also CA 117; 168; DLB 123

Sciascia, Leonardo 1921-1989 **CLC 8, 9, 41**
See also CA 85-88; 130; CANR 35; DLB 177; MTCW 1

Scoppettone, Sandra 1936- **CLC 26**

See also AAYA 11; CA 5-8R; CANR 41, 73; SATA 9, 92

Scorsese, Martin 1942- **CLC 20, 89**
See also CA 110; 114; CANR 46

Scotland, Jay
See Jakes, John (William)

Scott, Duncan Campbell 1862-1947 **TCLC 6; DAC**
See also CA 104; 153; DLB 92

Scott, Evelyn 1893-1963 **CLC 43**
See also CA 104; 112; CANR 64; DLB 9, 48

Scott, F(rancis) R(eginald) 1899-1985 **CLC 22**
See also CA 101; 114; DLB 88; INT 101

Scott, Frank
See Scott, F(rancis) R(eginald)

Scott, Joanna 1960- **CLC 50**
See also CA 126; CANR 53

Scott, Paul (Mark) 1920-1978 **CLC 9, 60**
See also CA 81-84; 77-80; CANR 33; DLB 14; MTCW 1

Scott, Sarah 1723-1795 **LC 44**
See also DLB 39

Scott, Walter 1771-1832 **NCLC 15, 69; DA; DAB; DAC; DAM MST, NOV, POET; PC 13; SSC 32; WLC**
See also AAYA 22; CDBLB 1789-1832; DLB 93, 107, 116, 144, 159; YABC 2

Scribe, (Augustin) Eugene 1791-1861 **N C L C 16; DAM DRAM; DC 5**
See also DLB 192

Scrum, R.
See Crumb, R(obert)

Scudery, Madeleine de 1607-1701 **LC 2**

Scum
See Crumb, R(obert)

Scumbag, Little Bobby
See Crumb, R(obert)

Seabrook, John
See Hubbard, L(afayette) Ron(ald)

Sealy, I. Allan 1951- **CLC 55**

Search, Alexander
See Pessoa, Fernando (Antonio Nogueira)

Sebastian, Lee
See Silverberg, Robert

Sebastian Owl
See Thompson, Hunter S(tockton)

Sebestyen, Ouida 1924- **CLC 30**
See also AAYA 8; CA 107; CANR 40; CLR 17; JRDA; MAICYA; SAAS 10; SATA 39

Secundus, H. Scriblerus
See Fielding, Henry

Sedges, John
See Buck, Pearl S(ydenstricker)

Sedgwick, Catharine Maria 1789-1867 **N C L C 19**
See also DLB 1, 74

Seelye, John (Douglas) 1931- **CLC 7**
See also CA 97-100; CANR 70; INT 97-100

Seferiades, Giorgos Stylianou 1900-1971
See Seferis, George
See also CA 5-8R; 33-36R; CANR 5, 36; MTCW 1

Seferis, George **CLC 5, 11**
See also Seferiades, Giorgos Stylianou

Segal, Erich (Wolf) 1937- **CLC 3, 10; DAM POP**
See also BEST 89:1; CA 25-28R; CANR 20, 36, 65; DLBY 86; INT CANR-20; MTCW 1

Seger, Bob 1945- **CLC 35**

Seghers, Anna **CLC 7**
See also Radvanyi, Netty
See also DLB 69

Seidel, Frederick (Lewis) 1936- **CLC 18**

See also CA 13-16R; CANR 8; DLBY 84

Seifert, Jaroslav 1901-1986 **CLC 34, 44, 93**
See also CA 127; MTCW 1

Sei Shonagon c. 966-1017(?) **CMLC 6**

Selby, Hubert, Jr. 1928- **CLC 1, 2, 4, 8; SSC 20**
See also CA 13-16R; CANR 33; DLB 2

Selzer, Richard 1928- **CLC 74**
See also CA 65-68; CANR 14

Sembene, Ousmane
See Ousmane, Sembene

Senancour, Etienne Pivert de 1770-1846 **NCLC 16**
See also DLB 119

Sender, Ramon (Jose) 1902-1982 **CLC 8; DAM MULT; HLC**
See also CA 5-8R; 105; CANR 8; HW; MTCW 1

Seneca, Lucius Annaeus 4B.C.-65 **CMLC 6; DAM DRAM; DC 5**

Senghor, Leopold Sedar 1906- **CLC 54; BLC 3; DAM MULT, POET**
See also BW 2; CA 116; 125; CANR 47, 74; MTCW 1

Serling, (Edward) Rod(man) 1924-1975 **C L C 30**
See also AAYA 14; AITN 1; CA 162; 57-60; DLB 26

Serna, Ramon Gomez de la
See Gomez de la Serna, Ramon

Serpieres
See Guillevic, (Eugene)

Service, Robert
See Service, Robert W(illiam)
See also DAB; DLB 92

Service, Robert W(illiam) 1874(?)-1958 **TCLC 15; DA; DAC; DAM MST, POET; WLC**
See also Service, Robert
See also CA 115; 140; SATA 20

Seth, Vikram 1952- **CLC 43, 90; DAM MULT**
See also CA 121; 127; CANR 50, 74; DLB 120; INT 127

Seton, Cynthia Propper 1926-1982 **CLC 27**
See also CA 5-8R; 108; CANR 7

Seton, Ernest (Evan) Thompson 1860-1946 **TCLC 31**
See also CA 109; DLB 92; DLBD 13; JRDA; SATA 18

Seton-Thompson, Ernest
See Seton, Ernest (Evan) Thompson

Settle, Mary Lee 1918- **CLC 19, 61**
See also CA 89-92; CAAS 1; CANR 44; DLB 6; INT 89-92

Seuphor, Michel
See Arp, Jean

Sevigne, Marie (de Rabutin-Chantal) Marquise de 1626-1696 **LC 11**

Sewall, Samuel 1652-1730 **LC 38**
See also DLB 24

Sexton, Anne (Harvey) 1928-1974 **CLC 2, 4, 6, 8, 10, 15, 53; DA; DAB; DAC; DAM MST, POET; PC 2; WLC**
See also CA 1-4R; 53-56; CABS 2; CANR 3, 36; CDALB 1941-1968; DLB 5, 169; MTCW 1; SATA 10

Shaara, Michael (Joseph, Jr.) 1929-1988 **C L C 15; DAM POP**
See also AITN 1; CA 102; 125; CANR 52; DLBY 83

Shackleton, C. C.
See Aldiss, Brian W(ilson)

Shacochis, Bob **CLC 39**
See also Shacochis, Robert G.

Shacochis, Robert G. 1951-

DA; DAB; DAC; DAM MST, NOV, POET;
PC 18; WLC
See also CA 104; 132; CDALB 1917-1929;
DLB 4, 54, 86; DLBD 15; MTCW 1

Steinbeck, John (Ernst) 1902-1968CLC 1, 5, 9,
13, 21, 34, 45, 75; DA; DAB; DAC; DAM
DRAM, MST, NOV; SSC 11; WLC
See also AAYA 12; CA 1-4R; 25-28R; CANR
1, 35; CDALB 1929-1941; DLB 7, 9; DLBD
2; MTCW 1; SATA 9

Steinem, Gloria 1934-   CLC 63
See also CA 53-56; CANR 28, 51; MTCW 1

Steiner, George 1929-   CLC 24; DAM NOV
See also CA 73-76; CANR 31, 67; DLB 67;
MTCW 1; SATA 62

Steiner, K. Leslie
See Delany, Samuel R(ay, Jr.)

Steiner, Rudolf 1861-1925   TCLC 13
See also CA 107

Stendhal 1783-1842NCLC 23, 46; DA; DAB;
DAC; DAM MST, NOV; SSC 27; WLC
See also DLB 119

Stephen, Adeline Virginia
See Woolf, (Adeline) Virginia

Stephen, SirLeslie 1832-1904   TCLC 23
See also CA 123; DLB 57, 144, 190

Stephen, Sir Leslie
See Stephen, SirLeslie

Stephen, Virginia
See Woolf, (Adeline) Virginia

Stephens, James 1882(?)-1950   TCLC 4
See also CA 104; DLB 19, 153, 162

Stephens, Reed
See Donaldson, Stephen R.

Steptoe, Lydia
See Barnes, Djuna

Sterchi, Beat 1949-   CLC 65

Sterling, Brett
See Bradbury, Ray (Douglas); Hamilton,
Edmond

Sterling, Bruce 1954-   CLC 72
See also CA 119; CANR 44

Sterling, George 1869-1926   TCLC 20
See also CA 117; 165; DLB 54

Stern, Gerald 1925-   CLC 40, 100
See also CA 81-84; CANR 28; DLB 105

Stern, Richard (Gustave) 1928-   CLC 4, 39
See also CA 1-4R; CANR 1, 25, 52; DLBY 87;
INT CANR-25

Sternberg, Josef von 1894-1969   CLC 20
See also CA 81-84

Sterne, Laurence 1713-1768   LC 2, 48; DA;
DAB; DAC; DAM MST, NOV; WLC
See also CDBLB 1660-1789; DLB 39

Sternheim, (William Adolf) Carl 1878-1942
TCLC 8
See also CA 105; DLB 56, 118

Stevens, Mark 1951-   CLC 34
See also CA 122

Stevens, Wallace 1879-1955 TCLC 3, 12, 45;
DA; DAB; DAC; DAM MST, POET; PC
6; WLC
See also CA 104; 124; CDALB 1929-1941;
DLB 54; MTCW 1

Stevenson, Anne (Katharine) 1933-CLC 7, 33
See also CA 17-20R; CAAS 9; CANR 9, 33;
DLB 40; MTCW 1

Stevenson, Robert Louis (Balfour) 1850-1894
NCLC 5, 14, 63; DA; DAB; DAC; DAM
MST, NOV; SSC 11; WLC
See also AAYA 24; CDBLB 1890-1914; CLR
10, 11; DLB 18, 57, 141, 156, 174; DLBD
13; JRDA; MAICYA; SATA 100; YABC 2

Stewart, J(ohn) I(nnes) M(ackintosh) 1906-
1994   CLC 7, 14, 32
See also CA 85-88; 147; CAAS 3; CANR 47;
MTCW 1

Stewart, Mary (Florence Elinor) 1916-CLC 7,
35, 117; DAB
See also CA 1-4R; CANR 1, 59; SATA 12

Stewart, Mary Rainbow
See Stewart, Mary (Florence Elinor)

Stifle, June
See Campbell, Maria

Stifter, Adalbert 1805-1868NCLC 41; SSC 28
See also DLB 133

Still, James 1906-   CLC 49
See also CA 65-68; CAAS 17; CANR 10, 26;
DLB 9; SATA 29

Sting 1951-
See Sumner, Gordon Matthew
See also CA 167

Stirling, Arthur
See Sinclair, Upton (Beall)

Stitt, Milan 1941-   CLC 29
See also CA 69-72

Stockton, Francis Richard 1834-1902
See Stockton, Frank R.
See also CA 108; 137; MAICYA; SATA 44

Stockton, Frank R.   TCLC 47
See also Stockton, Francis Richard
See also DLB 42, 74; DLBD 13; SATA-Brief
32

Stoddard, Charles
See Kuttner, Henry

Stoker, Abraham 1847-1912
See Stoker, Bram
See also CA 105; 150; DA; DAC; DAM MST,
NOV; SATA 29

Stoker, Bram 1847-1912TCLC 8; DAB; WLC
See also Stoker, Abraham
See also AAYA 23; CDBLB 1890-1914; DLB
36, 70, 178

Stolz, Mary (Slattery) 1920-   CLC 12
See also AAYA 8; AITN 1; CA 5-8R; CANR
13, 41; JRDA; MAICYA; SAAS 3; SATA 10,
71

Stone, Irving 1903-1989   CLC 7; DAM POP
See also AITN 1; CA 1-4R; 129; CAAS 3;
CANR 1, 23; INT CANR-23; MTCW 1;
SATA 3; SATA-Obit 64

Stone, Oliver (William) 1946-   CLC 73
See also AAYA 15; CA 110; CANR 55

Stone, Robert (Anthony) 1937-CLC 5, 23, 42
See also CA 85-88; CANR 23, 66; DLB 152;
INT CANR-23; MTCW 1

Stone, Zachary
See Follett, Ken(neth Martin)

Stoppard, Tom 1937-CLC 1, 3, 4, 5, 8, 15, 29,
34, 63, 91; DA; DAB; DAC; DAM DRAM,
MST; DC 6; WLC
See also CA 81-84; CANR 39, 67; CDBLB
1960 to Present; DLB 13; DLBY 85; MTCW
1

Storey, David (Malcolm) 1933-CLC 2, 4, 5, 8;
DAM DRAM
See also CA 81-84; CANR 36; DLB 13, 14;
MTCW 1

Storm, Hyemeyohsts 1935-   CLC 3; DAM
MULT
See also CA 81-84; CANR 45; NNAL

Storm, Theodor 1817-1888   SSC 27

Storm, (Hans) Theodor (Woldsen) 1817-1888
NCLC 1; SSC 27
See also DLB 129

Storni, Alfonsina 1892-1938   TCLC 5; DAM

MULT; HLC
See also CA 104; 131; HW

Stoughton, William 1631-1701   LC 38
See also DLB 24

Stout, Rex (Todhunter) 1886-1975   CLC 3
See also AITN 2; CA 61-64; CANR 71

Stow, (Julian) Randolph 1935-   CLC 23, 48
See also CA 13-16R; CANR 33; MTCW 1

Stowe, Harriet (Elizabeth) Beecher 1811-1896
NCLC 3, 50; DA; DAB; DAC; DAM MST,
NOV; WLC
See also CDALB 1865-1917; DLB 1, 12, 42,
74, 189; JRDA; MAICYA; YABC 1

Strachey, (Giles) Lytton 1880-1932 TCLC 12
See also CA 110; DLB 149; DLBD 10

Strand, Mark 1934- CLC 6, 18, 41, 71; DAM
POET
See also CA 21-24R; CANR 40, 65; DLB 5;
SATA 41

Straub, Peter (Francis) 1943-   CLC 28, 107;
DAM POP
See also BEST 89:1; CA 85-88; CANR 28, 65;
DLBY 84; MTCW 1

Strauss, Botho 1944-   CLC 22
See also CA 157; DLB 124

Streatfeild, (Mary) Noel 1895(?)-1986CLC 21
See also CA 81-84; 120; CANR 31; CLR 17;
DLB 160; MAICYA; SATA 20; SATA-Obit
48

Stribling, T(homas) S(igismund) 1881-1965
CLC 23
See also CA 107; DLB 9

Strindberg, (Johan) August 1849-1912TCLC
1, 8, 21, 47; DA; DAB; DAC; DAM DRAM,
MST; WLC
See also CA 104; 135

Stringer, Arthur 1874-1950   TCLC 37
See also CA 161; DLB 92

Stringer, David
See Roberts, Keith (John Kingston)

Stroheim, Erich von 1885-1957   TCLC 71

Strugatskii, Arkadii (Natanovich) 1925-1991
CLC 27
See also CA 106; 135

Strugatskii, Boris (Natanovich) 1933-CLC 27
See also CA 106

Strummer, Joe 1953(?)-   CLC 30

Stuart, Don A.
See Campbell, John W(ood, Jr.)

Stuart, Ian
See MacLean, Alistair (Stuart)

Stuart, Jesse (Hilton) 1906-1984CLC 1, 8, 11,
14, 34; SSC 31
See also CA 5-8R; 112; CANR 31; DLB 9, 48,
102; DLBY 84; SATA 2; SATA-Obit 36

Sturgeon, Theodore (Hamilton) 1918-1985
CLC 22, 39
See also Queen, Ellery
See also CA 81-84; 116; CANR 32; DLB 8;
DLBY 85; MTCW 1

Sturges, Preston 1898-1959   TCLC 48
See also CA 114; 149; DLB 26

Styron, William 1925-CLC 1, 3, 5, 11, 15, 60;
DAM NOV, POP; SSC 25
See also BEST 90:4; CA 5-8R; CANR 6, 33,
74; CDALB 1968-1988; DLB 2, 143; DLBY
80; INT CANR-6; MTCW 1

Su, Chien 1884-1918
See Su Man-shu
See also CA 123

Suarez Lynch, B.
See Bioy Casares, Adolfo; Borges, Jorge Luis

Suckow, Ruth 1892-1960   SSC 18

Teresa de Jesus, St. 1515-1582   **LC 18**
Terkel, Louis 1912-
   See Terkel, Studs
   See also CA 57-60; CANR 18, 45, 67; MTCW
   1
Terkel, Studs   **CLC 38**
   See also Terkel, Louis
   See also AITN 1
Terry, C. V.
   See Slaughter, Frank G(ill)
Terry, Megan 1932-   **CLC 19**
   See also CA 77-80; CABS 3; CANR 43; DLB 7
Tertullian c. 155-c. 245   **CMLC 29**
Tertz, Abram
   See Sinyavsky, Andrei (Donatevich)
Tesich, Steve 1943(?)-1996   **CLC 40, 69**
   See also CA 105; 152; DLBY 83
Tesla, Nikola 1856-1943   **TCLC 88**
Teternikov, Fyodor Kuzmich 1863-1927
   See Sologub, Fyodor
   See also CA 104
Tevis, Walter 1928-1984   **CLC 42**
   See also CA 113
Tey, Josephine   **TCLC 14**
   See also Mackintosh, Elizabeth
   See also DLB 77
Thackeray, William Makepeace 1811-1863
   **NCLC 5, 14, 22, 43; DA; DAB; DAC; DAM
   MST, NOV; WLC**
   See also CDBLB 1832-1890; DLB 21, 55, 159,
   163; SATA 23
Thakura, Ravindranatha
   See Tagore, Rabindranath
Tharoor, Shashi 1956-   **CLC 70**
   See also CA 141
Thelwell, Michael Miles 1939-   **CLC 22**
   See also BW 2; CA 101
Theobald, Lewis, Jr.
   See Lovecraft, H(oward) P(hillips)
Theodorescu, Ion N. 1880-1967
   See Arghezi, Tudor
   See also CA 116
Theriault, Yves 1915-1983   **CLC 79; DAC;
   DAM MST**
   See also CA 102; DLB 88
Theroux, Alexander (Louis) 1939- **CLC 2, 25**
   See also CA 85-88; CANR 20, 63
Theroux, Paul (Edward) 1941- **CLC 5, 8, 11,
   15, 28, 46; DAM POP**
   See also BEST 89:4; CA 33-36R; CANR 20,
   45, 74; DLB 2; MTCW 1; SATA 44
Thesen, Sharon 1946-   **CLC 56**
   See also CA 163
Thevenin, Denis
   See Duhamel, Georges
Thibault, Jacques Anatole Francois 1844-1924
   See France, Anatole
   See also CA 106; 127; DAM NOV; MTCW 1
Thiele, Colin (Milton) 1920-   **CLC 17**
   See also CA 29-32R; CANR 12, 28, 53; CLR
   27; MAICYA; SAAS 2; SATA 14, 72
Thomas, Audrey (Callahan) 1935- **CLC 7, 13,
   37, 107; SSC 20**
   See also AITN 2; CA 21-24R; CAAS 19; CANR
   36, 58; DLB 60; MTCW 1
Thomas, D(onald) M(ichael) 1935- **CLC 13,
   22, 31**
   See also CA 61-64; CAAS 11; CANR 17, 45,
   74; CDBLB 1960 to Present; DLB 40; INT
   CANR-17; MTCW 1
Thomas, Dylan (Marlais) 1914-1953 **TCLC 1,
   8, 45; DA; DAB; DAC; DAM DRAM,
   MST, POET; PC 2; SSC 3; WLC**

   See also CA 104; 120; CANR 65; CDBLB
   1945-1960; DLB 13, 20, 139; MTCW 1;
   SATA 60
Thomas, (Philip) Edward 1878-1917 **TCLC
   10; DAM POET**
   See also CA 106; 153; DLB 19
Thomas, Joyce Carol 1938-   **CLC 35**
   See also AAYA 12; BW 2; CA 113; 116; CANR
   48; CLR 19; DLB 33; INT 116; JRDA;
   MAICYA; MTCW 1; SAAS 7; SATA 40, 78
Thomas, Lewis 1913-1993   **CLC 35**
   See also CA 85-88; 143; CANR 38, 60; MTCW
   1
Thomas, Paul
   See Mann, (Paul) Thomas
Thomas, Piri 1928-   **CLC 17**
   See also CA 73-76; HW
Thomas, R(onald) S(tuart) 1913- **CLC 6, 13,
   48; DAB; DAM POET**
   See also CA 89-92; CAAS 4; CANR 30;
   CDBLB 1960 to Present; DLB 27; MTCW 1
Thomas, Ross (Elmore) 1926-1995   **CLC 39**
   See also CA 33-36R; 150; CANR 22, 63
Thompson, Francis Clegg
   See Mencken, H(enry) L(ouis)
Thompson, Francis Joseph 1859-1907 **TCLC 4**
   See also CA 104; CDBLB 1890-1914; DLB 19
Thompson, Hunter S(tockton) 1939- **CLC 9,
   17, 40, 104; DAM POP**
   See also BEST 89:1; CA 17-20R; CANR 23,
   46, 74; DLB 185; MTCW 1
Thompson, James Myers
   See Thompson, Jim (Myers)
Thompson, Jim (Myers) 1906-1977(?) **CLC 69**
   See also CA 140
Thompson, Judith   **CLC 39**
Thomson, James 1700-1748   **LC 16, 29, 40;
   DAM POET**
   See also DLB 95
Thomson, James 1834-1882 **NCLC 18; DAM
   POET**
   See also DLB 35
Thoreau, Henry David 1817-1862 **NCLC 7, 21,
   61; DA; DAB; DAC; DAM MST; WLC**
   See also CDALB 1640-1865; DLB 1
Thornton, Hall
   See Silverberg, Robert
Thucydides c. 455B.C.-399B.C.   **CMLC 17**
   See also DLB 176
Thurber, James (Grover) 1894-1961 **CLC 5,
   11, 25; DA; DAB; DAC; DAM DRAM,
   MST, NOV; SSC 1**
   See also CA 73-76; CANR 17, 39; CDALB
   1929-1941; DLB 4, 11, 22, 102; MAICYA;
   MTCW 1; SATA 13
Thurman, Wallace (Henry) 1902-1934 **TCLC
   6; BLC 3; DAM MULT**
   See also BW 1; CA 104; 124; DLB 51
Ticheburn, Cheviot
   See Ainsworth, William Harrison
Tieck, (Johann) Ludwig 1773-1853 **NCLC 5,
   46; SSC 31**
   See also DLB 90
Tiger, Derry
   See Ellison, Harlan (Jay)
Tilghman, Christopher 1948(?)-   **CLC 65**
   See also CA 159
Tillinghast, Richard (Williford) 1940- **CLC 29**
   See also CA 29-32R; CAAS 23; CANR 26, 51
Timrod, Henry 1828-1867   **NCLC 25**
   See also DLB 3
Tindall, Gillian (Elizabeth) 1938-   **CLC 7**
   See also CA 21-24R; CANR 11, 65

Tiptree, James, Jr.   **CLC 48, 50**
   See also Sheldon, Alice Hastings Bradley
   See also DLB 8
Titmarsh, Michael Angelo
   See Thackeray, William Makepeace
**Tocqueville, Alexis (Charles Henri Maurice
   Clerel, Comte) de** 1805-1859 **NCLC 7, 63**
Tolkien, J(ohn) R(onald) R(euel) 1892-1973
   **CLC 1, 2, 3, 8, 12, 38; DA; DAB; DAC;
   DAM MST, NOV, POP; WLC**
   See also AAYA 10; AITN 1; CA 17-18; 45-48;
   CANR 36; CAP 2; CDBLB 1914-1945; DLB
   15, 160; JRDA; MAICYA; MTCW 1; SATA
   2, 32, 100; SATA-Obit 24
Toller, Ernst 1893-1939   **TCLC 10**
   See also CA 107; DLB 124
Tolson, M. B.
   See Tolson, Melvin B(eaunorus)
Tolson, Melvin B(eaunorus) 1898(?)-1966
   CLC 36, 105; BLC 3; DAM MULT, POET
   See also BW 1; CA 124; 89-92; DLB 48, 76
Tolstoi, Aleksei Nikolaevich
   See Tolstoy, Alexey Nikolaevich
Tolstoy, Alexey Nikolaevich 1882-1945 **TCLC
   18**
   See also CA 107; 158
Tolstoy, Count Leo
   See Tolstoy, Leo (Nikolaevich)
Tolstoy, Leo (Nikolaevich) 1828-1910 **TCLC 4,
   11, 17, 28, 44, 79; DA; DAB; DAC; DAM
   MST, NOV; SSC 9, 30; WLC**
   See also CA 104; 123; SATA 26
Tomasi di Lampedusa, Giuseppe 1896-1957
   See Lampedusa, Giuseppe (Tomasi) di
   See also CA 111
Tomlin, Lily   **CLC 17**
   See also Tomlin, Mary Jean
Tomlin, Mary Jean 1939(?)-
   See Tomlin, Lily
   See also CA 117
Tomlinson, (Alfred) Charles 1927- **CLC 2, 4, 6,
   13, 45; DAM POET; PC 17**
   See also CA 5-8R; CANR 33; DLB 40
Tomlinson, H(enry) M(ajor) 1873-1958 **TCLC
   71**
   See also CA 118; 161; DLB 36, 100, 195
Tonson, Jacob
   See Bennett, (Enoch) Arnold
Toole, John Kennedy 1937-1969 **CLC 19, 64**
   See also CA 104; DLBY 81
Toomer, Jean 1894-1967 **CLC 1, 4, 13, 22; BLC
   3; DAM MULT; PC 7; SSC 1; WLCS**
   See also BW 1; CA 85-88; CDALB 1917-1929;
   DLB 45, 51; MTCW 1
Torley, Luke
   See Blish, James (Benjamin)
Tornimparte, Alessandra
   See Ginzburg, Natalia
Torre, Raoul della
   See Mencken, H(enry) L(ouis)
Torrey, E(dwin) Fuller 1937-   **CLC 34**
   See also CA 119; CANR 71
Torsvan, Ben Traven
   See Traven, B.
Torsvan, Benno Traven
   See Traven, B.
Torsvan, Berick Traven
   See Traven, B.
Torsvan, Berwick Traven
   See Traven, B.
Torsvan, Bruno Traven
   See Traven, B.
Torsvan, Traven

See Traven, B.

Tournier, Michel (Edouard) 1924-**CLC 6, 23, 36, 95**
See also CA 49-52; CANR 3, 36, 74; DLB 83; MTCW 1; SATA 23

Tournimparte, Alessandra
See Ginzburg, Natalia

Towers, Ivar
See Kornbluth, C(yril) M.

Towne, Robert (Burton) 1936(?)-   **CLC 87**
See also CA 108; DLB 44

Townsend, Sue   **CLC 61**
See also Townsend, Susan Elaine
See also SATA 55, 93; SATA-Brief 48

Townsend, Susan Elaine 1946-
See Townsend, Sue
See also CA 119; 127; CANR 65; DAB; DAC; DAM MST

Townshend, Peter (Dennis Blandford) 1945-
CLC 17, 42
See also CA 107

Tozzi, Federigo 1883-1920   **TCLC 31**
See also CA 160

Traill, Catharine Parr 1802-1899   **NCLC 31**
See also DLB 99

Trakl, Georg 1887-1914   **TCLC 5; PC 20**
See also CA 104; 165

Transtroemer, Tomas (Goesta) 1931-**CLC 52, 65; DAM POET**
See also CA 117; 129; CAAS 17

Transtromer, Tomas Gosta
See Transtroemer, Tomas (Goesta)

Traven, B. (?)-1969   **CLC 8, 11**
See also CA 19-20; 25-28R; CAP 2; DLB 9, 56; MTCW 1

Treitel, Jonathan 1959-   **CLC 70**

Tremain, Rose 1943-   **CLC 42**
See also CA 97-100; CANR 44; DLB 14

Tremblay, Michel 1942- **CLC 29, 102; DAC; DAM MST**
See also CA 116; 128; DLB 60; MTCW 1

Trevanian   **CLC 29**
See also Whitaker, Rod(ney)

Trevor, Glen
See Hilton, James

Trevor, William 1928-**CLC 7, 9, 14, 25, 71, 116; SSC 21**
See also Cox, William Trevor
See also DLB 14, 139

Trifonov, Yuri (Valentinovich) 1925-1981
CLC 45
See also CA 126; 103; MTCW 1

Trilling, Lionel 1905-1975   **CLC 9, 11, 24**
See also CA 9-12R; 61-64; CANR 10; DLB 28, 63; INT CANR-10; MTCW 1

Trimball, W. H.
See Mencken, H(enry) L(ouis)

Tristan
See Gomez de la Serna, Ramon

Tristram
See Housman, A(lfred) E(dward)

Trogdon, William (Lewis) 1939-
See Heat-Moon, William Least
See also CA 115; 119; CANR 47; INT 119

Trollope, Anthony 1815-1882**NCLC 6, 33; DA; DAB; DAC; DAM MST, NOV; SSC 28; WLC**
See also CDBLB 1832-1890; DLB 21, 57, 159; SATA 22

Trollope, Frances 1779-1863   **NCLC 30**
See also DLB 21, 166

Trotsky, Leon 1879-1940   **TCLC 22**
See also CA 118; 167

Trotter (Cockburn), Catharine 1679-1749**LC 8**
See also DLB 84

Trout, Kilgore
See Farmer, Philip Jose

Trow, George W. S. 1943-   **CLC 52**
See also CA 126

Troyat, Henri 1911-   **CLC 23**
See also CA 45-48; CANR 2, 33, 67; MTCW 1

Trudeau, G(arretson) B(eekman) 1948-
See Trudeau, Garry B.
See also CA 81-84; CANR 31; SATA 35

Trudeau, Garry B.   **CLC 12**
See also Trudeau, G(arretson) B(eekman)
See also AAYA 10; AITN 2

Truffaut, Francois 1932-1984   **CLC 20, 101**
See also CA 81-84; 113; CANR 34

Trumbo, Dalton 1905-1976   **CLC 19**
See also CA 21-24R; 69-72; CANR 10; DLB 26

Trumbull, John 1750-1831   **NCLC 30**
See also DLB 31

Trundlett, Helen B.
See Eliot, T(homas) S(tearns)

Tryon, Thomas 1926-1991 **CLC 3, 11; DAM POP**
See also AITN 1; CA 29-32R; 135; CANR 32; MTCW 1

Tryon, Tom
See Tryon, Thomas

Ts'ao Hsueh-ch'in 1715(?)-1763   **LC 1**

Tsushima, Shuji 1909-1948
See Dazai Osamu
See also CA 107

Tsvetaeva (Efron), Marina (Ivanovna) 1892-1941   **TCLC 7, 35; PC 14**
See also CA 104; 128; CANR 73; MTCW 1

Tuck, Lily 1938-   **CLC 70**
See also CA 139

Tu Fu 712-770   **PC 9**
See also DAM MULT

Tunis, John R(oberts) 1889-1975   **CLC 12**
See also CA 61-64; CANR 62; DLB 22, 171; JRDA; MAICYA; SATA 37; SATA-Brief 30

Tuohy, Frank   **CLC 37**
See also Tuohy, John Francis
See also DLB 14, 139

Tuohy, John Francis 1925-
See Tuohy, Frank
See also CA 5-8R; CANR 3, 47

Turco, Lewis (Putnam) 1934-   **CLC 11, 63**
See also CA 13-16R; CAAS 22; CANR 24, 51; DLBY 84

Turgenev, Ivan 1818-1883   **NCLC 21; DA; DAB; DAC; DAM MST, NOV; DC 7; SSC 7; WLC**

Turgot, Anne-Robert-Jacques 1727-1781 **LC 26**

Turner, Frederick 1943-   **CLC 48**
See also CA 73-76; CAAS 10; CANR 12, 30, 56; DLB 40

Tutu, Desmond M(pilo) 1931-**CLC 80; BLC 3; DAM MULT**
See also BW 1; CA 125; CANR 67

Tutuola, Amos 1920-1997**CLC 5, 14, 29; BLC 3; DAM MULT**
See also BW 2; CA 9-12R; 159; CANR 27, 66; DLB 125; MTCW 1

Twain, MarkTCLC **6, 12, 19, 36, 48, 59; SSC 6, 26; WLC**
See also Clemens, Samuel Langhorne
See also AAYA 20; DLB 11, 12, 23, 64, 74

Tyler, Anne 1941- **CLC 7, 11, 18, 28, 44, 59,**
103; DAM NOV, POP
See also AAYA 18; BEST 89:1; CA 9-12R; CANR 11, 33, 53; DLB 6, 143; DLBY 82; MTCW 1; SATA 7, 90

Tyler, Royall 1757-1826   **NCLC 3**
See also DLB 37

Tynan, Katharine 1861-1931   **TCLC 3**
See also CA 104; 167; DLB 153

Tyutchev, Fyodor 1803-1873   **NCLC 34**

Tzara, Tristan 1896-1963   **CLC 47; DAM POET**
See also CA 153; 89-92

Uhry, Alfred 1936-   **CLC 55; DAM DRAM, POP**
See also CA 127; 133; INT 133

Ulf, Haerved
See Strindberg, (Johan) August

Ulf, Harved
See Strindberg, (Johan) August

Ulibarri, Sabine R(eyes) 1919-**CLC 83; DAM MULT**
See also CA 131; DLB 82; HW

Unamuno (y Jugo), Miguel de 1864-1936
TCLC 2, 9; DAM MULT, NOV; HLC; SSC 11
See also CA 104; 131; DLB 108; HW; MTCW 1

Undercliffe, Errol
See Campbell, (John) Ramsey

Underwood, Miles
See Glassco, John

Undset, Sigrid 1882-1949**TCLC 3; DA; DAB; DAC; DAM MST, NOV; WLC**
See also CA 104; 129; MTCW 1

Ungaretti, Giuseppe 1888-1970**CLC 7, 11, 15**
See also CA 19-20; 25-28R; CAP 2; DLB 114

Unger, Douglas 1952-   **CLC 34**
See also CA 130

Unsworth, Barry (Forster) 1930-   **CLC 76**
See also CA 25-28R; CANR 30, 54; DLB 194

Updike, John (Hoyer) 1932-**CLC 1, 2, 3, 5, 7, 9, 13, 15, 23, 34, 43, 70; DA; DAB; DAC; DAM MST, NOV, POET, POP; SSC 13, 27; WLC**
See also CA 1-4R; CABS 1; CANR 4, 33, 51; CDALB 1968-1988; DLB 2, 5, 143; DLBD 3; DLBY 80, 82, 97; MTCW 1

Upshaw, Margaret Mitchell
See Mitchell, Margaret (Munnerlyn)

Upton, Mark
See Sanders, Lawrence

Upward, Allen 1863-1926   **TCLC 85**
See also CA 117; DLB 36

Urdang, Constance (Henriette) 1922-**CLC 47**
See also CA 21-24R; CANR 9, 24

Uriel, Henry
See Faust, Frederick (Schiller)

Uris, Leon (Marcus) 1924- **CLC 7, 32; DAM NOV, POP**
See also AITN 1, 2; BEST 89:2; CA 1-4R; CANR 1, 40, 65; MTCW 1; SATA 49

Urmuz
See Codrescu, Andrei

Urquhart, Jane 1949-   **CLC 90; DAC**
See also CA 113; CANR 32, 68

Ustinov, Peter (Alexander) 1921-   **CLC 1**
See also AITN 1; CA 13-16R; CANR 25, 51; DLB 13

U Tam'si, Gerald Felix Tchicaya
See Tchicaya, Gerald Felix

U Tam'si, Tchicaya
See Tchicaya, Gerald Felix

Vachss, Andrew (Henry) 1942-   **CLC 106**

Literary Criticism Series
Cumulative Topic Index

This index lists all topic entries in Gale's *Classical and Medieval Literature Criticism, Contemporary Literary Criticism, Literature Criticism from 1400 to 1800, Nineteenth-Century Literature Criticism,* and *Twentieth-Century Literary Criticism.*

Topic Index

Topic Index

CMLC Cumulative Nationality Index

CMLC Cumulative Title Index

Title Index

Title Index

CMLC Cumulative Critic Index

Critic Index

Critic Index

Juvenal **8**:6

Gilder, Rosamond
Hroswitha of Gandersheim **29**:105

Giles, Lionel
Lieh Tzu **27**:93

Gillies, Marshall M.
Apollonius Rhodius **28**:9

Gilson, Etienne
Abelard **11**:17
Augustine, St. **6**:44
Averroes **7**:18, 26
Bacon, Roger **14**:86
Meister Eckhart **9**:42, 60

Gilula, Dwora
Terence **14**:389

Girard, Rene
The Book of Job **14**:191
Sophocles **2**:408

Gladdon, Samuel Lyndon
Hildegard von Bingen **20**:182

Gladstone, W. E.
Iliad **1**:297

Glover, T. R.
Herodotus **17**:67

Gnagy, Allan S.
Anaximander **22**:99

Godwin, William
Poem of the Cid **4**:225

Goethe, Johann Wolfgang von
Kalidasa **9**:130
Longus **7**:217
Menander **9**:227
Sophocles **2**:303

Goldberg, Harriet
Razon de Amor **16**:360

Goldberg, Sander M.
Menander **9**:276
Terence **14**:372

Goldin, Frederick
The Song of Roland **1**:251

Golding, Arthur
Ovid **7**:287

Goldsmith, Margaret E.
Beowulf **1**:134

Gollancz, I.
Sir Gawain and the Green Knight **2**:186

Gollancz, Israel
Pearl **19**:286

Goller, Karl Heinz
Morte Arthure **10**:418

Gombrowicz, Witold
Inferno **3**:131

Gomez-Lobo, Alfonso
Socrates **27**:382

Gomme, A. W.
Menander **9**:259
Thucydides **17**:261

Gomperz, Heinrich
Heraclitus **22**:126

Good, Edwin M.
The Book of Job **14**:206

Goodell, Thomas Dwight
Aeschylus **11**:112

Goodheart, Eugene
The Book of Job **14**:171

Goodrich, Norma Lorre
Arthurian Legend **10**:100, 108

Goodspeed, Edgar J.
Tertullian **29**:310

Goodyear, F. R. D.
Phaedrus **25**:365

Goold, G. P.
Catullus **18**:166

Gordis, Robert
The Book of Job **14**:175

Gordon, E. V.
Hrafnkel's Saga **2**:86

Gosse, Edmund
Beowulf **1**:73

Gottfried von Strassburg
Gottfried von Strassburg **10**:246, 249, 258
Wolfram von Eschenbach **5**:291

Gradon, Pamela
Beowulf **1**:138

Graham, A. C.
Lieh Tzu **27**:108

Grahn, Judy
Sappho **3**:494

Grane, Leifn
Abelard **11**:25

Granrud, John E.
Cicero, Marcus Tullius **3**:205

Gransden, Antonia
Anglo-Saxon Chronicle **4**:21

Grant, Michael
Aeschylus **11**:175
Apuleius **1**:26
Cicero, Marcus Tullius **3**:285, 291
Josephus, Flavius **13**:240
Livy **11**:367
Ovid **7**:405

Polybius **17**:176
Thucydides **17**:296

Graves, Robert
Aeneid **9**:394
Apuleius **1**:20
Iliad **1**:361
Menander **9**:236
Terence **14**:341

Gray, Cecile Crovatt Gay
Tain Bo Cualnge **30**:159

Gray, Vivienne
Xenophon **17**:371

Gray, V. J.
Xenophon **17**:369

Gray, Wallace
Iliad **1**:405

Grayson, Christopher
Xenophon **17**:346

Green, D. H.
Hartmann von Aue **15**:206
Wolfram von Eschenbach **5**:391

Green, Peter
Apollonius Rhodius **28**:102
Juvenal **8**:68
Ovid **7**:419
Sappho **3**:438

Green, William H.
Torah **30**:242

Greenberg, Moshe
The Book of Job **14**:196

Greene, Thomas
Aeneid **9**:399

Greenfield, Concetta Carestia
Petrarch **20**:265

Greenfield, Stanley B.
Beowulf **1**:119
Cynewulf **23**:39
The Dream of the Rood **14**:243

Greenwood, Thomas
Albert the Great **16**:17

Gregory, Eileen
Sappho **3**:495

Grene, David
Aeschylus **11**:220
Herodotus **17**:113
Thucydides **17**:280

Grierson, Herbert J. C.
Beowulf **1**:90

Grieve, Patricia E.
Razon de Amor **16**:364

Griffin, Jasper
Iliad **1**:392
Odyssey **16**:304

Grigson, Geoffrey
Sei Shonagon **6**:300

Grimm, Charles
Chretien de Troyes **10**:141

Grobman, Neil R.
Ossian **28**:349

Groden, Suzy Q.
Sappho **3**:436

Groos, Arthur
Wolfram von Eschenbach **5**:423

Grossman, Judith
Arabian Nights **2**:57

Grossvogel, Steven
Boccaccio, Giovanni **13**:114

Grube, G. M. A.
Aristophanes **4**:136
Cicero, Marcus Tullius **3**:258

Gruffydd, W. J.
Mabinogion **9**:159

Grundy, G. B.
Thucydides **17**:268

Grunmann-Gaudet, Minnette
The Song of Roland **1**:248

Guardini, Romano
Augustine, St. **6**:95
The Book of Psalms **4**:414

Guarino, Guido A.
Boccaccio, Giovanni **13**:52

Gudzy, N. K.
The Igor Tale **1**:485

Gulley, Norman
Socrates **27**:303
Poetics **31**:174

Gunderloch, Anja
Ossian **28**:377

Gunkel, Hermann
The Book of Psalms **4**:379

Gunn, Alan M. F.
Romance of the Rose **8**:402

Guthrie, W. K. C.
Anaximander **22**:68
Plato **8**:321, 360
Presocratic philosophy **22**:19, 32
Pythagoras **22**:275
Socrates **27**:320

Habel, Norman C.
Torah **30**: 281

Hackett, Jeremiah M. G.
Bacon, Roger **14**:99, 110

Hadas, Moses
Aeschylus **11**:150
Apuleius **1**:23

Critic Index

Critic Index

Critic Index

Critic Index